STANDARD DEDUCTION

Filing Status	Amount
Married individuals filing joint returns and surviving spouses	$5,700
Heads of households	5,000
Unmarried individuals (other than surviving spouses and heads of households)	3,400
Married individuals filing separate return	2,850
Additional standard deductions for age and blindness	
Individual who is married and surviving spouses	650
Individual who is unmarried and not a surviving spouse	850

Personal Exemption 1991: $2,150*
                                   1990: $2,050

Reduction in personal and dependency exemptions

The personal and dependency exemption deductions are reduced or eliminated for certain high-income taxpayers. When a taxpayer's AGI exceeds the threshold amount described below, the deduction is reduced by 2% for each $2,500 (or fraction thereof) by which AGI exceeds the threshold amount. For married persons filing separately, the exemption deduction is reduced by 2% for each $1,250 (or fraction thereof) by which AGI exceeds the threshold amount. The personal exemption deduction amount cannot be reduced below zero.

The threshold amounts are:

Filing Status	Threshold Amount
Married individuals filing joint returns and surviving spouses	$150,000
Heads of households	125,000
Unmarried taxpayers (other than surviving spouses and heads of households)	100,000
Married filing separate return	75,000

PRENTICE HALL'S FEDERAL TAXATION, 1992

*Corporations,
Partnerships,
Estates, and Trusts*

PRENTICE HALL'S FEDERAL TAXATION, 1992

Corporations, Partnerships, Estates, and Trusts

Editors

JOHN L. KRAMER
University of Florida

LAWRENCE C. PHILLIPS
University of Miami

Co-authors

ANNA C. FOWLER
University of Texas at Austin

SANDRA S. KRAMER
University of Florida

SUSAN L. NORDHAUSER
University of Texas at San Antonio

Annotations by

DAVE N. STEWART
Brigham Young University

PRENTICE HALL, Englewood Cliffs, New Jersey 07632

Editorial/production supervision: Barbara Grasso
Development editor: Marsha Leest
Managing editor: Robert Dewey
Interior design: Levavi & Levavi, Inc.
Cover design: Bruce Kenselaar
Prepress buyer: Trudy Pisciotti
Manufacturing buyer: Robert Anderson

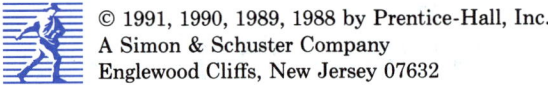
© 1991, 1990, 1989, 1988 by Prentice-Hall, Inc.
A Simon & Schuster Company
Englewood Cliffs, New Jersey 07632

All rights reserved. No part of this book may be
reproduced, in any form or by any means,
without permission in writing from the publisher.

ISSN 0898-2635

Printed in the United States of America
10 9 8 7 6 5 4 3 2 1

ISBN 0-13-677832-1

Prentice-Hall International (UK) Limited, *London*
Prentice-Hall of Australia Pty. Limited, *Sydney*
Prentice-Hall Canada Inc., *Toronto*
Prentice-Hall Hispanoamericana, S.A., *Mexico*
Prentice-Hall of India Private Limited, *New Delhi*
Prentice-Hall of Japan, Inc., *Tokyo*
Prentice-Hall of Southeast Asia Pte. Ltd., *Singapore*
Editora Prentice-Hall do Brasil, Ltda., *Rio de Janeiro*

Overview

	Preface xvii
CHAPTER 1	Tax Research 1-1
CHAPTER 2	Formation of the Corporation 2-1
CHAPTER 3	The Corporate Income Tax 3-1
CHAPTER 4	Corporate Nonliquidating Distributions 4-1
CHAPTER 5	Other Corporate Tax Levies 5-1
CHAPTER 6	Corporate Liquidating Distributions 6-1
CHAPTER 7	Corporate Acquisitions and Reorganizations 7-1
CHAPTER 8	Consolidated Tax Returns 8-1
CHAPTER 9	Partnership Formation and Operation 9-1
CHAPTER 10	Special Partnership Issues 10-1
CHAPTER 11	S Corporations 11-1
CHAPTER 12	The Gift Tax 12-1
CHAPTER 13	The Estate Tax 13-1
CHAPTER 14	Income Taxation of Trusts and Estates 14-1
CHAPTER 15	U.S. Taxation of Foreign-Related Transactions 15-1
CHAPTER 16	Administrative Procedures 16-1
APPENDIX	
A	Tax Research Working Paper File A-1
B	Completed Tax Forms B-1
C	Comparison of Tax Attributes for C Corporations, Partnerships, and S Corporations C-1
D	Credit for State Death Taxes D-1
E	Actuarial Tables E-1
F	Glossary F-1
G	Index of Code Sections G-1
H	Index of Treasury Regulations H-1
I	Index of Government Promulgations I-1
J	Index of Court Cases J-1
	Subject Index K-1

Contents

Preface xvii

CHAPTER 1
Tax Research 1-1

LEARNING OBJECTIVES 1-2
OVERVIEW OF TAX RESEARCH 1-2
STEPS IN THE TAX RESEARCH PROCESS 1-3
IMPORTANCE OF THE FACTS TO THE TAX RESULTS 1-5
    Facts of Case Where Taxpayer Won 1-6
    Facts of Case Where Taxpayer Lost 1-8
    Comparison of the Facts of the Two Cases 1-11
    Ability to Design Factual Situation Favoring the Taxpayer 1-11
THE SOURCES OF TAX LAW 1-12
    The Legislative Process 1-12
    The Internal Revenue Code 1-13
    Regulations 1-15
    Judicial Decisions 1-17
    Administrative Interpretations 1-26
    Tax Treaties 1-28
    Tax Periodicals 1-28
TAX SERVICES 1-29
    Federal Taxes 2d 1-29
    Standard Federal Tax Reporter 1-30
    Tax Coordinator 1-31
    Law of Federal Income Taxation (Mertens) 1-31
    Tax Management Portfolios 1-32
    Bender's Federal Tax Service 1-32
CITATORS 1-33
    Commerce Clearing House Citator 1-34
    Prentice Hall Information Services Citator 1-34
COMPUTERS AS A RESEARCH TOOL 1-39
SAMPLE WORK PAPERS AND CLIENT LETTER 1-40
PROBLEM MATERIALS 1-40
    Discussion Questions 1-40
    Problems 1-42
    Research Problems 1-45

CHAPTER 2
Formation of the Corporation 2-1

LEARNING OBJECTIVES 2-2
ORGANIZATION FORMS AVAILABLE 2-2
    Sole Proprietorships 2-2
    Partnerships 2-4
    Corporations 2-5
DEFINITION OF A CORPORATION 2-8
    Distinguishing Between a Partnership and a Corporation 2-8
    Distinguishing Between an Association and a Trust 2-9
    Disregard of the Corporate Entity 2-9
LEGAL REQUIREMENTS FOR FORMING A CORPORATION 2-10
TAX CONSIDERATIONS IN FORMING A CORPORATION 2-10
SECTION 351: DEFERRING GAIN OR LOSS UPON INCORPORATION 2-12
    The Property Requirement 2-13
    The Control Requirement 2-13
    Stock Requirement 2-17
    Effect of Sec. 351 on the Transferors 2-17
    Effect of Sec. 351 on Transferee Corporation 2-21
    Assumption of the Transferor's Liabilities 2-23
    Other Considerations in a Sec. 351 Exchange 2-25
CHOICE OF CAPITAL STRUCTURE 2-28
    Characterization of Obligations as Debt or Equity Capital 2-29
    Debt Capital 2-29
    Equity Capital 2-31
    Capital Contributions by Shareholders 2-32
    Capital Contributions by Nonshareholders 2-32
WORTHLESSNESS OF STOCK OR DEBT OBLIGATIONS 2-34
    Securities 2-34
    Unsecured Debt Obligations 2-35
CONTROVERSIAL ISSUE 2-36
    Obtaining Ordinary Loss Treatment for Advances to a Corporation 2-36
TAX PLANNING CONSIDERATIONS 2-37
    Avoiding Sec. 351 2-37

viii • Contents

      Obtaining an Ordinary Loss Deduction for Stock Losses   2-39
COMPLIANCE AND PROCEDURAL CONSIDERATIONS   2-39
      Reporting Requirements under Sec. 351   2-39
      Reasons for and Procedures to Obtain a Sec. 351 Ruling   2-40
PROBLEM MATERIALS   2-40
      Discussion Questions   2-40
      Problems   2-42
      Comprehensive Problem   2-46
      Case Study Problem   2-47
      Tax Research Problems   2-47

CHAPTER 3
The Corporate Income Tax   3-1

LEARNING OBJECTIVES   3-2
CORPORATE ELECTIONS   3-2
      Choosing a Calendar or Fiscal Year   3-2
      Accounting Methods   3-4
      General Formula for Determining the Corporate Tax Liability   3-5
COMPUTING A CORPORATION'S TAXABLE INCOME   3-6
      Differences Between Individual and Corporate Taxable Income   3-6
      Sales and Exchanges of Property   3-9
      Deductions   3-10
      Transactions Between a Corporation and Its Shareholders   3-22
      At-Risk Rules   3-23
      Passive Activity Limitation Rules   3-24
COMPUTING A CORPORATION'S INCOME TAX LIABILITY   3-24
      General Rules   3-25
      Personal Service Corporations   3-25
CONTROLLED GROUPS OF CORPORATIONS   3-26
      Why Special Rules Are Needed   3-26
      What Is a Controlled Group?   3-27
      Application of the Controlled Group Test   3-31
      Special Rules Applying to Controlled Groups   3-32
      Consolidated Tax Returns   3-32
COMPENSATION PLANNING FOR SHAREHOLDER-EMPLOYEES   3-34
      Advantage of Salary Payments   3-34
      Advantage of Fringe Benefits   3-35
      Limitation on Deductible Compensation Payments for Shareholder-Employees   3-35
TAX PLANNING CONSIDERATIONS   3-35
      Special Election to Allocate Reduced Tax Rate Benefits   3-35
      Using NOL Carryovers and Carrybacks   3-37
      Tax Planning to Avoid Controlled Group Status   3-38

COMPLIANCE AND PROCEDURAL CONSIDERATIONS   3-38
      Requirements for Filing and Paying Taxes   3-38
      Types of Tax Returns   3-38
      When the Return Must Be Filed   3-39
      Tax Return Schedules   3-39
      Estimated Taxes   3-42
PROBLEM MATERIALS   3-46
      Discussion Questions   3-46
      Problems   3-48
      Tax Form/Return Preparation Problem   3-53
      Case Study Problem   3-55
      Tax Research Problems   3-55

CHAPTER 4
Corporate Nonliquidating Distributions   4-1

LEARNING OBJECTIVES   4-2
DISTRIBUTIONS IN GENERAL   4-2
EARNINGS AND PROFITS (E&P)   4-3
      Current Earnings and Profits   4-3
      Distinction Between Current and Accumulated E&P   4-7
PROPERTY DISTRIBUTIONS   4-9
      Consequences of Property Distributions to Shareholders   4-9
      Consequences of Property Distributions to the Distributing Corporation   4-10
      Constructive Dividends   4-12
STOCK DIVIDENDS AND STOCK RIGHTS   4-14
      Tax-free Stock Dividends   4-15
      Tax-free Stock Rights   4-16
      Effect of Nontaxable Stock Dividends on the Distributing Corporation   4-17
      Taxable Stock Dividends and Stock Rights   4-17
STOCK REDEMPTIONS   4-17
      Effect of the Redemption on the Shareholder   4-18
      Attribution Rules   4-20
      Substantially Disproportionate Redemptions   4-21
      Complete Termination of the Shareholder's Interest   4-23
      Redemptions Not Essentially Equivalent to a Dividend   4-24
      Partial Liquidations   4-25
      Redemptions to Pay Death Taxes   4-27
      Effect of Redemptions on the Distributing Corporation   4-29
PREFERRED STOCK BAILOUTS   4-30
      Sec. 306 Stock Defined   4-31
      Dispositions of Sec. 306 Stock   4-31
      Redemptions of Sec. 306 Stock   4-32
      Exceptions to Sec. 306 Treatment   4-32
STOCK REDEMPTIONS BY RELATED CORPORATIONS   4-33
      Brother-Sister Corporations   4-33

Parent-Subsidiary Corporations 4-35
DISTRIBUTIONS OF STOCK AND SECURITIES OF A CONTROLLED CORPORATION 4-36
    Requirements of Sec. 355 4-38
    Tax Consequences to Shareholders and Security Holders 4-40
    Tax Consequences to the Distributing Corporation 4-43
CONTROVERSIAL ISSUES 4-44
    What Is a Complete Termination of Interest? 4-44
    What Is the Active Conduct of a Trade or Business? 4-45
TAX PLANNING CONSIDERATIONS 4-46
    Avoiding Unreasonable Compensation 4-46
    Bootstrap Acquisitions 4-47
    Timing of Distributions 4-48
COMPLIANCE AND PROCEDURAL CONSIDERATIONS 4-49
    Agreement to Terminate Interest under Sec. 302(b)(3) 4-49
PROBLEM MATERIALS 4-50
    Discussion Questions 4-50
    Problems 4-51
    Case Study Problem 4-57
    Tax Research Problems 4-57

CHAPTER 5
Other Corporate Tax Levies 5-1

LEARNING OBJECTIVES 5-2
THE CORPORATE ALTERNATIVE MINIMUM TAX 5-2
    The General Formula 5-2
    Definitions 5-3
    Tax Preference Items 5-3
    Adjustments to Taxable Income 5-5
    Disallowed Losses 5-7
    Adjusted Current Earnings (ACE) Adjustment 5-7
    Minimum Tax Credit 5-12
    Tax Credits and the AMT 5-12
SUPERFUND ENVIRONMENTAL TAX 5-14
PERSONAL HOLDING COMPANY TAX 5-15
    Personal Holding Company Defined 5-15
    Stock Ownership Requirement 5-15
    Passive Income Requirement 5-16
    Determining the PHC Penalty Tax 5-20
    Avoiding the PHC Designation and Tax Liability Through the Use of Dividend Distributions 5-21
    PHC Tax Calculation 5-24
ACCUMULATED EARNINGS TAX 5-25
    Corporations Subject to the Penalty Tax 5-25
    Proving a Tax Avoidance Purpose 5-26
    Evidence Concerning the Reasonableness of an Earnings Accumulation 5-26
    Determining the Accumulated Earnings Tax Liability 5-31
    Accumulated Earnings Tax Calculation 5-34
UNRELATED BUSINESS INCOME TAX 5-35
TAX PLANNING CONSIDERATIONS 5-36
    Special AMT Elections 5-36
    Eliminating the Adjusted Current Earnings Adjustment 5-37
    Avoiding the Personal Holding Company Tax 5-37
    Avoiding the Accumulated Earnings Tax 5-38
COMPLIANCE AND PROCEDURAL CONSIDERATIONS 5-38
    Alternative Minimum Tax 5-38
    Superfund Environmental Tax 5-39
    Personal Holding Company Tax 5-39
    Accumulated Earnings Tax 5-40
    Unrelated Business Income Tax 5-40
PROBLEM MATERIALS 5-40
    Discussion Questions 5-40
    Problems 5-43
    Tax Form/Return Preparation Problem 5-49
    Case Study Problem 5-49
    Tax Research Problems 5-50

CHAPTER 6
Corporate Liquidating Distributions 6-1

LEARNING OBJECTIVES 6-2
TAX CONSEQUENCES OF CORPORATE LIQUIDATIONS 6-3
    The Shareholder 6-3
    The Corporation 6-4
EFFECTS OF LIQUIDATING ON THE SHAREHOLDERS 6-5
    Definition of a Complete Liquidation 6-5
    General Liquidation Rules 6-5
    Liquidation of a Controlled Subsidiary Corporation 6-9
    Installment Obligations Received by a Shareholder 6-12
EFFECTS OF LIQUIDATING ON THE LIQUIDATING CORPORATION 6-13
    Recognition of Gain or Loss When Property Is Distributed in Redemption of Stock 6-13
    Recognition of Gain or Loss When Property Is Distributed in Retirement of Debt 6-17
    Expenses of the Liquidation 6-17
    Treatment of Net Operating Losses 6-18
    Tax Attribute Carryovers 6-18
DEEMED LIQUIDATION ELECTION 6-20
    Eligible Stock Acquisitions 6-20
    The Election 6-21
    Deemed Sale Transaction 6-22

Basis of the Assets After the Deemed Purchase 6-22
Tax Accounting Elections for the New Corporation 6-25
Liquidation of the Target Corporation 6-26
TAX PLANNING CONSIDERATIONS 6-28
Timing the Liquidation Transaction 6-28
Recognition of Ordinary Losses When a Liquidation Occurs 6-28
Using Sec. 332 to Obtain a Double Tax Exemption 6-29
Avoiding Sec. 332 in Order to Recognize Losses 6-30
COMPLIANCE AND PROCEDURAL CONSIDERATIONS 6-30
General Liquidation Procedures 6-30
Section 332 Liquidations 6-31
Section 338 Deemed Liquidations 6-31
Plan of Liquidation 6-31
PROBLEM MATERIALS 6-32
Discussion Questions 6-32
Problems 6-34
Case Study Problem 6-39
Tax Research Problems 6-40

CHAPTER 7
Corporate Acquisitions and Reorganizations 7-1

LEARNING OBJECTIVES 7-2
CHARACTERISTICS OF TAXABLE AND TAX-FREE TRANSACTIONS 7-3
Comparison of Taxable and Tax-Free Transactions 7-3
TAXABLE ACQUISITION TRANSACTIONS 7-5
Stock Acquisitions 7-5
Asset Acquisitions 7-6
TAX-FREE REORGANIZATIONS 7-7
Types of Reorganizations 7-7
TAX CONSEQUENCES OF REORGANIZATIONS 7-8
Target or Transferor Corporation 7-8
Acquiring or Transferee Corporation 7-9
Shareholders and Security Holders 7-10
ACQUISITIVE REORGANIZATIONS 7-14
Type A Reorganization 7-14
Type C Reorganization 7-21
Type D Reorganization 7-24
Type B Reorganization 7-26
Type G Reorganization 7-29
DIVISIVE REORGANIZATIONS 7-29
Type D Divisive Reorganization 7-29
Type G Divisive Reorganization 7-31
OTHER REORGANIZATION TRANSACTIONS 7-32
Type E Reorganization 7-32
Type F Reorganization 7-34
JUDICIAL RESTRICTIONS ON THE USE OF CORPORATE REORGANIZATIONS 7-34
Continuity of Proprietary Interest 7-35
Continuity of Business Enterprise 7-35
Business Purpose Requirement 7-36
Step Transaction Doctrine 7-37
TAX ATTRIBUTES 7-37
Assumption of Tax Attributes 7-37
Limitation on Use of Tax Attributes 7-38
TAX PLANNING CONSIDERATIONS 7-41
Why Use a Reorganization Instead of a Taxable Transaction? 7-41
Comparison of Consideration Used in Reorganizations 7-42
Avoiding the Reorganization Provisions 7-43
COMPLIANCE AND PROCEDURAL CONSIDERATIONS 7-44
Plan of Reorganization 7-44
Party to a Reorganization 7-44
Ruling Requests 7-44
Reporting Requirements 7-45
PROBLEM MATERIALS 7-45
Discussion Questions 7-45
Problems 7-47
Case Study Problems 7-53
Tax Research Problems 7-53

CHAPTER 8
Consolidated Tax Returns 8-1

LEARNING OBJECTIVES 8-2
SOURCE OF THE CONSOLIDATED TAX RETURN RULES 8-3
DEFINITION OF AN AFFILIATED GROUP 8-3
Requirements 8-3
Comparison with Controlled Group Definitions 8-4
CONSOLIDATED TAXABLE INCOME 8-6
Income Included in the Consolidated Tax Return 8-7
Affiliated Group Elections 8-8
Termination of the Affiliated Group 8-9
INTERCOMPANY TRANSACTIONS 8-11
Deferred Intercompany Transactions 8-11
Other Intercompany Transactions 8-16
DIVIDENDS RECEIVED BY GROUP MEMBERS 8-16
Elimination Procedure 8-16
Consolidated Dividends-Received Deduction 8-18
CONSOLIDATED CHARITABLE CONTRIBUTIONS DEDUCTION 8-19
NET OPERATING LOSSES (NOLs) 8-20

Contents • xi

  Current Year NOLs 8-20
  Carrybacks and Carryforwards of Consolidated NOLs 8-21
  Carryback of Consolidated NOL to Separate Return Year 8-22
  Carryforward of Consolidated NOL to Separate Return Year 8-24
  Special Loss Limitations 8-24
CONSOLIDATED CAPITAL GAINS AND LOSSES 8-28
  Section 1231 Gains and Losses 8-30
  Capital Gains and Losses 8-30
COMPUTATION OF THE AFFILIATED GROUP'S TAX LIABILITY 8-32
  Regular Tax Liability 8-32
  Corporate Alternative Minimum Tax Liability 8-33
CONSOLIDATED TAX CREDITS 8-34
  General Business Credit 8-34
  Foreign Tax Credit 8-35
TAX PLANNING CONSIDERATIONS 8-36
  Advantages of Filing a Consolidated Tax Return 8-36
  Disadvantages of Filing a Consolidated Tax Return 8-36
  Election Not to Defer Intercompany Gains and Losses 8-37
  100% Dividends-Received Deduction Election 8-37
  Estimated Tax Payments 8-37
COMPLIANCE AND PROCEDURAL CONSIDERATIONS 8-39
  The Basic Election 8-39
  Parent Corporation as Agent for the Affiliated Group 8-39
  Liability for Taxes Due 8-40
  Filing for NOL or Credit Refund 8-40
PROBLEM MATERIALS 8-41
  Discussion Questions 8-41
  Problems 8-43
  Tax Form/Return Preparation Problem 8-49
  Case Study Problem 8-50
  Tax Research Problems 8-50

CHAPTER 9
Partnership Formation and Operation 9-1

LEARNING OBJECTIVES 9-2
DEFINITION OF A PARTNERSHIP 9-2
  General and Limited Partnerships 9-3
OVERVIEW OF PARTNERSHIP TAXATION 9-4
  Taxation of Partnership Profits and Losses 9-4
  The Partner's Basis 9-5
  Partnership Distributions 9-6

TAX IMPLICATIONS OF FORMATION OF A PARTNERSHIP 9-6
  Contribution of Property 9-6
  Contribution of Services 9-12
  Syndication and Organizational Expenditures 9-14
PARTNERSHIP ELECTIONS 9-15
  Partnership Taxable Year 9-15
  Other Partnership Elections 9-19
PARTNERSHIP REPORTING OF INCOME 9-20
  Partnership Taxable Income 9-20
  Separately Stated Items 9-21
  Partnership Ordinary Income 9-22
PARTNER REPORTING OF INCOME 9-22
  Partner's Distributive Share 9-22
  Special Allocations 9-23
BASIS FOR PARTNERSHIP INTEREST 9-26
  Beginning Basis 9-26
  Effects of Liabilities 9-27
  Effects of Operations 9-29
LOSS LIMITATIONS 9-30
  At-Risk Loss Limitation 9-31
  At-Risk Rules and Current Distributions 9-32
  Passive Activity Limitations 9-33
TRANSACTIONS BETWEEN A PARTNER AND THE PARTNERSHIP 9-34
  Sales of Property 9-34
  Guaranteed Payments 9-35
FAMILY PARTNERSHIPS 9-37
  Capital Ownership 9-37
  Donor-Donee Allocations of Income 9-38
CONTROVERSIAL ISSUE 9-39
  Retroactive Allocation of Losses 9-39
TAX PLANNING CONSIDERATIONS 9-40
  Alternatives to Contributing Property 9-40
  Timing of Loss Recognition 9-40
COMPLIANCE AND PROCEDURAL CONSIDERATIONS 9-41
  Reporting to the IRS and the Partners 9-41
  IRS Audit Procedures 9-42
PROBLEM MATERIALS 9-43
  Discussion Questions 9-43
  Problems 9-44
  Tax Form/Return Preparation Problem 9-52
  Case Study Problem 9-53
  Tax Research Problems 9-54

CHAPTER 10
Special Partnership Issues 10-1

LEARNING OBJECTIVES 10-2
NONLIQUIDATING DISTRIBUTIONS 10-2
  Recognition of Gain 10-3
  Basis Effects of Distributions 10-4

xii • Contents

      Holding Period and Character of Distributed Property 10-6
NONLIQUIDATING DISTRIBUTIONS WITH SEC. 751 10-6
      Section 751 Assets Defined 10-6
      Exchange of Sec. 751 Assets and Other Property 10-8
TERMINATING AN INTERESET IN A PARTNERSHIP 10-11
      Liquidating Distributions 10-11
      Sale of a Partnership Interest 10-16
      Retirement or Death of a Partner 10-19
      Exchange of a Partnership Interest 10-22
      Abandonment of a Partnership Interest 10-22
      Gift of a Partnership Interest 10-23
      Income Recognition and Transfers of a Partnership Interest 10-23
      Termination of a Partnership 10-25
      Mergers and Consolidations 10-28
      Division of a Partnership 10-29
OPTIONAL BASIS ADJUSTMENTS 10-29
      Election to Make Basis Adjustments 10-30
      Optional Adjustments on Transfers 10-30
      Optional Adjustments on Distributions 10-35
      Special Adjustments on Distributions to Transferee Partners 10-38
TAX SHELTER PARTNERSHIPS 10-40
      Tax Shelters and Limited Partnerships 10-40
      Abusive Tax Shelters 10-40
      Publicly Traded Partnerships 10-41
TAX PLANNING CONSIDERATIONS 10-42
      Liquidating Distribution or Sale to Partners 10-42
COMPLIANCE AND PROCEDURAL CONSIDERATIONS 10-42
      Section 754 Election 10-42
      Section 732(d) Election 10-43
PROBLEM MATERIALS 10-44
      Discussion Questions 10-44
      Problems 10-45
      Case Study Problem 10-55
      Tax Research Problems 10-56

CHAPTER 11
S Corporations 11-1

LEARNING OBJECTIVES 11-2
S CORPORATION REQUIREMENTS 11-3
      Shareholder Requirements 11-3
      Corporate Requirements 11-4
ELECTION OF S CORPORATION STATUS 11-5
      Making the Election 11-5
      Termination of the Election 11-7
S CORPORATION OPERATIONS 11-11
      Taxable Year 11-11
      Accounting Method Elections 11-12
      Ordinary Income or Loss 11-12
      Special S Corporation Taxes 11-15
LIFO RECAPTURE TAX 11-18
RECAPTURE OF PREVIOUSLY CLAIMED INVESTMENT TAX CREDITS 11-18
TAXATION OF THE SHAREHOLDER 11-18
      Income Allocation Procedures 11-18
      Family S Corporations 11-20
      Loss and Deduction Pass-through to Shareholders 11-21
BASIS ADJUSTMENTS 11-25
      Basis Adjustments to S Corporation Stock 11-25
      Basis Adjustments to Shareholder Debt 11-26
S CORPORATION DISTRIBUTIONS 11-27
      Corporations Having No Earnings and Profits 11-27
      Corporations Having Accumulated Earnings and Profits 11-29
OTHER RULES 11-32
      Tax Preference Items and Other AMT Adjustments 11-32
      Transactions Involving Shareholders and Other Related Parties 11-33
      Fringe Benefits Paid to a Shareholder-Employee 11-34
CONTROVERSIAL ISSUES 11-35
      Second Class of Stock Requirement 11-35
TAX PLANNING CONSIDERATIONS 11-37
      Advantages of S Corporation Treatment 11-37
      Disadvantages of S Corporation Treatment 11-38
      Election to Allocate Income Based on S Corporation's Accounting Methods 11-39
      Increasing the Benefits from S Corporation Losses 11-39
      Passive Income Requirements 11-40
      Using an S Corporation When Liquidating 11-41
CONPLIANCE AND PROCEDURAL CONSIDERATIONS 11-42
      Making the Election 11-42
      Filing the Corporate Tax Return 11-42
      Estimated Tax Payments 11-43
      Administrative Rules 11-44
      Sample S Corporation Tax Return 11-45
PROBLEM MATERIALS 11-45
      Discussion Questions 11-45
      Problems 11-48
      Tax Form/Return Preparation Problem 11-53
      Case Study Problem 11-55
      Tax Research Problems 11-56

CHAPTER 12
The Gift Tax 12-1

LEARNING OBJECTIVES 12-2
CONCEPT OF TRANSFER TAXES 12-2

History and Purpose of Transfer Taxes 12-2
THE UNIFIED TRANSFER TAX SYSTEM 12-3
   Unified Rate Schedule 12-3
   Impact of Taxable Gifts on Death Tax Base 12-4
   Unified Credit 12-4
GIFT TAX FORMULA 12-4
   Determination of Gifts 12-5
   Exclusions and Deductions 12-6
   Gift-Splitting Election 12-6
   Cumulative Nature of Gift Tax 12-6
   Unified Credit 12-7
TRANSFERS SUBJECT TO THE GIFT TAX 12-8
   Transfers for Inadequate Consideration 12-8
   Statutory Exemptions from the Gift Tax 12-9
   Cessation of Donor's Dominion and Control 12-11
   Valuation of Gifts 12-13
   Gift Tax Consequences of Certain Transfers 12-15
EXCLUSIONS 12-18
   Amount of the Exclusion 12-18
   Present Interest Requirement 12-19
GIFT TAX DEDUCTIONS 12-20
   Marital Deduction 12-21
   Charitable Contribution Deduction 12-24
THE GIFT-SPLITTING ELECTION 12-25
COMPUTATION OF THE GIFT TAX LIABILITY 12-26
   Effect of Previous Taxable Gifts 12-26
   Unified Credit Available 12-27
COMPREHENSIVE ILLUSTRATION 12-27
   Background Data 12-28
   Calculation of Tax Liability 12-28
BASIS CONSIDERATIONS FOR A LIFETIME GIVING PLAN 12-28
   Property Received by Gift 12-29
   Property Received at Death 12-30
CONTROVERSIAL ISSUES 12-30
   Below Market Loans: Gift and Income Tax Consequences 12-30
   De Minimis Rules 12-31
TAX PLANNING CONSIDERATIONS 12-32
   Tax-Saving Features of *Inter Vivos* Gifts 12-32
   Negative Aspects of Gifts 12-33
COMPLIANCE AND PROCEDURAL CONSIDERATIONS 12-34
   Filing Requirements 12-34
   Due Date 12-34
   Gift-Splitting Election 12-35
   Short-Form Gift Tax Return 12-35
   Liability for Tax 12-35
   Determination of Value 12-35
   Statute of Limitations 12-36
PROBLEM MATERIALS 12-37
   Discussion Questions 12-37
   Problems 12-39
   Tax Form/Return Preparation Problems 12-42
   Case Study Problem 12-42
   Tax Research Problems 12-43

CHAPTER 13
The Estate Tax 13-1

LEARNING OBJECTIVES 13-2
ESTATE TAX FORMULA 13-2
   Gross Estate 13-2
   Deductions 13-4
   Adjusted Taxable Gifts and Tax Base 13-4
   Tentative Tax on Estate Tax Base 13-5
   Reduction for Post-1976 Gift Taxes 13-5
   Unified Credit 13-6
   Other Credits 13-6
THE GROSS ESTATE—VALUATION 13-6
   Date-of-Death Valuation 13-6
   Alternate Valuation Date 13-9
THE GROSS ESTATE—INCLUSIONS 13-10
   Comparison of Gross Estate with Probate Estate 13-10
   Property in Which the Decedent Had an Interest 13-10
   Dower or Curtesy Rights 13-11
   Transferor Provisions 13-11
   Annuities and Other Retirement Benefits 13-15
   Jointly Owned Property 13-16
   General Powers of Appointment 13-17
   Life Insurance 13-18
   Consideration Offset 13-19
   Recipient Spouse's Interest in QTIP Trust 13-20
DEDUCTIONS 13-21
   Debts and Funeral and Administration Expenses 13-21
   Losses 13-22
   Charitable Contribution Deduction 13-23
   Marital Deduction 13-24
COMPUTATION OF TAX LIABILITY 13-27
   Taxable Estate and Tax Base 13-27
   Tentative Tax and Reduction for Post-1976 Gift Taxes 13-27
   Unified Credit 13-28
   Other Credits 13-28
COMPREHENSIVE ILLUSTRATION 13-30
   Background Data 13-30
   Calculation of Tax Liability 13-31
LIQUIDITY CONCERNS 13-33
   Deferral of Payment of Estate Taxes 13-33
   Stock Redemptions to Pay Death Taxes 13-34
   Special Use Valuation of Farm Realty 13-35
GENERATION-SKIPPING TRANSFER TAX 13-35
TAX PLANNING CONSIDERATIONS 13-36
   Use of *Inter Vivos* Gifts 13-37
   Use of Exemption Equivalent 13-37
   What Size Marital Deduction Is Best? 13-37
   Use of Disclaimers 13-38
   Role of Life Insurance 13-39
   Qualifying the Estate for Installment Payments 13-39
   Where to Deduct Administration Expenses 13-40

xiv • Contents

      Flower Bonds   13-40
COMPLIANCE AND PROCEDURAL
  CONSIDERATIONS   13-40
      Filing Requirements   13-40
      Due Date   13-41
      Valuation   13-41
      Election of Alternate Valuation Date   13-41
      Documents to Be Included with Return   13-41
PROBLEM MATERIALS   13-42
      Discussion Questions   13-42
      Problems   13-43
      Comprehensive Problems   13-47
      Tax Form/Return Preparation Problems   13-48
      Case Study Problem   13-49
      Tax Research Problems   13-50

CHAPTER 14
Income Taxation of Trusts and Estates   14-1

LEARNING OBJECTIVES   14-2
BASIC CONCEPTS   14-2
      Inception of Trusts   14-2
      Inception of Estates   14-3
      Reasons for Creating Trusts   14-3
      Basic Principles of Fiduciary Taxation   14-4
PRINCIPLES OF FIDUCIARY ACCOUNTING   14-5
      The Importance of Identifying Income and
        Principal   14-5
      Effects of State Law or Terms of Trust
        Instrument   14-6
      Principal and Income—The Uniform Act   14-6
      Categorization of Depreciation   14-7
FORMULA FOR TAXABLE INCOME AND TAX
  LIABILITY   14-8
      Gross Income   14-9
      Deductions for Expenses   14-9
      Distribution Deduction   14-10
      Personal Exemption   14-11
      Credits   14-12
DISTRIBUTABLE NET INCOME   14-12
      Significance of DNI   14-12
      Definition of DNI   14-13
      Manner of Computing DNI   14-14
DETERMINING A SIMPLE TRUST'S TAXABLE
  INCOME   14-15
      Allocation of Expenses to Tax-Exempt
        Income   14-16
      Determination of DNI and the Distribution
        Deduction   14-17
      Tax Treatment for Beneficiary   14-17
      Short-Cut Approach to Proving Correctness of
        Taxable Income   14-18
      Effect of a Net Operating Loss   14-19
      Effect of a Net Capital Loss   14-19

COMPREHENSIVE ILLUSTRATION—
  DETERMINING A SIMPLE TRUST'S TAXABLE
  INCOME   14-20
      Background Data   14-20
      Trustee's Fee   14-20
      Distribution Deduction and DNI   14-21
      Trust's Taxable Income   14-22
      Categorizing a Beneficiary's Income   14-22
DETERMINING TAXABLE INCOME FOR COMPLEX
  TRUSTS AND ESTATES   14-22
      Determination of DNI and the Distribution
        Deduction   14-23
      Tax Treatment for Beneficiary   14-24
      Effect of a Net Operating Loss   14-28
      Effect of a Net Capital Loss   14-28
COMPREHENSIVE ILLUSTRATION—
  DETERMINING A COMPLEX TRUST'S TAXABLE
  INCOME   14-29
      Background Data   14-29
      Trustee's Fee   14-29
      Distribution Deduction and DNI   14-30
      Trust's Taxable Income   14-31
      Additional Observations   14-32
ACCUMULATION DISTRIBUTION RULES   14-32
      Purpose   14-32
      When Applicable   14-33
SECTION 644 TAX   14-34
      Purpose   14-34
      When Applicable   14-34
      Computation of the Tax   14-34
INCOME IN RESPECT OF A DECEDENT   14-35
      Definition and Common Examples   14-35
      Significance of IRD   14-36
GRANTOR TRUST PROVISIONS   14-38
      Purpose and Effect   14-38
      Revocable Trusts   14-39
      Clifford Trusts   14-39
      Post-1986 Reversionary Interest Trusts   14-40
      Retention of Administrative Powers   14-41
      Retention of Economic Benefits   14-41
      Control of Others' Enjoyment   14-42
TAX PLANNING CONSIDERATIONS   14-42
      Ability to Shift Income   14-43
      Timing of Distributions   14-43
      65-Day Rule   14-44
      Property Distributions   14-44
      Choice of Year-End for Estates   14-44
      Deduction of Administration Expenses   14-45
COMPLIANCE AND PROCEDURAL
  CONSIDERATIONS   14-45
      Filing Requirements   14-45
      Due Date for Return and Tax   14-46
      Section 644 Tax—Information About Grantor's
        Income   14-46
      Documents to Be Furnished to IRS   14-46
      Sample Simple and Complex Trust
        Returns   14-47
PROBLEM MATERIALS   14-47

Discussion Questions 14-47
Problems 14-48
Tax Form/Return Preparation Problems 14-51
Case Study Problem 14-52
Tax Research Problems 14-53

CHAPTER 15
U.S. Taxation of Foreign-Related Transactions 15-1

LEARNING OBJECTIVES 15-2
JURISDICTION TO TAX 15-2
TAXATION OF U.S. CITIZENS AND RESIDENT ALIENS 15-4
   Foreign Tax Credit 15-4
   Foreign-Earned Income Exclusion 15-8
   U.S. Citizens and Resident Aliens Employed in Puerto Rico and U.S. Possessions 15-14
TAXATION OF NONRESIDENT ALIENS 15-15
   Definition of Nonresident Alien 15-16
   Investment Income 15-16
   Trade or Business Income 15-18
TAXATION OF U.S. PERSONS DOING BUSINESS ABROAD 15-20
   Domestic Subsidiary Corporations 15-21
   Foreign Branches 15-21
   Foreign Corporations 15-21
   Controlled Foreign Corporations 15-25
   Special Foreign Corporation Forms 15-34
   Foreign Sales Corporations 15-34
   Domestic International Sales Corporations 15-39
   Possessions Corporations 15-40
TAX PLANNING CONSIDERATIONS 15-42
   Deduction Versus Credit for Foreign Taxes 15-42
   Election to Accrue Foreign Taxes 15-42
   Special Earned Income Elections 15-44
   Tax Treaties 15-45
   Special Resident Alien Elections 15-45
COMPLIANCE AND PROCEDURAL CONSIDERATIONS 15-46
   Reporting the Foreign Tax Credit 15-46
   Reporting the Earned Income Exclusion 15-47
   Filing Requirements for Aliens and Foreign Corporations 15-47
   FSC and DISC Filing Requirements 15-48
PROBLEM MATERIALS 15-48
   Discussion Questions 15-48
   Problems 15-50
   Tax Form/Return Preparation Problems 15-55
   Case Study Problem 15-55
   Tax Research Problems 15-56

CHAPTER 16
Administrative Procedures 16-1

LEARNING OBJECTIVES 16-2
ROLE OF THE INTERNAL REVENUE SERVICE 16-2
   Enforcement and Collection 16-2
   Interpretation of the Statute 16-3
   Organization of the IRS 16-3
AUDITS OF TAX RETURNS 16-3
   Percentage of Returns Audited 16-5
   Selection of Returns for Audit 16-5
   Alternatives for a Taxpayer Whose Return Is Audited 16-7
   Ninety-Day Letter 16-10
   Litigation 16-11
REQUESTS FOR RULINGS 16-12
   Information to Be Included in Taxpayer's Request 16-12
   Will the IRS Rule? 16-13
   When Rulings Are Desirable 16-14
DUE DATES 16-14
   Due Dates for Returns 16-14
   Extensions 16-15
   Due Dates for Payment of the Tax 16-15
   Interest on Tax Not Timely Paid 16-16
   Penalties 16-17
ESTIMATED TAXES 16-20
   Payment Requirements 16-20
   Penalty for Underpaying Estimated Taxes 16-21
   Exceptions to the Penalty 16-22
OTHER MORE SEVERE PENALTIES 16-23
   Negligence 16-23
   Substantial Understatement 16-24
   Civil Fraud 16-26
   Criminal Fraud 16-27
STATUTE OF LIMITATIONS 16-28
   General 3-Year Rule 16-29
   Six-Year Rule for "Substantial" Omissions 16-30
   When No Return Is Filed 16-31
   Other Exceptions to 3-Year Rule 16-31
   Refund Claims 16-32
LIABILITY FOR TAX 16-33
   Joint Returns 16-33
   Transferee Liability 16-35
TAX PRACTICE ISSUES 16-35
   Statements on Responsibilities in Tax Practice 16-35
   Statutory Provisions Concerning Tax Return Preparers 16-38
   Rules of *Circular 230* 16-39
   Other Penalties 16-40
CONTROVERSIAL ISSUE 16-40
   Concept of "Substantial Authority" 16-40
PROBLEM MATERIALS 16-41

Discussion Questions 16-41
Problems 16-43
Tax Research Problems 16-45

APPENDIX A
Tax Research Working Paper File A-1

APPENDIX B
Completed Tax Forms B-1

APPENDIX C
Comparison of Tax Attributes for C Corporations, Partnerships, and S Corporations C-1

APPENDIX D
Credit for State Death Taxes D-1

APPENDIX E
Actuarial Tables E-1

APPENDIX F
Glossary F-1

APPENDIX G
Index of Code Sections G-1

APPENDIX H
Index of Treasury Regulations H-1

APPENDIX I
Index of Government Promulgations I-1

APPENDIX J
Index of Court Cases J-1

Subject Index K-1

Preface

OBJECTIVES AND USE

These text materials are principally designed for use in a second course in federal taxation for undergraduate or graduate accounting students. A companion volume, entitled *Prentice Hall's Federal Taxation, 1992: Individuals,* has been published for use in the first course in federal taxation. The *Individuals* text may be used as a one-term survey course for undergraduate or graduate students. The Corporations, Partnerships, Estates, and Trusts text can then be used as a follow-up text in the second tax course to explore the taxation of various entity forms, the wealth transfer taxes, tax research, and tax administration.

We are especially pleased to again offer the *Prentice Hall's Federal Taxation, 1992: Comprehensive Volume.* The comprehensive text is designed for either a one- or two-term course for undergraduate or graduate students. Its content contains selected chapters and sections from the original two volumes.

A primary objective has been to provide a readable format without sacrificing a high level of technical content. This objective has been accomplished by including separate sections in each chapter for tax planning considerations, tax compliance and procedural considerations, and controversial issues, rather than including these materials in the main body of the text. We have also attempted to provide a more readable format by including minor exceptions in footnotes at the bottom of many pages. The text materials also include numerous examples to illustrate the concepts and technical rules that are discussed in the text.

The *Corporations, Partnerships, Estates, and Trusts* book is presented in the format of a mini-Masters of Taxation program. This book includes coverage of all of the major areas that are normally included in a Masters of Taxation program. These topics include: tax research, corporate taxation, partnership taxation, the wealth transfer taxes, income taxation of estates and trusts, international taxation, and tax administration. Adopters are provided with a wide variety of coverage, which permits them to select the topics they consider most appropriate for a second tax course.

UNIQUE FEATURES

Unique features of our text include the following:

- Chapter learning objectives which are highlighted and keyed to the text.

- The tax research chapter (Chapter 1) includes as an appendix a completed tax research file that permits the student to visualize the final product from a tax research assignment.
- The corporate taxation chapters are written using a life-cycle approach including (1) the formation of the corporation, (2) corporate operating activities, and (3) corporate liquidations, divisions, and reorganizations.
- A chapter is provided (Chapter 8) that examines the consolidated tax return concepts applicable to affiliated groups. Included is a completed consolidated Form 1120 tax return.
- A chapter is included (Chapter 15) that examines the U.S. tax rules that are applicable to individual and corporate taxpayers who conduct business abroad, as well as to individuals and corporations from abroad who conduct business in the United States.
- An appendix includes completed tax returns for a C corporation, a partnership, an S corporation, simple and complex trusts, the gift tax, and estate tax. Also included are forms for claiming the foreign tax credit and foreign earned income exlusion. All of these returns and forms are based on examples included in the body of the text or facts that are provided in the Instructor's Guide.
- A glossary of tax terms is included in an appendix. These terms are highlighted by bold type cross references in the text material. A full complement of indices by subject, code sections, regulations, government promulgations, and court cases is provided along with tax rate schedules.
- The text materials have been updated to incorporate changes made by the Revenue Reconciliation Act of 1990, and to reflect judicial and administrative changes in the Federal tax law.
- Each chapter includes discussion questions, problems, tax form and tax return preparation problems, case study problems, and tax research problems.
- Problem materials are identified and ordered by topic to facilitate student problem solving and to assist in the preparation of course syllabi.
- A special disk designation (shown at left) appears along side all chapter-ending problems that can be solved using Lotus 1-2-3 Template Software.
- Tax rate schedules for individuals, corporations, estates and trusts and the unified transfer tax system are provided on the inside front and back covers. Also included is information about the amount of the standard deduction, personal and special exemptions, and unified transfer tax credit.

NEW TO THIS EDITION

This year we are offering, for the first time ever in a federal taxation textbook, a unique instructional tool that the students should find invaluable. Six different kinds of marginal notes are provided to enrich the students' learning experience. These include:

- **Key Points**—emphasize those areas where students require repetition and reinforcement.
- **Typical Misconceptions**—identify those concepts that students are likely to

misunderstand, and help them to correct their thinking before they take a wrong approach.
- **Real World Examples**—provide facts and anecdotes about actual companies and real life strategies.
- **Additional Comments**—supporting comments which elaborate on the materials presented in the text.
- **Self-Study Questions**—questions for the student to think about. Each question is accompanied by a full solution. The student will obtain a reliable indicator of their understanding of the text material.
- **Historical Notes**—Offer more comprehensive understanding of the concepts by examining them in their historical context.

Turn to virtually any page in the text and you will notice one or more of these annotations. We are confident that students will find this material a valuable aid in their course preparation.

New to the three texts this year are topic reviews. Each chapter contains two to four topic reviews. A topic review is presented when a major area of topical coverage has been completed. This topic review permits students to organize their thoughts about the concepts presented about a topic before proceeding on to the next topic. Many of these topic reviews are in chart or tabular form.

More emphasis is being placed on oral and written communication by the various accounting professional organizations (e.g., American Institute of CPAs and Accounting Education Change Commission). Fifteen of the chapters in this volume contain a case study problem. The case study problem incorporates facts likely to be encountered in a tax practice situation. The student is required to consider a number of alternatives and present a written or oral solution to the problem. Most often this solution is presented in the form of a memorandum. Unlike the tax research problems, all case study problems can be solved with only the materials that are contained in the textbook.

One-hundred fifty new problems were added this year. All examples and problems have been rewritten to incorporate the current year (1991) and actual individual and entity names. This will eliminate some confusion which may have existed in prior editions.

In prior editions, a series of completed tax returns were provided in an appendix. A number of these tax returns were tied into examples presented in the text materials. This year additional facts have been provided for those returns not previously tied to the basic text material so that a faculty member can use all of the completed tax returns to explain various concepts contained in the text materials.

The ordering of the chapters has been changed slightly. Chapters 4 and 5 in the 1992 Edition have been reversed. The editors felt that it was necessary to cover certain dividend concepts prior to teaching the alternative minimum tax, personal holding company tax, and accumulated earning tax concepts. We hope that this reordering will enhance the students' understanding of these corporate tax concepts.

SUPPLEMENTAL MATERIALS

The text includes a full complement of supplementary and ancillary materials. Adopters are encouraged to use these materials to enhance their teaching effectiveness and the students' learning experience. The following aids are available for instructor and student use:

Instruction Aids

- **Prentice Hall Course Manager, free upon adoption**—This three-ring binder contains the textbook along with tabs and a sleeve for software disks, allowing the professor complete flexibility in course customization.
- **Instructor's Guide with Test Bank**—The perfect companion to the Prentice Hall Course Manager, this specially crafted Instructor's Guide includes: a sample syllabus for semester- and quarter-length courses, instructor outlines, test bank, and solutions to the tax return/tax form and tax research problems. This year the instructor outlines are available in ASCII computer files to enable faculty members to make their own modifications to the master outlines prior to using them in class without having to retype the entire outline. Also new this year is a cross-reference table which cross-references problems in the 1991 and 1992 Editions as well as indicates the nature of the change (if any) to the problems from the 1991 Edition.
- **Solutions Manual**—Prepared by the authors and thoroughly reviewed by the editors and a pool of graduate tax students, this volume includes solutions to the discussion questions, problems, comprehensive problems, and case study problems.
- **Solutions to Prentice Hall's Tax Practice Problems for Individuals, Corporations and Partnerships, 1992 Edition**—Contains completed forms to solve the Tax Practice Problems for both volumes.
- **Transparencies to Prentice Hall's Federal Taxation Series, 1992 Edition**—Approximately 100 transparencies to enrich the teaching experience.
- **Prentice Hall DataManager**—Unmatched by other computerized testing software, Prentice Hall DataManager is a state-of-the-art classroom management system designed to take the tedium out of running classes.

In addition, adopting professors are eligible to enroll in Prentice Hall's TAX INCENTIVES PROGRAM which entitles them to the following:

- **Newsletter Subscription**—Choose a free three-month subscription to one of the following: ACCOUNTANTS' WEEKLY TAX REPORT; PRENTICE HALL TAX LETTER; TAX RETURN PREPARER'S LETTER; TAX COURSE LETTER or TAX PROFESSIONALS' CASSETTE.
- **Tax Return Problems Update**—Because even annual revisions become outdated when the new tax rates and deductions go into effect, we prepare an updated tax form/return preparation problem solution set keyed into the PRENTICE HALL'S FEDERAL TAXATION series so that professors will have solutions tied into the most current tax forms.
- **Supplemental Tax Law Update**—Whenever major tax legislation is passed, we immediatley provide an updating supplement; available free in quantity for students.

Student Aids

Our foremost goal has been to provide students with a perspective that stresses readability, accuracy, and familiarity with technical aids to tax practice. The following student aids are curently available:

- **Study Guide**—This study guide is designed to give students a better understanding of the laws and concepts presented in the textbook through use of extensive cross-referencing to tables and figures in the textbook.

- **Prentice Hall's Tax Practice Problems for Corporations and Partnerships, 1992 Edition**—This practice set includes three comprehensive problems with all supporting IRS forms and instructions needed to file returns for a C Corporation, S Corporation, and Partnership. The tax practice problems are published annually in March.
- **Income Tax Applications Using Lotus 1-2-3**—This practical book/disk package integrates income tax concepts with a student tutorial on how to use the electronic spreadsheet, giving students the opportunity to simultaneously learn about numerous tax concepts and issues as they learn Lotus 1-2-3.
- **Free Blank Forms**—Selected IRS forms are available free in quantity for students.
- **Specimen Returns Books**—This booklet walks the students through the appropriate tax forms and schedules by presenting filled-in entries for a sample business. A book of problems relating to this return is also available.
- **Tax Tips for Graduates**—This booklet includes several hints designed to help the recent graduate pay the lowest possible tax.

SERVICE HOTLINE

To ensure that you are never more than a phone call away from information about our text and its extensive supplements package, Prentice Hall has installed a special ACCOUNTING AND TAXATION SERVICE HOTLINE. Keep this toll-free number on hand—it's your assurance of first-rate service: 800-227-1816.

ACKNOWLEDGMENTS

Our policy is to provide annual editions and to prepare timely updated supplements when major tax revisions occur. We are most appreciative of the suggestions made by outside reviewers for the 1992 Edition because these extensive review procedures have been valuable to the authors and editors during the revision process.

We wish to acknowledge the following reviewers, whose contributions over the past several years have helped shape the 1992 Edition:

Becky Andrews	Roane State Community College
John Beehler	University of Texas at Arlington
Ron Blasi	SUNY Buffalo
Rodger Bolling	Northern Illinois University
Ann Burstein Cohen	SUNY Buffalo
Julie Collins	University of North Carolina
Larry Cozort	Central Missouri State University
Nina Crimm	George Washington University
Shirley Dennis-Escoffier	University of Miami
Karen Fortin	University of Miami
Michael Gallagher	George Washington University
John Gardner	University of Wisconsin at LaCrosse
Larry Garrison	University of Missouri at Kansas City
Deborah Garvin	University of Florida

Howard Godfrey	University of North Carolina at Charlotte
Vance Grange	Utah State University
Patricia Janes	San Jose State University
John Karayan	California State University at Los Angeles
Ernest Larkins	Georgia State University
Andrew Laviano	University of Rhode Island
Brian Levinson	SUNY Binghamton
John McGowan	Saint Louis University
Ken Milani	University of Notre Dame
Thomas Pope	University of Kentucky
Steven Rice	University of Washington
David Ryan	Temple University
Kathleen Sinning	Western Michigan University
Paul Streer	University of Georgia
Charles Swenson	University of Southern California
Ella Ann Topham	University of Iowa
James Trebby	Marquette University
Joanne Turner	Rochester Institute of Technology
Mark Vogel	University of Denver
William Wallace	University of Mississippi
Richard White	University of South Carolina
Michael Whiteman	University of Massachusetts
Earl Zachry	University of Houston—Clear Lake

We are also grateful to the various graduate assistants, doctoral students, and colleagues who have reviewed the text and supplementary materials and checked solutions in order to maintain a high level of technical accuracy. In particular, we would like to acknowledge the following colleagues who assisted in the preparation of supplemental materials for this text:

Arthur D. Cassill	University of North Carolina at Greensboro
John J. Connors	University of Wisconsin-Milwaukee
Larry Cozort	Central Missouri State University
Deborah R. Garvin (Supplements Coordinator)	University of Florida
Debra M. Hopkins	University of Texas at Arlington
Ken Milani	University of Notre Dame
Cherie J. O'Neil	University of South Florida
Dave N. Stewart	Brigham Young University
Caroline D. Strobel	University of South Carolina

John L. Kramer
Lawrence C. Phillips

1 Tax Research

CHAPTER OUTLINE

LEARNING OBJECTIVES 1-2
OVERVIEW OF TAX
  RESEARCH 1-2
STEPS IN THE TAX RESEARCH
  PROCESS 1-3
IMPORTANCE OF THE FACTS
  TO THE TAX RESULTS 1-5
  Facts of Case Where Taxpayer
    Won 1-6
  Facts of Case Where Taxpayer
    Lost 1-8
  Comparison of the Facts of the
    Two Cases 1-11
  Ability to Design Factual
    Situation Favoring the
    Taxpayer 1-11

THE SOURCES OF TAX
  LAW 1-12
  The Legislative Process 1-12
  The Internal Revenue Code 1-13
  Regulations 1-15
  Judicial Decisions 1-17
  Administrative
    Interpretations 1-26
  Tax Treaties 1-28
  Tax Periodicals 1-28
TAX SERVICES 1-29
  Federal Taxes2d 1-29
  *Standard Federal Tax
    Reporter* 1-30
  Tax Coordinator 1-31
  Law of Federal Income Taxation
    (Mertens) 1-31

  Tax Management Portfolios 1-32
  *Bender's Federal Tax
    Service* 1-32
CITATORS 1-33
  *Commerce Clearing House
    Citator* 1-34
  *Prentice Hall Information
    Services Citator* 1-34
COMPUTERS AS A RESEARCH
  TOOL 1-39
SAMPLE WORK PAPERS AND
  CLIENT LETTER 1-40
PROBLEM MATERIALS 1-40
  Discussion Questions 1-40
  Problems 1-42
  Research Problems 1-45

> **LEARNING OBJECTIVES**
>
> *After studying this chapter, you should be able to*
>
> 1. Describe the steps in the tax research process
> 2. Explain how the facts affect the tax results
> 3. Enumerate the sources of tax law and understand the authoritative value of each
> 4. Use the tax services to research an issue
> 5. Use the citator to assess authorities
> 6. Prepare work papers and communications to clients

This chapter introduces the reader to the tax research process. The major focus is the sources of the "tax law" (i.e., the statutory and other authorities that constitute the federal tax laws) and the relative weights that are given to these sources. The steps in the tax research process are described, and particular emphasis is placed on the importance of the facts to the tax results. The chapter also describes how to use the citator and the most frequently used tax services.

The end product of the tax research process—written communication of the results to an interested party in the form of a client letter—is also discussed. This text uses a hypothetical set of facts to provide a comprehensive illustration of the research process. Sample work papers demonstrating how to document the results of the research efforts are included in Appendix A.

OVERVIEW OF TAX RESEARCH

Tax research is the process of solving a specific tax-related question on the basis of both tax law sources and the specific circumstances surrounding the particular situation. Sometimes this involves researching several issues. Tax research can also be aimed at determining tax policy. For example, policy-oriented research would determine the extent (if any) to which the amount of charitable contributions made would be likely to change if they were no longer deductible. This type of tax research is usually done by economists in order to assess the effect of actions by the government.

Tax research can also be conducted to determine the tax consequences of a particular action in a given set of circumstances. For example, client-oriented research would determine whether Smith Corporation could deduct a particular expenditure as a trade or business expense. This type of research is generally conducted by accounting and law firms for the benefit of their clients. Thus, for purposes of this book, only this type of tax research is considered.

Client-oriented tax research is performed in one of two contexts:

1. **Closed-fact situations:** The client contacts the tax advisor after a transaction has occurred or a question arises while the tax return preparer is preparing the client's tax return. Unfortunately, in such situations, the tax consequences can be costly because the facts cannot be restructured to obtain more favorable tax results.

Key Point
Closed-fact situations allow the tax advisor the least amount of flexibility. Because the facts are already established, the tax advisor must develop the best solution possible within certain predetermined constraints.

Example 1-1 ■

Key Point
Open-fact or tax-planning situations allow a tax advisor the flexibility to help structure the transaction to accomplish the client's objectives. In this type of situation, a creative tax advisor can often save taxpayers considerable tax dollars through effective tax planning. Of course, even the best tax plan must be tempered against the client's nontax objectives.

Tom advises Carol, his tax advisor, that on November 4, 1991, he sold land held as an investment for $500,000 cash. His basis in the land was $50,000. On November 9, 1991, Tom reinvested the sales proceeds in another plot of investment land costing $500,000. This is a closed-fact situation. Tom wants to know what are the amount and character of the gain (if any) he must recognize. Because the tax advisor's advice is solicited after the sale and reinvestment occur, the opportunity for tax planning is limited. The opportunity to defer taxes by using a like-kind exchange or an installment sale has been lost.

2. **Open-fact** or **tax-planning situations:** The client contacts the tax advisor before the transaction has been finalized. Sometimes, the tax advisor is even approached to discuss the available tax strategies before any particular transaction is decided upon. Tax-planning situations are generally more difficult and challenging because the tax advisor must keep in mind both the client's tax and nontax objectives. Most clients will not be interested in a transaction that minimizes their taxes if it is inconsistent with their nontax objectives. ■

Example 1-2 ■

Additional Comment
It is important to consider nontax objectives as well as tax objectives. In many situations, the nontax considerations outweigh the tax considerations. Thus, the plan that is eventually adopted by a taxpayer may not always be the best when viewed strictly from a tax perspective.

Diane seeks advice from Carol, her tax advisor, about how to minimize her estate taxes. Diane indicates she is a widow with three children and five grandchildren and at present has property valued at $10,000,000. This is an open-fact situation. Carol could advise Diane to leave all but a few hundred thousand dollars of her property to a charitable organization so that her estate would owe no estate taxes. Although this recommendation would minimize Diane's estate taxes, Diane would likely reject it. Diane probably wants her children and/or grandchildren to receive the majority of her assets. Thus, reducing estate taxes to zero is inconsistent with her other objectives. ■

STEPS IN THE TAX RESEARCH PROCESS

OBJECTIVE 1
Describe the steps in the tax research process

In both the open-fact and closed-fact situation, the tax research process consists of the following five basic steps.

1. Determine the facts.
2. Determine the issues (questions).
3. Determine which authorities are applicable.
4. Assess and evaluate the authorities and choose which to follow in situations where the authorities are in conflict.
5. Communicate your conclusions and recommendations to the client.

Additional Comment
The steps of tax research, as outlined on this page, also provide an excellent format for a written tax communication. For example, a good format for a client memo includes: (1) statement of facts, (2) identification of issues, (3) discussion of relevant authority, and (4) recommendations to the client of appropriate actions based on the results of the research.

Although the steps are listed in the preferred order, the tax research process is often circular. That is, it does not always proceed step-by-step from the first through the fifth steps. Figure 1-1 illustrates the steps in the process.

In a closed-fact situation, the facts are often self-evident. But, if one is researching the tax consequences in an open-fact context, a number of the facts have not yet occurred, and the tax advisor's task is to determine which facts are likely to result in a particular tax outcome. This goal is accomplished by reviewing the authorities, especially court cases, and denoting which facts accompanied a favorable outcome and which produced an unfavorable result. For example, if a client hopes to achieve ordinary loss treatment from the anticipated sale of several plots of land in the same

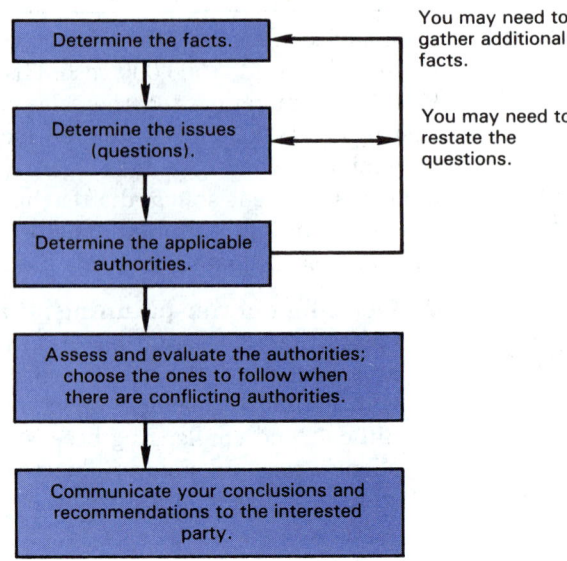

FIGURE 1-1   Steps in the Tax Research Process

year, the advisor might compare and contrast the facts that were present in cases dealing with this type of situation. The advisor should consider cases both won and lost by the taxpayer.

Often, the research deals with a "gray area" (i.e., an issue for which no clear-cut, unequivocally correct solution exists). In such situations, it is best to pursue the issue through a specifically tailored set of detailed questions. For example, in researching whether the taxpayer may deduct an ordinary loss instead of a capital loss, the tax advisor may need to investigate whether the presence of any investment motive precludes classifying a loss as ordinary.

Deciding upon the particular issues that need to be researched is one of the most challenging aspects of the research process. At times, the client may raise an explicit question, such as "May I deduct the costs of a winter trip to Florida recommended by my physician?" Often, however, the tax advisor must read the pertinent documents and other papers submitted by the taxpayer to formulate the issues for which an investigation is appropriate. Thus, one must have a fairly extensive knowledge of tax law in order to be able to determine which issues need to be researched.[1]

The following example illustrates how once the tax advisor becomes more familiar with tax law, he must request additional information from the client. Example 1-3 assumes that all of the tax authorities are in agreement.

Typical Misconception

Many taxpayers think that the tax law is all black and white. However, most tax research deals with gray areas. Ultimately, the ability, when confronted with tough issues, to develop strategies that favor the taxpayer and then to find relevant authority to support those strategies will make a tax advisor successful.

Example 1-3 ■

Mark calls his tax advisor Al and states that (1) he incurred a loss on renting his beach cottage during 1991 and (2) he wonders if he may deduct the loss. He also states that he, his wife, and their minor child occupied the cottage only 8 days during 1991.

Assume that this is the first time that Al has worked with the Sec. 280A vacation home rules. Upon reading Sec. 280A, Al learned that a loss is *not* deductible if

---

[1] Often supervisors will explain to a relatively new staff person the questions that they think are appropriate issues to be researched. Based upon the supervisor's past experience and knowledge, the specific authorities that the supervisor thinks will likely offer insight with respect to the tax consequences will also be indicated.

Mark used the cottage as a residence for personal purposes for longer than the greater of (1) 14 days or (2) 10% of the number of days the unit was rented at a fair rental value. He also learned that the property is *deemed* to be used by the taxpayer for personal purposes on any days on which it is used by any member of his family (as defined in Sec. 267(c)(4)). The Sec. 267(c)(4) definition of family members includes brothers, sisters, spouse, ancestors, or lineal descendants (i.e., children and grandchildren).

Mark's 8-day use is not enough days to make the rental loss nondeductible. However, Al must inquire about the number of days, if any, Mark's brothers, sisters, or parents used the property. (He already has information about use by Mark, his spouse, and his lineal descendants.) In addition, Al must find out how many days the cottage was rented to other persons at a fair rental value. Upon obtaining such additional facts, Al proceeds to determine how to calculate the deductible expenses. Al then reaches his conclusion concerning the deductible loss, if any, and communicates it to Mark. Assume that the passive activity and at-risk rules restricting a taxpayer's ability to deduct losses from real estate activities will not pose a problem for Mark. (See Chapter 8 of *Prentice Hall's Federal Taxation: Individuals* for a comprehensive discussion of this topic.) ∎

Key Point
When a written communication is impractical due to time or cost constraints, the tax advisor should, at a minimum, retain adequate notes or working papers to support the verbal communication provided to his client.

With respect to tax advisors' communication of their conclusions, many firms require conclusions to be communicated to their clients in writing. Members or employees of such firms can answer questions orally, but their oral conclusions must be followed up with a written communication. According to the American Institute of Certified Public Accountants' (AICPA's) *Statements on Responsibilities in Tax Practice,*

> Although oral advice may serve a client's needs appropriately in routine matters or in well-defined areas, written communications are recommended in important, unusual, or complicated transactions. In the judgment of the CPA, oral advice may be followed by a written confirmation to the client.[2]

IMPORTANCE OF THE FACTS TO THE TAX RESULTS

OBJECTIVE 2
Explain how the facts affect the tax results

Additional Comment
The Cox and Gardin cases are used to illustrate how slightly different facts can result in very different tax consequences. The two cases must be carefully read to identify the subtle differences.

At times, the statute is difficult to interpret, and a dilemma arises concerning the tax results. For example, one of the requirements a taxpayer must meet to claim a personal exemption for another person is to provide more than half of such person's support.[3] Neither the Code nor the Regulations define support. Consequently, if a taxpayer purchased a used automobile costing $5,000 for an elderly parent whose only source of income was $4,800 of social security, a question would arise with respect to whether the expenditure for the car constitutes support. The tax advisor would need to consult court cases and revenue rulings in order to find an interpretation of the word "support."

In other situations, the statutory language may be quite clear, but there might be a question as to whether the taxpayer's transaction falls within the realm of the facts necessary to obtain the favorable tax consequences. The following discussion of two actual cases focuses on the importance of facts in determining the tax results. In each

---

[2] AICPA, *Statements on Responsibilities in Tax Practice,* No. 8, "Form and Content of Advice to Clients," Sec. .06.
[3] Sec. 152(a).

case the taxpayer was arguing for a deduction of his travel expenses based upon the rationale that he incurred such costs while traveling "away from home" in his trade or business.

Facts of Case Where Taxpayer Won

Excerpts of the *David L. Cox* case appear below.[4] The Tax Court concluded that Mr. Cox was entitled to a deduction for his 1974 travel expenses. In the case, the taxpayer is referred to as the "petitioner" and the government as the "respondent."

FINDINGS OF FACT

Some of the facts have been stipulated and are found accordingly.

David L. Cox . . . and his wife, Dorothy K. Cox . . . filed a joint Federal income tax return for the calendar year 1974.

David L. Cox (hereinafter petitioner) is an electrician by trade. In 1970 petitioner accepted employment in Wilmington, North Carolina and moved his family from Jacksonville, Florida, where they had been living and petitioner had been working, to Wilmington, North Carolina. When petitioner initially came to Wilmington he worked for a cable television company and later began to work as an electrician on a plant that Davis Electrical Constructors, Inc. (Davis) was building for duPont near Wilmington, North Carolina. In December 1973, petitioner's work at the duPont plant near Wilmington was terminated and the superintendent of the project offered him a job with Davis in Florence, South Carolina.

In December 1973 petitioner began working on the job in Florence, South Carolina. When he took the job in Florence he was told that the electrical work on that project would be completed about July 1974. While petitioner was working in Florence, South Carolina his family continued to live in the home they had been living in since approximately 1970 in Wilmington, North Carolina.

Petitioner was told by an employee of Davis at the Florence, South Carolina project that there were jobs for electricians on a Virginia Electric Power Company plant being built by Brown and Root, Inc. in Virginia. In early February of 1974 petitioner contacted the superintendent of Brown and Root who was in charge of the electrical work on the plant in Virginia and was offered employment there. At the time of the offer petitioner was told that the work on the power plant would be completed July 1, 1975. Petitioner accepted the work in Virginia even though it was 300 miles from Wilmington since the project would last for approximately a year longer than the project at Florence was expected to last. In late 1973 and early 1974 work as an electrician on construction projects was difficult to obtain. Petitioner had no contract with respect to his employment by Brown and Root as an electrician on the power plant. Petitioner was not a member of a labor union.

When petitioner accepted the job in Virginia he considered the advisability of moving his family to a location near the Virginia site for the period of approximately 16 months that he was informed would be the maximum length of his employment on the power plant project. Petitioner considered Wilmington, North Carolina to be his home. At that time petitioner had two teenage daughters who were enrolled in school in Wilmington and active in church work there. He did not want to disrupt their lives by moving them near the job site in Virginia for a period of about 16 months. Therefore, petitioner's wife and two daughters remained in the home in Wilmington, North Carolina during the entire period of petitioner's employment in Virginia from March 1974 until July 1975. His employment with Brown and Root in Virginia was terminated in July of 1975 because of completion of the power plant project. Petitioner returned to Wilmington, North Carolina where he obtained employment on a construction project. Petitioner

---

[4] 1979 PH T.C. Memo ¶ 79,033, 38 TCM 136. In this and all other Tax Court cases, the **petitioner** is the person who originates the case—the taxpayer—and the government is the **respondent.** For an excellent discussion of how critical facts are for the outcome, see Ray M. Sommerfeld, et al., *Tax Research Techniques,* 3rd. Ed., Rev. (New York: AICPA, 1989), pp. 11-53.

continued to live in Wilmington and to work on the construction project there until March of 1976.

On their joint Federal income tax return for the calendar year 1974, petitioners claimed as an employee business expense a deduction of $3,825 as travel expenses and a deduction of $4,696 as expenses for food and lodging and incidental items while away from home in pursuit of a trade or business.

Respondent, in his notice of deficiency, disallowed $3,396 of the travel expense deduction claimed by petitioners and disallowed $4,275 of the claimed deduction for food and lodging while away from home. Respondent, in his notice of deficiency, explains each of these disallowances as being because the amounts did not constitute ordinary and necessary business expenses and because it has not been shown that the amounts were expended for the purposes designated. At the trial, respondent's counsel conceded that the amounts were expended by petitioner and that they were properly deductible if petitioner's employment in Virginia was considered temporary rather than indeterminate or indefinite.

OPINION

Section 162(a)(2) provides for a deduction for traveling expenses while away from home in the pursuit of a trade or business. It has long been settled that in order to be entitled to a deduction under this provision, the expenses incurred must be ordinary and necessary, incurred while away from home and incurred in the pursuit of a trade or business. . . . The only issue between the parties is whether petitioner was "away from home" within the meaning of section 162(a)(2).

As we pointed out in *Bochner v. Commissioner,* 67 T.C. 824 (1977), this and other courts have recognized that a taxpayer ordinarily is expected to maintain his home in the vicinity of his principal place of employment and, if for personal reasons he elects to maintain his residence in another location, his expenses of traveling to his place of employment and his expenses for food and lodging incurred at his place of employment are personal expenses and not deductible. Section 262. However, this rule is not applicable where the taxpayer's employment is temporary and of short duration, as distinguished from indefinite or indeterminate. . . . [It] has been held in a number of cases that the purpose of allowing the deduction of living expenses while a taxpayer is away from home is "to mitigate the burden of the taxpayer who, because of the exigencies of his trade or business, must maintain two places of abode and thereby incur additional and duplicate living expenses."

The cases involving the issue of whether a taxpayer's employment is temporary rather than indefinite or indeterminate are legion. However, no rule of thumb has been developed in these cases for ascertaining whether employment is temporary. Each case has been decided on the basis of its particular facts. Some of the facts that have been considered have been whether the employment was for a limited period and, if so, the duration of that period, the nature of the taxpayer's work and the reasonableness of the taxpayer's decision not to move his residence. Weighed in the light of the criteria laid down in the various cases, we conclude that petitioner's employment at the power plant in Virginia was temporary. The record is completely clear that petitioner knew the project would be completed by July 1, 1975, and therefore the maximum duration of his employment at the power plant in Virginia would be approximately 16 months. However, since petitioner had no contract with his employer and was not a member of a union, his employment might terminate before the project was completed if there was a reduction in the number of electricians employed at the project.

The record also shows that petitioner's family had been living for over 3 years in Wilmington, North Carolina and that petitioner viewed Wilmington as his home. His daughters were teenage and were well located in school in Wilmington and well adjusted to their community life there. Petitioner hoped to find employment in the Wilmington area upon completion of the power plant project in Virginia, and in fact, he did so.

Whether, under different circumstances, a period of 16 months might be considered sufficiently long as to reasonably expect that a taxpayer would move his home to the area of his work, we need not decide. . . . Under the facts of this particular case, we conclude that petitioner's employment at the power plant in Virginia was temporary.

> **Key Point**
> *Based on the facts in Cox, the Tax Court held that a time period as long as 16 months could be considered temporary. However, as evidenced in Gardin, under different facts the Tax Court held that a much shorter period of time was not considered temporary. Thus, in analyzing these two cases, a tax advisor would need to determine what other facts existed that caused the Tax Court to reach different conclusions.*

Decision will be entered for the petitioners.

Note that in the last paragraph, the court hinted that in a different factual setting it *might* conclude that 16 months was too long a time period for a taxpayer to be viewed as temporarily working away from home. That is, the court was commenting on how it might decide a case with different facts. Comments of a court on facts or an issue it does not have to rule on are referred to as *dictum*. In building an argument in favor of a particular tax result, a party may reference *dictum* as support for the argument. For example, another case may be litigated in which the taxpayer contends that he was away from home while working at a location for 16 months. The Internal Revenue Service (IRS) might cite the *dictum* from *Cox* and contend that the court should carefully examine the facts in deciding whether a deduction for travel-away-from-home expenses was justified in these circumstances. Not all such factual circumstances would survive the scrutiny.

Facts of Case Where Taxpayer Lost

Ronald L. Gardin lost his case dealing with the deductibility of his 1971 travel expenses.[5] The Tax Court held that Gardin did not incur such expenses while traveling away from home. Rather, his "tax home" was the city in which he paid the expenses.

FINDINGS OF FACT

Ronald L. and Cecelia A. Gardin are husband and wife. . . . At the time their petition was filed, they resided in Tucson, Ariz.

From 1966 to 1969, petitioner attended the University of Arizona in Tucson. He played varsity football there during the 1968 and 1969 seasons and was considered to be one of the best players on the team.

Petitioner's chances for success as a professional football player were affected by the fact that he was 25 years of age after his last year of college football, 3 or 4 years older than most players just out of college, was somewhat smaller than the average player in terms of height and weight, and had previously broken his leg. Nevertheless, in 1970 he was drafted by the Baltimore Colts. . . . In March of that year, he signed . . . standard player contracts with the Colts covering the 1970, 1971, and 1972 seasons. Besides the basic compensation, each contract provided that petitioner would earn bonuses on certain conditions. . . .

With a portion of the money received on the signing of these contracts, petitioners purchased a residence in Tucson.

In June 1970, petitioner traveled to Baltimore and began training with the Colts. He made the team, and played football for the Colts through the 1970 season. That season lasted until January 1971, when the Colts won the Super Bowl championship. Petitioner dropped a punt in that game. Petitioner played almost exclusively on the "special teams" and never made the starting team.

Cecelia Gardin remained in and around Tucson throughout 1970, except for short trips to Baltimore to visit her husband. In January 1971, petitioner returned to Tucson where he resided until he again went to the Colts' training camp in July 1971. At that time, his wife accompanied him to Baltimore and stayed there through September of 1971. At the commencement of training for the 1971 season, he felt that his position with the team was fairly secure, though later, during training, he found that he was given less desirable assignments and that he could not play well without the use of a hearing aid installed in his helmet.

Petitioner played for the Colts until September 26, 1971, at which time he was traded to the New England Patriots. The Colts assigned the rights in his contracts to the

---

[5] *Ronald L. Gardin,* 64 T.C. 1079 (1975).

Patriots on October 1, 1971. Petitioner traveled to the Patriots' franchise location in Needham Heights, Mass., immediately after the trade. His wife returned to Tucson where she resided for the rest of the year.

Petitioner considered the reputation of the Patriots at that time to be such that the trade jeopardized his future as a football player. Shortly after his arrival . . . he had a dispute with the team's head coach which led him to ask to be traded to another team. He felt he was being treated unfairly because of the coach's personal animosity toward him. The second or third week that he played for the Patriots, petitioner dropped two punts. . . . The next day the Patriots placed him on injured waivers, which meant that he could not play but was still under salary and could be reactivated at any time. He remained on injured waivers throughout the remainder of the season. . . . At the end of the season, he returned to Tucson.

Before the 1972 season, petitioner was traded again, the rights in his contract being assigned to the Pittsburgh Steelers. He attended the Steelers' training camp and played one regular season game with them before he was traded to the Miami Dolphins. Petitioner stayed with the Dolphins on the reserve list for the rest of the season and was released by them in December 1972. . . . He again returned to Tucson.

Petitioner engaged in a number of activities in Tucson when he was not playing football. He held jobs with a construction company and a department store in 1970 before attending training camp. From January to July 1971, he attended the University of Arizona part time, studying correctional administration. In connection with his studies, he took on-the-job training at. . . . a correctional institution for juveniles. He reported no income from this activity on his 1971 return.

Because of the local fame which he acquired as a star player for the University of Arizona and a member of the 1971 Super Bowl champions, petitioner was in some demand in Tucson as a promoter of athletic ventures. He was involved in the establishment of a boys' instructional sports camp during the 1971 off-season. This was conceived as a moneymaking enterprise, but was unsuccessful both in 1971 and in 1972, after which it was abandoned. At the same time, he engaged in discussions which in later years led to the formation of the Tucson Athletic Club. . . . Beginning in 1972, petitioner successfully solicited membership subscriptions for the club. Since his release by the Dolphins, petitioner has held various jobs in Tucson and has continued his education there.

The football teams which employed petitioner paid his living expenses only during training camp and while away from the franchise cities. The expenses here in issue, totaling $4,243, were living expenses incurred by petitioner while residing in Baltimore during August and September of 1971, and thereafter in Needham Heights until the middle of December 1971. None of the expenses were incurred by or on behalf of his wife.

OPINION

The parties have agreed that the expenses claimed by petitioner are deductible under section 162(a)(2) if they were incurred while he was "away from home in the pursuit of a trade or business." The question before us is: Where was petitioner's "home" within the meaning of section 162(a)(2) during 1971?

At the outset, the possibility of petitioner pursuing his chosen career in Tucson was nil—no professional football team was located in the area. . . . His other activities in Tucson during 1971 were minimal and at most constitute preparations for entering into business there at some future date. . . . It is thus apparent that Tucson cannot be considered petitioner's "home" for tax purposes during 1971.

We think it clear that, in respect of petitioner's employment with the Colts, Baltimore was his "home" for tax purposes during 1971 until his transfer to the Patriots at the end of September of that year. He had been employed by the Colts in 1970 under contracts covering 3 successive seasons. He had played for the Colts throughout the 1970 season, albeit on the "special teams" rather than as a regular player, and in the Super Bowl in January of 1971. In the summer of 1971, his employment by the Colts had 2 more years to run. He participated in the 1971 training sessions and in the early part of the regular season. We believe these specific objective facts are more significant in demonstrating a sufficient degree of permanence in his employment by the Colts than those relied upon by petitioner to show generally that his playing future was uncertain, such as his age, size, previous injuries, hearing difficulties, and playing assignments which he considered inferior or undesirable. Concededly, such latter factors imparted some aura of potential impermanence to petitioner's employment. But we do not believe that there was such a "quality of impermanence" in petitioner's employment by the Colts as to support the conclusion that "he could reasonably expect his employment to terminate within a fixed or short period of time." . . .

The fact that petitioner's employment with the Colts was terminated shortly after the start of the 1971 season is not enough retroactively to make his employment by the Colts for that season temporary. As a general rule, the permanent or temporary nature of employment is judged at the time it begins and is not changed by subsequent events. . . . We see nothing in the facts of this case to justify a departure from that rule. Nor does the fact that petitioner's employment by the Colts was seasonal justify the conclusion that such employment was temporary. . . .

With regard to amounts spent by petitioner in Needham Heights, the issue is less clear cut. Petitioner considered the trade to the Patriots unfavorable and, subjectively at least, this was a circumstance tending to undermine the probability that he would remain with that team for a long or indefinite period. Moreover, we recognize that, shortly *after* he joined the Patriots, certain circumstances arose which caused him to conclude that he might not remain with that team for the duration of his outstanding contract arrangements. On the other hand, petitioner clearly intended to make a go of his new position, and he was not traded to the Dolphins until after the 1971 season. Here again, we are not persuaded that, on the objective facts, petitioner's employment had that degree of impermanence which would justify characterizing it as "temporary."

Petitioner's exposure to being traded during his 3-year period of employment does not compel a decision for petitioners. The potentiality of transfer does not necessarily require that an employment be characterized as "temporary." . . . To hold otherwise would cause most players of professional sports to be engaged in a series of temporary employments, so that their living expenses at franchise locations would be deductible. We do not believe that Congress intended section 162(a)(2) to produce such a result.

. . . Even applying the somewhat modified test of determining "home" for tax purposes articulated by the Ninth Circuit Court of Appeals (to which an appeal from our decision herein would lie), we think that the facts, which we have found and analyzed, are sufficient to fit the standard of those cases that there was "a reasonable probability known to petitioner" that he would continue to be employed by the Colts and the Patriots during the 1971 season with the result that first Baltimore and then Needham Heights was his tax home during 1971. . . . In short, we are satisfied that petitioner's expenses in these two locations should be disallowed. . . .

This Court consistently held that a taxpayer should be expected to make his home in the vicinity of his permanent business or employment and that only the expenses of traveling from a home so situated are deductible as a business expense under section 162(a)(2). If for personal reasons he fails to move his home to the vicinity of his permanent business or employment, his expenses of traveling from the home are incurred for personal, not business, reasons and are not deductible.***

Petitioner's claimed deductions for living expenses must be disallowed. Accordingly, Decision will be entered for the respondent.

Under the *Golsen* rule (see page 1-24), the Tax Court follows opinions of the circuit courts to which the Tax Court decision in question would be appealable. Because of the *Golsen* rule, the Tax Court in *Gardin* followed decisions of the Ninth Circuit. It acknowledged the *Golsen* rule by stating, "Even applying the somewhat modified test of determining 'home' for tax purposes articulated by the Ninth Circuit Court of Appeals."[6] This language also illustrates that statutory interpretations may vary from one court to another.

Typical Misconception
In reading any Tax Court decision, it is important to understand the Golsen rule. This rule states that the Tax Court follows the opinions of the circuit court to which the particular decision is appealable. Since the Tax Court is a national court, Tax Court cases tried in different parts of the U.S. are appealable to different circuit courts. Thus, if conflicting precedents exist between circuits, the Tax Court can be forced into issuing inconsistent opinions in cases with identical facts.

---

[6] Ibid., at 1085.

Comparison of the Facts of the Two Cases

Table 1-1 provides a summary comparison of the two cases. Both taxpayers were married, but their occupations differed. Each contended that his tax home was in a city different from the one in which he was employed during the year in question. From 1970 through 1973, Mr. Cox was employed in Wilmington, North Carolina, the location that he contended was his tax home. Then he worked briefly in South Carolina prior to accepting employment in Virginia, where he incurred the expenses in question. At the time Mr. Cox accepted employment in Virginia, he knew that the maximum employment period there would be 16 months. He hoped to return to Wilmington for employment after the Virginia job ended.

Mr. Gardin contended that Tucson, Arizona, was his tax home. He, however, had not been employed in professional football there before he began his employment with the Baltimore Colts. Tucson, in fact, did not have a professional football team. Mr. Gardin signed a 3-year contract with the Colts.[7] Upon being traded to the Patriots, he intended to have a nontemporary relationship with that team.

Mr. Cox's wife and children remained in Wilmington, North Carolina, where they had lived for more than 3 years. His children were well settled into that community. Mrs. Gardin lived in Baltimore with her husband for 3 months during the year in question. She lived in Tucson the rest of the time.

The court allowed Mr. Cox to claim a travel-away-from-home deduction because it deemed his employment in Virginia to be temporary. On the other hand, Mr. Gardin's positions with the Colts and the Patriots were not viewed as temporary. Consequently, the court disallowed Mr. Gardin's deductions.

> **Typical Misconception**
> Many taxpayers believe tax practitioners spend most of their time simply preparing tax returns. Point out that designing factual situations that favor the taxpayer is one of the most important responsibilities of a tax advisor.

Ability to Design Factual Situation Favoring the Taxpayer

By using tax research, a taxpayer might be able to design the facts of a particular situation in a manner that should increase the likelihood of his expenses being deductible. For example, suppose a taxpayer anticipates working for several months in a different location and then returning to the city (City X) where he was formerly employed. The taxpayer would like to deduct both the expenses incurred at the new location and the cost of travel thereto. To do so, he must establish that City X is his tax home. Tax research reveals an IRS ruling that states that a taxpayer's tax home is City X if the following conditions are present:

1. The taxpayer performed part of his business in the vicinity of City X while living there.
2. Living expenses at City X are duplicated because business requires the taxpayer to be away.
3. The taxpayer has not abandoned the vicinity in which City X is located because members of the taxpayer's family reside in City X or the taxpayer often spends the night in City X.[8]

The ruling also states that if the taxpayer meets two out of the three tests, the IRS may deem City X to be the taxpayer's tax home, depending upon the facts and circumstances.

By meeting the three conditions described above, the taxpayer can practically guarantee the deductibility of his travel expenses and expenses incurred in the new

---

[7] The temporary or permanent nature of an employment relationship is determined as of the date the employment begins and is usually not altered by later developments.

[8] Rev. Rul. 83-82, 1983-1 C.B. 45.

TABLE 1-1 Summary Comparison of Facts in Cox and Gardin

Situation	Decision Cox	Gardin
Marital status	Married	Married
Occupation	Construction worker	Professional football player
Was employment prior to year in question in the same occupation in the location claimed as his tax home?	Yes	No
Before the fact, did employment in the new location appear to be of limited duration?	Yes	No
Did family remain at the claimed tax home for the entire period the taxpayer was away?	Yes	No
Did the taxpayer eventually return to employment in the same occupation at the location claimed as the tax home?	Yes	No

location. Some of the conditions may be undesirable from a nontax standpoint, however. For example, the taxpayer may not be able to afford to pay living expenses in two different locations or may prefer to move his family to the new location.

THE SOURCES OF TAX LAW

OBJECTIVE 3
Enumerate the sources of tax law and understand the authoritative value of each

Key Point
One of the reasons the tax law is so complex is that it comes from a variety of sources. This chapter highlights the three principal sources of the tax law: statutory, judicial, and administrative.

When tax advisors speak of "tax law," they generally refer to more than simply the tax statutes that are passed by Congress. For the most part, tax statutes (legislation) contain very general language. Congress is not capable of anticipating every type of transaction in which taxpayers might engage. Moreover, even if Congress could do so, it would not be feasible for the statute (known as the *Internal Revenue Code*) to contain details addressing the tax consequences of all such transactions.

Because of the general language contained in the statute, interpretations—both administrative and judicial—are necessary. Administrative interpretations include, for example, Treasury regulations, revenue rulings, and revenue procedures. Judicial interpretations consist of court decisions. The term *tax law* as used by most tax advisors encompasses administrative and judicial interpretations in addition to the statute. It also includes committee reports issued by the Congressional committees involved in the legislative process.

The Legislative Process

Chapter 1 of *Prentice Hall's Federal Taxation: Individuals* describes the legislative process. That process is summarized here as well. All tax legislation must begin in the House of Representatives. The committee responsible for initiating statutory changes dealing with taxation is the Ways and Means Committee. Once proposed legislation is approved by the Ways and Means Committee, it goes to the floor of the House for consideration by the full membership. Legislation approved by a majority vote in the

House then goes to the Senate, where it is considered by the Senate Finance Committee. The bill moves from the Finance Committee to the full Senate. Upon being approved by the Senate, the bill goes to the President for approval or veto, provided the House and Senate versions of the bill are in complete agreement. If the President signs the bill, it becomes law. If the President vetoes the bill, Congress can override the veto by a vote of at least two-thirds of the members of each house.

Often, the House and Senate versions are not in complete agreement. Whenever the two versions of a bill are not identical, the bill goes to a Conference Committee,[9] comprised of members of each house. One example of a discrepancy worked out by the Conference Committee arose in 1978. The issue involved was the preferential treatment of long-term capital gains. The House approved a provision for indexing the basis of capital assets. The Senate authorized a 70% long-term capital gain deduction. The Conference Committee agreed upon a compromise that increased the long-term capital gain deduction from 50% to 60% but did not ratify indexing an asset's basis.

Key Point

Committee Reports can be most helpful in interpreting new legislation because these reports indicate the intent of Congress. Due to the recent proliferation of tax legislation, Committee Reports play an even greater role in the administration of the tax law because the Treasury is often unable to draft the needed regulations in a timely manner.

Prior to embarking on drafting statutory changes, both the House of Representatives and the Senate often hold hearings at which various persons testify. Often the Secretary of the Treasury or another member of the Treasury Department offers extensive testimony. Generally persons testifying express their opinions concerning provisions that should or should not be enacted. The Government Printing Office publishes the statements made at the hearings.

Most major legislation is also accompanied by Committee Reports. These reports, which are published by the Government Printing Office as separate publications and appear in the *Cumulative Bulletin,* explain Congress's purpose in drafting legislation.[10] Because Committee Reports give clues to Congressional intent, they can be invaluable aids in interpreting the statute, especially in situations where there are no regulations concerning the statutory language in question.

Example 1-4 ■ In 1984 Congress enacted Sec. 7872 concerning the tax treatment of below-market interest rate loans. One subset of such rules applies to "gift loans," defined in Sec. 7872(f)(3) as "any below-market loan where the foregoing of interest is in the nature of a gift." The Conference Report elaborates on the transactions classified as gift loans as follows: "In general, there is a gift if property (including foregone interest) is transferred for less than full and adequate consideration under circumstances where the transfer is a gift for gift tax purposes. A sale, exchange, or other transfer made in the ordinary course of business . . . generally is considered as made for full and adequate consideration. A loan between unrelated persons can qualify as a gift loan."[11] This definition can be quite important to a tax advisor because it may be many months until the Treasury issues regulations that elaborate on an issue (e.g., proposed regulations were issued on the Sec. 7872(f)(3) definition ten months after the statute was enacted). Until such regulations are issued, this may be the only "authoritative" interpretation of the "gift loans" term that is available. ■

The Internal Revenue Code

The Internal Revenue Code (the Code), which constitutes Title 26 of the federal statutes, is the foundation of all tax law. First codified (i.e., organized into a single

---

[9] The size of the Conference Committee can vary. It is comprised of an equal number of members from the House and the Senate.

[10] The *Cumulative Bulletin* is described in the discussion of revenue rulings at page 1-27.

[11] H. Rept. No. 98-861, 98th Cong., 2d Sess., p. 1,018 (1984).

Typical Misconception

Not all of the contents of a tax statute are necessarily contained in the Code. For example, transition rules contained in new legislation are not usually included. Thus, tax advisors need to be prepared to refer to the actual statutes if questions arise pertaining to effective dates or transition rules of new legislation.

compilation of the internal revenue statutes) in 1939, the law was recodified in 1954. The Code was known as the Internal Revenue Code of 1954 until 1986, when its name was changed to the Internal Revenue Code of 1986. Whenever changes to the statute are approved, the old language is deleted and the new language added. Thus, the statutes are organized as a single document, and a researcher does not have to read through the applicable parts of all previous tax bills to find the most current law.

The Code contains provisions addressing income taxes, estate and gift taxes, employment taxes, alcohol and tobacco taxes, and other excise taxes. For purposes of organization, the Code (Title 26) is subdivided into subtitles, chapters, subchapters, parts, subparts, sections, subsections, paragraphs, subparagraphs, and clauses. Subtitle A contains the rules concerning income taxes, and Subtitle B focuses on estate and gift taxes. A set of provisions concerned with one general area generally constitutes a subchapter. For example, the topics of corporate distributions and adjustments and partners and partnerships appear in Subchapters C and K, respectively. Figure 1-2 presents the organizational scheme of the Code.

A section is the organizational category that tax advisors refer to most often. For example, they speak of "Sec. 351 transactions," "Sec. 306 stock," and "Sec. 1231 gains and losses." Although it is generally not important to differentiate between a section and a paragraph or a part, one must be familiar with the Code's organizational scheme in order to read and interpret it correctly. The language of the Code is replete with cross-referencing to titles, paragraphs, subparagraphs, etc.

Example 1-5 ■ Section 7701, a definitional section, begins by stating, "When used in this title . . ." and then lists a series of definitions. Thus, a definition in Sec. 7701 controls for all of Title 26—for purposes of the income tax, estate and gift tax, excise tax, etc. ■

Example 1-6 ■ Section 302(b)(3) allows taxpayers whose stock holdings are completely terminated in a redemption (i.e., an acquisition of stock from a shareholder by the issuing corporation) to receive capital gain treatment on the excess of the redemption proceeds over basis instead of ordinary income treatment on the entire proceeds.

Key Point

When attempting to read a provision in the Code, the tax advisor must understand the organization of a Code section. Example 1-6 shows that in order to properly understand Sec. 318, the tax advisor must understand how references to terms such as subsections and subparagraphs can limit the application of the particular phrase being examined.

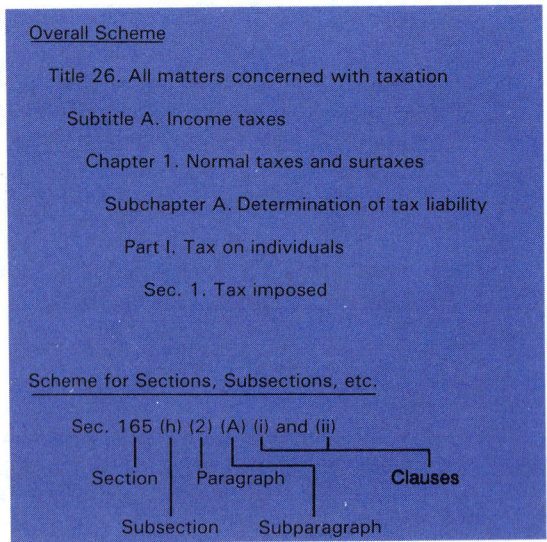

FIGURE 1-2 Organizational Scheme of the Internal Revenue Code

Section 302(c)(2)(A) states, "In the case of a distribution described in subsection (b)(3), section 318(a)(1) shall not apply if ..." Further, Sec. 302(c)(2)(C)(i) indicates, "Subparagraph (A) shall not apply to a distribution to any entity unless ..." Thus, in determining whether a taxpayer will receive capital gain treatment for a stock redemption transaction, a tax advisor must be able to locate various sections, subsections, paragraphs, and subparagraphs and interpret them.

Regulations

Key Point
Because the Treasury often has difficulty promulgating regulations in a timely manner, the previously discussed Committee Reports may provide the only authoritative information for a tax advisor attempting to understand recent legislation.

The Treasury Department (the Treasury) issues regulations as interpretations of the statute. The Regulations often give extensive examples complete with computations providing invaluable assistance in understanding the statutory language.

Because of the frequency of statutory changes, the Treasury Department is not always able to update the regulations in a timely manner. Consequently a tax advisor should consult the introductory note when referring to a regulation in order to determine when the regulation was adopted. If the regulation was adopted prior to the most recent statutory revision of this section, the regulation should be applied with the understanding that it does not reflect the most recent version of the statute.

Proposed, Temporary, and Final Regulations. Generally, regulations are first issued to the public in so-called proposed form. The public is given the opportunity to comment on them and suggest changes thereto. The persons most likely to issue comments are tax accountants and tax attorneys. In general, such comments are to the effect that the proposed treatment affects the taxpayer more adversely than warranted by Congressional intent. In drafting final regulations, Treasury usually takes the tax advisors' remarks into consideration and modifies the proposed regulations somewhat.

Proposed regulations are just that—proposed—and, consequently, do not have authoritative weight. They do, however, provide guidance concerning Treasury's interpretation of the statute. Thus, if the proposed regulations take a fairly protaxpayer approach, one can be sure that tax advisors will not attack them as being too lenient. Therefore, the final regulations will likely take the same approach as the proposed regulations. On the other hand, if Treasury receives considerable criticism about proposed regulations, it will likely adopt a more moderate approach in drafting the final regulations.

Self-Study Question
How long can a temporary regulation remain in effect?

Answer
According to the Technical Amendments and Miscellaneous Revenue Act of 1988, temporary regulations may remain effective for up to three years. Also, a temporary regulation must be issued concurrently as a proposed regulation.

Often Treasury issues temporary regulations soon after a major statutory change in order to give taxpayers and their advisors guidance with respect to procedural or computational matters. For example, in 1980 Congress essentially rewrote the law concerning the qualification for, and the tax results of, installment sales. In January 1981, Treasury issued temporary regulations interpreting the amended statute. Temporary regulations have the same authoritative value as final regulations.

Treasury drafts final regulations after the public has had time to comment on the proposed regulations. Most of the time, the final regulations differ at least slightly from the proposed version. As discussed under the next heading, final regulations have the same authoritative weight as the statute. Final regulations generally take effect retroactive to the effective date of the statutory language that they interpret.

Interpretative and Statutory Regulations. In addition to being classified as proposed, temporary, or final, regulations are categorized as interpretative or statutory. As the name implies, interpretative regulations merely make the statutory language easier to understand and apply. In addition, they may provide illustrations about how to perform certain computations. With respect to statutory (or legislative)

Typical Misconception

Regulations may be interpretative or legislative. Occasionally, Congress abdicates its rule-making authority to the Treasury. In such cases, the regulations are elevated from being an interpretation of the statute to being treated as the statute.

regulations, in comparison with interpretative regulations, Congress has delegated its rule-making duties to Treasury. Because Congress feels it lacks the expertise necessary to deal with a highly technical matter, it instructs Treasury to write the rules in the form of statutory regulations.

Whenever the statute contains language such as "The Secretary shall prescribe such regulations as he may deem necessary" or "under regulations prescribed by the Secretary," the regulations interpreting such a statute are legislative regulations. Perhaps the consolidated tax return regulations are the most dramatic example of statutory regulations. In Sec. 1502 Congress delegated to Treasury the responsibility for writing regulations that would enable the tax liability of a group of affiliated corporations filing consolidated returns to be determined. As a requirement of electing the privilege of filing a consolidated tax return, the corporations must consent to following the consolidated return regulations.[12] By consenting to follow the regulations, a taxpayer generally gives up the chance to argue that provisions in the regulations should be overturned by the courts.

Authoritative Weight. The presumption is that final regulations have the same authoritative weight as the statute. Section 7805 expressly grants to the Secretary of the Treasury the right to prescribe regulations for enforcing the tax laws and to prescribe the extent, if any, to which the regulations are to be applied without retroactive effect. Despite the presumption concerning the validity of final regulations, occasionally taxpayers can successfully argue that a regulation is invalid and, consequently, should not be followed.

A court will not conclude that an interpretative regulation is invalid unless, in its opinion, such regulation is "unreasonable and plainly inconsistent with the revenue statutes."[13] The courts are less likely to conclude that a legislative regulation is invalid because Congress has abdicated its rule-making authority with respect to such regulations to Treasury. However, the courts have held that legislative regulations were invalid in situations where the courts concluded the regulations exceeded the scope of the power delegated to Treasury,[14] were contrary to the statute,[15] or were unreasonable.[16]

Key Point

The older a regulation becomes, the less likely a court will invalidate the regulation. The "legislative reenactment" doctrine holds that if a regulation did not reflect the intent of Congress, lawmakers would have changed the statute in subsequent legislation to obtain their desired objectives.

In assessing the validity of regulations, courts often apply the **legislative reenactment doctrine.** Under this doctrine, a regulation is deemed to have received Congressional approval if such regulation was finalized many years earlier and during the interim period Congress did not amend the statutory language that the regulation addresses. In other words, if Congress had deemed the regulatory language to be an inappropriate interpretation, it could have changed the words of the statute to achieve a different result. Congress's failure to change the wording in the Code signifies its approval of the regulatory provisions.

Citations. Citations to regulations are relatively easy to understand. One or more numbers appear before a decimal place, and several numbers follow the decimal place. The numbers immediately following the decimal place indicate the Code section being interpreted. The numbers preceding the decimal place indicate the general subject matter of the regulation. Numbers that frequently appear before the decimal place and their general subject matter are as follows:

---

[12] Sec. 1501.
[13] *CIR v. South Texas Lumber Co.,* 36 AFTR 604, 48-1 USTC ¶ 5922 (USSC, 1948). In *U.S. v. Douglas B. Cartwright, Executor,* 31 AFTR 2d 73-1461, 73-1 USTC ¶ 12,926 (USSC, 1973), the Supreme Court concluded that a regulation dealing with the valuation of mutual fund shares for estate and gift tax purposes was invalid.
[14] *Panama Refining Co. v. U.S.,* 293 U.S. 388 (USSC, 1935).
[15] *M. E. Blatt Co. v. U.S.,* 21 AFTR 1007, 38-2 USTC ¶ 9599 (USSC, 1938).
[16] *Joseph Weidenhoff, Inc.,* 32 T.C. 1222 (1959).

Number	General Suject Matter
1	Income tax
20	Estate tax
25	Gift tax
301	Administrative and procedural matters
601	Procedural rules

The number appearing immediately to the right of the decimal place refers to the Code section being interpreted. The number following the Code section number indicates the number of the regulation, such as the fifth regulation. There is no relationship between this number and the subsection of the Code being interpreted. An example of a citation to a final regulation is

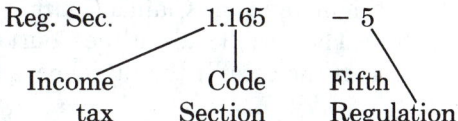

Citations to proposed or temporary regulations are in the same format. They are referenced as Prop. Reg. Sec. or Temp. Reg. Sec.

According to its caption, the topic of Reg. Sec. 1.165-5 is worthless securities, a topic addressed in subsection (g) of Code Sec. 165. Section 165 itself refers to losses. Parenthetical information following the caption to this regulation indicates that this regulation was last amended December 5, 1972 by Treasury Decision (T.D.) 7224. Section 165(g) was last revised in 1971.

When referencing a regulation, the researcher should "fine tune" the citation as much as possible to indicate the precise wording that provides the basis for his conclusion. An example of such a detailed citation is Reg. Sec. 1.165-5(i), Ex. 2(i), which refers to the first portion of Example 2 that is contained in the ith portion of the fifth regulation interpreting Sec. 165.

Judicial Decisions

Judicial decisions constitute important sources of tax law. Judges are unbiased persons who decide the appropriate tax result for a given set of facts or the proper interpretation of ambiguous language in the statute. Judges, like other persons, do not always agree on the tax consequences; therefore, tax advisors must often reach their conclusions against the background of conflicting judicial authorities. For example, a district court decision may differ from a Tax Court decision, or different circuit courts may have disagreed on an issue.

Typical Misconception
The three trial courts are sometimes referred to as the "triers-of-fact." Thus, the original trial courts, not the appellate courts, delineate the relevant facts to be considered in a tax case.

Overview of the Court System. With respect to tax matters, there are three trial courts—the U.S. Tax Court, the U.S. Claims Court, and U.S. District Courts. The taxpayer may begin litigation in any of the three. Precedents of the various courts are an important factor in a taxpayer's decision process of where to begin litigation (see page 1-26). Another important influence is the timing of the cash flow to pay the deficiency. If the taxpayer wants to litigate either in a U.S. District Court or in the U.S. Claims Court, he must first pay the additional tax that the IRS contends is due. The taxpayer then files a claim for refund, which the IRS will deny. This denial must be followed by a suit for obtaining a refund of the taxes. If the taxpayer wins the refund suit, he receives a refund of the taxes in question plus interest thereon. If the taxpayer begins litigation in the Tax Court, however, payment of the deficiency need

Self-Study Question

What are some of the factors that should be considered when deciding in which court to initiate the litigation of a tax case?

Answer

(1) Each court's published precedent pertaining to the issue, (2) desirability of a jury trial, (3) tax expertise of each court, and (4) whether the tax deficiency has already been paid.

not occur until the case has been decided. If the taxpayer loses in the Tax Court, he must pay the deficiency plus any interest and penalties.[17] A taxpayer who thinks that a jury trial would be especially favorable should litigate in a U.S. District Court, the only place where a jury trial is possible.

Regardless of which party loses at the trial court level, such party can appeal the decision. Appeals from Tax Court and U.S. District Court decisions are made to the Court of Appeals for the taxpayer's circuit (i.e., geographical area). There are 11 numbered circuits plus the circuit for the District of Columbia. The map in Figure 1-3 denotes which states lie in the various circuits. California, for example, is in the Ninth Circuit. Instead of saying the "Court of Appeals for the Ninth Circuit," one generally says the "Ninth Circuit." All decisions of the U.S. Claims Court are appealable to one court—the Court of Appeals for the Federal Circuit—irrespective of the taxpayer's geographical location.[18] The only cases that the Federal Circuit hears are those that originate in the Claims Court.

The party losing at the Court of Appeals level can request that the Supreme Court hear the case. If the Supreme Court agrees to consider the issue, it issues a **writ of**

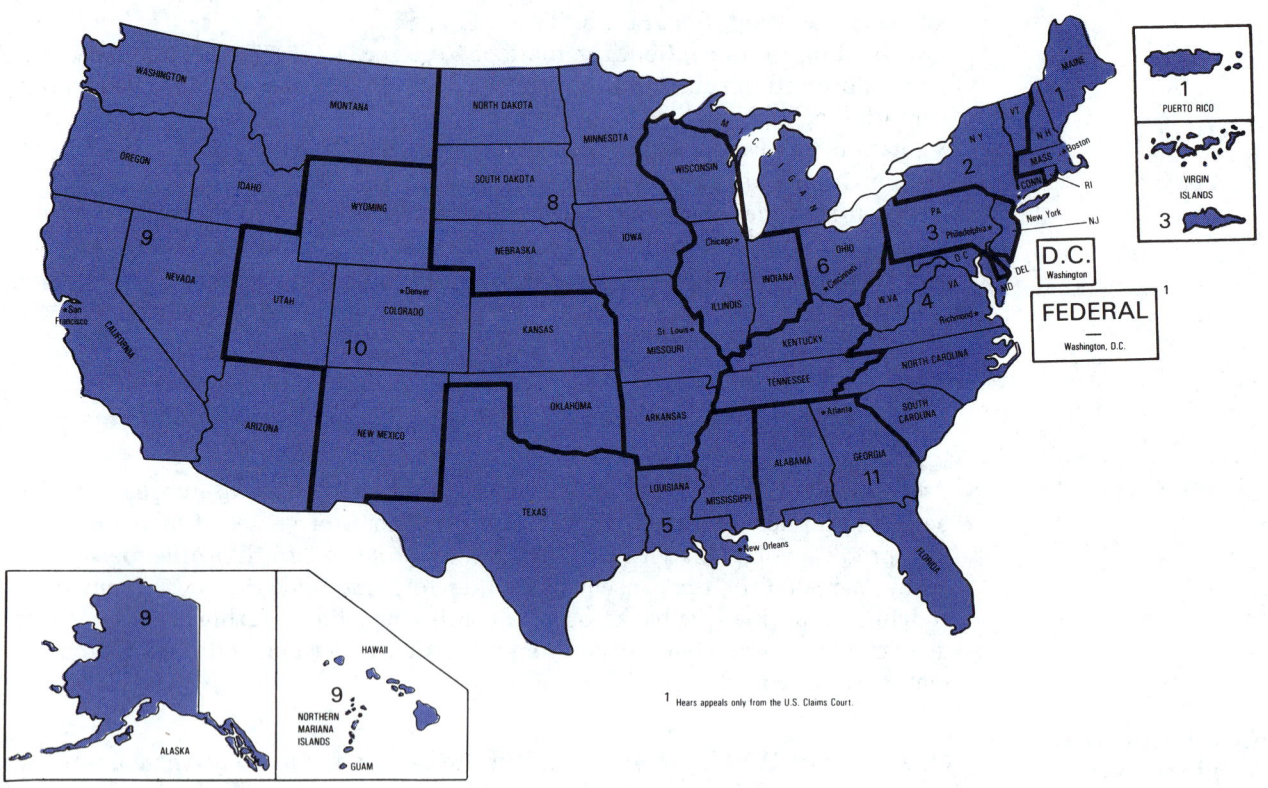

FIGURE 1-3 Map of the Geographical Boundaries of the Circuit Courts of Appeal
Source: The Federal Reporter, Second Series (West Publishing Co., 1989).

---

[17] Revenue Procedure 84-58 (1984-2 C.B. 501) provides procedures for taxpayers to make remittances in order to stop the running of interest on deficiencies. This action is more important now that the deduction for personal interest has been eliminated.

[18] Prior to the restructuring of the Court of Claims in 1982, the only possible appeal was to the Supreme Court.

certiorari.[19] In a given year, the Court hears only about six to ten tax cases. Figure 1-4 provides an overview of the court system with respect to tax matters.

The U.S. Tax Court. The U.S. Tax Court originated in 1942 as a successor to the Board of Tax Appeals. It is a court of national jurisdiction that hears cases dealing only with tax matters. Regardless of a taxpayer's state of residence, all litigated Tax Court cases end up in the same court. There are 19 Tax Court judges, including one chief judge.[20] The President, with the consent of the Senate, appoints the judges for 15 years and may reappoint them for an additional term. The judges periodically travel to various major cities to hear cases. At present, the Tax Court hears cases in approximately 100 cities. Only one judge hears a particular case.

The Tax Court issues both regular and memorandum (memo) decisions. The chief judge decides whether each opinion is to be published as a memo or regular decision. Generally, the first time the Tax Court decides a particular legal issue, its decision appears as a **regular decision. Memo decisions** usually deal with some factual variation on a matter for which the interpretation of the law was decided in an earlier case. Regular and memo decisions have the same precedential value.

At times the chief judge determines that a particular decision deals with a very important matter that the entire Tax Court should have a chance to consider. In such a situation, the words "reviewed by the court" will appear at the end of the majority decision. If there are any concurring or dissenting opinions, they will appear after the opinion of the majority.[21]

Other language sometimes appearing at the end of a Tax Court decision is *"Entered under Rule 155."* These words signify that the court has reached a decision

Key Point
Since the Tax Court deals only with tax cases, the Tax Court presumably has a higher level of tax expertise than do other courts. Tax Court judges are appointed by the President in part, due to their considerable tax experience.

Key Point
If a particular case is considered important enough, the chief judge will instruct the other 18 judges to review the case. In those situations in which a case is considered by the entire court, the phrase "reviewed by the court" is inserted immediately following the text of the majority opinion. Consequently, a reviewed decision provides an opportunity for Tax Court judges to express their dissenting opinions.

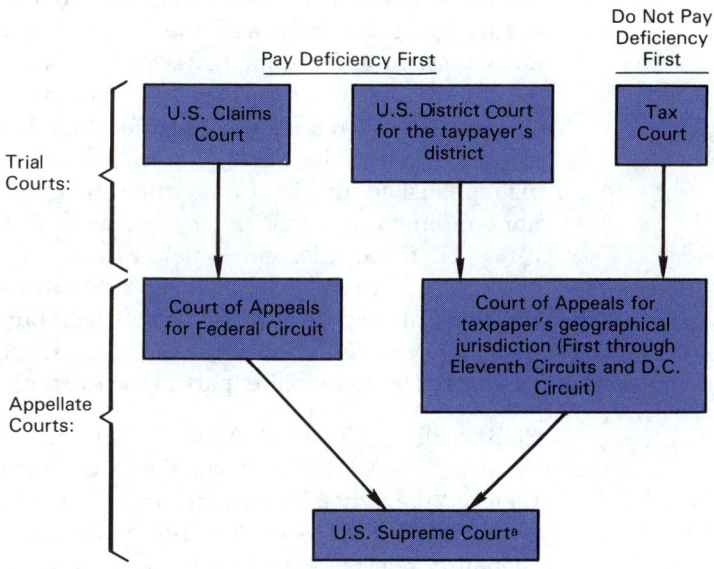

ªCases are heard only if the Supreme Court grants a writ of certiorari.

FIGURE 1-4 Overview of Court System—Tax Matters

---

[19] In issuing a writ of certiorari, the Supreme Court denotes its granting of an appellate review.
[20] The Tax Court's membership was expanded from 16 to 19 in 1981.
[21] A judge who issues a concurring opinion agrees with the basic outcome of the majority's decision but not with its rationale. A judge who issues a dissenting opinion believes that the majority decided upon an inappropriate outcome.

Self-Study Question

What are some of the advantages of the small cases procedure of the Tax Court?

Answer

The small cases procedure allows a taxpayer the advantage of having his "day in court" without the expense of an attorney. But, if the taxpayer loses, the disadvantage is that the decision cannot be appealed.

Typical Misconception

Taxpayers often get confused about the types of court decisions to which the IRS applies its acquiescence-policy. The only cases to which the IRS will consider publishing an acquiescence or nonacquiescence are those "regular" Tax Court decisions that the government loses. Since the vast majority of Tax Court cases are won by the government, the acquiescence policy actually applies to a small number of cases.

---

concerning the appropriate tax treatment of an issue but it has left the computation of the exact amount of the deficiency to the two litigating parties.

SMALL CASES PROCEDURE. The Tax Court has a special policy concerning small cases. Taxpayers have the option of having their cases heard under the **small cases procedure** if the amount in question for a particular year does not exceed $10,000.[22] Such procedures are less formal than the regular Tax Court procedures, and taxpayers can appear without an attorney.[23] The cases are heard by special commissioners instead of by one of the 19 Tax Court judges. For the losing party, a disadvantage of the small case procedure is that the decision cannot be appealed. The opinions in the small cases are not published and have no precedential value.

ACQUIESCENCE POLICY. Years ago the IRS adopted the policy of announcing whether it agreed or disagreed with Tax Court cases decided in favor of the taxpayer. This policy is known as the **acquiescence policy.** If the IRS wants to announce that it agrees with a Tax Court decision, it acquiesces to the decision. If it wishes to go on record as disagreeing with a decision, it issues a nonacquiescence to such decision. The acquiescence policy extends to regular Board of Tax Appeals and Tax Court decisions only.[24] The IRS does not, however, make a formal statement, an acquiescence or nonacquiescence, to every regular decision decided in favor of a taxpayer.

The IRS's decision to acquiesce or nonacquiesce has important implications for taxpayers. For example, suppose the IRS has nonacquiesced to a particular decision, and another taxpayer in similar circumstances files a return that adopts the Tax Court position. If the taxpayer's return is audited and the examining agent discovers that the taxpayer's return was prepared on the basis of the Tax Court holding rather than the nonacquiescence statement, the agent must argue that the taxpayer owes more tax. Because an acquiescence or nonacquiescence statement is binding on the agent, about the only way the taxpayer can prevail is by litigation. If the IRS acquiesces to a decision, however, the implication is that the IRS will no longer oppose the taxpayer's position on this issue.

When the IRS issues an acquiescence or nonacquiescence, information to this effect appears in the weekly *Internal Revenue Bulletin* (I.R.B.). Such information is also published in the *Cumulative Bulletin* (C.B.) for the period in which the announcement was made.[25] If the case dealt with more than one issue, the acquiescence or nonacquiescence may extend to only one issue. Sometimes the IRS acquiesces "in result only," meaning that it agrees with the ultimate outcome (for example, an expenditure is deductible) but not with the court's rationale. The *Cumulative Bulletin,* by way of footnotes, contains details about whether the IRS's acquiescence is complete, partial, or in result only.

PUBLISHED OPINIONS AND CITATIONS. Regular decisions of the Tax Court are published by the Government Printing Office in a bound volume known as the *Tax Court of the United States Reports.* Soon after a decision is made public, it is also published by Maxwell Macmillan/Prentice Hall Information Services Division (hereafter referred to as Prentice Hall Information Services) and Commerce Clearing

---

[22] Sec. 7463. The $10,000 limitation on the amount in dispute includes penalties but excludes interest.

[23] Taxpayers can represent themselves in regular Tax Court proceedings also, even though they are not an attorney. In situations where taxpayers represent themselves, the words *pro se* appear after their name.

[24] Board of Tax Appeals decisions can serve as precedent for current Tax Court decisions, although it is less likely than in prior years. It is also less likely that the IRS will acquiesce or nonacquiesce to a Board of Tax Appeals decision today.

[25] *Internal Revenue Bulletins* and the *Cumulative Bulletin* are described in the discussion of revenue rulings on p. 1-27.

The Sources of Tax Law • 1-21

House in their looseleaf reporters of Tax Court decisions. An official citation to a Tax Court decision is as follows:[26]

J. Simpson Dean, 35 T.C. 1083 (1961).

The information in the citation indicates that this case appears on page 1083 in Volume 35 of the official *Tax Court of the United States Reports* and that the case was decided in 1961. When a decision is first made public, however, it is impossible to know the page of the official reporter on which the opinion begins. Therefore, each new decision is assigned a case number which appears as part of the citation. An example of a citation to a relatively recent decision is

Lucky Stores, Inc., 92 T.C. ——— No. 75 (1989).

The blank space indicates that the page number is unknown. This case is the seventy-fifth case that appears in Volume 92 of the *Tax Court of the United States Reports;* it is a 1989 decision. When the bound volume was published, the case appeared on page 1151. Thus, after the publication of the bound volume, the citation became

Lucky Stores, Inc., 92 T.C. 1151 (1989).

Regular decisions of the Board of Tax Appeals were published by the Government Printing Office in the *United States Board of Tax Appeals Reports* from 1924-1942. A reference to a Board of Tax Appeals case can be cited as follows:

J. W. Wells Lumber Co. Trust A, 44 B.T.A. 551 (1941).

This case is printed in Volume 44 of the *United States Board of Tax Appeals Reports* at page 551. It is a 1941 decision.

If the IRS has acquiesced or nonacquiesced to a regular Tax Court or Board of Tax Appeals decision, information concerning the IRS's action should appear as part of the citation. At times the IRS's announcement may not occur until several years after the date of the court decision. An example of a citation involving an acquiescence is as follows:

Estate of John A. Moss, 74 T.C. 1239 (1980), *acq.* 1981-1 C.B. 2.

The case appears at page 1239 of Volume 74 of the *Tax Court of the United States Reports* and the acquiescence is reported on page 2 of Volume 1 of the 1981 *Cumulative Bulletin.* The IRS acquiesced to this 1980 decision in 1981.

A citation to a decision to which the IRS has nonacquiesced is as follows:

Warren Jones Co., 60 T.C. 663 (1973), *nonacq.* 1980-1 C.B. 2.

The case appears in Volume 60 of the *Tax Court of the United States Reports* on page 663. The nonacquiescence is reported on page 2 of Volume 1 of the 1980 *Cumulative Bulletin.* The IRS nonacquiesced to this 1973 decision in 1980.

Tax Court memorandum decisions are not published by the Government Printing Office. The decisions are available in bound form from Prentice Hall Information Services in *PH T.C. Memorandum Decisions* and from Commerce Clearing House in

> **Key Point**
> Once the IRS has acquiesced to a Tax Court position, it generally will not litigate the same issue again. The IRS can, however, change its mind and revoke a previous acquiescence or nonacquiescence. References regarding acquiescences or nonacquiescences to Tax Court decisions can be found in the citators.

---

[26] In a Tax Court case only the plaintiff (taxpayer) is listed. The defendant is understood to be the Commissioner of Internal Revenue and sometimes is not shown in the citation. In cases litigated outside the Tax Court, the plaintiff is listed first and the defendant second. In our footnotes and text for cases outside of the Tax Court the Commissioner of Internal Revenue is listed as *CIR.*

Typical Misconception
To have access to all Tax Court cases, a tax advisor must refer to two different publications. The regular opinions are found in the Tax Court of the United States Reports published by the Government Printing Office, and the memorandum decisions are published in bound form by both PH and CCH.

CCH Tax Court Memorandum Decisions. In addition, soon after an opinion is completed, it is published in loose-leaf form by the two publishers. Following are the citations to a Tax Court memorandum decision.

Edith G. McKinney, 1981 PH T.C. Memo ¶ 81,181, 41 TCM 1272.

McKinney is reproduced in Prentice Hall Information Service's 1981 *PH T.C. Memorandum Decisions* reporter at paragraph 81,181, and in Volume 41, page 1272, of Commerce Clearing House's *Tax Court Memorandum Decisions.* The 181 in the PH citation denotes that the case is the Tax Court's 181st memorandum decision of 1981.

U.S. District Courts. Each state has at least one U.S. district court, and more populous states have more than one. Each district court is a separate entity and is free to reach its own decision, subject to the precedential constraints discussed later (see pages 1-24 through 1-26). Many different types of cases—not just tax cases—are heard in this forum. A district court is the only forum in which the taxpayer has an opportunity for a jury trial. Depending upon the particular taxpayer and the circumstances involved, a jury trial might or might not be perceived as beneficial.[27]

District court decisions are officially reported in the *Federal Supplement* (cited as F. Supp.) published by West Publishing Co. Some decisions are not officially reported. They are referred to as **unreported decisions.** Decisions by U.S. district courts on the topic of taxation are also published by Prentice Hall Information Services and Commerce Clearing House in secondary reporters that include only tax-related cases. The Prentice Hall Information Services reporter is called *American Federal Tax Reports* (cited as AFTR),[28] and the Commerce Clearing House reporter is known as *U.S. Tax Cases* (cited as USTC). Even though a case is not officially reported, it may nevertheless be published in the AFTR and USTC. An example of a citation to a U.S. district court decision is as follows:

Margie J. Thompson v. U.S., 429 F. Supp. 13, 39 AFTR 2d 77-1485, 77-1 USTC ¶ 9343 (D.C. Pa., 1977).

Key Point
A variety of ways exist to properly cite judicial cases. A cite, at a minimum, must contain the following information: (1) the name of the case, (2) the reporter that contains the case along with both a volume and page (or paragraph) number, (3) the year the case was decided, and (4) the court that decided the case.

In the example above, the citation to the *Federal Supplement* is referred to as the **primary cite.** The case appears on page 13 of Volume 429 of the *Federal Supplement.* **Secondary cites** are to Volume 39 of the second series of the AFTR, page 77-1485 (meaning page 1485 in the volume containing 1977 cases) and to Volume 1 of the 1977 USTC at paragraph 9343. The parenthetical information denotes that the case was decided by a district court in Pennsylvania in 1977. Because some judicial decisions have greater value as precedents (i.e., a Supreme Court decision versus a District Court decision), it is useful to the reader to know which court decided the case.

U.S. Claims Court. The U.S. Claims Court is another trial court that addresses tax matters. It is a court with nationwide jurisdiction. Originally this trial court was named the U.S. Court of Claims (cited as Ct. Cl.), and its decisions were appealable to the Supreme Court only. In a restructuring, effective as of October 1, 1982, the court was renamed the U.S. Claims Court (cited as Cl. Ct.), and its decisions became appealable to the Circuit Court of Appeals for the Federal Circuit.

---

[27] Taxpayers will likely prefer to have a jury trial if they think that a jury will be sympathetic to their circumstances.

[28] The *American Federal Tax Reports* (AFTR) comes in two series. The first series is cited as "AFTR." The second series, which includes decisions published after 1957, is cited as "AFTR 2d." The *Thompson* decision cited as an illustration of a District Court decision is from the second *American Federal Tax Reports* series.

The Sources of Tax Law • 1-23

Typical Misconception
The U.S. Claims Court handles any claims (including suits to recover federal income taxes) against the U.S. government. Unlike the Tax Court, which travels to various cities across the United States, the U.S. Claims Court usually hears cases only in Washington, D.C.

At present, U.S. Claims Court decisions are reported officially in the *Claims Court Reporter,* a reporter published by West Publishing Co. since 1982.[29] An example of a citation for a U.S. Claims Court decision appears below.

Benjamin Raphan v. U.S., 3 Cl. Ct. 457, 52 AFTR 2d 83-5987, 83-2 USTC ¶ 9613 (1983).

The *Raphan* case appears in Volume 3 of the *Claims Court Reporter* at page 457. Secondary cites are to Volume 52, page 83-5987 of the AFTR, second series, and to Volume 2 of the 1983 USTC at paragraph 9613.

Circuit Court of Appeals. Trial court decisions are appealable by the losing party to a circuit court of appeals. The applicable circuit is a function of where the litigation originated. Generally, if the case began in the Tax Court or a U.S. district court, the case is appealable to the circuit for the taxpayer's residence as of the date of the appeal. In the case of a corporation, the case is appealable to the circuit where the corporation's principal place of business is located. As mentioned above, the Federal Circuit now handles all appeals of cases originating in the U.S. Claims Court.

Key Point
Either the taxpayer or the government can appeal a tax case to the circuit court of appeals in which the trial court is geographically located. The U.S. is divided into 13 circuits: 11 numbered circuits, the circuit for the District of Columbia, and the Federal Circuit for the U.S. Claims Court.

There are 11 geographical circuits designated by numbers, the circuit for the District of Columbia, and the Federal Circuit. A map of the circuits and their jurisdictions appears in Figure 1-3. The 11 numbered circuits and the D.C. circuit hear appeals of persons or firms from their locality. In October 1981, the Eleventh Circuit was created by moving Alabama, Georgia, and Florida from the Fifth to the new Eleventh Circuit. The Eleventh Circuit voluntarily adopted the policy that it will follow as precedent all decisions made by the Fifth Circuit during the time the states presently constituting the Eleventh Circuit were part of the Fifth Circuit.[30]

Example 1-7 ■ The Eleventh Circuit first faced a particular issue in 1990; the case concerns a Florida taxpayer. In 1970 the Fifth Circuit had ruled on this issue in a case involving a Louisiana taxpayer. Because Florida was part of the Fifth Circuit in 1970, under the policy adopted by the Eleventh Circuit, it will follow the Fifth Circuit's earlier decision. If the Fifth Circuit's decision had been rendered in 1982—after the creation of the Eleventh Circuit—the Eleventh Circuit would not have been bound by the Fifth Circuit's decision. ■

As the later discussion of precedential value points out, different circuits may reach different conclusions with respect to the same issue.

Circuit court of appeals decisions—regardless of the topic (e.g., civil rights, securities law, taxation, etc.)—are reported officially in the *Federal Reporter, Second Series* (cited as F.2d) published by West Publishing Co. The *Federal Reporter, Second Series* is the primary citation. In addition, tax decisions of the circuit courts appear in the *American Federal Tax Reports* and *U.S. Tax Cases.* Below is an example of a citation to a decision by a circuit court.

Horace B. Rickey, Jr. v. U.S., 592 F.2d 1251, 43 AFTR 2d 79-1023, 79-1 USTC ¶ 9323 (5th Cir., 1979).

---

[29] Prior to the creation of the U.S. Claims Court (and the *Claims Court Reporter*), the decisions of the U.S. Court of Claims were reported in either the *Federal Supplement* (F.Supp.) or the *Federal Reporter, Second Series* (F.2d). The *Federal Supplement* was used as the primary reference for the U.S. Court of Claims from 1932 through January 19, 1960. From January 20, 1960 to October 1982, these decisions were reported in the *Federal Reporter, Second Series.*

[30] *Bonner v. City of Prichard,* 661 F.2d 1206 (11th Cir., 1981).

The *Rickey* case appears on page 1251 of Volume 592 of the *Federal Reporter, Second Series*. It is also reported in Volume 43, page 79-1023 of the AFTR, second series, and in Volume 1, paragraph 9323, of the 1979 USTC. Parenthetical information indicates that the Fifth Circuit decided the case in 1979.

Supreme Court. Whichever party loses at the appellate court level can request that the Supreme Court hear the case. The Supreme Court, however, hears very few tax cases. Unless the circuits are divided on the proper treatment, or the issue is deemed to be of great significance, the Supreme Court probably will not hear the case.[31] Supreme Court decisions are "the law of the land." As a practical matter, a Supreme Court ruling on an interpretation of the Code has the same effect as if the interpretative language was added to the Code. If Congress does not approve of the Court's interpretation, it can amend the statutory language to achieve a result to the contrary. From time to time Congress has reacted to Supreme Court decisions by amending the Code.[32] If a Supreme Court decision dealing with the constitutionality of a particular statute concludes that it is unconstitutional, the provision is ineffective and must be revised.

All Supreme Court decisions, regardless of the subject matter, are published in the *United States Supreme Court Reports* (U.S.), by the Government Printing Office, the *Supreme Court Reporter* (S.Ct.), by West Publishing Co., and the *United States Reports, Lawyers' Edition* (L. Ed.) by Lawyer's Co-Operative Publishing Co. In addition, the AFTR and USTC reporters published by Prentice Hall Information Services and Commerce Clearing House, respectively, contain Supreme Court decisions concerned with taxation. An example of a citation to a Supreme Court case appears below.

U.S. v. Maclin P. Davis, 397 U.S. 301, 25 AFTR 2d 70-827, 70-1 USTC ¶ 9289 (1970).

According to the primary cite, this case appears at Volume 397, page 301, of the *United States Supreme Court Reports.* It is also reported at Volume 25, page 70-827, of the AFTR, second series, and at Volume 1, paragraph 9289, of the 1970 USTC.

Table 1-2 provides a summary of how court decisions, revenue rulings, revenue procedures, and other administrative interpretations should be cited. Primary citations are to the reporters published by West Publishing Co. or the Government Printing Office, and secondary citations are to the AFTR and USTC reporters.

Precedential Value of Various Decisions.

TAX COURT. The Tax Court is a court of national jurisdiction. Consequently, in general it rules uniformly for all taxpayers, regardless of their geographical location. It follows Supreme Court decisions and its own earlier decisions. It is not bound by cases decided by the U.S. Claims Court or a U.S. district court, even if the district court is the one for the taxpayer's jurisdiction.

In 1970 the Tax Court voluntarily adopted what has become known as the *Golsen* rule.[33] Under the *Golsen* rule, the Tax Court departs from its general policy of ruling uniformly for all taxpayers and instead follows decisions to the contrary made by the court of appeals to which the case in question is appealable. Stated differently, the

---

[31] *Vogel Fertilizer Co. v. U.S.,* 49 AFTR 2d 82-491, 82-1 USTC ¶ 9134 (USSC, 1982), is an example of a case the Supreme Court decided to hear to settle the controversy existing in the courts. The Fifth Circuit, the Tax Court, and the Court of Claims had reached one interpretation, whereas the Second, Fourth, and Eighth Circuits had ruled to the contrary.

[32] For an example of a situation where Congress enacted legislation to achieve a result contrary to that of a Supreme Court decision, see *U.S. v. Marian A. Byrum,* 30 AFTR 2d 72-5811, 72-2 USTC ¶ 12,859 (USSC, 1972).

[33] The *Golsen* rule is based on the decision in *Jack E. Golsen,* 54 T.C. 742 (1970).

TABLE 1-2 Summary of Format for Citations

COURT CASES	
Court	Citation
Tax Court—regular decisions	J. Simpson Dean, 35 T.C. 1083 (1961).
Tax Court—memo decisions	Edith G. McKinney, 1981 PH T.C. Memo ¶ 81,181, 41 TCM 1272.
Board of Tax Appeals—regular decisions	J. W. Wells Lumber Co. Trust A, 44 B.T.A. 551 (1941).
U.S. District Court	Margie J. Thompson v. U.S., 429 F. Supp. 13, 39 AFTR 2d 77-1485, 77-1 USTC ¶ 9343 (D.C. Pa., 1977).
U.S. Claims Court	Benjamin Raphan v. U.S., 3 Cl. Ct. 457, 52 AFTR 2d 83-5987, 83-2 USTC ¶ 9613 (1983).
Circuit Court of Appeals	Horace B. Rickey, Jr. v. U.S., 592 F.2d 1251, 43 AFTR 2d 79-1023, 79-1 USTC ¶ 9323 (5th Cir., 1979).
Supreme Court	U.S. v. Maclin P. Davis, 397 U.S. 301, 25 AFTR 2d 70-827, 70-1 USTC ¶ 9289 (1970).
ADMINISTRATIVE INTERPRETATIONS	
Revenue Rulings—prior to publication in *Cumulative Bulletin*	Rev. Rul. 90-99, I.R.B. 1990-49, 6.
Revenue Rulings—after publication in *Cumulative Bulletin*	Rev. Rul. 80-265, 1980-2 C.B. 378.
Revenue Procedures	Rev. Proc. 65-19, 1965-2 C.B. 1002.
Letter Rulings	Ltr. Rul. 8511075.
Information Release	I.R. 86-70.
Announcement	Ann. 86-128, I.R.B. 1986-51, 22.

Typical Misconception
A judge is required to follow prior court precedent only to the extent that the judge's decision is appealable to that court. Also, a court usually follows its own prior precedent except for situations in which the Golsen rule requires the Tax Court to issue inconsistent opinions. Thus, the Tax Court, the U.S. district courts, and the U.S. Claims Court are not required to follow each other's decisions. Neither is a circuit court required to follow the decision of a different circuit court.

Golsen rule provides that the Tax Court rules consistently with decisions of the circuit court for the taxpayer's jurisdiction.

Example 1-8 ■ In 1990, the first time the issue was litigated, the Tax Court decided that the expenditure in question was deductible. The government appealed the case to the Tenth Circuit and won a reversal. If and when the Tax Court faces this issue again, it will hold, with one exception, that the expenditure is deductible. The sole exception involves taxpayers of the Tenth Circuit; for them the Tax Court applies the *Golsen* rule and denies the deduction. ■

U.S. DISTRICT COURT. Because each U.S. district court is a separate court, district court decisions have precedential value only for subsequent cases before that same U.S. district court. District courts must follow decisions of the Supreme Court and the circuit court to which the case is appealable.

Example 1-9 ■ The U.S. District Court for Rhode Island, the Tax Court, and the Eleventh Circuit have ruled on a particular issue. Any U.S. district court within the Eleventh Circuit must follow that circuit's decision. Similarly, the U.S. District Court for Rhode Island must rule consistently with the way it ruled earlier. Tax Court decisions are not binding precedents for district courts. Thus, all district courts other than the one for Rhode Island and those within the Eleventh Circuit are free to reach their own independent decisions. ■

U.S. CLAIMS COURT. In reaching decisions today, the U.S. Claims Court must rule consistently with Supreme Court cases, cases decided by the Circuit Court of Appeals for the Federal Circuit, and its own earlier decisions. It need not follow decisions of other circuit courts. Because the Federal Circuit did not exist prior to October 1982, it has rendered very few decisions to date.

Example 1-10 ■ Assume the same facts as in Example 1-9. In a later year the same issue is litigated in the U.S. Claims Court. The Claims Court is not bound by any of the authorities that have addressed the issue. Thus, it has complete flexibility to reach its own answer. ■

CIRCUIT COURTS OF APPEAL. A circuit court is bound by Supreme Court cases and earlier cases decided by that particular circuit. If neither the Supreme Court nor the circuit in question has already faced the issue, there is no precedent that the circuit court must follow, regardless of whether other circuits have ruled on this point. In such a situation, the circuit court is said to be "writing on a clean slate." In reaching a decision, the judges may adopt the viewpoint reflected in another circuit's opinion if they deem it appropriate.

Example 1-11 ■ Assume the same facts as in Example 1-9. Any circuit other than the Eleventh would be "writing on a clean slate" if it faced the same issue. After reviewing the Eleventh Circuit's decision, another circuit court might or might not decide to rule the same way. ■

FORUM SHOPPING. Not surprisingly, courts are not always unanimous in their conclusions concerning the appropriate tax treatment. Consequently, conflicts sometimes exist among the courts—trial courts and appellate courts. Because taxpayers have the flexibility of choosing where to begin their litigation, part of their decision-making process should be the consideration of the precedents applicable in the various courts. The ability to consider differing precedents in choosing the forum for litigation is sometimes referred to as **forum shopping.**

Administrative Interpretations

The IRS uses several forums as a means of interpreting the statute. The IRS's interpretations are referred to generically as **administrative interpretations.** Some of the most important categories of interpretations are discussed below.

Typical Misconception

Even though revenue rulings do not have the same weight as regulations or court cases, one should not underestimate their importance. Most taxpayer confrontations involve an IRS revenue agent. And, since a revenue ruling is the official published position of the IRS, the revenue agent will place considerable weight on any applicable revenue rulings.

Revenue Rulings. In **revenue rulings,** the IRS indicates the tax consequences of a particular transaction in which a number of taxpayers might be interested. For example, a revenue ruling might indicate whether certain expenditures constitute support for purposes of claiming a dependency exemption for another individual.

The IRS issues several hundred revenue rulings a year. Revenue rulings do not rank as high as regulations and court cases in the hierarchy of authorities. They simply represent the viewpoint of the IRS. Taxpayers do not have to follow revenue rulings if they have sufficient authority for different treatment.[34] However, the IRS presumes that the tax treatment specified in a revenue ruling is correct. Consequently, if an examining agent discovers in an audit that a taxpayer did not adopt the position espoused in a revenue ruling, the agent will contend that the taxpayer's tax liability should be adjusted to reflect the tax results prescribed in the ruling.

---

[34] Chapter 16 discusses in depth the authoritative support that taxpayers and tax advisors should have for positions they adopt on a tax return.

Soon after the IRS issues a revenue ruling, it appears in the weekly *Internal Revenue Bulletin* (cited as I.R.B.), published by the Government Printing Office. Revenue rulings are also published in the *Cumulative Bulletin* (cited as C.B.), a bound publication issued semiannually by the Government Printing Office. An example of a citation to a revenue ruling appearing in the *Cumulative Bulletin* is as follows:

Rev. Rul. 80-265, 1980-2 C.B. 378.

This is the two hundred and sixty-fifth ruling issued during 1980, and it appears on page 378 of Volume 2 of the 1980 *Cumulative Bulletin*. Prior to the issuance of the appropriate volume of the *Cumulative Bulletin*, citations are given to the *Internal Revenue Bulletin*. An example of such a citation follows:

Rev. Rul. 90-99, I.R.B. 1990-49, 6.

The ruling is the ninety-ninth issued during 1990. It was published on page 6 of the *Internal Revenue Bulletin* for the forty-ninth week of 1990. Once a revenue ruling has been published in the *Cumulative Bulletin*, the citation to the *Cumulative Bulletin* should be used.

Revenue Procedures. As the name suggests, **revenue procedures** are pronouncements by the IRS that generally deal with the procedural aspects of tax practice. For example, in a revenue procedure the IRS provides guidance concerning the reporting of tip income. Another revenue procedure describes the requirements for reproducing paper substitutes for informational returns such as Form 1099.

Revenue procedures are published first in the *Internal Revenue Bulletin* and later in the *Cumulative Bulletin*. An example of a citation to a revenue procedure appearing in a *Cumulative Bulletin* is as follows:

Rev. Proc. 65-19, 1965-2 C.B. 1002.

This item was published in Volume 2 of the 1965 *Cumulative Bulletin* on page 1002; it was the nineteenth revenue procedure issued during 1965.

> **Self-Study Question**
> *Do letter rulings provide precedential value for taxpayers?*
>
> **Answer**
> *Not really. A letter ruling is binding only on the taxpayer to whom the ruling was issued. However, letter rulings can be very beneficial in tax research because they provide insight as to the IRS's opinion about the tax consequences of various transactions.*

Letter Rulings. **Letter rulings** are initiated by taxpayers who write and ask the IRS to explain the tax consequences of a particular transaction.[35] The IRS provides its explanation in the form of a letter ruling, that is, a personal response to the individual or corporation requesting an answer. Only the taxpayer to whom the ruling is addressed may rely on it as an authority. Nevertheless, letter rulings can furnish significant information to other taxpayers and to tax advisors because they lend insight into the IRS's opinion about the tax consequences of particular transactions.

Originally the public did not have access to letter rulings issued to other taxpayers. As a result of Sec. 6110, enacted in 1976, letter rulings, with any confidential information deleted, are accessible to the general public. Both Prentice Hall Information Services and Commerce Clearing House publish letter rulings in a letter rulings service.[36] An example of a citation to a letter ruling appears below.

Ltr. Rul. 8511075.

All letter rulings consist of seven digits.[37] The first two digits indicate that this ruling was made public during 1985. The next two digits denote the week it was made public, here the eleventh. The last three numbers reflect that it was the seventy-fifth ruling that week.

---

[35] Chapter 16 provides a more in-depth discussion of letter rulings.
[36] Prentice Hall Information Services' publication is entitled *Private Letter Rulings,* and Commerce Clearing House's is entitled *IRS Letter Rulings.*
[37] Sometimes letter rulings are cited as PLR (i.e., private letter ruling) instead of Ltr. Rul.

Other Interpretations.

Typical Misconception
A technical advice memorandum is published as a letter ruling. While a taxpayer-requested letter ruling deals with prospective transactions, a technical advice memorandum is obtained after a transaction has already occurred.

TECHNICAL ADVICE MEMORANDA. When a taxpayer's return is being audited with respect to a complicated, technical matter, the taxpayer may request that the matter be referred to the IRS National Office in Washington, D.C., for technical advice concerning the appropriate tax treatment. The answer from the National Office, in the form of a **technical advice memorandum**,[38] is made available to the public as a letter ruling. Researchers are able to recognize technical advice memos because they generally begin with language such as, "In response to a request for technical advice. . . ."

INFORMATION RELEASES. If the IRS thinks that vast numbers of the general public will be interested in a particular interpretation, it may issue an **information release.** Information releases are written in lay terms and are dispatched to thousands of newspapers throughout the United States for publication therein. The IRS may, for example, write an information release to announce the amount of the standard mileage rate applicable to taxpayers who deduct this standard allowance per mile instead of deducting their actual automobile expenses for business travel. An example of a citation to an information release is

    I.R. 86-70.

This is the seventieth information release issued in 1986.

Additional Comment
Announcements are used to summarize new tax law or publicize procedural matters. Announcements are generally aimed at tax practitioners and are "the equivalent of revenue rulings and revenue procedures" [Rev. Rul. 87-138, 1987-2, C.B. 287].

ANNOUNCEMENTS. The IRS also issues a form of information release which is more technical in nature and generally aimed at tax practitioners. These documents are called **announcements** and provide technical explanations of a certain tax issue which is of current importance. The IRS used a number of announcements to provide technical interpretations of the Tax Reform Act of 1986 prior to the time that they were able to issue either proposed or temporary regulations. An example of a citation to an announcement is

    Ann. 86-128, I.R.B. 1986-51, 22.

This is the one-hundred-twenty-eighth announcement issued in 1986. It can be found on page 22 of the fifty-first Internal Revenue Bulletin of 1986.

Tax Treaties

Key Point
A tax treaty is the equivalent of a statute. A tax advisor needs to be aware of provisions in tax treaties that will reduce a taxpayer's worldwide tax liability.

The United States has reached treaty agreements with numerous foreign countries. These treaties address tax and other matters. As a result, a tax advisor addressing the U.S. tax results of a U.S. corporation's business operations in another country, for example, Sweden, should determine whether there is a treaty between Sweden and the United States, and, if there is, the applicable provisions of the treaty. (See Chapter 15 for a more extensive discussion of treaties.)

Tax Periodicals

Writings of experts in tax periodicals can lend informative assistance in interpreting the tax law. For example, such writings can be especially helpful if they address a recently enacted statutory provision and it is too early for there to be any regulations, cases, or rulings on point.

---

[38] Technical advice memoranda are discussed in more depth in Chapter 16.

Key Point

Tax articles can be used to help find answers to tax questions. In such an instance, the statutory, administrative, or judicial authority used in the tax article should be cited as the authority and not the author of the article. The Courts and the IRS will place little, if any, reliance on mere editorial opinion.

Tax experts also frequently write articles in which they discuss the judicial authorities—often conflicting ones—with respect to a particular issue. The experts who most frequently write articles concerning technical tax matters are attorneys, accountants, and professors. Some periodicals that are devoted to providing in-depth discussions of tax matters are listed below.

— *The Journal of Taxation*
— *The Tax Adviser*
— *Taxation for Accountants*
— *Taxes—the Tax Magazine*
— *Tax Law Review*
— *The Journal of Corporate Taxation*
— *The Journal of Partnership Taxation*
— *The Journal of Real Estate Taxation*
— *The Review of Taxation of Individuals*
— *Estate Planning*
— *Tax Notes*

The first five journals listed above contain articles dealing with a variety of topical areas. As the names of the next five suggest, these publications deal with specialized areas. All of these publications (other than *Tax Notes* which is published weekly) are monthly or quarterly publications. Daily tax reports, such as the *Daily Tax Reporter* published by the Bureau of National Affairs, are sometimes used by tax professionals where more timely updates on tax matters are needed than can be provided by monthly and quarterly publications.

Published articles and tax services (discussed below) are examples of secondary sources of authority. The Code and administrative and judicial interpretations are primary sources of authority. Your research efforts should always involve citing primary authorities.

TAX SERVICES

OBJECTIVE 4
Use the tax services to research an issue

Key Point

Tax services are often where the research process begins. A tax service helps identify which of the tax authorities pertain to a particular tax issue. Again, the actual tax authorities, and not the tax service, are generally cited as support for a particular tax position.

Multivolume commentaries on the tax law are published by several publishers. These commentaries are known generically as **tax services.** Each of these tax services is encyclopedic in scope and most come in looseleaf form so that information concerning current developments can be easily added. The organizational scheme differs from one service to another; some are updated more frequently than others. Each one has its own special features and unique way of presenting certain material. The only way to become familiar with the various tax services is to use them in researching hypothetical or actual problems.

As with almost any other activity, the more familiar one becomes with the organizational scheme with which one is working, the more comfortable one feels. The following discussion provides an overview of the most commonly used tax services.

Federal Taxes2d

Federal Taxes2d, the tax service published by Prentice Hall Information Services (PH), consists of a 12-volume series devoted to income taxes, a 2-volume series covering estate and gift taxes, and a single volume dealing with excise taxes. This service also contains 2 volumes that reproduce the Internal Revenue Code and a volume containing a topical index and tables. In addition, a 2-volume set called *Cumulative Changes* denotes details about how the Code and regulations have been amended over the years. This set can be quite helpful if, for example, the tax advisor is researching a tax issue on a return currently under audit where the statute has been revised for years subsequent to the year in question.

> **Key Point**
>
> *Both the PH and CCH services are organized by code section. Accordingly, most tax advisors find both of these services easy to use.*

The *Federal Taxes2d* service is organized by Code section (i.e., its commentary begins with Sec. 1 of the Code and proceeds in numerical order through the last section of the Code). Researchers familiar with the Code section applicable to their problem can begin their research process by turning directly to the paragraphs discussing this section. Another technique for beginning the research process is to think of key words that capture the flavor of the problem and consult the index. The topical index appears in a separate volume. It refers the researcher to the paragraph number(s) of the service where the topics of interest are discussed. If the researcher knows which Code section addresses the issue (e.g., Sec. 280A), he can go immediately to whichever volume provides commentary on that section.

For each Code section, the *Federal Taxes2d* service reproduces verbatim the statutory language and the regulations, provides an editorial explanation of the provisions, and furnishes brief summaries of cases and rulings interpreting the Code section. It provides citations to the full text of each case or ruling. The summaries are categorized into fairly explicit topical areas, such as the deductibility as a medical expense of the cost of special food and beverages and food supplements.

The *Federal Taxes2d* service is updated weekly; the most recent developments are discussed in Volume 12 in a cross-reference section. The cross-reference section is organized by paragraph number. To determine whether there are any recent developments affecting your question, look for entries for the paragraph number at which you found helpful information in the main body of the service. If any additional authorities have arisen since the main body of the service was published, there will be a reference to the paragraphs where these new authorities are discussed. Because of the need to consult the cross-reference table, it is helpful to take note as you go along of the paragraph numbers that proved fruitful in your research process.

Standard Federal Tax Reporter

Commerce Clearing House (CCH) publishes the *Standard Federal Tax Reporter* (referred to in this text as the *CCH* service). This service is also organized by Code section. It contains separate services devoted to excise taxes and estate and gift taxes, as well as the multivolume income tax service. The CCH service reproduces the statute and the regulations for each Code section and summarizes and provides citations to other authorities in much the same way as the *Federal Taxes2d* service does.[39]

An index volume contains a topical index that lists references by paragraph number. Because the volumes are organized by Code section number, one can bypass the index if the number of the relevant Code section is known.

The approach for looking for any recent authorities on an issue is the same as for the *Federal Taxes2d* service. Consult the Cumulative Index table in Volume 13 and search for entries applicable to the paragraph numbers in the main body of the service where you found relevant authorities. The CCH service publishes supplements with current developments weekly.

---

[39] Citations for the two primary tax services are not often used. If one wanted to cite these services, it might be as follows: (1991) 6 *Fed. Taxes2d* (PH) ¶ 5,432 and (1991) 6 *Std. Fed. Tax Rep.* (CCH) ¶ 3329.43.

Tax Services • 1-31

Tax Coordinator

> **Additional Comment**
> *The RIA service is a larger service than either the PH or CCH services because RIA has more editorial commentary. The RIA updates are placed in the back of each corresponding volume, and the service is not replaced each year. In contrast, both the PH and CCH services put their updates in one volume. CCH is the only one of the publishers that replaces its entire service at the beginning of each calendar year.*

The *Tax Coordinator* is published by the Research Institute of America (RIA), referred to here as the *RIA* service. The RIA service is a multi-volume looseleaf publication organized by fairly broad topics. For example, Volume K explores the tax law with respect to the following deductions: taxes, interest, charitable contributions, medical, and other. The topical index, contained in a separate volume, refers to the paragraph numbers where the matters of interest are discussed. Another volume indexes where the various sections and regulations are discussed in the commentary volumes.

The RIA service reproduces all of the Code sections and regulations applicable to a particular volume behind a tab marker entitled "Code & Regs." Using detailed captions, the various volumes provide an editorial-type commentary about the tax results. References to cases, including citations, appear in footnote form. The RIA service does not compile information about new developments for all topics in a single volume. Instead, each volume has a tab marker entitled "Developments," where information concerning current developments for this volume is included. Explanations about the new developments are reported by paragraph number, using the same paragraph number applicable to the discussion of the topic in the main commentary section. The RIA service publishes current developments once a week.

Law of Federal Income Taxation (Mertens)

> **Additional Comment**
> *Mertens has the reputation of being the most scholarly tax service. For this reason, it is the only service cited by the judiciary with any regularity.*

The *Law of Federal Income Taxation,* published by Callaghan & Co., was originally edited by Jacob Mertens and is usually called Mertens by tax practitioners. Mertens is generally deemed to be the most authoritative tax service. It is the service most frequently cited by the courts, and, in fact, the only service cited by the judiciary with any regularity. Like the RIA service, Mertens is organized by general topical area. Volume 7, for example, provides a comprehensive discussion of taxes, losses, and net operating losses. The commentary is in narrative form and reads like an article. References to the authorities appear in footnotes.

One volume is devoted to a topical index. References are to section numbers (assigned by Mertens) instead of to paragraph numbers. Another volume, entitled *Tables,* discloses where Code sections, regulations, and rulings are discussed within the commentary volumes. The *Table of Cases* volume does the same with respect to cases.

Mertens is updated monthly to reflect current developments. Similar to the RIA service, the supplementary material for a particular volume is filed in that volume. The new material is organized by Mertens' section numbers and is reported under the section number assigned to the topic in question in the main body of the service. The volume entitled *Current Materials* contains in-depth articles on current developments as well as monthly updates that complement the supplementary material included in the treatise volumes.

Mertens devotes separate volumes to reproducing the Code and the regulations, and these items do not appear in the commentary volumes. A special feature of Mertens is its *Rulings Volume.* This volume contains a Code-Rulings Table organized by Code section number. The table lists the numbers of all of the revenue rulings that have been issued after 1953 with respect to a particular Code section. For example, for the period 1954 through 1990, the table lists one ruling interpreting Sec. 1034(b)(1).

Another part of the rulings volume consists of a Rulings Status Table. With respect to all of the post-1953 revenue rulings, this table denotes any subsequent action taken concerning each ruling. Examples of actions the IRS could have taken include revoking, modifying, and superseding a ruling. The citators published by

Prentice Hall Information Services and Commerce Clearing House contain the same information, but in a different format.[40]

Tax Management Portfolios

Key Point
The Tax Management Portfolios are popular with many tax advisors because they are very readable yet still provide a good understanding of the pertinent tax issues. But because the published portfolios do not cover all areas of the tax law, another service is necessary to supplement the gaps in the portfolio coverage.

The Bureau of National Affairs (BNA) publishes booklets of approximately 100 pages each called *Tax Management Portfolios* (referred to as BNA portfolios by many practitioners and in this text). Each portfolio provides an in-depth discussion of a relatively narrow issue, for example, involuntary conversions or the estate tax marital deduction. Thus, when the research question has been narrowed down to a very precise issue, consultation of a BNA portfolio can be quite helpful.

BNA provides a master binder or notebook that contains a Code section index and a key words or topical index. Each index references appropriate page numbers.

Each portfolio contains a narrative discussion called *Detailed Analysis,* and a section called *Working Papers.* In the Detailed Analysis portion, citations to authorities appear in the footnotes. The Working Papers section often contains items such as excerpts from committee reports, copies of tax forms applicable to the matter under discussion, and sample language for making a particular election. Each portfolio also has a bibliography and a list of references where relevant articles are listed and revenue rulings and letter rulings on the topic are summarized.

BNA portfolios are updated a few times a year with pink sheets filed in the front of the applicable booklet. The current developments material is organized according to which page number of the Detailed Analysis it supplements. From time to time, a portfolio may be revised or a new portfolio published to reflect major changes in the law.

Bender's Federal Tax Service

Additional Comment
Bender's Federal Tax Service is the newest of the major tax services. Therefore, not all libraries will have this service, and to most tax advisors, the characteristics of this service are yet unknown.

The newest of the major tax services is the *Bender's Federal Tax Service* which is published by Matthew Bender & Company. This service is a multi-volume looseleaf publication that, like the RIA and Mertens services, is organized by fairly broad topics. For example, Volume 5 refers to income taxation of estates, trusts and beneficiaries, sales and exchanges, and real estate while Volume 7 refers to partnerships and corporations.

The topical index, contained in Volume 1, refers to the Chapter and section number where the topical coverage can be found. The Chapter and section numbers are assigned by the Bender editors. Volume 2 provides Finding Tables that index where the 8 commentary volumes contain references to particular Internal Revenue Code provisions, Treasury Regulations, government promulgations, and judicial decisions. Volume 2 also contains tax rates and tables including valuation tables and withholding tables and practice aids.

The *Bender's Federal Tax Service* does not reproduce the Code and Treasury Regulations in the volumes with the topical commentary. Instead, it devotes 8 volumes to the Internal Revenue Code and proposed, temporary, and final Treasury Regulations. A Code section and the related Treasury Regulations will appear together in the same volume. Additional volumes provide sample completed tax forms, blank tax forms, and periodic updates.

The *Bender's Federal Tax Service* is updated at least monthly to reflect current developments. In addition, a weekly newsletter is provided in the Bender's *Federal Tax Week* volume to update subscribers between the monthly (or more often) updates to the tax service. The current developments material is organized according to the Chapter and section number to which it relates.

---

[40] Citators are described elsewhere in this chapter.

CITATORS

OBJECTIVE 5
Use the citator to assess authorities

Figure 1-5 provides an overview of the steps to follow in using the tax services to research a tax question.

Citators serve two functions: (1) they give a history of the case (i.e., if the case in question is an appeals court decision, the citator lists the trial court decision and the Supreme Court decision, if any, for the case); and (2) they list the other authorities (i.e., cases and revenue rulings) that have cited the case in question. Both Prentice

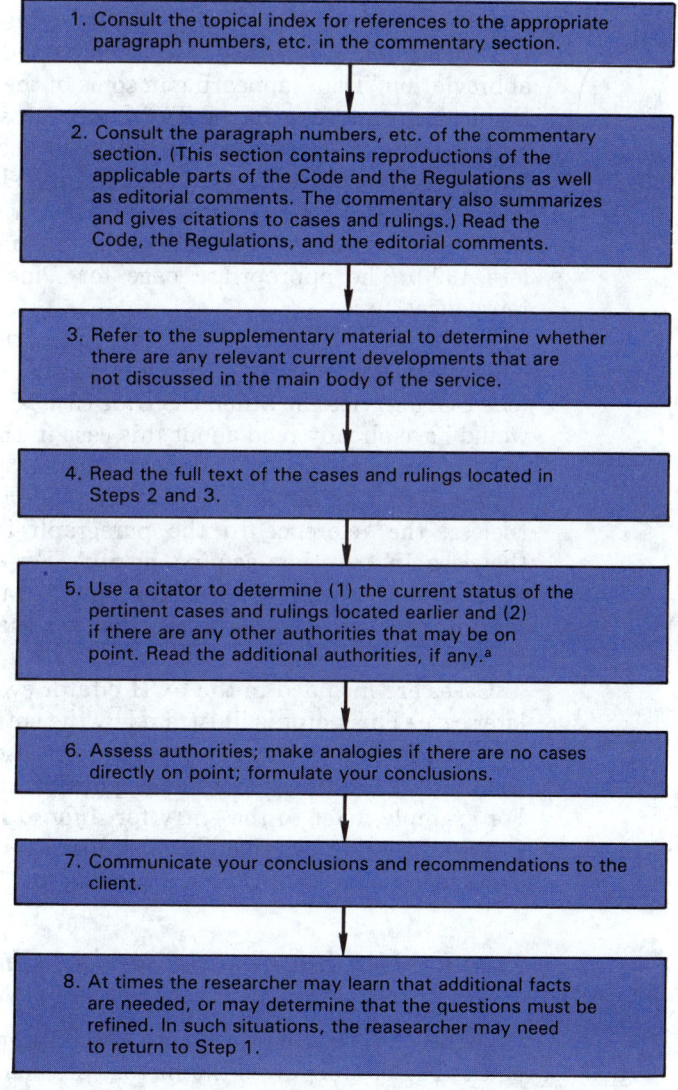

ᵃCitators are described and discussed elsewhere in this chapter.

FIGURE 1-5 Use of Tax Services to Research a Tax Question

Key Point

Citators are useful to (1) obtain the history of a tax case and (2) find additional cases and rulings that have cited the particular case in question.

Hall Information Services and Commerce Clearing House publish citators of judicial decisions.

Commerce Clearing House Citator

The Commerce Clearing House Citator (herein referred to as the CCH citator) consists of two loose-leaf volumes, one for cases with names beginning with the letters A through L and the other for cases with names starting with the letters M through Z, revenue rulings, and other government promulgations. This citator lists only the cases that the editors feel are the most important ones citing the case in question. A sample page from the CCH citator appears in Figure 1-6.

Refer to Figure 1-6 and find the *Leonarda C. Diaz* case. The information in darker print with bullets to the left denotes that *Diaz* was a decision of the Second Circuit and the Tax Court and that the Second Circuit affirmed (upheld) the Tax Court's decision. The two cases listed beneath the Second Circuit decision (i.e., *Kuh* and *Damm*) cited the *Diaz* decision. The three cases listed beneath the Tax Court decision (i.e., *Schwerm, Wassenaar,* and *Toner*) cited the Tax Court's opinion in *Diaz*. The abbreviation "Dec." appearing in some of the citations stands for decision. CCH lists the decision numbers of the Tax Court cases.

The basic CCH citator is published once a year. The first volume contains an update section, entitled "Current Citator Table," which shows listings for new court decisions and additional citations of earlier court decisions. The *Diaz* decision has not been cited by any additional decisions since the CCH citator was last published in late 1990. The appropriate page for *Diaz* in the Current Citator Table is not reproduced here.

The entry "¶ 1360.3876" appears to the right of the name of the case in question. This entry denotes the paragraph number of the *Standard Federal Tax Reporter* (the CCH service) at which the *Diaz* case is summarized. In most cases, a researcher would have already read about this case in the tax service and decided it was helpful for the research question before consulting the citator. In such situations, the citator is used to determine whether there are other cases that are relevant. Nevertheless, the reference to the paragraph in the CCH tax service summarizing the case in question can be helpful. For example, if a researcher who learned about the case from a source other than the tax service wants to read about the general topical area of the case in the tax service, the discussion can be easily located.

Cases are included in the CCH citator even though they have not been cited by a later case. This point is illustrated by the entry for *Albert N. Dibs,* a Tax Court memo decision, for which no subsequent case citations are listed. The citator also indicates whether the Commissioner has acquiesced or nonacquiesced to Tax Court decisions. For example, refer to the entry for *Alfonso Diaz;* the capital "A" following the Tax Court citation shows that the Commissioner's acquiescence is reported on page 2 of Volume 2 of the 1972 *Cumulative Bulletin.*

Prentice Hall Information Services Citator

Like the CCH citator, the Prentice Hall Information Services citator (referred to here as the PH citator) gives the history of each case and ruling and lists the cases and rulings that have cited the authority in question. The PH citator, however, conveys more extensive information than the CCH citator. Specifically, the citator includes information about the following:

Key Point

The history of a case may be easier to find in CCH because each of the courts that tried the case are listed in a single volume in **bold face print.** *For example, see the Isabel K. Dibblee case from the CCH citator reproduced on this page.*

———CCH——— 93,063 DIC

Diamond, Sol—continued
Kessler, Dec. 39,226(M), 44 TCM 624, T.C.Memo. 1982-432
Tooke, Dec. 34,336(M), 36 TCM 396, T.C.Memo. 1977-91
Pierson, Dec. 34,009(M), 35 TCM 1256, T.C.Memo. 1976-281
● **TC**—56 TC 530; Dec. 30,838
Manchester Music Co., Inc., DC--NH, 90-1 USTC ¶ 50,168, 733 FSupp 473
Miller, Jr., TC, Dec. 45,977(M), 57 TCM 1419, TC Memo. 1989-461
McNulty, Dec. 44,857(M), 55 TCM 1138, TC Memo. 1988-274
Greater Display & Wire Forming, Inc., Dec. 44,802(M), 55 TCM 922, TC Memo. 1988-231
National Oil Co., Dec. 43,557(M) 52 TCM 1223 TC Memo. 1986-596
Goodwin, David C., TC, Dec. 36,413, 73 TC 215
Schaevitz, Dec. 30,925(M), 30 TCM 823, T.C.Memo. 1971-197
Diamond, Solomon .... ¶ 1360.68
● 22 TCM 229; Dec. 25,981(M); T.C.Memo. 1963-57
Diamond T Motor Car Co.: Allen v. ..... ¶ 39,060.82
● **CA-10**—(rev'g DC), 61-1 USTC ¶ 9484; 291 F.2d 115
Randall, 76-2 USTC ¶ 9770, 542 F2d 270
Jefferson Bank and Trust, DC, 89-1 USTC ¶ 9221
Rodkey, 87-1 USTC ¶ 9218, DC
Nevada Rock & Sand Co., DC, 74-2 USTC ¶ 9617
Nomellini Construction Co., 71-2 USTC ¶ 9510, 328 F.Supp. 1281
● **DC**—Colo., 60-2 USTC ¶ 9557
Diamondhead Corp. v. Fort Hope Development, Inc.
.... ¶ 41,520.1945
● **DC**—Ga, 78-2 USTC ¶ 9718
Diamondstone, I. A. (See Kann, William L.)
DiAndrea, Inc. .... ¶ 2425.60, 2477.25, 2907.108
● **TC**—47 TCM 731; Dec. 40,697(M); T.C.Memo. 1983-768
Diaz, Alfonso .... ¶ 631.195
● 58 TC 560; Dec. 31,442; A. 1972-2 CB 2
Kong, TC, Dec. 46,090(M), 58 TCM 378, TC Memo. 1989-560
Caglia, E. Bonnie, TC, Dec. 45,585(M), 57 TCM 1, TC Memo. 1989-143
Ettig, Dec. 44,736(M), 55 TCM 720, TC Memo. 1988-182
Heller, Dec. 44,083(M), 53 TCM 1486 TC Memo. 1987-376
Anastasato, Dec. 43,309(M), 52 TCM 293 TC Memo. 1986-400
Stevenson, Dec. 43,068(M), 51 TCM 1050 TC Memo. 1986-207
Wilhelm, Dec. 42,813(M), 51 TCM 261, TC Memo. 1986-12
Branson, Dec. 38,026(M), 42 TCM 281, T.C.Memo. 1981-338
Calloway, Dec. 37,019(M), 40 TCM 495, T.C.Memo. 1980-211
Greenfield, Dec. 35,253(M), 37 TCM 1082, T.C.Memo. 1978-251
Leong, Dec. 34,232(M), 36 TCM 89, T.C.Memo. 1977-19
Dougherty, Dec. 32,138, 60 TC 917
Diaz, Antonio A. v. Southern Drilling Corp. .....
.... ¶ 42,298.45
● CA-5, (aff'g unreported DC), 71-1 USTC ¶ 9236
Diaz, Frank .... ¶ 29,762.9911
● **TC**—51 TCM 594; Dec. 42,922(M); TC Memo. 1986-98
Diaz, Humberto (See Flicker, Marvin)
Diaz, Juan (See Setal, Manuel G.)
Diaz, Leonarda C. .... ¶ 1360.3876
● **CA-2**—(aff'g TC), 79-2 USTC ¶ 9473; 607 F2d 995
Kuh, Dec. 40,461(M), 46 TCM 1405, TC Memo. 1984-572
Damm, Dec. 37,861(M), 41 TCM 1359, T.C.Memo. 1981-203
● **TC**—70 TC 1067; Dec. 35,436
Schwerm, Dec. 42,817(M), 51 TCM 270, TC Memo. 1986-16
Wassenaar, Dec. 36,359, 72 TC 1195
Toner, Dec. 35,877, 71 TC 772
Diaz, Miguel A. (See Powers (Belcher), Sandra L.)
Dibble, Leon N., Exr. .... ¶ 29,625.442
● 6 BTA 732; Dec. 2320; A. VI-2 CB 2
Dibble, Phillip A. .... ¶ 25,424.415
● **TC**—49 TCM 32; Dec. 41,602(M); TC Memo. 1984-589
Ogden, 86-1 USTC ¶ 9368, 788 F2d 252
Elrod, TC, Dec. 43,486, 87 TC 1046

Dibblee, Isabel K. .... ¶ 32,263.381
● **Sup. Ct.**—(rev'g CA-9), 36-1 USTC ¶ 9008; 296 U.S. 102; 56 S.Ct. 54
● **CA-9**—(aff'g BTA), 35-1 USTC ¶ 9128; 75 F.2d 617
● **BTA**—29 BTA 1070; Dec. 8415
Di Benedetto, Frank R. .... ¶ 40,580.038
● **DC**—RI, 75-1 USTC ¶ 9503
Continental Illinois Nat'l Bk. and Trust Co., Chicago, 87-2 USTC ¶ 9442, DC
Swift, 86-1 USTC ¶ 9109, DC
Rebelle, 85-2 USTC ¶ 9493, DC
Rebelle, III, 84-2 USTC ¶ 9717, DC
Moats, 83-2 USTC ¶ 9735, 564 FSupp 1330
Garity, 81-2 USTC ¶ 9598, DC
Garity, 80-1 USTC ¶ 9407, DC
Hanhauser, 80-1 USTC ¶ 9139, 85 FRD 89
Geiger, 78-1 USTC ¶ 9395, DC
DiBenedetto, Jack F. .... ¶ 42,018.0961, 42,033.112
● **CA-8**—(aff'g unreported DC), 76-2 USTC ¶ 9705; 542 F2d 490
Vannelli, 79-1 USTC ¶ 9257, 595 F2d 402
DiBernardo, Robert (See Grama, Nathan)
Di Blanco, Emilio v. Folson .. ¶ 652.0775, 33,878.26
● DC, N.Y., 57-1 USTC ¶ 9544
Dible, Leonard F. .... ¶ 669C.18, 1020.243
● **TC**—Dec. 46,122(M); 58 TCM 556; TC Memo. 1989-589
Di Bona, Donald R. .... ¶ 1179.083
● **TC**—27 TCM 1055; Dec. 29,149(M); T.C.Memo. 1968-214
Meehan, Dec. 33,949, 66 TC 794
Jamieson, Dec. 29,423, 51 TC 635
Di Borgo, Valerie N. P. .... ¶ 2006.55
● **TC**—23 TC 76; Dec. 20,609
Whittemore, 67-2 USTC ¶ 9670, 383 F.2d 824
Whittemore, 66-2 USTC ¶ 9663, 257 F.Supp. 1008
Dibrell Bros., Inc. ...... (Expired Excess Profits Tax)
● 18 BTA 1046; Dec. 5801
Dibs, Albert N. .... ¶ 1340.627, 1864.636, 2294N.30
● 29 TCM 897; Dec. 30,247(M); T.C.Memo. 1970-204
Dicello, Francis P. (See Koscot Interplanetary, Inc.)
Dicenso, Felilpo .... ¶ 2767.295
● **BTA**—11 BTA 620; Dec. 3826; A. VII-2 CB 11
Papineau, Dec. 18,044, 16 TC 130
DiCesare, Pasquale v. Chernenko ...... ¶ 40,191.09, 42,018.055
● **CA-4**, (aff'g unreported DC), 62-1 USTC ¶ 9482; 303 F.2d 423
Dichiarinte, Anthony J. .... ¶ 42,018.1134, 42,018.1244, 42,018.2557
● **CA-7**, (rev'g and rem'g unreported DC), 71-1 USTC ¶ 9460; 445 F.2d 126
Roberts, 80-2 USTC ¶ 16,344, 619 F2d 379
Mason, 77-2 USTC ¶ 9579, 557 F2d 426
Tirado, Dec. 36,875, 74 TC 14
Dick & Bros., Quincy Brewing Co. .... ¶ 1535.38
● Ct. Cls., 1929 CCH D-9205; 1925 CCH Fed. Cts. Vol. page CL-6649; Ct. D. 69, VIII-1 CB 254; 67 Ct.Cls. 505
Dick Brothers, Inc. .... ¶ 2657D.70, 2657D.75
● **CA-3**—(rev'g TC), 53-1 USTC ¶ 9423; 205 F.2d 64
Williams Co., 77-1 USTC ¶ 9221, 429 US 569
Sachs, 53-2 USTC ¶ 9634, 208 F.2d 313
Wilger Tire Co., Inc., In re, Dec. 35,904(M), 38 TCM 287, T.C.Memo. 1979-66
● **TC**—18 TC 832; Dec. 19,126
Dick, Fairman R. (See Roosevelt & Son Investment Fund)
Dick, Grace W. .... ¶ 29,663.22
● **Sup. Ct.**—Cert. denied, 296 U.S. 588; 56 S.Ct. 99
● **CA-10**—(aff'g BTA), 35-1 USTC ¶ 9252; 76 F.2d 265
Shepard, 58-2 USTC ¶ 9645, 163 F.Supp. 313
Rev. Rul. 58-341, 1958-2 CB 400
● **BTA**—30 BTA 1303; Dec. 8653
Dick, James .... ¶ 1242.103
● DC, Wis., 63-2 USTC ¶ 9594; 218 F.Supp. 839
Dick, Julia T. .... ¶ 2346.90, 2503.193
● **BTA**—20 BTA 637; Dec. 6279; A. X-1 CB 17 Cord, Dec. 10,532, 38 BTA 1372
Dick, Randall G. .... ¶ 37,814.8046
● **DC**—Ill, 79-1 USTC ¶ 9315
Dick, Randall G. .... ¶ 37,814.8046
● **DC**—DofC, 78-1 USTC ¶ 9173
Dick, Robert (See National Advertising Co., Inc.)
Dick, Robert M. .... ¶ 43,727.5098
● **CA-8**—(aff'g unreported DC per curiam), 82-2 USTC ¶ 9715; 694 F2d 1117
Dick, Ronald .... ¶ 42,205.0222
● **CA-DC**—(aff'g unreported DC per curiam), 87-1 USTC ¶ 9188

FIGURE 1-6 Excerpt from Commerce Clearing House Citator

Reproduced with permission from *Standard Federal Tax Reports,* published and copyrighted by Commerce Clearing House, Inc., 4025 W. Peterson Ave., Chicago, Illinois 60646.

1. Cases that have referenced the case in question, including whether the citing cases commented in a favorable or unfavorable manner or distinguished the cited cases.[41]
2. The specific issue in the case in question for which the citing authorities have referenced the case.

The PH Information Services citator consists of five bound volumes plus a softback cumulative supplement. The first hard-bound volume denotes citations made to cases during the period 1919 through 1941; the second volume contains citations made from 1942 through September 30, 1948; the third volume gives citations made from October 1, 1948 through July 29, 1954; the fourth volume contains citations made from July 30, 1954 through December 15, 1977; and the fifth volume lists citations made from December 15, 1977 through December 20, 1989. The softback cumulative supplement contains citations made after December 20, 1989. Thus, if a researcher is interested in determining how the courts have subsequently looked upon a 1945 case, they should consult all volumes of the citator except the first. If the case in question is a 1980 case, the researcher need consult only the most recent bound volume plus the supplement.

As mentioned, the PH Information Services citator discloses how the citing cases commented on the case in question. The nature of the comment is denoted by letters that appear to the left of the name of the citing case. Letters are also used to denote the history of the cited case (i.e., whether it was affirmed, etc.).[42] Figure 1-7 indicates what the various abbreviations symbolize.

The PH citator is especially helpful if the cited case deals with more than one issue. As mentioned, the citator reports the issue(s) for which the case was cited. The numbers to the left of the citing authority denote the issue number of the cited case for which the citation is made. The designation is not universally associated with a particular topic. Instead, the issue number refers to the number used to designate a particular issue in the court decision of interest. Issue numbers appear in the headnotes to the case (at the top of the first page of the case). To save time, researchers should take note of the applicable issue number when reading cases.

Part of a sample page from the 1977-89 citator appears in Figure 1-8. Refer to Figure 1-8 and locate the Tax Court decision for *Leonarda C. Diaz*. All of the cases citing the Tax Court's *Diaz* decision after 1977 and through 1989 are listed. (*Diaz* was decided by the Tax Court in 1978 so no earlier references will be found.) *Diaz* has been cited with respect to both the first and second issues in the case. If the case was concerned with additional issues, it has not been cited for them.

The "a" on the first line beneath the name of the case indicates that the Tax Court's decision was affirmed by the Second Circuit. The Tax Court's opinion has been explained and followed in various cases, but it has not been cited in an unfavorable manner. Thus, its authoritative value is strong.

The Second Circuit's decision appears as a separate entry. The letters "sa" signify that the circuit court affirmed the Tax Court decision in the *Diaz* case. The cases that have cited the circuit court's opinion are listed under the entry for such opinion. The appellate decision has not been questioned or criticized; thus, it is a relatively strong decision.

Recall that for the *Alfonso Diaz* case, the CCH Citator reported that in 1972 the Commissioner acquiesced to the decision (see Figure 1-6). Because the page from the 1977–1989 PH Citator reproduced in Figure 1-8 includes developments from

---

[41] When a court distinguishes its conclusion in one case from an earlier decision, it points out that the two different outcomes are justifiable because the facts in the two cases are not the same.

[42] If a case is *affirmed,* the decision of the lower court is upheld. *Reversed* means that the higher court arrived at the opposite decision of the court from which the case was appealed. *Remanded* signifies that the higher court sent the case back to the lower court with instructions to address certain matters not earlier addressed.

a	affirmed by a higher court (Note: When available, the official cite to the affirmance is provided; if the affirmance is by unpublished order or opinion, the date of the decision and the court deciding the case are provided.)
App auth	appeal authorized by the Treasury
App	appeal pending (Note: Later volumes may have to be consulted to determine if the appellate case was decided.)
cert gr	petition for certiorari was granted by the U.S. Supreme Court
d	appeal dismissed by the court or withdrawn by the party filing the appeal
(G)	following an appeal notation, this symbol indicates that it was the government filing an appeal.
m	the earlier decision has been modified by the higher court, or by a later decision.
r	the decision of the lower court has been reversed on appeal
rc	related case arising out of the same taxable event or concerning the same taxpayer.
reh den	rehearing has been denied by the same court in which the original case was heard.
remd	the case has been remanded for proceedings consistent with the higher court decision.
remg	the cited case is remanding the earlier case
reinst	a dismissed appeal has been reinstated by the appellate court and is under consideration again.
sa	the cited case is affirming the earlier case
sm	the cited case is modifying the earlier case
sr	the cited case is reversing the earlier case
sx	the cited case is an earlier proceeding in a case for which a petition for certiorari was denied
(T)	an appeal was filed from the lower court decision by the taxpayer
vacd	the lower court decision was vacated on appeal or by the original court on remand.
widrm	the original opinion was withdrawn by the court
x	petition for certiorari was denied by the U.S. Supreme Court
•	Supreme Court cases are designated by a bold-faced bullet (•) before the case line for easy location.

Certain notations appear at the end of the cited case line. These notations include:

(A)	the government has acquiesced in the reasoning or the result of the cited case
(NA)	the government has refused to acquiesce or to adopt the reasoning or the result of the cited case, and will challenge the position adopted if future proceedings arise on the same issue
on rem	the case has been remanded by a higher court and the case cited is the resulting decision

Evaluation of Cited Cases

iv	on all fours (both the cited and citing cases are virtually identical)
f	the reasoning of the court in the cited case is followed by the later decision
e	the cited case is used favorably by the citing case court
k	the cited and citing case principles are reconciled
l	the rationale of the cited case is limited to the facts or circumstances surrounding that case (this can occur frequently in situations in which there has been an intervening higher court decision or law change)
n	the cited case was noted in a dissenting opinion
g	the cited and citing cases are distinguished from each other on either facts or law
q	the decision of the cited case is questioned and its validity debated in relation to the citing case at issue
c	the citing case court has adversely commented on the reasoning of the cited case, and has criticized the earlier decision.
o	the later case directly overrules the cited case (use of the evaluation is generally limited to situations in which the court notes that it is specifically overturning the cited case, and that the case will no longer be of any value)

The evaluations used for the court decisions generally are followed by a number. That number refers to the headnoted issue in the American Federal Tax Reports (AFTR) or Tax Court decision to which the citing case relates. If the case is not directly on point with any headnote, a bracketed notation at the end of the citing case line directs the researcher to the page in the cited case on which the issue appears.

FIGURE 1-7 Abbreviations Used After 1977 in Prentice Hall Information Services Citator

Additional Comment

The PH citators have the advantage of providing the most citations for a given case. This is obvious when one compares PH's five volumes plus supplement with CCH's two volumes. Also, PH numbers each tax issue litigated in a court case. This allows the tax advisor to identify those cases dealing specifically with the issue being researched. For example, if one is interested in the 2nd issue in the Leonarda Diaz case, the citator reproduced on this page provides three cases that deal specifically with issue 2.

DIAMONDHEAD CORP. v NORTHCUTT, SUSAN RUTH JARREL, 42 AFTR2d 78-6038 (DC Ga) (See Diamondhead Corp v Ft. Hope Development, Inc.)
DIAMONDHEAD CORP. v NORTHCUTT, THOMAS JAMES, 42 AFTR2d 78-6038 (DC Ga) (See Diamondhead Corp v Ft. Hope Development, Inc.)
DIAMONDHEAD CORP. v U.S., 42 AFTR2d 78-6038 (DC Ga) (See Diamondhead Corp. v Ft. Hope Development, Inc.)
DiANDREA, ARTHUR, TRANSFEREE, 1983 PH TC Memo ¶ 83,768 See DiAndrea, Inc.)
DiANDREA, ARTHUR & YOLANDA, 1983 PH TC Memo ¶ 83,768 (See DiAndrea, Inc.)
DiANDREA, INC., 1983 PH TC Memo ¶ 83,768
  1—Godbold, Percy E., Jr. & Grace F., 82 TC 82, 82 PH TC 43
DiANDREA, YOLANDA, TRANSFEREE, 1983 PH TC Memo ¶ 83,768 See DiAndrea, Inc.)
DIAZ, ALFONSO & MARIA de JESUS, 58 TC 560, ¶ 58.57 PH TC
  Reilly, Peter W., Est. of, 76 TC 374, 76 PH TC 201 [See 58 TC 565, n. 2]
  e—Greenfield, Stuart & Eileen, 1978 PH TC Memo 78-1070 [See 58 TC 564]
  e—Calloway, Johnny T., 1980 PH TC Memo 80-952 [See 58 TC 564]
  e—Branson, David L., 1981 PH TC Memo 81-1199 [See 58 TC 564, 565]
  e—Cohen, Robert B. & Marilyn W., 1983 PH TC Memo 83-1042 [See 58 TC 564]
  e—Patton, Luther R., 1985 PH TC Memo 85-629 [See 58 TC 564]
  e—Malek, Theresa M. & Edward J., Sr., 1985 PH TC Memo 85-1905 [See 58 TC 574]
  e—Wilhelm, Mary R., 1986 PH TC Memo 86-39 [See 58 TC 564]
  e—Stevenson, Wayne E. & Marilyn J., 1986 PH TC Memo 86-866, 86-873 [See 58 TC 564]
  e—Anastasato, Pano & Janice, 1986 PH TC Memo 86-1811 [See 58 TC 564]
  e—Shih-Hsieh, Marilan, 1986 PH TC Memo 86-2429 [See 58 TC 562]
  e—Heller, Jacob W. & Esther R., 1987 PH TC Memo 87-1881 [See 58 TC 562]
  e—Ettig, Tobin R., 1988 PH TC Memo 88-953 [See 58 TC 564]
  e—Belli, Melia, 1989 PH TC Memo 89-1950 [See 58 TC 564]
  f—Kong, Young E. & Jeen K., 1989 PH TC Memo 89-2781 [See 58 TC 564-565]
  e-1—Caglia, E. Bonnie, 1989 PH TC Memo 89-689
DIAZ, FRANK & AMPARO R., 1986 PH TC Memo ¶ 86,098
DIAZ, LEONARDA C., 70 TC 1067, ¶ 70.95 PH TC
  a—Diaz, Leonarda C. v Comm., 44 AFTR2d 79-6027 (USCA 2)
  e—Stazer, Alan K. & Katalin V., 1981 PH TC Memo 81-505 [See 70 TC 1076]
  e—Damm, Marvin V. & Nina M., 1981 PH TC Memo 81-673 [See 70 TC 1074-1075]
  e—Stuart, Ian & Maria, 1981 PH TC Memo 81-1311, 81-1312 [See 70 TC 1076]
  e—Olsen, Randy B. & Deborah R., 1981 PH TC Memo 81-2409 [See 70 TC 1076]
  f—Kuh, Johannes L. & Adriana, 1983 PH TC Memo 83-2311 [See 70 TC 1075, 1076]
  f-1—Wassenaar, Paul R., 72 TC 1200, 72 PH TC 659
  f-1—Browne, Alice Pauline, 73 TC 726, 73 PH TC 402 [See 70 TC 1074]
  f-1—Rehe, William G. & Suzanne M., 1980 PH TC Memo 80-1426
  g-1—Schwerm, Gerald & Joyce J., 1986 PH TC Memo 86-54, 86-55
  e-1—Baist, George A. & Janice, 1988 PH TC Memo 88-2859
  f-2—Toner, Linda M. Liberi, 71 TC 778, 779, 781, 71 PH TC 435, 436, 437 [See 70 TC 1075]
  2—Toner, Linda M. Liberi, 71 TC 782, 783, 71 PH TC 437, 438
  n-2—Toner, Linda M. Liberi, 71 TC 790, 71 PH TC 441
  f-2—Robinson, Charles A. & Elaine M., 78 TC 552, 78 PH TC 290 [See 70 TC 1074]

DIAZ—contd.
  2—Gruman, David T., 1982 PH TC Memo 82-1700 [See 70 TC 1074]
DIAZ, LEONARDA C. v COMM., 44 AFTR2d 79-6027 (USCA 2, 6-25-79)
  sa—Diaz, Leonarda C., 70 TC 1067, ¶ 70.95 PH TC
  e—Stazer, Alan K. & Katalin V., 1981 PH TC Memo 81-505
  e—Damm, Marvin V. & Nina M., 1981 PH TC Memo 81-673
  e—Olsen, Randy B. & Deborah R., 1981 PH TC Memo 81-2409
  f—Kuh, Johannes L. & Adriana, 1983 PH TC Memo 83-2311
  e—Malek, Theresa M. & Edward J., Sr., 1985 PH TC Memo 85-1905
  f-1—Rehe, William G. & Suzanne M., 1980 PH TC Memo 80-1426
  g-1—Schwerm, Gerald & Joyce J., 1986 PH TC Memo 86-54, 86-55
  e-1—Baist, George A. & Janice, 1988 PH TC Memo 88-2859
DIAZ, MIGUEL A. & FELICIA N., 1981 PH TC Memo ¶ 81,069 (See Powers, Sandra L.)
DIBBLE, LEON N., EXEC. (EST. OF DIBBLE, LOUIS N.), 6 BTA 732
  McShain, John & Mary, 71 TC 1009, 71 PH TC 564
DIBBLE, PHILLIP A. & PHYLLIS K., 1984 PH TC Memo ¶ 84,589
  e—Frink, Gary R. & Sherry R., 1984 PH TC Memo 84-2729 [See 1984 PH TC Memo 84-2378]
  1—Ogden, Mary K. S., 84 TC 888, 84 PH TC 464
  e-1—Elrod, Johnie Vaden, 87 TC 1085, 87 PH TC 553
  g-1—Young, William & Ruby, 1987 PH TC Memo 87-2041
  e-1—McGuffey, Jack D. & Mary J., 1989 PH TC Memo 89-1321
DiBENEDETTO, FRANK R. v U.S., 35 AFTR2d 75-1502 (DC RI)
  f-1—Geiger, William T. v U.S., 41 AFTR2d 78-1231 (DC Md)
  f-1—Hanhauser, Marjorie M. v U.S., 45 AFTR2d 80-473 (DC Pa)
  e-1—Garity, Thomas P. v U.S., 46 AFTR2d 80-5144 (DC Mich)
  e-1—Garity, Thomas P. v U.S., 47 AFTR2d 81-548 (DC Mich)
  f-1—Moats, Robert L. v U.S., 52 AFTR2d 83-6240, 83-6241, 564 F Supp 1341 (DC Mo)
  f-1—Rebelle, Julius L., III v U.S., 54 AFTR2d 84-5700, 588 F Supp 51 (DC La)
  e-1—Swift, Wilbert v Levesque, Roger, 56 AFTR2d 85-6159, 85-6163, 614 F Supp 173, 177 (DC Conn)
  e-1—Continental Ill. Nat. Bk. & Tr. Co. of Chicago v U.S., 60 AFTR2d 87-5164 (DC Ill)
DiBENEDETTO, JACK F.; U.S. v, 38 AFTR2d 76-6013, 542 F2d 490 (USCA 8)
  e-1—Vannelli, Leonard J.; U.S. v, 43 AFTR2d 79-893, 595 F2d 405 (USCA 8)
  f-2—Bowman, Paul V.; U.S. v, 44 AFTR2d 79-5299, 602 F2d 165 (USCA 8)
DiBERNARDO, ROBERT & LINDA, 1985 PH TC Memo ¶ 85,608 (See Grama, Nathan & Francis)
DIBLE, LEONARD F. & BARBARA H., 1989 PH TC Memo ¶ 89,589
DICHIARINTE; U.S. v, 27 AFTR2d 71-1469, 445 F2d 126 (USCA 7)
  g—Tirado, Jacque, 74 TC 24, 74 PH TC 14 [See 27 AFTR2d 71-1470, 445 F2d 129 n. 2]
DICK BROS., INC., 18 TC 832, ¶ 18.102 PH TC 1952
  q-1—Wilger, Walt, Tire Co., Inc., 1979 PH TC Memo 79-284
DICK BROS., INC. v COMM., 205 F2d 64, 43 AFTR 1093 (USCA 3)
  g-1—Wilger, Walt, Tire Co., Inc., 1979 PH TC Memo 79-284
DICK v COMM., 23 AFTR2d 69-1186, 408 F2d 378 (USCA 2)
  e-1—Dick, Ronald Stewart, 1984 PH TC Memo 84-6
DICK, RANDALL G. v I.R.S., 41 AFTR2d 78-639 (DC DC, 1-10-78)
  g-1—Taxation With Representation Fund v I.R.S., 47 AFTR2d 81-1038, 646 F2d 682 (CADC)

FIGURE 1-8 Excerpt from Prentice Hall Information Services Citator, 1977–1989
Reproduced with permission from Maxwell Macmillan Professional and Business Reference Publishing.

December 15, 1977 through December 20, 1989, it does not report the acquiescence. The bound citator for 1954-1977 reports the 1972 acquiescence. In order to locate the most recent references to the *Leonarda C. Diaz* case, one would need to refer to the cumulative supplement. The appropriate excerpt from the supplement is illustrated here and indicates one subsequent case cited for the *Leonarda C. Diaz* decision by the Second Circuit.[43]

```
DIAZ, LEONARDA C., 70 TC 1067, ¶ 70.95 PH TC
    f—Wiertzema, Vance v U.S., 66 AFTR2d 90-5371 (DC
        ND) [See 70 TC 1074-1075]
DIAZ, LEONARDA C. v COMM., 44 AFTR2d 79-6027
    (USCA 2)
    e—Wiertzema, Vance v U.S., 66 AFTR2d 90-5371 (DC
        ND)
DICKERSON, CHERYL ANNE v U.S., 65 AFTR2d
    90-963 (DC Calif, 2-16-90)
DICKERSON, JERALD W. v U.S., 65 AFTR2d 90-963
    (DC Calif) (See Dickerson, Cheryl Anne v U.S.)
DICKEY, RAYMOND L., 1985 PH TC Memo ¶ 85,478
    e—Hill, Robert E. & Charmaine D, 1990 PH TC Memo
        90-1736 [See 1985 PH Memo TC 85-2145]
    e—Berry, Edward F. & Dorothy M., 1990 PH TC Memo
        90-1873 [See 1985 PH Memo TC 85-2145]
```

COMPUTERS AS A RESEARCH TOOL

Key Point

The use of computers in tax research is clearly increasing. With the technological advances in computer hardware and software, large data bases are becoming more accessible and less costly. In the coming years, computer-assisted tax research will become an even more important tool for the tax advisor.

Computers are now being used by more tax professionals as a tax research tool. Four computer-based legal data bases are now available. These data bases cover federal and state income tax matters as well as other federal and state legal matters. The names of the services and their providers are indicated below.

Name of Data Base[44]	Provider
ACCESS	Commerce Clearing House
LEXIS	Mead Data Central
PHINet	Prentice Hall Information Services
WESTLAW	West Publishing

A data base will include full texts of cases, revenue rulings, and other sources of the tax law. Unlike the tax services, these data bases generally do not contain an index. Rather, the researcher locates applicable authorities by using "key-word" search requests. That is, he instructs the computer to locate all of the authorities containing certain words or phrases. Researchers need to be imaginative in thinking of search requests; the service will not locate an authority unless it contains the exact wording the researcher specifies, even though it contains synonymous terms.

Example 1-12 ■ A researcher is interested in whether a certain expenditure for clothing is deductible under Sec. 162 as a uniform expense. The researcher might instruct the computer to retrieve all cases containing the words "uniform" and "Sec. 162" in close proximity to each other. This search will turn up only cases containing those words. Cases using the words "work clothing" will not be retrieved. A more comprehensive search will take place if the researcher instructs the computer to look for either "uniform" or "work clothing" within close proximity of "Sec. 162." ■

---

[43] No additional references have been reported as of March 17, 1991.

[44] PHINet and WESTLAW contain the index and text for the *Federal Taxes2d* tax service, while LEXIS contains the index and text for RIA's *Federal Tax Coordinator*.

These data bases can be especially valuable as a backup to the research one has conducted manually through the tax services. After researchers have located some authorities through the tax services, they can use the computer and the data base to determine whether there are additional authorities on point. Each of the data bases is updated for new developments on a very timely basis.

Bender's Federal Tax Service, published by Matthew Bender, Inc., is available not only as a looseleaf tax service but also on compact disc, known as CD ROM (compact disc read-only memory). The tax service is organized by topical area and separate volumes are devoted to the Code and regulations. Both the looseleaf service and the compact discs are updated monthly. Information is retrieved from the compact discs by typing key words into the computer. The compact discs, of course, allow pages and pages of information to be stored in practically no space.

SAMPLE WORK PAPERS AND CLIENT LETTER

OBJECTIVE 6
Prepare work papers and communications to clients

A sample set of work papers, including a draft of a client letter and a memo to the file describing the facts on which the research is based, are presented in Appendix A. The purpose of the work papers is to denote the issues to be researched, the authorities addressing the issues, and the researcher's conclusions concerning the appropriate tax treatment, with rationale therefor.

The format and other details of a set of work papers differ from firm to firm. The sample in this text is designed to give general guidance concerning the content of work papers. In practice, work papers may include less detail.

PROBLEM MATERIALS

DISCUSSION QUESTIONS

1-1. Explain the difference between closed-fact and open-fact situations.

1-2. List the steps of the tax research process.

1-3. Explain why the five steps in the tax research process are sometimes circular.

1-4. In what circumstances do the AICPA's *Statements on Responsibilities in Tax Practice* recommend that tax advisors communicate with their clients in writing instead of orally?

1-5. a. What does *dictum* mean?
   b. Refer to the *Cox* case reproduced in part on pages 1-6 to 1-8 and indicate which language in the case is *dictum*.

1-6. a. Refer to the *Gardin* case reproduced in part on pages 1-8 to 1-10 and indicate which language in the case is *dictum*.
   b. Do you agree with the decisions in *Cox* and *Gardin*?

1-7. Explain what is encompassed by the term *tax law* when tax advisors use this phrase.

1-8. The Government Printing Office publishes both hearings on proposed legislation and committee reports. Distinguish between these two publications.

1-9. Explain why committee reports can be valuable research aids.

1-10. Why has the tax researcher's job been simplified as a result of the codification of the tax statutes?

1-11. A friend notices that you are reading from the *Internal Revenue Code of 1986*. Your friend inquires why you are consulting a 1986 publication, especially given that tax laws change so frequently. What is your response?

1-12. Is Title 26 restricted to statutory provisions dealing with income taxation only? Explain.

1-13. Refer to Sec. 301 of the Code.
   a. Which subsection discusses the general rule for the tax treatment of a distribution of property?
   b. Where should one look for exceptions to the general rule?
   c. What type of Regulations would relate to subsection (e)?

1-14. Why should tax researchers take note of the date on which a regulation was adopted?

1-15. a. Distinguish between proposed, temporary, and final regulations.
   b. Distinguish between interpretative and statutory regulations.

1-16. Which type of regulation is more difficult for a taxpayer to successfully challenge, and why?

1-17. Explain the legislative reenactment doctrine.

1-18. a. In which courts may litigation dealing with tax matters begin?
   b. Discuss the factors that would likely be important to a taxpayer who is deciding in which trial court to begin litigation.
   c. What appeals court structure exists for the various trial courts?

1-19. Can a taxpayer appeal a case litigated under the Small Cases Procedures of the Tax Court?

1-20. Explain whether the following decisions have the same precedential value: (1) Tax Court regular decisions, (2) Tax Court memorandum decisions, (3) decisions under the Small Cases Procedures of the Tax Court.

1-21. Does the IRS potentially issue acquiescences to decisions of a U.S. district court?

1-22. Explain the *Golsen* rule. Create an example to illustrate its application.

1-23. Which courts' decisions are reported in the AFTR? In the USTC?

1-24. Who publishes regular decisions of the Tax Court? Memo decisions?

1-25. Assume the only litigation to date on a particular issue has been as follows:
Tax Court—decided for the taxpayer
Eighth Circuit Court of Appeals—decided for the taxpayer (affirming the Tax Court)
District Court of Louisiana—decided for the taxpayer
Fifth Circuit Court of Appeals—decided for the government (reversing the District Court)
   a. Discuss the precedential value of the cases listed above with respect to your client who is a California resident.
   b. If your client, a Texas resident, litigates in the Tax Court, how will the court rule? Explain.

1-26. a. Discuss the authoritative weight of revenue rulings.
   b. As a practical matter, what will happen if a taxpayer does not follow a revenue ruling and his return is audited?

1-27. When might a tax advisor need to consult the provisions contained in a tax treaty?

1-28. When may a tax advisor find it helpful to consult "writings of experts"?

1-29. Compare the tax services listed below with respect to (a) how they are organized and (b) where current developments appear.
   a. *Federal Taxes2d*
   b. *Standard Federal Tax Reporter*
   c. *Tax Coordinator*
   d. *Law of Federal Income Taxation* (Mertens)
   e. *Tax Management Portfolios*

1-30. What two functions does a citator serve?

1-31. Describe two types of information reported in the Prentice Hall Information Services citator but not in the Commerce Clearing House citator.

1-32. Explain how your research approach might differ if you were using a computerized data base instead of a standard tax service (e.g., the *Federal Taxes2d* service) at the beginning of your research.

PROBLEMS

1-33. *Interpretation of the Code.* Under a divorce instrument executed in 1986, an ex-wife receives cash of $25,000 per year for 8 years from her former husband. The instrument does not state that the payment is not includable in income.
  a. Does the ex-wife have gross income? If so, how much?
  b. Does the former husband receive a tax deduction? If so, is it for or from AGI?
  Refer only to the Internal Revenue Code in answering this problem.

1-34. *Interpretation of the Code.* Refer to Code Sec. 385 and answer the questions below.
  a. Whenever regulations are adopted, what type will they be—statutory or interpretative? Explain.
  b. Assume regulations have been finalized for Sec. 385. Will they have any relevance to estate tax matters? Explain.

1-35. *Determination of Acquiescence.*
  a. What official action did the Commissioner take in 1986 with respect to the Tax Court case of *John McIntosh*? (Hint: Consult the 1986-1 *Cumulative Bulletin*.)
  b. Did such action concern *all* the issues in the case? If not, explain. (Consult the headnote to the case before answering this part of the question.)

1-36. *Determination of Acquiescence.*
  a. What original action (acquiescence or nonacquiescence) did the Commissioner take with respect to *Streckfus Steamers, Inc*, 19 T.C. 1 (1952)?
  b. Was the action complete or partial?
  c. Did the Commissioner subsequently change his mind? If so, when?

1-37. *Determination of Acquiescence.*
  a. What original action (acquiescence or nonacquiescence) did the Commissioner take with respect to *Pittsburgh Milk Co.*, 26 T.C. 707 (1956)?
  b. Did the Commissioner subsequently change his mind? If so, when?

1-38. *Assessing a Case.* Look up the decision for *Everett J. Gordon*, 85 T.C. 309 (1985), and answer the questions below.
  a. Was the decision reviewed by the court? If so, was it a unanimous decision? Explain.
  b. Was the decision entered under Rule 155?
  c. Consult a citator. Was the case heard by an appellate court? If so, which court?

1-39. *Assessing a Case.* Look up the decision for *Bush Brothers & Co.*, 73 T.C. 424 (1979), and answer the questions below.
  a. Was the decision reviewed by the court? If so, was it a unanimous decision? Explain.
  b. Was the decision entered under Rule 155?
  c. Consult a citator. Was the case heard by an appellate court? If so, which court?

1-40. *Writing Citations.* Give the proper citations (including both primary and secondary cites where applicable) for the authorities listed below. (For secondary cites, give both the AFTR and USTC cites.)
  a. *Ruth K. Dowell v. U.S.*, a 10th Circuit decision
  b. *Thomas M. Dragoun v. CIR*, a Tax Court memo decision
  c. *John M. Grabinski v. U.S.*, a District Court of Minnesota decision
  d. *John M. Grabinski v. U.S.*, an Eighth Circuit decision
  e. *L. W. Hardy Co., Inc. v. U.S.*, a Claims Court decision
  f. *Hillsboro National Bank v. CIR*, a Supreme Court decision
  g. Rev. Rul. 78-129

1-41. *Writing Citations.* Give the proper citations (including both primary and secondary cites where applicable) for the authorities listed below. (For secondary cites, give both the AFTR and USTC cites.)
  a. Rev. Rul. 69-125
  b. *Frank H. Sullivan,* a Board of Tax Appeals decision.
  c. *Lloyd Weaver,* a Tax Court decision.
  d. *Ralph L. Rogers v. U.S.,* an Ohio District Court decision.
  e. *Norman Rodman v. CIR,* a Second Circuit Court decision.

1-42. *Interpreting Citations.* Following are some actual citations. For each case, indicate which court decided the case. In addition, for each authority, indicate on which pages and in which publications the authority was reported.
  a. *Lloyd M. Shumaker v. CIR,* 648 F.2d 1198, 48 AFTR 2d 81-5353 (9th Cir., 1981).
  b. *Dean R. Shore,* 69 T.C. 689 (1978).
  c. *Real Estate Land Title & Trust Co. v. U.S.,* 309 U.S. 13, 23 AFTR 816 (USSC, 1940).
  d. *J. B. Morris v. U.S.,* 441 F. Supp. 76, 41 AFTR 2d 78-335 (D.C. Tex., 1977).
  e. Rev. Rul. 83-3, 1983-1 C.B. 72.
  f. *Malone & Hyde, Inc. v. U.S.,* 568 F.2d 474, 78-1 USTC ¶ 9199 (6th Cir., 1978).

1-43. *Using the Cumulative Bulletin.* Consult any *Cumulative Bulletin.* In what order are revenue rulings arranged?

1-44. *Using the Cumulative Bulletin.* Which Code section does Rev. Rul. 85-44 interpret? (Hint: Consult the 1985-1 *Cumulative Bulletin.*)

1-45. *Using the Cumulative Bulletin.* Refer to the 1989-1 Cumulative Bulletin (C.B.).
  a. What time period is covered by this bulletin?
  b. What do you find on page 1?
  c. What items are printed in Part I of the bulletin?
  d. In what order are the items presented in Part I?
  e. What items are printed in Part II?
  f. What items are printed in Part III?

1-46. *Using the Cumulative Bulletin.* Refer to the 1990-1 Cumulative Bulletin (C.B.).
  a. For the time period covered by the bulletin, to which cases did the IRS issue a nonacquiescence?
  b. What is the topical area of Rev. Rul. 90-10?
  c. Does this bulletin contain any revenue ruling that interprets Sec. 162? If so, list it.

1-47. *Using a Tax Service.* Use the topical index of the *Federal Taxes2d* tax service to locate authorities dealing with the deductibility of the cost of a facelift.
  a. At which paragraph(s) does the *Federal Taxes2d* service give a synopsis of these authorities and citations to them?
  b. List the authorities.
  c. Have there been any recent non-statutory developments concerning the tax consequences of facelifts? ("Recent" means authorities appearing in the cross-reference section.)
  d. May a taxpayer deduct the cost of a facelift paid for in 1991? Explain.

1-48. *Using a Tax Service.* Refer to Reg. Sec. 1.302-1 in the *Federal Taxes2d* service. Does the regulation interpret today's version of the Code? Explain.

1-49. *Using a Tax Service.* Use the topical index of the *Standard Federal Tax Reporter* to locate authorities dealing with whether termite damage qualifies for a casualty loss deduction.
  a. At which paragraph(s) does the *Standard Federal Tax Reporter* service give a synopsis of these authorities and citations to them?
  b. List the authorities.
  c. Have there been any recent developments concerning the tax consequences of termite damage? ("Recent" means authorities appearing in the cumulative index section.)

1-50. *Using a Tax Service.*
  a. Locate in the *Standard Federal Tax Reporter* service the place where Sec. 303(b)(2)(A) is

reproduced. This provision states that Sec. 303(a) applies only if the stock meets a certain percentage test. What is the applicable percentage?

b. Locate Reg. Sec. 1.303-2(a) in the same tax service as in Part a. Does this regulation interpret today's version of the Code with respect to the percentage test addressed in Part a? Explain.

1-51. Using a Tax Service. The questions below deal with the *Tax Management Portfolios* published by the Bureau of National Affairs.
a. What is the portfolio number of the volume that provides a detailed examination of only the topic of the sale or exchange of a personal residence?
b. On which pages is the concept of a "principal residence" discussed?
c. What is the purpose of Worksheet 13 of this portfolio?
d. Refer to the bibliography. List the numbers (e.g., 68-5) of the 1968 revenue rulings that, according to the portfolio, dealt with the sale or exchange of a personal residence.

1-52. Using a Tax Service. This problem deals with the Mertens' *Law of Federal Income Taxation* tax service.
a. Refer to Volume 5. What broad, general topics does it discuss?
b. Which section of Volume 5 is devoted to a discussion of the principal methods of determining depreciation?
c. In Volume 5, what is the purpose of the yellow and white sheets appearing before (in front of) the tab labeled "Text"?
d. Refer to the Ruling Status Table in the Rulings volume. What is the current status of Rev. Ruls. 79-433 and 75-335?
e. Refer to the Code-Rulings Table in the Rulings volume. List the numbers (e.g., Rev. Rul. 84-88) of all 1984 revenue rulings and revenue procedures interpreting Sec. 121.

1-53. Using a Tax Service. The questions below deal with the *Tax Coordinator* published by The Research Institute of America.
a. Use the topical index to locate authorities dealing with the deductibility of the cost of work clothing by ministers (clergymen). List the authorities.
b. Does the supplementary material contain any authorities dealing with this issue?

1-54. Using a Tax Service. Refer to the *Federal Taxes2d* and *Standard Federal Tax Reporter* services. Then for each tax service, answer the following questions.
a. In which volume is the index located?
b. Is the index arranged by topic or by Code section?
c. If all you know is a Code section, how do you locate additional materials?
d. If all you know is a court decision, how do you locate additional materials?

1-55. Using a Citator. Trace *Biltmore Homes, Inc.*, a 1960 Tax Court memo decision, through both citators discussed in the text.
a. According to the PH citator, how many times has the Tax Court decision been cited by other courts on Issue Number 5?
b. How many issues were involved in the trial court litigation? (Hint: Refer to the headnote of the case.)
c. Did an appellate court hear the case? If so, which court?
d. According to the CCH citator, how many times has the Tax Court decision been cited by other courts?
e. According to the CCH citator, how many times has the Tax Court decision been cited by other courts on Issue Number 5?

1-56. Using a Citator. Trace *Steven Bolaris*, 776 F.2d 1428, through both citators discussed in the text.
a. According to the PH citator, how many times has the Ninth Circuit's decision been cited?
b. With how many issues, at a minimum, did the case deal?
c. Was the case ever commented on in an unfavorable manner? Explain.
d. According to the CCH citator, how many times has the Ninth Circuit's decision been cited?
e. According to the CCH citator, how many times has the Tax Court's decision been cited with respect to Issue Number 1?

1-57. *Interpreting a Case.* Consult the *Levin Metals Corporation* case (92 T.C. 307).
    a. In which year was the case decided?
    b. What was the issue?
    c. Who won the case?
    d. Was the case reviewed?
    e. Is there an appellate decision?
    f. Has the case been cited in other cases?

RESEARCH PROBLEMS

1-58. Josh contributes $5,000 toward the support of his widowed mother, aged 69. His mother, a U.S. citizen and resident, has $2,000 of gross income and spends it all on her own support. In addition, $3,200 of her medical expenses are paid for by Medicare. She does not receive any support from sources other than those described above. Must the Medicare payments be counted as support that Josh's mother provides for herself?

    Prepare work papers and a client letter (to Josh) dealing with the question about the Medicare payments.

1-59. Karen, who received her M.B.A. in 1961, was elected county treasurer in 1964. She holds this position until 1971, when she successfully ran for the state legislature. She is a member of the state legislature until early this year, when she is appointed state treasurer. State treasurer is normally an elected position, but the elected treasurer died 2 months after beginning his 4-year term. Karen is approved to serve the remaining time of the 4-year term. In connection with the confirmation hearings to be appointed state treasurer, she incurs $12,320 of legal and other fees. What is the tax treatment of her $12,320 expenditure?

    Prepare work papers and a client letter (to Karen) dealing with the tax consequences of the expenditure related to her confirmation hearings.

1-60. Amy owns a vacation cottage in Maine. She estimates that use of the cottage during the current year will be as follows:

By Amy, solely for vacation	16 days
By Amy, making repairs 10 hours per day and vacationing the rest of the day	3 days
By her sister, who paid fair rental value	7 days
By her cousin, who paid fair rental value	5 days
By her friend, who paid a token amount of rent	2 days
By three families from the Northeast, who paid fair rental value for 40 days each	120 days
Not used	212 days

Determine the ratio to be used to allocate the following expenses against the rental income received with respect to the cottage: interest, taxes, repairs, insurance, and depreciation.

    Prepare working papers in which you address the ratio(s) to be used in the allocations.

2 Formation of the Corporation

CHAPTER OUTLINE
- LEARNING OBJECTIVES 2-2
- ORGANIZATION FORMS AVAILABLE 2-2
  - Sole Proprietorships 2-2
  - Partnerships 2-4
  - Corporations 2-5
- DEFINITION OF A CORPORATION 2-8
  - Distinguishing Between a Partnership and a Corporation 2-8
  - Distinguishing Between an Association and a Trust 2-9
- LEGAL REQUIREMENTS FOR FORMING A CORPORATION 2-10
- TAX CONSIDERATIONS IN FORMING A CORPORATION 2-10
- SECTION 351: DEFERRING GAIN OR LOSS UPON INCORPORATION 2-12
  - The Property Requirement 2-13
  - The Control Requirement 2-13
  - Stock Requirement 2-17
  - Effect of Sec. 351 on the Transferors 2-17
  - Effect of Sec. 351 on Transferee Corporation 2-21
  - Assumption of the Transferor's Liabilities 2-23
  - Other Considerations in a Sec. 351 Exchange 2-25
- CHOICE OF CAPITAL STRUCTURE 2-28
  - Characterization of Obligations as Debt or Equity Capital 2-29
  - Debt Capital 2-29
  - Equity Capital 2-31
  - Capital Contributions by Shareholders 2-32
  - Capital Contributions by Nonshareholders 2-32
- WORTHLESSNESS OF STOCK OR DEBT OBLIGATIONS 2-34
  - Securities 2-34
  - Unsecured Debt Obligations 2-35
- CONTROVERSIAL ISSUE 2-36
  - Obtaining Ordinary Loss Treatment for Advances to a Corporation 2-36
- TAX PLANNING CONSIDERATIONS 2-37
  - Avoiding Sec. 351 2-37
  - Obtaining an Ordinary Loss Deduction for Stock Losses 2-39
- COMPLIANCE AND PROCEDURAL CONSIDERATIONS 2-39
  - Reporting Requirements under Sec. 351 2-39
  - Reasons for and Procedures to Obtain a Sec. 351 Ruling 2-40
- PROBLEM MATERIALS 2-40
  - Discussion Questions 2-40
  - Problems 2-42
  - Comprehensive Problem 2-46
  - Case Study Problem 2-47
  - Tax Research Problems 2-47

> **LEARNING OBJECTIVES**
>
> *After studying this chapter, you should be able to*
> 1. Explain the tax advantages and disadvantages of using each of the alternative business forms
> 2. Determine the tax characteristics that distinguish partnerships, corporations, and trusts
> 3. Determine the legal requirements for forming a corporation
> 4. Explain the requirements for deferring gain or loss upon incorporation
> 5. Determine the tax consequences of alternative capital structures
> 6. Determine the tax consequences of worthless stock or debt instruments

When a business is started, its owners must decide whether to operate it as a sole proprietorship, a partnership, or a corporation. This chapter discusses the advantages and disadvantages of each of these business entities. Since many businesses find it advantageous to operate as a corporation, this chapter looks at the definition of a corporation for federal income tax purposes. It also discusses the tax consequences of incorporating a business. The chapter closes by looking at the selection of the corporation's capital structure and the tax advantages and disadvantages of alternative capital forms.

The corporate taxation discussion takes a life cycle approach. The corporate life cycle starts in this chapter with its formation. Once it is formed, the corporation is in operation and its taxable income (or loss), its federal income tax liability, and the tax consequences of any distributions to its shareholders must be determined. Finally, at some point the corporation may outlive its usefulness and be liquidated, thus ending the life of the corporation. The corporate life cycle is too complex to discuss in one chapter, however, so more detailed coverage follows in Chapters 3 through 8.

ORGANIZATION FORMS AVAILABLE

OBJECTIVE 1
Explain the tax advantages and disadvantages of using each of the alternative business forms

Business can be conducted in several entities or forms, the most common of which are

- Sole proprietorships
- Partnerships
- Corporations

An overview of each type of entity is presented below.

Sole Proprietorships

A **sole proprietorship** is a business that is owned by a single individual. The sole proprietorship form of business is often selected by individuals who are beginning a new business. It is not a separate entity. The income or loss from a sole proprietorship is reported directly on the proprietor's individual tax return. The proprietor must report all of the business's income and expenses for the year on Schedule C (Profit or (Loss) from Business or Profession) of Form 1040. If the business is profitable, the profit is added to the proprietor's other income and is taxed at his marginal tax rate.

Organization Forms Available • 2-3

Example 2-1 ■ John is single and owns a computer store, which he operates as a sole proprietorship. John reports a $15,000 profit from the store for the year. Assuming he is taxed at a 28% marginal tax rate, his tax on the $15,000 of profits from the store is $4,200 (0.28 × $15,000). ■

If the business operates at a loss, the loss reduces the proprietor's taxable income and provides a tax savings based on the proprietor's marginal tax rate.

Example 2-2 ■ Assume the same facts as in Example 2-1, except that John reports a $15,000 loss on his computer business instead of a $15,000 profit. Assuming he is taxed at a 28% marginal tax rate, the $15,000 loss produces a $4,200 (0.28 × $15,000) tax savings. ■

Typical Misconception
While this chapter emphasizes the tax consequences of selecting the entity in which a business will be conducted, other issues are often more important in making such a decision. For example, the amount of legal liability assumed by an owner is very important and can vary substantially between the different business entities.

Self-Study Question
What is involved in reporting the activities of a sole proprietorship?

Answer
The income/loss of a sole proprietorship is reported on Schedule C. This schedule is simply a summary of the income and expense items of the sole proprietorship. The net income/loss is then carried to Form 1040 and included in the computation of the individual's taxable income.

Tax Advantages. The tax advantages of doing business as a sole proprietorship include

- The entity itself is not subject to taxation. Any income is taxed to the sole proprietor at his marginal tax rate. The marginal tax rate may be lower than the corporation's marginal tax rate that would be imposed on the same amount of income.
- The owner can contribute money to, or withdraw money from, the business without any tax consequences. Although the owner usually maintains separate books and records and a separate bank account for his business, the money in that bank account is still the owner's. He may withdraw money from the business bank account or put money into the business bank account without any tax consequences. He can also contribute property to the business or withdraw property from the business for his personal use without any tax consequences. However, he is taxed on the profits of the business whether those profits are retained in the business or distributed for his own use.
- Losses can be used to offset income from other sources such as interest, dividends, or the salary of the taxpayer's spouse.

Tax Disadvantages. The tax disadvantages of doing business as a sole proprietorship include

- All of the proprietor's profits are taxed to the proprietor when they are earned, even if they are not distributed to him but are reinvested in the business. A corporation's earnings, however, are only taxed to its shareholders when they are distributed. Corporate tax rates may be lower than those imposed on a sole proprietor.
- A sole proprietor is not considered to be an employee of the business. Therefore, the proprietor must pay self-employment taxes on the self-employment income derived from the business. Tax-exempt fringe benefits (e.g., premiums paid on accident and health insurance[1] and group term life insurance) generally are not available to a sole proprietor.
- A sole proprietor must use the same reporting period for both business and individual tax returns. Income cannot be deferred by choosing a fiscal year for the business that is different from the proprietor's own tax year.

---

[1] For tax years beginning between January 1, 1987 and December 31, 1991, Sec. 162(l) permits self-employed individuals to deduct 25% of the health insurance costs incurred on behalf of themselves, their spouses, and their dependents as a trade or business expense. Costs in excess of the 25% ceiling can be deducted as an itemized deduction if they exceed 7.5% of AGI.

Partnerships

Key Point
A partnership is not a taxpaying entity, but rather a tax-reporting entity. The income, loss, and tax credits of the partnership flow through to the respective partners, and the partners determine the tax implications of these particular items.

A **partnership** is a business carried on by two or more individuals or other entities. The partnership form is often used by friends or relatives who decide to go into business together and by groups of investors who want to share the profits and expenses of some type of business or investment such as a real estate project.

A partnership is a tax reporting, but not generally a taxpaying entity. The partnership acts as a conduit. Its income, expenses, losses, credits, and so on flow through to the partners who report those items on their own tax returns. Tax payments are required only of those partnerships that elect a fiscal year reporting period. These payments are based on the amount of the income deferral that is claimed by the partnership.

A partnership must file a tax return every year (Form 1065) to report the results of its operations. When the partnership return is filed, the preparer must send each partner a statement (Schedule K-1, Form 1065) that reports the partner's share of the partnership's income, expenses, losses, credits, and so on. The partners must then report these items on their individual tax returns.

Just as with a sole proprietorship, if the business is profitable, the partners' allocable shares of the profit are added to the partners' other income and taxed at the partners' marginal tax rates.

Example 2-3 ■ Bob is single and owns a 50% interest in the BT Partnership, a calendar year taxpayer. The BT Partnership reports $30,000 of profits for the year, of which $15,000 is Bob's share. Assuming Bob is taxed at a 28% marginal tax rate, his tax on his $15,000 share of partnership profits is $4,200 (0.28 × $15,000). Bob owes the $4,200 in taxes whether the BT Partnership distributes any of its profits to him or not. ■

If a partnership reports a loss, the partners' allocable shares of the loss reduce the partners' other income and provide a tax savings based on the partners' marginal tax rates.

Example 2-4 ■ Assume the same facts as in Example 2-3, except that the BT Partnership reports a $30,000 loss for the year instead of a profit. Assuming Bob is taxed at a 28% marginal tax rate, his $15,000 share of the loss produces a $4,200 (0.28 × $15,000) tax savings. ■

The advantages and disadvantages of doing business as a partnership are similar to those of a sole proprietorship.

Tax Advantages. The tax advantages of doing business as a partnership are

- The partnership itself is exempt from taxation. The income of the partnership is taxed directly to the partners. Their individual tax rates may be lower than the corporate marginal tax rate on the same amount of taxable income.
- The partners can generally contribute money to or withdraw money from the partnership without any adverse tax consequences.
- Profits are taxed only when they are earned. Additional taxes are not imposed on withdrawals made by the partners. Although the partners usually maintain a separate bank account for the partnership, the money in that account belongs to

Organization Forms Available • 2-5

them. They can withdraw money from the partnership account or put money into the partnership account without any tax consequences. They can also contribute property to the partnership or withdraw property from the partnership without any tax consequences.

- Losses can be used by partners to offset income from other sources.

Key Point

If two or more owners exist, obviously a business cannot be conducted as a sole proprietorship. From a compliance and recordkeeping perspective, conducting a business as a partnership is clearly more complicated than conducting the business as a sole proprietorship.

Tax Disadvantages. The tax disadvantages of doing business as a partnership are

- All of the partnership's profits are taxed to the partners when they are earned, even if they are reinvested in the business. The partners' tax rates may be higher than the marginal tax rate that applies to a corporation.
- A partner is not considered to be an employee of the partnership. Therefore, partners must pay self-employment taxes on their share of the partnership's self-employment income. Tax-exempt fringe benefits (e.g., premiums paid on accident and health insurance and group term life insurance) are not generally available to the partners. When such amounts are paid by the partnership on behalf of a partner, the payments are considered to be a property distribution to the partner or taxable compensation.
- Partners generally cannot defer income by choosing a fiscal year for the partnership that is different from the tax year of the partners who own a majority interest in the capital and profits of the partnership. A fiscal year can be elected by the partnership in certain situations which results in a limited income deferral.

Partnerships are discussed in detail in Chapters 9 and 10 of this volume.

Corporations

Key Point

Unlike a sole proprietorship and a partnership, a C corporation is a separate taxpaying entity. In prior years, the maximum corporate rates were lower than the maximum individual rates. Currently, however, corporate rates are 3 percentage points (34% versus 31%) higher than individual rates.

Corporations can be divided into two categories. A regular corporation, or C corporation, is taxed annually on its earnings. These earnings are taxed to the corporation's shareholders when distributed as a dividend. A special S corporation election is also available that permits a corporation to be taxed similarly to a partnership.

C Corporations. A **C corporation** is a separate taxpaying entity which is taxed on its taxable income at rates ranging from 15% to 34%. A corporation must report all of its income and expenses and compute its tax liability on Form 1120 (U.S. Corporation Income Tax Return). Shareholders are not taxed on the corporation's earnings unless they are distributed as dividends. Thus, income is taxed twice: first to the corporation and then to its shareholders when it is distributed as a dividend.

Example 2-5 ■ Jane owns 100% of the stock of York Corporation. York reports taxable income of $50,000 for the year. The first $50,000 of taxable income is taxed at a 15% rate, so York pays a corporate income tax of $7,500 (0.15 × $50,000). If no distributions are made to Jane during the year, she pays no additional tax on York's earnings. However, if York distributes its current after-tax earnings to Jane, she must pay tax on $42,500 ($50,000 − $7,500) of dividend income. Assuming she is in the 28% marginal tax bracket, the tax on the dividend income paid by Jane is $11,900 (0.28 × $42,500). The total tax on York's $50,000 of profits is $19,400 ($7,500 paid by York + $11,900 paid by Jane). ■

Even when a corporation doesn't distribute its profits, double taxation can occur. The profits are taxed to the corporation when they are earned. Then they may be taxed a second time when the shareholder sells his stock or the corporation is liquidated.

Example 2-6 ■ On January 1, 1991, Ken purchases 100% of the stock of York Corporation for $50,000. York Corporation reports taxable income of $50,000 in 1991, on which it pays tax of $7,500. None of the remaining $42,500 is distributed to Ken. However, on January 1, 1992, Ken sells his stock to Mary for $92,500. Ken must report a gain of $42,500 ($92,500 − $50,000). Thus, York's $50,000 profit is taxed twice—once at the corporate level and again at the shareholder level when the stock is sold. ■

TAX ADVANTAGES. The tax advantages of the C corporation form of doing business are

- Corporations (other than personal service corporations) are taxed at rates starting at 15%. Because a corporation is an entity independent from its owners, its marginal tax rate may be lower than the shareholder's marginal tax rate for the first $75,000 of taxable income. As long as the earnings are not distributed and taxed to both the shareholder and the corporation, considerable tax savings may result. As a result, more earnings may be available for reinvestment and the retirement of debt. This advantage is limited, however, by the accumulated earnings tax and the personal holding company tax (see Chapters 3 and 5 for a discussion of personal service corporations and the two penalty taxes).
- Shareholders who are employed by their own corporation are treated as employees for tax purposes. As employees, they are entitled to tax-free fringe benefits (e.g., premiums paid on group term life insurance and accident and health insurance). These fringe benefits can be provided by the corporation with *before-tax* dollars (instead of after-tax dollars). Sole proprietors and partners are not considered to be employees and, therefore, generally are ineligible for such benefits. They must pay for these items with *after-tax* dollars.
- A C corporation is allowed to use a fiscal year instead of a calendar year as its reporting period. A fiscal year may enable a corporation to defer income to a later reporting period. A personal service corporation, however, generally must use a calendar year as its tax year.[2]

Self-Study Question
How are corporate earnings subject to double taxation?

Answer
Corporate earnings are initially taxed to the corporation. In addition, once these earnings are distributed to the shareholders (dividends), these earnings are taxed again. Since the corporation does not receive a deduction for the distribution, these earnings have been taxed twice.

TAX DISADVANTAGES. The tax disadvantages of the C corporation form of doing business are

- "Double taxation" of income when corporate earnings are distributed as dividends to shareholders or the stock is sold or exchanged.
- Shareholders generally cannot withdraw money or property from the corporation without tax consequences. Any distribution to a shareholder is taxable to the shareholder if the corporation has sufficient earnings and profits (E&P).[3]
- Net operating losses can only be carried back or carried forward to offset the corporation's income in other years. For corporations in the start-up phase of operations, these losses cannot provide any tax benefits until a profit is earned in a subsequent year. Shareholders cannot use these losses to offset their income from other sources.
- Capital losses cannot offset any ordinary income of the corporation or of its

---

[2] Sec. 441. See Chapter 3 for the special tax year restrictions applying to personal service corporations.

[3] The term *earnings and profits* is a technical term that is defined generally as the corporations's after-tax earnings and represents the corporation's ability to pay a dividend. The term is discussed in Chapter 5.

shareholders. These losses must be carried back or carried forward to offset capital gains reported in other years.

S Corporations. **S corporations** are corporations that elect to be taxed like a partnership for federal income tax purposes. If the shareholders elect S corporation status, the corporation generally pays no tax. Instead, the corporation acts as a conduit that passes the corporation's income, expenses, losses, and credits through to the individual shareholders just as a partnership does.

Example 2-7 ■ Chuck owns 50% of the stock of Maine Corporation, a qualifying S corporation that is a calendar year taxpayer. For the current year, Maine reports $30,000 of taxable income, all of it ordinary income. Maine pays no tax. Chuck must pay tax on his share of Maine's income, $15,000 (0.50 × $30,000), whether it is distributed to him or not. If Chuck's marginal tax rate is 28%, he pays $4,200 (0.28 × $15,000) of tax on his share of Maine's income. If Maine instead reports a $30,000 loss, Chuck's $15,000 share of the loss reduces his tax liability by $4,200 (0.28 × $15,000). ■

Typical Misconception

An S corporation is still a corporation for legal purposes, and has simply elected to be taxed as an S corporation. One benefit of this election is that an S corporation not only enjoys the corporate attribute of limited liability but also is treated as a flowthrough entity for tax purposes.

TAX ADVANTAGES. The tax advantages of doing business as an S corporation are

- S corporations are generally exempt from taxation. Income is taxed to the shareholders. The shareholders' marginal tax rates may be lower than the corporation's marginal tax rate. An S corporation pays a tax levy only if it formerly was a C corporation and has either substantial passive income, or realizes a net built-in gain.
- Losses flow through to shareholders and can be used to offset income earned from other sources. This is particularly important to corporations just commencing their operations.
- Capital gains are taxed to individual shareholders as though they were earned by the individual. An individual may be able to offset those gains with capital losses from other sources or have them taxed at the 28% maximum rate applicable to individuals.
- Shareholders generally can contribute money to or withdraw money from an S corporation without any adverse tax consequences. Shareholders are taxed only on the annual income of the S corporation.
- Profits are taxed only when they are earned. Additional taxes are generally not imposed on distributions of profits to the S corporation's shareholders.

TAX DISADVANTAGES. The tax disadvantages of doing business as an S corporation are

- All of the corporation's distributed and undistributed profits are taxed to the shareholders. If the shareholders' marginal tax rates exceed those for a C corporation, the capital that is available for reinvestment and debt retirement may be reduced.
- Corporate fringe benefits generally are not available to S corporation shareholders who are employed by the business. Fringe benefits provided by an S corporation are generally treated as a distribution of profits or taxable compensation. The S corporation's shareholder-employees are treated as employees for purposes of social security tax payments on their salary income.
- S corporations generally cannot defer income by choosing a fiscal year for the S corporation that is different from the tax year of the individual shareholders. An

S corporation that elects fiscal year reporting also may have to make a special payment that is based on the amount of the income deferral that is claimed.

S corporations are discussed in detail in Chapter 11 of this volume. In addition, a detailed comparison of the tax rules for partnerships, C corporations, and S corporations is found in Appendix C.

DEFINITION OF A CORPORATION

OBJECTIVE 2
Determine the tax characteristics that distinguish partnerships, corporations, and trusts

The Internal Revenue Code includes "associations, joint stock companies and insurance companies" in its definition of a corporation.[4] In some cases, business trusts[5] and professional associations have been held to be associations taxed as corporations.[6] An entity is classified as an **association,** and thus taxed as a corporation, if it possesses certain corporate characteristics, including[7]

1. Associates
2. An objective to carry on a business and divide the gains therefrom (i.e., joint profit motive)
3. Continuity of life (i.e., the death, insanity, bankruptcy, retirement, resignation, or expulsion of any member will not cause a dissolution of the organization)
4. Centralized management (i.e., any person [or any group of persons which does not include all of its members] has continuing exclusive authority to make the management decisions necessary to the conduct of the business for which the organization was formed)
5. Limited liability (i.e., under local law there is no member who is personally liable for the debts or claims against the organization)
6. Free transferability of interests (i.e., each of its members or those members owning substantially all of the interests in the organization have the power, without the consent of the other members, to substitute for themselves in the same organization a person who is not a member of the organization)

Typical Misconception
State law determines whether an entity is a corporation or a partnership. However, an entity may be taxed for federal income tax purposes as a corporation even though for state law purposes it is organized as some other type of entity.

The laws of the state of incorporation are used to determine whether each of these characteristics is present or not.

Distinguishing Between a Partnership and a Corporation

Partnerships and corporations both have associates (i.e., partners or shareholders) and a joint profit motive. Therefore, only the last four characteristics are considered relevant in distinguishing between a partnership and a corporation for tax purposes. The question of classification is important primarily for partnerships that do not

---

[4] Sec. 7701(a)(3).
[5] *T. A. Morrissey* v. *CIR,* 16 AFTR 1274, 36-1 USTC ¶ 9020 (USSC, 1935).
[6] *U.S.* v. *Arthur R. Kintner,* 46 AFTR 995, 54-2 USTC ¶ 9626 (9th Cir., 1954).
[7] Reg. Sec. 301.7701-2.

Definition of a Corporation • 2-9

conform to the Uniform Partnership Act (UPA) or the Uniform Limited Partnership Act (ULPA). Most states have adopted the UPA or the ULPA or laws that are equivalent to these acts. Therefore, the importance of this question has diminished in recent years. In most cases, a partnership can ensure that it will be treated as a partnership for federal tax purposes by complying with the partnership act of the state in which it operates.

According to Reg. Sec. 301.7701-2(a)(3), an unincorporated organization is classified as an association that is taxed as a corporation if it has at least three of the four distinguishing characteristics. If an organization has only two of the four distinguishing characteristics of a corporation, other characteristics may be used to determine whether the organization should be treated as a corporation or as a partnership for federal tax purposes.[8]

Example 2-8 ■

Self-Study Question

How many corporate characteristics have to exist before the government treats the entity as a corporation?

Answer

In distinguishing between a partnership and a corporation, the "associates" and "joint profit motive" characteristics are ignored because they are common to both. An entity is taxed as a corporation if it possesses any three of the remaining four characteristics listed on the prior page.

A group of 10 individuals form a partnership to engage in the farming business. Under their agreement, the partnership is to have a 25-year life. Management consists of 3 members elected by the partners. The partners may sell their interests to anyone they choose without the approval of the remaining partners. Because the partnership has a fixed 25-year life that is not ended by the death, insanity, bankruptcy, retirement, resignation, or expulsion of any member, the partnership is deemed to have continuity of life. Since the partnership has continuity of life, centralized management, and free transferability of interests, it is classified as an association for federal tax purposes, even though it may be a partnership under state law. Thus, the entity is treated as a C corporation for tax purposes. ■

The 1980s saw a new partnership form emerge as a major investment vehicle whose interests are publicly traded like shares of corporate stock. These partnerships, known as master limited partnerships, have been taxed under the partnership rules, although they possessed a number of the six corporate characteristics. For 1988 and later tax years, these partnerships are taxed as corporations unless 90% or more of the partnership's income is passive-type income. This rule applies even if the entity is classified as a partnership under the general classification rules outlined above (see Chapter 10 for additional coverage of master limited partnerships).

Distinguishing Between an Association and a Trust

Trusts and corporations both have continuity of life, centralized management, limited liability, and free transferability of interests. Therefore, only the first two characteristics (i.e., associates and a joint profit motive) are considered relevant in distinguishing between a trust and an association. A **trust** is classified as an association—and is taxed as a corporation—if it has associates whose objective is to carry on a business and divide the gains therefrom.[9]

---

[8] Revenue Ruling 79-106 (1979-1 C.B. 448) states which other characteristics are *not* used to determine whether an organization should be taxed as an association.

[9] Reg. Sec. 301.7701-2(a)(2).

LEGAL REQUIREMENTS FOR FORMING A CORPORATION

OBJECTIVE 3
Determine the legal requirements for forming a corporation

Key Point
In general, the IRS respects the corporate form for tax purposes. However, it is possible for the IRS to hold that a corporate entity is not taxed as a corporation or that a non-corporate entity is to be taxed as a corporation. Recently, attention has been focused on large publicly traded partnerships and whether they should be taxed as corporations.

Additional Comment
States are not consistent in how they tax corporations. Certain states have no state income taxes. Other states will not recognize an S election, and thus tax an S corporation like a C corporation.

The legal requirements for forming a corporation depend on state law. These requirements may include, for example,

- A minimum amount of capital
- The filing of the articles of incorporation
- The granting of a corporate charter by the state
- The issuance of stock
- The payment of incorporation fees to the state

One of the first decisions that must be made when plans are made to form a corporation is selecting the state in which the organization is to be incorporated. A particular state may provide certain advantages to the corporation or its shareholders because its laws provide smaller legal capital minimums, a smaller incorporation fee, a lower annual franchise tax liability, or a lower corporate income tax liability. Most corporations, however, are incorporated in the state in which they initially conduct their primary business activities.

Regardless of which state is selected for incorporation, the laws of that state must be followed in the incorporation process. Normally, articles of incorporation must be filed with the appropriate state agency. The articles must contain such information as the name of the corporation, the purpose of the corporation, the amount and types of stock the corporation is authorized to issue, and the names of the individuals on the corporation's board of directors. A fee is charged by the state at the time of the incorporation. In addition, an annual franchise tax may be imposed for the privilege of doing business as a corporation.

Yet, even if all the state law requirements are met, an entity is not necessarily treated as a corporation for tax purposes. If, for example, an entity organized as a corporation is found to be a mere agent for its shareholders that does not engage in any significant business activity of its own, its status as a separate entity may be ignored for tax purposes.[10] Conversely, an entity may be taxed as a corporation even if it does *not* qualify as a corporation under state law. If, for example, a corporation has not been properly organized and has failed one or more of the state's requirements for corporation status, but is an "association" under the Internal Revenue Code, it will be taxed as a corporation.

TAX CONSIDERATIONS IN FORMING A CORPORATION

Once a decision has been reached to use the corporate form for conducting a business, the investors generally must transfer money, property (e.g., equipment, furniture, inventory, and receivables), or services (e.g., accounting, legal, or architectural

---

[10] *Florenz R. Ourisman*, 82 T.C. 171 (1984).

Tax Considerations in Forming a Corporation • 2-11

Typical Misconception
Sec. 351 is an example of a nontaxable exchange. However, a nontaxable exchange really means that the recognition of gain/loss is merely deferred. In other words, any gain realized by the transferor shareholders is deferred and will be recognized by such shareholders in subsequent taxable dispositions of the transferee corporation stock.

services) to the corporation in exchange for a debt or equity interest in the corporation. These transfers may have tax consequences to both the transferor and the corporation. For instance, an exchange of property for stock is usually a taxable exchange.[11] However, if Sec. 351(a) (which considers certain transferred business assets to be "changed in form" rather than "disposed of") applies, any gain or loss realized on the exchange is deferred. Thus, the answers to the following questions must be considered carefully in relation to the tax consequences of incorporation:

1. What property should be transferred to the corporation?
2. What services should be provided to the corporation by the transferors or by third parties?
3. What liabilities should be transferred to the corporation in connection with the transferred property?
4. How should the property be transferred to the corporation (e.g., sale, contribution to capital, or loan)?

The tax consequences of taxable and tax-free asset transfers are compared in Example 2-9.

Example 2-9 ■

Brad has operated a successful manufacturing business as a sole proprietorship for several years. For good business reasons, he decides to incorporate his business. Immediately preceding the formation of the corporation, the balance sheet for his sole proprietorship, which uses the accrual method of accounting, is as follows:

		Adjusted Basis	Fair Market Value
Assets:			
Cash		$ 10,000	$ 10,000
Accounts receivable		15,000	15,000
Inventory		20,000	25,000
Equipment	$120,000		
Minus: Depreciation	(35,000)	85,000	100,000
Total		$130,000	$150,000
Liabilities and Owner's Equity:			
Accounts payable		$ 30,000	$ 30,000
Note payable on equipment		50,000	50,000
Owner's equity		50,000	70,000
Total		$130,000	$150,000

If the transfer of all of these assets and liabilities to Block Corporation is a taxable event, Brad must recognize a $5,000 ordinary gain on the transfer of the inventory ($25,000 FMV − $20,000 basis) and a $15,000 ordinary gain on the transfer of the equipment ($100,000 FMV − $85,000 basis). However, if the transaction meets the requirements of Sec. 351(a), the exchange is tax-free; any gain realized on the transfer of the assets and liabilities of the sole proprietorship to the corporation is not recognized. ■

If all exchanges of property for corporate stock were taxable, many business owners would find the tax cost of incorporating prohibitively expensive. In Example 2-9, for

[11] Sec. 1001.

example, Brad would recognize a $20,000 gain on the exchange of his assets for the corporate stock.

A second problem is that losses also are recognized in an ordinary exchange transaction. Therefore, taxpayers might be able to exchange loss properties for stock and securities and recognize a loss while maintaining an economic interest in the property through stock ownership.

Section 351 was enacted to respond to these two problems: (1) to allow taxpayers to incorporate without incurring adverse tax consequences; and (2) to prevent taxpayers from recognizing losses while maintaining ownership of loss assets through stock ownership.

SECTION 351: DEFERRING GAIN OR LOSS UPON INCORPORATION

OBJECTIVE 4
Explain the requirements for deferring gain or loss upon incorporation

Section 351(a) provides that no gain or loss is recognized when property is transferred to a corporation in exchange for the corporation's stock, provided that, immediately after the exchange, the transferors are in control of the corporation.[12] Section 351 does not apply to a transfer of property to an investment company, nor does it apply in certain bankruptcy cases.[13]

Underlying this rule is the belief that, when property is transferred to a controlled corporation, the transferors have merely exchanged direct ownership for indirect ownership by means of having a stock interest in the transferee corporation. If the transferors of property receive anything in addition to stock, such as cash or securities, they may be required to recognize some or all of their realized gain under the provisions of Sec. 351(b).

A transferor's gain or loss that goes unrecognized when Sec. 351 applies is not permanently exempt from taxation; it is only *deferred* until the stock received in the exchange is sold or exchanged. Shareholders who receive stock in an exchange qualifying under Sec. 351 must adjust the basis of their investment to reflect the deferred gain or loss. Thus, to obtain the adjusted basis of the stock, the deferred gain amount must be deducted from (or the deferred loss must be added to) the FMV of the stock issued to the shareholders.

Self-Study Question
What rationale exists for treating a Sec. 351 transaction as a nontaxable exchange?

Example 2-10 ■

Answer
A Sec. 351 transaction is nontaxable because a taxpayer merely exchanges a direct ownership in assets for an indirect ownership in those same assets through stock ownership in the transferee corporation. Also, the wherewithal to pay doctrine suggests that if the transferor does not receive liquid assets in the exchange, then the transaction is not an appropriate taxing event.

Assume the same facts as in Example 2-9. If Sec. 351 applies, Brad does not recognize any gain or loss when the assets and liabilities of his sole proprietorship are transferred to Block Corporation. The $20,000 realized gain ($15,000 gain on equipment + $5,000 gain on inventory) is deferred until Brad sells his Block stock. Brad's basis for the Block stock is decreased to reflect the deferred gain. Thus, Brad's basis in the Block stock is $50,000 ($70,000 FMV of Block stock − $20,000 deferred gain). ■

The specific requirements for complete deferral of gain and loss under Sec. 351(a) are

- Property must be transferred to the corporation in an exchange transaction.

[12] For transfers taking place prior to October 3, 1989, transferors were permitted to receive long-term debt instruments (securities) and stock tax-free in exchange for property. Under the Revenue Reconciliation Act of 1989, securities are no longer permitted to be received tax-free. All debt instruments are treated as boot and taxed under Sec. 351(b).
[13] Secs. 351(e)(1) and (2).

Section 351: Deferring Gain or Loss Upon Incorporation • 2-13

Self-Study Question

How is the contribution of services treated in a Sec. 351 transaction?

Answer

When a corporation is formed, it is not uncommon for some shareholders to contribute property and for other shareholders to contribute services. The contribution of services does not qualify for nonrecognition treatment under Sec. 351. Thus, the FMV of property received by shareholders who contribute their services to a corporation is treated as compensation income.

- The transferors of the property must be in control of the corporation immediately after the exchange.
- The transferors must receive stock of the transferee corporation in exchange for their property.

Each of these requirements is explained below.

The Property Requirement

Nonrecognition of gain or loss applies only to those transfers of property to a corporation that are in exchange for the corporation's stock. Section 351 does not define the term *property*. However, the courts and the government have defined the term *property* to include money and almost any other kind of property including installment obligations, accounts receivable, inventory, equipment, patents, and other intangibles representing "know how," trademarks, trade names, and computer software.[14]

Statutorily excluded from the property definition are

- Services (such as legal or accounting services) received in exchange for stock in a corporation[15]
- Indebtedness of the transferee corporation that is not evidenced by a security[16]
- Interest on an indebtedness of the transferee corporation that accrued on or after the beginning of the transferor's holding period for the debt[17]

The first of these exclusions is perhaps the most important. A person receiving stock as compensation for services must recognize the stock's FMV as compensation (ordinary income) for tax purposes. In other words, an exchange of services for stock is a taxable transaction.[18] A shareholder's basis in the stock received as compensation for services is the stock's FMV.

Example 2-11 ■ Amy and Bill form West Corporation. Amy exchanges cash and other property for 90 shares (90% of the outstanding shares) of West stock. The exchange is tax-free because Sec. 351(a) applies. Bill performs accounting services in exchange for 10 shares of West stock worth $10,000. Bill's exchange is *not* tax-free under Sec. 351. Thus, Bill must recognize $10,000 of ordinary income—the FMV of the West stock received—as compensation for services. Bill's basis in the West stock received is $10,000, its FMV. ■

Key Point

The control requirement is satisfied if, immediately after the transfer, the transferor shareholders own at least 80% of the aggregate voting power and at least 80% of each class of nonvoting stock. While this is the same control test that is used in the corporate reorganization area (Chap. 7), it is different than the affiliated group control requirement (Chap. 8).

The Control Requirement

Section 351 requires the transferors, as a group, to be in control of the transferee corporation immediately after the exchange. A transferor can be any type of tax entity (i.e., an individual, a partnership, another corporation, a trust, and so on). Under Sec. 368(c), *control* is defined as ownership of at least 80% of the total combined voting power of all classes of stock entitled to vote and at least 80% of the total number of shares of all other classes of stock (e.g., nonvoting preferred stock).[19] The minimum

---

[14] For an excellent discussion of the definition of *property*, see footnote 6 of *D. N. Stafford v. U.S.*, 45 AFTR 2d 80-785, 80-1 USTC ¶ 9218 (5th Cir., 1980).
[15] Sec. 351(d)(1).
[16] Sec. 351(d)(2).
[17] Sec. 351(d)(3).
[18] Sec. 61.
[19] In determining whether the 80% requirements are satisfied, the constructive ownership rules of Sec. 318 do not apply (see Rev. Rul. 56-613, 1956-2 C.B. 212).

ownership levels for nonvoting stock are applied to each class of stock rather than to the nonvoting stock in total.[20]

Example 2-12 ■ Dan exchanges property having a $22,000 adjusted basis and a $30,000 FMV for 60% of newly created Sun Corporation's single class of stock. Ed exchanges $20,000 cash for the remaining 40% of the Sun stock. The transaction qualifies under Sec. 351 because the transferors, Dan and Ed, together own at least 80% of the Sun stock immediately after the exchange. Therefore, Dan defers recognition of his $8,000 ($30,000 − $22,000) gain on the exchange. ■

Since services do not qualify as property, stock received by a transferor in exchange for services does not count in determining whether the 80% control test has been met. Unless 80% of the corporation's stock is owned by those transferors who exchanged property for stock, Sec. 351 does not apply and the entire transaction is taxable.

Example 2-13 ■ Dana exchanges property having an $18,000 adjusted basis and a $35,000 FMV for 70 shares of newly created York Corporation's stock. Ellen exchanges legal services worth $15,000 for the remaining 30 shares of York stock. Because Ellen does not transfer any property to York Corporation, her stock is not counted for purposes of the control requirement. Only Dana transfers property to York and is counted for purposes of the control test. However, Dana is not in control of York immediately after the exchange, since he owns only 70% of the York stock. Therefore, Sec. 351 does not apply to the transaction. Dana must recognize $17,000 ($35,000 − $18,000) of gain on the exchange. Dana's basis in the York stock received is $35,000, its FMV. Ellen must recognize $15,000 of ordinary income, the FMV of the stock received for her services. The tax consequences to Ellen are the same whether Sec. 351 applies to Dana or not. Ellen's basis in the York stock is $15,000. ■

Typical Misconception
If a shareholder contributes both services and more than a minimum amount of property, the stock received for the services can be counted in satisfying the 80% control requirement. However, the FMV of stock received for services is still considered compensation to the shareholder.

If the transferors of property own at least 80% of the stock after the exchange, Sec. 351 applies to them, even if it does not apply to a transferor of services.

Example 2-14 ■ Assume the same facts as in Example 2-13, except that a third individual, Fred, provides $35,000 of cash for 70 shares of the York stock. Now Dana and Fred together own more than 80% of the York stock (140 ÷ 170 = 0.82). Therefore, Sec. 351 applies to the transaction. Neither Dana nor Fred recognizes any gain on the exchange. Ellen still must recognize $15,000 of ordinary income, the FMV of the stock she receives for her services. ■

Transferors of Both Property and Services. If a person transfers both services *and* property to a corporation in exchange for the corporation's stock, all of the stock received by that person is counted in determining whether the transferors of property have acquired control.[21]

Example 2-15 ■ Assume the same facts as in Example 2-13, except that in addition to legal services worth $15,000, Ellen also contributes property worth at least $1,500. In such case, all of Ellen's stock counts in determining whether the 80% minimum stock ownership requirement has been met. Since Dana and Ellen together own 100% of the Sun stock, the exchange meets the control requirement of Sec. 351. Therefore,

---

[20] Rev. Rul. 59-259, 1959-2 C.B. 115.
[21] Reg. Sec. 1.351-1(a)(2), Ex. (3).

Dana does not recognize any gain on the exchange. However, Ellen still must recognize $15,000 of ordinary income, the FMV of the stock received as compensation for services. ∎

When a person transfers both property and services in exchange for a corporation's stock, the property must be of more than nominal value in order for that person's stock to count toward the 80% control requirement.[22] The IRS generally requires that the FMV of the transferred property must have a value equal to at least 10% of the value of the services provided. If the value of the transferred property is less than 10% of the value of the services provided, the IRS will not issue an advance ruling stating that the transaction meets the requirements of Sec. 351.[23]

Example 2-16 ∎

Typical Misconception

Taxpayers often think that Sec. 351 applies only to contributions of property to newly formed corporations. This is not true. Sec. 351 can apply to contributions of property to existing corporations as long as the transferor shareholders have control of the transferee corporation immediately after the transaction.

Assume the same facts as in Example 2-15, except that Ellen contributes only $1,000 worth of property in addition to $15,000 of legal services. In such case, the IRS will not issue an advance ruling that the transaction meets the requirements of Sec. 351 because the FMV of the property transferred ($1,000) is less than 10% of the value of the services provided ($1,500 = 0.10 × $15,000). Since the transaction does not meet the IRS requirement for an advance ruling, it is likely to be challenged by the IRS if Ellen treats the transfer as coming under Sec. 351 and her tax return for the year of transfer is audited. ∎

Transfers to Existing Corporations. Section 351 can apply to transfers to an existing corporation as well as transfers to a newly created corporation. The same requirements apply in both cases. Property must be transferred in exchange for stock, and the transferors of the property must be in control of the corporation immediately after the exchange.

Example 2-17 ∎

Jack and Karen own 75 shares and 25 shares of Texas Corporation stock, respectively. Jack transfers property with a $15,000 adjusted basis and a $25,000 FMV to Texas Corporation in exchange for an additional 25 shares of Texas stock. Section 351 applies because, after the transaction, Jack owns 80% (100 ÷ 125 = 0.80) of the Texas stock and is in control of Texas Corporation. Therefore, Jack does not recognize any gain on the exchange. ∎

If a shareholder transfers property to an existing corporation for additional stock but does not own at least 80% of the stock after the exchange, Sec. 351 does not apply. The 80% control requirement precludes many transfers of property to an existing corporation by a new shareholder from qualifying as tax-free. A transfer to an existing corporation is tax-free for a new shareholder only if (1) an 80% interest in the corporation is acquired, or (2) enough existing shareholders also transfer property to the corporation to permit the 80% requirement to be satisfied by the transferors as a group.

Example 2-18 ∎

Alice owns all 100 shares of Local Corporation's stock valued at $100,000. Beth owns property that has a $15,000 adjusted basis and a $100,000 FMV. Beth contributes the property to Local Corporation in exchange for 100 shares of newly issued Local stock. Section 351 does not apply because Beth owns only 50% of the Local stock after the exchange and is not in control of Local Corporation. Beth must recognize an $85,000 ($100,000 − $15,000) gain on the exchange. ∎

---

[22] Reg. Sec. 1.351-1(a)(1)(ii).
[23] Rev. Proc. 77-37, 1977-2 C.B. 568, Sec. 3.07.

If an existing shareholder exchanges property for additional stock in order to help another shareholder qualify under Sec. 351, the stock received must be of more than nominal value.[24] For advance ruling purposes, the IRS requires that the value of the property transferred must be at least 10% of the value of the stock and securities already owned.[25]

Example 2-19 ■ Assume the same facts as in Example 2-18, except that Alice transfers additional property worth $10,000 for an additional 10 shares of Local stock. Now Alice and Beth are both considered to be transferors and Sec. 351 does apply. Neither Alice nor Beth recognize any gain on the exchange. If Alice transfers property worth less than $10,000, the IRS will not issue an advance ruling that Sec. 351 applies to the exchange. ■

Disproportionate Exchanges of Property and Stock. Section 351 does not require that the value of the stock received by the transferors be proportional to the value of the property transferred. However, if the value of the stock received is *not* proportional to the value of the property transferred, the exchange must be treated in accordance with its true nature; that is, a proportional exchange followed by a gift, payment of compensation, or payment of a liability owed by one shareholder to another.[26] If the true nature of the transaction is a gift from one transferor to another transferor, for example, the donor is treated as though he received stock equal in value to the property contributed to the corporation and then gave some of his stock to the donee.

Example 2-20 ■ Don and his son John transfer property worth $75,000 (adjusted basis to Don of $42,000) and $25,000 (adjusted basis to John of $20,000), respectively, to the newly formed Star Corporation in exchange for all 100 shares of Star stock. Don and John receive 25 and 75 shares of Star stock, respectively. Since Don and John are in control of Star Corporation immediately after the transaction, Sec. 351 applies and no gain or loss is recognized on the exchange. However, since the stock was not received by Don and John in proportion to the FMV of their property contributions, it is likely that Don has received 75 shares of Star stock and made a gift of 50 shares of Star stock (worth $50,000) to John. If a gift has in fact been made, Don may be required to pay gift taxes on the gift to John. Don's basis in the 25 shares of Star stock is $14,000 ([25 ÷ 75] × $42,000 basis in the property transferred). John's basis in the 75 shares is $48,000 ($20,000 basis in the property transferred by John + [$42,000 − $14,000] basis in the shares received from John). ■

Additional Comment

If one shareholder has a prearranged plan to dispose of his stock, and the disposition drops the ownership of the transferor shareholders below the required 80% control, such disposition can disqualify the Sec. 351 transaction for all of the shareholders. Thus, as a possible protection, all shareholders should be required to provide a written representation that they do not currently have a plan to dispose of their stock.

Immediately after the Exchange. Section 351 requires that the transferors be in control of the transferee corporation "immediately after the exchange." This requirement does not mean that all transferors must exchange their property for stock simultaneously. The exchanges must all be agreed to beforehand, and the agreement must be executed in an expeditious and orderly manner.[27]

Example 2-21 ■ Art, Beth, and Charles agree to form New Corporation. Art and Beth each transfer property worth $25,000 for one-third of the New stock. Charles contributes $25,000 cash for one-third of the New stock. Art and Charles exchange their property and cash, respectively, for stock on January 10, 1991. Beth exchanges her property for

---

[24] Reg. Sec. 1.351-1(a)(1)(ii).
[25] Rev. Proc. 77-37, 1977-2 C.B. 568, Sec. 3.07.
[26] Reg. Sec. 1.351-1(b)(1).
[27] Reg. Sec. 1.351-1(a)(1).

stock on March 3, 1991. Since all three of the exchanges are part of the same prearranged transaction, the Sec. 351 nonrecognition rules apply to all three exchanges. ∎

Section 351 does not require the transferors to retain control of the transferee corporation for any specific length of time after the exchange takes place. Control is only required "immediately after the exchange." However, the transferors must not have a prearranged plan to dispose of their stock outside the group. If they have such an arrangement, they are not considered to be in control immediately after the exchange.[28]

Example 2-22 ∎ Alan, Bill, and Carl form White Corporation. Each contributes appreciated property worth $25,000 for one-third of the White stock. Prior to the exchange, Alan arranges to sell his stock to Dana as soon as he receives it. This prearranged plan means that Alan, Bill, and Carl do *not* have control immediately after the exchange. Therefore, Sec. 351 does not apply to the transaction. ∎

Stock Requirement

Under Sec. 351, no gain or loss is recognized by those transferors who exchange property solely for stock of the transferee corporation. Under Sec. 351 any type of stock of the controlled corporation—voting or nonvoting stock, preferred or common stock—may be received by the transferors. However, stock does not include stock rights or stock warrants.[29]

Topic Review 2-1 presents a summary of the major requirements to achieve a tax-free transfer under Sec. 351.

Effect of Sec. 351 on the Transferors

If all the requirements of Sec. 351 have been met, the transferors do not recognize any gain or loss on the exchange of their property for stock in the corporation to which they have contributed their property. The receipt of property other than stock does not completely disqualify the transaction from coming under Sec. 351. However, the

TOPIC REVIEW 2-1

Major Requirements of Sec. 351

1. Nonrecognition of gain or loss applies only to transfers of **property** in **exchange** for a corporation's stock. It does not apply to an exchange of services for stock.
2. The transferors of property must be in **control** of the transferee corporation immediately after the exchange. Control means ownership of at least 80% of the voting power and 80% of all other classes of stock.
3. The transferors must be in control **immediately** after the exchange. There must not be any prearranged plan to dispose of the stock after the exchange.
4. Nonrecognition applies to an exchange of property for **stock**. If anything other than stock is received, it is considered boot. Gain is recognized to the extent of the lesser of the FMV of any boot received or the realized gain.

---

[28] Rev. Rul. 79-70, 1979-1 C.B. 144.
[29] Reg. Sec. 1.351-1(a)(1)(ii).

receipt of property other than stock may require the transferor to recognize part or all of their realized gain under Sec. 351(b).

Key Point

If boot property is received by a transferor shareholder, he must recognize gain to the extent of the lesser of (1) realized gain or (2) FMV of boot received. However, no matter how much boot is received, realized losses are not recognized in a Sec. 351 transaction.

Receipt of Boot. If a transferor receives any money or property other than stock of the transferee corporation, the additional property is considered to be **boot.** Boot may include, for example, cash, short-term notes, securities, or stock in another corporation. When boot is received, gain must be recognized to the extent of the lesser of (1) the transferor's realized gain or (2) the FMV of the boot property received.[30] A loss, however, is never recognized in an exchange qualifying under Sec. 351 whether boot is received or not.

The character of the gain recognized when boot is received in a Sec. 351 transaction depends upon the type of property that is transferred. For example, if a capital asset such as stock of another corporation is transferred, the recognized gain is a capital gain. If a Sec. 1231 property such as equipment or a building is transferred, the recognized gain is Sec. 1231 gain, except for any ordinary income that is recaptured under Secs. 1245 or 1250.[31] If inventory is transferred, the recognized gain is ordinary income. Note that depreciation recapture is *not* required unless boot is received by the transferor and a gain must be recognized.[32]

Example 2-23 ■ Pam, Rob, and Sam form East Corporation. Pam transfers machinery (Sec. 1231 property) that has a $10,000 adjusted basis and a $12,500 FMV in exchange for 25 shares of East stock. Rob transfers land (a capital asset) with an $18,000 adjusted basis and a $25,000 FMV for 40 shares of East stock and a $5,000 short-term note. Sam transfers $17,500 in cash for 35 shares of East stock. The transaction meets the requirements of Sec. 351 except that, in addition to East stock, Rob receives boot of $5,000 (the FMV of the short-term note). Rob realizes a $7,000 ($25,000 − $18,000) gain on the exchange. Rob must recognize $5,000 of gain—the lesser of the $7,000 realized gain or the $5,000 boot received. The gain is capital gain because the property transferred was a capital asset in Rob's hands. Pam realizes a $2,500 gain on her exchange of machinery for East stock. But, even though Pam might be required to recapture depreciation taken on the machinery as ordinary income if the machinery were sold or exchanged, Pam does not recognize any gain on the exchange because Sec. 351 applies to the exchange and Pam does not receive any boot. Sam does not realize or recognize any gain on his cash purchase of the East stock. ■

Typical Misconception

If multiple assets are contributed by a transferor, the gain/loss realized in the exchange must be computed on an asset-by-asset basis. If all the assets were aggregated into one computation, then any built-in losses would be netted against the gains. Such a result is inappropriate since losses cannot be recognized in a Sec. 351 transaction.

Computing Gain When Several Assets Are Transferred. If more than one asset is transferred, Rev. Rul. 68-55 adopts a "separate properties approach" for computing gain or loss.[33] The gain or loss realized and recognized is computed separately for each property transferred. The transferor is assumed to have received a proportionate share of the stock, securities, and boot for each property transferred based upon the assets' relative FMVs.

Example 2-24 ■ Joan transfers three properties to newly created North Corporation in a transaction qualifying under Sec. 351. The total FMV of the assets transferred is $110,000. The consideration received by Joan consists of $100,000 of North stock and

---

[30] Sec. 351(b).
[31] Section 1239 may also require some gain to be characterized as ordinary income. See Chapter 13 of *Prentice Hall's Federal Taxation: Individuals* companion text.
[32] Secs. 1245(b)(3) and 1250(c)(3).
[33] 1968-1 C.B. 140.

Section 351: Deferring Gain or Loss Upon Incorporation • 2-19

$10,000 in cash. The following summary shows how Joan determines her realized and recognized gain using the procedure outlined in Rev. Rul. 68-55.

	Asset 1	Asset 2	Asset 3	Total
FMV of asset transferred	$22,000	$33,000	$55,000	$110,000
Percent of total FMV	20%	30%	50%	100%
FMV of North stock received in exchange for the asset (FMV of stock × percent of total FMV)	$20,000	$30,000	$50,000	$100,000
Cash received in exchange (Cash × percent of total FMV)	2,000	3,000	5,000	10,000
Total proceeds	$22,000	$33,000	$55,000	$110,000
Minus: Adjusted basis of asset	(40,000)	(20,000)	(25,000)	(85,000)
Gain (or loss) realized	($18,000)	$13,000	$30,000	$25,000
Allocation of boot received	$ 2,000	$ 3,000	$ 5,000	$10,000
Gain recognized (lesser of realized gain or boot received)	None	$ 3,000	$ 5,000	$ 8,000

Under the separate properties approach, the loss realized on the transfer of asset 1 does not offset the gains realized on the transfer of assets 2 and 3. Therefore, only $8,000 of the total $25,000 realized gain is recognized, even though Joan receives $10,000 of boot. It may be advisable to sell asset 1 to North Corporation. See, however, the possible loss limitation under Sec. 267 if Joan is a controlling shareholder (page 2-37). ■

Computing a Shareholder's Basis.

BOOT PROPERTY. A transferor's basis for any boot property received is the property's FMV.[34]

STOCK. A shareholder's adjusted basis for stock received in an exchange qualifying under Sec. 351 is computed as follows:[35]

> Adjusted basis of property transferred to the corporation
> Plus: Any gain recognized by the transferor
> Minus: FMV of boot received from the corporation
> Money received from the corporation (including the amount of any liabilities assumed or acquired by the corporation)
> Adjusted basis of stock received

Example 2-25 ■ In 1991 Bob transfers Sec. 1231 property acquired in 1990 having a $50,000 basis and an $80,000 FMV to South Corporation. Bob receives all 100 shares of South stock having a $70,000 FMV and a $10,000 90-day South Corporation note (boot property). Bob realizes a $30,000 gain on the exchange, computed as follows:

---

[34] Sec. 358(a)(2).
[35] This method follows the provisions of Sec. 358(a)(1).

Key Point

Since Sec. 351 is a deferral provision, any unrecognized gain must be reflected in the basis of the stock received by the transferor shareholder. This is accomplished by substituting the transferor's basis in the property given up (plus certain adjustments) for the basis of the stock received.

FMV of stock received	$70,000
Plus: FMV of 90-day note	10,000
Amount realized	$80,000
Minus: Adjusted basis of property transferred	(50,000)
Realized gain	$30,000

Bob's recognized gain is the lesser of the $30,000 realized gain or the $10,000 FMV of the boot property, or $10,000 of Sec. 1231 gain. The Sec. 351 rules thus require Bob to defer $20,000 ($30,000 − $10,000) of gain. Bob's basis for the South stock is $50,000, computed as follows:

Adjusted basis of property transferred	$50,000
Plus: Gain recognized by Bob	10,000
Minus: FMV of boot received	(10,000)
Adjusted basis of stock to Bob	$50,000

■

If a transferor receives more than one class of stock, his basis for the stocks received must be allocated among the classes of stock received in accordance with their relative FMVs.[36]

Example 2-26 ■

Self-Study Question

What is the simplest method of determining the basis of the assets received by the transferor shareholder?

Answer

The basis of all boot property is its FMV, and the basis of stock received is the stock's FMV minus any deferred gain plus any deferred loss.

Assume the same facts as in Example 2-25, except that Bob receives 100 shares of South common stock with a $50,000 FMV, and 50 shares of South preferred stock with a $20,000 FMV, and a South Corporation 90-day note with a $10,000 FMV. The recognized gain remains $10,000. The total adjusted basis of the stocks is $50,000 ($50,000 basis of property transferred + $10,000 gain recognized − $10,000 FMV of boot received). This basis must be allocated between the common and preferred stocks that are received in accordance with their relative FMVs, as follows:

$$\text{Basis of common stock} = \frac{\$50,000}{\$50,000 + \$20,000} \times \$50,000 = \$35,714$$

$$\text{Basis of preferred stock} = \frac{\$20,000}{\$50,000 + \$20,000} \times \$50,000 = \$14,286$$

Bob's basis for the short-term note is $10,000, its FMV. ■

Transferor's Holding Period. The transferor's holding period for any stock received in exchange for a capital asset or Sec. 1231 property includes (i.e., is "tacked onto") the holding period for the property transferred.[37] If any other kind of property (i.e., inventory) is exchanged for the stock, the transferor's holding period for the stock received begins on the day after the exchange. The holding period for boot property begins on the day after the exchange.[38]

---

[36] Sec. 358(b)(1) and Reg. Sec. 1.358-2(b)(2).

[37] Sec. 1223(1). Revenue Ruling 85-164 (1985-2 C.B. 117) illustrates the holding period determination when multiple properties are transferred in an exchange coming under Sec. 351. Under this ruling, it is possible that a single share of stock may have two holding periods; that is, a carryover holding period for the portion of such share received in exchange for a capital asset or a Sec. 1231 property and a holding period that commences on the day after the exchange for the portion of such share received for inventory or other property.

[38] Sec. 1223(2).

Section 351: Deferring Gain or Loss Upon Incorporation • 2-21

Example 2-27 ■ Assume the same facts as in Example 2-25. Bob's holding period for the stock starts in 1990, when the Sec. 1231 property was purchased. His holding period for the note starts on the day after the exchange in 1991. ■

Topic Review 2-2 presents a summary of the tax consequences of a tax-free asset transfer to the transferor and the transferee corportion.

Effect of Sec. 351 on Transferee Corporation

The transferee corporation needs to determine (1) the amount of gain or loss (if any) it must recognize when it issues stock or debt instruments in exchange for property or services and (2) the basis for any property or services that are acquired.

Gain or Loss Recognized by the Transferee Corporation. Corporations do not recognize any gain or loss when they exchange their own stock for property.[39] This rule applies whether the exchange is subject to Sec. 351 or not. It is irrelevant whether the stock the corporation is exchanging is newly issued stock or treasury stock.

Self-Study Question
What is the tax consequence of a Sec. 351 transaction to the transferee corporation?

Answer
A corporation does not recognize gain/loss when it acquires property in exchange for its own stock. This general rule applies not only to Sec. 351 transfers but also to other acquisitions of property when the consideration given is the corporation's own stock.

TOPIC REVIEW 2-2

Tax Consequences of a Sec. 351 Transaction		
To Shareholders:		
General Rule:		1. No gain or loss is recognized when property is exchanged for stock.
Exception:		2. Gain is recognized equal to the lesser of the realized gain or the sum of any money received plus the FMV of any other boot property received. The character of the gain recognized depends on the type of property given up.
		3. The basis of the stock received equals the adjusted basis of the property transferred plus the gain recognized minus the FMV of the boot property received minus any money received (including liabilities assumed or acquired by the transferee corporation).
		4. The holding period of the stock received for capital assets or Sec. 1231 property includes the holding period for the transferred property. The holding period of stock received for other property begins on the day after the exchange.
To Transferee Corporation:		
General Rule:		1. No gain or loss is recognized by a corporation when it exchanges its own stock for property.
		2. The corporation's basis in any property received in a Sec. 351 exchange is the transferor's basis plus any gain recognized by the transferor.
		3. The corporation's holding period for property received in a Sec. 351 exchange includes the transferor's holding period.

[39] Sec. 1032.

Example 2-28 ▪

West Corporation acquires 100 shares of treasury stock for $10,000. The next year West exchanges the 100 shares for land having a $15,000 FMV. West realizes a $5,000 ($15,000 − $10,000) gain on the exchange. None of this gain is recognized. ▪

Corporations do not recognize any gain or loss when they exchange their own debt instruments for property or services.

A corporation must recognize gain (but not loss) if it transfers appreciated property to a transferor as part of a Sec. 351 exchange. The amount and character of the gain that is recognized is determined as though the property had been sold by the transferee corporation immediately before the transfer.

Example 2-29 ▪

Key Point
Since Sec. 351 transfers are nontaxable exchanges, the transferee corporation takes a carryover basis (plus gains recognized by the transferor shareholder) in the assets received. Thus, any of the built-in gains or losses in the contributed property may be subsequently recognized by the transferee corporation.

Alice transfers land having a $100,000 FMV and a $60,000 adjusted basis to Ace Corporation in a tax-free transfer coming under Sec. 351. In return Alice receives 75 additional shares of Ace common stock having a $75,000 FMV and Zero Corporation common stock having a $25,000 FMV. The Zero stock, a capital asset, has a $10,000 basis on Ace Corporation's books. Alice realizes a $40,000 gain ([$75,000 + $25,000] − $60,000) on the land transfer, of which $25,000 must be recognized. In addition, Ace Corporation must recognize a $15,000 capital gain ($25,000 − $10,000) when transferring the Zero stock to Alice.[40] ▪

Typical Misconception
If built-in gain property is contributed in a Sec. 351 transfer, such built-in gain is actually duplicated. This occurs since the transferee corporation assumes the potential gain through its carryover basis in the assets it receives. The transferor shareholder also assumes the potential gain through its substituted basis in the transferee corporation stock. Obviously, a similar duplication occurs for built-in loss property.

Transferee Corporation's Basis for Property Received. A corporation that purchases property by exchanging its stock in a transaction that is taxable to the transferor uses the property's acquisition cost (i.e., its FMV) as its basis for the property. However, if the exchange qualifies for nonrecognition treatment under Sec. 351 and is wholly or partially tax-free to the transferor, the corporation's basis for the property is computed as follows:[41]

Transferor's adjusted basis for property
transferred to the corporation
Plus: Gain recognized by transferor
―――――――――――――――――――――――
Transferee corporation's basis for property

The transferee corporation's holding period for property acquired in a transaction satisfying the Sec. 351 requirements includes the period of time the property was held by the transferor.[42] This general rule applies to all properties without regard to their character in the transferor's hands or the amount of gain recognized by the transferor.

Example 2-30 ▪

Top Corporation exchanges 100 shares of its stock for land having a $15,000 FMV. The land is held by Tina, whose adjusted basis for the land is $12,000. If the exchange satisfies the Sec. 351 requirements, Tina does not recognize any gain on the exchange. Top Corporation's basis in the land is $12,000, the same basis that Tina had in the land. Top Corporation's holding period includes the period of time the land was held by Tina. However, if the exchange does *not* satisfy the Sec. 351 requirements, Tina must recognize $3,000 of gain. Top Corporation's basis in the land is its $15,000 acquisition cost. Its holding period for the land begins on the day after the acquisition date. ▪

---

[40] Sec. 351(f).
[41] Sec. 362.
[42] Sec. 1223(2).

Assumption of the Transferor's Liabilities

Self-Study Question
Does the assumption of debt by the transferee corporation constitute a boot payment to the transferor shareholder?

Answer
The general rule is no, with two exceptions: (1) if the liabilities assumed are created for tax avoidance purposes or (2) if the liabilities assumed are in excess of the basis of the contributed property.

When property is transferred to a controlled corporation, the transferor's liabilities are often assumed (or the property is taken subject to a mortgage) by the corporation as well. The question arises as to whether the assumption of liabilities by the transferee is equivalent to a cash payment to the transferor and, therefore, is boot. In many other kinds of transactions, the assumption of a transferor's liability by the transferee is treated as a payment of cash to the transferor. For example, in a like-kind exchange, if a transferor's liability is assumed by a transferee, the transferor is treated as though he received a cash payment equal to the amount of the liability assumed. However, if a transaction satisfies the Sec. 351 requirements, the special rules of Sec. 357 apply and the liability transfer is not treated as a cash payment.

General Rule—Sec. 357(a). The assumption of liabilities by a transferee corporation in a property transfer qualifying under Sec. 351 is *not* considered to result in the receipt of money by the transferor. Therefore, the transferee corporation's assumption of liabilities does not cause the transferor to have to recognize part or all of his realized gain.

Example 2-31 ▪ Roy and Sam form Palm Corporation. Roy transfers property having a $15,000 adjusted basis and a $32,000 FMV to Palm Corporation for 50 shares of Palm stock. The property has an $8,000 mortgage, which Palm Corporation assumes. Sam transfers $24,000 cash for the remaining 50 shares of Palm stock. The transaction meets the requirements of Sec. 351. Roy realizes a $17,000 ([$24,000 + $8,000] − $15,000) gain on the exchange but recognizes none of this gain because Sec. 351 applies and Roy received no boot. The mortgage assumption is not considered to be money paid to Roy. ▪

There are, however, two exceptions to the general rule of Sec. 357(a). These exceptions, which are discussed below, are (1) transfers that are made for the purpose of tax avoidance or that have no bona fide business purpose, and (2) transfers where the liabilities assumed or acquired by the corporation are in excess of the basis of the properties transferred by the transferor.

Typical Misconception
If any of the assumed liabilities are created for tax avoidance purposes, this taints all *of the assumed liabilities.*

Tax Avoidance or No Bona Fide Business Purpose—Sec. 357(b). All liabilities assumed by a controlled corporation (or taken subject to the property) *are* considered money received by the transferor (and, therefore, are considered boot) if the principal purpose of the transfer of any portion of such liabilities is to avoid tax or if there is no bona fide business purpose for the transfer.

Liabilities whose transfer might be considered to have tax avoidance as the principal purpose are those that were incurred shortly before the property and liability were transferred to the corporation. Perhaps the most important factor in determining whether a tax avoidance purpose is present when liabilities are transferred is the length of time between the incurrence of the liability and the transfer of the liability to the corporation.

The assumption of liabilities is normally considered to have a business purpose if the liabilities were incurred by the transferor in the normal course of business or in the course of acquiring business property. Examples of liabilities that have no business purpose and whose transfer would cause all liabilities transferred to be considered boot are personal obligations of the transferor, including a home mortgage or any other loans of a personal nature.

Example 2-32 ▪ David owns land having a $100,000 FMV and a $60,000 adjusted basis. The land is not encumbered by any liabilities. In order to obtain cash for his personal use,

David transfers the land to his wholly owned corporation in exchange for additional stock and $25,000 cash. Since the cash received is considered boot, David must recognize $25,000 of gain. Assume instead that David mortgages the land for $25,000 to obtain the needed cash. If shortly after obtaining the mortgage, David transfers the land and the mortgage to his corporation for additional stock, and if David can show a business purpose for the transfer of the mortgage, the assumption of the mortgage is not considered to be money received by David and no gain is recognized. If, however, there is no business purpose for the transfer of the mortgage, the $25,000 mortgage assumed by the corporation would be considered boot. David's recognized gain is the lesser of the boot received ($25,000) or his realized gain ($40,000), or $25,000. ■

Self-Study Question

Is the excess liability amount treated as boot under Sec. 357(c)?

Answer

The amount by which the assumed liabilities exceeds the basis of contributed property is not merely considered boot. Instead, this excess amount is considered to be gain recognized regardless of whether any realized gain exists. Thus, this exception is more punitive to the transferor shareholder than the tax avoidance exception.

Liabilities in Excess of Basis—Sec. 357(c). Under Sec. 357(c), if the total amount of liabilities transferred to a controlled corporation by a transferor exceeds the total adjusted basis of all properties transferred by such transferor, the excess liability amount is a gain that is taxable to the transferor. This rule applies irrespective of whether there is any realized gain or loss. The rule recognizes the fact that the transferor has received a benefit (in the form of a release from liabilities) that is greater than his original investment in the transferred property. Therefore, the excess amount is taxable. The character of the recognized gain depends on the types of properties that were transferred to the transferee corporation. The transferor's basis in any stock received is zero.

Example 2-33 ■

Key Point

Because of the "liabilities in excess of basis" exception, many cash basis transferor shareholders could inadvertently create recognized gain in a Sec. 351 transaction. However, a special exception exists that protects cash basis taxpayers. This exception provides that liabilities that would give rise to a deduction when paid are not treated as liabilities for this purpose.

Judy transfers land (a capital asset) having a $70,000 adjusted basis and a $125,000 FMV and $10,000 cash to Duke Corporation in exchange for all of its stock. Duke Corporation assumes the $100,000 mortgage on the land. There is no tax-avoidance purpose in the mortgage assumption, and the liability assumption does have the requisite business purpose. Although Judy does not receive any boot, Judy must recognize a $20,000 ($100,000 − $80,000) capital gain, the amount by which the liabilities assumed by Duke Corporation exceeds the basis of the land and the cash transferred by Judy. Judy's basis for the Duke stock is zero computed as follows:

	Judy's basis in the land transferred	$70,000
Plus:	Cash transferred	10,000
	Gain recognized	20,000
Minus:	Boot received (i.e., liabilities assumed by Duke)	(100,000)
	Judy's basis in the Duke stock	–0–

Note that if it were not for the Sec. 357(c) requirement to recognize a $20,000 gain, Judy's basis in the Duke stock would be a negative $20,000 ($80,000 − $100,000). ■

Liabilities of a Taxpayer Using the Cash Method of Accounting—Sec. 357(c)(3). Special problems arise when a taxpayer using the cash or hybrid method of accounting transfers the properties and liabilities of an ongoing business to a corporation in a tax-free exchange under Sec. 351.[43] Quite often, the main assets that are transferred are accounts receivable that have a zero basis. Liabilities are usually transferred as well. Consequently, the amount of liabilities transferred often exceeds the total basis of the properties transferred.

Under Sec. 357(c), gain equal to the amount by which the liabilities assumed or acquired exceed the total basis of the properties transferred would have to be

---

[43] Sec. 357(c)(3).

recognized. However, a special exception to Sec. 357(c) provides that the term *liabilities* does *not* include any amount that (1) would give rise to a deduction when paid or (2) any amount payable under Sec. 736(a) (i.e., amounts payable to a retiring partner or to liquidate a deceased partner's interest).[44] These amounts are also not considered to be liabilities for purposes of applying the Sec. 358 basis rules to determine the shareholder's basis for any stock items.[45] Therefore, they do not reduce the shareholder's basis in his stock.

Example 2-34 ■ Tracy operates an accounting practice as a sole proprietorship. She transfers the assets of her cash basis accounting practice to Prime Corporation in exchange for all of the Prime stock. The items transferred are

	Adjusted Basis	FMV
Cash	$ 5,000	$ 5,000
Furniture	5,000	8,000
Accounts receivable	—0—	50,000
Total	$10,000	$63,000
Accounts payable (expenses)	$—0—	$25,000
Note payable (on furniture)	2,000	2,000
Owner's equity	8,000	36,000
Total	$10,000	$63,000

If the accounts payable were considered *liabilities*, the $27,000 of liabilities transferred (i.e., the $25,000 of accounts payable and the $2,000 note payable) would exceed the $10,000 basis for the properties that are transferred. However, since payment of the $25,000 of accounts payable gives rise to a deduction, they are not considered liabilities for purposes of applying Sec. 357(c). The $2,000 note payable *is* considered a liability because paying it would *not* give rise to a deduction. Thus, for purposes of applying Sec. 357(c), the total liabilities transferred to Prime Corporation amount to $2,000. Since that amount does not exceed the $10,000 basis of the properties transferred, no gain is recognized. The accounts payable are not considered liabilities for purposes of computing Tracy's basis for the Prime stock. Therefore, Tracy's basis for her stock is $8,000 ($10,000 − $2,000). ■

Topic Review 2-3 presents a summary of the liability assumption and acquisition rules of Sec. 357.

Other Considerations in a Sec. 351 Exchange

Key Point
Unless gain is recognized by the transferor, any potential depreciation recapture follows the contributed property into the transferee corporation. When such property is subsequently disposed of, the depreciation recapture rules must be applied at that time.

Recapture of Depreciation. If a Sec. 351 exchange is completely nontaxable (i.e., no boot is received by the transferor), no depreciation recapture is required.[46] Instead, the entire amount of the transferor's recapture potential is transferred to the transferee corporation. Where part of the depreciation recapture is recognized by the transferor as ordinary income (e.g., under Sec. 351(b)), the remaining recapture potential is transferred to the transferee corporation. If the transferee corporation subsequently disposes of the property, it is subject to the depreciation recapture rules on all depreciation that it has claimed plus the recapture potential transferred by the transferor.

---

[44] Sec. 357(c)(3)(A).
[45] Sec. 358(d)(2).
[46] Secs. 1245(b)(3) and 1250(d)(3).

TOPIC REVIEW 2-3

Liability Assumption and Acquisition Rules of Sec. 357

1. *General Rule (Sec. 357(a))*: The assumption or acquisition of liabilities by a transferee corporation in a Sec. 351 exchange is *not* considered to result in the receipt of money/boot by the shareholder for gain recognition purposes. The liabilities are treated as money for purposes of determining the basis of the stock received.
2. *Exception 1 (Sec. 357(b))*: All liabilities assumed or acquired by a transferee corporation *are* considered money/boot received by the transferor if the principal purpose of the transfer of any of the liabilities was tax avoidance or if there is no bona fide business purpose for the transfer.
3. *Exception 2 (Sec. 357(c))*: If the total amount of liabilities assumed or acquired by a transferee corporation exceeds the total basis of properties transferred by a transferor, the excess liability amount is recognized as gain by the transferor.
4. *Special Rule (Sec. 357(c)(3))*: For purposes of Exception 2, the term liabilities for a cash or hybrid method of accounting transferor does not include any amount that (1) would give rise to a deduction when paid, or (2) any amount payable to a retiring partner or to liquidate a deceased partner's interest.

Example 2-35 ■ Ken transfers machinery having an $18,000 adjusted basis and a $35,000 FMV for all 100 shares of Wheel Corporation's stock. Before the transfer, Ken used the machinery in his business. He originally paid $25,000 for the machinery and claimed $7,000 of depreciation before transferring the machinery. Ken does not recapture any depreciation on the transfer. Instead, the $7,000 recapture potential is transferred to Wheel Corporation. After claiming an additional $2,000 of depreciation on the machinery, Wheel's basis in the machinery is $16,000. If Wheel Corporation now sells the machinery for $33,000, it must recognize a $17,000 ($33,000 − $16,000) gain on the sale. Of this gain, $9,000 is ordinary income recaptured under Sec. 1245. The remaining $8,000 is Sec. 1231 gain. ■

Computing Depreciation. When a shareholder transfers depreciable property to a corporation in a nontaxable Sec. 351 exchange, and the shareholder has been depreciating the property, the corporation must continue to use the same depreciation method and recovery period with respect to the shareholder's basis in the property.[47] For the year of the transfer, the depreciation must be allocated between the transferor and the transferee corporation according to the number of months the property was held by each. The transferee corporation is assumed to have held the property for the entire month in which the property was transferred.[48]

Example 2-36 ■

Key Point

Not only does the basis of contributed property carry over to the transferee corporation, but so also does the depreciation method and recovery period for such property. However, if the transferee corporation's basis is higher than the transferor's basis, such excess is treated as new property subject to the MACRS rules.

On June 10, 1990, Carla purchases a computer (5-year property for Modified ACRS purposes) for $6,000, which she uses in her sole proprietorship. She claims $1,200 (0.20 × $6,000) of depreciation for 1990. On February 10, 1991, she transfers the computer and other assets of her sole proprietorship to King Corporation in exchange for all of the King stock. No gain or loss is recognized on the exchange. For the year 1991, King Corporation must use the same Modified ACRS recovery period and method that Carla used in 1990. Depreciation for the year is $1,920 (0.32 × $6,000). That amount must be allocated between Carla and King Corporation. The computer is considered to have been held by Carla for 1 month and by King Corporation for 11 months (including the month of transfer).

[47] Sec. 168(i)(7).
[48] Prop. Reg. Secs. 1.168-5(b)(4)(i) and 1.168-5(b)(2)(i)(B).

Thus, $160 ($\frac{1}{12} \times$ $1,920) of depreciation is allocated to Carla, and $1,760 ($\frac{11}{12} \times$ $1,920) of depreciation is allocated to King Corporation. King Corporation's basis in the computer on the transfer date is $4,640 ($6,000 − [$1,200 + $160]). ■

If the transferee corporation's basis for the depreciable property exceeds the transferor's basis, the corporation treats the excess amount as a newly purchased Modified ACRS property and may select whatever recovery period and method it desires.[49]

Example 2-37 ■ Assume the same facts as in Example 2-36, except that, in addition to King stock, Carla also receives cash and is required to recognize $1,000 of gain on the transfer of the computer. King Corporation's basis in the computer is $5,640 ($6,000 − $1,200 − $160 + $1,000). The additional $1,000 of basis is depreciated as though it is a separate, newly purchased Modified ACRS property. Thus, King Corporation claims depreciation of $200 (0.20 × $1,000) on this portion of the basis in addition to the $1,760 of depreciation on the $4,640 of carryover basis. ■

Assignment of Income Doctrine. The **assignment of income doctrine** is a judicial requirement that income be taxed to the person who earns it.[50] Income may not be assigned to another taxpayer. The question arises as to whether the assignment of income doctrine applies when a taxpayer using the cash method of accounting transfers uncollected accounts receivable to a corporation in a Sec. 351 exchange. The question is who must recognize the income when it is collected—the taxpayer who earned it and transferred the receivable to the corporation before the income was recognized or the corporation who owns the receivable and collects it. The IRS has ruled that the doctrine does *not* apply in a Sec. 351 exchange if (1) the transferor transfers substantially all the business assets and liabilities and (2) a business purpose exists for the transfer. Instead, the accounts receivable take a zero basis in the corporation's hands and are included in the corporation's income when collected.[51]

Example 2-38 ■ For good business reasons, Ruth, a lawyer who uses the cash method of accounting, transfers all of the assets and liabilities of her legal practice to Video Corporation in exchange for all of Video's stock. The assets include $30,000 of accounts receivable. The assignment of income doctrine does not apply to the accounts receivable. Video Corporation's basis in the receivables is zero, and the corporation includes the receivables in income as they are collected. ■

There have been many cases disputing whether a transferee corporation could deduct the accounts payable transferred to it in a nontaxable transfer.[52] Normally, expenses are deductible only by the party who incurred those liabilities in the course of its trade or business. However, the IRS has ruled that the transferee corporation is allowed deductions for the payments it makes to satisfy otherwise deductible business expenses incurred by a transferor.[53]

Comprehensive Example. On March 3 of the current year, John, Eric, and Martha form Chip Corporation with the following investment:

---

[49] Prop. Reg. Sec. 1.168-5(b)(7).
[50] See, for example, *Lucas v. Guy C. Earl,* 8 AFTR 10287, 2 USTC ¶ 496 (USSC, 1930).
[51] Rev. Rul. 80-198, 1980-2 C.B. 113.
[52] See, for example, *Wilford E. Thatcher* v. *CIR,* 37 AFTR 2d 76-1068, 76-1 USTC ¶ 9324 (9th Cir., 1976), and *John P. Bongiovanni* v. *CIR,* 31 AFTR 2d 73-409, 73-1 USTC ¶ 9133 (2nd Cir., 1972).
[53] Rev. Rul. 80-198, 1980-2 C.B. 113.

Transferor	Asset	Basis to Transferor	FMV	Number of Shares of Stock Issued
John	Cash	$10,000	$10,000	
	Building	40,000	60,000	
	Mortgage on building	55,000	55,000	
	Equipment	—0—	25,000	40
Eric	Truck	8,000	6,000	
	Cash	34,000	34,000	30
Martha	Services	—0—	10,000	10

Eric also receives a Chip Corporation note for $10,000 due in two years. The building and equipment were used in John's business and the truck was inventory to Eric. The building was depreciated under the Modified ACRS rules and had $12,000 of depreciation recapture potential under Sec. 1250. The equipment was fully depreciated under the Modified ACRS rules.

The transaction satisfies the Sec. 351 requirements. John and Eric transferred property in exchange for stock and they received 87.5% (70 of 80) of the Chip Corporation stock. John must recognize a $5,000 gain on the transfer of the building because the liability transferred ($55,000) exceeds the total basis of all assets transferred ($50,000) by $5,000. Since the liability relates solely to the mortgage, the character of the gain is Sec. 1250 ordinary income. John's basis in the stock is zero ($50,000 basis of assets transferred − $55,000 liabilities assumed by Chip + $5,000 gain). His holding period for each share of stock is divided into three parts—$25/40$ths (based on relative FMVs of the assets) includes John's holding period for the equipment, $5/40$ths includes John's holding period for the building, and $10/40$ths commences on the exchange date. Chip's basis in the building is $55,000 ($50,000 + $5,000) and its basis for the equipment is zero. The holding period for the building and equipment includes John's holding period.

Eric does not recognize any loss on the transfer or the truck even though $10,000 in boot property is received. His basis in the Chip note received is its FMV, or $10,000. Eric's basis in the Chip stock received is $32,000 ($8,000 + $34,000 − $10,000). Eric's holding period for each share of stock is divided into two parts—$6/40$ths includes Eric's holding period for the truck and $34/40$ths commences on the exchange date.

Martha must recognize $10,000 of ordinary income, the value of the stock received for the services. Her basis in the stock is $10,000, the amount of ordinary income recognized. Martha's holding period begins on the day after the date she received it.

CHOICE OF CAPITAL STRUCTURE

OBJECTIVE 5
Determine the tax consequences of alternative capital structures

When a corporation is formed, decisions must be made as to the capital structure of the corporation. The corporation may derive its capital from shareholders, nonshareholders, and creditors. In exchange for their capital, shareholders may receive common stock or preferred stock; nonshareholders may receive benefits such as employment for a city's residents or special rates on products produced by the corporation; creditors may receive long-term or short-term debt obligations. Each of these alternatives has tax consequences and other advantages and disadvantages for the shareholders, the creditors, and the corporation itself.

Characterization of Obligations as Debt or Equity Capital

Self-Study Question
From a tax perspective, why is the distinction between debt and equity important?

Answer
Interest paid with respect to a debt instrument is deductible by the payor corporation. Dividends paid with respect to an equity instrument are not deductible by the payor corporation. Thus, the determination of whether an instrument is debt or equity can provide very different results to the payor corporation.

The tax laws provide a strong incentive for many corporations to use as much debt financing as possible (because of the deduction allowed for annual interest payments). Debt financing often resembles equity obligations (i.e., preferred stock), and the IRS and the courts have refused in some cases to accept the form of the obligation as controlling.[54] In some cases, obligations labeled as debt that possessed more characteristics of equity than debt have been reclassified as common or preferred stock. No single factor has been relied upon by the courts in making this determination. In *O. H. Kruse Grain & Milling v. CIR*, for example, the Ninth Circuit Court of Appeals listed the following factors that it felt were generally relied upon by the courts in determining whether an amount advanced to the corporation would be characterized as debt or equity capital:

- Names given to the certificates evidencing the indebtedness
- Presence or absence of a maturity date
- Source of the payments
- Right to enforce the payment of interest and principal
- Participation of the debt holders in management
- Status for the issue equal to or inferior to that of regular corporate creditors
- Intent of the parties
- Thin or adequate capitalization
- Identity of interest between creditors and stockholders
- Payment of interest only out of dividend money
- Ability of the corporation to obtain loans from outside lending institutions[55]

In addition to these factors, the IRS also examines the corporation's debt-to-equity ratio. No acceptable ceiling has been established for the debt-to-equity ratio, but generally the courts have accepted debt obligations as borrowed capital when this ratio does not exceed 4 or 5 to 1. Higher debt-to-equity ratios have been accepted by the courts and the IRS when the corporation has sufficient assets and cash flows to permit timely payment of interest and principal.

In 1969 Congress enacted Sec. 385 in an attempt to establish a workable standard for determining whether an obligation is debt or equity capital. Unfortunately, regulations have still not been issued, and taxpayers are forced to rely on prior judicial decisions. Section 385 was amended in 1989 to give Treasury the authority to characterize a corporate instrument that has significant debt and equity characteristics as part debt and part equity. This change may make it easier to develop a final set of Sec. 385 Regulations.

Historical Note
To illustrate the difficulty of distinguishing between debt and equity, note that the Treasury at one time issued proposed and final regulations covering Sec. 385. These regulations were the subject of so much criticism that the Treasury eventually withdrew them. The 1989 amendment to Sec. 385 makes it clear that Congress wants the Treasury to make another attempt at clarifying the debt-equity issue.

Debt Capital

Tax laws impact on the use of debt capital (1) when the debt is issued; (2) annually as the interest is paid on the obligation; and (3) when the debt is satisfied, retired, or declared worthless. The tax implications for each of these three events are examined below.

---

[54] See, for example, *Aqualane Shores, Inc. v CIR*, 4 AFTR 2d 5346, 59-2 USTC ¶ 9632 (5th Cir., 1959) and *Sun Properties, Inc. v. U.S.*, 47 AFTR 273, 55-1 USTC ¶ 9261 (5th Cir., 1955).

[55] 5 AFTR 2d 1544, 60-2 USTC ¶ 9490 (9th Cir., 1960).

Issuance of Debt. Under Sec. 351, appreciated assets may be exchanged tax-free for stock provided the transferors have control of the transferee corporation immediately after the exchange. However, if assets are exchanged for debt instruments whether part of the same transaction or not, the FMV of the debt received is treated as boot. Therefore, the receipt of debt by the transferor may result in the recognition of gain.

When Interest Is Paid. Interest paid on an indebtedness is deductible by the corporation in arriving at taxable income.[56] Dividends paid on equity capital are not deductible. A corporation is not subject to the limitations on interest deductions that apply to individual taxpayers (e.g., investment interest or personal interest limitations). Individual investors who borrow funds in order to invest in a corporation generally are subject to the investment interest limitation, or if the investment is a passive activity, the interest expense may be subject to the passive activity limitation rules.

If a debt instrument is issued at a discount, Sec. 163(e) requires that the original issue discount be determined and amortized by the holder under the rules of Secs. 1272 through 1275. The debtor corporation amortizes the original issue discount over the life of the obligation and treats the discount as an additional cost of borrowing.[57] If a corporate debt obligation is repurchased by the corporation for more than the issue price (plus any original issue discount deducted as interest), the excess of the purchase price over the issue price (adjusted for any amortization of original issue discount) is deductible by the corporation as interest expense.[58]

If the debt instrument is issued at a premium, Sec. 171 permits the holder to elect to amortize the premium over the life of the obligation and treat the premium as a reduction in the interest income earned from the obligation. The debtor corporation must amortize the premium over the life of the obligation and report such amount as additional interest income.[59] If a debt obligation is repurchased at a price in excess of the issue price (minus any premium reported as income), the excess of the purchase price over the issue price (adjusted for any amortization of premium) is deductible as interest expense.[60]

When an Indebtedness Is Satisfied. Generally, the repayment of an indebtedness (such as an accounts receivable) is not considered an exchange transaction. Thus, an obligation that is repaid by a corporation does not result in a gain or loss being recognized by the creditor. Section 1271(a) considers amounts received by the holder of a debt instrument (e.g., note, bond, or debenture) at the time of its retirement to be received in exchange for the obligation. Thus, if the obligation is a capital asset in the holder's hands, the holder will recognize a capital gain or loss if the amount received in retirement of the obligation is different from its adjusted basis.

Example 2-39 ■ Titan Corporation issues a 10-year obligation at its $1,000 face amount. The obligation is purchased by Rick for $1,000 on the issue date. Due to a decline in interest rates, Titan Corporation calls the obligation by paying $1,050 to each of the holders of the 10-year obligations. Rick will recognize a $50 capital gain on the repayment of the debt instrument. The premium paid by Titan Corporation is deductible as interest expense. ■

---

[56] Sec. 163(a).
[57] Sec. 163(e).
[58] Prop. Reg. Sec. 1.163-7(f).
[59] Reg. Sec. 1.61-12(c)(2).
[60] Prop. Reg. Sec. 1.163-7(f).

Choice of Capital Structure • 2-31

Typical Misconception
The characteristics of preferred stock can be similar to those of a debt security. Often, a regular dividend is required at a stated rate much like what would be required with respect to a debt obligation. The holder of preferred stock, similar to a debt holder, may have preferred liquidation rights over holders of common stock. Also, it is not required that preferred stock possess voting rights. Thus, where preferred stock is concerned, it is easy to see that whether an instrument is debt or equity can be confusing.

TABLE 2-1 *Tax Advantages of Stock*

1. A 70%, 80% or 100% dividends-received deduction is available for a corporate shareholder receiving dividends. A special deduction is not available for interest payments (see Chapter 3).
2. Common and preferred stock can be received by a shareholder participating in a tax-free corporate formation coming under Sec. 351 or a tax-free reorganization coming under Sec. 368 without any need to recognize gain (see Chapters 2 and 7, respectively). Receipt of debt obligations in each of these two types of transactions generally triggers the recognition of gain by the shareholder.
3. Common and preferred stock can be distributed tax-free to the shareholders of a corporation as a stock dividend. Some common and preferred stock distributions may be taxable to the shareholders under Sec. 305(b). Distributions of obligations of the distributing corporation are taxable as a dividend (see Chapter 4).
4. Common or preferred stock that is sold, exchanged, or becomes worthless is eligible for ordinary loss treatment under the Sec. 1244 rules (see pages 2-34 and 2-35). The loss recognized on similar transactions involving debt obligations is generally a capital loss.
5. Common and preferred stock used in an acquisition does not count toward the interest expense limitation that is imposed by Sec. 279 on "corporate acquisition indebtedness."

Additional Comment
Even though debt is often thought of as a preferred instrument because of the deductibility of the interest paid on the debt, it should be noted that the debt must be repaid at its maturity, whereas stock has no such specified maturity date. Also, interest usually must be paid at regular intervals, whereas dividends do not have to be declared if sufficient funds are not available.

Equity Capital

Equity capital issues come in a variety of forms. Some corporations have only a single class of stock, whereas others have a number of outstanding classes of stock. Reasons for the use of multiple classes of stock include

- Permitting the employees of family-owned corporations to obtain an equity interest in the business while keeping voting control in the hands of the family members.
- Permitting a closely held corporation (1) to acquire outside financing from a corporate investor or wealthy individual who acquires a preferred stock interest and (2) to enable the existing shareholders to retain their voting control by owning the common stock.

Because of the wide variety of situations that can occur and the unlimited number of equity issues that can be issued, it is impossible to list all of the tax and nontax advantages of each type of equity issue. Therefore, a list of the major tax advantages and disadvantages of common and preferred stock issues is presented in Tables 2-1 and 2-2.

TABLE 2-2 *Tax Disadvantages of Stock*

1. Dividends are not deductible in determining taxable income.
2. Redemption of common or preferred stock is generally taxable as a dividend. Under this general rule, none of the distribution offsets the shareholder's basis for the stock investment. No gain or loss is generally recognized from the retirement of a debt obligation. Redemption of common and preferred stock by the issuing corporation is eligible for exchange treatment only in specific situations contained in Secs. 302 and 303 (see Chapter 4).
3. Preferred stock that is received by a shareholder as a tax-free stock dividend can be labeled Sec. 306 stock. Sale, exchange, or redemption of such stock can result in the recognition of ordinary income or dividend income instead of capital gains (see Chapter 4).

Self-Study Question

Does the transferee corporation recognize gain on the receipt of appreciated property from a shareholder?

Answer

No. A corporation does not recognize gain when it receives property from its shareholders, regardless of whether or not it exchanges its own stock. However, if the shareholder contributes appreciated property, the transfer must qualify as a Sec. 351 exchange or the transaction will be taxable to the shareholders.

Topic Review 2-4 presents a summary comparison of the advantages and disadvantages of using debt and equity in the capital structure.

Capital Contributions by Shareholders

A corporation does not recognize any income when it receives money or property as a capital contribution from a shareholder.[61] If the shareholders make voluntary pro rata payments to a corporation but do not receive any additional stock, the payments are regarded as an additional price paid for the stock already owned.[62] The shareholders' bases in their stock is increased by (1) the amount of money contributed, plus (2) the basis of any nonmoney property contributed, plus (3) any gain recognized by the shareholders. The corporation's basis in any property received as a capital contribution from a shareholder equals the shareholder's basis increased by any gain recognized by the shareholder.[63] Normally, the shareholders do not recognize any gain when property is contributed to a corporation as a capital contribution.

Example 2-40 ■ Dot and Fred own equally all of Trail Corporation's stock, and each has a $50,000 basis in that stock. Later, as a voluntary contribution to capital, Dot contributes $40,000 in cash and Fred contributes property having a $25,000 basis and a $40,000 FMV. Trail Corporation recognizes no gross income because of the contributions. However, Dot's basis in her stock is increased to $90,000 ($50,000 + $40,000), and Fred's basis in his stock is increased to $75,000 ($50,000 + $25,000). Trail's basis in the property contributed by Fred is $25,000—the same as Fred's basis in the property. ■

An involuntary contribution of property by a shareholder in satisfaction of an assessment made by the corporation is treated by the tax laws as an exchange transaction. Therefore, the shareholder must recognize gain or loss equal to the FMV of the property contributed minus its basis to the shareholder. The shareholder's basis for his stock is increased by the FMV of the transferred property. The transferee corporation's basis in the contributed property is its FMV on the exchange date.

If a shareholder gratuitously forgives an indebtedness of the corporation, the transaction generally represents a contribution to the corporation's capital equal to the principal amount of the indebtedness. The determination of whether a forgiveness is a capital contribution or not is based upon the facts and circumstances surrounding the situation.

Self-Study Question

What basis does a transferee take in capital contributions of property from nonshareholders?

Answer

Capital contributions by nonshareholders are not common. In those unusual occurrences that do qualify as nonshareholder contributions, the transferee corporation takes a zero basis in any property received.

Capital Contributions by Nonshareholders

Nonshareholders sometimes make capital contributions in the form of money or property. For example, a city government might contribute land to a corporation to induce the corporation to locate within the city and provide jobs for its citizens. Such contributions are excluded from gross income if the money or property contributed is neither a payment for goods or services rendered nor a subsidy to induce the corporation to limit production.[64]

---

[61] Sec. 118(a).
[62] Reg. Sec. 1.118-1.
[63] Sec. 362(a).
[64] Reg. Sec. 1.118-1.

TOPIC REVIEW 2-4

Advantages and Disadvantages of Using Debt and Equity in the Capital Structure

Equity
1. No gain or loss is recognized when stock is received in exchange for property.
2. A corporation cannot deduct dividend payments on its stock.
3. If a shareholder incurs a loss on selling or exchanging stock, it is usually a capital loss. However, if the stock qualifies as Sec. 1244 stock, the loss may be an ordinary loss.

Debt
1. If a shareholder receives a debt instrument in exchange for property at the time the corporation is formed or a later capital contribution is made, the debt is considered boot and the realized gain must be recognized to the extent of the lesser of the boot received or the realized gain.
2. A corporation can deduct interest payments made on debt instruments.
3. Shareholders do not have to recognize income when an amount is received in repayment of debt as they would in the case of a stock redemption.
4. If debt becomes worthless or is sold at a loss, the loss is generally a nonbusiness bad debt (short-term capital loss) or a capital loss. Section 1244 ordinary loss treatment applies only to stock.

If a nonshareholder contributes property other than money to a corporation, the basis of such property to the corporation is zero.[65] The zero basis that is assigned to the property prevents the transferee corporation from claiming either a depreciation or capital recovery deduction with respect to the contributed property.

If a nonshareholder contributes money, the basis of any property acquired with the money during a 12-month period beginning on the day the contribution was received is reduced by the amount of the contribution. This limits the corporation's deduction to the amount of funds it invested to purchase the property. The amount of any monies received from nonshareholders that are not spent to purchase property during the 12-month period reduces the basis of any other property held by the corporation on the last day of the 12-month period.[66]

The basis reduction is applied to the corporation's properties in the following order:

1. Depreciable property
2. Amortizable property
3. Depletable property
4. All other property

A property's basis may not be reduced below zero as a result of these downward basis adjustments.

Example 2-41 ■ The city of San Antonio contributes $100,000 in cash and a tract of land having a $500,000 FMV to Circle Corporation to induce the company to locate there. Because of a downturn in Circle's business, only $70,000 of the contributed funds are spent in the next 12 months. Circle does not have any gross income on account of the contribution. Circle's basis in the land and the properties purchased with the

---

[65] Sec. 362(c)(1).
[66] Sec. 362(c)(2).

contributed funds are zero. The basis of Circle's remaining properties must be reduced by the $30,000 ($100,000 − $70,000) that was contributed but not spent, starting with its depreciable properties.

WORTHLESSNESS OF STOCK OR DEBT OBLIGATIONS

OBJECTIVE 6
Determine the tax consequences of worthless stock or debt instruments

Investors who invest or lend money to a corporation ususally intend to earn a profit and recover their investment. Unfortunately, some investments do not provide a good return and an investor may lose part or all of his investment. This section of the chapter examines the tax consequences of stock or debt becoming worthless.

Securities

Typical Misconception
Probably the most difficult aspect of deducting a loss on a worthless security is establishing that the security is actually worthless. A mere decline in value is not sufficient to create a loss. The burden of proof of showing that total worthlessness has occurred rests with the taxpayer.

A debt or equity investment that is evidenced by a security and that becomes worthless results in a capital loss for the investor on the last day of the tax year in which worthlessness occurs.[67] A security includes (1) a share of stock in the corporation; (2) a right to subscribe for, or the right to receive, a share of stock in the corporation; or (3) a bond, debenture, note, or other evidence of indebtedness issued by a corporation with interest coupons or in registered form.[68]

In some situations, investors can report an ordinary loss when a security becomes worthless. These situations include

- *Securities that are noncapital assets.* Ordinary loss treatment results when a security that is a noncapital asset is sold, exchanged, or becomes totally worthless. Securities fitting into this category include those held as inventory by a securities dealer. Whether stock is a capital asset depends upon the investor's motive for making the investment. Generally, the courts have found that stock is a capital asset when a substantial investment motive exists for acquiring and holding the stock.[69]

Key Point
No taxpayer invests in stock with the intention of losing his investment. However, since this is always a possibility, the taxpayer should, if possible, structure the investment so that any losses will qualify as ordinary losses. For example, Sec. 1244 does provide ordinary loss treatment for individual taxpayers as long as certain requirements are satisfied.

- *Affiliated corporations.* A domestic corporation is permitted to claim an ordinary loss incurred in connection with any security of an affiliated corporation that becomes worthless during the tax year. The domestic corporation must own (1) at least 80% of the total voting power of all classes of stock entitled to vote, and (2) at least 80% of each class of nonvoting stock (other than stock that is limited and preferred as to dividends). At least 90% of the aggregate gross receipts of the loss corporation for all tax years must come from sources other than passive income.[70]

- *Section 1244 stock.* The Sec. 1244 rules permit an ordinary loss to be claimed for qualifying stock issued by small business corporations that is sold, exchanged, or becomes worthless.[71] Ordinary loss treatment is available only to (1) an individual who sustains a loss and was issued the qualifying stock by an eligible small business corporation, or (2) to an individual who was a partner in a

---

[67] Sec. 165(g)(1).
[68] Sec. 165(g)(2).
[69] Rev. Rul. 78-94, 1978-1 C.B. 58. See also *W. W. Windle Co.*, 65 T.C. 694 (1976); and *Bell Fibre Products Corp.*, 1977 PH T.C. Memo ¶ 77,042, 36 TCM 182.
[70] Sec. 165(g)(3).
[71] Sec. 1244(a). Eligible small business corporations are defined in the Tax Planning Considerations section of this chapter.

partnership at the time the partnership acquired the stock from the issuing corporation and whose distributive share of partnership losses includes the loss sustained by the partnership on such stock. Thus, ordinary loss treatment is not available for stock acquired in a secondary market. The ordinary loss is limited to $50,000 per year (or $100,000 if the taxpayer is married and files a joint return). Losses in excess of the dollar ceiling in any given year are considered capital losses.[72]

Example 2-42 ■ Tammy and her husband purchase 25% of the single class of stock of Minor Corporation for $175,000. Minor Corporation is a qualifying small business corporation, and the Minor stock satisfies all of the Sec. 1244 requirements. On September 1, 1989, Minor Corporation files for bankruptcy. After substantial litigation, the shareholders are notified in 1991 that the Minor stock is worthless. Tammy and her husband can deduct $100,000 of their loss as an ordinary loss. The remaining $75,000 loss is a capital loss. ■

If the stock is issued for property whose adjusted basis exceeds its FMV immediately before the exchange, the basis of the stock is reduced to the property's FMV for purposes of determining the amount of ordinary loss claimed under Sec. 1244.

Example 2-43 ■ Penny exchanges property having a $40,000 adjusted basis and a $32,000 FMV for 100 shares of Bear Corporation stock in a transaction qualifying under Sec. 351. The stock qualifies as Sec. 1244 stock. Penny's basis in her Bear stock is $40,000. However, for Sec. 1244 purposes only, her basis in the stock is the transferred property's FMV, or $32,000. If the stock is sold for $10,000, Penny's recognized loss is $30,000 ($10,000 − $40,000). Her ordinary loss under Sec. 1244 is $22,000 ($10,000 − $32,000 Sec. 1244 basis). The remaining $8,000 loss is a capital loss. ■

Unsecured Debt Obligations

Key Point
Unsecured shareholder advances to a corporation may be treated as either additional paid-in capital or as an unsecured loan. If the advance is treated as paid-in capital and becomes worthless, this will increase the amount of the worthless security loss. If the advance is treated as an unsecured debt, when it becomes worthless it is treated as a bad debt.

Shareholders may lend money to the corporation in addition to their stock investment. The type of loss allowed if these advances are not repaid depends upon the nature of the loan or advance. If the advance is treated as additional paid-in capital, the worthless security loss claimed by the shareholder for his stock investment is increased.

If the unpaid loan was not evidenced by a security (i.e., an unsecured debt obligation) it is either a business or nonbusiness bad debt. Most advances to the corporation by a shareholder are considered to be incurred outside of the taxpayer's conduct of a trade or business. If the advance is made by a noncorporate taxpayer, the nonbusiness bad debt rules of Sec. 166(d) treat the loss as a short-term capital loss. Such losses are limited to $3,000 in a tax year.

A loss sustained by a shareholder who acts as a guarantor on a loan made by a third party to the corporation is generally considered to be a nonbusiness bad debt. The loss can be claimed only to the extent that the shareholder actually makes a payment to the third party and is unable to collect any amount due from the debtor corporation.[73]

---

[72] Ordinary loss treatment is also available for securities held by banks under Sec. 582(a), stocks held by small business investment companies under Sec. 1243, and stock of small business investment companies under Sec. 1242.

[73] Reg. Sec. 1.166-8(a).

CONTROVERSIAL ISSUE

Key Point

In many closely held corporations, the shareholders are also employees. Thus, when a shareholder/employee makes a loan to the corporation, a question arises whether the loan is being made in the individual's capacity as an employee or a shareholder. The distinction is important because an employee loan that is determined to be worthless is entitled to ordinary loss treatment, whereas a shareholder loan that is determined to be worthless is treated as a nonbusiness bad debt (short-term capital loss).

Obtaining Ordinary Loss Treatment for Advances to a Corporation

Under Code Sec. 166, nonbusiness bad debts receive less favorable tax treatment than business bad debts. Nonbusiness bad debts are deductible only as short-term capital losses up to a $3,000 annual limit when the debt is determined to be totally worthless. Business bad debts are deductible without limit when they are either partially or totally worthless. The IRS generally treats a loan made by a shareholder to a corporation in connection with his stock investment as a nonbusiness activity.[74] It is simple to see why a shareholder might like to rebut this presumption and say that there is a business purpose behind the making of the loan.

An advance made in connection with the shareholder's trade or business, such as a loan made to protect the shareholder's employment with the corporation, may be treated as an ordinary loss under the business bad debt rules. Regulation Sec. 1.166-5(b) indicates that whether the loss is treated as a business or nonbusiness bad debt depends upon the taxpayer's motive for making the advance. The debt qualifies as a business bad debt only if the necessary relationship between the loss and the conduct of the taxpayer's trade or business exists at the time the debt becomes worthless.

In *U.S. v. Edna Generes,* the Supreme Court held that when multiple motives exist for making an advance to a corporation, such as when a shareholder is also an employee of the corporation, the distinction between whether a business or nonbusiness loan exists is based upon the "dominant motivation" for making the loan.[75] If only a "significant motivation" exists relating the debt and the taxpayer's trade or business, this is usually insufficient to satisfy the proximate relationship required between the bad debt and the taxpayer's trade or business under Reg. Sec. 1.166-5(b) in order to have a business bad debt. The *Generes* decision did not completely settle the question of whether a shareholder advance is a business bad debt, however, since the IRS and the taxpayer often view the motivation behind the making of the loan differently.

Factors that have proven to be important in making the business bad debt determination include the relative dollar amounts of the taxpayer's stock investment in the corporation, compensation from the corporation, and other compensation. A small salary and a large stock investment would be indicative of an investment purpose for making the loan. A large salary and a small stock investment would be indicative of a business purpose for making the loan. Because these factors are subjective in nature and the dollars that are involved may be substantial, this issue still remains open to litigation.

Example 2-44 ■ Mary is employed by Top Corporation as its legal counsel. Her annual compensation from Top Corporation is $100,000. Top Corporation is experiencing financial problems, and Mary lends the corporation $50,000 in 1989 in an attempt to help it through its financial difficulties. Top Corporation subsequently declares bankruptcy, and in 1991 Mary and the other creditors receive 10 cents on each dollar that they are owed. Mary's $45,000 ($50,000 × 0.90) loss is an ordinary loss and is fully deductible in the year the loss is incurred if Mary can prove that the dominant

---

[74] The assumption is made here that the loan is not considered to be an additional capital contribution. In such a case, the worthless security rules of Sec. 165 apply instead of the Sec. 166 bad debt rules.

[75] 29 AFTR 2d 72-609, 72-1 USTC ¶ 9259 (USSC, 1972).

motivation for making the loan is in connection with her employment. If there is a significant relationship between Mary's loan and her investment in the Top stock, it is likely that the loss will be a nonbusiness bad debt, of which only $3,000 can be deducted each year.

TAX PLANNING CONSIDERATIONS

Typical Misconception

Even though Sec. 351 is generally considered a beneficial taxpayer provision, it is not an elective provision. Therefore, even if a shareholder wants to recognize gain on a transfer of property to a controlled corporation, such gains must be deferred unless one of the requirements of Sec. 351 can be violated.

Avoiding Sec. 351

Section 351 is not an elective provision. If its provisions are met, Sec. 351 applies even if the taxpayer does not want it to apply. Most often, Sec. 351 treatment is desired by taxpayers since it enables them to defer gains when transferring property to a corporation. In some cases, however, shareholders find it disadvantageous and seek to avoid it. Sometimes shareholders have gains or losses that they want to recognize.

Avoiding Nonrecognition of Losses under Sec. 351. If a shareholder is transferring property, on which he has a loss, to a corporation, he may want to recognize the loss on that property so that income from other sources can be offset. However, the loss is not recognized if Sec. 351 applies to the transfer. The shareholder can recognize his loss only if Sec. 351 does not apply to the exchange.

To avoid Sec. 351 entirely requires that one or more of its requirements not be met. The best way to accomplish this is to make sure that the transferors of property do not receive 80% of the voting stock.

Even if a shareholder avoids Sec. 351, he still may not be able to recognize his losses because of the Sec. 267 related party transaction rules. Under Sec. 267(a)(1), if the shareholder owns more than 50% of the corporation's stock, directly or indirectly, he cannot recognize any losses on an exchange of his property for the corporation's stock or other property.

Self-Study Question

Which tax provisions may potentially limit a transferor shareholder from recognizing a loss on the transfer of property to a corporation?

Thus, to recognize a loss when property is exchanged for stock, the shareholder must avoid both Sec. 351 and Sec. 267. If the transferors of property receive less than 80% of the voting stock of the corporation and the transferor of the loss property does not own any more than 50% of the corporate stock, the transferor of the loss property may recognize the loss.

Example 2-45 ■

Answer

(1) Such transfer cannot be to a controlled corporation or Sec. 351 will defer the loss. (2) Even if Sec. 351 can be avoided, losses on sales between a corporation and a more than 50% shareholder are disallowed under Sec. 267. Thus, to recognize a loss on the sale of property, such shareholders must, directly or indirectly, own 50% or less of the stock of the transferee corporation.

Lynn owns property that has a $100,000 basis and a $60,000 FMV. If Lynn transfers the property to White Corporation in a transaction qualifying under Sec. 351, her loss is not recognized. It is postponed until she sells her stock in the corporation. If Sec. 351 does not apply, she may be able to recognize a loss of $40,000 in the year the property is transferred. If Lynn receives 50% of the White stock in exchange for her property; and Cathy, an unrelated individual, receives 25% of the stock in exchange for $30,000 cash; and John, another unrelated individual, receives the remaining 25% of stock for services performed, Sec. 351 does not apply because less than 80% of the stock was received by transferors of property. Moreover, since Lynn does not own more than 50% of the stock either directly or indirectly, Sec. 267 does not apply to the exchange. Therefore, Lynn recognizes a $40,000 loss on the exchange of her property for the White stock. ■

Avoiding Nonrecognition of Gain under Sec. 351. Sometimes a transferor wants to recognize a gain when appreciated property is transferred to a corporation so

Key Point

As pointed out previously, any potential built-in gain on property transferred to the transferee corporation is duplicated because such gain may be recognized at the corporate level and at the shareholder level. This may be another reason for avoiding the nonrecognition of gain under Sec. 351.

that the transferee corporation has a higher basis in the transferred property. Some other possible reasons for this are as follows:

- The transferor's gain is capital gain that he can offset with capital losses from other sources.
- For 1991 and later years individual long-term capital gains are taxed at a maximum 28% rate. This rate is below the 34% marginal tax rate generally applicable to corporate capital gains.
- The corporation's highest marginal tax rate (34% or 39%) is higher than the highest marginal tax rate applicable to a noncorporate transferor (31%). In such case, it might be beneficial for the transferor to recognize gain on the transfer so that the corporation can obtain a higher basis in the property. A higher basis would either (1) reduce the corporation's gain when it sells the property or (2) allow the corporation to claim higher depreciation deductions on the property while it is using it.

A transferor who cannot recognize a gain on a transfer of appreciated property because of Sec. 351 may be able to avoid Sec. 351 and recognize the gain by using one of the following methods:

- The transferor can sell the property to the controlled corporation for cash, thereby avoiding Sec. 351 altogether.
- The transferor can sell the property to the controlled corporation for cash and debt. This method requires less cash than the previous method. However, the sale may be treated as a transfer coming under Sec. 351 if the debt instruments received are considered equity.[76]
- The transferor can arrange to receive sufficient boot property so that, even if Sec. 351 applies to the transaction, gain is recognized.
- The transferors can fail one or more of the Sec. 351 provisions. If the transferors of property do not obtain control of the corporation (i.e., 80% of the voting stock), Sec. 351 does not apply and gain is recognized.
- The transferors may transfer to the corporation either (1) sufficient debt so that the debt exceeds the basis of all properties transferred or (2) debt that lacks a business purpose in order to trigger the gain recognition provisions of Secs. 357(b) and (c).

Example 2-46 ■ John owns land purchased as an investment 10 years ago for $100,000. The land is now worth $500,000. John plans to transfer the land to Bell Corporation in exchange for all of its stock. Bell Corporation will subdivide the land and sell individual parcels. Its gain on the land sales will be ordinary income. John has a large capital loss in the current year and would like to recognize a capital gain on the transfer of the land to Bell Corporation. One way for John to accomplish this is to transfer the land to Bell Corporation in exchange for all of the Bell stock plus a note for $400,000. John recognizes $400,000 of gain even though Sec. 351 applies to the exchange. ■

The transferor can postpone recognition of the gain while still allowing the transferee corporation to obtain a step-up in basis for the transferred property by having the debt made payable several years in the future. Under the installment sale rules of Sec. 453, gain generally is not recognized until the note is actually collected.

---

[76] See, for example, *Aqualane Shores, Inc. v. CIR*, 4 AFTR 2d 5346, 59-2 USTC ¶ 9632 (5th Cir., 1959) and *Sun Properties, Inc. v. U.S.*, 47 AFTR 273, 55-1 USTC ¶ 9261 (5th Cir., 1955).

Example 2-47 ◼ In Example 2-46, if the note is due in 4 years, John can postpone recognition of the gain for 4 years until the note is collected by treating the exchange as an installment sale. ◼

Obtaining an Ordinary Loss Deduction for Stock Losses

Small businesses have a high failure rate. Investors who advance monies to an unsuccessful corporation, either in the form of equity or debt capital, will generally find it advantageous if the loss is an ordinary deduction. Ordinary losses are not subject to the $3,000 annual limitation on capital losses. Ordinary losses are deductible against any ordinary income reported on the investor's tax return. Ordinary losses that produce an NOL on the investor's tax return can be carried back or forward under the general NOL rules.

An ordinary loss deduction up to $50,000 ($100,000 if the investor is married and files a joint return with a spouse) is allowed for losses on stock of closely held corporations under the small business corporation stock rules of Sec. 1244. No special election is required to take advantage of Sec. 1244. Investors should be aware of the special requirements that must be satisfied. Failure to satisfy any of these requirements will disqualify the stock from Sec. 1244 treatment and generally cause the shareholder's loss to be a capital loss. The special requirements include

- The issuing corporation must be a small business corporation at the time the stock is issued. A small business corporation is one whose aggregate money and other property received for stock is $1 million or less.[77]
- The stock must be issued for money or property (other than stock and securities).
- The issuing corporation must have derived more than 50% of its aggregate gross receipts from "active" sources (i.e., other than royalties, rents, dividends, interest, annuities, and gains on sales of stock and securities) during the 5 most recent tax years ending before the date on which the stock is sold, exchanged, or becomes worthless.

Self-Study Question
Why would a shareholder want his stock to qualify as Sec. 1244 stock?

Answer
Sec. 1244 is a provision that may help the taxpayer but that can never hurt. If the requirements of Sec. 1244 are satisfied, the individual shareholders of a small business corporation may treat losses from the sale or worthlessness of their stock as ordinary rather than capital losses. If Sec. 1244 requirements are not satisfied, such losses are capital losses.

COMPLIANCE AND PROCEDURAL CONSIDERATIONS

Key Point
The required information provided to the IRS by both the transferor shareholders and the transferee corporation should be consistent. For example, the FMVs assigned to the stock and other properties included in the exchange must be the same for both sides of the transaction.

Reporting Requirements under Sec. 351

Every person who receives stock or other property in an exchange qualifying under Sec. 351 must attach a statement to his tax return for the period that includes the date of the exchange.[78] The statement must include all the facts pertinent to the exchange, including

1. A description of the property transferred and its adjusted basis to the transferor
2. A description of the stock received in the exchange including its kind, number of shares, and FMV

---

[77] Special rules are provided in Reg. Sec. 1.1244(c)-2 for designating which shares of stock are eligible for Sec. 1244 treatment when more than $1 million of stock has been issued by the corporation.
[78] Reg. Sec. 1.351-3(a).

3. A description of the securities received in the exchange including principal amount and terms, and FMV
4. The amount of money received
5. A description of any other property received including its FMV
6. A statement on the liabilities transferred to the corporation including the nature of the liabilities, when and why they were created, and the corporate business reason for their transfer

The transferee corporation must attach a statement to its tax return for the year in which the exchange took place.[79] The statement must include

1. A complete description of all property received from the transferors
2. The adjusted basis of the property to the transferors
3. A description of the stock issued to the transferors
4. A description of the securities issued to the transferors
5. The amount of money distributed to the transferors
6. A description of any other property distributed to the transferors
7. Information regarding the transferor's liabilities that are assumed by the corporation

Additional Comment

If the nonrecognition of gain on a transfer of property to a controlled corporation is critical, an advance ruling from the National Office of the IRS may be desirable. If a favorable ruling cannot be obtained, other acquisition techniques discussed in subsequent chapters might provide the desired tax result. For example, see Chpt. 7.

Reasons for and Procedures to Obtain a Sec. 351 Ruling

In some cases, taxpayers may be uncertain as to whether a proposed transfer to a controlled corporation satisfies the Sec. 351 requirements. In such a case, the taxpayers may want to ask the IRS for an advance ruling. An advance private letter ruling informs them as to whether a proposed transaction satisfies the requirements of Sec. 351. If the ruling is favorable, they can proceed with the transaction. If the ruling is unfavorable, they can abandon the transaction or modify it so that it does comply with Sec. 351.

Advance rulings are generally requested before a proposed transaction takes place. Revenue Procedure 83-59 contains a detailed listing of the information that must be submitted with a Sec. 351 ruling request.[80]

The IRS will not issue an advance ruling as to whether Sec. 351 has been satisfied in some cases. It will not rule, for example, if a transaction involves an exchange of widely held oil or gas properties for stock of a transferee corporation that is readily tradable.[81]

PROBLEM MATERIALS

DISCUSSION QUESTIONS

2-1. What entities or business forms are available for a new business? Explain the advantages and disadvantages of each.

2-2. Alice and Bill are planning to go into business together. They anticipate losses for the first 2 or 3 years which they would like to use to offset income from other sources. They are also

---

[79] Reg. Sec. 1.351-3(b).
[80] 1983-2 C.B. 575. Advance rulings may in some situations be requested after a transaction takes place, but before the return is filed.
[81] Rev. Proc. 91-3, I.R.B. 1991-1, 52, Sec. 5.12.

concerned about exposing their personal assets to the business liabilities. What business form would best satisfy their concerns?

2-3. What circumstances will result in an entity that qualifies as a partnership under state law being taxed as a corporation?

2-4. What circumstances are likely to cause an entity that qualifies as a trust under state law to be taxed as a corporation?

2-5. Explain the importance of state law in determining the status of a corporation.

2-6. Explain the Congressional intent of Sec. 351.

2-7. What are the tax consequences of Sec. 351 for the transferor and transferee when property is transferred to a newly created corporation?

2-8. What requirements must be satisfied for the Sec. 351(a) nonrecognition rules to apply?

2-9. What items are included in the "property" definition for purposes of Sec. 351(a)? What items are statutorily excluded from the "property" definition?

2-10. How is the *control* requirement defined for purposes of Sec. 351(a)?

2-11. Explain how the IRS has interpreted the phrase "in control immediately after the exchange" for purposes of a Sec. 351 exchange.

2-12. John and Mary each exchange property worth $50,000 for 100 shares of New Corporation stock. Peter exchanges services for 98 shares of stock and $1,000 in money for 2 shares of stock. Does Sec. 351 apply to the exchange? Explain why or why not.

2-13. Does Sec. 351 require shareholders to receive stock equal in value to the property transferred? Suppose Fred and Susan each transfer property worth $50,000 of Spade Corporation. Fred receives 25 shares of Spade stock and Susan receives 75 shares. Does Sec. 351 apply? Explain the tax consequences of the transaction.

2-14. Can Sec. 351 apply to property transferred to an existing corporation? Suppose Ken and Lynn each own 50 shares of North Corporation stock. Ken transfers property worth $50,000 to North for an additional 25 shares of stock. Does Sec. 351 apply? Explain why or why not.

2-15. When must gain be recognized in a Sec. 351 exchange? How is the amount and character of the gain determined when multiple properties are transferred to the controlled corporation?

2-16. How are a transferor's basis and holding period for stocks and other property (boot) received in a Sec. 351 exchange determined? How does the assumption of liabilities by the transferee corporation affect the transferor's basis for the stock?

2-17. How are the transferee corporation's basis and holding period for property received in a Sec. 351 exchange determined?

2-18. Under what circumstances is the assumption of liabilities by a corporation considered boot in a Sec. 351 exchange?

2-19. Mark transfers all the properties of his sole proprietorship to newly formed Utah Corporation in exchange for all of the Utah stock. Some of the properties are depreciable properties on which Mark has claimed depreciation. Under what circumstances is Mark required to recapture previously claimed depreciation deductions? What happens if Utah Corporation sells the depreciable properties?

2-20. How does the assignment of income doctrine affect a Sec. 351 exchange?

2-21. What factors do the courts utilize in determining whether an indebtedness is classified as debt or equity for tax purposes? Explain the implications on the classification process of Congress having enacted Sec. 385.

2-22. What are the advantages and disadvantages of using debt as part of a firm's capital structure?

2-23. How are capital contributions by shareholders and nonshareholders treated by the recipient corporation?

2-42 • Ch. 2 / Formation of the Corporation

2-24. What are the advantages of qualifying for Sec. 1244 loss treatment when a stock investment becomes worthless? What requirements must be satisfied in order to be able to take advantage of the Sec. 1244 benefits?

2-25. What are the advantages of business bad debt treatment when a shareholder's loan or advance to a corporation is unable to be repaid? How can one avoid having such a loss treated as a nonbusiness bad debt?

2-26. Under what circumstances is the corporate form of a business entity likely to be disregarded by the IRS?

2-27. Why might shareholders want to avoid Sec. 351? Explain how they can accomplish this.

2-28. What are the reporting requirements under Sec. 351?

2-29. Explain the reasons why some shareholders request an advance ruling when a Sec. 351 transaction is planned.

PROBLEMS

2-30. *Transfer of Property and Services to a Controlled Corporation.* In 1991 Alice, Bob, and Charles form Star Corporation. Alice contributes land purchased in 1989 for $15,000 that has a $40,000 FMV in exchange for 40 shares of Star stock. Bob contributes machinery purchased in 1988 that has a $45,000 adjusted basis and a $40,000 FMV in exchange for 40 shares of Star stock. Charles contributes services worth $20,000 in exchange for 20 shares of Star stock.
   a. What is the amount of Alice's recognized gain or loss?
   b. What is Alice's basis in her Star shares? When does her holding period begin?
   c. What is the amount of Bob's recognized gain or loss?
   d. What is Bob's basis in his Star shares? When does his holding period begin?
   e. What is Star Corporation's basis in the land and the machinery? When does its holding period begin?
   f. How much income, if any, must Charles recognize?
   g. What is Charles's basis in his Star shares? When does his holding period begin?

2-31. *Transfer of Property and Services to a Controlled Corporation.* In 1991 Ed, Fran, and George form Jet Corporation. Ed contributes land he purchased as an investment in 1987 for $15,000 that has a $35,000 FMV in exchange for 35 shares of Jet stock. Fran contributes machinery purchased in 1987 and used in her business having a $45,000 adjusted basis and a $35,000 FMV in exchange for 35 shares of Jet stock. George contributes services worth $30,000 in exchange for 30 shares of Jet stock.
   a. What is the amount of Ed's recognized gain or loss?
   b. What is Ed's basis in his Jet shares? When does his holding period begin?
   c. What is the amount of Fran's recognized gain or loss?
   d. What is Fran's basis in her Jet shares? When does her holding period begin?
   e. What is Jet Corporation's basis in the land and the machinery? When does its holding period begin?
   f. How much income, if any, must George recognize?
   g. What is George's basis in his Jet shares? When does his holding period begin?
   h. How would your answers to Parts a through g change if George instead contributed $5,000 cash and services worth $25,000 for his 30 shares of Jet stock?

2-32. *Control Test.* In which of the following independent situations is the Sec. 351 control requirement met?
   a. Olive transfers property to Quick Corporation for 75% of Quick's stock, and Mary provides services to Quick Corporation for the remaining 25% of Quick's stock.
   b. Pete transfers property to Target Corporation for 60% of Target's stock, and Robert transfers property worth $15,000 and performs services worth $25,000 for the remaining 40% of Target's stock.
   c. Herb and his wife, Wilma, each have owned 50 of the 100 outstanding shares of Vast Corporation stock since it was formed in 1988. In 1991, their son, Sam, transfers property to Vast Corporation for 50 newly issued shares of Vast stock.
   d. Charles and Ruth develop a plan to form Tiny Corporation. On June 3, 1991, Charles

transfers property worth $50,000 for 50 shares of Tiny stock. On August 1, 1991, Ruth transfers $50,000 cash for 50 shares of Tiny stock.
  e. Assume the same facts as in Part d, except that Charles has a prearranged plan to sell 30 of his shares to Sam on October 1, 1991.

2-33. *Sec. 351 Requirements.* To which of the following exchanges does Sec. 351 apply?
  a. Fred exchanges property worth $50,000 and services worth $50,000 for 100 shares of New Corporation stock. Greta exchanges $100,000 cash for the remaining 100 shares of New stock.
  b. Maureen exchanges property worth $2,000 and services worth $48,000 for 100 shares of Gemini Corporation stock. Norman exchanges property worth $50,000 for the remaining 100 shares of Gemini stock.

2-34. *Incorporating a Sole Proprietorship.* Tom incorporates his sole proprietorship by transferring all of its assets to newly formed Total Corporation for all 100 shares of Total stock with a $125,000 FMV and four $10,000 notes that mature consecutively on the first four anniversaries of the incorporation date. The assets transferred are

Assets		Adjusted Basis	FMV
Cash		$ 5,000	$ 5,000
Equipment	$130,000		
Minus: Accumulated depreciation	(70,000)	60,000	40,000
Building	$100,000		
Minus: Accumulated depreciation[a]	(49,000)	51,000	90,000
Land		24,000	30,000
Total		$140,000	$165,000

[a] $14,000 of this amount represents excess depreciation subject to recapture under Sec. 1250.

  a. What are the amount and character of Tom's recognized gain or loss?
  b. What is Tom's basis in his Total stock and notes?
  c. What is Total Corporation's basis in the properties received from Tom?

2-35. *Transfer to an Existing Corporation.* For the last 5 years, Ann and Fred have each owned 50 of the 100 outstanding shares of Zero Corporation's stock. Ann transfers land having a $10,000 basis and a $25,000 FMV to Zero Corporation for an additional 25 shares of Zero stock. Fred transfers $1,000 cash to Zero Corporation for 1 additional share of Zero stock. What is the amount of the gain or loss that Ann must recognize on the exchange? If the transaction does not comply with the Sec. 351 requirements, suggest ways in which the transaction can be made to comply.

2-36. *Transfer to an Existing Corporation.* For the last 3 years, Lucy and Marvin have each owned 50 of the 100 outstanding shares of Lucky Corporation's stock. Lucy transfers property that has an $8,000 basis and a $12,000 FMV to Lucky Corporation for an additional 10 shares of Lucky stock. How much gain or loss must Lucy recognize on the exchange? If the transaction does not comply with the Sec. 351 requirements, suggest ways in which the transaction can be made to comply.

2-37. *Disproportionate Receipt of Stock.* Jerry transfers property with a $28,000 adjusted basis and a $50,000 FMV to Texas Corporation for 75 shares of Texas stock. Frank, Jerry's father, transfers property with a $32,000 adjusted basis and a $50,000 FMV to Texas Corporation for the remaining 25 shares of Texas stock.
  a. What is the amount of each transferor's recognized gain or loss?
  b. What is Jerry's basis for his Texas stock?
  c. What is Frank's basis for his Texas stock?

2-38. *Receipt of Bonds for Property.* Joe, Karen, and Larry form Gray Corporation. Joe contributes land having an $8,000 adjusted basis and a $15,000 FMV to Gray Corporation in exchange for a similar dollar amount of its 10-year bonds. Karen contributes property having an $18,000 adjusted basis and a $25,000 FMV for 50 shares of Gray stock. Larry contributes $25,000 cash for 50 shares of Gray stock.

   a. What is the amount of Joe, Karen, and Larry's recognized gain or loss on the transaction?
   b. What basis do Joe, Karen, and Larry take in the stock or bonds that they receive?
   c. What basis does Gray Corporation take in the land and property?

2-39. Transfer of Depreciable Property. Dana transfers depreciable machinery that originally cost $25,000 and has a $15,000 adjusted basis to Booth Corporation in exchange for all 100 shares of Booth's stock having an $18,000 FMV and a short-term Booth Corporation note having a $7,000 FMV.

   a. What are the amount and character of Dana's recognized gain or loss?
   b. What are Dana's bases for the stock and note she received?
   c. What is Booth Corporation's basis for the depreciable machinery received from Dana?

2-40. Transfer of Personal Liabilities. Jim owns 80% of the stock of Gold Corporation. He transfers a business automobile to Gold Corporation in exchange for additional Gold stock worth $2,000 and its assumption of his $6,000 education loan. The automobile originally cost Jim $12,000, has a $4,500 adjusted basis, and has an $8,000 FMV on the transfer date.

   a. What are the amount and character of Jim's recognized gain or loss?
   b. What is Jim's basis for his additional Gold shares?
   c. When does Jim's holding period start for the additional shares?
   d. What basis does Gold Corporation take in the automobile?

2-41. Liabilities in Excess of Basis. Barbara transfers machinery that has a $15,000 basis and a $35,000 FMV and $10,000 in money to Moore Corporation in exchange for 50 shares of Moore stock. The machinery was used in Barbara's business, originally cost Barbara $50,000, and is subject to a $28,000 liability which Moore Corporation assumes. Sam exchanges $17,000 cash for the remaining 50 shares of Moore stock.

   a. What are the amount and character of Barbara's recognized gain or loss?
   b. What is her basis in the Moore stock?
   c. What is Moore Corporation's basis in the machinery?
   d. What are the amount and character of Sam's recognized gain or loss?
   e. What is Sam's basis in the Moore stock?
   f. When does Barbara and Sam's holding periods for their stock begin?
   g. How would your answers to Parts a through f change if Sam received $17,000 of Moore stock for legal services (instead of for money)?

2-42. Transfer of Business Properties. Marty transfers property that has a $28,000 adjusted basis and a $45,000 FMV to Silver Corporation in exchange for all of its stock worth $30,000, and for Silver Corporation's assumption of a $15,000 mortgage on the property.

   a. What is the amount of Marty's recognized gain or loss?
   b. What is Marty's basis in his Silver stock?
   c. What is Silver Corporation's basis in the property?
   d. How would your answers to Parts a through c change if the mortgage assumed by Silver was instead $30,000 and the Silver stock was instead worth $15,000?

2-43. Incorporating a Cash Basis Proprietorship. Ted decides to incorporate his medical practice. He uses the cash method of accounting. On the date of incorporation, the practice has the following balance sheet:

	Basis	FMV		Basis	FMV
Assets:			Liabilities and		
Cash	$ 5,000	$ 5,000	Owner's Equity:		
Accounts receivable	—0—	65,000	Current liabilities	$—0—	$ 35,000
Equipment			Note payable on		
(net of $15,000			equipment	15,000	15,000
depreciation)	35,000	40,000	Owner's equity	25,000	60,000
Total	$40,000	$110,000	Total	$40,000	$110,000

All of the current liabilities would be deductible by Ted if he paid them. Ted transfers

all the assets and liabilities to a professional corporation in exchange for all of its stock.
   a. What are the amount and character of Ted's recognized gain or loss?
   b. What is Ted's basis in the shares he receives?
   c. What is the corporation's basis in the properties it receives?
   d. Who must recognize the income from the receivables when they are collected? Can the corporation obtain a deduction for the liabilities when they are paid?

2-44. *Contribution to Capital by a Nonshareholder.* The City of San Antonio donates land worth $500,000 to Ace Corporation to induce it to locate in San Antonio and provide 2,000 jobs for its citizens.
   a. How much income (if any) must Ace Corporation report because of the land contribution?
   b. What basis does the land have to Ace Corporation?
   c. Assume the same facts except that the City of San Antonio also donated $100,000 cash to Ace Corporation, which the corporation used to acquire equipment. How much income (if any) must Ace Corporation report because of the cash contribution? What basis does the equipment that was purchased have to Ace Corporation?

2-45. *Sec. 351 Requirements.* Al, Bob, and Carl form West Corporation with the following assets:

Transferor	Asset	Transferor's Basis	FMV	Shares Received by Transferor
Al	Patent	—0—	$25,000	1,000 common
Bob	Cash	$25,000	25,000	250 preferred
Carl	Services	—0—	7,500	300 common

   a. Does the transaction qualify as tax-free under Sec. 351? Explain the tax consequences of the transaction to Al, Bob, Carl, and West Corporation.
   b. How would your answer to Part a change if Bob had instead received 200 shares of common stock and 200 shares of preferred stock?
   c. How would your answer to Part a change if Carl had instead contributed property having an $800 FMV as well as services worth $6,700?

2-46. *Sec. 351: Boot Property Received.* Jane transfers land (a capital asset) having a $50,000 adjusted basis to Jones Corporation in a transaction qualifying under Sec. 351. In exchange, Jane receives the following consideration:

Consideration	FMV
100 shares of Jones Corporation common stock	$100,000
Jones Corporation bond due in 10 years	30,000
Jones Corporation note due in 3 years	20,000
Total	$150,000

   a. What are the amount and character of Jane's recognized gain or loss?
   b. What is Jane's basis for her stock, bond, and note?
   c. What is Jones Corporation's basis for the land?

2-47. *Avoiding Sec. 351 Treatment.* Donna purchased land 6 years ago as an investment. The land cost her $150,000 and is now worth $480,000. Donna plans to transfer the land to Data Corporation. Data Corporation will subdivide the land and sell individual parcels. Data Corporation's profit on the land sales will be ordinary income.
   a. What are the tax consequences of the asset transfer and land sales if Donna contributes the land to Data Corporation in exchange for all of its stock?
   b. What alternative methods can be used to structure the transaction in order to achieve better tax consequences?

2-48. *Transfer of Depreciable Property.* On January 10, 1991, Mary transfers to Green

Corporation a machine purchased on March 3, 1988, for $100,000. The machine has a $60,000 adjusted basis and a $110,000 FMV on the transfer date. Mary receives all 100 shares of Green stock worth $100,000 and a 2-year Green Corporation note worth $10,000.

a. What are the amount and character of Mary's recognized gain or loss?
b. What is Mary's basis in the stock and note? When does her holding period begin?
c. What are the amount and character of Green Corporation's gain or loss?
d. What is Green Corporation's basis for the machine? When does Green Corporation's holding period begin?

2-49. Choice of Capital Structure. Jackson Corporation is being formed by a group of 25 investors. The total capital to be raised from these investors is $3,000,000. Explain the tax consequences of the following three alternative financing proposals:

a. The 25 investors will receive common stock worth $3,000,000.
b. The 25 investors will receive a package of common stock worth $1,500,000 and preferred stock worth $1,500,000.
c. The 25 investors will receive a package of $1,500,000 of common stock and $1,500,000 of Jackson Corporation notes.

In preparing your answer, consider the following items: (1) Amounts paid to investors; (2) the repayment of the notes, and (3) the worthlessness of the debt or stock.

2-50. Worthless Stock or Securities. Tom and Vicki each purchase one-half of the stock of Guest Corporation, for which they each pay $75,000. Tom is employed full time by Guest Corporation and is paid $100,000 in salary annually. Because of Guest Corporation's financial difficulties, Tom and Vicki each loan Guest Corporation an additional $25,000. The $25,000 is secured by a note and is to be repaid in 12 months with interest being charged at a rate acceptable to the IRS. Guest Corporation's financial difficulties continue and bankruptcy is declared. Tom and Vicki receive nothing for their Guest stock or for their Guest Corporation notes.

a. What are the amount and character of each shareholder's loss on the worthless stock and note?
b. How would your answer to Part a change if the liability is not secured by a note?
c. How would your answer to Part a change if the advances by Tom and Vicki are classified as additional capital contributions?

2-51. Worthless Stock. Duck Corporation is owned equally by Harry, Susan, and Big Corporation. Harry, Tom, and Big Corporation, the original investors in Duck Corporation, each paid $125,000 for their Duck stock in 1985. Susan purchased her stock from Tom in 1988 for $175,000. No adjustments to basis occur after the stock acquisition date. Duck Corporation suffers some financial difficulties as the result of losing a large judgment in a lawsuit brought by a person who purchased a product that was defective, resulting in a serious personal injury. Duck Corporation files for bankruptcy, and all of its assets are ultimately paid to its creditors in 1991. What are the amount and character of each shareholder's loss?

2-52. Sale of Sec. 1244 Stock. Lois, who is single, transfers property with an $80,000 basis and a $120,000 FMV to Water Corporation in exchange for all of Water's 100 shares of stock. The Water stock qualifies as Sec. 1244 stock. Two years later, Lois sells the stock for $28,000.

a. What is the amount and character of Lois's recognized gain or loss?
b. How would your answer to part a change if the FMV of the property transferred was instead $70,000?

2-53. Transfer of Sec. 1244 Stock. Assume the same facts as in Problem 2-52 except that Lois gave the Water stock to her daughter, Sue, 6 months after she received it. The stock had a $120,000 FMV when Lois received it and when she made the gift. Sue sold the stock two years later for $28,000. How is the loss treated for tax purposes?

COMPREHENSIVE PROBLEM

2-54. On March 1, 1991, Alice, Bob, Carla, and Dick form Bear Corporation with the following investment:

Transferor	Asset	Basis to Transferor	FMV	Number of Common Shares Issued
Alice	Land	$12,000	$30,000	
	Building	38,000	70,000	400
	Mortgage on the building	60,000		
Bob	Equipment	25,000	40,000	300
Carla	Van	15,000	10,000	50
Dick	Accounting services	—0—	10,000	100

Bob also receives a Bear Corporation note for $10,000 due on March 1, 1993. The note bears interest at a rate acceptable to the IRS. The equipment was purchased by Bob on March 1, 1988. Carla also receives $5,000 cash. The van was purchased by Carla on January 10, 1990.

a. Does the transaction satisfy the requirements of Sec. 351?
b. What are the amount and character of the recognized gain or loss of Alice, Bob, Carla, and Dick, and Bear Corporation?
c. What is each shareholder's basis for their Bear stock? When does the holding period for the stock begin?
d. What is Bear Corporation's basis for its properties and services? When does its holding period begin for each property?

CASE STUDY PROBLEM

2-55. Bob Jones has approached you for advice. He has a small repair shop that he has run for several years as a sole proprietorship. The proprietorship has used the cash method of accounting and the calendar year as its tax year. He is in need of additional capital for expansion and knows two people who might be interested in investing in the business. One would like to work in the business. The other would be an investor only.

Bob wants to know what the tax consequences of incorporating his business are. His business assets include a small building, equipment, accounts receivable, and cash. There is a mortgage on the building and a small amount of accounts payable.

Required: Write a memorandum to Bob explaining the tax consequences of the incorporation. As part of your memorandum examine the possibility of having the corporation issue common and preferred stock and debt for the shareholders' property and money.

TAX RESEARCH PROBLEMS

2-56. Alice, Bob, and Carol are partners in the ABC Partnership. David is an employee of the partnership. The partnership owes David $25,000 for services rendered to the partnership during the past 2 years. On June 10, 1991, Alice, Bob, and Carol contribute their interests in the ABC Partnership to North Corporation in exchange for North stock. David receives North stock in satisfaction of the amount he is owed by the partnership. Alice, Bob, Carol, and David each receive 25% of the North stock. Explain the tax consequences of the transaction to Alice, Bob, Carol, and David, North Corporation, and the ABC Partnership.

A partial list of research sources is

- Reg. Sec. 1.351-1(b)(2).
- *G & W. H. Corson, Inc.,* 1954 PH T.C. Memo ¶ 71,149, 12 TCM 753 (1953).
- Rev. Rul. 84-111, 1984-2 C.B. 88.

2-57. Anne exchanges land held for investment for like-kind property. Six months later, in a Sec. 351 transaction, Anne transfers the like-kind property to Blue Corporation in exchange for all of Blue's stock. What are the tax consequences of the two exchanges?

A partial list of research sources is

- Sec. 1031.
- Rev. Rul. 75-292, 1975-2 C.B. 333.

2-58. Bob and Carl transfer property to Stone Corporation for 90% and 10% of the Stone stock, respectively. Pursuant to a binding agreement entered into before the transfer, Bob sells half of his stock to Carl. Does Sec. 351 apply to the exchange?

A partial list of research sources is

- Sec. 351.
- Reg. Sec. 1.351-1.
- Rev. Rul. 79-194, 1979-1 C.B. 145.

2-59. In an exchange qualifying under Sec. 351, Greta receives 100 shares of White Corporation stock plus a contingent right to receive another 25 shares. The shares are contingent on the determination of the value of a patent contributed by Greta. The licensing of the patent is pending and consequently the patent cannot be valued for several months. Are the contingent shares considered "stock" for purposes of Sec. 351? What are the tax consequences to Greta of her receipt of the contingent shares?

A partial list of research sources is

- Rev. Rul. 66-112, 1966-1 C.B. 68.
- *James C. Hamrick v. CIR,* 17 AFTR 2d 66-357, 66-1 USTC ¶ 9322 (4th Cir., 1966).

3
The Corporate Income Tax

CHAPTER OUTLINE
LEARNING OBJECTIVES 3-2
CORPORATE ELECTIONS 3-2
- Choosing a Calendar or Fiscal Year 3-2
- Accounting Methods 3-4
- General Formula for Determining the Corporate Tax Liability 3-5

COMPUTING A CORPORATION'S TAXABLE INCOME 3-6
- Differences Between Individual and Corporate Taxable Income 3-6
- Sales and Exchanges of Property 3-9
- Deductions 3-10
- Transactions Between a Corporation and Its Shareholders 3-22
- At-Risk Rules 3-24
- Passive Activity Limitation Rules 3-24

COMPUTING A CORPORATION'S INCOME TAX LIABILITY 3-24
- General Rules 3-25
- Personal Service Corporations 3-25

CONTROLLED GROUPS OF CORPORATIONS 3-26
- Why Special Rules Are Needed 3-26
- What Is a Controlled Group? 3-27
- Application of the Controlled Group Test 3-31
- Special Rules Applying to Controlled Groups 3-32
- Consolidated Tax Returns 3-32

COMPENSATION PLANNING FOR SHAREHOLDER-EMPLOYEES 3-34
- Advantage of Salary Payments 3-34
- Advantage of Fringe Benefits 3-35
- Limitation on Deductible Compensation Payments for Shareholder-Employees 3-35

TAX PLANNING CONSIDERATIONS 3-35
- Special Election to Allocate Reduced Tax Rate Benefits 3-35
- Using NOL Carryovers and Carrybacks 3-37
- Tax Planning to Avoid Controlled Group Status 3-38

COMPLIANCE AND PROCEDURAL CONSIDERATIONS 3-38
- Requirements for Filing and Paying Taxes 3-38
- Types of Tax Returns 3-38
- When the Return Must Be Filed 3-39
- Tax Return Schedules 3-39
- Estimated Taxes 3-42

PROBLEM MATERIALS 3-46
- Discussion Questions 3-46
- Problems 3-48
- Tax Form/Return Preparation Problem 3-53
- Case Study Problem 3-55
- Tax Research Problems 3-55

LEARNING OBJECTIVES

After studying this chapter, you should be able to

1. Determine the basic tax elections a new corporation is required to make
2. Compute a corporation's taxable income
3. Compute a corporation's income tax liability
4. Explain what a controlled group is and the tax consequences of being a controlled group
5. Explain how compensation planning can reduce taxes for corporations and their shareholders
6. Determine the requirements for filing a corporate tax return and paying corporate income taxes

A **corporation** is a separate taxpaying entity that must file a tax return every year, even if it has no income or loss for the year. This chapter covers the tax rules for **domestic corporations** (i.e., corporations that are incorporated in one of the 50 states or under federal law).[1] It explains the rules for (1) determining a corporation's taxable income, loss, and tax liability and (2) for filing corporate tax returns.

The corporations discussed in this chapter are sometimes referred to as regular or C corporations. Such corporations do not have any special tax status and are taxed under the provisions of Subchapter C of the Internal Revenue Code. Corporations that have a special tax status include S corporations and affiliated groups of corporations that file consolidated returns.[2] A comparison of the tax treatments of C corporations, S corporations, and partnerships is presented in Appendix C.

CORPORATE ELECTIONS

OBJECTIVE 1
Determine the basic tax elections a new corporation is required to make

When a corporation is formed, certain elections must be made. The corporation must select its **tax year,** whether calendar year or fiscal year. It must also select its basic accounting method, either cash, accrual, or hybrid method of accounting. These elections are made on the corporation's first tax return. They are important and should be considered carefully because, once made, they generally can be changed only with permission from the Internal Revenue Service (IRS).

Choosing a Calendar or Fiscal Year

Key Point
Whereas partnerships and S corporations must generally adopt a calendar year, regular C corporations (other than personal service corporations) have the added flexibility of adopting a fiscal year. The fiscal year must end on the last day of the month.

A new corporation may elect to use either a calendar year or a fiscal year as its accounting period. The election is made by filing the corporation's first tax return for the selected period. A calendar year is a 12-month period ending on December 31. A

---

[1] Sec. 7701(a)(4). The tax rules for foreign corporations doing business in the United States are covered in Chapter 15 of this book.
[2] The rules for affiliated groups electing to file consolidated tax returns and for S corporations are covered in Chapters 8 and 11, respectively.

fiscal year is a 12-month period ending on the last day of any month other than December (e.g., March 31 or September 30).[3] Examples of acceptable fiscal years are February 1, 1991, to January 31, 1992; and October 1, 1991, to September 30, 1992. A fiscal year that runs from September 16, 1991, through September 15, 1992, is not an acceptable tax year since it does not end on the last day of the month. The IRS will require a corporation using an unacceptable tax year to change to a calendar year.[4]

Self-Study Question

If a corporation files a short-period tax return in its initial or final tax year, must it annualize its income?

Answer

No. The corporation treats the short period as a regular tax year. Not only does income not have to be adjusted, but the corporation is entitled to use the entire graduated rate structure available to a C corporation.

Short Tax Period. A corporation's first tax year may not cover a full 12-month period. If, for example, a corporation begins business on March 10, 1991, and elects a fiscal year ending on September 30, its first tax year covers the period from March 10, 1991, through September 30, 1991. Its second tax year covers the period from October 1, 1991, through September 30, 1992. The corporation must file a **short-period tax return** for its first tax year.[5] From then on, its tax returns cover a full 12-month period. The last year of a corporation's life may also be a short period for tax purposes covering the period of time from the beginning of the last tax year through the date that the corporation goes out of existence.

Restrictions on Adopting a Tax Year. Some corporations are subject to restrictions in their choice of a tax year. An S corporation generally must use a calendar year (see Chapter 11). A corporation that is a member of an affiliated group that elects to file a consolidated return must use the same tax year as the group's parent corporation (see Chapter 8).

A personal service corporation generally must use a calendar year as its tax year. A **personal service corporation** (PSC) is defined for this purpose as a corporation whose principal activity is the performance of personal services. A corporation is not a PSC unless its employee-owners own more than 10% of the stock (by value) on any day of the year and the personal services are substantially performed by employee-owners. An employee-owner is any employee who owns any of the corporation's stock on any day of the tax year.[6]

Self-Study Question

What choices does a PSC have relative to its taxable year?

Answer

In general, a PSC is limited to a calendar year, but if it can show a business purpose, a fiscal year can be selected. Finally, similar to partnerships and S corporations, a PSC can elect under Sec. 444 a fiscal year that can provide as much as a three-month deferral.

A PSC is allowed to adopt or retain a fiscal tax year if it can establish a business purpose for such a year. It may, for example, be able to establish a natural business year and use that year as its tax year.[7] Deferral of income by shareholders is not an acceptable business purpose.

A PSC may elect under Sec. 444 to use a fiscal year that does not satisfy the normal business purpose requirement. Under this election, a new corporation may elect to use a September 30, October 31, or November 30 year-end. An existing corporation that has a fiscal year may elect under Sec. 444 to retain that year or change to one whose deferral period is shorter than its current one. The deferral period is the number of months from the beginning of the corporation's fiscal year to December 31st.

If a PSC elects a fiscal year under Sec. 444, it must meet certain minimum distribution requirements to employee-owners during the deferral period. If these distribution requirements are not met, the PSC's deduction for amounts paid to employee-owners and which are includible in the employee's gross income (other than gains from the sale of property between the owner and the corporation and dividends)

---

[3] Sec. 441. Accounting periods of either 52 or 53 weeks that always end on the same day of the week (such as Friday) are also permitted under Sec. 441.

[4] Sec. 441(i).

[5] Sec. 443(a)(2).

[6] Sec. 441(i).

[7] The natural business year exception requires that the year-end used for tax purposes must coincide with the end of the taxpayer's peak business period. (See Chapters 9 and 11 and Rev. Proc. 87-32, 1987-2 C.B. 396, for a further explanation of this exception.)

is limited. Any excess deduction amount is deferred to the corporation's next fiscal year.[8]

Example 3-1 ◼

Typical Misconception

In contrast to partnerships and S corporations, a PSC does not have to make a Sec. 7519 payment if a fiscal year is elected under Sec. 444. However, a PSC must meet minimum distribution requirements in the deferral period or be denied a deduction for certain payments to its owner-employees.

Cole Corporation is created by Alice and Bob, who each own 50% of its stock. Alice and Bob use the calendar year as their tax year. Alice and Bob are both active in the business and along with a professional staff of 30 are the new corporation's primary employees. The new corporation performs engineering services for the automotive industry. Cole Corporation is restricted to using a calendar year as its tax year unless it qualifies to use a fiscal year based upon either the natural business year or business purpose exceptions. Alternatively, it can elect under Sec. 444 to adopt a fiscal year with a three-month or shorter deferral period. If such an election is made, the minimum distribution requirements of Sec. 280H must be complied with. ◼

Changing the Annual Accounting Period. A corporation that desires to change its annual accounting period must secure the prior approval of the IRS unless the change is authorized under the Regulations. Such a change usually results in a short period running from the end of the old annual accounting period to the beginning of the new accounting period. A request for approval of an accounting period change must be filed on Form 1128 (Application for Change in Annual Accounting Period) on or before the fifteenth day of the second calendar month following the close of the short period.

Key Point

Normally, a corporation must obtain permission from the IRS before changing its tax year. This usually requires that the corporation establish a substantial business purpose for the change of accounting period. However, the regulations do allow a corporation, in limited situations, to change its accounting period without prior IRS approval.

In general, a request for change is approved if there is a substantial business purpose for the change. But, if the change would result in a substantial distortion of income, the taxpayer and the IRS must agree to the terms, conditions, and adjustments necessary to prevent the substantial distortion of income before the change can be effected. A substantial distortion of income includes, for example, a change that causes the "deferral of a substantial portion of the taxpayer's income or shifting of a substantial portion of deductions from one year to another so as to reduce substantially the taxpayer's tax liability."[9]

Under the Regulations, a corporation may change its annual accounting period without the prior approval of the IRS if all of the following conditions are met: (1) the corporation has not changed its annual accounting period within the prior 10 years; (2) the resulting short period does not have a net operating loss (NOL); (3) the taxable income in the resulting short period is, if annualized, at least 80% of the corporation's taxable income for the tax year preceding the short period; (4) if the corporation has a special status (i.e., personal holding company or exempt status) for the short period or the tax year prior to the short period, it has the same status for both; and (5) the corporation does not elect S corporation status in the year following the short period.[10]

Accounting Methods

A new corporation must select the overall **accounting method** it will use to keep its books and records. The method chosen must be indicated on the corporation's initial return. The same method must be used to compute its financial accounting income and its taxable income. The three possible accounting methods are: (1) accrual, (2) cash, and (3) hybrid.[11]

---

[8] Sec. 280H.
[9] Reg. Sec. 1.442-1(b)(1).
[10] Reg. Sec. 1.442-1(c).
[11] Sec. 446.

Key Point

Whereas partnerships and S corporations are generally allowed to be cash method taxpayers, most C corporations must use the accrual method of accounting. This restriction can prove an inconvenience for many small corporations that would rather employ the less complicated cash method of accounting.

Accrual Method. Income is reported when it has been earned; expenses are reported when they have been incurred. C corporations must use this method unless they come under one of the following exceptions:[12]

1. A qualified family farming corporation.
2. A qualified personal service corporation: a corporation (a) substantially all of whose activities involve the performance of services in the fields of health, law, engineering, architecture, accounting, actuarial science, performing arts, or consulting; and (b) substantially all of whose stock is held by current (or retired) employees performing the services listed above, their estates, or (for 2 years only) persons who inherited their stock from such employees.
3. Corporations with gross receipts of $5,000,000 or less for all prior tax years beginning after December 31, 1985. A corporation meets this test for any prior tax year if its average gross receipts for the 3-year period ending with that prior tax year do not exceed $5,000,000. If the corporation was not in existence for the entire 3-year period, the period during which the corporation *was* in existence may be used.

If a corporation meets one of the exceptions listed above, it may use either the accrual method or one of the following two methods.

Cash Method. Income is reported when it is received; expenses are reported when they are paid. Corporations in service industries such as engineering, medicine, law, and accounting generally use this method because they do not want to report their income until they actually receive it. This method may not be used if inventories are a material income-producing factor. In such case, the corporation must use either the *accrual* method or the *hybrid* method of accounting.

Hybrid Method. Under this method, a corporation uses the accrual method of accounting for its sales, cost of goods sold, inventories, accounts receivable, and accounts payable, and the cash method of accounting for all other income and expense items. Small businesses with inventories (e.g., retail stores) frequently use this method. Although they must use the accrual method of accounting for sales-related income and expense items, they often find it less burdensome to use the cash method of accounting for other income and expense items, such as utilities, rents, salaries, taxes, and so on.

Historical Note

Before the Tax Reform Act of 1986, corporations were subject to a rather insignificant minimum tax. To ensure that most corporations would pay some taxes, Congress enacted a formidable 20% corporate alternative minimum tax. For some corporations, the alternative minimum tax is their primary tax system.

General Formula for Determining the Corporate Tax Liability

Each year, C corporations are responsible for determining their federal tax liability under both the corporate income (or regular) tax and the corporate alternative minimum tax rules. In addition to these two primary taxes, a C corporation may owe one or more special tax levies (i.e., the accumulated earnings tax, the personal holding company tax, or the Superfund environmental tax). A corporation's total tax liability equals the sum of its two primary corporate tax liabilities plus the amount of any special tax levies that it owes. The general formula for determining a corporation's tax liability is outlined in Table 3-1.

---

[12] Sec. 448. Certain family farming corporations having gross receipts of less than $25 million may use the cash method of accounting. Section 447 requires farming corporations with gross receipts in excess of $25 million to use the accrual method of accounting.

This chapter explains how to compute a corporation's income (or regular) tax liability. Chapter 5 explains the computation of the corporate alternative minimum tax, personal holding company tax, accumulated earnings tax, and Superfund environmental tax.

Topic Review 3-1 reviews the basic tax year and accounting method elections for C corporations, personal service corporations, and S corporations.

COMPUTING A CORPORATION'S TAXABLE INCOME

OBJECTIVE 2
Compute a corporation's taxable income

The rules for computing a C corporation's taxable income are similar to those for computing an individual's taxable income. The differences are explained in the first part of this section. Some rules for computing a C corporation's taxable income are unique to C corporations and require a detailed explanation. The second part of this section presents detailed coverage of the C corporation rules.

Typical Misconception
Taxpayers usually have a difficult time understanding the relationship between the regular income tax and the alternative minimum tax. Table 3-1 illustrates that, in total, a taxpayer ends up paying the higher of (1) the regular income tax liability or (2) the tentative minimum tax reduced by the AMT investment tax credit.

Differences Between Individual and Corporate Taxable Income

The computation of a corporation's taxable income is outlined in Table 3-2. The primary differences between the individual and corporate tax rules for computing gross income and deductions are explained below.

Gross Income. Gross income is computed in much the same way for a corporation as it is for an individual. A corporation's gross income includes most of the same items that an individual's gross income includes such as receipts for services, gross profits on sales, rents, gains on sales of property, interest, dividends, and commissions. A corporation's gross income also excludes most of the same items that are excluded from an individual's gross income, such as tax-exempt interest on state and municipal bonds and proceeds from life insurance policies.

Some exclusions that apply to individuals do not apply to corporations; for example, corporations are not eligible to exclude employee fringe benefits such as premiums on $50,000 of group term life insurance. Conversely, some exclusions that apply to corporations do not apply to individuals; for example, a corporation excludes from its gross income amounts contributed to its capital.

Key Point
Corporations do not make the distinction between "for" and "from" AGI deductions. For corporations, all ordinary and necessary business expenses are deductions from gross income.

Deductions and Losses. A corporation's deductions are similar to an individual's *for* AGI (above the line) deductions. But a corporation does not have the equivalent of an individual's itemized deductions since all of its deductions are deducted directly from gross income. All of a corporation's business deductions must be ordinary and necessary trade or business expenses under Sec. 162. The distinction between an individual's expenses deductible under Sec. 162 (trade or business expenses) and those deductible under Sec. 212 (expenses for the production of income) does not apply to corporations. A corporation is not eligible to deduct expenses incurred for the production of income under Sec. 212. A corporation has no standard deduction amount and no personal or dependency exemptions. C corporations are not subject to the hobby loss limitations of Sec. 183, or the investment interest limitations of Sec. 163(d) as an individual taxpayer would be. Closely held C corporations, however, are

TOPIC REVIEW 3-1

Basic Corporate Tax Elections

1. Tax Year Election
   a. Any fiscal year or a calendar year can be elected by a C corporation so long as it is the same as the taxpayer's annual accounting period.
   b. A calendar year is generally required for S corporations and personal service corporations. A fiscal year can be elected if the business purpose requirement is satisfied (e.g., a natural business year). A special election is available under Sec. 444 which permits a deferral period of up to three months unless the tax year is grandfathered under pre-1987 tax law. If a Sec. 444 election is made, a special required payment must be made annually by an S corporation, or a minimum distribution requirement must be met by a personal service corporation, to maintain the election.
   c. All corporations that join in the filing of a consolidated tax return must use the parent corporation's tax year.
2. Overall Accounting Method
   a. General rule: C Corporations must use the accrual method of accounting.
   b. Exceptions: Qualified farming corporations
      Qualified personal service corporations
      C corporations with average gross receipts of $5,000,000 or less for the most recent three-year period.
      S corporations

   If a corporation meets one of the exceptions it may use the cash method of accounting except where inventories are a material income producing factor. The accrual method of accounting is required for the sales-related activities in such a situation. Alternatively, the hybrid method of accounting can be elected.

TABLE 3-1 *General Rules for Determining the Corporate Tax Liability*

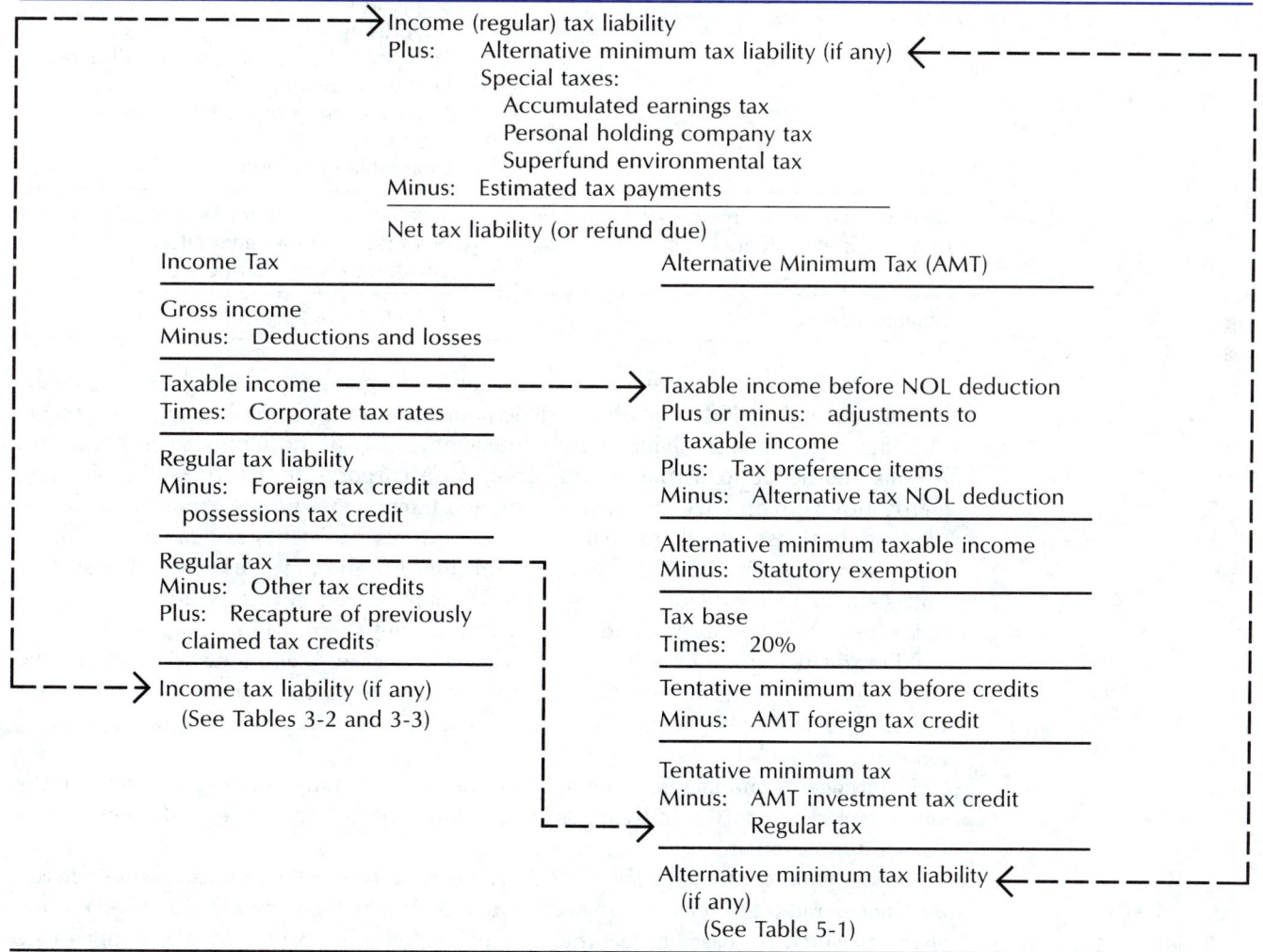

Additional Comment

Most expenditures made by large corporations are either legitimate deductions or are capitalized. Expenditures made by closely held corporations are subject to close IRS scrutiny because the potential exists that the payments may be made for personal shareholder expenses.

TABLE 3-2 *Computation of Corporate Taxable Income*

General Formula	Specific Examples
Gross income	Receipts from services
	Gross profits
	Dividends
	Interest
	Rents
	Royalties
	Gains from sales or exchanges of property
	Other income
Minus: Deductions and losses	Losses from sales or exchanges of property
	Compensation of officers
	Other salaries and wages
	Repairs
	Bad debts
	Rents
	Taxes
	Interest
	Depreciation
	Depletion
	Advertising
	Pension and profit-sharing contributions
	Employee benefit costs
	Amortization of organization and start-up costs
	Charitable contributions
Taxable income before special deductions	Taxable income before special deductions
Minus: Special deductions	Net operating loss deduction
	Dividends-received deduction
Taxable income	Taxable income

subject to the at risk rules of Sec. 465 and the passive activity loss and credit limitations of Sec. 469 in much the same manner as an individual taxpayer would be.

Some deductions available to individuals obviously do not apply to corporations. Among the deductions that do not apply to a corporation are those for alimony, contributions to an IRA or a Keogh plan, and moving expenses. Corporations do not have nonbusiness bad debts. All of a corporation's bad debts are considered to be business related. On the other hand, corporations are allowed some special deductions not available to individuals. These include amortization of organizational expenditures (Sec. 248) and a dividends-received deduction (Secs. 243 to 245).

Many deductions are available both to corporations and to individuals. But in some cases, the computation of the deduction is different for corporations than for individuals (e.g., the deductions for charitable contributions and net operating losses).

Capital gains and losses are computed on sales or exchanges of capital assets in the same way they are for individuals, but capital losses are treated differently on a corporate tax return.

Casualty losses are deductible in full by a corporation. All corporate casualty losses are considered to be business related. They are not reduced by a $100 offset nor are they restricted to losses exceeding 10% of AGI as are an individual's nonbusiness casualty losses.

Sales and Exchanges of Property

Sales and exchanges of property are generally treated the same way for corporations as they are for an individual. However, (1) special rules apply in the case of capital losses; and (2) corporations are subject to an additional 20% depreciation recapture rule under Sec. 291 on sales of Sec. 1250 property.

Capital Gains and Losses. Corporations compute capital gains and losses the same way that individuals do. A corporation has a capital gain or loss if it sells or exchanges a capital asset. A corporation must net all of its capital gains and losses together to obtain its net capital gain or loss position.

NET CAPITAL GAIN. All of a corporation's net capital gains for the tax year are included in gross income. A corporation's capital gains receive no special tax treatment and are taxed in the same manner as any other ordinary income item.

> **Typical Misconception**
> The (1) definition of capital assets, (2) mechanics of calculating capital gains and losses, (3) distinction between long-term and short-term, and (4) method of netting the capital gains and losses are all the same for individuals and corporations.

Example 3-2 ■ Beta Corporation has a net capital gain of $40,000, gross profits on sales of $110,000, and deductible expenses of $28,000. B's gross income is $150,000 ($40,000 + $110,000). Its taxable income is $122,000 ($150,000 − $28,000). The $40,000 of net capital gain receives no special treatment and is taxed in the same manner as any other ordinary income item. ■

NET CAPITAL LOSSES. If a corporation has a net capital loss, the loss may not be deducted in the current year. A corporation's capital losses may be used only to offset capital gains. They may *never* be used to offset the corporation's ordinary income.

A net capital loss must be carried back to the 3 previous tax years and be used to offset net capital gains in the earliest year possible (i.e., the losses must be carried to the third previous year first). If the loss is not totally absorbed as a carryback, the remainder may be carried forward for 5 years. Any losses that remain unused at the end of the carryforward period are lost.

Example 3-3 ■ For 1991 East Corporation reports gross profits of $150,000, deductible expenses of $28,000, and a net capital loss of $10,000. East reported the following net capital gains during 1988-1990:

Year	Net Capital Gains
1988	$6,000
1989	—0—
1990	3,000

> **Self-Study Question**
> How does the use of a net capital loss differ for individual taxpayers and corporate taxpayers?
>
> **Answer**
> Net capital losses are treated differently by individuals and corporations. Individuals (1) may use up to $3,000 per year of net capital losses to offset ordinary income, (2) cannot carry back net capital losses, and (3) can carry forward net capital losses indefinitely. In contrast, corporations (1) may not use any net capital losses to offset ordinary income, (2) can carry back net capital losses 3 years, and (3) can carry forward net capital losses for only 5 years.

East has gross income of $150,000 and taxable income of $122,000 ($150,000 − $28,000) for 1991. East also has a $10,000 net capital loss that can be carried back. This loss is carried back to 1988 first and offsets the $6,000 net capital gain reported in that year. East receives a refund for the taxes paid on the $6,000 of capital gains in 1988. The $4,000 ($10,000 − $6,000) remainder of the loss carryback is carried to 1990 and offsets East's $3,000 net capital gain reported in that year. East still has a $1,000 net capital loss to carry forward to 1992. ■

Sec. 291: Tax Benefit Recapture Rule. If Sec. 1250 property is sold at a gain, Sec. 1250 requires that the recognized gain be reported as ordinary income to the extent the depreciation taken exceeds the depreciation that would have been allowed if the straight-line method had been used. This ordinary income is known as "Sec. 1250 depreciation recapture." For individuals, any remaining gain is characterized as Sec.

1231 gain. However, corporations must recapture as ordinary income an additional amount equal to 20% of the additional ordinary income that would have been recognized had the property been Sec. 1245 property instead of Sec. 1250 property.

Example 3-4 ■

Additional Comment

Section 291 results in the recapture, as ordinary income, of an additional 20% of the gain on sales of Sec. 1250 property. Section 291 was enacted strictly as a revenue enhancement provision. However, with capital gains currently being taxed at the same rates as ordinary income, the provision has little impact on a corporation's bottom-line tax liability.

Texas Corporation purchased residential real estate in January, 1988 for $125,000, of which $25,000 is allocated to the land and $100,000 to the building. Texas took straight-line MACRS depreciation deductions of $10,757 on the building in the years 1988 through 1990. In 1991, Texas sells the property for $155,000, of which $45,000 is allocated to the land and $110,000 to the building. Texas has a $20,000 ($45,000 − $25,000) gain on the land sale, all of which is Sec. 1231 gain. This gain is not affected by Sec. 291, since land is not Sec. 1250 property. Texas has a $20,757 ($110,000 sales price − [$100,000 original cost − $10,757 depreciation]) gain on the sale of the building. If Texas were an individual taxpayer, the entire $20,757 recognized gain would be Sec. 1231 gain. But as a *corporate* taxpayer, $2,151 of gain must be reported as ordinary income. This amount is computed as follows:

Recapture amount for Sec. 1245 property:
Lesser of:
$10,757 (Depreciation claimed)
or
$20,757 (Recognized gain) $10,757
Times: Sec. 291 percentage   × 0.20
Recapture under Sec. 291 $ 2,151

Thus, Texas Corporation's recognized gain on the sale of the building is reported as $2,151 of ordinary income and $18,606 ($20,757 − $2,151) of Sec. 1231 gain. ■

Deductions

Corporations may deduct most of the same business expenses that a sole proprietor may deduct on Schedule C of an individual return. Deductions are allowed for ordinary and necessary business expenses including salaries paid to officers and other employees of the corporation, rent, repairs, insurance premiums, advertising, interest, taxes, losses on sales of inventory or other property, bad debts, and depreciation.[13]

No deductions are allowed for interest on amounts borrowed to purchase tax-exempt securities, illegal bribes or kickbacks, fines or penalties imposed by a government, or insurance premiums incurred to insure the lives of officers and key employees when the corporation is the beneficiary.

Key Point

Without the election available under Sec. 248, organizational expenditures would be capitalized and would not be recovered until the corporation is liquidated. Thus, the election to amortize organizational expenditures over a period of 60 months is certainly preferable to the alternative.

Organizational Expenditures. When a corporation is formed, it may incur some organizational expenditures such as legal fees and accounting fees incident to the incorporation process. These expenditures must be capitalized. Unless an election is made under Sec. 248, however, these expenditures cannot be amortized because they have an unlimited life. A Sec. 248 election allows organizational expenditures to be amortized over a period of 60 or more months beginning with the month in which the corporation begins its business. The election must be made in a statement attached to the first return filed by the corporate entity. The return and statement must be filed no later than the due date of the tax return (including any permitted extensions).[14] If

---

[13] Sec. 162.
[14] Sec. 248(c).

an amortization election is not made, organizational expenditures cannot be deducted until the corporation is liquidated.

The election applies only to expenditures incurred before the end of the tax year in which the corporation begins business. A corporation begins business when it starts the business operations for which it was organized.[15] In determining when an organizational expenditure has been incurred, it is immaterial whether the corporation uses the cash or accrual method of accounting. Expenditures incurred *after* the first tax year has ended (e.g., legal expenses incurred to modify the corporate charter) must be capitalized and cannot be deducted until the corporation is liquidated.[16]

Organizational expenditures are defined by Sec. 248(b) to include any expenditure that is (1) incident to the creation of the corporation; (2) chargeable to the corporation's capital account; and (3) of a character which, if expended incident to the creation of a corporation having a limited life, would be amortizable over that life.

Organizational expenditures include:

- Legal services incident to the organization of the corporation (e.g., drafting the corporate charter and bylaws, minutes of organizational meetings, and terms of original stock certificates)
- Accounting services necessary to the creation of the corporation
- Expenses of temporary directors and of organizational meetings of directors and stockholders
- Fees paid to the State of incorporation.[17]

Organizational expenditures do not include any expenditures connected with the issuing or selling of the corporation's stock or other securities (e.g., commissions, professional fees, and printing costs) and expenditures related to the transfer of assets to the corporation.

Example 3-5 ■ Heart Corporation is incorporated on July 1, 1991; starts in business on August 1, 1991; and elects a tax year ending on September 30. Heart incurs the following expenditures during its first 12 months:

Date	Type of Expenditure	Amount
June 10, 1991	Legal expenses to draft charter	$ 2,000
July 17, 1991	Commission to stockbroker for issuing and selling stock	40,000
July 18, 1991	Accounting fees to set up corporate books	2,400
July 20, 1991	Temporary directors' fees	1,000
August 25, 1991	Directors' fees	1,500
October 9, 1991	Legal fees to modify corporate charter	1,000

Heart's first tax year begins July 1, 1991, and ends on September 30, 1991. Heart may amortize organizational expenditures of $5,400 ($2,000 legal expenses + $2,400 accounting expenses + $1,000 temporary directors' fees). The legal expenses to modify the corporate charter incurred on October 9, 1991, may not be

---

[15] Reg. Sec. 1.248-1(a)(3).
[16] Reg. Sec. 1.248-1(a)(2).
[17] Reg. Sec. 1.248-1(b)(2).

amortized because they were not incurred during Heart's first tax year. The commission for selling the Heart stock is not an organizational expenditure and is treated as a reduction in the amount of Heart's paid-in capital. The directors' fees incurred in August 1991 may be deducted as a trade or business expense under Sec. 162 since Heart has commenced in business by that date. If Heart elects to amortize its organizational expenditures over 60 months, it deducts $90 ($5,400 ÷ 60) per month. A $180 deduction can be claimed in 1991 ($90 per month × 2 months). ∎

If the business is discontinued or disposed of before the end of the amortization period, any remaining organizational expenditures may be deducted as a loss.[18]

Self-Study Question
What are start-up expenditures?

Answer
Start-up expenditures usually occur prior to the actual operation of a trade or business and involve those costs incurred in investigating and creating an active trade or business.

Start-Up Expenditures. A distinction must be made between a corporation's organizational expenditures and its start-up expenditures. Start-up expenditures are ordinary and necessary business expenses that are paid or incurred by an individual or corporate taxpayer:[19]

- To investigate the creation or acquisition of an active trade or business
- To create an active trade or business
- To conduct an activity engaged in for profit or the production of income before the time the activity becomes an active trade or business.

Examples of start-up expenditures are the costs incurred for a survey of potential markets; an analysis of available facilities; advertisements relating to the opening of the business; the training of employees; travel and other expenses for securing prospective distributors, suppliers, or customers; and the hiring of management personnel and outside consultants.

The expenditures must be such that if they were incurred in connection with the operation of an existing active trade or business they would be allowable as a deduction for the year in which paid or incurred. In addition, they must be capitalized.

Under Sec. 195, a separate election may be made to amortize start-up expenditures over a period of 60 or more months starting with the month in which an active trade or business begins. If the business is discontinued or disposed of before the end of the amortization period, any remaining start-up expenditures may be deducted as a loss.[20]

Key Point
Accrual method corporate taxpayers have some flexibility on the timing of their charitable contribution deductions. The charitable contributions are deducted in the year paid or when accrued if (1) the board of directors authorizes the contribution and (2) the contribution is made by the 15th day of the third month following the end of the accrual year.

Charitable Contributions. The treatment of charitable contributions by individual and corporate taxpayers differs in three ways: (1) the timing of the deduction; (2) the amount of the deduction permitted for the contribution of certain nonmoney properties; and (3) the maximum deduction permitted in any given year.

TIMING OF THE DEDUCTION. Corporations are allowed a deduction for contributions to "qualified charitable organizations" just as individuals are.[21] Generally, the contribution must have been *paid* during the year (not just pledged) for a deduction to be allowed for a given year. A special rule applies to corporations using the accrual method of accounting (corporations using the cash or hybrid methods of accounting are not eligible).[22] These corporations may elect to treat part or all of a charitable contribution as having been made in the year in which it was accrued (instead of being deducted in the year paid) if

---

[18] *Malta Temple Association,* 16 B.T.A. 409 (1929), acq. XIII-2 C.B. 12.
[19] Sec. 195(c)(1).
[20] Sec. 195(b).
[21] Sec. 170(a)(1). For a definition of qualified charitable organizations, see Chapter 7 of *Prentice Hall's Federal Taxation: Individuals.*
[22] Sec. 170(a)(2).

1. The board of directors authorizes the contribution in the year it was accrued;
2. The contribution is paid on or before the 15th day of the third month following the end of the tax year.

Any portion of the contribution for which the election is not made is deducted in the year that it is paid. The election is made by deducting the contribution on the corporation's tax return for the year it was accrued and attaching a copy of the board of director's resolution to the return.[23]

Example 3-6 ■ Echo Corporation is a calendar-year taxpayer using the accrual method of accounting. In 1991, its board of directors authorizes a $10,000 contribution to the Girl Scouts. The contribution is paid on March 10, 1992. Echo may elect to treat part or all of the contribution as having been paid in 1991. If the contribution is not paid by March 15, 1992, it may not be deducted in 1991 but may be deducted in 1992. ■

Key Point

Congress has provided corporations with added incentive to help support charitable organizations that care for the ill, needy, or infants. If corporations donate ordinary income property to such charities, the corporation gets to deduct not only the usual adjusted basis in the property but also an additional 50% of the appreciation in the contributed property. This incentive also applies to property contributed to educational institutions or research organizations for use in research or experimentation.

DEDUCTING CONTRIBUTIONS OF ORDINARY INCOME PROPERTY. If money is donated to a qualified charitable organization, the amount of the charitable contribution deduction equals the amount of money donated. If property is donated, the amount of the charitable contribution deduction generally equals the property's fair market value (FMV). However, special rules apply to donations of "ordinary income property" and to certain donations of appreciated "capital gain property."

"**Ordinary income property**" is defined as property whose sale would have resulted in a gain other than a long-term capital gain (i.e., ordinary income or short-term capital gain).[24] Examples of ordinary income property include investment property held for one year or less, inventory property, and property subject to recapture under Secs. 1245 and 1250. The deduction allowed for a donation of such property is generally limited to the greater of (1) the property's FMV minus the amount of ordinary income or short-term capital gain that would have been recognized if the property had been sold or (2) the property's adjusted basis. For certain inventory properties, however, the corporate donor is allowed to deduct the property's adjusted basis plus one-half of the excess of the property's FMV over its adjusted basis if:

1. The use of the property is related to the donee's exempt function, and it is used solely for the care of the ill, the needy, or infants
2. The property is not transferred to the donee in exchange for money, other property, or services
3. The donor receives a statement from the charitable organization stating that conditions (1) and (2) will be complied with[25]

The amount of the deduction cannot exceed twice the property's adjusted basis.

A similar rule applies to contributions of scientific research property if:

1. The contribution is to a college or university or tax-exempt scientific research organization
2. The property was constructed by the taxpayer
3. The contribution is made not later than 2 years after the property is substantially completed
4. The donee is the original user of the property
5. The property is scientific equipment or an apparatus substantially all of which is used by the donee for research or experimentation

[23] Reg. Sec. 1.170A-11(b)(2).
[24] Sec. 170(e)(1)(A).
[25] Sec. 170(e)(3).

6. The property is not sold or exchanged by the donee for money, property, or services
7. The corporation receives from the donee a written statement that the property will be used in accordance with the conditions listed in Items 5 and 6[26]

Example 3-7 ■ King Corporation donates inventory having a $26,000 adjusted basis and a $40,000 FMV to a qualified public charity. A $33,000 ($26,000 + [0.50 × $14,000]) deduction is allowed for the contribution of the inventory if the inventory is to be used by the charitable organization for the care of the ill, needy, or infants, or if the donee is an educational institution or research organization that will use the scientific research property for research or experimentation. Otherwise the deduction is limited to the property's $26,000 adjusted basis. If the inventory's FMV is instead $100,000 and the donation meets either of the two sets of requirements outlined above, the charitable contribution deduction is limited to the lesser of the property's adjusted basis plus one-half of the appreciation {$63,000 = $26,000 + (0.50 × [$100,000 − $26,000])} or twice the property's adjusted basis ($52,000 = $26,000 × 2), or $52,000. ■

DEDUCTING CONTRIBUTIONS OF CAPITAL GAIN PROPERTY. When a corporation donates appreciated property whose sale would result in long-term capital gain (also known as **capital gain property**) to a charitable organization, the amount of the contribution deduction generally equals the property's FMV. However, special restrictions apply if:

1. A corporation donates tangible personal property to a charitable organization and the organization's use of the property is unrelated to its tax-exempt purpose or
2. A corporation donates appreciated property to certain private nonoperating foundations.[27]

In both cases, the amount of the corporation's contribution is limited to the property's FMV minus the long-term capital gain that would have resulted from the property's sale.[28]

Example 3-8 ■ Fox Corporation donates an artwork to the MacNay Museum. The artwork, purchased 2 years earlier for $15,000, is worth $38,000 on the date of the gift. At the time of the donation, it is known that the MacNay Museum intends to sell the work to raise funds to conduct its activities. Fox's deduction for the gift is limited to $15,000. If the artwork is to be displayed by the MacNay Museum to be viewed by the public, the entire $38,000 deduction is permitted. Fox Corporation can avoid the loss of a portion of its charitable contribution deduction by placing restrictions on the sale or use of the property at the time that it is donated. ■

Self-Study Question
What happens to excess charitable contributions?

Answer
Corporations may not deduct charitable contributions in excess of 10% of adjusted taxable income. Excess charitable contributions cannot be carried back, but are eligible for a 5-year carryforward. Excess charitable contributions are subject to the same 10% limitation in future years.

MAXIMUM DEDUCTION PERMITTED. As is the case with individuals, there is a limit on the amount of charitable contributions that a corporation can deduct in a given year. The limit is calculated differently for corporations than for individuals. Contribution deductions by corporations are limited to 10% of adjusted taxable income. Adjusted taxable income is the corporation's taxable income computed without regard to any of the following:

---

[26] Sec. 170(e)(4).
[27] Sec. 170(e)(5). The restriction on contributions of appreciated property to private nonoperating foundations does not include contributions of stock for which market quotations are readily available.
[28] Sec. 170(e)(1)(B).

Computing a Corporation's Taxable Income • 3-15

- The charitable contribution deduction
- An NOL carryback
- A capital loss carryback
- Any dividends-received deduction[29]

Contributions that exceed the 10% limit are not deductible in the current year. Instead, they are carried forward to the next 5 tax years. Any excess contributions not deducted within those 5 years are lost. Excess contributions may be deducted in the carryover year only after any contributions that were made in that year have been deducted. The total charitable contribution deduction (including any deduction for contribution carryovers) is limited to 10% of the corporation's adjusted taxable income in the carryover year.[30]

Example 3-9 ■ Golf Corporation reports the following results in 1990 and 1991:

	1990	1991
Adjusted taxable income	$200,000	$300,000
Charitable contributions	35,000	25,000

Golf's 1990 contribution deduction is limited to $20,000 (0.10 × $200,000). Golf has a $15,000 ($35,000 − $20,000) contribution carryover to 1991. The 1991 contribution deduction is limited to $30,000 (0.10 × $300,000). Golf's deduction for 1991 is composed of the $25,000 that is donated in 1991 and $5,000 of the 1990 carryover. A $10,000 carryover from 1990 may be carried over to 1992, 1993, 1994, and 1995. ■

Topic Review 3-2 summarizes the basic corporate charitable contribution deduction rules.

Dividends-Received Deduction. Any dividend that a corporation receives because of owning stock in another corporation is included in its gross income. As was described in Chapter 2, the taxation of dividend payments to a shareholder generally results in double taxation. When the dividend payment is made to a corporate shareholder, and the distributee corporation subsequently pays these earnings out to its shareholders, triple taxation of the earnings can result.

Example 3-10 ■ Adobe Corporation owns stock in Bell Corporation. Bell Corporation reports taxable income of $100,000 and pays federal income taxes on its income. Bell distributes its after-tax income to its shareholders. The dividend that Adobe Corporation receives from Bell must be included in its gross income and, to the extent that it reports a profit for the year, Adobe will pay taxes on the dividend. Adobe Corporation distributes its remaining after-tax income to its shareholders. The shareholders must include Adobe's dividends in their gross income and generally end up paying federal income taxes on the distribution. Thus, Bell's income in this example is eventually taxed three times. ■

Key Point

To avoid the possibility of triple taxation, corporate shareholders are entitled to a dividends-received deduction. The amount of this deduction differs depending on the amount of stock ownership:

Stock Ownership

Less than 20%–70% DRD. At least 20% but less than 80%–80% DRD. 80% or more–100% DRD.

To partially mitigate the effects of the multiple taxation, domestic corporations are allowed a dividends-received deduction for dividends received from other domestic corporations.

[29] Sec. 170(b)(2).
[30] Sec. 170(d)(2).

GENERAL RULE FOR DIVIDENDS-RECEIVED DEDUCTION. Corporations that own less than 20% of the distributing corporation's stock may deduct 70% of the dividends received. If the shareholder corporation owns 20% or more of the distributing corporation's stock, it may deduct 80% of the dividends received.[31]

Example 3-11 ■ In 1991, Hale Corporation reports the following results:

Gross income from operations	$300,000
Dividends from 15%-owned domestic corporation	100,000
Expenses	280,000

Hale's dividends-received deduction is $70,000 (0.70 × $100,000). Thus, Hale's taxable income is computed as follows:

Gross income	$400,000
Minus: Expenses	(280,000)
Taxable income before special deductions	$120,000
Minus: Dividends-received deduction	(70,000)
Taxable income	$ 50,000

■

LIMITATION ON DIVIDENDS-RECEIVED DEDUCTION. In the case of dividends received from a 20% or more owned corporation, the dividends-received deduction is limited to the lesser of (1) 80% of dividends received or (2) 80% of taxable income computed without regard to any NOL deduction, any capital loss carryback, or the dividends-received deduction itself. In the case of dividends from corporations that are less than 20% owned, the deduction is limited to the lesser of (1) 70% of dividends received or (2) 70% of taxable income computed without regard to any NOL deduction, any capital loss carryback, or the dividends-received deduction itself.[32]

Example 3-12 ■

Typical Misconception

The 70% dividends-received deduction is limited to 70% of a corporation's taxable income unless, by taking the entire dividends-received deduction, the deduction creates or adds to an NOL (a similar rule also exists for the 80% dividends-received deduction). This limitation can produce unusual results. Example 3-13 illustrates how $21,000 of additional deductions can provide a $28,000 reduction in taxable income.

Assume the same facts as in Example 3-11 except that Hale Corporation's expenses for the year are $310,000. Hale's taxable income before the dividends-received deduction is $90,000 ($300,000 + $100,000 − $310,000). The dividends-received deduction is limited to the lesser of 70% of dividends received ($70,000 = $100,000 × 0.70) or 70% of taxable income before the dividends-received deduction ($63,000 = $90,000 × 0.70). Thus, the dividends-received deduction is $63,000. Hale's taxable income is $27,000 ($90,000 − $63,000). ■

A corporation that receives both dividends eligible for the 80% dividends-received deduction and the 70% dividends-received deduction must reduce taxable income by the aggregate amount of dividends eligible for the 80% deduction before computing the 70% deduction.

EXCEPTION TO THE LIMITATION. The limitation noted above does not apply if, after taking into account the full dividends-received deduction, the corporation has an NOL for the year.[33]

Example 3-13 ■ Assume the same facts as in Example 3-11, except that Hale Corporation's expenses for the year are $331,000. Hale's taxable income before the dividends-received deduction is $69,000 ($300,000 + $100,000 − $331,000). The tentative dividends-received deduction is $70,000 (0.70 × $100,000). Hale's dividends-

---

[31] Sec. 243(a).
[32] Sec. 246(b)(1).
[33] Sec. 246(b)(2).

TOPIC REVIEW 3-2

Corporate Charitable Contribution Rules

1. Timing of the contribution deduction
   a. General Rule: A deduction is allowed for contributions paid during the year.
   b. Accrual method of accounting corporations are permitted to accrue contributions approved by their board of directors prior to the end of the tax year and paid within 2½ months of the end of the tax year.
2. Amount of the contribution deduction
   a. General Rule: A deduction is allowed for the amount of money and the FMV of property donated.
   b. Exceptions for Ordinary Income Property:
      1. If property is donated that would result in ordinary income or short-term capital gain being recognized when sold, the deduction is limited to the greater of the property's FMV minus the ordinary income or short-term capital gain that would be recognized if the property were sold, or (2) the property's adjusted basis.
      2. Special Rule: For donations of inventory used for the care of the ill, needy, or infants, or scientific research property, a corporate donor is allowed to deduct the property's basis plus one-half of the excess of the property's FMV over its adjusted basis. The deduction may not exceed twice the property's adjusted basis.
   c. Exceptions for Capital Gain Property: If tangible personal property is donated to a charitable organization for a use unrelated to its tax-exempt purpose, or appreciated property is donated to a private nonoperating foundation, the corporation's contribution is limited to the property's FMV minus the long-term capital gain that would result if the property were instead sold.
3. Limitation on contribution deduction
   1. The amount of the contribution deduction is limited to 10% of the corporation's taxable income computed without regard to the charitable contribution deduction, any net operating loss or capital loss carry back, and any dividends-received deduction.
   2. Excess contributions can be carried over for a 5-year period.

received deduction is not restricted by the limitation of 70% of taxable income before the dividends-received deduction because, after taking into account the tentative $70,000 dividends-received deduction, the corporation has a $1,000 ($69,000 − $70,000) NOL for the year. ∎

The results of Examples 3-11, 3-12, and 3-13 are compared in the following table:

	Example 3-11	Example 3-12	Example 3-13
Gross income	$400,000	$400,000	$400,000
Minus: Expenses	(280,000)	(310,000)	(331,000)
Taxable income before special deductions	$120,000	$ 90,000	$ 69,000
Minus: Dividends-received deduction	(70,000)	(63,000)	(70,000)
Taxable income	$ 50,000	$ 27,000	$ (1,000)

The only case where the dividends-received deduction is not equal to the full 70% of the $100,000 dividend is Example 3-12. In that case, the deduction is limited to $63,000 because taxable income before special deductions is less than the $100,000 dividend *and* the full $70,000 deduction would not result in an NOL. The special exception to the dividends-received deduction can create interesting situations. For example, the additional $21,000 of deductions incurred in Example 3-13 resulted in a $28,000 reduction in taxable income. Corporate taxpayers should be cognizant of these rules and consider deferring income or recognizing expenses to ensure being able to deduct the full 70% or 80% dividends-received deduction. If the taxable income limitation applies, there is no carryover of unused dividends-received deductions.

Typical Misconception
Corporations that are affiliated receive basically the same benefits relative to dividends, regardless of whether a consolidated return is filed or not. If a consolidated return is filed, the dividend is eliminated. If a separate return is filed, the shareholder is still entitled to a 100% dividends-received deduction.

MEMBERS OF AN AFFILIATED GROUP. Members of an affiliated group of corporations can claim a 100% dividends-received deduction with respect to dividends received from other group members.[34] A group of corporations is affiliated if (1) a parent corporation owns at least 80% of the stock (both voting power and value) of at least one subsidiary corporation and (2) at least 80% of the stock (both voting power and value) of each other corporation is owned by other group members. There is no taxable income limitation on the 100% dividends-received deduction.[35] (See Chapter 8 for a more detailed discussion of affiliated groups and the 100% dividends-received deduction.)

DIVIDENDS RECEIVED FROM FOREIGN CORPORATIONS. The dividends-received deduction applies primarily to dividends received from domestic corporations. A dividends-received deduction is not allowed on dividends received from a foreign corporation because its income is not taxed by the U.S. government and, therefore, is not subject to the multiple taxation illustrated above.[36]

Key Point
Stock purchased on which a dividend has been declared has an increased value. This value will drop again when the dividend is paid. If the dividend is eligible for a dividends-received deduction and the drop in value also creates a capital loss, corporate shareholders could use this as a tax-planning device. To prohibit this result, no dividends-received deduction is available for stock held less than 45 days.

STOCK HELD 45 DAYS OR LESS. A dividends-received deduction is not allowed for dividends received on any share of stock that the corporate shareholder has held for 45 days or less.[37] This rule prevents a corporation from claiming a dividends-received deduction if it purchases stock immediately before an ex-dividend date and sells the stock immediately thereafter. (The ex-dividend date is the first day on which a purchaser of stock is not entitled to a previously declared dividend.) Absent this rule, such a purchase and sale would allow the corporation to receive dividends at a low tax rate—a maximum of a 10.2% ([100% − 70%] × 0.34) effective tax rate—and to obtain a capital loss on the sale of stock that could offset capital gains taxed at a 34% tax rate.

Example 3-14 ■ Rose Corporation purchases 100 shares of Maine Corporation's stock (less than 1% of the outstanding stock) for $100,000 one day before Maine's ex-dividend date. Rose receives a $5,000 dividend on which a tax of $510 {0.34 × ($5,000 − [0.70 × $5,000])} is paid. Rose sells the stock for $95,000 on the forty-fifth day *after* the dividend payment date. (Since the stock is worth $100,000 immediately before the $5,000 dividend is paid, the stock is worth $95,000 ($100,000 − $5,000) after the dividend is paid.) The sale results in a $5,000 ($100,000 − $95,000) capital loss that may offset a $5,000 capital gain, thereby producing a $1,700 (0.34 × $5,000) tax savings. Thus, Rose has a $1,190 ($1,700 − $510) profit on the purchase and sale, ignoring any changes in the stock's value. This type of tax planning is not available if Rose sells the stock shortly after receiving the dividend, since Rose must hold the Maine stock for at least 46 days to obtain the dividends-received deduction. ■

---

[34] Sec. 243(a)(3).
[35] Secs. 243(b)(5) and 1504.
[36] Sec. 245. A limited dividends-received deduction is allowed on dividends received from a foreign corporation that earns income by conducting a trade or business in the United States and, therefore, is subject to U.S. taxes.
[37] Sec. 246(c)(1).

DEBT-FINANCED STOCK. The dividends-received deduction is not allowed to the extent that the stock on which a dividend is paid is debt-financed (i.e., purchased with borrowed money).[38] This rule prevents a corporation from deducting interest paid on money borrowed to purchase the stock, while paying little or no tax on the dividends received on the stock.

Example 3-15 ■

Key Point
If money is borrowed by a corporation to acquire stock, a significant tax advantage could result. The interest on the debt would be deductible and the dividend income from the stock investment would be eligible for a dividends-received deduction. Thus, the statute does not allow a dividends-received deduction on debt-financed stock.

Peach Corporation borrows $100,000 at a 10% interest rate to purchase 30% of Sun Corporation's stock. The Sun stock pays an $8,000 annual dividend. If a dividends-received deduction were allowed for this investment, Peach would have a net gain of $856 annually on owning the Sun stock. This gain is computed as follows:

Dividends	$ 8,000
Minus: Tax on dividend	(544)[a]
Dividend (after taxes)	$ 7,456
Interest paid (0.10 × $100,000)	$10,000
Minus: Tax savings (0.34 × $10,000)	(3,400)
Net cost of borrowing	$ 6,600
Dividend (after taxes)	$ 7,456
Minus: net cost of borrowing	(6,600)
Net profit on transaction	$ 856

[a] ($8,000 − [0.80 × $8,000]) × 0.34 = $544

Because the Sun stock is completely debt-financed, Peach is not allowed a dividends-received deduction. The tax on the dividend is instead $2,720 (0.34 × $8,000) and a $1,320 ([$8,000 dividend − $2,720 tax] − $6,600 net cost of borrowing) net *loss* results. ■

Net Operating Losses (NOLs). If a corporation's deductions exceed its gross income for the year, the corporation has a **net operating loss** (NOL). The NOL is the amount by which the corporation's deductions (including any dividends-received deduction) exceeds its gross income.[39] In computing an NOL for a given year, no deduction is permitted for a carryover or carryback of an NOL from a preceding or succeeding year. However, unlike an individual's NOL, no other adjustments are required to compute a corporation's NOL.

A corporation's NOL may be carried back 3 years and carried forward 15 years. It is carried to the earliest of the 3 preceding years first and used to offset the taxable income reported in that year. If the loss cannot be used in that year it is carried to the second preceding year, then to the immediately preceding year, and then to the next 15 years in order. The corporation may elect to relinquish the carryback period entirely and instead carry the loss forward to the next 15 years.

Example 3-16 ■

In 1991, Gray Corporation has gross income of $150,000 (including $100,000 from operations and $50,000 in dividends from a 30% owned corporation) and $180,000 of expenses. Gray has a $70,000 ($150,000 − $180,000 − [0.80 × $50,000]) NOL.

[38] Sec. 246A.
[39] Sec. 172(c).

The loss is carried back to 1988 unless Gray elects to relinquish the carryback period. If Gray had $20,000 of taxable income in 1988, $20,000 of Gray's 1991 NOL is used to offset that income. Gray receives a refund of all taxes paid on its $20,000 of taxable income in 1988. Gray carries the remaining $50,000 of NOL from 1988 to 1989. ∎

> **Typical Misconception**
>
> *The election to forgo the 3-year carryback must be made on a timely filed return (including extensions). Some taxpayers are not very concerned about filing their tax returns in NOL years. If a timely election is not made and the losses must be carried back to years with expiring tax credits, the NOLs are wasted.*

A corporation might elect not to carry an NOL back because (1) its income was taxed at a low marginal tax rate in the carryback period and the corporation anticipates income being taxed at a higher marginal tax rate in later years or (2) it utilized tax credit carryovers in the earlier year that were about to expire. This election must be made by the due date (including any permitted extensions) for filing the return for the year in which the NOL was incurred. It is made by attaching a statement to that year's tax return as prescribed by Reg. Sec. 1.172-1(c). Once made for a tax year, the election is irrevocable.[40] However, if the corporation has an NOL in another year, the decision as to whether that NOL should be carried back is a separate decision. In other words, each year's NOL is treated separately and is subject to a separate election.

To obtain a refund due to carrying an NOL back to a preceding year, a corporation must file either Form 1120X (Amended U.S. Corporation Income Tax Return) or Form 1139 (Corporation Application for a Tentative Refund).

> **Typical Misconception**
>
> *The sequencing of deductions is normally straightforward. However, if an NOL carryforward exists, the NOL deduction must be computed twice. The NOL must first be calculated in determining taxable income for the charitable contribution limitation. The NOL deduction is then added back to taxable income and recomputed after both the charitable contribution and dividends-received deductions have been computed.*

The Sequencing of the Deduction Calculations. The rules for charitable contributions deductions, dividends-received deductions, and NOL deductions require that these deductions be taken in the correct sequence. Otherwise, the computation of the amount of these deductions allowed for the year may be incorrect. The correct order for taking deductions is:

1. All deductions other than the charitable contributions deduction, the dividends-received deduction, and the NOL deduction
2. The charitable contributions deduction
3. The dividends-received deduction
4. The NOL deduction

As stated previously, the charitable contributions deduction is limited to 10% of taxable income before the charitable contributions deduction, any NOL or capital loss carryback, or any dividends-received deduction, but *after* any NOL carryover deduction. Once the charitable contributions deduction has been computed, any NOL carryover deduction must be added back and the charitable contributions deduction subtracted before the dividends-received deduction is computed and subtracted. Then the NOL deduction is subtracted.

Example 3-17 ∎

East Corporation reports the following results:

Gross income from operations	$150,000
Dividends from 30% owned domestic corporation	100,000
Operating expenses	100,000
Charitable contributions	30,000

In addition, East has a $40,000 NOL carryover available. East's taxable income before the charitable contributions deduction, dividends-received deduction, and any NOL or capital loss carrybacks is computed as follows:

---

[40] Sec. 172(b)(3)(C).

Gross income from operations	$150,000
Plus: Dividends	100,000
Gross income	$250,000
Minus: Operating expenses	(100,000)
NOL carryover	(40,000)
Taxable income before charitable contributions deduction	$110,000

East's charitable contributions deduction is limited to $11,000 (0.10 × $110,000). The $11,000 limitation means that East also has a $19,000 ($30,000 − $11,000) contribution carryover that may be carried over for 5 years. East Corporation computes its taxable income as follows:

Taxable income before charitable contributions deduction	$110,000
Plus: NOL carryover	40,000
Minus: Charitable contributions deduction	(11,000)
Taxable income before special deductions	$139,000
Minus: Dividends-received deduction	(80,000)
NOL deduction	(40,000)
Taxable income	$19,000

The NOL carryover increases taxable income before the charitable contributions deduction since Sec. 170 requires NOL carryovers to reduce the contributions deduction limitation but the NOL deduction must be reported as a special deduction. East's dividends-received deduction is $80,000 (0.80 × $100,000). The entire NOL carryover is deductible as an NOL deduction since taxable income before the NOL deduction is $59,000 ($139,000 − $80,000). ∎

Key Point

NOL carrybacks do not affect either the charitable contribution or dividends-received deductions. This rule certainly simplifies the calculation of the NOL deduction created by a NOL carryback.

Note that, if an NOL is carried *back* from a later year, it is *not* taken into account in computing East's charitable contributions deduction limitation. The charitable contributions deduction is different if we assume that the $40,000 NOL is carried back from a later tax year instead of being carried over from an earlier year. In this case, the charitable contributions deduction is increased from $11,000 to $15,000. This change is illustrated in Example 3-18.

Example 3-18 ∎ Assume the same facts as in Example 3-17 except that East instead has a $40,000 NOL carryback from a later year. East's taxable income before the charitable contributions deduction, dividends-received deduction, and any NOL or capital loss carrybacks is computed as follows:

Gross income from operations	$150,000
Plus: Dividends	100,000
Gross income	$250,000
Minus: Operating expenses	(100,000)
Taxable income before charitable contributions deduction	$150,000

East's charitable contributions deduction is limited to $15,000 (0.10 × $150,000). The $15,000 limitation means that East also has a $15,000 ($30,000 − $15,000) contribution carryover. East Corporation computes its taxable income as follows:

Taxable income before charitable contributions deduction	$150,000
Minus: Charitable contributions deduction	(15,000)
Taxable income before special deductions	$135,000
Minus: Dividends-received deduction	(80,000)
NOL deduction	(40,000)
Taxable income	$ 15,000

East's dividends-received deduction remains $80,000 as in the preceding example. The entire NOL carryback is deductible since taxable income before the NOL deduction is $55,000 ($135,000 − $80,000). ■

Limitation on Deductions for Accrued Compensation. If a corporation accrues an obligation to pay compensation, the payment must be made within 2½ months after the close of the corporation's tax year. Otherwise, the deduction cannot be taken until the year of payment.[41] The reason is that, if a payment is delayed beyond 2½ months, the IRS treats it as a deferred compensation plan. Deferred compensation cannot be deducted until the year payment is made and the recipient includes the payment in income.[42]

Example 3-19 ■ On December 10, 1991, Bell Corporation (a calendar-year taxpayer) accrues an obligation for a $100,000 bonus to Marge, a sales representative who has had an outstanding year. The payment must be made by March 15, 1992. Otherwise, Bell Corporation cannot deduct the $100,000 on its 1991 tax return but must wait until the year the payment is made. ■

Transactions Between a Corporation and Its Shareholders

Special rules apply to transactions between a corporation and a controlling shareholder. Section 1239 may convert a capital gain realized on the sale of depreciable property between a corporation and a controlling shareholder into ordinary income. Section 267(a)(1) denies a deduction for losses realized on property sales between a corporation and a controlling shareholder. Section 267(a)(2) defers a deduction for accrued expenses and interest on certain transactions involving a corporation and a controlling shareholder.

In all 3 of the preceding situations, a controlling shareholder is defined as one who owns more than 50% (in value) of the corporation's stock.[43] In determining whether a shareholder owns more than 50% of a corporation's stock, certain constructive stock ownership rules apply.[44] Under these rules, a shareholder is considered to own not only his own stock, but stock owned by family members (e.g., brothers, sisters, spouse, ancestors, and lineal descendants) and entities in which the shareholder has an ownership or beneficial interest (e.g., corporations, partnerships, trusts, and estates).

Gains on Sale or Exchange Transactions. If a controlling shareholder sells depreciable property to a controlled corporation (or vice versa) and the property is

---

[41] Reg. Sec. 1.404(b)-1T.
[42] Sec. 404(b).
[43] Sec. 267(b)(2).
[44] Sec. 267(e)(3).

depreciable in the purchaser's hands, any gain on the sale is treated as ordinary income under Sec. 1239(a).

Example 3-20 ■

Key Point
Section 1239 states that if a sale or exchange of property is (1) between a corporation and a more than 50% shareholder and (2) the property is depreciable to the purchaser, then the character of any gain recognized on the sale must be ordinary income.

Ann owns all of the stock of Cape Corporation. Ann sells a building to Cape Corporation and recognizes a $25,000 gain, which would ordinarily be Sec. 1231 gain. However, because Ann owns more than 50% of the Cape stock and the building is a depreciable property in Cape Corporation's hands, Sec. 1239 causes the entire $25,000 gain to be ordinary income to Ann. ■

Losses on Sale or Exchange Transactions. Section 267(a)(1) denies a deduction for losses realized on a sale of property by a corporation to a controlling shareholder or on a sale of property by the controlling shareholder to the corporation. If the purchaser later sells the property to another party at a gain, gain is recognized only to the extent that it exceeds the disallowed loss.[45] Should the purchaser instead sell the property at a loss, the disallowed loss is never recognized.

Example 3-21 ■

Hope Corporation sells an automobile to Juan, its sole shareholder, for $6,500. The corporation's adjusted basis for the automobile is $8,000. Hope realizes a $1,500 ($6,500 − $8,000) loss on the sale. Section 267(a)(1) disallows the loss to the corporation. If Juan later sells the auto for $8,500, he realizes a $2,000 ($8,500 − $6,500) gain. He recognizes only $500 of that gain, the amount by which his $2,000 gain exceeds the $1,500 loss that was disallowed to Hope Corporation. If Juan instead sells the auto for $4,000, he realizes and recognizes a $2,500 ($4,000 − $6,500) loss. In this case, the $1,500 loss disallowed to Hope Corporation is permanently lost. ■

Key Point
Section 267(a)(2) is primarily aimed at the situation involving an accrual method corporation that accrues compensation to a cash method shareholder/employee. This provision forces a matching of the income and expense recognition by deferring the deduction to the day the shareholder recognizes the income.

Corporation and Controlling Shareholder Using Different Accounting Methods. Section 267(a)(2) defers a deduction for accrued expenses or interest owed by a corporation to a controlling shareholder or by a controlling shareholder to a corporation when (1) the two parties use different accounting methods and (2) the payee will include the accrued expense as part of gross income at a date that is later than when it is accrued by the payor. Under this rule, accrued expenses or interest owed by a corporation to a controlling shareholder may not be deducted until the day the shareholder includes the payment in gross income.

Example 3-22 ■

Hill Corporation uses the accrual method of accounting. Hill's sole shareholder, Ruth, uses the cash method of accounting. Both taxpayers use the calendar year as their tax year. The corporation accrues a $25,000 interest payment to Ruth on December 20, 1991. The payment is made on March 20, 1992. Hill Corporation cannot deduct the interest in 1991 but must wait until Ruth reports the income in 1992. Thus the expense and income are matched. ■

At-Risk Rules

If 5 or fewer shareholders own more than 50% of the value of the outstanding stock of a C corporation at any time during the last half of the corporation's tax year, it is subject to the at-risk rules.[46] In such a case the corporation's losses for any activity are

---

[45] Sec. 267(d).
[46] Sec. 465(a).

Typical Misconception
Closely held corporations and PSCs are subject to the passive activity limitation rules. Certain closely held corporations (other than PSCs) can offset their net active income (but not portfolio income) for the tax year with passive losses. This offset of passive losses against net active income is unique to closely held C corporations.

deductible only to the extent that the corporation is at risk for that activity at the close of its tax year. Any losses not deductible because of the at-risk rules must be carried over and deducted in a succeeding year when the corporation's risk with respect to the activity has increased. (See Chapter 9 for additional discussion of the at-risk rules and the risk amount.)

Passive Activity Limitation Rules

Personal service corporations (PSCs) and closely-held C corporations (those subject to the at-risk rules described above) may be subject to the passive activity limitations.[47] If a PSC does not meet the material participation requirements, its net passive losses and credits must be carried over to a year when it has passive income. In the case of closely-held C corporations that do not meet material participation requirements, passive losses and credits are allowed to offset the corporation's net active income but not its portfolio income (i.e., interest, dividends, annuities, royalties, and capital gains on the sale of investment property).[48]

COMPUTING A CORPORATION'S INCOME TAX LIABILITY

OBJECTIVE 3
Compute a corporation's income tax liability

Once a corporation's taxable income has been computed, the next step is to compute the corporation's tax liability for the year. Table 3-3 outlines the steps in the computation of a corporation's regular (income) tax liability. This section explains the steps involved in arriving at a corporation's income tax liability in detail.

TABLE 3-3 *Computation of the Regular Corporate Income Tax Liability for 1988 and Later Years*

Taxable Income
Times: Income tax rates
    15% for taxable income from $1–$50,000[a]
    25% for taxable income from $50,001–$75,000
    34% for taxable income from $75,001–$100,000
    39% for taxable income from $100,001–$335,000
    34% for taxable income in excess of $335,000
Regular tax liability
Minus: Foreign tax credit (Sec. 27)
    Puerto Rico and U.S. Possessions credit (Sec. 936)
Regular tax
Minus: General business credit (Sec. 38)
    Minimum tax credit (Sec. 53)
    Drug testing credit (Sec. 28)
    Nonconventional fuels production credit (Sec. 29)
    Nonhighway use of gasoline and special fuels credit (Sec. 34)
Plus: Recapture of previously claimed tax credits
Income tax liability

[a] The size of the tax rate brackets change for corporations that are members of a controlled group (see pages 3-26 to 3-32).

[47] Sec. 469(a)(2)(B) and (C).
[48] Sec. 469(e)(2).

General Rules

Historical Note

In contrast to prior years, after 1986 the highest marginal rate for a corporation is 3 percentage points (34–31) higher than the highest marginal rate for an individual. This change in the relative tax rates of individuals and corporations has significantly changed the choice of entity in which small businesses are conducted.

All C corporations (other than members of controlled groups of corporations and personal service corporations) use the same tax rate schedule to compute their income or regular tax liability. The tax rates for a corporate taxpayer are[49]

Taxable Income	Tax Rates for Tax Years Beginning on or after July 1, 1987
0 to $50,000	15%
$50,001 to 75,000	25%
Over $75,000	34%

Reduced tax rates on the first $75,000 of taxable income result in an $11,750 tax savings for corporations that have taxable income between $75,000 and $100,000.

Example 3-23 ■ Copper Corporation reports taxable income of $100,000. Copper's regular tax liability is computed as follows:

Tax on first $50,000:	0.15 × $50,000 =	$7,500
Tax on second $25,000:	0.25 × 25,000 =	6,250
Tax on remaining $25,000:	0.34 × 25,000 =	8,500
Regular tax liability		$22,250

■

In addition to the tax computed above, a surcharge of 5% of the corporation's taxable income in excess of $100,000 is imposed. The maximum surcharge is $11,750. The surcharge phases out the lower graduated tax rates that apply to the first $75,000 of taxable income for corporations earning between $100,000 and $335,000 ($11,750 = [$335,000 − $100,000] × 0.05) of taxable income.

Example 3-24 ■ Delta Corporation has taxable income of $200,000. Delta's regular tax liability is computed as follows:

Tax on first $50,000:	0.15 × $ 50,000 =	$ 7,500
Tax on next $25,000:	0.25 × 25,000 =	6,250
Tax on remaining $125,000:	0.34 × 125,000 =	42,500
Surcharge (income over $100,000):	0.05 × 100,000 =	5,000
Regular tax liability		$61,250

■

A corporation whose taxable income is at least $335,000 pays a 34% tax rate on all of its taxable income.

Example 3-25 ■ Elgin Corporation has taxable income of $350,000. Elgin's regular tax liability is $119,000 (0.34 × $350,000). ■

Personal Service Corporations

Personal service corporations are denied the benefit of the graduated corporate tax rates. All of the income of personal service corporations is taxed at a flat 34% rate.

[49] Sec. 11(b).

Self-Study Question

Does the selection of a corporate entity ever make sense based on a desire for lower tax marginal tax rates?

Answer

Entities with projected income of $50,000 or less may still be better off with the selection of the corporate entity because the first $50,000 of corporate taxable income is taxed at a 15% rate. Once the income level increases above $75,000, the C corporation marginal rate jumps to 34% (ignoring the 5% surcharge). In contrast, if the corporation made an S election, income above $75,000 would be taxed at a maximum marginal rate of 31%.

A personal service corporation is defined in Sec. 448(d) as a corporation that meets the following two tests:

1. Substantially all of its activities involve the performance of services in the fields of health, law, engineering, architecture, accounting, actuarial science, performing arts, and consulting.
2. Substantially all of its stock (by value) is held directly or indirectly by employees performing the services or retired employees who performed the services in the past, their estates, or persons who hold stock in the corporation by reason of the death of an employee or retired employee within the past two years.

This rule encourages employee-owners of personal service corporations to withdraw earnings from the corporation as salary rather than have the corporation retain them or make an S corporation election. The maximum marginal tax rate on salary income or the income earned by an S corporation and passed through to its shareholders is 31% which is less than the 34% corporate tax rate.

CONTROLLED GROUPS OF CORPORATIONS

OBJECTIVE 4
Explain what a controlled group is and the tax consequences of being a controlled group

Special tax rules apply to corporations that are under common control to prevent them from being used to avoid taxes that would otherwise be due. The rules apply to corporations that meet the definition of a "controlled group of corporations." This section explains why special rules apply to controlled groups, how controlled groups are defined, and what special rules apply to controlled groups.

Why Special Rules Are Needed

Special controlled group rules are needed to prevent shareholders from using multiple corporations to avoid having corporate income taxed at a 34% rate. If these rules were not in effect, the owners of a corporation could divide the corporation's income among two or more corporations and take advantage of the lower 15% and 25% rates on the first $75,000 of corporate income for each corporation.

The following example demonstrates how a group of shareholders could obtain a significant tax advantage by dividing a business enterprise among several corporate entities. Each corporation then would be able to take advantage of the graduated corporate tax rates. To prevent a group of shareholders from using multiple corporations to gain such tax advantages, Congress enacted laws that limit the tax benefits of multiple corporations.[50]

Example 3-26 ■ Axle Corporation has taxable income of $450,000. Axle's regular tax liability on that income is $153,000 (0.34 × $450,000). If Axle's taxable income could be divided equally among six corporations ($75,000 apiece), each corporation's federal income tax liability would be $13,750 ([0.15 × $50,000] + [0.25 × $25,000]), or a total regular tax liability of $82,500 for all of the corporations. Thus, Axle could save $70,500 ($153,000 − $82,500) in federal income taxes if it could arrange to

---
[50] Secs. 1561 and 1563.

have its $450,000 of taxable income divided among itself and five other corporations. ∎

The law governing controlled corporations operates by requiring special treatment for two or more corporations controlled by the same shareholder or group of shareholders. The most important restrictions on a controlled group of corporations are that the entire group must (1) share the tax benefits from the progressive corporate tax rate schedule and (2) pay a surtax of 5% on the group's total taxable income that exceeds $100,000 (up to $335,000 for a maximum surcharge of $11,750 in 1991). If the group's total taxable income is $335,000 or more, each group member will have a regular income tax liability equal to 34% times its taxable income.

Example 3-27 ∎

Self-Study Question
What are the tax consequences of being a member of a controlled group?

Answer
Several of the different tax consequences that can result from being a member of a controlled group are mentioned in this chapter. The most important purpose of the controlled group rules is to prevent shareholders from using multiple corporations to proliferate the benefits of the 15% and 25% graduated rate structure for corporations. Example 3-26 illustrates what could be accomplished without the controlled group rules.

White, Blue, Yellow, and Green Corporations belong to a controlled group. Each corporation has $100,000 of taxable income (a total of $400,000). Only one $50,000 amount is taxed at 15% and only one $25,000 amount is taxed at 25%. Furthermore, the group is subject to the maximum $11,750 surtax since its total taxable income exceeds $335,000. This surcharge is levied on the group member(s) that received the benefit of the 15 and 25% rates. Therefore, the group's regular income tax liability is $136,000 (0.34 × $400,000), the same as though the entire $400,000 was earned by one corporation. ∎

What Is a Controlled Group?

A **controlled group** is a group of two or more corporations that are owned directly or indirectly by the same shareholder or group of shareholders. There are three types of controlled groups: a parent-subsidiary controlled group; a brother-sister controlled group; and a combined controlled group. Each of these groups is subject to the limitations described above. That is, if a group of corporations meets any of the following three definitions, the group must share the benefits of the progressive corporate tax rate schedule and pay a surtax of 5% on the group's taxable income exceeding $100,000 up to a maximum surtax of $11,750.

Key Point
The statute identifies three types of controlled groups: (1) parent-subsidiary, (2) brother-sister, and (3) combined. A group of corporations which satisfy the definition of any of these three controlled groups must share one corporate graduated rate structure.

Parent-Subsidiary Controlled Groups. A **parent-subsidiary controlled group** is a group of two or more corporations where one corporation (the parent corporation) owns directly at least 80% of the voting power of all classes of voting stock, or 80% of the total value of all classes of stock of a second corporation (the subsidiary corporation).[51] There can be more than one subsidiary corporation in the group. If the parent corporation, the subsidiary corporation, or any other members of the controlled group in total own at least 80% of the voting power of all classes of voting stock, or 80% of the total value of all classes of stock of another corporation, that other corporation is included in the parent-subsidiary controlled group.

Example 3-28 ∎

Parent Corporation owns 80% of Axle Corporation's single class of stock and 40% of Wheel Corporation's single class of stock. Axle Corporation also owns 40% of Wheel's stock. Parent, Axle, and Wheel are members of the same parent-subsidiary

---

[51] Sec. 1563(a)(1). Section 1563(d)(1) requires that certain attribution rules apply to determine stock ownership for parent-subsidiary controlled groups. If any person has an option to acquire stock, such stock is considered as owned by such person. Certain types of stock are excluded by Sec. 1563(c) from the controlled group definition of stock.

controlled group because (1) Parent directly owns 80% of Axle's stock and is therefore its parent corporation, and (2) Wheel's stock is 80% owned by Parent (40%) and Axle (40%). (See Figure 3-1.)

If Parent and Axle together only owned 70% of Wheel's stock and the remaining 30% was owned by an unrelated shareholder, Wheel would not be included in the parent-subsidiary group. The controlled group then would consist only of Parent and Axle Corporations. ∎

To have a parent-subsidiary controlled group, there must be a direct ownership by one corporation of 80% or more of the voting power or value of a second corporation.

Example 3-29 ∎

Typical Misconception

*Two items about the parent-subsidiary controlled group definition must be clarified: (1) The 80% stock requirement is an **or** test. This means that either 80% of the voting power or 80% of the FMV of all classes of stock will satisfy the requirement. (2) The 80% requirement must be satisfied through direct ownership by the parent with respect to at least one of the subsidiaries.*

Beta Corporation owns 70% of Cove Corporation's single class of stock and 60% of Red Corporation's single class of stock. Blue Corporation owns the remaining stock of Cove Corporation (30%) and Red Corporation (40%). No combination of these corporations forms a parent-subsidiary group since there is no direct stock ownership by one corporation of at least 80% of any other corporation's stock. ∎

Brother-Sister Controlled Groups. A group of two or more corporations is a **brother-sister controlled group** if five or fewer individuals, trusts, or estates own

1. At least 80% of the voting power of all classes of voting stock (or at least 80% of the total value of the outstanding stock) of each corporation, and
2. More than 50% of the voting power of all classes of stock (or more than 50% of the total value of the outstanding stock) of each corporation, taking into account only the stock ownership that each person has that is identical with respect to each corporation.[52] A shareholder's identical ownership is the percentage of stock the shareholder owns in common in each of the corporations. If, for example, a shareholder owns 30% of New Corporation and 70% of Old Corporation, his identical ownership is 30%.

Example 3-30 ∎

Typical Misconception

The application of the 50% identical ownership test for purposes of the brother-sister controlled group definition is confusing. Examples 3-30 and 3-31 illustrate a case when the 50% test is satisfied and one when it is not satisfied. Also note that both the 80% and the 50% tests must be satisfied for a brother-sister controlled group to exist.

North and South Corporations have only one class of stock outstanding. Their stock is owned by the following individuals:

	Stock Ownership Percentages		
Shareholder	North Corp.	South Corp.	Identical Ownership
Walt	30%	70%	30%
Gail	70%	30%	30%
Total	100%	100%	60%

Five or fewer individuals (Walt and Gail) own at least 80% (they own 100%) of each corporation's stock, and the same individuals own more than 50% (they own 60%) of each corporation's stock, taking into account only their identical

---

[52] Sec. 1563(a)(2). Section 1563(d)(2) requires that certain attribution rules apply to determine stock ownership for brother-sister controlled groups. If any person has an option to acquire stock, such stock is considered as owned by such person. A proportionate amount of stock owned by a partnership, estate, or trust is attributed to partners having an interest of 5% or more in the capital or profits of the partnership or beneficiaries having a 5% or more actuarial interest in the estate or trust. A proportionate amount of stock owned by a corporation is attributed to shareholders owning 5% or more of the corporate stock. Family attribution rules can also cause an individual to be considered to own the stock of a spouse, child, grandchild, parent, or grandparent.

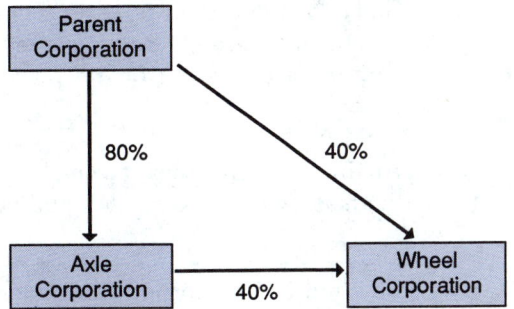

FIGURE 3-1 Parent-Subsidiary Controlled Group (Example 3-28)

ownership. Since both tests are satisfied, North and South Corporations are a brother-sister controlled group (see Figure 3-2). ■

It is not sufficient for five or fewer shareholders to own 80% or more of the stock of two corporations. The shareholders must also have more than 50% identical ownership in the corporations for them to be brother-sister corporations.

Example 3-31 ■ East and West Corporations have only one class of stock outstanding. Their stock is owned by the following individuals:

	Stock Ownership Percentages		
Shareholder	East Corp.	West Corp.	Identical Ownership
John	80%	20%	20%
Sara	20%	80%	20%
Total	100%	100%	40%

Five or fewer individuals (John and Sara) own at least 80% (they own 100%) of the stock of East and West Corporations. But those same individuals own only 40% of each corporation's stock, taking into account only their identical ownership.

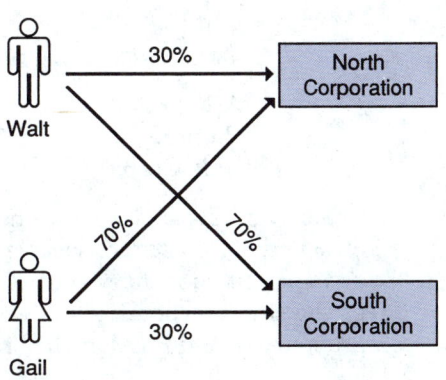

FIGURE 3-2 Brother-Sister Controlled Group (Example 3-30)

Since the more-than-50% test is not satisfied, East and West Corporations are not a controlled group. Because they are not members of a controlled group, each corporation is taxed on its own income without regard to the earnings of the other. ∎

An individual's stock ownership can be counted for the 80% test only if that individual owns stock in each and every corporation in the controlled group.[53]

Example 3-32 ∎

> **Typical Misconception**
> If a shareholder does not own stock in each member of the brother-sister controlled group, that shareholder's stock ownership is not only ignored for purposes of the 50% test, but that shareholder's stock ownership cannot be included for purposes of the 80% test either. Example 3-32 provides a good illustration of this concept.

Toy and Robot Corporations each have only a single class of stock outstanding. Their stock is owned by the following individuals:

Stock Ownership Percentages

Shareholder	Toy Corp.	Robot Corp.	Identical Ownership
Alex	50%	40%	40%
Beth	20%	60%	20%
Carol	30%	—	—
Total	100%	100%	60%

Carol's stock is not counted for purposes of Toy's 80% stock ownership requirement because she does not own any stock in Robot Corporation. Only Alex and Beth's stock holdings are counted and together they own only 70% of Toy Corporation's stock. Thus, the 80% test is failed and Toy and Robot Corporations are *not* a controlled group of corporations. ∎

Combined Controlled Groups. A **combined controlled group** is a group of three or more corporations where the following criteria are met:

1. Each corporation is a member of a parent-subsidiary controlled group or a brother-sister controlled group
2. At least one of the corporations is (a) the parent corporation of a parent-subsidiary controlled group and (b) a member of a brother-sister controlled group.[54]

Example 3-33 ∎

> **Key Point**
> The combined controlled group definition does just what its name implies: it combines a parent-subsidiary controlled group and a brother-sister controlled group. Thus, instead of trying to apply the controlled group rules to two different groups, the combined group definition simplifies the issue by combining the groups into one controlled group.

Able, Best, and Coast Corporations each have a single class of stock outstanding. Their stock is owned by the following shareholders:

Stock Ownership Percentages

Shareholder	Able Corp.	Coast Corp.	Best Corp.
Art	50%	50%	—
Barbara	50%	50%	—
Able Corp.	—	—	100%

Able and Coast Corporations are a brother-sister controlled group since both the 80% and 50% tests are satisfied by Art and Barbara. Able and Best Corporations are a parent-subsidiary controlled group, since Able owns all of Best's stock. Each of the three corporations is a member of either the parent-subsidiary controlled group (Able and Best) or the brother-sister controlled group (Able and Coast), and

---

[53] Reg. Sec. 1.1563-1(a)(3).
[54] Sec. 1563(a)(3).

Key Point

A corporation is included in a controlled group if (1) the corporation is a member of a group on December 31 or (2) is a member of a group for at least one-half of its tax year that precedes December 31. Thus, a corporation would still be included in a controlled group even though such corporation was disposed of just prior to the end of the tax year.

the parent corporation (Able) of the parent-subsidiary controlled group is also a member of the brother-sister controlled group. Therefore, Able, Coast, and Best Corporations are members of a combined controlled group (see Figure 3-3). ∎

Application of the Controlled Group Test

The controlled group test is generally applied on December 31. A corporation is included in the controlled group (i.e., is a component member of the group) if it is a member on December 31 or if it has been a member of that group for at least one-half of the days in its tax year which precede December 31 even though it is not a group member on December 31. A corporation is excluded from the group (i.e., is an excluded member) if it is a member on December 31 but it has been a member of the controlled group for less than one-half of the days in its tax year which precede December 31.

Example 3-34 ∎ Ace and Copper Corporations are members of a parent-subsidiary controlled group of which Ace is the common parent corporation. Both corporations are calendar-year taxpayers and have been group members for the entire year. They do not file a consolidated return. Bell Corporation, which has a fiscal year ending on August 31, becomes a group member on December 1, 1991. Although Bell is a group member on December 31, 1991, it has been a group member for less than half of the days in its tax year which precede December 31—only 30 of 121 days starting on September 1. Therefore, Bell is *not* a component member of the Ace-Copper controlled group for its tax year beginning on September 1, 1991. ∎

If a corporation is a component member of the group on December 31, it must share the tax benefits of the Sec. 11(b) progressive corporate tax rate schedule. If a corporation is *not* a component member of the group (i.e., an excluded member) on December 31, it is excluded from the controlled group for that year and can take full advantage of the reduced 15% and 25% corporate tax rates on its first $75,000 of taxable income.

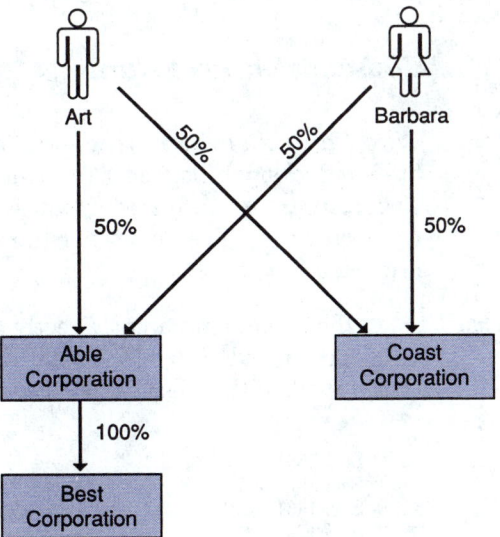

FIGURE 3-3 Combined Controlled Group (Example 3-33)

Key Point

The controlled group definition is important in a number of areas other than the corporate graduated rate structure. For example, Sec. 267 treats members of a controlled group as "related parties." For purposes of the superfund tax, a controlled group is entitled to one $2,000,000 exemption. Examples of other items affected by the controlled group definition are listed on this page.

Special Rules Applying to Controlled Groups

If two or more corporations are members of a controlled group, the member corporations are limited to a total of $50,000 being taxed at 15% and $25,000 being taxed at 25%—the reduced tax rates found in Sec. 11(b). All other income is taxed at 34%.

In addition, a controlled group must apportion certain other tax benefits among its group members. Among the items requiring allocation are:

- The $250,000 minimum accumulated earnings tax credit[55]
- The 100% general business tax credit offset for the first $25,000 of income taxes[56]
- The $40,000 statutory exemption for the alternative minimum tax[57]
- The $10,000 of depreciable assets that can be expensed annually[58]
- The $100,000 exemption for the 5% surcharge on taxable income[59]

Furthermore, under Sec. 267(a)(1), no deduction is allowed for any loss on the sale or exchange of property between two members of the same controlled group.[60] The loss realized on the sale of property between members of a controlled group receives special treatment. A loss realized on a transaction between members of a controlled group is deferred (instead of being disallowed). The deferred loss is recognized by the selling member when the property that is sold or exchanged in the intragroup transaction is sold outside the group. The entire deferred loss is recognized at the time the property is disposed of outside the controlled group. Under Sec. 267(a)(2), no deduction is allowed for certain accrued expenses or interest owed by one member of a controlled group to another member of the same controlled group when the two corporations use different accounting methods so that the payments would be reported in different tax years. (See p. 3-23 for a detailed discussion of Sec. 267 and page 3-38 for a discussion of tax planning to avoid controlled corporation status.) The Sec. 1239 rules that convert capital gain into ordinary income when (1) property is sold by a controlling shareholder to a corporation or by a corporation to a controlling shareholder and (2) such property is depreciable in the purchasing party's hands also apply to sales or exchanges involving two members of the same controlled group.

Typical Misconception

The definitions of a parent-subsidiary controlled group and an affiliated group are similar, but not identical. For example, the 80% stock ownership test for controlled group purposes is satisfied if 80% of the voting power or 80% of the FMV of a corporation is owned. For purposes of an affiliated group, 80% of both the voting power and value must be owned.

Consolidated Tax Returns

Who Can File a Consolidated Return. Some groups of related corporations (i.e., affiliated groups) may elect to file a single income tax return called a **consolidated tax return.** An affiliated group is one or more chains of includible corporations connected through stock ownership with a common parent,[61] but only if the following criteria are met:

1. The common parent directly owns stock with at least 80% of the total voting power and 80% of the total value of at least one includible corporation.
2. Stock with at least 80% of the total voting power and 80% of the total value of

---

[55] Sec. 1561(a)(2).
[56] Sec. 38(c)(3)(B).
[57] Sec. 1561(a)(3).
[58] Sec. 179(d)(6).
[59] Sec. 1561(a).
[60] Sec. 267(b)(3).
[61] Includible corporations are those eligible to join in the consolidated tax return election under Sec. 1504(b).

each other corporation included in the affiliated group is owned directly by one or more group members.[62]

Most parent-subsidiary controlled groups are eligible to file a single consolidated return in place of separate tax returns for each corporation. The parent-subsidiary portion of a combined group generally can also file a consolidated tax return. Brother-sister controlled groups are not eligible to file consolidated returns because the requisite parent-subsidiary relationship has not been established.

An affiliated group makes the election to file a consolidated tax return by filing Form 1120, which includes all of the income and expenses of each of its members. Each corporate member of the affiliated group must consent to the election.

Advantages of Filing a Consolidated Return. A consolidated return is, in effect, one tax return for the entire affiliated group of corporations. The main advantages of filing a consolidated return are

- Income of a profitable member of the group can be offset against losses of another member of the group.
- Capital gains of one member of the group can be offset against capital losses of another member of the group.
- Profits or gains reported on intercompany transactions are deferred generally until a sale outside the group takes place (i.e., if one member sells property to another member, the gain is postponed until the property is sold to someone outside the affiliated group).

If the group members file separate returns, members with NOLs or capital losses must either carry back these losses to earlier years or carry them forward to future years. Although the losses of one group member can be offset against the profits of another group member when a consolidated return is filed, there are some important limitations on the use of a member corporation's NOL. These limitations are designed to prevent one corporation from purchasing another corporation's NOL carryovers to offset its own taxable income or purchasing a profitable corporation to facilitate the use of its NOL carryovers. (See Chapter 8 for an explanation of these loss limitations.)

The following example illustrates the advantage of a consolidated return election.

Self-Study Question
What is probably the most often used reason for making a consolidated return election?

Answer
Filing consolidated returns allows the group to offset losses of one corporation against the income of other members of the group.

Example 3-35 ■

Self-Study Question
What are some of the disadvantages of filing consolidated returns?

Answer
Taxpayers may think that it would reduce administrative costs to file one consolidated return rather than a number of separate returns. Once they have had the chance to study Chapter 8, they will realize this is not the case. Also, since a consolidated return election is binding for all subsequent tax years, the election should not be made without first evaluating all the possible advantages and disadvantages.

Parent Corporation owns 100% of the stock of Subsidiary Corporation. Parent Corporation reports $110,000 of taxable income including a $10,000 capital gain. Subsidiary Corporation has a $100,000 NOL and a $10,000 capital loss. If Parent and Subsidiary file separate returns, Parent has a $26,150 ([$50,000 × 0.15] + [$25,000 × 0.25] + [$25,000 × 0.34] + [$10,000 × .39]) tax liability. Subsidiary has no tax liability but may be able to use its $100,000 NOL and $10,000 capital loss to offset taxable income in other years. If Parent and Subsidiary file a consolidated return, the group's consolidated taxable income is zero and the group has no tax liability. By filing a consolidated return, the group saves $26,150 in taxes for the year. ■

Disadvantages of Filing a Consolidated Return. The main disadvantages of a consolidated return election are

- The election is binding on all subsequent tax years unless the IRS grants permission to discontinue filing consolidated returns or the affiliated group is terminated.

[62] Sec. 1504(a).

- Losses on intercompany transactions are deferred generally until a sale outside the group takes place.
- Losses of an unprofitable member of the group may reduce the deduction or credit limitations of the group below what would be available if separate tax returns were filed.
- Additional administrative costs may be incurred in maintaining the records needed to file a consolidated return.

Affiliated groups and consolidated returns are discussed and explained in more detail in Chapter 8.

COMPENSATION PLANNING FOR SHAREHOLDER-EMPLOYEES

OBJECTIVE 5
Explain how compensation planning can reduce taxes for corporations and their shareholders

Compensation paid to a shareholder-employee in the form of salary carries with it the advantage of single taxation; that is, the salary is taxable to the employee and deductible by the payor corporation. A dividend payment, however, is taxed twice. The corporation is taxed on its income when it is earned, and the shareholder is taxed on the profits paid out in the form of dividends. Some owners of closely held corporations elect to be taxed under the rules of Subchapter S in order to avoid double taxation. Other owners of closely held corporations retain C corporation status to benefit from tax-free fringe benefits such as health and accident insurance. These fringe benefits are nontaxable to the employee and deductible by the payor corporation. Closely-held corporations must determine the appropriate level of (1) earnings to be withdrawn from the business in the form of salary and fringe benefits and (2) earnings to be retained in the business for tax and nontax reasons.

Key Point
The basic objective of compensation planning is to provide employees with the greatest possible benefits for the least amount of cost to the employer. If the employer is a C corporation, the compensation package of a shareholder-employee usually includes salary, fringe benefits, and some type of deferred compensation arrangement. In contrast, the least desirable method of getting money out of the corporation and into the hands of a shareholder-employee is through the payment of corporate dividends.

Advantage of Salary Payments

If all corporate profits are paid out as salary and fringe benefit payments, the problem of double taxation is eliminated. However, the following four constraints limit the tax planning that can be undertaken in the salary and fringe benefits area:

- Regulation Sec. 1.162-7(a) requires salary or fringe benefit payments to be reasonable in amount and to be paid for services rendered by the employee. Compensation deemed to be unreasonable is generally characterized as a dividend (see Chapter 5) and results in double taxation.
- A corporation is a tax-paying entity independent of its owners. The first $75,000 of a corporation's earnings are taxed at 15% and 25% corporate tax rates, which may be lower than the top 28% or 31% individual tax rates.
- The highest individual tax rate (31%) is eight percentage points below the highest corporate tax rate (39%). For corporations having large amounts of income taxed at the highest tax rate, it may be better to have the income taxed at the lower individual tax rates.
- A combined employee-employer social security tax rate of 15.30% applies in 1991. Both employers and employees are liable for a 7.65% tax up to the first $53,400 of wages for 1991, or a total of 15.30%. This 7.65% social security tax is actually comprised of a 6.20% old age security and disability insurance tax and a 1.45% Medicare hospital insurance tax. Starting in 1991 the cap on wages that is

Key Point
In determining the amount of monies that should be paid by a closely held corporation as salary payments and fringe benefits versus the amount that should be retained, a number of factors need to be considered: (1) the marginal tax rates of the corporation, (2) the marginal tax rates of the shareholder-employees, (3) the amount of employment taxes that may be incurred, and (4) the possibility that excessive salary and fringe benefits payments will be reclassified as constructive dividends.

Additional Comment
A fringe benefit is probably the most cost effective form of compensation because the amount of the benefit is deductible by the employer and never taxed to the employee. Thus, where possible, fringe benefits are an excellent compensation planning tool. For closely held corporations, however, the tax savings to shareholder-employees are reduced because the fringe benefit must be offered to all employees without discrimination.

taken into account in calculating the Medicare hospital insurance portion of the social security taxes is larger than that for the old age security and disability insurance. The 1991 cap on this 2.90% portion of the employee-employer tax is $125,000. Increasing salaries paid to owner-employees increases social security taxes until the $125,000 overall cap is reached. In addition to these taxes, state and federal unemployment taxes of up to a 6.2% combined rate may be required to be paid on the first $7,000 of wages paid.

Each of the items listed above can limit the tax planning that would otherwise be possible for the owners of a closely held corporation concerning salaries or fringe benefits.

Advantage of Fringe Benefits

Fringe benefits may provide two types of tax advantages—a tax deferral and/or an exclusion. Qualified pension, profit-sharing, and stock bonus plans generally provide a tax deferral; that is, the value of the corporation's contribution to the plan is nontaxable to the employees when the contribution is made, but the benefits from the plan are taxed to the employees when they are received. Other fringe benefits commonly provided by closely-held corporations such as group term life insurance, accident and health insurance, and disability insurance are exempt from tax altogether; that is, the employee is never taxed on the value of these fringe benefits. (For a more detailed summary of the requirements for and tax treatment given fringe benefits, see Chapter 9 of *Prentice Hall's Federal Taxation: Individuals* companion text.)

The value of fringe benefits is excluded from an employee's gross income. The marginal individual tax rate applicable to these employee benefits is zero. The conversion of a salary payment into a fringe benefit provides a tax savings for the shareholder-employee equal to the amount paid times the marginal individual tax rate.

Limitation on Deductible Compensation Payments for Shareholder-Employees

The amount of compensation that is determined to be reasonable for a shareholder-employee of a closely held corporation depends upon the facts and circumstances of the situation. The portion of the compensation considered to be unreasonable is generally treated as a constructive dividend. The corporation bears the burden of proof to show that the amount of cash and deferred compensation plus fringe benefits paid to a shareholder-employee is reasonable. Further discussion on the tax consequences of paying an unreasonable amount of compensation is presented in Chapter 4.

TAX PLANNING CONSIDERATIONS

Special Election to Allocate Reduced Tax Rate Benefits

A controlled group may elect to apportion the tax benefits of the 15% and 25% tax rates to the member corporations in any manner that they choose. If no election of a special apportionment is made, the $50,000 and $25,000 amounts for the two reduced tax rate brackets are divided equally among all the corporations in the group.[63] When a controlled group has one or more group members that report little or no taxable income, a special apportionment of the reduced tax benefits is needed in order to obtain the full $11,750 tax savings.

Example 3-36 ■ North and South Corporations are members of the North-South controlled group. The corporations file separate tax returns for 1991 and report the following results:

Corporation	Taxable Income (NOL)
North	$(25,000)
South	100,000

If no special apportionment plan is elected, North and South are limited to $25,000 each that is taxed at a 15% rate and $12,500 each that is taxed at a 25% rate, and their tax liability is determined as follows:

Corporation	Calculation	Tax
North		—0—
South	15% tax bracket: 0.15 × $25,000	$ 3,750
	25% tax bracket: 0.25 × $12,500	3,125
	34% tax bracket: 0.34 × $62,500	21,250
	Subtotal for South Corporation	$28,125
	Total for North-South controlled group	$28,125

If a special apportionment plan is elected, North and South may apportion the full $50,000 and $25,000 amounts for each of the reduced tax rate brackets to South Corporation. The tax owed by each corporation is determined as follows:

Corporation	Calculation	Tax
North		—0—
South	15% tax bracket: 0.15 × $50,000	$ 7,500
	25% tax bracket: 0.25 × $25,000	6,250
	34% tax bracket: 0.34 × $25,000	8,500
	Subtotal for South Corporation	$22,250
	Total for North-South controlled group	$22,250

Use of the special apportionment election reduces the total tax liability for the North-South group by $5,875 ($28,125 − $22,250). ■

If a controlled group's total taxable income exceeds $100,000, the 5% surcharge that is imposed to recapture the benefits of the reduced tax rates must be paid by the component member (or members) that took advantage of the lower tax rates.

Self-Study Question
A shareholder-employee recognizes the same amount of income even if a portion of his salary payments is treated as unreasonable. If so, what is the concern about unreasonable compensation?

Answer
Salary payments that are considered to be unreasonable in amount are reclassified as constructive dividends. Thus, while this reclassification may not alter the tax liability of the shareholder-employee, the portion of the payments treated as constructive dividends affects the corporate tax liability because such payments are no longer deductible by the corporation.

Key Point
A special apportionment of the 15% and 25% tax rates can reduce a controlled group's overall tax liability. Example 3-36 illustrates how the North-South controlled group can save $5,875 of taxes through a special apportionment plan. Without the special apportionment, all of the benefits of the reduced rates are not utilized.

[63] Sec. 1561(a).

Example 3-37 ■ Hill, Jet, and King Corporations are members of the Hill-Jet-King controlled group. The corporations file separate tax returns and report the following results:

Corporation	Taxable Income
Hill	$200,000
Jet	100,000
King	100,000
Total	$400,000

All of the reduced tax rate benefits are allocated to Hill Corporation under a special apportionment plan. Hill's income tax is calculated as follows:

15% tax bracket: 0.15 × $50,000	$ 7,500
25% tax bracket: 0.25 × $25,000	6,250
34% tax bracket: 0.34 × $125,000	42,500
Surtax: .05 × ($335,000 − $100,000)	11,750
Hill's total tax liability	$68,000

Jet and King each have a regular tax liability of $34,000 (0.34 × $100,000). Thus the group's regular tax liability is $136,000 ($68,000 + $34,000 + $34,000). Because Hill, Jet, and King each report taxable income in excess of $75,000, the group would have the same total regular tax liability if the special apportionment plan apportioned all of the tax benefit to Jet or King Corporations or divided it evenly among the three corporations. ■

Using NOL Carryovers and Carrybacks

Typical Misconception
Another situation in which a corporation may elect to forgo the NOL carryback is when tax credit carryovers are being utilized in the earlier years. If the NOLs are carried back, the tax credits may simply expire. Thus, before deciding to carry back NOLs, the prior tax returns should be carefully examined to ensure that expiring tax credits do not exist.

When a corporation incurs an NOL for the year, it has two choices:

1. Carry the NOL back to the third, second, and first preceding years in that order, and then forward to the succeeding 15 years in order until it is exhausted.
2. Forgo the carryback and just carry the NOL forward to the 15 succeeding years.

A corporation might elect to forgo the NOL carryback, because it will offset income that was taxed at a low rate so that the tax refund that is obtained due to the NOL is not as great as is anticipated if the NOL is carried forward instead.

Example 3-38 ■ Boyd Corporation incurs a $25,000 NOL in 1991. Boyd's 1988 taxable income was $50,000. If Boyd carries the NOL back to 1988, Boyd's tax refund is computed as follows:

Original tax on $50,000 (using 1988 rates)		$7,500
Minus: Recomputed tax on $25,000 ([$50,000 − $25,000] × 0.15)		(3,750)
Tax refund		$3,750

If Boyd anticipates taxable income (before reduction for any NOL carryovers) of $75,000 or more in 1992, carrying the NOL foward will result in the entire loss offsetting taxable income that would otherwise be taxed at a 34% or 39% marginal tax rate. The refund is computed as follows:

Tax on $100,000	$22,250
Minus: Tax on $75,000 ($100,000 − $25,000)	(13,750)
Tax savings in 1992	$ 8,500

Thus, if Boyd expects taxable income to be $100,000 in 1992, it might elect to forgo the NOL carryback and obtain the additional $4,750 tax benefit. Of course, by carrying the NOL over to 1992, Boyd loses the value of having the funds immediately available. However, the NOL may be used to reduce Boyd's estimated tax payments for 1992. ∎

Tax Planning to Avoid Controlled Group Status

Key Point
For purposes of the brother-sister controlled group definition, a shareholder's ownership is not included unless the shareholder owns stock in each member of the controlled group. Thus, controlled group status can be avoided if at least 21% of the stock of one of the corporations is in the hands of one or more key employees who do not also own stock in the other members of the group.

If an individual owns 100% of the stock of each of two corporations, the corporations are a brother-sister controlled group. As such, they must share the reduced tax rates on the first $75,000 of income. If, however, another unrelated individual owns at least 21% of the stock of one of the corporations, the corporations are not brother-sister corporations since the unrelated individual's stock is not counted if he does not own stock in both corporations. In some cases, it might be advisable for an individual who owns the stock of two corporations to issue 21% of the stock of one corporation to one or more key employees to avoid the controlled corporation classification. In addition to the tax saving that accrues from the reduced tax rates, the stock could serve as a performance and retention incentive to the employees. This might be an especially attractive option in the case of a start-up company where cash flows are limited and key employees can be attracted with a stock offer even when salaries are relatively low.

COMPLIANCE AND PROCEDURAL CONSIDERATIONS

Requirements for Filing and Paying Taxes

OBJECTIVE 6
Determine the requirements for filing a corporate tax return and paying corporate income taxes

A corporation must file a tax return even if it has no taxable income for the year.[64] If the corporation was not in existence for its entire annual accounting period (either calendar year or fiscal year), it must file a return for that part of the year during which it was in existence. A corporation is not in existence after it ceases business and dissolves, retaining no assets, even if, under state law, it is treated as continuing as a corporation for purposes of winding up its affairs.[65]

Types of Tax Returns

Corporations must use Form 1120 (U.S. Corporation Income Tax Return) or Form 1120-A (U.S. Corporation Short-Form Income Tax Return) to file their tax returns. A corporation is eligible to use Form 1120-A if *all* of the following requirements are satisfied:

1. The corporation's gross receipts do not exceed $500,000.
2. Its total income does not exceed $500,000.
3. Its total assets do not exceed $500,000.

[64] Sec. 6012(a)(2).
[65] Reg. Sec. 1.6012-2(a)(2).

4. It does not own any stock in a foreign corporation.
5. It does not have foreign shareholders who as a group own, directly or indirectly, 50% or more of its stock.
6. It is not a member of a controlled group of corporations.
7. It is not a personal holding company.
8. It does not file a consolidated tax return.
9. It is not a corporation undergoing a dissolution or liquidation.
10. It is not filing its final tax return.
11. Its only dividend income is from domestic corporations and those dividends qualify for the 70% (in 1990) dividends-received deduction.
12. It has no nonrefundable tax credits other than the general business credit and credit for prior year minimum tax.
13. It is not an S corporation, a life insurance company, political organization, or any other organization required to file a specialized form.
14. It is not subject to the superfund environmental tax.
15. It has no liability for interest relating to certain installment sales or installment payments of tax from installment sales or LIFO inventory recapture.

A completed corporate income tax return Form 1120 and a completed Form 1120-A are reproduced in Appendix B.

When the Return Must Be Filed

Corporate returns must be filed by the fifteenth day of the third month following the close of the corporation's tax year.[66] A corporation can obtain an automatic 6-month extension of time to file its tax return by filing Form 7004 by the original due date for the return. Corporations that fail to file a timely tax return can be subject to the failure to file penalty. A discussion of this penalty is presented in Chapter 16.

Typical Misconception
Corporate returns are due by the 15th day of the third month following a corporation's year-end. An automatic 6-month extension is available. Remember that an extension merely extends the time for filing the return, not the time for payment of the corporate income tax liability.

Example 3-39 ■ Perry Corporation uses a fiscal year ending on September 30 as its tax year. Its corporate tax return for the year ending September 30, 1991, is due on or before December 15, 1991. If Perry files a Form 7004 by December 15, 1991, it can obtain an automatic extension of time to file until June 15, 1992. ■

Additional extensions beyond the automatic 6-month period are not available. The IRS can rescind the extension period by mailing a 10-day notice to the corporation before the end of the 6-month period.[67]

Self-Study Question
Is the balance sheet that is required on Schedule L a tax balance sheet or a financial balance sheet?

Answer
Schedule L requires a financial balance sheet rather than a tax balance sheet. However, for many smaller corporations, the tax balance sheet is the same as the financial balance sheet.

Tax Return Schedules

Schedule L (of Form 1120) or Part II (of Form 1120-A): The Balance Sheet.
Both Forms 1120 and 1120-A require a balance sheet showing the financial accounting results at the beginning and end of the tax year. The balance sheets must be provided on Schedule L of Form 1120 or on Part II of Form 1120-A. Both forms also require the reconciliation of the corporation's financial accounting income (also known as *book income*) and its taxable income (before NOL deduction and special deductions). The reconciliation must be provided on Schedule M-1 of Form 1120 or on Part III of Form 1120-A. Form 1120 also requires an analysis of the unappropriated retained earnings account on Schedule M-2.

[66] Sec. 6072(b).
[67] Reg. Sec. 1.6081-3.

Self-Study Question

Why might the IRS be interested in reviewing a corporation's Schedule M-1?

Answer

Since the Schedule M-1 adjustments reconcile book income to taxable income, this schedule can prove illuminating to an IRS agent who is auditing a corporate return. Since Schedule M-1 highlights each departure from the financial accounting rules, the schedule sometimes helps the IRS identify tax issues that it may want to examine further.

Schedule M-1 (of Form 1120) or Part III (of Form 1120-A): Reconciliation of Book Income and Income Per Return. A corporation's book income usually differs from the corporation's taxable income. These differences arise because

- Some book income is not taxable (e.g., tax-exempt interest)
- Some gross income is not reflected in book income for the current period (e.g., prepaid rent)
- Some financial accounting expenses are not deductible for tax purposes (e.g., federal income taxes)
- Some deductions allowed for tax purposes are not expenses in determining book income in the current period (e.g., asset costs expensed under Sec. 179)

Some book income items that are nontaxable in the current year will never be taxed; some book expense items that are nondeductible in computing taxable income for the current year will never be deductible. These income and deduction items are called **permanent differences.** They include tax-exempt interest and penalty taxes.

Some book income items that are nontaxable in the current year will be taxed in a later year or were taxed in an earlier year. Some book expense items that are nondeductible in computing taxable income for the current year will be deductible in a later year or were deductible in an earlier year. These differences are called **temporary differences.** They include, for example, prepaid rent and charitable contributions in excess of the 10% of taxable income limitation.

The reconciliation of book income to taxable income starts with net book income. The result of the reconciliation is the corporation's taxable income before NOL and special deductions (e.g., dividends-received deductions).

The items that must be added to the book income amount in order to arrive at the reconciling figure are listed on the left side of Schedule M-1 and include

1. *Federal income tax expense.* This amount is deducted in arriving at book income but is not deductible for tax purposes.
2. *Excess of capital losses over capital gains.* This amount is deducted in arriving at book income but is not deductible for tax purposes. (The loss, however, may be carried back or forward and will "reverse" when utilized.)
3. *Income subject to tax but not recorded on the books this year.* This item includes prepayments received during the current year (e.g., prepaid rent or prepaid interest) that must be included in gross income during the current year but will be included in book income in a later year.
4. *Expenses recorded on the books but not deductible for tax purposes this year.* Among the items included are
   a. Contributions in excess of the 10% of taxable income limitation
   b. Book depreciation expense in excess of that allowed for tax purposes
   c. Life insurance premiums on key personnel where the corporation is the beneficiary of the policy
   d. Interest payments on money borrowed to purchase tax-exempt securities
   e. Estimated costs of warranty service
   f. Political contributions

The items that must be deducted from book income in order to arrive at the reconciling figure are listed on the right side of Schedule M-1 and include

1. *Income recorded on books this year that is not taxable in the current year.* Among the items included are
   a. Prepaid rent or interest that was received and reported for tax purposes in an earlier year

b. Life insurance proceeds received on the death of key personnel
  c. Tax-exempt interest
2. *Deductions or losses claimed in the tax return that do not reduce book income in the current year.* Among the items included are
  a. Depreciation, cost recovery deductions, and asset costs expensed under Sec. 179 that are in excess of the depreciation taken for book purposes
  b. Charitable contribution carryovers from an earlier year deducted on this year's tax return
  c. Capital losses from another year used to offset capital gains on this year's tax return
  d. Amortization of organizational expenditures in excess of the amortization allowed for book purposes

TEMPORARY DIFFERENCES. The effects of a temporary difference on the reconciliation of book income to taxable income can be illustrated by examining the adjustments required for the amortization of organizational expenditures. For book purposes, organizational expenditures are generally amortized over a period of 10 years. For tax purposes, organizational expenditures generally are amortized over a 5-year period. Thus, the monthly deduction claimed in determining taxable income for the first 5 years is twice the expense claimed in determining book income. For the next 5 years, no expense may be claimed for tax purposes, while the expense reported for book income purposes is the same as it was for the first 5 years. Therefore, to reconcile taxable income and book income, a downward adjustment must be made to book income during each of the first 5 years in which such expenditures are amortized. An upward adjustment must be made to book income during the sixth through tenth years in order to arrive at the taxable income amount.

Example 3-40 ■ Ace Corporation is incorporated and begins business on January 1, 1989. In 1991, Ace Corporation's book income is $25,000. For book purposes, Ace is amortizing its $7,200 of organizational expenditures over 10 years. For tax purposes, the organizational expenditures are being amortized over 5 years. To arrive at taxable income for 1991, Ace must deduct $720—one-tenth of the total organizational expenditures—from book income. Because Ace has already deducted $720 ($7,200 ÷ 10) of amortization in arriving at book income, an additional $720 deduction is required to equal the $1,440 ($7,200 ÷ 5) of amortization allowed for tax purposes. If no other adjustments are required, Ace's taxable income for 1991 is $24,280 ($25,000 − $720). After its first 5 tax years, Ace's taxable income will be $720 *more* than its book income for 5 years because amortization of organizational expenditures for book purposes is $720 each year for the first 10 years, whereas amortization of organizational expenditures for tax purposes is $1,440 for the first 5 years and zero from then on. ■

The following example illustrates the reconciliation required on Schedule M-1:

Example 3-41 ■ Valley Corporation reports the following results:

Net income per books	$121,700
Federal income taxes	27,250
Prepaid rent	10,000
Net capital loss	10,750
Tax-exempt interest income	12,500

Key Point
Turn to Figure 3-4. The Schedule M-1 can be used to summarize the adjustments needed to reconcile book and taxable income. The general adjustments on lines 4, 5, 7, and 8, along with federal income tax expense and excess capital losses, represent all of the required adjustments. A review of Schedule M-1 is an excellent way to review the financial accounting and tax accounting differences in a corporation.

Key Point
Schedule M-2 requires an analysis of a corporation's retained earnings. Retained earnings is a financial accounting number that has little relevance to tax accounting. It would seem much more worthwhile for the IRS to require an analysis of a corporation's earnings and profits, which is an extremely important number in determining the taxation of a corporation and its shareholders.

Insurance premiums on life of key employee where Valley is the beneficiary	800
Proceeds of insurance policy on life of key employee	50,000
Interest paid on loan to buy tax-exempt bonds	15,000
MACRS deductions in excess of book depreciation deduction (straight-line depreciation was used for book purposes)	2,000

Valley's Schedule M-1 reconciliation is shown in Figure 3-4.

Schedule M-2 (of Form 1120). Schedule M-2 on Form 1120 requires an analysis of the changes in the unappropriated retained earnings account from the beginning of the year to the end of the year. The schedule supplies the IRS with information regarding dividends paid during the year and any special transactions that caused a change in retained earnings for the year.

Schedule M-2 starts with the balance in the unappropriated retained earnings account at the beginning of the year. The following items, which must be added to the beginning balance amount, are listed on the left side of the schedule:

1. Net income per books
2. Other increases (e.g., refund of federal income taxes paid in a prior year taken directly to the retained earnings account instead of used to reduce federal income tax expense)

The following items, which must be deducted from the beginning balance amount, are listed on the right side of the schedule:

1. Dividends (e.g., cash or property)
2. Other decreases (e.g., appropriation of retained earnings made during the tax year)

The result is the balance in the unappropriated retained earnings account at the end of the year.

Example 3-42 ■ In 1991, Beta Corporation reports net income and other capital account items as follows:

Unappropriated retained earnings, January 1, 1991	$400,000
Net income	350,000
Federal income tax refund for 1989	15,000
Cash dividends paid in 1991	250,000
Unappropriated retained earnings, December 31, 1991	515,000

Beta Corporation's Schedule M-2 is shown in Figure 3-5. ■

Estimated Taxes

Every corporation must pay four installments of estimated tax, each equal to 25% of its required annual payment. For corporations that are not large corporations (defined below) the required annual payment is the lesser of 90% of the tax shown on the return for the current year or 100% of the tax shown on the return for the preceding year. The estimated tax amount is defined as the corporation's income tax liability

Compliance and Procedural Considerations • 3-43

1 Net income per books		121,700	7 Income recorded on books this year not included in this return (itemize):		
2 Federal income tax		27,250			
3 Excess of capital losses over capital gains		10,750	a Tax-exempt interest $ 12,500		
4 Income subject to tax not recorded on books this year (itemize):			*Insurance proceeds* 50,000		62,500
Prepaid rent		10,000	8 Deductions in this tax return not charged against book income this year (itemize):		
5 Expenses recorded on books this year not deducted in this return (itemize):			a Depreciation . . . $ 2,000		
a Depreciation $			b Contributions carryover $		
b Contributions carryover $					
c Travel and entertainment $					
Insurance premiums 800					2,000
Interest on loan 15,000		15,800	9 Total of lines 7 and 8		64,500
6 Total of lines 1 through 5		185,500	10 Income (line 28, page 1)—line 6 less line 9		121,000

FIGURE 3-4 Valley Corporation's Schedule M-1 (Example 3-41)

including any alternative minimum tax liability and Superfund environmental tax in excess of its estimated tax credits.[68] The amount of estimated tax due may be computed on Schedule 1120-W.

Estimated Tax Payment Dates. A calendar year corporation must deposit estimated tax payments in a Federal Reserve bank or authorized commercial bank on or before April 15th, June 15th, September 15th, and December 15th.[69] This schedule differs from that of an individual taxpayer. The final estimated tax installment for a calendar-year corporation is due in December of the tax year, rather than in January of the following tax year, as is the case for individual taxpayers.

Example 3-43 ■ Garden Corporation uses a calendar year as its tax year. For 1991 Garden expects to report the following results:

Regular tax	$119,000
Alternative minimum tax	25,000
General business credit	4,000

Garden's 1991 estimated tax liability is $140,000 ($119,000 regular tax liability + $25,000 AMT liability − $4,000 tax credit). Garden's tax liability for 1990 was $120,000. Assuming Garden is not a large corporation, its required annual payment for 1991 is the lesser of its 1990 liability ($120,000) or 90% of its 1991 tax

Schedule M-2 Analysis of Unappropriated Retained Earnings per Books (line 25, Schedule L) (This schedule does not have to be completed if the total assets on line 15, column (d), of Schedule L are less than $25,000.)

1 Balance at beginning of year	400,000	5 Distributions: a Cash		250,000
2 Net income per books	350,000	b Stock		
3 Other increases (itemize):		c Property		
Federal income tax refund for 1989	15,000	6 Other decreases (itemize):		
		7 Total of lines 5 and 6		
4 Total of lines 1, 2, and 3	765,000	8 Balance at end of year (line 4 less line 7)		515,000

FIGURE 3-5 Beta Corporation's Schedule M-2 (Example 3-42)

[68] Secs. 6655(c)(1) and (g)(1).
[69] Sec. 6655(c)(2). Fiscal year taxpayers are required by Sec. 6655(i)(1) to deposit their taxes on the 15th day of the 4th, 6th, 9th, and 12th month of their tax year.

Typical Misconception

The easiest method of determining a corporation's estimated tax payments is to pay 100% of last year's tax liability. Unfortunately, for "large corporations," other than for its first quarterly payment, last year's tax liability is not an acceptable method of determining the required estimated tax payments. Also, last year's tax liability cannot be used if no tax liability existed in the prior year or a short-year return was filed for the prior year.

return liability ($126,000 = 0.90 × $140,000), or $120,000. Garden will not incur any penalty if it deposits four equal installments of $30,000 ($120,000 ÷ 4) on or before April 15, June 15, September 15, and December 15, 1991. ■

Different estimated tax payment rules are used for large corporations. A large corporation's required annual payment is 90% of the tax shown on the return for the year.[70] The estimated tax payments for a large corporation cannot be based on the prior year's tax liability, although a large corporation can base its first installment payment for the year on last year's tax liability. If a large corporation elects to base its first estimated tax payment on the prior year's liability, any shortfall between the required payment based on the current year's tax liability and the actual payment must be made up when the second payment is made.[71] A large corporation is one whose taxable income was $1 million or more in any of its 3 immediately preceding tax years.[72] Controlled groups of corporations are required to allocate the $1 million amount among its group members.[73]

Example 3-44 ■

Self-Study Question

What is the consequence of underpaying a corporation's estimated taxes?

Answer

A nondeductible penalty is assessed if estimated taxes are not timely paid. The amount of the penalty is dependent on three factors: (1) the underpayment rate in Sec. 6621, (2) the amount of the underpayment, and (3) the amount of time that lapses until payment is actually made.

Assume the same facts as in Example 3-43 except that Garden is a large corporation (i.e., it had more than $1 million in taxable income in 1989). Garden can base its first estimated tax payment based on either 22.5% (22.5% = 0.25 × 90%) of its 1991 tax liability, or 25% of 1990's tax liability. Garden should elect to use its 1990 tax liability as the basis for its first installment since it can reduce the needed payment from $31,500 (0.225 × $140,000) to $30,000 (0.25 × $120,000). It must also recapture the shortfall of $1,500 ($31,500 − $30,000) when it pays its second installment. Therefore, the total second installment is $33,000 ($31,500 second installment + $1,500 recapture from first installment). ■

Penalties for Underpayment of Estimated Tax. A nondeductible penalty is assessed if a corporation does not deposit its required estimated tax installment on or before the due date for that installment. The penalty is the underpayment rate found in Sec. 6621 times the amount by which the installment(s) due by a payment date exceed the payment(s) actually made.[74] The penalty is owed from the payment date for the installment until the earlier of the date the payment is actually made or the due date for the tax return (excluding extensions).

Example 3-45 ■

Globe Corporation is a calendar-year taxpayer that owes an estimated tax liability for 1991 of $100,000. It was required to make estimated tax payments of $22,500 ([0.90 × $100,000] ÷ 4) on or before April 15, June 15, September 15, and December 15, 1991. Assume the underpayment rate prescribed by Sec. 6621 for 1991 and 1992 remains at 10%. No penalty is assessed if Globe deposits at least $22,500 on or before each of the four dates. If, for example, a deposit of only $15,000 ($7,500 less than the $22,500 required), is made on April 15, 1991, and the

---

[70] Sec. 6655(d)(2)(A).
[71] Sec. 6655(d)(2)(B). A revision to the required estimated tax payment amount also can occur if the corporation is basing its quarterly payments on the current year's tax liability. The amount of the installment to be paid after the estimate of the current year's liability has been revised must take into account any shortage or excess in previous installment payments resulting from the change in the original estimate.
[72] Sec. 6655(g)(2)(A).
[73] Sec. 6655(g)(2)(B)(ii).
[74] Sec. 6621. This interest rate is the short-term federal rate as determined by the Secretary of the Treasury plus 3 percentage points. It is subject to change every 3 months. For the period January 1, 1990 through March 31, 1991 the rate for underpayments has been 11%. For periods after December 31, 1990, the interest rate for large corporations is the short-term federal rate plus 5 percentage points. This higher interest rate commences 30 days after the issuance of either a 30-day or 90-day deficiency notice.

remaining $7,500 is not deposited before the due date for the 1991 return, Globe must pay a penalty at a 10% annual rate on the $7,500 underpayment for the period of time from April 15, 1991, until March 15, 1992. The penalty is $706 (0.10 × $7,500 × [330 days ÷ 365 days]). If Globe deposits $30,000 on the second installment date (June 15, 1991), so that a total of $45,000 has been paid by the due date for the second installment, the 10% penalty runs only from April 15, 1991, through June 15, 1991. ■

Exceptions to Penalty Provisions. There are three exceptions to the penalty provisions for failure to pay the amount of estimated taxes calculated in the prior section. A corporation will not owe any penalty for underpaying an installment if:

- the corporation bases its installment on its "annualized income"
- the corporation bases its installment on its "adjusted seasonal income" or
- the corporation's tax for the year is less than $500.

Key Point
Both the "annualized income exception" and the "seasonal income exception" are complicated computations. However, due to the large amounts of money involved in making estimated tax payments along with the possible underpayment penalties, a great deal of time and effort is spent in determining the least amount necessary for a required estimated tax payment.

The Annualized Income Exception. A corporation does not owe a penalty for a given estimated tax installment date if it paid at least the amount computed by multiplying the applicable percentage (22.5% for the first installment, 45% for the second installment, 67.5% for the third installment, and 90% for the fourth installment) by the tax liability that is attributable to the *annualized income* for the appropriate period and subtracting any prior estimated tax payments.[75]

HOW TO ANNUALIZE INCOME. Taxable income for a period of months less than 12 months (short period) is placed on an annual basis by (1) multiplying the taxable income for the short period by 12 and (2) dividing the resulting amount by the number of months in the short period.

Under the annualized income exception, annualized income for:

1. the first installment is based on taxable income for the first three months of the taxable year
2. the second installment is based on taxable income for the first three or the first five months of the taxable year
3. the third installment is based on taxable income for the first six or the first eight months of the taxable year and
4. the fourth installment is based on taxable income for the first nine or eleven months of the taxable year

A corporation may use the annualized income exception for an installment payment only if it is less than the regular required installment. It must recapture any reduction in an earlier required installment resulting from use of the annualized income exception by increasing the amount of the next installment that does not qualify for the annualized income exception.

For small corporations, the best way to ensure that no penalty will be imposed for the underpayment of estimated tax is to make sure that the current year's estimated tax payments are based on 100% of last year's tax. This is not possible, however, for large corporations or for corporations that did not owe any tax in the prior year or who filed a short period tax return for the prior year.

SEASONAL INCOME EXCEPTION. A corporation may base its installments on its adjusted seasonal income. This rule permits corporations that earn seasonal income to annualize their income by assuming income earned in the current year is earned in the same pattern as in preceding years. As in the case of the annualized income

---

[75] Sec. 6655(e)(1) and (2).

TOPIC REVIEW 3-3

Requirements for Filing Tax Returns and Paying Taxes Due

1. Filing Requirements
   a. The corporate tax return is due 2½ months after the end of the tax year.
   b. A corporate taxpayer may request an automatic 6-month extension.
2. Estimated Tax Requirement
   a. Every corporation must pay 4 installments of estimated tax, each equal to 25% of its required annual payment.
   b. If a corporation is not a large corporation, its required annual payment is the lesser of 90% of the tax shown on the current year's return or 100% of the tax shown on the preceding year's return.
   c. Taxes for which estimated payments are required of a C corporation include: regular tax, alternative minimum tax, and Superfund Environmental tax minus any available tax credits.
   d. No estimated tax payment is required if the tax due for the tax year is less than $500.
   e. If a corporation is a large corporation, its required annual payment is 90% of the tax shown on the current year's return. Its first estimated tax payment may be based on the preceding year's tax liability, but any shortfall must be made up when the second installment is due.
   f. Special rules apply if the corporation bases its estimated tax payments on its annualized income, or its adjusted seasonal income.

exception, the seasonal income exception may be used only if the resulting installment payment is less than the regular required installment. Once the exception no longer applies, any savings resulting from its use for prior installments must be recaptured.[75]

Paying the Remaining Tax Liability. A corporation must pay all of its remaining tax liability for the year when it files its corporate tax return. An extension of time to file the tax return does *not* extend the time to pay the tax liability. If any amount of tax is not paid by the original due date for the tax return, interest at the underpayment rate prescribed by Sec. 6621 must be paid from the due date until the tax is paid. In addition to interest, a penalty is assessed if the tax is not paid on time, and the corporation cannot show reasonable cause for the failure to pay. Reasonable cause is presumed if the corporation requests an extension of time to file its tax return and the amount of tax shown on the request for extension (Form 7004) or the amount of tax paid by the original due date of the return is at least 90% of the corporation's final tax liability.[77] A discussion of the failure-to-pay penalty and the interest calculation can be found in Chapter 16.

Topic Review 3-3 summarizes the requirements for filing the corporate tax return and paying the taxes due.

PROBLEM MATERIALS

DISCUSSION QUESTIONS

3-1. High Corporation is incorporated on May 1, 1991, and commences business on May 10, 1991. What alternative tax years can High elect to report its initial year's income?

---

[75] Sec. 6655(e)(3).
[77] Reg. Sec. 301.6651-1(c)(4).

3-2. What restrictions limit the closely-held C corporation's selection of a tax year?

3-3. Rome Corporation manufactures digital circuits. What overall accounting method(s) can Rome elect to use to keep its books and records?

3-4. What restrictions limit the closely-held C corporation's selection of an overall accounting method?

3-5. Port Corporation wants to change its tax year from a calendar year to a fiscal year ending June 30. Port is a C corporation owned by 100 shareholders none of whom own more than 5% of the stock. Can Port Corporation change its tax year? If so, how can the change be accomplished?

3-6. Compare the tax treatment of capital gains and losses by a corporation and by an individual.

3-7. Explain the effect of the Sec. 291 recapture rule when a corporation sells depreciable real estate.

3-8. What are organizational expenditures? How are they treated for tax purposes?

3-9. What are start-up expenditures? How are they treated for tax purposes?

3-10. Describe three ways in which the treatment of charitable contributions by individual and corporate taxpayers differs.

3-11. Zero Corporation contributes inventory (computers) to State University for use in their mathematics program. The computers have a $350 cost basis and an $800 fair market value. How much is Zero Corporation's charitable contribution deduction for the computers? (Ignore the 10% limit.)

3-12. Carver Corporation uses the accrual method of accounting and the calendar year as its tax year. Its board of directors authorizes a cash contribution on November 3, 1991, that is paid on March 10, 1992. In what year(s) is it deductible? What happens if the contribution is not paid until April 20, 1992?

3-13. Why are corporations allowed a dividends-received deduction? What dividends are eligible for this special deduction?

3-14. Why is a dividends-received deduction disallowed if the stock on which the dividend is paid is debt-financed?

3-15. What special restrictions apply to the deduction of a loss realized on the sale of property between a corporation and a shareholder who owns 60% of the corporation's stock? What restrictions apply to the deduction of expenses accrued by a corporation for expenses owed to a cash method of accounting shareholder who owns 60% of the corporation's stock?

3-16. Explain how the at-risk and passive activity limitation rules restrict the closely-held C corporation's deduction of losses against its other income.

3-17. Budget Corporation is a personal service corporation. Its taxable income for the current year is $75,000. What is Budget Corporation's income tax liability for the year?

3-18. Deer Corporation is a C corporation. Its taxable income for the current year is $200,000. What is Deer Corporation's income tax liability for the year?

3-19. Why do special restrictions on using the progressive corporate tax rates apply to controlled groups of corporations?

3-20. Describe the three types of controlled groups.

3-21. List five restrictions on the claiming of multiple tax benefits that apply to controlled groups of corporations.

3-22. What are the advantages and disadvantages of filing a consolidated tax return?

3-23. What are the tax advantages of substituting fringe benefits for salary paid to a shareholder-employee?

3-24. Explain the tax consequences to both the corporation and a shareholder-employee of an IRS determination that a portion of the compensation paid in a prior tax year exceeds the reasonable compensation limit. What steps can be taken by the corporation and the shareholder-employee to avoid the double taxation usually associated with such a determination?

3-25. What is the advantage of a special apportionment plan for the benefits of the 15% and 25% tax rates to members of a controlled group?

3-26. Describe the circumstances when a corporation should consider electing *not* to carry a net operating loss back to its 3 preceding tax years.

3-27. Describe the situations in which a corporation must file a tax return.

3-28. When is a corporate tax return due for a calendar-year taxpayer? What extension(s) of time in which to file the return are available?

3-29. List four types of differences that can cause a corporation's book income to differ from its taxable income.

3-30. What corporations must pay estimated taxes? When are the estimated tax payments due?

3-31. What penalties are assessed for the underpayment of estimated taxes? The late payment of the remaining tax liability?

PROBLEMS

3-32. *Computing a Corporation's Income Tax Liability.* What is Booker Corporation's income tax liability assuming its taxable income is: (i) $75,000; (ii) $175,000; and (iii) $375,000. How would your answers change if Booker Corporation is characterized as a personal service corporation?

3-33. *Organizational and Start-up Expenditures.* Delta Corporation is incorporated on January 1, 1991, commences business on July 1, 1991, and elects to have its initial tax year end on October 31, 1991. Delta incurs the following expenses related to its organization during 1991:

January 30, 1991	Travel to investigate potential business site	$2,000
May 15, 1991	Legal expenses to draft corporate charter	2,500
May 30, 1991	Commissions to stockbroker for issuing and selling stock	4,000
May 30, 1991	Temporary directors' fees	2,500
June 5, 1991	Accounting fees to set up corporate books	1,500
June 10, 1991	Training expenses for employees	5,000
June 15, 1991	Rent expense for June	1,000
July 15, 1991	Rent expense for July	1,000

a. What alternative treatments are available for Delta's expenditures?
b. What amount of organizational expenditures can Delta Corporation deduct on its first tax return for the year ending October 31, 1991?

3-34. *Charitable Contribution of Property.* Yellow Corporation donates the following properties to the State University:

- ABC Corporation stock purchased two years ago for $18,000. The stock has a $25,000 FMV on the contribution date.
- Inventory with a $17,000 adjusted basis and a $22,000 FMV. The inventory is to be used for scientific research and qualifies under Sec. 170(e)(4).
- An antique vase purchased two years ago for $10,000 and having an $18,000 FMV. State University plans to sell the vase to obtain funds for educational purposes.

Yellow Corporation's taxable income before any charitable contributions deduction, NOL or capital loss carryback, or dividends-received deduction is $250,000.

a. What is Yellow Corporation's charitable contributions deduction for the current year?
b. What is the amount of its charitable contributions carryover (if any)?

3-35. *Charitable Contribution Deduction Limitation.* Zeta Corporation reports the following results for 1991 and 1992:

	1991	1992
Adjusted taxable income	$180,000	$125,000
Charitable contributions (cash)	20,000	12,000

The adjusted taxable income is before any charitable contributions deduction, NOL or capital loss carryback, or dividends-received deduction is claimed.

a. How much is Zeta Corporation's charitable contributions deduction in 1991? in 1992?
b. What is Zeta Corporation's contribution carryover to 1993, if any?

3-36. Taxable Income Computation. Old Corporation reports the following results for the current year:

Gross profits on sales	$100,000
Dividends from less than 20% owned domestic corporations	50,000
Operating expenses	80,000
Charitable contributions (cash)	10,000

a. What is Old Corporation's charitable contributions deduction for the current year and its charitable contributions carryover to next year, if any?
b. What is Old Corporation's taxable income for the current year?

3-37. Dividends-Received Deduction. Theta Corporation reports the following results for the current year:

Gross profits on sales	$220,000
Dividends from less than 20% owned domestic corporations	100,000
Operating expenses	218,000

a. What is Theta Corporation's taxable income for the current year?
b. How would your answer to Part a change if Theta's operating expenses are instead $234,000?
c. How would your answer to Part a change if Theta's operating expenses are instead $252,000?

3-38. Stock Held 45 Days or Less. Beta Corporation purchased 100 shares of Gamma Corporation stock (less than 5% of the outstanding stock) two days before the ex-dividend date for $200,000. Beta receives a $10,000 dividend from Gamma. Beta sells the Gamma stock one week after purchasing it for $190,000. What are the tax consequences of these three events?

3-39. Debt-financed Stock. Cheers Corporation borrowed $500,000 to purchase 5,000 shares of Beer Corporation stock (less than 5% of the outstanding Beer stock) at the beginning of the current year. Cheers paid $50,000 of interest on the debt this year. Cheers received a $40,000 dividend on the Beer stock on September 1 of the current year.

a. What is the amount that Cheers can deduct for the interest paid on the loan?
b. What is the amount of the dividends-received deduction that Cheers can claim with respect to the dividend?

3-40. Net Operating Loss Carrybacks and Carryovers. In 1991, Ace Corporation reports gross income of $200,000 (including $150,000 of profit from its operations and $50,000 in dividends from less than 20% owned domestic corporations) and $220,000 of operating expenses. Ace's 1988 taxable income (all ordinary income) was $75,000, on which taxes of $13,750 were paid.

a. What is Ace's NOL for 1991?
b. What is the amount of Ace's tax refund if the 1991 NOL is carried back to 1988?
c. Assume that Ace expects 1992's taxable income to be $400,000. What election could Ace make in order to maximize the tax benefit from its NOL?

3-41. Sale to a Related Party. Union Corporation sells a truck for $18,000 to Jane, who owns 70% of its stock. The truck has a $24,000 adjusted basis on the sale date. Jane sells the truck to an unrelated party, Mike, for $25,000 two years later after $6,000 in depreciation has been claimed.

a. What is Union Corporation's realized and recognized gain or loss on selling the truck?
b. What is Jane's realized and recognized gain or loss on selling the truck to Mike?

c. How would your answers to Part b change if Jane instead sells the truck for $8,000?

3-42. Payment to a Cash Basis Employee/Shareholder. Value Corporation is a calendar-year taxpayer that uses the accrual method of accounting. On December 10, 1991, Value accrues a bonus payment of $100,000 to Brett, its president and sole shareholder. Brett is a calendar-year taxpayer who uses the cash method of accounting.
   a. When can Value Corporation deduct the bonus if it is paid to Brett on March 13, 1992? on March 16, 1992?
   b. How would your answers to Part a change if Brett is an employee of Value Corporation who owns no stock in the corporation?

3-43. Depreciation Recapture. Young Corporation purchased residential real estate in 1987 for $225,000, of which $25,000 was allocated to the land and $200,000 was allocated to the building. Young took straight-line MACRS deductions of $50,000 during the years 1987–1991. In 1991 Young sells the property for $275,000, of which $50,000 is allocated to the land and $225,000 is allocated to the building. What are the amount and character of Young's recognized gain or loss on the sale?

3-44. Capital Gains and Losses. North Corporation reports the following results for the current year:

Gross profits on sales	$100,000
Long-term capital gain	10,000
Long-term capital loss	(5,000)
Short-term capital gain	3,000
Short-term capital loss	(5,000)
Operating expenses	32,000

What are North's taxable income and regular tax liability (before credits) for the current year?

3-45. Computing the Corporate Tax Liability. Brodie Corporation, a C corporation, paid no dividends and had no capital gains or losses in the current year. What is its income tax liability assuming its taxable income for the year was:
   a. $75,000.
   b. $175,000.
   c. $335,000.
   d. Assume the same facts as in Part a except the corporation had a $10,000 capital loss for the year and paid $20,000 in dividends to its sole shareholder.

3-46. Computing Taxable Income and Tax Liability. Pace Corporation reports the following results for the current year:

Gross profits on sales	$120,000
Long-term capital loss	(10,000)
Short-term capital loss	(5,000)
Dividends from more than 20% owned domestic corporation	30,000
Operating expenses	65,000
Charitable contributions	10,000

   a. What are Pace's taxable income and regular tax liability (before credits)?
   b. What carrybacks and carryovers (if any) are available and to what years must they be carried?

3-47. Computing Taxable Income and Tax Liability. Roper Corporation reports the following results for the current year:

Gross profits on sales	$80,000
Short-term capital gain	40,000
Long-term capital gain	25,000
Dividends from 25% owned domestic corporation	10,000
NOL carryover from the preceding tax year	8,000
Operating expenses	45,000

What are Roper's taxable income and regular tax liability (before credits)?

3-48. *Ordering of Deductions.* Beta Corporation reports the following results for the current year:

Gross income from operations	$180,000
Dividends from less than 20% owned domestic corporations	100,000
Operating expenses	150,000
Charitable contributions	20,000

In addition, Beta has a $50,000 NOL carryover from the preceding tax year.
a. What is Beta's taxable income for the current year?
b. What carryovers are available (if any) to next year?

3-49. *Controlled Groups.* Which of the following groups constitute controlled groups? (Any stock not listed below is held by unrelated individuals each owning less than 1% of the outstanding stock.)
a. Judy owns 90% of the single classes of stock of Hot and Ice Corporations.
b. Jones and Kane Corporations each have only a single class of stock outstanding. The stock is owned by two controlling individual shareholders as follows:

	Stock Ownership Percentages	
Shareholder	Jones Corp.	Kane Corp.
Tom	60%	80%
Mary	30%	0%

c. Link, Model, and Name Corporations each have a single class of stock outstanding. The stock is owned as follows:

	Stock Ownership Percentages	
Shareholder	Model Corp.	Name Corp.
Link Corp.	80%	50%
Model Corp.		40%

Link Corporation's stock is widely held by over 1,000 shareholders, none of whom owns directly or indirectly more than 1% of Link's stock.
d. Oat, Peach, Rye, and Seed Corporations each have a single class of stock outstanding. The stock is owned as follows:

	Stock Ownership Percentages			
Shareholder	Oat Corp.	Peach Corp.	Rye Corp.	Seed Corp.
Bob	100%	90%		
Oat Corp.			80%	30%
Rye Corp.				60%

3-50. *Controlled Groups of Corporations.* Sally owns 100% of the outstanding stock of Eta, Theta, Phi, and Gamma Corporations, each of which files a separate return for the current year. During the current year, the corporations report taxable income as follows:

Corporation	Taxable Income
Eta	$40,000
Theta	(25,000)
Phi	50,000
Gamma	10,000

a. What are each corporation's separate tax liabilities, assuming no special apportionment plan governing the reduced Sec. 11(b) corporate tax rates has been elected?
b. What are each corporation's separate tax liabilities, assuming a special election is made for apportioning the Sec. 11(b) reduced corporate tax rates that minimizes the group's total tax liability?

3-51. *Compensation Planning.* Marilyn owns all of the stock of Bell Corporation. Bell Corporation is taxed as a C corporation. She is married, has two children, and files a joint tax return with her husband. In the past Marilyn has not itemized her deductions. She projects that Bell Corporation will report $400,000 of pretax profits for the current year. Five salary levels are being considered by Marilyn as follows:

Total Income	Salary Paid to Marilyn	Earnings Retained by Bell Corporation	Tax Liability Marilyn	Bell Corporation	Total
$400,000	—0—	$400,000			
400,000	$100,000	300,000			
400,000	200,000	200,000			
400,000	300,000	100,000			
400,000	400,000	—0—			

a. Determine the total tax liability for Marilyn and Bell Corporation for each of the five proposed salary levels.

b. What recommendations can you make about a salary level for Marilyn that will minimize the total tax liability? Assume salaries paid up to $400,000 are considered reasonable compensation.

c. What possible disadvantage could accrue to Marilyn if Bell Corporation retains funds in the business and must distribute some of the accumulated earnings as a dividend in a later tax year?

3-52. *Fringe Benefits.* Refer to the facts in Problem 3-51. Marilyn has read an article explaining the advantages of paying tax-free fringe benefits (e.g., premiums on group term life insurance, accident and health insurance, etc.) and having deferred compensation plans (e.g., qualified pension and profit-sharing plans). Provide Marilyn with information on the tax savings associated with converting $3,000 of her salary into tax-free benefits. What additional costs may be incurred by Bell Corporation with the adoption of a fringe benefit plan?

3-53. *Schedule M-1.* Zero Corporation reports the following results for the current year:

Net income per books	$33,000
Federal income taxes	12,000
Tax-exempt interest income	6,000
Interest on loan to purchase tax-exempt bonds	8,000
Modified ACRS depreciation in excess of book depreciation	3,000
Net capital loss	6,000

Schedule M-1 Reconciliation of Income per Books With Income per Return (You are not required to complete this schedule if the total assets on line 14, column (d), of Schedule L are less than $25,000.)

1 Net income per books	
2 Federal income tax	
3 Excess of capital losses over capital gains . .	
4 Income subject to tax not recorded on books this year (itemize): _____	
5 Expenses recorded on books this year not deducted in this return (itemize):	
a Depreciation . . . $ _____	
b Contributions carryover $ _____	
c Travel and entertainment . $ _____	
6 Total of lines 1 through 5	
7 Income recorded on books this year not included in this return (itemize):	
a Tax-exempt interest $ _____	
8 Deductions in this tax return not charged against book income this year (itemize):	
a Depreciation . . . $ _____	
b Contributions carryover $ _____	
9 Total of lines 7 and 8	
10 Income (line 28, page 1)—line 6 less line 9	

FIGURE 3-6 Schedule M-1 for Problem 3-53

Insurance premium on life of corporate officer where Zero is the beneficiary	10,000
Excess charitable contributions	2,500

Using the Schedule M-1 presented in Figure 3-6, compute Zero's current year taxable income before special deductions.

3-54. *Schedule M-2.* White Corporation's financial accounting records disclose the following results for the period ending December 31 of the current year:

Retained earnings balance on January 1st	$246,500
Net income for year	259,574
Contingency reserve established on December 31st	60,000
Cash dividend paid on July 23rd	23,000

Using the Schedule M-2 presented in Figure 3-7, compute White's unappropriated retained earnings balance on December 31st of the current year.

3-55. *Filing the Tax Return and Paying the Tax Liability.* Wright Corporation's taxable income for calendar years 1988, 1989, and 1990 was $120,000, $150,000, and $100,000, respectively. Its total tax due for 1991 is $22,250. Wright estimates that its 1992 taxable income will be $500,000, on which it will owe federal income taxes of $170,000. 1992's taxable income is assumed to be earned evenly throughout the year.
   a. What are Wright's minimum quarterly estimated tax payments for 1992 in order to avoid an underpayment penalty?
   b. When is Wright's 1992 tax return due?
   c. When are any remaining taxes due?
   d. How would your answer to Part c change if Wright's tax liability for 1991 was $200,000?

3-56. *Estimated Tax Requirement.* Zeta Corporation's taxable income for the preceding year was $1,500,000, on which federal income taxes of $510,000 were paid. Zeta estimates the current year's taxable income to be $2,000,000, on which it will pay $680,000 in federal income taxes.
   a. What are Zeta's minimum quarterly estimated tax payments for the current year in order to avoid an underpayment penalty?
   b. When is Zeta's current year tax return due?
   c. When are any remaining taxes due?
   d. If Zeta obtains an extension, when is its tax return due? Will the extension permit Zeta to delay making its final tax payments?

TAX FORM/RETURN PREPARATION PROBLEM

3-57. Packer Corporation, incorporated on January 3, 1984, is a calendar-year taxpayer that uses the accrual method of accounting. Its employer identification number is 74-1234567. Its address is 1010 West Avenue, San Antonio, Texas 78213. Packer operates a bookstore. Bob Parks (social security number 000-45-3000) owns 100% of the single class of stock. He receives $65,000 in

FIGURE 3-7 Schedule M-2 for Problem 3-54

salary from Packer in the current year. During the current year, Packer reports the following income and expense items:

Gross receipts		$595,000
Purchases		300,000
Salaries:	Officers	65,000
	Other employees	50,000
Rent payments		48,000
Taxes:	Payroll	9,000
	Franchise	250
Interest payments		250
Charitable contributions (cash)		8,000
Depreciation (see schedule below)		38,820
Advertising		15,000
Telephone		500
Utilities		17,080
Officer's life insurance premium (firm is the beneficiary)		1,500

Depreciation Schedule

Asset	Cost	Prior Depreciation	Method	Current Year Depreciation
Light truck	$ 20,000	$10,400	MACRS	$ 3,840
Fixtures	200,000	77,560	MACRS	34,980
Total	$220,000	$87,960		$38,820

A truck purchased seven years earlier for $8,000 which was fully depreciated using the regular ACRS tables was sold on May 10 for $3,500. Packer uses the same depreciation method for tax purposes and for book purposes. The corporation made estimated tax payments on April 14, June 15, September 10, and December 15 of the current year of $2,000 each (total of $8,000). Its prior year tax liability was $8,000. Packer's balance sheet at the beginning and end of the current year is as follows:

Assets	January 1	December 31
Cash	$ 34,000	$ 32,420
Other current assets	—0—	48,075
Depreciable assets	228,000	220,000
Minus: Accumulated depreciation	(95,960)	(126,780)
Inventory	125,000	145,000
Total assets	$291,040	$318,715

Liabilities and Stockholders' Equity

Accounts payable	$ 68,900	$ 39,475
Common stock	60,000	60,000
Retained earnings (unappropriated)	162,140	219,240
Total liabilities and equity	$291,040	$318,715

Packer Corporation uses the first-in, first-out inventory method. The corporation does not claim any deduction for expenses connected with entertainment facilities, living accommodations, or employees attending foreign conventions. The corporation does not own any stock in any other corporation and has no interest in or authority over any foreign bank account or other foreign assets. Packer Corporation maintains its accounting records on a computerized system. The corporation does not pay any dividends in the current year. Prepare Form 1120 for Packer Corporation for the current year.

CASE STUDY PROBLEM

3-58. Marquette Corporation, a tax client since its creation three years ago, has requested that you prepare a memorandum explaining their estimated tax requirements for 1992. The corporation is in the fabricated steel business. Its earnings have been growing each year. Marquette's taxable income for the last three years has been $500,000, $1,500,000, and $2,500,000, respectively. The Chief Financial Officer expects its taxable income this year to be approximately $3,000,000.

Required: Prepare a one-page client memorandum explaining Marquette's estimated tax requirements for 1992 providing the necessary supporting authorities.

TAX RESEARCH PROBLEMS

3-59. Wicker Corporation makes estimated tax payments of $6,000 in 1990. On March 15, 1991, it files its 1990 tax return, showing a tax liability of $20,000, and it pays the balance of $14,000. On April 15, 1992, it discovers an error and files an amended return for 1990 showing a reduced tax liability of $8,000. Can Wicker Corporation base its estimated payments for 1991 on the $8,000 tax liability for 1990, or must it use the $20,000 tax liability reported on its original return?

A partial list of research sources is

- Sec. 6655(d)(1).
- Rev. Rul. 86-58, 1986-1 C.B. 365.

3-60. King Corporation is owned equally by three individuals—Alice, Bill, and Charles, who purchased King stock when King Corporation was created. King Corporation has used the cash method of accounting since its inception in 1984. Alice, Bill, and Charles operate an environmental engineering firm of 60 employees, which had gross receipts of $4,000,000 in 1990. Gross receipts have grown by about 15% in each of the last 3 years and were just under $5,000,000 in 1991. The 15% growth rate is expected to continue for at least 5 years. Outstanding accounts receivable average about $600,000 at the end of each month. Forty-four of the employees (including Alice, Bill, and Charles) are actively engaged in providing engineering services on a full-time basis. Sixteen of the employees serve in a clerical and support capacity (e.g., secretarial staff, accountants, etc.). Bill reads about the special restrictions on the use of the cash method of accounting and requests information from you about the impact that these rules will have on King Corporation's continued use of the cash method of accounting. If the corporation should change over to the accrual method of accounting, what kinds of adjustments must be made? Would an S corporation election prevent King Corporation from having to make a change? If so, what factors should enter into the decision about whether to make an S corporation election or not?

A partial list of research sources is

- Secs. 446 and 448.
- Temp. Reg. Secs. 1.448-1T and -2T.
- H. Rept. No. 99-841, 99th Cong., 2d Sess., pp. 285-289 (1986).

4 Corporate Nonliquidating Distributions

CHAPTER OUTLINE
LEARNING OBJECTIVES 4-2
DISTRIBUTIONS IN GENERAL 4-2
EARNINGS AND PROFITS (E&P) 4-3
   Current Earnings and Profits 4-3
   Distinction Between Current and Accumulated E&P 4-7
PROPERTY DISTRIBUTIONS 4-9
   Consequences of Property Distributions to Shareholders 4-9
   Consequences of Property Distributions to the Distributing Corporation 4-10
   Constructive Dividends 4-12
STOCK DIVIDENDS AND STOCK RIGHTS 4-14
   Tax-free Stock Dividends 4-15
   Tax-free Stock Rights 4-16
   Effect of Nontaxable Stock Dividends on the Distributing Corporation 4-17
   Taxable Stock Dividends and Stock Rights 4-17
STOCK REDEMPTIONS 4-17
   Effect of the Redemption on the Shareholder 4-18
   Attribution Rules 4-20
   Substantially Disproportionate Redemptions 4-21
   Complete Termination of the Shareholder's Interest 4-23
   Redemptions Not Essentially Equivalent to a Dividend 4-24
   Partial Liquidations 4-25
   Redemptions to Pay Death Taxes 4-27
   Effect of Redemptions on the Distributing Corporation 4-29
PREFERRED STOCK BAILOUTS 4-30
   Sec. 306 Stock Defined 4-31
   Dispositions of Sec. 306 Stock 4-31
   Redemptions of Sec. 306 Stock 4-32
   Exceptions to Sec. 306 Treatment 4-32
STOCK REDEMPTIONS BY RELATED CORPORATIONS 4-33
   Brother-Sister Corporations 4-33
   Parent-Subsidiary Corporations 4-35
DISTRIBUTIONS OF STOCK AND SECURITIES OF A CONTROLLED CORPORATION 4-36
   Requirements of Sec. 355 4-38
   Tax Consequences to Shareholders and Security Holders 4-40
   Tax Consequences to the Distributing Corporation 4-43
CONTROVERSIAL ISSUES 4-44
   What Is a Complete Termination of Interest? 4-44
   What Is the Active Conduct of a Trade or Business? 4-45
TAX PLANNING CONSIDERATIONS 4-46
   Avoiding Unreasonable Compensation 4-46
   Bootstrap Acquisitions 4-47
   Timing of Distributions 4-48
COMPLIANCE AND PROCEDURAL CONSIDERATIONS 4-49
   Agreement to Terminate Interest under Sec. 302(b)(3) 4-49
PROBLEM MATERIALS 4-50
   Discussion Questions 4-50
   Problems 4-51
   Case Study Problem 4-57
   Tax Research Problems 4-57

LEARNING OBJECTIVES

After studying this chapter, you should be able to

1. Explain how current E&P is calculated
2. Explain the difference between current and accumulated E&P
3. Determine the tax consequences of property distributions
4. Determine the tax consequences of stock dividends and distributions of stock rights
5. Distinguish between a stock redemption treated as a sale and one treated as a dividend
6. Explain the tax treatment for preferred stock bailouts
7. Determine when Sec. 304 applies to a stock sale and its tax consequences
8. Determine when Sec. 355 applies to a stock distribution and its tax consequences

A corporation may distribute money, property, or stock to its shareholders. Shareholders who receive such distributions may have ordinary income, capital gain, or no taxable income at all. The distributing corporation may or may not be required to recognize gain or loss when the distribution is made. How distributions are treated for tax purposes by shareholders and by the distributing corporation depends not only on what is distributed but also on the circumstances surrounding the distribution. Was the corporation in the process of liquidating? Was the distribution made in exchange for some of the shareholder's stock?

This chapter discusses distributions made when a corporation is not in the process of liquidating. It discusses the tax consequences of the following types of distributions:

- Distributions of cash or other property where the shareholder does not surrender any stock
- Distributions of stock or rights to acquire stock of the distributing corporation
- Distributions of property in exchange for the corporation's own stock (i.e., stock redemptions)
- Distributions of the stock of a controlled subsidiary corporation

Chapter 6 discusses liquidating distributions.

Self-Study Question
How does a shareholder classify a distribution for tax purposes?

Answer
Distributions are treated as follows: (a) dividends to the extent of E&P, (b) return of capital to the extent of stock basis and, finally, (c) gain from the sale of stock.

DISTRIBUTIONS IN GENERAL

Section 301 requires a shareholder to include in gross income the amount of any distribution from a corporation to the extent that it is a dividend. A **dividend** is defined by Sec. 316(a) as a distribution of property made by a corporation out of its earnings and profits (E&P). The term *E&P* is defined in the next section of this chapter. **Property** is defined broadly by Sec. 317(a) to include money, securities, and any other property except stock or stock rights of the distributing corporation.

Distributed amounts that exceed a corporation's E&P are treated as a return of capital. They reduce the shareholder's basis in his stock. If such distributions exceed the shareholder's basis, the remainder is treated as gain from the sale of the stock. If the stock is a capital asset in the shareholder's hands, the gain is a capital gain.

Example 4-1 ■ On March 1 Gamma Corporation distributes $60,000 to each of its two equal shareholders, Ellen and Bob. At the time of the distribution, Gamma's E&P is $80,000. Ellen's basis in her stock is $25,000, and Bob's basis in his stock is $10,000. Ellen and Bob each must recognize a $40,000 (0.50 × $80,000) taxable dividend. The additional $20,000 that each one receives is treated as follows. In Ellen's case, the $20,000 is a return of capital that reduces her basis in the stock to $5,000 ($25,000 − $20,000). In Bob's case, $10,000 is a return of capital that reduces his basis in the stock to zero. The remainder is reported as a $10,000 capital gain. ■

EARNINGS AND PROFITS (E&P)

Typical Misconception
Since E&P is such an important concept in many corporate transactions, one would assume that corporations know exactly what their E&P is. However, most corporations do not compute their E&P on a regular basis.

The term *E&P* is not specifically defined in the Code. Its meaning must be construed from its function in judicial decisions, Treasury Regulations, and some rules provided in the Code regarding how certain transactions affect E&P.

The function of E&P is to provide a measure of the corporation's economic ability to pay dividends to shareholders. Distributions are considered to come from the corporation's E&P unless the corporation can show that it has no E&P. A corporation at the time it is formed, for example, has no E&P. Any payments made to shareholders by such a corporation are simply a return of the capital contributed by the shareholders until it reports E&P. If, however, a corporation has $10,000 of E&P, the first $10,000 of cash or property distributed to its shareholders is treated as a dividend.

Current Earnings and Profits

E&P consists of two parts—current E&P and accumulated E&P. **Current E&P** is calculated annually as explained below. **Accumulated E&P** is the sum of the undistributed current E&P balances for all previous years reduced by the sum of (1) all previous current E&P deficits and (2) any distributions that have been made out of accumulated E&P.

Example 4-2 ■ Zeta Corporation is formed in 1988. Its current E&P (or current E&P deficit) and distributions for each year through 1991 are as follows:

Year	Current E&P (Deficit)	Distributions
1988	$(10,000)	—0—
1989	15,000	—0—
1990	18,000	$9,000
1991	8,000	—0—

The $9,000 distribution is made from 1990's current E&P. At the beginning of 1991, Zeta's accumulated E&P is $14,000 (− $10,000 + $15,000 + $18,000 −

OBJECTIVE 1
Explain how current E&P is calculated

$9,000). At the beginning of 1992, Zeta's accumulated E&P is $22,000 ($14,000 + $8,000). ∎

Computing Current E&P. Current E&P is computed on an annual basis at the end of each year. The starting point for computing current E&P is the corporation's taxable income or net operating loss (NOL) for the year. Taxable income or loss must be adjusted to obtain the corporation's economic income or loss for the year. For example, federal income taxes must be deducted from taxable income when determining E&P. Since these taxes must be paid to the U.S. government, they reduce the amount available to pay dividends to shareholders. On the other hand, tax-exempt income must be added to taxable income since, even though it is not taxable, it increases the corporation's ability to pay dividends.

A partial listing of the adjustments that must be made is presented in Table 4-1. Some of the adjustments that must be made to taxable income to derive current E&P are explained below.[1]

Income Excluded from Taxable Income. Although certain income is specifically excluded from taxable income, any income received by the corporation must be included in its E&P if it (1) increases the corporation's ability to pay a dividend and (2) is not a contribution to capital. Thus, a corporation's current E&P includes both

Key Point
Many of the prominent adjustments to E&P (listed in Table 4-1) are recognition of cash outflows/inflows that don't affect taxable income but do affect the ability of the corporation to pay dividends.

TABLE 4-1 *Computation of Current E&P*

Taxable income
Plus: Income excluded from taxable income:
　　　　Tax-exempt interest income
　　　　Life insurance proceeds where the corporation is the beneficiary
　　　　Recoveries of bad debts and other deductions from which the corporation received no tax benefit
　　　　Federal income tax refunds from prior years
Plus: Income deferred to a later year when computing taxable income:
　　　　Deferred gain on installment sales
Plus or minus: Adjustments for items that must be recomputed:
　　　　Income on long-term contracts based on percentage of completion method rather than completed contract method
　　　　Excess of accelerated depreciation over straight-line depreciation
　　　　Excess of ACRS deductions claimed over straight-line ACRS calculation using an extended recovery period
　　　　Excess of percentage depletion claimed over cost depletion
Plus: Deductions not allowed in computing E&P:
　　　　Dividends-received deduction
　　　　NOL carryovers, charitable contribution carryovers, and capital loss carryovers used in the current year
Minus: Expenses and losses not deductible in computing taxable income:
　　　　Federal income taxes
　　　　Life insurance premiums where corporation is the beneficiary
　　　　Excess capital losses that are not deductible
　　　　Excess charitable contributions that are not deductible
　　　　Expenses related to production of tax-exempt income
　　　　Nondeductible losses on sales to related parties
　　　　Nondeductible penalties and fines
　　　　Nondeductible political contributions

Current E&P (or E&P deficit)

---

[1] The adjustments required are based on rules found in Code Sec. 312 and the related regulations.

tax-exempt interest income and life insurance proceeds. Current E&P also includes any recovery of an item deducted in a previous year if the deduction did not result in a tax benefit to the corporation, and therefore was excluded from taxable income.

Example 4-3 ■ Ace Corporation deducted $10,000 of bad debts in 1990. Because Ace Corporation had a NOL in 1990 which it was unable to carry back or forward, it received no tax benefit from the deduction. Ace Corporation recovers $8,000 of the amount due in 1991. Ace excludes the $8,000 from its gross income for 1991 because it received no tax benefit from the bad debt deduction in 1990. In addition, Ace must add the $8,000 to its taxable income when determining current E&P for 1991. ■

Income Deferred to a Later Period. Gains and losses on property transactions are generally included in E&P in the same year they are recognized for tax purposes. For example, gain deferred in a like-kind exchange is deferred for E&P purposes as well.

Example 4-4 ■ Stone Corporation exchanges investment property that has a $12,000 basis and an $18,000 fair market value (FMV) for investment property worth $17,000 and $1,000 cash. Stone recognizes a $1,000 gain on the like-kind exchange—the amount of boot received. $5,000 of gain is deferred. The recognized gain is included in taxable income and in current E&P. The deferred gain is not included in taxable income or in current E&P. ■

Additional Comment
Both installment sales and long-term contracts are examples of the government ignoring regular accounting methods in an attempt to ensure that the maximum E&P possible exists to characterize distributions as dividends.

In the case of an installment sale, the entire gain on the sale must be included in current E&P in the year of the sale.[2] This rule applies to sales made by dealers and nondealers.

Example 4-5 ■ In 1991, Tally Corporation sells land that has a $12,000 basis and a $20,000 FMV to Rick, an unrelated individual. Rick makes a $5,000 down payment in 1991 and will pay Tally an additional $5,000 in 1992, 1993, and 1994, plus interest at a rate acceptable to the IRS on the unpaid balance. Tally's realized gain is $8,000 ($20,000 − $12,000). Tally recognizes its gain on the sale using the installment method of accounting. In 1991, Tally recognizes $2,000 of gain ([$8,000 ÷ $20,000] × $5,000). Thus, only $2,000 of gain is included in taxable income, but all $8,000 of Tally's realized gain must be included in current E&P for 1991. In computing current E&P for 1991, Tally's taxable income must be increased by $6,000. ■

Self-Study Question
In determining taxable income and E&P, different depreciation methods are often used. What happens on the sale of such an asset?
Answer
The taxpayer must calculate a different gain/loss for both tax and E&P purposes. This is an added complexity in making E&P calculations.

Adjustments for Items That Must Be Recomputed. Some deductions must be computed differently for E&P purposes than they are for taxable income purposes. Therefore, an adjustment must be made for the difference between the two computations.

- E&P must be computed using the percentage of completion method even if the corporation uses the completed contract method of accounting for tax purposes.[3]
- Depreciation must be recomputed. For tangible personal property depreciated using the Modified ACRS rules, the alternative depreciation system of Sec. 168(g) must be used for E&P purposes. Property expensed under Sec. 179 is expensed ratably over a 5-year period for E&P purposes starting with the month

---

[2] Sec. 312(n)(5).
[3] Sec. 312(n)(6).

it is deductible for Sec. 179 purposes. For personalty, Sec. 168(g) requires the use of straight-line depreciation over the property's class life using a half-year convention. Realty must be depreciated over a 40-year period for E&P purposes using the straight-line method and mid-month covention.[4]

Example 4-6 ■ In January 1990, R Corporation purchased equipment with a 10-year class life for $5,000. R expensed the entire cost of the equipment in 1990 under Sec. 179. R's cost-recovery deduction for E&P purposes is $1,000 ($5,000 ÷ 5) in every year from 1990 through 1991.

- Cost depletion must be used for E&P purposes even if percentage depletion is used for computing taxable income.[5]
- Intangible drilling costs must be capitalized and amortized over 60 months for E&P purposes.[6] ■

Deductions Not Allowed in Computing E&P. Some deductions claimed when computing taxable income are not allowed when computing current E&P.

- The dividends-received deduction is not permitted for E&P purposes because it does not reduce the corporation's ability to pay dividends. Therefore, it must be added back to taxable income to compute E&P.[7]
- NOL carryovers, charitable contribution carryovers, and capital loss carryovers that reduce taxable income for the current year cannot be deducted when determining E&P. These losses or excess deductions reduce E&P in the year they are incurred.

Example 4-7 ■ Thames Corporation's taxable income is $50,000 after deducting a NOL carryover from two years ago of $10,000. Thames must add $10,000 to its taxable income to compute current E&P. The $10,000 NOL reduced current E&P in the year it was incurred. ■

Expenses and Losses Not Deductible in Computing Taxable Income. Some expenses and losses that are not deductible in computing taxable income are deductible when computing current E&P.

- Federal income taxes are not deductible when taxable income is computed. For E&P purposes, federal income taxes are deductible in the year they accrue if the corporation uses the accrual method of accounting and in the year they are paid if the corporation uses the cash method of accounting.

Example 4-8 ■ Perch Corporation, which uses the accrual method of accounting, has taxable income of $100,000 on which it owes $22,250 of federal income taxes. In computing its current E&P, it must reduce taxable income by $22,250.

- Charitable contributions are deductible in full for E&P purposes without regard to the 10% limitation on such deductions. Thus, taxable income must be reduced by any charitable contributions that were disallowed because of the 10% limitation when current E&P is computed. ■

---

[4] Sec. 312(k)(3). When determining the taxability of a distribution made to a 20% corporate shareholder (and the distributee corporation's basis for its investment in the distributing corporation's stock), the distributing corporation does not have to make the adjustments otherwise required by Secs. 312(k) and (n) (Sec. 301(e)).

[5] Reg. Sec. 1.312-6(c)(1).

[6] Sec. 312(n)(2).

[7] *R. M. Weyerhaeuser,* 33 B.T.A. 594 (1935).

Example 4-9 ■ Dot Corporation has $25,000 of taxable income before any charitable contribution deduction. Dot contributed $10,000 to the Red Cross. Although Dot's contribution deduction is limited to $2,500 in computing taxable income because of the 10% of taxable income limitation on charitable contribution deductions, Dot deducts the entire $10,000 in computing current E&P. Therefore, $7,500 must be deducted from taxable income of $22,500 to compute current E&P. In a later year(s) when the $7,500 carryover is deducted in determining taxable income, a positive adjustment must be made to taxable income in arriving at E&P so as not to deduct the excess contributions in two different years in arriving at current E&P.

Key Point
After reviewing some of the complex calculations needed to compute E&P, one can begin to appreciate why most corporations resist incurring the costs necessary to compute E&P regularly.

- Life insurance premiums paid on policies to insure the lives of key corporate personnel (net of any increase in the cash surrender value of the policy) are not deductible when taxable income is computed but are deductible when E&P is computed.
- Capital losses in excess of capital gains cannot be deducted when taxable income is computed but are deductible when computing current E&P.
- Nondeductible expenses related to the production of tax-exempt income (e.g., interest charges to borrow money to purchase tax-exempt securities) are deductible when computing E&P.
- Losses on sales to related parties that are disallowed under Sec. 267 are deductible when current E&P is computed.
- Nondeductible fines, penalties, and political contributions are deductible for E&P purposes. ■

The adjustments listed in Table 4-1 and described above are only a partial list of the adjustments that must be made to taxable income in order to compute current E&P. The basic rule is that adjustments are made so that current E&P represents the corporation's economic ability to pay dividends out of its current earnings.

Distinction Between Current and Accumulated E&P

OBJECTIVE 2
Explain the difference between current and accumulated E&P

A distinction must be made between current and accumulated E&P. Corporate distributions are deemed to come from current E&P first and then from accumulated E&P only if current E&P is insufficient.[8] If current E&P is sufficient to cover all distributions made during the year, each distribution is treated as a taxable dividend. This rule applies even if there is a deficit in accumulated E&P. Current E&P is computed on the last day of the tax year. No reduction is made for distributions made during the year.

Example 4-10 ■
Key Point
Distributions are deemed to come from current E&P first. If current E&P is not adequate, then accumulated E&P is utilized.

At the beginning of 1991, Water Corporation has a $30,000 accumulated E&P deficit. For the year 1991, Water has current E&P of $15,000. Water distributes $10,000 to its shareholders during 1991. The $10,000 distribution is a taxable dividend to the shareholders since it is deemed to come from current E&P. At the beginning of 1992, Water has an accumulated E&P deficit of $25,000 (− $30,000 E&P deficit + $5,000 undistributed current E&P). ■

If distributions made during the year exceed current E&P, current E&P is allocated to those distributions on a pro rata basis regardless of when during the year the distributions were made. Remaining distributions are deemed to come from accumu-

---
[8] The distinction between current and accumulated E&P is explained in Reg. Sec. 1.316-2.

Key Point
If multiple distributions exist, current E&P is allocated pro rata and accumulated E&P is allocated chronologically.

lated E&P (if any) in chronological order. Distributions in excess of current and accumulated E&P are treated as a return of capital and reduce the shareholder's basis on a dollar-for-dollar basis. However, these distributions cannot create an E&P deficit. These rules are important if the stock changes hands during the year and total E&P is insufficient to cover all distributions.

Example 4-11 ■ At the beginning of the current year, Cole Corporation has $25,000 of accumulated E&P. For the current year, Cole's current E&P is $30,000. On April 10, Cole distributes $20,000 to Bob, its sole shareholder. On July 15, Cole distributes an additional $24,000 to Bob. On August 1, Bob sells all of his Cole stock to Lynn. On September 15, Cole distributes $36,000 to Lynn. Cole's current and accumulated E&P must be allocated to the three distributions made during the year as follows:

Date	Distribution Amount	Current E&P	Accumulated E&P	Dividend Income	Return of Capital
April 10	$20,000	$ 7,500	$12,500	$20,000	$—0—
July 15	24,000	9,000	12,500	21,500	2,500
September 15	36,000	13,500	—0—	13,500	22,500
Total	$80,000	$30,000	$25,000	$55,000	$25,000

The current E&P allocated to the April 10 distribution is calculated as follows:

$$\$30{,}000 \text{ (Current E\&P)} \times \frac{\$20{,}000 \text{ (April 10 distribution)}}{\$80{,}000 \text{ (Total distributions)}}$$

Self-Study Question
When is E&P measured for purposes of determining if a distribution is a dividend?

Answer
Usually at year-end. However, if a current deficit exists, the E&P available for measuring dividend income is determined at the date of the distribution.

Note that the total amount of dividends paid by Cole equals $55,000, the sum of $30,000 of current E&P and $25,000 of accumulated E&P. Current E&P is allocated to all three distributions on a pro rata basis, whereas accumulated E&P is allocated first to the April 10 distribution ($12,500). The remaining accumulated E&P is allocated to the July 15 distribution, so that none is available to allocate to the September 15 distribution. Thus, Bob's dividend income from Cole is $41,500 ($20,000 + $21,500). He also has a $2,500 return of capital payment that reduces his basis for his stock. Lynn's dividend income from Cole is $13,500. She also has a $22,500 return of capital payment that reduces the basis for her stock. Note that Bob cannot determine his gain on the sale of his stock until the end of the year. He must wait until he knows how much of the two distributions he received reduced the basis for his stock. ■

If there is a current E&P deficit and an accumulated E&P deficit, none of the distributions are treated as dividends. Instead, all distributions are a return of capital until the basis of a shareholder's stock is reduced to zero. Any additional amounts received are taxable as a capital gain.

Example 4-12 ■ At the beginning of 1991, Rose Corporation has a $15,000 accumulated E&P deficit. Rose's current E&P deficit is $20,000. Rose distributes $10,000 on July 1. The distribution is not a dividend, but a return of capital and/or a capital gain for amounts in excess of the shareholder's basis in his stock. Rose's accumulated E&P deficit at January 1, 1992 is $35,000. ■

If there is a current E&P deficit and a positive accumulated E&P balance, the two accounts must be netted at the time of the distribution to determine the amount of any distribution that comes from E&P. The deficit in current E&P that has been accrued up through the day before the distribution reduces the accumulated E&P balance on that date. If the balance remaining after the reduction is made is positive, the distribution is a dividend to the extent of the lesser of the distribution amount or the E&P balance. If the balance is zero or negative, the distribution is a return of capital. If the actual deficit in current E&P to the date of distribution cannot be determined, the current E&P deficit is prorated on a daily basis to the day before the distribution date. (See additional discussion on the timing of distributions in the Tax Planning Considerations section of this chapter.)

PROPERTY DISTRIBUTIONS

OBJECTIVE 3
Determine the tax consequences of property distributions

The term *property* is defined by Sec. 317(a) as money, securities, and any other property except stock in the corporation making the distribution (or rights to acquire such stock). When a property distribution is made to shareholders, the following questions must be answered:

- What is the amount of the distribution?
- To what extent is the amount distributed a dividend to the shareholder?
- What is the basis of the property to the shareholder, and when does its holding period begin?
- Does the distributing corporation recognize any gain or loss on the distribution?
- What effect does the distribution have on the distributing corporation's E&P account?

For cash distributions, these questions are easy to answer. The distribution amount is the amount of cash distributed. This amount is a dividend to the extent that it comes from the corporation's current and accumulated E&P, and the E&P account is reduced by the amount of the cash dividend. The shareholder's basis in the cash received is its face amount. The distributing corporation does not recognize any gain or loss on the distribution of cash.

When property such as land or inventory is distributed to a shareholder, these questions are more difficult to answer. Neither the amount of the distribution nor the basis of the property to the shareholder are immediately apparent. The corporation may be required to recognize gain or loss on the distribution, and the amount of reduction in the corporation's E&P must be determined. The following sections explain the rules that govern the answers to these questions.

Consequences of Property Distributions to Shareholders

Key Point
The amount of the distribution is measured by the FMV of the property less liabilities assumed (but not below zero) because this represents the real economic value received by the shareholder.

When property is distributed to a shareholder, the amount of the distribution is the FMV of the property distributed.[9] The value is determined on the date of the distribution. The amount of any liability assumed by the shareholder in connection with the distribution, or to which the distributed property is subject, reduces the amount of the distribution. However, the amount of the distribution cannot be reduced below zero. The amount of the distribution is a dividend to the shareholder to the extent of the distributing corporation's E&P.

The shareholder's basis in any property received is the property's FMV. The basis is not reduced by any liabilities assumed by the shareholder or to which the property

[9] Sec. 301(b).

is subject.[10] The holding period of the property begins on the day after the day on which the property is received. It does not include the holding period of the distributing corporation.[11]

Example 4-13 ■

Key Point

Distributions may trigger income both at the shareholder and the corporate level. This is another example of the double taxation that exists in our corporate tax structure.

Self-Study Question

How is the corporate gain determined if the property being sold is subject to a liability in excess of the FMV of the property?

Answer

If property is subject to a liability in excess of its FMV, the property is deemed sold at the liability amount because this relief of debt represents the economic benefit recognized by the corporation on the distribution.

Post Corporation has $100,000 of current and accumulated E&P. On March 1, Post distributes land with a $60,000 FMV and a $35,000 adjusted basis to Meg, its sole shareholder. The land is subject to a $10,000 liability, which Meg assumes. The amount of the distribution is $50,000 ($60,000 − $10,000), all of which is a dividend to Meg since it does not exceed Post's E&P balance. Meg's basis in the property is $60,000, its FMV, and her holding period for the property begins on March 2. ■

Consequences of Property Distributions to the Distributing Corporation

Two questions must be answered with respect to a corporation that distributes property:

- What are the amount and character of the gain or loss that the distributing corporation must recognize on the distribution?
- What effect does the distribution have on the corporation's E&P?

Corporate Gain or Loss on Property Distributions. A corporation must recognize gain when it distributes property that has appreciated in value just as though the corporation had sold the property. However, a corporation does not recognize any loss when it makes a nonliquidating distribution of property even if a sale of the property would have yielded a loss.[12]

Example 4-14 ■

Silver Corporation distributes land (a capital asset) worth $60,000 to Mark, a shareholder. The land has a $20,000 adjusted basis to Silver. Silver must recognize a $40,000 ($60,000 − $20,000) capital gain, the same as though Silver had sold the property. If the land instead has a $12,000 FMV, Mark does not recognize any loss on the distribution. ■

If the distributed property is subject to a liability or the shareholder assumes a liability in connection with the distribution, the property's FMV for purposes of determining gain on the distribution is deemed to be no less than the amount of the liability.[13]

Example 4-15 ■

Assume the same facts as in Example 4-14, except that the land's FMV is instead $25,000 and the land is subject to a $35,000 mortgage. The land's FMV for purposes of calculating the gain recognized on the distribution is deemed to be $35,000 because it cannot be less than the amount of the liability. Thus, Silver Corporation's gain is $15,000 ($35,000 − $20,000), the amount by which the land's deemed FMV exceeds its basis. ■

Effect of Property Distributions on the Distributing Corporation's E&P. Distributions have two effects on E&P:

[10] Sec. 301(d).
[11] Sec. 1223(2).
[12] Sec. 311(a).
[13] Sec. 311(b)(2).

1. When a corporation distributes appreciated property to its shareholders, it must recognize gain as though it had sold the property. This results in an increase in E&P equal to the appreciation in value.[14]
2. A corporation's E&P is reduced by (a) the amount of money distributed plus (b) the greater of the FMV or the adjusted basis of any nonmoney property distributed, minus any liabilities that the property is subject to or that are assumed by a shareholder in connection with the distribution.[15]

Example 4-16 ■ Brass Corporation distributes property with a $25,000 adjusted basis and a $40,000 FMV to Joan, a shareholder. The property is subject to a $12,000 mortgage which Joan assumes. Brass must recognize a $15,000 ($40,000 − $25,000) gain on the distribution. Brass's E&P is increased by $15,000 (the appreciation in value) and is reduced by $28,000 ($40,000 FMV − $12,000 liability) plus the amount of income taxes that are paid or accrued by Brass on the gain. ■

A special rule applies when a corporation distributes its own obligation (e.g., its notes, bonds, or debentures) to a shareholder. In such case, the distributing corporation's E&P is reduced by the principal amount of the obligation distributed.[16]

Topic Review 4-1 presents a summary of the tax consequences of a nonliquidating distribution to the shareholders and the distributing corporation.

TOPIC REVIEW 4-1

Tax Consequences of a Nonliquidating Distribution

Consequences to Shareholders:
1. The amount of a distribution is the amount of money plus the FMV of any nonmoney property received reduced by any liabilities assumed or acquired by the shareholder.
2. The amount of the distribution is a dividend to the extent of the distributing corporation's current and accumulated E&P.
3. The shareholder's basis in the property received is its FMV.
4. The shareholder's holding period begins on the day after the day the property is received.

Consequences to Distributing Corporation:
1. A corporation must recognize gain when it distributes appreciated property as though the property had been sold immediately before the distribution.
2. For gain recognition purposes, a property's FMV is deemed to be at least equal to any liability to which the property is subject or which the shareholder assumes in connection with the distribution.
3. A corporation does not recognize a loss when it distributes property to its shareholders.
4. A corporation's E&P is increased by any gain (net of taxes) recognized on a distribution of appreciated property.
5. A corporation's E&P is reduced by (a) the amount of money distributed plus (b) the greater of the FMV or adjusted basis of any nonmoney property distributed, minus (c) any liabilities that the property is subject to or that are assumed by the shareholder in connection with the distribution.

---

[14] Sec. 312(b). The appreciation in value is included in the distributing corporation's taxable income and, of course, will effect the amount of federal income taxes owed at year-end.
[15] Secs. 312(a) and (c).
[16] Sec. 312(a)(2).

Constructive Dividends

Key Point
In general, taxpayers are most vulnerable to the assertion of a constructive dividend in a closely held corporation context.

A **constructive dividend** (or undeclared distribution) is an indirect payment made to a shareholder without the benefit of a formal declaration. Ordinarily, a corporate dividend payment is formally declared by the board of directors and is paid in cash or property on a specified date. A formal declaration is not required, however. Constructive dividends may be treated as dividends for income tax purposes even though they have not been formally authorized by the corporation's board of directors. It is not even necessary that the distribution be pro rata. Any economic benefit provided by a corporation to a shareholder may be treated as a constructive dividend to the shareholder.

Constructive dividends are most likely to arise in the context of a closely held corporation where the shareholders and management groups overlap. In such situations, the dealings between the corporation and its shareholders are likely to be less structured and subject to less review than they would be in a publicly held corporation. Constructive dividends can arise, however, in a publicly held corporation as well.

Intentional Efforts to Avoid Dividend Treatment. Constructive dividends may arise from intentional attempts (1) to bail out a corporation's E&P without subjecting it to taxation at the shareholder level or (2) to obtain a deduction at the corporate level for distributions to shareholders that should not be deductible. If a corporation has sufficient E&P, dividend distributions are fully taxable to the shareholder, but are not deductible by the distributing corporation. Shareholders may try to disguise a dividend as a salary payment. If successful, the payment is taxable to the shareholder-employee, and is deductible by the distributing corporation as long as the amount is reasonable. Shareholders may try to disguise a dividend as a loan to the shareholder. If successful, the payment is neither deductible by the corporation nor taxable to the shareholder. If the IRS reclassifies either payment as a dividend, it is taxable to the shareholder and nondeductible by the distributing corporation.

Unintentional Constructive Dividends. Some constructive dividends are unintentional. Shareholders may not realize that the benefits they receive from the corporation in which they own stock are actually taxable dividends until the transactions are examined by a tax consultant or by the IRS. A transaction that is found to be a dividend rather than a salary payment, loan, and so on will be recast as a dividend. Appropriate adjustments must then be made to the corporation's and shareholder's books. This may mean an increase in the shareholder's taxable income (e.g., because the distribution is a dividend rather than a loan) or an increase in the distributing corporation's taxable income (i.e., because of reduced deductions). Transactions most likely to be recast and treated as dividends are summarized below.

Additional Comment
The government has requirements that when loans exist between a corporation and its shareholders, they must charge a reasonable interest rate. If a "below-market" interest rate loan exists, the service will impute a reasonable rate of interest [Sec. 7872].

Loans to Shareholders. Loans to shareholders may be considered disguised dividends unless they are bona fide loans. Whether a loan is considered as bona fide ordinarily depends upon the shareholder's intent when the loan is made. To prove that the loan is bona fide (and to avoid having the loan treated as a dividend), the evidence must show that the shareholder intends to repay the loan. Evidence of an intent to repay includes

1. Recording the loan on the corporate books.
2. Evidencing the loan by a written note.
3. Charging a reasonable rate of interest.
4. Scheduling regular payments of principal and interest.

Evidence that the loan is *not* bona fide includes

1. Maintaining a continuing "open account" loan to the shareholder. An open account loan is one where the shareholder borrows from the corporation whenever money is required and with no fixed schedule for repayment.
2. Failing to charge interest on the loan.
3. Failing to enforce the payment of interest and principal.
4. Making advances in proportion to stockholdings.
5. Making advances to a controlling shareholder.

If the corporation lends money to a shareholder and then, after a period of time, cancels the loan, the amount cancelled is treated as a dividend distribution under Sec. 301.[17] If inadequate interest is charged, interest is imputed and the imputed interest is treated as a dividend paid to the shareholder.

Self-Study Question
Since either compensation or a dividend is taxable to a shareholder-employee, what is the concern over excessive compensation?

Answer
The concern is not at the shareholder-employee level, but rather at the corporation level. Compensation is deductible to the paying corporation, whereas dividend distributions are not deductible.

Excessive Compensation Paid to Shareholder-Employees. Shareholders may receive compensation for services in the form of salary, bonus, or fringe benefits. Such compensation payments are deductible by the distributing corporation as long as they are ordinary and necessary expenses and are reasonable in amount. However, if they are found to be excessive, the excess amounts may be considered to be constructive dividends to the shareholders. In such cases, the payments are not deductible by the corporation but they are still taxable to the shareholder as dividend income. There are no hard and fast rules as to when compensation is excessive. As a result, there has been much controversy and many court cases in this area.

Reasonableness of compensation paid must be determined on a case-by-case basis. Some factors considered important in determining whether compensation is reasonable were cited in *Mayson Manufacturing Co.,* a 1949 Sixth Circuit Court of Appeals case.[18] These factors include the following:

- The employee's qualifications
- The nature, extent, and scope of the employee's work
- The size of the business
- The complexities of the business
- A comparison of the salaries paid with the gross and net income of the corporation
- The prevailing general economic conditions
- Whether the corporation has paid any dividends
- Compensation for comparable positions in comparable concerns
- The salary policy of the corporation to all of its employees
- The amount of compensation paid to the particular employee in previous years
- The amount of compensation voted by the board of directors

Excessive Compensation Paid to Shareholders for the Use of Shareholder Property. Like salary payments, payments to shareholders for the use of property (i.e., rents, interest, and royalties) are deductible by a corporation under Sec. 162(a) if they are ordinary, necessary, and reasonable in amount. To the extent they exceed the amounts that would have been paid to an unrelated party, the excess amount may be recast as a constructive dividend to the shareholder.

[17] Reg. Sec. 1.301-1(m).
[18] *Mayson Manufacturing Co. v. CIR,* 38 AFTR 1028, 49-2 USTC ¶ 9467 (6th Cir., 1949).

Corporate Payments for the Shareholder's Benefit. If a corporation pays a personal obligation of a shareholder, the amount of the payment may be treated as a constructive dividend to the shareholder. Such payments may include payment by the corporation of the shareholder's personal debt obligations, expenses in connection with the shareholder's personal residence, expenses incurred for the improvement of the shareholder's land and property, and debt obligations personally guaranteed by the shareholder.

If a corporate expenditure is disallowed as a deduction by the corporation, it may be a constructive dividend to the shareholder if it provides the shareholder with an economic benefit. Examples of such constructive dividends are unsubstantiated travel and entertainment expenses; club dues; and automobile, airplane, and yacht expenses related to the shareholder-employee's personal use of the property.

Bargain Purchase of Corporate Property. If a shareholder is allowed to purchase corporate property at a price less than the property's FMV, the discount from the FMV may be a constructive dividend to the shareholder.

Shareholder Use of Corporate Property. If a shareholder is allowed to use corporate property (i.e., hunting lodge, yacht, airplane, and so on) without paying adequate compensation to the corporation, the FMV of such use may be a constructive dividend to the shareholder.

STOCK DIVIDENDS AND STOCK RIGHTS

OBJECTIVE 4
Determine the tax consequences of stock dividends and distributions of stock rights

Typical Misconception
Stock dividends generally are nontaxable as long as the shareholders' proportionate interests in the corporation do not increase. If a shareholder's stock interest increases, Sec. 305(b) causes this transaction to be taxable.

In 1919, the Supreme Court ruled in *Eisner v. Macomber* that a stock dividend was not income to the shareholder because it took nothing from the property of the corporation and added nothing to the property of the shareholder.[19] Subsequently, the Revenue Act of 1921 provided that stock dividends are nontaxable. This general rule still applies today. But some exceptions have been enacted to prevent perceived abuses.

Code Sec. 305(a) provides, "Except as otherwise provided in this section, gross income does not include the amount of any distribution of the stock of a corporation made by such a corporation to its shareholders with respect to its stock." Thus, a distribution of additional common stock that is made with respect to a shareholder's common stock is a tax-free stock dividend. However, to circumvent the tax-avoidance schemes fostered by the tax-free stock dividend rule, Sec. 305(b) provides for some exceptions.

As a general rule, whenever a stock dividend changes or has the potential to change the shareholders' proportionate interests in the distributing corporation, the distribution is taxable. Taxable distributions include those where

- The shareholder can elect to receive either stock of the distributing corporation or other property (e.g., money).
- Some shareholders receive property and other shareholders receive an increase in their proportionate interests in the distributing corporation's assets or E&P.
- Some holders of common stock receive preferred stock and others receive additional common stock.
- The distribution is on preferred stock (other than an increase in the conversion

---
[19] *Eisner v. Myrtle H. Macomber*, 3 AFTR 3020, 1 USTC ¶ 32 (USSC, 1919).

ratio of convertible preferred stock that is made solely to take into account a stock dividend or stock split with respect to the stock into which such convertible stock is convertible).

- Convertible preferred stock is distributed unless it can be established that there will not be a disproportionate effect.

The following example illustrates how these exceptions work.

Example 4-17 ▪ Peach Corporation has $100,000 of current E&P. Two shareholders, Al and Beth, each own 100 of the 200 outstanding shares of Peach stock. Al has a high marginal tax rate and does not want any additional income in the current year. Beth has a low marginal tax rate and needs additional cash. Peach Corporation declares a dividend payable in stock or money. Each taxpayer can receive one share of Peach stock (valued at $100) or $100 for each share of Peach stock already owned. Al, who elects to receive stock, receives 100 additional shares of Peach stock. Beth, who elects to receive money, receives $10,000. Beth's distribution is taxable as a dividend. But, absent any exceptions to Sec. 305, Al would have a nontaxable stock dividend because he chose to receive Peach stock. However, Al has received something of value. After the distribution, he owns 200 of the 300 outstanding shares of Peach stock, whereas before the distribution he owned only one-half of the Peach stock. One of the exceptions to the general rule of Sec. 305(a) applies here, so that Al has a taxable stock dividend equal to the value of the additional shares he received. Even if both shareholders were to elect to receive stock, they have a taxable dividend since they had the option to receive cash. ▪

Self-Study Question

What, if any, tax issues exist when a stock dividend is tax free?

Answer

The basis of the stock received must be determined. A portion of the basis of the old stock is allocated to the new stock received in the distribution.

Tax-free Stock Dividends

If a stock dividend is nontaxable, the basis of the stock with respect to which the distribution was made must be allocated between the old and the new stocks in proportion to their relative FMVs on the distribution date.[20] The holding period of the new shares includes the holding period of the old shares.[21]

If the old shares and the new shares are identical, the basis of each share is determined by dividing the basis of the old shares by the total number of shares held by the shareholder after the distribution.

Example 4-18 ▪ Barbara owns 1,000 shares of Axle Corporation common stock with a $66,000 basis, or $66 per share. Barbara receives a nontaxable 10% common stock dividend and now owns 1,100 shares of common stock. The basis for each share of common stock is now $60 ($66,000 ÷ 1,100). ▪

If the old shares and the new shares are not identical, the allocation of the old shares' basis is based on the relative FMVs of the old and the new shares.

Example 4-19 ▪ Mark owns 1,000 shares of Axle Corporation common stock with a $60,000 basis. Mark receives a nontaxable stock dividend payable in preferred stock. At the time of the distribution, the common stock has a $90,000 FMV ($90 × 1,000 shares) and the preferred stock has a $10,000 FMV ($200 × 50 shares). After the distribution Mark owns 50 shares of preferred stock with a basis of $6,000 ([$10,000 ÷ $100,000] × $60,000). Thus, $6,000 of the basis of the common stock is allocated to

---

[20] Sec. 307(a) and Reg. Sec. 1.307-1 and -2.
[21] Sec. 1223(5).

the preferred stock, and the basis of the common stock is reduced from $60,000 to $54,000. ■

Tax-free Stock Rights

A distribution of stock rights is also tax-free under Sec. 305 unless it changes, or has the potential to change, the shareholders' proportionate interests in the distributing corporation. The same exceptions to tax-free treatment for stock dividends enumerated in Sec. 305(b) also apply to distributions of stock rights.

If the value of the stock rights is less than 15% of the value of the stock with respect to which the rights were distributed (i.e., the underlying stock), the basis of the rights is zero unless the shareholder elects to allocate basis to those rights.[22] If the taxpayer plans to sell the rights, it might be desirable to allocate basis to the rights so as to minimize the amount of gain recognized on the sale. The election to allocate basis to the rights must be made in the form of a statement attached to the shareholder's return for the year in which the rights are received.

Example 4-20 ■ Linda owns 100 shares of Yale Corporation common stock with a $27,000 basis and a $50,000 FMV. Linda receives 100 nontaxable stock rights with a $4,000 FMV. Since the FMV of the stock rights is less than 15% of the FMV of the stock (0.15 × $50,000 = $7,500), the basis of the stock rights is zero unless Linda elects to make an allocation. Should Linda elect to allocate the $27,000 basis of the Yale common stock between the stock and the stock rights, the basis of the rights is $2,000 ([$4,000 ÷ $54,000] × $27,000) and the basis of the stock is $25,000 ($27,000 − $2,000). ■

If the value of the stock rights is 15% or more of the value of the underlying stock, the basis of the underlying stock must be allocated between the stock and the stock rights. In such a case, or in the case of a shareholder who elects to allocate basis to the rights, the same allocation procedure must be used as is used to allocate basis when a tax-free stock dividend is received. The holding period for the rights includes the holding period for the underlying stock.[23]

Example 4-21 ■ Kay owns 100 shares of Minor common stock with a $14,000 basis and a $30,000 FMV. Kay receives 100 stock rights with a total FMV of $5,000. Since the FMV of the stock rights is at least 15% of the stock's FMV, the $14,000 basis must be allocated between the stock rights and the stock. The basis of the stock rights is $2,000 ([$5,000 ÷ $35,000] × $14,000) and the basis of the stock is $12,000 ($14,000 − $2,000). ■

Typical Misconception
Taxpayers often get confused about what happens to a stock right. A stock right can (a) be sold or (b) be exercised—which means the actual stock is acquired. If nothing is done, the right will eventually (c) lapse or be terminated.

If the stock rights are sold, gain or loss is measured by subtracting the allocated basis of the rights (if any) from the sale price. If the rights lapse, the allocated basis is added back to the basis of the underlying stock. If the rights are exercised, the basis allocated to the rights is added to the basis of the stock purchased with those rights.[24] The holding period for the stock acquired with the rights begins on the exercise date.[25]

Example 4-22 ■ Jeff receives 10 stock rights in a nontaxable distribution. No basis is allocated to the stock rights. With each stock right Jeff may acquire one share of Jackson stock for $20. If Jeff exercises all 10 stock rights, the new Jackson stock acquired has a

---
[22] Sec. 307(b)(1).
[23] Sec. 1223(5).
[24] Reg. Sec. 1.307-1(b).
[25] Sec. 1223(6).

$200 (10 rights × $20) basis. If instead the 10 rights are sold for $135 each, Jeff has a recognized gain of $1,350 ([$135 × 10 rights] − -0- basis) on the sale. Alternatively, if the rights are permitted to lapse, no loss can be claimed by Jeff. ∎

Effect of Nontaxable Stock Dividends on the Distributing Corporation

Nontaxable distributions of stock and stock rights have no effect on the distributing corporation. The corporation does not recognize any gain or loss on the distribution, nor will any reduction in its E&P occur.[26]

Taxable Stock Dividends and Stock Rights

If a distribution of stock or stock rights is taxable, the amount of the distribution equals the FMV of the stock or stock rights on the distribution date. The distribution is treated the same as any other property distribution. It is a dividend to the extent it is made out of the distributing corporation's E&P. The basis of the stock or stock rights to the recipient shareholder is its FMV.[27] The holding period of the stock or stock rights begins on the day after the distribution date. No adjustment is made to the basis of the underlying stock with respect to which the distribution was made. The distributing corporation does not recognize any gain or loss on the distribution.[28] The distributing corporation reduces its E&P by the FMV of the stock or stock rights on the distribution date.

STOCK REDEMPTIONS

OBJECTIVE 5
Distinguish between a stock redemption treated as a sale and one treated as a dividend

A **stock redemption** is defined as the acquisition by a corporation of its own stock in exchange for property. The property exchanged may be money, securities, or any other property that the corporation wants to use in order to acquire its own stock.[29] The corporation may cancel the acquired stock, retire it, or hold it as treasury stock.

There are many reasons for a stock redemption. Some of these are as follows:

1. A shareholder may want to withdraw from a corporation and sell his stock. In such a case, the shareholder may prefer that the corporation, rather than an outsider, purchase the stock so that the remaining shareholders (who may be family members) retain complete control and ownership of the corporation after his withdrawal.

2. A shareholder may be required to sell the stock back to the corporation by the terms of an agreement that he has entered into with the corporation.

3. A shareholder may want to sell some stock to reduce his ownership in a corporation, but he may be unwilling or unable to sell that stock to outsiders. There may be no market for the shares or there may be restrictions on sales to outsiders.

---

[26] Secs. 311(a) and 312(d).
[27] Reg. Sec. 1.301-1(h)(2)(i).
[28] Sec. 311(a). Gain may have to be recognized when the shareholder has the ability to elect to receive either appreciated property or stock or stock rights of the distributing corporation.
[29] Sec. 317.

4. A shareholder may want to withdraw some assets from a corporation prior to a sale of the business. A potential purchaser of the business may not be (a) interested in acquiring all the assets of the business or (b) able to pay the full value for the stock. A withdrawal of some assets by the seller in exchange for some of his stock allows the purchaser to acquire the remaining stock and business assets for a lower total price.

5. After the death of a major shareholder, a corporation may have an agreement to purchase the decedent's stock from either the estate or a beneficiary so that they will have sufficient funds to pay death taxes and administrative expenses.

6. Management may feel that its stock is selling at a low price and that the best use for the corporation's available cash would be to acquire the corporation's own stock on the open market.

> **Key Point**
> Taxpayers should get into the habit of addressing each of these tax questions as they relate to both the shareholders and the redeeming corporation in order to better understand the tax consequences of a redemption.

Whatever the reason for the redemption, the shareholder must answer the following questions:

- What are the amount and character of the income, gain, or loss recognized as a result of the stock redemption?
- What basis does the shareholder take in any property received in redemption of his stock?
- When does the holding period for the property begin?
- What basis does the shareholder take for any stock of the distributing corporation that he holds after the redemption?

The distributing corporation must answer the following questions:

- What are the amount and character of the gain or loss recognized when nonmoney property is used to redeem its stock?
- What effect does the redemption have on the corporation's E&P?

Effect of the Redemption on the Shareholder

> **Key Point**
> As far as a shareholder is concerned, the basic issue in a stock redemption is whether the redemption is treated as a dividend or a sale.

The general rule when a shareholder sells or exchanges stock in a corporation is that any gain or loss on the transaction is treated as a capital gain or loss. In some cases, a redemption is treated the same as any other sale or exchange of stock. In other cases, the entire amount received by a shareholder in exchange for his stock is treated as a dividend. The reason for this difference is that some redemptions more closely resemble a sale of stock to a third party, whereas others are essentially equivalent to a dividend. The following two examples illustrate the difference between a redemption that is treated as a dividend distribution and a redemption that is treated as a sale or exchange.

Example 4-23 ■ John owns all 100 outstanding shares of Tango Corporation stock. John's basis for his stock is $50,000. Tango has E&P of $100,000. If Tango redeems 25 of John's shares for $25,000, John still owns all of the Tango stock. Since John's ownership of Tango Corporation is not affected by the redemption, the redemption is essentially equivalent to a dividend and John is deemed to have received a $25,000 dividend. ■

Example 4-24 ■ Carol has owned 3 of the 1,000 outstanding shares of Water Corporation's stock for 2 years. Her basis in the stock is $1,000. Water Corporation has E&P of $100,000. If Water redeems all 3 of Carol's shares for $3,000, Carol has a $2,000 ($3,000 − $1,000) capital gain. She is in essentially the same position as though she had sold the stock to a third party. She has received $3,000 for her stock and has no further interest in Water Corporation. This redemption is treated the same as any other sale or exchange. It is not essentially equivalent to a dividend. ∎

Example 4-23 is an extreme case that should clearly be treated as a dividend to the shareholder. Example 4-24 is an extreme case that should clearly be treated as a sale of stock by the shareholder. There are many cases in between where it is not immediately apparent which treatment is correct. The problem for Congress and the courts has been distinguishing those redemptions that should be treated as a sale or exchange from those that should be treated as a dividend. Under current law, a redemption qualifies for sale or exchange treatment if it satisfies *any* of the following conditions:

- The redemption is substantially disproportionate.
- The redemption is a complete termination of the shareholder's interest.
- The redemption is not essentially equivalent to a dividend.
- The redemption is a partial liquidation of the distributing corporation in redemption of a noncorporate shareholder's stock.
- The redemption is made in order to pay death taxes.

If a redemption qualifies as a sale or exchange, the shareholder is treated as though the stock was sold to an outside party. Gain or loss is equal to the FMV of the property received less the shareholder's adjusted basis for the stock surrendered. The gain or loss is capital gain or loss if the stock is a capital asset. The shareholder's basis for any property received is its FMV. The holding period for the property begins on the day following the date of the exchange.

A redemption distribution that does not satisfy any of the five conditions necessary for sale or exchange treatment is treated by the shareholder as a property distribution under Sec. 301. This means that the entire amount of the distribution is a dividend to the extent of the distributing corporation's E&P.[30] The surrender of stock by the shareholder is ignored in determining the amount of the dividend. The basis of the surrendered stock is added to the basis of any remaining shares owned by the shareholder. If all of the shareholder's stock has been redeemed, the basis of the redeemed shares is added to the basis of shares owned by those whose ownership is attributed to the shareholder under the constructive stock ownership rules described below.[31]

Example 4-25 ∎ Amy and Rose each own 50 of the 100 outstanding shares of York stock. York Corporation has $100,000 of E&P. On May 10, York redeems 20 of Amy's shares with property worth $25,000. Amy's adjusted basis for those shares is $20,000. If the redemption distribution satisfies one of the conditions necessary for sale treatment, Amy has $5,000 ($25,000 − $20,000) of capital gain. Her basis for the property received is $25,000, its FMV. Its holding period begins on May 11. If the redemption does not satisfy any of the conditions necessary for sale treatment, the distribution in redemption of the stock follows the same rules as any other property distribution. Amy reports a $25,000 dividend. Her $20,000 basis for the surrendered stock is added to her basis for her remaining 30 shares of York stock. ∎

Although the Tax Reform Act of 1986 eliminated the preferential tax treatment for long-term capital gains, structuring a stock redemption as a sale or exchange still

---

[30] Sec. 302(d).
[31] Reg. Sec. 1.302-2(c).

Self-Study Question

Why does it matter if a redemption is treated as a dividend or a sale?

Answer

One major difference is that the basis of the redeemed stock reduces the gain if the tax treatment is a sale. If the tax treatment is a dividend, no such reduction occurs. Capital gains also can be offset by capital losses from other transactions. Starting in 1991, the maximum tax rate on an individual taxpayer's long-term capital gains is 3 percentage points below the rate applying to ordinary income.

provides an advantage. In a sale or exchange, the basis of the shares redeemed reduces the amount of gain that is recognized. If a redemption is treated as a dividend, the basis of the shares redeemed does not reduce the dividend income that is recognized, but reduces the gain (or increases the loss) recognized on a later sale or exchange of the distributing corporation stock that is held by the shareholder following the redemption. In 1991 and subsequent years, the 28% maximum tax rate imposed on an individual's net capital gain will again provide an additional incentive to structure a redemption to achieve sale or exchange treatment.

Attribution Rules

Three of the five tests used to determine whether a redemption distribution should be treated as a dividend depend on the shareholder's stock ownership before and after the redemption. The purpose of the tests is to determine whether the shareholder's ownership of the corporation has been substantially reduced.

In general, if the shareholder's ownership is substantially reduced, the redemption is treated as a sale. If the ownership interest remains substantially the same or increases, the redemption is treated as a dividend distribution.

In determining stock ownership for this purpose, the constructive ownership or attribution rules of Sec. 318 must be taken into account.[32] These rules provide that a shareholder is considered to own not only the shares he owns directly, but also shares owned by his spouse, other family members, and related entities. Furthermore, entities such as corporations, partnerships, trusts, and estates are considered to own shares that are owned by their shareholders, partners, or beneficiaries.

Stock once attributed to a person is not further reattributed from that person to another person under the same rules. Thus, stock attributed to one family member cannot be reattributed from that family member to a second family member.[33] However, stock once attributed to a person under an attribution rule may be reattributed from that person to another person under a different attribution rule. For example, stock attributed by the corporate attribution rule from a corporation to its shareholder (H) may be reattributed from the shareholder (H) to the shareholder's spouse (W) under the family attribution rules.

Additional Comment

The concept of stock attribution can come up in many different contexts. In the corporate area, Sec. 318 is often the provision that is used when attribution rules are needed.

Key Point

The attribution rules are designed to treat a taxpayer as owning not only that stock which is directly owned, but also all the stock owned by other related parties.

The basic purpose of the attribution rules is to prevent shareholders from either taking advantage of favorable tax rules or avoiding unfavorable rules by having family members or related entities own stock that the shareholder is not permitted to own. All stock ownership tests would be subject to potential abuse if only direct ownership of stock were considered.

Four types of attribution rules are prescribed by Sec. 318(a): family attribution, attribution from entities, attribution to entities, and option attribution. These rules are discussed below.

Family Attribution. An individual is considered to own all stock owned by or for a spouse, children, grandchildren, and parents.[34] The individual is not considered to own stock owned by brothers, sisters, or grandparents.

Example 4-26 ■ Harry; his wife, Wilma; their son, Steve; and Harry's father, Frank, each own 25 of the 100 outstanding shares of Strong Corporation stock. Harry is considered to own all 100 Strong shares (25 directly plus the shares owned by Wilma, Steve, and Frank). Wilma is considered to own 75 shares (25 directly plus the shares owned by

---

[32] Sec. 302(c).
[33] Sec. 318(a)(5)(B).
[34] Sec. 318(a)(1).

> **Additional Comment**
> The family attribution rules of Sec. 318 are not as inclusive as the family attribution rules of Sec. 267 (covered in Chap. 3).

Harry and Steve). The shares owned by Frank that are attributed to Harry are not reattributed to Wilma. Steve is considered to own 75 shares (25 directly plus the shares by Harry and Wilma). Steve is not considered to own the shares owned by his grandfather (Frank), nor are the shares owned by Frank attributed to Harry and then reattributed to Steve. Frank is considered to own 75 shares (25 directly plus the shares owned by Harry and Steve (his grandson)). The shares owned by Wilma and that are attributed to Harry are not reattributed to Frank. ∎

Attribution from Entities. Stock owned by or for a partnership is considered to be owned proportionately by the partners, and stock owned by or for an estate is considered to be owned proportionately by the beneficiaries. Stock owned by or for a trust is considered to be owned by the beneficiaries in proportion to their actuarial interests. Stock owned by or for a corporation is considered to be owned proportionately by any shareholders owning (directly or indirectly) 50% or more in value of the stock.[35]

▪ **Example 4-27** ▪

> **Key Point**
> Stock is attributed from a shareholder to a corporation or from a corporation to a shareholder only if the shareholder owns at least 50% (directly or indirectly) of the corporation.

Bill, an individual, has a 50% interest in a partnership. The partnership owns 40 of the 100 outstanding shares of Yellow Corporation stock, the remaining 60 shares being owned by Bill. Bill is considered to own 80 shares, 60 directly and 20 (0.50 × 40 shares) indirectly. Reattribution is also possible in this situation since the stock attributed to Bill under the partnership attribution rules may be reattributed to Bill's spouse under the family attribution rules. ∎

Attribution to Partnerships, Estates, Trusts, and Corporations. All stock owned by or for a partner in a partnership is considered to be owned by the partnership. All stock owned by or for a beneficiary of an estate or a trust is considered to be owned by the estate or trust. All stock owned by or for a shareholder who owns (directly or indirectly) 50% or more in value of a corporation's stock is considered to be owned by the corporation.[36]

▪ **Example 4-28** ▪

Assume the same facts as in Example 4-27. The partnership in which Bill is a partner is considered to own all 100 shares of Yellow stock (40 directly and 60 owned by Bill). No reattribution of the stock that is owned by Bill and that is attributed to the partnership can occur from the partnership to another of Yellow's partners. ∎

Option Attribution. A person who has an option to purchase stock is considered to own the stock.[37]

▪ **Example 4-29** ▪

John owns 25 of the 100 outstanding shares of Yard Corporation stock. He has an option to acquire an additional 50 shares. John is considered to own 75 Yard shares (25 directly plus the 50 shares he has an option to buy). ∎

Substantially Disproportionate Redemptions

If a stock redemption qualifies as substantially disproportionate under Sec. 302(b)(2), the redemption qualifies as a sale. This Code provision, then, provides a safe haven for capital gain treatment rather than dividend treatment. A redemption is "substantially disproportionate" with respect to a shareholder if all of the following hold true:

---

[35] Sec. 318(a)(2).
[36] Sec. 318(a)(3).
[37] Sec. 318(a)(4).

Key Point
The mechanical (substantially disproportionate) test was added to the more subjective "not equivalent to a dividend" test in order to give taxpayers a "safe harbor" provision that can be used for tax planning purposes.

- After the redemption, the shareholder owns less than 50% of the total combined voting power of all classes of voting stock
- After the redemption, the shareholder owns less than 80% of his percentage ownership of voting stock before the redemption
- After the redemption the shareholder owns less than 80% of his percentage ownership of common stock (voting or nonvoting) before the redemption

These tests are applied mechanically to each shareholder individually. A redemption may be substantially disproportionate with respect to one shareholder but not disproportionate with respect to another. If only one class of stock is outstanding, requirements 2 and 3 are the same.

Example 4-30 ■ Long Corporation has 400 shares of common stock outstanding of which individuals Ann, Bob, Carl, and Dana (all unrelated) each own 100 shares. Long redeems 55 shares from Ann, 25 shares from Bob, and 20 shares from Carl.

	Before Redemption			After Redemption	
Shareholder	No. of Shares Owned	Percentage of Ownership	Shares Redeemed	No. of Shares Owned	Percentage of Ownership
	(1)		(2)	(1) − (2)	
Ann	100	25%	55	45	15.00%
Bob	100	25%	25	75	25.00
Carl	100	25%	20	80	26.67
Dana	100	25%	—	100	33.33
Total	400	100%	100	300	100.00%

Typical Misconception
The substantially disproportionate rules must be applied separately to each shareholder. In Example 4-30, Ann treats the redemption as a sale, whereas both Bob and Carl treat the redemption as a distribution that is generally taxed as a dividend.

The redemption is substantially disproportionate with respect to Ann because after the redemption, she owns less than 50% of Long's stock, and her stock ownership percentage (15%) is less than 80% of her stock ownership percentage before the redemption (0.80 × 25% = 20%). The redemption is not substantially disproportionate with respect to Bob, because he does not have the necessary reduction in his stock ownership percentage. Bob owns the same percentage of stock (25%) after the redemption as he did before the redemption (25%). The redemption is not substantially disproportionate for Carl either, since his stock ownership percentage increases from 25% to 26.67%. ■

The constructive ownership rules of Sec. 318(a) must be applied in determining whether the shareholder has met the three requirements for a substantially disproportionate redemption.[38]

Example 4-31 ■ Assume the same facts as in Example 4-30, except that Ann and Bob are mother and son. In this case, the redemption is not substantially disproportionate for either Ann or Bob. Ann and Bob are each considered to own 200 shares, or 50%, of the Long stock before the redemption, and each is considered to own 120 shares, or 40%, after the redemption. Although the 50% test is met, neither Ann nor Bob satisfies the requirement that after the redemption the shareholder must own *less* than 80% of the percentage of stock owned before the redemption. After the redemption each owns *exactly* 80% of the percentage owned before the redemption (0.80 × 50% = 40%). ■

---

[38] Reg. Sec. 1.302-3(a).

Several individual redemption transactions, with each qualifying as an exchange transaction, may be deemed to be a series of related redemptions so as to become a single transaction and thereby denying exchange treatment to certain of the individual parts.

Complete Termination of the Shareholder's Interest

If a stock redemption qualifies as a complete termination of the shareholder's interest in the corporation under Sec. 302(b)(3), the redemption qualifies as a sale. This rule does not appear to offer any additional route to sale treatment for the shareholder. If a corporation redeems all of a shareholder's stock, the requirements for a substantially disproportionate redemption under Sec. 302(b)(2) would seem to have been satisfied. However, the complete termination rule does extend sale treatment to certain redemptions not covered by the substantially disproportionate redemption rules of Sec. 302(b)(2).

These transactions include:

1. If a shareholder's interest in a corporation consists of nonvoting stock, a redemption of all of the stock qualifies for sale treatment under Sec. 302(b)(3).
2. If a shareholder owns some voting stock and his entire interest in the corporation is completely terminated by a redemption, the family attribution rules of Sec. 318(a)(1) may be waived and the redemption can qualify for sale treatment even if other family members continue to own some or all of the corporation's stock.[39]

To have the family attribution rules waived, all of the following requirements must be met:[40]

- The shareholder must not retain any interest in the corporation after the redemption except as a creditor. This includes any interest as an officer, director, or employee.
- The shareholder must not acquire any such interest (other than by bequest or inheritance) for at least 10 years from the date of the redemption.
- The shareholder must file a written agreement with the IRS that the Service will be notified if any prohibited interest is acquired.

Example 4-32 ■ Father and Son each own 50 of the 100 outstanding shares of Short Corporation stock. Short Corporation redeems all of Father's shares. Under the family attribution rules, Father is considered to own 100% of the Short stock both before and after the redemption. Thus, the redemption is not substantially disproportionate. However, if Father files the necessary agreement not to retain or acquire any interest in Short Corporation for 10 years (except as a creditor or an interest acquired by bequest or inheritance), the family attribution rules are waived and the redemption is treated as a stock sale. It qualifies as a complete termination of Father's interest in Short Corporation. ■

Waiver of the family attribution rules is not permitted in two situations involving related parties. These are when:

1. Part or all of the stock redeemed was acquired, directly or indirectly, within the

[39] Sec. 302(c)(2).
[40] Sec. 302(c)(2)(A).

10-year period ending on the date of the distribution by the distributee from a person whose stock ownership would be attributable (at the time of the distribution) to the distributee under Sec. 318.
2. Any person owns (at the time of the distribution) stock of the redeeming corporation the ownership of which is attributable to the distributee under Sec. 318 and such person acquired any stock in the redeeming corporation, directly or indirectly, from the distributee within the 10-year period ending on the distribution date.

The first situation prevents an individual from transferring stock to a related party (e.g., family member or controlled entity) and then having the related party use the complete termination exception to recognize a capital gain when the stock that was transferred is redeemed. The second situation prevents an individual from transferring a portion of their stock to a related party and then using the complete termination exception to recognize a capital gain when their remaining stock is redeemed. These prohibitions against waiving the family attribution rules do not apply if the transfer took place more than 10 years preceding the redemption or the distributee can show that the acquisition or disposition of the stock of the redeeming corporation did not have as one of its purposes the avoidance of federal income taxes. The family attribution rules can also be waived in the second situation above if the stock acquired by the related party from the distributee is redeemed in the same transaction.

Note that only the family attribution rules can be waived. However, entities are permitted to have the family attribution rules waived if both the entity and the individual whose stock is attributed to the entity agree not to have any prohibited interest in the corporation for at least 10 years.[41]

Example 4-33 ■ The A Trust, which was created by Andrew, owns 30% of the stock of Wide Corporation. Andrew's wife, Wanda, is the sole beneficiary of the trust. The remaining 70% of the Wide stock is owned by their son Steve. Wide Corporation redeems all of its stock owned by the A Trust. The redemption is not treated as a sale because the trust is deemed to own all of the stock owned by its beneficiary (Wanda) and Wanda is deemed to own all of the stock owned by her son (Steve). However, if A Trust and Wanda both agree not to have any interest in the corporation for 10 years, the family attribution rules can be waived, the redemption will be treated as a complete termination of the trust's interest in Wide Corporation and eligible for sale treatment. ■

Key Point
Sec. 302(b)(1) has generally been interpreted to require that a shareholder incur a "meaningful reduction" of its stock interest. What constitutes a "meaningful reduction" is the subject of controversy.

Redemptions Not Essentially Equivalent to a Dividend

Code Sec. 302(b)(1) provides that a redemption of stock is treated as a sale if the redemption is not essentially equivalent to a dividend. There is no mechanical test to determine when a redemption is not essentially equivalent to a dividend. The question depends upon the facts and circumstances of each case.[42] Therefore, Sec. 302(b)(1) does not provide the safe haven provided by the rules for substantially disproportionate redemptions or redemptions that are a complete termination of a shareholder's interest. This exception was added to the Code in 1954 to prevent the rules on redemptions from being too restrictive, especially in the case of redemptions of preferred stock.

---

[41] Sec. 302(c)(2)(C).
[42] Reg. Sec. 1.302-2(b).

The Supreme Court's decision in *Maclin P. Davis* helped to define some of the criteria to be used in determining when a redemption is not essentially equivalent to a dividend.[43] The Supreme Court held that (1) a business purpose is irrelevant in determining whether a redemption is essentially equivalent to a dividend, (2) the Sec. 318 attribution rules must be used to determine dividend equivalency, and (3) a redemption of part of a sole shareholder's stock is always essentially equivalent to a dividend. The court said that there had to be a "meaningful reduction" in the shareholder's proportionate interest in the corporation after taking into account the constructive ownership rules of Sec. 318(a) in order for Sec. 302(b)(1) to apply. However, the definition of "a meaningful reduction in interest" is still not clear today.

Because of the uncertainty involved in determining when Sec. 302(b)(1) applies, it generally is applied only to (1) a redemption of nonvoting preferred stock when the shareholder does not own any common stock[44] or (2) redemptions resulting in a substantial reduction in the shareholder's right to vote and exercise control over the corporation, right to participate in earnings, and right to share in net assets on liquidation. Generally, the IRS allows sale treatment if a controlling shareholder reduces his interest to a noncontrolling position[45] or a noncontrolling shareholder reduces his minority interest.[46] A shareholder does not qualify for sale treatment if he has control both before and after the redemption,[47] or if he assumes a controlling position.

Example 4-34 ■ All of Thyme Corporation's single class of stock is owned by four unrelated individuals in the following manner: Alan, 27%; Betty, 24.33%; Clem, 24.33%, and David, 24.33%. Some of Alan's stock holdings are redeemed by Thyme resulting in Alan's interest being reduced to 22.27%. Betty, Clem, and David own equally the remaining 77.73% of the Thyme stock. The redemption of Alan's stock does not qualify as substantially disproportionate since Alan's stock interest is not reduced below 21.6% (0.80 × 27% = 21.6%). Nor will the redemption qualify as a complete termination of Alan's interest. The IRS has indicated in Rev. Rul. 76-364 that the redemption of Alan's stock will be treated as a sale transaction under Sec. 302(b)(1) since the transaction results in a meaningful reduction of Alan's noncontrolling interest in Thyme Corporation. ■

Self-Study Question
When does a partial liquidation qualify for sale treatment?

Answer
A partial liquidation qualifies for sale treatment if the distribution is (a) to a noncorporate shareholder, (b) not essentially equivalent to a dividend, and (c) made during the tax year (or the succeeding tax year) in which the plan of partial liquidation is adopted.

Partial Liquidations

Under Sec. 302(b)(4), a redemption is treated as a sale if the distribution qualifies as a partial liquidation and is made to a noncorporate shareholder. A **partial liquidation** occurs when a corporation discontinues one line of business, distributes the assets related to that business to its shareholders, and continues in at least one other line of business. A distribution also qualifies as a partial liquidation if the distribution is (1) not essentially equivalent to a dividend and (2) made within the tax year in which a plan of partial liquidation has been adopted or within the succeeding tax year.

Determination Made at the Corporate Level. For purposes of the partial liquidation definition, whether a distribution is not essentially equivalent to a

---

[43] *U.S. v. Maclin P. Davis*, 25 AFTR 2d 70-827, 70-1 USTC ¶ 9289 (USSC, 1970).
[44] Reg. Sec. 1.302-2(a).
[45] A reduction in stock ownership from 57% to 50% where the shareholder no longer had control was considered a meaningful reduction in interest in Rev. Rul. 75-502 (1975-2 C.B. 111).
[46] A reduction in stock ownership from 27% to 22% was considered a meaningful reduction in interest in Rev. Rul. 76-364 (1976-2 C.B. 91).
[47] See *Jack Paparo* (71 T.C. 692 [1979]), where a reduction in stock ownership from 100% to 81.17% and from 100% to 74.15% were not considered meaningful reductions in interest.

dividend is determined at the corporate level.[48] The distribution must be the result of a bona fide contraction of the corporate business. Guidance as to what constitutes a genuine corporate contraction comes from relevant regulations and revenue rulings. Some examples of genuine corporate contractions include

- The distribution of insurance proceeds obtained as a result of a fire that destroys part of a business.[49]
- Termination of a contract representing 95% of the gross income of a domestic corporation.[50]
- Change in a corporation's business from a full-line department store to a discount apparel store resulting in the elimination of certain departments and most forms of credit and a reduction in inventory, floor space, employees, and so on.[51]

Safe Harbor Rule. Under Sec. 302(e)(2), a distribution satisfies the not essentially equivalent to a dividend requirement and qualifies as a partial liquidation if:

1. the distribution (a) is attributable to the distributing corporation's ceasing to conduct a qualified trade or business, or (b) consists of the assets of a qualified trade or business; and
2. immediately after the distribution, the distributing corporation is engaged in the active conduct of at least one qualified trade or business.

A qualified trade or business is any trade or business that:

1. has been actively conducted throughout the 5-year period ending on the date of the redemption; and
2. was not acquired by the corporation within such 5-year period in a partially or wholly taxable transaction.

The definition of a trade or business is the same as used for Sec. 355 (corporate division) purposes and which is described on page 4-39.

Example 4-35 ■ Sage Corporation has been engaged in the manufacture of hats and gloves for the past 5 years. In 1991, Sage discontinues the manufacture of hats, sells all of its hat-making machinery, and distributes the proceeds to its shareholders in redemption of part of their stock. The corporation continues to manufacture gloves. The distribution constitutes a partial liquidation of Sage. ■

A partial liquidation does not have to be pro rata.

Typical Misconception
Sale treatment is not always preferable to dividend treatment. A corporate shareholder would generally prefer dividend treatment due to the availability of the dividends-received deduction.

Effect of a Partial Liquidation on the Shareholders. If a distribution qualifies as a partial liquidation, a noncorporate shareholder treats the redemption of his stock as a sale. However, a corporate shareholder treats the redemption distribution as a dividend unless the shareholder qualifies under one of the other tests for sale treatment (i.e., Secs. 302(b)(1)-(3) or 303). In determining whether stock is held by a corporate or noncorporate shareholder, stock held by a partnership, trust, or estate is considered to be held proportionately by its partners or beneficiaries. Dividend treatment may be more advantageous than sale treatment for a corporate shareholder

---

[48] Sec. 302(c)(1)(A).
[49] Reg. Sec. 1.346-1.
[50] Rev. Rul. 75-3, 1975-1 C.B. 108.
[51] Rev. Rul. 74-296, 1974-1 C.B. 80.

because a corporation is eligible for a 70%, 80% or 100% dividends-received deduction.

Example 4-36 ▪ Assume the same facts as in Example 4-35, except that Sage Corporation is owned by Ted and by Jolly Corporation, each of whom owns 50 shares of Sage stock. Each shareholder has a $10,000 basis in his stock. Sage has $100,000 of current and accumulated E&P. Sage distributes $18,000 to each of the shareholders in redemption of 10 shares of Sage stock worth $18,000. Since the redemption qualifies as a partial liquidation, Ted treats the transaction as a sale. He has a $16,000 ($18,000 − $2,000) capital gain. Jolly Corporation cannot treat the transaction as a sale. Therefore, Jolly must report $18,000 of dividend income. Jolly is eligible for a $14,400 (0.80 × $18,000) dividends-received deduction. Jolly's $2,000 basis in the redeemed stock is added to its basis in its remaining stock. Therefore, Jolly has a $10,000 basis in its 40 remaining Sage shares. ▪

Redemptions to Pay Death Taxes

Key Point
Sec. 303 is meant as a relief provision to lessen the tax impact of the death of a shareholder of a closely held corporation. Without this provision, an estate could find it very costly to redeem enough stock to pay the estate taxes.

If corporate stock represents a substantial portion of a decedent's gross estate, a redemption of the stock from the estate or its beneficiaries may be eligible for sale treatment under Sec. 303. This Code section is intended to help those shareholders who inherit stock in a closely held corporation and who are required to sell some of their stock in order to pay estate taxes, inheritance taxes, and funeral and other administrative expenses. If the stock is not readily marketable, a stock redemption may be the only way to provide the estate and beneficiaries with sufficient liquidity to meet their cash needs. In most cases, the Sec. 318 attribution rules would prevent such a redemption from qualifying as substantially disproportionate or as a complete termination of the shareholder's interest. The redemption would then be treated as a dividend were it not for the special provisions of Sec. 303. However, the Sec. 318 attribution rules do not apply to the portion of a stock redemption that qualifies under Sec. 303.

Section 303 provides that a redemption of stock that was included in a decedent's gross estate is treated as a sale of stock by the shareholder (either the estate or the beneficiary of the estate) if the following conditions are met:

1. The value of the redeeming corporation's stock is more than 35% of the adjusted gross estate. The adjusted gross estate is the total gross estate (i.e., the FMV of all property owned by the decedent on the date of death) less allowable deductions for funeral and administrative expenses, claims against the estate, debts, and casualty and other losses.[52]

Example 4-37 ▪ The gross estate of a decedent is valued at $2,900,000. It includes Pepper Corporation stock worth $1,200,000 and $1,700,000 in cash. Funeral expenses, debts, and other administrative expenses allowable as estate tax deductions amount to $900,000, so that the decedent's adjusted gross estate is $2,000,000 ($2,900,000 − $900,000). Since the value of the Pepper stock included in the gross estate is more than 35% of the adjusted gross estate ($1,200,000 is more than $700,000 [0.35 × $2,000,000]), a redemption of some of Pepper's stock can qualify as a stock sale under Sec. 303. ▪

2. The maximum amount of the redemption distribution that can qualify for sale treatment under Sec. 303 is the sum of all federal and state estate and inheritance

---

[52] Sec. 303(b)(2)(A).

taxes, plus any interest due on those taxes, and all funeral and administrative expenses that are allowable as deductions on the federal estate tax return. The redemption must be of stock held by the estate or by heirs who are liable for the estate taxes and other administrative expenses.

3. Section 303 applies to a redemption distribution only to the extent that the recipient shareholder's interest in the estate is reduced by the payment of taxes and other expenses. The maximum distribution to any shareholder that is eligible for sale treatment under Sec. 303 is the amount of estate taxes and expenses that the shareholder is obligated to bear.[53]

Example 4-38 ■ Assume the same facts as in Example 4-37, except that all of the stock is bequeathed to the decedent's son, Sam. The remainder of the estate is bequeathed to decedent's wife, Wilma, and she is liable for all taxes and expenses. In such case, Sec. 303 could not be used by Sam. He is not liable for any of the estate taxes or administrative expenses. If instead $800,000 is bequeathed to Wilma and the remainder of the estate to Sam, Sam would be liable for all estate taxes and administrative expenses. He could use Sec. 303 to receive sale treatment on a redemption of enough of his stock to pay the estate taxes and administrative expenses. ■

4. Section 303 applies only to distributions made within certain time limits.[54]

  a. In general, the redemption must take place within 90 days after the expiration of the period for the assessment of the federal estate tax. Since the statute of limitations for the federal estate tax expires 3 years after the estate tax return is due and the return is due 9 months after the date of death, the redemption generally must take place within 4 years after the date of death.

  b. If a petition for redetermination of an estate tax deficiency is filed with the Tax Court, the distribution period is extended to 60 days after the Tax Court's decision becomes final.

  c. If the taxpayer made a valid election under Sec. 6166 to defer payment of federal estate taxes under an installment plan, the distribution period is extended to the time the installment payments are due.

5. The stock of two or more corporations may be aggregated in order to satisfy the 35% requirement, provided that 20% or more of the value of each corporation's outstanding stock is included in the gross estate.[55]

Example 4-39 ■ The gross estate of a decedent is valued at $2,900,000. It includes 80% of the stock of Curry Corporation valued at $400,000 and 90% of the stock of Brodie Corporation valued at $450,000. Allowable estate tax deductions for administrative expenses and debts amount to $900,000, so that the decedent's adjusted gross estate is $2,000,000. Although neither the Curry stock nor the Brodie stock has a value greater than 35% of the $2,000,000 adjusted gross estate, the value of the stock of both corporations taken together is greater than 35% of the adjusted gross estate ($850,000 [$400,000 + $450,000] is greater than $700,000 [0.35 × $2,000,000]). Therefore, a redemption of sufficient Curry stock and/or Brodie stock to pay estate taxes and administrative expenses is eligible for sale treatment under Sec. 303. ■

---

[53] Sec. 303(b)(3).
[54] Sec. 303(b)(1).
[55] Sec. 303(b)(2)(B).

Stock Redemptions • 4-29

Typical Misconception

Sec. 303 is quite flexible in that the favorable sale or exchange treatment is allowed even though the redemption proceeds are not used to pay the estate taxes.

Although the basic purpose of Sec. 303 is to provide liquidity for the payment of estate taxes when a major portion of the estate consists of stock in a closely held corporation, a redemption can qualify under Sec. 303 even when the estate has sufficient liquid assets to pay estate taxes and other expenses. The redemption proceeds do not have to be used for this purpose.

The advantage of qualifying a redemption under Sec. 303 is that, generally, the redeeming shareholder has little or no capital gain to report. This is because his basis in the redeemed stock is the stock's FMV on the date of death of the decedent from whom the stock was inherited (or an alternate valuation date, if applicable). On the other hand, if the redemption does *not* qualify as a sale, the redeeming shareholder may have dividend income equal to the entire distribution from the redeeming corporation.

Example 4-40 ■

Self-Study Question

How much gain is the redeeming shareholder likely to recognize in a qualifying Sec. 303 redemption?

Answer

Probably none. The basis in the redeemed stock equals its FMV at the date of the death of the decedent (or an alternate valuation date).

Chili Corporation redeems 100 shares of its stock for $105,000 from Art, who inherited the stock from his father, Fred. The stock's FMV on Fred's date of death was $100,000. Chili Corporation has an E&P balance of $500,000. If the redemption qualifies as a sale under Sec. 303, Art recognizes a $5,000 capital gain ($105,000 − $100,000). However, if the redemption does not qualify as a sale under Sec. 303 or one of the other sale treatment exceptions, Art has $105,000 of dividend income. ■

Thus, Sec. 303 can make a large difference in the amount of income a redeeming shareholder must report as well as the character of that income.

Effect of Redemptions on the Distributing Corporation

As in the case of property distributions that are not in redemption of a shareholder's stock, two questions must be answered with respect to a corporation that distributes property in redemption of its stock:

- What are the amount and character of the gain or loss recognized by the distributing corporation on the distribution?
- What effect does the distribution have on the corporation's E&P?

Each of these questions is addressed below.

Key Point

Consistent with the rules in the distribution area, using appreciated property in a stock redemption will create income and a corresponding increase in the E&P of the redeeming corporation.

Corporate Gain or Loss on Property Distributions. The rules for the recognition of gain or loss by a corporation that distributes property in redemption of its stock are the same as the rules for property distributions that are not in redemption of the corporation's stock. Under Sec. 311,

1. The corporation recognizes gain when it distributes appreciated property in redemption of its stock. The character of the gain depends on the character of the distributed property in the corporation's hands.
2. The corporation does not recognize any loss when it distributes property that has declined in value.

Effect of Redemptions on E&P. A stock redemption affects a corporation's E&P accounts in two ways. First, if appreciated property is distributed, the gain is included in the corporation's gross income and increases the corporation's E&P account. Next, the corporation's E&P balance must be reduced because of the distribution. The amount of the reduction depends on whether the redemption distribution is treated as a sale or as a dividend distribution by the shareholder whose stock is redeemed.

If the redemption does not qualify for sale treatment, the corporation must reduce its E&P by the amount of money, the principal amount of any obligations, and the greater of the adjusted basis or FMV of any other property distributed, the same as it does for a property distribution that is not a redemption distribution.

If the redemption qualifies for sale treatment under Secs. 302(a) or 303, E&P is reduced by only a portion of the distribution. E&P is reduced by the portion of the E&P that is attributable to the redeemed stock. In other words, E&P is reduced by a percentage that is equal to the percentage of the stock that was redeemed. The remainder of the distribution reduces the capital account.[56]

Example 4-41 ■ Teddy Corporation has 100 shares of stock outstanding, 30 of which are owned by Mona. All 30 shares are redeemed by Teddy for $30,000 in a redemption qualifying as a sale under Sec. 302(b)(3). At the time of the redemption, Teddy has $60,000 in paid-in capital and $40,000 of E&P. Since 30% of the outstanding stock was redeemed, the distribution reduces Teddy's E&P by $12,000 (0.30 × $40,000). The remaining $18,000 ($30,000 − $12,000) of the distribution reduces the paid-in capital amount to $42,000 ($60,000 − $18,000). ■

PREFERRED STOCK BAILOUTS

OBJECTIVE 6
Explain the tax treatment for preferred stock bailouts

The rules with respect to stock redemptions were added to the Code to permit sale treatment for stock redemptions under certain specific circumstances and to require dividend treatment in all other situations. Taxpayers, however, devised methods to circumvent Congress's intentions.

One such method, devised by taxpayers prior to the enactment of the Internal Revenue Code of 1954, is known as the **preferred stock bailout**. In general, the preferred stock bailout scenario operated as follows:

Additional Comment
When the term "bailout" is used in the corporate context, this generally refers to some scheme that allows a corporation to make a dividend distribution, but for tax purposes the transaction is treated as a sale of a capital asset.

1. A tax-free stock dividend of nonvoting preferred stock was issued with respect to a corporation's common stock. Under the rules for nontaxable stock dividends, a portion of the common stock's basis is allocated to the preferred stock. Its holding period includes the holding period for the common stock.

2. The preferred stock was sold to an unrelated third party at its FMV. The sale resulted in a capital gain equal to the difference between the preferred stock's sale price and its allocated basis.

3. The corporation redeemed the preferred stock from the third-party purchaser (at a small premium to reward the third party for his cooperation in the scheme).

The result was that the shareholder was able to receive the corporation's earnings as a long-term capital gain without changing his equity position in the company.

In order to prevent this tax-avoidance possibility, Congress enacted Sec. 306. Section 306 operates by "tainting" certain stock (usually preferred stock) when it is distributed. The tainted stock is not taxed at the time of its distribution, but a subsequent sale or other disposition of the stock generally results in the recognition of ordinary or dividend income rather than capital gain.

---
[56] Sec. 312(n)(7).

Section 306 is less important today than it was when capital gains received more preferential treatment. But it still prevents taxpayers from using a preferred stock bailout to recover part or all of their stock basis tax-free and/or creating capital gains that can be offset by capital losses from other sources.

Sec. 306 Stock Defined

Section 306 stock is defined by Sec. 306(c) as follows:

1. Stock (other than common stock issued with respect to common stock) which is received as a nontaxable stock dividend.
2. Stock (other than common stock) received in a tax-free corporate reorganization or corporate division if the effect of the transaction was substantially the same as the receipt of a stock dividend, or if the stock was received in exchange for Sec. 306 stock.
3. Stock which has a basis determined by reference to the basis of Sec. 306 stock (i.e., a substituted or transferred basis).
4. Stock (other than common stock) acquired in an exchange to which Sec. 351 applies if the receipt of money (in lieu of the stock) would have been treated as a dividend.

Note that preferred stock issued by a corporation having no current or accumulated E&P in the year the stock is issued cannot be Sec. 306 stock.[57] Also, stock that is inherited is not Sec. 306 stock, because the basis of such stock is its FMV on the date of death (or alternate valuation date) and, therefore, is not determined by reference to the basis that the stock had in the hands of the decedent.[58]

Typical Misconception

Even though the amount of ordinary income recognized in a sale of Sec. 306 stock is measured by the E&P existing in the year the Sec. 306 stock was distributed, the E&P of the distributing corporation is not reduced by the amount of Sec. 306 ordinary income.

Dispositions of Sec. 306 Stock

If a shareholder sells or otherwise disposes of Sec. 306 stock (except in a redemption), the amount realized is treated as ordinary income to the extent that the shareholder would have had a dividend at the time of the distribution if money in an amount equal to the FMV of the stock was distributed instead of the stock itself.[59] The shareholder's ordinary income is measured by reference to the corporation's E&P in the year the Sec. 306 stock was distributed. Any additional amount received for the Sec. 306 stock generally constitutes a return of capital. If the amount received exceeds the shareholder's basis in the Sec. 306 stock, the excess is a capital gain. If the amount received is less than the shareholder's basis, the unrecovered basis is added back to the shareholder's basis in his common stock. It is not recognized as a loss.

Example 4-42 ■ Carlos owns all 100 outstanding shares of Adobe Corporation's stock. His basis in those shares is $100,000. Adobe Corporation, which has $150,000 of E&P, distributes 50 shares of nonvoting preferred stock to Carlos as a nontaxable stock dividend. The preferred stock has a $50,000 FMV on the distribution date, while the common stock has a $200,000 FMV. Carlos must allocate $20,000 of his basis {($50,000 ÷ [$200,000 + $50,000]) × $100,000} in the common stock to the preferred stock. Carlos sells the preferred stock to Dillon for $50,000. The $50,000 realized when the stock is sold is all ordinary income because Adobe Corporation's E&P in the year the preferred stock dividend was issued exceeds the FMV of the preferred stock. Carlos's $20,000 basis in the preferred stock is added back to his

---

[57] Sec. 306(c)(2).
[58] Reg. Sec. 1.306-3(e).
[59] Sec. 306(a)(1).

basis in his common stock so that his basis in his common stock is restored to $100,000. If instead Carlos sells the preferred stock for $100,000, he has $50,000 of ordinary income, the lesser of Adobe Corporation's E&P in the year the preferred stock dividend was issued or the stock's FMV on the distribution date. The next $20,000 is treated as a return of capital. Carlos also has a $30,000 capital gain, the amount by which the $100,000 proceeds exceeds the sum of the $50,000 dividend income and his $20,000 basis in the preferred stock. ∎

Redemptions of Sec. 306 Stock

Key Point

The amount realized in a redemption of Sec. 306 stock is a dividend to the extent of E&P existing in the year of redemption. Unlike a sale of Sec. 306 stock, E&P is reduced as a result of a redemption.

If Sec. 306 stock is redeemed by the issuing corporation, the total amount realized by the shareholder is a distribution to which the Sec. 301 dividend distribution rules apply.[60] It is, therefore, a dividend to the extent of the redeeming corporation's E&P *in the year of the redemption*. Amounts received in excess of the corporation's E&P are treated as a recovery of the shareholder's basis in his Sec. 306 stock, and then as a capital gain once the basis has been recovered. If the shareholder's basis in the redeemed stock is not recovered, the unrecovered basis is added to the basis of the common stock owned by the shareholder.

Example 4-43 ∎ Don owns all 100 shares of Brigham Corporation's common stock and has a $300,000 adjusted basis in the stock. On January 1, 1990, Brigham issues 50 shares of preferred stock to Don. The preferred stock and common stock have $100,000 and $400,000 FMVs, respectively, on the distribution date. Brigham's current and accumulated E&P for 1990 is $200,000. Don's allocated basis in the preferred stock is $60,000 [($100,000 ÷ [$100,000 + $400,000]) × $300,000]. The basis of Don's common stock is reduced to $240,000 ($300,000 − $60,000) as a result of the basis allocation. On January 2, 1991, Brigham redeems the preferred shares for $250,000. In the year of the redemption, Brigham's E&P is $400,000. Don has dividend income of $250,000 (because Brigham's E&P is at least $250,000 in the year of the redemption). If Brigham's E&P is instead $200,000 in the year of the redemption, Don has $200,000 of dividend income and a $50,000 tax-free return of capital. Because his basis in his preferred stock is $60,000, the $10,000 unrecovered basis is added to his basis in the common stock, increasing it to $250,000 ($240,000 + $10,000). ∎

Exceptions to Sec. 306 Treatment

Section 306(b) provides that Sec. 306 does not apply in the following situations.

1. A shareholder sells all of his common and preferred stock in a corporation, thus completely terminating his interest in the corporation. Sec. 306 does not apply even if some of the stock sold is Sec. 306 stock. The sale cannot be to a related party as defined by Sec. 318(a) (i.e., a family member or related entity).

2. The corporation redeems all of the shareholder's common and preferred stock, completely terminating the shareholder's interest in the corporation.

3. The corporation redeems an individual shareholder's stock in a partial liquidation qualifying under Sec. 302(b)(4).

4. A shareholder disposes of Sec. 306 stock in a way in which gain or loss is not recognized (e.g., a gift of Sec. 306 stock). Although no income is recognized when Sec.

---

[60] Sec. 306(a)(2).

306 stock is disposed of by gift, the stock retains its taint and remains Sec. 306 stock in the donee's hands.

5. Section 306 does not apply if it is demonstrated to the IRS's satisfaction that the distribution and subsequent disposition of Sec. 306 stock did not have tax avoidance as one of its principal purposes.

STOCK REDEMPTIONS BY RELATED CORPORATIONS

OBJECTIVE 7
Determine when Sec. 304 applies to a stock sale and its tax consequences

If a shareholder sells stock in one corporation to a second corporation, the sale usually results in the recognition of a capital gain or loss by the shareholder. However, if the shareholder controls both the corporation whose stock is sold (the issuing corporation) and the corporation that purchases the stock (the acquiring corporation), the net result may be more similar to a dividend than to a sale.

Example 4-44 ■ Arnie owns all 100 shares of the stock of Par and Birdie Corporations. Arnie sells 25 shares of the Par stock to Birdie Corporation for $25,000. The net result of this transaction is that Arnie has received a $25,000 cash distribution from Birdie and he still has complete control of both corporations. ■

Example 4-45 ■ Bonnie owns all 100 shares of Parent Corporation stock. Parent owns all of Sub Corporation's stock. Bonnie sells 25 shares of Parent stock to Sub Corporation for $25,000. The net result of this transaction is that Bonnie has received a $25,000 cash distribution from Sub. Bonnie still controls Parent Corporation, and Parent Corporation still owns all of the Sub stock. ■

Key Point
Sec. 304 is a backstop to Sec. 302. Sec. 304 prevents a shareholder from using related corporations to get assets out of corporate solution as capital gains when they should be taxed as dividends.

As Examples 4-44 and 4-45 demonstrate, the potential exists to use two commonly controlled corporations to bail out the E&P of a corporation at capital gains rates. To prevent this kind of tax avoidance, Sec. 304 requires that a sale of stock of one controlled corporation to a second controlled corporation be treated as a stock redemption. If one of the provisions of Sec. 302(b) or Sec. 303 applies to the redemption (e.g., if the redemption is substantially disproportionate), the transaction is treated as a sale. Otherwise, the redemption is treated as a Sec. 301 distribution, which implies a dividend if there is sufficient E&P.

Section 304 applies to two types of sales. The first is a sale of stock involving two brother-sister corporations. The second is a sale of a parent corporation's stock to one of its subsidiary corporations. The following sections define brother-sister groups, parent-subsidiary groups, and explain how Sec. 304 applies to each type of group.

Brother-Sister Corporations

Typical Misconception
In a brother-sister relationship, Sec. 304 creates a hypothetical redemption of stock and a contribution to capital to enable the provisions of Sec. 302 to be applied. Sec. 302 is applied with respect to the stock of the issuing corporation.

Two corporations are called brother-sister corporations when one or more shareholders is in control of each of the corporations and a parent-subsidiary relationship is not present. Control means ownership of at least 50% of the voting power or 50% of the total value of all stock of the corporation. The shareholder(s) who have such ownership are called controlling shareholders. If a controlling shareholder (or shareholders) transfers stock in one such corporation to the other corporation in exchange for property, the exchange is recast as a redemption by the acquiring corporation of its own stock. In other words, (1) the acquiring corporation is deemed to receive the issuing corporation's stock as a contribution to capital; in exchange, it is deemed to give the controlling shareholder some of its own stock; (2) the acquiring corporation is deemed to have redeemed its own newly-issued stock from the controlling shareholder for the amount that was actually paid.

To determine whether the redemption is a sale or a dividend, reference is made to the shareholder's stock ownership in the issuing corporation. For purposes of making this test under Sec. 302(b), the attribution rules of Sec. 318(a) must be applied.[61]

Redemption Treated as a Distribution. If the redemption does not qualify as a sale, it is treated as a Sec. 301 distribution. The distribution is assumed to have been made first by the acquiring corporation to the extent of its E&P, and then by the issuing corporation to the extent of its E&P.[62] The shareholder's basis in the issuing corporation's stock that was sold is added to his basis for the acquiring corporation's stock. The acquiring corporation takes the same basis in the issuing corporation's shares that the shareholder had.

Example 4-46 ■ Bert owns 60 of the 100 outstanding shares of Frog Corporation stock and 60 of the 100 outstanding shares of Tree Corporation stock. Frog and Tree Corporations have $50,000 and $20,000 of E&P, respectively. Bert sells 20 shares of Frog stock (for which his adjusted basis is $10,000) to Tree Corporation for $20,000. Since Frog and Tree are both controlled by Bert (because of his ownership of at least 50% of each corporation's stock), Sec. 304 applies. The transaction is recast as a contribution by Bert of his Frog stock to Tree Corporation in exchange for Tree stock and a redemption by Tree of its own stock from Bert. To determine whether the transaction qualifies as a sale, reference is made to Bert's ownership of Frog stock. Before the redemption, Bert owned 60% of the Frog stock. After the redemption, Bert owns 52% of the Frog stock (40 shares directly and 12 [0.60 × 20] shares indirectly through Tree). The redemption is treated as a Sec. 301 distribution, since it is not substantially disproportionate or a complete termination, and it is not likely to meet the other tests for sale treatment. The entire distribution is a dividend since it does not exceed the $70,000 total of Frog and Tree Corporations' E&P. All $20,000 of the distribution is treated as coming out of Tree's E&P. Tree's basis in the Frog stock is $10,000, the same as Bert's basis in the stock. Bert's basis in his Tree stock is increased by $10,000, his basis in the Frog stock that he is deemed to have contributed to Tree Corporation. ■

Redemption Treated as a Sale. If the redemption qualifies as a sale under Sec. 302(b) or Sec. 303, the shareholder's recognized gain or loss is measured by the difference between the amount received from the acquiring corporation and the shareholder's basis in the acquiring corporation's stock that was deemed to have been issued to him. The shareholder's basis in those shares is the same as his basis in the issuing corporation's shares that were contributed to the acquiring corporation. The acquiring corporation is treated as having purchased the issuing corporation's shares and takes a cost basis for such shares.

Example 4-47 ■ Assume the same facts as in Example 4-46, except that Bert sells 40 shares of Frog stock (for which his adjusted basis is $20,000) to Tree Corporation for $40,000. After the redemption, Bert owns 44 shares of Frog stock (20 shares directly and 24

---

[61] The attribution rules of Sec. 318(a) are modified for Sec. 304 purposes so that a shareholder is considered to own a proportionate amount of stock owned by any corporation of which he owns 5% or more (instead of 50% or more) of the value of the stock.

[62] Sec. 304(b)(2).

[0.60 × 40] shares indirectly through Tree). Therefore, he meets both the 50% and the 80% tests for a substantially disproportionate redemption, and he treats the redemption as a sale. He has a $20,000 ($40,000 received from Tree − $20,000 adjusted basis in the Tree shares) capital gain. Tree's basis in the Frog shares acquired from Bert is $40,000, its acquisition cost for the shares. ∎

Parent-Subsidiary Corporations

If a shareholder sells stock in a parent corporation to a subsidiary of the parent corporation, the exchange is treated as a distribution in redemption of part or all of the shareholder's stock in the parent corporation. For this purpose, a parent-subsidiary relationship exists if one corporation owns at least 50% of the voting power or 50% of the total value of all stock in the subsidiary.

To determine whether the redemption is to be treated as a sale or as a Sec. 301 distribution, reference is made to the shareholder's ownership of the parent corporation stock before and after the redemption. The constructive ownership rules of Sec. 318 must be taken into account in making this determination.

Redemption Treated as a Dividend. If the redemption does not qualify as a sale, the distribution is treated as having been made by the subsidiary corporation to the extent of its E&P and then from the parent corporation to the extent of its E&P. The effect of this rule is to make the E&P of both corporations available in determining the portion of the distribution that is a dividend. The shareholder's basis in his remaining parent corporation stock is increased by his basis in the stock transferred to the subsidiary. The subsidiary's basis in the parent corporation stock is the amount it paid for the stock.[63]

> **Typical Misconception**
> When a shareholder sells stock of a parent corporation to its subsidiary, Sec. 304 recasts the transaction as a redemption of the parent stock. This allows the provisions of Sec. 302 to be applied.

Example 4-48 ∎ Brian owns 60 of the 100 shares of Parent Corporation stock and has a $15,000 basis in his shares. Parent Corporation owns 60 of the 100 shares of Sub Corporation stock. Parent and Sub Corporations have $10,000 and $30,000 of E&P, respectively. Brian sells 10 of his Parent shares to Sub Corporation for $12,000. The sale is recast as a redemption. Parent Corporation is deemed to have redeemed its stock from Brian. Brian owned 60% of the Parent stock before the redemption. After the redemption he owns 53 shares (50 shares directly and 3 [0.60 × 0.50 × 10] shares indirectly). Because the 80% test is not met (Brian does not own less than 48 (0.80 × 60) shares after the redemption), the redemption is not substantially disproportionate. The redemption does not qualify as a sale under Sec. 302(b)(1) since Brian remains in control of Parent after the redemption, and no other test for sale treatment is met. Therefore, Brian has a dividend distribution under Sec. 301. The $12,000 distribution is deemed to have been distributed from Sub's E&P. Brian's $2,500 basis in the redeemed shares is added to his $12,500 basis in his remaining Parent shares, so that his total basis in those shares remains at $15,000. Sub's basis in the 10 Parent shares acquired from Brian is $12,000, the amount that Sub paid for the shares. ∎

Redemption Treated as a Sale. If the redemption of the parent corporation's stock qualifies as a sale, gain or loss is computed in the usual fashion. The basis of the stock transferred to the subsidiary is subtracted from the amount received in the distribution to determine the shareholder's recognized gain.

[63] Rev. Rul. 80-189, 1980-2 C.B. 106.

Example 4-49 ■ Assume the same facts as in Example 4-48, except that Brian sells 40 shares of Parent stock to Sub Corporation for $48,000. Since Brian owns 60% of the Parent stock before the redemption and he owns 24.8% (20 shares directly and 4.8 [0.60 × 0.20 × 40] shares indirectly after the redemption), the redemption meets the 50% and 80% tests for a substantially disproportionate redemption. In this case, Brian has a $38,000 ($48,000 − $10,000 adjusted basis in the 40 shares sold) capital gain. Brian's adjusted basis for his remaining 20 shares of Parent stock is $5,000. Sub Corporation's basis for the 40 Parent shares purchased from Brian is $48,000, the amount that Sub paid for the shares. ■

Topic Review 4-2 presents a summary of the methods by which a redemption transaction can be characterized as a sale or exchange as well as the special stock redemption rules.

DISTRIBUTIONS OF STOCK AND SECURITIES OF A CONTROLLED CORPORATION

OBJECTIVE 8
Determine when Sec. 355 applies to a stock distribution and its tax consequences

Key Point
If the provisions of Sec. 355 can be satisfied, a corporation or corporations can be separated without the recognition of gain. If Sec. 355 is not applicable, gains may be recognized at both the corporate and shareholder levels.

Under Sec. 355, special rules apply when a corporation distributes the stock and securities of a subsidiary corporation to its shareholders and security holders.[64] If the requirements of Sec. 355 are met, the distribution is tax-free. The shareholders are not taxed as they are when other types of property are distributed. If the requirements are not met, the distribution of stock and securities is taxed to the shareholders as a property distribution.

Three types of distributions can be tax-free under Sec. 355:

1. The parent corporation distributes the stock and securities of a subsidiary to its shareholders without receiving anything in exchange. Such a distribution, called a **spinoff,** may occur because of a court order to the parent corporation to divest itself of the subsidiary (see Figure 4-1).

2. The parent corporation distributes the stock and securities of a subsidiary to some of its shareholders in exchange for part or all of their stock and securities in the

TOPIC REVIEW 4-2

Alternative Treatments of Stock Redemptions

Redemptions Treated as Sales or Exchanges
1. Redemptions that are not essentially equivalent to a dividend (Sec. 302(b)(1))
2. Substantially disproportionate redemptions (Sec. 302(b)(2))
3. Complete terminations of a shareholder's interest (Sec. 302(b)(3))
4. Partial liquidation of a corporation in redemption of a noncorporate shareholder's stock (Sec. 302(b)(4))
5. Redemption to pay death taxes (Sec. 303)

Special Redemption Rules
1. Redemptions of Sec. 306 stock are generally treated as dividends to the shareholder (Sec. 306).
2. A sale of stock in one controlled corporation to another controlled corporation is treated as a redemption (Sec. 304).

---

[64] For this purpose, securities means long-term debt instruments.

Distributions of Stock and Securities of a Controlled Corporation ◆ 4-37

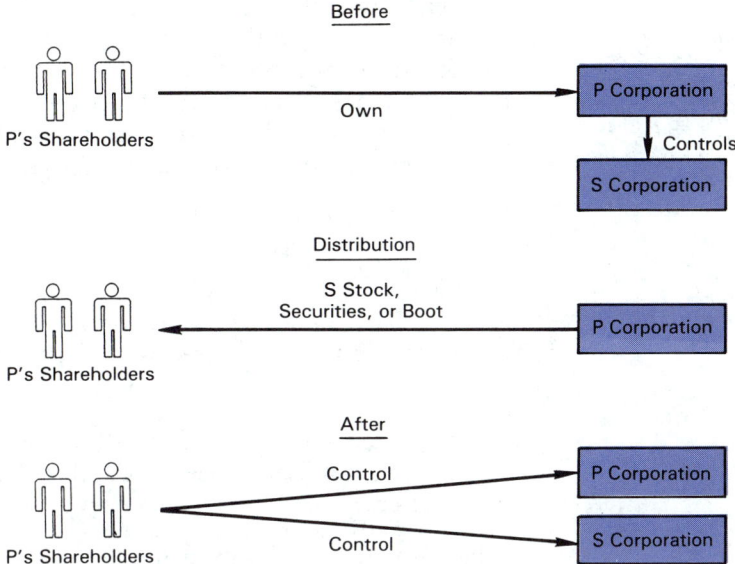

FIGURE 4-1 Spinoff of Stock of a Controlled Subsidiary Corporation

Key Point

A Sec. 355 distribution takes one of the following forms: spinoff (dividend), split-off (redemption), or split-up (liquidation).

parent corporation. Such a distribution, called a **split-off,** may occur in order to eliminate a group of dissenting shareholders (see Figure 4-2).

3. The parent corporation distributes the stock and securities of two or more subsidiaries to its shareholders in exchange for all of their stock and securities in the parent corporation. The parent corporation goes out of existence. Such a distribution,

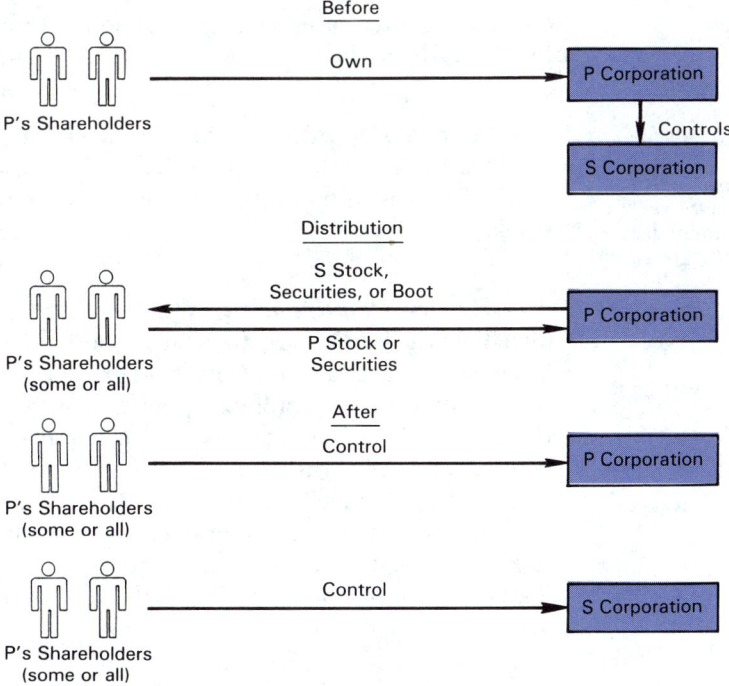

FIGURE 4-2 Split-off of Stock of a Controlled Subsidiary Corporation

Typical Misconception
For future reference, in a spinoff the shareholder does not give up anything in the transaction, whereas in both a split-off and a split-up the shareholder surrenders stock in the distributing corporation.

called a **split-up,** may occur to eliminate a holding company arrangement and permit the shareholders to own the stock of each corporation directly (see Figure 4-3).

The requirements of Sec. 355 must be met in order for any of these distributions of a subsidiary's stock to be tax-free. If the Sec. 355 requirements are *not* met, a spinoff is taxed as a dividend to the shareholders, a split-off is taxed as a stock redemption to the shareholders, and a split-up is taxed as a liquidation to the shareholders.

Requirements of Sec. 355

Under Sec. 355, a parent corporation's distribution of the stock and securities of a subsidiary corporation is tax-free to the shareholders if the following six requirements are met:[65]

1. The property distributed must consist solely of stock or securities of a corporation that was controlled by the distributing corporation immediately before the distribution.

2. The distribution must not have been used principally as a device to distribute the E&P of the distributing corporation, the controlled corporation, or both.

3. Immediately after the distribution, the distributing corporation and the controlled corporation must both be engaged in the active conduct of a trade or business.

4. The distributing corporation must distribute either (a) all of the stock and securities in the controlled corporation held by it immediately before the distribution or (b) an amount of stock in the controlled corporation constituting control.

5. The distribution must have a substantial business purpose.

6. The persons who directly or indirectly owned the corporation prior to its division must maintain a continuing equity interest in one or more of the corporations following the division.

Key Point
The control requirement for Sec. 355 is the same control requirement previously discussed relating to the formation of a corporation under Sec. 351 (Chap. 2).

The Control Requirement. For purposes of Sec. 355, control requires ownership of stock possessing at least 80% of the total combined voting power of all classes of stock entitled to vote and at least 80% of the total number of shares of all other classes of stock.[66]

The Device Requirement. Whether a transaction has been used as a device to distribute the E&P of the distributing corporation, the controlled corporation, or both is a matter of the facts and circumstances in each case. A sale or exchange of stock of the distributing or controlled corporation after the distribution is evidence of a device. If such sale is prearranged, it is considered substantial evidence. The nature, kind, amount, and use of the assets of the distributing or controlled corporation immediately after the distribution is also considered. The existence of assets not used in a trade or business is evidence of a device. The absence of earnings and profits, the presence of a corporate business purpose, or a transaction that qualifies as an exchange under Secs. 302 or 303 for each distributee means that a distribution is generally not a device.[67]

---

[65] Sec. 355(a) and Reg. Secs. 1.355-2(b) and (c).
[66] Sec. 368(c).
[67] Reg. Sec. 1.355-2(d).

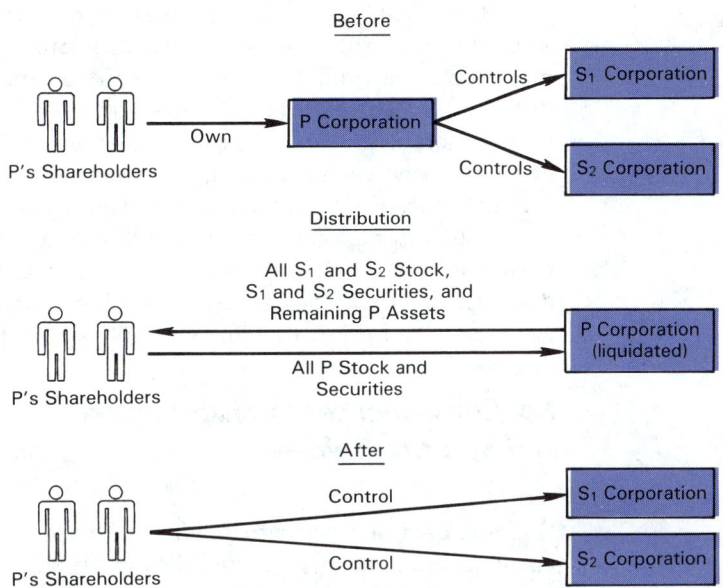

FIGURE 4-3 Split-up of Stock of Controlled Subsidiary Corporations

Typical Misconception
The active trade or business requirement has two parts: (1) a predistribution 5-year history and (2) after the distribution, active engagement by both corporations in a trade or business.

The Active Conduct of a Trade or Business Requirement. Immediately after the distribution, the distributing corporation and the controlled corporation must each be engaged in a business that was actively conducted for at least 5 years prior to the distribution. The main reason for this requirement is to prevent a corporation from spinning off a newly formed subsidiary whose only assets are unneeded cash and other liquid assets. The shareholders could then sell or liquidate the subsidiary and obtain the liquid assets in an exchange transaction rather than as a dividend.

For purposes of this requirement, it is not necessary that the distributing corporation or the controlled corporation, as the case may be, have been conducting the business itself during the entire 4-year period. However, they must not have acquired the business in a transaction in which any gain or loss was recognized by the seller. Furthermore, control of a corporation conducting the business must not have been acquired in a taxable transaction within the 4-year period ending on the distribution date.[68]

The Distribution Requirement. The distributing corporation must distribute sufficient stock of the controlled corporation to constitute control (i.e., at least 80% of the total combined voting power of all classes of stock entitled to vote and at least 80% of the total number of shares of all other classes of stock). Under Sec. 355(a)(1)(D), it may be allowed to retain some of the stock and securities if it can establish to the satisfaction of the IRS that they were not retained as part of a tax-avoidance plan.

Key Point
Even though business purpose is a requirement in a number of different corporate transactions, the IRS scrutinizes business purpose very closely in a Sec. 355 distribution.

The Business Purpose Requirement. The distribution must have a substantial corporate business purpose. Qualifying distributions include those made to comply with antitrust litigation and those made to separate businesses where the shareholders have major disagreements.[69]

---

[68] Sec. 355(b)(2).
[69] Reg. Sec. 1.355-2(b)(5), Exs. (1) and (2).

The Continuity of Interest Requirement. The shareholders that directly or indirectly own the stock of the distributing corporation prior to the division must maintain a continuing equity interest in one or more of the corporations following the division.[70] Not all shareholders need to maintain an equity interest in the distributing corporation or the controlled corporation(s) following the division. Some shareholders may receive cash in exchange for their shares, provided a substantial portion of the original shareholders maintain a continuing equity interest. The distribution of stock and securities also does not have to be pro rata. Disproportionate distributions are permitted by the Code, and can be used to eliminate the stock ownership of a dissenting shareholder group by exchanging the stock of a controlled subsidiary corporation for their stock interest in the parent corporation in a split-off transaction.

Tax Consequences to Shareholders and Security Holders

Shareholders and security holders who receive stock and securities of a controlled corporation must answer the following two questions:

1. What are the amount and character of the gain, loss, or income that must be recognized on the distribution?
2. What basis does the shareholder take in the stock and securities received?

Self-Study Question

Does the receipt of boot make the entire Sec. 355 transaction taxable to the shareholders?

Answer

No. The shareholders may have a partial recognition of gain. The amount and type of gain depends on whether the shareholders surrender stock of the distributing corporation in the transaction.

Recognition of Gain by the Shareholders and Security Holders. If a distribution of the stock and securities of a controlled subsidiary meets all the requirements of Sec. 355, the shareholders and security holders do not recognize any income or gain or loss on the distribution. If, however, they receive any property in addition to the stock and securities permitted under Sec. 355, the transaction is not necessarily completely taxable. Under Sec. 356, the distribution may still be at least partially tax-free. However, shareholders and security holders may be required to recognize some dividend income or capital gain on the transaction.

Property that cannot be received tax-free under Sec. 355 is referred to as *boot*. **Boot** may consist of money, short-term debt, any property other than the stock or securities of a controlled corporation, any stock of the controlled corporation that was purchased within the previous 5 years in a taxable transaction, securities of the controlled corporation to the extent the principal amount of the securities received exceeds the principal amount of the securities surrendered by the shareholder, and stock or securities attributable to accrued interest.[71] When boot is received, the amount of income or gain that must be recognized depends on whether the shareholder surrendered stock and securities in the parent corporation (i.e., a split-off or split-up) or did not surrender any stock or securities (i.e., a spinoff).

Typical Misconception

In a spinoff, the FMV of the boot received is treated as a Sec. 301 distribution to the shareholder. In a split-off or split-up, the shareholders recognize gain to the extent of the lesser of (a) boot received or (b) gain realized.

SPINOFFS. When boot is received in a spinoff, the FMV of the boot is considered to be a property distribution under Sec. 301. Thus, it is a dividend to the extent of the shareholder's ratable share of the distributing corporation's E&P. Any securities of the controlled corporation that the shareholders receive are boot, because the shareholders do not surrender any securities in a spinoff transaction. Thus, the FMV of such securities is a dividend to the extent of the shareholder's ratable share of the distributing corporation's E&P.

---

[70] Reg. Sec. 1.355-2(c).
[71] Secs. 355(a)(3) and 356(b).

Example 4-50 ■ Parent Corporation has $100,000 of E&P. In a transaction qualifying under Sec. 355 except that boot property is distributed, Parent Corporation distributes all the stock of its controlled subsidiary corporation Sub worth $50,000 to its sole shareholder, Belinda. In addition, Parent Corporation distributes a $10,000 10-year Sub Corporation note worth $9,000 to Belinda. The receipt of the Sub stock is tax-free to Belinda. However, she has a $9,000 dividend because of the receipt of the security (i.e., the 10-year note). ■

SPLIT-OFFS AND SPLIT-UPS. In a split-off or a split-up, a shareholder surrenders stock and securities in the parent corporation in exchange for stock and securities of the controlled corporation plus, in some cases, boot property. The shareholder may have realized a gain or loss on the exchange. If the shareholder has realized a loss on the exchange, the loss is not recognized whether boot was received or not.[72] If the shareholder realized a gain on the exchange, the gain is recognized to the extent of the FMV of any boot received.

If the exchange has the effect of a distribution of a dividend under the stock redemption rules of Sec. 302, the gain recognized must be treated as a dividend to the extent of the shareholder's ratable share of the distributing corporation's E&P.[73] The IRS applies the tests of Sec. 302 to determine whether the boot distribution has the effect of a dividend. In doing so, the shareholder is treated as though he continued to own stock in the distributing corporation and surrendered only the portion of his shares equal in value to the amount of the boot received. This hypothetical redemption is tested under the rules of Sec. 302(b).[74]

Example 4-51 ■ Parent Corporation has $60,000 of E&P. The corporation owns assets with a $60,000 FMV plus all of the outstanding shares of Sub Corporation. The Sub stock is worth $40,000. Parent is owned by individuals Carl and Diane, each of whom owns 100 shares of Parent stock. Parent distributes all of the Sub stock to Carl in exchange for Carl's 100 shares of Parent stock in a transaction which qualifies as a split-off under the provisions of Sec. 355, except for the fact that Carl also receives $10,000 in cash. Carl's basis in the Parent shares that he surrenders is $25,000. Carl has a $25,000 realized gain determined as follows:

FMV of Sub stock	$40,000
Plus: Cash received	10,000
Amount realized	$50,000
Minus: Basis of Parent stock	(25,000)
Realized gain	$25,000

$10,000 of this gain must be recognized (i.e., the lesser of the $25,000 realized gain or the $10,000 boot received). If Carl surrenders Parent stock solely for the $10,000 boot, he would be surrendering 20 shares worth $10,000. Before this hypothetical redemption, he owns 50% of the outstanding Parent shares (100 ÷ 200), and afterward he owns 44% (80 ÷ 180). Thus, the hypothetical redemption is not substantially disproportionate under Sec. 302(b)(2) since the 44% post-redemption stock ownership is more than 80% of the pre-redemption stock ownership (50% × 0.80 = 40%). Unless the exchange can meet one of the other

---

[72] Sec. 356(c).
[73] Sec. 356(a)(2).
[74] Rev. Rul. 74-516, 1974-2 C.B. 121.

> **Typical Misconception**
> Securities (long-term debt) can be exchanged in a Sec. 355 transaction without the recognition of gain as long as the principal amount surrendered is equal to or greater than the principal amount received.

tests for sale treatment, the $10,000 is a dividend. Otherwise it is a capital gain. ∎

In a split-off or a split-up, securities of the controlled corporation may be distributed to a shareholder tax-free but only if the shareholder surrenders securities in the distributing corporation with an equal or larger principal amount. To the extent the principal amount of the securities received by a shareholder exceeds the principal amount of the securities surrendered by that shareholder, the FMV of the excess principal amount is boot.

Example 4-52 ∎ Brett exchanges 60 shares of Parent Corporation stock and a Parent Corporation security with a principal amount of $1,000 for 100 shares of Sub Corporation stock and a Sub Corporation security with a principal amount of $1,200 and a FMV of $1,100. The exchange qualifies as a tax-free split-off except for the receipt of boot. The FMV of the $200 excess principal amount is treated as boot. The FMV of the boot is computed as follows:

$$\frac{\$1{,}200 - \$1{,}000 \text{ (Excess principal amount)}}{\$1{,}200 \text{ (Principal amount received)}} \times \$1{,}100 \text{ (FMV of security received)} = \$183.33$$ ∎

> **Key Point**
> Since Sec. 355 is a deferral provision, any unrecognized gain must be reflected in the shareholders' basis for the nonrecognition property received in the transaction. This is accomplished through the substituted basis rules of Sec. 358.

Basis of Property Received by Shareholders and Security Holders. Section 358 prescribes the basis of property received by a shareholder in a Sec. 355 or Sec. 356 distribution. The shareholder's basis in any boot property received is the property's FMV. The shareholder's basis in the stock and securities received that are not considered to be boot property is determined as follows:

Basis of stocks and securities owned before the distribution
Minus: FMV of boot received (including money)
Plus: Dividend income or gain recognized by the shareholder on the distribution
―――
Basis of stocks and securities (other than boot) owned after the distribution

The shareholder must allocate the basis computed above to all the stocks and securities (other than boot) that he owns after the distribution, both in the distributing corporation and in the subsidiary corporation, in accordance with their relative FMVs.

Example 4-53 ∎ Allie owns 50 shares of Parent Corporation stock. The shares have a $10,000 adjusted basis and a $60,000 FMV. In a transaction qualifying under Sec. 355 except for the receipt of boot, Allie receives 25 shares of Sub Corporation stock (a controlled subsidiary) worth $25,000, and $5,000 worth of other property (boot) in exchange for 25 shares of his Parent stock. Allie has a $25,000 realized gain on the exchange, computed as follows:

FMV of Sub shares	$25,000
Plus: FMV of other property	5,000
Amount realized	$30,000
Minus: Basis of Parent shares surrendered	(5,000)
Realized gain	$25,000

Allie must recognize $5,000 of gain (the FMV of the boot received). Allie's basis in the Parent and Sub stock held after the transaction is $10,000 ($10,000 basis of

Self-Study Question

Would the answer in Example 4-53 be any different if Allie did not surrender any Parent stock in the transaction?

Answer

Yes. Allie would be treated as receiving a $5,000 Sec. 301 distribution (dividend income to the extent of E&P) rather than a gain from the sale of stock.

Parent stock + $5,000 gain recognized − $5,000 FMV of boot property). This basis must be allocated to the Parent and Sub shares held after the distribution, in accordance with their relative FMVs. The basis of the Parent stock is computed as follows:

$$\frac{\$30{,}000 \text{ (FMV of Parent stock)}}{\$30{,}000 + \$25{,}000 \text{ (FMVs of Parent and Sub stock)}} \times \$10{,}000 \text{ (basis)} = \$5{,}454$$

The basis of the Sub stock is computed as follows:

$$\frac{\$25{,}000 \text{ (FMV of Sub stock)}}{\$30{,}000 + \$25{,}000 \text{ (FMVs of Parent and Sub stock)}} \times \$10{,}000 \text{ (basis)} = \$4{,}546$$

Allie's basis in the other property (boot) received is its FMV of $5,000. ∎

The taxpayer's holding period for any nonrecognition property received in a Sec. 355 or Sec. 356 distribution is tacked onto the holding period of the stock that was surrendered in a split-off or split-up, or the stock that was retained in a spinoff.[75]

Tax Consequences to the Distributing Corporation

Additional Comment

Sec. 355 represents a vehicle for distributing appreciated stock and securities without triggering a gain to the distributing corporation. This is different than both the distribution and redemption rules which have been covered in this chapter.

Recognition of Gain or Loss. A corporation generally does not recognize any gain or loss when it distributes nonrecognition property (i.e., stock or securities in a controlled corporation) to its shareholders in a distribution that qualifies under Sec. 355 or Sec. 356.[76] If other property is distributed as part of the transaction (i.e., boot), gain must be recognized under the provisions of Sec. 311 just as it would for any other property distribution.

In 1990 a new rule was enacted that requires a distributing corporation to recognize gain when it distributes a subsidiary's stock under some circumstances. The new law was passed to prevent a perceived abuse. Prior to the enactment of this new provision, a person could purchase a corporation's stock and, as a result of a Sec. 355 distribution, obtain a basis in the stock of a distributed subsidiary corporation greater than the distributing corporation's basis, while the distributed corporation recognized no gain.

Additional Comment

However, this new rule does not impose a tax at the shareholder level. This is because no tax would have resulted to the shareholder if the shareholder had acquired the stock directly in a purchase.

Under the new provision, a distributing corporation must recognize gain on the distribution of subsidiary stock if, immediately after the distribution, any person holds a 50% disqualified stock interest in either the distributing corporation or any subsidiary corporation whose stock was distributed. Gain is recognized by the distributing corporation under Sec. 355(c)(2) as if it had sold the controlled subsidiary corporation's stock and securities for their FMV.

Disqualified stock is defined by Sec. 355(c) as (1) any stock in the distributing corporation purchased after October 9, 1990, and during the five-year period ending on the distribution date, or (2) any stock in any controlled subsidiary corporation that was either (a) purchased after October 9, 1990, and during the five-year period ending on the distribution date, or (b) received in the distribution to the extent it is attributable to distributions made with respect disqualified stock in the distributing corporation or attributable to any of the distributing corporation's securities that were purchased after October 9, 1990, and during the five-year period ending on the distribution date.

---

[75] Sec. 1223(1).
[76] Sec. 355(c)(1).

Example 4-54 ■ On January 1, 1991, Beth purchased a 30% interest in Parent Corporation and a 10% interest in its subsidiary Junior Corporation. One year later, 40% of the Junior stock is distributed to Beth in exchange for her Parent stock. The rest of the Junior stock is distributed to other shareholders. Both distributions are part of a Sec. 355 split-off where 90% of the junior stock is distributed to a group of Parent shareholders in exchange for all of their Parent stock. Parent Corporation must recognize gain on the distribution of the Junior shares because Beth's entire 50% interest is disqualified stock; that is, the 10% that was acquired directly by purchase and the 40% that Beth received as a result of owning the Parent stock that she had purchased. ■

Earnings and Profits. Regulation Secs. 1.312-10 and -11 provide special rules to allocate the E&P of the distributing parent corporation between the parent corporation and the controlled subsidiary whose stock is distributed. These rules are beyond the scope of this text.

CONTROVERSIAL ISSUES

What Is a Complete Termination of Interest?

Key Point

Any time a shareholder is relying on the waiver of the family attribution rules for purposes of Sec. 302(b)(3), such former shareholder would be well advised not to be too aggressive in the retention of any interest in the redeeming corporation.

According to Sec. 302(c)(2), the family attribution rules may be waived if a shareholder completely terminates his interest in a corporation and retains no interest other than that of a creditor. Unfortunately, the forbidden interests are not clearly named. Regulation Sec. 1.302-4(d) states that a former shareholder is permitted to retain a creditor interest but cannot retain any equity interest. The debt involved must be a true debt of the corporation and not a disguised equity interest. If (1) the amount or the certainty of a debt repayment to a former shareholder depends upon the corporation's earnings, or (2) the rate of interest depends upon the corporation's earnings, the holder of such an instrument may not be considered a creditor, and the family attribution rules will not be waived.

A former shareholder is permitted to collect rent from the corporation for the use of property that he owns. Such an interest is similar to that of a creditor.[77] A former shareholder is also permitted to serve as the executor of the estate of a deceased shareholder of the corporation.[78] A former shareholder may not serve as either trustee of a voting trust for stock of the corporation[79] or as a custodian for stock of the corporation under the Uniform Gifts to Minors Act.[80]

The IRS holds that the performance of any service such as consulting or advisory services for the corporation, even without compensation, constitutes an interest in the corporation that is not permitted.[81] The Tax Court, in a case affirmed by the Fourth Circuit Court of Appeals, has ruled that a taxpayer who signed a broad contract to manage properties held by the firm that redeemed all of his shares acquired a forbidden interest.[82] However, the Tax Court has held that a father who, after redemption of all his stock in a family corporation, continued to render accounting

---

[77] Rev. Rul. 77-467, 1977-2 C.B. 92.
[78] Rev. Ruls. 72-380, 1972-2 C.B. 201 and 79-334, 1979-2 C.B. 127.
[79] Rev. Rul. 71-426, 1971-2 C.B. 173.
[80] Rev. Rul. 81-233, 1981-2 C.B. 83.
[81] Rev. Rul. 70-104, 1970-1 C.B. 66.
[82] *Jack O. Chertkof,* 72 T.C. 1113 (1979), *aff'd.* 48 AFTR 2d 81-5194, 81-1 USTC ¶ 9462 (4th Cir., 1981).

TOPIC REVIEW 4-3

Requirements for a Sec. 355 Tax-Free Distribution

1. The distribution must consist solely of stock or securities of a controlled corporation.
2. The distribution must not be a device for the distribution of E&P.
3. Both the distributing and controlled corporations must be engaged in the active conduct of a trade or business immediately after the distribution.
4. The distributing corporation must distribute at least 80% of the stock of the controlled corporation. No stock and securities may be retained if the retention is part of a tax avoidance plan.
5. The distribution must have business purpose.
6. Some shareholders must maintain a continuing interest in the distributing or controlled corporation or both.

Tax Consequences of a Sec. 355 Distribution

To the Shareholders and Security Holders:

1. No income, gain, or loss is recognized when stock and securities are received that are permitted to be distributed tax-free under Sec. 355.
2. If additional property (e.g., excess securities, money, or other property) is received in a spinoff, the FMV of the boot property is a dividend under Sec. 301.
3. If additional property is received in a split-off or split-up, gain must be recognized to the extent of lesser of the realized gain or the FMV of the property received. The character of gain is determined by applying the Sec. 302(b) rules.

To the Distributing Corporation:

1. No gain or loss or loss is recognized when nonrecognition property (e.g., stock and securities) is distributed to the shareholders.
2. Gain is recognized on the distribution of a controlled subsidiary corporation's stock if, immediately after the exchange, any person holds a 50% disqualified stock interest in either the distributing corporation or the former controlled subsidiary corporation. Disqualified stock is, in general, stock purchased during the five-year period prior to the distribution.
3. Gain is also recognized under Sec. 311 when property other than nonrecognition property (e.g., boot property) is distributed.

services on an independent contractor basis did *not* retain an interest in the corporation. The family attribution rules were waived; but the IRS still does not agree with this decision.[83]

What Is the Active Conduct of a Trade or Business?

The term *active conduct of a trade or business* is important in connection with both a partial liquidation and a distribution of the stock and securities of a controlled corporation. A distribution can qualify as a partial liquidation only if the distribution is attributable to the distributing corporation's ceasing to conduct a trade or business which was actively conducted throughout the 5-year period ending on the date of the distribution. A distribution of a controlled corporation's stock can qualify as tax-free under Sec. 355 only if, immediately after the distribution, both the distributing corporation and the controlled corporation are each engaged in the active conduct of a

---

[83] *Estate of Milton S. Lennard*, 61 T.C. 554 (1974), nonacq. 1978-2 C.B. 3. See also *William M. Lynch v. CIR*, 58 AFTR 2d 86-5970, 86-2 USTC ¶ 9731 (9th Cir., 1986) where a former shareholder, who acted as an independent consultant, maintained an office in the corporate facilities, and was covered by the corporate medical plan, was held to have retained a prohibited interest.

Typical Misconception
What constitutes a trade or business would seem to be a somewhat simple determination. However, the rules and regulations under Sec. 302(b)(4) and Sec. 355 clearly indicate otherwise.

trade or business. However, there has been a good deal of controversy about what constitutes the active conduct of a trade or business. According to Reg. Sec. 1.355-3(b)(2)(ii) issued in January 1989, a corporation is considered to be engaged in the active conduct of a trade or business

> if a specific group of activities is being carried on by the corporation for the purpose of earning income or profit, and the activities included in such group include every operation that forms a part of, or a step in, the process of earning income or profit. Such group of activities ordinarily must include the collection of income and the payment of expenses.

The regulations state that whether a corporation is actively conducting a trade or business is a question of fact to be determined from all the facts and circumstances.

In general, a corporation must perform active and substantial management and operational functions if it is to be considered as conducting an active trade or business. Under the regulations, the active conduct of a trade or business does not include (1) the holding of stock, securities, land, or other property for investment purposes, or (2) the ownership and operation (including leasing) of real or personal property used in a trade or business unless the owner performs significant services with respect to the operation and management of the property.

TAX PLANNING CONSIDERATIONS

Avoiding Unreasonable Compensation

The advantage of using salary and fringe benefit payments to permit a shareholder of a closely held corporation to withdraw funds from the corporation and still be taxed at a single level was discussed in Chapter 3. If a corporation pays too large a salary to a shareholder-employee, some of the salary may be reclassified as a dividend. In such case, double taxation results.

Corporations can avoid the double taxation problem associated with a constructive dividend by entering into a **hedge agreement** with a shareholder-employee, which obligates the shareholder to repay any portion of the salary that is disallowed by the IRS as a deduction. The shareholder-employee deducts the amount of the repayment under Sec. 162 in the year the repayment is made, provided that a legal obligation exists under state law to make the payment.[84] If a hedge agreement is not in effect, voluntary repayment of the salary is not deductible by the shareholder-employee.[85]

Example 4-55 ■ Theresa owns one-half of the stock of Marine Corporation and serves as its president. The remaining Marine stock is owned by eight investors, none of whom owns more than 10% of the outstanding shares. Theresa enters into a hedge agreement with Marine Corporation in 1988 requiring all salary payments that are declared unreasonable compensation by the IRS to be repaid. Marine Corporation pays Theresa a salary and bonus of $750,000 in 1991. The IRS subsequently holds that $300,000 of the salary is unreasonable compensation and should be taxed as a dividend. Marine Corporation and the IRS agree that $180,000 of the compensation is, in fact, unreasonable. The $180,000 is repaid in 1994. The entire $750,000

---

[84] Rev. Rul. 69-115, 1969-1 C.B. 50; and *Vincent E. Oswald,* 49 T.C. 645 (1968), *acq.* 1968-2 C.B. 2.
[85] *Ernest H. Berger,* 37 T.C. 1026 (1962); and *John G. Pahl,* 67 T.C. 286 (1976).

is taxable to Theresa in 1991. She can deduct the $180,000 as a trade or business expense in 1994. ∎

Hedge agreements have also been used in connection with other payments involving a corporation and its shareholders (e.g., travel and entertainment expenses). Some firms shy away from hedge agreements because the IRS is likely to consider the existence of such an agreement as evidence of unreasonable compensation.

Bootstrap Acquisitions

A prospective purchaser who wants to acquire the stock of a corporation may not have sufficient cash to make the purchase. Instead, corporate funds may be used to make the purchase. This can be accomplished by having the seller sell part of his stock to the purchaser and having the corporation redeem the remainder of the seller's stock. Such an arrangement is called a **bootstrap acquisition.**

Example 4-56 ∎ Ted owns all 100 shares of Dragon Corporation stock. The stock has a $100,000 FMV. Vickie wants to purchase the stock from Ted but has only $60,000. Dragon Corporation has a large cash balance which it does not need for its operations. Ted sells Vickie 60 shares of Dragon stock for $60,000 and then causes Dragon Corporation to redeem his remaining shares for $40,000. The redemption qualifies as a complete termination of interest for Ted under Sec. 302(b)(3) and, therefore, is eligible for capital gain treatment. ∎

Court cases have established that redemptions qualify for exchange treatment as long as the sale and redemption are all part of an integrated plan to terminate the seller's entire interest. It does not matter whether the redemption precedes the sale.[86] In such situations, however, the purchaser must be careful to avoid having dividend income. For example, a purchaser who contracts to acquire all the stock of a corporation on the installment plan and then uses corporate funds to pay the installment obligations will have dividend income. The use of corporate funds constitutes a constructive dividend to the purchaser when the corporation discharges a purchaser's legal obligation. Even if the corporation uses its own funds to redeem the seller's shares, a purchaser who was legally obligated to purchase the shares is considered to have received a constructive dividend.[87]

Example 4-57 ∎ Assume the same facts as in Example 4-56 except that after Vickie purchases the 60 shares from Ted she is legally obligated to purchase the remaining 40 shares from Ted. After entering into the contract, Vickie causes Dragon Corporation to redeem Ted's 40 shares. Since Dragon Corporation has paid Vickie's legal obligation, a constructive dividend to Vickie of $40,000 results. No constructive dividend would result from the redemption if Vickie were legally obligated only to purchase 60 shares from Ted. ∎

Key Point
The IRS will allow a bootstrap redemption to occur without the recognition of dividend income as long as the buyer does not have an unconditional obligation to purchase the stock and the corporation redeems the stock at no more than its FMV.

Rev. Rul. 69-608 contains guidelines for the buyer of stock in a bootstrap redemption transaction to avoid the constructive dividend situation.[88] The guiding principle is that the buyer does not have a constructive dividend when the corporation redeems some of the seller's shares, as long as the buyer does not have a primary and unconditional obligation to purchase the stock, and as long as the corporation pays no

---

[86] See, for example, *U.S. v. Gerald Carey,* 7 AFTR 2d 1301, 61-1 USTC ¶ 9428 (8th Cir., 1961).
[87] *H. F. Wall v. U.S.*, 36 AFTR 423, 47-2 USTC ¶ 9395 (4th Cir., 1947).
[88] Rev. Rul. 69-608, 1969-2 C.B. 42.

4-48 • Ch. 4 / Corporate Nonliquidating Distributions

more than the FMV for the stock that is redeemed. A stock purchaser who has an option—not a legal obligation—to purchase the seller's remaining stock, and who assigns the option to the corporation, is not stuck with a constructive dividend.[89]

Timing of Distributions

Dividends can only be paid out of a corporation's E&P. Therefore, if distributions can be timed to be made when the corporation has little or no E&P, the distributions are treated as a return of capital rather than as a dividend.

If a corporation has a current E&P deficit, the deficit reduces accumulated E&P evenly throughout the year unless the corporation can demonstrate that the deficits arose at particular dates. Thus, if a distribution is made in a year in which there is a deficit in current E&P, but there is some accumulated E&P, the timing of the distribution may determine whether it is a dividend or a return of capital.

Example 4-58 ■ Major Corporation has a $30,000 accumulated E&P balance at the beginning of the year and incurs a $50,000 deficit during the year. Because of its poor operating performance, Major Corporation pays only two of its usual $5,000 quarterly dividend payments to its sole shareholder—those ordinarily paid on March 31 and June 30. The source of the distributions is determined as follows:

E&P balance, January 1		$30,000
Minus:	Reduction for first quarter loss	(12,500)
	Reduction for March 31, distribution	(5,000)
E&P balance, April 1		$12,500
Minus:	Reduction for second quarter loss	(12,500)
E&P balance, June 30		—0—

The first and second quarter losses are computed as follows:

$$(\$50,000) \times 0.25 = (\$12,500)$$

The operating loss reduces the accumulated E&P balance evenly throughout the year. All of the March 31 distribution is taxable because sufficient losses have not been incurred to offset the accumulated E&P amounts at the beginning of the year. The second quarter loss makes the June 30 distribution and any other distributions made before the end of the year tax-free returns of the shareholder's capital investment (assuming that the shareholder's basis in his stock is in excess of the distribution amount). Delaying all of the distributions until late in the year could have made any cash payments to the shareholders tax-free. ■

Typical Misconception
The timing of distributions can affect the amount that is treated as dividend income as opposed to return of capital or capital gain. This is the case in a year when deficits in current E&P exist because such deficit is allocated evenly throughout the year.

The timing of a distribution can also be of critical importance in determining its tax treatment if the distributing corporation has an accumulated E&P deficit and is accruing a positive current E&P balance.

Example 4-59 ■ Yankee Corporation has an accumulated E&P deficit of $250,000 at the beginning of 1991. During 1991 and 1992, Yankee Corporation reports the following current E&P balances and makes the following distributions to Joe, its sole shareholder:

---

[89] *Joseph R. Holsey v. CIR*, 2 AFTR 2d 5660, 58-2 USTC ¶ 9816 (3rd Cir., 1958).

Year	Current E&P	Distributions	Distribution Date
1991	$100,000	$75,000	December 31, 1991
1992	—0—	—0—	

The $75,000 distribution made in 1991 is taxable as a dividend. The $25,000 of current E&P that is not distributed reduces Yankee's accumulated E&P deficit to $225,000. Had Yankee delayed making the $75,000 distribution until January 1, 1992, or later in 1992, the distribution would have been tax-free to the shareholder as a return of Joe's investment in Yankee Corporation. ■

COMPLIANCE AND PROCEDURAL CONSIDERATIONS

Agreement to Terminate Interest under Sec. 302(b)(3)

Key Point
The statute of limitation extends to one year beyond the date a shareholder notifies the IRS that a forbidden interest has been acquired. Otherwise, it would be an almost impossible job for the IRS to administer this provision.

If a shareholder's interest in a corporation is completely terminated by a redemption, the family attribution rules of Sec. 318(a)(1) may be waived. In order to have the rules waived, the shareholder must file a written agreement with the Treasury that he will notify the IRS if any prohibited interest is acquired within the 10-year period following the redemption. A copy of this agreement (which should be in the form of a statement in duplicate signed by the distributee) must be attached to the first return filed by the shareholder for the tax year in which the redemption occurs. If the agreement is not filed on time, the District Director of the IRS is permitted to grant an extension. Regulation Sec. 1.302-4(a) provides that an extension will be granted only if there is reasonable cause for failure to file the agreement on time and if the request for such an extension is filed within such time as the District Director considers reasonable in the circumstances.

The Regulations do not indicate (1) what constitutes a reasonable cause for failure to file, or (2) what constitutes a reasonable extension of time. In *Edward J. Fehrs* the Court of Claims held that late filing of a 10-year agreement is permissible (1) where a taxpayer could not reasonably have expected a filing would be necessary, (2) where the taxpayer files the agreement promptly after he has noticed that it is required, and (3) where the agreement is filed before the issues in question are presented for trial.[90] However, in *Robin Haft Trust*, an agreement was filed *after* an adverse court ruling. In an appeal for a rehearing, the judge ruled that the filing of the agreement after the case came to trial was too late and the appeal for a rehearing was denied.[91]

If the shareholder *does* acquire a forbidden interest in the corporation within the 10-year period following the redemption, additional taxes may be due. Such an acquisition ordinarily results in the redemption being treated as a dividend distribution rather than a sale. The limitation period for assessing additional taxes extends to one year following the date the shareholder files notice of the acquisition of the forbidden interest with the IRS.[92]

---

[90] *Edward J. Fehrs v. U.S.*, 40 AFTR 2d 77-5040, 77-1 USTC ¶ 9423 (Ct. Cl., 1977).
[91] *Robin Haft Trust*, 62 T.C. 145 (1974).
[92] Sec. 302(c)(2)(A).

PROBLEM MATERIALS

DISCUSSION QUESTIONS

4-1. Why must a corporation compute its E&P?

4-2. Explain how a corporation computes its current E&P and its accumulated E&P.

4-3. Why is it necessary to distinguish between current and accumulated E&P?

4-4. Describe the effect of a $100,000 cash distribution paid on January 1 to the sole shareholder of a calendar-year corporation whose stock basis is $25,000 when the corporation has
  a. $100,000 of current E&P and $100,000 of accumulated E&P
  b. A $50,000 accumulated E&P deficit and $60,000 of current E&P
  c. A $60,000 accumulated E&P deficit and a $60,000 current E&P deficit
  d. An $80,000 current E&P deficit and $100,000 of accumulated E&P
  Answer Parts a to d again, assuming that the distribution is made on October 1.

4-5. Zero Corporation owns a building with a $160,000 adjusted basis and a $120,000 FMV. Should the corporation sell the property and distribute the proceeds to its shareholders or distribute the property to its shareholders and let them sell the property? Why?

4-6. Walnut Corporation owns a building with a $120,000 adjusted basis and a $160,000 FMV. Should the corporation sell the property and distribute the proceeds to its shareholders or distribute the property to its shareholders and let them sell the property? Why?

4-7. Pecan Corporation distributes land to a shareholder. Explain how the following are computed:
  a. The amount of the distribution
  b. The amount of the dividend
  c. The basis of the property to the shareholder
  d. When the holding period for the property begins

4-8. Under what circumstances does a corporation recognize gain or loss when property is distributed to its shareholders in a nonliquidating distribution?

4-9. What effect does a property distribution have on a corporation's E&P?

4-10. Why are stock dividends generally nontaxable? Under what circumstances are stock dividends taxable?

4-11. How is a distribution of stock rights treated by a shareholder for tax purposes? by the distributing corporation?

4-12. What is a stock redemption? What are some reasons for making a stock redemption? Why are some redemptions treated as a sale and some as a dividend?

4-13. Field Corporation redeems 100 shares of stock from Andrew for $10,000. Andrew's basis in those shares is $8,000. Explain the possible tax treatments of the $10,000 received by Andrew.

4-14. What conditions are necessary for a redemption to be treated as a sale by the redeeming shareholder?

4-15. Explain the purpose of the attribution rules in determining stock ownership in a redemption. Describe the four types of attribution rules that apply to redemptions.

4-16. Under what circumstances does a corporation recognize gain or loss when it distributes property in redemption of its stock? What effect does a redemption distribution have on the distributing corporation's E&P?

4-17. What is a preferred stock bailout? How does Sec. 306 operate to prevent a shareholder from realizing the planned advantages of a preferred stock bailout?

4-18. Define Sec. 306 stock.

4-19. Bill owns all 100 of the outstanding shares of Plum Corporation stock and 80 of the 100 outstanding shares of Cherry Corporation stock. He sells 20 Plum Corporation shares to Cherry Corporation for $80,000. Explain why this transaction is treated as a redemption and how the tax consequences of the transaction are determined.

4-20. Describe a spinoff, a split-off, and a split-up.

4-21. When is the distribution of a controlled corporation's stock tax-free to the distributing corporation's shareholders?

4-22. When does the distributing corporation recognize gain or loss on a distribution of stock and securities in a controlled corporation to its shareholders?

4-23. What is a constructive dividend? Under what circumstances are constructive dividends most likely to arise?

4-24. Define the term *active conduct of a trade or business*. Why is the term important in connection with partial liquidations and distributions of the stock of a controlled corporation?

4-25. Explain the tax consequences to both the corporation and a shareholder-employee of an IRS determination that a portion of the compensation paid in a prior tax year exceeds the reasonable compensation limit. What steps can be taken by the corporation and the shareholder-employee to avoid the double taxation usually associated with such a determination?

4-26. What is a bootstrap acquisition? What are the tax consequences of such a transaction?

PROBLEMS

4-27. *Current E&P Calculation.* Beach Corporation reports the following results using the accrual method of accounting:

Income:	
Gross profit from manufacturing operations	$250,000
Dividends received from 25%-owned domestic corporation	20,000
Interest income: Corporate bonds	10,000
Municipal bonds	12,000
Proceeds from life insurance policy on key employee	100,000
Section 1231 gain on sale of land	8,000
Expenses:	
Administrative expenses	110,000
Bad debt expense	5,000
Depreciation[a]	86,000
NOL carryover	40,000
Charitable contributions: Current year	8,000
Carryover from last year	3,500
Capital loss on sale of stock	1,200
Penalty on late payment of federal taxes	450

[a]Depreciation under the alternative depreciation system of Sec. 168(g) would have been $42,000.

    a. What is Beach Corporation's taxable income?
    b. What is Beach Corporation's current E&P?

4-28. *Current E&P Computation.* Water Corporation reports $500,000 of taxable income for the current year. The following additional information is available:

    1. Water Corporation reported a long-term capital loss of $80,000 for the current year. No capital gains were reported this year.
    2. $80,000 of dividends from a 10%-owned domestic corporation are included in taxable income.
    3. Water Corporation paid fines and penalties of $6,000 that were not deducted in computing taxable income.

4. Water Corporation deducted a $30,000 NOL carryover from a prior tax year in computing this year's taxable income.
5. Taxable income includes a deduction for $40,000 of depreciation that is in excess of the depreciation allowed for E&P purposes.

What is Water Corporation's current E&P for this year?

4-29. *Consequences of a Single Cash Distribution.* Yellow Corporation is a calendar-year taxpayer. All of the stock is owned by Edna. Her basis for the stock is $25,000. On March 1, Yellow Corporation distributes $60,000 to Edna. Determine the tax consequences of the cash distribution to Edna in each of the following independent situations:

	Current E&P	Accumulated E&P
a.	$15,000	$50,000
b.	25,000	(25,000)
c.	(36,500)	65,000
d.	(10,000)	(25,000)

4-30. *Consequences of Multiple Cash Distributions.* At the beginning of the current year, Charles owns all of Pearl Corporation's outstanding stock. His basis in the stock is $80,000. On July 1, he sells all of his stock to Donald for $125,000. During the current year, Pearl Corporation, a calendar-year taxpayer, makes two cash distributions: $60,000 on March 1 to Charles and $90,000 on September 1 to Donald. How are these distributions treated in the following independent situations?

	Current E&P	Accumulated E&P
a.	$ 40,000	$ 30,000
b.	100,000	(50,000)
c.	(36,500)	120,000

4-31. *Distribution of Appreciated Property.* In the current year, Ruby Corporation has $100,000 of current and accumulated E&P. On March 3, Ruby Corporation distributes a parcel of land worth $60,000 to Barbara, a shareholder. The land has a $30,000 adjusted basis to Ruby Corporation and is subject to an $8,000 mortgage, which Barbara assumes.
   a. What are the amount and character of the income recognized by Barbara as a result of the distribution?
   b. What is Barbara's basis for the land?
   c. What are the amount and character of Ruby Corporation's gain or loss as a result of the distribution?
   d. What effect does the distribution have on Ruby Corporation's E&P?

4-32. *Distribution of Property Subject to a Liability.* On May 10 of the current year, Stowe Corporation distributes land (a capital asset) worth $50,000 to Arlene, a shareholder. The land has a $15,000 adjusted basis and is subject to a $60,000 mortgage, which Arlene assumes.
   a. What are the amount and character of the income recognized by Arlene as a result of the distribution?
   b. What is Arlene's basis for the land?
   c. What are the amount and character of Stowe Corporation's gain or loss as a result of the distribution?
   d. What effect does the distribution have on Stowe Corporation's E&P?

4-33. *Property Distribution-Comprehensive Problem.* On May 15, 1991, Quick Corporation distributes a building worth $250,000 to Calvin, a shareholder. The building originally cost $180,000 in 1988. Straight-line depreciation was taken in the amount of $30,000, so that the adjusted basis on the date of distribution is $150,000. The building is subject to an $80,000 mortgage, which Calvin assumes. Assume Quick Corporation has an E&P balance in excess of the amount distributed.
   a. What are the amount and character of the income recognized by Calvin as a result of the distribution?

b. What is Calvin's basis for the building?
c. What are the amount and character of Quick Corporation's gain or loss as a result of the distribution?
d. What effect does the distribution have on Quick Corporation's E&P?

4-34. ***Property Distribution-Comprehensive Problem.*** During the current year, Zeta Corporation distributes the items listed below to its sole shareholder, Susan. For each item listed below, determine the gross income recognized by Susan, her basis in the item, the amount of gain or loss recognized by Zeta Corporation, and the effect of the distribution on Zeta Corporation's E&P. Assume that Zeta Corporation has an E&P balance in excess of the amount distributed.
   a. A parcel of land used in Zeta Corporation's business that has a $200,000 FMV and a $125,000 adjusted basis.
   b. Assume the same facts as Part a, except that the land is subject to a $140,000 mortgage.
   c. Inventory having a $25,000 FMV and an $18,000 adjusted basis.
   d. A building used in Zeta's business having a $450,000 FMV and a $150,000 adjusted basis. $75,000 of depreciation has been taken with respect to the building using the straight-line method.
   e. An automobile used in Zeta's business having an $8,000 FMV, a $5,760 adjusted basis, on which $6,240 of MACRS depreciation was taken.
   f. Installment obligations having a $35,000 face amount and FMV and a $24,500 adjusted basis.

4-35. ***Stock Dividend Distribution.*** Wilton Corporation has a single class of common stock outstanding. Robert owns 100 shares, which he purchased in 1989 for $100,000. In 1991, when the stock is worth $1,200 per share, Wilton Corporation declares a 10% stock dividend payable in common stock. Robert receives 10 additional shares on December 10, 1991. On January 30, 1992, he sells 5 of the new shares for $7,000.
   a. How much income must Robert recognize when he receives the stock dividend?
   b. How much gain (or loss) must Robert recognize when he sells the common stock?
   c. What is Robert's basis in his remaining common stock? When does his holding period in the new common stock begin?

4-36. ***Stock Dividend Distribution.*** Moss Corporation has a single class of common stock outstanding. Tillie owns 1,000 shares, which she purchased in 1988 for $100,000. Moss Corporation declares a stock dividend payable in 8% preferred stock having a $100 par value. Each shareholder receives 1 share of preferred stock for each 10 shares of common stock held. On the distribution date—November 10, 1990—the common stock is worth $180 per share and the preferred stock is worth $100 per share. On April 1, 1991, Tillie sells half of her preferred stock for $5,000.
   a. How much income must Tillie recognize when she receives the stock dividend?
   b. How much gain (or loss) must Tillie recognize when she sells the preferred stock? (Ignore the implications of Sec. 306.)
   c. What is Tillie's basis in her remaining common and preferred stock? When does her holding period for the preferred stock begin?

4-37. ***Stock Rights Distribution.*** Trusty Corporation has a single class of stock outstanding. Jim owns 200 shares of the common stock, which he purchased for $50 per share on March 1, two years ago. On April 10 of the current year, Trusty Corporation distributes to its shareholders one right to purchase a share of common stock at $60 per share for each share of common stock held. At the time of the distribution, the common stock is worth $75 per share and the rights are worth $15 per right. On September 10, Jim sells 100 rights for $2,000 and exercises the remaining 100 rights. He sells 60 of the shares acquired with the rights for $80 each on November 10.
   a. What are the amount and character of the income recognized when the rights are received?
   b. What are the amount and character of the gain (or loss) recognized when the rights are sold?
   c. What are the amount and character of the gain (or loss) recognized when the rights are exercised?
   d. What are the amount and character of the gain (or loss) recognized when the new common stock is sold?

e. What basis does Jim have in the remaining shares?

4-38. *Redemption from a Sole Shareholder.* Paul owns all 100 shares of Presto Corporation's stock. His basis in the stock is $10,000. Presto Corporation has $100,000 of E&P. Presto Corporation redeems 25 of Paul's shares for $25,000. What are the tax consequences of the redemption to Paul and to Presto Corporation?

4-39. *Multiple Redemptions.* Moore Corporation has 100 shares of stock outstanding that is owned by four unrelated shareholders as indicated below. Moore redeems 100 shares from the shareholders as shown below for $300 per share. Each shareholder has a $180 per share basis for their stock. Moore Corporation's current and accumulated E&P at the end of the tax year is $150,000.

Shareholder	Shares Held Before the Redemption	Shares Redeemed
Ann	100	70
Beth	100	20
Carol	100	10
David	100	–0–
Total	400	100

a. What are the tax consequences (e.g., amount and character of income, gain, or loss recognized and basis of remaining shares) of the redemptions to Ann, Beth, and Carol?
b. How does your answer to Part a change if Ann is Carol's mother?

4-40. *Attribution Rules.* George owns 100 shares of Polar Corporation's 1,000 shares of outstanding common stock. Under the family attribution rules of Sec. 318, to which of the following individuals will George's stock be attributed?

a. George's wife
b. George's father
c. George's brother
d. George's mother-in-law
e. George's daughter
f. George's son-in law
g. George's grandfather
h. George's grandson
i. George's mother's brother (his uncle)

4-41. *Redemption—Comprehensive Illustration.* Andrew, Bill, Carl, and Carl, Jr. (Carl's son), and Tetra Corporation own all of the single class of Excel Corporation stock as follows:

Shareholder	Shares Held	Adjusted Basis
Andrew	20	$3,000
Bea	30	6,000
Carl	25	4,000
Carl, Jr.	15	3,000
Tetra Corporation	10	2,000
Total	100	

Andrew, Bea, and Carl are unrelated. Bea owns 75% of the Tetra stock, and Andrew owns the remaining 25% of the Tetra stock. Excel Corporation's E&P is $100,000. Determine the tax consequences to the shareholders and Excel Corporation of the following independent redemptions:

a. Excel Corporation redeems 10 of Bea's shares for $10,000.
b. Excel Corporation redeems 25 of Bea's shares for $30,000.
c. Excel Corporation redeems all of Carl's shares for $25,000.
d. Assume the same facts as in Part c, except that the stock is redeemed from Carl's estate in order to pay death taxes. The entire redemption qualifies under Sec. 303.

e. Excel Corporation redeems all of Andrew's shares for land having a $6,000 basis to Excel Corporation and a $20,000 FMV.

4-42. *Partial Liquidation.* Unrelated individuals Amy, Beth, and Carla, and Delta Corporation each own 25 of the 100 outstanding shares of Axle Corporation's stock. Axle distributes $20,000 to each shareholder in exchange for 5 shares of Axle stock in a transaction that qualifies as a partial liquidation. Each share redeemed has a $1,000 basis to the shareholder and a $4,000 FMV. How does each shareholder treat the distribution?

4-43. *Effect of Redemption on E&P.* White Corporation has 100 shares of stock outstanding, 40 of which are owned by Ann. The remaining 60 shares are owned by unrelated shareholders. White Corporation redeems 30 of Ann's shares for $30,000. In the year of the redemption, White Corporation has $30,000 of paid-in capital and $80,000 of E&P.
   a. How does the redemption affect White Corporation's E&P balance if the redemption qualifies for sale treatment?
   b. How does the redemption affect White Corporation's E&P balance if the redemption does *not* qualify for sale treatment?

4-44. *Comprehensive Redemption Problem.* Alan, Barbara, and Dave are all unrelated. Each has owned 100 shares of Time Corporation stock for five years and each has a $60,000 basis in those 100 shares. Time's E&P is $240,000. Time redeems all 100 of Alan's shares for $100,000, their FMV.
   a. What are the amount and character of Alan's recognized gain? What basis do Barbara and Dave have in their remaining shares? What effect does the redemption have on Time's E&P?
   b. Assuming that Alan is instead Barbara's son, answer the questions in Part a again.
   c. Assume the same facts as in Part b, except that Alan signs an agreement under Sec. 302(c)(2)(A) to waive the family attribution rules. Answer the questions in Part a again.

4-45. *Redemption to Pay Death Taxes.* John died on March 3. His gross estate of $2,500,000 includes 400 of the 1,000 outstanding shares of First Corporation stock worth $1,500,000. The remaining 600 shares are owned by John's wife, Myra. Funeral and administrative expenses deductible under Secs. 2053 and 2054 amount to $250,000. John, Jr. is the sole beneficiary of John's estate. Estate taxes amount to $350,000.
   a. Does a redemption of First stock from John's estate; John. Jr.; or John's wife qualify for sale treatment under Sec. 303?
   b. On September 10, First Corporation redeems 200 shares of its stock from John's estate for $800,000. How is this redemption treated by the estate?

4-46. *Preferred Stock Bailout.* Fran owns all 100 shares of Star Corporation stock for which her adjusted basis is $60,000. On December 1, 1991, Star Corporation distributes 50 shares of preferred stock to Fran as a nontaxable stock dividend. In the year of the distribution, Star Corporation's E&P is $100,000, the preferred shares are worth $150,000, and the common shares are worth $300,000.
   a. What are the tax consequences to Fran and to Star Corporation if Fran sells her preferred stock to Ken for $200,000 on January 10, 1992? In 1992, Star Corporation's E&P is $75,000.
   b. How would your answer to Part a change if Fran sells her preferred stock to Ken for $110,000 instead of $200,000?
   c. How would your answer to Part a change if Star Corporation redeems Fran's preferred stock for $200,000 on January 10, 1992?

4-47. *Preferred Stock Bailout.* In each of the following situations, does Sec. 306 apply? If so, what is its effect?
   a. Beth sells her Sec. 306 stock to Marvin in a year when the issuing corporation has no E&P.
   b. Zero Corporation redeems Sec. 306 stock from Jim in a year in which it has no E&P.
   c. Zero Corporation redeems Sec. 306 stock from Ruth in a year in which it has a large E&P balance.
   d. Joan gives 100 shares of Sec. 306 stock to her nephew, Barry.
   e. Ed completely terminates his interest in Zero Corporation by having all of his common stock and preferred stock (the Sec. 306 stock in question) redeemed by Zero.

f. Carl inherits 100 shares of Sec. 306 stock from his uncle Ted.

4-48. *Parent-Subsidiary Redemptions.* Jane owns 150 of the 200 outstanding shares of Parent Corporation's stock. Parent owns 160 of the 200 outstanding shares of Subsidiary Corporation's stock. Jane sells 50 shares of her Parent stock to Subsidiary for $40,000. Jane's basis in her Parent shares is $15,000 ($100 per share). Subsidiary Corporation and Parent Corporation have E&P of $60,000 and $25,000, respectively, at the end of the year in which the redemption occurs.
   a. What are the amount and character of Jane's gain or loss on the sale?
   b. What is Jane's basis in her remaining shares of Parent stock?
   c. How does the sale affect the E&P of Parent and Subsidiary Corporations?
   d. What basis does Subsidiary Corporation take in the Parent shares it purchases?
   e. How would your answer to Part a change if Jane instead sells 100 of her Parent shares to Subsidiary Corporation for $80,000?

4-49. *Brother-Sister Redemptions.* Bob owns 60 of the 100 outstanding shares of Dazzle Corporation's stock and 80 of the 100 outstanding shares of Razzle Corporation's stock. Bob's basis in his Dazzle shares is $12,000, and his basis in his Razzle shares is $8,000. On December 20, 1991, Bob sells 30 of his Dazzle shares to Razzle Corporation for $50,000. In the year of the sale, Dazzle and Razzle Corporations have E&P of $25,000 and $40,000, respectively.
   a. What are the amount and character of Bob's gain or loss on the sale?
   b. What is Bob's basis in his remaining shares of the Dazzle and Razzle stock?
   c. How does the sale affect the E&P of Dazzle and Razzle Corporations?
   d. What basis does Razzle Corporation take in the Dazzle shares it purchases?
   e. How would your answer to Part a change if Bob owns only 50 of the 100 outstanding shares of Razzle stock?

4-50. *Spinoff.* Parent Corporation has been in the business of manufacturing and selling trucks for the past 8 years. Its subsidiary, Tiny Corporation, has been in the business of manufacturing and selling diesel engines for the past 7 years. Parent acquired control of Tiny Corporation 6 years ago when it purchased 100% of its stock from Large Corporation. Parent has been ordered to divest itself of Tiny Corporation by a federal court. Consequently, Parent distributes all of its Tiny Corporation stock to its shareholders. Alan owns 10% of Parent's outstanding stock having a $40,000 basis. He receives 25 shares of Tiny stock having a $25,000 FMV as a result of Parent's distribution. Parent's E&P at the end of the year in which the spinoff occurs is $250,000. The Parent stock held by Alan has a $75,000 FMV immediately after the distribution.
   a. What are the amount and character of the gain, loss, or income that Alan must recognize as a result of distributing the Tiny stock?
   b. What basis does Alan take for the Tiny stock that he receives?
   c. When does Alan's holding period for the Tiny stock commence?
   d. How would your answer to Part a change if Parent had been in the truck business for only 3 years prior to making the distribution?

4-51. *Split-off.* Parent Corporation has owned all 100 shares of the Subsidiary Corporation stock since 1980. Parent Corporation has been in the business of manufacturing and selling light fixtures, and Subsidiary Corporation has been in the business of manufacturing and selling light bulbs. Amy and Bill are the two equal shareholders of the Parent stock. Amy's basis in her 50 shares of Parent stock is $80,000, and Bill's basis in his 50 shares of Parent stock is $60,000. On April 10, 1991, Parent distributes all 100 shares of Subsidiary stock to Bill in exchange for all of his Parent stock (which is cancelled). The distribution has an acceptable business purpose. In the year of the distribution, Parent has $150,000 of E&P. Immediately after the distribution, the FMVs of the Parent and Subsidiary stocks are $1,600 and $800 per share, respectively.
   a. How much gain, loss, or income must Bill recognize?
   b. What basis does Bill take in the Subsidiary stock?
   c. When does Bill's holding period for the Subsidiary stock begin?
   d. How would your answer to Part a change if the Subsidiary stock had instead been purchased by Parent Corporation in 1989?

4-52. *Distribution of Stock and Securities.* Elgin Corporation has 100 shares of stock outstanding. Fred, a shareholder of Elgin Corporation, exchanges his 25% interest in the Elgin stock for Garnet Corporation stock and securities. Elgin purchased 80% of the Garnet stock 10 years ago for $25,000. At the time of the exchange, Fred has a $50,000 basis in his Elgin stock, and the stock has an $80,000 FMV. Fred receives Garnet stock that has a $60,000 FMV and a Garnet Corporation security that has a $20,000 FMV. Elgin has $50,000 of E&P. Assume that all the requirements of Sec. 355 are met except for the receipt of boot.
   a. What are the amount and character of Fred's recognized gain or loss on the exchange?
   b. What is Fred's basis for the Garnet stock and the Garnet security?
   c. What are the amount and character of Elgin Corporation's recognized gain or loss on the distribution?
   d. When does Fred's holding period begin for the Garnet stock and the Garnet security?
   e. How would your answer to Part a change if the exchange did not meet the requirements of Sec. 355 or Sec. 356?

4-53. *Disguised Dividends.* King Corporation is a very profitable manufacturing corporation with $800,000 of E&P. It is owned equally by Harry and Wilma, who are husband and wife. Determine the tax consequences of the following independent events:
   a. In reviewing a prior year King Corporation tax return, the IRS determines that the $500,000 of salary and bonuses paid to Wilma is unreasonable compensation. Reasonable compensation would be $280,000.
   b. King has loaned Harry $400,000 over the past 3 years. None of the money is ever repaid. Harry does not pay any interest on the loans.
   c. King sells a building to Wilma for $150,000 in cash. The property has an adjusted basis of $90,000 and is subject to a $60,000 mortgage, which Wilma also assumes. The FMV of the building is $350,000.
   d. Harry leases a warehouse to King for $50,000 per year. Similar warehouses can be leased for $35,000 per year.
   e. Wilma sells some land to King for $250,000 on which King intends to build a factory. The land is appraised at $185,000.
   f. The corporation owns an airplane that it uses to fly executives to business sites and business meetings. When it is not being used for business, Harry and Wilma use it to fly to their ranch in Texas. The approximate cost of their trips to the ranch in the current year is $8,000.

4-54. *Unreasonable Compensation.* Forward Corporation is owned by a group of 15 shareholders. During the current year Forward Corporation pays $450,000 in salary and bonuses to Alvin, its president and controlling shareholder. The IRS audits Forward's tax return and determines that reasonable compensation for Alvin would be $250,000. Forward Corporation agrees to the adjustment.
   a. What are the effects of the disallowance of part of the deduction for Alvin's salary and bonuses to Forward Corporation and Alvin?
   b. What tax savings could have been obtained by Forward Corporation and Alvin if an agreement had been in effect that required Alvin to repay Forward Corporation the monies that were determined by the IRS to be unreasonable compensation?

CASE STUDY PROBLEM

4-55. Amy, Beth, and Meg each own 100 of the 300 outstanding shares of Theta Corporation stock. Amy wants to sell her shares which have a $40,000 basis and a $100,000 FMV. Either Beth or Meg can purchase her shares (50 shares each) or Theta can redeem all of Amy's shares. Theta Corporation has a $150,000 E&P balance.

Required: Write a memorandum to the three sisters, who are active in the management of Theta, comparing the tax consequences of the two options.

TAX RESEARCH PROBLEMS

4-56. Hatch Corporation, a manufacturing business, was owned by Mike and his son, Steve. Hatch Corporation redeems all of Mike's stock in a transaction qualifying as a complete termination of Mike's interest in Hatch Corporation. To qualify, Mike must file an agreement not to acquire any interest in Hatch Corporation for 10 years. After the redemption, Mike starts a new career as owner of a counseling firm for employees who are about to retire. Two years later, Steve wants to use Mike's firm to counsel some of his employees who are close to retirement. Mike's company charges a fixed fee for each employee counseled, and Hatch Corporation is to pay the same amount as all of Mike's other customers. Does such an arrangement violate Mike's agreement not to acquire any interest in Hatch Corporation?

A partial list of research sources is:

- Sec. 302(c)(2).
- Reg. Sec. 1.302-4.
- Rev. Rul. 70-104, 1970-1 C.B. 66.
- *Est. of Milton S. Lennard,* 61 T.C. 554, *nonacq.* 1978-2 C.B. 3.

4-57. When Winter Corporation is audited on its 1990 tax return, $10,000 of travel and entertainment expenses incurred by Charles, an officer-shareholder, are disallowed because of inadequate documentation. The IRS asserts that the $10,000 expenditure was a constructive dividend to Charles. Charles asserts that the expense was a business expense and that he derived no personal benefit from the expenditure and therefore should not be charged with any dividend income. Who is correct?

A partial list of research sources is:

- Secs. 162 and 274.
- Reg. Secs. 1.274-1 and -2.
- *Henry Schwartz Corp.,* 60 T.C. 728 (1973), *nonacq.* 1981-1 C.B. 2.

4-58. Ann owns 30% of the outstanding Summer Corporation stock. The remainder is owned by unrelated individuals. Summer Corporation owns land with a $100,000 adjusted basis and a $60,000 FMV. In the current year, Summer Corporation sells the land to Ann for $50,000. What are the tax consequences of this sale to Summer Corporation and to Ann?

A partial list of research sources is:

- Secs. 301, 311, 316, and 1001.
- Reg. Secs. 1.301-1(j) and (k).
- *Jason L. Honigman v. CIR,* 30 AFTR 2d 72-5360, 72-2 USTC ¶ 9613 (6th Cir., 1972).

4-59. Sara is the owner of 60% of the single class of stock of Mayfield Corporation, a calendar-year domestic corporation that uses the accrual method of accounting. The remaining 40% of Mayfield Corporation stock is owned by a group of five family members and three key employees. Sara uses the cash method of accounting. She is an officer and a member of the board of directors of Mayfield Corporation. During the period 1990-1992, Sara draws the following amounts as salary and tax-free fringe benefits from Mayfield Corporation: 1990, $160,000; 1991, $240,000; and 1992, $290,000. The amounts are earned evenly throughout the tax years in question. A revenue agent upon auditing M's tax returns for 1990-1992 determines in 1994 that reasonable compensation for Sara's services for the 3 years in question is $110,000, $165,000, and $175,000, respectively. The bylaws of Mayfield Corporation were amended on December 15, 1991, to provide that

> Any payments made to an officer of the corporation, including salary, commissions, bonuses, or other forms of compensation, interest, rent, or travel and entertainment expense that is incurred, and which shall be disallowed in whole or in part as a deductible expense by the Internal Revenue Service, shall be reimbursed by such officer to the corporation to the full extent of such disallowance.

Following the disallowance of the salary expense, the board of directors meets and requests payment of the aforementioned amounts from Sara. Because of the large amount of money involved, the board of directors approves an installment plan whereby the $240,000 would be repaid in 5 annual installments of $48,000 each over the period 1994-1998. No interest will be required to be paid on the unpaid balance of the $240,000. What salary and fringe benefits are taxable to Sara in the period 1990-1992, and what repayments are deductible by Sara during the period 1994-1998?

A partial list of research sources is

- Sec. 162(a)(1).
- Reg. Sec. 1.162-7.
- Rev. Rul. 69-115, 1969-1 C.B. 50.
- *Vincent E. Oswald,* 49 T.C. 645 (1968), acq. 1968-2 C.B. 2.
- *John G. Pahl,* 67 T.C. 286 (1976).

5 Other Corporate Tax Levies

CHAPTER OUTLINE
LEARNING OBJECTIVES 5-2
THE CORPORATE ALTERNATIVE MINIMUM TAX 5-2
  The General Formula 5-2
  Definitions 5-3
  Tax Preference Items 5-3
  Adjustments to Taxable Income 5-5
  Disallowed Losses 5-7
  Adjusted Current Earnings (ACE) Adjustment 5-7
  Minimum Tax Credit 5-12
  Tax Credits and the AMT 5-12
SUPERFUND ENVIRONMENTAL TAX 5-14
PERSONAL HOLDING COMPANY TAX 5-15
  Personal Holding Company Defined 5-15
  Stock Ownership Requirement 5-15
  Passive Income Requirement 5-16
  Determining the PHC Penalty Tax 5-20
  Avoiding the PHC Designation and Tax Liability Through the Use of Dividend Distributions 5-21
  PHC Tax Calculation 5-24
ACCUMULATED EARNINGS TAX 5-25
  Corporations Subject to the Penalty Tax 5-25
  Proving a Tax-Avoidance Purpose 5-26
  Evidence Concerning the Reasonableness of an Earnings Accumulation 5-26
  Determining the Accumulated Earnings Tax Liability 5-29
  Accumulated Earnings Tax Calculation 5-34
UNRELATED BUSINESS INCOME TAX 5-35
TAX PLANNING CONSIDERATIONS 5-36
  Special AMT Elections 5-36
  Eliminating the Adjusted Current Earnings Adjustment 5-37
  Avoiding the Personal Holding Company Tax 5-37
  Avoiding the Accumulated Earnings Tax 5-38
COMPLIANCE AND PROCEDURAL CONSIDERATIONS 5-38
  Alternative Minimum Tax 5-38
  Superfund Environmental Tax 5-39
  Personal Holding Company Tax 5-39
  Accumulated Earnings Tax 5-40
  Unrelated Business Income Tax 5-40
PROBLEM MATERIALS 5-40
  Discussion Questions 5-40
  Problems 5-43
  Tax Form/Return Preparation Problem 5-49
  Case Study Problem 5-49
  Tax Research Problems 5-50

LEARNING OBJECTIVES

After studying this chapter, you should be able to

1. Calculate the amount of the corporation's alternative minimum tax liability (if any)
2. Determine whether a corporation is subject to the Superfund environmental tax or not
3. Determine whether a corporation is a personal holding company (PHC) or not
4. Calculate the amount of the corporation's PHC tax liability
5. Evaluate whether a corporation has an accumulated earnings tax problem or not
6. Calculate the amount of the corporation's accumulated earnings tax liability
7. Determine whether a corporation is subject to the unrelated business income tax or not
8. Explain how a corporation can avoid being subject to the personal holding company tax
9. Explain how a corporation can avoid being subject to the accumulated earnings tax

Chapter 3 examined the general corporate tax liability formula and the procedures for calculating, reporting and paying the corporate income tax liability. Chapter 5 continues this examination of the corporate tax liability formula by examining a series of additional tax levies that may be imposed upon a C corporation. These include the corporate alternative minimum tax, the personal holding company penalty tax, the accumulated earnings penalty tax, the superfund environmental tax and the unrelated business income tax. Each of these additional tax liabilities may be imposed in different situations. This chapter examines when each of these levies are likely to be incurred, and means by which a corporate taxpayer can avoid having to pay the additional tax liability (e.g., by making a dividend distribution).

THE CORPORATE ALTERNATIVE MINIMUM TAX

OBJECTIVE 1

Calculate the amount of the corporation's alternative minimum tax liability (if any)

The General Formula

The **alternative minimum tax** (AMT) for corporations is similar to that for individuals. The objective of the tax is to ensure that every corporation with substantial economic income pays a significant amount of tax despite the use of exclusions, deductions, and credits.

The starting point for computing a corporation's AMT is its taxable income. Taxable income is increased by tax preference items, modified by adjustments, and reduced by a statutory exemption amount. The resulting tax base is multiplied by 20% to yield the **tentative minimum tax** (TMT). If the TMT exceeds the corporation's regular (income) tax, the excess is the corporation's AMT liability. If the TMT does not exceed the corporation's regular tax, no AMT is owed. The computation of a corporation's AMT is outlined in Table 5-1.

Definitions

This section defines the terms used in the computation of the AMT.[1]

Alternative Minimum Taxable Income (AMTI). **Alternative minimum taxable income** is the corporation's taxable income (1) increased by tax preference items (2) adjusted (either up or down) for income, gain, deduction, and loss items that have to be recomputed under the AMT system and (3) reduced by the alternative tax NOL deduction.

Tentative Minimum Tax. The tentative minimum tax is calculated by (1) multiplying 20% times the corporation's alternative minimum taxable income less an exemption amount, and (2) deducting foreign tax credits allowable under the AMT (AMT FTCs).[2]

Regular Tax. A corporation's **regular tax** is its tax liability for income tax purposes as defined in Sec. 26(b) (see Chapter 3 for the computation of a corporation's regular tax liability) reduced by foreign tax credits and possession tax credits allowable for income tax purposes under Sec. 27.

Alternative Minimum Tax. The AMT equals the amount by which a corporation's TMT exceeds its regular tax for the year.

Statutory Exemption Amount. The exemption amount is $40,000, but it is reduced by 25% of the amount by which AMTI exceeds $150,000.[3] The statutory exemption is phased out when AMTI equals $310,000.

> **Additional Comment**
> Application of the AMT results in an acceleration of the recognition of income as compared to the regular tax system. This acceleration is accomplished by adding back tax preference items and making other adjustments to taxable income in arriving at AMTI. Even though the AMT rate (20%) is lower than the top corporate tax rate (34%), the AMT system often results in a higher federal tax liability because the tax base under the AMT is larger than the tax base for regular taxable income.

Example 5-1 ■ Yellow Corporation's AMTI is $200,000. Its exemption amount is $27,500 {$40,000 − (0.25 × [$200,000 − $150,000])}. ■

The following example illustrates the computation of the AMT.

Example 5-2 ■ In 1991, Badger Corporation has $400,000 of taxable income. It also has $350,000 of tax preferences and $250,000 of positive adjustments for purposes of the AMT. It has no tax credits available. Badger's regular tax liability is $136,000 (0.34 × $400,000). Its AMT exemption is zero since AMTI exceeds $310,000. Therefore, its AMT tax base is $1,000,000 ($400,000 + $350,000 + $250,000), and its TMT is $200,000 (0.20 × $1,000,000). Badger's AMT is $64,000 ($200,000 − $136,000). Thus, Badger must pay a total federal tax liability of $200,000 ($136,000 + $64,000) for 1991. ■

Tax Preference Items

The tax preference items that must be added to a corporation's taxable income to compute its AMTI include[4]

> **Typical Misconception**
> One distinction between tax preference items and adjustments is that tax preference items always increase AMTI, whereas an adjustment can result in an increase or a decrease in AMTI.

---
[1] Sec. 55.
[2] Sec. 55(b). The tentative minimum tax amount can be reduced by up to 25% of the regular investment tax credit amount (and any carryovers). Although the investment tax credit was generally repealed for tax years after 1985, certain transitional rules and carryover provisions can permit an investment tax credit offset to be claimed in 1991 and 1992.
[3] A closely held corporation having income in excess of the statutory exemption can avoid the AMT by electing to be taxed as an S corporation. An S corporation's shareholders are subject to the individual AMT (see Chapter 11).
[4] Sec. 57(a).

TABLE 5-1 Determination of the Corporate Alternative Minimum Tax Liability

Taxable income or loss before NOL deduction
Plus: Tax preference items:
1. Excess percentage depletion
2. Excess intangible drilling costs
3. Excess bad debt deductions of financial institutions
4. Tax-exempt interest on private activity bonds
5. Charitable contribution deduction claimed on donations of appreciated property
6. Excess depreciation on pre-1987 real property acquisitions
7. Excess depreciation on pre-1987 leased personal property acquisitions (personal holding companies only)[a]
8. Excess amortization on pre-1987 pollution control facility acquisitions

Plus or minus: Adjustment to taxable income for:
1. Depreciation on post-1986 property acquisitions
2. Excess mining exploration and development costs
3. Circulation expenditures (personal holding companies only)
4. Long-term contracts
5. Amortization of pollution control facilities
6. Installment sales of inventory and stock-in-trade
7. Basis adjustment
8. Adjusted current earnings adjustment

Plus: Losses disallowed under the passive loss limitation and at-risk rules
Minus: Alternative tax NOL deduction
Alternative tax energy preference deduction

Alternative minimum taxable income (AMTI)
Minus: Statutory exemption

Tax base
Times: 0.20

Tentative minimum tax before credits
Minus: AMT foreign tax credit (AMT FTC)

Tentative minimum tax (TMT)
Minus: Regular (income) tax liability before credits net of foreign tax credits and possessions tax credits

Alternative minimum tax (if any) owed (AMT)

---

[a] A personal holding company is a closely held corporation that earns primarily passive income. Further discussion of this corporate form is contained in a later section of this chapter.

- The excess of the depletion deduction allowable for the tax year over the adjusted basis of the depletable property at the end of the tax year (excluding the current year's depletion deduction).

- The amount by which excess intangible drilling and development costs incurred in connection with oil, gas, and geothermal wells exceeds 65% of the net income from such properties.[5]

- The excess of the reserve for bad debts deducted by a financial institution over the amount that would have been allowable based on actual experience.

- Tax-exempt interest on private activity bonds issued after August 8, 1986. Although the interest on private activity bonds is tax-exempt for income tax

---

[5] Excess intangible drilling and development costs are the amount by which intangible drilling and development costs arising in the tax year with respect to productive oil, gas, and geothermal properties exceeds the deduction that would have been allowable for the tax year if such costs had been capitalized and amortized using the straight-line method over a 10-year period commencing with the month in which production begins.

purposes it can increase the corporation's total tax liability by being included as a preference item in determining AMTI and the AMT liability.

- The excess of the deduction allowable for charitable contributions of capital gain properties over total of the properties' adjusted bases.

Example 5-3 ■ Bell Corporation contributes appreciated capital gain property to the American Red Cross. The property has a $300 FMV and a $100 adjusted basis. The entire $300 amount is deductible as a charitable contribution for income tax purposes. A $200 positive adjustment resulting from the appreciation being considered a tax preference item reduces the "net" charitable contribution deduction for AMT purposes to $100 ($300 contribution deduction − $200 preference item). ■

- The excess of accelerated depreciation claimed on real property for the tax year over a hypothetical straight-line depreciation allowance based on the property's useful life or a special ACRS recovery period for property placed in service prior to 1987.
- The excess of accelerated depreciation claimed on personal property placed in service by the corporation prior to 1987 (and leased by the corporation to others) for the tax year over a hypothetical straight-line depreciation allowance based on the property's useful life or a special ACRS recovery period. This preference item applies only to personal holding companies.
- The excess of rapid amortization claimed on certified pollution control facilities placed in service prior to 1987 over the depreciation deduction otherwise available.

Additional Comment
The accelerated depreciation on pre-1987 assets, which is in excess of straight-line depreciation, is considered a tax preference item. Since a tax preference item never decreases AMTI, when the straight-line depreciation eventually is in excess of the accelerated depreciation, no adjustment is made. Thus, pre-1987 assets are not fully depreciated for AMT purposes. The adjustment for post-1986 property is more equitable because it allows both increases and decreases to AMTI. Thus, post-1986 assets can be fully depreciated for AMT purposes.

Adjustments to Taxable Income

While tax preferences always *increase* AMTI, adjustments require a recomputation of certain income, gain, loss and deduction items and may either *increase* or *decrease* AMTI. The adjustments that must be made to taxable income to obtain AMTI are as follows:[6]

- Depreciation on property placed in service after 1986 and depreciated using the Modified ACRS system must be recomputed using the alternative depreciation system of Sec. 168(g). For AMT purposes, the depreciation method for all personal property is the 150% declining balance method, switching to the straight-line method in the first year in which it results in a larger allowance. The recovery period for personal property is the property's class life determined under the asset depreciation range (ADR) system. If personal property has no class life, the recovery period is 12 years. The depreciation method for real property is straight-line. The recovery period for commercial real property and residential rental property is 40 years. AMTI is increased (or decreased) by the amount by which the total depreciation deduction for regular tax purposes exceeds (or is less than) the total depreciation allowance for AMT purposes.[7]
- Separate gain or loss calculations must be made for regular tax and AMT purposes when a disposition of real or personal property occurs. A depreciable property's basis for regular tax purposes is adjusted downward by the amount of

---

[6] Sec. 56(a).
[7] Sec. 56(a)(1). The recovery periods and annual depreciation rates for making the AMT depreciation calculation are contained in Appendix C of the *Prentice Hall's Federal Taxation: Individuals* companion volume.

the regular tax depreciation allowance. A depreciable property's basis for AMT purposes is adjusted downward by the amount of the AMT depreciation allowance. Therefore, an asset may have different bases amounts for regular tax and AMT purposes. An adjustment to the amount of gain or loss that was recognized for regular tax purposes must be made for the difference in these two basis amounts when computing AMTI. This amount is commonly called the "basis adjustment" by tax practitioners.[8] The adjustment process is illustrated in the following example.

Example 5-4 ■

Key Point

When different depreciation methods are used for regular tax and AMT purposes, the adjusted bases for the depreciable assets are affected. Thus, when these assets are disposed of, an adjustment to AMTI will be required to reflect the difference in the regular tax recognized gain or loss as compared to the AMT recognized gain or loss.

Bulldog Corporation places into service depreciable personal property costing $3,000. The property's regular tax recovery period is 3 years under MACRS. The property's ADR life is 4 years. At the end of 3 years Bulldog Corporation sells the property for $1,500. The depreciation allowances claimed for regular tax and AMT purposes, adjusted basis for the property at the beginning of the year for each taxing system, and the positive or negative AMT adjustment for each of the years is presented in the table below.

Year	Regular Tax Adj. Basis	Depreciation	AMT Adj. Basis	Depreciation	AMT Adjustment
1	$3,000	$1,000	$3,000	$563	$437
2	2,000	1,334	2,437	914	420
3	666	444	1,523	609	(165)

A $1,278 ($1,500 proceeds − $222 adjusted basis) gain is recognized for regular tax purposes. A $586 ($1,500 proceeds − $914 adjusted basis) gain is recognized for AMT purposes. This necessitates a $692 negative basis adjustment when computing AMTI to take into account the difference resulting from the claiming of different depreciation allowances in the three years. This amount equals the net of the positive and negative depreciation allowance adjustments for years 1 through 3. ■

- Mine exploration and development costs that are expensed must be capitalized and amortized using the straight-line method over a 10-year period.
- Circulation expenditures must be amortized over a 3-year period instead of being expensed. This adjustment applies only to personal holding companies.
- Any long-term contracts entered into after March 1, 1986, must be accounted for using the percentage of completion method. Corporations using the percentage of completion—capitalized cost method or cash method for regular tax purposes will be required to make adjustments when determining AMTI. Repeal of the percentage of completion—capitalized cost method for long-term contracts entered into after July 11, 1989, for regular tax purposes over time will reduce the need for making this adjustment in future years.
- Pollution control facilities placed in service after December 31, 1986, and being amortized over a 60-month period must be depreciated using the alternative depreciation system of Sec. 168(g).
- The installment method may not be used to report gains on certain items for AMT purposes. Nondealers may use the installment method for AMT purposes. No adjustment is therefore required of nondealers when computing AMTI. Dealers cannot use the installment method of accounting on sales of inventory-type items for AMT purposes except when the corporation is paying an interest

---

[8] An asset also may have different bases amounts for E&P and state income tax purposes. Different gain or loss amounts, from that reported for regular tax purposes, may have to be recognized when computing E&P or the state tax liability.

charge to defer taxes. Therefore, an adjustment is generally required of dealers when computing AMTI.

- The NOL deduction must be replaced with the alternative tax NOL deduction. To compute the alternative tax NOL deduction, the NOL deduction must be adjusted in the same way that taxable income is adjusted in arriving at AMTI, and the NOL must be reduced by adding back any tax preference items and any losses disallowed under the passive activity limitations and at risk rules. Generally the alternative tax NOL is a different amount from the regular tax NOL because of these adjustments. The resulting alternative tax NOL will be carried back three years and forward 15 years. The alternative tax NOL deduction cannot exceed 90% of AMTI before the alternative tax NOL deduction and the alternative tax energy preference deduction.

For tax year 1991 and later years, taxpayers (other than integrated oil producers) are allowed a special adjustment based on energy preferences. This deduction equals the lesser of the alternative tax energy preference deduction or 40% of AMTI (excluding this deduction and the alternative tax NOL).[9] The alternative tax energy preference deduction equals the sum of (1) 75% of the intangible drilling cost (IDC) preference attributable to qualified exploratory costs, (2) 15% of the IDC preference over the portion of the IDC preference attributable to qualified exploratory costs, and (3) 50% of the marginal production depletion preference. A detailed discussion of this adjustment is beyond the scope of this text.

The following example illustrates the computation of AMTI.

Example 5-5 ■ Marion Corporation engages in copper activities. During 1991 it reported taxable income of $300,000, which includes deductions of $70,000 for percentage depletion and $80,000 for depreciation under the MACRS rules. $30,000 of the percentage depletion claimed was in excess of the adjusted basis of the depletable properties. The hypothetical depreciation deduction under the alternative depreciation system of Sec. 168(g) would have been only $55,000. AMTI is determined as follows:

Taxable income		$300,000
Plus:	Percentage depletion claimed in excess of basis	30,000
	MACRS depreciation claimed	80,000
Minus:	AMT depreciation	(55,000)
AMTI		$355,000

The recomputation needed for depreciation results in an increase in AMTI of $25,000. Since AMTI exceeds $310,000, no statutory exemption is available to Marion. ■

Disallowed Losses

Closely held corporations and personal service corporations must refigure losses coming under the at risk and passive activity limitation rules taking into account the corporation's AMTI adjustments and tax preference items.

Adjusted Current Earnings (ACE) Adjustment

For 1990 and later tax years a corporation is required to make a positive adjustment equal to 75% of the excess of its ACE over its AMTI (before this adjustment and the

---

[9] Sec. 56(h).

Historical Note

*The ACE adjustment is a complex computation. However, the ACE adjustment, as initially enacted by the Tax Reform Act of 1986, would have been much more complicated. The single most important simplification is that the ACE depreciation computation will **not** include present value computations.*

alternative tax NOL deduction).[10] ACE is a concept based on the traditional earnings and profits (E&P) definition found in Sec. 312 that has been used for years to determine whether a corporate distribution is a dividend or a return of capital (see Chapter 4). ACE equals AMTI for the tax year plus or minus a series of special adjustments described below and excluding the ACE adjustment and the alternative tax NOL deduction. However, it is emphasized that ACE is not the same as E&P, even though many items are treated in the same manner for both purposes. The ACE adjustment is not required of an S corporation.[11]

A negative adjustment is also permitted equal to 75% of the excess of the corporation's pre-adjustment AMTI over its ACE. The negative adjustment, however, cannot exceed the cumulative amount of its prior year positive ACE adjustments minus any negative ACE adjustments made in prior years.[12] Any excess of pre-adjustment AMTI over ACE that is not allowed as a negative adjustment because of the limitation cannot be carried over to a later year to reduce a required positive ACE adjustment.

Example 5-6 ■ Bravo Corporation reports the following ACE and AMTI (excluding the ACE adjustment and alternative tax NOL deduction) amounts for 1990-1992.

	1990	1991	1992
ACE	$2,000	$1,500	$1,000
Pre-adjustment AMTI	1,500	1,500	1,500

A $375 ([$2,000 − $1,500] × 0.75) positive ACE adjustment is made in 1990. No ACE adjustment is made in 1991 since ACE and AMTI are equal. A $375 ([$1,000 − $1,500] × 0.75) negative ACE adjustment is made in 1992. ■

Example 5-7 ■ Assume the same facts as in Example 5-6 except that the pre-adjustment AMTI amount in 1992 is $2,000. The tentative negative ACE adjustment is $750 ([$1,000 − $2,000] × 0.75). Only a $375 negative ACE adjustment can be made because the negative ACE adjustment may not exceed the total cumulative net positive ACE adjustments made in prior years, or $375. ■

Additional Comment

Since MACRS Sec. 1250 property is depreciated for AMT purposes using the straight-line method over 40 years, no ACE adjustment should be required. If taxpayers wish to avoid the ACE adjustment for newly acquired Sec. 1245 property, an election can be made to depreciate such property using the straight-line method for both regular tax and AMT purposes [Sec. 168(g)(7)]. This election is discussed in the Tax Planning Considerations section of the chapter.

Both the AMTI and ACE amounts may be either positive or negative. In determining whether an excess amount exists, a positive amount exceeds a negative amount by the sum of the absolute numbers, and a smaller negative amount exceeds a larger negative amount by the difference between the absolute numbers.[13]

A summary of the adjustments that need to be made to AMTI to arrive at ACE is presented below. Like with the general AMT adustments presented above these items require a recomputation of certain income, gain, and deduction items and may either increase or decrease AMTI. Unless otherwise indicated these changes are effective for tax years beginning after 1989.

- Depreciation on property placed in service in a tax year beginning after 1989 is determined using the alternative depreciation system of Sec. 168(g). Property

---

[10] Sec. 56(g)(1). AMTI determined without the ACE adjustment and alternative tax NOL deduction is known as **pre-adjustment AMTI.** For tax years 1987 through 1989 a book underreported profits (BURP) adjustment was required of corporate taxpayers. This positive adjustment equalled 50% of the excess of the corporation's **adjusted net book income (ANBI)** over AMTI before this adjustment and the alternative tax NOL deduction but after all other adjustments and tax preference items. Some parallels can be drawn between ANBI and ACE. A number of differences exist between these two concepts. Regulation Sec. 1.56-1 has been issued which goes into substantial technical detail concerning the BURP adjustment.

[11] Sec. 56(g)(6).
[12] Sec. 56(g)(2).
[13] Prop. Reg. Sec. 1.56(g)-1(a)(3).

placed in service under MACRS in a tax year beginning after 1987 and before 1990 is depreciated by taking the property's adjusted basis for *AMTI* purposes at the close of the last pre-1990 tax year and using the straight-line method over the remainder of the alternative depreciation system recovery period. Property placed in service under ACRS in a tax year beginning after 1980 and before 1990 is depreciated by taking the property's adjusted basis for *regular tax* purposes at the close of the last pre-1990 tax year and using the straight-line method over the remainder of the alternative depreciation system recovery period. Property placed in service in a tax year beginning before 1981 or placed in service after 1980 and not subject to ACRS and MACRS is depreciated in the same manner as for regular tax purposes.[14]

- The adjusted basis of an asset is determined by using the depreciation, depletion, or amortization rules appropriate for the ACE calculation. As a result, a basis adjustment similar to that described above for the AMTI calculation may be required when an asset is sold, exchanged, or otherwise disposed of.[15]

- Any amount that is permanently excluded from gross income when computing AMTI, but which is taken into account in determining E&P, is included in gross income for ACE purposes (e.g., interest on tax-exempt bonds other than private activity bonds, certain interest on employee stock ownership plan loans, and the proceeds of life insurance contracts). The adjustment is reduced by any deduction that would have been allowable in computing AMTI had the excluded income amount been included in gross income for AMTI purposes. No adjustment is required for any timing differences. Thus a taxpayer who uses the completed contract method of accounting for long-term contracts does not take any income or expense into account for determining either pre-adjustment AMTI or ACE before the tax year that the contract is completed. Income arising from the discharge of an indebtedness that is excluded from gross income for AMTI purposes under Sec. 108 is also excluded for ACE purposes.[16]

- Build-ups in life insurance contracts (net of premiums paid on the contracts) are included in gross income for ACE purposes.[17]

- The installment method cannot be used to compute ACE with respect to any installment sale made in a tax year beginning after December 31, 1989. An exception is available for nondealers which permits the use of the installment method for ACE purposes when an interest charge is paid under Sec. 453A for the right to defer payment of the tax.[18]

- A deduction cannot be claimed when computing ACE for any item that would not be deductible in the tax year when computing E&P even if the item would be deductible in determining pre-adjustment AMTI. These items increase ACE to the extent that they are deductible in determining pre-adjustment AMTI. The 80% and 100% dividends-received deductions are permitted to be claimed for ACE purposes though they cannot be deducted when computing E&P. The 70% dividends-received deduction, however, cannot be claimed for either ACE or E&P purposes. A partial list of items not deductible in computing E&P and which are nondeductible for ACE purposes, and deduction items that are treated the same for computing pre-adjustment AMTI and ACE is presented in Reg. Sec. 1.56(g)-1(d)(3) and (4).[19]

Key Point

Even if a corporation is not currently subject to the AMT, it may make sense to compute both the AMT and ACE depreciation amounts. A less efficient and more costly approach is to wait until the AMT applies and then try to recreate the numbers for past years.

Typical Misconception

Interest on certain state and local government obligations has traditionally not been subject to federal income tax. However, to the extent that tax-exempt income is not already included in AMTI, through an adjustment or preference item (e.g., private activity bonds), 75% of such income will be subjected to the AMT through the E&P adjustment. State and local governments have expressed concern over this aspect of the ACE adjustment, which they view as an impairment to their ability to finance their operations.

Key Point

In general, no deduction is allowed in determining the ACE adjustment for items that are not deductible in computing E&P. One important exception to this rule is the dividends-received deduction for 20%-or-more and 80%-or-more corporate shareholders.

---

[14] Sec. 56(g)(4)(A).
[15] Sec. 56(g)(4)(I).
[16] Sec. 56(g)(4)(B)(i).
[17] Sec. 56(g)(4)(B)(ii).
[18] Sec. 56(g)(4)(D)(iv).
[19] Sec. 56(g)(4)(C)(i) and (ii).

- Items deductible in computing E&P but not deductible in computing pre-adjustment AMTI, such as Federal income taxes and capital losses in excess of capital gains, are not deductible in computing ACE.[20]
- Intangible drilling costs and mine exploration and development costs must be amortized over 60 months commencing with the month in which they are paid or incurred.[21]
- Circulation and organizational expenditures that are otherwise amortizable under Secs. 173 and 248, respectively, are not permitted to be amortized for ACE purposes if incurred after December 31, 1989.[22]
- The increase or decrease in the LIFO recapture amount that takes place during the tax year increases or decreases ACE.[23] The LIFO recapture amount is the amount by which the inventory amount under the first-in, first-out (FIFO) inventory method exceeds the inventory amount under the last-in, first-out (LIFO) method.[24]
- Depletion with respect to any property placed in service in a tax year beginning after December 31, 1989, is determined by using the cost depletion method.[25]
- The Uniform Capitalization rules (instead of the E&P rules) apply for purposes of determining the expenditures that must be capitalized. Thus, the de minimis exceptions of Sec. 263A may permit certain corporations to avoid having to use the Uniform Capitalization rules for AMT purposes.[26]

Comprehensive Example. The following comprehensive example provides a side-by-side comparison of the taxable income, AMTI, and ACE calculations. The example is based on the following operating results for Glidden Corporation for 1991. Assume a $60,000 ACE adjustment was made in 1990.

Facts:		
	Gross profit from sales	$300,000
	Proceeds from life insurance policy	130,000
	Tax-exempt bond interest	15,000
	Dividends:	
	From 20% owned corporation	10,000
	From 10% owned corporation	20,000
	Gain of sale or exchange of property:	
	Installment sale of land	60,000
	Depreciable property	12,778
	Operating expenses	175,000
	Depreciation	40,000
	Amortization of organizational expenditures	2,500

Notes:

1. The build-up (cash surrender value net of premiums paid and increased by any prior ACE adjustments) on the life insurance plicy at the time of death was $30,000.

---

[20] Reg. Sec. 1.56(g)-1(e).
[21] Sec. 56(g)(4)(D)(i).
[22] Sec. 56(g)(4)(D)(ii).
[23] Sec. 56(g)(4)(D)(iii).
[24] Sec. 312(n)(4).
[25] Sec. 56(g)(4)(G).
[26] Reg. Sec. 1.56(g)-1(a)(5).

2. The tax-exempt interest is not from private activity bonds.
3. The land was sold at the end of the current year with a total gain of $60,000. Under the installment sale method, Glidden (a nondealer) reports only $25,000 of gain.
4. The gains reported for AMTI and ACE purposes on the sale of the depreciable property are $5,860 and $3,750, respectively.
5. Depreciation for AMTI and ACE purposes is $32,500 and $26,000, respectively.
6. The difference between the inventory carrying amounts using the FIFO and LIFO methods (or the LIFO recapture amount) increased from $35,000 to $52,000 this year.
7. Organizational expenditures are being amortized over a 60-month period.

	Taxable Income	Pre-Adjustment AMTI	Adjusted Current Earnings
Gross profit from sales	$300,000	$300,000	$300,000
Proceeds from life insurance policy	—0—	—0—	100,000
Tax-exempt bond interest	—0—	—0—	15,000
Dividends from:			
10%-owned corporation	20,000	20,000	20,000
20%-owned corporation	10,000	10,000	10,000
Gain on sale of depreciable property	12,778	5,860	3,750
Gain on sale of land	25,000	25,000	60,000
LIFO recapture amount	—0—	—0—	17,000
Total gross income	$367,778	$360,860	$525,750
Operating expenses	$175,000	$175,000	$175,000
Depreciation	40,000	32,500	26,000
Amortization of organizational expenditures	2,500	2,500	—0—
Dividends-received deduction	22,000	22,000	8,000
Total deductions	$239,500	$232,000	$209,000
Taxable Income/Preadjustment AMTI/Adjusted Current Earnings	$128,278	$128,860	$316,750
ACE Adjustment		140,917	
Alternative Minimum Taxable Income		$269,777	
Minus: Statutory exemption		(10,056)	
AMT Tax Base		$259,721	
Times: 20% rate		× .20	
Tentative minimum tax		$ 51,944	
Minus: Regular tax		(33,278)	
Alternative minimum tax		$ 18,666	

The proceeds from the life insurance policy (net of build-up) and tax-exempt bond interest are inclusions only for ACE. The gain on the sale of the depreciable property is smaller for pre-adjustment AMTI and ACE because smaller amounts of depreciation were claimed prior to the sale. Part of the gain on the sale of the land is included in taxable income and pre-adjustment AMTI under the installment method. An installment sale adjustment is not required for pre-adjustment AMTI since the land is not held as inventory by Glidden. The entire gain is reported for ACE purposes in the year of sale since the installment method is not permitted for ACE purposes for dealers or nondealers except where interest is paid for the privilege of a tax deferral. Depreciation is smaller for AMTI and ACE purposes because each calculation requires different depreciation calculations from that used for taxable income purposes. No deduction is allowed for ACE purposes for the organizational expenditures and the dividends from the 10% owned corporation. The ACE adjustment equals 75% of the excess of ACE ($316,750) over pre-adjustment AMTI ($128,860), or $140,917. A reduced statutory exemption is available because of the phase-out that occurs when AMTI is in excess of $150,000. The AMT liability is the excess of the tentative minimum tax ($51,944) over the regular tax liability ($33,278), or $18,666.

Minimum Tax Credit

Key Point
Since the purpose of the AMT is to ensure that all profitable corporations pay tax, the use of tax credits is also limited. For example, the general business credit cannot reduce the regular tax below the TMT.

The AMT is simply an acceleration of the payment of a corporation's income taxes. When an AMT liability is paid, a corporation may be eligible to take a minimum tax credit (MTC) that can be offset against its regular (income) tax liability. The minimum tax credit is necessary to prevent the same item from being taxed twice: once as part of the AMT and a second time as part of the regular income tax liability.

For tax years beginning after December 31, 1989, the entire amount of the AMT liability may be claimed as a credit. This includes the portion of the AMT liability that is due to deferral adjustments and preference items which represent timing differences that will reverse in another tax year as well as the AMT liability that is due to permanent preference items that will never reverse.[27]

Example 5-8 ■ In 1991, Seminole Corporation has $400,000 of taxable income plus $250,000 of deferral adjustments plus $350,000 of exclusion preferences. Its regular tax liability is $136,000 (0.34 × $400,000). Its AMT is $64,000 ([0.20 × $1,000,000] − $136,000). Seminole's minimum tax credit is the entire amount of its AMT liability, or $64,000. ■

The credit may be carried forward indefinitely and used to offset regular tax liabilities in future years, but only to the extent the regular tax liability exceeds the corporation's TMT in the carryforward year.

Tax Credits and the AMT

A corporation is allowed to reduce its regular tax liability by any available tax credits. Among the tax credits that a corporation can claim are:

1. Foreign tax credits (FTCs)
2. Puerto Rican and U.S. possessions tax credit
3. Drug testing credit
4. Nonconventional fuel credit
5. General business credit, which is the sum of

---

[27] Sec. 53. The three exclusion preferences are percentage depletion, charitable contributions of appreciated property, and tax-exempt bond interest. All of the other AMT adjustments and preference items result in a deferral of the regular tax liability rather than a permanent reduction.

a. Investment tax credit (rehabilitation credit, energy credit, and reforestation credit)
b. Alcohol fuels credit
c. Targeted jobs credit
d. Research credit
e. Low-income housing credit
f. Enhanced oil recovery credit
g. Disabled access credit

> **Additional Comment**
> Since the general business credit limitation is tied to the TMT, **every** corporation with excess general business credits will have to compute the TMT, even though such corporation may have few if any tax preference adjustments.

AMT and the General Business Credit. Several limitations have been placed on the use of the general business credit to prevent it from offsetting all of a corporation's regular tax liability and certain other taxes. The general business credit may not be used to offset the alternative minimum tax, the accumulated earnings tax, or the personal holding company (PHC) tax.

The following rule prevents the general business credit from offsetting all of a corporation's tax (if the tax exceeds $25,000), and it also prevents the credit from offsetting any of the corporation's AMT. Under Sec. 38(c), the general business credit for a tax year is limited to the excess (if any) of the corporation's net income tax over the greater of (1) its tentative minimum tax or (2) 25% of its net regular tax liability in excess of $25,000.

A corporation's net income tax is the sum of its regular tax and AMT liabilities reduced by any credits allowed under Secs. 21-29 (which includes foreign tax credits, possessions credits, drug testing credits, and nonconventional fuel credits). A corporation's net regular tax liability is its regular tax liability reduced by any credits allowed under Secs. 21-29. Any business credits that cannot be used in the current year may be carried back 3 years and forward 15 years.[28]

The result of this limitation is that the general business credit can offset only the portion of the regular tax that exceeds the TMT, not all of a corporation's regular tax.

Example 5-9 ■ In 1991, Scientific Corporation's net income tax liability before credits is $125,000. Its TMT is $50,000. Scientific's only available credit for the year is a general business credit (consisting solely of a research credit) of $140,000. Scientific's net regular tax liability is $125,000 since its income tax liability ($125,000) is greater than its TMT ($50,000). As computed below, Scientific's general business credit for 1991 is limited to $75,000. The tax credit limitation is the lesser of:

(1) Allowable portion of net regular tax liability:
Net income tax liability	$125,000
Minus: 25% of net regular tax liability in excess of $25,000 (0.25 × [$125,000 − $25,000])	(25,000)
Total	$100,000

or

(2) Net income tax liability minus the tentative minimum tax ($125,000 − $50,000) ..... $ 75,000

Scientific's net 1991 tax liability is $50,000 ($125,000 − $75,000). Scientific has a general business credit carryback or carryover of $65,000 ($140,000 − $75,000), which can be carried back 3 years and forward 15 years. ■

AMT and the Foreign Tax Credit. For purposes of computing the AMT, foreign tax credits (AMT FTCs) are limited to 90% of the TMT before FTCs and NOLs.

---

[28] Sec. 39.

TOPIC REVIEW 5-1

Alternative Minimum Tax (AMT)

1. The AMT is levied in addition to the regular (income) tax.
2. The starting point for the AMT calculation is taxable income. Taxable income is increased by tax preference items and increased or decreased by adjustments to arrive at alternative minimum taxable income (AMTI).
3. AMTI is reduced by a $40,000 statutory exemption. The statutory exemption is phased-out between $150,000 and $310,000 of AMTI to arrive at the AMT tax base.
4. A 20% tax rate is applied to the tax base to arrive at the tentative minimum tax.
5. The tentative minimum tax amount is reduced by the AMT foreign tax credit. Other tax credits, such as the general business credit, do not reduce the tentative minimum tax amount. The AMT foreign tax credit, the alternative tax NOL deduction, and the alternative tax energy preference deduction cannot offset more than 90% of the tentative minimum tax liability.
6. The excess of the AMT liability over the regular tax liability may be claimed as a minimum tax credit. This credit may be carried over to a later year to offset the excess of the regular tax liability (reduced by other available tax credits) over the tentative minimum tax.
7. The AMT liability, as well as the regular tax liability, are subject to the estimated tax requirements.

Credits that cannot be used in the current year may be carried back 2 years and forward 5 years and used to offset the TMT in those years.[29]

Example 5-10 ■ White Corporation's TMT before FTCs and NOLs is $100,000, and the corporation has $120,000 of FTCs available. Its AMT FTC is limited to $90,000 (0.90 × $100,000). Its remaining $30,000 of FTCs may be carried back 2 years or carried forward 5 years and used to offset any TMT in those years. ■

Topic Review 5-1 presents an overview of the alternative minimum tax.

SUPERFUND ENVIRONMENTAL TAX

OBJECTIVE 2
Determine whether a corporation is subject to the Superfund environmental tax or not

Key Point
Some corporations may choose not to compute AMTI because they realize they do not have an AMT liability. However, if a corporation's AMTI is greater than $2,000,000, it still must compute AMTI in order to calculate its Superfund Environmental Tax.

The Superfund Environmental Tax was enacted to assist in paying for certain governmental actions in environmental matters. Code Sec. 59A(a) imposes the tax on corporate taxpayers (other than regulated investment companies, real estate investment trusts, and S corporations) for tax years 1987 through 1992. The tax is levied at a 0.12% rate times the amount by which modified AMTI exceeds $2 million. Modified AMTI is defined by Code Sec. 59A(b) as AMTI excluding (1) any alternative tax NOL deduction, (2) the alternative tax energy preference deduction, and (3) any deduction for the Superfund Environmental Tax. The $2 million exemption is aggregated for all members of a controlled group of corporations. The Superfund Environmental Tax is imposed whether the corporation is subject to the AMT or not. Section 164(a)(5) permits the Superfund Environmental Tax to be deducted against gross income. No credits are permitted against the Superfund Environmental Tax. The estimated tax, interest, and penalty provisions that apply to the corporate income tax also apply to the Superfund Environmental Tax.

[29] Sec. 59(a)(2).

PERSONAL HOLDING COMPANY TAX

Historical Note

The PHC penalty tax was enacted in 1934 and was aimed at the so-called "incorporated pocketbook." Prior to the Tax Reform Act of 1986, corporate tax rates were less than individual tax rates. This created a natural incentive for individuals to place their investment property into a corporation. However, now that individual rates are 3 percentage points less than corporate rates, the benefits of having income-producing property held by a corporation have been greatly reduced.

Additional Comment

Remember that in at least two cases, individuals may still prefer their investment assets to be incorporated. First, if the investment income is $75,000 or less, the corporate rates are only 15% and 25%. This could prove advantageous if the individual is being taxed at a 31% rate. Second, due to the dividends-received deduction, a corporate investor benefits more from dividend income than does an individual investor.

Typical Misconception

The PHC penalty tax applies to any corporation that meets the definition of a personal holding company. No improper intent is necessary. Thus, the PHC penalty tax truly fits into the category of "a trap for the unwary."

OBJECTIVE 3

Determine whether a corporation is a personal holding company or not

A corporation that satisfies both the stock ownership test and the income test is classified as a **personal holding company** (PHC) for the tax year. The PHC penalty tax was enacted to prevent taxpayers from using closely held corporations to shelter passive income from the higher individual tax rates. This penalty tax is levied at a 28% tax rate on the PHC's undistributed personal holding company income (UPHCI). A corporation that is classified as a PHC must pay either the corporate income tax or the corporate alternative minimum tax and the PHC penalty tax. Corporations can avoid the PHC tax by (1) failing either the stock ownership or income tests or (2) reducing UPHCI to zero by making dividend distributions.

The importance of the PHC tax was diminished by the Tax Reform Act of 1986. Under pre-1986 Tax Act law, the top marginal tax rate for individual taxpayers was generally higher than the top marginal tax rate for a C corporation. The Tax Reform Act of 1986 marked the first time in the history of the modern income tax when the top individual tax rate (31% for 1991) is below the top corporate tax rate (34% for 1991). This inversion has diminished the attractiveness of using a C corporation to hold investment property that could otherwise be held by an individual investor or a conduit-type entity (e.g., partnership or S corporation). Although the PHC tax is less important than under prior law, it still can result in a substantial penalty. This portion of the chapter emphasizes (1) determining whether a corporation is a PHC or not and (2) finding ways in which the PHC tax can be avoided.

Personal Holding Company Defined

A personal holding company is any corporation that (1) has 5 or fewer shareholders who own more than 50% of the corporation's outstanding stock at any time during the last half of its tax year; and (2) has personal holding company income that is at least 60% of its adjusted ordinary gross income for the tax year.[30]

Corporations that retain special tax statuses are excluded from the PHC definition. These include:

- S corporations
- Corporations exempt from tax under Secs. 501 through 504
- Banks and domestic building and loan associations
- Life insurance companies
- Surety companies
- Lending and finance companies that satisfy the Sec. 543(a)(6) exception
- Corporations subject to court jurisdiction in a Title 11 or similar case (i.e., bankruptcy or receivership)
- Small business investment companies.[31]

Stock Ownership Requirement

Section 542(a)(2) provides that a corporation satisfies the PHC stock ownership requirement if more than 50% of the value of its outstanding stock is directly or indirectly owned by 5 or fewer individuals at any time during the last half of its tax year. Any corporation having fewer than 10 individual shareholders at any time

---

[30] Sec. 542(a).

[31] Sec. 542(c). Additional exceptions apply to foreign corporations. See Secs. 543(c)(5), (7), and (10).

during the last half of its tax year, and which is not an excluded corporation, will meet the stock ownership requirement.[32]

For purposes of determining whether the 50% requirement is met, stock owned directly or indirectly by or for an individual shareholder is considered to be owned by the individual. The Sec. 544 stock attribution rules are used for this purpose. The Sec. 544 attribution rules provide that:

- Stock owned by a family member is considered to be owned by the other members of his family. Family members include brothers and sisters, spouse, ancestors, and lineal descendants.
- Stock owned directly or indirectly by or for a corporation, partnership, estate or trust is considered to be owned proportionately by its shareholders, partners, or beneficiaries.
- A person who holds an option to acquire stock is considered to own such stock without regard to whether such individual intends to exercise the option or not.
- Stock owned by a partner is considered to be owned by his partners.
- The family, partnership, and option rules can be used only to make a corporation a PHC. They cannot be used to prevent a corporation from retaining PHC status.[33]

Passive Income Requirement

Key Point
A corporation must satisfy two tests to be considered a PHC: a stock ownership test and a passive income test. Since most closely held corporations satisfy the stock ownership test, PHC status is usually determined by the passive income test.

A corporation whose shareholders satisfy the stock ownership requirement is not a PHC unless it also earns predominantly passive income. The passive income requirement is met if at least 60% of the corporation's **adjusted ordinary gross income** (*AOGI*) for the tax year is personal holding company income (*PHCI*). The following text defines the terms AOGI and PHCI and outlines ways in which a corporation can take steps to avoid satisfying the passive income requirements.

Key Point
The PHC penalty tax is aimed at those corporations who earn predominantly passive income. The passive income test is satisfied if at least 60% of its AOGI for the taxable year is PHCI.

Adjusted Ordinary Gross Income Defined. The first step in calculating AOGI is calculating the corporation's gross income for the tax year (see Figure 5-1). Gross income is determined using the same accounting methods used to compute taxable income. Any income item that is excluded in determining taxable income is also excluded in determining AOGI. Gross receipts from sales transactions are reduced by the corporation's cost of goods sold.

The next step in determining the AOGI requires the calculation of the corporation's **ordinary gross income** (*OGI*). To do this, the corporation's gross income is reduced by the amount of its capital gains and Sec. 1231 gains.[34] When a trade or business property is sold, only the Sec. 1231 gain is excluded from OGI. The exclusion of capital gains and Sec. 1231 gains from OGI (and, later, from AOGI) means that these items are neutral factors in determining whether a corporation is a PHC; that is, the realization and recognition of a large Sec. 1231 gain or capital gain cannot cause a corporation to be a PHC.

Key Point
Computing AOGI is a three-step process. Gross income is determined and then adjusted to arrive at OGI. Finally, certain other adjustments are made in arriving at AOGI. In calculating OGI, both capital gains and Sec. 1231 gains are eliminated. Thus, capital gains and Sec. 1231 gains are neutral factors in determining whether a corporation is a PHC.

OGI is reduced for certain expenses. These expenses relate to the production of rental income; mineral, oil, and gas (M, O, & G) royalties; and income from working interests in oil or gas wells.[35] The rental income adjustment is described below.

---

[32] The PHC stock ownership test is also used to determine if a closely held C corporation is subject to the at-risk rules (Sec. 465) or the passive activity loss and credit limitation rules (Sec. 469). Thus, a closely held corporation that is not a PHC may be subject to other special rules because of satisfying the PHC stock ownership requirement.
[33] Sec. 544(a)(4)(A).
[34] Sec. 543(b)(1).
[35] Sec. 543(b)(2).

FIGURE 5-1 Determining Adjusted Ordinary Gross Income

Gross income reported for taxable income purposes Plus: Gross losses from tangible and intangible property transactions that reduce gross income (i.e., losses on stocks, securities, and commodities transactions and Sec. 1231 property)
Gross income (for PHC purposes) Minus: Gross gains from the sale of capital assets   Gross gains from the sale of Sec. 1231 properties

Ordinary gross income
Minus: Certain expenses incurred in connection with gross income from rents; mineral, oil, and gas royalties; and working interests in oil or gas wells
           Interest received on certain U.S. obligations held for sale to customers by dealers
           Interest received due to condemnation awards, judgments, or tax refunds
           Rents from tangible personal property manufactured or produced by the corporation, provided it has engaged in substantial manufacturing or production of the same type of personal property in the tax year

Adjusted ordinary gross income

REDUCTION BY RENTAL INCOME EXPENSES. Gross income from rents is reduced by the deductions claimed for depreciation or amortization, property taxes, interest, and rent. This net amount is known as the **adjusted income from rents** (*AIR*).[36] No other Sec. 162 expenses incurred in the production of rental income reduce OGI. The expense adjustment that is made cannot exceed the total gross rental income.

Example 5-11 ■ All of Keno Corporation's single class of stock is owned by Milt. Both Milt and Keno Corporation use the calendar year as their tax years. Keno Corporation reports the following results for 1991:

Rental income	$100,000
Depreciation	15,000
Interest expense	9,000
Real estate taxes	4,000
Maintenance expenses	8,000
Administrative expenses	12,000

Keno Corporation's AIR is $72,000 ($100,000 − [$15,000 + $9,000 + $4,000]). The maintenance and administrative expenses are deductible in determining taxable income and UPHCI, but do not reduce the AIR amount. ■

Additional Comment

Income not included in AOGI cannot be PHCI. In calculating the 60% passive income test, PHCI is the numerator and AOGI is the denominator. Since the passive income test is purely objective, to whatever extent possible both the numerator and denominator should be manipulated. When the ratio is close to 60%, one planning opportunity would be to accelerate income which is AOGI but not PHCI.

Personal Holding Company Income Defined. **Personal holding company income** includes the following 12 categories: dividends; interest; annuities; royalties (other than M, O, and G, computer software, and copyright royalties); adjusted income from rents; adjusted income from M, O, and G royalties or working interests in oil or gas wells; computer software royalties; copyright royalties; produced film rents; income from personal service contracts involving a 25% or more shareholder; rental income for corporate property used by a 25% or more shareholder; and distributions from estates or trusts.

PHCI is determined according to the following general rules:

- *Dividends:*   Includes only distributions made out of E&P. Any amounts that are tax exempt (e.g., return of capital distributions) or that are eligible for capital gain treatment (e.g., liquidating distributions) are excluded from PHCI.[37]

---

[36] Sec. 543(b)(3).
[37] Reg. Sec. 1.543-1(b)(1).

Key Point

The exception for royalties on computer software was added by the Tax Reform Act of 1986. Without this exception, most computer software companies would almost certainly be classified as PHCs.

- *Interest income:* Includes any amount that is received for the use of money loaned that must be included in gross income. Excluded from PHCI is any interest that is excluded from gross income.[38]
- *Annuity proceeds:* Includes only amounts that are included in gross income. Any annuity amount excluded from gross income as a return of capital is excluded from PHCI.[39]
- *Royalty income:* Includes amounts received for the use of intangible property (e.g., patents, copyrights, trademarks, and so on). Special rules apply to copyright royalties, M, O, and G royalties, active business computer software royalties, and produced film rents. Each of these four special types of royalty income constitutes a separate PHCI category that may be excluded under one of the exceptions described below and shown in Table 5-2.[40]
- *Distributions from an estate or trust:* Included in PHCI. Since an interest in an estate or trust is generally a capital asset, however, any gain recognized on the sale of such an interest is excluded from PHCI.[41]

Self-Study Question

What is the effect of the two-pronged test that allows the exclusion from PHCI of certain AIR?

Answer

The effect of this two-pronged test is to make it difficult to use rents to shelter other passive income. For example, the 50% test would require at least $100 of AIR to shelter $100 of interest income. The 10% test is even more restrictive. To satisfy this test, it would be necessary to generate $900 of OGI (AIR and other items) to shelter the same $100 of interest income.

Special exclusions apply to adjusted income from rents; adjusted income from M, O, and G royalties; copyright royalties; produced film rents; rental income from the use of property by a 25% or more shareholder; and active business computer software royalties. These exclusions, which are summarized in Table 5-2, reduce the probability that a corporation will be a PHC. The two most commonly encountered exclusions, the ones for rental income and personal service contract income, are explained below.

EXCLUSION FOR RENTS. Adjusted income from rents is included in PHCI unless the special exception applies for corporations earning predominantly rental income. PHCI does not include rents if (1) AIR is at least 50% of AOGI and (2) the dividends-paid deduction equals or exceeds the amount by which nonrental PHCI exceeds 10% of OGI.[42] The special exception permits corporations earning predominantly rental income and having very little nonrental PHCI to avoid PHC status. The dividends-paid deduction is available for dividends paid during the tax year, dividends paid within 2½ months of the end of the tax year for which a special "throwback" election is made to treat the distribution as having been paid on the last day of the preceding tax year, and consent dividends (see pages 5-22 and 5-23). Nonrental PHCI includes all PHCI (determined without regard to the exclusions for copyright royalties and M, O, & G royalties) *other than* adjusted income from rents and rental income earned from leasing property to a shareholder owning 25% or more of the stock.

Example 5-12 ■

All of Texas Corporation's single class of stock is owned by Ted. Both Ted and Texas Corporation use the calendar year as their tax years. Texas Corporation reports the following results for 1991:

Rental income	$100,000
Operating profit from sales	40,000

---

[38] Reg. Sec. 1.543-1(b)(2).
[39] Reg. Sec. 1.543-1(b)(4).
[40] Reg. Sec. 1.543-1(b)(3).
[41] Sec. 543(a)(8).
[42] Sec. 543(a)(2). The AIR term does not include rental income earned from leasing property to a shareholder owning 25% or more of the stock which is included in PHCI under its own separate category, copyright royalties, produced film rents, and rents from tangible personal property manufactured or produced by the corporation provided it has engaged in substantial manufacturing or production of the same type of personal property in the tax year.

Personal Holding Company Tax • 5-19

TABLE 5-2 *Exclusions Permitted in Computing Personal Holding Company Income*

Type of PHCI	Percent of Income Requirement	Maximum Level of Other PHCI	Minimum Level of Business Expenses
Rents	≥50% of AOGI[a]	≤10% of OGI (unless reduced by distributions)	—
Mineral, oil, and gas royalties	≥50% of AOGI[a]	≤10% of OGI	≥15% of AOGI
Copyright royalties	≥50% of OGI	≤10% of OGI	≥25% of OGI
Produced film rents	≥50% of OGI	—	—
Compensation for use of property by a shareholder owning at least 25% of the outstanding stock	—	≤10% of OGI	—
Active business computer software royalties	≥50% of OGI	≤10% of OGI (unless reduced by distributions)	≥25% of OGI[b]

[a] Measured in terms of adjusted income from rents or mineral, oil, and gas royalties, respectively.
[b] The deduction test can be applied to either the single tax year in question or the 5-year period ending with the tax year in question.

Dividend income	15,000
Interest income from corporate bonds	10,000
Depreciation	15,000
Interest expense	9,000
Real estate taxes	4,000
Other expenses	20,000

No dividends are paid by Texas Corporation during 1991 or during the 2½ month throwback period in 1992. Because all of the Texas stock is owned by a single shareholder, Texas Corporation satisfies the stock ownership requirement. Texas Corporation's AOGI is calculated as follows:

Rental income		$100,000
Operating profit from sales		40,000
Dividends		15,000
Interest		10,000
Gross income and OGI		$165,000
Minus: Depreciation	$15,000	
Interest	9,000	
Taxes	4,000	(28,000)
AOGI		$137,000

The first test for exclusion of AIR from PHCI is met, since AIR ($100,000 − $28,000 = $72,000) exceeds 50% of AOGI ($137,000 × 0.50 = $68,500). Nonrental PHCI of $25,000 ($15,000 dividends + $10,000 interest) exceeds 10% of Texas Corporation's OGI ($165,000 × 0.10 = $16,500). Since Texas Corporation paid no dividends, the second test for exclusion of AIR from PHCI is not met. As a result, AIR is included in PHCI. Texas Corporation's PHCI is $97,000 ($72,000 AIR + $15,000 dividends + $10,000 interest). The $97,000 of PHCI exceeds 60% of AOGI ($137,000 AOGI × 0.60 = $82,200). Therefore, Texas Corporation is a PHC.

Texas Corporation could avoid PHC status by paying a sufficient amount of dividends during 1991 and/or during the 2½ month throwback and consent dividend periods of 1992 for the AIR exclusion to be satisfied. The necessary amount of dividend payments would be the amount by which nonrental PHCI

($25,000) exceeds 10% of OGI ($16,500), or $8,500. An $8,500 cash dividend paid during 1991 or early 1992 would permit Texas Corporation to exclude the $72,000 of AIR from PHCI. PHCI would then be $25,000 ($15,000 + $10,000), which is less than 60% of AOGI ($82,200).

Additional Comment

The provision for personal service contracts was enacted to prevent entertainers, athletes, and other highly compensated professionals from incorporating their activities and, after taking a below-normal salary, having the rest of the income taxed at the corporate rates. Even if it is apparent that a 25% shareholder will perform the services, as long as no one other than the corporation has the right to designate who performs the services, the income is not PHCI. Thus, the careful drafting of contracts is important in this area.

EXCLUSION FOR PERSONAL SERVICE CONTRACTS. Income earned from contracts under which the corporation is to perform personal services and income earned from the sale of such contracts is included in PHCI if the following two conditions are met:

1. (a) Some person other than the corporation has the right to designate (by name or by description) the individual who is to perform the services or (b) the individual who is to perform the services is designated (by name or by description) in the contract.
2. 25% or more of the value of the corporation's outstanding stock is directly or indirectly owned by the person who has performed, is to perform, or is designated as the person to perform the services.[43]

The 25% or more requirement only needs to be satisfied at some point during the tax year and is determined by using the Sec. 544 constructive stock ownership rules. This provision was enacted to prevent professionals, entertainers, and sports figures from incorporating their activities, paying themselves a below-normal salary, and sheltering at the lower corporate tax rates the difference between their actual earnings and their below-normal salary.

Example 5-13 ■ Dr. Kellner owns all of the stock of a professional corporation that provides medical services. The professional corporation has an employment contract with Dr. Kellner that specifies the terms of his employment and his salary. Dr. Kellner is the only doctor under contract with the professional corporation. The corporation provides office space for Dr. Kellner and employs the necessary office staff to enable Dr. Kellner to perform the medical services. The income earned by Dr. Kellner does not constitute PHCI because (1) the normal patient-physician relationship does not generally involve a contract that includes a designation of the doctor who will perform the services, nor will the patient generally be permitted to designate the doctor who will perform the services; and (2) the professional corporation will be able to substitute a qualified replacement when Dr. Kellner is not on duty (i.e., when he is on vacation or not on call).[44]

The compensation received by the corporation for Dr. Kellner's services would constitute PHCI if the contract with the patient specified that only Dr. Kellner would provide the services, or if the services provided by Dr. Kellner were so unique that only he could provide them. Any portion of the corporation's income from the personal service contract that is attributable to "important and essential" services provided by persons other than Dr. Kellner is not to be included in PHCI.[45] ■

OBJECTIVE 4
Calculate the amount of the corporation's PHC tax liability

Determining the PHC Penalty Tax

Determination of the PHC penalty tax is illustrated in Figure 5-2. First, the amount of undistributed personal holding company income (UPHCI) must be determined. Then the 28% PHC tax rate is applied to the UPHCI. If the PHC tax is owed, a corporation can avoid paying the tax if it makes a timely deficiency dividend distribution.

[43] Sec. 543(a)(7).
[44] Rev. Rul. 75-67, 1975-1 C.B. 169. See also Rev. Ruls. 75-249, 1975-1 C.B. 171 (relating to a composer), and 75-250, 1975-1 C.B. 172 (relating to an accountant).
[45] Reg. Sec. 1.543-1(b)(8)(B)(ii).

> **Key Point**
> The PHC penalty tax is assessed at a 28% rate. This tax is in addition to the corporate income tax. Thus, the existence of both taxes eliminates any advantage obtained by interposing a corporation between the taxpayer and his income-producing assets.

Calculating the UPHCI. The starting point for the UPHCI calculation is the corporation's taxable income. A series of adjustments must be made to taxable income to arrive at UPHCI. The most important of these adjustments are described below.

POSITIVE ADJUSTMENTS TO TAXABLE INCOME. A PHC may not claim a dividends-received deduction. Thus, its taxable income must be increased by the amount of any dividends-received deductions claimed.[46]

Since PHCs are restricted to deducting only the NOL for the immediately preceding tax year, two compensating adjustments must be made for NOLs. First, the amount of the NOL deduction claimed in determining taxable income must be added back to taxable income. Second, the entire amount of the corporation's NOL (computed without regard to the dividends-received deduction) for the immediately preceding tax year is deducted. It does not matter whether that amount was carried back to an earlier year or carried over to the current year for federal income tax purposes.[47]

> **Key Point**
> The negative adjustments made to taxable income in arriving at UPHCI represent items that do not affect taxable income but reduce the amount of PHCI available for distribution to shareholders. For example, federal income taxes reduce UPHCI because such taxes represent monies not available for distribution to shareholders. In contrast, positive adjustments made to taxable income in arriving at UPHCI (e.g., the dividends-received deduction) are not allowed in arriving at UPHCI because they do not represent monies that are unavailable for distribution to shareholders.

NEGATIVE ADJUSTMENTS TO TAXABLE INCOME. Charitable contribution deductions can only be claimed up to the 20% and 50% of adjusted gross income limitations for individuals. Thus two adjustments may be required: (1) the deduction of charitable contributions in excess of the 10% corporate limitation (but not in excess of the individual limitation); (2) the addition of charitable contribution carryovers deducted (for income tax purposes) in the current year, but which were deducted for PHC tax purposes in an earlier year.[48]

Income taxes (i.e., federal income taxes [including the alternative minimum tax], foreign income taxes, and U.S. possessions' income taxes) accrued by the corporation reduce UPHCI. The corporation's method of accounting is irrelevant in making this adjustment.[49]

Capital gains and losses reduce UPHCI. A PHC is permitted a deduction for the amount of its net capital gain (i.e., net long-term capital gain over net short-term capital loss), minus the amount of income taxes attributable to the net capital gain.[50] The federal income taxes that are attributable to the net capital gain equal the taxes imposed on the corporation's taxable income minus the taxes imposed on the corporation's taxable income as computed by excluding the net capital gain.

The capital gains adjustment that is made when determining AOGI prevents a large capital gain from causing a corporation to be taxed as a PHC. Even if the corporation is a PHC, the capital gains adjustment made in determining UPHCI prevents the corporation from paying the PHC tax on the amount of its long-term (but not its short-term) capital gains.

Avoiding the PHC Designation and Tax Liability Through the Use of Dividend Distributions

Types of Dividends. The PHC can claim a dividends-paid deduction for the following types of distributions:

- Current year dividends
- Throwback dividends
- Consent dividends

---

[46] Sec. 545(b)(3).
[47] Sec. 545(b)(4) and Rev. Rul. 79-59, 1979-1 C.B. 209.
[48] Sec. 545(b)(2). The 20% and 50% limitations on individual charitable contributions are explained in Chapter 7 of the *Prentice Hall's Federal Taxation: Individuals* companion text.
[49] Sec. 545(b)(1).
[50] Sec. 545(b)(5).

FIGURE 5-2 Determination of the Personal Holding Company Tax

Taxable income
Plus: Dividends-received deduction claimed
NOL deduction claimed
Excess charitable contributions carried over from a preceding tax year and deducted in determining taxable income
Net loss attributable to the operation or maintenance of property leased by the corporation
Minus: Accrued U.S. and foreign income taxes
Charitable contributions in excess of the 10% corporate limitation
NOL (computed without regard to the dividends-received deduction) incurred in the immediately preceding tax year
Net capital gain minus the amount of any income taxes attributed to it
Dividends-paid deduction claimed

Undistributed personal holding company income (UPHCI)
Times: 0.28

Personal holding company tax

Additional Comment

The intent of the PHC rules is not to collect taxes from a corporation at a combined rate of 52.5% {34 + [(1 − .34) × .28]}. Instead, the rules are meant to compel the distribution of income by a closely held investment corporation so that such income will be taxed at the shareholders' individual tax rates. This purpose is evident when they consider the flexibility of the dividends-paid deduction.

- Liquidating dividends
- Deficiency dividends

In addition, a dividend carryover is permitted for certain dividends paid in prior years.

CURRENT YEAR DIVIDENDS. Distributions made during the current year are eligible for a **dividends-paid deduction** if they are made out of the corporation's current or accumulated E&P.[51]

A dividends-paid deduction is not available for **preferential dividends.** A dividend payment is preferential when (1) the amount distributed to a shareholder exceeds his ratable share of the distribution as determined by the number of shares of stock that are owned or (2) the amount received by a class of stock is more or less than its rightful amount.[52] In either case, the entire distribution (and not just any excess distributions) is a preferential dividend. The preferential dividend rule prevents a corporation from avoiding the PHC penalty tax by making dividend distributions solely to tax-exempt entities or to taxpayers who have low marginal tax rates.

THROWBACK DIVIDENDS. **Throwback dividends** are distributions paid in the first 2½ months after the close of the tax year. A dividend distribution made in the first 2½ months of the next tax year is treated as a throwback distribution for PHC tax purposes only if the PHC makes the appropriate election.[53] Otherwise, the dividends-paid deduction is claimed in the tax year in which the distribution is made. Throwback dividends made by a PHC are limited to the lesser of (1) the PHC's UPHCI or (2) 20% of the amount of any dividends (other than consent dividends) paid during the tax year. Thus, a PHC that fails to make any dividend distributions during its tax year is prevented from paying a throwback dividend.

CONSENT DIVIDENDS. **Consent dividends** are hypothetical dividends deemed paid to shareholders on the last day of the corporation's tax year. Consent dividends permit a corporation to reduce its PHC tax liability when it is prevented from making an actual dividend distribution because of a lack of available money, a restrictive loan covenant, and so on. A consent dividend election can be made by a shareholder who owns stock on the last day of the corporation's tax year.[54] For tax purposes, the

---

[51] Secs. 561(a) and 562(a).
[52] Sec. 562(c).
[53] Sec. 563(b).
[54] Sec. 565.

making of the election results in a hypothetical money dividend being paid on the last day of the PHC's tax year for which the dividends-paid deduction is claimed. The consent dividend is treated by the shareholder as being received on the distribution date and immediately contributed by the shareholder to the distributing corporation's capital account. The contribution increases the basis for the shareholder's stock investment. The consent dividend election can be made through the due date for the corporation's income tax return (including any permitted extensions).

Example 5-14 ■ Assume the same facts as in Example 5-12, except that Texas Corporation obtains a 6-month extension to file its corporate income tax return, which it files on September 15, 1991. Ted can make a consent dividend election specifying the payment of an $8,500 consent dividend between January 1, 1991, and September 15, 1991, and permit Texas Corporation to exclude the AIR from its PHCI. The consent dividend is considered to have been distributed on December 31, 1990, regardless of the date Ted makes the election. The dividend is included in Ted's 1990 gross income and increases his basis for the Texas stock by $8,500. ■

DIVIDEND CARRYOVERS. Dividends that are paid in the preceding two tax years can be used as a dividend carryover to reduce the amount of the current year's PHC tax liability.[55] Section 564 permits a PHC to deduct the amount by which its dividend distributions that were eligible for a dividends-paid deduction in each of the two preceding tax years exceeds the corporation's taxable income for such a year. These "excess" dividend amounts are claimed as a dividends-paid deduction in the current year.

LIQUIDATING DIVIDENDS. A dividends-paid deduction is available for liquidating distributions that are made by a PHC within 24 months of the adoption of a plan of liquidation.[56] Special rules are contained in Sec. 562(b)(2) which determine the amount of the dividends-paid deduction. These rules are beyond the scope of this text.

Self-Study Question

When would a deficiency dividend be beneficial to a corporation?

Answer

If a corporation fails to eliminate its UPHCI, either under the erroneous assumption that it was not a PHC or due to a miscalculation of its UPHCI, a deficiency dividend can be very beneficial. If certain requirements are satisfied, a special deficiency dividend can be distributed and designated as a retroactive dividend deductible against UPHCI earned in a previous year.

DEFICIENCY DIVIDENDS. A corporation that determines that it owes the PHC penalty tax can avoid paying the tax by electing to pay a **deficiency dividend** under Sec. 547. The deficiency dividend procedures substitute an income tax levy on the dividend payment at the shareholder level for the payment of the PHC tax. The distributing corporation's shareholders include the deficiency dividend in their gross income for the tax year in which it is received, not the tax year for which the PHC claims a dividends-paid deduction. Payment of a deficiency dividend does not relieve the PHC from any interest and penalties owed with respect to the PHC tax.

The following requirements must be satisfied in order to claim a dividends-paid deduction for a deficiency dividend:

- A determination (e.g., judicial decision or agreement entered into by the taxpayer with the IRS) must be made that establishes the amount of the PHC tax liability.
- A dividend must be paid within 90 days of establishing the PHC tax liability.
- A claim for a dividends-paid deduction based upon the payment of the deficiency dividend must be filed within 120 days of the determination date.[57]

Example 5-15 ■ Boston Corporation files its 1991 tax return reporting a $200,000 distribution received pursuant to a stock redemption as a capital gain. Upon an IRS audit of Boston's 1991 income tax return, both parties agree that the capital gain

---

[55] Sec. 561(a)(3).
[56] Sec. 562(b).
[57] Secs. 547(c) through (e).

classification is erroneous and that dividend treatment for the distribution is indeed correct. This change causes Boston to be classified as a PHC for 1991. If Boston pays a deficiency dividend within 90 days of signing the agreement with the IRS establishing the existence of the PHC tax liability, the liability for the payment of the PHC tax is eliminated. ■

PHC Tax Calculation

The following example illustrates the calculation of the PHC's UPHCI and the determination of the PHC's income tax and penalty tax liabilities.

Example 5-16 ■ Marlo Corporation is classified as a PHC for 1991, reporting $227,000 of taxable income on its 1991 federal income tax return:

Operating profit	$100,000
Long-term capital gain	60,000
Short-term capital gain	30,000
Dividends (20% owned corporation)	200,000
Interest	100,000
Gross income	$490,000
Dividends-received deduction	(160,000)
Salaries	(40,000)
General and administrative expenses	(20,000)
Charitable contributions	(43,000)[a]
Taxable income	$227,000

[a] $43,000 = 0.10 × ($490,000 − $40,000 − $20,000).

Federal income taxes (using 1991 rates and ignoring any alternative minimum tax liability) accrued by Marlo are $71,780. Actual charitable contributions made by Marlo are $60,000 in 1991. $50,000 in dividends are paid in August 1991. Calculation of the PHC tax liability is as follows:

Taxable income			$227,000
Plus:	Dividends-received deduction		160,000
Minus:	Excess charitable contributions		(17,000)[b]
	Federal income taxes		(71,780)
	Dividends-paid deduction		(50,000)
	Long-term capital gain	$60,000	
	Minus: Federal income taxes	(20,400)	
	LTCG adjustment		(39,600)
UPHCI			$208,620
Times:	Tax rate		× 0.28
PHC tax			$ 58,414

[b] $60,000 − $43,000 = $17,000.

Marlo's total federal tax liability is $130,194 ($71,780 + $58,414). Payment of the PHC tax ($58,414) can be avoided by paying a timely deficiency dividend in the amount of $208,620. ■

TOPIC REVIEW 5-2

Personal Holding Company (PHC) Tax

1. The personal holding company tax only applies to corporations qualifying as PHCs. A PHC has (1) 5 or fewer shareholders owning more than 50% of the corporation's stock at any time during the last half of the tax year and (2) PHC income that is at least 60% of its adjusted ordinary gross income for the tax year.
2. Two special exemptions exist for the PHC test. First, certain special corporate forms are excluded from the penalty tax (e.g., S corporations). Second, certain income forms (e.g., rents and active business computer software royalties) are able to be excluded if the percent of income, maximum level of other PHC income, and minimum level of business expense requirements are met. The excludable income forms are summarized in Table 5-2.
3. The PHC tax equals 28% of the undistributed PHC income. Undistributed PHC income equals taxable income plus certain positive adjustments (e.g., dividends-received deduction) and minus certain negative adjustments (e.g., federal income taxes, excess charitable contribution deductions, and net capital gain reduced by federal income taxes attributable to the gain).
4. Undistributed PHC income can be reduced by a dividends-paid deduction claimed for cash and property dividends paid during the tax year and consent and throwback dividends paid after year-end.
5. A PHC tax liability can be eliminated by the payment of a deficiency dividend. This distribution substitutes an income tax levy at the shareholder level for the PHC tax.
6. The PHC tax is not subject to the estimated tax requirements.

Topic Review 5-2 presents an overview of the personal holding company penalty tax.

ACCUMULATED EARNINGS TAX

Additional Comment
The accumulated earnings tax is a penalty tax imposed on corporations who accumulate unreasonable amounts of earnings for the purpose of avoiding shareholder taxes. With corporate tax rates currently higher than individual tax rates, little incentive exists for a corporation to retain earnings with the hope of paying less tax than if the earnings were paid out.

Key Point
The accumulated earnings tax theoretically applies to both large and small corporations. However, as a practical matter, this tax applies only to closely held corporations where shareholders control the corporate dividend policy.

Corporations that are not subject to the personal holding company tax may be subject to the accumulated earnings tax. The **accumulated earnings tax** attempts "to compel the company to distribute any profits not needed for the conduct of its business so that, when so distributed, individual stockholders will become liable" for taxes on the dividends received.[58] Unlike its name, the tax is not levied on the corporation's total accumulated earnings balance, but only on its current year addition to the balance. In other words, the tax is levied on accumulated earnings earned currently that are not needed for a reasonable business purpose.

Corporations Subject to the Penalty Tax

Section 532(a) states that the accumulated earnings tax applies "to every corporation . . . formed or availed of for the purpose of avoiding the income tax with respect to its shareholders . . . by permitting earnings and profits to accumulate instead of being divided or distributed." Three special corporate forms are statutorily excluded from the accumulated earnings tax:

- Personal holding companies
- Corporations that are exempt from tax under Secs. 501 through 504

[58] *Helvering v. Chicago Stock Yards Co.*, 30 AFTR 1091, 43-1 USTC ¶9379 (USSC, 1943).

- S corporations[59]

Theoretically, the accumulated earnings tax applies to both large and small corporations.[60] In practice, however, the accumulated earnings tax only applies to closely held corporations where management can utilize the corporate dividend policy to reduce the tax liability of the shareholder group.

Proving a Tax-Avoidance Purpose

OBJECTIVE 5
Evaluate whether a corporation has an accumulated earnings tax problem or not

Section 533(a) provides that the accumulation of E&P by a corporation beyond the reasonable needs of the business indicates a tax-avoidance purpose unless the corporation can prove that the earnings are not being accumulated merely to avoid taxes. This burden of proof may be shifted to the IRS under the rules outlined in Sec. 534.

The existence of a tax-avoidance purpose is based upon the facts and circumstances of each situation. Under Reg. Sec. 1.533-1(a)(2), the following circumstances indicate a tax-avoidance purpose.

Additional Comment
If the IRS determines that the accumulation of earnings is unreasonable, the presumption is that the IRS determination is correct. To rebut this presumption, the taxpayer must be able to show that the IRS's determination is improper by "a preponderance of the evidence."

- Dealings between the corporation and its shareholders (e.g., loans made by the corporation to its shareholders or funds expended by the corporation for the shareholders' benefit).
- Investments made by the corporation of undistributed earnings in assets having no reasonable connection to the corporation's business.
- The extent to which the corporation has distributed its E & P (e.g., a low dividend payout rate, low salaries, and a large earnings accumulation may indicate a tax-avoidance purpose).

Holding or investment companies are held to a different standard than operating companies. Section 533(b) provides that the fact that a corporation is a holding or investment company is prima facie evidence of the requisite tax-avoidance purpose.[61] Holding companies, like operating companies, can rebut this presumption by showing that it was neither formed or availed of for the purpose of avoiding shareholder income taxes.

The presence or absence of a tax-avoidance purpose may be only one of several motives for the corporation's accumulation of corporate earnings. In *U.S. v. The Donruss Company,* the Supreme Court held that tax avoidance does not have to be the dominant motive for the accumulation of earnings in order for the accumulated earnings tax to be imposed. According to the court, the corporation must know about the tax consequences of accumulating corporate earnings in order for a tax avoidance purpose to be present.[62] Such knowledge does not need to be the dominant motive or purpose for the accumulation of the earnings.

Evidence Concerning the Reasonableness of an Earnings Accumulation

The courts have not held a single factor to be indicative of an unreasonable amount of accumulated earnings. Instead, some factors have been found to exhibit evidence of a tax-avoidance motive. Other factors have gained acceptance from the IRS and

---

[59] Secs. 532(b) and 1363(a). Certain foreign corporations are also exempt from the accumulated earnings tax.
[60] Sec. 532(c).
[61] Regulation Sec. 1.533-1(c) defines a holding or investment company as "a corporation having no activities except holding property and collecting income therefrom or investing therein."
[62] *U.S. v. The Donruss Company,* 23 AFTR 2d 69-418, 69-1 USTC ¶ 9167 (USSC, 1969).

Typical Misconception
The statute refers to the existence of a tax-avoidance purpose, which would appear to be a subjective test. However, the existence of the tax-avoidance purpose really hinges on the more-objective determination of whether a corporation has accumulated earnings beyond the reasonable needs of the business.

the courts as reasonable needs of the business for an accumulation of earnings and profits.

Evidence of a Tax-Avoidance Motive. A corporation that wants to avoid problems concerning the accumulated earnings tax should be careful to act defensively. Exposure to the accumulated earnings tax can be avoided by minimizing the presence of the following factors:

- Loans to shareholders
- Expenditure of corporate funds for the personal benefit of the shareholders
- Loans having no reasonable relation to the conduct of business (e.g., loans made to relatives or friends of shareholders)
- Loans to a corporation controlled by the same shareholders that control the taxpayer corporation
- Investments in properties or securities unrelated to the activities of the taxpayer corporation
- Protection against unrealistic hazards[63]

Loans to shareholders or the expenditure of corporate funds for the personal benefit of shareholders act as substitutes for dividend payments to the shareholders. Similarly, loans made to relatives or friends of shareholders by the taxpayer corporation are substitutes for paying dividends to shareholders, who then make personal loans to their friends and relatives. All three actions may indicate an unreasonable accumulation of corporate earnings which should instead be distributed as dividends.

Loans or corporate expenditures made for the benefit of a corporation controlled by the shareholder (or the shareholder group) who controls the payor corporation may be considered to have a tax-avoidance purpose. The taxpayer corporation could instead make a dividend payment to the shareholder and then have the shareholder make a capital contribution of the funds to the related corporation.

Other factors not mentioned in the Regulations that are indicative of a tax-avoidance motive include corporations that are run as holding or investment companies and that have a poor dividend payment record.

Key Point
In determining if an accumulation of earnings is reasonable, the regulations specify the adoption of a "prudent businessman" standard. In applying this standard, the courts are reluctant to substitute their judgment for that of corporate management unless the facts and circumstances clearly suggest that the accumulations of earnings are not for reasonable business needs.

Evidence of Reasonable Business Needs. Code Sec. 537 defines **reasonable business needs** as

- Reasonably anticipated needs of the business
- Sec. 303 (death tax) redemption needs
- Excess business holdings redemption needs

Regulation Sec. 1.537-1(a) elaborates on this standard by indicating

An accumulation of the earnings and profits . . . is in excess of reasonable needs of the business if it exceeds the amount that a prudent businessman would consider appropriate for the present business purposes and for the reasonably anticipated future needs of the business. The need to retain earnings and profits must be directly connected with the needs of the corporation itself and must be for bona fide business purposes.

SPECIFIC, DEFINITE, AND FEASIBLE PLANS. A corporation can justify an accumulation of earnings as being for reasonably anticipated future needs only if there is an

---
[63] Reg. Sec. 1.537-2(c).

indication that the future needs of the business require such an accumulation. The corporation must usually have specific, definite, and feasible plans for the use of such accumulations.

NO SPECIFIC TIME LIMITATIONS. The earnings accumulation does not need to be used within a short period of time after the close of the tax year, but the plans must provide that the accumulation will be used within a reasonable period of time after the close of the tax year based upon all the facts and circumstances associated with the future needs of the business.

IMPACT OF SUBSEQUENT EVENTS. Determination of the reasonably anticipated needs of the business is based on the facts and circumstances that exist at the end of the tax year. Regulation Sec. 1.537-1(b)(2) indicates that subsequent events cannot be used to show that an earnings accumulation is unreasonable if all the elements of reasonable anticipation are present at the close of the tax year. Subsequent events, however, can be used to determine whether the taxpayer actually intended to consummate the plans for which the earnings are accumulated.

A number of reasons are mentioned in the Regulations, or have been accepted by the courts, as representing reasonable needs of the business for accumulating earnings.

- Expansion of a business or replacement of plant
- Acquisition of a business enterprise
- Debt retirement
- Working capital
- Loans to suppliers or customers
- Product liability losses
- Stock redemptions
- Business contingencies

Some of the more important reasons are now examined.

Additional Comment
The courts have allowed accumulations for the acquisition or expansion of property, plant, or equipment if the taxpayer establishes specific, definite, and feasible plans for the proposed outlay. If the expansion is into a new business, taxpayers should be careful to make the investment substantial enough so that it will not be considered simply a passive investment.

EXPANSION OF A BUSINESS OR REPLACEMENT OF PLANT. The expansion of a corporation's present business facilities or the replacement of existing plant and equipment have always been accepted by the IRS and the courts as reasonable needs of a business. Taxpayers have only encountered problems when the plans are undocumented, indefinite, vague, or infeasible.[64] Although the plans do not need to be reduced to writing, it is probably best to provide sufficient written documentation.

ACQUISITION OF A BUSINESS ENTERPRISE. The acquisition of a business enterprise can involve either the same business or expansion into a new business. It can involve the purchase of either the stock or the assets of the new business. Taxpayers should be careful to acquire a sufficient interest in the new business so that it will not be considered a passive investment.

WORKING CAPITAL: THE BARDAHL FORMULA. Providing for the needed amount of working capital is considered a reasonable need of a business. The needs of a manufacturing business for working capital differ from those of a service business. At one time, the courts used certain rules of thumb (e.g., a current ratio of 2 to 1 or 3 to 1 or the accumulation of funds to cover a single year's operating expenses) to determine an adequate amount of working capital. However, in the first of two *Bardahl* cases, the Tax Court established a mathematical formula for determining an operating cycle.

---

[64] See, for example, *Myron's Enterprises v. U.S.*, 39 AFTR 2d 77-693, 77-1 USTC ¶ 9253 (9th Cir., 1977); *Atlas Tool Co., Inc. v. CIR*, 45 AFTR 2d 80-645, 80-1 USTC ¶ 9177 (3rd Cir., 1980).

Key Point

Working capital is generally defined as the excess of current assets over current liabilities. The Bardahl formula attempts to measure the amount of working capital necessary for an operating cycle. The operating cycle usually includes the period of time needed for acquisition of the inventory, sale of the goods, and collection of the accounts receivable. Thus, the amount of earnings accumulated to cover one full operating cycle is considered a reasonable business need.

This formula is now used to ascertain the appropriate amount of working capital in many situations.

For purposes of a manufacturing business, an operating cycle is defined as the "period of time required to convert cash into raw materials, raw materials into an inventory of marketable Bardahl products, the inventory into sales and accounts receivable, and the period of time to collect its outstanding accounts."[65]

In the second *Bardahl* case, the Tax Court determined that monies advanced to a corporation by its suppliers in the form of short-term credit (e.g., trade payables) reduce the required amount of working capital.[66] The **Bardahl formula** for determining the amount of required working capital is as follows:

$$\text{Average operating cycle} = \text{Inventory period} + \text{Accounts receivable period} - \text{Credit period}$$

The *inventory period* in the formula is the time (as a percent of a year) from the acquisition of the raw materials inventory to the sale of the finished goods inventory. The *accounts receivable period* is the time (as a percent of a year) from the sale date to the collection of the accounts receivable. The *credit period* is the time (as a percent of a year) from when an expense is incurred or inventory is purchased to the payment of the liability.

The average operating cycle can be expressed with the following equation:

$$\left[\frac{\text{Inventory amount}}{\text{Annual cost of goods sold}} + \frac{\text{Accounts receivable amount}}{\text{Annual sales}} - \frac{\text{Accounts payable amount}}{\text{Annual operating expenses and purchases (less noncash expenses)}}\right] \times 100$$

$$= \text{Average operating cycle (as a percent of a year)}$$

The average operating cycle and the cash needs of the business for the year are combined to determine the working capital requirements, as follows:

$$\text{Average operating cycle (as a percent of a year)} \times \left[\text{Cost of goods sold} + \text{Operating expenses}\right] = \text{Working capital requirements}$$

The cost of goods sold amount is generally determined on a "full cost" basis (i.e., including both direct and indirect expenses). Operating expenses exclude noncash expenses such as depreciation, amortization, depletion, charitable contributions, and so on, as well as capital expenditures. The Tax Court has allowed federal income taxes (e.g., quarterly estimated tax payments) to be included as operating expenses as well as permitting an adjustment to the operating cycle calculation for an inflation factor.[67]

The working capital requirements of the business must be compared with the actual working capital available at year-end. If the working capital requirements exceed the corporation's actual working capital, this need for additional working capital can be used to justify accumulating a portion of the corporation's earnings. If the working capital requirements are less than the corporation's actual working capital, the excess working capital is available for distribution to the shareholders

---

[65] *Bardahl Manufacturing Corp.*, 1965 PH T.C. Memo ¶ 65,200, 24 TCM 1030, at 1044.
[66] *Bardahl International Corp.*, 1966 PH T.C. Memo ¶ 66,182, 25 TCM 935.
[67] *Doug-Long, Inc.*, 72 T.C. 158 (1979).

unless some other justification for its accumulation can be determined (e.g., plant replacement).

The *Bardahl* formula may provide a false sense of mathematical exactness in calculating working capital because the IRS and the courts have interpreted it differently. Some courts have used the "peak month" inventory, accounts receivable, and trade payables turnover amounts (instead of an annual average) to determine the length of an operating cycle.[68] This method generally lengthens the corporation's operating cycle. Use of these two different methods in calculating the *Bardahl* formula can lead to very different estimates of working capital needs. As a result, significant disputes have arisen over what constitutes an appropriate amount of working capital.

Example 5-17 ■

Typical Misconception

There is no exact method for determining the working capital needs of a corporation. The Bardahl formula is merely a "rule of thumb" adopted by the Tax Court. Even the correct measurement of the components (peak cycle approach versus the average cycle approach) of the Bardahl formula is subject to dispute among the courts.

The management of Austin Corporation feels that it may have an accumulated earnings tax problem and asks that its working capital requirements on December 31, 1991, be determined using the *Bardahl* formula. The following information is available from Austin's records for 1991.

Cost of goods sold	$2,700,000
Average inventory	675,000
Purchases	3,000,000
Sales (all on account)	6,000,000
Average accounts receivable	750,000
Operating expenses (including depreciation and other noncash expenditures)	875,000
Depreciation and other noncash expenditures	75,000
Average trade payables	350,000
Federal income taxes	100,000
Working capital on December 31, 1991	825,000

Calculation of the operating cycle takes place as follows:

Inventory turnover = ($675,000 ÷ $2,700,000) × 365 = 91.25 days

Receivables turnover = ($750,000 ÷ $6,000,000) × 365 = 45.625 days

$$\text{Payables turnover} = \left[\frac{\$350,000}{\$3,000,000 + \$800,000}\right] \times 365 = 33.62 \text{ days}$$

$$\text{Operating cycle} = \left[\frac{91.25 + 45.625 - 33.62}{365}\right] \times 100 = 28.3\% \text{ of a year}$$

Annual cash expenses = $2,700,000 + $875,000 − $75,000 + $100,000 = $3,600,000

Working capital requirement = $3,600,000 × 0.283 = $1,018,800[a]

[a] Removal of the estimated federal income tax payments from the annual expenses would reduce the amount calculated.

The working capital requirement is $193,800 ($1,018,800 − $825,000) in excess of the actual working capital available on December 31, 1991. This permits Austin to justify the accumulation of additional earnings by its need to expand its current amount of working capital. ■

The *Bardahl* formula is also used to estimate the working capital needs of service companies. Since service companies do not have the same needs for inventory, a different calculation is used. For service companies, one looks primarily to the

[68] *State Office Supply, Inc.*, 1982 PH T.C. Memo ¶ 82,292, 43 TCM 1481.

company's need to finance its accounts receivables. Because the maintenance of an adequate labor supply is important, service companies also need to maintain adequate working capital to be able to retain key personnel when a below-normal level of business is expected. Therefore, some amount may be added to the basic working capital needs to cover the cost of retaining this part of the labor force for a period of time.[69]

Real World Example
Apparently, an accumulation of funds to redeem stock where a buy-sell agreement exists is not an acceptable business need. Even though a 50% shareholder was killed in a plane crash shortly after the year-end, the Tax Court refused to recognize the validity of an accumulation to redeem such shareholder's stock [Wilcox Manufacturing Co., 1979 PH T.C. Memo ¶ 79,092, 38 TCM 378].

STOCK REDEMPTIONS. Section 537(a) permits corporations to accumulate earnings for two types of stock redemptions—Sec. 303 (death tax) redemptions and excess business holdings redemptions. In the first situation, monies can be accumulated after the death of the shareholder to redeem stock from the shareholder's estate or a beneficiary of the estate. These monies cannot exceed the amount that can be redeemed under the Sec. 303 rules. In the second situation, monies can be accumulated by a corporation to redeem stock held by a private foundation in excess of the business holdings limit of Sec. 4943.

BUSINESS CONTINGENCIES. The courts have permitted earnings to be accumulated for a number of business contingencies that were not specifically sanctioned in the Sec. 537 Regulations. Among the events recognized by the IRS audit guidelines and the courts as business contingencies for which earnings can properly be accumulated are actual or potential litigation, a decline in business activities following the loss of a major customer, a reserve for self-insurance against a particular loss, a threatened strike, and an employee retirement plan.

Determining the Accumulated Earnings Tax Liability

OBJECTIVE 6
Calculate the amount of the corporation's accumulated earnings tax liability

Determination of the accumulated earnings tax liability is illustrated in Figure 5-3. The accumulated earnings tax is levied at a 28% rate. As with the PHC penalty tax, a corporation can reduce its tax base by making dividend distributions. However, corporations generally do not avail themselves of this tax planning strategy, other than by maintaining a particular dividend payout ratio, because the accumulated earnings tax issue usually is not raised by the IRS auditors until one or more years after the tax return is filed. Unlike the PHC penalty tax, once the IRS or the courts have determined that the accumulated earnings tax is owed, its payment cannot be avoided by deficiency dividends.

FIGURE 5-3 *Determining the Accumulated Earnings Tax Liability*

Taxable income
Plus: Dividends-received deduction
        NOL deduction claimed
        Excess charitable contributions carried over from preceding tax year and deducted in determining taxable income
Minus: Accrued U.S. and foreign income taxes
        Charitable contributions made in excess of the 10% corporate limitation
        Nondeductible capital losses
        Net capital gain minus the amount of any income taxes attributed to it
        Dividends-paid deduction
Accumulated earnings credit

Accumulated taxable income
Times: 0.28

Accumulated earnings tax

---

[69] See, for example, *Simons-Eastern Co. v. U.S.,* 31 AFTR 2d 73-640, 73-1 USTC ¶ 9279 (D.C. Ga., 1972).

> **Key Point**
> Accumulated taxable income should not be confused with current E&P. In fact, the accumulated earnings tax has been assessed in years where there was no increase in the E&P of a corporation.

> **Key Point**
> Accumulated taxable income equals taxable income (with certain adjustments) minus both the dividends-paid deduction and the accumulated earnings credit. These adjustments are primarily for the purpose of deriving an amount that more closely corresponds to the corporation's actual economic income and thus better measures the dividend-paying capability of the corporation.

Accumulated Taxable Income. The starting point for the accumulated taxable income calculation is the corporation's taxable income. A series of positive and negative adjustments to taxable income are needed to arrive at the accumulated taxable income.

POSITIVE ADJUSTMENTS TO TAXABLE INCOME. As with the PHC penalty tax, a corporation is prohibited from claiming a dividends-received deduction. Taxable income must be increased by the amount of the dividends-received deduction that was claimed when determining the regular tax liability.[70]

The amount of any NOL deduction claimed when determining taxable income must be added back to determine accumulated taxable income. Unlike with the PHC tax, no special deduction is provided for an NOL incurred in the immediately preceding year.[71]

NEGATIVE ADJUSTMENTS TO TAXABLE INCOME. Charitable contributions are deductible without regard to either the 10% corporate limitation or the individual charitable contribution limitations. The same adjustments required for PHC tax purposes are required here.[72]

U.S. and foreign income taxes accrued by the corporation reduce accumulated taxable income, whether the corporation uses the accrual or the cash method of accounting.[73]

A corporation is permitted a deduction for the amount of its net capital gain, minus the income taxes attributable to the net capital gain.[74] The capital gains adjustment prevents a corporation having large capital gains from paying the accumulated earnings tax on the portion of the gains that were retained in the business.

Net capital losses in excess of net capital gains for the tax year are a negative adjustment to taxable income. This deduction is determined without regard to any capital loss carryovers from a preceding year or capital loss carrybacks from a succeeding year. Also, it must be reduced by the lesser of (1) the aggregate amount of net capital gain deductions taken in previous tax years (minus any recapture of such deductions occurring in earlier years) or (2) the amount of the corporation's accumulated E&P as of the end of the preceding tax year.[75]

> **Key Point**
> The dividends-paid deduction is very helpful in avoiding the PHC penalty tax. However, deficiency dividends cannot reduce accumulated taxable income. In addition, since the accumulated earnings tax is usually asserted in subsequent years during an IRS audit, the throwback and consent dividends are of limited benefit.

DIVIDENDS-PAID DEDUCTION. The dividends-paid deduction is available for four types of dividends:

- Dividends paid during the tax year
- Throwback dividends
- Consent dividends
- Liquidating distributions

With some minor exceptions, the rules for the dividends-paid deduction are the same as for the PHC tax. Nonliquidating distributions paid during the tax year are eligible for the dividends-paid deduction only if they are paid from the corporation's E&P. A dividends-paid deduction is not available for preferential dividends.[76]

Throwback dividends are distributions made out of E&P in the first 2½ months following the close of the tax year. The accumulated earnings tax rules require that

---

[70] Sec. 535(b)(3).
[71] Sec. 535(b)(4).
[72] Sec. 535(b)(2).
[73] Sec. 535(b)(1).
[74] Sec. 535(b)(6).
[75] Secs. 535(b)(5) and (7).
[76] Sec. 562(c).

any distribution made in the first 2½ months following the close of the tax year be treated as if it were paid on the last day of the preceding tax year without regard to the amount of actual dividends that were paid during the preceding tax year.[77] Because the accumulated earnings tax issue is not usually raised until the IRS audits the corporation's tax return, throwback dividends have limited value in avoiding the accumulated earnings tax.

The consent dividend rules for the accumulated earnings tax are the same as for the PHC tax. Consent dividends are of limited value in avoiding the accumulated earnings tax since they must be paid on or before the due date for the corporate tax return (including extensions) and the taxpayer is usually reluctant to pay consent dividends in anticipation of an accumulated earnings tax assessment.

Liquidating distributions made by corporations are eligible for the dividends-paid deduction. Eligible distributions include those made in connection with a complete liquidation, a partial liquidation, or a stock redemption.[78]

ACCUMULATED EARNINGS CREDIT. Unlike other credits, the **accumulated earnings credit** does not offset the accumulated earnings tax liability on a dollar-for-dollar basis. Instead, it serves to reduce the accumulated taxable income amount. Different rules for the accumulated earnings credit exist for operating companies, service companies, and holding or investment companies.[79]

Additional Comment
The minimum accumulated earnings credit is $250,000 ($150,000 for certain PSC corporations) reduced by the accumulated E&P at the close of the preceding year. In many situations, however, corporations that have been in existence for some time have accumulated E&P in excess of $250,000. Thus, the minimum credit is often of little practical significance.

Typical Misconception
The maximum accumulated earnings credit is the amount of current E&P retained to meet the reasonable needs of the business minus an adjustment for net capital gains. This amount does not include the entire accumulation needed for business needs, rather, only the accumulation in the current taxable year. Thus, to calculate the maximum credit, it is necessary to first determine how much of the prior accumulations are retained for reasonable business needs.

- Operating companies can claim a credit equal to the greater of (1) $250,000 minus the accumulated E&P at the end of the preceding tax year, or (2) the portion of the current E&P (after the reduction for the dividends-paid deduction) retained to meet the reasonable needs of the business minus the net capital gain for the current year (reduced by any taxes attributable to such gain).

- Service companies providing services in the fields of health, law, engineering, architecture, accounting, actuarial science, performing arts, or consulting are limited to the greater of (1) a $150,000 statutory exemption or (2) the reasonable needs of the business.

- Holding and investment companies can claim a credit equal to $250,000 minus the accumulated E&P amount at the end of the preceding tax year. An increased credit is not available to a holding or investment company based upon the reasonable needs of the business.

The accumulated E&P balance used in computing the credit is reduced by the amount of any throwback distributions paid during the current year that are considered to have been paid out of the preceding year's E&P. Section 1561(a)(2) limits controlled groups to a single statutory exemption.

Example 5-18 ■

Midway Corporation is formed in 1989. During its first 2 years it reports $175,000 of start-up losses connected with its manufacturing activities. In the third year it reports a $400,000 profit. No dividends have been paid in any of the first 3 years. At the end of 1991, Midway's accumulated E&P is $225,000 ($400,000 − $175,000). All of these earnings are needed because of plans for expansion of the plant over the next 3 years. Midway's management does not have an accumulated earnings tax problem at the end of 1991, since its E&P balance is less than the $250,000 minimum exemption. Assuming a similar level of profits in 1992, management will

---

[77] Sec. 563(a).
[78] Sec. 562(b)(1)(B).
[79] Sec. 535(c).

exhaust its statutory exemption and only be able to rely on the reasonable business needs exception. ∎

Accumulated Earnings Tax Calculation

The following example illustrates the calculation of accumulated taxable income and the determination of the accumulated earnings tax liability.

Example 5-19 ∎ Pasadena Corporation is a closely held family corporation that has conducted highly successful manufacturing operations for a number of years. At January 1 of the current year, Pasadena Corporation has a $750,000 accumulated E&P balance. The following information is available about the current year's operations:

Operating profit	$650,000
Long-term capital gain	30,000
Dividends (20% owned corporation)	150,000
Interest	70,000
Gross income	$900,000
Dividends-received deduction	(120,000)
Salaries	(100,00)
General and administrative expenses	(200,000)
Charitable contributions	(60,000)[a]
Taxable income	$420,000

[a] $60,000 = { 0.10 × ($900,000 − [$100,000 + $200,000])}.

Federal income taxes (using 1991 rates and ignoring any alternative minimum tax liability) accrued by Pasadena Corporation are $142,800. Actual charitable contributions are $70,000. Cash dividends of $20,000 were paid on June 30 of the current year. Pasadena's increase in the earnings retained for the reasonable needs of the business during the current year is $160,000.

If an IRS agent challenges Pasadena on the accumulated earnings tax issue, and the facts as noted above are held to be correct, the accumulated earnings tax liability would be calculated as follows:

Taxable income			$420,000
Plus:	Dividends-received deduction		120,000
Minus:	Excess charitable contributions		(10,000)[a]
	Federal income taxes		(142,800)
	Long-term capital gain	$30,000	
	Minus: Federal income taxes	(10,200)[b]	(19,800)
	Dividends-paid deduction		(20,000)
	Accumulated earnings credit		(160,000)
Accumulated taxable income			$187,400
Times:	Tax rate		× 0.28
Accumulated earnings tax liability			$ 52,472

[a] $70,000 total contributions − $60,000 limitation = $10,000 excess contributions.
[b] $10,200 = $30,000 × 0.34

Pasadena's total federal tax liability for the current year is $195,272 ($142,800 + $52,472). ∎

TOPIC REVIEW 5-3

Accumulated Earnings Tax

1. The accumulated earnings tax applies to all corporations except ones that are specially excluded (e.g., S corporations). In practice, the accumulated earnings tax only applies to closely-held corporations.
2. Transactions that provide evidence of a tax avoidance motive generally lead IRS auditors to conclude that an accumulated earnings tax problem exists. These transactions include loans made by the corporation to shareholders, expenditures of corporate funds for the personal benefit of the shareholders, and investments in properties or securities unrelated to the corporation's activities.
3. Earnings accumulated for the reasonable needs of the business are exempt from the accumulated earnings tax. Business needs for retention of earnings include acquisition of a business enterprise, debt retirement, and working capital. A $250,000 lifetime exemption from the accumulated earnings tax is available. This amount is reduced to $150,000 for personal service corporations.
4. The accumulated earnings tax equals 28% of accumulated taxable income. Accumulatd taxable income equals taxable income plus certain positive adjustments (e.g., dividends-received deduction) and minus certain negtive adjustments (e.g., federal income taxes, excess charitable contributions, and net capital gain reduced by federal income taxes attributable to the gain). An accumulated earnings credit is also available equal to the greater of the unused lifetime earnings exemption or the earnings accumulated during the year for the reasonable needs of the business.
5. Accumulated taxable income can be reduced by a dividends-paid deduction for cash and property dividends paid during the year and consent and throwback dividends paid after the year-end. The deficiency dividend opportunity available to PHCs is not available for accumulated earnings tax purposes.
6. The accumulated earnings tax is not subject to the estimated tax requirements.

Topic Review 5-3 presents an overview of the accumulated earnings penalty tax.

UNRELATED BUSINESS INCOME TAX

OBJECTIVE 7
Determine whether a corporation is subject to the unrelated business income tax or not

Code Sec. 501 generally exempts a variety of nonprofit organizations that are organized as corporations from the corporate income tax. Section 511(a) extends the corporate income tax levy to the unrelated business taxable income that is earned by tax-exempt organizations (other than those that are taxed as trusts). However, the unrelated business income tax does not extend to governmental organizations, except for colleges and universities that are agencies of a governmental organization. Code Sec. 513(a) indicates that unrelated business taxable income must be derived from an activity that (1) constitutes a trade or business, (2) is carried on regularly by the organization, and (3) is not substantially related to the organization's charitable, educational, or other purpose or function upon which the organization's exempt purpose is based.

Unrelated business taxable income means the gross income derived by an organization from an unrelated trade or business meeting the three requirements of the preceding paragraph minus any business deductions that are directly connected with such trade or business. Code Sec. 512(b) contains a number of specific exemptions from the unrelated business income tax for certain income forms. Among the income forms exempted from the unrelated business income tax are: royalties, dividends, interest, and annuities unless derived from debt-financed property; rents from real property; rents from personalty rented with real property when such rents are incidental to the total rental income; and gains and losses from the sale, exchange, or other disposition of property other than inventory or property held primarily for sale to customers in the ordinary course of the trade or business. The deductions permitted to be claimed against gross income include those expenses and losses that are otherwise deductible by a regular corporation that is engaged in a trade or business. Charitable contributions are permitted to be deducted up to 10% of the corporation's unrelated business taxable income. Net operating losses are permitted to be carried back and forward. In addition, a specific exemption is provided in Sec. 512(b)(12) for the first $1,000 of unrelated business taxable income.

TAX PLANNING CONSIDERATIONS

This section examines three areas of tax planning: (1) making special accounting method elections for AMT purposes, (2) avoiding the personal holding company (PHC) tax, (3) avoiding the accumulated earnings tax.

Key Point

Not only can these special AMT elections reduce a taxpayer's AMT liability, but these elections should also reduce compliance costs by eliminating the need to keep an additional set of depreciation records.

Special AMT Elections

Two special elections are available under the AMT rules which permit taxpayers to defer the claiming of certain deductions for income tax purposes. The deferral of these deductions will increase the taxpayer's regular tax liability, but can provide an overall savings by reducing the taxpayer's AMT liability.

Code Sec. 59(e) permits the extended writeoff period to apply to certain expenditures that would otherwise be a tax preference item. If the extended writeoff period is elected, Code Sec. 59(e)(6) exempts each expenditure from being a tax preference item under Sec. 57, or prevents an adjustment from having to be made for the expenditure under Sec. 56. The expenditures for which the special election can be made and the writeoff periods that apply are as follows:

Code Section	Type of Expenditure	Writeoff Period
173	Circulation	3 yrs.
174	Research and Experimental	10 yrs.
263	Intangible Drilling and Development	5 yrs.
616	Mining and Natural Resource Development	10 yrs.
617	Mining Exploration	10 yrs.

The special election can be made with respect to any portion of a qualified expenditure, and can be revoked only with IRS consent.[80]

The second election permits a taxpayer to elect to use the depreciation method generally required for AMT purposes—the 150% declining balance method over the property's class life—in computing their regular tax liability. Such an election permits the taxpayer to change the depreciation method from the 200% declining

[80] Secs. 59(e)(4)(A) and (B).

balance method to the 150% declining balance method, and the depreciation period from the property's recovery period specified in the MACRS rules to its class life. Such an election can not be made with respect to nonresidential real property or residential rental property. This election may be made with respect to 1 or more classes of property for any tax year and once made with respect to a class of property shall apply to all property in such class placed in service during the tax year. The election must be made by the due date for the taxpayer's return (including any extensions that are permitted).[81]

Eliminating the Adjusted Current Earnings Adjustment

C corporations are required to increase their alternative minimum taxable income by the amount of the adjusted current earnings adjustment. This adjustment can be significant for some C corporations, although it will generally be smaller than the book underreported profits adjustment that was required under the pre-1990 AMT rules. If the C corporation is closely held by individual shareholders and certain trusts, it can elect to be taxed under the S corporation rules and this adjustment can be avoided.[82]

Avoiding the Personal Holding Company Tax

Five types of tax planning can be used to avoid the PHC tax, as discussed in the following sections.

OBJECTIVE 8
Explain how a corporation can avoid being subject to the personal holding company tax

Making Changes in the Corporation's Stock Ownership. Additional stock can be sold to unrelated parties in order to avoid having 5 or fewer shareholders owning more than 50% (in value) of the stock at any time during the last half of the tax year. Sales of either common or preferred stock can be made. The sale of nonvoting preferred stock to unrelated parties permits the corporation's stock ownership to be spread among a larger number of individuals without diluting the voting power of the current shareholder group.

Changing the Amount and Type of Income Earned by the Corporation. Several tax planning options are available to change the amount and type of corporate income. These include

- Adding additional "operating" activities to the corporation's line of business. Passive income will become a smaller portion of the corporation's total income.
- Converting taxable interest or dividend income earned on an investment portfolio into nontaxable interest income or long-term capital gains. Nontaxable interest income and long-term capital gains are not included in the PHCI definition and, therefore, cannot cause a corporation to be a PHC.
- Adding additional passive income of a type that either (1) is eligible to be excluded from PHCI or (2) reduces the amount of other PHCI that is earned. A corporation might increase the proportion of its income that is earned from rents in order to exceed the 50% of OGI requirement to exclude adjusted income from rents from PHCI.

---

[81] Secs. 168(b)(2) and (5).
[82] Sec. 56(g)(6).

5-38 • Ch. 5 / Other Corporate Tax Levies

> **Key Point**
> One of the easiest methods of avoiding the PHC penalty tax is through a dividend distribution. If a corporation lacks the funds to pay a dividend, a consent dividend (which is a hypothetical dividend) may be useful. In addition, certain dividends can be declared after year-end to help in after-the-fact tax planning.

Making Dividend Distributions. Dividends reduce the tax base used to levy the PHC tax. The inclusion in PHCI of certain income forms (e.g., adjusted income from rents) can be avoided by paying enough dividends to reduce the amount of other PHCI to 10% of OGI or less. Some of these dividends (e.g., throwback dividends, consent dividends, and deficiency dividends) can be paid after year-end in order to engage in last-minute tax planning.

Making an S Corporation Election. An S corporation election prevents the imposition of the PHC tax, since S corporations are statutorily exempt from the penalty tax. Such an election is particularly advantageous because the individual tax rates are now generally below the corporate tax rates (see Chapter 11).

Liquidating the Corporation. A PHC could be liquidated and have the assets held by the shareholders instead. The liquidating distributions are eligible for the dividends-paid deduction and can reduce the UPHCI amount. This alternative offers an additional advantage because the individual tax rates are now generally below the corporate tax rates.

Avoiding the Accumulated Earnings Tax

> **OBJECTIVE 9**
> Explain how a corporation can avoid being subject to the accumulated earnings tax

The primary defense against an IRS position that the corporation has accumulated an unreasonable amount of earnings is to document that the earnings accumulations are necessary to meet the future capital needs of the business. The existence of these business plans must be documented each year. The plans, which should be as specific as possible, should be revised periodically. Completed projects should be documented. Abandoned projects should be eliminated from the plan. A tentative timetable for the current set of projects is a positive factor for the corporation should an IRS challenge be encountered. Such plans might be incorporated into the minutes of one or more of the board of directors meetings.

> **Key Point**
> An S election can be useful in avoiding both the PHC penalty tax and the accumulated earnings tax since an S corporation is statutorily exempt from both taxes. The S corporation election cannot eliminate potential accumulated earnings tax problems arising in prior C corporation tax years.

Transactions that are indicative of an unreasonable earnings accumulation (e.g., loans to shareholders or large investment portfolios) should be avoided. The business purpose for engaging in any transaction that has the appearance that the corporation is maintaining an unreasonable earnings accumulation should be thoroughly documented.

Corporations that have a potential accumulated earnings tax problem should consider making an S corporation election. Corporations making an S corporation election are only able to avoid accumulated earnings tax problems on a prospective basis. The making of the election does not eliminate the possibility that the penalty tax might be imposed for a tax year prior to the election year in which a determination is made that an unreasonable earnings accumulation exists.

COMPLIANCE AND PROCEDURAL CONSIDERATIONS

Alternative Minimum Tax

The corporate AMT liability is reported on Form 4626 (Alternative Minimum Tax—Corporations). A completed Form 4626 is included in Appendix B which utilizes the facts in the following example.

Example 5-20 ■ Miami Corporation reports the following results for 1990:

Taxable income	$350,000
Regular tax liability	119,000
Depreciation adjustment for personal property placed in service after 1986	17,500
Depreciation preference for real property placed in service in 1984	10,000
Basis adjustment (regular tax gain is in excess of AMTI gain on sale of depreciable property)	(16,500)
Adjusted current earnings	900,000

Miami Corporation's AMTI is determined as follows:

Taxable income		$350,000
Plus:	Depreciation adjustment	17,500
Plus:	Depreciation preference	10,000
Minus:	Basis adjustment	(16,500)
AMTI before ACE adjustment		$361,000
Plus:	ACE adjustment	404,250[a]
AMTI		$765,250
Times:	Tax rate	× 0.20
Tentative minimum tax		$153,050
Minus:	Regular tax liability	(119,000)
Alternative minimum tax liability		$ 34,050

[a]($900,000 − $361,000) × 0.75 = $404,250 ■

Chapter 3 discussed the corporate estimated tax payment requirements. Section 6655(g) includes the corporate AMT liability as part of the required annual payment. Corporations must, therefore, estimate their AMT liability properly when making their quarterly payments or possibly be subject to the underpayment penalties described in Sec. 6655.

Superfund Environmental Tax

The Superfund Environmental Tax is reported on Line 17 of Form 4626 (Alternative Minimum Tax—Corporations). Since this additional tax is based upon the corporation's AMTI (excluding the alternative tax NOL deduction), the Form 4626 can be used to report both taxes. Section 6665(g) includes the Superfund Environmental Tax as part of the required annual payment. Corporations must, therefore, estimate their Superfund Environmental Tax properly when making their quarterly payments or possibly be subject to the underpayment penalties described in Sec. 6655.

Personal Holding Company Tax

Filing Requirements for Tax Returns. A PHC must file a corporate income tax return (Form 1120). Schedule PH must accompany the return. Schedule PH includes the steps necessary to determine whether the corporation is a PHC and to calculate the UPHCI and PHC tax amounts. Regulation Sec. 301.6501(f)-1 extends the statute of limitations for the PHC penalty tax from 3 to 6 years if a PHC fails to file the Schedule PH, even though no additional tax may be owed.

Payment of the Tax, Interest, and Penalties. Corporations ordinarily pay the PHC tax (1) when they file their Form 1120 and Schedule PH or (2) when a determination is made by the IRS or the courts that the tax is owed. The penalty tax is not part of the corporation's required estimated tax payments. Corporations that pay the PHC penalty tax after the due date for filing their return (without regard to any extensions) will generally also owe interest and penalties on the unpaid PHC tax from the date that the return is originally due (without regard to any extensions) until the tax is paid.[83] The payment of a deficiency dividend eliminates the additional tax that is owed, but does not prevent the corporation from having to pay the interest and penalties.

Accumulated Earnings Tax

No formal schedule or return is required of a corporation that owes the accumulated earnings tax. Because of the subjective nature of this tax, a firm generally will not pay the penalty tax until some time after the IRS has audited their income tax return. Since the tax is not paid when the return is filed, Sec. 6601(b) requires interest to be charged on the accumulated earnings tax from the date that the return is originally due (without regard to any extensions) until the date that the tax payment is received.[84] The penalty for negligent underpayment of taxes imposed by Sec. 6653 may be assessed in accumulated earnings tax situations.[85]

Unrelated Business Income Tax

Determination and reporting of the unrelated business income tax liability occurs on Form 990-T (Exempt Organization Business Income Tax Return). The return is filed at the same time as the organization's annual information return. Quarterly payments of the unrelated business income tax liability must be made using the same rules as for regular corporations.

PROBLEM MATERIALS

DISCUSSION QUESTIONS

5-1. Explain the legislative intent behind enacting the alternative minimum tax.

5-2. Define the following terms:
  a. Tax preference item
  b. Adjustment item
  c. Alternative minimum taxable income
  d. Statutory exemption amount
  e. Tentative minimum tax

5-3. Explain the steps in making the alternative minimum tax liability calculation.

---

[83] *Hart Metal Products Corp. v. U.S.*, 38 AFTR 2d 76-6118, 76-2 USTC ¶ 9781 (Ct. Cls., 1976).
[84] Rev. Rul. 87-54, 1987-1 C.B. 349.
[85] Rev. Rul. 75-330, 1975-2 C.B. 496.

5-4. What tax preference items must be added to taxable income, and what adjustments must be made to taxable income, in order to compute AMTI?

5-5. Identify the following items as adjustments to taxable income (A) or as tax preference items (P):
  a. Depletion claimed in excess of a property's adjusted basis at the end of the tax year.
  b. Accelerated depreciation claimed on real estate placed in service before 1987.
  c. Accelerated depreciation claimed on tangible property placed in service after 1986.
  d. Tax-exempt interest on private activity bonds.
  e. Appreciation connected with a contribution made to a charitable organization.
  f. Difference between adjusted current earnings (ACE) and pre-adjustment AMTI.

5-6. Determine whether the following statements are true or false. If false, explain why the statement is false.
  a. Tax preference items may either increase or decrease AMTI.
  b. The same NOL carryover amount is used for regular tax and AMT purposes.
  c. The minimum tax credit is the entire amount by which the AMT exceeds the regular tax.
  d. A taxpayer's general business credit can offset not only its regular tax liability but also its AMT liability.
  e. The ACE adjustment is able to increase and decrease pre-adjustment AMTI.

5-7. Explain the adjusted current earnings (ACE) concept. How does the ACE adjustment differ from the book underreported profits adjustment used in tax years 1987 through 1989?

5-8. What adjustment must be made if ACE exceeds pre-adjustment AMTI? is less than pre-adjustment AMTI?

5-9. What restrictions are placed on negative ACE adjustments?

5-10. Indicate whether the following items are included in taxable income, pre-adjustment AMTI, and ACE.
  1. Tax-exempt interest on private activity bonds.
  2. Proceeds of a life-insurance policy on a corporate officer which has no cash surrender value.
  3. Profit on sale of inventory which a dealer reports using the installment method of accounting.
  4. Gain on sale of Sec. 1231 property which a nondealer reports using the installment method of accounting.
  5. Intangible drilling costs that were deducted in the year in which they were incurred.
  6. Amortization of organizational expenditures.
  7. Dividends-received deduction.

5-11. Dunn Corporation has taxable income of less than $40,000. The CPA preparing the corporate tax return does not calculate the AMT liability because he knows that taxable income is less than the AMT statutory exemption. Is he correct in his action? Explain.

5-12. Calculate Samuel Corporation's tax base for determining its tentative minimum tax amount for the current year given that AMTI (before the exemption) is:
  a. $30,000.
  b. $180,000.
  c. $400,000.

5-13. Jerome Corporation owes an $800,000 income tax liability but no AMT liability. Can Jerome Corporation owe a Superfund Environmental Tax liability?

5-14. The personal holding company tax and the accumulated earnings tax were enacted to prevent individuals from using corporations to avoid taxation. Explain the Congressional intent behind both of these levies. How have the individual and corporate rate changes in the Tax Reform Act of 1986 affected the importance of these two penalty taxes?

5-15. Which of the following special corporate forms are exempt from the PHC tax? The accumulated earnings tax?
  a. Closely held corporations

b. S corporations
c. Professional corporations
d. Tax-exempt organizations

5-16. Define the following terms used in connection with the PHC tax:
  a. Ordinary gross income
  b. Adjusted ordinary gross income
  c. Personal holding company income
  d. Adjusted income from rents

5-17. Which of the following types of income are included in the definition of personal holding company income (PHCI) when received by a corporation? Indicate if any special circumstances would exclude a type of income that is generally included in PHCI.
  a. Dividends
  b. Interest from a corporate bond
  c. Interest from a bond issued by a state government
  d. Rental income from a warehouse leased to a third party
  e. Rental income from a warehouse leased to the corporation's sole shareholder
  f. Royalty income from a book whose copyright is owned by the corporation
  g. Royalty income from a computer software copyright developed by the corporation and leased to a software marketing firm
  h. Accounting fees earned by a professional corporation offering public accounting services that has three equal shareholders
  i. Long-term capital gain earned on the sale of a stock investment

5-18. Which of the following dividend payments are eligible for a dividends-paid deduction when computing the PHC tax? The accumulated earnings tax?
  a. Cash dividend paid on common stock during the tax year
  b. Cash dividend paid on preferred stock where no dividend is paid to the common stock shareholders
  c. Property dividend payable in the stock of an unrelated corporation
  d. Property dividend payable in the stock of the distributing corporation
  e. Cash dividend paid two months after the close of the tax year

5-19. Define the term *consent dividend*. What requirements must be satisfied by the PHC or its shareholders before a consent dividend is eligible for a dividends-paid deduction? What are the tax consequences of a consent dividend to the shareholders and the distributing corporation?

5-20. Explain the advantages of paying a deficiency dividend. What requirements must be satisfied by the PHC and its shareholders before a deficiency dividend can be used to reduce or eliminate the PHC tax liability? Can a deficiency dividend eliminate the interest and penalties imposed in addition to the PHC penalty tax?

5-21. Determine whether the following statements about the PHC tax are true or false:
  a. A corporation may not owe any PHC tax liability for a tax year even though it is classified as a PHC.
  b. A sale of a large tract of land that is held for investment purposes can cause a corporation to be classified as a PHC.
  c. Federal income taxes (including the alternative minimum tax) accrued by the PHC reduce the UPHCI amount for the tax year.
  d. Consent dividends can be paid any time from the first day of the tax year through the due date for the corporation's tax return (including any extensions permitted) and reduce the UPHCI amount.
  e. The payment of a deficiency dividend permits a PHC to eliminate its PHC tax liability as well as any interest and penalties that are imposed in addition to the liability.
  f. A corporation that is classified as a PHC for a tax year can also be liable for the accumulated earnings tax for that year.

5-22. Explain the following statement: Although the accumulated earnings tax can be imposed upon both publicly held and closely held corporations, it is likely to be imposed only on closely held corporations.

5-23. The accumulated earnings tax is imposed only when the corporation is "formed or availed of for the purpose of avoiding the income tax." Does tax avoidance have to occur at the corporate or the shareholder level in order for the penalty tax to be imposed? Does tax avoidance have to be the sole motivation for the earnings accumulation before the penalty tax is imposed?

5-24. List six reasons a corporation can give for accumulating earnings to rebut an IRS presumption that an unreasonable accumulation of earnings has occurred.

5-25. Explain the operation of the *Bardahl* formula. Why have some tax authorities said that this formula implies a greater amount of mathematical accuracy than, in fact, actually may be present when determining working capital needs.

5-26. Different rules apply to operating companies, holding and investment companies, and service companies when determining the accumulated earnings credit. Explain these differences.

5-27. Determine whether the following statements about the accumulated earnings tax are true or false:
   a. Before the IRS can impose the accumulated earnings tax, it only needs to show that tax avoidance was one of the motives for the corporation's unreasonable accumulation of earnings.
   b. Long-term capital gains are included in the tax base for the accumulated earnings tax.
   c. Each corporation that is a member of a controlled group can claim a separate $150,000 or $250,000 accumulated earnings credit.
   d. A dividends-paid deduction can be claimed for both cash and property distributions (other than nontaxable stock dividends) paid by a corporation.
   e. The accumulated earnings tax liability cannot be eliminated by paying a deficiency dividend.
   f. Interest and penalties on the accumulated earnings tax deficiency are imposed only from the date that a "determination" is made by the IRS or the courts that the liability is owed.

5-28. For each of the following statements, indicate whether the statement is correct for the PHC tax only, the accumulated earnings tax only, both penalty taxes, or neither penalty tax.
   a. The penalty tax is imposed only if the corporation satisfies certain stock ownership and income requirements.
   b. The penalty tax applies to both closely held and publicly held corporations.
   c. The penalty tax is subjective in nature.
   d. Long-term capital gains are a neutral factor in determining the amount of the penalty tax levy.
   e. Tax-exempt interest income is excluded in determining the tax base used to levy the penalty tax.
   f. A credit is available that reduces the penalty tax liability on a dollar-for-dollar basis.
   g. Throwback dividends are permitted to be paid without limit.
   h. Consent dividends are eligible for a dividends-paid deduction.
   i. Throwback and consent dividends are effective tools for reducing or eliminating the penalty tax liability.
   j. The penalty tax can be avoided by making a deficiency dividend distribution.

5-29. What is the legislative intent behind the unrelated business income tax? Explain briefly how the tax is imposed on an incorporated charitable organization.

PROBLEMS

5-30. *Alternative Minimum Tax Calculation.* Whitaker Corporation reports taxable income of $600,000 for the current year. It had positive AMTI adjustments of $500,000 and tax preference items of $200,000.
   a. What is Whitaker's AMTI?
   b. What is Whitaker's tentative minimum tax?
   c. What is Whitaker's regular tax liability?
   d. What is Whitaker's AMT liability?

5-31. *Depreciation Calculations.* Water Corporation purchased a machine for $10,000 on June 1

of the current year. The machine is 5-year property under the Modified ACRS rules. The machine has a 7-year class life. Calculate the annual depreciation deductions for purposes of determining:
a. Taxable income.
b. Alternative minimum taxable income.
c. Adjusted current earnings.

5-32. Basis Adjustment. Assume the same facts as in Question 5-31. Water Corporation sells the machine for $5,000 on August 1, 1995.
a. What gain is reported for purposes of determining taxable income, AMTI, and adjusted current earnings?
b. If you were using taxable income as the starting point for calculating AMTI, what type of adjustment is needed to properly report the transaction for AMTI purposes?

5-33. ACE Adjustment. Calculate the ACE Adjustment for Towne Corporation for the period 1990-1994.

	1990	1991	1992	1993	1994
ACE	500	500	500	500	(500)
Minus: Pre-adjustment AMTI	600	(100)	900	—0—	(300)
ACE Adjustment	?	?	?	?	?

5-34. ACE Adjustment. Bronze Corporation reports the following information about its 1991 operations:

Taxable income	$600,000
Dividends from 10% owned corporation	60,000
Capital losses in excess of capital gains	10,000
Tax-exempt bond interest (not from private activity bonds)	20,000
Installment sale of land (a capital asset)	
Total realized gain	160,000
Gain reported in 1991	32,000
Depreciation:	
For regular tax purposes	120,000
For AMTI purposes	85,000
For ACE purposes	60,000
Sec. 1245 property sold in 1991:	
Recognized gain for regular tax purposes	30,000
Basis for regular tax purposes	24,000
Basis for AMTI purposes	30,000
Basis for ACE purposes	34,000

a. What is Bronze Corporation's ACE adjustment?
b. What is Bronze Corporation's AMTI?
c. What is Bronze Corporation's AMT liability?

5-35. Regular Tax and AMT Calculations. Campbell Corporation has taxable income of $200,000 for 1991. The following items were taken into consideration in arriving at this number.

1. Equipment acquired in 1987 was depreciated using the MACRS rules. MACRS depreciation for 1987–1991 was $90,000. Depreciation under the alternative depreciation system for AMT purposes would have been $60,000.
2. $12,000 of Sec. 1245 gain is recognized for income tax purposes on the sale of an asset. The asset's income tax basis is $9,000 less than its AMT basis.
3. Campbell's adjusted current earnings for 1991 are $420,000.

a. What is Campbell Corporation's AMTI?

b. What is Campbell Corporation's AMT liability? Is any minimum tax credit carryback or carryover available?

5-36. AMTI Calculation. Alabama Corporation conducts mining activities. During the current year it reported taxable income of $400,000 which included a $100,000 deduction for percentage depletion. The depletable property's adjusted basis at year-end (before reduction for the current year's depletion) was $40,000. Cost depletion had it been taken would have been $30,000. Depreciation on post-1986 property acquisitions under the MACRS rules was $140,000. Under the alternative depreciation system only $90,000 could have been claimed. In addition, $12,000 of accelerated depreciation was claimed on real property placed in service in 1985. Straight-line depreciation would have been $7,000. Alabama Corporation sold an asset for a $12,000 gain that was included in taxable income. The asset's adjusted basis was $5,000 higher for AMT purposes than it was for regular tax purposes. Alabama Corporation's adjusted current earnings is $800,000. What is Alabama Corporation's AMTI for the current year? What is its AMT liability?

5-37. Regular Tax and AMT Calculations. What is Middle Corporation's regular tax liability, AMT liability, and minimum tax credit (if any) in the following three independent situations?

	Situation		
	No. 1	No. 2	No. 3
Taxable income	$200,000	$ 50,000	$300,000
Tax preference items and adjustments (other than the ACE adjustment)	100,000	25,000	100,000
Adjusted Current Earnings	500,000	150,000	400,000

5-38. Regular Tax and AMT Calculations. Delta Corporation reports taxable income of $2,000,000, tax preference items of $100,000 and net adjustments for the AMT of $600,000 before the ACE adjustment. Its adjusted current earnings is $4,000,000. What is Delta Corporation's regular tax liability and AMT liability? What is Delta Corporation's minimum tax credit (if any)?

5-39. Minimum Tax Credit. Jones Corporation has $600,000 of taxable income plus $400,000 of positive adjustments and $200,000 of tax preference items.
a. What is Jones Corporation's regular tax liability and AMT liability?
b. What is Jones Corporation's minimum tax credit (if any)? To what years can it be carried back or carried over?

5-40. Minimum Tax Credit. Gulf Corporation reports the following tax liabilities for the period 1990-1992:

Tax Liability	1990	1991	1992
Regular tax	$75,000	$100,000	$150,000
Tentative minimum tax	40,000	140,000	120,000

In what years does a minimum tax credit originate? To what years can the credit be carried? Do any credit carryovers remain to 1993?

5-41. AMT Foreign Tax Credit. Phoenix Corporation reports a tentative minimum tax liability (before foreign tax credits and alternative tax NOL) of $200,000 for the current year. The corporation has paid or accrued $200,000 of creditable foreign taxes. No NOL deduction is claimed. What is the maximum amount of foreign tax credits that Phoenix can claim (ignoring the Sec. 904 limitation)?

5-42. General Business Credit. Edge Corporation's regular tax liability before credits is $180,000 in the current year. Its tentative minimum tax is $100,000. The only credit Edge Corporation earns in the current year is a $200,000 general business credit relating to research expenditures.
a. What amount of this credit may Edge Corporation use to reduce its current year liability?

b. What carryovers and carrybacks are available, and to what years may they be carried?

5-43. *Estimated Tax Payments.* Dallas Corporation reports the following information with respect to its 1990 and 1991 tax liabilities:

Type of Liability	1990	1991
Regular tax liability	$100,000	$120,000
AMT liability	—0—	15,000

Both tax years cover 12-month periods. Dallas Corporation is not a large corporation and it made $23,000 of estimated tax payments for each quarter of 1991.
  a. What is the amount of tax that is owed when Dallas files its 1991 tax return?
  b. Is Dallas potentially liable for any estimated tax underpayment penalties? If so, how much is underpaid for each quarter?

5-44. *Estimated Tax Requirement.* Ajax Corporation anticipates owing a $120,000 income tax liability and a $60,000 alternative minimum tax liability for the current year. Last year it owed a $200,000 income tax liability and no alternative minimum tax liability. What is its minimum estimated tax payment for the current year?

5-45. *PHC Definition.* In which of the following situations will Small Corporation be a PHC? Assume that personal holding company income constitutes more than 60% of Small's adjusted ordinary gross income.
  a. Art owns all of Parent Corporation's stock. Parent Corporation owns all of the Small stock. Parent and Small Corporations file separate tax returns.
  b. Art owns one-third of the Small stock. The PRS Partnership, of which Phil, Robert, and Sue each have a one-third interest in both capital and profits, also owns one-third of the Small stock. The remaining Small stock is owned by 50 individuals unrelated to Art, Phil, Robert, and Sue.
  c. Art and his wife, Becky, each own 20% of the Small stock. The remaining Small stock is owned by the Whitaker Family Trust. Becky and her three sisters each have a one-fourth beneficial interest in the trust.

5-46. *PHC Definition.* In which of the following situations will Total Corporation, a corporation that is owned equally by Amy, Len, and Milt at all times during the tax year, be a PHC?
  a. Total Corporation reports $75,000 of gross profit from manufacturing activities; $40,000 of interest income; $60,000 of dividend income; and $25,000 of long-term capital gains.
  b. Total Corporation reports $100,000 of rental income; $14,000 of interest income; and $6,000 of dividend income. Depreciation, interest, and property taxes on the rental properties are $40,000. No dividends are paid by Total during the tax year.
  c. Assume the same facts as in Part b, except that Total Corporation instead pays $9,000 of dividends during the year.

5-47. *PHC Definition.* Random Corporation is owned equally by two individual shareholders. During 1991 Random reports the following results:

Income:	Rentals	$200,000
	Dividends (from a 25%-owned domestic corporation)	25,000
	Interest	15,000
	Long-term capital gains	25,000
Expenses related to rental income:		
	Interest	30,000
	Depreciation	27,000
	Property taxes	8,000
	Other Sec. 162 expenses	50,000
General and administrative expenses		10,000
Dividend paid on June 30, 1991		15,000

  a. What is Random's gross income?
  b. What is Random's ordinary gross income?
  c. What is Random's adjusted income from rents?

d. What is Random's adjusted ordinary gross income?
e. What is Random's personal holding company income?
f. Is Random Corporation a PHC?

5-48. *PHC Tax Liability.* Mouse Corporation is a PHC for 1991. The following results are reported by Mouse for 1991:

Taxable income:	$150,000
Dividend received by Mouse from a 25%-owned domestic corporation	40,000
Dividends paid by Mouse during 1991	60,000

a. What is Mouse's federal income tax liability (ignoring any alternative minimum tax implications)?
b. What is Mouse's PHC tax liability?
c. What actions can be taken by Mouse to eliminate its PHC tax liability before its tax return is filed? After its tax return is filed?

5-49. *PHC Tax Liability.* Kennedy Corporation is a PHC for the current year. The following results were reported for the current year:

Taxable income	$400,000
Federal income taxes	136,000
Dividends paid to Marlene, Kennedy's sole shareholder	75,000

The following information is available about the federal income tax calculation:

1. $100,000 of dividends were received from a 25% owned domestic corporation.
2. $30,000 of tax-exempt interest income was received.
3. $175,000 of long-term capital gains were realized on the sale of land (a Sec. 1231 asset).

a. What is Kennedy Corporation's PHC tax liability?
b. What can be done after the year-end and before the tax return is filed to reduce the PHC tax liability? After the tax return is filed?

5-50. *PHC Tax Liability.* Victor Corporation is classified as a PHC for 1991. The following results are reported by Victor for 1991:

Taxable income	$250,000
Federal income taxes	80,750
Dividends paid during 1991	30,000

The following information is available about Victor's taxable income calculation:

1. Taxable income includes $25,000 of net capital gain.
2. A charitable contributions carryover of $5,000 from 1990 is deducted in 1991.
3. A dividends-received deduction of $20,000 is claimed by Victor for dividends received from a 30%-owned domestic corporation.

a. What is Victor's PHC tax liability?
b. What action can be taken by Victor to eliminate the PHC tax liability before the tax return is filed? After the tax return is filed?

5-51. *Unreasonable Accumulation of Earnings.* Indicate for each of the following independent situations why an unreasonable accumulation of earnings by Adobe Corporation may exist. Assume that all of the Adobe stock is owned by Tess.
a. Adobe Corporation established a sinking fund 10 years ago in order to retire its short-term notes. Monies have been added to the fund annually. Six months ago a decision was made to refinance the notes when they come due with a new series of notes that will be sold only to an insurance company. The monies in the sinking fund remain invested in stocks and bonds.

b. Adobe Corporation regularly lends monies to Tess at a rate slightly below the rate charged by a commercial bank. Some of these monies have been repaid. The current balance on the loans is $500,000, which approximates one year's net income for Adobe Corporation.
c. Adobe Corporation has made substantial investments in stocks and bonds. The current market value of its investments is $2,000,000. The investment portfolio constitutes approximately one-half of Adobe Corporation's assets.
d. Tess owns three corporations other than Adobe Corporation, which, together with Adobe Corporation, form a brother-sister controlled group. Adobe Corporation regularly lends monies to Tess's other corporations. The current loans amount to $500,000. The interest rate that is charged is below the commercial interest rate for similar loans.

5-52. Bardahl Formula. Lion Corporation is concerned over a possible accumulated earnings tax problem. It accumulates E&P to maintain the working capital necessary to conduct its manufacturing activities. The following information about Lion Corporation's financial position is taken from its 1991 balance sheet.

Account	January 1, 1991 Balance	December 31, 1991 Balance	Peak Balance for the Year
Accounts receivable	$300,000	$400,000	$400,000
Inventory	240,000	300,000	375,000
Accounts payable	150,000	200,000	220,000

The following information about operations is taken from Lion Corporation's 1991 income statement:

Sales	$3,200,000
Cost of goods sold	1,500,000
Purchases	1,200,000
Operating expenses (other than cost of goods sold)	1,000,000

Included in operating expenses are depreciation of $150,000 and federal income taxes of $100,000.
a. What is Lion's operating cycle in days? As a decimal percentage?
b. What is Lion's working capital needs as determined with the *Bardahl* formula?
c. What steps must Lion take in order to justify a larger accumulation than is indicated by the *Bardahl* formula?

5-53. Accumulated Earnings Credit. For each of the following independent situations, calculate the amount of the available accumulated earnings credit. Assume that the corporation in question is an operating company that uses a calendar year as its tax year unless otherwise stated.
a. Frank Corporation was started in 1990 when it reported E&P of $50,000. E&P reported in 1991 totals $150,000. The reasonable needs of the business increase from $50,000 to $180,000 during 1991.
b. How would your answer to Part a change if Frank is instead a service company?
c. Hall Corporation's accumulated E&P balance at January 1, 1991, is $200,000. During 1991 Hall reports $100,000 of current E&P. The reasonable needs of the business increase from $200,000 to $275,000 during 1991.

5-54. Accumulated Earnings Tax Liability. Tara Corporation has conducted manufacturing operations for a number of years. It has an accumulated E&P balance of $150,000 on January 1, 1991. The following results of operations are presented for 1991:

Taxable income	$450,000
Federal income taxes	153,000
Dividends paid on June 1, 1991	60,000

Tara can justify an increase in the reasonable needs of the business from $150,000 to $275,000 during 1991.
a. What is Tara's accumulated taxable income?
b. What is Tara's accumulated earnings tax liability?

5-55. **Accumulated Earnings Tax Liability.** Howard Corporation conducts manufacturing activities and has a substantial need to accumulate earnings. Its January 1, 1991, E&P balance is $600,000. The following results of operations are presented for 1991:

Taxable income		$500,000
Federal income taxes		170,000
Dividends paid:	July 15, 1991	125,000
	February 10, 1992	100,000

Other information about Howard's operations for 1991 is as follows:

NOL carryover from 1990 deducted in 1991	$100,000
Net capital gain	80,000
Dividends-received from 10%-owned domestic corporation	75,000

a. What is Howard's accumulated taxable income?
b. What is Howard's accumulated earnings tax liability?

TAX FORM/RETURN PREPARATION PROBLEM

5-56. King Corporation, I.D. No. 38-1534789, reports the following results for the current year:

Taxable income	$800,000
Regular tax liability (before credits)	272,000
Accelerated depreciation on real property placed in service in 1985	15,000
Depreciation adjustment for personal property placed in service after 1986	36,000
Basis adjustment for personal property acquired in 1987 and sold in the current year	(12,000)
Adjusted current earnings	1,800,000
General business credit (targeted jobs credit)	10,000

Taxable income includes a charitable contribution deduction for appreciated stock donated to a public charity. The stocks had a $75,000 FMV and a $10,000 adjusted basis. Also included is a land sale which resulted in $40,000 of Sec. 1231 gain being reported on the installment method. King's realized gain on the sale was $200,000. Prepare Form 4626 for King Corporation to report its alternative minimum tax liability (if any) for the current year.

CASE STUDY PROBLEM

5-57. Eagle Corporation is a family corporation created by Edward Eagle, Sr. 10 years ago. Edward Eagle, Sr. dies, and the Eagle stock passes to his children and grandchildren. The corporation is primarily an investment company with its assets consisting of rental property, highly appreciated stocks, and corporate bonds. The profit or loss projection for 1991 that was made by the tax advisor who regularly handles Eagle Corporation's tax matters is as follows:

Rentals	$260,000
Dividend income (from a 40%-owned domestic corporation)	80,000
Interest income	20,000
Gross income	$360,000
Rental expenses:	
Depreciation expense	$ 70,000
Interest expense	100,000
Property taxes	10,000
Other Sec. 162 expenses	20,000
General and administrative expenses	15,000
Total expenses	$215,000
Net profit	$145,000

Dividends of $40,000 have been paid in each of the past 3 years. The stock investment has appreciated substantially in value in the past 6 months. As a result, dividend income is expected to increase from $10,000 to $80,000 this year. Assume that Eagle Corporation has not been a PHC in prior years.

Required: Prepare a memorandum to Edward Eagle, Jr. regarding the possible PHC problem. As part of your discussion, make sure you discuss the following two questions.

a. Is Eagle Corporation projected to be a PHC for 1991?

b. If Eagle Corporation is projected to be a PHC for 1991, what actions (if any) should be taken prior to year-end to eliminate the PHC problem?

TAX RESEARCH PROBLEMS

5-58. Brown Corporation purchased two assets in January 1988, its initial year of operation. The first asset, a commercial factory building, cost $200,000 with $40,000 of the acquisition price being allocated to the land. The second, a machine which is a 7-year MACRS property, cost $80,000. The class life for the machine under the Asset Depreciation Range System is 10 years. Both assets were sold in March, 1991 in connection with a relocation of their manufacturing activities. The sale price for the factory building was $225,000, with $45,000 of the sale price being allocated to the land. The sale price for the machine was $70,000. The maximum amount of depreciation was claimed on both assets for regular tax purposes. What is the amount and character of the gain reported by Brown Corporation for regular tax and alternative minimum tax purposes?

A partial list of research sources is:

- Secs. 56(a)(1), 56(g)(4)(A)(ii), 168(a)-(g).

5-59. Camp Corporation is owned by Hal and Ruthie, who have owned their stock since the corporation was formed in 1986. The corporation has filed each of its prior tax returns using the calendar year as its tax year and the accrual method of accounting. In 1991 Camp Corporation borrows $4,000,000 from a local bank at a 12% annual rate. The loan is secured by a lien against some of its machinery. Ninety percent of the borrowings are lent by Camp Corporation to Vickers Corporation at a 12% annual rate. Vickers Corporation is also owned equally by Hal and Ruthie. Vickers Corporation sells parts to the automobile industry that are manufactured by Camp Corporation and other unrelated manufacturers. A downturn is experienced by Camp Corporation due to a slowdown in the automobile industry, and the gross margin from its sales activities declines from $1,000,000 in 1990 to $200,000 in 1991. Interest income accrued by Camp on the loan to Vickers Corporation is $432,000 in 1991. Other passive income earned by Camp Corporation is $40,000. Camp Corporation's accountant feels that the corporation is not a personal holding company since the interest income Camp Corporation earns can be netted against the interest expense paid to the bank for the monies lent to Vickers Corporation. Is he correct in his assumption?

A partial list of research sources is

- Secs. 542(a) and 543(a)(1).
- Reg. Sec. 1.543-1(b)(2).
- *Bell Realty Trust,* 65 T.C. 766 (1976).
- *Blair Holding Co., Inc.,* 1980 PH T.C. Memo ¶ 80,079, 39 TCM 1255.

5-60. William Queen owns all of the stock of Able and Baker Corporations. Able Corporation has been quite successful and has excess working capital in the amount of $3 million. Baker Corporation is still in its developmental stages and has had tremendous needs for capital. To help provide for Baker Corporation's capital needs, William Queen has had Able Corporation lend Baker Corporation $2 million over the past two years. These loans are secured by Baker Corporation notes, but not by any Baker Corporation properties. Able Corporation has charged Baker Corporation interest at a rate acceptable to the IRS. Upon reviewing Able Corporation's books as part of an audit of its 1987 income tax return, an IRS agent indicates that Able Corporation has an accumulated earnings tax problem because of its accumulation of excess working capital and its loans to Baker Corporation. You are about to meet with the agent for a third time. Prior to this meeting you need to research whether loans to a related corporation in order to provide needed working capital are a reasonable need of the business for retaining earnings.

A partial list of research sources is:

- Secs. 532 and 537.
- Reg. Secs. 1.537-2(c) and -3(b).
- *Latchis Theatres of Keene, Inc. v. CIR*, 45 AFTR 1836, 54-2 USTC ¶ 9544 (1st Cir., 1954).
- *Bremerton Sun Publishing Co.*, 44 T.C. 566 (1965).

6. Corporate Liquidating Distributions

CHAPTER OUTLINE

LEARNING OBJECTIVES 6-2
TAX CONSEQUENCES OF
  CORPORATE
  LIQUIDATIONS 6-3
  The Shareholder 6-3
  The Corporation 6-4
EFFECTS OF LIQUIDATING ON
  THE SHAREHOLDERS 6-5
  Definition of a Complete
    Liquidation 6-5
  General Liquidation Rules 6-5
  Liquidation of a Controlled
    Subsidiary Corporation 6-9
  Installment Obligations Received
    by a Shareholder 6-12
EFFECTS OF LIQUIDATING ON
  THE LIQUIDATING
  CORPORATION 6-13
  Recognition of Gain or Loss
    When Property Is Distributed
    in Redemption of Stock 6-13
  Recognition of Gain or Loss
    When Property Is Distributed
    in Retirement of Debt 6-17
  Expenses of the
    Liquidation 6-17
  Treatment of Net Operating
    Losses 6-18
  Tax Attribute Carryovers 6-18
DEEMED LIQUIDATION
  ELECTION 6-20
  Eligible Stock Acquisitions 6-20
  The Election 6-21
  Deemed Sale Transaction 6-22
  Basis of the Assets After the
    Deemed Purchase 6-22
  Tax Accounting Elections for the
    New Corporation 6-25
  Liquidation of the Target
    Corporation 6-26
TAX PLANNING
  CONSIDERATIONS 6-28
  Timing the Liquidation
    Transaction 6-28
  Recognition of Ordinary Losses
    When a Liquidation
    Occurs 6-28
  Using Sec. 332 to Obtain a
    Double Tax Exemption 6-29
  Avoiding Sec. 332 in Order to
    Recognize Losses 6-30
COMPLIANCE AND
  PROCEDURAL
  CONSIDERATIONS 6-30
  General Liquidation
    Procedures 6-30
  Section 332 Liquidations 6-31
  Section 338 Deemed
    Liquidations 6-31
  Plan of Liquidation 6-31
PROBLEM MATERIALS 6-32
  Discussion Questions 6-32
  Problems 6-34
  Case Study Problem 6-39
  Tax Research Problems 6-40

LEARNING OBJECTIVES

After studying this chapter, you should be able to

1. Explain the tax consequences of a corporate liquidation
2. Explain the difference between a complete liquidation and a dissolution
3. Explain the general shareholder gain and loss recognition rules for a corporate liquidation
4. Explain the different tax treatments for open and closed liquidation transactions
5. Determine when the Sec. 332 nonrecognition rules apply to the liquidation of a subsidiary corporation
6. Determine when gains and losses must be recognized by the liquidating corporation on making a liquidating distribution
7. Determine when gains and losses must be recognized on the retirement of debt by a liquidating corporation
8. Determine the effect of a liquidation on the liquidating corporation's tax attributes
9. Explain when an acquisition qualifies for a step-up in basis under Sec. 338
10. Determine the amount of gain or loss that is recognized on a deemed sale transaction
11. Determine the basis of the target corporation's assets following a deemed purchase transaction

Additional Comment

Under Sec. 351, usually no tax cost is involved in forming a corporation. However, as this chapter will illustrate, the tax costs of liquidating a corporation may be substantial. The tax consequences of liquidating a corporation should be a consideration in the initial decision whether to use the corporate form to conduct a business.

As part of the corporate life cycle, management may decide to discontinue the operations of either a profitable or unprofitable corporation by liquidating it. As a result of this decision, the shareholders may receive liquidating distributions of the corporation's assets. Preceding the formal liquidation of the corporation, management may sell part or all of the corporation's assets. The sale may be undertaken to dispose of assets which the shareholder(s) may not want to own on an individual basis or to obtain cash which can be used to pay off the corporation's liabilities.

Ordinarily the liquidation transaction is motivated by a combination of tax and business reasons. However, sometimes it is undertaken principally for tax reasons.

- By liquidating the corporation and having its shareholders hold the assets in an unincorporated form (e.g., sole proprietorship, partnership, and so on), the top marginal tax rate applying to the earnings can be reduced from 39% to 31%.
- If the assets are producing operating and/or capital losses, it may be advantageous for the shareholders to hold the assets in an unincorporated form and deduct the losses on their personal tax returns.
- Corporate earnings are taxed once under the corporate income tax rules and a second time when distributed as a dividend or realized by selling or exchanging the corporate stock. Liquidation of the corporation permits the assets to be held in an unincorporated form, thereby avoiding double taxation of the corporate earnings.

This chapter explains the tax consequences of liquidating distributions to both the shareholders and the distributing corporation and the special provisions that can eliminate the recognition of gain for both the shareholders and the distributing corporation. It also examines the special "deemed liquidation" election, which permits a corporation to acquire the stock of a target corporation, make a special election, and step-up the basis of the target corporation's assets to the amount paid for the stock.

TAX CONSEQUENCES OF CORPORATE LIQUIDATIONS

OBJECTIVE 1
Explain the tax consequences of a corporate liquidation

This chapter initially presents an overview of the tax consequences of a corporate liquidation to both the shareholders and the distributing corporation.

The Shareholder

Three questions must be answered in order to determine the tax consequences of the liquidation transaction to the liquidating corporation's shareholders. These are:

1. What are the amount and character of the shareholders' recognized gain or loss?
2. What is the adjusted basis of the property that is received by the shareholders?
3. When does the holding period commence for the property that is received by the shareholders?

Key Point
The same basic questions posed in any sale or disposition need to be answered for the shareholders in a corporate liquidation. These basic questions are: (1) realized gain/loss? (2) recognized gain/loss? (3) character of gain/loss? (4) adjusted basis of property received? and (5) holding period of property received?

When a corporation is liquidated under the general rule, the liquidating distribution(s) is treated as an amount received in exchange for the shareholder's stock. The shareholder recognizes the excess of the money received plus the fair market value (FMV) of the nonmoney property received over the adjusted basis of their stock as a capital gain or loss (see Table 6-1). The bases of the properties that are received are stepped-up or stepped-down to the property's FMV on the liquidation date. The holding period for the assets commences on the day after the liquidation date. Special rules apply to liquidations of subsidiary corporations that permit part or all of the shareholders' realized gains or losses to go unrecognized. Special carryover basis and holding period rules apply to liquidations of subsidiary corporations.

TABLE 6-1 *Tax Consequences of a Liquidation to the Shareholders*

	Amount of Gain or Loss Recognized	Character of Gain or Loss Recognized	Adjusted Basis of Property Received	Holding Period of Property Received
General Rule	Shareholder's realized gain or loss (cash + FMV of other property − adjusted basis of stock) is recognized (Sec. 331).	Long-term or short-term capital gain or loss (Sec. 1222). Ordinary loss (Sec. 1244).	FMV of the property (Sec. 334(a)).	Commences on the day after the liquidation date (Sec. 1223(1)).
Exception:	No gain or loss is recognized when an 80% controlled subsidiary corporation is liquidated into its parent corporation (Sec. 332).[a]	Not applicable.[a]	Basis of property carries over from the books of the subsidiary corporation (Sec. 334(b)).[a]	Includes the holding period of the subsidiary corporation (Sec. 1223(2)).[a]

[a] Minority shareholders use general rule.

The Corporation

Key Point
As illustrated in Table 6-1, there are two different possibilities with respect to a shareholder in a corporate liquidation. Either the shareholder is considered to be involved in a taxable exchange with a corresponding FMV basis for the liquidated assets **or** the transaction is nontaxable (parent-subsidiary liquidation) with a corresponding carryover basis for the liquidated assets.

Typical Misconception
In a complete liquidation other than a liquidation of a controlled subsidiary, there is a potential tax at both the shareholder and corporate levels. Assuming a 34% rate at the corporate level and the 28% maximum capital gains rate at the shareholder level, the effective tax cost of a complete liquidation would be approximately 52.5%. Clearly, a decision to liquidate should be carefully considered.

Two questions must be answered to determine the tax consequences of the liquidation transaction for the corporation being liquidated. These are:

1. What are the amount and character of the corporation's recognized gain or loss?
2. What happens to the corporation's tax attributes upon liquidation?

When a liquidation occurs under the general rule, the liquidating corporation must recognize gain or loss on the distribution of property to its shareholders (see Table 6-2). The amount of gain or loss recognized is the same as what would be recognized if the property were instead sold to the distributee. An exception to the general rule is provided for gain or loss recognition when an 80%-controlled subsidiary corporation is liquidated into its parent corporation. Three other special rules restrict the recognition of losses in special situations that are described in Table 6-2.

The tax attributes (e.g., net operating loss [NOL] carryovers) of the liquidating corporation disappear when the liquidation takes place under the general liquidation rule. As a result, any loss carryovers that have not been used by the liquidation date are lost. On the other hand, the tax attributes of a controlled subsidiary corporation generally carry over to the parent corporation.

Section 338 permits a parent corporation that acquires a controlling interest in a target (acquired) corporation's stock to make a special **deemed liquidation election** to increase the basis of the target corporation's assets to the price paid by the acquiring corporation for the target corporation's stock. Such an election requires the target corporation to engage in a "deemed sale" transaction and recognize the amount of gain or loss that would otherwise be recognized in an actual sale. The target corporation is then treated as a new corporation for tax purposes.

TABLE 6-2 Tax Consequences of a Liquidation to the Corporation

	Amount and Character of Gain, Loss, or Income Recognized	Treatment of the Liquidating Corporation's Tax Attributes
General Rule:	Gain or loss is recognized when a corporation distributes property as part of a complete liquidation (Sec. 336(a)).	Tax attributes disappear when the liquidation is completed.
Exception 1:	No gain or loss is recognized when property of a controlled subsidiary corporation is distributed to its parent corporation in a liquidation to which the Sec. 332 nonrecognition of gain or loss rules apply (Sec. 337(a)).	Tax attributes of a controlled subsidiary corporation are assumed by its parent corporation in a liquidation to which the Sec. 332 nonrecognition of gain or loss rules apply (Sec. 381(a)).
Exception 2:	No loss is recognized when a distribution of property is made to minority shareholders in a liquidation to which the Sec. 332 nonrecognition of gain or loss rules apply.	
Exception 3:	No loss is recognized when a distribution of property is made to a related person, unless such property is distributed ratably to all shareholders *and* the property was not acquired by the liquidating corporation in a Sec. 351 transaction or as a contribution to capital during the 5 years preceding the distribution.	
Exception 4:	No loss is recognized when a sale, exchange, or distribution of property occurs and such property was acquired by the liquidating corporation in a Sec. 351 transaction or as a contribution to capital having a principal purpose being the recognition of loss.	

EFFECTS OF LIQUIDATING ON THE SHAREHOLDERS

Three different sets of rules can apply to the shareholders of the liquidating corporation. This discussion examines the general liquidation rules (Sec. 331), the controlled subsidiary corporation liquidation rules (Sec. 332), and the special rules that apply to shareholders who receive installment obligations resulting from the sale of corporate assets (Sec. 453(h)).

OBJECTIVE 2
Explain the difference between a complete liquidation and a dissolution

Definition of a Complete Liquidation

The term *complete liquidation* is not defined in the Code, but Reg. Sec. 1.332-2(c) indicates that distributions made by a liquidating corporation must (1) completely cancel or redeem all of its stock in accordance with a plan of liquidation, or (2) be one of a series of distributions that completely cancels or redeems all of its stock in accordance with a plan of liquidation (see pages 6-31 and 6-32 for a discussion of plans of liquidation).

When there is more than one distribution, the corporation must be in a liquidation status at the time that the first liquidating distribution is made under the plan, and such status must continue until the liquidation is completed. A distribution that is made before a plan of liquidation is adopted will generally be taxed under the dividend distribution or stock redemption rules.

A liquidation status exists when the corporation ceases to be a going concern and its activities are merely for the purpose of winding up its affairs, paying its debts, and distributing any remaining properties to its shareholders. A liquidation is completed when the liquidating corporation has divested itself of all properties. The retention of a nominal amount of assets (e.g., to retain the corporation's name) does not prevent a liquidation from occurring under the tax rules.

Key Point
A corporation can go through a complete liquidation without undergoing dissolution. If it is desirable to keep the corporate charter alive, this is possible as long as certain state requirements are satisfied.

The liquidation of a corporation does not mean that a corporation has undergone dissolution. **Dissolution** is a legal term that implies that the corporation has surrendered the charter that it originally received from the state. A corporation may complete its liquidation prior to surrendering its charter to the state and undergoing dissolution. Dissolution may never occur if the corporation retains its charter in order to protect the corporate name from being acquired by another party.

Example 6-1 ■ Thomas Corporation adopts a plan of liquidation in December 1990. All but a nominal amount of Thomas's assets are distributed to its shareholders in January 1991. The nominal assets are retained to preserve the corporation's existence under state law and to prevent others from acquiring the corporation's name. The retention of the nominal amount of assets does not prevent Thomas from having been liquidated for tax purposes in January 1991. ■

OBJECTIVE 3
Explain the general shareholder gain or loss recognition rules for a corporate liquidation

General Liquidation Rules

The coverage of the general liquidation rules is divided into four parts: (1) amount and timing of gain or loss recognition, (2) character of the recognized gain or loss, (3) basis of property received in the liquidation, and (4) the open versus closed transaction concept. Each of these points is discussed below.

6-6 • Ch. 6 / Corporate Liquidating Distributions

Amount of Recognized Gain or Loss. Section 331(a) requires that amounts received by a shareholder as a distribution in complete liquidation of a corporation be treated as full payment in exchange for the stock. The amount of the shareholder's recognized gain or loss equals the difference between the amount realized and his basis for the stock. If a shareholder assumes or acquires liabilities of the liquidating corporation, the amount of these liabilities reduces the amount realized by the shareholder.

Example 6-2 ■ Red Corporation is liquidated with Mike receiving (1) $10,000 in money and (2) other property having a $12,000 FMV. Mike's basis in his Red stock is $16,000. Mike's amount realized is $22,000 ($12,000 + $10,000). He must recognize a $6,000 ($22,000 − $16,000) gain on the liquidation. ■

Example 6-3 ■ Assume the same facts as in Example 6-2, except that Mike also assumes a $2,000 mortgage attaching to the other property. Mike's amount realized is reduced by the $2,000 liability assumed and is $20,000 ($22,000 − $2,000). The recognized gain on the liquidation is $4,000 ($20,000 − $16,000). ■

Self-Study Question

How is the gain/loss calculated if a shareholder has acquired stock at different times and at varying prices?

Answer

A shareholder who has purchased blocks of stock at different times and at varying prices must calculate the gain/loss on each of the blocks separately. Calculating the gain/loss separately on each block may result in (a) both gains and losses existing in the same liquidating distribution and (b) the character of the various gains/losses being different.

Impact of Accounting Method. A shareholder who uses the accrual method of accounting reports the gain or loss using the accrual concepts (i.e., the gain or loss is recognized when all the events have occurred that fix the amount of the liquidating distribution and when the shareholders are entitled to receive the distribution upon surrender of their shares). A shareholder who uses the cash method of accounting reports the gain or loss when there has been actual or constructive receipt of the liquidating distribution(s).[1]

When Stock Is Acquired. The shareholder's stockholdings may have been acquired at different times or for different per-share amounts. If this occurs, the shareholder must compute the gain or loss separately for each share or block of stock that is owned.[2]

Partially Liquidating Distributions. Liquidating distributions are often received in the form of a series of partially liquidating distributions. Section 346(a) indicates that a series of partially liquidating distributions received in complete liquidation of the corporation are taxed under the Sec. 331 liquidation rules instead of under the Sec. 302 rules applying to redemptions in partial liquidation. The IRS (1) permits the shareholder's basis to be recovered first and (2) requires the recognition of gain once the basis of a particular share or block of stock has been fully recovered. A loss cannot be recognized with respect to a share or block of stock until the final liquidating distribution has been received, or until it becomes clear that there will be no more liquidating distributions.[3]

Example 6-4 ■ Diane owns 1,000 shares of Adobe Corporation stock purchased for $40,000 in 1988. Diane receives the following liquidating distributions: July 23, 1989, $25,000; March 12, 1990, $17,000; and April 5, 1991, $10,000. No gain is recognized in 1989,

---

[1] Rev. Rul. 80-177, 1980-2 C.B. 109.
[2] Reg. Sec. 1.331-1(e).
[3] Rev. Ruls. 68-348, 1968-2 C.B. 141; 79-10, 1979-1 C.B. 140; and 85-48, 1985-1 C.B. 126.

since Diane's $40,000 basis is not fully recovered by year-end. The $15,000 ($40,000 − $25,000) unrecovered basis that exists after the first distribution is less than the $17,000 liquidating distribution that is received on March 12, 1990, so a $2,000 gain must be recognized at this time. An additional $10,000 gain is recognized in 1991 when the final liquidating distribution is received. ∎

Example 6-5 ∎ Assume the same facts as in Example 6-4, except that Diane pays $60,000 for her Adobe stock. The receipt of each of the liquidating distributions is tax-free, since Diane's $60,000 basis exceeds the $52,000 ($25,000 + $17,000 + $10,000) total of the distributions. An $8,000 loss ($52,000 − $60,000) is recognized in 1991 when Diane receives the final liquidating distribution. ∎

Key Point
Since stock is normally a capital asset in the hands of the shareholder, with several minor exceptions, the gain/loss recognized by a shareholder in a corporate liquidation is capital gain or capital loss.

Character of the Recognized Gain or Loss. Generally, the liquidating corporation's stock is a capital asset in the shareholder's hands. The gain or loss that is recognized is, therefore, a capital gain or loss for most shareholders. Some exceptions to these rules are indicated below.

- Gain recognized upon the liquidation of a collapsible corporation is ordinary income.[4]

- Gains and losses recognized by a securities dealer on any shares held in inventory are ordinary in nature.

- Loss recognized by an individual shareholder on Sec. 1244 stock is ordinary loss (see Chapter 2).

- Loss recognized by a corporate shareholder on the worthlessness of the stock of a controlled subsidiary (as defined in Sec. 165(g)(3)) is ordinary loss (see Chapter 2).

Key Point
As in other taxable exchanges, the basis of property received by a shareholder in a corporate liquidation is its FMV. Likewise, since the assets have in effect been purchased in the transaction, the holding period of such assets begins on the day after the distribution.

Basis of Property Received in the Liquidation. Section 334(a) provides that the basis of any property received under the general liquidation rules is its FMV on the distribution date. The holding period for the asset starts on the day after the distribution date.

Subsequent Assessments Against the Shareholders. The shareholders may be required at a date subsequent to the liquidation to pay a contingent liability of the corporation or a liability that is not anticipated at the time of the liquidating distribution (e.g., an income tax deficiency determined after the liquidation is completed or a judgment that is contingent at the time the final liquidating distribution is made). The additional payment does not affect the reporting of the initial liquidating transaction. The tax treatment for the additional payment depends

Self-Study Question
If a cash-method shareholder is subsequently obligated to pay a contingent liability of the liquidated corporation, what are the tax consequences of such a payment?

---

[4] Gain recognized on a sale or exchange of the stock of a collapsible corporation, a distribution of corporate assets made as part of a partial or complete liquidation of a collapsible corporation, or an ordinary distribution made by a collapsible corporation that is treated as gain from the sale or exchange of the stock is characterized as ordinary income under the collapsible corporation rules instead of being treated as long-term capital gain. A collapsible corporation is defined by Sec. 341(b) as a corporation formed or availed of principally for the manufacture, construction, or production of property, or for the purchase of certain assets, with the intention of either (1) selling or exchanging the stock of the corporation or (2) distributing the property to its shareholders before the corporation has realized a substantial portion of the taxable income to be derived from the property. Restoration of preferential tax treatment for long-term capital gains in 1991 will provide a tax advantage to using collapsible corporations and may lead the IRS to again argue that a corporation is a collapsible corporation.

6-8 • Ch. 6 / Corporate Liquidating Distributions

Answer
First, the prior tax year return is not amended. The additional payment results in a loss recognized in the year of payment. The character of the loss is dependent on the nature of the gain or loss recognized by the shareholder in the year of liquidation.

on the nature of the gain or loss that was originally reported by the shareholder and not on the type of loss or deduction that would have been reported by the liquidating corporation if it had instead paid the liability.[5] If the liquidation results in a capital gain or loss being recognized, the additional payment is deductible as a capital loss by a shareholder who uses the cash method of accounting in the year of payment (i.e., an amended tax return is not filed for the year in which the gain or loss from the liquidation was originally reported). An accrual method of accounting shareholder will recognize the additional deduction at the time that the liability is incurred.

Example 6-6 ■

Coastal Corporation is liquidated in 1989, with Tammy reporting a $30,000 long-term capital gain on the exchange of her Coastal stock. In 1991 Tammy is required to pay $5,000 as her part of the settlement of a lawsuit against Coastal. An additional amount must be paid by all shareholders, because the settlement exceeds the amount of funds that Coastal placed into an escrow account as a result of the litigation. The $5,000 additional payment is reported in 1991 by Tammy as a long-term capital loss. ■

OBJECTIVE 4
Explain the different tax treatments for open and closed liquidation transactions

Open Versus Closed Transactions. Sometimes the value of a property received in a corporate liquidation cannot be determined by the usual valuation techniques. Property that can only be valued on the basis of uncertain future payments falls into this category. In such a case, the shareholders may attempt to rely upon the **open transaction doctrine** of *Burnet v. Logan* and treat the liquidation as an open transaction.[6] Under this doctrine, the shareholder's gain or loss from the liquidation is not determined until the assets that cannot be valued are subsequently sold, collected, or able to be valued. Any assets that cannot be valued are assigned a zero value.

The shareholder's receipt of those properties that can be valued is reported using the general liquidation rules. Thus, a shareholder must report a gain on the liquidation if the FMV of those properties that can be valued exceeds the shareholder's basis for the stock. A loss is not recognized if the FMV of such properties is less than the basis of the stock. If the assets that cannot be valued are subsequently sold, collected, or able to be valued, the additional payments or amounts are initially treated as a return of capital on the liquidation transaction (or as additional gain if some amount of gain was previously recognized). The character of any additional gain that is reported is the same as was originally reported when the other properties were received.

Example 6-7 ■

Mesa Corporation is owned by Walt. Mesa's properties include $10,000 of cash, $30,000 of land, and a royalty agreement with a coal company that will pay Mesa a royalty only as the coal is produced. No coal has ever been produced on the property, and there is no minimum royalty amount mentioned in the agreement. According to a qualified appraisal company, no FMV can be assigned to the lease agreement. Walt's basis in his Mesa stock is $50,000. Mesa Corporation liquidates on December 13, 1989, with Walt receiving the cash, land, and lease agreement. Relying on the open transaction doctrine, the $40,000 that is received would be reported as a recovery of his investment in the Mesa stock. Walt would have

---

[5] *F. Donald Arrowsmith v. CIR*, 42 AFTR 649, 52-2 USTC ¶ 9527 (USSC, 1952).
[6] *Burnet v. Edith A. Logan*, 9 AFTR 1453, 2 USTC ¶ 736 (USSC, 1931).

Effects of Liquidating on the Shareholders • 6-9

$10,000 of unrecovered basis against which subsequent royalty payments could be offset before reporting any capital gain on the receipt of such payments. If Walt's basis for the Mesa stock were instead $25,000, Walt would report a $15,000 ($40,000 − $25,000) long-term capital gain on the liquidation and any additional amounts that were received under the royalty agreement would also be long-term capital gain. ∎

Key Point
The position of the IRS is that the FMV of almost any asset should be able to be determined. Thus, the IRS assumes that the open transaction method should be used only in rare and extraordinary circumstances.

The IRS's position is that a taxpayer may use the open transaction method to report a corporate liquidation only in unusual circumstances. Generally the IRS opts for a **closed transaction.** All of the assets in a closed transaction have a basis equal to their FMV on the distribution date. If a transaction is closed, gain or loss is determined on the liquidation date based upon the FMV of all of the assets. When the liquidated property with the uncertain value is ultimately sold or collected by the former shareholder, gain or loss is determined by comparing the sale price or amount collected with respect to the property to its basis in the former shareholder's hands. This is typically the value established at the date of liquidation. The character of the gain or loss depends upon whether it is a capital asset or not in the hands of the former shareholder. The closing of the transaction typically accelerates the reporting of the shareholder's gain from the transaction.

Example 6-8 ∎

Assume the same facts as in Example 6-7, except that the FMV of the royalty agreement is determined to be $12,000 and the royalty payments received under the agreement are: 1990, $9,000; and 1991, $8,000. Walt reports a $2,000 ([$10,000 + $30,000 + $12,000] − $50,000) long-term capital gain on the liquidation. The basis of the royalty agreement is $12,000 to Walt. 1990's $9,000 royalty payment is a tax-free return of capital and reduces Walt's basis in the royalty agreement to $3,000 ($12,000 − $9,000). 1991's $8,000 royalty payment would recover the remaining basis and result in Walt recognizing $5,000 ($8,000 − $3,000) of ordinary income.[7] The closed transaction requirement has accelerated the recognition of the capital gain on the liquidation, as well as converted $5,000 of long-term capital gain into ordinary income. ∎

OBJECTIVE 5
Determine when the Sec. 332 nonrecognition rules apply to the liquidation of a subsidiary corporation

Liquidation of a Controlled Subsidiary Corporation

Section 332(a) provides that no gain or loss is recognized when a controlled subsidiary corporation is liquidated into its parent corporation. This liquidation rule permits a corporation to modify its corporate structure without incurring any adverse tax consequences. Section 332 only applies to the parent corporation. Shareholders owning a minority interest are taxed under the general liquidation rules of Sec. 331.

Under this exception, a subsidiary corporation can be liquidated and operated as a division of its parent corporation. Gain or loss realized from the transaction is not recognized.

Example 6-9 ∎

Parent Corporation owns all of the stock of Subsidiary Corporation. Subsidiary Corporation's assets have a $1,000,000 FMV. Parent Corporation's basis for its Subsidiary stock is $250,000. The liquidation of Subsidiary Corporation results in a $750,000 ($1,000,000 − $250,000) realized gain for Parent Corporation, none of

---

[7] Ordinary income is reported since the liquidation transaction is closed in 1989. The coal company's payment represents a royalty and not a liquidating distribution.

which is recognized. If Sec. 332 were not available, Parent Corporation would recognize a $750,000 capital gain on the liquidation. ■

Requirements. The following requirements must all be met for a liquidation transaction to come under the Sec. 332 nonrecognition rules:

- The parent corporation must own at least (1) 80% of the total combined voting power of all classes of stock entitled to vote and (2) 80% of the total value of all classes of stock (other than certain nonvoting preferred stock issues) from the date on which the plan of liquidation is adopted until receipt of the property of the subsidiary corporation.[8]
- The distribution of the property must be in complete cancellation or redemption of all of its stock.
- Distribution of the property must (1) occur within a single tax year, or (2) be one of a series of distributions that is completed within 3 years from the close of the tax year during which the first of the series of liquidating distributions is made.

If all of these requirements are met, the nonrecognition of gain or loss rules contained in Sec. 332 are mandatory. If one or more of the conditions listed above is not met, the parent corporation is taxed under the previously discussed general liquidation rules.

STOCK OWNERSHIP. For Sec. 332 to apply, the parent corporation must own the requisite amount of voting and nonvoting stock. In applying this requirement, the Sec. 318 attribution rules for stock ownership are not applied (see Chapter 4).[9] The requisite 80% ownership of the voting and nonvoting stock must be owned from the date on which the plan of liquidation is adopted until the liquidation is completed. Failure to satisfy this requirement denies the transaction the benefits of Sec. 332. (See pages 6-29 through 6-30 for further discussion of the stock ownership question.)

CANCELLATION OF THE STOCK. The subsidiary corporation must distribute its properties in complete cancellation or redemption of all of its stock in accordance with a plan of liquidation. There may be more than one liquidating distribution. When more than one liquidating distribution occurs, the subsidiary corporation must have adopted a plan of liquidation and be in a status of liquidation when the first distribution is made. This status must continue until the liquidation is completed. Regulation Sec. 1.332-2(c) indicates that a liquidation is completed when the liquidating corporation has divested itself of all properties.

The distribution of all the subsidiary corporation's assets within one tax year of the liquidating corporation in complete cancellation or redemption of all its stock is considered a complete liquidation.[10] Although a formal plan of liquidation can be adopted, the shareholders' adoption of a resolution authorizing the distribution of the corporation's assets in complete cancellation or redemption of its stock is considered to be the adoption of a plan of liquidation when the distribution occurs within a single tax year. The tax year in which the liquidating distribution occurs does not have to be the same as the one in which the plan of liquidation is adopted.[11]

---

[8] The definition of stock that is used for Sec. 332 purposes excludes any stock which is not entitled to vote, is limited and preferred as to dividends and does not participate in corporate growth to any significant extent, has redemption and liquidation rights which do not exceed its issue price (except for a reasonable redemption or liquidation premium), and is not convertible into another class of stock.
[9] Sec. 332(b)(1).
[10] Sec. 332(b)(2) and Reg. Sec. 1.332-3.
[11] Rev. Rul. 76-317, 1976-2 C.B. 98.

Additional Comment

The liquidation of a subsidiary into its parent is an exception to the general gain/loss recognition treatment of liquidating distributions. The nonrecognition rule of Sec. 332 is due to the fact that the transaction is a mere change in form and the assets remain in the corporate group.

Typical Misconception

The 80% stock ownership requirement of Sec. 332 is not the same stock ownership requirement covered with respect to Sec. 351 in Chap. 2. Instead, the Sec. 332 ownership requirement is the same requirement that exists for affiliated groups and will be discussed in Chap. 8.

Key Point

If the liquidating distributions are completed within one tax year, a formal plan is not required. Otherwise, a formal plan is required and the liquidating distributions must be completed within three years. If these and the other Sec. 332 requirements are satisfied, the application of Sec. 332 is mandatory.

Effects of Liquidating on the Shareholders • 6-11

The subsidiary corporation can carry out the plan of liquidation by making a series of distributions that extend over a period of more than one tax year to cancel or redeem its stock. A formal plan of liquidation must be adopted when the liquidating distributions extend beyond a single tax year of the liquidating corporation. The liquidating distributions must include all of the corporation's properties and must be completed within 3 years from the close of the tax year during which the first distribution is made under the plan.[12]

Recognition of Gain or Loss. The Sec. 332(a) nonrecognition rules apply only to a parent corporation that receives a liquidating distribution from a solvent subsidiary. Section 332(a) does not apply to a parent corporation that receives a liquidating distribution from an insolvent subsidiary, to minority shareholders who receive liquidating distributions, or to a parent corporation that receives a payment to satisfy the subsidiary's indebtedness to the parent. All of these exceptions are discussed below.

> **Self-Study Question**
> What are the tax consequences if the liquidating subsidiary is insolvent?
>
> **Answer**
> Sec. 332 is not applicable because the distribution is not in exchange for stock. Instead, the parent is generally entitled to an ordinary loss deduction under Sec. 165(g)(3) to the extent that the parent's basis in the subsidiary stock exceeds the liquidation proceeds.

INSOLVENT SUBSIDIARY. Section 332 does not apply if the subsidiary corporation is insolvent at the time of the liquidation. An insolvent subsidiary is one that has liabilities in excess of the FMV of its assets. Regulation Sec. 1.332-2(b) requires the parent corporation to receive at least partial payment for the stock which it owns in the subsidiary corporation in order to qualify for nonrecognition under Sec. 332. If the subsidiary is insolvent, the special worthless security rules of Sec. 165(g)(3) for affiliated corporations will generally apply and permit the parent corporation to recognize an ordinary loss with respect to its investment in the subsidiary's stock or debt obligations (see Chapter 2).

Example 6-10 ■ Parent Corporation owns all of the stock of Subsidiary Corporation, which it established to produce and market a product that proved unsuccessful. Parent Corporation has a $1,500,000 basis in its Subsidiary stock. In addition, it made a $1,000,000 advance to Subsidiary that is secured by a note. Under a plan of liquidation, Subsidiary distributes all of its assets, having a $750,000 FMV, to Parent in partial satisfaction of the advance after having paid all third-party creditors. No assets remain to pay the remainder of the advance or to redeem the outstanding stock. Because Subsidiary is insolvent immediately before the liquidating distribution is made, none of its assets are considered to have been distributed in redemption of the Subsidiary stock. Therefore, the liquidation cannot qualify under the Sec. 332 rules. Parent Corporation can claim a $250,000 business bad debt with respect to the unpaid portion of the advance and a $1,500,000 ordinary loss for its stock investment. ■

> **Typical Misconception**
> Sec. 332 is applicable only to the parent corporation. If a minority interest exists, the general liquidation rules of Sec. 331 apply to those minority shareholders.

MINORITY SHAREHOLDERS RECEIVING LIQUIDATING DISTRIBUTIONS. Liquidating distributions made to minority shareholders are taxed under the Sec. 331 general liquidation rules. These rules require the minority shareholders to recognize gain or loss—which is generally capital—upon the redemption of their stock in the subsidiary corporation.

Example 6-11 ■ Parent Corporation and Jane own 80% and 20%, respectively, of Subsidiary Corporation's single class of stock. Parent Corporation and Jane have adjusted bases of $100,000 and $15,000, respectively, for their stock interests. Subsidiary Corporation adopts a plan of liquidation on May 30, 1991, and makes liquidating

---
[12] Sec. 332(b)(3) and Reg. Sec. 1.332-4.

distributions of two parcels of land having $250,000 and $62,500 FMVs to Parent Corporation and Jane, respectively, on November 1, 1991, in exchange for their stock. Parent Corporation's $150,000 gain ($250,000 − $100,000) is not recognized because of Sec. 332. Jane's $47,500 gain ($62,500 − $15,000) is recognized as a capital gain under Sec. 331. ∎

Self-Study Question

What bases do both the parent and minority shareholders take in the assets received in a Sec. 332 liquidation?

Answer

Since the parent corporation recognizes no gain/loss in the transaction, the parent corporation takes a carryover basis in its assets. However, since the minority shareholders are involved in a taxable exchange, the minority shareholders take a FMV basis in their assets.

SATISFACTION OF THE SUBSIDIARY'S DEBT OBLIGATIONS. The Sec. 332(a) nonrecognition rules apply only to amounts received by the parent corporation in its role as a shareholder. Gain or loss must generally be recognized by the parent corporation upon the receipt of property in payment of a subsidiary corporation indebtedness.[13]

Basis of Property Received. Section 334(b)(1) provides that the parent corporation's basis for the property received in the liquidating distribution is equal to its basis to the subsidiary corporation. This rule is consistent with the principle that no gain or loss is recognized by the liquidating corporation when it distributes the property and that the property's tax attributes (e.g., the depreciation recapture potential) carry over from the subsidiary corporation to the parent corporation. The parent corporation's basis for its stock investment in the subsidiary corporation is ignored in determining the basis for the distributed property. Property received by minority shareholders takes a basis equal to its FMV because gain or loss is recognized by the minority shareholders.

Example 6-12 ∎ Assume the same facts as in Example 6-11 and that the two parcels of land received by Parent Corporation and Jane have adjusted bases of $175,000 and $40,000, respectively. Parent Corporation takes a $175,000 carryover basis for its land. Jane takes a stepped-up $62,500 basis for her land. ∎

Installment Obligations Received by a Shareholder

Shareholders who receive an installment obligation as part of their liquidating distribution ordinarily report the FMV of their obligation as part of the consideration received to calculate the amount of the recognized gain or loss. Shareholders who receive an installment obligation that was acquired by the liquidating corporation in connection with a sale or exchange of property are eligible for special treatment in reporting their gain on the liquidating transaction if (1) the sale or exchange takes place during the 12-month period beginning on the date a plan of complete liquidation is adopted and (2) the liquidation is completed during such 12-month period. These shareholders may report their gain as the installment payments are received.[14]

The special tax deferral does not apply to the portion of the gain attributable to the sale of the inventory or property held for sale to customers in the ordinary course of its trade or business, unless such sale is to one person in one transaction and involves substantially all of the inventory-type properties attributable to a trade or business of the corporation.[15] Installment obligations arising from the sale of depreciable property by the corporation to the shareholder's spouse or a person related to the shareholder are also ineligible for the special tax deferral.[16]

---

[13] Sec. 1001(c).
[14] Sec. 453(h)(1)(A).
[15] Sec. 453(h)(1)(B).
[16] Sec. 453(h)(1)(C). A related party is defined by Sec. 1239(b).

EFFECTS OF LIQUIDATING ON THE LIQUIDATING CORPORATION

This portion of the chapter is divided into three parts: (1) the recognition of gain or loss by the liquidating corporation when it distributes property, (2) the deductibility of the expenses of liquidating, and (3) the carryover of tax attributes in liquidation transactions.

OBJECTIVE 6
Determine when gains and losses must be recognized by the liquidating corporation on making a liquidating distribution

Recognition of Gain or Loss When Property Is Distributed in Redemption of Stock

Section 336(a) provides that gain or loss must be recognized by the liquidating corporation when property is distributed in a complete liquidation. The amount and character of the gain or loss are determined as if the property is sold to the distributee at its FMV.

Example 6-13 ■

Key Point
The general rule is that the liquidating corporation recognizes gain/loss on distributions in a complete liquidation. The gain/loss is computed as if the liquidating corporation had sold all of its assets to the distributee shareholder for the property's FMV.

Under West Corporation's plan of liquidation, land is distributed to one of its shareholders, Arnie. The land, which is used in West's trade or business, has a $40,000 adjusted basis to West and a $120,000 FMV on the distribution date. West must recognize an $80,000 Sec. 1231 gain ($120,000 − $40,000) when it makes the liquidating distribution. Arnie must recognize a gain to the extent that the land's FMV exceeds his basis for the West stock. Arnie's basis for the land is its $120,000 FMV. The distribution of the land to Arnie produces the same tax burden as if West Corporation had sold the land and distributed the cash proceeds. ■

With limited exceptions, the liquidating corporation can now recognize a loss when property that has declined in value is distributed to its shareholders. This change eliminates the need for a liquidating corporation to sell properties that have declined in value in order to recognize its losses.

Example 6-14 ■

Typical Misconception
A significant difference between a liquidating and a nonliquidating distribution is that, under Sec. 336, the distributing corporation may recognize losses on a liquidating distribution, whereas the same corporation cannot recognize a loss on a nonliquidating distribution of the same assets.

Assume the same facts as in Example 6-13, except that the FMV of the land is instead $10,000. West Corporation is permitted to recognize a $30,000 Sec. 1231 loss ($10,000 − $40,000 adjusted basis) when the land is distributed to Arnie. Arnie's basis for the land is $10,000. ■

The Sec. 336 rules apply only to property that is distributed in exchange for the liquidating corporation's stock as part of a complete liquidation. These rules do not apply to distributions of appreciated property as part of a partial liquidation, or when a debt of the liquidating corporation is retired in exchange for appreciated property.

Liabilities Assumed or Acquired by the Shareholders. Property that is distributed by the liquidating corporation is treated for purposes of determining the amount of the gain or loss recognized under Sec. 336 as having been sold to the distributee for its FMV on the distribution date. Section 336(b) contains a special restriction on valuing a liquidating property distribution when liabilities are assumed or acquired by the shareholders. According to this rule, the FMV of the distributed property cannot be less than the amount of the liability assumed or acquired. The Sec. 336(b) exception applies for gain and loss recognition purposes only and not for purposes of determining a property's basis in the shareholder's hands.

Example 6-15

Key Point
If the distributed property is subject to a liability, for purposes of determining the amount of gain/loss, the value of the property is treated as being not less than the amount of the liability. This is consistent with other corporate distribution provisions.

Jersey Corporation owns an apartment complex costing $3,000,000 and which has been depreciated so that its adjusted basis is $2,400,000. The property is secured by a $2,700,000 mortgage. A plan of liquidation is adopted, and the property and the mortgage are distributed to Jersey's sole individual shareholder at a time when the property's FMV is $2,200,000. Jersey Corporation must recognize a $300,000 gain ($2,700,000 − $2,400,000) on distributing the property since its FMV cannot be less than the $2,700,000 mortgage on the property. The property's basis is $2,200,000 in the shareholder's hands. ∎

Exceptions to the General Gain or Loss Recognition Rule. Four exceptions to the general rule of Sec. 336(a) have been enacted. Each of these exceptions is examined below.

LIQUIDATION OF A SUBSIDIARY CORPORATION. An exception is provided for liquidating transfers within a parent-subsidiary group because the property (together with the other attributes of the liquidated subsidiary) is retained within the economic unit of the parent-subsidiary group. Section 337(a) provides that no gain or loss is recognized by the liquidating corporation on the distribution of property to the 80% distributee in a complete liquidation to which Sec. 332 applies.[17] The term *80% distributee* is defined by Sec. 337(c) as a corporation that meets the 80% stock ownership requirement specified in Sec. 332 (see page 6-10).[18]

Example 6-16

Typical Misconception
A corporation that sells, exchanges, or distributes the stock of a subsidiary may elect to treat the sale of stock as a sale of the subsidiary's assets. This election could prove beneficial when the assets of the subsidiary corporation are substantially less appreciated than the subsidiary stock itself.

Parent Corporation owns all of the stock of Subsidiary Corporation. Pursuant to a plan of complete liquidation, Subsidiary Corporation distributes land having a $200,000 FMV and a $60,000 basis to Parent. Section 337(a) prevents Subsidiary Corporation from having to recognize gain with respect to the distribution. Parent Corporation takes a $60,000 basis for the land. ∎

The depreciation recapture provisions in Secs. 1245, 1250, and 291 do not override the Sec. 337(a) nonrecognition rule if a controlled subsidiary corporation is liquidated into its parent corporation. The depreciation recapture potential associated with the property distributed is assumed by the parent corporation and is recaptured when the parent corporation sells or exchanges the property.[19]

The Sec. 337(a) nonrecognition rule applies only to distributions that are made to the parent corporation. Liquidating distributions that are made to minority shareholders are not eligible for the protection of Sec. 337(a). The liquidating corporation must recognize gain under Sec. 336(a) when appreciated property is distributed to the minority shareholders. Section 336(d)(3), however, prevents the subsidiary corporation from recognizing loss on distributions made to minority shareholders. Liquidating distributions made to minority shareholders are, thus, treated in the same way as nonliquidating distributions.

Self-Study Question
Can a subsidiary corporation recognize losses on distributions to either the parent or minority shareholders in a Sec. 332 liquidation?

Answer
No. Sec. 332 liquidations are an exception to the general rule that losses can be recognized by the liquidating corporation. Losses are not recognized on distributions to either the parent or the minority shareholders.

---

[17] Section 336(e) permits a corporation to sell, exchange, or distribute the stock of a subsidiary corporation and to elect to treat such a transaction as a disposition of all the subsidiary corporation's assets. No gain or loss is recognized on the sale, exchange, or distribution of the stock. The economic consequences of making this election for a stock sale are essentially the same as if the parent corporation instead liquidates the subsidiary in a transaction to which Sec. 332 applies and then immediately sells the properties to the purchaser.

[18] An exception to the general rule of Sec. 337(a) applies when the distribution is made to a tax-exempt distributee and the property that is distributed is used in an activity that produces income which is subject to the unrelated business income tax. In such case, Sec. 337(b)(2)(B) requires the distributing corporation to recognize gain on the distribution of appreciated property and recognize loss when property that has declined in value is distributed.

[19] Secs. 1245(b)(3) and 1250(d)(3).

Example 6-17 ■ Assume the same facts as in Example 6-16, except that Parent Corporation owns 80% of the Subsidiary stock, Chuck owns the remaining 20% of such stock, and that two parcels of land are being distributed to Parent Corporation and Chuck. The parcels have FMVs of $160,000 and $40,000, and adjusted bases of $50,000 and $10,000, respectively. The $110,000 gain ($160,000 − $50,000) realized by Subsidiary Corporation on the distribution to Parent Corporation is not recognized. The $30,000 gain ($40,000 − $10,000) realized on the distribution to Chuck must be recognized since the Sec. 337(a) nonrecognition rule applies only to distributions made to the parent corporation. ■

Key Point

Another exception to the general rule is that losses cannot be recognized by the liquidating corporation if property is distributed to a related party and (a) the distribution is nonpro rata or (b) the distribution consists of "disqualified property." The disqualified property rule prohibits a shareholder from infusing loss property into the liquidating corporation and generating losses at both the corporate and shareholder levels.

DISTRIBUTIONS TO RELATED PERSONS. Section 336(d)(1)(A) prevents the recognition of loss in connection with distributions of property to a related person if (1) the distribution is other than pro rata or (2) the property being distributed is disqualified property. A related person is defined under Sec. 267(b) as including, for example, an individual and a corporation whose stock is more than 50% owned (in terms of value) by such individual, as well as two corporations who are members of the same controlled group. Disqualified property is defined by Sec. 336(d)(1)(B) as (1) any property that is acquired by the liquidating corporation in a transaction to which Sec. 351 applies, or as a contribution to capital, during the 5-year period ending on the distribution date, or (2) any property having an adjusted basis that carries over from a disqualified property.

Thus, a nonpro rata distribution of any property or a pro rata distribution of a disqualified property, that has declined in value, to a related party will prevent the liquidating corporation from being able to recognize a loss for tax purposes.

Example 6-18 ■ Mesa Corporation is 60% owned by Al and 40% owned by Betty. A plan of liquidation is adopted by Mesa Corporation. Pursuant to the plan, Mesa distributes stocks and securities purchased 3 years ago to Al. The stocks and securities, which are not disqualified properties, have a $40,000 FMV and a $100,000 adjusted basis. The nonpro rata distribution of the stocks and securities, however, prevents Mesa Corporation from claiming a $60,000 capital loss when the distribution is made. If the stocks and securities are instead distributed 60% to Al and 40% to Betty, the capital loss is deductible by Mesa Corporation. ■

Example 6-19 ■ Assume the same facts as in Example 6-18, except that the stocks and securities were acquired as a capital contribution from Al and are distributed 60% to Al and 40% to Betty. The stocks and securities are now disqualified properties and, even though they are distributed ratably to Al and Betty, Mesa cannot deduct the $60,000 capital loss. ■

Key Point

Certain built-in loss property acquired by the liquidating corporation within two years of the liquidation (either as a contribution to capital or in a Sec. 351 transaction) is deemed to have been acquired for tax avoidance purposes. Consequently, such built-in losses are not allowed to be recognized by the liquidating corporation.

SALES HAVING A TAX-AVOIDANCE PURPOSE. Section 336(d)(2) restricts the claiming of a loss with respect to the sale, exchange, or distribution of property acquired in a Sec. 351 transaction, or as a contribution to capital, where the acquisition of the property by the liquidating corporation is part of a plan that has as a principal purpose the recognition of a loss by the corporation in connection with the liquidation. The limiting of the loss that can be claimed prevents a taxpayer from transferring loss properties into a corporation in order to reduce or eliminate the amount of gain from the sale of other appreciated properties that would otherwise have to be recognized by the liquidating corporation.

Properties acquired by the liquidating corporation in any Sec. 351 transaction or as a contribution to capital any time after the date two years before the date that a plan of complete liquidation is adopted are treated as part of a plan having a tax-avoidance purpose unless exempted by forthcoming regulations.[20] According to the Conference Committee Report, the Sec. 336(d)(2) regulations should not prevent corporations from deducting losses associated with dispositions of assets used in a trade or business (or a line of business) that are contributed to the corporation, or dispositions occurring during the first 2 years of a corporation's existence.[21]

The basis of the contributed property for loss purposes equals its adjusted basis on the liquidating corporation's books reduced (but not below zero) by the excess (if any) of the property's adjusted basis over its FMV immediately after its acquisition. No adjustment occurs to the contributed property's adjusted basis when determining the corporation's recognized gain.

Example 6-20 ■ Terry makes a capital contribution of a widget maker having a $1,000 adjusted basis and a $100 FMV to Pirate Corporation in exchange for additional stock on January 10, 1990. On April 1, 1991, Pirate Corporation adopts a plan of liquidation. During the time period between January 10, 1990, and the date the plan of liquidation is adopted, the widget maker is not used in connection with the conduct of Pirate's trade or business. A liquidating distribution is made on July 1, 1991, and Pirate Corporation distributes the widget maker and a second property that has a $2,500 FMV and a $900 adjusted basis. Because the widget maker is contributed to Pirate after the date that is two years before the date it adopted its plan of complete liquidation and the widget maker is not used in the conduct of Pirate's trade or business, the presumption is that the acquisition and distribution of the widget maker were motivated by a desire to recognize the $900 loss. Unless Pirate Corporation can prove otherwise, Sec. 336(d)(2) will apply to the distribution of the widget maker. Pirate's basis for purposes of determining its loss will be $100 ($1,000 − [$1,000 − $100]). Thus, Pirate Corporation cannot claim a loss on the liquidating distribution of the widget maker. Pirate Corporation is thereby prevented from offsetting the $1,600 ($2,500 − $900) gain recognized on distributing the second property by the $900 loss realized on distributing the widget maker. ■

The basis adjustment also affects sales, exchanges, or distributions of property made prior to the adoption of the plan of liquidation or in connection with the liquidation. Thus, losses that are claimed in a tax return filed before the adoption of the plan of liquidation may be restricted by Sec. 336(d)(2). The liquidating corporation may recapture these losses in the tax return for the tax year in which the plan of liquidation is adopted, or it can file an amended tax return for the tax year in which the loss was originally claimed.

Example 6-21 ■ Assume the same facts as in Example 6-20, except that Pirate Corporation sells the widget maker for $200 on July 10, 1990. An $800 loss ($200 − $1,000) is reported on Pirate's 1990 tax return. The adoption of the plan of liquidation causes the loss on the sale of the widget maker also to be covered by the Sec. 336(d)(2) rules. Pirate Corporation can file an amended 1990 tax return showing the $800 loss being

---

[20] H. Rept. No. 99-841, 99th Cong., 2d Sess., p. II-201 (1986). The Conference Committee Report for the 1986 Tax Act indicates that property transactions occurring more than 2 years in advance of the adoption of the plan of liquidation will be disregarded unless there is no clear and substantial relationship between the contributed property and the conduct of the corporation's current or future business enterprises.

[21] Ibid.

disallowed, or it can file its 1991 tax return reporting $800 of income under the loss recapture rules.[22]

Recognition of Gain or Loss When Property Is Distributed in Retirement of Debt

OBJECTIVE 7
Determine when gains and losses must be recognized on the retirement of debt by a liquidating corporation

Key Point
No gain/loss is recognized by a liquidating subsidiary on the distribution of its assets in retirement of an indebtedness owed to its parent corporation in a Sec. 332 liquidation.

Generally, the use of property to satisfy an indebtedness results in the debtor recognizing gain or loss at the time it transfers the property.[23] Section 337(b) prevents a subsidiary corporation in the midst of a complete liquidation from recognizing gain or loss when it transfers appreciated property to its parent corporation in satisfaction of an indebtedness. The exception is provided because the property is retained within the economic unit of the parent-subsidiary group.

Section 337(b) applies only to an indebtedness of the subsidiary corporation that is owed to a parent corporation on the date the plan of liquidation is adopted and that is satisfied by the transfer of property pursuant to a complete liquidation of the subsidiary corporation. It does not apply to liabilities owed to other shareholders or third party creditors, or liabilities incurred after the plan of liquidation is adopted. In addition, if the subsidiary corporation is able to satisfy the indebtedness for less than its face amount, it may have to recognize income from the discharge of an indebtedness.

Example 6-22 ■ Parent Corporation owns all of Subsidiary Corporation's single class of stock. At the time of its acquisition of the Subsidiary stock, Parent Corporation purchases $1,000,000 of Subsidiary bonds. Subsidiary Corporation adopts a plan of liquidation on April 5, 1991. Subsequently Subsidiary distributes property having a $1,000,000 FMV and a $400,000 adjusted basis to Parent Corporation in cancellation of the bonds. Subsidiary Corporation also distributes its remaining properties to Parent Corporation in exchange for all of its outstanding stock. Subsidiary Corporation recognizes no gain on the transfer of the property in cancellation of the bonds. Parent Corporation recognizes no gain when the liability is satisfied because the property's FMV equals the purchase price of the bonds. Section 334(b)(1) provides that Parent Corporation takes a $400,000 carryover basis for the property it receives in cancellation of the bonds. ■

Expenses of the Liquidation

The corporation is permitted to deduct the general liquidation expenses incurred in connection with the liquidation transaction. These costs include attorneys' and accountants' fees, costs incurred in drafting the plan of liquidation and obtaining shareholder approval, and so on.[24] Such amounts are ordinarily deductible in the corporation's final tax return.

The specific liquidation expenses associated with selling the corporation's properties are treated as an offset against the sales proceeds. When a corporation sells an asset pursuant to its liquidation, the selling expenses reduce the amount of gain or increase the amount of loss reported by the corporation.[25]

---

[22] The property has a $1,000 basis for purposes of determining Pirate's gain on the sale and a $100 ($1,000 − $900) basis for purposes of determining Pirate's loss on the sale. Therefore, no gain or loss is reported since the $200 sale price lies between the gain and loss basis amounts.

[23] Sec. 61(a)(12).

[24] *Pridemark, Inc. v. CIR*, 15 AFTR 2d 853, 65-1 USTC ¶ 9388 (4th Cir., 1965).

[25] See, for example, *J. T. Stewart III Trust*, 63 T.C. 682 (1975), acq. 1977-1 C.B. 1.

Example 6-23 ■ Madison Corporation adopts a plan of liquidation on July 15, 1991, and shortly thereafter sells a parcel of land on which it realizes a $60,000 gain (excluding the effects of a $6,000 sales commission). Madison Corporation pays its legal counsel $1,500 to draft the plan of liquidation. All of Madison's remaining properties are distributed to its shareholders in December 1991. The $1,500 paid to legal counsel is deductible as a general liquidation expense in Madison's 1991 income tax return. The sales commission reduces the $60,000 gain realized on the land sale, so that M's recognized gain is reduced to $54,000 ($60,000 − $6,000). ■

Any amounts of deferred expenses that are unamortized at the time of liquidation should be deducted if they have no further value to the corporation (e.g., unamortized organizational costs).[26] Deferred expenses that have value must be allocated to the shareholders receiving the benefit of such an outlay (e.g., prepaid insurance, prepaid rent, etc.).[27] Expenses related to the issuing of the corporation's stock are nondeductible, even at the time of liquidation because they are treated as a reduction in paid-in capital. Unamortized bond premiums are deductible, though, at the time that the corporation retires the bonds.

Treatment of Net Operating Losses

Additional Comment

If a liquidating corporation creates a NOL in the year of liquidation or already has NOL carryovers, these losses may well disappear with the liquidated corporation. If the liquidation is a Sec. 332 liquidation, then the parent corporation will acquire the NOLs. If the liquidation is to be taxed under Sec. 331, the liquidating corporation may want to consider an S corporation election for the liquidation year so any NOLs created in that year can flow through to the shareholders.

If little or no income is reported in the liquidating corporation's final income tax return, the corporation may create a NOL when it deducts its expenses of liquidation and any remaining deferred expenses. The NOL is carried back to offset taxes paid in prior years. This federal income tax refund receivable may be distributed to a liquidating trust and then paid by the trust to the shareholders when it is collected. This additional payment will increase (decrease) the gain (loss) previously reported by the shareholder. Alternatively, the shareholders might consider having the corporation elect to be taxed under the S corporation provisions for the tax year of the liquidation and have the loss reported on the shareholders' tax returns. (See Chapter 11 for a discussion on the taxation of an S corporation.)

The need for a liquidating corporation to recognize gains when distributing appreciated properties can be partially or fully offset by expenses incurred in carrying out the liquidation or any available NOL carryovers. Losses that are recognized by the liquidating corporation when distributing property that has declined in value can be used to offset operating profits earned in the year in which the liquidation occurs. Should such losses produce an NOL, the NOL may be able to be carried back and provide a refund of taxes paid in a prior year, or passed through to the corporation's shareholders if an election to be taxed under the S corporation provisions has been made for the tax year.

Tax Attribute Carryovers

OBJECTIVE 8

Determine the effect of a liquidation on the liquidating corporation's tax attributes

The tax attributes of the liquidating corporation disappear when the liquidation is completed. They only carry over in the case of a controlled subsidiary corporation that is liquidated into its parent corporation under Sec. 332.[28] Included among the carried-over attributes are:

---
[26] Reg. Sec. 1.248-1(b)(3).
[27] *Koppers Co., Inc. v U.S.*, 5 AFTR 2d 1597, 60-2 USTC ¶ 9505 (Ct. Cls., 1960).
[28] Sec. 381(a).

- NOL carryovers
- Earnings and profits
- Capital loss carryovers
- General business and other tax credit carryovers

The amount of each of these carryovers is determined as of the close of the day on which the distribution of all of the subsidiary corporation's properties is completed. Further discussion of these rules is contained in Chapter 7.

Topic Review 6-1 presents a summary of the general corporate liquidation rules and the special rules applicable to the liquidation of a controlled subsidiary corporation.

TOPIC REVIEW 6-1

Tax Consequences of a Corporate Liquidation

General Corporate Liquidation Rules

1. The shareholder's recognized gain or loss equals the amount of cash plus the FMV of the other property received minus the adjusted basis of the stock redeemed. Corporate liabilities assumed or acquired by the shareholder reduce the amount realized.
2. The gain or loss is capital in nature if the stock investment is a capital asset. If a loss is recognized on the liquidation, Sec. 1244 permits ordinary loss treatment for qualifying individual shareholders.
3. The adjusted basis of the property received is its FMV on the distribution date.
4. The shareholder's holding period for the property commences on the day after the liquidation date.
5. With certain limited exceptions, the distributing corporation recognizes gain or loss when making the distribution. The amount and character of the gain or loss is determined as if the property had been sold for its FMV immediately before the distribution. Special rules apply when corporate liabilities are assumed or acquired by the shareholders and the amount of such liabilities exceed the property's FMV.
6. The liquidated corporation's tax attributes disappear at the time of liquidation.

Liquidation of a Controlled Subsidiary Corporation

1. Specific requirements must be met with respect to: (a) stock ownership; (b) distribution of the property in complete cancellation or redemption of all of its stock; and (c) distribution of all property within a single tax year or a three-year period. To satisfy the stock ownership requirement, at least 80% of the total voting power of all voting stock and at least 80% of the value of all classes of stock must be owned.
2. No gain or loss is recognized when property is distributed to an 80% distributee (i.e., parent corporation). Section 332 does not apply to liquidations of insolvent subsidiaries and distributions to minority shareholders.
3. The basis of the distributed property carries over to the parent corporation from the books of the subsidiary corporation.
4. The parent corporation's holding period includes the subsidiary corporation's holding period.
5. The subsidiary corporation does not recognize gain or loss when making a distribution to an 80% distributee. Gain (but not loss) is recognized on distributions made to minority shareholders. Gain is also not recognized by the distributing corporation when appreciated property is distributed in satisfaction of certain subsidiary debts to the parent corporation.
6. The subsidiary corporation's tax attributes are acquired by the parent corporation as part of the liquidation.

DEEMED LIQUIDATION ELECTION

The sale of all of the outstanding stock of a target corporation generally results in the recognition of a capital gain or loss by the shareholders of the acquired (i.e., target) corporation. The acquiring corporation takes a basis in the stock equal to its cost. Stock sales have proven to be popular with sellers since they are easier to accomplish than a sale of the individual assets. The stock sale may be less costly than an asset sale, since only a single level of taxation is encountered. Double taxation results when the assets are sold by the target corporation and a subsequent liquidation of the target corporation occurs.

No adjustment occurs to the basis of the target corporation's assets following a stock sale, even though the basis of the stock that was acquired may be substantially higher than the total basis of the assets that is reported for tax purposes by the target corporation. Thus, one of the tax advantages of actually purchasing the assets of the target corporation—the higher basis for the properties for tax purposes—is not available when a stock purchase occurs.

Liquidation of the target corporation shortly after its acquisition is tax-free, both for the target corporation and its parent corporation, under the rules of Secs. 332 and 337. The act of liquidating the target corporation does not permit a basis adjustment, since the basis of the assets on the books of the subsidiary (target) corporation carries over to the parent corporation.

Additional Comment

A Sec. 338 election allows the purchase of stock to be treated as a purchase of assets. This election treats the "old" target as if it sold all of its assets to the "new" target corporation. This deemed asset sale is then treated as a taxable sale. Therefore, in most situations it makes little sense to pay a tax to obtain a step-up in basis when such additional basis is recovered only in future years.

The Sec. 338 deemed liquidation rules permit the acquiring and target corporations to elect an indirect acquisition of the assets by first having the target corporation's shareholders sell their stock to the acquiring corporation and then having the acquiring corporation make a deemed liquidation election with respect to the target corporation. This election permits the basis of the target corporation's assets to be increased to the amount paid by the acquiring corporation for the target corporation's stock. Corporate purchasers generally no longer prefer Sec. 338 treatment because of the significant upfront tax cost associated with the basis step-up. The making of a Sec. 338 election can be desired in certain situations. The making of a protective carryover basis election to avoid a deemed Sec. 338 election can also be desired in other situations. The discussion that follows examines the Sec. 338 basics and when a Sec. 338 election or a protective carryover basis election may be desired.

Eligible Stock Acquisitions

OBJECTIVE 9

Explain when an acquisition qualifies for a step-up in basis under Sec. 338

In this type of election, Sec. 338 requires the acquiring corporation to make a qualified stock purchase (i.e., to purchase 80% or more of the target corporation's voting stock and 80% of the total value of all classes of stock [except certain nonvoting preferred stock issues] during a 12-month acquisition period).[29] The 12-month acquisition period must be a continuous period commencing on the date on which the acquiring corporation first purchases stock in the target corporation and ending on the date that the qualified stock purchase occurs.[30] If the acquiring corporation does not acquire the necessary 80% minimum within a continuous 12-month period, the Sec. 338 election cannot be made.

Key Point

If more than one corporation is purchased from an affiliated group during the consistency period, Sec. 338 must be applied to all or none of the acquisitions. This eliminates acquiring corporations in an affiliated group applying Sec. 338 in only those situations in which it is advantageous to the taxpayers involved.

---

[29] The basic Sec. 332 stock definition outlined in footnote 8 is also used for Sec. 338 purposes.

[30] The deemed liquidation election must be made for all or none of the corporations that are members of an affiliated group and whose stock is acquired during the consistency period. The **consistency period** includes the 12-month period that precedes the acquisition period, the 12-month or shorter acquisition period, and the 12-month period that follows the acquisition period. The affiliated group definition used here is the same 80% of voting stock and 80% of value of all stock used for consolidated tax return purposes except that the includable corporation requirement is not imposed. See Chapter 8 for an explanation of this definition.

Example 6-24 ■ Missouri Corporation purchases a 25% block of Target Corporation's single class of stock on each of four dates—April 1, 1990; July 1, 1990; December 1, 1990; and February 1, 1991. Since at least 80% of Target's stock is acquired within a 12-month period (April 1, 1990, through February 1, 1991), Missouri Corporation can elect to report the transaction under the Sec. 338 deemed liquidation rules. ■

Example 6-25 ■ Assume the same facts as in Example 6-24, except that Missouri Corporation instead makes the final 25% purchase on May 15, 1991. In this case, only 75% of the Target stock is acquired in any 12-month period. Two possible 12-month periods are involved—April 1, 1990, through March 31, 1991, and May 16, 1990, through May 15, 1991. The 80% stock ownership minimum is not met in either period. A Sec. 338 election is unavailable to Missouri Corporation. ■

Stock acquisitions that are not treated as purchases for the purpose of meeting the 80% requirement include the following:

- Stock whose adjusted basis is determined in whole or in part by its basis in the hands of the person from whom it was acquired (e.g., stock acquired as a capital contribution).
- Stock whose basis is determined under Sec. 1014(a) (i.e., FMV on the date of death or an alternative valuation date) that is acquired from a decedent.
- Stock acquired in a tax-free transaction where nonrecognition of gain or loss is permitted by Secs. 351, 354, 355, or 356 (e.g., corporate formations, corporate divisions, or tax-free reorganizations).
- Stock acquired from a related party where stock ownership would be attributed to the purchaser under the attribution rules in Secs. 318(a)(1) through (3).

The Election

A Sec. 338 election must be made not later than the fifteenth day of the ninth month following the acquisition date. The acquisition date is the first date during the 12-month acquisition period on which the 80% stock ownership requirement is met.[31]

Example 6-26 ■ Arizona Corporation purchases 40% of Target Corporation's single class of stock on April 1, 1991. An additional 50% of Target's stock is purchased on October 20, 1991. The acquisition date is October 20, 1991. The Sec. 338 election must be made on or before July 15, 1992. ■

Key Point
If an asset of the target corporation is purchased during the consistency period by the purchasing corporation, a Sec. 338 election is deemed to have been made. Thus, the purchaser cannot achieve a cost basis for some assets and a higher carryover basis for other assets.

A purchasing corporation is treated as having made a Sec. 338 election with respect to a target corporation if, at any time during the consistency period, it acquires any asset of the target corporation. This rule prevents the acquiring corporation from selectively stepping-up the basis of certain assets by purchasing them while retaining a higher carryover basis for other properties. An exception to the deemed election rules permits the acquiring corporation to acquire the assets of the target corporation (or an affiliate of the target corporation) in the ordinary course of its business.[32]

---

[31] Secs. 338(g) and 338(h)(2).
[32] Sec. 338(e).

If a corporation makes a qualified stock purchase and a Sec. 338 election is not desirable, it is important that a corporation make a protective carryover basis election under Temp. Reg. Sec. 1.338-4T(f)(6). The protective carryover basis election prevents the IRS from claiming that a deemed Sec. 338 election occurred should the purchasing corporation, for example, make a tainted asset acquisition during the consistency period. The protective carryover basis election must be filed by the last day for making a Sec. 338 election. If the IRS is successful in its claim and no protective carryover basis election was filed, then the target corporation must recognize the appropriate gain or loss on the deemed sale and step-up or step-down the basis of its assets. It will also lose its tax attributes.

Deemed Sale Transaction

> **OBJECTIVE 10**
> Determine the amount of gain or loss that is recognized on a deemed sale transaction

When a Sec. 338 election is made, the target corporation is treated as having sold all of its assets at their FMV in a single transaction at the close of the acquisition date. The asset sale is a taxable transaction with gain or loss being recognized by the target corporation.

Since the Sec. 338 election was originally designed for transactions in which the acquisition price of the target corporation's stock was in excess of the adjusted basis of the target corporation's assets, it is likely that the amount of gain recognized by the target in many of these transactions may be substantial. The size of this tax cost may result in companies forgoing the Sec. 338 election when target corporation stock is purchased or lowering the price that they are willing to pay for the target corporation's stock if they intend to make a Sec. 338 election. Alternatively the company may acquire the assets in a tax-free reorganization that is not eligible for a Sec. 338 election but which permits the acquiring corporation to use its stock (instead of cash) to make the acquisition. The tax-free transaction, however, requires the use of a carryover basis for the assets on the acquiring corporation's books.

Basis of the Assets After the Deemed Purchase

> **OBJECTIVE 11**
> Determine the basis of the target corporation's assets following a deemed purchase transaction

Although the target corporation's assets are treated as having been sold by the old target corporation for their FMV, the basis for the assets on the new target corporation's books is based on the amount paid by the acquiring corporation for the target corporation's stock. This amount is called the **adjusted grossed-up basis** for the target corporation's stock. The adjusted grossed-up basis amount equals the sum of (1) the basis of the purchasing corporation's stock interest in the target corporation plus (2) an adjustment for the target corporation's liabilities on the day following the acquisition date, and plus or minus (3) other relevant items.[33] The adjusted grossed-up basis amount is determined at the beginning of the day following the acquisition date (except for certain adjustment events described below).

Typical Misconception
All of the target's assets are deemed acquired even if less than 100% of the target stock is acquired. Thus, the purchase price of the target stock is "grossed-up" to a hypothetical value that reflects ownership of all the target's stock. However, only the recently purchased stock is grossed up. The actual basis of any nonrecently purchased stock is also reflected in the basis of the target's assets.

Valuation of the Stock. The target corporation's stock that is held by the acquiring corporation is divided into two categories: recently purchased stock and nonrecently purchased stock. This division is necessary to compute the basis of the target corporation's assets. Recently purchased stock is any target corporation stock that is held on the acquisition date and that was purchased by the acquiring corporation during the 12-month (or shorter) acquisition period. Nonrecently purchased stock is all other target corporation stock that is held by the acquiring corporation on the

---

[33] Secs. 338(b)(1) and (2).

acquisition date.[34] The basis of the purchasing corporation's stock interest equals the sum of the grossed-up basis of the recently purchased stock plus the basis of the nonrecently purchased stock.

Example 6-27 ■ Apple Corporation purchases all of Target Corporation's single class of stock on July 23, 1991. All of the Target stock is considered to be recently purchased stock since it is purchased in a single transaction. The acquisition date is July 23, 1991. ■

Example 6-28 ■ Assume the same facts as in Example 6-27, except that Apple Corporation already owns 10% of the Target stock (purchased in 1988) and only purchases the remaining 90% of the Target stock. The original block of Target stock is nonrecently purchased stock, since it is acquired more than 12 months before the acquisition date (July 23, 1991). ■

GROSSED-UP BASIS FOR STOCK. When the acquiring corporation does not own all of the target corporation's stock, the basis of the acquiring corporation's recently purchased stock must be increased or grossed-up to a hypothetical value that reflects ownership of all the target corporation's stock. The following formula is used to gross up the basis of the recently purchased stock.[35]

$$\text{Grossed-up basis of recently purchased target corporation stock} = \text{Basis of recently purchased target corporation stock} \times \frac{100\% - \text{the percentage of the target corporation's stock (by value) attributable to the purchasing corporation's nonrecently purchased stock}}{\text{Percentage of the target corporation's stock (by value) attributable to the purchasing corporation's recently purchased stock}}$$

The acquiring corporation's basis for the nonrecently purchased target corporation stock is its cost basis to the acquiring corporation. No gross-up is generally permitted for the nonrecently purchased stock.

Example 6-29 ■ Austin Corporation purchases 10% of Target Corporation's single class of stock for $200,000 on April 5, 1988. An additional 80% of Target's single class of stock is acquired by Austin on March 12, 1991, for $2,000,000 in cash. The 1991 acquisition is treated as a qualified stock purchase. The basis of the recently purchased stock is grossed up as follows:

$$\text{Grossed-up basis of recently purchased target corporation stock} = \$2,000,000 \times \frac{100\% - 10\%}{80\%} = \$2,250,000$$

The total basis for the Target Corporation stock component of the asset basis calculation is $2,450,000 ($2,250,000 + $200,000). ■

---

[34] Sec. 338(b)(6).
[35] Sec. 338(b)(4).

Key Point

The basis of the new target's assets is equal to the amount paid for the stock plus the liabilities of the target. This liability adjustment is necessary to reflect the fact that if the acquisition had truly been an asset purchase, the assumption of the liabilities would have been reflected in the total purchase price.

LIABILITIES OF THE TARGET CORPORATION. The basis of the stock is increased by the face amount of any target corporation liabilities that were outstanding at the beginning of business on the day following the acquisition date plus any tax liability resulting from gain being recognized on the deemed sale.[36]

Contingent liabilities are not generally included in the basis calculation but are treated as a subsequent adjustment to the adjusted grossed-up basis of the stock. These rules are described in the next section.

OTHER RELEVANT ITEMS. The adjusted grossed-up basis of the target corporation stock may be increased or decreased by other relevant items. The IRS has indicated that this category includes only items that arise from adjustment events that occur after the close of the new target's first tax year and items discovered as a result of an IRS examination of a tax return.[37] Items that are indicated by Temp. Reg. Sec. 1.338(b)-3T(a)(1) as being in this category include, for example, the payment of contingent amounts for recently or nonrecently purchased stock, the change in a contingent liability of the old target corporation to one that is fixed and determinable, reductions in amounts paid for recently or nonrecently purchased stock, and reductions in liabilities of the new target corporation that were taken into account for purposes of determining the adjusted grossed-up basis of the stock.

Key Point

The acquiring corporation would obviously like to allocate as much basis as possible to depreciable, depletable, or amortizable assets. To curtail this potential abuse, Sec. 338 requires a residual approach to allocating basis. This approach first allocates the purchase price to the balance sheet assets to the extent of their FMV. Any remaining basis is allocated to goodwill or other nonamortizable assets.

Allocation of Basis to Individual Assets. The adjusted grossed-up basis of the stock is allocated among four classes of assets by using the residual method.[38] The residual method requires that the adjusted grossed-up basis amount be allocated to the corporation's tangible and intangible properties (other than goodwill and going concern value) on a priority basis. Any amount not allocated to specific tangible and intangible properties is then allocated to the target corporation's goodwill and going concern value.

The four classes of assets used in allocating the basis are:

1. Class I—cash, demand deposits, and similar accounts in banks, savings and loan associations, etc.
2. Class II—certificates of deposit, U.S. government securities, readily marketable stocks and securities, foreign currency, etc.
3. Class III—all assets other than Class I, II, and IV assets. Included here would be tangible and intangible properties without regard to whether they are depreciable, depletable, or amortizable.
4. Class IV—intangible assets in the nature of goodwill and going concern value.[39]

Because the Class IV assets are generally nonamortizable, taxpayers should attempt to minimize the portion of the adjusted grossed-up basis amount that is allocated to the Class IV assets.

The adjusted grossed-up basis amount is first allocated to the individual Class I assets based upon their actual dollar amounts.[40] Any amount remaining after the allocation to the Class I assets is assigned to the Class II assets (but not in excess of their FMV). Any amount remaining after the allocation to the Class II assets is allocated to the Class III assets (but not in excess of their FMV). Finally, any amount remaining after the allocation to the Class III assets is allocated to the Class IV assets. The total basis amounts allocated to the Class II, III, and IV asset categories is allocated to individual assets within the class based upon relative FMVs. When

---

[36] Sec. 338(b)(2) and Temp. Reg. Secs. 1.338(b)-1T(f)(1) and (2).
[37] Temp. Reg. Sec. 1.338(b)-1T(g).
[38] Temp. Reg. Sec. 1.338(b)-2T(a).
[39] Temp. Reg. Sec. 1.338(b)-2T(b)(2).
[40] Ibid.

Example 6-30

Parent Corporation purchases all of the stock of Target Corporation for $100,000 on August 8, 1991, and makes a timely Sec. 338 deemed liquidation election. Target Corporation's assets have the following adjusted bases and FMVs at the beginning of the day after the acquisition date:

Asset Class	Asset	FMV	Adjusted Basis
I	Cash	$ 10,000	$ 10,000
II	Marketable securities	15,000	13,000
III	Inventory	15,000	10,000
III	Accounts receivable	30,000	30,000
III	Building[a]	40,000	23,000
III	Land	10,000	7,000
III	Machinery and equipment[a]	22,500	15,000
	Total	$142,500	$108,000

[a] The machinery, equipment, and building are Sec. 1245 properties.

Target Corporation's secured (i.e., mortgage) and unsecured liabilities as of the beginning of the day after the acquisition date (excluding income tax liabilities arising on the deemed sale) amount to $35,000. Target's assets are considered to have been sold for their FMV. Target must recognize the following gains on the deemed sale: marketable securities, $2,000 capital gain; inventory, $5,000 ordinary income; building, $17,000 ordinary income; land, $3,000 Sec. 1231 gain; and machinery and equipment, $7,500 ordinary income. Assuming a 34% marginal tax rate, Target's income tax liability on the sale is $11,730 ($34,500 × 0.34).

The adjusted grossed-up basis for the Target stock is determined as follows:

Adjusted basis of Target stock		$100,000
Plus:	Income tax liability	11,730
	Other liabilities	35,000
Adjusted grossed-up basis		$146,730

Allocation of the adjusted grossed-up basis occurs in the following manner:

Step 1: Allocate $10,000 to the cash (Class I asset).

Step 2: Allocate $15,000 to the marketable securities (Class II asset).

Step 3: Allocate $117,500 to the inventory, accounts receivable, building, land, and machinery and equipment (Class III assets). Since the total basis that remains after the allocation in Step 2 ($121,730) exceeds the FMV of the Class III assets ($117,500), each asset will take a basis equal to its FMV.

Step 4: Allocate $4,230 [$146,730 −($10,000 + $15,000 + $117,500] to goodwill. This amount is not amortizable. ■

Tax Accounting Elections for the New Corporation

The "new" target corporation continues to file a tax return (separate from that of the acquiring corporation unless a consolidated return is filed) since it is still a separate legal entity. However, in many respects, the "new" target corporation is treated as a

---

Additional Comment

The residual method is specifically aimed at making sure that any premium paid for the target stock is reflected in goodwill. With the residual method now being the only acceptable allocation method, the area of controversy shifts from which allocation methods are acceptable to the determination of what are the FMVs of the assets listed in categories I, II, and III.

Self-Study Question

What are some of the tax consequences of a Sec. 338 election?

Answer

The effects of a Sec. 338 election include: (a) termination of the "old" target corporation, (b) creation of a new target corporation with the option of a new tax year and different accounting methods, (c) elimination of tax attributes of the old target (i.e., NOL carryforwards), and (d) new depreciation elections without regard to anti-churning rules.

new entity. For example, the target corporation may adopt, without obtaining prior approval from the IRS, any tax year that meets the requirements of Sec. 441 and any accounting method that meets the requirements of Sec. 446.

The new target corporation is permitted to claim depreciation deductions under the Modified ACRS rules without regard to the elections made by the old target corporation and without regard to the anti-churning rules (see Chapter 10 of the *Prentice Hall's Federal Taxation: Individuals* text).[41] The holding period for the new target corporation's assets begins on the day after the acquisition date.

The new target corporation is not considered to be a continuation of the old target corporation for purposes of the tax attribute carryover rules.[42] As a result, any tax attribute carryovers that exist on the acquisition date are permanently lost when a Sec. 338 deemed liquidation election is made. Gain recognized on the deemed sale transaction can be used to reduce the amount of any target corporation loss and credit carryovers that might otherwise be lost. The acquiring corporation must therefore carefully consider the relative benefit of obtaining a step-up in basis for the individual assets versus the value of the available tax attributes (e.g., NOL carryovers).

Liquidation of the Target Corporation

The acquiring corporation can purchase the target corporation's stock and then liquidate the target corporation. If at least 80% of the target corporation's voting stock and 80% of the total value of the outstanding stock (except certain nonvoting preferred stock issues) is owned, the liquidation can take place tax-free under Sec. 332. In such a case, the acquiring corporation (1) receives the target corporation's assets and utilizes the target corporation's basis for those assets,[43] and (2) assumes all of the target corporation's tax attributes. Thus, there is no step-up or step-down of the target corporation's assets as when a Sec. 338 election is made. This treatment for the acquisition can prove advantageous if the target corporation either has assets with an adjusted basis in excess of their FMV or possesses substantial loss or credit carryovers.

The target corporation recognizes no gain or loss when it is liquidated.[44] As a result, the gains recognized when a Sec. 338 election is made will not have to be recognized. Thus, the liquidation transaction is generally tax-free to both the acquiring and target corporations.

Example 6-31 ■ Acme Corporation purchases all of Target Corporation's single class of stock for $400,000 on January 4, 1991. At the time of the acquisition, Target has assets with a $600,000 adjusted basis, a $450,000 FMV, and $150,000 in liabilities. In addition, Target has $500,000 of NOL carryovers from 1987 through 1990. If Acme makes a Sec. 338 election, Target's NOL carryovers are lost, and the basis of Target's assets will be $550,000 ($400,000 basis for the stock plus $150,000 in liabilities). If the Sec. 338 election is not made and Target is liquidated under Sec. 332, Target receives a $600,000 adjusted basis for the assets and the $500,000 NOL carryover. ■

The additional tax benefits enjoyed by Target Corporation in Example 6-31 may be lost under Sec. 269(b). This provision permits the IRS to disallow any deduction, credit, or other allowance, in whole or in part, when:

---

[41] Temp. Reg. Sec. 1.338-4T(1)(2), Question 2.
[42] Sec. 381(a)(1).
[43] Sec. 334(b). See footnote 8 for a summary of the excluded preferred stock issues.
[44] Sec. 337(a).

- A qualified purchase of a target corporation's stock by a second corporation occurs.
- A Sec. 338 election is not made with respect to the acquisition.
- The acquired corporation is liquidated pursuant to a plan of liquidation adopted less than 2 years after the acquisition date.
- The principal purpose for the liquidation is the evasion or avoidance of federal income tax by securing the benefit of a deduction, credit, or allowance which the acquiring corporation would not otherwise enjoy.

The principal problem that the IRS faces in applying Sec. 269(b) is showing that the principal purpose requirement is met. When the taxpayer can show a significant business purpose for engaging in the liquidation, the IRS should be prevented from disallowing the deductions, credits, and so on.[45]

Topic Review 6-2 presents a summary of the requirements for, and tax consequences of, having made a Sec. 338 deemed liquidation election.

TOPIC REVIEW 6-2

Section 338 Deemed Liquidation Election

Election Requirements

1. The acquiring corporation must have made a qualified stock purchase (i.e., a purchase of 80% or more of the target corporation's voting stock and 80% or more of the total value of all stock within a 12-month period). Certain nonvoting preferred stock issues are excluded from the 80% requirements.
2. Stock acquisitions involving carryover basis (e.g., tax-free reorganizations, corporate formations, gifts, etc.), transfers at death, or related parties do not count towards the 80% minimum.
3. A deemed Sec. 338 election can be made by acquiring assets of the target corporation during the consistency period. Similarly, a Sec. 338 election with respect to one member of an affiliated group may trigger a deemed Sec. 338 election for other members of the affiliated group.
4. The election must be made not later than the 15th day of the 9th month following the acquisition date. The acquisition date is the first date on which the 80% stock ownership requirement is met.

Tax Consequences of a Sec. 338 Election

1. The old target corporation is treated as having sold all of its assets to the new target corporation at their FMV in a single transaction at the close of the acquisition date. Gain or loss is recognized on the sale by the old target corporation.
2. The new target corporation takes a basis for the assets equal to the sum of (1) the acquiring corporation's basis for the stock interest in the target corporation on the acquisition date, (2) the target corporation's liabilities on the day following the acquisition date, and (3) other relevant items (e.g., contingent liabilities that become fixed).
3. This total basis is allocated to the individual assets using the residual method. The residual method allocates the basis first to cash and near-cash items, other tangible and intangible assets, and finally to goodwill and going concern value.
4. The tax attributes of the old target corporation disappear with the deemed liquidation.
5. The new target corporation makes new tax year and accounting method elections.

[45] See, for example, *Hawaiian Trust Co., Ltd. v. U.S.*, 7 AFTR 2d 1553, 61-1 USTC ¶ 9481 (9th Cir., 1961).

TAX PLANNING CONSIDERATIONS

Additional Comment

Timing the distribution of loss property so that the losses generated may be used to offset high-bracket taxable income at the corporate level makes good tax sense if the general liquidation rules are applicable. However, this planning possibility would not exist in a Sec. 332 parent-subsidiary liquidation since losses cannot be recognized by the liquidating subsidiary.

Timing the Liquidation Transaction

Sometimes a plan of liquidation is adopted in one year, but the liquidation is not completed until a subsequent year. Corporations that are planning to distribute properties that have both increased in value and decreased in value may find it to their advantage to sell or distribute properties that have declined in value in a tax year in which they also conducted business activities. As such, the loss recognized when making the liquidating distribution can offset profits that are taxed at higher rates. Deferring the sale or distribution of properties that have appreciated in value may delay the recognition of the gain for one tax year and also place it in a year in which the marginal tax rate is lower.

Example 6-32 ■   Miami Corporation adopts a plan of liquidation in November 1991, a tax year in which it earns $150,000 in profits from its operating activities. Miami's operating activities are discontinued before the end of 1991. Pursuant to the liquidation it distributes assets, which results in the recognition of $40,000 of ordinary losses. In January 1992, Miami distributes assets that have appreciated in value, which results in the recognition of $40,000 of ordinary income. Distributing the loss property in 1991 results in a $15,600 tax savings ($40,000 × [34% + 5%]). Only $6,000 ($40,000 × 0.15) in taxes are owed with respect to the distribution of the appreciated properties in 1992. The rate differential provides a $9,600 ($15,600 − $6,000) net savings to Miami. ■

Timing the liquidating distributions should not proceed without also considering the tax position of the various shareholders. Taxpayers should be careful about timing the liquidating distributions to avoid placing a taxpayer in a higher marginal tax rate, although this problem has been reduced with the enactment of the 28% maximum tax rate for long-term capital gains starting in 1991. If the liquidation results in a loss being recognized, shareholders should take advantage of the opportunity to offset the loss against realized and unrealized capital gains, as well as to attempt to increase the portion of the loss eligible for ordinary loss treatment under Sec. 1244.

Key Point

Losses recognized on a liquidating distribution by individual shareholders may qualify for ordinary loss treatment due to Sec. 1244; corporate shareholders with 80% stock ownership may qualify for ordinary loss treatment due to Sec. 165(g)(3); but corporate shareholders with less than 80% stock ownership are most likely limited to capital loss treatment.

Recognition of Ordinary Losses When a Liquidation Occurs

Losses are sometimes recognized when a liquidation occurs. Individual shareholders should recognize that, because a complete liquidation is treated as an exchange transaction, Sec. 1244 ordinary loss treatment is available when a small business corporation is liquidated. This treatment permits $50,000 of ordinary loss to be claimed when the stock is surrendered, or $100,000 if the taxpayer is married and filing a joint return.

Ordinary loss treatment is also available for a domestic corporation that owns stock in a subsidiary corporation. Since the rules in Sec. 332 regarding nonrecognition of gain or loss do not apply when a subsidiary corporation is insolvent (see page 6-11), the parent corporation is permitted to recognize a loss when the subsidiary corporation's stocks and securities are determined to be worthless. This loss is an ordinary loss (instead of a capital loss) if (1) at least 80% of the voting stock and 80% of each class of nonvoting stock are owned by the domestic corporation and (2) more

Tax Planning Considerations • 6-29

than 90% of the liquidating corporation's gross income for all tax years has been other than passive income.[46]

Using Sec. 332 to Obtain a Double Tax Exemption

The 80% stock ownership requirement provides the taxpayer with an opportunity to engage in tax planning when a subsidiary corporation is liquidated. A parent corporation seeking to come under the Sec. 332 nonrecognition rules may acquire additional shares of the subsidiary corporation's stock prior to the adoption of the plan of liquidation. This acquisition serves to help the parent corporation meet the 80% minimum and avoid having to recognize any gain on the liquidation. If these additional shares of stock are purchased from other shareholders, Sec. 332 will not apply when the 80% minimum is satisfied by acquiring these shares after the plan of liquidation is adopted.[47]

Example 6-33 ■ Parent Corporation owns 75% of Subsidiary Corporation's single class of stock. On March 12, 1991, Parent Corporation purchases for cash the remaining 25% of the Subsidiary stock from three individual shareholders pursuant to a tender offer. A plan of liquidation is approved by Subsidiary's shareholder on October 1, 1991. Subsidiary Corporation's assets are distributed to Parent Corporation on December 1, 1991, in exchange for all of Subsidiary's outstanding stock. Parent Corporation does not recognize any gain or loss on the redemption of its Subsidiary stock in the liquidation, since all of the Sec. 332 requirements have been satisfied. ■

Alternatively, the parent corporation might cause the subsidiary corporation to redeem some of the shares held by its minority shareholders before the plan of liquidation is adopted. The IRS originally held that the intention to liquidate is present once the subsidiary corporation agrees to redeem the shares of the minority shareholders. Thus, the redemption of a 25% minority interest did not permit Sec. 332 to be used, even though the parent corporation owned 100% of the outstanding stock after the redemption.[48]

In *George L. Riggs, Inc.*, the Tax Court held that a tender offer to minority shareholders by the parent corporation and the calling of the subsidiary's preferred stock does not invalidate the Sec. 332 liquidation, since "the formation of a conditional intention to liquidate in the future is not the adoption of a plan of liquidation."[49] The IRS has acquiesced to the *Riggs* decision.

By having the transaction qualify under Sec. 332(a), the parent corporation can receive nonmoney distributions in liquidation of the subsidiary corporation that are nontaxable to both corporations. As discussed above, Sec. 337(a) permits the liquidating subsidiary corporation to avoid recognizing gain or loss when it distributes property to its parent corporation. Because the exemption found in Sec. 337(a) applies only to the 80% distributee, property distributions to minority shareholders result in recognition of gain (but not loss) to the liquidating subsidiary corporation.

Example 6-34 ■ Parent Corporation owns 80% of the single class of stock of Subsidiary Corporation. The remaining 20% of the Subsidiary stock is owned by Rachel. Parent and Rachel have adjusted bases of $200,000 and $50,000, respectively, for their

---
[46] Sec. 165(g)(3).
[47] Rev. Rul. 75-521, 1975-2 C.B. 120.
[48] Rev. Rul. 70-106, 1970-1 C.B. 70.
[49] *George L. Riggs, Inc.*, 64 T.C. 474 (1975), *acq.* 1976-2 C.B. 2.

Subsidiary stock. Subsidiary Corporation distributes land having a $250,000 adjusted basis and a $400,000 FMV to Parent Corporation and $100,000 in cash to Rachel. No gain or loss is recognized by Subsidiary Corporation on the distribution of the land or the cash. Parent Corporation recognizes no gain on the liquidation and takes a $250,000 basis for the land. Rachel must recognize a $50,000 ($100,000 − $50,000) capital gain on the receipt of the money. Distribution of the land and cash ratably to Parent and Rachel would have required Subsidiary Corporation to recognize as gain the appreciation on the portion of the land distributed to Rachel. ∎

Avoiding Sec. 332 in Order to Recognize Losses

Key Point
If the liquidating subsidiary corporation primarily has loss property to distribute, Sec. 332 should be avoided since those losses cannot be recognized. To avoid Sec. 332 treatment, consider having the parent corporation dispose of enough of its subsidiary stock to drop below the requisite 80% threshold. In such a case, the general liquidation rules which allow recognition of the liquidating corporation's losses are applicable.

A parent corporation may desire to avoid the Sec. 332 nonrecognition rules in order to recognize a loss when a solvent subsidiary corporation is liquidated. Because the stock ownership requirement must be met during the entire liquidation process, the parent corporation can apparently sell some of its stock in the subsidiary corporation to reduce its stock ownership below the 80% level at any time during the liquidation process and be able to recognize the loss.[50] Such a sale would permit the parent corporation to recognize a capital loss when it surrenders its stock interest in the subsidiary corporation.

Since the sale of a portion of the subsidiary's stock after the plan of liquidation is adopted prevents Sec. 332 from applying to the parent corporation, the Sec. 337 rules, which prevent the subsidiary corporation from recognizing gain or loss when a liquidating distribution is made to an 80% distributee, also do not apply. Thus, the subsidiary corporation is permitted to recognize a loss when it distributes properties that have declined in value.

COMPLIANCE AND PROCEDURAL CONSIDERATIONS

General Liquidation Procedures

Section 6043(a) requires a corporation to file a Form 966 (Information Return under Sec. 6043) within 30 days after the adoption of any resolution or plan calling for the liquidation or dissolution of the corporation. This form is filed with the district director of the IRS for the district in which the liquidating corporation's income tax return is filed. Any amendment or supplement to the resolution or plan must be filed on an additional Form 966 within 30 days of making the amendment or supplement. Form 966 must be filed by the liquidating corporation whether the shareholders' realized gain is recognized or not. The information that must be included with the Form 966 is described in Reg. Sec. 1.6043-1(b).

Regulation Sec. 1.6043-2(a) requires every corporation that makes a distribution of $600 or more during a calendar year to any shareholder in liquidation of part or all of its capital stock to file a Form 1099-DIV (U.S. Information Return for Recipients of Dividends and Distributions). A separate Form 1099-DIV is required for each

---

[50] *CIR v. Day & Zimmerman, Inc.*, 34 AFTR 343, 45-2 USTC ¶ 9403 (3rd Cir., 1945).

shareholder. The information that must be included with the Form 1099-DIV is described in Reg. Secs. 1.6043-2(a) and (b).

A corporation that is in existence for part of a year is required by Reg. Sec. 1.6012-2(a)(2) to file a corporate tax return for the portion of the tax year that it was in existence. A corporation that ceases business and dissolves, while retaining no assets, is not considered to be in existence for federal tax purposes, even though under state law it may be considered for certain purposes to be continuing its affairs (e.g., for purposes of suing or being sued).

Section 332 Liquidations

Regulation Sec. 1.332-6 requires every corporation receiving distributions in a complete liquidation that comes within the purview of the Sec. 332 nonrecognition rules to maintain permanent records. A complete statement of all facts pertinent to the nonrecognition of gain or loss includes the following: a certified copy of the plan of liquidation, a list of all the properties received upon the distribution, a statement of any indebtedness of the liquidating corporation to the recipient corporation, and a statement of stock ownership that must be included in the corporate distributee's return for the tax year in which a liquidating distribution is received.

A special waiver of the general 3-year statute of limitations is required when the liquidation covers more than one tax year.[51] The recipient corporation must file a waiver of the statute of limitations on assessment for each of its tax years which falls partially or wholly within the liquidation period. This waiver must be filed at the time the recipient corporation files its income tax return. This waiver must extend the assessment period to a date not earlier than one year after the last date of the period for assessment of such taxes for the last tax year in which the liquidation may be completed under Sec. 332.

Additional Comment

As evidenced by these several pages, the compliance and procedural requirements of complete liquidations and Sec. 338 deemed liquidations are formidable. Any taxpayer contemplating either of these types of corporate transactions should consult competent tax and legal advisors to ensure that the proposed results will be accomplished.

Section 338 Deemed Liquidations

The statement of election under Sec. 338 must be made by the acquiring corporation on Form 8023 (Election under Sec. 338(g)). This election must be made by the fifteenth day of the ninth month following the acquisition date. The information about the acquiring corporation, the target corporation, and the election that must be filed with Form 8023 is contained in Temp. Reg. Sec. 1.338-1T(d).

Additional information must be filed with the final tax return of the target corporation. This information is specified in Temp. Reg. Sec. 1.338-1T(e)(1) and includes the following: identification of each corporation subject to the election; FMV of the consideration paid by the purchasing corporation for the stock of each corporation subject to the election; portion of the consideration represented by cash, purchase money debt, and other items; and liabilities of each target corporation as of the close of the acquisition date. Other information may be required if various special elections are made under Sec. 338. This information is specified in Temp. Reg. Secs. 1.338-1T(d) and (e).

Plan of Liquidation

A **plan of liquidation** is generally a written document detailing the steps to be undertaken while carrying out the complete liquidation of the corporation. The date of adoption of a plan of complete liquidation ordinarily is the date that the shareholders adopt a resolution authorizing the distribution of all the corporation's

---

[51] Reg. Sec. 1.332-4(a)(2).

assets (other than those assets retained to meet creditor claims) in redemption of all of its stock.[52] Although generally a written document, the IRS and the courts have accepted informal shareholder agreements and resolutions as equivalent to the adoption of a formal plan of liquidation.[53]

Although a formal plan of liquidation is not required, it may assist the corporation in determining when it enters a liquidation status and, therefore, when distributions to the shareholders qualify for exchange treatment under Sec. 331 (instead of possibly being treated as a dividend under Sec. 301). The adoption of a formal plan of liquidation can provide the liquidating corporation or its shareholders additional benefits under the tax laws. For example, the adoption of a plan of liquidation permits a parent corporation to have a 3-year period of time (instead of 1 tax year) to carry out the complete liquidation of a subsidiary corporation.

PROBLEM MATERIALS

DISCUSSION QUESTIONS

6-1. What is a complete liquidation? A partial liquidation? Explain the difference in the tax treatment accorded these two different events.

6-2. Texas Corporation is liquidated by making a series of distributions to its shareholders after a plan of liquidation has been adopted. How are these distributions taxed?

6-3. Explain the following statement: A corporation may be liquidated for tax purposes even though dissolution has not occurred under state corporation law.

6-4. Explain why a shareholder receiving a liquidating distribution would prefer to receive either capital gain treatment or ordinary loss treatment.

6-5. What event or occurrence determines when a cash or accrual method of accounting taxpayer reports a liquidating distribution?

6-6. Hill Corporation's shareholders are called upon to pay an assessment that was levied against them as a result of a liability not anticipated at the time of liquidation. When will the deduction for the additional payment be claimed? What factors determine the character of the deduction claimed?

6-7. What is an open transaction? What advantages accrue to the shareholders when a liquidation is treated as an open transaction? As a closed transaction?

6-8. Explain the IRS's position regarding whether a liquidation transaction will be considered to be open or closed.

6-9. Explain the Congressional intent behind the enactment of the Sec. 332 rules regarding the liquidation of a subsidiary corporation.

6-10. Compare the general liquidation rules with the Sec. 332 rules for liquidation of a subsidiary corporation with respect to the following items:
  a. Recognition of gain or loss by the distributee corporation
  b. Recognition of gain or loss by the liquidating corporation
  c. Basis of assets in the distributee corporation's hands
  d. Treatment of the liquidating corporation's tax attributes

6-11. What requirements must be satisfied for the Sec. 332 rules to apply to a corporate shareholder?

---

[52] Reg. Sec. 1.337-2(b).
[53] Rev. Rul. 65-235, 1965-2 C.B. 88, and *Badias & Seijas, Inc.*, 1977 PH T.C. Memo ¶ 77,118, 36 TCM 518.

6-12. Parent Corporation owns 80% of the stock of an insolvent subsidiary corporation. The remaining 20% of the stock is owned by Tracy. Subsidiary Corporation is determined to be bankrupt by the courts. Each shareholder receives nothing for their investment. How do they report their loss for tax purposes?

6-13. Parent Corporation owns all of the stock of Subsidiary Corporation and a substantial amount of Subsidiary Corporation bonds. Subsidiary Corporation proposes to transfer appreciated property to Parent Corporation in redemption of its bonds pursuant to the liquidation of Subsidiary Corporation. Explain the tax consequences of the redemption to Parent and Subsidiary Corporations.

6-14. Explain the circumstances under which a shareholder who receives an installment obligation as part of a liquidating distribution is permitted to defer recognition of part or all of their gain on the liquidation.

6-15. What are the differences in the tax treatment for nonliquidating and liquidating distributions made by the distributing corporation?

6-16. Explain the circumstances when a liquidating corporation does not recognize gain or loss when making a liquidating distribution.

6-17. Kelly Corporation makes a liquidating distribution. One of the properties that is distributed is land that is subject to a mortgage. The amount of the mortgage exceeds both the adjusted basis and FMV for the land. How is the amount of Kelly's recognized gain or loss on the distribution determined? How is the shareholder's basis for the land determined?

6-18. Explain the differences in the tax rules applying to distributions made to the parent corporation and a minority shareholder when a controlled subsidiary corporation is liquidated.

6-19. Parent Corporation owns all of the stock of Subsidiary Corporation. Subsidiary Corporation distributes appreciated property to Parent Corporation in redemption of an outstanding bond issue held by Parent. Does the distribution come under the nonrecognition rules of Secs. 332 and 337? Explain.

6-20. Describe the tax treatment accorded the following expenses associated with a liquidation:
  a. Commissions paid on the sale of the liquidating corporation's assets
  b. Accounting fees paid to prepare the corporation's final income tax return
  c. Unamortized organizational expenditures
  d. Prepaid rent for office space that will be occupied by one of the shareholders following the liquidation

6-21. What happens to a corporation's tax attributes when it liquidates?

6-22. Why might a parent corporation elect to treat the acquisition of a subsidiary corporation's stock as a deemed liquidation coming under Sec. 338? When would such an election not be advisable?

6-23. What is a protective carryover basis election? Why might it be advisable to make such an election?

6-24. Explain the following items related to a Sec. 338 election:
  a. The rule used to determine the time period within which a Sec. 338 election can be made.
  b. The stock acquisition transactions that are counted when determining if a qualified stock purchase has been made.
  c. The method for determining the sale price for the target corporation's assets.
  d. The method for determining the total basis for the target corporation's assets.

6-25. How does the residual method allocate the total cost or basis of a group of assets to individual properties?

6-26. What happens to the target corporation's tax attributes when a Sec. 338 election is made?

6-27. Keith Corporation, a calendar-year taxpayer, adopts a plan of liquidation on April 1, 1991. The final liquidating distribution is made on January 5, 1992. Must Keith Corporation file a tax return for 1991? For 1992?

6-28. What is a plan of liquidation? Why is it advisable for a corporation to adopt a formal plan of liquidation?

6-29. Indicate whether each of the following statements about a liquidation is true or false. If the statement is false, explain why.
  a. Liabilities assumed by a shareholder when a corporation liquidates reduce the amount realized by the shareholder on redemption of their stock.
  b. The loss recognized by a shareholder on a liquidation is generally characterized as an ordinary loss.
  c. A shareholder's basis for property received in a liquidation is the same as the property's basis in the liquidating corporation's hands.
  d. The holding period for the property received in a liquidation includes the period of time that it is held by the liquidating corporation.
  e. The tax attributes of a liquidating corporation are assumed by its shareholders.
  f. A parent corporation can elect to recognize gain or loss when it liquidates a controlled subsidiary corporation.
  g. No gain or loss is recognized by a liquidating subsidiary corporation when its properties are distributed to its parent corporation.
  h. A parent corporation's basis for the assets received in a liquidation where gain is not recognized remains the same as it was on the books of the liquidating subsidiary corporation.

PROBLEMS

6-30. *Shareholder Gain or Loss Calculation.* Florida Corporation is owned by Alan and Sally. The corporation has been engaged in real estate rental activities for a number of years. Alan's basis in his stock is $60,000. Sally's basis in her stock is $40,000. Alan receives a liquidating distribution of $100,000 in cash. Sally receives an apartment building having a $100,000 FMV.
  a. What are the amount and character of Alan and Sally's gain or loss on the transaction?
  b. How would your answer to Part a change if the apartment building was subject to a $30,000 mortgage which Sally assumed?

6-31. *Shareholder Gain or Loss Calculation.* Monaco Corporation is owned entirely by Stacy and Mary, who are husband and wife. Stacy and Mary have a $165,000 basis in their jointly-owned Monaco stock. The Monaco stock is Sec. 1244 stock. They receive the following assets in liquidation of their corporation: accounts receivable, $25,000 FMV; a car, $16,000 FMV; office furniture, $6,000 FMV; and $5,000 cash. What are the amount and character of their gain or loss?

6-32. *Shareholder Gain or Loss Calculation.* Diamond Corporation is owned by Arlene and Billy. Arlene and Billy have $40,000 and $20,000 adjusted bases, respectively, for their Diamond stock. Each shareholder receives a $30,000 liquidating distribution in exchange for their Diamond stock. What are the amount and character of each shareholder's recognized gain or loss?

6-33. *Series of Liquidating Distributions.* Union Corporation is owned equally by Ron and Steve. Ron and Steve purchased their stock in 1985 and 1987 and have adjusted bases for their Union stock of $15,000 and $27,500, respectively. Each shareholder receives two liquidating distributions. The first liquidating distribution made in 1991 results in each shareholder receiving a one-half interest in a parcel of land that has a $40,000 FMV and an $18,000 adjusted basis to Union Corporation. The second liquidating distribution made in 1992 results in each shareholder receiving $20,000 in money.
  a. What are the amount and character of Ron and Steve's recognized gain or loss for 1991? For 1992?
  b. What is the basis of the land in Ron and Steve's hands?
  c. How would your answers to Parts a and b change if the land instead has a $12,000 FMV?

6-34. *Subsequent Assessment Upon the Shareholders.* Meridian Corporation is owned equally by five individual shareholders. A plan of liquidation is adopted by Meridian Corporation, and each shareholder receives a liquidating distribution. Tina, a cash method of accounting taxpayer, reports a $30,000 long-term capital gain in 1986 on the redemption of her stock.

Pending the outcome of a lawsuit which Meridian Corporation is a party to, $5,000 of Tina's liquidating distribution is held back and placed in escrow. Settlement of the lawsuit in 1991 requires that the escrowed funds be paid out and that each shareholder pay an additional $2,500. Tina pays the amount due in 1992. How does Tina report the settlement of the lawsuit and the payment of the additional amount?

6-35. *Open vs. Closed Transactions.* Hilton Corporation is owned by Gordon, who has a $40,000 basis for his Hilton stock. Gordon receives a liquidating distribution in 1989 of $12,000 in money, a patent having a $15,000 FMV, and a contingent claim for $125,000 against Tide Corporation for infringement on the patent. According to Hilton's legal counsel, no reliable valuation can be placed on the $125,000 claim.
  a. What are the amount and character of Gordon's gain or loss on the liquidation?
  b. How would your answer to Part a change if the claim is settled by having Tide Corporation pay Gordon $50,000 in 1991?
  c. How would your answers to Parts a and b change if litigation of the claim commences in 1989 and legal counsel places a $30,000 valuation on the contingent claim against Tide Corporation?

6-36. *Installment Sale of Assets.* White Corporation is owned by Bob, who has a $300,000 basis for his White stock. On June 15, 1990, White Corporation adopts a plan of liquidation and sells a group of assets realizing a $600,000 gain, all of which must be recognized. White Corporation distributes $1,200,000 in cash to Bob as a liquidating distribution.
  a. What are the amount and character of the gain recognized by Bob?
  b. How would your answer to Part a change if Bob had instead received an installment obligation of $1,200,000? The obligation (and interest at a rate reasonable to the IRS) is to be paid in 4 equal installments starting in 1991.

6-37. *Gain or Loss on Making a Liquidating Distribution.* What is the amount and character of the gain or loss that is recognized by the distributing corporation when making liquidating distributions in the following situations? In any situation where a loss is disallowed, indicate what changes would be necessary to improve the tax consequences of the transaction.
  a. Best Corporation distributes land having a $200,000 FMV and a $100,000 adjusted basis to Cecil, its sole shareholder. The land, a capital asset, is subject to a $40,000 mortgage which Cecil assumes.
  b. Jordan Corporation distributes marketable securities having a $100,000 FMV and a $175,000 adjusted basis to Brad, a 66.67% shareholder. The marketable securities were purchased by Jordan three years ago. A cash payment in the amount of $50,000 is made to Ann, a 33.33% shareholder.
  c. Assume the same facts as in Part b, except that the securities were acquired by Jordan as a capital contribution from Brad three years ago.
  d. Wilkins Corporation distributes depreciable property to its two equal shareholders. Robert receives a milling machine having a $50,000 adjusted basis and a $75,000 FMV. $30,000 depreciation had been claimed on the machine. Sharon receives an automobile that originally cost $40,000 and has a $26,000 FMV. $20,000 in depreciation had been claimed on the automobile.

6-38. *Gain or Loss Recognition by a Distributing Corporation.* Melon Corporation adopts a plan of liquidation in which it plans on distributing the following properties:
  - Land having a $30,000 FMV and a $12,000 adjusted basis.
  - Depreciable personal property having a $15,000 FMV and a $9,000 adjusted basis. Depreciation in the amount of $10,000 has been claimed on the property during the 3 years since its acquisition.
  - Installment obligations having a $30,000 FMV and face amount and a $21,000 adjusted basis acquired when a Sec. 1231 property was sold.
  - Supplies that cost $6,000 and which were expensed in the preceding tax year. The supplies have a $7,500 FMV.
  - Marketable securities having a $15,000 FMV and an $18,000 adjusted basis.

  a. Which of the properties when distributed by Melon Corporation to an individual shareholder will require the recognition of gain or loss by the distributing corporation?

b. How will your answer to Part a change if the distribution is made to Melon's parent corporation as part of a complete liquidation meeting the Sec. 332 requirements?

c. How will your answer to Part b change if the distribution is made to a minority shareholder?

6-39. *Distribution of Property Subject to a Mortgage.* Titan Corporation adopts a plan of liquidation on August 8, 1991. It distributes an apartment building having a $4,000,000 FMV and a $2,400,000 adjusted basis to the MNO Partnership in exchange for all of the outstanding Titan stock. The MNO Partnership agrees to assume the $3,000,000 mortgage on the building.

a. What is Titan's recognized gain or loss on the distribution?

b. How would your answer to Part a change if the apartment building is instead worth $2,700,000?

6-40. *Sale of Loss Property by a Liquidating Corporation.* Mike contributes land having a $75,000 adjusted basis and a $50,000 FMV to Kansas Corporation in exchange for additional Kansas stock. The land is used as a parking lot by Kansas's employees for 2 years before it is sold for $45,000. One month after the sale, Kansas Corporation adopts a plan of liquidation.

a. What is Kansas's recognized gain or loss on the sale?

b. How would your answer to Part a change if the land was not used in the conduct of Kansas's trade or business and if it is held for only 1 year prior to being sold?

c. How would your answer to Part b change if the land were instead sold for $80,000?

6-41. *Tax Consequences of a Corporate Liquidation.* King Corporation is owned by Lynn and by Tiger Corporation, each of which has a $100,000 basis in their King stock. Tiger Corporation is owned equally by Lynn and Mark. A plan of liquidation is adopted by King Corporation on February 1, 1991, and Lynn receives the following property as a liquidating distribution on March 12, 1991: money, $40,000; land, $75,000 FMV; and Blue Corporation securities, $30,000 FMV. The land is subject to a $15,000 mortgage. The land and securities (both capital assets) have adjusted bases of $50,000 and $70,000, respectively, in King Corporation's hands. The securities were purchased 8 years ago by King Corporation. King's E&P is $30,000 on the liquidation date. After payment of all liabilities, Tiger Corporation receives $130,000 in cash as a liquidating distribution.

a. What are the amount and character of King Corporation's recognized gain or loss on the liquidating distributions?

b. What are the amount and character of Lynn's and Tiger Corporation's recognized gain or loss?

c. What are the bases of the land and securities in Lynn's hands?

6-42. *Liquidation of a Subsidiary Corporation.* Parent Corporation owns all of the stock of Subsidiary Corporation. Its stock investment is $175,000. A plan of liquidation is adopted and assets having a $300,000 FMV and a $200,000 adjusted basis (to Subsidiary) are distributed to Parent Corporation.

a. What are the amount and character of Subsidiary Corporation's recognized gain or loss on the distribution?

b. What are the amount and character of Parent Corporation's recognized gain or loss on the distribution?

c. What is the basis of the assets on Parent Corporation's books?

6-43. *Liquidation of a Subsidiary Corporation.* Assume the same facts as in Problem 6-42 except that Parent Corporation also assumes $40,000 in Subsidiary Corporation liabilities. How will your answers to Parts a through c change?

6-44. *Liquidation of a Subsidiary Corporation.* Parent Corporation owns all of Subsidiary Corporation's single class of stock. Its adjusted basis for the stock is $150,000. After adopting a plan of liquidation, Subsidiary Corporation distributes the following properties to Parent Corporation: money, $20,000; LIFO inventory, $200,000 FMV; and equipment, $150,000 FMV. The inventory has a $125,000 adjusted basis, and its FIFO adjusted basis is $160,000. The equipment originally cost $280,000. Depreciation in the amount of $160,000 has been claimed on the property. Subsidiary Corporation has a $150,000 E&P balance and a $40,000 NOL carryover on the liquidation date.

a. What are the amount and character of Subsidiary Corporation's recognized gain or loss when the liquidating distributions are made?

b. What are the amount and character of Parent Corporation's recognized gain or loss on the redemption of the Subsidiary stock?
c. What is the basis of each nonmoney property on the books of Parent Corporation?
d. What happens to the E&P balance and NOL carryover of Subsidiary Corporation following the liquidation?
e. What happens to Parent's $150,000 basis in the Subsidiary stock?

6-45. *Liquidation of a Subsidiary Corporation.* Parent Corporation owns all of Subsidiary Corporation's single class of stock and $2,000,000 of Subsidiary Corporation debentures. The debentures were purchased in small blocks from various unrelated parties at a $100,000 discount from their face amount. Subsidiary Corporation adopts a plan of liquidation whereby it distributes property having a $3,000,000 FMV and a $2,400,000 adjusted basis in redemption of the Subsidiary stock. The debentures are redeemed for Subsidiary Corporation property having a $2,000,000 FMV and a $1,500,000 adjusted basis.
a. What income or gain is recognized by Subsidiary Corporation as a result of making the liquidating distributions?
b. What gain or loss is recognized by Parent Corporation on the redemption of the Subsidiary stock? The Subsidiary debentures?
c. What is Parent Corporation's basis for the property received from Subsidiary Corporation?

6-46. *Liquidation of a Subsidiary Corporation.* Parent Corporation owns 80% of the single class of Subsidiary Corporation stock. The remaining 20% of the Subsidiary stock is owned by Janice. Parent and Janice have adjusted bases of $100,000 and $25,000, respectively, for their Subsidiary stock. Parent Corporation has also purchased all $200,000 of Subsidiary Corporation's debentures. These debentures were purchased in small blocks from various unrelated parties at their face amount. After adopting a plan of liquidation on January 30, 1991, Subsidiary Corporation is left with three properties: (1) land having a $40,000 adjusted basis and a $160,000 FMV, (2) marketable securities having a $90,000 adjusted basis and a $200,000 FMV, and (3) $40,000 in money. Subsidiary Corporation has a $50,000 E&P balance on the liquidation date.
a. What are the tax consequences to Parent and Subsidiary Corporations and Janice of the following: distributing the land to Parent in redemption of its Subsidiary stock, distributing the money to Janice in redemption of her Subsidiary stock, and distributing the marketable securites to Parent Corporation in redemption of the debentures?
b. How would your answer to Part a change if the land and the money are instead distributed ratably to Parent Corporation and Janice in retirement of the Subsidiary stock? (Assume the marketable securities are still distributed in exchange for the debentures.)

6-47. *Basis of Assets Received in a Liquidation.* Parent Corporation owns all of the Subsidiary Corporation stock. Parent has a $200,000 basis in its stock investment. What are the tax consequences to Parent of the following liquidating distributions made by Subsidiary?
a. Assets having a $250,000 FMV and a $200,000 adjusted basis (to Subsidiary) are distributed.
b. Assets having a $250,000 FMV and a $150,000 adjusted basis are distributed.
c. Assets having a $150,000 FMV and a $250,000 adjusted basis are distributed.

6-48. *Tax Consequences of a Corporate Liquidation.* Pueblo Corporation is owned by Art and Peggy. Art owns 80% of the Pueblo stock while Peggy owns the remainder. Art and Peggy have $320,000 and $80,000 adjusted bases, respectively, for their Pueblo stock. Pueblo Corporation owns the following assets: cash, $25,000; inventory, $150,000 FMV and $100,000 adjusted basis; marketable securities, $100,000 FMV and $125,000 adjusted basis; and equipment, $325,000 FMV and $185,000 adjusted basis. The equipment was purchased four years ago and subsequently $215,000 of Modified ACRS depreciation was claimed. On July 1 of the current year Pueblo Corporation adopts a plan of liquidation at a time when it has $250,000 of E&P and no liabilities. The equipment, marketable securities, and $55,000 of the inventory are distributed to Art before year-end as a liquidating distribution. The remaining inventory and the cash are distributed to Peggy before year-end as a liquidating distribution.
a. What are the tax consequences of the liquidation to Pueblo Corporation and Art and Peggy?
b. Can you offer any suggestions to Pueblo Corporation's management that could improve the tax consequences of the liquidation? Explain.

c. How would your answers to Parts a and b change if Art and Peggy were instead domestic corporations?

6-49. Qualified Stock Purchase. Acquiring Corporation purchased 20% of Target Corporation's stock on each of the following dates: January 1, 1991, April 1, 1991, June 1, 1991, and October 1, 1991, and January 1, 1992.
   a. Has a qualified stock purchase occurred? When must an election be made by Acquiring to have the stock purchase treated as an asset acquisition under Sec. 338?
   b. How would your answer to part a change if the purchase dates were instead January 1, 1991, April 1, 1991, September 1, 1991, January 3, 1992, and April 15, 1992?

6-50. Sec. 338 Election. Acquiring Corporation acquires 20% of the Target Corporation stock from Milt on August 10, 1991. An additional 30% of the stock is acquired from Nick on November 15, 1991. The remaining 50% of the Target stock is acquired from Phil on April 10, 1992. The total price paid for the stock is $1,500,000. Target Corporation's balance sheet on April 10, 1992, shows assets with a $2,500,000 FMV, a $1,800,000 adjusted basis, and $750,000 in liabilities.
   a. What is the acquisition date for the Target stock for purposes of Sec. 338? By what date must the Sec. 338 election be made?
   b. If a Sec. 338 election is made, what is the deemed sale price?
   c. What is the total basis of the assets following the deemed sale, assuming a tax liability attributable to the deemed sale of $238,000?
   d. How does the tax liability attributable to the deemed sale affect the price Acquiring Corporation is willing to pay for the Target stock?
   e. What happens to Target's tax attributes following the deemed sale?

6-51. Sec. 338 Election. Rain Corporation is considering the purchase of Water Corporation's stock. Water Corporation's adjusted basis for its assets is $1,250,000. Sale of the Water Corporation assets at their FMV would result in $400,000 of depreciation recapture taking place under Sec. 1245; $250,000 of ordinary income being recognized on the sale of its LIFO inventory; and $1,600,000 of capital gain being recognized on the sale of its investment assets. Water Corporation's E&P balance is $750,000. No other carryovers are owned by Water Corporation.
   a. What advantages would accrue to Rain Corporation if a Sec. 338 election is made?
   b. What tax costs would accrue to Water Corporation if the Sec. 338 election is made (assume a 34% corporate tax rate)? How would these tax costs affect the price Rain Corporation would be willing to pay for the Water stock?
   c. Under what circumstances might the Sec. 338 election be ill-advised?

6-52. Sec. 338 Basis Allocation. Apache Corporation purchases all of Target Corporation's stock for $276,000 cash on January 8, 1991. A timely Sec. 338 election is made by Apache. Target's balance sheet at the close of business on the acquisition date is as follows:

Assets	Adjusted Basis	FMV	Liabilities	Amount
Cash	$ 50,000	$ 50,000	Accounts payable	$ 40,000
Marketable securities	18,000	38,000	Note to bank	60,000
Accounts receivable	66,000	65,000	Owner's equity	300,000
Inventory (FIFO)	21,000	43,000		
Equipment[a]	95,000	144,000		
Land and building[b]	30,000	60,000		
Total	$280,000	$400,000	Total	$400,000

[a] The equipment cost $200,000 when purchased.
[b] The building is Sec. 1250 property. $10,000 of depreciation recapture would be recognized if the property were sold.

   a. What is the deemed sale price for Target's assets?
   b. What are the amount and character of the gain or loss that Target Corporation must recognize on the deemed sale?
   c. What is the adjusted grossed-up basis for the Target stock (assume a 34% corporate tax rate)? How is this amount allocated to the individual properties?

6-53. *Timing of Liquidation Transaction.* Beaumont Corporation is owned by Renee, who has a $200,000 basis for her Beaumont stock. Renee has been employed as President of Beaumont Corporation since she founded the corporation 20 years ago. Her annual salary from Beaumont is $200,000. Because Beaumont has consumed most of her time and monies, she has little other investment income. Beaumont has become very prosperous, but Renee decides that she wants to retire to Hawaii. Therefore, she plans to negotiate the sale of Beaumont's assets and adopts a plan of liquidation in November 1991, selling the assets for $6,000,000 (a $2,000,000 profit) and distributing the money received from the sale in January 1992. Under Sec. 1245, $300,000 of Beaumont's profit must be recognized as ordinary income. The remainder is Sec. 1231 gain or long-term capital gain. Beaumont Corporation's 1991 operating profit is $150,000 (after the payment of Renee's $200,000 salary).
   a. What suggestions can you offer Renee about structuring the sale of the assets?
   b. Are there any advantages which Renee could achieve if she sells the Beaumont Corporation stock instead of its assets?

6-54. *Tax Attribute Carryovers.* Bell Corporation is owned by George, who has a $400,000 basis for his Bell stock. The activities of Bell Corporation have been unprofitable in recent years, small NOLs have been incurred, and its operating assets currently have a $300,000 FMV and a $500,000 adjusted basis. George is approached in early 1991 by Time Corporation, which wants to purchase Bell's assets for $300,000. Approximately $200,000 in money is expected to remain after the payment of Bell Corporation's liabilities.
   a. What are the tax consequences of the transaction if Bell Corporation adopts a plan of liquidation, sells the assets, and distributes the money in redemption of the Bell stock within a 12-month period?
   b. What advantages (if any) would accrue to Bell Corporation and George if Bell remains in existence to conduct a new trade or business after the sale?

6-55. *Sale of Corporate Assets.* Federal Corporation was formed 20 years ago by Fred, who has a $20,000 basis in the Federal stock. The corporation holds two tracts of land. One tract of land has been leased by an oil company for many years and is producing a small amount of operating income each year. The other tract of land is located near Boomtown, Texas, and has substantial value as a commercial property. The first tract of land and the leases have a $50,000 FMV and a $5,000 basis. The second tract of land has a $1,000,000 FMV and a $15,000 basis. Fred has been approached by a number of commercial developers who want to purchase the second tract of land. All have been willing to pay the $1,000,000 market value. No contracts have been entered into by Fred to sell either tract of land. Fred has indicated that he should probably liquidate Federal Corporation if he sells the second tract of land. What suggestions can you offer Fred about the tax consequences of selling the land and liquidating the corporation?

6-56. *Open vs. Closed Transaction.* Kane Corporation is owned equally by Maria and Martha. Both individuals are investors who, through Kane Corporation, hold a number of patents on their inventions. Kane Corporation holds the patent on a special manufacturing process used in the production of plastics. This process has been the subject of litigation with a competitor about infringement of rights that Kane has under the patent. Kane Corporation is suing for $500,000 in royalties, which would have been earned had the competitor been licensed to use the patent. Because of a disagreement, Martha and Maria have adopted a plan to liquidate Kane Corporation. As part of the liquidation plan, Maria is to receive the patent in question (valued at $1,000,000) and any amounts to be collected under the lawsuit. Martha is to receive other patents and money totaling $1,000,000. Kane Corporation's attorneys are unable to make a definite statement as to what Maria can expect to receive from the lawsuit. Each shareholder's basis for their Kane stock is $50,000. What is the appropriate treatment of the liquidating distribution by Kane Corporation and Maria?

CASE STUDY PROBLEM

6-57. Paul, a long-time client of yours, has operated an automobile repair shop (as a C corporation) for most of his life which has been fairly successful in recent years. His children do not have an interest in continuing the business. Paul is age 62 and has accumulated approximately $500,000 in assets outside of his business, most of which are in his personal residence and retirement plan. A recent balance sheet for the business shows the following:

Assets	Adjusted Basis	FMV	Liabilities	Amount
Cash	$ 25,000	$ 25,000	Accounts payable	$ 30,000
Inventory	60,000	75,000	Mortgage payable	70,000
Equipment	200,000	350,000		
Building	100,000	160,000		
Land	40,000	60,000		
Goodwill	0	100,000		
Total	$425,000	$770,000	Total	$100,000

The inventory is accounted for using the first-in, first-out inventory method. Depreciation in the amount of $250,000 has been claimed on the equipment. The building was acquired in 1987 and has been depreciated in the amount of $25,000 under the Modified ACRS rules. The goodwill is an estimate that Paul feels reflects the value of his business over and above the other assets that are listed.

Paul has received an offer of $800,000 from a competing automobile repair company for the assets of his business which will be used to establish a second location for the competing company. The sale will be made in cash within 60 days. The purchaser has obtained the necessary bank financing to make the acquisition.

Required: Prepare a memorandum for Paul outlining the tax consequences of the sale transaction and liquidation of the corporation.

TAX RESEARCH PROBLEMS

6-58. Parent Corporation owns 85% of the common stock and 100% of the preferred stock of Subsidiary Corporation. The common stock and preferred stock have adjusted bases of $500,000 and $200,000, respectively. Subsidiary Corporation adopts a plan of liquidation on July 3, 1991, when its assets have a $1,000,000 market value. Liabilities on that date amount to $850,000. On November 9, 1991, Subsidiary Corporation pays off its creditors and distributes $150,000 to Parent Corporation with respect to its preferred stock. No monies are left to be paid to Parent with respect to the remaining $50,000 of its liquidation preference for the preferred stock, or with respect to any of the common stock. In each of Subsidiary Corporation's tax years, less than 10% of its gross income has been passive income. What are the amount and character of Parent's loss on the preferred stock? The common stock?

A partial list of research sources is

- Secs. 165(g)(3) and 332(a).
- Reg. Sec. 1.332-2(b).
- *Spaulding Bakeries, Inc.,* 27 T.C. 684 (1957).
- *H. K. Porter Co., Inc.,* 87 T.C. 689 (1986).

6-59. Parent Corporation has owned 60% of the single class of Subsidiary Corporation stock for a number of years. The remaining 40% of the Subsidiary stock is owned by Bill. On August 10, 1991, Parent Corporation purchases Bill's Subsidiary Corporation stock for cash. On September 15, 1991, Subsidiary Corporation adopts a plan of liquidation. Subsidiary Corporation makes a single liquidating distibution on October 1, 1991. The activities of Subsidiary Corporation are continued as a separate division. Does the liquidation of Subsidiary Corporation qualify for nonrecognition treatment under Secs. 332 and 337? Must Parent Corporation assume the Subsidiary Corporation earnings and profits?

A partial list of research sources is

- Secs. 332(b) and 381.
- Reg. Sec. 1.332-2(a).
- Rev. Ruls. 70-106, 1970-1 C.B. 70, and 75-521, 1975-2 C.B. 120.

6-60. Able Corporation, a calendar-year taxpayer, is owned by 25 individual shareholders. A recent balance sheet shows Able Corporation with assets having a $3,500,000 FMV and a $2,150,000 adjusted basis. Able Corporation's management is contemplating the sale of the assets followed by a complete liquidation of the corporation. Such a sale would result in $950,000 of ordinary income and $400,000 of capital gain being recognized. An unrelated purchaser has proposed to pay $350,000 the first year, and to provide a note covering the balance. $350,000 would be paid by the purchaser annually on the note plus interest at a rate acceptable to the IRS. Explain the tax consequences of the following alternative plans being considered by management.

- Sell the assets and have the corporation hold the installment obligation. Collections on the obligation would be distributed by the corporation to the shareholders. Following receipt of the last payment, the corporation would be liquidated.
- Adopt a plan of liquidation, sell the assets, and distribute the installment obligation to the shareholders as a liquidating distribution. The shareholders would collect the interest and annual payments.
- Adopt a plan of liquidation, sell the assets, and transfer the installment obligation to a liquidating trust, and liquidate the corporation. The trust would collect the interest and annual payments and remit them to the former shareholders.

A partial list of research sources is:

- Secs. 331, 336, and 541.
- Reg. Sec. 301.7701-4(d).
- Rev. Rul. 75-379, 1975-2 C.B. 505.

7 Corporate Acquisitions and Reorganizations

CHAPTER OUTLINE

LEARNING OBJECTIVES 7-2
CHARACTERISTICS OF TAXABLE AND TAX-FREE TRANSACTIONS 7-3
  Comparison of Taxable and Tax-Free Transactions 7-3
TAXABLE ACQUISITION TRANSACTIONS 7-5
  Stock Acquisitions 7-5
  Asset Acquisitions 7-6
TAX-FREE REORGANIZATIONS 7-7
  Types of Reorganizations 7-7
TAX CONSEQUENCES OF REORGANIZATIONS 7-8
  Target or Transferor Corporation 7-8
  Acquiring or Transferee Corporation 7-9
  Shareholders and Security Holders 7-10
ACQUISITIVE REORGANIZATIONS 7-14
  Type A Reorganization 7-14
  Type C Reorganization 7-21
  Type D Reorganization 7-24
  Type B Reorganization 7-26
  Type G Reorganization 7-29
DIVISIVE REORGANIZATIONS 7-29
  Type D Divisive Reorganization 7-29
  Type G Divisive Reorganization 7-31
OTHER REORGANIZATION TRANSACTIONS 7-32
  Type E Reorganization 7-32
  Type F Reorganization 7-34
JUDICIAL RESTRICTIONS ON THE USE OF CORPORATE REORGANIZATIONS 7-34
  Continuity of Proprietary Interest 7-35
  Continuity of Business Enterprise 7-35
  Business Purpose Requirement 7-36
  Step Transaction Doctrine 7-37
TAX ATTRIBUTES 7-37
  Assumption of Tax Attributes 7-37
  Limitation on Use of Tax Attributes 7-38
TAX PLANNING CONSIDERATIONS 7-41
  Why Use a Reorganization Instead of a Taxable Transaction? 7-41
  Comparison of Consideration Used in Reorganizations 7-42
  Avoiding the Reorganization Provisions 7-43
COMPLIANCE AND PROCEDURAL CONSIDERATIONS 7-44
  Plan of Reorganization 7-44
  Party to a Reorganization 7-44
  Ruling Requests 7-44
  Reporting Requirements 7-45
PROBLEM MATERIALS 7-45
  Discussion Questions 7-45
  Problems 7-47
  Case Study Problems 7-53
  Tax Research Problems 7-53

LEARNING OBJECTIVES

After studying this chapter, you should be able to

1. Explain the differences between taxable and tax-free acquisition transactions
2. Determine the tax consequences of taxable acquisition transactions
3. Explain the types of tax-free reorganizations
4. Determine the tax consequences of a tax-free reorganization to the target corporation
5. Determine the tax consequences of a tax-free reorganization to the acquiring corporation
6. Determine the tax consequences of a tax-free reorganization to the target corporation's shareholders and security holders
7. Explain the requirements of a Type A reorganization
8. Explain the requirements of a Type C reorganization
9. Explain the requirements of an acquisitive Type D reorganization
10. Explain the requirements of a Type B reorganization
11. Explain the requirements of a divisive Type D reorganization
12. Explain how judicial doctrines can restrict a taxpayer's ability to use a corporate reorganization
13. Determine which reorganization forms permit the carryover of tax attributes
14. Explain how NOL carryovers are restricted following an acquisition

The management of a corporation may decide to acquire a second corporation. Alternatively, these same individuals may decide to divest themselves of part or all of the corporate assets, such as the assets of an operating division or the stock of a subsidiary corporation. These acquisitions or divestitures can be either taxable or tax-free transactions. In a taxable transaction, the entire amount of the realized gain must be recognized. To qualify as a tax-free transaction, however, a specific set of statutory and judicial requirements must be met. If the transaction satisfies these requirements, part or all of the realized gain generally goes unrecognized. The amount of unrecognized gain is deferred until the assets or stock involved are subsequently sold or exchanged in a taxable transaction.[1] The rationale behind the tax-free reorganization rules is that gain should not be recognized until the taxpayer has the wherewithal to pay any tax liability; that is, until property other than stock or securities (e.g., money) has been received.

This chapter presents an overview of the tax consequences of taxable and tax-free acquisitions and divestitures. It also examines the statutory provisions and judicial doctrines that apply to determine the tax consequences for these transactions.

---

[1] The tax deferral can be permanent if the stocks and securities are held until death by the shareholder. At death, the carryover or substituted basis is stepped-up to its fair market value (FMV) without incurring any income tax liability.

CHARACTERISTICS OF TAXABLE AND TAX-FREE TRANSACTIONS

OBJECTIVE 1
Explain the differences between taxable and tax-free acquisition transactions

Comparison of Taxable and Tax-Free Transactions

One way to illustrate the difference between taxable and tax-free transactions is to compare the tax consequences. For purposes of our discussion, assume that (1) Acquiring Corporation acquires all of the assets and liabilities of Target Corporation and (2) immediately following the acquisition, Target Corporation is liquidated. If Acquiring Corporation uses cash and debt obligations to make the purchase, the acquisition is taxable. If Acquiring Corporation acquires all of Target's assets using its voting stock and long-term debt obligations to effect the transaction, the acquisition is a tax-free reorganization.

Key Point
Determining whether a transaction is taxable or nontaxable is doubly important to Target because it is involved in two taxable exchanges: (1) the exchange between Target and Acquiring and (2) the exchange between Target and Target's shareholders.

Tax Consequences for Target Corporation. Code Sec. 1001(c) indicates that with certain exceptions the entire amount of the gain or loss realized on a sale or exchange must be recognized. All gains and losses realized by Target Corporation on selling its assets are recognized. The character of the recognized gain or loss depends on the nature of the assets that are sold or exchanged.

A tax-free reorganization is one exception to the Sec. 1001(c) general rule. Gains realized by Target Corporation in a tax-free disposition of its assets are recognized equal to the sum of the money plus the FMV of the nonmoney boot property that is received in the reorganization and retained. Losses realized on asset dispositions are not recognized. When Target Corporation is liquidated, it recognizes no gain or loss when making a distribution to its shareholders or creditors of either (1) its stock, stock rights, or obligations, or (2) the stock, stock rights, or obligations of another corporation, which is a party to the reorganization, that are received in the reorganization. It must recognize gain (but not loss) when other property (e.g., nonmoney boot property or property that has been retained by the target corporation) is distributed to a shareholder or creditor.

Self-Study Question
Why would Acquiring want an acquisition to be tax-free if it gets only a carryover basis rather than a step-up in basis for the acquired assets?

Answer
Usually the motivation for an acquisition to be tax-free comes from Target and Target's shareholders. However, two reasons that Acquiring may desire a tax-free acquisition are: (1) Acquiring has no cash to acquire the assets so it must use stock as the consideration for the purchase and (2) Target may have favorable tax attributes (e.g., a NOL) that Acquiring would like to utilize.

Tax Consequences for Acquiring Corporation. Acquiring Corporation does not recognize gain or loss when its stock is issued in exchange for property in either a taxable or tax-free transaction. The assets that are received in a taxable transaction have their tax basis adjusted upward or downward to their acquisition cost. The holding period for the acquired assets commences on the day after the transaction date. If the assets are acquired in a tax-free reorganization, their basis carries over from Target Corporation's books and is increased by any gain recognized by Target Corporation on the exchange. Acquiring Corporation's holding period tacks on to Target Corporation's holding period.

Because a taxable acquisition is treated as a purchase transaction, all of Target Corporation's tax attributes (e.g., a net operating loss (NOL) carryover) disappear when it is liquidated. On the other hand, the tax attributes are acquired in a tax-free reorganization. This difference can be important when Target Corporation has incurred substantial NOLs that have not been used prior to the acquisition.

Tax Consequences for Target Corporation's Shareholders. When Target Corporation is liquidated as part of a taxable acquisition, its shareholders recognize gain or loss from the surrender of their stock. The gain or loss (normally capital in nature) is measured by the difference between the adjusted basis of the shareholder's stock and the FMV of the assets received in the liquidating distribution. A tax-free reorganization requires the shareholder to recognize gain only to the extent that boot

TOPIC REVIEW 7-1

Comparison of Taxable and Tax-Free Asset Acquisitions

Variable	Taxable Acquisition	Tax-free Reorganization
1. Consideration employed to effect acquisition	Primarily cash and debt instruments; may involve some stock of the acquiring corporation or its parent corporation	Primarily stock and securities of the acquiring corporation or its parent corporation
2. Target Corporation		
a. Amount of gain or loss	All gains and losses are recognized	Gain realized on an asset transfer is recognized only when boot property is received and retained by the target corporation. Gain may be recognized on the distribution of boot property or other property that has been retained by the target corporation.
b. Character of gain or loss	Depends on nature of each asset transferred or distributed	Depends on nature of each asset transferred or distributed.
c. Recapture provisions	Sec. 1245 or 1250 gains are recaptured	Secs. 1245 or 1250 do not apply.
3. Acquiring Corporation		
a. Gain or loss when stock is issued for property	None recognized	None recognized
b. Basis of acquired assets	Cost	Carryover from target corporation
c. Holding period of acquired assets	Commences on day after the transaction date	Includes holding period of the target corporation
d. Acquisition of target corporation's tax attributes	No	Yes
e. Accounting for the acquisition	"Purchase" accounting is generally used	"Pooling" accounting is generally used; transaction may require that purchase accounting be used.
4. Shareholders of Target Corporation		
a. Amount of gain or loss	Realized gain or loss is recognized	Gain is recognized to the extent of boot received; realized losses are not recognized.
b. Character of gain or loss	Capital gain	Dividend income and/or capital gain
c. Basis of stock and securities received	Cost; generally FMV of stock, securities, or property received	Carries over from the stock and securities surrendered
d. Holding period of stock and securities received	Commences on day after the transaction date	Carries over from the stock and securities surrendered

is received. A pro rata distribution of the boot generally causes the gain to be taxed as a dividend. A nonpro rata distribution of boot can permit the gain to be taxed as a capital gain. In a taxable acquisition, the shareholder may receive some Acquiring Corporation's stock, securities, or other property. These assets take a basis equal to their FMV. Most of the consideration received in a tax-free reorganization is stock or securities of Acquiring Corporation. The stocks and securities that are received take a carryover basis that references the basis of the Target Corporation stocks and securities that were surrendered.

Accounting for the Acquisition. Not all of the variables used in choosing between taxable or tax-free acquisitions relate to the tax consequences. A taxable acquisition generally is reported for financial accounting purposes using "purchase" accounting.[2] A tax-free reorganization generally is reported by using the "pooling" method. However, because of the stringent pooling requirements, many tax-free reorganizations are not eligible for pooling treatment. These two methods can result in substantial differences in the way Acquiring Corporation reports the prior and future results of the combined activities. These reporting differences can influence how the acquisition transaction is structured.

Topic Review 7-1 presents a comparison of taxable and tax-free asset acquisition transaction.

Additional Comment
For publicly traded companies, the "pooling" method usually is more desirable because it provides a higher net income. Consequently, in the planning of the transaction, qualifying for a particular financial accounting treatment may be more important than the tax consequences.

TAXABLE ACQUISITION TRANSACTIONS

OBJECTIVE 2
Determine the tax consequences of taxable acquisition transactions

Taxable acquisition transactions can be divided into two major categories:

- Purchase of the target corporation's stock
- Purchase of the target corporation's assets

The asset acquisition transaction can occur directly by having the acquiring corporation purchase the target corporation's assets or indirectly by a purchase of the target corporation's stock that is followed by maintaining the target corporation as a subsidiary corporation or by an actual or a deemed liquidation of the target corporation. The tax ramifications of the actual and deemed liquidation transactions were discussed earlier in Chapter 6. The tax ramifications of taxable stock and asset purchase transactions from both the buyer and seller's points of view are examined below.

Stock Acquisitions

The stock acquisition is the simplest of the acquisition transactions. The gain recognized on the sale receives capital gain treatment if the stock is a capital asset in the seller's hands. If part or all of the consideration is deferred into a later tax year, the seller's gain can be reported using the installment method of accounting.[3] If part of the total consideration received by the seller of the stock represents an agreement with the purchaser not to compete for a specified time period, the consideration received for the agreement is taxed as ordinary income.[4]

The purchaser's basis for the stock is its acquisition cost.[5] The target corporation's basis for its assets does not change as a result of the stock sale. Any payment for the

---

[2] For a discussion of the purchase and pooling methods of accounting, see F.A. Beams, *Advanced Accounting*, 4th ed. (Englewood Cliffs, N.J.: Prentice Hall, 1988), Chap. 1.
[3] Sec. 453.
[4] The purchaser can deduct any amounts paid to the seller with respect to the agreement not to compete.
[5] Sec. 1012.

stock that is in excess of the book value of the net assets of the acquired company cannot be reflected in a stepped-up basis for the assets. Any potential for depreciation recapture that exists on the transaction date stays with the target corporation's assets and is, therefore, assumed by the purchaser. If the target corporation has loss or credit carryovers, these carryovers are subject to special limitations following an acquisition where more than 50 percentage point change in stock ownership occurs (see pages 7-38 through 7-41).

Example 7-1 ■

Key Point

In Example 7-1, the built-in gain in Target's assets is not recognized in a stock acquisition. However, Target's assets are not stepped-up in basis even though A Corporation pays $300,000 for the Target stock.

Target Corporation's stock is owned equally by Ann, Bob, and Cathy. Acquiring Corporation extends a tender offer whereby it will purchase the Target stock at a price of $50 per share. Each shareholder agrees to tender their 2,000 shares of Target stock to Acquiring Corporation. The tendered shares were acquired 6 years ago by Ann, Bob, and Cathy at a price of $10 per share. At the time of the sale, Target's assets have an adjusted basis of $280,000 and a FMV of $400,000. Its liabilities are $100,000. Ann, Bob, and Cathy must each report an $80,000 long-term capital gain ([$50 − $10] × 2,000 shares) on the sale. Acquiring Corporation takes a $300,000 basis for the stock. Target Corporation becomes a wholly-owned subsidiary of Acquiring Corporation and does not adjust the basis of its assets as a result of the sale unless a Sec. 338 deemed liquidation election is made (see Chapter 6). ■

Key Point

In a stock acquisition, only the shareholders of Target recognize gain. In an asset acquisition, both Target and Target's shareholders may recognize gain. As Examples 7-1 and 7-2 illustrate, the stock acquisition generates $240,000 of gain, whereas the asset acquisition generates $319,200 of gain. However, the basis in Target's assets are stepped-up to $400,000. Which is the better result depends upon the comparative marginal tax rates of Target and Target's shareholders.

Asset Acquisitions

The asset acquisition is not a difficult transaction for the acquiring and target corporations to accomplish. The sale transaction is reported by determining the gain or loss recognized on the sale of each individual asset. Sales of depreciable assets (e.g., Sec. 1245 and 1250 property) result in previously claimed depreciation being recaptured.

The purchaser's bases for the assets are their acquisition cost.[6] The purchaser can claim depreciation based upon the property's total acquisition cost.

A taxable asset acquisition offers the purchaser two major advantages. First, a significant portion of the acquisition can be debt-financed, whereas the tax-free reorganization requirements either restrict or prohibit the use of debt. The interest expense that is incurred with respect to the debt is deductible for tax purposes. Second, only those assets and liabilities that are designated in the purchase-sale agreement are acquired. The purchaser need not acquire all or substantially all of the target corporation's assets, as is the case when the target corporation's stock is acquired in either a taxable transaction or a tax-free reorganization or when an asset-for-stock tax-free reorganization takes place. Similarly, only those liabilities that are specified in the purchase-sale agreement are assumed by the purchaser. Contingent or unknown liabilities remain the responsibility of the seller.

The target corporation may be liquidated after the asset sale takes place. The target corporation recognizes gain or loss with respect to the assets that are sold. Any properties that are retained by the target corporation are distributed to the shareholders as part of the liquidation. The liquidating corporation must recognize gain or loss at the time the distribution occurs as if such properties were instead sold. The target corporation's shareholders report their gain or loss on the liquidation as capital gain or loss.

[6] Ibid.

Example 7-2 ■ Assume the same facts as in Example 7-1, except that Acquiring Corporation instead purchases the assets and liabilities of Target Corporation for $250,000 of Acquiring stock (5,000 shares × $50 per share) plus $50,000 of money. Target Corporation must recognize a $120,000 gain ([$250,000 + $50,000 + $100,000] − $280,000 basis) on the sale. The character of the gains and losses recognized depends upon the nature of the individual properties that are sold. Assuming a 34% marginal corporate tax rate, Target's income tax liability on the gain is $40,800 ($120,000 × 0.34). Acquiring Corporation takes a $400,000 basis for the assets that are acquired. Ann, Bob, and Cathy each report a $66,400 capital gain {0.333 × ([$250,000 + $50,000 − $40,800] −$60,000 basis)} upon the liquidation. This capital gain is smaller than in Example 7-1 because of the need for Target Corporation to recognize a gain when the assets were sold. Ann, Bob, and Cathy will take a $50 basis for each share of Acquiring stock held. ■

TAX-FREE REORGANIZATIONS

OBJECTIVE 3
Explain the types of tax-free reorganizations

Types of Reorganizations

Section 368(a)(1) authorizes seven types of reorganizations. Generally, tax practitioners refer to the specific type of reorganization by the subparagraph of Sec. 368(a)(1) that contains its definition. For example, a merger transaction is referred to as a *"Type A"* reorganization because it is defined in Sec. 368(a)(1)(A). The seven types of reorganizations can also be classified according to the nature of the transaction, with the most common forms being acquisitive transactions and divisive transactions. An **acquisitive reorganization** is a transaction where the acquiring corporation obtains part or all of the assets of a target (or transferor) corporation. Types A, B, C, D, and G reorganizations can be classified as acquisitive transactions. A **divisive reorganization** is a transaction in which part of a transferor corporation's assets are transferred to a second corporation that is controlled by either the transferor or its shareholders. The controlled (or transferee) corporation's stock or securities that are received in exchange for the assets are distributed as part of a reorganization plan to the transferor corporation's shareholders. The transferor corporation can either remain in existence or be liquidated. If the transferor corporation remains in existence, its assets end up being divided between at least two corporations. Types D and G reorganizations can be either acquisitive or divisive transactions.

Two reorganization forms are neither acquisitive or divisive. Types E and F reorganizations involve a single corporation that does *not* acquire additional assets or does *not* transfer a portion of its assets to a transferee corporation. The Type E reorganization—a recapitalization—involves changes to a corporation's capital structure. Type F reorganizations—a change in identity, legal form, or state of incorporation—may involve the transfer of the assets of an existing corporation to a new corporation, but the shareholders of the transferor corporation generally retain the same equity interest in the transferee corporation.

Not all reorganization transactions fit neatly into one of the seven classifications. In fact, some reorganizations may satisfy the requirements for two or more of the classifications. If this occurs, the Code or the IRS generally determines which reorganization rules prevail. In other transactions, a reorganization may satisfy the

Typical Misconception
For an acquisition to qualify for tax-free treatment, the transaction must be a reorganization. The term *reorganization* includes only those transactions specifically enumerated in Sec. 368. Other transactions that may constitute reorganizations in a more general context are not considered tax-free reorganizations.

Typical Misconception
One perplexing aspect of the tax-free reorganization provisions is the overlap between the different statutory reorganizations. One transaction can often qualify as more than one type of reorganization.

TAX CONSEQUENCES OF REORGANIZATIONS

OBJECTIVE 4
Determine the tax consequences of a tax-free reorganization to the target corporation

This portion of the chapter examines the tax consequences of a tax-free reorganization to the target (or transferor) corporation, the acquiring (or transferee) corporation, and the shareholders and security holders.[7]

Target or Transferor Corporation

Additional Comment
Since most of the asset reorganizations require Target to liquidate, gain is not usually recognized on the exchange between Acquiring and Target.

Recognition of Gain or Loss on Asset Transfer. Section 361(a) prevents the target corporation from having to recognize gain or loss on any exchange of property that occurs as part of a tax-free reorganization where solely stock or securities of another corporation that is a party to the reorganization (also known as nonrecognition property) is received. No gain is recognized under Sec. 361(b) if the target corporation also receives money or nonmoney boot property as part of the reorganization and it distributes such property to its shareholders or creditors. The realized gain is recognized equal to the amount of money plus the FMV of any nonmoney boot property received in the exchange that is not distributed. Since most acquisitive and divisive reorganizations require the target or transferor corporation to be liquidated, gain is not generally recognized as a result of the target corporation's retention of boot property.

Example 7-3

Self-Study Question
Target realizes a $100,000 gain on the exchange with Acquiring. If Target receives $120,000 of boot property, how much gain must Target recognize if it distributes only $100,000 of the boot property to its shareholders?

Answer
$20,000. The rule states that Target must recognize any realized gain to the extent that boot property is not distributed. The fact that the realized gain is $100,000 and $100,000 of boot is distributed is not the relevant issue.

Target Corporation transfers assets having a $175,000 adjusted basis to Acquiring Corporation in exchange for $400,000 of Acquiring common stock as part of a tax-free reorganization. Target realizes a $225,000 gain ($400,000 − $175,000) on the asset transfer. Because no boot is received by Target, none of the gain must be recognized. Even if Target instead receives $350,000 of Acquiring common stock and $50,000 of money, no gain is recognized by Target if the boot property is distributed to its shareholders.

Depreciation Recapture. The depreciation recapture rules of Secs. 1245 and 1250 do not override the nonrecognition of gain or loss rules of Sec. 361.[8] The recapture potential that accrues prior to the asset transfer carries over to the acquiring

---

[7] The corporation that transfers its assets as part of a reorganization is referred to as either a **target** or **transferor corporation.** The term *target corporation* is generally used with an acquisitive reorganization where substantially all of a corporation's assets are acquired by the acquiring corporation. The term *transferor corporation* is used with divisive and other reorganizations where only part of a corporation's assets are transferred to a transferee corporation and the transferor corporation may remain in existence. Tax law provisions are generally applied the same to target or transferor corporations and acquiring or transferee corporations, therefore, only a single reference to the target or acquiring corporation is generally provided in connection with an explanation. (See page 2-34 for a definition of a security item.) The owner of a security is known as a **security holder.**

[8] Secs. 1245(b)(3) and 1250(d)(3). Similar provisions are found as part of the other recapture rules.

Key Point
Section 357(c) gain is recognized by Target even though it may distribute all of the boot property received in the transaction.

Typical Misconception
Often taxpayers do not realize that Sec. 361 applies to two exchanges. Section 361(a) applies to the exchange between Acquiring and Target (which has already been discussed). Section 361(c) deals with the exchange between Target and Target's shareholders. Therefore, Target is the only party to the reorganization that may recognize two separate gains.

Self-Study Question
How can Target distribute appreciated boot property to its shareholders if Target receives a FMV basis in all such property received from Acquiring?

corporation and is recognized at the time the acquiring corporation sells or exchanges the assets in a taxable transaction.[9]

Assumption of Liabilities. Neither the acquiring corporation's assumption of the target corporation's liabilities nor the acquisition of the target corporation's property subject to a liability will trigger the recognition of gain on the asset transfer. Section 357(c) requires the target corporation to recognize gain if the sum of the liabilities assumed or acquired exceeds the total adjusted bases of the properties that are transferred *and* the tax-free reorganization is either an acquisitive or a divisive Type D reorganization. An additional explanation of the Sec. 357(c) rules is presented in connection with the discussion of the acquisitive Type D reorganization.

Recognition of Gain or Loss on Distribution of Stock and Securities. No gain or loss is recognized by the target corporation when it distributes either (1) its stock, stock rights, or obligations or (2) any stock, stock rights, and obligations of a party to a reorganization that are received in the reorganization to its shareholders or creditors as part of the plan of reorganization (see page 7-44 for an explanation of a plan of reorganization).[10] Distributions of nonmoney boot property made pursuant to the reorganization plan require the recognition of gain (but not loss) in the same manner as if such property were sold by the target corporation at its FMV.[11] Normally the amount of the gain that is recognized when boot property is distributed is small because of the short amount of time that passes between when it is received from the acquiring corporation (and takes a basis equal to its FMV) and when it is distributed to a shareholder or security holder. If any property distributed to a shareholder or creditor is subject to a liability, or if the shareholder or creditor assumes such a liability, then for purposes of determining gain or loss, the FMV of the property shall be treated as not less than the amount of such liability.[12]

Example 7-4 ■

Answer
If the property appreciates in the hands of Target before it is distributed, gain will result. In addition, Target may retain some of its own assets and distribute these assets to its shareholders. Consistent with the repeal of the General Utilities doctrine, this will also result in gain being recognized.

Target Corporation transfers all of its assets and liabilities to Acquiring Corporation as part of its being merged into Acquiring (a Type A reorganization). To effect the merger, Acquiring transfers $300,000 of its common stock and $100,000 of money to Target in exchange for Target's assets. Target's basis for the assets is $250,000. Target realizes a $150,000 gain on the asset transfer ([$300,000 + $100,000] − $250,000). None of this gain is recognized by Target, even though boot is received, since Target must be liquidated as part of the merger transaction. Target's distribution of the Acquiring stock to its shareholders as part of the reorganization does not trigger the recognition of any gain by Target. ■

Distributions made by the target or transferor corporation pursuant to the reorganization plan carry with them an exemption from the gain or loss recognition requirements of Secs. 311, 336, and 337 (see Chapters 4 and 6).[13]

Acquiring or Transferee Corporation

OBJECTIVE 5
Determine the tax consequences of a tax-free reorganization to the acquiring corporation

Amount of Gain or Loss Recognized. Section 1032 prevents the acquiring corporation from recognizing gain or loss when it receives money or other property in exchange for its stock as part of a tax-free reorganization. Similarly, no gain or loss is

---

[9] Reg. Secs. 1.1245-4(c) and 1.1250-3(c).
[10] Secs. 361(c)(1)-(c)(3).
[11] Sec. 361(c).
[12] Sec. 361(c)(2)(C).
[13] Sec. 361(c)(4).

recognized when a corporation receives money or other property in exchange for its securities as part of a tax-free reorganization.

Basis of Acquired Property. Section 362(b) requires property acquired in a tax-free reorganization to assume the basis of the property in the target corporation's hands, increased by the amount of gain recognized by the target corporation on the exchange. Since no gain or loss is generally recognized on the asset transfer, no step-up in basis is ordinarily obtained.

Self-Study Question
Since Acquiring is merely purchasing assets, can Acquiring ever recognize gain or loss in the transaction?

Example 7-5 ■

Answer
Yes. If Acquiring uses nonmoney boot property, gain or loss will be recognized to the extent of the built-in gain or loss in such property [Prop. Reg. Sec. 1.1032-2(c)].

Assume the same facts as in Example 7-4. Acquiring's basis for the acquired properties is the same as Target Corporation's basis, or $250,000. ■

Holding Period of Acquired Property. The acquiring corporation's holding period for the acquired properties includes the period of time that the target corporation held the properties.[14]

Shareholders and Security Holders

OBJECTIVE 6

Determine the tax consequences of a tax-free reorganization to the target corporation's shareholders and security holders

Amount of Gain or Loss Recognized. Section 354(a) requires that no gain or loss be recognized if stock or securities in a corporation that is a party to a reorganization are, in pursuance of a plan of reorganization, exchanged solely for stock or securities in the same corporation, or for stock or securities of another corporation that is a party to the reorganization. The receipt of property other than stock or securities does not automatically disqualify the transaction from tax-free treatment. Section 356(a) requires that the shareholder or security holder recognize gain to the extent of the lesser of (1) the realized gain or (2) the amount of money received plus the FMV of any property (other than money) received. Gain is thus recognized to the extent that nonqualifying property is received that does not represent a continuation of the former equity interest.

Example 7-6 ■

Additional Comment
Acquiring may increase its basis in the assets received only by the gain recognized by Target on its exchange with Acquiring. Any gain recognized by Target on its exchange with Target's shareholders is not reflected anywhere.

Typical Misconception
Section 354 is applied to each shareholder individually. Therefore, it is possible for one shareholder to recognize gain while another shareholder recognizes no gain.

Brian exchanges 1,000 shares of Target Corporation stock having a $13,000 basis for Acquiring Corporation stock having a $28,000 FMV as part of a tax-free reorganization. Brian's realized gain is $15,000 ($28,000 − $13,000), none of which is recognized. If Brian had instead received $25,000 of Acquiring stock and $3,000 of cash, his realized gain would remain $15,000, but Brian must now recognize a $3,000 gain. ■

With some limitations, the general rule of Sec. 354(a) permits a tax-free exchange of stocks and securities. The receipt of securities is completely tax-free only if the principal amount of the securities that are surrendered equals or exceeds the principal amount of the securities that are received. If the principal amount of the securities received exceeds the principal amount of the securities surrendered, the FMV of the "excess" principal amount of the securities that are received constitutes boot.[15] If no securities are surrendered by the shareholder or security holder, the FMV of the entire principal amount of the securities received constitutes boot. Determination of the FMV of the boot securities was explained in connection with the discussion of distributions of stock and securities of controlled corporations contained in Chapter 4.

---

[14] Sec. 1223(1).
[15] Secs. 354(a)(2) and 356(d)(2)(B).

Tax Consequences of Reorganizations • 7-11

Key Point

As with other nonrecognition provisions, a shareholder's recognized gain is the lesser of his realized gain or boot (money or other property) received.

Character of the Recognized Gain. Section 356(a)(2) requires that the recognized gain be characterized as dividend income if the receipt of the boot property has the same effect as the distribution of a dividend. The amount of dividend income that is recognized equals the lesser of (1) the shareholder's recognized gain or (2) the shareholder's ratable share of the target corporation's current and accumulated earnings and profits (E&P). Any additional gain that must be recognized is reported as a capital gain.

The Sec. 302(b) stock redemption rules are employed to test whether the exchange has the effect of a dividend distribution.[16] (See Chapter 4 for a review of the Sec. 302(b) rules.) Tax-free reorganizations do not generally involve actual redemptions of the stock of the target company's shareholders. Instead, the shareholder is treated as having exchanged his target corporation stock in a tax-free reorganization solely for stock in the acquiring corporation. After having received the acquiring corporation's stock, a hypothetical redemption of a portion of the acquiring corporation's stock occurs. Capital gain treatment results only if the boot that is received causes the hypothetical redemption to be substantially disproportionate, a complete termination, or not essentially equivalent to a dividend.

Application of the dividend equivalency test that is used when boot is received in a tax-free reorganization is illustrated in the following example.

Example 7-7 ■

Self-Study Question

In addition to receiving stock in Acquiring, shareholder Sue receives securities with a FMV of $120,000 and a principal amount of $100,000. In the exchange, Sue surrenders securities of Target with a FMV and principal amount of $80,000. Is Sue treated as having received any boot?

Answer

Yes. $100,000 − $80,000 = $20,000 of excess principal amount received. The boot received is $24,000. This amount represents the FMV of the excess principal amount ($20,000/$100,000 × $120,000).

Betty owns all 60 of the outstanding shares of Fisher Corporation stock. Fisher Corporation is merged with Gulf Corporation in a tax-free reorganization, with Betty receiving 35 shares of Gulf stock worth $350,000 and Gulf cash in the amount of $250,000. The remaining Gulf stock is owned by 4 individuals each of whom owns 25 shares of stock worth $250,000. The Fisher stock held by Betty has a basis of $200,000. Fisher and Gulf Corporations have E&P balances of $300,000 and $500,000, respectively, at the time of the reorganization. Betty's realized gain is $400,000 ([$350,000 + $250,000]− $200,000), of which $250,000 must be recognized due to the receipt of money that is treated as boot under Sec. 356. Since the Fisher stock is worth $600,000 and the Gulf stock is worth $10,000 per share ($350,000 ÷ 35), the Fisher stock is treated as having been exchanged for 60 shares of Gulf stock. After this exchange, Betty owns 60 of the 160 shares of Gulf stock that are supposedly outstanding immediately after the stock-for-stock swap, or 37.5% of the outstanding Gulf stock. Since the 60 shares of Gulf stock are worth $600,000, the money that Betty receives is treated as having been exchanged for 25 shares ($250,000 ÷ $10,000 per share) of Gulf stock. Because Betty owns 37.5% of the Gulf stock before the hypothetical redemption and 25.92% (35 shares ÷ 135 shares) after the hypothetical redemption, the $250,000 gain is characterized as capital gain under the substantially disproportionate redemption rules. ■

The Sec. 302(b) test would be applied in the same manner if securities were received in the reorganization. In such a case, the boot portion of the transaction would equal the FMV of the "excess" principal amount that is received by the shareholder or security holder.

Whether capital gain treatment is available for boot received in a reorganization depends upon the relative sizes of the target and acquiring corporations. If the

---

[16] *CIR v. Donald E. Clark*, 63 AFTR 2d 89-1437, 89-1 USTC ¶ 9230 (USSC, 1989), aff'g. 60 AFTR 2d 87-5160, 87-2 USTC ¶ 9504 (4th Cir., 1987). Because the stock being redeemed in the hypothetical redemption is that of the acquiring corporation, the amount of dividend income recognized by the shareholder if the Sec. 302(b) exception does not apply is apparently based upon the shareholder's ratable share of the acquiring corporation's E&P.

acquiring corporation is larger than the target corporation, then generally the Sec. 302(b)(2) [substantially disproportionate redemption] or Sec. 301(b)(1) [not essentially equivalent to a dividend] rules will provide for capital gain treatment. If the acquiring corporation is smaller than the target corporation, it is possible that the target corporation's shareholder may be considered as having received dividend income or a combination of dividend income or capital gain (e.g., if the boot received exceeds the shareholder's ratable share of E&P).

Capital gain treatment may be preferred by individual shareholders for the recognized gain since a 28% maximum tax rate applies to long-term capital gains starting in 1991. Dividend income treatment may be preferred by a corporate shareholder since they can claim a 70%, 80%, or 100% dividends-received deduction to reduce their tax burden. In addition, capital gains that are recognized in the reorganization are permitted to offset capital losses recognized by corporate and noncorporate shareholders in other transactions. Finally, Sec. 453(f)(6)(C) permits a corporate or noncorporate shareholder involved in a tax-free reorganization to use the installment method of accounting to defer the reporting of the recognized gain, provided the gain is not characterized as a dividend.[17]

> **Self-Study Question**
>
> *From the point of view of the Target shareholder, what is the preferable answer to the Clark case?*
>
> **Answer**
>
> *It depends. If the Target shareholder is a corporate shareholder, the best result is generally going to be a dividend because of the dividends-received deduction. Currently, with a small differential rate for capital gains, the Target shareholder who is an individual will have a small preference for capital gain treatment.*

Basis of Stocks and Securities Received. The basis of the stocks and securities that are received by the target corporation's shareholders and security holders is determined according to the Sec. 358 rules that were introduced in Chapter 2. The basis of these properties is determined as follows:

```
         Adjusted basis of the property exchanged
Plus:    Any gain recognized on the exchange
Minus:   Money received in the exchange
         FMV of any property (other than money) received in
           the exchange
         ─────────────────────────────────────────────────
         Basis of the nonrecognition property received
```

If no gain or loss is recognized by the shareholder or security holder, the stocks and securities will take a carryover basis from the stocks and securities that are exchanged. If a gain must be recognized, the basis of the stocks and securities that are exchanged is increased by the amount of such gain and then reduced by the amount of money plus the FMV of any nonmoney boot property that is received in the reorganization. The basis of any nonmoney boot property that is received is its FMV.

> **Key Point**
>
> *When a reorganization is tax-free, shareholders defer their realized gain. Consequently, they take a substituted basis in the new nonrecognition property received (i.e., any deferred gain is reflected in the basis of the nonrecognition property received).*

Example 7-8 ■ Ken owns Target Corporation stock having a $10,000 adjusted basis. As part of a tax-free reorganization involving Target and Acquiring Corporations, Ken exchanges his Target stock for $12,000 of Acquiring stock and $4,000 of Acquiring securities. Ken realizes a $6,000 gain ([$12,000 + $4,000] − $10,000), of which $4,000 must be recognized. The basis of the Acquiring securities is $4,000. The basis of the Acquiring stock is $10,000 ($10,000 basis of Target stock + $4,000 gain recognized − $4,000 FMV of Acquiring securities). ■

When the target corporation owns a single class of stock (or a single class of securities) and ends up owning two or more classes of stock and/or securities as a result of a tax-free reorganization, the total basis for the nonrecognition property determined above must be allocated between the stocks and/or the securities owned in proportion to the relative FMVs of the classes.[18]

---

[17] *King Enterprises, Inc. v. U.S.*, 24 AFTR 2d 69-5866, 69-2 USTC ¶ 9720 (Ct. Cls., 1969).
[18] Reg. Sec. 1.358-2(a)(2)-(4).

Holding Period. The holding period of the stocks and securities that are nonrecognition property carries over from the stocks and securities that are surrendered. The holding period for boot property commences on the day following the transaction date.[19]

Topic Review 7-2 presents a summary of the tax consequences of a tax-free reorganization to the target corporation, the acquiring corporation, and the target corporation's shareholders.

TOPIC REVIEW 7-2

Tax Consequences of a Tax-Free Reorganization

Target Corporation

1. No gain or loss is recognized by the target corporation on the asset transfer except to the extent that money or other boot property is received and retained by the target corporation. Generally this does not occur since the target corporation is usually liquidated.
2. The character of any gain or loss that is recognized depends on the nature of the asset transferred.
3. The acquiring corporation's assumption or acquisition of target corporation liabilities does not trigger the recognition of gain on the asset transfer except to the extent that Sec. 357(c) applies to "excess" liability situations involving Type D reorganizations.
4. No gain or loss is recognized by the target corporation when it distributes qualified property (i.e., stock and securities) to its shareholders and security holders. Gain or loss may be recognized when boot property or retained assets are distributed to shareholders or security holders.

Acquiring Corporation

1. The acquiring corporation does not recognize gain or loss when it receives money or property in exchange for its stock or debt obligations.
2. The basis of the acquired property equals its basis in the transferor's hands increased by any gain recognized by the transferor.
3. The acquiring corporation's holding period for the acquired properties includes the transferor's holding period.

Shareholders and Security Holders

1. No gain or loss is recognized if only stock is received. Gain (but not loss) is recognized when money, excess securities, or other boot property is received. The amount of the recognized gain equals the lesser of (1) the realized gain or (2) the amount of money plus the FMV of any nonmoney boot property received.
2. The character of the gain recognized is determined by applying the Sec. 302(b) rules to the acquiring corporation. Dividend income recognized, however, cannot exceed the shareholder's ratable share of the acquiring corporation's E&P.
3. The total basis of the stocks and securities received equals the adjusted basis of the property exchanged plus any gain recognized on the exchange minus the sum of the money and FMV of nonmoney boot property received. This basis is allocated to the stocks and securities received based on their relative FMVs. The basis of boot property is its FMV.
4. The holding period of stocks and securities received carries over from the stocks and securities surrendered. The holding period for boot property commences on the day following the exchange date.

[19] Sec. 1223(1).

ACQUISITIVE REORGANIZATIONS

This portion of the chapter is devoted to the Types A, B, C, D, and G acquisitive reorganizations. Each of these types of reorganizations is explained below. A summary of their requirements is presented in Topic Review 7-3 on pages 7-16 and 7-17.

Type A Reorganization

OBJECTIVE 7
Explain the requirements of a Type A reorganization

The Code permits four kinds of **Type A reorganizations:** mergers, consolidations, triangular mergers, and reverse triangular mergers. Each of these transactions is described below, although the first two are the most important.

Key Point
The "A" reorganization is unique in comparison to the other statutory reorganizations because state law, rather than federal law, determines if a transaction qualifies as a statutory merger.

Merger or Consolidation. A Type A reorganization is a **merger** or a **consolidation** that satisfies the corporation laws of the United States, a state, or the District of Columbia.[20] Figure 7-1 illustrates a merger. Two types of mergers have been accepted by the IRS. The first involves the acquiring corporation transferring its stock, securities, and other consideration (boot) to the target corporation in exchange for its assets and liabilities. The acquiring corporation stock and securities and other consideration received by the target corporation are distributed to its shareholders and security holders in exchange for their target corporation stock and securities. The target corporation then goes out of existence. This type of merger is illustrated in Figure 7-1. The second type of merger requires the acquiring corporation to exchange its stock, securities, and other consideration directly for the stock and securities held by the target corporation's shareholders and security holders. The acquiring corporation then liquidates the target corporation and acquires all of its assets and liabilities.[21]

A consolidation, illustrated in Figure 7-2, involves two or more corporations having their assets acquired by a new corporation. The stock, securities, and other consideration transferred by the acquiring corporation is distributed by each target corporation to its shareholders and security holders pursuant to its liquidation in exchange for their stock and securities. This type of consolidation is illustrated in Figure 7-2. As with a merger, an alternative form of consolidation, in which the acquiring corporation directly transfers its stock, securities, and other consideration to the target corporations' shareholders and security holders in exchange for their stock and securities is permitted. In this case, each target corporation is then liquidated with the acquiring corporation receiving all of its assets and liabilities.

Key Point
The Type A reorganization is the most flexible reorganization with respect to the type of consideration that must be used. The only requirement is the continuity of interest doctrine, which will be discussed later in the chapter.

REQUIREMENTS FOR MERGERS AND CONSOLIDATIONS. The Type A reorganization provides the acquiring corporation with the greatest flexibility in selecting the consideration to be used to effect the reorganization. The Internal Revenue Code places no restrictions on the types of consideration that can be used in a merger. The IRS interpretation of the continuity of interest judicial doctrine for a tax-free reorganization requires stock of the acquiring corporation to be at least 50% of the total consideration used.[22] The stock that is used can be voting stock, nonvoting

---

[20] Sec. 368(a)(1)(A) and Reg. Sec. 1.368-2(b)(1).
[21] Rev. Rul. 69-6, 1969-1 C.B. 104.
[22] Rev. Proc. 77-37, 1977-2 C.B. 568, Sec. 3.02.

Additional Comment

The actual exchange of Acquiring stock for Target stock may be different than the illustrations provided in this chapter. These illustrations represent how the Internal Revenue Code construes the steps in each of the reorganizations. As a practical matter, the exchange of stock between Acquiring and Target is usually performed by an independent stock transfer agent rather than flowing from Acquiring to Target and finally to Target's shareholders.

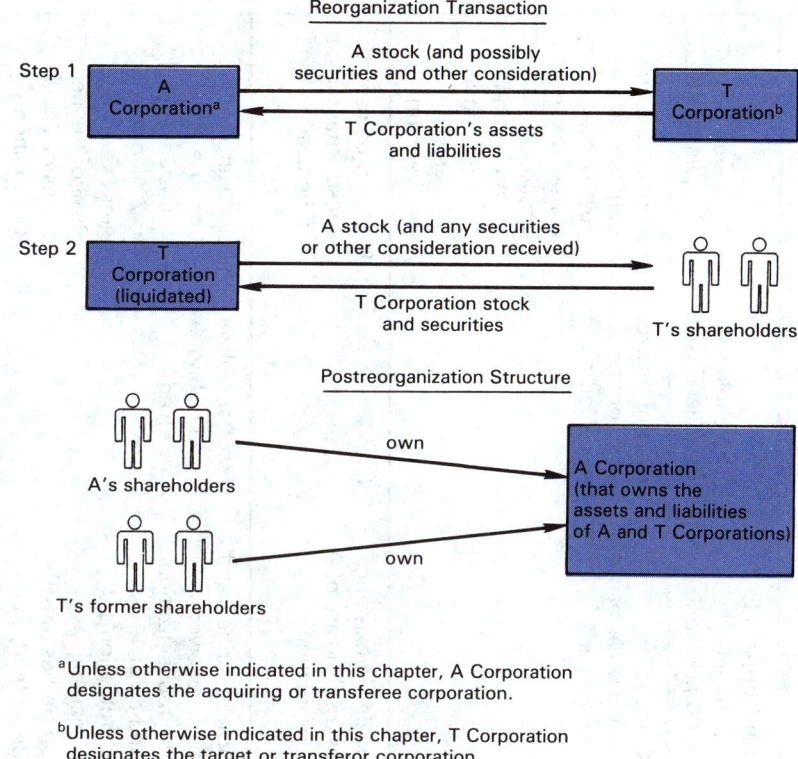

FIGURE 7-1 Type A Reorganization—Merger

stock, or a combination of the two. Either common or preferred stock may be used. The 50% minimum must be met only if the taxpayer desires to obtain a favorable advance ruling regarding the tax consequences of the transaction (see page 7-44).

Additional Comment

Shareholder approval is time consuming, expensive, and not always possible to obtain.

Because a merger or consolidation transaction must comply with state or federal corporation laws, transactions that qualify as mergers or consolidations, and the procedures that must be followed to effect them, vary according to the law of the states in which the acquiring and target corporations are incorporated. Generally, these laws require a favorable vote by a majority of the shareholders of the corporations that are involved in the merger. State law dictates the procedures that must be followed. Where the stock of one or both of the companies is publicly traded, the need to hold a shareholder's meeting, solicit proxies, and obtain the necessary approval may make the procedure both costly and time consuming.

The rights of any dissenting shareholders are also dictated by the state law. These shareholders may have the right to dissent and have their shares valued and purchased for cash. A substantial number of dissenting shareholders may necessitate a large cash outlay in order to purge their interests.

A transaction that fails to satisfy the state laws does not qualify as a merger or consolidation.[23] Generally, this failure causes the acquisition to be a taxable transaction.

ADVANTAGES AND DISADVANTAGES OF A MERGER TRANSACTION. A number of advantages and disadvantages exist with a merger transaction.

---

[23] *Edward H. Russell v. CIR*, 15 AFTR 2d 1107, 65-2 USTC ¶ 9448 (5th Cir., 1965).

TOPIC REVIEW 7-3

Tax-Free Reorganization Summary

Type of Reorganization	Target (T) Corporation Property Acquired	Consideration That Can Be Employed	What Happens to the Target (T) Corporation?	Shareholders' Recognized Gain	Other Requirements
1. A—Merger or consolidation	Assets and liabilities of T Corporation[a]	Stock, securities, and other property of A Corporation[b]	T Corporation liquidates as part of the merger	Lesser of realized gain or boot received	For advance ruling purposes, at least 50% of the consideration employed must be A Corporation stock (continuity of interest requirement)
2. B—Stock for stock	At least 80% of the voting and 80% of the nonvoting T stock	Voting stock of A Corporation	Remains in existence as a subsidiary of A Corporation	None	Boot can be used to cause a transaction to be taxable
3. C—Assets for stock	Substantially all of the assets of T Corporation (and possibly some or all of its liabilities)	Stock, securities, and other property of A Corporation, provided at least 80% of the assets are acquired for voting stock	Stock, securities, and boot received in the reorganization and all of T Corporation's remaining properties must be distributed; as a practical matter, T is usually liquidated	Lesser of realized gain or boot received	For advance ruling purposes, "substantially all" is 70% of the gross assets and 90% of the net assets of T Corporation
4. D—Acquisitive	Substantially all of the assets of T Corporation (and possibly some or all of its liabilities) are acquired by a "controlled" transferee corporation (A Corporation)	Stock, securities, and other property of A Corporation	Stocks, securities, and boot received in the reorganization and all of T Corporation's remaining properties must be distributed; as a practical matter, T is usually liquidated.	Lesser of realized gain or boot received	"Substantially all" is defined as it was for a Type C reorganization; the continuity of interest requirement also applies here for advance ruling purposes; control is defined as 50%

					of the voting power or 50% of the value of A Corporation's stock
5. D—Divisive	Part or all of the assets of T Corporation (and possibly some or all of its liabilities) are transferred to a "controlled" transferee (A Corporation)	Stock, securities, and other property of A Corporation	Stock, securities, and boot received in the reorganization must be distributed; T Corporation may be liquidated, but can remain in existence	Lesser of realized gain or boot received	Transactions can take on three forms—spinoff, split-off or split-up. Control is defined as it was for an acquisitive Type D reorganization.
6. E—Recapitalization	A change to the capital structure of a single corporation (T Corporation) takes place	Stock, securities, and other property of T Corporation	T Corporation remains in existence	Lesser of realized gain or boot received	May involve stock-for-stock, bond-for-bond, bond-for-stock, or stock-for-bond exchanges
7. F—Change in form, identity, or place of organization	Assets or stock of old T Corporation are transferred to a new corporation (new T Corporation)	Stock, securities, and other property of new T Corporation	Old T Corporation is liquidated	Lesser of realized gain or boot received	Must involve only a single operating company.
8. G—Acquisitive or divisive	Part or all of the assets of T Corporation (and possibly some or all of its liabilities) are transferred to another corporation in a Title 11 (bankruptcy) case	Stock, securities, and other property of A Corporation	T Corporation may be liquidated but can remain in existence	Lesser of realized gain or boot received	Stock and securities of A Corporation received by T Corporation must be distributed to its shareholders, security holders, or creditors.

[a] T Corporation refers to the target or transferor corporation.
[b] A Corporation refers to the acquiring or controlled transferee corporation.

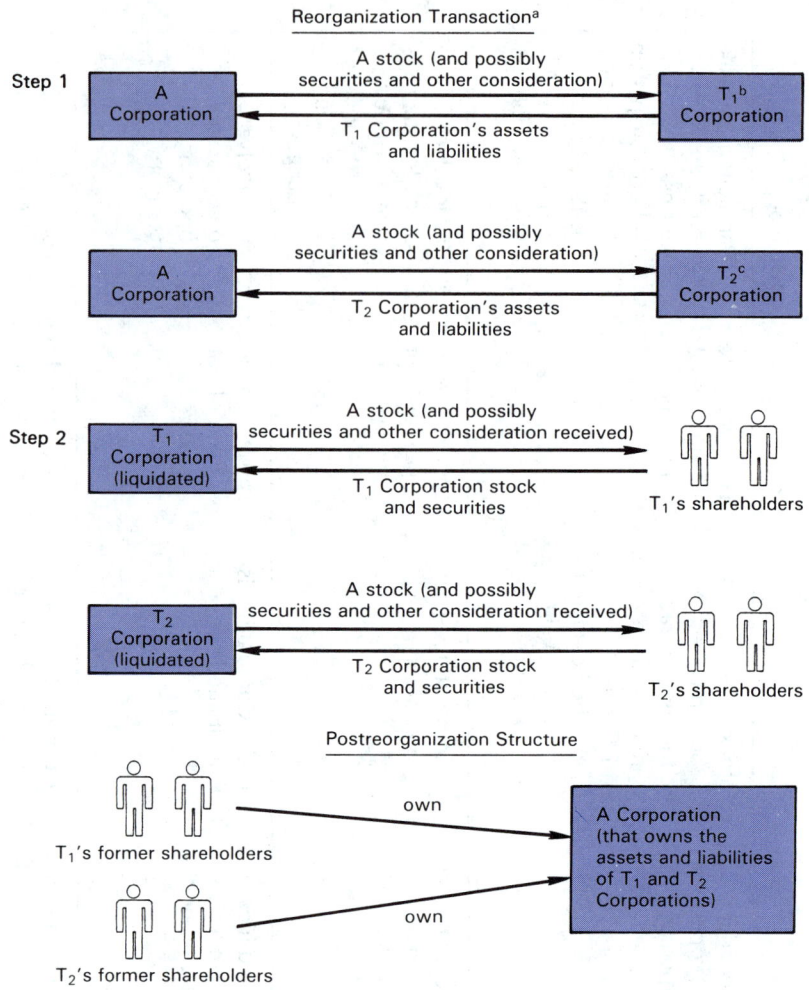

FIGURE 7-2 Type A Reorganization-Consolidation

Advantages:

- A merger allows greater flexibility than other types of reorganizations because there is no restriction that the consideration be solely voting stock as in the case of some other reorganization forms. Money, securities, assumption of liabilities, and other property can be 50% of the consideration used.
- There is no requirement that "substantially all" of the assets of the target corporation be acquired. Dispositions of unwanted assets generally do not prevent a merger from being a tax-free reorganization as in the case of a Type C reorganization.

Disadvantages:

- Compliance with state corporation laws is required. In most states, the shareholders of both the acquiring and target corporations have to approve the plan. Such approvals can take time and can be costly. Dissenting shareholders of both corporations also have the right to have their shares appraised and purchased for cash which may require a substantial cash outlay.

- All liabilities of the target corporation must be assumed including unknown and contingent liabilities.
- The target corporation may have contracts, rights, or other privileges which are nontransferable.

TAX CONSEQUENCES OF A MERGER TRANSACTION. The following example illustrates the tax consequences of a merger transaction.

Example 7-9 ■ Acquiring Corporation acquires all of Target Corporation's assets in a merger transaction that qualifies as a Type A reorganization. Target transfers assets having a FMV and an adjusted basis of $2,000,000 and $1,300,000, respectively, and $400,000 in liabilities to Acquiring in exchange for $1,000,000 of Acquiring's nonvoting preferred stock and $600,000 of Acquiring securities. At the time of the transfer, Acquiring's E&P balance is $1,000,000. Target Corporation distributes the Acquiring stock and securities to its sole shareholder Millie in exchange for all of her Target stock, which has a $175,000 basis. If Millie had received only Acquiring stock in the reorganization, she would have held 12% of the Acquiring stock (in value) immediately after the reorganization. Target realizes a $700,000 gain ([$1,000,000 + $600,000 + $400,000] − $1,300,000) on the asset transfer. None of the gain is recognized by Target. Acquiring takes a $1,300,000 carryover basis for the assets that it receives. No gain is recognized by Target when it distributes the stock and securities to Millie. Millie realizes a $1,425,000 gain on the exchange ([$1,000,000 + $600,000] − $175,000), of which $600,000 must be recognized because of the "excess" securities that are received. Because Millie received only nonvoting preferred stock, the hypothetical redemption of Millie's Acquiring Corporation stock required under the *Clark* decision qualifies as an exchange under Sec. 302(b)(1) as not essentially equivalent to a dividend and the gain is characterized as capital gain. Millie's basis for her Acquiring stock is $175,000 ($175,000 basis of Target stock + $600,000 gain recognized − $600,000 value of securities received). Her basis for the Acquiring securities is their FMV of $600,000. ■

Key Point

Since there is not a "substantially all" requirement in an "A" reorganization, the unwanted assets of Target may be disposed of either before or after the transaction without disqualifying the tax-free reorganization.

The tax-free reorganization rules permit the acquiring corporation to transfer part or all of the assets and liabilities acquired in the merger or consolidation to a controlled subsidiary corporation.[24] The asset transfer does not affect the tax-free nature of the transaction. No gain is recognized by either the parent or subsidiary corporation on the transfer. The bases of the individual assets will carry over to the subsidiary corporation.

Triangular Mergers. **Triangular mergers** are authorized by Sec. 368(a)(2)(D). They are similar to the conventional Type A merger (previously discussed) except that the parent corporation uses a controlled subsidiary corporation to serve as the acquiring corporation. The target corporation is then merged into the subsidiary

---

[24] Sec. 368(a)(2)(C). As defined in Sec. 368(c), **control** requires the parent corporation to own at least 80% of the voting power and 80% of each class of nonvoting stock. The ability to "drop down" the assets that were acquired to a subsidiary corporation without recognizing any gain also applies to Type B, C, and G reorganizations.

Historical Note

Although most state laws allow triangular mergers, the IRS initially ruled that the parent corporation was not a party to the reorganization. This caused the transaction to be taxable. In response to this IRS position, in 1968 and 1971, Congress added the two triangular mergers to Sec. 368's list of tax-free reorganizations.

Key Point

The Sec. 368(a)(2)(D) triangular merger is very popular because the consideration that may be used is still very flexible and yet the parent corporation does not have to assume the actual or contingent liabilities of Target. Rather, these liabilities are assumed by the controlled subsidiary.

corporation using one of the two alternative merger forms described earlier (see Figure 7-3).

Triangular mergers must satisfy the same state law requirements as basic merger transactions. In addition, the stock used to carry out the reorganization is limited to that of the parent corporation. However, the subsidiary corporation's cash and securities can be used as part of the transaction, and the subsidiary corporation can assume the target corporation's liabilities.

THE "SUBSTANTIALLY ALL" REQUIREMENT. The subsidiary corporation must acquire "substantially all" of the target corporation's assets as part of the plan of reorganization. For advance ruling purposes, "substantially all" has been defined by the IRS to be at least 70% of the FMV of the target corporation's gross assets and 90% of the FMV of its net assets.[25]

ADVANTAGES OF A TRIANGULAR MERGER. The tax treatment accorded a triangular merger is the same as for the conventional Type A merger transaction. The triangular merger provides three additional advantages (over the conventional Type A merger):

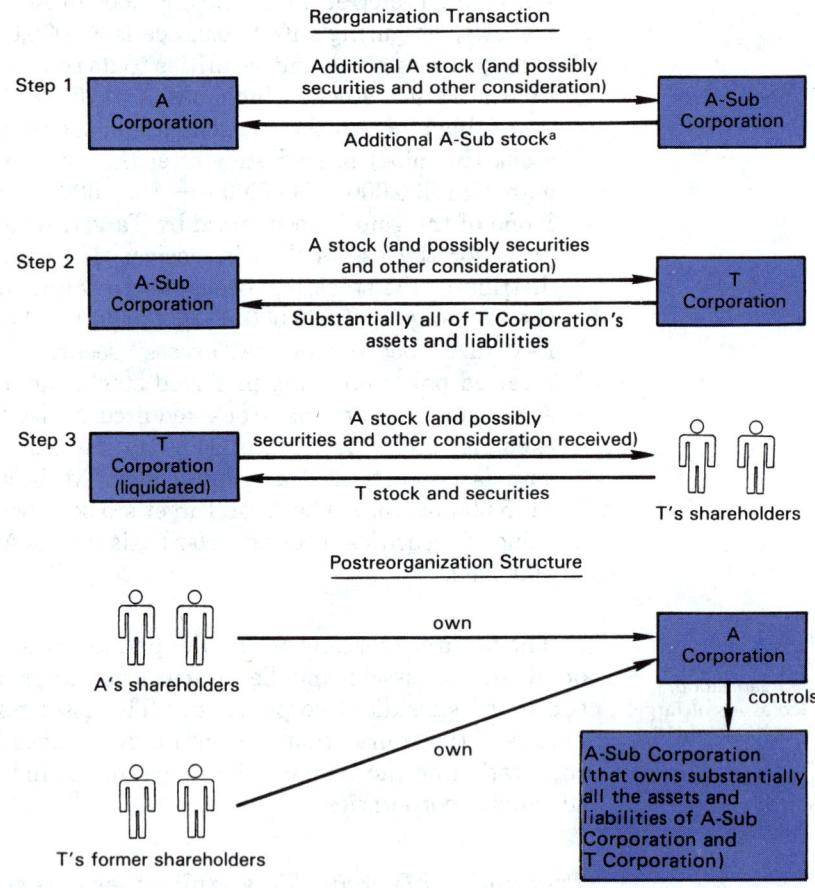

[a] A Corporation must control, as defined in Sec. 368(c), A-Sub Corporation. If A already owns 100% of A-Sub, the A stock may be treated as additional paid-in capital for its shares that are already outstanding.

FIGURE 7-3 Triangular Type A Reorganization

---

[25] Rev. Proc. 77-37, 1977-2 C.B. 568, Sec. 3.01.

- The target corporation's assets and liabilities become the property of the subsidiary corporation. Thus, the parent corporation cannot be held liable for either any liabilities that are not known to the acquiring corporation at the time of the transfer or any contingent liabilities. Creditor claims against the parent corporation's assets are thus minimized.
- Shareholder approval on behalf of the acquiring subsidiary corporation comes from its parent corporation. Thus, if the parent corporation's stock is widely held, the cost of obtaining approval of the shareholders may be reduced.
- The target corporation's shareholders may prefer to receive parent corporation stock because of its increased marketability. By receiving marketable stock, the target corporation's shareholders can sell off a portion of the parent corporation stock over an extended period of time and recognize the gain as if they were using the installment method of accounting.

Key Point
In addition to the "B" reorganization, which will be discussed later, the reverse triangular merger is an acquisitive reorganization that keeps Target in existence.

Reverse Triangular Mergers. **Reverse triangular mergers** are authorized by Sec. 368(a)(2)(E). They are similar to the triangular merger illustrated in Figure 7-3, except that the subsidiary corporation (A-Sub Corporation) is merged into the target corporation (T Corporation), and the target corporation stays alive as a subsidiary of the parent corporation (A Corporation). This type of transaction permits the target corporation to continue its corporate existence. This action may be desirable from a business standpoint (e.g., to maintain a special authorization or a special license owned by the target corporation).

OBJECTIVE 8
Explain the requirements of a Type C reorganization

Type C Reorganization

A **Type C reorganization** is an asset-for-stock or a practical merger transaction. This type of transaction, illustrated in Figure 7-4, requires the acquiring corporation to obtain substantially all of the target corporation's assets in exchange for its voting stock and a limited amount of other consideration.[26]

Key Point
Because of the solely-for-voting-stock requirement, a "C" reorganization is much less flexible than an "A" reorganization relative to the consideration that can be used.

The substantially all requirement is not defined in the Code or the Regulations. For advance ruling purposes, the same standard holds here that applies to triangular Type A mergers (i.e., the 70% of the FMV of gross assets and 90% of the FMV of net assets standard).[27] The courts have employed a flexible standard for the substantially all requirement, which has varied depending on the nature of the assets retained by the acquired corporation, the reason for retaining the assets, and whether such assets are to be used in a new trade or business or distributed pursuant to the liquidation of the target corporation.[28]

The acquired corporation in a Type C reorganization must distribute the stock, securities, and other property it receives in the reorganization, plus any other property that it retained, to its shareholders as part of the plan of reorganization. Although the corporation does not have to formally be dissolved, as a practical matter it has been liquidated.[29] Because the Type C reorganization produces the same economic result as a merger (i.e., the acquisition of the target corporation's assets) without requiring the dissolution of the target corporation under state law, many tax practitioners call it a practical merger transaction.

The acquired corporation may (1) retain its corporate charter in order to prevent others from using its corporate name, and (2) obtain a special IRS waiver to the

---
[26] Sec. 368(a)(1)(C).
[27] Rev. Proc. 77-37, 1977-2 C.B. 568, Sec. 3.01.
[28] See, for example, *CIR v. First National Bank of Altoona*, 23 AFTR 119, 39-2 USTC ¶ 9568 (3rd Cir., 1939), and *James Armour, Inc.*, 43 T.C. 295 (1964), where the courts used asset percentages below those specified in the letter ruling guideline.
[29] Sec. 368(a)(2)(G).

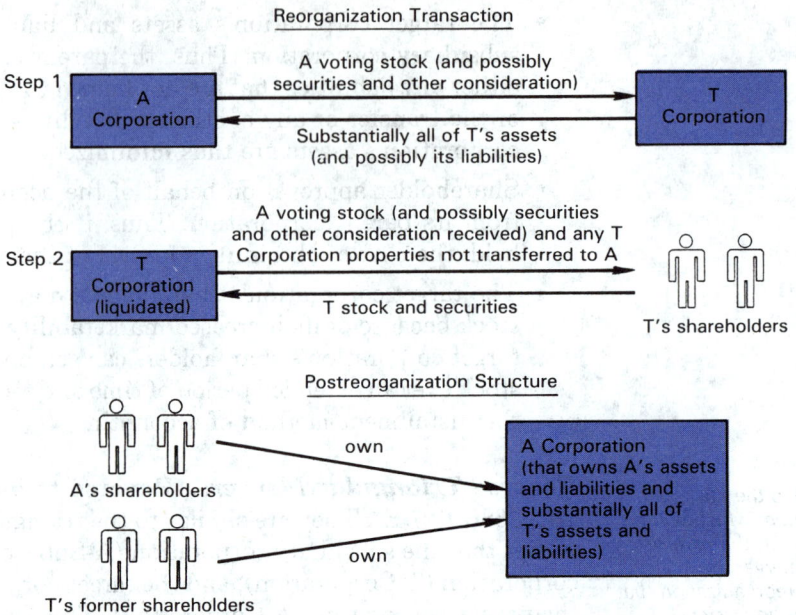

FIGURE 7-4 Type C (asset-for-stock) Reorganization

distribution requirement. The latter is generally granted in cases where the needed distribution would cause a hardship. In such a case, a deemed distribution of the property to the shareholders followed by a contribution of the properties back to the corporation is permitted. The procedures for asking the IRS for advance approval to waive the distribution requirement are explained in Rev. Proc. 89-50. In general, this Rev. Proc. permits the target corporation to retain only its corporate charter and other assets, if any, needed to satisfy the minimum capital requirements under state law to maintain its corporate existence.[30]

Consideration Used to Effect the Reorganization. Section 368(a)(1)(C) requires the consideration used to effect the reorganization be solely voting stock of the acquiring corporation. Both the acquiring corporation's assumption of part or all of the target corporation's liabilities and the acquisition of a property subject to a liability are disregarded for purposes of the solely-for-voting-stock requirement.

Section 368(a)(2)(B) permits other consideration to be used in the reorganization, provided the acquiring corporation obtains at least 80% of the target corporation's properties solely for its voting stock. This rule permits money, securities, nonvoting stock, or other property to be used to acquire up to 20% of the target corporation's properties. Liabilities that are assumed or acquired reduce the amount of money that can be used in the reorganization on a dollar-for-dollar basis. If the liabilities that are assumed or acquired exceed 20% of the FMV of the target corporation's assets, the transaction can take place as a Type C reorganization only if no money, securities, nonvoting stock, or other property is used.

Example 7-10 ■ Acquiring Corporation wants to acquire all of Target Corporation's assets and liabilities as part of a Type C reorganization. The following illustrates the application of the solely-for-voting-stock requirement for four different situations:

---

[30] 1989-1 C.B. 631.

Additional Comment

Target's liabilities assumed by Acquiring are not a problem unless boot is received by Target as part of the consideration. In this case, when applying the 20% boot relaxation rule, liabilities are treated as money. Situation 4 in Example 7-10 illustrates that if Target has liabilities in excess of 20% of the FMV of its assets, the boot relaxation rule is of no benefit in attempting to satisfy the solely-for-voting-stock requirement.

	Situation 1	Situation 2	Situation 3	Situation 4
FMV of Target's assets	$200,000	$200,000	$200,000	$200,000
Target's liabilities assumed by Acquiring	-0-	30,000	100,000	100,000
Consideration given by Acquiring:				
FMV of Acquiring voting stock	160,000	160,000	100,000	99,900
Money	40,000	10,000	-0-	100

In Situation 1, the FMV of the Acquiring stock equals 80% of the total assets, so the transaction qualifies as a Type C reorganization. The liabilities that are assumed in Situation 2 reduce the money that can be exchanged by Acquiring, but the transaction is still a Type C reorganization since the money and liabilities, in total, do not exceed 20% of the FMV of Target's total assets. In Situation 3, the high percentage of liabilities does not prevent the transaction from being a Type C reorganization since Acquiring used no money to effect the reorganization.[31] In Situation 4, the transaction is disqualified from being a Type C reorganization since some money is used along with the Acquiring stock and the total money given by Acquiring and liabilities assumed by Acquiring are more than 20% of the total FMV of Target's assets. ∎

Self-Study Question

Must Acquiring assume all liabilities of Target in a "C" reorganization?

Answer

No. Unlike a regular "A" merger, Acquiring may leave Target's liabilities in Target. These liabilities would then have to be satisfied with assets retained by Target or as part of the liquidating distribution required in a "C" reorganization.

Advantages and Disadvantages of a Type C Reorganization. A number of advantages and disadvantages exist when comparing a Type C reorganization and a merger.

- The acquiring corporation acquires only the assets specified in the purchase agreement in a Type C reorganization. However, it needs to acquire "substantially all" of the target corporation's assets. Unwanted assets that are sold or otherwise disposed, and assets that are retained, by the target corporation are not included in determining if the "substantially all" requirement has been met. A disposition of a substantial amount of assets shortly before an asset-for-stock acquisition may prevent the transaction from being a Type C reorganization. The "substantially all" requirement does not apply to a merger, and dispositions of unwanted assets generally will not prevent an acquisition from being a merger.

- The acquiring corporation acquires only the liabilities that are specified in the purchase agreement. Unknown and contingent liabilities are not acquired as is the case in a merger.

- Shareholders of the acquiring corporation generally do not have to approve the acquisition thus reducing the cost to accomplish the transaction.

- For many target corporations, the liabilities that are acquired or assumed will be so large (i.e., in excess of 20% of total consideration) as to prevent the acquiring corporation from using any consideration other than voting stock. Merger transactions permit 50% nonstock consideration to be used, and do not require the stock to have voting rights.

- Dissenting shareholders of the target corporation may have the right under state law to have their shares appraised and purchased for cash.

Tax Consequences of a Type C Reorganization. The tax consequences of a Type C reorganization are illustrated by the following example.

---

[31] The IRS may attempt to treat a transaction as a purchase when the amount of liabilities assumed or acquired is high relative to the FMV of the assets acquired.

Example 7-11 ■ Acquiring Corporation acquires all of Target Corporation's assets and liabilities in exchange for $1,200,000 of Acquiring common stock. Target distributes the Acquiring stock to its sole shareholder Andrew in exchange for all of his Target stock. Target's assets have a $1,400,000 FMV and a $600,000 adjusted basis. Liabilities in the amount of $200,000 are assumed by Acquiring. Target has a $500,000 E&P balance at the time of the transfer. Andrew's basis for his Target stock is $400,000. Target Corporation realizes an $800,000 gain ([$1,200,000 + $200,000] − $600,000), none of which must be recognized. Acquiring Corporation recognizes no gain when it exchanges its stock for the assets and takes a $600,000 basis in the acquired assets. Andrew realizes an $800,000 ($1,200,000 − $400,000) gain on the transfer of the Target stock, none of which must be recognized. Andrew's basis for the Acquiring stock is $400,000. Acquiring Corporation assumes all of Target Corporation's tax attributes including the $500,000 E&P balance. ■

Typical Misconception
As with an "A" reorganization, a "C" reorganization can be structured as a triangular acquisition. Although this provides greater flexibility in tax planning, it makes the area more confusing because of the substantial overlap between the different types of reorganizations.

Section 368(a)(2)(B) permits the acquiring corporation in a Type C reorganization to transfer part or all of the assets and liabilities acquired in the reorganization to a controlled subsidiary corporation without destroying the tax-free nature of the transaction. Section 368(a)(1)(C) permits a triangular Type C reorganization to be used whereby voting stock of the parent corporation is used by a subsidiary corporation to acquire substantially all of the target corporation's assets. The triangular Type C reorganization requirements are the same as for the basic Type C reorganization except that the voting stock used to acquire the assets must consist solely of the stock of the acquiring corporation's parent corporation. The subsidiary corporation can, however, provide additional consideration in the form of securities, money, or other property.

OBJECTIVE 9
Explain the requirements of an acquisitive Type D reorganization

Type D Reorganization

Type D reorganizations can be either acquisitive or divisive. (Divisive Type D reorganizations are discussed on pages 7-29 through 7-31.) An acquisitive Type D reorganization involves the transfer by a corporation of substantially all of its assets to a controlled corporation in exchange for such corporation's stock and securities (and possibly other consideration) pursuant to a plan of reorganization. The exchange must be followed by a distribution to the shareholders and security holders of the stock, securities, and other consideration that is received in the reorganization, plus any other properties retained by the transferor corporation, pursuant to a complete liquidation of the transferor corporation.[32] (See Figure 7-5 for an illustration of an acquisitive Type D reorganization.)

Key Point
A Type D reorganization is not often used as an acquisitive reorganization. It is more often used by the government either as a tool to fight the abusive "liquidation-reincorporation" transaction or as part of a divisive reorganization under Sec. 355 (discussed later in this chapter).

The substantially all requirement is based on the facts and circumstances of the situation. For advance ruling purposes, the 70% of the FMV of gross assets and 90% of the FMV of net assets standard employed in the triangular Type A and Type C reorganizations is applied.[33]

Control Requirements. The transferor corporation or one or more of its shareholders must control the transferee corporation immediately after the asset transfer. Control is defined in Sec. 368(a)(2)(H) as either 50% or more of the total combined voting power of all classes of voting stock, or 50% or more of the total value of all classes of stock.

---

[32] Secs. 368(a)(1)(D) and 354(b)(1).
[33] Rev. Proc. 77-37, 1977-2 C.B. 568, Sec. 3.01.

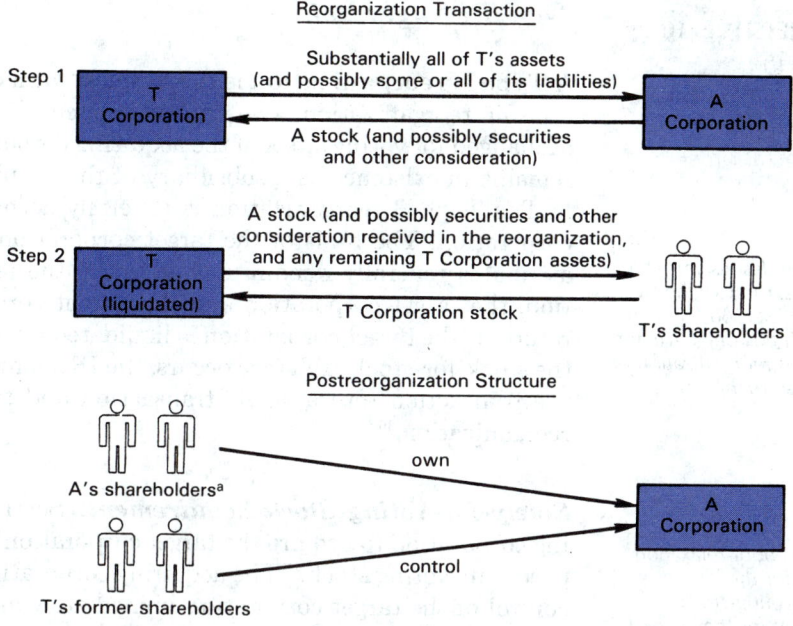

FIGURE 7-5 Acquisitive Type D Reorganization

Self-Study Question

Why does a Type D reorganization use the 50% control requirement when the rest of the Sec. 368 reorganizations use the higher 80% control requirement?

Answer

The use of the 50% control requirement is the result of a recent change in the statute. This change was made to make the Type D reorganization a more useful tool in fighting the "liquidation-reincorporation" tax avoidance transaction (rather than a more flexible acquisitive reorganization).

Type D reorganizations are not often found because of this control requirement. Type C reorganizations (where the transferor does not control the transferee corporation) and Type A reorganizations (where the transaction satisfies the state law merger requirements) are more common.[34]

The Sec. 368(a)(1)(D) rules do not limit the consideration that may be exchanged in the transaction. The IRS and the courts require that the transferor corporation's shareholders maintain a continuing equity interest in the transferee corporation. For advance ruling purposes, the IRS requires that the transferor corporation's shareholders receive transferee corporation stock equal to at least 50% of the value of the transferor corporation's outstanding stock in order to satisfy this requirement.[35]

Tax Consequences of a Type D Reorganization. The Type C and acquisitive Type D reorganization requirements and tax consequences are quite similar. If the reorganization satisfies both the Type C and Type D reorganization requirements, Sec. 368(a)(2)(A) requires that the transaction be treated as a Type D reorganization. The basic tax consequences of a Type D reorganization for the target corporation, the acquiring corporation, and the target corporation's shareholders are the same as for a Type C reorganization except in the application of Sec. 357(c) "excess" liability rule. Section 357(c) requires the transferor corporation in a Type D reorganization to recognize gain equal to the amount by which the liabilities assumed or acquired by the transferee corporation exceeds the total adjusted basis of the transferor corporation's assets that were transferred. Such gain does not have to be recognized if the asset acquisition only qualifies as a Type C reorganization (e.g., when the transferor corporation does not control the transferee corporation).

---

[34] One example of a Type D reorganization is a merger transaction involving two foreign corporations that fails to satisfy either state or federal corporation laws.

[35] Rev. Proc. 77-37, 1977-2 C.B. 568, Sec. 3.02.

OBJECTIVE 10
Explain the requirements of a Type B reorganization

Key Point
If Acquiring desires Target to remain in existence, the two choices in Sec. 368 that can accomplish this objective are (1) a Type B reorganization or (2) a reverse triangular merger.

Key Point
There is no boot relaxation exception for the solely-for-voting-stock requirement for the Type "B" reorganization. Thus, the Type "B" reorganization has the least flexible consideration requirement of any of the reorganizations.

Type B Reorganization

A **Type B reorganization** is the simplest form of acquisitive reorganization. In this type of reorganization, two things happen: (1) the target corporation's stock is exchanged for voting stock of the acquiring corporation and (2) the target corporation remains in existence as a subsidiary of the acquiring corporation (see Figure 7-6).

The Type B reorganization is generally accomplished independent of the target corporation. The basis of the target corporation's assets and the amount of its tax attributes generally remain unchanged by the reorganization. After the reorganization, the target corporation and the parent corporation can file a consolidated tax return. If the target corporation is liquidated into the parent corporation shortly after the stock-for-stock exchange occurs, the IRS may attempt to collapse the two parts of the transaction into a single transaction and treat it as a Type C asset-for-stock reorganization.[36]

Solely-for-Voting-Stock Requirement. Section 368(a)(1)(B) requires the acquiring corporation to acquire the target corporation's stock "in exchange solely for all or part of its voting stock." The acquiring corporation must own sufficient stock to be in control of the target corporation immediately after the exchange.

The solely-for-voting-stock requirement generally precludes the use of other property to effect the transaction. However, the voting stock used can be either common or preferred stock. If consideration other than voting stock is used to effect the reorganization (e.g., nonvoting preferred stock), the transaction does not qualify

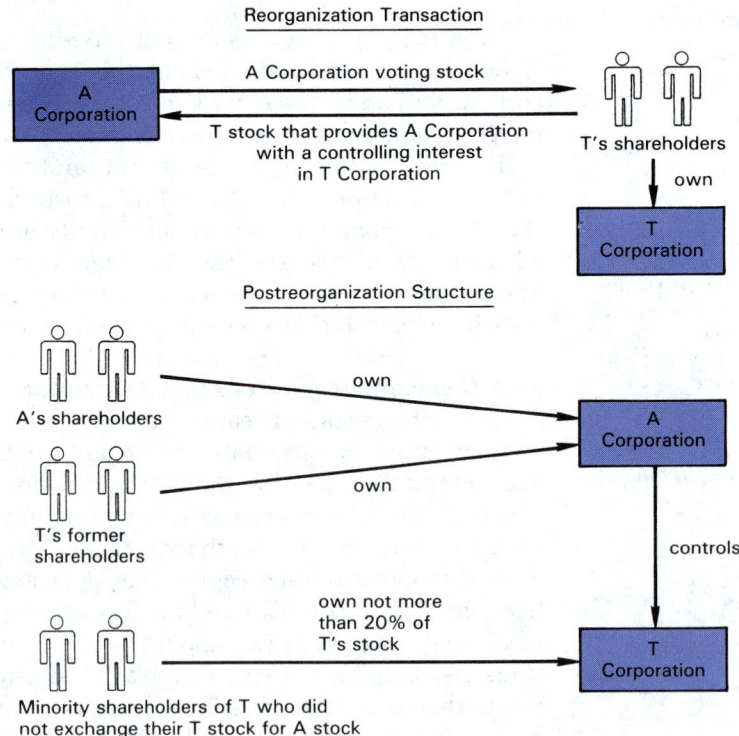

FIGURE 7-6 Type B (stock-for-stock) Reorganization

[36] Rev. Rul. 67-274, 1967-2 C.B. 141.

as a Type B reorganization and the transaction is taxable to the target corporation's shareholders (see page 7-43).

EXCEPTIONS. Cash can be used in limited circumstances without violating this requirement. For example:

- The target corporation's shareholders can receive cash in exchange for their right to receive a fractional share of the acquiring corporation's stock.[37]
- Expenses of the reorganization (such as legal expenses, accounting fees, and administrative costs) can also be paid by the acquiring corporation without violating the solely-for-voting-stock requirement.[38]

Key Point
These limited exceptions to the solely-for-voting-stock requirement apply to Type "C" reorganizations as well as Type "B" reorganizations.

Self-Study Question
Is there any way to take care of dissenters in a Type B reorganization?

Answer
Yes. Even though Acquiring cannot use any boot in acquiring the stock of Target, it is possible for Target to redeem out the dissenters prior to the reorganization. Also, Target's nondissenting shareholders could buy out the stock of the dissenters.

CONTROL. For purposes of this requirement, control is defined here by the rules of Sec. 368(c) as 80% of the total combined voting power of all classes of voting stock and 80% of each class of nonvoting stock. Because the acquiring corporation does not have to acquire all of the target corporation's stock, it is possible that a minority interest of up to 20% may be present. Minority shareholders can have their shares acquired for cash without destroying the tax-free nature of the transaction. For example, the target corporation can use its cash to redeem the stock of the minority shareholders prior to or after the reorganization. A cash acquisition by the acquiring corporation of the shares of a group of dissenting minority shareholders either prior to or as part of the reorganization prevents the transaction from being tax-free.[39]

TIMING OF THE TRANSACTION. Some Type B reorganizations are accomplished by simply exchanging stock of the acquiring corporation for 100% of the target corporation's shares in a single transaction. In other cases, the reorganization is accomplished in a series of transactions taking place over an extended period of time. Regulation Sec. 1.368-2(c) states that a cash purchase of stock may be disregarded for purposes of the solely-for-voting-stock requirement if it was independent of the stock-for-stock exchange. Stock acquisitions that are made over a relatively short period of time—12 months or less—are, according to this regulation, to be aggregated for purposes of applying the solely-for-voting-stock requirement.

Example 7-12 ■ Acquiring Corporation acquires 12% of Target Corporation's single class of stock for cash in July 1991. The remaining 88% is acquired by Acquiring in January 1992 in a stock-for-stock exchange. The cash and stock-for-stock acquisitions will likely be aggregated by the IRS since they occur within a 12-month period. Even though 80% control is acquired in a single stock-for-stock transaction, the transaction does not meet the Type B reorganization requirements because the solely-for-voting-stock requirement is not met if the two transactions are aggregated. The transaction could qualify as a Type B reorganization if (1) Acquiring unconditionally sold its 12% holding of the Target stock and then acquired the necessary 80% interest in a single stock-for-stock exchange, or (2) Acquiring delayed the stock-for-stock exchange until some time after July 1992, when it would likely be considered a separate transaction.[40] ■

Example 7-13 ■ Acquiring Corporation acquires 85% of Target Corporation's single class of stock in April 1986 in a transaction that qualifies as a Type B reorganization. Acquiring acquires the remaining 15% of Target's stock in December 1991 in a stock-for-

---

[37] Rev. Rul. 66-365, 1966-2 C.B. 116.
[38] Rev. Rul. 73-54, 1973-1 C.B. 187.
[39] Rev. Rul. 68-285, 1968-1 C.B. 147.
[40] See, for example, *Eldon S. Chapman et al. v. CIR*, 45 AFTR 2d 80-1290, 80-1 USTC ¶ 9330 (1st Cir., 1980).

Additional Comment

"Creeping acquisitions" are allowed in a Type B reorganization since the requirement is merely that 80% must be owned after the transaction. Transactions within 12 months are generally considered to be related transactions. This can be either an advantage or a disadvantage depending on what consideration was used in the various steps of the acquisition.

stock exchange. Even though Acquiring already controls Target, the second acquisition is treated as a Type B reorganization. ■

Tax Consequences of a Type B Reorganization. The tax consequences of a Type B reorganization are straightforward.

- The target corporation's shareholders recognize no gain or loss on the exchange unless fractional shares of stock are acquired for cash or the target corporation redeems some of its stock.
- The shareholders carry over their basis and holding period in the target corporation's stock to the acquiring corporation's stock that they receive.
- The acquiring corporation recognizes no gain or loss when it issues its stock for the target corporation's stock.
- The acquiring corporation's basis for the target corporation's stock is the same as it was in the hands of the target corporation's shareholders.

Example 7-14 ■ Target Corporation's single class of stock is owned entirely by Mark, who has a $400,000 basis for his stock. Mark exchanges his Target stock for $700,000 of Acquiring Corporation common stock. Mark realizes a $300,000 gain ($700,000 − $400,000), none of which is recognized. Mark's basis for the Acquiring stock is $400,000. Acquiring Corporation recognizes no gain or loss when it issues its stock and takes a $400,000 basis for the Target stock. ■

Advantages of a Type B Reorganization. The Type B reorganization has a number of advantages. First, as explained earlier, it can usually be accomplished quite simply and without formal shareholder approval. The acquiring corporation can acquire the necessary shares with a tender offer made directly to the target corporation's shareholders, even if the target corporation's management does not approve of the transaction. Second, the target corporation remains in existence and its tax attributes are not lost or reduced, as in some reorganizations (see pages 7-38 through 7-41).[41] Third, the corporate name, goodwill, licenses, and rights of the target company can continue on after the acquisition. Fourth, the acquiring corporation does not acquire the target corporation's liabilities as is the case of some other reorganizations.

Disadvantages of a Type B Reorganization. Offsetting the advantages noted above are a number of disadvantages. First, the sale consideration that may be used to effect the transaction is voting stock. The issuing of the additional voting stock can dilute the voting power of the acquiring corporation's shareholders and restrict their flexibility to structure the transaction in order to retain control of the acquiring corporation. Second, at least 80% of the target corporation's stock must be acquired, even though effective control of the acquired company might be obtained with ownership of less than 80%. Third, the acquisition of less than 100% of the target corporation's stock may lead to a vocal group of dissenting minority shareholders. These shareholders have the right to have their shares appraised and purchased for cash. Fourth, the bases of the target corporation's stock and assets are not stepped-up

---

[41] A Type B reorganization can result in an ownership change that restricts the ability of the target corporation's NOL carryovers to be used under Sec. 382 but which does not, in total, diminish the amount of its carryovers (see page 7-39).

to their FMVs when the change in ownership occurs, as would be the case in a taxable acquisition.

Triangular Type B Reorganizations. As with the other acquisitive reorganizations, a triangular Type B reorganization or a drop-down of the target corporation's stock into a subsidiary corporation can be accomplished tax-free. In a triangular reorganization, the stock of the acquiring corporation's parent corporation is exchanged for a controlling stock interest in the target corporation. Similar to the basic Type B reorganization, the target corporation remains in existence as a subsidiary of the acquiring (subsidiary) corporation.

Type G Reorganization

Section 368(a)(1)(G) defines a **Type G reorganization** as "a transfer by a corporation of part or all of its assets to another corporation in a title 11 [bankruptcy] or similar case, but only if, in pursuance of the plan, stock or securities of the corporation to which the assets are transferred are distributed in a transaction that qualifies under sections 354, 355, or 356." Use of a Type G reorganization is quite limited since the reorganization must take place according to a court-approved plan in a bankruptcy, receivership, or other similar situation.

In an acquisitive Type G reorganization, the financially troubled corporation might transfer substantially all of its assets to an acquiring corporation according to a court-approved plan (e.g., a bankruptcy reorganization plan) and then distribute all the stock, securities, and other property received in the exchange, plus any properties that it had retained, to its shareholders and creditors in exchange for their stock and debt interests.

Historical Note
The Type G reorganization is the newest of the Sec. 368 reorganizations. Previously reorganizations used in restructuring corporations involved in bankruptcy proceedings had their own statutory provisions. As part of the Bankruptcy Tax Act of 1980, the old provisions were repealed and the Type G reorganization was enacted. This change was made to allow more flexibility in restructuring bankrupt corporations.

DIVISIVE REORGANIZATIONS

A **divisive reorganization** involves the transfer of *part* of a transferor corporation's assets to a controlled corporation in exchange for its stock and securities (and possibly some boot property).[42] The stock and securities (and possibly some boot property) are then distributed to the transferor's shareholders. The primary divisive reorganization comes under the Type D reorganization rules, although a divisive reorganization involving a financially troubled corporation could be a Type G reorganization.

Type D Divisive Reorganization

OBJECTIVE 11
Explain the requirements of a divisive Type D reorganization

The Type D reorganization must take place as part of a plan of reorganization and satisfy the requirements of both Secs. 368(a)(1)(D) and 355.[43] There are three forms of Type D divisive reorganizations—spinoffs, split-offs, and split-ups (see Figure 7-31).

---

[42] In a divisive Type D reorganization, control is most always defined by Sec. 368(c). Section 368(c) requires ownership of at least 80% of the voting and nonvoting stock to constitute control. An acquisitive Type D reorganization, on the other hand, requires only 50% of the voting and nonvoting stock to be owned to constitute control (see page 7-24).

[43] The requirements of the divisive Type D reorganization may be contrasted with the acquisitive Type D reorganization (previously discussed) where substantially all of the transferor's assets must be transferred to a controlled corporation.

Typical Misconception
The existence of a good corporate business purpose is necessary before the stock of a controlled subsidiary can be distributed to the shareholders of the distributing corporation. This requirement is much more difficult to satisfy in a Sec. 355 distribution than it is in an acquisitive reorganization.

A distribution of a controlled corporation's stock can be tax-free under Sec. 355, even if none of the distributing corporation's assets are transferred to the controlled corporation. For a transaction to constitute one of the three divisive Type D reorganization forms both the asset transfer and the Sec. 355 distribution must take place as part of a single transaction that is governed by a plan of reorganization. Because of our previous definition and coverage of the three types of Sec. 355 distributions (see Chapter 4), our discussion here is restricted to an examination of the asset transfer and the overall tax consequences of the transaction.

A divisive Type D reorganization can be used to accomplish a number of types of business adjustments, including

- Dividing up a business into two corporations to separate a high-risk business from a low-risk business
- Dividing up a single business between two shareholders that have a major disagreement
- Dividing up a corporation's business activities according to its separate functions or the geographical areas in which it operates

Key Point
The tax consequences of a divisive reorganization are basically the same as the tax consequences of an acquisitive reorganization. The general rule is that no gain or loss is recognized by any of the parties to the reorganization and the controlled corporation takes a carryover basis in the assets it receives. In addition, the transferor's shareholders take a substituted basis in the controlled corporation stock which they receive.

Asset Transfer. The transferor corporation recognizes no gain or loss on the asset transfer, except when (1) boot property is received by the transferor and retained, or (2) the transferee corporation acquires or assumes liabilities of the transferor corporation and the total of the liabilities acquired or assumed exceeds the total adjusted bases of the assets transferred.[44] No gain or loss is recognized by the controlled corporation when it exchanges its stock for the transferor corporation's property. The transferor corporation's basis and holding period for the property carry over to the controlled corporation.

Distribution of Stock. No gain or loss is recognized by the transferor corporation when it distributes the controlled corporation's stock (or securities) to its shareholders.[45] No gain or loss is recognized by the shareholders on the receipt of the stock (and securities), except to the extent that boot property is received. A shareholder's basis in the stock (or securities) held after the distribution equals his basis in the stock (or securities) that are held prior to the distribution, increased by any gain that is recognized and decreased by the sum of the money received and the FMV of any other boot property received. If more than one class of stock or securities is held before or after the distribution, the total basis is allocated to each class based upon their relative FMVs. The holding period for the stock and securities received includes the holding period of the stock and securities surrendered. The holding period for boot property begins on the day after the distribution date.

Example 7-15 ■ Transferor Corporation transfers assets having a $600,000 FMV and a $350,000 adjusted basis to Acquiring Corporation in exchange for $600,000 of Acquiring stock. Transferor Corporation is owned equally by Ruth and Pat. Pat's basis for her shares is $400,000. The Acquiring stock, which represents a controlling interest of

---

[44] Sec. 357(c)(1)(B).
[45] Sec. 361(c)(1). Gain (but not loss) is recognized when boot property is distributed to the transferor corporation's shareholders as part of the reorganization, and when a disqualified distribution of stock or securities in the controlled corporation is made (see Chapter 4).

Divisive Reorganizations • 7-31

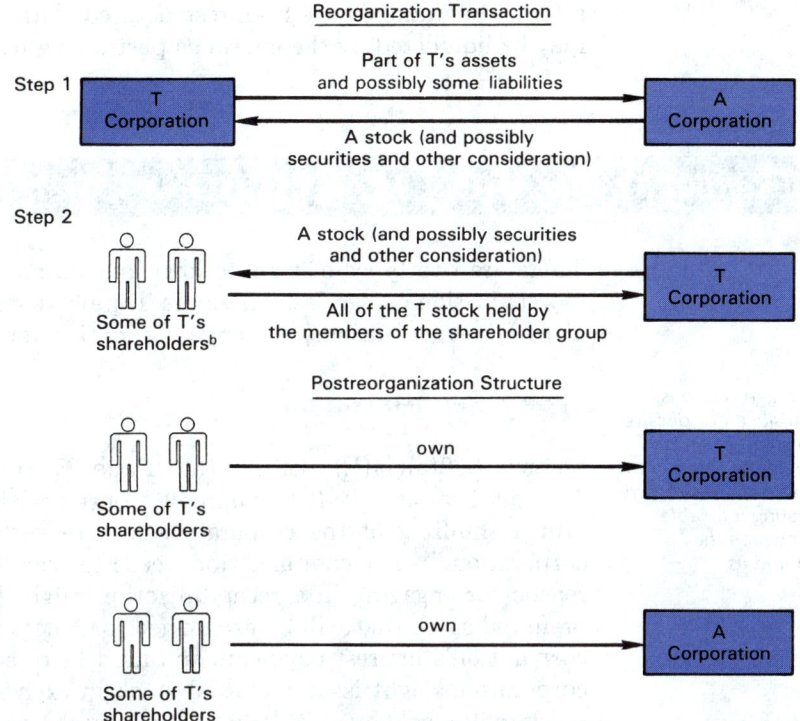

FIGURE 7-7 Divisive Type D Reorganization (split-off form)

80% or more, is exchanged by Transferor Corporation for all of Pat's shares. Transferor Corporation realizes a $250,000 gain ($600,000 − $350,000) on the asset transfer, none of which is recognized. Transferor Corporation also does not recognize any gain upon the distribution of the Acquiring shares to Pat. Pat realizes a $200,000 gain ($600,000 − $400,000) on exchanging the Transferor shares, none of which is recognized. Her basis in the Acquiring stock is $400,000. Acquiring Corporation does not recognize any gain when it issues its stock for Transferor's assets and takes a $350,000 basis for the assets that were acquired. ∎

Type G Divisive Reorganization

The divisive Type G reorganization involves the transfer of *part* of the assets of a corporation to a second corporation according to a court-approved plan. The transferee corporation's stock and securities are then distributed by the transferor corporation to its shareholders, security holders, and creditors. The transferor corporation may then continue in business separate from the transferee corporation

OTHER REORGANIZATION TRANSACTIONS

There are two types of transactions that do not fit into the acquisitive or divisive reorganization categories. These are Type E reorganizations, a recapitalization, and Type F reorganizations, a change in identity, form, or state of incorporation.

Type E Reorganization

Key Point
A Type E reorganization is neither acquisitive nor divisive in nature. Instead, it simply allows a single corporation to restructure its capital structure without creating a taxable exchange between the corporation and its shareholders.

Section 368(a)(1)(E) defines the **Type E reorganization** quite simply as a "recapitalization." A 1942 Supreme Court decision defined a **recapitalization** as "the reshuffling of the corporate structure within the framework of an existing corporation."[46] A recapitalization needs to have a bona fide business purpose. One reason for engaging in a recapitalization might be to issue additional common or preferred stock that will be exchanged for outstanding bonds in order to reduce the corporation's interest payments and its debt to equity ratio. Alternatively, a family corporation might issue preferred stock in exchange for part or all of the common stock that is held by an elderly, controlling shareholder to permit that shareholder to turn over active management of the corporation to his children and to engage in estate planning (see page 7-33).

Four types of adjustments to the corporate capital structure can qualify for tax-free treatment as a Type E reorganization. These are a stock-for-stock exchange, a bond-for-stock exchange, a bond-for-bond exchange, and a stock-for-bond exchange. Normally, these exchanges do not result in an increase or decrease in the corporation's assets except to the extent that a distribution of money or other property is made to the shareholders as part of the transaction.

Stock-for-Stock Exchange. An exchange of common stock for common stock or preferred stock for preferred stock within a single corporation can qualify as a recapitalization if it is made pursuant to a plan of reorganization. Code Sec. 1036 also permits the same types of exchanges to take place outside of the reorganization rules. In either case, shareholders (1) recognize no gain or loss and (2) carry over their basis in the shares given up to the shares that are received.

Example 7-16 ■ The shareholders of Pilot Corporation exchange all of their nonvoting Class B common stock for additional shares of Pilot's Class A common stock. The Class A stock retains voting rights. The exchange is tax-free under Sec. 1036, even if no plan of reorganization has been created. An exchange of some of Pilot's Class A preferred stock for Class B preferred stock would also be tax-free under Sec. 1036. ■

Section 1036 does not apply to an exchange of common stock for preferred stock, or preferred stock for common stock, within the same corporation, or an exchange of stock involving two corporations. The recapitalization rules, however, apply to an exchange of two different classes of stock (e.g., common for preferred) in the same

---

[46] *Helvering v. Southwest Consolidated Corp.*, 28 AFTR 573, 42-1 USTC ¶ 9248 (USSC, 1942).

corporation if the exchange is made as part of a plan of reorganization. The exchange is tax-free for the shareholders under the Sec. 354(a) nonrecognition rules, except to the extent that boot property is received. If the FMV of the stock that is received is different from that of the stock surrendered, the difference may be a gift, a contribution to capital, compensation for services, a dividend, or a payment made to satisfy a debt obligation, depending upon the facts and circumstances of the situation.[47] The tax consequences of that portion of the exchange will fall outside the reorganization rules.

Example 7-17 ■   John owns 60% of Boise Corporation's common stock and all of its preferred stock. The remainder of Boise's common stock is held by 80 unrelated individuals. John's basis for his preferred stock is $400,000. John exchanges his preferred stock for additional common stock and $100,000 in money. The preferred and common stock that are exchanged are both valued at $400,000. John realizes a $100,000 gain ([$400,000 + $100,000] − $400,000) on the exchange that must be recognized as dividend income (assuming that Boise Corporation has sufficient E&P), since none of the Sec. 302(b) exceptions that permit capital gain treatment apply. John's basis for the common stock received is $400,000 ($400,000 + $100,000 gain − $100,000 money received). ■

A recapitalization is often used as an estate planning device whereby a parent's controlling interest in a corporation's common stock is exchanged for both common stock and preferred stock. The common stock is often gifted to a child (or children) who following the recapitalization will own a controlling interest in the common stock and manage the company. The parent will receive annual income from the preferred stock's cash dividends. The preferred stock's value will not increase over time, thereby freezing the value of the parent's estate and reducing his or her estate tax liability. The capital appreciation will accrue to the child (children) who owns the common stock.

Substantial income tax and estate and gift tax planning opportunities exist when recapitalizing a closely-held corporation. In order to prevent abuses in this area, Code Secs. 2701-2704 were added by the Revenue Reconciliation Act of 1990. These rules provide procedures for more accurately valuing, for transfer tax purposes, interests that are transferred and retained in corporations and partnerships. Among the areas that these rules apply to are the valuation of certain retained rights in corporations and partnerships and split interests in property, as well as the effects of buy-sell agreements, purchase options, and options that lapse on the valuation of interests in a corporation or a partnership. Additional coverage of this topic is presented in Chapter 12.

Bond-for-Stock Exchange. A bond-for-stock exchange is tax-free to the shareholder except to the extent that a portion of the stock is received in satisfaction of the corporation's liability for accrued interest on the bonds.[48]

Bond-for-Bond Exchange. These exchanges are tax-free only when the principal amount of the bonds received does not exceed the principal amount of the bonds surrendered. If the principal amount of the bonds received exceeds the principal amount of the bonds surrendered, the FMV of the "excess" principal amount that is received is taxed to the bondholder as boot. (See pages 7-10 and 7-11 for a discussion of the boot rules.)

---

[47] Rev. Ruls. 74-269, 1974-2 C.B. 87 and 83-120, 1983-2 C.B. 170.
[48] Sec. 354(a)(2)(B).

Stock-for-Bond Exchange. An exchange of stock for bonds is generally taxable because receipt of the principal amount of the bonds represents boot.[49] The shareholder must recognize gain equal to the bonds' FMV. If the shareholder ends up owning no stock after the exchange, the IRS has held that a stock-for-bond exchange is treated as a redemption of the stock under Sec. 302.[50] The FMV of any additional bonds that are received in satisfaction of the corporation's liability for accrued interest on the bonds that were surrendered is taxable as interest income.

Type F Reorganization

Historical Note
The statute was changed in 1982 to limit a Type F reorganization to one corporation. Since that time, the importance of a Type F reorganization has been greatly diminished.

A **Type F reorganization** is defined by Sec. 368(a)(1)(F) as a "mere change in identity, form, or place of organization of one corporation, however effected." Traditionally, Type F reorganizations are used to change either the state in which the business is incorporated or the name of a corporation, without requiring the old corporation or its shareholders to recognize any gain or loss. In a Type F reorganization, the assets and liabilities of the old corporation become the property of the new corporation. Thus, the shareholders and creditors of the old corporation exchange their stock and debt interests for similar interests in the new corporation.

Example 7-18 ■ Rider Corporation is incorporated in the State of Illinois. Its management decides to change its state of incorporation to Delaware because of the more favorable securities and corporation laws in the latter state. Old Rider Corporation exchanges its assets for all of the stock of new Rider Corporation. The shareholders of old Rider Corporation then exchange their stock for new Rider Corporation stock. Old Rider Corporation then goes out of existence. Neither the shareholders nor the two corporations involved in the reorganization recognize any gain on the transaction. Each shareholder's basis and holding period for the old Rider Corporation stock carries over to the new Rider Corporation stock. Old Rider Corporation's basis for its assets and its tax attributes also carry over to new Rider Corporation. ■

The reorganization illustrated in Example 7-18 could also take place by having old Rider Corporation's shareholders exchange their stock for new Rider Corporation stock. Old Rider Corporation would then be liquidated into new Rider Corporation. The tax consequences are the same for either transaction form.

JUDICIAL RESTRICTIONS ON THE USE OF CORPORATE REORGANIZATIONS

OBJECTIVE 12
Explain how judicial doctrines can restrict a taxpayer's ability to use corporate reorganizations

The Supreme Court holds that literal compliance with the statutory requirements for a reorganization transaction is not enough for a transaction to receive tax-free treatment.[51] As a result, the courts have placed four primary restrictions on reorganization transactions:

- Continuity of the investor's proprietary interest
- Continuity of the business enterprise
- A business purpose for the transaction

---

[49] Sec. 356(d)(2)(B) and *J. Robert Bazley v. CIR*, 35 AFTR 1190, 47-2 USTC ¶ 9288 (USSC, 1947).
[50] Rev. Rul. 77-415, 1977-2 C.B. 311.
[51] *Evelyn F. Gregory v. Helvering*, 14 AFTR 1191, 35-1 USTC ¶ 9043 (USSC, 1935).

Typical Misconception

The continuity of interest requirement has nothing to do with the relative sizes of Acquiring and Target. Target's shareholders may end up with a minimal amount of the total outstanding stock of Acquiring, and yet the acquisition will still be a good reorganization as long as 50% of the consideration received by Target's shareholders is an equity interest in Acquiring.

- The collapsing of a series of related transactions down into a single transaction that reflects their economic substance

Each of these requirements is explained below.

Continuity of Proprietary Interest

The requirement for the continuity of the investor's proprietary interest is based upon the principal that the tax deferral associated with a reorganization is available because the shareholder has changed his investment from one form to another rather than liquidating it. According to Reg. Sec. 1.368-1(b), this test is met by (1) continuity of the business enterprise under a modified corporate form and (2) continuity of interest on the part of those persons who, directly or indirectly, own the enterprise prior to its reorganization. In a series of decisions, the courts have held that the continuing proprietary interest must be a common or preferred stock interest.[52] Thus, a transaction that involves the target corporation receiving only cash or short-term securities does not qualify as a tax-free reorganization. The Code does not specify how much stock constitutes the required proprietary interest. For advance ruling purposes, however, the IRS requires the former shareholders of the target corporation to receive at least 50% of their total consideration in the form of acquiring corporation stock. The 50% rule applies only for advance ruling purposes, and the courts have accepted lesser percentages.[53] Despite the existence of judicial support, few taxpayers are willing to proceed with a reorganization without the receipt of an advance ruling because of the risk associated with a possible disallowance of the tax-free status. Thus, the IRS exercises substantial power through its ruling position in the reorganization area.

Example 7-19 ■

Self-Study Question

For which reorganizations is the continuity of interest requirement most important?

Answer

The only limitation on consideration used for both the Type A and the triangular Type A mergers is the continuity of interest requirement. The other reorganizations have statutory requirements for the consideration that must be used that are even more restrictive than 50%.

Target Corporation transfers all of its assets to Acquiring Corporation in a merger transaction in exchange for $100,000 in cash, $100,000 in Acquiring stock, and $800,000 of 5-year notes issued by Acquiring. The cash, stock, and notes are distributed by Target Corporation to its sole shareholder Nancy in exchange for all of its outstanding stock. Even though the transaction meets the statutory requirements for a Type A reorganization, the IRS will most likely attempt to hold that the transaction is not a reorganization because the continuity of proprietary interest requirement is not met (i.e., only 10% of the total consideration received by Nancy represents an equity interest in Acquiring). ■

Continuity of Business Enterprise

The requirement for continuity of the business enterprise necessitates that the acquiring corporation either (1) continue the acquired corporation's historic business or (2) use a significant portion of the acquired corporation's historic business assets in a new business.[54] This restriction limits tax-free reorganizations to transactions involving *continuing interests* in the target corporation's business or property under a modified corporate form. The continuity of interest doctrine, however, does not require that the target corporation's historic business be continued.[55]

Whether the requirements for continuity of the business enterprise are satisfied depends on the facts and circumstances of the particular situation. The historic

---

[52] See, for example, *V. L. LeTulle v. Scofield*, 23 AFTR 789, 40-1 USTC ¶ 9150 (USSC, 1940).
[53] Rev. Proc. 77-37, 1977-2 C.B. 568, Sec. 3.02. See also *John A. Nelson Co. v. Helvering*, 16 AFTR 1262, 37-1 USTC ¶ 9019 (USSC, 1935), where the Supreme Court permitted a tax-free reorganization to take place where the stock exchanged constituted only 38% of the total consideration.
[54] Reg. Sec. 1.368-1(d)(2).
[55] Rev. Rul. 81-25, 1981-1 C.B. 132.

business requirement can be satisfied if the acquiring corporation continues one or more of the acquired corporation's significant lines of business.

Example 7-20

Self-Study Question

Does Acquiring have to continue its own historic business?

Answer

No. The IRS has specifically ruled that the continuity of business enterprise test requires only that the historic business of Target be continued [Rev. Rul. 81-25, 1981-1 C.B. 132].

Target Corporation is merged into Acquiring Corporation. Immediately preceding the merger, Target is manufacturing resins and chemicals and distributing chemicals for other products. All three lines of business are approximately the same size. Two months after the merger, Acquiring sells the resin manufacturing activities to an unrelated party for cash. The transaction satisfies the requirement for the continuity of the business enterprise since Acquiring is continuing at least one of Target's three significant lines of business.[56]

The asset continuity requirement is satisfied if the acquiring corporation uses a significant portion of the assets that were used in the acquired corporation's historic business in its business. The significance of the assets that are used is based on the relative importance of the assets to the operation of the historic business of the acquired company.

Example 7-21

Additional Comment

Since Target and its shareholders have the most to lose, they should protect themselves by stipulating that Acquiring retain the historic assets. If not, there is nothing to stop Acquiring from unilaterally disposing of the historic assets and busting the reorganization.

Acquiring and Target Corporations are both computer manufacturers. Target Corporation is merged into Acquiring Corporation. Acquiring terminates Target's manufacturing activities and maintains Target's equipment as a backup source of supply for its components. Acquiring satisfies the requirement for the continuity of the business enterprise by continuing to use Target's historic business assets. If Acquiring had instead sold Target's assets for cash and invested the proceeds in an investment portfolio, the requirement for the continuity of the business enterprise would not be met. Acquiring does not need to continue Target's business in order to satisfy the continuity of business enterprise requirement.[57]

Business Purpose Requirement

Key Point

Business purpose is much more difficult to establish in divisive (Sec. 355) transactions than it is in acquisitive (Sec. 354) transactions.

A transaction must serve a bona fide business purpose to qualify as a reorganization.[58] Regulation Sec. 1.368-1(c) states that a transaction that takes "the form of a corporate reorganization as a disguise for concealing its real character, and the object and accomplishment of which is the consummation of a preconceived plan having no business or corporate purpose, is not a plan of reorganization."

Example 7-22

Transferor Corporation transfers some highly appreciated stock from its investment portfolio to Subsidiary Corporation in exchange for all of its stock. The Subsidiary stock is distributed to Transferor's sole shareholder Kathy in exchange for part of her Transferor stock. Shortly after the stock transfer, Subsidiary Corporation is liquidated with Kathy receiving the appreciated stock. Treating the liquidation of Subsidiary Corporation as a separate event, Kathy recognizes a capital gain on the liquidation, which she uses to offset capital loss carryovers from other tax years, and is able to step-up the basis of the appreciated stock to its FMV without incurring a tax liability. Even though the stock transfer to Subsidiary Corporation fits within the statutory definition of a divisive Type D reorganization, the IRS will likely rely on *Gregory v. Helvering* and hold that the series of transactions serves no business purpose, thereby treating Kathy's receipt of the appreciated stock from Subsidiary Corporation as a dividend.

---

[56] Reg. Secs. 1.368-1(d)(3) and -1(d)(5), Ex. (1).
[57] Reg. Secs. 1.368-1(d)(4) and -1(d)(5), Ex. (2).
[58] *Evelyn F. Gregory v. Helvering*, 14 AFTR 1191, 35-1 USTC ¶ 9043 (USSC, 1935).

Step Transaction Doctrine

The **step transaction doctrine** may be used by the IRS to collapse a multistep reorganization into a single taxable transaction. Alternatively, the IRS may attempt to take a series of steps, which the taxpayer calls independent events, and collapse them into a single tax-free reorganization transaction (e.g., a liquidation-reincorporation where a corporation's assets are distributed to its shareholders and then part or all of such assets are transferred to a new corporation after the passage of a short period of time).[59] Both of these IRS actions are intended to prevent the taxpayer from arranging a series of business transactions in order to obtain a tax result that is not available if only a single transaction is used.

Example 7-23 ■ Jody transfers business properties from his sole proprietorship to his wholly owned Smith Corporation. Three days after the incorporation, Smith Corporation transfers all of its assets to Brown Corporation in a Type C reorganization in which the Brown stock is distributed to Jody pursuant to Smith Corporation's liquidation. After the liquidation, Jody owns 15% of the Brown stock. The IRS will likely attempt to collapse the two transactions (the Sec. 351 transfer of assets by Jody to Smith Corporation and the Type C asset-for-stock reorganization) into a single transaction—an asset transfer by Jody to Brown Corporation. Under the IRS's position, the Sec. 351 rules do not apply because Jody does not own at least 80% of the Brown stock immediately after the transfer. Jody, therefore, must recognize gain or loss on the transfer of assets from his sole proprietorship to Brown Corporation.[60] ■

TAX ATTRIBUTES

Section 381(a) requires the acquired or transferor corporation's tax attributes (e.g., loss or tax credit carryovers) to be assumed by the acquiring or transferee corporation in certain types of reorganizations. Sections 269, 382, 383 and 384 restrict the taxpayer's ability to use certain tax attributes (e.g., NOL carryovers) of an acquired company through the acquisition of its stock or assets.

OBJECTIVE 13
Determine which reorganization forms permit the carryover of tax attributes

Assumption of Tax Attributes

In the Type A, C, acquisitive D, F, and acquisitive G reorganizations, the acquiring corporation obtains both the tax attributes and the assets. The tax attributes do not change hands in either the Type B or Type E reorganization because there is no transfer of assets from one corporation to another. Even though there is a division of assets between a transferor corporation and a controlled corporation in the divisive Type D and G reorganizations, the only tax attribute that is allocated between the two entities is the transferor corporation's E&P.[61]

Some of the tax attributes that are carried over under Sec. 381(c) include

- Net operating losses
- Capital losses

---

[59] Liquidation-reincorporation transactions became less prevalent after the 1986 Tax Act because the distributing corporation now must recognize gain and loss when a liquidating distribution is made, and individual shareholders receive only a small capital gains preference.
[60] Rev. Rul. 70-140, 1970-1 C.B. 73.
[61] Reg. Sec. 1.312-10.

- Earnings and profits
- General business credits
- Inventory methods

Key Point
The thrust of Sec. 381, as it relates to NOLs, is to allow Target's NOL carryforwards to offset only the post-acquisition income of Acquiring.

The acquired corporation's NOL carryover is determined as of the transaction's acquisition date and is carried over to tax years ending after such date. Generally, the acquisition date for a tax-free reorganization is the date on which the assets are transferred by the transferor or target corporation. When loss carryovers from more than one tax year are present, the loss from the earliest ending tax year is used first. NOLs cannot be carried back from the time period following the acquisition date by the acquiring corporation to offset profits earned by the acquired corporation in its tax years preceding the acquisition date.[62]

Example 7-24 ■ Target Corporation is merged into Acquiring Corporation at the close of business on June 30, 1991. Both corporations use the calendar year as their tax year. At the beginning of 1991, Target reports a $200,000 NOL carryover. Target must file a final tax return for the period January 1, 1991 through June 30, 1991. Assume that Target reports $60,000 of taxable income (before any NOL deductions) in its tax return for the short period. Target's taxable income for the January 1 through June 30, 1991 period reduces its NOL carryover to $140,000 ($200,000 − $60,000). This carryover is acquired by Acquiring. ■

Section 381(c) restricts the acquiring corporation's use of the NOL carryover in its first tax year that ends after the acquisition date. The NOL deduction is limited to the portion of the acquiring corporation's taxable income that is allocable on a daily basis to the postacquisition period.

Example 7-25 ■ Assume the same facts as in Example 7-24, except that it is now known that Acquiring Corporation's taxable income is $150,000 in 1991. Acquiring Corporation can use Target's NOL carryover to offset its taxable income that is attributable to the 184 days in the July 1 through December 31, 1991 postacquisition period, or $75,616 ([184 ÷ 365] × $150,000). The remainder of Target's NOL carryover of $64,384 ($140,000 − $75,616) is carried forward to offset Acquiring's taxable income in 1992. ■

OBJECTIVE 14
Explain how NOL carryovers are restricted following an acquisition.

Limitation on Use of Tax Attributes

Sections 382 and 269 prevent the purchasing of the assets or stock of a corporation having loss carryovers (known as the **loss corporation**) primarily to acquire the corporation's tax attributes. Similarly, Secs. 382 and 269 prevent a corporation having loss carryovers (also known as a loss corporation) from acquiring the assets or stock of a profitable corporation primarily to enable the loss corporation to use its carryovers. Section 383 provides similar restrictions for acquisitions intended to facilitate the use of capital loss and tax credit carryovers. Section 384 additionally restricts the use of pre-acquisition losses to offset built-in gains.

Section 382. Section 382 restricts the use of NOLs in purchase transactions and tax-free reorganizations when a substantial change in the stock ownership of the loss corporation occurs.

---

[62] Special rules apply to Type F reorganizations. Because only a change in form or identity occurs in such a transaction, NOLs incurred following the acquisition date can be carried back to offset profits earned in pre-acquisition tax years after a Type F reorganization has occurred.

Typical Misconception

To create an ownership change, the 5% shareholders must increase their stock ownership by more than 50 percentage points. Thus, if shareholder A increases his stock ownership from 10% to 20%, this alone is not an ownership change even though it represents a 100% increase in A's ownership.

STOCK OWNERSHIP CHANGE. The requisite stock ownership change is considered to have taken place when (1) any shift in the stock ownership involving any person(s) owning 5% or more of a corporation's stock occurs or (2) a tax-free reorganization (other than a divisive Type D or G reorganization or a Type F reorganization) has taken place *and* the percentage of stock of the new loss corporation owned by one or more 5% shareholders has increased by more than 50 percentage points over the *lowest* percentage of stock in the old loss corporation owned by such shareholders at *any* time during the preceding 3-year (or shorter) "testing" period.[63] The 5% shareholder test is based upon the value of the loss corporation's stock. Nonvoting preferred stock is excluded from the calculation.

An **old loss corporation** is any corporation that is entitled to use a NOL carryover or has a NOL for the tax year in which the ownership change occurs and which undergoes the requisite stock ownership change. A **new loss corporation** is any corporation that is entitled to use a NOL carryover after the stock ownership change.[64] For most acquisitions (e.g., the purchase of a loss corporation's stock by a new shareholder group), the old and new loss corporations are the same. The old and new loss corporations are different in many acquisitive reorganizations (e.g., a merger transaction where an unprofitable target [old loss] corporation is merged into the acquiring [new loss] corporation).

Key Point

One of the burdensome aspects of Sec. 382 is that each time the stock ownership of a 5% shareholder is changed, all 5% shareholders must be tested at that date to see if an ownership change has occurred.

Ownership changes must be tested any time that a stock transaction occurs affecting the stock that is owned by a person who owns 5% or more of the stock either before or after the change. Such change may occur because of a stock transaction involving a 5% shareholder or involving a person who does not own a 5% interest in the loss corporation but that affects the size of the stock interest owned by a 5% shareholder (i.e., a stock redemption). For purposes of applying this rule, all persons who own less than 5% of the loss corporation's stock are considered to be a single shareholder.

Example 7-26 ■

Additional Comment

The reason that the new loss corporation's use of the old loss corporation's NOLs is limited annually to the FMV of the old loss corporation multiplied by the long-term tax-exempt rate is that this limitation is supposed to approximate the rate at which the old loss corporation could have used the NOLs. Thus, the underlying theory of Sec. 382 is one of neutrality.

Acquiring Corporation (the old and new loss corporation) is a publicly traded corporation with no single individual owning more than 5% of its outstanding stock. A series of NOLs have been incurred by Acquiring in recent years, substantial amounts of which are available as carryovers. On July 3, 1991, Barry acquires 80% of Acquiring's single class of stock pursuant to a tender offer. Barry had not owned any of the Acquiring stock prior to making the acquisition. Acquiring Corporation has experienced a stock ownership change because it now has a 5% shareholder (Barry), who owns 80 percentage points more stock than he owned at any time during the testing period (Barry owned 0% during the testing period). Acquiring Corporation's NOLs are subject to the Sec. 382 limitations. ■

In many acquisitive tax-free reorganizations, the Sec. 382 stock ownership test is applied against the old loss (or target) corporation and then against the new loss (or acquiring) corporation.

Example 7-27 ■

Target Corporation is a publicly held corporation with a single class of stock outstanding. None of its shareholders owns more than 1% of the outstanding stock. Target has incurred substantial NOLs in recent years. Pursuant to a merger agreement, Target Corporation is merged into Acquiring Corporation, also a

---

[63] Sec. 382(g). Special rules permit the use of a testing period of less than 3 years for applying the 50 percentage point ownership change rule. One such situation is when a recent change in the stock ownership has occurred involving a 5% shareholder. In such case, the testing period goes back only to the date of the earlier ownership change.

[64] Secs. 382(k)(1)-(3).

publicly held corporation with a single class of stock outstanding and no single shareholder owning more than 1% of its outstanding stock. None of Target Corporation's shareholders owns any of the Acquiring stock prior to the merger. After the merger, Target Corporation's shareholders own 40% of the outstanding Acquiring stock. All of Acquiring Corporation's shareholders are aggregated for purposes of the Sec. 382 stock ownership test. Because Acquiring Corporation's shareholders owned none of the old loss corporation (Target Corporation) stock prior to the reorganization, and owned 60% of the new loss corporation (Acquiring Corporation) stock after the reorganization, the Sec. 382 loss limitation rules apply to limit the use of Target's NOL carryovers. ■

Divisive Type D and G reorganizations or Type F reorganizations may be subject to the Sec. 382 limitations if the transaction results in a more than 50 percentage point shift in stock ownership for the transferor corporation.

LOSS LIMITATION. The Sec. 382 loss limitation for any tax year ending after the stock ownership change equals the value of the old loss corporation's stock (including nonvoting preferred stock) immediately before the ownership change multiplied by the long-term tax-exempt federal rate.[65] The long-term tax-exempt federal rate is determined by the IRS and is the highest of the adjusted federal long-term rates in effect for any month in the 3-calendar-month period ending with the month in which the stock ownership change occurs.[66]

A new loss corporation is permitted to claim its current year deductions and any of its NOL and other deduction carryovers from postchange tax years. Then any NOLs from the old loss corporation (prechange tax years) can be deducted. If the amount of the NOL carryovers from the old loss corporation exceeds the Sec. 382 loss limitation, the unused carryovers are deferred until the following year, provided the end of the 15-year NOL carryforward period has not been reached. If the amount of the Sec. 382 loss limitation exceeds the new loss corporation's taxable income for the current year, the unused loss limitation is carried forward and increases the Sec. 382 loss limitation for the next year.[67] A new loss corporation that does not continue the business enterprise of the old loss corporation at all times during the 2-year period beginning on the stock ownership change date must use a zero Sec. 382 limitation for any postchange year. This zero limitation, in effect, disallows the use of the NOL carryovers.[68]

Typical Misconception
Section 382 does not disallow NOLs. Section 382 merely limits the amount of NOL carryovers that the new loss corporation can utilize on an annual basis.

Key Point
If the old loss corporation is a very large corporation relative to its NOL carryovers, Sec. 382 will not be a real obstacle in the use of the NOLs by the new loss corporation. Only when the old loss corporation has a small FMV relative to its NOL carryovers does Sec. 382 represent a major obstacle.

Example 7-28 ■ Peter purchased all of the stock of Taylor Corporation (the old and new loss corporation) from Karl in a taxable transaction that took place at the close of business on December 31, 1990. Taylor Corporation is engaged in the manufacture of brooms and has a $1,000,000 NOL carryover from 1990. Taylor continues to manufacture brooms after Peter's acquisition of a controlling interest and earns $300,000 of taxable income for 1991. The value of the Taylor stock immediately before the acquisition is $3,500,000. The applicable long-term tax-exempt federal rate is assumed to be 7%. The requisite stock ownership change has taken place since Peter has increased his ownership from zero during the testing period to 100% immediately after the acquisition. The Sec. 382 loss limitation for 1991 is $245,000 ($3,500,000 × 0.07). Taylor Corporation can claim a $245,000 NOL

---

[65] Sec. 382(b)(1).
[66] Sec. 382(f). The long-term tax-exempt federal rate for April 1991 is 6.62% (Rev. Rul. 91-23, I.R.B. 1991-13, 17). The highest long-term tax-exempt federal rate for April 1991 and the two preceding months is 6.83%.
[67] Sec. 382(b)(2).
[68] Sec. 382(c).

deduction in 1991, thereby reducing its taxable income to $55,000. The remaining $755,000 ($1,000,000 − $245,000) of NOL is carried over to 1992 and later years. ∎

Special rules apply for the year in which the stock ownership change occurs. Taxable income earned before the change is not subject to the Sec. 382 limitation. Taxable income earned after the change, however, is subject to the limitation. Allocation of income earned during the tax year to the time periods before and after the change is based on the number of days in each of the two time periods.

Old loss corporation NOLs incurred prior to the date of the stock ownership change are limited by Sec. 382. These include NOLs incurred in tax years ending prior to the date of change plus the portion of the NOL for the tax year that includes the date of change that is considered to have been incurred prior to the change. Allocation of an NOL for the tax year which includes the date of change is based on the number of days before and after the change.[69]

Section 383. Section 383 restricts the use of tax credit and capital loss carryovers when stock ownership changes occur that come under the purview of Sec. 382. The same restrictions that apply to NOLs are applied to the general business credit, the minimum tax credit, and the foreign tax credit.

Section 384. Section 384 prevents pre-acquisition losses of either the acquiring or target corporation (the loss corporation) from offsetting built-in gains recognized during the 5-year post-acquisition recognition period by another corporation (the gain corporation). Such gains can offset pre-acquisition losses of the gain corporation. This limitation applies if a corporation acquires either a controlling stock interest or the assets of another corporation and either corporation is a gain corporation.

Section 269. Section 269 applies to transactions where (1) control of a corporation is secured and (2) the principal purpose of the acquisition is "the evasion or avoidance of federal income tax by securing the benefit of a deduction," credit, and so forth. Control is defined as 50% of the voting power or 50% of the value of the outstanding stock. The IRS can use this provision to disallow a loss or credit carryover in situations where Sec. 382 does not apply. The IRS's primary problem in applying these rules is being able to show that the requisite "principal purpose" is present.

Additional Comment
While the legislative intent of Sec. 382 has not been seriously opposed, the complexity of the statute with its accompanying regulations is of some concern.

Additional Comment
Section 269 represents the IRS's oldest and broadest weapon in dealing with trafficking in NOLs. However, because of the subjectivity of the statute, Secs. 382 and 383 have turned out to be the Service's main statutory weapon in this area.

TAX PLANNING CONSIDERATIONS

Why Use a Reorganization Instead of a Taxable Transaction?

The choice between a taxable and tax-free transaction can be a difficult one. The advantages and disadvantages of the tax-free reorganization are important considerations for the buyer and seller. Depending upon their relative importance to each party, they may serve as points for negotiation and compromise when attempting to structure the transaction.

From the point of view of the acquired company's shareholders, there are a number of considerations that need to be evaluated. First, a tax-free reorganization permits a

[69] Sec. 382(b)(3).

Self-Study Question

Is a tax-free reorganization always preferable to a taxable acquisition?

Answer

No. The determination of what form an acquisition should take involves the resolution of a whole myriad of issues that relate to the parties to the reorganization. A number of these issues are discussed on this page.

deferral of tax to the shareholders unless boot is received. This permits a shareholder to retain a higher percentage of the capital after payment of any income tax liability. A second factor is that a taxable transaction permits the shareholders of the target company to convert their former equity interests into liquid assets (e.g., when cash or property other than stock or securities of the acquiring company is received). These funds can be invested in whatever manner the shareholder chooses. In a reorganization, the shareholders of the target company must retain a continuing proprietary interest in the acquiring corporation. Future success by the acquiring corporation is likely to enhance the value of this interest. If the acquiring corporation encounters financial problems, the value of the shareholder's investment may diminish. Third, losses that are realized as part of a tax-free reorganization cannot be recognized. A taxable transaction permits an immediate recognition of the loss. Fourth, gains recognized as part of a tax-free reorganization are taxed as dividend income if the effect of the boot distribution is equivalent to a dividend payment. Taxable transactions generally result in the shareholder recognizing only capital gains. This difference takes on increased importance now that capital gains are taxed at a 28% maximum tax rate. Finally, there is a difference in the treatment of the shareholder's basis. A taxable transaction permits the shareholder to step-up the basis of the stock and securities that are received to their FMV. A tax-free transaction, however, requires a lower carryover basis to be used.

From the transferor corporation's point of view, a tax-free reorganization permits the assets to be exchanged with no gain being recognized. The rules for depreciation recapture do not apply to a reorganization. In each case the recapture burden is shifted to the purchasing party.

From the purchaser's point of view, a tax-free reorganization permits an acquisition to take place without the use of substantial amounts of cash or securities. Because the shareholders of the target company do not have to recognize any gain unless boot is received, they may be willing to accept a lower sales price than would be required if the transaction is structured as a taxable purchase transaction. The purchaser must use a carryover basis for the properties acquired in a tax-free reorganization. This inability to step-up the basis of the assets to their cost or FMV reduces the attractiveness of a tax-free reorganization. This, in turn, may lower the price that the purchaser is willing to offer.

Typical Misconception

It is important to realize that when a plan for an acquisition is developed, the tax consequences are only one of many considerations that must be addressed. Often, the form of the final acquisition plan will not be optimal from a tax perspective because other factors were deemed more important.

The cost of using a taxable asset or stock acquisition transaction was increased dramatically by the Tax Reform Act of 1986. Prior to the 1986 Tax Act, a corporation that sold its assets was able to avoid recognizing its gains on the transaction by liquidating within 12 months of adopting its plan of liquidation. Similarly, a corporation that purchases the stock of a target corporation and causes the target corporation to make a Sec. 338 election ends up recognizing the same gains and losses as if the target corporation had sold the assets in a taxable transaction. These additional tax costs make the tax exemption that is available for the target corporation in a tax-free reorganization even more attractive.

A tax-free reorganization permits the purchaser to acquire the benefits of NOL, tax credit, and other carryovers from the target corporation. Such tax attributes do not carry over to the buyer in a taxable transaction.

Comparison of Consideration Used in Reorganizations

Tax-free reorganizations generally involve an exchange of the acquiring corporation's stock and securities for the assets, stock, or securities of the target corporation. The consideration that can be used in the various types of tax-free reorganizations is quite varied. The Type A reorganization (i.e., mergers and consolidations) permits the acquiring corporation the greatest flexibility. In general, the only restriction is that at least 50% of the total consideration employed be the acquiring corporation's stock. This means that cash, other property, assumption of liabilities, and securities can be used to acquire up to 50% of the assets or stock of the target corporation. In addition, the stock that is used can be either common stock or voting or nonvoting preferred stock.

The Type B reorganization (i.e., a stock-for-stock reorganization) is subject to the greatest restrictions. The acquiring corporation must exchange solely voting stock to acquire a controlling interest in the target corporation. This voting stock can be either common or preferred stock. Cash can be used only sparingly to acquire fractional share interests, to pay certain expenses of the reorganization, or to have the acquired corporation redeem some of its outstanding stock.

The Type C reorganization (i.e., an asset-for-stock reorganization) can involve the use of a wider variety of consideration than a Type B reorganization, but is not permitted the same latitude as a Type A reorganization. In a Type C reorganization, the acquiring corporation must obtain at least 80% of the target corporation's properties in exchange for its voting stock. Money, securities, nonvoting stock, and other property can be used to acquire up to 20% of the target corporation's properties. Liabilities that are assumed reduce the amount of consideration other than voting stock that can be used. Because the balance sheet of most businesses contains liabilities that are in excess of 20% of the FMV of the corporation's total assets, very few Type C reorganizations can be structured to include the payment of money and other boot property.

Because of the restrictions that are imposed on the consideration that can be used in these three primary reorganization forms, corporate management may be precluded from using certain combinations of stock, securities, and other property to effect an acquisition. For example, a corporation that wants to acquire a target corporation's stock is generally restricted to using its voting stock unless it wants to comply with the state laws for a merger transaction. Likewise, a corporation that wants to acquire the assets of a target corporation that owes a substantial amount of liabilities may be precluded from using a common stock and cash combination unless the transaction can qualify as a merger.

> **Key Point**
> The Type A reorganization is much more flexible with respect to consideration that must be used than either the Type B or Type C reorganizations. As such, the Type A reorganization is the more often used acquisition tool of these three reorganizations.

Avoiding the Reorganization Provisions

An acquisition can be changed from a tax-free reorganization to a taxable transaction if the restrictions on the use of consideration for the particular type of reorganization are not met. This change can be advantageous for the taxpayers involved. For example, the Type B reorganization rules can be avoided if the acquiring corporation makes a tender offer to the target corporation's shareholders involving an exchange of both stock of the acquiring corporation and cash for the target corporation's stock. Since this transaction does not meet the solely-for-voting-stock requirement, it is a taxable transaction for the shareholders. It is also considered to be a purchase of the target corporation's stock, thereby permitting the acquiring corporation to make a Sec. 338 deemed liquidation election and step-up the basis of the target corporation's assets to the price that was paid for the stock.

> **Typical Misconception**
> The tax-free reorganization provisions are not elective. If a transaction qualifies as a Sec. 368 reorganization, it must be treated as such. But, if the desire is for a taxable acquisition, it is usually not difficult to bust a tax-free reorganization.

Example 7-29 ■ Acquiring Corporation offers to exchange one share of its common stock (valued at $40) plus $10 cash for each share of Target Corporation's single class of common stock (valued at $50). All of Target's shareholders agree to the proposal, and exchange a total of 2,000 shares of Target stock for 2,000 shares of Acquiring common stock and $20,000 cash. At the time of the acquisition, Target's assets have a $35,000 adjusted basis, and a $110,000 FMV. Target Corporation recognizes no gain or loss with respect to the exchange. The basis of its assets remains at $35,000 unless a Sec. 338 election is made. Its shareholders must recognize the entire amount of their realized gain or loss on the exchange of their Target stock. ■

COMPLIANCE AND PROCEDURAL CONSIDERATIONS

Plan of Reorganization

One requirement for nonrecognition of gain by a transferor corporation on an asset transfer (Sec. 361) or by a shareholder on a stock transfer (Sec. 354) is that there be a plan of reorganization. A written plan is not needed but it is safest for all parties involved in the reorganization when it is reduced to writing either as a communication to the shareholders, as part of the corporate records, or as part of a written agreement between the parties. If a plan of reorganization does not exist, or a transfer or distribution is not part of the plan, it is generally a taxable event.[70] A **plan of reorganization** is defined as a consummated transaction that is specifically defined as a reorganization. Nonrecognition of gain or loss is limited to exchanges or distributions that are (1) a direct part of a reorganization and (2) undertaken for reasons germane to the continuance of the business of a corporation that is a party to a reorganization.[71]

Party to a Reorganization

Sections 354 and 361 require that a shareholder or a transferor be a party to a reorganization to have the asset or stock transfer be tax-free. Section 368(b) defines a **party to a reorganization** as "including any corporation resulting from a reorganization, and both corporations involved in a reorganization where one corporation acquires the stock or assets of a second corporation." In the case of a triangular reorganization, the corporation controlling the acquiring corporation and whose stock is used to effect the reorganization is also a party to a reorganization.

Additional Comment
The IRS has announced that it will no longer issue "comfort rulings" as to whether a transaction qualifies as a Type A, (a)(2)(D), (a)(2)(E), B, E, or F reorganization [Rev. Proc. 91-3].

Ruling Requests

Before proceeding with a taxable or tax-free acquisition or disposition, most taxpayers usually request an advance ruling from the IRS on the tax consequences of the transaction. Advance rulings are generally requested because of the complexity of the tax law in the reorganization area and because these transactions involve dollar amounts that are generally quite large. A subsequent redetermination by the IRS or the courts that a completed reorganization is taxable might have substantial adverse tax consequences to the parties involved in the transaction. Note that an advance ruling is only issued for reorganizations that conform with the guidelines that have been promulgated by the IRS in Rev. Proc. 77-37.[72] However, these guidelines do not have the force of law, and in many cases may be stricter than the court precedents.

---

[70] *A. T. Evans*, 30 B.T.A. 746 (1934), acq. XIII-2 C.B. 7; and *William Hewitt*, 19 B.T.A. 771 (1930).
[71] Reg. Sec. 1.368-2(g).
[72] 1977-2 C.B. 568.

To obtain an advance ruling, the taxpayer makes a written request indicating all of the facts regarding the transaction. The IRS sends the taxpayer a written response indicating the tax treatment that will be accorded the transaction and the authority for this treatment. If the response does not meet with the taxpayer's expectations, the taxpayer can either restructure the transaction to achieve the desired tax results, abandon the transaction, or proceed with the transaction as originally planned. However, a taxpayer who proceeds with a reorganization transaction in spite of a negative ruling should be prepared to have the transaction challenged.

The tax consequences of certain reorganization issues are under review by the IRS at all times. As a result, the IRS refuses to issue advance rulings on the tax consequences of similar transactions until the questions under review have been resolved. Information on the types of reorganization issues that are under review is periodically made available to taxpayers through the publication of revenue procedures.[73]

Reporting Requirements

Persons who are involved in the acquisition of control of a corporation in a single transaction or a series of transactions, or who engage in a recapitalization or other change to the capital structure of a corporation, are required to make an information return filing (Form 8820) with the IRS that sets forth the identity of the parties to the transaction, the type of transaction, the consideration used, the fees paid to persons in connection with the transaction, the changes in the capital structure involved, and any other information required by the IRS. Failure to comply with this requirement will result in a $500 per day penalty. A special exemption will be provided by the IRS for small corporations in forthcoming regulations.[74]

PROBLEM MATERIALS

DISCUSSION QUESTIONS

7-1. Compare the tax consequences arising from a taxable asset acquisition transaction and an asset-for-stock tax-free reorganization, giving consideration to the following points:
   a. Consideration employed to effect the transaction
   b. Recognition of gain by the target corporation
   c. Basis of property to the acquiring corporation
   d. Gain or loss recognized when the target corporation is liquidated.

7-2. What advantages exist for the buyer when he acquires the assets of a corporation in a taxable transaction? For the seller when he exchanges his stock in a taxable transaction?

7-3. Which of the following events that occur as part of a tax-free reorganization require the target corporation to recognize gain? Assume that in all cases the target corporation is liquidated as part of the reorganization.
   a. Transfer of appreciated target corporation property in exchange for stock and short-term notes

---

[73] Rev. Proc. 91-3, I.R.B. 1991-1, 52. See Sec. 3.01.25-29 of this revenue procedure concerning the IRS's indication that it will not issue an advance ruling regarding whether a transaction constitutes a Type A, B, E, or F reorganization and whether the taxpayer is subject to the consequences of qualifying as a reorganization when such issues are adequately discussed by statute, regulation, Supreme Court decision, or government promulgation. This position is designed to reduce the number of "comfort" rulings issued by the IRS in the reorganization area.

[74] Sec. 6043(c).

     b. Transfer of appreciated target corporation property in exchange for stock and the assumption of the target corporation's liabilities
     c. Transfer of appreciated target corporation property in exchange for stock and cash. The cash is distributed to the target corporation's shareholders.
     d. Transfer of appreciated target corporation property in exchange for stock and cash. The cash is used to pay off the target corporation's liabilities.

7-4. Explain the boot rule as it applies to the shareholders in a tax-free reorganization.

7-5. How is the character of the shareholders' recognized gain determined in a tax-free reorganization?

7-6. Evaluate the following statement: Individual shareholders that must recognize gain as the result of receiving boot in a corporate reorganization generally will prefer to report capital gain income while corporate shareholders generally will prefer to report dividend income.

7-7. How is the basis for the stocks and securities received by a shareholder determined? How is the basis determined for boot property?

7-8. Which tax-free reorganizations are acquisitive transactions? Divisive transactions?

7-9. Compare the type of consideration that can be employed to effect Type A, B, and C reorganizations.

7-10. How does the IRS interpret the continuity of interest doctrine for a Type A merger transaction?

7-11. What is a triangular reorganization?

7-12. Compare the tax consequences of a triangular Type A merger transaction with a regular Type A merger transaction that is followed by a transfer of the assets to a newly created, controlled subsidiary corporation.

7-13. What is a reverse triangular merger? What advantage does a reverse triangular merger provide over a regular merger?

7-14. What are the advantages of using an asset-for-stock reorganization instead of a Type A merger transaction? The disadvantages?

7-15. How does the IRS interpret the "substantially all" of the assets requirement for a Type C reorganization?

7-16. Explain why an acquiring corporation is generally prohibited from using cash as part of the consideration it uses to accomplish a Type C reorganization.

7-17. Some transactions may be characterized as either a Type C or a Type D reorganization. Which reorganization provision controls in the case of an overlap?

7-18. Explain the circumstances in which money and other property can be used in a Type B reorganization.

7-19. Acquiring Corporation has purchased for cash a 5% interest in Target Corporation's stock. Acquiring Corporation's management desires to make a tender offer to acquire the remaining Target stock in exchange for Acquiring stock. Can this tender offer be accomplished as a Type B reorganization? What problems may be encountered in structuring the acquisition as a tax-free reorganization?

7-20. Acquiring Corporation wants to exchange its voting common stock for all of Target Corporation's single class of stock in a tender offer. Only 85% of Target Corporation's shareholders agree to tender their shares. Assuming the reorganization is accomplished, what options exist for Acquiring to acquire the remaining shares as part of the reorganization? at a later date?

7-21. The tax consequences to a corporation distributing the stock of a controlled subsidiary corporation to its shareholders was explained in Chapter 4. Explain the difference between such a distribution and a divisive Type D reorganization.

7-22. What is a recapitalization?

7-23. Explain why a transaction might satisfy a literal interpretation of the Sec. 368 requirements for a tax-free reorganization, yet fail to be treated as a reorganization.

7-24. Explain the following judicial doctrines as they apply to a reorganization:
   a. Continuity of proprietary interest doctrine
   b. Continuity of business enterprise doctrine
   c. Business purpose doctrine
   d. Step transaction doctrine

7-25. Which of the seven types of reorganizations result in a carryover of the target (or transferor) corporation's tax attributes?

7-26. What restrictions are placed on the acquisition of the tax attributes of a loss corporation?

7-27. Define the following terms:
   a. Stock ownership change
   b. Old loss corporation
   c. New loss corporation

7-28. Explain why Sec. 382 will not be an obstacle to the use of NOL carryovers following a purchase transaction taking place if the old loss corporation is large relative to its NOL carryovers.

7-29. What is a plan of reorganization?

7-30. Why is it generally advantageous for a taxpayer to secure an advance ruling regarding a reorganization transaction?

PROBLEMS

7-31. *Amount of Shareholder Gain or Loss.* Silvia exchanges all of her Victory Corporation stock for $300,000 of Market Corporation stock pursuant to Victory's merger into Market Corporation. Immediately after the stock-for-stock exchange Silvia owns 25% of the Market stock. Silvia's adjusted basis in the Victory stock is $175,000 before the merger.
   a. What is the amount of Silvia's recognized gain or loss?
   b. What is Silvia's basis for the Market stock?
   c. How would your answers to Parts a and b change if Silvia instead receives Victory stock worth $250,000 and $50,000 cash?

7-32. *Amount of Corporate Gain or Loss.* Turtle Corporation transfers all of its assets and $100,000 of its liabilities in exchange for Beach Corporation stock having a $600,000 FMV as part of a transaction in which Turtle is liquidated. Turtle Corporation's basis for its assets is $475,000.
   a. What is the amount of Turtle's recognized gain or loss?
   b. What is Beach's basis for the assets?
   c. What is the amount of Turtle's recognized gain or loss when it distributes the stock to its shareholders?
   d. How would your answers to Parts a through c change if Turtle's basis for the assets had instead been $750,000?

7-33. *Amount and Character of Shareholder Gain or Loss.* Stan owns 100% of the stock of Dolphin Corporation having a $600,000 adjusted basis. As part of the merger of Dolphin Corporation into Bear Corporation, Stan exchanges his Dolphin stock for Bear Corporation common stock having a $3,000,000 FMV and $750,000 in cash. Stan retains a 60% interest in Bear Corporation immediately after the merger.
   a. What is the amount and character of Stan's recognized gain?

b. What is Stan's basis in the Bear stock?

7-34. *Amount and Character of Shareholder Gain or Loss.* Black Corporation exchanges $375,000 of its preferred stock for all of White Corporation's assets pursuant to White's merger into Black Corporation. The assets have an adjusted basis of $225,000. White Corporation's sole shareholder, Lois, exchanges her White stock having an adjusted basis of $200,000 for the preferred stock. Lois, owns none of Black's voting stock, and owns only 4% (by value) of the Black stock immediately after the reorganization.
a. What is the amount of White Corporation's recognized gain or loss on the asset transfer? On the distribution of the stock to Lois?
b. What is Black Corporation's basis for the assets received?
c. What is the amount and character of Lois's recognized gain or loss?
d. What is Lois's basis for the Black stock?

7-35. *Characterization of the Shareholder's Gain or Loss.* Turbo Corporation has 1,000,000 shares of common stock and 200,000 shares of nonvoting preferred stock outstanding. Pursuant to a merger agreement, Kelly Corporation exchanges its common stock worth $15,000,000 for the Turbo common stock and $10,000,000 in cash for the Turbo preferred stock. Some shareholders of Turbo Corporation received only Kelly common stock for their common stock, some shareholders received only cash for their preferred stock, and some shareholders received both cash and Kelly common stock for their Turbo preferred and common stock, respectively. Shareholders owning approximately 10% of the Turbo common stock also owned Turbo preferred stock. The total cash received by these shareholders amounted to $1,500,000. The Turbo Corporation common stockholders end up owning 15% of the Kelly stock. What is the tax treatment of the common stock and cash received by each of the three groups of Turbo Corporation shareholders?

7-36. *Requirements for a Type A Reorganization.* Union Corporation is planning to acquire all of the assets of Federal Corporation in a merger transaction. Federal's assets have a $5,000,000 FMV and a $2,200,000 adjusted basis. Which of the following transactions qualify as a Type A reorganization assuming that Federal Corporation is liquidated?
a. The assets are exchanged for $5,000,000 of Union common stock.
b. The assets are exchanged for $5,000,000 of Union nonvoting preferred stock.
c. The assets are exchanged for $5,000,000 of Union securities.
d. The assets are exchanged for $3,500,000 of Union preferred stock and $1,500,000 in cash.
e. The assets are exchanged for $3,000,000 of Union common stock and Union's assumption of $2,000,000 of Federal liabilities.

7-37. *Tax Consequences of a Merger.* Gould Corporation exchanges $1,000,000 of its common stock and $250,000 of Gould Corporation bonds for all of Fox Corporation's outstanding stock. Fox Corporation is then merged into Gould Corporation with Gould receiving assets having a $1,250,000 FMV and an $875,000 adjusted basis. As part of the merger, Brett exchanges his 15% interest in Fox Corporation's single class of stock, having an adjusted basis of $80,000, for $150,000 in Gould stock and $37,500 in Gould bonds. Following the reorganization, Brett owns 6% of Gould's stock. Fox Corporation's E&P balance is $300,000.
a. What is the amount of Fox Corporation's recognized gain or loss on the asset transfer?
b. What is Gould Corporation's basis for the assets received in the exchange?
c. What are the amount and character of Brett's recognized gain or loss?
d. What is Brett's basis for the Gould stock? For the Gould bonds?

7-38. *Requirements for a Type C Reorganization.* Heart Corporation is planning to acquire all of the assets of Diamond Corporation in an asset-for-stock (Type C) tax-free reorganization. Diamond's assets have an adjusted basis of $600,000 and a $1,000,000 FMV. Which of the following transactions qualify as a Type C reorganization (assuming that Diamond is liquidated as part of the reorganization)?
a. The assets are exchanged for $800,000 of Heart common stock and $200,000 of cash.
b. The assets are exchanged for $800,000 of Heart common stock and $200,000 of Heart bonds.
c. The assets are exchanged for $1,000,000 of Heart nonvoting preferred stock.
d. The assets are exchanged for $700,000 of Heart common stock and Heart's assumption of $300,000 of Diamond's liabilities.

e. The assets are exchanged for $700,000 of Heart common stock, Heart's assumption of $200,000 of Diamond's liabilities, and $100,000 in cash.

7-39. *Tax Consequences of a Type C Reorganization.* Ash Corporation exchanges $250,000 of its voting common stock and $50,000 of its bonds for all of Bush Corporation's assets as part of a Type C tax-free reorganization. Bush Corporation is liquidated, with each of its two shareholders receiving equal amounts of the Ash Corporation stock and bonds. Barbara has a $50,000 basis in her stock, and George has a $200,000 basis in his stock. George and Barbara each own 8% of Ash's stock immediately after the reorganization. At the time of the reorganization, Bush Corporation's E&P balance is $75,000, and its assets have an adjusted basis of $225,000.
  a. What is the amount of Bush Corporation's recognized gain or loss on the asset transfer? On the distribution of the stock and bonds?
  b. What are the amount and character of each shareholder's recognized gain or loss?
  c. What is the basis of each shareholder's Ash stock? Ash bonds?

7-40. *Tax Consequences of a Type C Reorganization.* Space Corporation exchanges its noncash assets having a $300,000 FMV and a $175,000 adjusted basis for $250,000 of Dale Corporation voting stock and Dale Corporation's assumption of $50,000 of Space's liabilities as part of a Type C tax-free reorganization. Space is liquidated with its sole shareholder, Michelle, receiving all of the Dale stock in exchange for her Space stock having an adjusted basis of $100,000. Michelle owns 12% of Dale's stock immediately after the reorganization.
  a. What is the amount of Space's recognized gain or loss on the asset transfer? On the distribution of the stock?
  b. What is Dale's basis for the assets it receives?
  c. What effect would the transfer of Space's assets to Subsidiary Corporation (a subsidiary controlled by Dale Corporation) have on the reorganization?
  d. What are the amount and character of Michelle's recognized gain or loss?
  e. What is Michelle's basis for her Dale stock?

7-41. *Tax Consequences of a Divisive Type D Reorganization.* West Corporation is owned equally by four shareholders. Its activities are conducted in two operating divisions—the road construction division and meat packing division. In an attempt to separate the two activities into separate corporations, the assets and liabilities of the road construction division (60% of West's total net assets) are transferred to East Corporation in exchange for all of East's single class of stock. The assets of the road construction division have a $2,750,000 FMV and a $1,100,000 adjusted basis. A total of $500,000 of liabilities are transferred to East. The $2,250,000 of East stock is distributed ratably to each of the four shareholders.
  a. What is the amount of West Corporation's recognized gain or loss on the asset transfer? On the distribution of the East stock?
  b. What are the amount and character of each shareholder's recognized gain or loss on the distribution if each shareholder's basis in the West stock is $200,000?
  c. What is the basis of each shareholder's West and East stock after the reorganization? (Assume the West stock is worth $1,500,000 immediately after the distribution.)

7-42. *Tax Consequences of a Divisive Type D Reorganization.* Light Corporation is owned equally by two individual shareholders. The shareholders no longer can agree on matters concerning Light's operations. Tom agrees to a plan whereby $500,000 of Light's assets (having an adjusted basis of $350,000) and $100,000 of Light's liabilities are transferred to TJ Corporation in exchange for all of its common stock. Tom will exchange all of his Light stock having a $150,000 adjusted basis for the $400,000 of TJ stock.
  a. What is the amount of Light Corporation's recognized gain or loss on the asset transfer? On the distribution of the TJ stock?
  b. What are the amount and character of Tom's recognized gain or loss?
  c. What is Tom's basis for his TJ stock?

7-43. *Requirements for a Type B Reorganization.* Bear Corporation is planning to acquire all of the stock of Bull Corporation in a stock-for-stock (Type B) tax-free reorganization. Which of the following transactions will qualify as a Type B reorganization?
  a. All of Bull's stock is exchanged for $1,000,000 of Bear voting preferred stock.

b. All of Bull's stock is exchanged for $750,000 of Bear voting common stock and $250,000 of Bear bonds.
c. All of Bull's stock is exchanged for $1,000,000 of Bear voting common stock, and the shareholders of Bull end up owning less than 1% of Bear's stock.
d. Ninety percent of Bull's stock is exchanged for $900,000 of Bear voting common stock. One shareholder who owns 10% of the Bull stock exercises his right under state law to have his shares redeemed for cash by Bull Corporation and receives $100,000.

7-44. *Tax Consequences of a Type B Reorganization.* Crown Corporation's single class of stock is owned equally by Paul and Andy who are unrelated. Each shareholder has a $125,000 basis for their 1,000 shares of Crown stock. Hill Corporation exchanges 2,500 shares of its voting common stock having a $100 per share FMV for each shareholder's Crown stock in a single transaction. Immediately after the reorganization each shareholder owns 15% of the Hill stock.
a. What are the amount and character of each shareholder's recognized gain or loss?
b. What is each shareholder's basis for their Hill stock?
c. What is Hill Corporation's basis for the Crown stock?
d. How would your answers to Parts a through c change if Hill Corporation instead exchanged 2,000 shares of Hill common stock and $50,000 in cash for each shareholder's Crown stock?

7-45. *Tax Consequences of a Type B Reorganization.* Daisy Corporation exchanges $1,500,000 of its voting common stock for all of Rose Corporation's single class of stock. Pam owns all of the Rose stock, which has a basis of $375,000. Pam owns 25% of the Daisy stock after the reorganization.
a. What are the amount and character of Pam's recognized gain or loss?
b. What is Pam's basis for her Daisy stock?
c. What is Daisy Corporation's basis for the Rose stock?
d. What are the tax consequences for all parties to the acquisition if Daisy Corporation liquidates Rose Corporation as part of the plan of reorganizaton?

7-46. *Tax Consequences of a Type B Reorganization.* Ski Corporation purchases 10% of the Slope Corporation stock from Cathy for $250,000 in cash on January 30, 1990. Andrea and Bill each exchange one-half of the remaining 90% of the Slope stock for $1,800,000 of Ski stock on May 30, 1991. Andrea and Bill each have a $200,000 basis for their Slope stock. Andrea and Bill together own 30% of the Ski stock immediately after the reorganization.
a. What are the amount and character of Andrea and Bill's recognized gain or loss?
b. What are Andrea and Bill's bases for their Ski stock?
c. What is Ski Corporation's basis for the Slope stock?
d. How would your answer to Parts a through c change if Ski Corporation had instead acquired the remaining Slope stock on May 30, 1990?

7-47. *Requirements for a Type E Reorganization.* Master Corporation is planning to undertake a recapitalization. Explain the tax consequences of each of the three independent transactions.
a. A class of nonvoting preferred stock is exchanged for common stock. $300,000 of dividends for the current year and prior years on the preferred stock are paid in cash.
b. Master Corporation bonds in the amount of $3,000,000 will be exchanged for a similar dollar amount of preferred stock. In addition, $180,000 of unpaid interest will be paid by issuing Master preferred stock to the former bondholders.
c. Ron owns all of the Master Corporation's single class of common stock. He is planning on exchanging 75% of his stock for a new class of nonvoting, preferred stock. The remaining 25% of the common stock will be gifted to his three children. Ron's three children, who have worked for the company for a number of years, will assume all management duties for the company.

7-48. *Tax Consequences of a Type E Reorganization.* Tyrone, age 70, owns 80% of the single class of Alpha Corporation stock. Tyrone's daughter owns the remaining Alpha stock. Pursuant to the advice of his accountant, Tyrone agrees to exchange all of his common stock for a new class of Alpha Corporation voting preferred stock. Both the common stock that is surrendered and the preferred stock that is received are valued at $2,500,000. Tyrone's basis for his common stock is $400,000. Alpha Corporation's E&P balance immediately preceding the reorganization is $300,000.

a. What are the amount and character of Tyrone's recognized gain or loss?
b. What is Tyrone's basis for the preferred stock?
c. How would your answer to Parts a and b change if Tyrone instead received preferred stock valued at $2,200,000 and $300,000 in cash?
d. What possible transfer tax implications might the recapitalization that is suggested by the accountant have for Tyrone?

7-49. *Tax Consequences of a Type E Reorganization.* Milan Corporation is owned by four individual shareholders. Andy and Bob each own 40% of the outstanding common and preferred stock while Chris and Doug each own 10% of the two classes of stock. The shareholders desire to retire the preferred stock that was issued five years ago when the corporation was in the midst of a major expansion. Retirement of the preferred stock will obviate the need to pay annual dividends on the preferred stock. Explain the tax consequences of the following two alternatives to the shareholders:

(1) The $100 par preferred stock is redeemed for its $120 call price. Each shareholder purchased his preferred stock at par five years ago.
(2) Each share of the $100 par preferred stock is exchanged for $120 of additional common stock.

What nontax advantages might exist for selecting one alternative over the other?

7-50. *Reorganization Requirements.* Discuss the tax consequences of the following corporate reorganizations to the parties to the reorganization:
a. Adobe Corporation and Bullet Corporation are merged under the laws of the State of Florida. The shareholders of Adobe Corporation receive $300,000 of Bullet stock and $700,000 of Bullet securities for their Adobe stock.
b. Tyler Corporation exchanges $1,000,000 of its voting common stock for all of the noncash assets of Indiana Corporation. The transaction meets all the requirements for a Type C reorganization. Indiana Corporation is divided into two operating divisions—meat packing and meat distribution. Tyler Corporation retains the meat packing division's assets and continues to conduct its activities, but sells the assets of the meat distribution division.
c. Parent Corporation transfers $500,000 of investment securities to Subsidiary Corporation in exchange for all of its single class of stock. The Subsidiary stock is exchanged for one-third of the stock held by each of Parent Corporation's shareholders. Six months after engaging in the reorganization, the investment securities are distributed to Subsidiary Corporation's shareholders pursuant to the liquidation of Subsidiary.

7-51. *Determining the Type of Reorganization Transaction.* For each of the following transactions indicate its reorganization designation (e.g., Type A, Type B, etc.). Assume all common stock is voting stock.
a. Anderson and Brown Corporations exchange their assets for common stock of newly created Computer Corporation. Following the exchange, Anderson and Brown Corporations are liquidated. The transaction satisfies the State of Michigan corporation law requirements.
b. Price Corporation (incorporated in the State of Texas) exchanges all of its assets for all of the single class of stock of Price Corporation (incorporated in the State of Delaware). Following the exchange, Price Corporation (Texas) is liquidated.
c. All of Gates Corporation's noncumulative, 10% preferred stock is exchanged for Gates Corporation common stock.
d. Hobbs Corporation exchanges its common stock for 90% of the outstanding common stock and 80% of the outstanding nonvoting preferred stock of Calvin Corporation. The remaining Calvin stock is held by about 30 individual investors.
e. Sailor Corporation transfers the assets of its two operating divisions to Major and Minor Corporations in exchange for all of each corporation's single class of stock. The Major and Minor stocks are distributed pursuant to the liquidation of Sailor.
f. Hall Corporation has $3,000,000 of assets and $1,000,000 of liabilities. Elf Corporation exchanges $2,000,000 of its common stock for all of Hall Corporation's assets and liabilities. Hall Corporation is liquidated, and its shareholders end up owning 11% of Elf's stock following the transaction.

7-52. *Tax Attribute Carryovers.* Ocean Corporation exchanges $2,000,000 of its common stock for all of the noncash assets of Creek Corporation at the close of business on June 30, 1991. Creek Corporation uses its cash to pay off its liabilities and then liquidates. Creek and Ocean Corporations report the following taxable income amounts:

Tax Year Ending	Ocean Corp.	Creek Corp.
December 31, 1988	($100,000)	($75,000)
December 31, 1989	60,000	10,000
December 31, 1990	70,000	(90,000)
June 30, 1991	XXX	(40,000)
December 31, 1991	72,000	XXX

a. What tax returns must be filed by Ocean and Creek for 1991?
b. What is the amount of the NOL carryover that is acquired by Ocean?
c. Ignoring any implications of Sec. 382, what amount of Creek Corporation's NOL can be used by Ocean Corporation in 1991 (assume all months have 30 days)?

7-53. Sec. 382 Limitation—Purchase Transaction. Murray Corporation's stock is owned by about 1,000 shareholders, none of whom own more than 1% of the stock. Pursuant to a tender offer, Keith purchases all of the Murray stock for $4,000,000 cash at the close of business on December 31, 1990. Prior to the acquisition, Keith did not own any Murray stock. Murray Corporation had incurred substantial NOLs, which at the end of 1990 totaled $1,000,000. Murray Corporation's taxable income is expected to be $200,000 and $600,000, respectively, for 1991 and 1992. Assuming that the long-term tax-exempt federal rate is 8% and Murray Corporation continues in the same trade or business, what amount of NOLs can be used by Murray Corporation in 1991 and 1992?

7-54. Sec. 382 Limitation—Tax-Free Reorganization. Jones Corporation is a profitable publicly traded corporation. None of its shareholders own more than 1% of its stock. On July 1, 1990, Jones Corporation exchanges $6,000,000 of its stock for all of the stock of Turner Corporation as part of a merger transaction. Turner Corporation is owned by a single shareholder Tara, who receives 15% of the Jones stock as part of the reorganization. Tara owns none of the Jones stock prior to the merger. Turner Corporation has accumulated $2,500,000 in NOL carryovers prior to being merged into Jones. Jones Corporation expects to earn $1,000,000 and $1,500,000 in taxable income during 1990 and 1991, respectively. Assuming that the long-term tax-exempt federal rate is 8%, what amount of NOLs can be used by Jones Corporation in 1990 and 1991?

7-55. Sec. 382 Limitation—Alternative Transaction Forms. Progress Corporation, 100% owned by Julie, has assets with a $3,000,000 FMV, a $1,750,000 adjusted basis, and $1,000,000 in liabilities. Because of a general business slowdown, Progress has accumulated $350,000 of NOL carryovers from the past 3 years. Voyles Corporation approaches Julie about acquiring the Progress Corporation business activities. Julie is in the 31% marginal tax bracket. Evaluate the following acquisition alternatives from both the buyer's and seller's points of view:

- Acquisition of the Progress stock for $2,000,000 in cash
- Acquisition of the Progress stock for $2,000,000 of Voyles 8%, cumulative, voting preferred stock
- Acquisition of the Progress assets for $3,000,000 cash

7-56. Successive Reorganization Transactions. Small Corporation is owned equally by Alice and Betty. Each shareholder has a $100,000 basis in their stock. Small Corporation exchanges all of its assets and liabilities for $500,000 of U.S. Manufacturing Corporation common stock. Following the exchange, Small Corporation is liquidated, and Alice and Betty each end up owning approximately 2% of the U.S. Manufacturing stock. Three years later, U.S. Manufacturing Corporation is merged into Worldwide Manufacturing Corporation. Each of the U.S. Manufacturing shareholders receive Worldwide stock in exchange for their stockholdings. Alice and Betty each receive $1,000,000 of Worldwide stock in exchange for their U.S. Manufacturing stock. Following the exchange, Alice and Betty each end up owning less than 1% of the Worldwide stock.

a. What are the tax consequences of the transfer of the Small Corporation assets?

b. What are the tax consequences of the exchange of the U.S. Manufacturing stock?

CASE STUDY PROBLEMS

7-57. *Comparative Acquisition Forms.* Bailey Corporation owns a number of automotive parts shops. Bill Smith owns an automotive parts shop that has been in existence for 40 years and has competed with one of Bailey's locations. Bill is thinking about retirement and would like to sell his business. He has his CPA prepare a balance sheet which he takes to the President of Bailey Corporation that has been a long-time friend.

Assets	Adjusted Basis	FMV
Cash	$250,000	$250,000
Accounts receivable	75,000	70,000
Inventories (FIFO)	600,000	1,750,000
Equipment	200,000	250,000
Building and Land	60,000	400,000
Total	$1,185,000	$2,720,000

Should Bailey Corporation make the acquisition, it intends to operate the automotive parts shop using its own tradename in the location that Bill has used for 40 years. The President has asked you to prepare a summary of the tax consequences of a purchase of all of the assets or stock of Bill's corporation using cash and Bailey Corporation notes and the consequences of an asset-for-stock tax-free reorganization using solely Bailey stock. Upon interviewing Bill, you find out the following additional information: Bill's business is operated as a C corporation. $200,000 of accounts payable are outstanding. Bill has depreciated the building using the straight-line method. The equipment is Sec. 1245 property. The after-tax profits for each of the last three years has been in excess of $300,000, and Bill suspects that there is some goodwill value that is not shown on the balance sheet.

Required: Prepare a memorandum which outlines the tax consequences of each of the three alternative acquisition transactions assuming that $2,800,000 is the anticipated cash purchase price for the assets and $2,600,000 for the stock.

7-58. Assume the same facts as in the preceding case study except that you are to prepare the memorandum which outlines the tax consequences of each of the three methods of selling the business for Bill Smith. Assume that Bill has a net worth of $1,000,000 of real estate holdings excluding the parts business and that he has about $500,000 in his pension plan.

TAX RESEARCH PROBLEMS

7-59. Indigo Corporation acquires 8% of Wool Corporation's single class of stock for cash on January 10, 1991. On August 25, 1991, Indigo Corporation makes a tender offer to exchange Indigo common stock for the remaining Wool stock. Wool Corporation shareholders tender 85% of the outstanding Wool stock. The exchange is completed on September 25, 1991. Do part or all of the two acquisition transactions qualify as a tax-free reorganization? If part or all of either transaction is taxable to Wool Corporation's shareholders, can you offer any suggestions for restructuring the acquisitions to improve the tax consequences of the transaction, assuming that Indigo Corporation does not desire to make a Sec. 338 election?

A partial list of research sources is

- Sec. 368(a)(1)(B).
- Reg. Sec. 1.368-2(c).
- *Eldon S. Chapman, et al. v. CIR*, 45 AFTR 2d 80-1290, 80-1 USTC ¶ 9330 (1st Cir., 1980).
- *Arden S. Heverly, et al. v. CIR*, 45 AFTR 2d 80-1122, 80-1 USTC ¶ 9322 (3rd Cir., 1980).

7-60. Jordan Corporation's single class of stock is entirely owned by Michelle. On August 15, 1990, Michelle exchanges her 300,000 shares of Jordan stock, having an adjusted basis of $900,000, for 100,000 shares of Basic Corporation common stock pursuant to a plan of reorganization. The Basic stock has a $3,000,000 market value. Basic Corporation has a single class of stock outstanding, and Michelle owns 18% of this stock immediately after the reorganization. Jordan Corporation is operated as a separate subsidiary after the acquisition. On December 1, 1990,

Jordan Corporation adopts a plan of liquidation. The assets and liabilities of Jordan Corporation are distributed to Basic Corporation on February 10, 1991. Following the liquidation, the activities of Jordan Corporation are operated as a separate division of Basic Corporation. What are the tax consequences of the acquisition and subsequent liquidation of Jordan Corporation?

A partial list of resources is

- Secs. 332, 368(a)(1)(B), and 368(a)(1)(C).
- Rev. Rul. 67-274, 1967-2 C.B. 141.

7-61. Diversified Corporation is a successful bank with approximately ten branches. Al, Bob, and Cathy created Diversified Corporation 6 years ago and own all of the Diversified stock. Diversified has constructed a new building in downtown Metropolis which houses a banking facility on the first floor, offices for its employees on the second and third floors, and office space to be leased out to third parties on the fourth through twelfth floors. Since the building was completed 6 months ago, approximately 20% of the floor space on the upper floors has been occupied. Pursuant to a plan of reorganization, Diversified proposes to transfer the building to Metropolis Real Estate (MRE) Corporation in exchange for all of the MRE common stock. The building will be the only property owned by MRE following the reorganization. Diversified owns no other real estate since it currently leases the locations for its ten retail banking branches. The MRE common stock will be distributed by Diversified ratably to Al, Bob, and Cathy, who will end up holding all of the Diversified and MRE common stocks. Does the proposed transaction satisfy the requirements for a tax-free reorganization?

A partial list of resources is

- Secs. 355 and 368(a)(1)(D).
- Reg. Sec. 1.355-3(b).
- *Theodore F. Appleby v. CIR*, 9 AFTR 372, 62-1 USTC ¶ 9178 (3rd. Cir., 1962).

8: Consolidated Tax Returns

CHAPTER OUTLINE

LEARNING OBJECTIVES 8-2
SOURCE OF THE CONSOLIDATED TAX RETURN RULES 8-3
DEFINITION OF AN AFFILIATED GROUP 8-3
  Requirements 8-3
  Comparison with Controlled Group Definitions 8-4
CONSOLIDATED TAXABLE INCOME 8-6
  Income Included in the Consolidated Tax Return 8-7
  Affiliated Group Elections 8-8
  Termination of the Affiliated Group 8-9
INTERCOMPANY TRANSACTIONS 8-11
  Deferred Intercompany Transactions 8-11
  Other Intercompany Transactions 8-16
DIVIDENDS RECEIVED BY GROUP MEMBERS 8-16
  Elimination Procedure 8-16
  Consolidated Dividends-Received Deduction 8-18
CONSOLIDATED CHARITABLE CONTRIBUTIONS DEDUCTION 8-19
NET OPERATING LOSSES 8-20
  Current Year NOLs 8-20
  Carrybacks and Carryforwards of Consolidated NOLs 8-21
  Carryback of Consolidated NOL to Separate Return Year 8-22
  Carryforward of Consolidated NOL to Separate Return Year 8-24
  Special Loss Limitations 8-24
CONSOLIDATED CAPITAL GAINS AND LOSSES 8-28
  Section 1231 Gains and Losses 8-30
  Capital Gains and Losses 8-30
COMPUTATION OF THE AFFILIATED GROUP'S TAX LIABILITY 8-32
  Regular Tax Liability 8-32
  Corporate Alternative Minimum Tax Liability 8-33
CONSOLIDATED TAX CREDITS 8-34
  General Business Credit 8-34
  Foreign Tax Credit 8-35
TAX PLANNING CONSIDERATIONS 8-36
  Advantages of Filing a Consolidated Tax Return 8-36
  Disadvantages of Filing a Consolidated Tax Return 8-36
  Election Not to Defer Intercompany Gains and Losses 8-37
  100% Dividends-Received Deduction Election 8-37
  Estimated Tax Payments 8-37
COMPLIANCE AND PROCEDURAL CONSIDERATIONS 8-39
  The Basic Election 8-39
  Parent Corporation as Agent for the Affiliated Group 8-39
  Liability for Taxes Due 8-40
  Filing for NOL or Credit Refund 8-40
PROBLEM MATERIALS 8-41
  Discussion Questions 8-41
  Problems 8-43
  Tax Form/Return Preparation Problem 8-49
  Case Study Problem 8-50
  Tax Research Problems 8-50

LEARNING OBJECTIVES

After studying this chapter, you should be able to

1. Determine whether a group of corporations is an affiliated group
2. Calculate consolidated taxable income for an affiliated group
3. Determine whether a transaction is an intercompany transaction or not
4. Explain the reporting of a deferred intercompany transaction
5. Explain the reporting of an other intercompany transaction
6. Calculate an affiliated group's consolidated NOL
7. Calculate the carryback or carryover of a consolidated NOL
8. Determine how the special loss limitations restrict the use of separate and consolidated NOL carrybacks and carryovers
9. Calculate the consolidated regular tax liability for an affiliated group
10. Calculate the consolidated alternative minimum tax liability for an affiliated group
11. Explain the advantages and disadvantages of filing a consolidated tax return
12. Explain the procedures for making an initial consolidated return election

Additional Comment
Filing a consolidated tax return does not affect the reporting of other taxes such as payroll, sales, or property taxes. Also, some states do not allow the filing of consolidated tax returns for state income tax purposes.

Affiliated corporations (i.e., a parent corporation and at least one subsidiary corporation) have two options for filing their federal income tax returns:

1. Each member of the group can file separate tax returns that report its own income and expenses. No special treatment is provided for transactions between group members. However, the group can elect to claim a 100% dividends-received deduction for intragroup dividends.
2. The affiliated group can file a single tax return, called a **consolidated tax return,** that reports the results for all its group members. A number of special treatments are applied to transactions between group members (e.g., deferring gains and losses on intercompany transactions and eliminating intragroup dividends).

Some consolidated tax returns include as few as two corporations. Other consolidated tax returns include hundreds of corporations. The importance of the consolidated tax return election to the corporate taxing system is illustrated for 1986 where 81,956 consolidated tax returns were filed. Those consolidated tax returns represented only 2.39% of the 3.43 million corporate federal income tax returns that were filed. These affiliated corporations, who were part of a consolidated tax return, reported taxable income (net of deficits) of $159.3 billion (59.1% of total taxable income (net of deficits) for all corporations) and paid $84.5 billion in taxes (76.0% of total taxes paid by all corporations).[1] The importance of the consolidated tax return election to the larger corporate taxpayers is illustrated by the much higher proportion of total taxable income and total taxes that were reported by corporations filing on a consolidated basis than did their counterparts who filed separately.

---

[1] IRS, *Statistics of Income—1986 Corporation Income Tax Returns* (Washington, D.C.: U.S. Government Printing Office, 1990), p. 65.

This chapter considers the advantages and disadvantages of filing a consolidated tax return. It also examines the basic requirements for computing the consolidated tax liability.

SOURCE OF THE CONSOLIDATED TAX RETURN RULES

Key Point
Most of the requirements for filing consolidated tax returns are contained in the Treasury regulations rather than in the Internal Revenue Code.

Code Secs. 1501 through 1504 are the primary statutory provisions governing the filing of a consolidated tax return. These four sections are very general and primarily define the composition of the affiliated groups that are eligible to elect to file a consolidated tax return. This topic is quite complex. Therefore, responsibility for drafting the Regulations needed to (1) determine the consolidated tax liability and (2) file a consolidated tax return generally was delegated by Sec. 1502 to the Treasury Department. Since it is unusual for the Treasury Department to have the authority to draft both statutory and interpretative regulations for a particular topical area, Sec. 1501 requires that all affiliated groups filing a consolidated tax return must consent to all of the consolidated tax return regulations in effect when the return is filed. The purpose of Sec. 1501 is to reduce or avoid conflicts in applying the statutory and interpretative regulations.

DEFINITION OF AN AFFILIATED GROUP

OBJECTIVE 1
Determine whether a group of corporations is an affiliated group

Requirements

Stock Ownership Requirement. Only an affiliated group of corporations can elect to file a consolidated return. Section 1504(a) outlines the stock ownership requirements that must be satisfied, as follows:

Self-Study Question
What issues determine if an affiliated group exists?

Answer
In determining if an affiliated group exists, three questions must be addressed: (a) Does a corporation (common parent) own directly 80% or more of at least one subsidiary? (b) What are the includible corporations? (c) What chains of corporations are connected by at least 80% ownership?

- A parent corporation must directly own stock having at least 80% of the total voting power of all classes of stock entitled to vote and at least 80% of the total value of all outstanding stock in at least one includible corporation.
- For *each* other corporation eligible to be included in the affiliated group, stock having at least 80% of the total voting power of all classes of stock entitled to vote and at least 80% of the total value of all outstanding stock must be owned directly by the parent corporation and the other group members.

The term *stock* does not include any nonvoting preferred stock that is limited and preferred as to its dividends (and which does not participate in corporate growth to any significant extent), has redemption or liquidation rights limited to its issue price (plus a reasonable redemption or liquidation premium), and is not convertible into another class of stock.

Example 8-1 ■ P Corporation owns 90% of S_1 Corporation's single class of stock and 30% of S_2 Corporation's single class of stock.[2] S_1 Corporation owns 50% of S_2's stock. The remainder of S_1 and S_2's stock is owned by 100 individual shareholders. P, S_1, and

---
[2] All corporations referred to in the examples are includible corporations unless otherwise indicated. See definition of includible corporation later in this chapter.

S_2 Corporations form the P-S_1-S_2 affiliated group because P owns more than the 80% of the S_1 stock needed to satisfy the direct ownership requirement and P and S_1 together own 80% (50% + 30%) of S_2's stock. The P-S_1-S_2 group can elect to file a consolidated tax return. ∎

Example 8-2 ∎ Ted owns all of the stock of Alpha and Beta Corporations. Alpha and Beta Corporations do not constitute an affiliated group, even though each corporation is directly owned by the same individual shareholder. Because a parent-subsidiary relationship is not present, they are ineligible to make a consolidated return election.[3] ∎

Includible Corporation Requirement. As few as two corporations may satisfy the affiliated group definition. In many of the nation's largest affiliated groups, however, the number of related corporations runs into the hundreds. Some of these corporate groups may have a number of subsidiary corporations that are not able to participate in the consolidated tax return election because they are not includible corporations under Sec. 1504(b). By not being an includible corporation, their stock ownership cannot be counted toward satisfying the 80% stock ownership requirement, nor can their operating results be reported as part of the consolidated tax return. In general, each excluded corporation must file its own separate corporate tax return.

The following special tax status corporations are not includible corporations:

- Corporations exempt from tax under Sec. 501
- Insurance companies subject to tax under Sec. 801[4]
- Foreign corporations
- Corporations electing to claim the Sec. 936 possessions tax credit
- Regulated investment companies
- Real estate investment trusts
- Domestic international sales corporations
- S corporations[5]

If both the stock ownership and includible corporation requirements are satisfied, the subsidiary corporation must be included in the consolidated return election made by a parent corporation.

Example 8-3 ∎ P Corporation owns all of the single class of stock of S_1 and S_2 Corporations. S_1 Corporation owns all of S_3 Corporation's stock. S_2 Corporation owns all of S_4 Corporation's stock. P, S_1, and S_3 are domestic corporations. S_2 and S_4 are foreign corporations. P, S_1 and S_3 Corporations constitute the P-S_1-S_3 affiliated group. S_2 and S_4 are not members of the affiliated group because as foreign corporations they are not includible corporations. ∎

Additional Comment

Even if S_4 were an includible corporation, S_4 would not be part of the P-S_1-S_3 affiliated group. The chain is broken since S_2 is not an includible corporation.

Comparison with Controlled Group Definitions

Three types of controlled groups—brother-sister groups, parent-subsidiary groups, and combined groups—were defined in Chapter 3. As illustrated in Example 8-2, the brother-sister category of controlled groups cannot elect to file a consolidated tax

---

[3] See page 8-5 for a discussion of brother-sister controlled groups.
[4] Two or more Sec. 801 domestic life insurance companies may join together to form an affiliated group. If an affiliated group contains one or more Sec. 801 domestic life insurance companies, Sec. 1504(c)(2)(A) permits the parent corporation to elect to treat all such companies that have met the affiliated group stock ownership test for the 5 immediately preceding tax years as includible corporations.
[5] Sec. 1361(b)(2)(A).

Definition of an Affiliated Group • 8-5

return since they do not satisfy the direct stock ownership requirement. However, most parent-subsidiary controlled groups and the parent-subsidiary portion of a combined controlled group can elect to file a consolidated tax return.

Typical Misconception
The terms affiliated group, consolidated group, *and* controlled group *are sometimes used interchangeably. These terms, however, each have very different definitions and purposes.*

Difference Between Definitions. A number of differences between the definitions of Sec. 1504 (affiliated group) and Sec. 1563 (parent-subsidiary controlled group) do exist. These differences, which are listed below, cause some members of a controlled group to be excluded from the affiliated group.

- Section 1563 requires only the 80% of total voting power test *or* the 80% of total value test to be satisfied. Section 1504 requires *both* the 80% of total voting power and 80% of total value tests to be satisfied.
- Section 1563 has a series of constructive stock ownership rules that are applied to determine whether the 80% minimum requirements are met. Section 1504 does not.
- Section 1504 has a series of special-status corporations that cannot be included in the affiliated group. These corporations are not generally excluded from the controlled group definition because of their special filing status which excludes them from the affiliated group.
- The Sec. 1563 controlled group definition is determined December 31 of each tax year. The Sec. 1504 definition is applied each day to determine if a corporation is a member of an affiliated group.

Controlled Group Restrictions. A controlled group of corporations is restricted by Sec. 1561 in claiming certain tax benefits (e.g., the tax savings resulting from the reduced corporate tax rates of Sec. 11(b)). These benefits must be allocated equally to all the members of the controlled group unless a different apportionment method is elected. (See Chapter 3 for the special Sec. 11(b) apportionment rules.) Thus, when an affiliated group files a consolidated tax return that does not include all of the members of a controlled group, the amount of each tax benefit that is restricted by Sec. 1561 must be allocated among all the corporations of the controlled group whether they are included in or excluded from the affiliated group. Only the portion of the tax benefit allocated to the affiliated group members (under the equal or special apportionment rules) may be used to determine the consolidated tax liability.

Example 8-4 ■ Michelle owns all of the stock of P and Beta Corporations. P Corporation owns all of the stock of S Corporation. P, S, and Beta Corporations are a combined controlled group. Because P and S Corporations also constitute an affiliated group, they can elect to file a consolidated tax return. Thus, unless a special apportionment election is made, the $11,750 tax savings produced by the 15% and 25% corporate tax rates (in 1991) must be allocated equally among the three members of the controlled group. P and S would receive a $7,833 (0.667 × $11,750) allocation to reduce their consolidated tax liability under the equal apportionment method. ■

Topic Review 8-1 presents a summary of the requirements for making a consolidated tax return election.

TOPIC REVIEW 8-1

Requirements for Making a Consolidated Return Election

Requirement	Method for Satisfying Requirement
Stock ownership	1. Parent corporation must directly own stock having at least 80% of the voting power and 80% of the value of the outstanding stock of one includible corporation. 2. For each other includible corporation to be included in the affiliated group, at least 80% of the voting power and 80% of the value of the outstanding stock must be owned by other group members.
Includible corporation	Common corporate forms excluded from affiliated groups are: tax-exempt corporations, life insurance companies, foreign corporations, and S corporations.
Election	1. If both the stock ownership and includible corporation requirements are satisfied, a consolidated return election can be made. 2. Election is made by filing timely consolidated tax return (Form 1120) that includes income and expenses for all members. 3. Parent's consent to election is made by filing Form 1120. Each subsidiary must file Form 1122 (Authorization and Consent of Subsidiary Corporation to be Included in Consolidated Return). Affiliated group also must file Form 851 (Affiliations Schedule). 4. Election to file consolidated return also requires consent to consolidated return regulations in place at time return is filed.

CONSOLIDATED TAXABLE INCOME

OBJECTIVE 2
Calculate consolidated taxable income for an affiliated group

The heart of the computation of the consolidated federal income tax liability is the calculation of **consolidated taxable income.** The calculation of consolidated taxable income is divided into the following 5 steps. An overview of the 5-step consolidated taxable income calculation is presented in Table 8-1.

STEP 1. The starting point is the determination of each member's taxable income. The amount of a group member's taxable income is determined as if the group member were filing a separate tax return.

STEP 2. Once each group member's taxable income has been determined, a series of adjustments (e.g., elimination of gain on certain intercompany transactions) must be made to take into account the special treatment that certain transactions receive in consolidated returns.

STEP 3. Any income, loss, or deduction items that must be reported on a consolidated basis are eliminated from the taxable income calculation. The resulting amount is the group member's **separate taxable income.**

STEP 4. The separate taxable income amounts of the individual group members are aggregated into a **combined taxable income** amount.

STEP 5. Each of the tax attributes that are stated on a consolidated basis (and which were eliminated in Step 3) are added to or subtracted from the combined taxable income amount. The resulting amount is the affiliated group's consolidated taxable income.[6]

Consolidated taxable income is multiplied by the appropriate tax rates of Sec. 11 to determine the consolidated regular tax liability. This amount may be increased if the affiliated group is found to owe an additional amount under the corporate alternative minimum tax, one of the other special tax levies, or as the result of recapturing previously claimed tax credits. Any tax credits and estimated tax payments are subtracted from the regular tax liability to determine the consolidated regular tax liability that is owed.

Income Included in the Consolidated Tax Return

Key Point
Two basic rules exist for determining what income must be included in a consolidated tax return: (a) common parent's income for the entire tax year and (b) a subsidiary's income only for the period the subsidiary is a member of a group.

A consolidated tax return includes the parent corporation's income for its entire tax year, except for any portion of the year that it was a member of another affiliated group that filed a consolidated tax return. A subsidiary corporation's income is included in the consolidated tax return only for the portion of the affiliated group's tax year for which it was a group member and for which it did not elect to be excluded from the affiliated group under a 30-day rule (discussed below). When a corporation is a member of an affiliated group for only a portion of its tax year, the member's income for the remainder of its tax year is included in a separate tax return or the consolidated tax return of another affiliated group.[7]

Example 8-5 ■

P and S Corporations file separate tax returns for calendar year 1990. At the close of business on April 30, 1991, P Corporation acquires all of S Corporation's stock. If the P-S affiliated group files a consolidated tax return for 1991, P's income is included in the consolidated tax return for all of 1991, and S's income is included only for the period May 1 through December 31, 1991. S Corporation must file a separate tax return to report its income for the pre-affiliation period January 1 through April 30, 1991. ■

Self-Study Question
What possible benefits exist to making a 30-day election?

Answer
No short-period return, no additional closing of books, and an extra year is not used for purposes of determining carryforwards (e.g., NOLs and NCLs).

Thirty-Day Rules. Two 30-day rules exist. The first 30-day rule permits a corporation to be a member of an affiliated group from the beginning of its tax year if, within the first 30 days of its tax year, it becomes a member of an affiliated group that files a consolidated tax return for a tax year including such time period.[8] By electing to use this 30-day rule, a corporation does not have to file a short-period (separate) tax return for the period of time from the beginning of its tax year to the date it joins the affiliated group.

The second 30-day rule permits a corporation that has been a group member for 30 or fewer days in the consolidated return year[9] to be considered a nonmember of the

---

[6] Reg. Sec. 1.1502-12.
[7] Reg. Sec. 1.1502-76(b)(2).
[8] Reg. Sec. 1.1502-76(b)(5)(i).
[9] **A consolidated return year** is defined by Reg. Sec. 1.1502-1(d) as a tax year for which a consolidated return is filed or is required to be filed by the affiliated group. A **separate return year** is defined by Reg. Sec. 1.1502-1(e) as a tax year for which a corporation (1) files a separate return or (2) joins in the filing of a consolidated tax return with a different affiliated group.

Typical Misconception
This table illustrates that the filing of consolidated tax returns instead of separate tax returns is clearly not easier from a compliance point of view.

TABLE 8-1 **Consolidated Taxable Income Calculation**

Step 1: Compute each group member's taxable income (or loss) based upon the member's own accounting methods as if the corporation is filing its own separate tax return.

Step 2: Adjust each group member's taxable income as follows:
1. The following income and deduction items must be eliminated:
   a. Intercompany dividends (dividends received by one member from another member)
   b. Disallowed built-in deductions
2. Gains and losses on certain intercompany transactions are deferred. If a restoration event occurs during the year, then gains and losses previously deferred must be restored.
3. An inventory adjustment may be required.
4. An adjustment for an excess loss (negative investment basis) account of an affiliate may be required.

Step 3: The following gains, losses, and deductions are eliminated from each member's taxable income because they must be computed on a consolidated basis:
1. Net operating loss (NOL) deductions
2. Capital gains and losses
3. Section 1231 gains and losses (including net casualty gain)
4. Charitable contribution deductions
5. Dividends-received deductions
6. Percentage depletion under Sec. 613A

The result of making the adjustments noted above to a member's taxable income is the member's separate taxable income.

Step 4: Combine the members' separate taxable income amounts. This amount is referred to as the group's combined taxable income.

Step 5: Adjust the group's combined taxable income for the following consolidated items:
1. Deduct the consolidated Sec. 1231 net loss.
2. Deduct the consolidated net casualty loss.
3. Add the consolidated capital gain net income (taking into account capital loss carrybacks and carryovers and Sec. 1231 gains).
4. Deduct the consolidated NOL deduction (taking into account any allowable NOL carryovers and carrybacks).
5. Deduct the consolidated charitable contribution deduction.
6. Deduct the consolidated dividends-received deductions.
7. Deduct the consolidated percentage depletion deduction.

Consolidated taxable income (or Consolidated NOL)

Additional Comment
By making the second 30-day election, a corporation is not considered to be a member of the group for that taxable year. Therefore, the IRS can't hold that corporation severally liable for the consolidated tax liability.

group for the entire year.[10] By electing to use this rule, the corporation may file a single tax return for a calendar year in which two or more tax returns may otherwise be required.

Allocation of income between the consolidated tax return and a member's separate tax return takes place according to the accounting methods employed by the individual corporation. If this allocation cannot be readily determined, the amounts included in each tax return can be based upon the relative number of days included in each tax year.

Affiliated Group Elections

Tax Years. An affiliated group's consolidated tax return must be filed using the parent corporation's tax year. Beginning with the initial consolidated return year for

---

[10] Reg. Sec. 1.1502-76(b)(5)(ii).

Consolidated Taxable Income • 8-9

which it is includible in the consolidated tax return, each subsidiary corporation must adopt the parent corporation's tax year. The requirement for a common tax year applies to affiliated group members both when an initial consolidated tax return is being filed and when the stock of a new member is acquired.[11]

Example 8-6 ■

Self-Study Question
When a subsidiary leaves a consolidated group, may it select any year-end it wishes?

Answer
Without permission from the IRS to do otherwise, a subsidiary must retain the group's year-end (if filing a separate tax return) or adopt the year-end of the acquiring consolidated group, if applicable.

P and S Corporations file separate tax returns for 1990. P Corporation uses a calendar year as its tax year. S Corporation uses a fiscal year ending June 30 as its tax year. At the close of business on April 30, 1991, P Corporation acquires all of S Corporation's stock. If the P-S affiliated group files a consolidated tax return for 1991, S must change its tax year so that it ends on December 31. S must file a short-period tax return for the period July 1, 1990, through April 30, 1991. P's income for all of 1991 and S's income for the period May 1, 1991, through December 31, 1991, are included in the initial consolidated tax return. ■

Methods of Accounting. Unless the IRS grants permission for a change in accounting method, the accounting methods used by each group member are determined by using the same rules as if the member were filing a separate tax return.[12] This holds true when a consolidated tax return election is made or a new corporation joins an existing affiliated group. Thus, one group member may use the cash method of accounting and another group member may use the accrual method of accounting during a consolidated return year.

Key Point
Even though members of a consolidated group must use the same year-end, members are not required to use the same accounting methods.

The possibility of finding members of an affiliated group using the cash method of accounting is reduced by the Sec. 448 limitation placed on its use. C corporations can use the cash method of accounting only if they conduct a farming business, are qualified personal service corporations, have gross receipts of less than $5 million for all prior post-1985 tax years, or have average annual gross receipts of less than $5 million for a three-year period ending with the immediately preceding tax year. Because the gross receipts of all related entities are aggregated for purposes of applying the $5 million test, the possibility of an affiliated group qualifying under this exception is substantially reduced. An affiliated group of qualified personal service corporations can, however, qualify without regard to the $5 million exception.

Termination of the Affiliated Group

An affiliated group that elects to file a consolidated tax return must continue to file on a consolidated basis as long as the affiliated group exists unless the IRS grants permission for them to do otherwise. An affiliated group exists as long as the parent corporation and at least one subsidiary corporation remain affiliated. It does not matter whether the parent corporation owns the *same* subsidiary throughout the entire tax year or even whether the continuing subsidiary exists at the beginning of the year.

Example 8-7 ■

P and S_1 Corporations have filed a consolidated tax return for several calendar years. At the close of business on August 31, 1991, P purchases all of S_2 Corporation's stock. S_2 Corporation uses the calendar year as its tax year. At the close of business on September 30, 1991, P sells its entire holding of S_1 stock. The affiliated group, with P as the parent corporation, must file a consolidated tax

---
[11] Reg. Sec. 1.1502-76(a).
[12] Reg. Sec. 1.1502-17(a).

return for 1991, because P remained the parent corporation of at least one subsidiary corporation (first S_1, later S_2) at all times during the year. If the order of the purchase and sale transactions is reversed, the affiliated group would have been terminated following the sale of the S_1 stock (on August 31, 1991). A new affiliated group would have been created with the purchase of the S_2 stock (on October 1, 1991). The creation of the new affiliated group would require a new consolidated return election. If such an election were made, the consolidated return for the P-S_2 affiliated group would contain the income of P and S_2 Corporations from October 1, 1991 through December 31, 1991. ∎

Example 8-8 ∎

Self-Study Question

In the second half of Example 8-7, the order of the transactions is reversed. In this case, what tax returns are due, and what income is included in these returns?

Answer

(a) Final P-S_1 consolidated tax return that includes P's income from 1/1-9/30 and S_1's income from 1/1-8/31. (b) New P-S_2 consolidated tax return with P-S_2's income from 10/1-12/31. (c) Short-period separate tax return for S_1 from 9/1-12/31. (d) Short-period separate tax return for S_2 from 1/1 through 9/30.

P and S Corporations have filed a consolidated tax return for several calendar years. At the close of business on August 31, 1991, P Corporation sells its entire holding of S stock to Artie. P's income is included in the 1991 consolidated tax return for the entire calendar year. S's income is included only for the period January 1 through August 31, 1991. S must also file a separate tax return to report its income for the period September 1 through December 31, 1991. ∎

Good Cause Request to Discontinue Status. Permission to discontinue filing a consolidated tax return is sometimes granted by the IRS in response to a "good cause" request initiated by the taxpayer. A good cause reason for discontinuing the consolidated tax return election includes a "substantial adverse effect" on the consolidated tax liability for the tax year (relative to what the aggregate tax liability would be if the group members filed separate tax returns) originating from amendments to the Code or Regulations having effective dates in the tax year in question.[13]

Effects on Former Members. The termination of an affiliated group affects its former members in several ways, each of which is examined in subsequent sections of this chapter.

1. Any gains and losses that have been deferred on intercompany transactions (e.g., intercompany profits on sales of inventory between group members) may have to be recognized.
2. Consolidated tax attributes (such as NOL carryovers, capital loss carryovers, tax credit carryovers, and excess charitable contributions) must be allocated among the former group members.
3. The amount of any negative investment account (known as the **excess loss account**) attaching to an investment in a lower-tier subsidiary corporation may have to be taken into income.

Additional Comment

Permission to discontinue the filing of consolidated tax returns is seldom granted by the IRS.

In addition, disaffiliation of a corporation from an affiliated group prevents the corporation from being included in a consolidated return with the same affiliated group, or any other affiliated group having the same common parent, until 5 years after the beginning of its first tax year in which it ceased to be a group member. The IRS can waive the 5-year requirement and permit the departing group member to join in a consolidated return at an earlier date.[14]

---

[13] See Rev. Proc. 91-11, I.R.B. 1991-6, 9. The IRS recently determined that amendments to its rules regarding the recognition of loss when a subsidiary corporation's stock is sold or exchanged may have an adverse effect on the filing of consolidated tax returns. It granted all affiliated groups blanket permission to discontinue filing consolidated returns for the tax year that includes November 19, 1990 (the effective date of the Regulations) provided the election is made before July 1, 1991. This election prevents the former group members from filing a consolidated return for 60 months.

[14] Rev. Proc. 90-53 (I.R.B. 1990-42, 13) details the circumstances of when an early election will be permitted and the procedures for obtaining approval of such a request.

INTERCOMPANY TRANSACTIONS

OBJECTIVE 3
Determine whether a transaction is an intercompany transaction or not

An **intercompany transaction** is defined as a transaction taking place during a consolidated return year between corporations that are members of the same group immediately after the transaction.[15] Specifically excluded from this definition are

1. Dividend distributions by one group member to a second group member with respect to the distributing corporation's stock
2. Capital contributions on which no gain is realized
3. Distributions in redemption or liquidation of a group member's stock
4. Sales of, exchanges and redemptions of, or the worthlessness of, obligations of other group members

Additional Comment
The deferral and restoration rules that can apply to intercompany transactions are an excellent example of the additional recordkeeping necessary to filing consolidated tax returns.

Two special treatments, both of which are discussed below, are accorded intercompany transactions under the consolidated tax return regulations. First, gains and losses on "deferred intercompany transactions" are not reported in the year in which they take place, but instead are deferred until a restoration event (e.g., a sale of property outside the affiliated group) occurs. Second, the deduction for expenses incurred in "other intercompany transactions" must be deferred by a group member until the second group member reports the income from the transaction.

Deferred Intercompany Transactions

OBJECTIVE 4
Explain the reporting of a deferred intercompany transaction

A **deferred intercompany transaction** is an intercompany transaction involving (1) a sale or exchange of property; (2) the performance of services in which the acquiring party capitalizes the amount of the expenditure for the services; or (3) any other transaction involving an expenditure that is capitalized by the acquiring party (e.g., under the Sec. 263A Uniform Capitalization Rules). Intercompany transactions not meeting any of these three requirements fall into the "other" intercompany transaction category.

Any gain or loss recognized on a deferred intercompany transaction must be deferred by the selling group member. Deferral of a gain or loss takes place by excluding the gain or loss amount from the selling group member's gross income or total losses. The selling member restores all or a portion of the deferred gain or loss at the time a restoration event occurs. Restoration of the gain or loss takes place by including the gain or loss in the selling group member's gross income or total losses. In a deferred intercompany transaction, the selling member is not permitted to use the installment method for reporting any deferred gain. The deferred gain must be reported according to the rules applicable to restoration events.[16]

Self-Study Question
What is the basis of property acquired by the purchasing member in a deferred intercompany transactiion?

Answer
Since the gains/losses are deferred rather than eliminated, the purchasing member takes a cost basis in any assets acquired in a deferred intercompany transaction.

Amount and Character of the Deferred Gain or Loss. At the time of the transaction, the amount and character of the deferred gain or loss are determined as if the transaction had occurred in a separate return year. The amount of the deferred gain or loss includes all direct and indirect costs that are part of the cost of goods sold, the cost of the services performed, or the cost of the property sold.

Basis and Holding Period. The basis and holding period for a property acquired in a deferred intercompany transaction are determined as if the acquisition occurred in a separate return year. Thus, the adjusted basis for an asset is the property's acquisition

---

[15] Reg. Sec. 1.1502-13(a)(1).
[16] Reg. Secs. 1.1502-13(c)(1)-(2).

cost if the property is purchased by a group member for cash from a second group member. The holding period for such property begins on the day after the acquisition date.

Example 8-9 ■ P and S Corporations have filed consolidated tax returns for several years. P acquires a parcel of land in 1986 for $39,000 and uses the unimproved land to provide additional parking for its employees. On August 8, 1989, P sells the land to S for $75,000 in cash. P's deferred Sec. 1231 gain is $36,000 ($75,000 − $39,000). S's basis for the land is $75,000. Its holding period for determining the character of the gain or loss on a subsequent sale of the land commences on August 9, 1989. P will recognize the deferred gain when one of the restoration events described below occurs. ■

Key Point
If property is transferred in a deferred intercompany transaction, any investment tax credit recapture potential on the property is assumed by the purchasing member.

Investment Tax Credit Recapture. The investment tax credit recapture rules for an affiliated group filing a consolidated tax return are similar to those for a corporation filing a separate tax return. Recapture of unearned credits is not required for transfers of qualifying property between group members during a consolidated return year. If the transferred property is disposed of by the acquiring group member (other than to another group member) before the end of the property's recovery period, any investment tax credit recapture increases the affiliated group's tax liability provided the disposition occurs in a consolidated return year. The holding period used in determining the recapture amount includes the time that both the transferor and transferee corporations held the property.[17]

Typical Misconception
If more than one restoration event applies to the same deferred intercompany gain, the earliest restoration event is applied to determine the timing of the restored gain.

Determining the Restored Gain or Loss. A number of events involving the selling and acquiring group members are treated as restoration events and thereby trigger recognition of any deferred gain or loss on the property involved. The restoration event date is the earliest of the following events:[18]

1. The claiming of a depletion, depreciation, or amortization deduction with respect to a property, a capital expenditure made for services, or any other form of capital expenditure made by the acquiring group member
2. The collection, satisfaction, discharge, or disposition (outside the affiliated group) of an installment obligation of a nonmember of the group originating from a group member's disposition of property (acquired in a deferred intercompany transaction) in a transaction in which the installment method of accounting is employed
3. The collection, satisfaction, or worthlessness of an installment obligation of a nonmember of the group that has been transferred between group members in an intercompany transaction
4. The disposition (including abandonment) outside the affiliated group of a property acquired in a deferred intercompany transaction[19]

---

[17] Reg. Sec. 1.1502-3(f).
[18] Reg. Secs. 1.1502-13(d)-(f).
[19] Section 267(f)(2) requires a realized loss to be deferred when a sale of property occurs between members of a controlled group. Temporary Reg. Sec. 1.267(f)-2T provides special rules for property sales involving members of a controlled group. A sale of property at a loss by a member of the affiliated group to a corporation that is part of the selling member's controlled group, but which cannot join in a consolidated return election, is not a restoration event. Nor does a restoration event occur when there is the departure from the affiliated group of a corporation, which owns property that it acquired in a deferred intercompany transaction where a loss was deferred, that remains a member of the controlled group. A discussion of these rules is beyond the scope of this text.

5. The writing down of inventory that is accounted for by the lower of the cost or market method to its market value
6. The redemption or worthlessness of the stock of a member or nonmember of the affiliated group
7. The departure from an affiliated group of the group member that either sells or owns a property that is acquired in a deferred intercompany transaction other than in a transaction where the tax attributes carry over to the acquiring corporation under Sec. 381
8. The first day of a separate return year for the parent corporation[20]

Key Point

Section 1239 also applies to many deferred intercompany transactions. If so, any gain is automatically ordinary income.

The character of the restored gain is generally the same as that which is deferred when the intercompany transaction took place. There is one exception to this rule: Deferred gains and losses are treated as ordinary income or loss if they are recognized as a result of the acquiring corporation's depreciation, depletion, or amortization of a property or the acquiring corporation's abandonment of a property.

Example 8-10 ■ Assume the same facts as in Example 8-9, except that S sells the land to a third party for $120,000 in cash in 1991. P's $36,000 deferred Sec. 1231 gain is recognized in 1991 because S has sold the land to a nonmember of the group. S also reports its $45,000 gain ($120,000 − $75,000) in 1991. ■

Example 8-11 ■ Assume the same facts as in Example 8-10, except that S's $120,000 sale proceeds are to be collected in three equal, annual installments starting in 1991. Interest at a rate acceptable to the IRS is charged on the unpaid balance. After selling the land, S reports the transaction using the installment sale provisions of Sec. 453 applicable to nondealers. P must defer the gain on the sale and recognize it as S collects the amounts due under the installment contract.

Typical Misconception

Even though the restoration event illustrated in Example 8-11 is based on the receipt of installment obligations, remember that intercompany sales cannot be reported on the installment method.

The following formula is used to determine P's recognized gain:

$$\frac{\text{Amount of the installment payment received}}{\text{Total contract price}} \times \text{Deferred gain or loss} = \text{Restored gain or loss}$$

P must restore $12,000 of the deferred gain ([$40,000 ÷ $120,000] × $36,000) in 1991, 1992, and 1993. S reports its $45,000 gain in three installments of $15,000 each ($45,000 ÷ 3) over the life of the contract plus reporting any interest income earned on the unpaid balance. ■

Recovery property that is sold between two group members in a deferred intercompany transaction results in a continuation of the selling group member's recovery period and recovery method under the Sec. 168(i)(7) anti-churning rules to the extent that the purchasing group member's basis equals or is less than the selling group member's adjusted basis. To the extent that the purchasing group member's basis for the property exceeds the selling group member's adjusted basis, the amount

---

[20] Reg. Secs. 1.1502-13(d)-(f). In this restoration event, the selling member must recognize only those deferred gains relating to inventory and property held primarily for sale to customers on the first day of its first separate return year (or on the first day of the first separate return year for the member that owns the property), provided consolidated tax returns have been filed for at least 3 consecutive tax years preceding the separate return year. Under this exception, deferred gains and losses attributable to the other property categories are recognized in separate return years only when another of the restoration events has occurred.

is treated under Temp. Reg. Sec. 1.1502-13T(l)(1) as a separate property that was acquired from an unrelated party.

If a transaction took place after December 31, 1986 and involved ACRS property placed in service before 1987 in which a gain was recognized by the selling party, the anti-churning rules of Sec. 168(i)(7) would treat the purchasing party as continuing the ACRS depreciation on the portion of the asset's cost basis equal to the seller's adjusted basis. The purchasing party would treat the step-up in basis (i.e., excess of the purchase price minus seller's adjusted basis for the property) as a new property and use the appropriate MACRS depreciation method and recovery period. The purchaser's depreciation for the carryover portion of the basis is the same each year as the seller's depreciation would have been if the seller had not sold the property. The amount of the deferred gain attributable to the sale that the seller must restore in any year (that is, the amount of the increased depreciation deduction to the group) is the amount of the depreciation deduction attributable to the portion of the purchaser's basis which exceeds the carryover portion.

The same procedures would apply if a property was placed in service after 1987 under the MACRS rules and was sold to another group member. The only difference is that both the carryover portion of the basis and the step-up in basis are depreciated using the MACRS rules. This scenario is illustrated in the following example.

Example 8-12 ∎

P and S Corporations form the P-S affiliated group. On January 1, 1987, P pays $10,000 to a nonmember of the group for machinery which under the Modified Accelerated Cost Recovery System (MACRS) rules is 5-year property. P claims the following depreciation deductions:

Year	Deduction
1987	$2,000 ($10,000 × 0.20)
1988	$3,200 ($10,000 × 0.32)

On January 1, 1989, P sells the machinery to S for $9,000. P's $4,200 Sec. 1245 gain ($9,000 proceeds − $4,800 adjusted basis) is deferred by P until S depreciates the asset.

Temp. Reg. Sec. 1.1502-13T(l)(1) requires S to be treated as continuing the MACRS depreciation on the $4,800 portion of the acquisition price that equals the carryover portion of P's adjusted basis for the machinery. The MACRS provisions would also apply to the $4,200 portion of the acquisition price that represents a step-up in basis (or gain portion of the basis) on S Corporation's books. S recovers the asset's $4,200 step-up in basis over 5 years under the MACRS rules. The amount of the capital-recovery deductions claimed by S and the restored gain or loss recognized by P during S's holding period for the asset are as follows:[21]

Year		P's Basis	Depreciation Step-Up	Total	Restoration of P's Deferred Gain
1989	$10,000 × .1920	$1,920		$1,920	
	$4,200 × 0.2000		$ 840	840	$840
				$2,760	

Key Point
Depending on when an asset is placed in service and then sold in a deferred intercompany transaction, an asset can be divided into two pieces for depreciation purposes. These situations are covered by special anti-churning rules.

[21] Reg. Sec. 1.1502-13(c)(4). Intercompany sales of property, that will be depreciated in the purchasing group member's hands, will generally result in the recognition of ordinary income under Sec. 1239 since the selling and purchasing group members are usually also members of a controlled group and, therefore, are related parties under Sec. 1239(b).

Year	P's Basis	Depreciation Step-Up	Total	Restoration of P's Deferred Gain
1990	$10,000 × 0.1152 1,152		$1,152	
	$4,200 × 0.3200	1,344	1,344	1,344
			$2,496	
1991	$10,000 × 0.1152 1,152		$1,152	
	$4,200 × 0.1920	806	806	806
			$1,958	
1992	$10,000 × 0.0576 576		$576	
	$4,200 × 0.1152	484	484	484
			$1,060	
1993	$4,200 × 0.1152	484	484	484
1994	$4,200 × 0.0576	242	242	242
Total depreciation and restoration	$4,800	$4,200	$9,000	$4,200

The $4,200 deferred gain is recognized by P as ordinary income under Sec. 1245. If on January 15, 1995, S sells the asset to a third party for $1,000, it will recognize a $1,000 Sec. 1245 gain ($1,000 proceeds − 0 adjusted basis). ∎

Inventory Adjustments. Inventory sales between group members are treated as deferred intercompany transactions. Gain or loss on these sales is deferred until the occurrence of a restoration event such as the inventory being sold outside the affiliated group or the inventory being written down to its market value.[22]

A series of special inventory adjustments are required if

1. The selling corporation is a member of an affiliated group that files a consolidated tax return for the current tax year
2. The selling corporation was a member of the affiliated group for its immediately preceding tax year
3. The selling corporation filed a separate tax return for the preceding tax year
4. Sales of inventory occurred between the selling corporation and other group members during the separate return year(s) immediately preceding the consolidated return year and
5. Some of the inventory items remain unsold at the beginning of the initial consolidated return year and are subsequently disposed of outside the affiliated group during a consolidated return year

These adjustment rules require that the selling member's profit on the goods that make up ending inventory for the final separate return year be added to its income for the consolidated return year(s) during which such goods are disposed of outside the group. The inventory adjustment procedures enable a group member to defer from taxation only the additional profits arising from intercompany sales of inventory that take place after the beginning of the initial consolidated return year. The application of these rules is beyond the scope of this text.

Additional Comment

The special inventory rules are extremely complex. As a practical matter, it would appear that these adjustments are generally avoided by making the consolidated return election when affiliation occurs or by adopting the LIFO inventory method so the initial inventory never leaves the affiliated group.

---

[22] Reg. Sec. 1.1502-13(f)(1).

OBJECTIVE 5
Explain the reporting of an other intercompany transaction

Other Intercompany Transactions

Any income, gain, deduction, or loss realized or incurred on other intercompany transactions is included in the income and expense classifications for the tax year in which the transaction is ordinarily reported. Both parties report their side of the transaction in determining separate taxable income.[23] These amounts net to zero since both are included in consolidated taxable income.

Code Sec. 267(a)(2) imposes a special rule on related party transactions requiring the matching of the recognition of the payor's deduction item and the payee's income item. Thus, when two group members would ordinarily report the income and deduction items in different consolidated return years under their regular accounting methods, they must both report the income and deduction items in the year that the payee member reports the income.

Section 267(b)(3) includes two corporations which are members of the same controlled group as related parties. This definition includes most members of affiliated groups whether separate returns or consolidated returns are filed. It may also include certain corporations that are not included in the affiliated group because they are not includible corporations.

Example 8-13 ■

Self-Study Question

Why are the "other intercompany transactions" not deferred or eliminated?

Answer

Since both sides of the transaction are reported in the same consolidated return, they simply net each other out. If, due to accounting methods, the items would be reported in different tax periods, both the income and deduction must be reported in the year the payee member reports the income.

P and S Corporations have filed calendar-year consolidated tax returns for several years. P Corporation uses the cash method of accounting, and S Corporation uses the accrual method of accounting. P lends S $100,000 on March 1, 1991; this debt and the related interest are unpaid at the end of 1991. Interest is charged by P at an annual rate of 12%. The $10,000 interest charge owed at year-end is paid by S on March 1, 1992. Ordinarily, P, a cash-basis corporation, would report no interest income and S, an accrual-basis corporation, would report $10,000 of interest expense in the computation of their separate taxable incomes for 1991's consolidated tax return. Because there is a timing difference in reporting the intercompany transaction, S must defer the reporting of the interest expense until 1992. Thus, the income and expense items are "matched" within the 1992 consolidated tax return. ■

Topic Review 8-2 presents a summary of the intercompany transaction rules.

DIVIDENDS RECEIVED BY GROUP MEMBERS

Self-Study Question

Are dividends received from members of the same consolidated group entitled to a dividends-received deduction?

Answer

No. Intercompany dividends are eliminated, hence no dividends-received deduction is necessary.

Dividends received by group members are treated differently depending on whether they come from corporations within the affiliated group or from firms outside it. In determining consolidated taxable income, the dividends received from other group members are eliminated, while those received from nonmembers of the group are eligible for a 70%, 80%, or 100% dividends-received deduction.

Elimination Procedure

A dividend distribution from one group member to a second group member during a consolidated return year is eliminated. The elimination process is a negative adjustment made to the separate taxable income reported by the recipient group

---

[23] Reg. Sec. 1.1502-13(b)(1). This procedure may be contrasted with financial accounting, in which both sides of the transaction are eliminated in preparing the consolidated financial statements.

TOPIC REVIEW 8-2

Reporting Intercompany Transactions
Definition
1. An intercompany transaction is a transaction taking place during a consolidated return year between corporations that are members of the same group immediately after the transaction.
2. Certain transactions or events are excepted from this rule including: dividends, distributions in redemption or liquidation of a member's stock, and capital contributions.
3. Two sets of intercompany transaction rules exist: deferred intercompany transactions and other intercompany transactions.
Deferred Intercompany Transactions
1. **Definition:** an intercompany transaction involving (a) sale or exchange of property; (b) performance of services in which the acquiring party capitalizes the amount of the expenditure for the services; or (3) any other transaction involving an expenditure that is capitalized by the acquiring party.
2. Gains and losses on deferred intercompany transactions are recognized in the separate returns of the group members and then deferred. A special election is available to recognize deferred gains and losses currently.
3. Gain or loss is calculated as if separate returns were to be filed. Deferral of the gain or loss is mandatory and is accomplished by excluding the gain or loss amount from the selling member's gross income or total losses.
4. Restoration occurs by including the deferred gain or loss in the selling member's gross income or total losses. The character of the restored gain generally is the same as when the property initially was sold.
5. Common events which trigger restoration of a deferred gain or loss include:
a. Depreciation, depletion, or amortization of the property or expenditure by the purchasing member.
b. Collection of an installment obligation of a nonmember of a group resulting from the sale outside the affiliated group of property originally transferred in a deferred intercompany transaction.
c. Disposition of property acquired in a deferred intercompany transaction outside the affiliated group.
f. Departure from an affiliated group of a member that either sells or owns property that was transferred in a deferred intercompany transaction.
g. Termination of the affiliated group.
Other Intercompany Transactions
1. **Definition:** intercompany transactions that are not deferred intercompany transactions.
2. Any income, gain, deduction, or loss realized or incurred on an other intercompany transaction is included in the income and expense classifications for the tax year in which the transaction is ordinarily reported if separate returns were filed.
3. Many of these transactions will involve the related party rules of Sec. 267(a)(2) since they involve members of the same controlled group. When different accounting methods are used by the two parties that would result in reporting the two parts of the transaction in different tax years, the payor member's deduction is reported in the year that the payee member's income is reported.

Typical Misconception
One difference between consolidated tax returns and separate tax returns is that in a consolidated setting, intercompany distributions in excess of both E&P and basis in the owning member's stock do not create a capital gain, but rather create an excess loss account (i.e., a negative basis account).

member that removes the dividend from the affiliated group's consolidated taxable income.[24] (See Table 8-1 and the eliminating entry illustrated in the sample calculation of consolidated taxable income in Appendix B.)

Within an affiliated group, nondividend distributions (e.g., a distribution made when there is no earnings and profits balance) reduce the shareholder corporation's basis in the distributing corporation's stock. If the amount of the distribution exceeds the shareholder corporation's adjusted basis in the stock, the excess either creates a new, or increases an existing, excess loss account (i.e., a negative investment account). However, the shareholder corporation does not recognize any gain from the portion of the distribution that exceeds its basis in the distributing corporation's stock (as it would with nonaffiliated corporations).[25]

The amount of any distribution received by one group member from another equals the money distributed plus the sum of the adjusted basis of any property distributed and the gain recognized by the distributing corporation. Since under Sec. 311(b) gain is recognized on most distributions of appreciated property, the amount distributed and the adjusted basis of the distributed property will generally equal its fair market value where a distribution of appreciated property takes place between group members. Gain recognized by the distributing corporation under Sec. 311 due to the distribution of property to another group member is treated as a deferred intercompany transaction. The deferred gain is included in consolidated taxable income by the distributing corporation when a restoration event occurs (e.g., the shareholder corporation begins to depreciate the property).[26]

Consolidated Dividends-Received Deduction

The dividends-received deduction for dividends received from nonmembers is computed on a consolidated basis. It is not applied to the separate taxable income of each group member. The consolidated dividends-received deduction equals the sum of (1) 70% of dividends received from unaffiliated domestic corporations in which a less than 20% interest is held, (2) 80% of dividends received from unaffiliated domestic corporations in which a 20% or more interest is held, and (3) 100% of dividends received from a more than 80% owned domestic corporation that is not permitted to be included in the consolidated return election. The 70% and 80% dividends-received deductions are separately limited by consolidated taxable income. The 70% or 80% portion of this calculation cannot exceed 70% or 80% (as appropriate) of the consolidated taxable income excluding the consolidated dividends-received deductions and any consolidated NOL or capital loss carrybacks. The limitations do not apply if the full amount of the deduction creates or increases a consolidated NOL.[27]

Example 8-14 ■ P, S_1, and S_2 Corporations create the P-S_1-S_2 affiliated group. Consolidated taxable income (excluding all dividends-received exclusions and deductions, NOL carrybacks, and capital loss carrybacks) is $200,000. The following dividend income is received by the group from unaffiliated corporations that are less than 20% owned:

---

[24] Reg. Sec. 1.1502-14(a)(1).
[25] Reg. Sec. 1.1502-14(a)(2). The amount of the excess loss account's negative balance is reported as either ordinary income or capital gain when a disposition of the stock of the subsidiary corporation occurs.
[26] Reg. Secs. 1.1502-14(a)(3) and (c).
[27] Reg. Sec. 1.1502-26(a)(1).

Self-Study Question

What is the dividends-received deduction in Example 8-14, if the group has consolidated taxable income of (a) $95,000? (b) $94,999?

Answer

(a) $84,500 due to the consolidated taxable income limitation.
(b) All $95,000 is allowed because the full dividends-received deduction creates an NOL. Should $1 difference in consolidated taxable income make a $10,500 difference in the dividends-received deduction?

Shareholder Group Member	Dividend Amount
P	$ 6,000
S_1	10,000
S_2	34,000
Total	$50,000

In addition, P receives a $40,000 dividend from S_1, and S_1 receives a $60,000 dividend from a 100%-owned insurance company that cannot join in the consolidated return election. The $40,000 dividend that P receives from S_1 is eliminated in determining consolidated taxable income. S_1's dividend from the 100%-owned insurance company is eligible for a 100% dividends-received deduction. This $60,000 deduction is not subject to any limitation and reduces consolidated taxable income before applying the 70% limitation. The 70% dividends-received deductions are: P, $4,200 (0.70 × $6,000); S_1, $7,000 (0.70 × $10,000); and S_2, $23,800 (0.70 × $34,000), or a total of $35,000. The 70% dividends-received deduction ($35,000) is not restricted by the dividends-received deduction limitation ([$200,000 − $40,000 − $60,000] × 0.70 = $70,000). The consolidated dividends-received deduction is $95,000 ($35,000 + $60,000). ∎

CONSOLIDATED CHARITABLE CONTRIBUTIONS DEDUCTION

Key Point

Determining the charitable contribution deduction on a consolidated basis rather than by each corporation separately may or may not be beneficial. The outcome depends on the actual numbers in each individual situation.

The affiliated group's charitable contributions deduction is computed on a consolidated basis. The consolidated charitable contributions deduction equals the sum of the charitable contributions deductions of the individual group members for the consolidated return year (computed without regard to any individual group member's limitation) plus any charitable contribution carryovers from earlier consolidated or separate return years. The charitable contributions deduction is limited to 10% of adjusted consolidated taxable income. Consolidated taxable income is computed without regard to the dividends-received deduction, any consolidated NOL or capital loss carrybacks, and the consolidated charitable contributions deduction. Any charitable contributions made by the group in excess of the 10% limitation are carried over to the 5 succeeding tax years.[28] Any unused contribution amounts remaining at the end of the carryover period are lost.

A member leaving the affiliated group takes with it any excess contributions arising in a prior separate return year plus its allocable share of any excess consolidated charitable contributions for a consolidated return year. The excess consolidated charitable contributions are allocated to each group member based on the relative amount of their contributions (when compared to the total contributions of all group members) for the consolidated return year.

Example 8-15 ∎ P, S_1, and S_2 Corporations form the P-S_1-S_2 affiliated group. The group members report the following charitable contributions and "adjusted" consolidated taxable income for 1991:

---

[28] Reg. Sec. 1.1502-24(a).

Group Member	Charitable Contributions	Adjusted Consolidated Taxable Income
P	$12,500	$150,000
S_1	5,000	(40,000)
S_2	2,000	10,000
Total	$19,500	$120,000

The P-S_1-S_2 affiliated group's charitable contributions deduction is the lesser of (1) its actual charitable contributions ($19,500) or (2) 10% of its adjusted consolidated taxable income ($12,000). The $7,500 ($19,500 − $12,000) of excess charitable contributions can be carried over to tax years 1992 through 1996. ■

NET OPERATING LOSSES (NOLs)

OBJECTIVE 6
Calculate an affiliated group's consolidated NOL

Key Point
The most often quoted advantage of filing consolidated tax returns is the ability to offset losses of one member against the income of other members.

One advantage of filing a consolidated tax return is the ability of an affiliated group to offset one member's current NOLs against the taxable income of other group members. If these losses cause the affiliated group to report a consolidated NOL, the NOL may be carried back or carried forward to other consolidated return years of the affiliated group. In some cases part or all of the consolidated NOL can be carried back or carried over to separate return years of the individual group members. NOLs of group members arising in separate return years may also be carried back or carried over to consolidated return years, subject to the separate return limitation year (SRLY) limitations discussed in the text. In addition, NOLs, capital losses, and excess credits of a loss corporation that is a member of an affiliated group can be subject to the special consolidated Sec. 382-384 loss limitations. The rules that apply to these four types of carrybacks and carryovers are examined below.

Current Year NOLs

Each member's separate taxable income is combined to determine combined taxable income before any adjustment is made for NOL carryovers (see Table 8-1).[29] The combining process allows the losses of one group member to offset the taxable income of other group members. A group member cannot elect separately to carry back its own losses from a consolidated return year to one of its earlier profitable separate return years. Only the consolidated NOL of the group (if any) may be carried back or over.

Example 8-16 ■   P and S Corporations form the P-S affiliated group. During 1990, the initial year of operation, P and S file separate tax returns. Beginning in 1991, the P-S group elects to file a consolidated tax return. P and S report the following results for 1990 and 1991:

[29] Reg. Sec. 1.1502-12.

Group Member	Taxable Income	
	1990	1991
P	($15,000)	$40,000
S	250,000	(27,000)
Consolidated taxable income	XXX	$13,000

P's 1990 NOL may not be used to offset S's profits because separate returns were filed. This loss carryover may be used only to reduce the $13,000 of 1991 consolidated taxable income that is reported after S's 1991 loss is offset against P's separate taxable income. Because S's 1991 loss is fully offset against P's 1991 taxable income, S cannot carry its 1991 NOL back against its 1990 profits to increase the value of the tax savings obtained from the loss. ■

OBJECTIVE 7
Calculate the carryback or carryover of a consolidated NOL

Carrybacks and Carryforwards of Consolidated NOLs

The consolidated NOL rules are similar to the NOL rules applying to a corporation filing a separate tax return. A consolidated NOL is determined as follows:[30]

Separate taxable income of each group member
Plus: Consolidated capital gain net income
Minus: Consolidated Sec. 1231 net loss
Consolidated charitable contributions deduction
Consolidated dividends-received deduction

Consolidated NOL

The consolidated NOL may be carried back to the 3 preceding consolidated return years or carried over to the 15 succeeding consolidated return years. The parent corporation may also elect for the affiliated group to relinquish the entire carryback period for a consolidated NOL and use it only as a carryforward to succeeding years.[31] (See Chapter 3 for a discussion of how this election is made.)

A carryback or carryforward of the consolidated NOL to a tax year in which the members of the affiliated group have not changed poses no real problem. The amount of the consolidated NOL that is absorbed is determined according to the basic Sec. 172 rules for NOLs outlined in Chapter 3.

Determining the amount of the consolidated NOL that may be absorbed in a tax year is more difficult when the group members are not the same in the carryback or carryforward year. In such a case, the consolidated NOL is apportioned to each corporation that was both a member of the affiliated group and incurred a separate NOL during the loss year. When a loss corporation is not also a group member in the carryback or carryforward year, the rules relating to carrybacks and carryforwards to separate return years (discussed below) must be applied.

[30] Prop. Reg. Sec. 1.1502-21(e).
[31] Prop. Reg. Sec. 1.1502-21(b)(3)(i).

Carryback of Consolidated NOL to Separate Return Year

Typical Misconception
A consolidated NOL may be carried back 3 years and carried forward 15 years. This is not complicated unless the members of the group change before the loss is fully utilized.

A consolidated NOL may be carried back and absorbed against a member's taxable income from a preceding separate return year. To effect a carryback, part or all of the consolidated NOL must be apportioned to the member. To the extent that a member uses its allocable share of the consolidated NOL, such an amount is not available to the remaining members as a carryback or carryforward to a consolidated return year. The consolidated NOL is apportioned to a loss member in the following manner:[32]

$$\frac{\text{Separate NOL of the individual member}}{\text{Sum of the separate NOLs incurred by all members having such losses}} \times \text{Consolidated NOL} = \text{Portion of consolidated NOL attributable to member}$$

Example 8-17 ■ P and S Corporations form the P-S affiliated group. The P-S group files separate tax returns in 1988. S reports taxable income of $275,000 in 1988. The group elects to file consolidated tax returns for 1989 through 1991. The P-S group reports a $150,000 consolidated NOL for 1991, all of which is attributable to S. S carries the $150,000 NOL back to 1988 and uses the loss to partially offset the taxable income it reported in 1988. The loss is used up in 1988 and therefore cannot be used by the P-S group in any consolidated return year. Alternatively, an election by P to forgo the carryback permits the loss to be used in 1992 and subsequent consolidated return years. ■

Key Point
In Example 8-17, since P-S did not file a consolidated tax return in 1988, P must either forgo the 3-year carryback or allow all of the consolidated NOL to be carried back to S's 1988 separate tax return year.

Special Carryback Rule for New Members. When the consolidated NOL is apportioned to a member, it is normally carried back to the third preceding consolidated or separate return year. A special rule permits an affiliated group member to carry an NOL back to the equivalent separate or consolidated return year of another group member if

1. The member corporation with the loss carryback did not exist in the carryback year, and
2. The loss member was a member of the affiliated group immediately after its organization

If these two requirements are met, the portion of the consolidated NOL attributable to the loss member is carried back to the equivalent consolidated return year (or separate return year) as part of the other group members' consolidated NOL carryback (or separate NOL carryback). An equivalent consolidated return year is generally defined in the Regulations as a similarly numbered preceding tax year (e.g., the third preceding tax year of the loss member is considered equivalent to the third preceding tax year of the affiliated group).[33]

---

[32] Prop. Reg. Sec. 1.1502-21(b)(2)(iv). The member's separate NOL is determined in a manner similar to the calculation of separate taxable income except for a series of adjustments prescribed in Reg. Sec. 1.1502-79(a)(3) to account for the member's share of the consolidated charitable contributions and dividends-received deductions, the member's capital gain net income, and the member's net capital loss or Sec. 1231 net loss minus any portion of the consolidated amounts attributable to the member that was absorbed currently.

[33] Prop. Reg. Sec. 1.1502-21(a)(2).

Example 8-18

Self-Study Question

What is the reason for allowing S_2's portion of the consolidated NOL to be carried back to 1988?

Answer

Since the assets that comprise S_2 Corporation in 1991 were really P's assets in 1988, it only makes sense to allow the NOLs to be carried back against whatever tax return P filed in 1988.

P, S_1, and S_2 Corporations form the P-S_1-S_2 affiliated group. P and S_1 are affiliated for 1988 and 1989 and file consolidated tax returns. P acquires all of S_2 Corporation's stock on January 1, 1990, the date on which S_2 is created. P, S_1, and S_2 report the following results (excluding NOL deductions) for 1988 through 1991:

Group Member	Taxable Income			
	1988	1989	1990	1991
P	$10,000	$12,000	$14,000	$16,000
S_1	7,000	8,000	10,000	4,000
S_2	XXX	XXX	(20,000)	(30,000)
Consolidated taxable income	$17,000	$20,000	$4,000	($10,000)

All of the $10,000 consolidated NOL of 1991 is attributable to S_2. Two options are available with respect to this NOL: (1) The NOL may be carried over to subsequent tax years, or (2) the NOL may be carried back to the period 1988 through 1990. If the first alternative is elected, the NOL offsets consolidated taxable income amounts reported in 1992 and subsequent years. If the second alternative is selected, the $10,000 NOL is carried back to offset part of the 1988 consolidated taxable income. This result is possible because S_2 did not exist in 1988 and it joined the affiliated group immediately after it was created on January 1, 1990. ■

If the loss corporation is not a member of the affiliated group immediately after its organization, that member's portion of the consolidated NOL is carried back only to its prior separate return years.

Example 8-19

Self-Study Question

Is there any reason for P to elect not to carry back the NOL to S_2's separate tax return years?

Answer

Probably not. But, if S_2 has minority shareholders, since the refund is issued to S_2, the minority stock interest will share in the increase in fair market value of S_2's stock. Don't overlook minority shareholders!

Assume the same facts as in Example 8-18, except that S_2 Corporation files separate tax returns for 1988 and 1989 prior to its stock being acquired by P on January 1, 1990. P, S_1, and S_2 report the following results (excluding NOL deductions) for 1988 through 1991:

Group Member	Taxable Income			
	1988	1989	1990	1991
P	$10,000	$12,000	$14,000	$16,000
S_1	7,000	8,000	10,000	4,000
S_2	8,000	3,000	(20,000)	(30,000)
Consolidated taxable income	$17,000[a]	$20,000[a]	$ 4,000	($10,000)

[a] Including only the results of P and S_1.

All of the 1991 consolidated NOL can be carried back by S_2 to 1988 and 1989. The $10,000 NOL offsets all of S_2's 1988 separate return taxable income of $8,000, and the remaining loss carryback of $2,000 reduces its 1989 separate return taxable income to $1,000. Alternatively, the P-S_1-S_2 affiliated group could elect to carry the loss forward to offset 1992's taxable income. ■

Carryforward of Consolidated NOL to Separate Return Year

If a corporation ceases to be a member of the affiliated group during the current year, the portion of the consolidated NOL that is allocable to the departing member becomes the member's separate carryforward. However, the allocation of the NOL to the departing group member cannot be made until the available carryover is absorbed in the current consolidated return year. This requirement exists even when all of the carryover is attributable to the departing member. The departing member's share of the NOL carryforward then may be used in its first separate return year.[34]

Example 8-20 ■

Typical Misconception

In Example 8-20, it is important to understand that the group is entitled to use the consolidated NOL prior to S_1 determining its NOL carryforward. This can have an impact on negotiating the purchase price of S_1.

P, S_1, and S_2 Corporations form the P-S_1-S_2 affiliated group with P owning all the S_1 and S_2 stock. The group files consolidated tax returns for several years. At the close of business on September 30, 1991, P sells its investment in S_1. S_1 must file a separate tax return covering the period October 1, 1991, through December 31, 1991. During pre-1991 tax years, P, S_1, and S_2 incur substantial NOLs. At the beginning of 1991, a consolidated NOL carryforward of $100,000 is still available. Two-thirds of this loss is allocable to S_1; the remainder is allocable to S_2. The affiliated group reports the following results (excluding NOL deductions) for 1991:

Group Member		Taxable Income
P		$20,000
S_1:	January 1, 1991 through September 30, 1991	30,000
	October 1, 1991 through December 31, 1991	15,000
S_2		10,000
Total		$75,000

The consolidated NOL carryforward of $100,000 offsets the $60,000 of taxable income ($20,000 + $30,000 + $10,000) reported by P, S_1, and S_2 in their 1991 consolidated tax return. This leaves $40,000 of carryforward to be allocated to S_1 and S_2. S_1 receives $26,667 (0.667 × $40,000), and S_2 receives $13,333 (0.333 × $40,000) of the carryforward. $15,000 of S_1's carryforward can be used in its separate tax return for the period ending December 31, 1991. The affiliated group can carry forward S_2's allocable share of the NOL to 1992 and subsequent years. ■

Special Loss Limitations

OBJECTIVE 8

Determine how the special loss limitations restrict the use of separate and consolidated NOL carrybacks and carryovers

Two special loss limitations, the **separate return limitation year (SRLY) rules** and the **Sec. 382 loss limitation rules,** are imposed on affiliated groups.[35] The SRLY rules limit the separate return NOL amount that can be used by an affiliated group to a member's contribution to consolidated taxable income. This prevents the affiliated group from offsetting its current taxable income by purchasing loss corporations solely to use their NOLs. The Sec. 382 loss limitation rules, which were explained in Chapter 7 on a separate return basis, also apply to affiliated groups filing

---

[34] Prop. Reg. Sec. 1.1502-21(a)(2)(i) and (ii).

[35] Proposed Reg. Sec. 1.1502-21 applies to NOLs and other deductions and losses arising in tax years ending on or after January 29, 1991. Different regular NOL and SRLY NOL rules apply to tax years ending before January 29, 1991. In addition, the **consolidated return change of ownership (CRCO) rules** applied to that time period. The CRCO rules restricted the ability of an affiliated group that had (1) incurred NOLs and (2) had a major change in the parent corporation's stock ownership to acquire a profitable corporation whose profits could be used to offset its NOLs. These rules have been replaced by the proposed consolidated Sec. 382 loss limitation regulations.

Key Point
The SRLY rules are used to limit a group from acquiring already existing losses and offsetting those losses against the group's income.

consolidated returns. The special consolidated return rules restrict an affiliated group from using NOLs following an ownership change that results from a purchase transaction or a tax-free reorganization. These rules generally provide that an ownership change and the Sec. 382 limitation are determined with respect to the tax attributes of the affiliated group on a single entity basis and not for its members separately. Each of these sets of rules is explained below.

Separate Return Limitation Year Rules. A member incurring an NOL in a separate return year (that is available as a carryback or a carryforward to a consolidated return year) is subject to a limit on the use of the NOL when the loss year is designated a separate return limitation year. A **separate return limitation year** is defined as any separate return year, except

1. A separate return year of the group member that is designated as the parent corporation for the consolidated return year to which the tax attribute (e.g., NOL) is carried
2. A separate return year of any corporation that was a group member for every day of such loss year

Additional Comment
These two exceptions to the SRLY rules exist because in both cases the group has not acquired already existing NOLs.

NOL CARRYFORWARDS. An NOL incurred in an SRLY may be carried forward to offset consolidated taxable income in a consolidated return year only to the extent that the member incurring the SRLY loss contributes to the consolidated taxable income for such year.[36]

The aggregate of the NOL carrybacks and carryovers originating in SRLYs that are included in the consolidated NOL deduction for a particular tax year may not exceed the sum of the consolidated taxable income amounts for all prior consolidated return years of the group determined by taking into account only the loss member's items of income, gain, deduction, and loss. Any NOL carryovers or carrybacks that cannot be used currently because of the member's contribution to consolidated taxable income for an individual tax year or for all consolidated return tax years must be carried over to subsequent tax years.

Example 8-21 ■

Self-Study Question
What is the consequence of having losses subject to the SRLY limitations?

Answer
The effect of having a loss tainted as a SRLY loss is that it can be used only to offset taxable income of the subsidiary member (or possibly subgroup) that created the NOL.

P and S Corporations form the P-S affiliated group. P acquires the S stock shortly after its creation in mid-1987. P and S file separate tax returns for 1987 and begin filing a consolidated tax return in 1988. The group reports the following results (excluding NOL deductions) for 1987 through 1991:

Group Member	Taxable Income				
	1987	1988	1989	1990	1991
P	($ 9,000)	$17,000	$ 6,000	($6,000)	$ 1,000
S	(20,000)	(2,000)	5,000	5,000	17,000
Consolidated taxable income	$XXX	$15,000	$11,000	($1,000)	$18,000

S's 1987 NOL is incurred in a SRLY and is subject to the SRLY rules in 1988 and later consolidated return years. P's 1987 loss is not subject to the SRLY rules because it is the parent corporation in each of the carryforward years (1988

---

[36] Prop. Reg. Sec. 1.1502-21(b)(1). Any unused NOLs that are carried to the consolidated return year from tax years ending before the separate return limitation year reduce the SRLY limitation on a first-in, first-out (FIFO) basis. Tax years ending on the same date reduce the SRLY limitations on a pro rata basis. For an illustration of the adjustments that must be made to the member's separate taxable income to calculate the member's contribution to consolidated taxable income, see Prop. Reg. Sec. 1.1502-21A(c)(5) Ex. (1).

through 1991). As a result, its $9,000 loss is fully offset against the group's $15,000 1988 consolidated taxable income. None of S's 1987 loss may be used because its loss limitation for 1988 under the SRLY rules is zero (i.e., S makes no contribution to the consolidated taxable income in 1988). In 1989, $3,000 of the 1987 NOL—the lesser of S's $5,000 contribution to 1989 consolidated taxable income or its $3,000 total contribution to 1988 and 1989 consolidated taxable income—may be used. None of the 1987 loss may be used in 1990 because a consolidated NOL is reported. (This 1990 consolidated NOL can be carried back to 1988 or forward to 1991.) In 1991 the loss limitation is $17,000—the lesser of S's $17,000 contribution to 1991 consolidated taxable income or its $20,000 ($25,000 contribution − $5,000 loss used in 1989) net contribution to consolidated taxable income in 1988–1991. This permits the $15,000 remainder of S's 1987 NOL to reduce consolidated taxable income. ∎

The SRLY rules are generally applied to each individual corporation that has a loss carryover from a separate return limitation year. Alternatively, the SRLY rules can be applied to a subgroup of two or more corporations within an affiliated group that are continuously affiliated after ceasing to be members of a former affiliated group, where at least one of the corporations carries over losses from the former group to the current group. If the subgroup has remained continuously affiliated up to the beginning of the year to which the loss is carried, the subgroup's loss carryovers can be used to the extent that the subgroup contributes to consolidated taxable income.[37]

> **Key Point**
>
> The SRLY rules apply to both carryforwards and carrybacks. Remember that SRLYs stem from either a year in which a member files a separate tax return or a year in which a member joins in the filing of a different consolidated tax return.

NOL CARRYBACKS. The SRLY rules also apply to NOL carrybacks from a separate return limitation year to a consolidated return year. For example, assume that S Corporation in the preceding example leaves the P-S group at the end of 1991. Any NOL that S incurs in a subsequent separate return year and that could be carried back to the 1989 through 1991 consolidated return years is subject to the SRLY rules. Its use is restricted to S's contribution to consolidated taxable income in the carryback year, or S's contribution for all consolidated return tax years, whichever is less.

The use of built-in deductions is also limited by the SRLY rules. A **built-in deduction** is a deduction that accrues in a separate return year but which is recognized for tax purposes in a consolidated return year. One example of such a deduction is the depreciation connected with a subsidiary corporation's asset which declines in value between the time it was acquired in a separate return year and the beginning of the initial consolidated return year. Built-in deductions can also result from the sale of a capital or noncapital asset at a loss in a consolidated return year when the decline in value takes place in a separate return year and is recognized in a consolidated return year. A built-in deduction can be deducted only if the corporation's SRLY limitation equals or exceeds the built-in deduction amount.[38]

> **Additional Comment**
>
> The built-in deduction rules eliminate the ability to circumvent the SRLY rules by acquiring a corporation with losses that have economically accrued and having these losses recognized after the subsidiary is a member of the group.

Section 382 Loss Limitation. Section 382 prevents the purchasing of the assets or stock of a corporation having loss carryovers (known as the loss corporation) primarily to acquire the corporation's tax attributes.[39] Trafficking in NOLs and other tax attributes is prevented by applying the Sec. 382 loss limitation to any tax year ending after the ownership change. The 50 percentage point minimum stock

---

[37] Prop. Reg. Sec. 1.1502-21(c)(2).
[38] Prop. Reg. Sec. 1.1502-15.
[39] The Sec. 382 limitation rules apply to the tax attributes that are limited by Secs. 382-384 (e.g., NOLs, capital losses, foreign tax credits, general business credits, minimum tax credit, built-in gains, and built-in losses).

ownership change needed to trigger the Sec. 382 rules can occur in acquisitive transactions involving a single corporation or a group of corporations that are filing separate or consolidated returns.

The consolidated Sec. 382 rules generally provide that the ownership change and Sec. 382 limitation are determined with respect to the entire affiliated group (or an affiliated subgroup) and not for individual entities.[40] Following an ownership change for a loss group, the consolidated taxable income for a post-change tax year that may be offset by a pre-change NOL cannot exceed the consolidated Sec. 382 limitation. If the post-change tax year includes the ownership change date, the Sec. 382 limitation applies to the consolidated taxable income that is earned in the portion of the tax year following the ownership change date.

Additional Comment

Sec. 382 adopts a single entity approach in determining ownership changes and Sec. 382 limitations. This means that the members of a consolidated group are treated like divisions of a single taxpayer.

A loss group is an affiliated group that is entitled to use an NOL carryover (other than a SRLY carryover) to the tax year in which the ownership change occurs, or has a consolidated NOL for the tax year in which the ownership change occurs.[41] An affiliated group can have two forms of ownership changes—a parent ownership change and a subgroup ownership change. A parent ownership change is when the loss group's common parent corporation has a shift in stock ownership involving a 5% or more shareholder, or a tax-free reorganization takes place, and the percentage of stock of the new loss corporation owned by one or more 5% shareholders has increased by more than 50 percentage points over the lowest percentage of stock owned in the old loss corporation by such shareholders during the preceding 3-year (or shorter) testing period.[42] A parent ownership change is illustrated in the following example.

Example 8-22 ■ Dwayne owns all of the P Corporation stock. P owns 80% of the S Corporation stock. The remaining 20% of the S stock is owned by Mitzi. For 1991 the P-S group has a consolidated NOL that can be carried over to 1992. The P-S affiliated group is a loss group. On August 15, 1992 Dwayne sells 51% of the P stock to Carter. The Sec. 382 stock ownership requirements are applied to P to determine if an ownership change has occurred. The 51% increase in Carter's stock ownership is an ownership change that causes the Sec. 382 loss limitation to apply to the carryover of the 1991 NOL to 1992. If Carter had instead acquired only 49% of the P stock, the requisite ownership change would not have occurred and the Sec. 382 limit would not apply. ■

The preceding example applied the ownership change rules to a parent corporation. An ownership change can also occur with respect to a loss subgroup. A loss subgroup generally consists of two or more corporations that are continuously affiliated after ceasing to be members of one group when at least one of the corporations carries over losses from the first group to the second group.[43] The loss subgroup can have an ownership change if, for example, the common parent of the loss subgroup has an ownership change (e.g., when an acquisition of subsidiaries from another affiliated group occurs. The 50 percentage point ownership change test is applied to the common parent of the loss subgroup. Further discussion of this type of ownership change is beyond the scope of the text.

The consolidated Sec. 382 limitation (or subgroup limitation) for any post-change tax year equals the value of the loss group (or subgroup) times the highest adjusted Federal long-term tax-exempt rate that applies with respect to the three-month period ending in the month of the ownership change. The value of the loss group is the value,

---

[40] Prop. Reg. Sec. 1.1502-91(a).
[41] Prop. Reg. Sec. 1.1502-91(c).
[42] Prop. Reg. Sec. 1.1502-92(b)(1)(i).
[43] Prop. Reg. Sec. 1.1502-92(b)(1)(ii).

immediately before the ownership change, of the common and preferred stock of each member, other than stock owned by other group members.

Example 8-23 ■ Assume the same facts as in Example 8-22 except that the value of the P stock is $1,000,000 and the value of the S stock is $750,000. The value of the P-S affiliated group for purposes of applying the Sec. 382 limitation is $1,150,000 ($1,000,000 value of P stock + [0.20 × $750,000 value of S stock owned by Mitzi]). The $1,150,000 value is multiplied by the federal long-term tax-exempt rate to determine the portion of the 1991 consolidated NOL that can be used in 1992. ■

Additional Comment

In Example 8-23, if S leaves the group, the loss which is attributable to S will be subject to whatever amount of the Sec. 382 limitation P apportions to S. S's Sec. 382 limitation is zero if P chooses not to apportion any of the group's Sec. 382 limitation to S.

A number of special Sec. 382 rules that apply to affiliated groups deserve brief recognition here.

1. If the Sec. 382 limitation for a post-change tax year exceeds the consolidated taxable income that may be offset by a pre-change NOL, the excess amount is carried forward to the next tax year to increase that year's Sec. 382 limitation.[44]
2. A loss group is treated as a single entity for purposes of determining whether it satisfies the Sec. 382 continuity of enterprise requirement. Should the loss group not meet the continuity of enterprise requirement at any time in its first two years, the group's Sec. 382 limitation is zero.[45]
3. The Sec. 382 rules can apply to a new corporation joining the affiliated group that brings with it a loss carryover from a separate return limitation year. The Sec. 382 ownership change requirement is tested on a separate entity basis to see if the Sec. 382 limitation or the basic SRLY rules will apply to limit the use of the NOLs against consolidated taxable income. Separate tracking of SRLY carryovers ceases if an ownership change occurs when the loss corporation joins the affiliated group, if an ownership change occurs after joining the group, or when the loss corporation has been a member of the affiliated group for 5 years.[46]
4. When an affiliated group terminates or a member leaves the affiliated group, the Sec. 382 limitation is apportioned to the individual group members.[47]

The consolidated Sec. 382 regulations apply to any testing date commencing on or after January 22, 1991. A series of special transitional rules work towards ameliorating any problem that exists because of the timing of the release of the Regulations.[48]

Topic Review 8-3 presents a summary of the rules applying to carrybacks and carryovers of consolidated return and separate return NOLs. *Note:* The general principles that apply to NOLs also apply to other tax attributes.

CONSOLIDATED CAPITAL GAINS AND LOSSES

In the previous discussion of separate taxable income (see page 8-6), all capital gains and losses, Sec. 1231 gains and losses, and casualty and theft gains and losses were excluded. These three types of gains and losses are reported by the affiliated group on a consolidated basis. For a consolidated return year, the affiliated group's consolidated net capital gain or loss is composed of

[44] Prop. Reg. Sec. 1.1502-93(a).
[45] Prop. Reg. Sec. 1.1502-93(d).
[46] Prop. Reg. Sec. 1.1502-94(a).
[47] Prop. Reg. Sec. 1.1502-95(a).
[48] Prop. Reg. Sec. 1.1502-99.

TOPIC REVIEW 8-3

Rules Governing Affiliated Group NOL Carrybacks and Carryovers

Loss Year	Carryover Year	Rule and Special Limitations
CRY[a]	CRY	1. Consolidated NOLs are carried back 3 years and forward 15 years. Election to forgo carryback period is made by parent corporation. No special problems are encountered if the group members are the same in the loss year and carryback or carryover year. 2. Section 382 limitation can apply to the loss carryover if an ownership change has occurred.
CRY	SRY[b]	1. Carryback to a member's prior separate return year is only possible if part or all of loss is apportioned to the member. Offspring rule permits carryback of an offspring member's allocable share of consolidated NOL to a separate return or consolidated return tax year of the corporation which created the member. 2. A departing group member is allocated part of the consolidated NOL carryover. Consolidated loss is used first in the consolidated return year in which the departing member leaves the group before an allocation is made. The allocated share of the loss is first used in the departing member's first separate return year. Departing member may be allocated a portion of the Sec. 382 loss limitation by the common parent corporation.
SRY	CRY	1. Separate return year NOL can be carried over and used in a consolidated return year. SRLY rules will apply to NOLs other than those of a corporation that is the parent corporation in carryover year and a corporation that is a member of the affiliated group on each day of the loss year. 2. Carryback of a loss of a departed group member to a consolidated return year is a SRLY loss.

[a]Consolidated return year.
[b]Separate return year.

1. the aggregate amount of the capital gains and losses of the group members (determined without regard to any Sec. 1231 transactions or net capital loss carryovers or carrybacks).
2. the consolidated net Sec. 1231 gain.
3. the consolidated net capital loss carryovers or carrybacks to the year.[49]

Any consolidated capital gain net income that is part of the consolidated taxable income is taxed at the regular corporate tax rates. Any consolidated net capital loss is carried back 3 years or forward 5 years as a short-term capital loss.

---

[49] Prop. Reg. Sec. 1.1502-22(a)(1)-(3).

Key Point
Netting Sec. 1231 gains/losses on a consolidated basis rather than on a separate corporation basis can dramatically alter the amount of ordinary versus capital gain income.

Section 1231 Gains and Losses

A group member's Sec. 1231 gains and losses exclude any such gains recognized in deferred intercompany transactions. (These intercompany gains are reported at the time a restoration event occurs.) The consolidated Sec. 1231 net gain or loss for the tax year is determined by taking into account the aggregate gains and losses of the group members' Sec. 1231 transactions. If the group's total Sec. 1231 gains (including net gain from casualty and theft occurrences involving Sec. 1231 property and certain capital assets) exceed similar losses, the net gain from these transactions is the consolidated net Sec. 1231 gain and is eligible for long-term capital gain treatment. If the group reports a net loss either from Sec. 1231 transactions or from its casualty and theft occurrences, the net Sec. 1231 loss(es) is treated as an ordinary loss and is deductible in determining consolidated taxable income.

Example 8-24 ■ P and S Corporations form the P-S affiliated group. The P-S group files consolidated tax returns for several years. They report the following results for 1991:

Group Member	Ordinary Income	Sec. 1231 Gains and Losses
P	$ 70,000	$21,000
S	40,000	(7,000)
Total	$110,000	$14,000

The consolidated net Sec. 1231 gain is $14,000. This gain is combined with the group's capital gains and losses (if any). If S instead reports a $30,000 Sec. 1231 loss, the $9,000 ($21,000 − $30,000) net Sec. 1231 loss offsets the ordinary income reported. ■

Code Sec. 1231(c) requires that the Sec. 1231 losses claimed as an ordinary loss must be recaptured. The consolidated net Sec. 1231 gain,[50] accordingly, is recharacterized as ordinary income to the extent of the net Sec. 1231 losses[51] for the 5 most recent tax years that have not previously been recaptured.

Self-Study Question
How do deferred intercompany transactions affect the calculation of capital gains/losses?

Answer
Deferred intercompany gains/losses are included in the netting of capital gains/losses only when the restoration rules trigger their recognition.

Capital Gains and Losses

Determining the Amount of Gain or Loss. The amount of any group member's capital gains and losses excludes any such gains recognized on deferred intercompany transactions. These intercompany gains and losses are reported at the time a restoration event occurs. Once the recognized gains and losses of each group member are determined, each member's short- and long-term transactions (including any consolidated Sec. 1231 net gain that is not treated as ordinary income) are combined into separate net gain or net loss positions. The sum of these separate positions then determines the amount of the affiliated group's aggregate short- or long-term capital gain or loss. These aggregate amounts are combined to determine the group's consolidated capital gain net income.

---

[50] **Net Sec. 1231 gain** is defined by Sec. 1231(c)(3) as the excess of the Sec. 1231 gains over the Sec. 1231 losses.
[51] **Net Sec. 1231 loss** is defined by Sec. 1231(c)(4) as the excess of the Sec. 1231 losses over the Sec. 1231 gains.

Carrybacks and Carryforwards. The treatment of consolidated capital loss carrybacks and carryovers is similar to NOLs. The losses that are carried back or forward to other consolidated return years are treated as short-term capital losses and serve as a component of the consolidated capital gain or loss position.

The capital loss carrybacks or carryovers available to be used in a consolidated return year equal the sum of (1) the affiliated group's unused consolidated capital loss carrybacks or carryovers and (2) any unused capital loss carrybacks or carryovers of individual group members arising in separate return years. These capital loss carrybacks and carryovers are absorbed according to the same rules described above for NOLs (see pages 8-20 through 8-28).[52]

Example 8-25 ■ P, S_1, and S_2 Corporations form the P-S_1-S_2 affiliated group. This group has filed consolidated tax returns for several years. During 1991 the affiliated group reports $100,000 of ordinary income and the following property transaction results:

Group Member	Capital Gains and Losses		Sec. 1231 Gains and Losses
	Short-Term	Long-Term	
P	$2,000	($1,000)	($2,500)
S_1	(1,000)	7,000	2,000
S_2	(2,000)	3,000	2,000
Total	($1,000)	$9,000	$1,500

Typical Misconception
The allocation of net capital losses to the individual group members is based in part on each member's Sec. 1231 losses. Thus, it is possible for a member with only a Sec. 1231 loss to share in the net capital loss carryforward or carryback.

In addition, the group carries over a consolidated capital loss of $3,000 from 1990. No net Sec. 1231 losses have been recognized in prior years. The P-S_1-S_2 affiliated group reports a $1,500 consolidated net Sec. 1231 gain in 1991. This amount is combined with the $8,000 aggregate amount of capital gains and losses ($9,000 − $1,000) and the $3,000 consolidated net capital loss carryover to obtain the 1991 consolidated capital gain net income of $6,500 ($1,500 + $8,000 − $3,000). This entire amount is taxed at the regular corporate tax rates. ■

Additional Comment
There is no election to forgo the 3-year carryback for a net capital loss. This can complicate matters when the 3 prior years include separate tax return years of the members of the group.

CARRYBACK OF A CONSOLIDATED NET CAPITAL LOSS. A carryback of a member's apportionment of a consolidated capital loss to one of its preceding separate return years is required when capital gains are available in the carryback year against which the loss may be offset. However, no election to forgo the carryback and use the loss only as a carryover is available here, although such an election is possible with an NOL. Apportionment of the consolidated capital loss to the loss member(s) occurs in a manner similar to that described for NOLs.

SRLY LIMITATION. Carryovers or carrybacks of capital losses from a separate return limitation year invoke the SRLY rules. The amount of the loss carryback or carryover from a separate return limitation year that may be used in a consolidated return year equals the lesser of loss member's contribution to the current year consolidated capital gain net income or the loss member's contribution to the sum of the consolidated capital gain net income for all prior consolidated return years.

SEC. 382 LIMITATION. The Sec. 382 loss limitation rules apply to consolidated and separate return capital loss carryovers as well as consolidated and separate return NOLs. These two categories of losses, as well as credits also limited by Sec. 383, are subject to the general Sec. 382 limitation described earlier. Special ordering rules found in the Sec. 383 regulations determine whether pre-change losses and pre-change credits can be used in a particular tax year.

---

[52] Prop. Reg. Sec. 1.1502-22(b).

TAXABLE INCOME LIMITATION. In addition to the special capital loss limitations outlined above, Sec. 1212(a)(1)(A)(ii) contains a general limitation that prevents a capital loss from being carried back and creating or increasing the NOL for the tax year to which it is carried. Therefore, the utilization of a capital loss is also limited to the group's consolidated taxable income.

Departing Group Member's Losses. A member leaving the affiliated group may take with it an apportionment of any consolidated capital loss carryover and any of its unused capital loss carryovers that originated in a separate return year. These losses are used in subsequent years until they expire. Apportionment of the consolidated capital loss to the departing group member occurs in a manner similar to that described above for NOLs.

COMPUTATION OF THE AFFILIATED GROUP'S TAX LIABILITY

Regular Tax Liability

OBJECTIVE 9
Calculate the consolidated regular tax liability for an affiliated group

The consolidated regular (income) tax liability is determined by applying the tax rates found in Sec. 11 to consolidated taxable income. Section 1561(a) limits a controlled group of corporations to a single reduction in the corporate tax rates for the first $75,000 of taxable income under Sec. 11(b), regardless of the number of corporations that make up the controlled group. The benefits of the reduced tax rates must be apportioned equally among all the members of the controlled group (whether such members are included in or excluded from the consolidated return election) unless the controlled group's members elect to use an unequal method of apportionment. (See the apportionment discussion in Chapter 3.)

Recapture of the tax savings from the 15% and 25% tax rate brackets occurs when consolidated taxable income exceeds $100,000. To the extent that the members of the affiliated group are apportioned the savings from the reduced tax rate brackets and consolidated taxable income exceeds $100,000, an additional 5% tax is imposed until consolidated taxable income exceeds $335,000.[53]

Example 8-26 ■ The P-S affiliated group has filed consolidated tax returns for a number of years. Their 1991 results are as follows:

Group Member	Ordinary Income	Capital Gains Short-Term	Capital Gains Long-Term
P	$200,000	$4,000	$ 4,000
S	50,000	(6,000)	8,000
Total	$250,000	($2,000)	$12,000

The affiliated group's consolidated regular tax liability on $260,000 of taxable income ($250,000 + $10,000) is determined as follows:

---

[53] For purposes of applying the recapture tax, members of a controlled group are treated as a single corporation, and the recapture tax must be divided among them in the same manner as the benefits of the reduced rates were allocated. The $335,000 ceiling may be lower for an affiliated group if some of the reduced rate benefits are allocated to members of a controlled group that are ineligible to join in the consolidated return election.

Taxable Income	Rate	Tax Liability
First $50,000	15%	$ 7,500
Next $25,000	25%	6,250
Remaining $185,000	34%	62,900
Recapture of 15% and 25% tax rates	5%	8,000[54]
Regular tax liability		$84,650

Corporate Alternative Minimum Tax Liability

OBJECTIVE 10
Calculate the consolidated AMT liability for an affiliated group

Key Point
Determining the alternative minimum tax for corporations is discussed in Chapter 5. Determining the alternative minimum tax for a consolidated group merely adds to the complexity of this already difficult computation.

Additional Comment
The Revenue Reconciliation Act of 1989 has simplified to some extent the computation of ACE. The ACE adjustment may need to be calculated as soon as the first quarter of 1991 as part of determining 1991's quarterly estimated tax payments.

The corporate alternative minimum tax liability is determined on a consolidated basis for all group members. The starting point for the calculation is consolidated taxable income. The adjustments to consolidated taxable income required by Secs. 56 and 57 are made for all group members, including for post-1989 tax years 75% of the excess (if any) of the adjusted current earnings of the affiliated group over the alternative minimum taxable income (as determined without this adjustment and the alternative tax NOL deduction).[55] A downward adjustment is permitted for 75% of the excess (if any) of the affiliated group's alternative minimum taxable income (determined without this adjustment and the alternative tax NOL deduction) and its adjusted current earnings. The $40,000 statutory exemption that is available for the corporate alternative minimum tax must be allocated between all members of the controlled group. Section 1561(a) requires that this amount be divided equally among all group members, whether included in the consolidated return election or not, unless a special allocation is made by the controlled group. Determination of the actual corporate alternative minimum tax liability (if any) occurs by comparing the affiliated group's tentative minimum tax for the year to its regular tax liability. Excess alternative minimum tax payments from prior tax years that are attributable to timing and permanent differences can be carried over by the affiliated group and claimed as a minimum tax credit to reduce its regular tax liability. Section 6154(c) requires that the corporate alternative minimum tax amount be included in determining the affiliated group's estimated tax payments for the year.

Section 56(g) provides special rules for purposes of making the adjusted current earnings-alternative minimum taxable income adjustment. The consolidated alternative minimum taxable income (AMTI) of the affiliated group is increased or decreased by the consolidated adjusted current earnings (ACE) adjustment. The consolidated positive ACE adjustment equals 75% of the excess (if any) of (1) the consolidated ACE over (2) consolidated pre-adjustment AMTI.[56] The consolidated negative ACE adjustment decreases consolidated AMTI. The consolidated negative ACE adjustment equals 75% of the excess (if any) of (1) consolidated pre-adjustment AMTI over (2) consolidated ACE.[57] The negative adjustment is limited to the excess (if any) of (1) the aggregate positive ACE adjustments for the group in prior years over (2) the aggregate negative ACE adjustments for the group in prior years.

Consolidated pre-adjustment AMTI is consolidated taxable income of the affiliated group determined with all of the adjustments from Secs. 56-58 (except for the ACE and alternative tax NOL adjustments) and increased for all tax preference items.

---

[54] $260,000 taxable income − $100,000 = $160,000 × 0.05 = $8,000.

[55] For 1987 through 1989, corporate taxpayers made a positive adjustment for one-half of the difference between the adjusted net book income and the alternative minimum taxable income (determined without regard to this adjustment and the alternative tax NOL deduction). Affiliated groups of corporations electing to file a consolidated tax return calculated the amount of this adjustment on a consolidated basis.

[56] Prop. Reg. Sec. 1.56(g)-1(n)(1).

[57] Prop. Reg. Sec. 1.56(g)-1(n)(2).

Self-Study Question

In Example 8-27, what is AMTI if the sum of the ACE is $500,000?

Answer

Applying the ACE rules results in a downward adjustment of $112,500 [0.75 × ($650,000 − $500,000)] and an AMTI of $537,500. A downward adjustment is possible under the ACE adjustment. (This question assumes sufficient positive ACE adjustments have occurred in prior tax years.)

Consolidated ACE is consolidated pre-adjustment AMTI of the affiliated group increased or decreased for the ACE adjustments.[58]

The basic adjustments to move from preadjustment AMTI to adjusted current earnings were outlined in Chapter 5. These adjustments must be made by the affiliated group to arrive at consolidated adjusted current earnings. The Conference Committee report for the 1986 Tax Act indicates that appropriate adjustments are also required to prevent the double inclusion of any item of adjusted current earnings (e.g., elimination of intercompany profit) through the operation of the consolidated return regulations or otherwise. Similar types of adjustments will also need to be made to take into account corporations joining and leaving the affiliated group. Detailed ACE adjustment proposed regulations for corporations filing separate returns were issued in May 1990. A less-detailed version of the proposed ACE adjustment rules for affiliated groups filing consolidated tax returns was also issued at the same time. One may anticipate that more detailed ACE adjustment regulations specifically directed at affiliated groups filing consolidated returns will be forthcoming.

Example 8-27 ■ P, S_1, and S_2 Corporations are members of an affiliated group that files a consolidated tax return for 1991. Separate ACE amounts for the group members were: P, $400,000; S_1, $300,000; and S_2, $100,000. The consolidated pre-adjustment AMTI is $650,000. The ACE adjustment is $112,500 (0.75 × [($400,000 + $300,000 + $100,000) − $650,000]). AMTI for the P-S_1-S_2 group is $762,500 since the statutory exemption has been completely phased out. P-S_1-S_2's tentative minimum tax amount is $152,500 ($762,500 × .20). ■

CONSOLIDATED TAX CREDITS

The affiliated group can claim all tax credits available to corporate taxpayers. The discussion that follows examines the two major credits claimed by most affiliated groups—the general business credit and the foreign tax credit.

General Business Credit

The affiliated group's general business credit is determined on a consolidated basis (i.e., the group members' investment tax credit, targeted jobs credit, alcohol fuels credit, research credit, low-income housing credit, enhanced oil recovery credit, and disabled access credit amounts are combined into a single amount for the affiliated group). For these credits, an affiliated group is limited to the excess of (1) the affiliated group's net income tax over (2) the greater of (a) the affiliated group's tentative minimum tax for the year or (b) 25% of the affiliated group's net regular tax liability for the year in excess of $25,000.[59] Any unused general business tax credits may be carried back 3 years and forward 15 years under Sec. 39(a).

When determining the limitation, the amount of the consolidated net regular tax liability equals the consolidated regular tax liability minus its consolidated tax credits

---

[58] Prop. Reg. Sec. 1.56(g)-1(n)(3).
[59] Sec. 38(c).

claimed under Secs. 21-29 (e.g., foreign tax credit). The consolidated tentative minimum tax liability equals the consolidated tentative minimum tax amount before credits minus the consolidated AMT foreign tax credit. The consolidated net income tax amount equals the sum of the consolidated regular and AMT tax liabilities minus the consolidated tax credits claimed under Secs. 21-29. A profitable group member may find that use of the consolidated tax liability as the basis for the general business credit limitation may result in a reduced credit amount because the losses of other group members are used to offset its taxable income. An unprofitable member, however, may find its general business credit limitation increased by the taxable income of another member, so that credits that would otherwise have been carried back or forward if separate returns were filed may be used currently by the group.

Example 8-28 ■ The P-S affiliated group files a consolidated tax return for 1991. P and S Corporations contribute separate taxable income (or loss) amounts of $300,000 and ($100,000), respectively, to 1991's $200,000 consolidated taxable income. P and S can tentatively claim a $40,000 research credit and a $10,000 targeted jobs credit. The P-S group's regular tax liability is $61,250 ([$50,000 × 0.15] + [$25,000 × 0.25] + [$125,000 × 0.34] + [$100,000 × 0.05]). The P-S group's tentative minimum tax liability (assuming no differences between AMTI and taxable income other than the statutory exemption) is $34,500.[60] The group's general business credit limitation is the excess of the net income tax ($61,250 + -0- AMT) over the greater of (1) the tentative minimum tax for the year ($34,500) or (2) 25% of the group's net regular tax liability in excess of $25,000 ($9,062 = [$61,250 − $25,000] × 0.25), or $26,750 ($61,250 − $34,500). The $23,250 ($50,000 − $26,750) of unused general business credits can be carried back 3 years and forward 15 years. ■

Self-Study Question

How do the SRLY rules apply to general business credit carryforwards?

Answer

Assume the group's general business credit limitation is $100,000. Also assume that the general business credit limitation without the SRLY member is $80,000. Then that SRLY member can use $20,000 of its general business credit carryforward.

The amount of general business tax credits that an affiliated group claims in a consolidated return year can be increased by (1) the amount of the consolidated general business tax credit carryforwards and carrybacks to the tax year, and (2) any general business tax credit carryforwards that originate in a group member's separate return years. The absorption of these credit carryforwards occurs in a manner similar to the rules applicable to corporations filing separate tax returns. Credit carryforwards are utilized first, followed by credits originating in the current consolidated return year, and, finally, credit carrybacks from subsequent tax years. Unused credit carryforwards, which may originate in a separate return year or a consolidated return year, are absorbed in an FIFO manner, beginning with the earliest ending tax year. Like with NOLs, the affiliated group's general business credit carryovers are subject to the SRLY and Sec. 382 limitations.

Foreign Tax Credit

An affiliated group's foreign tax credit for a consolidated return year is determined on a consolidated basis. The parent corporation makes the election to claim either a deduction or a credit for foreign taxes. If the credit is chosen, the affiliated group's foreign tax credit limitation is computed by taking into account the group's income from U.S. and non-U.S. sources, the consolidated taxable income, and the consolidated regular and alternative minimum tax liability amounts in the general manner described in Chapter 15.[61]

---

[60] {$200,000 taxable income − [$40,000 statutory exemption − (0.25 × [$200,000 − $150,000])} × 0.20 = $34,500.

[61] Reg. Sec. 1.1502-4.

TAX PLANNING CONSIDERATIONS

OBJECTIVE 11
Explain the advantages and disadvantages of filing a consolidated tax return

Key Point
The elimination of intercompany dividends is an advantage of filing consolidated tax returns. However, even if consolidated tax returns are not filed, the owning member should be eligible for a 100% dividends-received deduction.

Advantages of Filing a Consolidated Tax Return

Filing a consolidated tax return offers a number of advantages and disadvantages, some of the more important of which are discussed below. Some of the advantages that may be gained by filing a consolidated tax return include the following:

- The separate return losses of one affiliated group member may be offset against the taxable income of other group members in the current tax year. Such losses provide an immediate tax benefit by reducing the tax due on other income or eliminating the need to carry a loss to a subsequent tax year.
- Capital losses of one group member may be offset against the capital gains of other group members in the current tax year. Again, this avoids carrying these losses to subsequent tax years.
- Dividends paid from one group member to a second group member are "eliminated" in the consolidated tax return.
- The various credit and deduction limitations are computed on a consolidated basis. This permits group members to use "excess" credits or "excess" deductions in the current tax year and avoids carrying them to subsequent years.
- Gains on intercompany transactions are deferred until a subsequent restoration event occurs. Similarly, depreciation and other recapture provisions (e.g., Secs. 1245 and 1250) do not apply to intercompany transactions.
- No investment tax credit recapture occurs when an asset is transferred between group members. Recapture, however, may be required at the time the property is transferred outside the group.
- Calculation of the alternative minimum tax liability takes place on a consolidated basis (rather than for each individual company) and may reduce the negative effects of the tax preference items and other adjustments (e.g., the ACE-AMTI adjustment) and eliminate the need for the affiliated group as a whole to pay an alternative minimum tax liability.

Typical Misconception
One significant disadvantage of filing consolidated tax returns that should be obvious after going through this chapter is the added recordkeeping costs necessary to file a consolidated tax return.

Disadvantages of Filing a Consolidated Tax Return

Some of the disadvantages of filing a consolidated tax return include the following:

- A consolidated return election is binding on all subsequent tax years unless (1) the IRS grants the group permission to discontinue filing a consolidated return or (2) the affiliated group is terminated.
- Losses and deductions on intercompany transactions are deferred until a subsequent restoration event occurs.
- Operating losses and capital losses of group members may reduce or eliminate the ability of profitable group members to take advantage of credits or deductions by lowering the applicable credit or deduction limitation.
- The initial inventory adjustment requirement results in a double counting of income and a double payment of taxes until (1) the intercompany profit amount becomes zero or (2) the selling and purchasing members terminate their affiliation.
- Additional administrative costs may be incurred in maintaining the necessary

records to account for deferred intercompany transactions and the initial inventory adjustments.

There is no general rule that can be applied to determine whether an affiliated group should elect to file a consolidated tax return. Each group should examine the long- and short-term advantages and disadvantages of filing a consolidated tax return before making a decision.

Election Not to Defer Intercompany Gains and Losses

The affiliated group can elect current recognition of gains and losses on deferred intercompany transactions involving either all or specific classes of property. This election is binding until the IRS grants permission to revoke the election.[62] The election, which eliminates the need for all the bookkeeping activities associated with the deferral and restoration of gains and losses on deferred intercompany transactions, must be made on or before the due date for the consolidated return.

Even though the consolidated return regulations permit an election to recognize intercompany gains and losses currently, deferred losses are not recognized currently for most intercompany sales. Section 267(f) provides that losses from the sale or exchange of property between members of the same controlled group will be deferred, rather than not being recognized, until the property is transferred outside the controlled group. Temporary Reg. Sec. 1.267(f)-2T(c), which outlines the deferral and recognition process for gains and losses arising from sales between members of the same controlled group, does not permit the IRS to grant permission to a taxpayer to not defer losses.

Key Point
Note that a 100% dividends-received deduction may be necessary for intercompany dividends for state income tax purposes if the state doesn't allow the filing of consolidated tax returns.

100% Dividends-Received Deduction Election

Intercompany dividends are eliminated when a consolidated tax return is filed. The 100% dividends-received deduction election may be used by the affiliated group to exempt from taxation any dividends received from corporations that are not eligible to be included in the consolidated return (e.g., a 100%-owned life insurance company).

If a state does not permit the filing of a consolidated tax return for state income tax purposes,[63] it may be necessary for an affiliated group to elect the 100% dividends-received deduction. In such a case, the state requires the filing of separate tax returns by each member of the affiliated group. Generally, the state also permits the claiming of any dividends-received deduction elected for federal income tax purposes. Since a consolidated tax return is not filed for state income tax purposes, no elimination of the dividends is possible and the 100% dividends-received deduction is substituted on the state income tax return.

Estimated Tax Payments

Once consolidated tax returns have been filed for two consecutive years, the affiliated group must pay estimated taxes on a consolidated basis.[64] The affiliated group is treated as a single corporation for this purpose. Thus, the estimated tax payments and any underpayment exceptions or penalties are based on the affiliated group's income

---

[62] Reg. Sec. 1.1502-13(c)(3). Rev. Proc. 82-36 (1982-1 C.B. 490) sets forth the requirements for making the election.
[63] Rev. Rul. 73-484, 1973-2 C.B. 78.
[64] Reg. Sec. 1.1502-5(a).

for the current year and the immediately preceding tax year without regard to the number of corporations that comprise the affiliated group. This treatment can be advantageous if new, profitable corporations are added to the affiliated group.

Example 8-29 ■ The P-S_1 affiliated group files consolidated tax returns for several years. During 1990 the P-S_1 group reports a $100,000 consolidated tax liability. The P-S_1 affiliated group acquires all of S_2 Corporation's stock during 1991. S_2 is very profitable and causes the P-S_1-S_2 group to report a $300,000 consolidated tax liability in 1991. Assuming the P-S_1-S_2 group does not come under the "large" corporation rules outlined below, its 1991 estimated tax payments can be based on the P-S_1 group's $100,000 consolidated tax liability for the prior tax year. No underpayment penalties are imposed provided the P-S_1-S_2 group makes $25,000 ($100,000 ÷ 4) estimated tax payments by the fifteenth day of the fourth, sixth, ninth, and twelfth months of the tax year, since the Sec. 6655(d)(1) exception to the underpayment rules (prior year's tax liability) is satisfied. The balance of the consolidated tax liability must be paid by the due date for the consolidated tax return (without regard to any extensions). ■

Underpayment Rules. Affiliated groups are also subject to the special underpayment rules of Sec. 6655(d)(2) for large corporations; that is, those corporations having taxable income of at least $1 million in any one of the 3 immediately preceding tax years. An affiliated group is considered one corporation when applying the large corporation rules. Only the actual members of the affiliated group for the 3 preceding tax years are used in applying the $1 million threshold. New members entering the group are ignored for the 3 preceding years test.[65]

Consolidated or Separate Basis. For the first 2 years for which a group files consolidated tax returns, the affiliated group may elect to make estimated tax payments on either a consolidated or separate basis. Starting in the third year, however, the affiliated group must make consolidated estimated tax payments. It must continue to do so until separate tax returns are again filed. During the first 2 tax years for which the election is in effect, the affiliated group sometimes can reduce its quarterly payments by making separate estimated tax payments in the first year and consolidated estimated tax payments in the second year or vice versa. Application of the exceptions to the penalty for underpayment of estimated taxes depends upon whether estimated taxes are paid on a separate or consolidated basis. Different exceptions (e.g., prior year's liability or annualization of current year's income) to the underpayment rules should be used by the individual group members if it will reduce the amount of the estimated tax payments that are required. Determination of the actual separate or consolidated limitations, however, is beyond the scope of this book.

Additional Comment
The final estimated tax payment for a member joining a consolidated tax return group is due the 15th day of the last month of the short taxable year. If a member is acquired after the 15th, the final estimated tax payment is already overdue.

Short-Period Return. If a corporation joins an affiliated group after the beginning of its tax year, a short-period return covering the preaffiliation time period must generally be filed. The payment rules covering the short-period return are found in Reg. Sec. 1.6655-3. If a corporation leaves an affiliated group, it must make the necessary estimated tax payments required of a corporation filing a separate tax return for the post-affiliation, short-period tax year, unless it joins in the filing of a consolidated tax return with another affiliated group. No estimated tax payment is required for a short tax year that is less than 4 months.

---

[65] Proposed Reg. Sec. 1.6655-4(e)(3) requires the $1 million threshold to be applied to all members of the controlled group. This could affect the application of the rule to controlled groups that contain one or more corporations that are ineligible to file on a consolidated basis.

COMPLIANCE AND PROCEDURAL CONSIDERATIONS

OBJECTIVE 12
Explain the procedures for making an initial consolidated return election

The Basic Election

An affiliated group makes an election to use the consolidated method for filing its tax return by filing a consolidated tax return (Form 1120) that includes the income, expenses, etc. of all of its members. (See Appendix B for a sample completed Form 1120 and supporting workpapers.) The election must be made no later than the due date for the common parent corporation's tax return, including any permitted extensions.[66] An affiliated group can change from a consolidated tax return to separate tax returns,[67] or from separate tax returns to a consolidated tax return, at any time on or before the last day for filing the consolidated tax return. Once that day has passed, no change can be made.

In addition to filing the necessary Form 1120 reflecting the consolidated results of operations, each corporation that is a member of the affiliated group during the initial consolidated return year must consent to the election. The parent corporation's consent is evidenced by its filing the consolidated tax return (Form 1120). Subsidiary corporations consent to the election by filing a Form 1122 (Authorization and Consent of Subsidiary to Be Included in a Consolidated Income Tax Return) and submitting it as a part of the initial consolidated tax return. Only new subsidiary corporations file Form 1122 with subsequent consolidated tax returns.

Each consolidated tax return must also include an Affiliations Schedule (Form 851). This form includes the name, address, and identification number of the corporations included in the affiliated group, the corporation's tax prepayments, the stock holdings at the beginning of the tax year, and all stock ownership changes occurring during the tax year.

The due date for the consolidated tax return is 2½ months after the end of the affiliated group's tax year. A 6-month extension for filing the consolidated tax return is permitted if the parent corporation files Form 7004 and pays the estimated balance of the consolidated tax liability. The due date for the tax return of a subsidiary corporation that is not included in the consolidated return depends upon whether the affiliated group's consolidated tax return has been filed by the due date for the subsidiary corporation's tax return. These rules are beyond the scope of this text, but can be reviewed in Reg. Sec. 1.1502-76(c).

Additional Comment
If a group is considering making a consolidated tax return election, a properly executed Form 1122 should be obtained before any corporation is sold during the election year. After the sale, the consent form may be difficult to obtain.

Parent Corporation as Agent for the Affiliated Group

The parent corporation acts as agent for each subsidiary corporation and for the affiliated group. As agent for each subsidiary, the parent corporation is authorized to act in its own name in all matters relating to the affiliated group's tax liability for the consolidated return year.[68]

No subsidiary corporation can act in its own behalf with respect to a consolidated return year except to the extent that the parent corporation is prohibited from acting in its behalf. Thus, a subsidiary corporation is prevented from making or changing any election that is used in computing separate taxable income, carrying on

---

[66] Reg. Sec. 1.1502-75(a)(1).
[67] Such a change can take place only for the initial consolidated return year or for a tax year for which the IRS has granted permission to discontinue the consolidated return election.
[68] Reg. Sec. 1.1502-77(a).

correspondence with the IRS regarding the determination of a tax liability, filing any requests for extensions of time in which to file a tax return, or filing a claim for a refund or credit relating to a consolidated return year.

The parent corporation cannot make certain elections on behalf of a subsidiary corporation. These include (1) initial consent to file a consolidated tax return and (2) the election for the subsidiary corporation to claim the Puerto Rican and U.S. Possessions tax credit under Sec. 936.

Liability for Taxes Due

> **Additional Comment**
> Each member corporation is severally liable for the entire tax liability of the consolidated group. Anyone purchasing a corporation out of a consolidated group should consider this factor when negotiating the purchase price of the target corporation.

The parent corporation and every other corporation that was a group member for any part of the consolidated return year are severally liable for that year's consolidated taxes.[69] Thus, the entire consolidated tax liability may be collected from one group member if, for example, the other group members are unable to pay their allocable portion. The IRS can ignore attempts made by the group members to limit their share of the liability by entering into agreements with one another or with third parties.

Thus, the potential consolidated tax liability and any deficiencies could accrue to a corporation that is a member of an affiliated group for even a few days during a tax year. This potential liability can be alleviated by electing to use the 30-day rule that permits a corporation to be excluded from the affiliated group for a partial year and to become a member of the group at the beginning of the next tax year.

An exception to this several liability principle occurs when a subsidiary corporation ceases to be a group member as a result of its stock being sold or exchanged prior to the date that a deficiency is assessed against the affiliated group. Thus, if the IRS believes that the assessment and collection of the balance of the deficiency from the other group members will not be jeopardized, it can opt to assess a former subsidiary corporation for its allocable portion of the total deficiency only.

Filing for NOL or Credit Refund

> **Key Point**
> An inequity can result when a corporation is purchased from a consolidated group. Tax refunds generated by loss carrybacks from a former member to the prior consolidated group will be sent to the common parent. The purchase agreement should provide for this inequity.

The rules regarding the carryback of a consolidated NOL, consolidated net capital loss, or consolidated excess credit amount are slightly more difficult for the affiliated group to apply than they are for corporations filing separate returns. The increased difficulty occurs because the losses can originate in a consolidated return year or separate return year and can be carried back to a consolidated return year or a separate return year. The rules regarding which corporation files the application for refund and which corporation receives the refund are summarized below.

Year in Which Carryback Arose	Year to Which Carryback Is Taken	Corporation Filing Claim	Corporation Receiving Refund
Consolidated return year	Consolidated return year	Parent corporation	Parent corporation
Consolidated return year	Separate return year	Individual group member	Individual group member
Separate return year	Consolidated return year	Individual group member	Parent corporation

The last situation above could originate, for example, when the affiliated group sells its investment in a member corporation and the group member then incurs a separate return NOL. In some cases, the purchaser may enter into an agreement with

---

[69] Reg. Sec. 1.1502-6(a)

the selling corporation that any tax refunds originating as a result of the loss carryback from a subsequent separate return year will be paid to the purchaser.[70] Lacking such an agreement, the parent corporation could refuse to remit the refund to the seller. This problem can be avoided for NOLs by having the loss corporation make an election to forgo the carryback period entirely and carry the loss forward for 15 years.[71]

PROBLEM MATERIALS

DISCUSSION QUESTIONS

8-1. What minimum level of stock ownership is required for a corporation to be included in an affiliated group?

8-2. Which of the following equity items are considered to be stock for purposes of the affiliated group definition?
   a. Common stock
   b. A second class of common stock
   c. Nonvoting preferred stock
   d. Voting preferred stock
   e. Nonvoting preferred stock convertible into common stock

8-3. Which of the following corporations are includible in an affiliated group?
   a. C corporation
   b. S corporation
   c. Foreign corporation
   d. Real estate investment trust
   e. Regulated investment company
   f. Life insurance company taxed under Sec. 801

8-4. Explain the difference between a controlled group and an affiliated group.

8-5. P, S_1, S_2, and S_3 Corporations form a controlled group of corporations. Since S_3 Corporation is a nonincludible corporation for affiliated group purposes, only P, S_1, and S_2 Corporations are permitted to file their income tax returns on a consolidated basis. Explain the alternatives available for allocating the tax savings from the 15% and 25% tax rates to the members of the controlled group.

8-6. Briefly explain how consolidated taxable income is calculated starting with the financial accounting (book) income information for each individual group member.

8-7. Explain how the consolidated taxable income calculation is different from the taxable income calculation for a corporation filing a separate tax return.

8-8. Explain the 30-day rules. What advantages can result from electing to use one of these provisions?

8-9. Determine whether each of the following statements is true or false:
   a. One member of an affiliated group may elect to utilize the accrual method of accounting, while another group member uses the cash receipts and disbursements method of accounting.
   b. A corporation that uses the calendar year as its tax year acquires all of the stock of another corporation that has for years used a fiscal year as its tax year. They both may continue to use their previous separate return tax years when filing their initial consolidated tax return.

---

[70] Reg. Sec. 1.1502-78(a). The carryback that originates in the separate return year is limited by the SRLY rules. As a result, the carryback can be used only to the extent of the member's contribution to consolidated taxable income, etc.

[71] Sec. 172(b)(3)(C) and Prop. Reg. Sec. 1.1502-21(b)(3).

c. A 30-day rule permits a corporation that leaves the affiliated group in the final 30 days of a consolidated return year to be included for the full tax year.

8-10. What events permit an affiliated group to terminate its consolidated tax return election?

8-11. The P-S_1-S_2 affiliated group has filed consolidated tax returns for a number of years. At the close of business on July 15, 1991 P Corporation sells all of its S_1 Corporation stock to Mickey. P Corporation retains its investment in S_2 Corporation. Explain what tax returns are required of the three corporations for 1991. What affect does the sale have on the P-S_2 group's deferred intercompany gains and losses and charitable contributions carryover which is unused in 1991's consolidated tax return?

8-12. Assume the same facts as in Question 8-11 except that the original affiliated group was just P and S_1 Corporations and that the S_1 stock was sold to Mickey on July 15, 1991. What affect does the sale have on the P-S_1 group's deferred intercompany gains and losses and charitable contributions carryover which is unused in the final consolidated tax return?

8-13. Define the following terms:
  a. Intercompany transaction
  b. Deferred intercompany transaction
  c. Restoration event

8-14. Explain how the rules governing depreciation recapture, basis, and depreciation operate when a 5-year recovery class property under Modified ACRS is sold at a profit by one group member to a second group member after the property has been held for 3 years.

8-15. Compare the reporting of interest income and interest expense for financial accounting and tax purposes when one group member lends money to a second group member.

8-16. P and S_1 Corporations constitute the P-S_1 affiliated group on January 1, 1991. S_1 Corporation acquires all of the stock of S_2 Corporation on April 1, 1991. Which of the following transactions are intercompany transactions?
  a. P Corporation sells inventory to S_1 Corporation throughout 1991.
  b. S_2 Corporation sells land (a capital asset) to P Corporation on March 15, 1991.
  c. S_1 Corporation sells machinery (a Sec. 1245 property) to S_2 Corporation on September 1, 1991.
  d. P Corporation sells inventory to the PS_1 Partnership that is owned equally by P and S_1 Corporations on July 23, 1991.

8-17. P, S_1, and S_2 Corporations constitute the P-S_1-S_2 affiliated group for all of 1991. The affiliated group members use the accrual method of accounting and the calendar year as their tax year. Determine whether each of the following transactions that take place during 1991 are deferred intercompany transactions or other intercompany transactions.
  a. P Corporation lends S_1 Corporation money. The money remains unpaid at the end of the tax year.
  b. S_1 Corporation sells inventory to P Corporation.
  c. P Corporation sells land (a Sec. 1231 property) to S_2 Corporation.
  d. S_2 Corporation pays a cash dividend to P Corporation.
  e. S_1 Corporation provides engineering services that are capitalized as part of the cost of S_1's new factory building.

8-18. Indicate for each of the following dividend payments the tax treatment that is available in computing consolidated taxable income:
  a. Dividend received from a C corporation that is 10% owned by the parent corporation
  b. Dividend received from a C corporation that is 100% owned by the parent corporation and included in the consolidated tax return election
  c. Dividend received from a foreign corporation that is 50% owned by the parent corporation
  d. Dividend received from an unconsolidated life insurance corporation that is 100% owned by the parent corporation

8-19. Explain the circumstances in which a consolidated NOL can be carried back to a preceding separate return year.

8-20. What advantages can accrue to an affiliated group or an individual group member by electing to forgo the carryback of an NOL that is incurred in a consolidated return year? A separate return year? Who makes the election to forgo the carryback?

8-21. Define SRLY and explain its significance to an affiliated group filing a consolidated tax return.

8-22. What is a Sec. 382 ownership change and explain its significance to an affiliated group filing a consolidated tax return.

8-23. Explain why an affiliated group that files a consolidated tax return may be able to avoid paying an alternative minimum tax liability that would be owed if separate returns were instead filed.

8-24. Determine if the following statements regarding the alternative minimum tax are true or false:
   a. An affiliated group calculates its alternative minimum tax liability on a separate company basis.
   b. Each member of an affiliated group receives a separate $40,000 statutory exemption.
   c. An affiliated group must make an adjustment for 75% of the difference between its consolidated adjusted current earnings and its alternative minimum taxable income (as determined without this adjustment and the alternative tax NOL deduction).

8-25. What are the advantages of filing a consolidated tax return? The disadvantages of filing a consolidated tax return?

8-26. Explain why an affiliated group might make an election to claim a 100% dividends-received deduction for a tax year even though all dividends received during that year are received from other members of the affiliated group.

8-27. What reasons might cause an affiliated group to elect not to defer intercompany gains and losses?

8-28. During what time period can an affiliated group elect to file a consolidated tax return? How is the election made?

8-29. Indicate for which of the following tax-related matters can the parent corporation act as the affiliated group's agent:
   a. Making an initial consent for a subsidiary corporation to participate in a consolidated return election
   b. Changing an accounting method election for a subsidiary corporation
   c. Carrying on correspondence with the IRS regarding a transaction entered into by a subsidiary corporation that impacts upon the group's determination of consolidated taxable income
   d. Requesting an extension of time within which to file a consolidated tax return

8-30. The consolidated tax return regulations represent an attempt by the taxing authorities to treat a group of separate but affiliated corporate entities as a single taxpaying entity. These regulations also permit the individual group members to retain a large degree of separate entity status. What are some of the tax provisions that illustrate each of these two opposing principles?

PROBLEMS

8-31. *Affiliated Group Definition.* Which of the following independent situations result in an affiliated group being created? In each case, indicate the corporations that are eligible to be included in the consolidated tax return election. All corporations are domestic corporations unless otherwise indicated.
   a. Zeke owns all of the stock of A and B Corporations.
   b. Kellye owns all of the stock of P and W Corporations. P Corporation owns all of the stock of both S_1 and S_2 Corporations.
   c. P Corporation owns all of the stock of S_1 and S_2 Corporations. S_1 Corporation owns 40% of the stock of S_3 Corporation. P Corporation owns the remaining S_3 stock. S_2 Corporation is a foreign corporation.

8-32. *Affiliated Group Definition.* Jane owns all of the stock of P Corporation. P Corporation owns all of S Corporation's stock. S Corporation owns all of the stock of F Corporation. P Corporation also owns all of T Corporation's stock and 70% of the U Corporation's stock. T Corporation owns the remaining 30% of U Corporation's stock and 80% of V Corporation's stock. F Corporation is a foreign corporation. All other corporations are domestic corporations. V Corporation is an insurance company taxed under Sec. 801 that has been owned for the past five years. All undisclosed minority interests are held by unrelated individuals. Which of the corporations can join in a consolidated tax return election?

8-33. Stock Ownership Requirement. P Corporation is the parent corporation of the P-S_1-S_2 affiliated group. P Corporation is conducting negotiations to purchase the stock of R Corporation. The management of P would like to include R in the affiliated group's consolidated tax return. R Corporation's outstanding shares are as listed.

Type of Stock	Number Outstanding	Par Value	Market Value
Common stock (1 vote per share)	100,000	$ 1	$30
Voting preferred stock (4 votes per share)	10,000	100	95
Nonvoting preferred stock	40,000	100	90

Determine a plan that permits P to acquire enough stock to include R in the affiliated group.

8-34. Consolidated Return Election. P and S Corporations have been in existence for a number of years. P uses the calendar year as its tax year. S Corporation uses a fiscal year ending June 30 as its tax year. At the close of business on August 31, 1991, P acquires all of the S stock and elects to file a consolidated tax return for 1991.
  a. What tax year must be used in filing the consolidated tax return?
  b. What is the last date on which the election to file a consolidated tax return can be made?
  c. What income of P and S is included in the consolidated tax return? In a separate return?

8-35. Income Included in Consolidated Return. P and S_1 Corporations form the P-S_1 affiliated group, which has filed consolidated tax returns on a calendar-year basis for a number of years. At the close of business on February 25, 1991, P Corporation sells all the stock of S_1 Corporation. P Corporation acquires all of the stock of S_2 Corporation on September 25, 1991. S_2 Corporation has always used the calendar year as its tax year. The new P-S_2 affiliated group elects to file a consolidated tax return for 1991. What tax returns are required of P, S_1, and S_2 Corporations with respect to reporting 1991's income?

8-36. Consolidated Return Election. The P-S_1 affiliated group has filed consolidated tax returns for several years. All P-S_1 returns have been filed using the calendar year as the tax year. At the close of business on August 8, 1991, P Corporation purchases all of the stock of S_2 Corporation. S_2 has been filing its separate tax returns using a fiscal year ending September 30. At the close of business on November 9, 1991, P Corporation sells all of its S_1 stock.
  a. What tax year must S_2 Corporation use after joining the affiliated group?
  b. What tax returns are required of S_2 Corporation to report its results from October 1, 1990, through December 31, 1991?
  c. What tax year must S_1 Corporation use after leaving the affiliated group?
  d. What action would be required (if any) should S_1 desire to change to a fiscal-year filing basis?

8-37. Deferred Intercompany Transactions. P, S_1 and S_2 Corporations form the P-S_1-S_2 affiliated group with P Corporation owning all of the stock of S_1 and S_2 Corporations. The P-S_1-S_2 group has filed consolidated tax returns for several years. In 1987, S_1 sells land that it has held for a possible expansion to S_2 for $180,000. The land originally cost S_1 $80,000 in 1982. S_2 constructs a new plant facility on the land. The land and the plant facility are sold to a third party in 1991 with $275,000 of the sales price attributable to the land.
  a. What is the amount and character of S_1's recognized gain or loss? In what year(s) is the gain or loss included in consolidated taxable income?
  b. What is the amount and character of S_2's recognized gain or loss? In what year(s) is the gain or loss included in consolidated taxable income?

8-38. Deferred Intercompany Transactions. P and S Corporations form the P-S affiliated group, which has filed consolidated tax returns for several years. On June 10, 1987, P purchases a new machine (5-year Modified ACRS property) for $20,000 cash. No special expensing elections under Sec. 179 were made. On April 4, 1989, P sells the machine to S for $15,000 cash. S uses the property for 2 years before selling it to an unrelated party on March 10, 1991, for $12,000.
  a. What are the amount and character of P's recognized gain or loss? In what year(s) is the gain or loss included in consolidated taxable income?
  b. What is S's basis for the equipment?
  c. When does S's holding period for the asset commence?
  d. What are the amount and character of S's recognized gain or loss? In what year(s) is the gain or loss included in consolidated taxable income?

8-39. Deferred Intercompany Transactions. P and S Corporations form the P-S affiliated group which has filed consolidated tax returns for a number of years. On January 1, 1987 P Corporation purchased a new machine (7-year MACRS property) for $50,000. No special expensing elections were made under Sec. 179. On June 30, 1990 P sells the machine to S for $35,000. The machine is still classified as 7-year MACRS property in S's hands. S holds the asset until March 15, 1993 when it is sold to an unrelated party for $20,000.
  a. What are the amount and character of P's recognized gain or loss? In what year(s) is it included in consolidated taxable income?
  b. What are the amount and character of S's recognized gain or loss? In what year(s) is it included in consolidated taxable income?

8-40. Deferred Intercompany Transactions. P and S Corporations form the P-S affiliated group. The P-S group has filed consolidated tax returns for several years. S acquires some land from P Corporation in 1986 for $60,000. P acquired the land in 1982 as an investment at a cost of $20,000. S uses the land for 3 years as additional parking space for its employees. No improvements are made to the land. The land is sold by S to an unrelated party in 1989 for $240,000. Terms of the sale require a 25% down payment and 5 equal installments to be paid annually in the years 1990 through 1994. Interest is charged at a rate acceptable to the IRS. Assume all payments are made in a timely fashion.
  a. What are the amount and character of P's recognized gain or loss? In what year(s) is it included in consolidated taxable income?
  b. What are the amount and character of S's recognized gain or loss? In what year(s) is it included in consolidated taxable income?

8-41. Other Intercompany Transactions. P Corporation has owned all of the stock of S Corporation since 1987. The P-S affiliated group commences filing a consolidated tax return in 1989 using the calendar year as its tax year. Both corporations use the accrual method of accounting. On July 1, 1990, P loans S $250,000 on a 1-year note. Interest is charged at a 12% simple rate. The loan and interest are paid on June 30, 1991.
  a. When does P report its interest income? When does S report its interest expense?
  b. How would your answer to Part a change if P instead uses the cash method of accounting?

8-42. Deferred Intercompany Transactions. P and S Corporations form the P-S affiliated group which has filed consolidated tax returns for a number of years. During 1990 P Corporation commenced selling inventory items to S Corporation. P and S use the first-in, first-out inventory method. The intercompany profit on P's sales to S was $125,000 in 1990. Goods remaining in S's inventory at the end of 1990 accounted for $35,000 of the intercompany profit. During 1991 all of S's beginning inventory of goods acquired from P in 1990 was sold to unrelated parties and the intercompany profit on P's current sales of inventory to S amounted to $240,000. Goods remaining in S's inventory at the end of 1991 accounted for $60,000 of the intercompany profit. Taxable income for the P-S affiliated group (excluding the intercompany inventory sales) is $100,000 in each year. What is consolidated taxable income for 1990 and 1991 for the P-S group?

8-43. Deferred Intercompany Transactions. P and S Corporations form the P-S affiliated group. P has owned all of the S Corporation stock since 1987. The affiliated group has filed consolidated tax returns since 1987. No intragroup inventory sales occurred prior to 1989.

During 1989 P sells S 100,000 widgets, earning $5 per unit profit on the sale. S uses the FIFO method to account for its inventories. On January 1, 1990, 25,000 widgets remain in S's inventory. During 1990 S sells the beginning widget inventory and purchases 175,000 additional widgets. P earns a $6 per unit profit on the sale. S retains 40,000 of these units in its 1990 ending inventory. No additional widgets are purchased in 1991. All widgets in beginning inventory are sold by S during 1991.

a. What intercompany profit amounts are deferred and restored in 1989? in 1990? in 1991?

b. How would your answer to Part a change if the LIFO inventory method were instead used?

8-44. Dividends-Received Deduction. P and S Corporations form the P-S affiliated group. The P-S group has filed consolidated tax returns for several years. In 1991 P and S report separate taxable income amounts (excluding any dividend payments) of $200,000 and ($80,000), respectively. Cash dividend payments received by P and S during 1991 are as follows:

Shareholder Corporation	Distributing Corporation	Amount
P	S	$60,000
P	100%-owned nonconsolidated domestic life insurance company	15,000
S	30%-owned domestic corporation	25,000

a. What is the amount of the 1991 dividends-received deduction?

b. Why might P elect to claim a 100% dividends-received deduction for the dividend received from S in 1991, even though a consolidated tax return is being filed?

8-45. Charitable Contributions Deduction. P and S Corporations form the P-S affiliated group. This group has filed consolidated tax returns for several years. The group reports consolidated taxable income (excluding charitable contributions) for 1991 of $60,000. Included in this amount are a consolidated dividends-received deduction of $8,000 and an NOL deduction of $25,000 that represents a carryover of the 1990 consolidated NOL. P and S Corporations make cash contributions to public charities of $18,000 and $10,000, respectively, during 1991.

a. What is the P-S group's consolidated taxable income?

b. What is the amount of the charitable contributions carryover to 1992?

8-46. NOL Carryover. P, S_1, and S_2 Corporations form the P-S_1-S_2 affiliated group, which has filed consolidated tax returns since the creation of all three corporations in 1989. At the close of business on July 10, 1991, P Corporation sells its entire interest in S_2 Corporation. The affiliated group remains in existence after the sale, since P Corporation still owns all of the S_1 stock. The P-S_1-S_2 group reports the following results for 1989 through 1991:

	Taxable Income		
Group Member	1989	1990	1991
P	$ 8,000	($12,000)	$16,000
S_1	9,000	(24,000)	(4,000)
S_2	10,000	(36,000)	6,000[a]
			8,000[b]
Consolidated taxable income (excluding NOL deduction)	$27,000	($72,000)	$18,000

[a] Taxable income earned from January 1, 1991, through July 10, 1991.

[b] Taxable income from July 11, 1991, through December 31, 1991, and included in S_2's separate tax return.

What amount of 1990's consolidated NOL can be carried over to 1992 by the P-S_1 affiliated group? By S_2?

8-47. NOL Carrybacks and Carryovers. P and S Corporations form the P-S affiliated group, which files consolidated tax returns for the period 1988 through 1991. The affiliated group reports the following results for this period:

		Taxable Income		
Group Member	1988	1989	1990	1991
P	$10,000	($6,000)	$20,000	$15,000
S	2,000	2,000	(30,000)	10,000
Consolidated taxable income (excluding NOL deduction)	$12,000	($4,000)	($10,000)	$25,000

No elections were made to forgo the NOL carrybacks.

a. What portion of the 1989 and 1990 consolidated NOLs can be carried back to 1988? Forward to 1991?

b. Which corporation files for the refund of the 1988 taxes?

c. Which corporation receives the refund of the 1988 taxes?

8-48. *Special NOL Limitation.* P, S_1, and S_2 Corporations have formed the P-S_1-S_2 affiliated group for a number of years and have always filed consolidated tax returns. S_1 and S_2 are wholly-owned subsidiaries of P. During 1988, 1989, and 1990 consolidated taxable income for this group was $35,000, $40,000, and $50,000, respectively, with no NOL carryovers available to 1991. On October 1, 1991 P Corporation acquired all of the S_3 Corporation stock. S_3 Corporation, which has always filed a separate tax return, reported the following results in its prior tax years: 1989, ($10,000); 1990, ($8,000); and 1991 (pre-affiliation), ($12,000). During 1991 the P-S_1-S_2-S_3 affiliated group reported the following results:

Group Member	Taxable Income
P	$35,000
S_1	8,000
S_2	(10,000)
S_3 (post-affiliation)	8,000
Consolidated taxable income (excluding NOL deduction)	$41,000

a. What are the amount of and source (by year) of any NOL carryforwards that can be used by the affiliated group in 1991? (Ignore the Sec. 382 loss limitation that might apply to the acquisition of S_3.)

b. What carryforwards are available to be used in 1992?

8-49. *Special NOL Limitation.* P, S_1, and S_2 Corporations form the P-S_1-S_2 affiliated group. P Corporation was created by Bart on January 1, 1989. P purchased all the S_1 and S_2 Corporation stock on September 1, 1989, after both corporations were in operation for about 6 months. All three corporations filed separate tax returns in 1989. The P-S_1-S_2 affiliated group elected to file a consolidated tax return starting in 1990. The P-S_1-S_2 group reports the following results for 1989 through 1991:

	Taxable Income		
Group Member	1989	1990	1991
P	($8,000)	$50,000	$10,000
S_1	(24,000)	20,000	(18,000)
S_2	(16,000)	(10,000)	15,000
Consolidated taxable income (excluding NOL deduction)	xxx	$60,000	$ 7,000

a. What loss carryovers are available to be used in 1992? (Ignore the Sec. 382 loss limitation that might apply to the acquisitions of S_1 and S_2.)

b. How would your answer to Part a change if Bart instead created P, S_1, and S_2 Corporations as an affiliated group on January 1, 1989?

8-50. Sec. 382 Loss Limitation. Mack owns all of the stock of P Corporation. P Corporation owns all of the stock of S_1 and S_2 Corporations. At the close of business on December 31, 1991, Mack sells his P Corporation stock to Jack for $6,000,000. The P-$S_1$-$S_2$ affiliated group has a consolidated NOL carryover to 1992 of $1,500,000 at the end of 1991.
  a. Has an ownership change occurred? Explain.
  b. What is the P-S_1-S_2 affiliated group's consolidated Sec. 382 limitation for 1992 if the federal long-term tax-exempt rate is 8%?
  c. How much of the consolidated NOL carryover can be used in 1992 if the affiliated group's taxable income is $750,000? In 1993 if the affiliated group's consolidated taxable income is $200,000?

8-51. Special NOL Limitation. P, S_1, and S_2 Corporations form the P-S_1-S_2 affiliated group. All three corporations were created by Jason in 1991, with P Corporation owning all of the stock of S_1 and S_2 Corporations. An election to file a consolidated tax return was made for the group's initial year of operation. On January 1, 1992, Jason sold all of the P stock to Tammy. S_2 Corporation purchases all of the stock of S_3 Corporation on June 1, 1993. The P-S_1-S_2-S_3 group's results for 1991 through 1993 are as follows:

	Taxable Income		
Group Member	1991	1992	1993
P	$100,000	$60,000	$100,000
S_1	75,000	40,000	(60,000)
S_2	(600,000)	30,000	140,000
S_3			200,000[a]
Consolidated taxable income (excluding NOL deduction)	($425,000)	$130,000	$380,000

[a] S_3's taxable income from June 1, 1993, through December 31, 1993.

Jason's sale price for the P-S_1-S_2 affiliated group on January 1, 1992 was $4,000,000. Assume the federal long-term tax-exempt rate is 7.50%.
  a. What portion of the 1991 consolidated NOL can be used in 1992 and 1993?
  b. What portion of the 1991 and 1993 losses can be carried over to 1994?

8-52. Capital Gains and Losses. The P-S_1-S_2 affiliated group has filed consolidated tax returns for a number of years. The affiliated group reports the following results from its 1991 operations:

Group Member	Ordinary Income	Capital Gains	
		Short-Term	Long-Term
P	$100,000		$ 6,000
S_1	(20,000)	($3,000)	1,000
S_2	60,000	(2,000)	4,000
Total	$140,000	($5,000)	$11,000

  a. What is the P-S_1-S_2 group's consolidated taxable income?
  b. Ignoring any alternative minimum tax implications, what is the P-S_1-S_2 group's consolidated regular tax liability?

8-53. Consolidated Taxable Income. P and S Corporations have filed consolidated tax returns for a number of years. P is an accrual method of accounting taxpayer and S is a cash method of accounting taxpayer. P and S report separate return taxable income for 1991 of $100,000 and $50,000, respectively. These numbers include the following transactions or events accounted for appropriately on a separate return basis.
  a. P sold land held for investment purposes to S at a $25,000 profit in 1988. S sold the land (a Sec. 1231 asset) to an unrelated corporation in 1991 for a $12,000 gain.
  b. S provides management services to P. P's taxable income amount includes a $25,000 charge for services provided by S that has been accrued by P but not paid by P at year-end.

c. P sold inventory to S in 1990 for which the deferred intercompany profit at year-end was $50,000. All of this inventory was sold outside the affiliated group in 1991. Additional inventory was sold by P to S in 1991 that remained unsold at year-end. The deferred intercompany profit on this inventory is $80,000.
d. P and S made charitable contributions of $10,000 and $12,000, respectively, in 1991.
e. The P-S group has a $20,000 NOL carryover available from 1990.

Calculate consolidated taxable income for the P-S affiliated group for 1991.

8-54. *Alternative Minimum Tax.* P and S Corporations are members of the P-S affiliated group that has filed consolidated tax returns for a number of years. Separate adjusted current earnings amounts for P and S in 1991 were $200,000 and $500,000, respectively. Consolidated alternative minimum taxable income (excluding the adjusted current earnings adjustment) is $400,000 for 1991. Consolidated taxable income for 1991 is $325,000. The consolidated general business credit amount (computed without regard to the overall limitation) is $10,000 for 1991. What is the P-S group's 1991 federal tax liability?

8-55. *Alternative Minimum Tax.* P and S Corporations have filed consolidated tax returns for a number of years. During 1991, the P-S group reports taxable income of $320,000 and alternative minimum taxable income of $620,000. The P-S group has a tentative general business credit of $6,000.
a. What is the P-S group's federal tax liability?
b. Does the P-S group have any credit carrybacks or carryovers?

TAX FORM/RETURN PREPARATION PROBLEM

8-56. The Flying Gator Corporation and it subsidiary, T Corporation, have filed consolidated tax returns for a number of years. Both corporations use the hybrid method of accounting. During the current year they report the operating results as listed in Table 8-2. Note the following additional information:

- Flying Gator and T Corporations are the only members of their controlled group.
- Flying Gator's address is: 2101 W. University Ave., Gainesburg, FL 32611. Its employer

TABLE 8-2 *Flying Gator Corporation's Current Year Operating Results (Problem 8-56)*

Income or Deductions	Flying Gator	T	Total
Gross receipts	$2,500,000	$1,250,000	$3,750,000
Cost of goods sold	(1,500,000)	(700,000)	(2,200,000)
Gross profit	$1,000,000	$ 550,000	$1,550,000
Dividends	100,000	50,000	150,000
Interest	15,000		15,000
Sec. 1231 gain		20,000	20,000
Sec. 1245 gain		25,000	25,000
Long-term capital gain (loss)	(5,000)	6,000	1,000
Short-term capital gain (loss)		(3,000)	(3,000)
Total income	$1,110,000	$ 648,000	$1,758,000
Salaries and wages	175,000	200,000	375,000
Repairs	25,000	40,000	65,000
Bad debts	10,000	5,000	15,000
Taxes	18,000	24,000	42,000
Interest	30,000	20,000	50,000
Charitable contributions	22,000	48,000	70,000
Depreciation (other than that included in cost of goods sold)	85,000	40,000	125,000
Other expenses	160,000	260,000	420,000
Total deductions	$ 525,000	$ 637,000	$1,162,000
Separate taxable income	$ 585,000	$ 11,000	$ 596,000

identification number is 38-2345678. Flying Gator was incorporated on June 11, 1984. Its total assets are $380,000. Flying Gator made estimated tax payments of $160,000 for the affiliated group in the current year. Stephen Marks is the Flying Gator's President.
- No NOL or other carryovers from preceding years are available.
- Flying Gator uses the last-in, first-out (LIFO) inventory method. T commenced selling inventory to Flying Gator in the preceding year that resulted in a $40,000 year-end deferred intercompany profit. An additional LIFO inventory layer was created by T's sales to Flying Gator during the current year that remained unsold at year-end. The deferred intercompany profit on this inventory is $30,000.
- All of Flying Gator's dividends are received from T. T's dividends are received from a 15% owned domestic corporation.
- Flying Gator's interest income is received from T. The interest is paid on March 31 of the current year on a loan that is outstanding from October 1 of the preceding year through March 31, of the current year.
- Officer's salaries are $80,000 for Flying Gator and $65,000 for T Corporation.
- Flying Gator's capital losses include a $10,000 loss on a sale of land that is made to T in the current year.
- T's Sec. 1245 gains include $20,000 recognized on the sale of equipment to Flying Gator in the current year. The asset cost $100,000 and had been depreciated for two years by T as 5-year property under the Modified ACRS rules. No depreciation was claimed by T in the current year. Flying Gator commences depreciating the property in the current year by using the Modified ACRS rules and a 5-year recovery period.

Determine the affiliated group's current year consolidated tax liability. Prepare the front page of the affiliated group's current year corporate income tax return. Hint: prepare a spreadsheet similar to the one included in Appendix B in order to arrive at consolidated taxable income.

CASE STUDY PROBLEM

8-57. P Corporation operates 6 fast-food restaurants in a metropolitan area. The restaurants have been a huge success in their first 3 years of operation and P's annual taxable income is in excess of $600,000. The real estate associated with the six restaurants is owned by J Corporation. P Corporation leases its restaurant locations from J Corporation. J Corporation is reporting large interest and MACRS depreciation deductions because of a highly leveraged operation. As a result J Corporation has reported NOLs in its first 3 years of operation.

Both corporations are owned by Carol who is in her late 20s. Carol sees the idea for the restaurant chain starting to really develop and expects to add 6 more locations each of the next two years. You and Carol have been friends for a number of years. Because of the rapid expansion that is planned, she feels that she has outgrown her father's accountant and needs to have new ideas to help her save tax dollars so that she can reinvest more monies in the business.

Required: Prepare a memorandum to the tax partner of your office outlining your thoughts about Carol's tax problems and the suggested solutions to those problems in preparation for next week's meeting with Carol.

TAX RESEARCH PROBLEMS

8-58. Angela owns all of the stock of A and P Corporations. P Corporation has owned all of the stock of S_1 Corporation for 6 years. The P-S_1 affiliated group has filed a consolidated tax return in each of these 6 years using the calendar year as its tax year. On July 10, 1991, Angela sells her entire stock investment in A Corporation, which uses the calendar year as its tax year. On November 25, 1991, S_1 Corporation purchases 90% of the common stock and 80% of the nonconvertible, nonvoting preferred stock (measured by value) of S_2 Corporation. A, P, S_1, and S_2 Corporations are domestic corporations that do not retain any special filing status. Which corporations are included in the affiliated group? In the controlled group? If no special allocations are made, what portion of the reduced tax rate benefits of Sec. 11(b) can be claimed by the affiliated group?

A partial list of research sources is

- Secs. 1504(a) and (b).
- Secs. 1563(a) through (c).

8-59. P Corporation has owned all of the stock of S_1 and S_2 Corporations for 15 years. The three corporations are calendar-year taxpayers and have filed separate tax returns for a number of years. P, S_1, and S_2 Corporations file separate tax returns for 1991 on March 1, 1992. P Corporation's new controller discovers that a substantial tax savings could be achieved if a consolidated return election is made for 1991. The P-S_1-S_2 affiliated group files an amended tax return for 1991 on a consolidated basis (including all necessary first-time elections) on March 15, 1992. Has the P-S_1-S_2 affiliated group made a valid consolidated return election for 1991?

A partial list of research sources is

- Sec. 1501.
- Reg. Sec. 1.1502-75(a)(1).
- Rev. Ruls. 56-67, 1956-1 C.B. 437, and 76-393, 1976-2 C.B. 255.

8-60. P Corporation owns all of the stock of S Corporation. P and S Corporations are part of the P-S-O combined controlled group. The P-S affiliated group has filed consolidated tax returns for a number of years. During 1987, P Corporation sells land having a $200,000 adjusted basis to S Corporation for $60,000. The $140,000 Sec. 1231 loss on the intercompany transaction is deferred when filing the 1987 consolidated tax return. On June 10, 1991, S Corporation sells the land, which was being held for investment purposes, to O Corporation for $100,000. How should P Corporation report the deferred loss when the land is sold outside the affiliated group? How should S Corporation report the gain on its sale of the land to O Corporation?

A partial list of research sources is

- Sec. 267(f).
- Reg. Sec. 1.1502-13.
- Temp. Reg. Secs. 1.267(f)-1T and 2T.

9 Partnership Formation and Operation

CHAPTER OUTLINE

LEARNING OBJECTIVES 9-2
DEFINITION OF A PARTNERSHIP 9-2
  General and Limited Partnerships 9-3
OVERVIEW OF PARTNERSHIP TAXATION 9-4
  Taxation of Partnership Profits and Losses 9-4
  The Partner's Basis 9-5
  Partnership Distributions 9-6
TAX IMPLICATIONS OF FORMATION OF A PARTNERSHIP 9-6
  Contribution of Property 9-6
  Contribution of Services 9-12
  Syndication and Organizational Expenditures 9-14
PARTNERSHIP ELECTIONS 9-15
  Partnership Taxable Year 9-15
  Other Partnership Elections 9-19

PARTNERSHIP REPORTING OF INCOME 9-20
  Partnership Taxable Income 9-20
  Separately Stated Items 9-21
  Partnership Ordinary Income 9-22
PARTNER REPORTING OF INCOME 9-22
  Partner's Distributive Share 9-22
  Special Allocations 9-23
BASIS FOR PARTNERSHIP INTEREST 9-26
  Beginning Basis 9-26
  Effects of Liabilities 9-27
  Effects of Operations 9-29
LOSS LIMITATIONS 9-30
  At-Risk Loss Limitation 9-31
  At-Risk Rules and Current Distributions 9-32
  Passive Activity Limitations 9-33
TRANSACTIONS BETWEEN A PARTNER AND THE PARTNERSHIP 9-34
  Sales of Property 9-34

Guaranteed Payments 9-35
FAMILY PARTNERSHIPS 9-37
  Capital Ownership 9-37
  Donor-Donee Allocations of Income 9-38
CONTROVERSIAL ISSUE 9-39
  Retroactive Allocation of Losses 9-39
TAX PLANNING CONSIDERATIONS 9-40
  Alternatives to Contributing Property 9-40
  Timing of Loss Recognition 9-40
COMPLIANCE AND PROCEDURAL CONSIDERATIONS 9-41
  Reporting to the IRS and the Partners 9-41
  IRS Audit Procedures 9-42
PROBLEM MATERIALS 9-43
  Discussion Questions 9-43
  Problems 9-44
  Tax Form/Return Preparation Problem 9-52
  Case Study Problem 9-53
  Tax Research Problems 9-54

> **LEARNING OBJECTIVES**
>
> *After studying this chapter, you should be able to*
>
> 1. Differentiate between general and limited partnerships
> 2. Explain the tax results of a contribution of property or services in exchange for a partnership interest
> 3. Determine the permitted tax years for a partnership
> 4. Differentiate between items that must be separately stated and those that are included in ordinary income or loss
> 5. Calculate a partner's distributive share of partnership income, gain or loss
> 6. Explain the requirements for a special partnership allocation
> 7. Calculate a partner's basis in a partnership interest
> 8. Determine the limitations on a partner's deduction of partnership losses
> 9. Determine the tax consequences of a guaranteed payment to a partner
> 10. Explain the requirements for the holder of a partnership interest to be recognized as a partner in a family partnership
> 11. Determine the allocation of partnership income between a donor and a donee of a partnership interest
> 12. Determine the requirements for filing a partnership tax return

Partnerships have long been one of the major entities for conducting business activities. Partnerships vary in complexity from the corner gas station owned and operated by two brothers to syndicated tax partnerships with their partnership interests traded on major security markets. Regardless of the simplicity or complexity of the partnership, a single set of rules determines the federal income tax consequences of the partnership operations. These rules are found in Subchapter K of the Code, which includes the material from Secs. 701 through 761.

Chapters 9 and 10 discuss the income tax rules applying to partnership business operations. In this chapter, a partnership is defined and the two kinds of partnerships are described. The formation of a partnership is discussed next. The remainder of this chapter deals with the ongoing operations of a partnership such as the annual taxation of partnership earnings, transactions between partners and the partnership, and a partner's basis in a partnership interest. Procedural matters are also considered such as reporting the annual partnership income and IRS audit procedures for partnerships and their partners. Chapter 10 continues by discussing distributions to the partners and the tax implications of the numerous transactions that can be used to terminate a partner's interest in a partnership. Chapter 10 also includes discussions of adjustments which may be made to the bases of partnership assets and the unique problems of limited partnerships.

DEFINITION OF A PARTNERSHIP

For tax purposes the definition of a partnership is much broader than two or more individuals working together. The term includes "a syndicate, group, pool, joint venture, or other unincorporated organization" which carries on a business or

Definition of a Partnership • 9-3

Key Point
Even though the formation of a partnership requires no legal documentation, to prevent subsequent disagreements and arguments, a formal written partnership agreement is needed.

financial operation or venture.[1] However, a trust, estate, or corporation cannot be taxed as a partnership. Unlike a corporation, which can exist only after incorporation documents are finalized, formation of a partnership requires no legal documentation. If two people (or business entities) work together to carry on any business or financial operation with the intention of making a profit and sharing that profit as co-owners, a partnership exists for federal income tax purposes.[2]

The Code and Regulations define a **partner** only as a member of a partnership. It is clear from years of case law and common business practice that a partner can be an individual, trust, estate, or corporation. The only restriction on the number of partners in a partnership is that there must be at least two partners, but there may be hundreds or even thousands of partners in a large syndicated partnership.[3]

General and Limited Partnerships

OBJECTIVE 1
Differentiate between general and limited partnerships

Each state has laws governing the rights and restrictions of partnerships. Virtually all of the state statutes are modeled on the Uniform Partnership Act (UPA) or the Uniform Limited Partnership Act (ULPA) and so have strong similarities to each other. There are two legal forms a partnership can take—a general partnership or a limited partnership. The differences between the two types are substantial and extend to the partners' legal rights and liabilities as well as the tax consequences to the partners of operations. Because of the importance of these differences, we examine these two partnership forms before proceeding with further discussion of the partnership tax rules.

Key Point
When deciding the form in which to conduct a business, probably the strongest argument against a general partnership is that each partner has unlimited liability for the partnership debts.

General Partnerships. A **general partnership** exists any time two or more partners join together and do not specifically provide that one or more of the partners is a limited partner (as defined below). In a general partnership, each partner has the right to participate in the management of the partnership. However, the general partnership form is flexible enough to allow the business affairs of the general partnership to be managed by a single partner chosen by the general partners.

While management may be exercised by only one (or a few) of the general partners, each **general partner** has the ability to make commitments for the partnership.[4] In a general partnership, each partner has unlimited liability for all partnership debts.[5] If the partnership fails to pay its debts, each partner may have to pay far more than the amount which he has invested in the venture. Thus, each partner faces the risk of losing personal assets if the partnership (and therefore the partner) incurs business losses. This fact is the single biggest drawback to the general partnership form of doing business.

Limited Partnerships. In a **limited partnership,** there are two classes of partners. There must be at least one general partner, who has essentially the same rights and liabilities as any general partner in a general partnership.[6] In addition, there are limited partners, who have very different rights and risks.

Even if a partnership becomes bankrupt, a **limited partner** can lose no more than his original investment plus any additional amount he has committed to contribute.[7]

---

[1] Sec. 761(a).
[2] Section 761(a) allows an election to avoid the Subchapter K rules for a very limited group of business owners.
[3] Under certain circumstances, a two-man partnership may be considered a partnership for a time after one of the partners dies or retires. See Chapter 10 for a further discussion of the death or retirement of a partner.
[4] Uniform Partnership Act, Sec. 9.
[5] Ibid., Sec. 15.
[6] Uniform Limited Partnership Act, Sec. 9.
[7] Ibid., Sec. 7.

Self-Study Question

Is it possible in a limited partnership to have all partners with limited liability?

Answer

No. A limited partnership must have at least one general partner. This general partner can be a corporation as long as it has a certain minimum amount of capitalization.

However, a limited partner has no right to be active in the partnership's management. In fact, any limited partner who does become active in the partnership's management loses the limited liability protection.[8]

Even with this rudimentary explanation of the rights of general and limited partners, it is clear that a general partnership is an unwieldy form for operating a business with a large number of owners. A limited partnership having one (or a small number of) general partners, however, can be useful for a business operation that needs to attract a large amount of capital. In fact, one common form for a tax shelter investment is a limited partnership having an undercapitalized corporation as its sole general partner. Such an arrangement allows the tax advantages of the partnership form (detailed in the remainder of this chapter and in the next chapter) while retaining the limited liability feature for virtually every investor.[9]

Many of these limited partnerships are so large and widely-held that in many ways they appear more like a corporation than a partnership. As discussed in Chapter 10, the tax laws provide that publicly-traded partnerships may be reclassified for tax purposes as corporations.

OVERVIEW OF PARTNERSHIP TAXATION

This overview gives a broad perspective of the entire area of partnership taxation. (A comparison of the tax characteristics of a partnership, a C corporation, and an S corporation is presented in Appendix C.) More detailed descriptions of each area follow the overview.

Self-Study Question

Does a partnership pay taxes?

Answer

No. A partnership is an information-reporting entity. Any income/loss flows through to its partners, and they pay the necessary taxes.

Additional Comment

Since most partnerships use the calendar year as their tax year, the K-1s are not due until April 15th. Since a calendar-year corporate partner's return is due on March 15th and an individual partner's return is due on April 15th, filing these tax returns without requesting extensions presents a real problem.

Taxation of Partnership Profits and Losses

A partnership is not a taxpaying entity. Instead, each partner reports a share of the partnership's income, gain, loss and credit items as a part of his income tax return.[10] The partnership, however, must file Form 1065, an information return, which provides the IRS with information about partnership earnings as well as how the earnings are allocated among the partners. In order to make this information available to the IRS and the partners, the partnership must elect a tax year[11] and accounting methods to calculate its earnings. The partnership return is due by the fifteenth day of the fourth month after the end of the partnership's tax year.[12] (Appendix B includes a completed partnership tax return that includes a Form 1065 and Form K-1 for a partner.)

Each partner receives a Form K-1 from the partnership, which informs the partner of the amount and character of his share of partnership income. The partner then combines his partnership earnings and losses with all other items of income or loss to be reported for the tax year, computes the amount of taxable income, and calculates the tax bill. Since each partner pays tax on a share of partnership income along with

---

[8] Under Sec. 9 of the ULPA only the general partner(s) are empowered to manage the partnership's business.

[9] The IRS has issued Rev. Proc. 89-12, 1989-1 C.B., 798, which lists several prerequisites to the issuance of an advance ruling confirming that a limited partnership having a sole corporate general partner is to be taxed as a partnership rather than as an association. See also Chapter 2 for a discussion of the partnership-association characterization question.

[10] Sec. 701.

[11] Sec. 706(b). Partnerships that elect under Sec. 444 to use a fiscal year as their tax year may be required to make tax payments under Sec. 7519. These payments are an exception to the general rule that partnerships do not make income tax payments (see page 9-17).

[12] Reg. Sec. 1.6031-1(e)(2).

all other income and loss items, it is not reasonable to determine a tax rate for partnership earnings. Partnership income is taxed at the applicable tax rate for its partners, which can range from 15% to 31% in 1991 for partners who are individuals, trusts, or estates. Corporate partners pay tax on partnership income at rates ranging from 15% to 39% in 1991.

One of the major advantages of the partnership form of doing business is that partnership losses are allocated among the partners.[13] If the loss limitation rules (explained later in this chapter) do not apply, these losses are combined with the partners' other income, and the result is an immediate tax savings for the partners. Of course, the amount of tax savings varies with each partner's marginal tax rate. The immediate tax saving that is available to the partner contrasts sharply with the net operating loss (NOL) carrybacks or carryforwards that result from a C corporation's tax loss.

Self-Study Question

When does a partner need to know his/her basis in his/her partnership interest?

Answer

Three important reasons for calculating a partner's basis in his partnership interest are (a) to determine the gain/loss on a sale of the partnership interest, (b) to determine the amount of partnership losses that a partner can deduct, and (c) to determine the amount of the distributions that are tax-free to the partner.

The Partner's Basis

A partner's basis in his partnership interest is a crucial element in partnership taxation. When a partner makes a contribution to a partnership or purchases a partnership interest, he establishes the beginning basis.[14] Since the partners are personally liable for partnership debts, a partner's basis in his partnership interest is increased by his share of any partnership liabilities.[15] Accordingly, the partner's basis fluctuates as the partnership borrows and repays loans or increases and decreases its accounts payable. In addition, a partner's basis in his partnership interest is increased by the partner's share of partnership income and decreased by his share of partnership losses.[16] Because a partner's basis in his partnership interest can never be negative, the basis serves as one limit on the amount of deductible partnership losses. (See the discussion on pages 9-30 through 9-34 about the various loss limitations.)

Example 9-1 ■ Tom purchases a 20% interest in the XY Partnership for $8,000 on January 1, 1991, and begins to materially participate in the partnership's business. The XY Partnership uses the calendar year as its tax year. At the time of the purchase, the XY Partnership has $2,000 in liabilities. Tom's basis in his partnership interest on January 1, 1991, is $8,400 ($8,000 + [0.20 × $2,000]). ■

Example 9-2 ■ Assume the same facts as in Example 9-1, except that the XY Partnership incurs $10,000 in losses and its liabilities increase by $4,000 during 1991. Tom's basis on December 31, 1991, is computed as follows:

January 1, 1991 basis	$8,400
Plus: Share of liability increase ($4,000 × 0.20)	800
Minus: Share of partnership losses ($10,000 × 0.20)	(2,000)
December 31, 1991 basis	$7,200

■

Example 9-3 ■ Assume the same facts as in Example 9-2, except that the XY Partnership incurs $50,000 in losses and its liabilities increase by $10,000 during 1992. Tom's share of the losses is $10,000 ($50,000 × 0.20), but the $9,200 maximum loss that he can deduct is calculated as follows:

---

[13] Sec. 702(a).
[14] Secs. 722 and 742.
[15] Secs. 752(a) and (b).
[16] Sec. 705(a).

January 1, 1992, basis	$7,200
Plus: Share of liability increase	2,000
December 31, 1992, basis before losses	$9,200
Minus: Maximum loss to be deducted	(9,200)
December 31, 1992, basis	—0—

Tom's remaining $800 in losses must be carried over to a later year and are deducted when he has sufficient basis in his partnership interest. ∎

Typical Misconception

Many taxpayers think that partners pay taxes when they receive distributions from the partnership. However, distributions are generally tax-free because they are merely the receipt of earnings that have already been taxed to the partners.

Partnership Distributions

When a partnership makes a current distribution, the distribution is generally tax-free to the partners since it represents the receipt of earnings that have already been taxed to the partners. Distributions reduce the partner's basis in his partnership interest.[17] If a cash distribution is so large that it exceeds a partner's basis in his partnership interest, the partner will recognize gain equal to the amount of the excess. When the partnership goes out of business or when a partner withdraws from the partnership, liquidating distributions are paid to the partner. Like current distributions, these distributions generally cause the partner to recognize gain only if the cash that is received exceeds the partner's basis in his partnership interest.[18] A loss may be recognized if the partner receives only cash, inventory, and unrealized receivables in complete liquidation of his partnership interest.[19] (Distributions are discussed in Chapter 10.)

TAX IMPLICATIONS OF FORMATION OF A PARTNERSHIP

When two or more individuals or entities decide to operate an unincorporated business together, a partnership is formed. In the following sections, the tax implications of property contributions, service contributions, and organization and syndication expenditures are examined.

Contribution of Property

OBJECTIVE 2

Explain the tax results of a contribution of property or services in exchange for a partnership interest

Nonrecognition of Gain or Loss. Formation of a partnership is governed by Sec. 721. In most cases, the statute provides that a partner who contributes property in exchange for a partnership interest does not recognize gain or loss on the transaction. Likewise, the partnership recognizes no gain or loss on the contribution of property. The partner's basis for his partnership interest and the partnership's basis for the property both reference the property's basis in the transferor's hands.[20]

The nonrecognition treatment is limited to transactions in which a partnership interest is received in exchange for a contribution of property. As in the corporate formation area, the term *property* includes cash, tangible property (e.g., buildings and

---

[17] Sec. 733.
[18] Sec. 731(a)(1).
[19] Sec. 731(a)(2).
[20] Secs. 722 and 723.

Tax Implications of Formation of a Partnership • 9-7

Key Point
The basic rule for formation of a partnership is that no gain/loss is recognized by the partners or partnership. The partner's basis in his partnership interest (known as outside basis) and the inside basis of the property to the partnership equal the basis of the property in the hands of the contributing partner for all partnerships other than investment partnerships.

land), and intangible property (e.g., franchise rights, trademarks, and leases).[21] The property must be contributed to the partnership in order to defer the recognition of gain under Sec. 721. Regulation Sec. 1.707-1(a) indicates that a transaction in which a partner allows the partnership to use the property for partnership purposes while retaining ownership (e.g., use of a franchise while the partner retains significant current or future interests) does not come under Sec. 721 and is treated as if the transaction occurred between unrelated parties. Note that services are specifically excluded from the definition of property, so a contribution of services for a partnership interest is not a tax-free transaction.

Recognition of Gain or Loss. The general rule of Sec. 721(a) provides that no gain or loss is recognized by the partnership or any partner when property is contributed in exchange for a partnership interest. Two exceptions to this general rule may require a partner to recognize a gain (but never a loss) on the contribution of property to a partnership in exchange for a partnership interest:

- Contribution of property to a partnership along with the partnership's assumption of liabilities previously owed by the partner.
- Contribution of property to a partnership which would be treated as an investment company if it were incorporated.

Typical Misconception
In order for contributions to a corporation to be nontaxable, the contributing shareholders must control (by at least 80%) the corporation immediately after the transaction. There is no such control requirement for contributions to a partnership to be nontaxable.

The investment company exception of Sec. 721(b) requires recognition of gain only if the exchange results in diversification of the transferor's property interest. This investment is only taxed when immediately after the exchange more than 80% of the value of the partnership's assets (excluding cash and nonconvertible debt obligations) are held for investment or are readily marketable stocks, securities, or interests in regulated investment companies or real estate investment trusts.[22] Clearly, the Sec. 721 provisions were enacted to permit tax-free combinations of business assets to be used to operate a business but not to allow tax-free diversification of the partners' investment portfolios. If the contribution of property is to an investment partnership, the contributing partner must recognize any gain realized on property transfers as if the stocks or securities were sold and the proceeds used to diversify the partner's portfolio.

Key Point
When a partner is relieved of debt, this is treated as if the partner receives a cash distribution. If a partner assumes debt, it is treated as if the partner makes a cash contribution. These two simple rules are critical to understanding transactions such as formations of partnerships, distributions from partnerships, and sales or liquidations of partnership interests.

Effects of Liabilities. As mentioned earlier, the role of liabilities in the partnership setting is unique. Because each general partner is liable for his share of partnership liabilities, increases and decreases in the partnership liabilities are reflected in each partner's basis. Specifically, Sec. 752 provides that two effects result from the contribution of property to a partnership if the partnership assumes any liabilities of the transferor.

- Each partner's basis is increased by his share of the partnership's liabilities as if he had contributed cash to the partnership in the amount of his share of partnership liabilities.
- The partner whose personal liabilities are assumed by the partnership has a reduction in the basis of his partnership interest as if the partnership distributed cash to him in the amount of the assumed liability.

The net effect of these two basis adjustments is seldom sufficiently large to cause a transferor partner to recognize gain when property is contributed to the partnership. The transferor partner is deemed first to have made a contribution of property plus a

---

[21] For an excellent discussion of the definition of the term *property*, see footnote 6 of *D.N. Stafford v. U.S.*, 45 AFTR 2d 80-785, 80-1 USTC ¶ 9218 (5th Cir., 1980).
[22] Reg. Sec. 1.351-1(c)(1).

contribution of cash equal to the partner's share of any partnership liabilities existing prior to his entrance into the partnership (or contributed by other partners concurrently with this transaction). The partner is deemed then to have received a cash distribution equal to the total amount of his own liability that is assumed by the *other* partners. (No basis adjustment is required for the portion of the liability transferred to the partnership by the transferor which he will retain in his new role as a partner.) The following examples help clarify the necessary basis adjustments.

Example 9-4 ■ In return for a 20% partnership interest, Mary contributes a machine having a $60,000 FMV and a $30,000 basis to the XY Partnership. The partnership assumes Mary's $15,000 liability arising from her purchase of the machine. The XY Partnership has $4,000 in liabilities immediately preceding her contribution. Mary's $18,800 basis in her partnership interest is calculated as follows:

Basis of contributed property		$30,000
Plus:	Mary's share of existing partnership liabilities ($4,000 × 0.20)	800
Minus:	Mary's liabilities that are assumed by the other partners ($15,000 × 0.80)	(12,000)
Mary's basis in her partnership interest		$18,800

Mary recognizes no gain on the partnership's assumption of her liability because the deemed cash distribution from the assumption of her $12,000 in liabilities by the partnership does not exceed her $30,800 basis in the partnership interest immediately preceding the fictional distribution. ■

Example 9-5 ■ Assume the same facts as in Example 9-4, except that the amount of the liability assumed by the XY Partnership is $50,000. Mary's zero basis in her partnership interest is calculated as follows:

Self-Study Question

Why does Mary recognize a $9,200 gain in Example 9-5?

Answer

The reason that Mary has a $9,200 gain in Example 9-5 is that Mary receives a 20% partnership interest in exchange for the machine. Thus, 80% of the debt is assumed by the other partners, which results in a deemed $40,000 cash distribution to Mary. Since the distribution is in excess of her basis in the partnership interest, Mary recognizes a $9,200 gain.

Basis of contributed property		$30,000
Plus:	Mary's share of existing partnership liabilities ($4,000 × 0.20)	800
Minus:	Mary's liabilities that are assumed by the other partners ($50,000 × 0.80)	(40,000)
Tentative basis for partnership interest		($9,200)
Basis (larger of zero or tentative basis)		—0—

The negative tentative basis amount means that Mary's deemed cash distribution from the assumption of her liability by the other partners exceeds her basis prior to the distribution. The cash that is distributed in excess of Mary's basis requires her to recognize a $9,200 gain. No matter what negative number results from the distribution, the partner's basis in the partnership interest can never be less than zero. ■

Example 9-5 illustrates one of several tax law differences between the formation of a corporation and a partnership. Note that in this example the liability assumed by the partnership is greater than Mary's basis in the property (but less than the property's FMV). If the property is instead contributed to a corporation in a transaction that otherwise qualifies under Sec. 351, the transferor would recognize a $20,000 gain (the excess of the $50,000 liability assumed over the property's $30,000 basis). In the partnership setting, the gain is only $9,200.

Tax Implications of Formation of a Partnership • 9-9

Typical Misconception
To contrast partnership formations with corporate formations, if Example 9-5 had involved a formation of the XY Corporation, Mary would have been treated as if relieved of the entire $50,000 of debt, which would have resulted in a $20,000 Sec. 357(c) gain to Mary.

Because the assumption of a partner's liabilities by the partnership is treated as a cash distribution, the character of any gain recognized by the partner is controlled by the partnership distribution rules. Cash distributions in excess of basis always result in gain recognition, and that gain is deemed to be gain from the sale of the partnership interest.[23] Since a partnership interest is usually a capital asset, the normal result is that gain arising from assumption of a partner's liabilities is a capital gain.

Partner's Basis in the Partnership Interest. In general, the transferor partner's beginning basis in the partnership interest equals the sum of the money contributed plus a carryover basis from the contributed property. If the partner recognizes any gain on the contribution because the partnership is an investment company, the amount of the recognized gain is added to his basis in the partnership interest.[24] Any gain recognized because of the effects of liabilities on the partner's basis does not increase the basis for the partnership interest since the Code mandates that in this situation the basis is zero.

It should be noted that valuable property having little or no basis may be contributed. For example, the accounts receivable of a partner using the cash method of accounting can be a valued contribution to a partnership, but if the receivables' bases are zero, the beginning basis of the partnership interest is also zero. Similarly, a note receivable from the contributing partner may be a valuable contribution to the partnership, but is likely to have a zero basis to carry over to the partnership interest.

Typical Misconception
If a partner contributes both ordinary income property and capital gain property to a partnership, the partner will have two different holding periods for his partnership interest.

Holding Period for Partnership Interest. The holding period for the partnership interest includes the transferor's holding period for the contributed property if that property is a capital asset or a Sec. 1231 asset in the transferor's hands.[25] If the contributed property is an ordinary income asset (e.g., inventory) to the partner, the holding period for the partnership interest begins on the day after the day of the contribution.[26]

Example 9-6 ■ On April 1, 1991, Sue contributes a building (a Sec. 1231 asset) to the ST Partnership in exchange for a 20% interest. Sue purchased the building on March 1, 1989. Her holding period for her partnership interest includes her holding period for the contributed building and commences on March 2, 1989. ■

Example 9-7 ■ On April 1, 1991, Ted contributes inventory to the ST Partnership in exchange for a 20% interest. No matter when Ted acquired the inventory, his holding period for his partnership interest begins on April 2, 1991, the day after the date of his contribution. ■

Partnership's Basis in Property. Under Sec. 723, the partnership's basis for contributed property is the same as the property's basis in the hands of the contributing partner. If the contributing partner recognizes gain because the partnership is an investment company, such gain increases the partnership's basis in the contributed property. Gain recognized by the contributing partner because of the assumption of a partner's liability does not increase the partnership's basis in the property.[27]

---

[23] Sec. 731(a).
[24] Sec. 722.
[25] Sec. 1223(1).
[26] Reg. Sec. 1.1223-1(a).
[27] Rev. Rul. 84-15, 1984-1 C.B. 158.

Typical Misconception

Example 9-5 illustrates another difference between partnership and corporate formations. In the example, XY Partnership does not increase its basis in the property for the gain recognized by Mary, but if XY were a corporation, it would increase its basis in the property by Mary's recognized gain.

Not only does the property's basis carry over to the partnership from the contributing partner, but for some properties the character of gain or loss on a subsequent disposition of the property by the partnership also references the character of the property in the contributing partner's hands. Section 724 prevents the transformation of ordinary income into capital gains (or capital losses into ordinary losses) when property is contributed to a partnership after March 31, 1984. Properties that were (1) unrealized receivables, inventory, or capital loss property in the hands of the contributing partner and (2) contributed to a partnership after March 31, 1984, retain their character for some subsequent partnership dispositions.[28]

UNREALIZED RECEIVABLES. The concept of unrealized receivables plays a key role for tax purposes in many different partnership transactions. An **unrealized receivable** is any right to payment for goods or services that has not been included in income because of the method of accounting being used.[29] The most common examples of unrealized receivables are the accounts receivable of a cash method of accounting taxpayer.

If a property is an unrealized receivable in the hands of the contributing partner and is contributed to a partnership after March 31, 1984, any gain or loss recognized on the partnership's later disposition of the property is treated as ordinary income or loss. Ordinary income or loss treatment is mandated without regard to the period of time the partnership holds the property before disposition or the character of the property in the partnership's hands.

INVENTORY. If a property was inventory in the hands of the contributing partner and is contributed to a partnership after March 31, 1984, its character cannot be changed for a 5-year period. Any gain or loss recognized by the partnership on the disposition of such property during the 5-year period beginning on the date of contribution is ordinary gain or loss. Ordinary gain or loss treatment is mandated even if the asset is a capital asset or Sec. 1231 asset in the partnership's hands.

Example 9-8 ■

Historical Note

Sec. 724 was enacted to eliminate the ability to transform the character of gain/loss on property by contributing such property to a partnership and having the partnership subsequently sell the property. A similar set of rules also limits the possibility of transforming the character of gain/loss by distributing property from a partnership and having the partners subsequently sell the property.

On June 1, 1987, Sam, a real estate developer, contributes 10 acres of land in an industrial park he developed to the Hi-Tech Partnership in exchange for a 30% interest in the partnership. Although Sam was holding the acreage in inventory, the land serves as the site for Hi-Tech's new research facility. Four years later Hi-Tech sells its research facility and the land. Gain on the sale of the land, which would ordinarily be taxed as Sec. 1231 gain, is reported as ordinary income under Sec. 724. ■

CAPITAL LOSS PROPERTY. The final type of property whose character is fixed at the time of the contribution is property that would generate a capital loss if it is sold by the contributing partner rather than contributed to the partnership. A loss recognized by the partnership on the disposition of the property within 5 years of the date it is contributed to the partnership is a capital loss. However, the amount of loss which is characterized as capital may not exceed the capital loss the contributing partner would recognize if the property were instead sold on the contribution date. The character of any loss that exceeds the difference between the property's FMV and its adjusted basis on the contribution date is determined by the property's character in the hands of the partnership.

---

[28] Sec. 724. The determination of whether a property is an unrealized receivable, inventory, or a capital loss property in the contributing partner's hands occurs immediately before the contribution.

[29] Section 724(d)(1) references the unrealized receivables definition found in Sec. 751(c). For distributions and sale transactions, the unrealized receivables definition is broadened to include certain recapture items, but this difference is discussed more fully in Chapter 10.

Example 9-9 ■ Pam holds investment land that she purchased for $50,000 in 1985. The FMV of the land is only $40,000 in 1987 when she contributes it to the PK Partnership, which is in the business of developing and selling lots. PK develops the contributed land and sells the lots four years after the contribution for a total of $28,000, or at a loss of $22,000. The $10,000 loss that accrued while Pam held the land as a capital asset retains its character as a capital loss. The remaining $12,000 of loss that accrues while the land is part of the partnership's inventory is an ordinary loss. ■

Partnership's Holding Period. Under Sec. 1223(2), the partnership's holding period for its contributed assets includes the holding period of the contributing partner. This rule applies without regard to the character of the property in the contributing partner's hands or the partnership's hands.

Key Point
Unless gain is recognized by the transferor partner on the contribution of property to a partnership, the Sec. 1245 and Sec. 1250 recapture potential carry over to the partnership.

Section 1245 and Sec. 1250 Recapture Rules. While the Sec. 1245 and Sec. 1250 depreciation recapture rules override most other nonrecognition of gain provisions in the Code, there is no depreciation recapture unless a gain is recognized when property is contributed in exchange for a partnership interest.[30] Instead, both the adjusted basis and depreciation recapture potential carry over to the partnership. If the property is later sold at a gain, the Sec. 1245 and 1250 provisions affect the character of the gain.

If a gain is recognized on the contribution of depreciable property under the investment company or the liability adjustment exceptions, such gain is ordinary income up to the total amount of recapture potential that exists at the time of the contribution.[31] The amount of the gain that exceeds the depreciation recapture amount generally is Sec. 1231 or capital gain.

Example 9-10 ■ Sara contributes equipment having a $9,000 adjusted basis and a $28,000 FMV to the RS Partnership in exchange for a 20% partnership interest. Sara claimed $8,000 of depreciation prior to the contribution. She recognizes no gain on the transaction, so the full $8,000 of Sec. 1245 recapture potential carries over to the partnership. ■

Example 9-11 ■ Assume the same facts as in Example 9-10, except that the property is encumbered with a $15,000 mortgage, which the partnership assumes. The partnership has no other liabilities. Sara's basis in her partnership interest is zero, and she must recognize $3,000 of gain under the Sec. 752(b) liability exception as determined below.

Basis of contributed property	$ 9,000
Minus: Sara's liabilities that are assumed by the other partners	(12,000)
Tentative basis for the partnership interest	($ 3,000)
Actual basis (greater of zero or tentative basis)	—0—

The $3,000 gain is Sec. 1245 ordinary income. The equipment retains $5,000 of recapture potential, which carries over to the partnership. The $9,000 basis for the

---

[30] Secs. 1245(b)(3) and 1250(d)(3). Property acquired as a capital contribution where gain is not recognized under Sec. 721 is subject to the Modified ACRS anti-churning rules of Sec. 168(i)(7)(A). See Chapter 2 for a discussion of these rules in connection with a corporate formation transaction.

[31] See *Frederick S. Klein*, 25 T.C. 1045 (1956), *acq.* 1956-2 C.B. 6.

Self-Study Question

Does the contribution of services to a partnership in exchange for an unrestricted partnership interest qualify for Sec. 721 nontaxable treatment?

Answer

No. The service partner recognizes income to the extent of the FMV of the partnership interest received less any cash or other property contributed by the partner.

equipment on the partnership's books is not increased by Sara's recognized gain (see page 9-9). ■

Other recapture provisions (e.g., Secs. 617, 1252, and 1254) operate much like the rules in Secs. 1245 and 1250 described above.

Contribution of Services

A partner who receives a partnership interest in exchange for services has been compensated as surely as if he receives cash and must recognize ordinary income. The amount and timing of the income to be recognized are determined under Sec. 83. Consequently, receipt of an unrestricted interest in a partnership requires the service partner to immediately recognize income equal to the FMV of the partnership interest less any cash or property contributed by the partner. Generally, no income is recognized from the receipt of a restricted interest in a partnership until the restriction lapses or the interest can be freely transferred. The income from receiving a restricted partnership interest equals the FMV of the interest at the time that either the restriction lapses or the interest becomes transferable minus any cash or property that the service partner contributed. If the partner elects, income from the receipt of a restricted partnership interest can be reported when the interest is received (thereby avoiding recognizing any increase in the value of the interest between the date that it is received and the date that the restrictions lapse as ordinary income).

While a partnership interest seems to be a unified interest, it is really made up of two components—a capital interest and a profits interest. A partner may receive both components or only a profits interest in exchange for his services. (It is rare to have a capital interest without a profits interest.) The Regulations indicate that a **capital interest** can be valued by determining the amount the partner would receive if the partnership liquidated on the day the partnership interest was received.[32] If the partner would receive proceeds from the sale of the partnership's assets or receive the assets themselves, then he is considered to own a capital interest. Alternatively, if the partner's only interest is in the future earnings of the partnership (with no interest in the current partnership assets), the partner owns a **profits interest** (but not a capital interest).

It has long been settled that receipt of a capital interest in a partnership in exchange for services is taxable under the rules outlined above. A profits interest is no more than a right to future income that will, of course, be taxed to the partner when it is earned. To the extent that the profits interest itself has a value, it is reasonable to expect that the value be taxed when the profits interest is received as any other property received for services would be taxed.

Example 9-12 ■ Carl arranges favorable financing for the purchase of an office building and receives a 30% profits interest in a partnership formed to own and operate the building. Less than 3 weeks later Carl sells his profits interest to his partner for $40,000. Carl must recognize $40,000 as ordinary income from the receipt of a partnership profits interest in exchange for services. ■

The facts in Example 9-12 approximate those of *Sol Diamond,* a landmark partnership taxation case, which was the first case to tax the partner when a profits interest was received.[33] Prior to this case, most tax practitioners agreed that the

---

[32] Reg. Sec. 1.704-1(e)(1)(v). The capital interest definition that is referenced relates to family partnerships. There is no reason to believe that such definition differs from the one used for this purpose.

[33] 33 AFTR 2d 74-852, 74-1 USTC ¶ 9306 (7th Cir., 1974), *aff'g.* 56 T.C. 530 (1971).

receipt of a profits interest was not a taxable event. The Tax Court, however, pointed out that Sec. 61 included all compensation for services, and no other provision contained in the Code or Regulations removed this transaction from taxation. The Seventh Circuit Court of Appeals seemed to limit the inclusion of a profits interest to situations in which the market value of the profits interest could be determined. In many situations, the market value of the profits interest is not determinable, and, therefore, taxation of the profits interest at the time it is received is unlikely. In those cases, an income tax is never levied on the profits interest separately, but all partnership profits that accrue to the partner are, of course, taxed under the normal rules of partnership taxation.[34]

Key Point
To the extent the service partner recognizes income, the partnership is entitled to a deduction or, if the services performed are a capital expenditure, the amount must be capitalized and amortized if appropriate.

Consequences to the Partnership. Normally, payments made by the partnership for services are either deductible as an expense or capitalized. This result is unchanged when the partnership pays for services with an interest in the partnership. The timing of the partnership's deduction for the expense generally matches the timing for the partner to include the value of his partnership interest in income.[35]

ALLOCATING THE EXPENSE DEDUCTION. The expense deduction or the amortization of the capital expenditure is allocated among the partners other than the service partner. This allocation occurs because it is these partners who make the outlay by relinquishing part of their interest in the partnership.

Example 9-13 ■ In June 1991, Jay, a lawyer, receives a 1% interest (valued at $4,000) in the JLK Partnership in return for providing legal services to JLK's employees during the first 5 months of 1991. The legal services were a fringe benefit for JLK's employees and were deductible by JLK. Jay must include $4,000 in his 1991 gross income and JLK can deduct the expense in 1991. ■

If the service performed is of a nature that should be capitalized, the partnership capitalizes the amount and amortizes it as appropriate. The asset's basis is increased at the same time and in the same amount as the partner's gross income inclusion.[36]

Example 9-14 ■ In June 1991, Rob, an architect, receives a 10% capital and profits interest in the KLB Partnership for his services in designing a new building to house the partnership's operations. The June 1991 value of the partnership interest is $24,000. Rob must recognize $24,000 of ordinary income in 1991 as a result of receiving the partnership interest. The KLB Partnership must capitalize the $24,000 as part of the building's cost and depreciate that amount (along with the building's other costs) over its recovery period. ■

BASIS ADJUSTMENTS. The partnership, in effect, pays its bill for services by transferring an interest in partnership property. Generally, when property is used to pay a debt, the payor must recognize gain or loss equal to the difference between the property's adjusted basis and FMV. Likewise, the partnership must recognize the gain or loss existing in the proportionate share of its assets deemed to be transferred to the service partner.[37] Furthermore, since the partnership must recognize gain, the partnership's bases in its assets are increased.

In order to accomplish this basis adjustment, a hypothetical transaction is created whereby payment to the service partner is deemed to be a proportionate interest in

---

[34] In *William G. Campbell*, 1990 PH T.C. Memo ¶ 90,162, 59 TCM 236, the Tax Court reaffirmed the principles of the *Sol Diamond* case.
[35] Reg. Sec. 1.83-6(a)(1).
[36] Reg. Sec. 1.83-6(a)(4).
[37] Reg. Sec. 1.83-6(b).

each partnership asset. Thus, the partner's income equals the total of his share of the FMV of each partnership asset. The partner's basis in each partnership asset equals the FMV of the portion of each asset which he is deemed to own. The partnership recognizes the gain or loss applicable to the share of each asset deemed distributed to the service partner. This hypothetical transaction continues with the service partner deemed to contribute his proportionate interest in each asset (now having a basis equal to its FMV) back to the partnership in exchange for his partnership interest. No gain or loss is recognized on the contribution portion of the hypothetical transaction. The service partner's basis for his partnership interest equals the FMV of his share of the partnership assets.

Example 9-15 ■

Key Point
To better understand the hypothetical transactions created by contribution of services to a partnership, the following is a summary of the resulting tax consequences for both the service partner and the partnership:

1. Income to the service partner to the extent of the FMV of an undivided interest in the partnership assets deemed received.
2. Deduction (or capital expenditure) for the partnership.
3. Gain/loss recognized by the partnership on the assets deemed transferred.
4. Service partner's basis in his partnership interest equals the amount of income recognized by the service partner.
5. The partnership adjusts (to their FMV), the inside basis of the portion of the assets deemed transferred. This adjustment reflects the gain/loss recognized by the partnership on the deemed asset transfer.

XYZ Partnership has the following assets on January 1, 1991, when Wendy is admitted as a 25% partner in exchange for services valued at $16,500. The partnership has no liabilities at the time.

Assets	Basis	FMV
Cash	$14,000	$14,000
Accounts receivable	8,000	8,000
Inventory	8,000	12,000
Land	20,000	32,000
Total	$50,000	$66,000

The transaction is taxed as if Wendy received an undivided one-fourth interest in each asset. She is taxed on the $16,500 FMV of the assets and takes a $16,500 basis in her shares of the assets. The partnership must recognize the $4,000 gain on the assets deemed distributed to Wendy.

	Fair Market Value Deemed Distributed (1)	Basis Deemed Distributed (2)	Gain Recognized by XYZ (3) = (1) − (2)	Partnership's Postcontribution Basis for Assets
Cash	$ 3,500	$ 3,500	$—0—	$14,000
Accounts receivable	2,000	2,000	—0—	8,000
Inventory	3,000	2,000	1,000	9,000
Land	8,000	5,000	3,000	23,000
Total	$16,500	$12,500	$ 4,000	$54,000

Wendy is deemed to contribute her undivided one-fourth interest in the assets back to the XYZ Partnership. The partnership, of course, simply takes a carryover basis of $16,500 in the assets she contributes. The partnership's original basis in its assets ($50,000) is reduced by the basis of assets deemed distributed to Wendy ($12,500) and increased by the carryover basis of the assets deemed contributed by Wendy ($16,500). This $54,000 ($50,000 − $12,500 + $16,500) postcontribution basis is allocated among the individual assets as shown above. Wendy's basis for her partnership interest is $16,500. ■

Syndication and Organizational Expenditures

The costs of organizing a partnership are treated as capital expenditures. The capitalized amount can be amortized on a straight-line basis and deducted over a period of not less than 60 months beginning with the month in which the partnership

Self-Study Question

What is the importance of the distinction between organizational expenditures and syndication expenditures?

Answer

Organizational expenditures can be amortized over a period of not less than 60 months, but syndication expenditures are not deductible.

begins business.[38] In order to amortize the organizational expenditures, the partnership must make an election that is included with the partnership tax return for the period including the month in which it begins business.

Organizational expenditures that can be capitalized and amortized must meet the same requirements as the costs incurred by a corporation making the Sec. 248 election to amortize organizational expenditures (see Chapter 3). The organizational expenditures must be (1) incident to the creation of the partnership, (2) chargeable to a capital account, and (3) of a character that would be amortizable over the life of the partnership if the partnership had a limited life. Eligible expenditures include legal fees for negotiating and preparing partnership agreements, accounting fees for establishing the initial accounting system, and filing fees. Syndication expenditures for the issuing and marketing of interests in the partnership are not organizational expenditures and cannot be included in this election.[39] Unamortized organizational expenditures are deducted when the partnership is terminated or liquidated.

Topic Review 9-1 summarizes the tax consequences of the formation of a partnership.

PARTNERSHIP ELECTIONS

Once the partnership is formed, the partnership must make a number of elections. For example, partnerships must select a taxable year and elect accounting methods for all but a few items affecting the computation of partnership taxable income or loss.

Partnership Taxable Year

OBJECTIVE 3
Determine the permitted tax years for a partnership

The election of the partnership's taxable year is critical because it determines when each partner reports his share of partnership income or loss. Under Sec. 706(a), each partner's tax return includes his share of partnership income, gain, loss, deductions, or credits for any taxable year of the partnership ending within or with the partner's taxable year.

Example 9-16 ■

Vicki is a member of a partnership having a November 30 year-end. In her tax return for the calendar year 1991, she must include her share of partnership items from the partnership tax year that ends November 30, 1991. Results of partnership operations in December 1991 are reported along with all other partnership items from the partnership year that ends on November 30, 1992, in Vicki's 1992 tax return. She receives, in essence, a 1-year deferral of the taxes due on December's partnership income. ■

Typical Misconception

A partnership tax year is determined by applying the statutory rules in the following order:

1. The majority partner(s)' (own in aggregate more than 50%) tax year.
2. If (1) is not applicable, then the tax year of all the principal partners (5% or more partners).
3. If neither (1) nor (2) is applicable, then a calendar year.

Section 706 Restrictions. Because the choice of a tax year for a partnership can provide a substantial opportunity for tax deferral, it is no surprise that partnerships are more restricted than C corporations in their ability to elect a fiscal year as their tax year. Section 706 severely restricts the available choices for a partnership's tax year. The partnership must use the same tax year as the one or more **majority partner(s)** who have an aggregate interest in partnership profits and capital in excess of 50%. This rule must be used only if these majority partners have a common tax year and have had this tax year for the shorter of the 3 preceding years or the partnership's period of existence. If the tax year of the partner(s) owning a majority

---

[38] Sec. 709(b).
[39] Reg. Sec. 1.709-2(a).

TOPIC REVIEW 9-1

Formation of a Partnership

	Contribution to a Partnership	
	Property	Services
Recognition of gain, loss, or income by partner	Tax-free unless: (1) liabilities assumed by the partnership exceed partner's tentative basis in partnership interest (gain recognized equals amount by which liabilities assumed by partnership exceed tentative basis), or (2) partnership formed is an investment partnership (gain recognized equals excess of FMV of partnership interest over basis of assets contributed).	Taxable to partner equal to FMV of partnership interest received.
Basis of partnership interest	Carryover basis from property contributed plus share of partnership liabilities assumed minus the partner's liabilities assumed by the partnership. Gain recognized because of investment company rules increases the basis of the partnership interest.	Amount of income recognized plus share of partnership liabilities assumed by the partner minus partner's liabilities assumed by the partnership.
Gain or loss recognized by the partnership	No gain or loss recognized by the partnership.	1. Deduction or capitalized expense is created depending on the nature of the service rendered. 2. Gain or loss recognized equals difference between FMV of portion of assets used to pay service partner minus the basis of such portion of the assets.
Basis of assets to the partnership	Carryover basis, increased by gain recognized by the partner from the formation of an investment partnership. No basis adjustment occurs due to assumption of partner's liabilities that results in recognition of gain due to distribution of money in excess of partner's basis in partnership interest.	Increased or decreased to reflect the FMV of the assets paid to the service partner.

interest cannot be used, the partnership must use the tax year of all its principal partners (or the tax year to which all of its principal partners are concurrently changing). A **principal partner** is defined as one who owns a 5% or more interest in capital or profits.[40] If the principal partners do not have a common tax year, the partnership is required to use a calendar year.

If the partnership has a business purpose for using some tax year other than the year prescribed by these rules, the IRS may approve use of another tax year. Rev. Proc. 74-33[41] states that an acceptable business purpose for using a different tax year is to end the partnership's tax year at the end of the partnership's "natural business year." This revenue procedure explains that a business having a peak period and a nonpeak period completes its natural business year at the end of its peak season (or shortly thereafter). For example, a ski lodge has a natural business year that ends in early spring. A second pronouncement, Rev. Proc. 87-32,[42] allows an alternate tax year if the following tests are met:

- 25% or more of the partnership's gross receipts for the 12-month period in question are recognized in the last 2 months of the period.
- This requirement has been met for the prior 3 consecutive 12-month periods.

Partnerships that do not have a peak period are not able to use the natural business year exception.

Key Point
Partnerships that are able to satisfy the stringent requirements of Rev. Proc. 87-32 are permitted to use their natural business year for tax purposes.

Example 9-17 ■ ABC Partnership is owned equally by Amy, Brad, and Chris. Each partner uses an October 31 tax year-end. ABC earns 30% of its gross receipts in July and August each year and has had this pattern of earnings for more than 3 years. The IRS would likely grant approval under the guidelines of Rev. Proc. 87-32 for the partnership to report using an August 31 tax year-end. ■

The taxable year restrictions enacted in the 1986 Tax Act forced many partnerships to change their tax year. As a result, income from a short tax year had to be reported and usually caused a bunching of income for the partner. Each partner could elect to include the short tax year's income ratably over the first 4 tax years beginning after December 31, 1986.[43]

Example 9-18 ■ ABC Partnership earns $160,000 during its tax year that ended on June 30, 1987. The partnership has no business purpose for its June 30 year-end, and all the partners have December 31 year-ends. The 1986 Tax Act requires ABC to change to a December 31 year-end. Income earned from the partnership's short tax year (July 1, 1987, through December 31, 1987) totals $80,000. Brian, a 50% partner, may elect to report $10,000 (0.25 × 0.50 × $80,000) of the partnership's income from the short tax year in his tax years ending December 31, 1987, 1988, 1989, and 1990. If no election is made, B reports $40,000 (0.50 × $80,000) in his 1987 tax return. ■

The Revenue Act of 1987 provides an election in Sec. 444 which permits a partnership to retain either the tax year used in 1986 or a year-end which results in a deferral of the lesser of the current deferral period or three months. The deferral period is the time from the beginning of the partnership's fiscal year to the close of the

---

[40] Sec. 706(b)(3).
[41] 1974-2 C.B. 489. The IRS in Rev. Rul. 87-57, 1987-2 C.B. 224, has provided a series of situations illustrating the business purpose requirement.
[42] 1987-2 C.B. 396. Use of this test was endorsed by the Conference Committee Report for the 1986 Tax Reform Act. See H. Rept. No. 99-841, 99th Cong., 2d Sess., p. II-319 (1986).
[43] H. Rept. No. 99-841, 99th Cong., 2d Sess., p. II-318 (1986).

first required tax year ending within such year (i.e., usually December 31). The Sec. 444 election is available to both new partnerships making an initial tax year election or existing partnerships that are changing tax years. A partnership which satisfies the Sec. 706 requirements described above or which has established a business purpose for its choice of a year-end (i.e., natural business year) does not need a Sec. 444 election.

A partnership that makes a Sec. 444 election is required by Sec. 7519 to make a required payment (see the Compliance and Procedural Considerations section of this chapter for a discussion of the Sec. 444 election and Sec. 7519 required payment requirements). The required payment has the effect of collecting a tax on the partnership's deferred income at the highest individual marginal tax rate. Willful failure to comply with the required payment rules results in cancellation of the partnership's Sec. 444 election effective for the tax year in which such failure occurs.

The required payment is calculated using the following formula:

$$\left[\left(\begin{array}{c}\text{Deferred}\\ \text{base year}\\ \text{net}\\ \text{income}\end{array} + \begin{array}{c}\text{Excess}\\ \text{applicable}\\ \text{payments}\end{array}\right) \times \begin{array}{c}\text{Adjusted}\\ \text{highest}\\ \text{Sec. 1}\\ \text{rate}\end{array}\right] - \begin{array}{c}\text{Net}\\ \text{required}\\ \text{payment}\\ \text{balance}\end{array} = \begin{array}{c}\text{Required}\\ \text{payment}\end{array}[44]$$

where:

- base year net income equals the partnership's net income (i.e., the aggregate [but not less than zero] of partnership items from Sec. 702(a) other than tax-exempt income and tax credits) for the preceding fiscal year;
- deferral ratio equals the number of months in the deferral period of the base year divided by the number of months in the base year (usually 12);
- deferred base year net income equals the base year net income times the deferral ratio;
- applicable payments equals the payments made to the partner that are deductible in the base year and which are includible at any time in the partner's gross income other than gains from the sale or exchange of property between the owner and the entity (e.g., rents, interest, and so on but not partnership guaranteed payments);
- excess applicable payments equals the applicable payments made during the base year times the deferral ratio minus any actual applicable payments;
- actual applicable payments are the aggregate of the applicable payments made during the deferral period of the base year;
- adjusted highest Sec. 1 rate is the highest tax rate under Sec. 1 (individual tax rates) plus one percentage point;
- net required payment balance equals the cumulative total of all prior payments under this provision less any refunds made in preceding election years.

A required payment does not have to be made if the total of such payments for the current year and all preceding years is $500 or less. Amounts less than the $500 threshold are carried over to succeeding years.

Calculation of the required payment for a partnership that makes an election under Sec. 444 is presented in the following example.

---

[44] The required payment procedures were phased-in over 1987–1989 by having an additional term called the "applicable percentage" which was multiplied by the product of the other three terms inside the brackets to determine the gross required payment. The applicable percentage was: 25% for 1987; 50% for 1988; and 75% for 1989. The phase-in was completed in 1990 when the applicable percentage became 100%. Since it now equals 1, we have omitted it from the calculation.

Key Point

Because of the Sec. 706 requirements, most partnerships are required to adopt a calendar year. As a compromise, a Sec. 444 election was introduced which allows a fiscal tax year as long as no more than a three-month deferral exists.

Historical Note

Sec. 444 was enacted, in part, as a concession to tax return preparers who already have the majority of their clients with calendar years. The Sec. 444 election allows a fiscal year for filing purposes but requires a Sec. 7519 required payment of any taxes deemed deferred by the partners.

Example 9-19 ■ The following information is about the XYZ Partnership, which has previously used a tax year ending on August 31st and elects under Sec. 444 to retain it. Required payments under Sec. 7519 for 1987, 1988, and 1989 were $5,400, $4,750, and $2,900, respectively.

	Fiscal year ending August 31:	
	1990	1991
Base year net income	$150,000	$180,000
Applicable payments:		
Rents to Partner Joe ($2,000 per month)	24,000	24,000
Interest to Partner Sue paid in equal amounts in January and June	60,000	60,000

The required payment under Sec. 7519 is determined as follows:

	1990	1991
Base year net income	$150,000	$180,000
Times: Deferral fraction	×4/12	×4/12
Deferred base year net income	$ 50,000	$ 60,000
Applicable payments	$ 84,000	$ 84,000
Times: Deferral fraction	×4/12	×4/12
	$ 28,000	$ 28,000
Minus: Payments made during deferral period (4 months × $2,000/month)	(8,000)	(8,000)
Excess applicable payments	$ 20,000	$ 20,000
Deferred base year net income	$ 50,000	$ 60,000
Plus: Excess applicable payments	20,000	20,000
Net base year income	$ 70,000	$ 80,000
Times: Adjusted highest Sec. 1 rate	×0.29	×0.32
	$ 20,300	$ 25,600
Minus: Net required payment balance	(13,050)	(20,300)
Required payment	$ 7,250	$ 5,300

The $7,250 required payment for 1990 is due on May 15, 1991. The $5,300 required payment for 1991 is due on May 15, 1992. ■

Code Sec. 7519(c) provides that a partnership is entitled to a refund if the net required payment balance exceeds the bracketed term in the equation. Similar refunds will also be available if the partnership terminates a Sec. 444 election or liquidates. The required payments are not deductible by the partnership and are not passed through and deducted or credited by a partner as federal income taxes. The required payments are in the nature of a refundable deposit.

Key Point
Since the Sec. 7519 required payment is in the nature of a refundable deposit, the partnership is entitled to a refund, if (a) the partnership terminates the Sec. 444 election, (b) the partnership liquidates, or (c) the Sec. 7519 required payment is less than last year's deposit.

Other Partnership Elections

With the exception of three specific elections that are reserved to the partners, Sec. 703(b) requires that all elections that can affect the computation of taxable income derived from the partnership must be made by the partnership.[45] The three elections reserved to the individual partners are

---

[45] The partnership does not include any depletion from oil or gas wells in its computation of income (Sec. 703(a)(2)(F)). Instead each partner elects cost or percentage depletion (Sec. 613A(c)(7)(D)).

TOPIC REVIEW 9-2

Allowable Tax Year for a Partnership

Code Sec. 706 requires that a partnership select the highest ranked tax year-end from the ranking which follows:
1. The tax year-end used by the partner(s) who own a majority of the partnership capital or profits.
2. The tax year-end used by all principal partners (i.e., a partner who owns at least 5% of the partnership capital or profits).
3. A calendar year-end.

If the partnership has a peak period, the IRS may grant permission for the partnership to use a fiscal year-end. This permission will allow a fiscal year-end to be used if the partnership has a natural business year; that is a tax year where 25% or more of the partnership's gross receipts for the 12-month period are reported in the last 2 months of the period.

If the partnership does not have a peak period, it must either
1. Use the tax year-end required by Sec. 706 or
2. Elect a fiscal year-end under Sec. 444 and make a required payment which approximates the tax due on the deferred income.

- Sec. 108(b)(5) relating to reducing basis of depreciable property (instead of other tax attributes) when excluding income from the discharge of indebtedness
- Sec. 617 relating to deduction and recapture of certain mining exploration expenditures
- Sec. 901 relating to the choice between deducting or crediting taxes paid or accrued to foreign countries or U. S. possessions.

Key Point
Except for the three exceptions listed on this page, partnerships make the tax elections for the partnership rather than the partners.

Other than these elections, an election can only be made by the partnership as an entity. Accordingly, the partnership elects its overall accounting method, which can differ from the methods used by its partners. The partnership also elects its inventory and depreciation methods.

Topic Review 9-2 presents a summary of the allowable partnership tax year elections.

PARTNERSHIP REPORTING OF INCOME

Partnership Taxable Income

OBJECTIVE 4
Differentiate between items that must be separately stated and those that are included in ordinary income or loss

Partnership taxable income is calculated much the same way as the taxable income of individuals with a few differences mandated by the statutes. First, taxable income is divided into (1) separately stated items and (2) ordinary income or loss. In Sec. 703(a), the Code specifies a list of deductions that are available to individuals but that cannot be claimed by a partnership. These forbidden deductions include the following:

1. Personal and dependency exemptions
2. Additional itemized deductions for individuals[46]
3. Taxes paid or accrued to a foreign country or to a U.S. possession
4. Charitable contributions
5. Oil and gas depletion
6. Net operating loss (NOL) carryback or carryover

[46] Additional itemized deductions are those deductible under Secs. 212 to 221.

Partnership Reporting of Income • 9-21

Key Point
The reasons why these six listed deductions are forbidden to partnerships are quite obvious. The first two items are individual deductions, the next three are separately stated and their deductibility is determined at the partner level, and the last item is not allowed because partnerships do not have NOLs.

The first two items in this list are inapplicable to a business entity. The next three items must be separately stated and may or may not be deductible by the partner. Since all losses are allocated to the partners for deduction on their tax returns, the partnership itself never has an NOL carryover or carryback. Instead, a single partner may have an NOL if his deductible share of partnership losses exceeds his other business income. These NOLs are utilized at the partner level without any further regard for the partnership entity.

Separately Stated Items

Each partner's distributive share of partnership income must be reported. However, Sec. 702 establishes a list of items that must be separately stated at the partnership level so that their character can remain intact at the partner reporting level. Section 702(a) lists the following items that must be separately stated:

- Net short-term capital gains and losses
- Net long-term capital gains and losses
- Sec. 1231 gains and losses
- Charitable contributions
- Dividends that are eligible for a dividends-received deduction
- Taxes paid or accrued to a foreign country or to a U.S. possession
- Any other item provided by the Regulations

Regulation Sec. 1.702-1(a)(8) adds several other items to the list begun by the Code. The additions from the Regulations include, among others, the following:

- Tax-exempt or partially tax-exempt interest
- Recoveries of bad debts, prior taxes, and delinquency amounts
- Gains and losses from wagering transactions
- Soil and water conservation expenditures
- Intangible drilling and development costs
- Certain mining exploration expenditures
- Any items subject to special allocations (discussed below)

As a general rule, an item must be separately stated if the income tax liability of any partner that would result from treating the item separately is different from the liability that would result if that item is included with partnership ordinary income.[47]

Example 9-20 ■ Amy and Big Corporation are equal partners in the AB Partnership, which purchases new equipment during 1991 at a total cost of $100,000. AB elects to expense $10,000 under the provisions of Sec. 179. Big Corporation has already expensed $6,000 under Sec. 179 in 1991. The Sec. 179 expense must be separately stated since Big Corporation is subject to a separate $10,000 limit in its use. ■

Once the item is separately stated and a distributive share is allocated to each partner, the separately stated items must be reported on each partner's tax return as if the partnership entity did not exist. The partner's share of partnership net long-term capital gains or losses is combined with the partner's personal long-term capital gains and losses to calculate the partner's net long-term capital gain or loss. Likewise, the partner's share of partnership charitable contributions is combined

[47] Reg. Sec. 1.702-1(a)(8)(ii).

Typical Misconception
The amount and character of any gain/loss are determined at the partnership level. How the gain/loss will be taxed is determined at the partner level.

with the partner's own charitable contributions. The total is subject to the partner's charitable contribution limitations. In summary, Sec. 702(b) requires that the character of each separately stated item be determined at the partnership level. The amount is then passed down to the partners and reported in each partner's return as if the partner directly realized the amount.

Partnership Ordinary Income

All items of income, gain, loss, or deduction that do not have to be separately stated are combined into a total called Sec. 702(a)(8) income or loss or **partnership ordinary income** or **loss.** It must be noted that this ordinary income amount is sometimes incorrectly referred to as **partnership taxable income.** Even though it is never totaled, partnership taxable income is, as outlined earlier, the sum of all taxable items among the separately stated items plus the partnership ordinary income. Therefore, partnership taxable income is often substantially greater than partnership ordinary income.

Typical Misconception
Partnership ordinary income/loss *is the sum of all income/loss items not separately stated. This amount is reported as a residual number on line 21 of Form 1065.* **Partnership taxable income** *includes both the separately stated items and the partnership ordinary income/loss. Students should not use these two terms interchangeably.*

Included in the partnership's ordinary income are items such as gross profit on sales, administrative expenses, and employee salaries. Such items are always ordinary income or expenses that are not subject to special limitations. Income recognized under the Sec. 1245 or 1250 depreciation recapture rules is also included in the ordinary income total because it is ordinary income that is not eligible for any preferential treatment.

A share of partnership ordinary income or loss is allocated to each partner. If the partner is an individual, his distributive share of ordinary income, or the deductible portion of his distributive share of ordinary loss, is reported on Schedule E of Form 1040. Schedule E includes rental and royalty income and income or losses from estates, trusts, S corporations, and partnerships. If the partner is a corporation, partnership ordinary income or loss is reported in the Other Income category on Form 1120.

PARTNER REPORTING OF INCOME

Partner's Distributive Share

OBJECTIVE 5
Calculate a partner's distributive share of partnership income, gain, or loss

After the partnership's separately stated income, gain, loss, deduction or credit items, and partnership ordinary income or loss is determined, the totals must be allocated among the partners. Each partner must report and pay taxes on his distributive share. Under Sec. 704(b), the partner's distributive share is normally determined by the terms of the partnership agreement or, if the partnership agreement is silent, by the partner's overall interest in the partnership as determined by taking into account all facts and circumstances.

Key Point
Once the amount and character of the partnership income/loss items have been determined, the distributive share, or amount that each partner will report, must be determined for each item. The distributive share is usually determined by the partnership agreement.

Note that the term **distributive share** is a misnomer since it has nothing to do with the amount actually distributed to a partner. A partner's distributive share is actually the portion of partnership taxable and nontaxable income that the partner has agreed to report for tax purposes. Actual distributions in a given year may be more or less than the distributive share reported by the partner.

Partnership Agreement. The **partnership agreement** may describe a partner's distributive share by indicating the partner's profits and loss interest, or it may indicate separate profits and loss interests. For example, the partnership agreement may state that a partner has a 10% interest in both partnership profits and losses or a partner has only a 10% interest in partnership profits (i.e., profits interest) but has a 30% interest in partnership losses (i.e., loss interest).

If only one interest percentage is stated, it is used to allocate both partnership profit and loss. If profit and loss percentages are stated separately, the partnership's taxable income for the year is first totaled to determine whether a net profit or net loss has been earned. Then the appropriate percentage (either profit or loss) is applied to each class of income for the year.[48]

Example 9-21 ■ The ABC Partnership reports the following income and loss items for 1991:

Net long-term capital loss	($100,000)
Net Sec. 1231 gain	90,000
Ordinary income	220,000

Beth has a 20% profits interest and a 30% loss interest in the ABC Partnership. Since the partnership earns a $210,000 (− $100,000 + $90,000 + $220,000) net taxable profit, Beth's distributive share is calculated using her 20% profits interest and is reported as follows:

Net long-term capital loss	($20,000)
Net Sec. 1231 gain	18,000
Ordinary income	44,000

Her loss percentage is used only in years when the partnership has a net taxable loss. ■

Varying Interest Rule. If a partner's ownership interest changes during the partnership tax year, the income or loss allocation takes into account the partner's varying interest.[49] This varying interest rule is applied for changes occurring to a partner's interest as a result of buying an additional interest in the partnership, selling part (but not all) of a partnership interest, giving or being given a partnership interest, or the admission of a new partner. The partner's ownership interest is generally applied to the income earned on a pro rata basis.

Example 9-22 ■ Maria owns 20% of the XYZ Partnership from January 1 through June 30, 1991. On July 1, 1991, she buys an additional 10% interest in the partnership. During 1991, XYZ Partnership has ordinary income of $120,000, which is earned evenly throughout the year. Maria's $30,049 ($11,901 + $18,148) distributive share of income is calculated as follows:

$$\text{Pre-July 1st:} \quad \$120,000 \times \frac{181 \text{ days}}{365 \text{ days}} \times 0.20 = \$11,901$$

$$\text{Post-June 30th:} \quad \$120,000 \times \frac{184 \text{ days}}{365 \text{ days}} \times 0.30 = \$18,148$$

Special Allocations

OBJECTIVE 6
Explain the requirements for a special partnership allocation

Special allocations are unique to partnerships and allow tremendous flexibility in sharing specific items of income and loss among the partners. Special allocations can provide a specified partner with more or less of an item of income, gain, loss, or

---

[48] This rule is derived from the House and Senate reports on the original Sec. 704(b) provisions. The two reports are identical and read, "The income ratio shall be applicable if the partnership has taxable income . . . and the loss ratio shall be applicable [if] the partnership has a loss." H. Rept. No. 1337, 83d Cong., 2d Sess., p. A223 (1954); S. Rept. No. 1622, 83d Cong., 2d Sess., p. 379 (1954).

[49] Sec. 706(c)(2)(B).

deduction than would be available using the partner's regular distributive share. There are two different kinds of special allocations. First, Sec. 704 requires certain special allocations with respect to contributed property. Second, other special allocations are allowed as long as they meet the tests laid out in the Regulations for having "substantial economic effect." If the substantial economic effect test is not met, the special allocation is lost, and the income, gain, loss, or deduction is allocated according to the partner's interest in the partnership as expressed in the actual operations and activities.

Allocations Related to Contributed Property. As previously discussed, when property is contributed to a partnership, it takes a carryover basis that references the contributing partner's basis. If there were no special allocations, this carryover basis rule would require the partnership (and each of the partners) to accept the tax burden of any gain or loss that accrues to the property before its contribution.

Example 9-23 ■ Elizabeth contributes land having a $4,000 basis and a $10,000 FMV to the DEF Partnership. Assuming the property continues to increase in value, or at least does not decline in value, DEF's gain on the ultimate sale of this property is $6,000 greater than the gain that actually accrues while the partnership owns the property. ■

Key Point
Sec. 704(c) limits the ability to use a partnership to shift income/loss between taxpayers. This provision requires precontribution gains/losses to be allocated to the contributing partner when recognized by the partnership.

Section 704(c) requires precontribution gains or losses to be allocated to the contributing partner for any property contributed to a partnership after March 31, 1984. In addition, income and deductions reported with respect to contributed property must be allocated to take into account the difference between the property's basis and FMV at the time of contribution. The allocation of depreciation is a common example of the special deduction allocation related to contributed property which is necessary under these rules.

Example 9-24 ■ Kay and Sam form an equal partnership when Sam contributes cash of $10,000 and Kay contributes a machine having a $6,000 basis and a $10,000 FMV. The machine is depreciated by the partnership on a straight-line basis over a 5-year recovery period. Both Kay and Sam may be considered to own a one-half interest in each of the partnership assets.

	Basis	FMV
Cash	$10,000	$10,000
Machine	6,000	10,000

Depreciation on the machine is $1,200 each year. Without any special allocation requirements, each partner reports $600 of depreciation. However, Sam paid $10,000 for a one-half interest in partnership assets worth $20,000. In effect, Sam purchased one-half of a $10,000 machine for $5,000 in cash. Had he purchased the interest in the machine outright, he would have been allocated $1,000 ($5,000 ÷ 5 years) of depreciation for each of the 5 years. Therefore, a special allocation of depreciation is needed to allocate $1,000 of the annual depreciation charge to Sam to properly reflect the difference between adjusted basis and FMV on the contribution date. The remaining $200 ($1,200 − $1,000) of depreciation is allocated to Kay. ■

Typical Misconception
Special allocations are unique to partnerships and allow tremendous flexibility. Even so, for a special allocation to be recognized it must have "substantial economic effect."

Substantial Economic Effect. Special allocations not related to contributed property must meet several specific criteria established by the Regulations. These criteria are designed to ensure that the allocations affect the partner's economic consequences and not just the tax consequences.

Example 9-25 ■ The AB Partnership earns $10,000 in tax-exempt interest income and $10,000 in taxable interest income each year. Andy and Becky each have 50% capital and profit interests in the partnership. An allocation of the tax-exempt interest income to Andy, a 31% tax bracket partner, and the taxable interest income to Becky, a 15% tax bracket partner, does not have substantial economic effect. ■

The allocation described in Example 9-25 affects only the tax consequences to the partners, since a 50% distributive share would not really change the partner's economic position.

In order to separate transactions only affecting taxes from those affecting the partner's economic position, the Regulations look at (1) whether the allocation has an economic effect and (2) whether the allocation's effect is substantial. Under the Sec. 704 regulations, the allocation has economic effect if it meets all three of the following conditions:

- It results in the appropriate increase or decrease in the partner's capital account.
- The proceeds of any liquidation, occurring at any time in the partnership's life cycle, are in accordance with the capital accounts.
- Partners are required to make up negative balances in their capital accounts upon the liquidation of the partnership and these contributions are used to pay partnership debts or are allocated to partners having positive capital account balances.[50]

Key Point
For an allocation to have economic effect, the regulations require that:
1. the allocation be reflected in the partner's capital account,
2. liquidation proceeds be distributed in accordance with the capital account, and
3. a partner be liable to the other partners for deficits in his capital account.

Example 9-26 ■ Arnie and Bonnie each contribute $100,000 to form the AB Partnership on January 1, 1991. These contributions plus a $1,800,000 mortgage are used to purchase a $2,000,000 office building. To simplify the calculations, assume the building is depreciated using the straight-line method over a 40-year life and that in each year income and expenses are equal before considering depreciation. AB makes a special allocation of depreciation to Arnie. The allocation reduces Arnie's capital account, and any liquidating distributions are made in accordance with the capital account balances.

	Capital Account Balance	
	Arnie	Bonnie
January 1, 1991 balance	$100,000	$100,000
1991 loss	(50,000)	—0—
1992 loss	(50,000)	—0—
1993 loss	(50,000)	—0—
December 31, 1993 balance	($50,000)	$100,000

If we assume that the property has declined in value in an amount equal to the depreciation claimed and that the partnership is now liquidated, the need for the requirement to restore negative capital account balances becomes apparent.

---

[50] Reg. Sec. 1.704-1(b)(2)(ii). The Regulations provide other alternatives for meeting this portion of the requirements, but those alternatives are beyond the scope of this text.

Sales price of property		$ 1,850,000
Minus: Mortgage principal		(1,800,000)
Partnership cash to be distributed to partners		$ 50,000

If Arnie does not have to restore his negative capital account balance, there is only $50,000 in cash that Bonnie can receive, even though her capital account balance is $100,000. In effect, Bonnie has borne the economic burden of the 1993 depreciation. Without the requirement to restore the negative capital account balance, the special allocation to Arnie will be ignored for 1993 and Bonnie will receive the depreciation deduction. If Arnie must restore any negative capital account balance, he will contribute $50,000 when the partnership liquidates at the end of 1993, and Bonnie will receive her full $100,000 capital account balance. The 1993 special allocation to Arnie would then have economic effect. ■

The second requirement for a special allocation to be accepted under the Regulations is that the economic effect must be substantial, which requires that there is a reasonable possibility that the allocation will substantially affect the dollar amounts to be received by the partners independent of tax consequences.[51] It should be noted that it is highly unlikely that a special allocation of a tax credit can pass this test.

BASIS FOR PARTNERSHIP INTEREST

OBJECTIVE 7
Calculate a partner's basis in a partnership interest

The calculation of a partner's basis in a partnership interest depends upon the method used to acquire the interest with different valuation techniques for a purchased interest, a gifted interest, and an inherited interest. The results of the partnership's operations and liabilities both cause adjustments to the beginning value. Additional contributions to the partnership and distributions from the partnership further alter the partner's basis.[52]

Beginning Basis

Self-Study Question
What are some of the more common methods of acquiring a partnership interest, and what is the beginning basis (ignoring liabilities)?

Answer
1. Purchase—cost basis
2. Inherit—FMV
3. Gift—usually donor's basis with a possible gift tax adjustment

A partner's beginning basis for a partnership interest received for a contribution of property or services has been discussed. It is possible to acquire a partnership interest by methods other than contributing property or services to the partnership. If the partnership interest is purchased from an existing partner, the new partner's basis (before adjustments for partnership liabilities) is simply the price paid for the partnership interest. If the partnership interest is inherited, the heir's basis (before adjustments for partnership liabilities) is the FMV of the partnership interest on the decedent's date of death or, if elected by the executor, the alternate valuation date. If a partnership interest is received as a gift, the donee's basis generally equals the donor's basis (including the donor's ratable share of partnership liabilities) plus the portion of any gift tax paid by the donor that relates to appreciation attaching to the gift

---

[51] Reg. Sec. 1.704-1(b)(2)(iii)(a). It should be noted that the substantial economic effect regulations go far beyond the rules covered in this text.

[52] An alternative basis calculation is provided in Sec. 705(b) which can be used when it is not possible to know the partnership's complete history of earnings, contributions, and distributions. This basis calculation is beyond the scope of this text.

property. In summary, the beginning basis for a partnership interest is calculated following the usual rules for the method of acquisition. This basis amount must then be adjusted for the effects of partnership liabilities.

Effects of Liabilities

The effect of partnership liabilities on the basis of a partnership interest was briefly discussed in connection with the contribution of property subject to a liability. However, a more complete explanation is necessary to fully understand the pervasive impact of liabilities on the system of partnership taxation.

Increases and Decreases in Liabilities. Two changes in a partner's liabilities are considered contributions of cash by the partner to the partnership. The first is an increase in the partner's share of partnership liabilities. This increase can arise from either an increase in the partner's profit or loss interests or from an increase in total partnership liabilities. Accordingly, if a partnership incurs a large debt, the partners' bases in their partnership interests increase. The second way to increase a partner's basis is to have the partner assume partnership liabilities in an individual capacity.[53]

There are also two liability changes that are treated for all purposes as a distribution of cash from the partnership to the partner. These changes are (1) a decrease in a partner's share of partnership liabilities, and (2) a decrease in the partner's individual liabilities caused by the partnership's assumption of a liability of the partner.[54] Frequently both an increase and a decrease result from a single transaction. The impact of these increases and decreases can be illustrated by the following example.

Example 9-27 ■ John, a 40% partner in the ABC Partnership, has a $30,000 basis in his partnership interest before receiving a partnership distribution. He receives land having a $15,000 basis and a $20,000 FMV. John assumes a $10,000 mortgage on the land. The basis for John's partnership interest must first be decreased by the $15,000 basis for the land distributed and by the $4,000 decline in John's share of partnership liabilities resulting from the partnership no longer owing the $10,000 mortgage. His basis in the partnership interest is also increased by $10,000, which is the partnership liability that he assumes in his individual capacity. His ending basis for the partnership interest is $21,000 ($30,000 − $15,000 − $4,000 + $10,000). ■

Additional Comment

The fact that a partner gets basis for his share of recourse debt is not controversial. The fact that a partner gets basis for debt on which the partner is not personally liable seems questionable. Yet, other rules do limit the benefit of the basis created by the nonrecourse debt.

A Partner's Share of Liabilities. Once the general impact of liabilities as increases and decreases in a partner's basis for his partnership interest is understood, the specific amount of the partner's share of the partnership's liabilities must be determined. In all examples until now we have considered only general partners who have the same interest in profits and losses. It is common to have one or more limited partners in a partnership, and it is not unusual for partners to have differing profit and loss ratios. The Regulations provide guidelines for allocating partnership liabilities to the individual partners.

RECOURSE AND NONRECOURSE LOANS. Before the allocation rules can be explained, it is necessary to define recourse and nonrecourse loans. A **recourse loan** is the usual kind of loan for which the borrower remains liable until the loan is paid. If the recourse loan is secured and payments are not made as scheduled, the lender can

---

[53] Sec. 752(a).
[54] Sec. 752(b).

be repaid by selling the security. If the sales proceeds are insufficient to repay a recourse loan, the borrower must make up the difference. Under recently issued temporary regulations, a recourse loan is one for which any partner or a related party will stand an economic loss if the partnership cannot pay the debt.[55] A **nonrecourse loan** is one in which the lender may sell the security if the loan is not paid, but no partner is liable for any deficiency. The lender has no recourse against the borrower for additional amounts. Nonrecourse debts most commonly occur in connection with the financing of real property that is expected to substantially increase in value over the life of the loan.

A nonrecourse loan is paid out of partnership profits and is allocated among the partners according to their profits interests. However, under the temporary regulations, recourse loans are allocated among the partners according to the amount of economic loss the partner could potentially bear.[56]

GENERAL AND LIMITED PARTNERS. Still further, it is necessary to consider the impact of the general and limited partner designations. A limited partner is not normally liable to pay partnership debts beyond (1) the original contribution (which is already reflected in basis) and (2) any additional amount the partner pledged to contribute. Therefore, recourse debt is added to a limited partner's basis to the extent the partner has a risk of economic loss. For liabilities that are paid only if the partnership is profitable (nonrecourse debt), the limited partners' earnings can be expected to be used to pay the debt. Therefore, these nonrecourse debts can be used to increase a limited partner's basis based on the profit ratio.

Logically, a general partner's share of nonrecourse liabilities is determined by his profit ratio. Because limited partners seldom receive an allocated share of the recourse liabilities, the general partners share all recourse liabilities beyond any amounts that the limited partners can claim according to their economic loss potential. Table 9-1 summarizes the allocations.

> **Typical Misconception**
> Nonrecourse debt is allocated among **all** partners according to their profit ratios. Recourse debt is allocated first to the limited partner(s) to the extent of any additional amounts those partners pledged to contribute. The remaining recourse debt is allocated among the general partners according to their loss ratios.

Example 9-28 ■

The ABC Partnership has two general partners (Anna and Bob) and a limited partner (Clay) with the following partnership interests:

	Anna (General)	Bob (General)	Clay (Limited)
Loss interest	35%	45%	20%
Profits interest	30%	30%	40%
Basis before liabilities	$100,000	$100,000	$100,000

Clay has an obligation to make an additional contribution of $5,000. He has made no other agreements or guarantees. The partnership has two liabilities at year-end: a $300,000 nonrecourse debt and a $400,000 debt with recourse to the partnership. The partners' year-end bases are calculated as follows:

TABLE 9-1 *Allocation of Partnership Liabilities*

Type of Partner	Recourse	Nonrecourse
Limited partners	Economic loss potential	Profits interest
General partners	Economic loss potential	Profits interest

---

[55] Reg. Sec. 1.752-1(e).

[56] This may be modified by the limited partner agreeing to assume some of the risk of economic loss despite his limited partner status. For example, a limited partner may guarantee the debt or may agree to reimburse the general partner some amount if the general partner has to pay the debt. These arrangements mean that the limited partner shares the risk of loss.

	Anna (General)	Bob (General)	Clay (Limited)
Year-end basis (before any liabilities)	$100,000	$100,000	$100,000
Share of recourse debt[a]	172,812	222,188	5,000
Share of nonrecourse debt	90,000	90,000	120,000
Year-end basis	$362,812	$412,188	$225,000

[a] $395,000 ($400,000 − $5,000 share for Clay) of the debt with recourse is shared by Anna and Bob.

$$\text{Anna: } \$395,000 \times \frac{35}{35 + 45} = \$172,812$$

$$\text{Bob: } \$395,000 \times \frac{45}{35 + 45} = \$222,188$$

Effects of Operations

Key Point

Basis in a partnership interest is increased by the partner's share of partnership income. This increase in basis is necessary so that when the previously taxed earnings are distributed, the partner is not taxed a second time.

A partner's basis is a summary of his contributions and the partnership's liabilities, earnings, losses, and distributions.[57] In many ways, basis serves as a history of the partner's holding period for his partnership interest. Basis serves the major role of preventing a second tax levy on income that was taxed as a partner's distributive share when that income is subsequently distributed. Section 705 mandates a basis increase for additional contributions made by the partner to the partnership plus the partner's distributive share for the current and prior tax years of the following items:

- Taxable income of the partnership (both separately stated items and partnership ordinary income)
- Tax-exempt income of the partnership

Basis is decreased (but not below zero) by distributions from the partnership to the partner plus the partner's distributive share for the current and prior tax years of the following items:

Self-Study Question

Why does a partner increase his basis in his partnership interest by his distributive share of tax-exempt income?

Answer

A partner's basis in his partnership interest must be increased for tax-exempt income to avoid the possibility of making such income taxable! For example, if a partner's basis were not increased, when the partner disposes of the partnership interest (which has now increased in FMV due to the receipt of the tax-exempt income), the gain on the sale would be inadvertently increased by the amount of the tax-exempt income.

- Losses of the partnership (both separately stated items and partnership ordinary loss)
- Expenditures that are not deductible for tax purposes and that are not capital expenditures

The positive basis adjustment for tax-exempt income and the negative basis adjustment for nondeductible expenses are made in order to preserve that tax treatment for the partner. If these adjustments are not made, tax-exempt income is taxable to the partner when a subsequent distribution is made or upon the sale or other disposition of the partnership interest. Likewise, the partner is in the position to deduct the nondeductible expense as a capital loss when the partnership interest is liquidated.

Example 9-29 ■ Steve and Mike each contribute $10,000 to create an equal partnership on January 1, 1991, and the partnership purchases a $20,000 State of Delaware bond. During 1991 the partnership has no income or losses except for $2,000 in tax-exempt

---

[57] Certain items related to depletion affect a partner's basis but are beyond the scope of this text.

interest income. Each partner is allocated $1,000 of the income, and no taxes are due from the partners. The partnership sells the bond in 1992 for $20,000, and no gain or loss is realized or recognized on the sale. The partnership then distributes the $22,000 cash equally to Mike and Steve. If the tax-exempt income did not increase the basis of their interests, each partner would recognize a $1,000 gain on the distribution, since the $11,000 cash distribution would exceed their $10,000 basis. In effect the tax-exempt income would be taxed as a capital gain when distributed. The basis increase for the tax-exempt income makes each partner's basis $11,000, so that no gain is recognized on the distribution. ∎

OBJECTIVE 8
Determine the limitations on a partner's deduction of partnership losses

Loss Limits. Each partner is allocated his distributive share of ordinary income or loss and separately stated income, gain, loss, or deduction items each year. The income and gain items are always reported in the partner's current tax year and increase the partner's basis in the partnership interest. However, the partner may not be able to use his full distributive share of losses, because Sec. 704(d) only allows losses to be deducted up to the amount of the partner's basis in the partnership interest prior to the loss. All positive basis adjustments for the year are made prior to determining the amount of the deductible loss.[58]

Example 9-30 ∎

Key Point
Prior to determining how much basis exists for purposes of limiting losses, all income/gain items are added to basis, and all distributions are deducted from basis.

On December 31, 1991, Matt has a $31,000 basis for his general interest in the MT Partnership before making adjustments for 1991 profits and losses. He materially participates in the partnership's business. His distributive share of MT's current items are a $4,000 net long-term capital gain and a $43,000 ordinary loss. Matt can deduct $35,000 ($31,000 beginning basis + $4,000 net long-term capital gain) of the ordinary loss. The remaining $8,000 of loss cannot be deducted in 1991. ∎

Any distributive share of loss that cannot be deducted because of the basis limit is simply noted in the partner's financial records. It is not reported on the partner's tax return, nor does it reduce the partner's basis. However, the losses can be carried forward until the partner has positive basis again from capital contributions, additional partnership borrowings, or partnership earnings.[59]

Example 9-31 ∎

Self-Study Question
What happens to losses that are disallowed due to lack of basis in a partnership interest?
Answer
The losses are indefinitely suspended until that partner obtains additional basis.

Assume the same facts as in Example 9-30. Matt makes no additional contributions in 1992, and the MT Partnership's liabilities are unchanged. Matt's distributive share of MT's 1992 partnership items is $2,500 of net short-term capital gain and $14,000 of ordinary income. These items restore his basis to $16,500 (0 + $2,500 + $14,000), and he can deduct the $8,000 loss carryover from 1991. At the beginning of 1993, Matt's basis is $8,500 ($16,500 − $8,000). ∎

Topic Review 9-3 summarizes the rules for determining the initial basis for a partnership interest and the annual basis adjustments required to determine the interest's adjusted basis.

LOSS LIMITATIONS

Three sets of rules limit the loss from a partnership interest that a taxpayer may deduct. The Sec. 704(d) rules explained earlier in this chapter limit losses to the partner's basis in the partnership interest. Two other rules establish more stringent

[58] Reg. Sec. 1.704-1(d)(2).
[59] Reg. Sec. 1.704-1(d)(1).

TOPIC REVIEW 9-3

Basis of a Partnership Interest

How Acquired	Beginning Basis
Property contributed	Carryover basis from property contributed plus gain recognized for contributions to an investment partnership
Services contributed	Amount of income recognized for services rendered
Gift	Donor's basis plus gift tax paid on appreciation
Inheritance	Fair market value at date of death or alternate valuation date

Liability Impact	
Increase basis for	Increases in the partner's share of partnership liabilities
	Liabilities of the partnership assumed by the partner in his individual capacity
Decrease basis for	Decreases in the partner's share of partnership liabilities
	Liabilities of the partner assumed by the partnership

Operations Impact	
Increase basis for	Partner's share of separately stated income and gain items (including tax-exempt items) and ordinary income
	Additional contributions of property to the partnership[a]
Decrease basis for	Partner's share of separately stated loss and deduction items (including items which are not deductible for tax purposes and that are not capital expenditures) and ordinary loss
	Distributions from the partnership to the partner[a]

[a] Increases and decreases in the partner's share of partnership liabilities are treated as contributions to and distributions from the partnership. However, since these changes have affected basis already when you adjusted the basis of the partnership interest for the impact of liabilities, do not again adjust the basis for the liability changes.

Typical Misconception

Before a loss can be deducted by a partner, the partner must be able to satisfy three different limitation provisions. In order of application, these limitations are (a) adequate partnership basis under Sec. 704(d), (b) the at-risk loss limitations, and finally (c) the passive activity limitations.

limits. The at-risk rules limit losses to an amount called *at-risk basis*. The passive activity loss or credit limitation rules disallow virtually all net passive activity losses.

At-Risk Loss Limitation

The Sec. 704(d) loss limitation rules were the only loss limits for many years. Congress, however, became increasingly uncomfortable with allowing partners to increase their basis by a portion of the partnership's nonrecourse liabilities and then offset this basis with partnership losses. Accordingly, Congress established the **at-risk rules,** which limit loss deductions to the partner's at-risk basis. The **at-risk basis** is essentially the same amount as the regular partnership basis with the exception that liabilities increase the at-risk basis only if the partner is at risk for such an amount.

While much of the complexity of the "at-risk" term is beyond the scope of this text, a simplified working definition is possible: A partner is at risk for an amount if he would lose that amount should the partnership suddenly become worthless. Since a partner would not have to pay a partnership's nonrecourse liabilities even if the partnership became worthless, the usual nonrecourse liabilities cannot be included in any partner's at-risk basis. Under the at-risk rules, the loss that a partner may deduct may be substantially less than the amount that was deductible when only the Sec. 704(d) rules applied.[60]

Example 9-32 ■ Joan is a limited partner in the JM Manufacturing Partnership. At the end of the partnership's tax year, her basis in the limited interest is $30,000 ($10,000 investment plus a $20,000 share of nonrecourse financing). Joan's distributive share of partnership losses for the tax year is $18,000. The at-risk rules limit her deduction to $10,000 because she is not at risk for the nonrecourse financing. ■

Typical Misconception

The at-risk rules severally limit the use of nonrecourse debt to obtain loss deductions except for certain qualified real estate financing. Yet, this loophole is more apparent than real because of the final set of rules that must be satisfied: the passive activity limitations.

There is one significant exception to the application of the at-risk rules. At-risk rules do not apply to qualified nonrecourse real estate financing. The partner is at risk for his share of nonrecourse real estate financing if all of the following requirements are met:

- The financing is secured by real estate used in the partnership's real estate activity.
- The financing is from a qualified person, is from any federal, state, or local government agency, or is guaranteed by any federal, state, or local government.
- A qualified person is an unrelated party who is in the trade or business of lending money (e.g., bank, financial institution, mortgage broker).
- A qualified person may be related to the partnership if the terms of the debt are commercially reasonable and substantially the same terms as loans made during the same time period between unrelated parties.
- The debt is not convertible to any kind of equity interest in the partnership.[61]

At-Risk Rules and Current Distributions

When a partner receives a current distribution from a partnership, the Sec. 705 basis is reduced. Normally, unless the money distributed exceeds the Sec. 705 basis, no gain is recognized on the distribution. However, a partner who is subject to the at-risk rules may simultaneously have a zero at-risk basis and a positive Sec. 705 basis. If a cash distribution is made when either the at-risk basis is zero or the cash distribution exceeds the at-risk basis, the partner must recognize income. To the extent that income must be recognized under this provision, the partner is allowed to carry the at-risk loss forward to a subsequent tax year.[62]

---

[60] Sec. 465(a).
[61] Sec. 465(b)(6).
[62] Sec. 465(e).

Example 9-33 ■ The LMN Partnership is engaged in manufacturing. Lisa, a general partner who materially participates in the business, has a $36,000 distributive share of ordinary losses for 1991. At the end of 1991, her Sec. 705 basis is $45,000, and her at-risk basis is $20,000. Her loss deduction is limited to $20,000 by her at-risk basis.

	Sec. 705 Basis	*At-Risk Basis*
Basis including liabilities	$45,000	$20,000
Minus: Loss	(36,000)	(20,000)
Ending basis	$ 9,000	$—0—

Lisa has a $16,000 ($36,000 − $20,000) loss carryforward. If she receives a $5,000 cash distribution in early 1992, $5,000 in income must be recognized because her at-risk basis is zero at the time of the distribution. After recognizing the $5,000 of income, Lisa is allowed to increase her loss carryover by $5,000 ($5,000 + $16,000 = $21,000) and treat it as if that much loss was never deducted. ■

Passive Activity Limitations

Key Point
Sec. 469 and its accompanying regulations are extremely complex. Their biggest impact in the partnership area is probably that limited partners generally fail the material participation test and, hence, their partnership losses are considered to be passive activity losses. Therefore, even if the partner has both Sec. 704(d) and at-risk basis, losses that are generated from passive activities may be utilized only to offset other passive income or gains.

The 1986 Tax Reform Act added still a third set of limits to the loss that a partner may deduct—the passive activity loss and credit limitations.

Under the passive activity limitation rules of Sec. 469, all income is divided into (1) amounts derived from passive activities; (2) active income such as salary, bonuses, and income from businesses in which the taxpayer materially participates; and (3) portfolio income such as dividends and interest. Generally, losses of an individual partner from a passive activity cannot be used to offset either active income or portfolio income. They can, however, be carried over to future years. These passive losses are allowed in full when a taxpayer disposes of the entire interest in the passive activity. However, passive losses generated by a rental activity in which an individual partner is an active participant may be deducted up to a maximum of $25,000 in a year. This deduction is phased out by 50% of the amount of the partner's adjusted gross income (AGI) in excess of $100,000, so that there is no deduction if the partner has AGI of $150,000 or more. (The phase-out begins at $200,000 for low-income housing or rehabilitation credits.) Losses disallowed under the phase-out become passive losses and are deductible to the extent of passive income or the amount allowable under the phase-in of the passive activity limitation.

Key Point
The $60,000 1991 loss in Example 9-34, which was disallowed because of the passive activity limitations, can be used in a subsequent year if passive income is generated. Since the $60,000 loss has already reduced basis for purposes of both Sec. 704(d) and the "at-risk" rules, the disallowed loss need not be tested against those rules a second time.

Most credits generated by a passive activity can only be used to offset tax due on income generated by a passive activity. However, credits generated by a rental activity in which an individual partner is an active participant may be claimed up to a deduction equivalent of $25,000 per year. Like the passive loss deductions allowed for rental activities, the rental activity credits are phased out as the partner's AGI exceeds $100,000 ($200,000 for low-income housing or rehabilitation credits). Note that a single $25,000 amount applies on an aggregate basis to credits and deductions from rental activities for a tax year. Unused credits generated by a passive activity can be carried forward but cannot be used when the taxpayer disposes of his or her entire interest in the passive activity. (See Chapter 8 of *Prentice Hall's Federal Taxation: Individuals* for a full discussion of the passive loss limitation rules.)

There are two types of passive activities: (1) any trade or business in which the taxpayer does not materially participate and (2) any rental activity. A taxpayer who owns a limited partnership interest in any activity generally fails the material participation test.[63] Accordingly, losses from most limited partnerships can only be used to offset income from other passive activities. These passive loss rules are applicable for all passive investments made after October 22, 1986, the enactment date of the 1986 Tax Act.

While passive activity limits may greatly affect the taxable income or loss reported by a partner, they have no unusual effect on basis. Basis is reduced (but not below zero) by the partner's distributive share of losses whether or not the losses may be deducted under the passive loss rules.[64] When the suspended passive losses later become deductible, the partner's basis in the partnership interest is not affected.

Example 9-34 ■ Chris purchases a 20% capital and profits interest in the CJ Partnership in 1991, but he does not participate in CJ's business. Chris owns no other passive investments. Chris's distributive share of the CJ Partnership's loss for 1991 is $60,000. His Sec. 704(d) basis in CJ is $80,000, and his at-risk basis is $70,000. Chris cannot deduct any of the CJ loss in 1991 because it is a passive activity loss. ■

TRANSACTIONS BETWEEN A PARTNER AND THE PARTNERSHIP

The partner and the partnership are treated as separate entities for many transactions. Section 707(b) restricts the use of sales of property between the partner and partnership by disallowing certain losses and converting certain capital gains into ordinary income. Section 707(c) permits a partnership to make guaranteed payments for capital and services to a partner that are separate from the partner's distributive share. Each of these rules is explored below.

Sales of Property

Key Point
Losses on sales between partners and certain related partnerships are disallowed similarly to the realted party rules of Sec. 267. The concern is that tax losses can be artificially recognized without the property being disposed of outside the economic group.

Loss Sales. Without restrictions to prevent it, a controlling partner could sell property to the partnership to recognize a loss for tax purposes while retaining a substantial interest in the property through the ownership of a partnership interest. This kind of transaction could provide significant opportunities to reduce the partner's tax bill. Congress closed the door to such loss recognition with the Sec. 707(b) rules.

The rules for partnership loss transactions are quite similar to the Sec. 267–related party rules discussed in Chapter 8 of *Prentice Hall's Federal Taxation: Individuals*. Under Sec. 707(b)(1), no loss can be deducted on the sale or exchange of property between a partnership and a person who directly or indirectly owns more than 50% of the partnership's capital or profits interests.[65] Similarly, losses are disallowed on sales or exchanges of property between two partnerships in which the same persons own, directly or indirectly, more than 50% of the capital or profits interests. If a loss is disallowed under Sec. 707(b)(1), any subsequent gain realized on a sale of the property by the purchaser can be reduced by the previously disallowed loss.

Key Point
One of the complicating factors of the loss disallowance rules is the application of the attribution rules of Sec. 267 in determining what percentage a partner is deemed to own in a partnership.

---

[63] Sec. 469(h)(2).
[64] S. Rept. No. 99-313, 99th Cong., 2d Sess., p. 723, footnote 4 (1986).
[65] For purposes of Sec. 267, related parties include among others, members of the taxpayer's family (spouse, brothers, sisters, lineal descendants, and ancestors), an individual and a more than 50%-owned corporation, and two corporations that are members of the same controlled group.

Example 9-35 ▪ Pat sold land having a $45,000 basis to the PTA Partnership for $35,000, its FMV. If Pat has a 60% capital and profits interest in the partnership, a $10,000 loss on the sale is realized, but not recognized by Pat. If Pat owns only a 49% interest, directly and indirectly, the loss can be recognized. ▪

Example 9-36 ▪ Assume the same facts as in Example 9-35, except that the land is later sold by the partnership for $47,000. The partnership's realized gain is $12,000 ($47,000 − $35,000 basis). If Pat has a 60% capital and profits interest, his previously disallowed loss of $10,000 reduces the partnership's recognized gain to $2,000. This $2,000 gain is then allocated to the partners according to the partnership agreement. Note that Pat receives only part of the benefit of his previously disallowed loss since the partnership's recognized gain is reduced for all partners and not only the selling partner. ▪

Key Point
If a gain is recognized on the sale of a capital asset between a partnership and a 50% or more partner (or between two commonly controlled partnerships), and the property is depreciable to the transferee, then the character of the gain is ordinary. The purpose of this provision is to stop taxpayers from merely selling depreciable assets inside the economic group and obtaining a step-up in basis.

Gain Sales. Section 707(b)(2) may modify the normal result of a sale between a partnership and a person who owns a controlling interest when a gain is recognized. This provision prevents the selling party from recognizing a capital gain (and requires ordinary income recognition) on a sale that is followed by the purchasing party claiming a deduction (e.g., depreciation) based on the property's increased basis.

Section 707(b)(2) applies only when the property that is sold or exchanged at a profit is not a capital asset in the transferee's hands. Sales or exchanges resulting in the application of Sec. 707(b)(2) include transfers between (1) a partnership and a person who owns, directly or indirectly, more than 50% of the partnership's capital or profits interests, or (2) two partnerships in which the same persons own, directly or indirectly, more than 50% of the capital or profits interests.[66]

Example 9-37 ▪ Sharon and Tony have the following capital and profits interests in two partnerships:

	ST Partnership (%)	QRS Partnership (%)
Sharon	42	58
Tony	42	30
Other unrelated partners	16	12
Total	100	100

The ST Partnership sells land having a $150,000 basis to the QRS Partnership for $180,000. The land was a capital asset for the ST Partnership, but QRS intends to subdivide and sell the land. Because the land is ordinary income property to the QRS Partnership and Sharon and Tony control both partnerships, the ST Partnership must recognize $30,000 of ordinary income on the land sale. ▪

Guaranteed Payments

OBJECTIVE 9
Determine the tax consequences of a guaranteed payment to a partner

A corporate shareholder can be an employee of the corporation. The shareholder-employee receives a salary and, with some restrictions, employee fringe benefits. However, a partner generally is not an employee of the partnership, and most fringe benefits are disallowed for a partner who is employed by his partnership.

It is only reasonable that a partner who provides services to the partnership in an ongoing relationship might be compensated much like any other employee. Code Sec. 707(c) provides for just this kind of payment and labels it a **guaranteed payment.**

---

[66] Sec. 707(b)(2).

Typical Misconception

If a partner, acting in his capacity as a partner, receives payments from the partnership that are determined without regard to the partnership's income, the partner is treated as having received a guaranteed payment. A partner can also deal with his partnership in a nonpartner capacity. If the partner is acting as a nonpartner, the partner is treated as any other outside contractor.

The term *guaranteed payment* also includes certain payments made to a partner for the use of invested capital that are similar to interest. Both types of guaranteed payments must be payments that are determined without regard to the partnership's income.[67] Conceptually, this requirement separates guaranteed payments from distributive shares. As indicated below, however, such a distinction may not be so clear in practice.

Determining the Guaranteed Payment. Sometimes the determination of the guaranteed payment is quite simple. For example, some guaranteed payments are expressed as specific amounts (e.g., $20,000 per year) with the partner also receiving his normal distributive share. Other times the guaranteed payment is expressed as a **guaranteed minimum.** However, these guaranteed minimum arrangements make it difficult to distinguish the partner's distributive share and guaranteed payment amounts, since there is no guaranteed payment under this arrangement unless the partner's distributive share is less than his guaranteed minimum.

Example 9-38 ■ Tina manages the real estate owned by the TAV Partnership in which she is also a partner. She receives 30% of all partnership income before guaranteed payments, but no less than $60,000 per year. In 1991 the TAV Partnership reports $300,000 in ordinary income. Tina's 30% distributive share is $90,000 (0.30 × $300,000), which is greater than her $60,000 guaranteed minimum amount. Therefore, she has no guaranteed payment. ■

Example 9-39 ■ Asssume the same facts as in Example 9-38, except that the TAV Partnership reports $150,000 of ordinary income. Tina has a guaranteed payment of $15,000, which represents the difference between her $45,000 distributive share (0.30 × $150,000) and her $60,000 guaranteed minimum.[68] ■

Tax Impact of Guaranteed Payments. Like salary or interest income, guaranteed payments are always ordinary income to the recipient. The guaranteed payment must be included in income for the recipient partner's tax year during which the partnership year ends and the partnership deducts or capitalizes the payments.[69]

Example 9-40 ■ In January 1992, a calendar-year taxpayer, Will, receives a $10,000 guaranteed payment from the WRS Partnership. WRS capitalizes the payment during its tax year ending on November 30, 1991. Will must report his guaranteed payment in his 1991 tax return since that return includes the 1991 partnership income that reflects the impact of the guaranteed payment. ■

Key Point

The effect of a guaranteed payment is that the partner recognizes income and the partnership deducts or capitalizes the payments. A cash-basis partner recognizes the income in the partner's tax year during which the partnership tax year ends regardless of when the payment is received. Example 9-40 illustrates this point.

Note that this timing rule is not altered by the fact that the partnership may be required to deduct the payment instead of capitalizing it.[70]

For the partnership, the guaranteed payment is treated as if it is made to an outsider. If the payment is for a service that is a capital expenditure (e.g., architectural services for designing a building for the partnership), the guaranteed payment must be capitalized and, if allowable, amortized. If the payment is for a service that is deductible under Sec. 162, the payment can be deducted from ordinary income.[71] Deductible guaranteed payments can offset the partnership's ordinary income but never its capital gains. If the guaranteed payment exceeds the partner-

---

[67] Sec. 707(c).
[68] Reg. Sec. 1.707-1(c), Exs. (1) and (2).
[69] Reg. Secs. 1.707-1(c) and 1.706-1(a).
[70] Rev. Rul. 80-234, 1980-2 C.B. 203.
[71] Sec. 707(c).

ship's ordinary income, the payment creates an ordinary loss that is allocated among the partners.[72]

Example 9-41 ▪ Tim is a partner in the STU Partnership. He is to receive a guaranteed payment for deductible services of $60,000 and 30% of partnership income computed after deducting the guaranteed payment. The partnership reports $40,000 of ordinary income and a $120,000 net long-term capital gain before deducting the guaranteed payment. Tim's income from the partnership is determined as follows:

	STU Partnership	Tim's Share Ratable Share	Tim's Share Amount
Ordinary income (before guaranteed payment)	$ 40,000		
Minus: Guaranteed payment	(60,000)	100%	$60,000
Ordinary loss	($20,000)	30%	(6,000)
Long-term capital gain	$120,000	30%	36,000

▪

Calculation of the distributive share for a partner who receives a guaranteed payment can be a great deal more complex than this example illustrates. Many guaranteed minimums and other such complex arrangements are beyond the scope of this book.

FAMILY PARTNERSHIPS

Capital Ownership

OBJECTIVE 10
Explain the requirements for the holder of a partnership interest to be recognized as a partner in a family partnership

Since each partner reports and pays taxes on a distributive share of partnership income, a family partnership is an excellent way to spread income among family members and minimize the family's tax bill. However, in order to accomplish this tax minimization goal, the family members must be accepted by the IRS as "real" partners. The question of whether someone is a partner in a family partnership is often litigated, but there are safe-harbor rules that provide clear answers if a capital interest is owned in a family partnership. Under Sec. 704(a), three tests must be met: (1) the partnership interest must be a capital interest; (2) capital must be a material income-producing factor in the partnership's business activity; and (3) the family member must be the true owner of the interest.

The definition of a capital interest discussed earlier in this chapter is applicable here. To reiterate, a capital interest gives the partner the right to receive assets if the partnership liquidates immediately.

Key Point

In certain situations, family partnerships provide an excellent tax-planning tool, but the family members must be "real" partners. The rules that determine who is a real partner in a family partnership are guided by the assignment-of-income principle.

Capital is a material income-producing factor if substantial portions of gross income are derived from the use of capital. For example, capital is a material income-producing factor if the business has substantial inventory or significant investment in plant or equipment. Capital is seldom considered to be a material income-producing factor in a service business.[73]

---

[72] Reg. Sec. 1.707-1(c), Ex. (4).
[73] Reg. Sec. 1.704-1(e)(1)(iv).

The remaining question is whether the family member is in fact the true owner of the interest. Ownership is seldom questioned if one family member purchases the interest at a market price from another family member. However, when the interest is gifted from one family member to another, the major question is whether the donor retains so much control over the partnership interest that the donor is still the owner of the interest. If the donor still controls the interest, the donor is taxed on the distributive share.

> **Key Point**
> A major problem in creating a family partnership is that when the donor gifts the partnership interest to the donee family member, the donor is often not willing to give up complete control of the gifted partnership interest.

Donor Retained Control. There is no mechanical test that indicates whether the donor has retained too much control, but there are several factors that may indicate a problem:[74]

- Retention of control over distributions of income can be a problem unless the retention occurs with the agreement of all partners or if the retention is for the reasonable needs of the business.
- Retention of control over assets that are essential to the partnership's business can indicate too much control by the donor.
- Limitation of the donee partner's right to sell or liquidate his interest, unless the donee accepts substantially less than the FMV, may indicate that the donor has not relinquished full control over the interest.
- Retention of management control that is inconsistent with normal partnership arrangements can be another sign that the donor retains control. This situation is not considered a fatal problem unless it occurs in conjunction with a significant limit on the donee's ability to sell or liquidate his interest.

If the donor has not directly or indirectly retained too much control, the donee is a full partner. As a partner, the donee must report his distributive share of income. A donee can be recognized as a partner even if the donee does not participate in the affairs of the partnership and only collects income from it.

> **Typical Misconception**
> A valid family partnership is a useful method for splitting income between family members. However, the distributive share of income from a partnership interest to a partner under age 14 is subject to the "kiddie tax."

Minor Donees. When income splitting is the goal of a family, the appropriate donee for the partnership interest is frequently a minor. With the problem of donor-retained controls in mind, it becomes obvious that gifts to minors should be made with great attention to detail. Further, note that net unearned income of a child under age 14 is taxed to the child at the parents' marginal tax rate. (See Chapter 2 of *Prentice Hall's Federal Taxation: Individuals* text.) This provision removes much of the incentive to transfer family partnership interests to young children, but there are still significant tax advantages to gifting partnership interests to minors who are age 14 or older.

Donor-Donee Allocations of Income

> **OBJECTIVE 11**
> Determine the allocation of partnership income between a donor and a donee of a partnership interest

Partnership income must be properly allocated between a donor and a donee in order to be accepted by the IRS. Note that only the allocation between the donor and donee is questioned, and there is no impact on the distributive shares of any other partners.

There are two requirements for the donor-donee allocations. First, the donor must be allocated reasonable compensation for services rendered to the partnership. Then, after reasonable compensation is allocated to the donor, any remaining partnership income must be allocated based on relative capital interests.[75] Note that this allocation scheme apparently overrides the partnership's general ability to make special allocations of income.

---

[74] Reg. Sec. 1.704-1(e)(2)(ii).
[75] Sec. 704(e)(2).

Example 9-42 ■ Andrew, a 40% partner in the ABC Partnership, gives one-half of his interest to his brother, John. During 1991 Andrew performs services for the partnership for which reasonable compensation is $65,000, but for which he accepts no pay. Andrew and John are each credited with a $100,000 distributive share, all of which is ordinary income. Reallocation between Andrew and John is necessary to reflect the value of Andrew's services.

Total distributive shares for the brothers	$200,000
Minus: Reasonable compensation for Andrew	(65,000)
Income to allocate	$135,000

John's distributive share: $\dfrac{20\%}{40\%} \times \$135{,}000 = \$67{,}500$

Andrew's distributive share: $\left(\dfrac{20\%}{40\%} \times \$135{,}000\right) + \$65{,}000 = \$132{,}500$ ■

CONTROVERSIAL ISSUES

Retroactive Allocation of Losses

Additional Comment

The use of "tiered partnerships" to effect a retroactive allocation of losses has been curtailed by Sec. 706(d). Nevertheless, a partner who buys into a partnership late in the year may be able to accomplish a similar result by using a special allocation of the partnership loss. Theoretically, if the allocation has "substantial economic effect," the allocation should be allowed.

Prior to 1976, partnerships with large losses could admit a new partner near the end of the partnership's tax year and allocate a substantial portion of the entire year's losses to that new partner. The Sec. 706(c)(2)(B) rule, which requires that a partnership must allocate losses and income based on the partner's varying interest during the year (discussed on page 9-23), seemed to close this loophole.

Soon, however, creative taxpayers decided to use a cash method of accounting partnership which could incur expenses during most of the tax year while deferring their payment as late in the year as feasible. A new partner was admitted near the end of the tax year, and the unpaid items were then paid and expensed. The Tax Court's decision in the *Cecil R. Richardson* case established the precedent that allowed this technique to be used and essentially permitted a retroactive allocation of losses.[76]

The Tax Reform Act of 1984 closed off much of this technique by adding Sec. 706(d), which requires that a partnership using the cash method of accounting accrue four types of expenses (interest, taxes, payments for services or for the use of property, and any other appropriate item specified by the Regulations) for purposes of determining distributive shares.

While this avenue for achieving a retroactive allocation appears closed, a later case provides a new technique. In the Tax Court's decision in the *Mary K. S. Ogden* case, a partner who was admitted late in the tax year received a one-time special allocation of the partnership's loss that accrued during the partnership's third quarter, which was after her admission but before the end of the partnership's tax year.[77] The Tax Court accepted the special allocation as meeting the tests for substantial economic effect. In fact, for this partner, receiving a special allocation of the postadmission loss gave her almost the same amount of loss that a retroactive allocation of her usual share of loss for the entire tax year would have provided. However, on appeal, the Fifth Circuit Court of Appeals ruled that the allocation lacked substantial economic effect because by agreement partners with deficit accounts did not have to restore the deficit nor

---

[76] 76 T.C. 512, *aff'd.*, 51 AFTR 2d 83-418, 83-1 USTC ¶ 9109 (5th Cir., 1982).
[77] 84 T.C. 871 (1985).

receive smaller distributions on termination of the partnership.[78] Nevertheless, the technique may still be valid if partnership agreements are drawn so that the requirements for special allocations are met. Use of a special allocation to obtain the same effect as a retroactive allocation is still a very controversial technique.

TAX PLANNING CONSIDERATIONS

Alternatives to Contributing Property

Because the contribution of property in exchange for a partnership interest is not a taxable transaction, it may not be a desirable alternative. The new partner may want to recognize a loss on the transfer of the property, or the partnership may desire to claim a higher basis for appreciated property. When a reason arises to avoid the nontaxable contribution, several alternatives do exist.

1. The new partner can sell the property to an outsider and buy a partnership interest with cash. This is the simplest alternative if loss recognition is desired. It is an excellent choice unless the partnership needs the specific property held by the new partner.

2. When the partnership needs the specific property, the new partner can sell the property to the partnership as if they were unrelated parties. If a sale occurs, the partner can recognize a loss unless he owns more than a 50% capital or profits interest in the partnership. Alternatively, the partner may recognize a capital gain on the sale of investment or Sec. 1231 property while the partnership obtains the advantage of a stepped-up basis for the property. However, the Sec. 1245 and Sec. 1250 depreciation recapture rules may convert some of the capital gain into ordinary income on the sale of depreciable property. One must also remember that a partner who owns more than a 50% capital or profits interest in the partnership is restricted to recognizing ordinary income on the sale when the property is not a capital asset in the partnership's hands.

3. The partner can lease the property to the partnership. As long as the transaction is structured in an arm's length manner, this lease is likely to be treated as if it involved the partnership and an unrelated party. In addition, the partner does not relinquish his ownership of the property.

Key Point

If a partner is unable to use all of his share of partnership losses due to lack of basis, contributions to capital or increasing partnership liabilities may provide the additional needed tax basis. If the passive activity limitation rules are the reason that the partnership losses cannot be used, then the possibility of investing in passive activities that generate passive income may be the best planning alternative.

Timing of Loss Recognition

The loss limitation rules provide a unique opportunity for tax planning. For example, if a partner knows that her distributive share of active losses from a partnership for a tax year will exceed the Sec. 704 limit for deducting losses, she should carefully examine the tax situation for the current and upcoming tax years. Substantial current personal income may make immediate use of the loss desirable. Current income may be taxed at a higher marginal tax rate than future income is likely to be taxed at because of, for example, an extraordinarily good current year, an expected retirement, or a decrease in future years' tax rates. If the partner chooses to use the loss in the current year, additional contributions can be made just before year-end (perhaps even from funds that the partner borrows, as long as the additional benefit exceeds the cost of the funds).

---

[78] 57 AFTR 2d 86-1333, 86-1 USTC ¶ 9368 (5th Cir., 1986).

Alternatively, one partner may convince the other partners to incur additional partnership liabilities so that each partner's basis increases. This last strategy should be exercised with caution unless there is a business reason (rather than solely a tax reason) for the borrowing.

Example 9-43 ▪ Ted, a 60% general partner in the ST Partnership, expects to be allocated partnership losses of $120,000 for 1991 from a partnership in which he materially participates, but his partnership basis is only $90,000. Because he has a marginal tax rate of 31% for 1991 (and anticipates only a 15% marginal tax rate for 1992), Ted wants to use the ST Partnership losses to offset his 1991 income. He could make a capital contribution to raise his basis by $30,000. Alternatively, he could get the partnership to incur $50,000 in additional liabilities, which would increase his basis by his $30,000 ($50,000 × 0.60) distributive share of the liability. The partnership's $50,000 borrowing must serve a business purpose for the ST Partnership. ▪

Alternatively, a partner may determine that it is better to delay the deduction of partnership losses that exceed the current year's loss limitation. This situation could occur if the partner has little current year income and expects substantial income in the following year. If the partner has loss, deduction, or credit carryovers that expire in the current year, a deferral of the distributive share of partnership losses to the following year may be desirable. If the partner opts to deduct the loss in a later year, she needs only to leave things alone so that her distributive share of losses exceeds her loss limitation for the current year.

COMPLIANCE AND PROCEDURAL CONSIDERATIONS

Reporting to the IRS and the Partners

OBJECTIVE 12
Determine the requirements for filing a partnership tax return

Historical Note
Turn to the partnership K-1 in Appendix B of this book. The staggering number of items that now have to be separately stated illustrates how certain tax laws, such as the passive activity limitation rules and the investment interest limitation rules, have complicated the preparation of Form 1065.

Forms. Within 3½ months after the end of the partnership tax year, the partnership must file a Form 1065 with the IRS. (See Appendix B for a completed Form 1065.) Since the partnership is only a conduit, Form 1065 is an information return and is not accompanied by any tax payment.[79] Included on Form 1065 are all the items of income, gain, loss and deduction that are not separately stated by the partners. Schedule K of Form 1065 reports both a summary of the ordinary income items as well as the partnership total of the items that are separately stated. Schedule K-1, which must be prepared for each partner in the partnership, reflects that partner's distributive share of partnership income including his special allocations. The partner's Schedule K-1 is notification of his share of partnership items for use in calculating income taxes and self-employment taxes.

Sec. 444 Election and Required Payments. A partnership can elect to use a tax year other than a required year by filing an election under Sec. 444. This election is made by filing Form 8716 [Election to Have a Tax Year Other Than a Required Tax Year] by the earlier of (1) the 15th day of the fifth month following the month that

---

[79] Reg. Sec. 301.6031-1(e)(2). While the partnership pays no income tax, it is still required to pay the employer's share of social security taxes and unemployment taxes as well as withhold income taxes from its employees' salaries.

includes the first day of the tax year for which the election is effective, or (2) the due date (without regard to extension) of the income tax return resulting from the Sec. 444 election. In addition, a copy of the Form 8716 must be attached to the partnership's Form 1065 for the first tax year for which the Sec. 444 election is made.

The Sec. 7519 required payment is due on or before May 15th of the calendar year following the calendar year in which the election year begins. The required payment is paid with Form 8752 [Required Payment or Refund Under Section 7519] along with a computational worksheet which is illustrated in the instructions to the Form 1065. Refunds of excess required payments are also obtained by filing the Form 8752.

Estimated Taxes. Because the partnership pays no income taxes, the partnership makes no estimated tax payments. However, the partners must make estimated tax payments based on their separate tax positions including their distributive share of partnership income or loss for the current year. It should be emphasized that the partners are not making separate estimated tax payments for their partnership income, but rather are including the effects of the partnership's results in the calculation of their normal estimated tax payments.

IRS Audit Procedures

Key Point
To alleviate the administrative nightmare of having to audit each partner of a partnership, Congress has authorized the IRS to conduct audits of partnerships in a unified proceeding at the partnership level. This process is more efficient and should provide greater consistency in the treatment of the individual partners than the earlier system.

Any questions arising during an IRS audit about a partnership item must be determined at the partnership level (instead of at the partner level).[80] Section 6231(a)(3) defines a **partnership item** as virtually all items that are reported by the partnership for the tax year including tax preference items, credit recapture items, guaranteed payments, and the at-risk amount. In fact, almost every item that can appear on the partnership return is treated as a partnership item. Each partner must either report partnership items in a manner consistent with the Schedule K-1 received from the partnership or notify the IRS of the inconsistent treatment.[81]

The IRS can bring a single proceeding at the partnership level to determine the characterization or tax impact of any partnership item. All partners have the right to participate in the administrative proceedings, and the IRS must offer a consistent settlement to all partners.

A **tax matters partner** is generally assigned (1) to facilitate communication between the IRS and the partners of a large partnership and (2) to serve as the primary representative of the partnership.[82] The tax matters partner is a partner designated by the partnership or, if no one partner is so designated, the general partner having the largest profits interest at the close of the partnership's tax year.

Either the tax matters partner or the other dissenting partners can appeal an administrative decision in the courts. However, in general only one court case will result from a partnership item about which a disagreement exists. A single court will have jurisdiction to review all the partnership items in question for the litigated tax year and the allocation of such items among the partners. The audit procedures are efficient and provide consistency of treatment for partnership items.

It should be noted, however, that these audit procedures do not apply to small partnerships. For this purpose, a small partnership is defined as one having no more than 10 partners who must be either natural persons (but excluding nonresident aliens) or estates. In counting partners, a husband and wife (or their estates) count as a single partner. In addition, there can be no special allocations if the partnership is to qualify under these rules.[83] Further, the IRS has announced in Rev. Proc. 84-35

---

[80] Sec. 6221. This section applies to partnership tax years that begin after September 3, 1982.
[81] Sec. 6222.
[82] Sec. 6231(a)(7).
[83] Sec. 6231(a)(1)(B).

that a partnership can be excluded from the audit procedures only if it can be established that all partners fully reported their shares of partnership items on timely filed tax returns.[84]

PROBLEM MATERIALS

DISCUSSION QUESTIONS

9-1. List four advantages of using a partnership (rather than a corporation) for conducting a business.

9-2. List four disadvantages of using a partnership (rather than a corporation) for conducting a business.

9-3. Explain the differences between a limited partner and a general partner.

9-4. Sam, a 31% tax bracket taxpayer, wants to help his brother, Lou, start a new business. Lou is a capable auto mechanic, but has little business sense, so he needs Sam to advise him regularly on business decisions. Should this partnership be arranged as a general partnership or as a limited partnership? Why?

9-5. Doug contributes services but no property to the CD Partnership when it is being formed. What are the tax implications of him receiving only a profits interest versus him receiving a capital and profits interest.

9-6. An existing partner wants to contribute property having a basis that is less than its FMV for an additional interest in a partnership.
   a. Should he contribute the property to the partnership?
   b. What are his other options?
   c. Explain the tax implications for the partner of these other options.

9-7. What are the tax implications to the service partner and the partnership of an individual being admitted to a new partnership in return for establishing the business's accounting system?

9-8. Jane contributes valuable property to a partnership in exchange for a general partnership interest. The partnership assumes the recourse mortgage which Jane incurred when she purchased the property 2 years ago.
   a. How will the liability affect the amount of gain that Jane must recognize?
   b. How will it affect her basis in the partnership interest?

9-9. Which of the following items can be amortized as part of a partnership's organizational expenditures?
   a. Legal fees for drawing up the partnership agreement
   b. Accounting fees for establishing an accounting system
   c. Fees for securing an initial working capital loan
   d. Filing fees required under state law to conduct business within the state
   e. Accounting fees for preparation of initial short-period tax return
   f. Transportation costs for acquiring machinery essential to the partnership's business
   g. Syndication expenses

9-10. Explain the difference between partnership ordinary income and partnership taxable income.

9-11. Which of the following items must be separately stated in determining partnership taxable income?
   a. Gambling income
   b. Sec. 1245 gains
   c. Tax-exempt interest

[84] 1984-1 C.B. 509.

d. Dividends
e. Investment interest income
f. Specially allocated depreciation
g. Ordinary loss from operations
h. Sec. 1231 gains

9-12. How will a partner's distributive share be determined if one-half of his beginning-of-the-year partnership interest is sold at the beginning of the tenth month of the partnership's tax year?

9-13. Can a recourse debt of a partnership increase the basis of a limited partner's partnership interest? Explain.

9-14. The ABC Partnership has a nonrecourse liability that it incurred by borrowing monies from an unrelated bank and which is secured by an apartment building owned and managed by the partnership. The liability is not convertible into an equity interest. How does this liability affect the at-risk basis of general partner Anna and limited partner Bob?

9-15. Is the Sec. 704(d) loss limitation rule more or less restrictive than the at-risk rules? Explain.

9-16. Is the Sec. 704(d) loss limitation rule more or less restrictive than the passive loss limitation rules? Explain.

9-17. Jeff, a 10% limited partner in the recently formed JRS Partnership, expects to have losses from the partnership for several more years. He is considering a purchase of an interest in a profitable general partnership in which he will materially participate. Will the purchase allow him to use his losses from the JRS Partnership?

9-18. Helen, a 55% partner in the ABC Partnership, owns land (a capital asset) having a $20,000 basis and a $25,000 FMV. She plans to sell the land to the ABC Partnership, which will subdivide the land and sell the lots. Would you advise Helen to make the sale? Why or why not?

9-19. What is a guaranteed payment? How does it effect partnership taxable income? Be specific.

9-20. What is the difference between a guaranteed payment which is a guaranteed amount and one which is a guaranteed minimum?

9-21. Compare the point in time when income must be included in the partner's tax return if the income is a distributive share versus a guaranteed payment.

9-22. What requirements must be met before a daughter, who receives a partnership interest as a gift from her father, will be considered a partner for tax purposes?

9-23. Roy's father gives him a profits interest in Family Partnership. Will the Sec. 704(e) family partnership rules apply to this interest?

9-24. Andrew gives his brother Steve a 20% interest in the AS Partnership and retains a 30% interest. Andrew works for the partnership but is not paid. How will this affect the income from the AS Partnership that is reported by Andrew and Steve?

9-25. Briefly explain the IRS audit procedures for a partnership.

PROBLEMS

9-26. *Formation of a Partnership.* Dan, Joe, and Sally decide to form the DJS Partnership. They make the following contributions in order to become equal partners in the general partnership:

Individual	Asset	Basis to Partner	FMV
Dan	Land	$35,000	$ 25,000
Joe	Building	65,000	100,000
Sally	Machinery	10,000	25,000

The building secures a $75,000 mortgage which DJS assumed. The building has been depreciated by using the straight-line method under MACRS. Sally has claimed $14,000 of MACRS depreciation on the machinery she contributes.

a. How much gain, loss, or income must each partner recognize as a result of the formation?
b. How much gain, loss, or income must the partnership recognize as a result of the formation?
c. What is each partner's basis in their partnership interest?
d. What is the partnership's basis in its assets?
e. What capital-recovery methods can the partnership use on the building and the machinery?
f. What effects do the depreciation recapture provisions have on the property contributions?

9-27. *Formation of a Partnership.* On May 31, 1991, six brothers decided to form the Grimm Brothers Partnership to publish and print children's stories. The contributions of the brothers and their partnership interests are listed.

Individual	Asset	Basis to Partner	FMV	Partnership Interest
Al	Cash	$15,000	$ 15,000	15%
Bob	Accounts receivable	—0—	30,000	20%
Clay	Office equipment	13,000	15,000	15%
Dave	Land	50,000	15,000	15%
Ed	Building	15,000	150,000	20%
Fred	Services	?	15,000	15%

Other information about the contributions may be of interest, as follows:

- Bob contributes accounts receivable from his proprietorship, which uses the cash method of accounting, and the partnership assumes $10,000 of the proprietorship's accounts payable.
- Clay uses the office equipment in a small business he owns. When he joins the partnership, he sells the remaining business assets to an outsider. MACRS depreciation of $8,000 was claimed on the office equipment.
- The partnership assumes a $130,000 mortgage on the building Ed contributes. Ed claimed $100,000 of ACRS depreciation on the commercial property. Straight-line depreciation on the property would have been $60,000.
- Fred, an attorney, drew up all the partnership agreements and filed the necessary paperwork. He receives a full 15% capital and profits interest for his services.

a. How much gain, loss, or income must each partner recognize as a result of the formation?
b. How much gain, loss, or income must the partnership recognize as a result of the formation?
c. What is each partner's basis in their partnership interest?
d. What is the partnership's basis in its assets?
e. What effects do the depreciation recapture provisions have on the property contributions?
f. How would your answer to Part a change if Fred received only a profits interest?
g. What are the tax consequences to the partners and the partnership when the land contributed by Dave is subsequently sold for $9,000?

9-28. *Formation of a Partnership.* On January 1, 1991, Julie, Kay, and Susan decide to form a partnership. The contributions of the three individuals are listed below. Julie and Susan each received a 30% partnership interest while Kay received a 40% partnership interest.

Individual	Asset	Basis to Partner	FMV
Julie	Accounts receivable	$—0—	$ 30,000
Kay	Land	50,000	20,000
	Building	30,000	110,000
Susan	Services	?	30,000

Kay has claimed $60,000 of accelerated ACRS depreciation. Straight-line depreciation on the building would have been $30,000. The building has a $90,000 mortgage which is assumed by the partnership. Susan is an attorney and the services she contributes are the drawing-up of all partnership agreements.

a. What is the amount and character of the gain, loss, or income recognized by each partner on the formation of the partnership?
b. What is each partner's basis in the partnership interest?

c. What is the partnership's basis in each of its assets?
d. If the partnership sells the land contributed by Kay for $18,000, what is each partner's distributive share?

9-29. *Contribution of Services.* Sean is admitted to the XYZ Partnership in December 1991 in return for his services managing the partnership's business during 1991. The partnership reports ordinary income of $100,000 for 1991 without considering this transaction.
   a. What are the tax consequences to Sean and the XYZ Partnership if Sean receives a 20% capital and profits interest in the partnership with a $75,000 FMV for the interest?
   b. What are the tax consequences to Sean and the XYZ Partnership if Sean receives only a 20% profits interest with no determinable FMV?

9-30. *Contributions of Services.* Carol received a 5% limited partnership interest in the CDE Partnership as payment for selling interests in the limited partnership. Her interest is a profits interest only. Similar interests sold for $20,000 for each 1% interest at approximately the same time Carol received her interest. What are the tax implications for Carol and the CDE Partnership of Carol's receipt of the partnership interest?

9-31. *Partnership Tax Year.* The BCD Partnership is being formed and will be owned equally by individuals Beth and Cindy and Delux Corporation. The partners' tax year-ends are June 30 for Beth, September 30 for Cindy, and October 31 for Delux. The BCD Partnership's natural business year ends on January 31.
   a. What tax year(s) can the partnership elect without IRS permission?
   b. What tax year(s) can the partnership elect with IRS permission?
   c. How would your answers to Parts a and b change if Beth, Cindy, and Delux own 4%, 4%, and 92%, respectively, of the partnership?

9-32. *Partnership Tax Year.* The JAS Partnership is formed in January of the current year. The equal partners Joan, Anne, and Susanna have had tax year-ends of June 30, August 31, and June 30, respectively, for the preceding five years. The JAS Partnership has no natural business year.
   a. What tax year-end is required under Sec. 706?
   b. Can JAS make a Sec. 444 election? If so, what are the possible tax year-ends that JAS could choose?

9-33. *Section 444 Election.* The BBB Partnership has a required calendar year-end but has properly elected an October 31 year-end under Sec. 444. The current year is the second year of partnership operations and a Sec. 7519 payment of $3,450 was made last year. Bob, a 40% general partner, receives an interest payment of $18,000 from the partnership in January and July of each year. Bill, a 40% general partner, receives rent payments from the partnership of $1,500 each month. Base year net income is $120,000 and there were 12 months in the base year. What is the required payment for BBB for the current year? When must the payment be made?

9-34. *Section 444 Election.* The MS Partnership has elected a March 31 year-end instead of the majority partner's June 30 year-end. Previous required payments under Sec. 7519 totaled $10,420 before the most recent two years. Information for the most recent two years is as follows.

	Fiscal Year Ending March 31	
	1990	1991
Base year net income	$180,000	$240,000
Applicable payments:		
Interest to partner Michael (paid in April and October each year)	24,000	24,000
Rent to partner Stephen ($3,000 each month)	36,000	36,000

What is the required Sec. 7519 payment for each of the two years?

9-35. *Reporting Partnership Income.* The KLM Partnership, which uses the accrual method of accounting, is owned equally by Karen, who uses the cash method of accounting, and LM Corporation, which uses the accrual method of accounting. Karen is a real estate developer.

Both materially participate in the business. KLM reported the following results for the current year:

Operating profit (excluding the items listed below)	$120,000
Dividends from a 10%-owned domestic corporation	19,000
Interest income:	
Municipal bonds (tax-exempt)	18,000
Corporate bonds	29,000
Gains and losses on property sales:	
Gain on sale of land contributed by Karen 2 years ago when its basis was $10,000 and FMV was $35,000. (The land was included in Karen's inventory but held by KLM as an investment property.)	40,000
Sec. 1231 loss	28,000
Long-term capital gains	17,000
Long-term capital losses	21,000
Short-term capital losses	5,000
Charitable contributions	23,000
Interest expense on loans to acquire taxable investments	16,000
Guaranteed payment to Karen for management services	37,000
ACRS and MACRS capital-recovery allowances	36,000
Rehabilitation expenditures on a certified historic dwelling placed in service on November 1 of the current year, as an office for the partnership.	164,000

a. What are KLM's separately stated items?
b. What is KLM's ordinary income (loss)?

9-36. *Reporting Partnership Income.* The JLK Partnership, which uses the accrual method of accounting, is owned equally by Jim, Liz and Ken. All three materially participate in the business. JLK reports the following results for the current year:

Operating profit (excluding the items listed below)	$ 94,000
Rental income	30,000
Interest income:	
Municipal bonds (tax-exempt)	15,000
Corporate bonds	3,000
Dividend income (all from less than 20% owned domestic corporations)	20,000
Gains and losses on property sales:	
Gain on sale of land held as an investment (contributed by Jim 6 years ago when its basis was $9,000 and its FMV was $15,000)	60,000
Long-term capital gains	10,000
Short-term capital losses	7,000
Sec. 1231 gain	9,000
Sec. 1250 gain	44,000
ACRS and MACRS capital-recovery allowances:	
Rental real estate	12,000
Machinery and equipment	27,000
Interest expense:	
Mortgages on rental property	18,000
Loans to acquire municipal bonds	5,000
Guaranteed payments to:	
Jim (for managing partnership operations)	30,000
Ken (for acquiring financing to purchase new rental property)	15,000
Low-income housing expenditures qualifying for credit	21,000

a. What are JLK's separately stated items?
b. What is JLK's ordinary income (loss)?

9-37. Partner's Distributive Shares. On January 1, 1991, the BCD Partnership is owned 20% by Becky, 30% by Chuck, and 50% by Dawn. During 1991 BCD reports the following results. All items occur evenly throughout the year unless otherwise indicated.

Ordinary income	$120,000
Long-term capital gain (recognized September 1, 1991)	18,000
Short-term capital loss (recognized March 2, 1991)	6,000
Charitable contribution (made October 1, 1991)	20,000

   a. What are the distributive shares for each partner for 1991, assuming they all continue to hold their interests on January 1, 1992?
   b. Assume that Becky purchases a 5% partnership interest from Chuck on July 1, 1991 so that Becky and Chuck each own 25% from that date through the end of the year. What are Becky and Chuck's distributive shares for 1991?

9-38. Distributive Share. On January 1, 1991, the ABC Partnership is owned by Amy (25%), Brad (35%) and Craig (40%). During the year the partnership earned the following amounts. Assume earnings were even throughout the year unless otherwise stated.

Ordinary loss	$120,000
Long-term capital gain—the transaction is entered into on 12/1/1991	190,000
Sec. 1231 gains	40,000
Short-term capital losses	30,000

   a. What is each partner's distributive share of 1991 partnership income assuming no change in ownership occurs during the year?
   b. Assume that on July 1, 1991, Craig sold one-half of his partnership interest to Brad. What are the distributive shares of Brad and Craig for 1991?

9-39. Allocation of Pre-contribution Gain. On January 1 of the current year, John and Andrew form the JA Partnership. On that date, John contributed a building with a $60,000 FMV and a $31,500 adjusted basis and Andrew contriubted $60,000 cash. The two were equal partners. Assume that the building should be depreciated using the straight-line method over a 31.5 year recovery period.
   a. How much depreciation should be allocated to Andrew in the current year?
   b. Assume the building is sold exactly one year after the partnership formation for $65,000. How much gain must the partnership recognize? How will the gain be allocated between John and Andrew? (Remaining pre-contribution gain to be allocated to John is $30,500, which is the difference between the building's FMV reduced by economic depreciation and the building's basis reduced by actual depreciation.)

9-40. Special Allocations. Diane and Ed have equal capital and profits interests in the DE Partnership. In addition, Diane has a special allocation of all depreciation on buildings owned by the partnership. The buildings are financed with recourse liabilities. The depreciation reduces Diane's capital account, and liquidation is in accordance with the capital account balances. Depreciation for the DE Partnership is $50,000 annually. Diane and Ed each have $50,000 capital account balances on January 1, 1991. Will the special allocation have substantial economic effect for 1991, 1992, and 1993 in the following independent situations?
   a. There is no obligation to repay negative capital account balances, and the partnership's operations (other than depreciation) each year have no net effect on the capital accounts.
   b. There is an obligation to repay negative capital account balances.
   c. There is no obligation to repay negative capital account balances. The partnership operates at its break-even point (excluding any depreciation that is claimed) and borrows $200,000 on a full recourse basis on December 31, 1992.

9-41. Basis of Partnership Interest. What is Kelly's basis for her partnership interest in each of the following independent situations?
   a. Kelly receives her 20% partnership interest for a contribution of property having a $14,000 basis and a $17,000 FMV. The partnership assumes her $10,000 liability but has no other debts.

b. Kelly receives her 20% partnership interest as a gift from a friend. The friend's basis (without considering partnership liabilities) is $34,000. The FMV of the interest at the time of the gift is $36,000. The partnership has liabilities of $100,000 when Kelly receives her interest. No gift tax was paid with respect to the transfer.

c. Kelly inherits her 20% interest from her mother. Her mother's basis was $140,000. The FMV of the interest is $120,000 on the date of death and $160,000 on the alternate valuation date. The executor chooses the date of death for valuing the estate. The partnership has no liabilities.

9-42. *Partnership Basis.* What is Kim's basis in her partnership interest for each of the independent situations below? Assume the partnership has no liabilities except those specifically mentioned.

a. Kim contributes $4,000 cash, land with a $3,000 basis and a $5,000 FMV, and services which cost $2,000 to Kim and had a $6,000 FMV.

b. Kim becomes a 20% partner when she contributes a building with a $40,000 basis and $60,000 FMV. A $50,000 mortgage is assumed by the partnership.

c. Kim inherits her partnership interest upon her aunt's death. Her aunt's basis was $10,000. At the date of death, the FMV was $47,000. Six months later the FMV was $53,000. The executor of her aunt's estate valued the estate at the date of death value.

d. Kim receives her 30% interest as a gift from a friend when its FMV was $45,000. The friend's basis was $36,000 and $1,000 of gift taxes were paid on the gift. The partnership has $90,000 in liabilities.

9-43. *Basis in Partnership Interest.* Tina purchases an interest in the TP Partnership on January 1, 1991, for $50,000. The partnership uses the calendar year as its tax year and has only $200,000 in recourse liabilities when Tina acquires her interest. Her distributive share of partnership items for 1991 is as follows:

Ordinary income (excluding items listed below)	$30,000
Long-term capital gains	10,000
Municipal bond interest income	8,000
Charitable contributions	1,000
Interest expense related to municipal bond investment	2,000

TP reports the following liabilities on December 31, 1991:

Recourse debt	$100,000
Nonrecourse debt	80,000

a. What is Tina's basis on December 31, 1991, if she has a 40% interest in profits and losses? TP is a general partnership and Tina has not guaranteed partnership debt nor has she made any other special agreements about partnership debt.

b. How would your answer to Part a change if Tina instead has a 40% interest in profits and a 30% interest in losses? Assume TP is a general partnership, and all other agreements continue in place.

c. How would your answer to Part a change if Tina is instead a limited partner having a 40% interest in profits and 30% interest in losses? There are no guarantees or special agreements.

9-44. *At-Risk Loss Limitation.* The KC Partnership is a general partnership that manufactures widgets. The partnership uses a calendar year as its tax year and is owned equally by Kerry and City Corporation, a widely held corporation. On January 1, 1991, Kerry and City Corporation each have a $300,000 basis in their partnership interests. Operations during 1991 provide the following results:

Ordinary loss	($900,000)
Long-term capital loss	(100,000)
Short-term capital gain	300,000

The only change in KC's liabilities during 1991 is KC's first borrowing—a $100,000 nonrecourse loan that is still outstanding at year-end.

a. What is each partner's deductible loss from the partnership's activities for 1991 before any passive loss limitation?

b. What is each partner's basis in the partnership interest after 1991's operations?
c. How would your answers to Parts a and b change if the KC Partnership's business is totally in real estate but is not a rental activity? Assume the loan is qualified real estate financing.

9-45. *At-Risk Loss Limitation.* Mary and Gary are partners in the MG Partnership. Mary owns a 40% capital and profits interest while Gary owns the remaining interest. Both materially participate in partnership activities. At the beginning of the current year, MG's only liabilities are $30,000 in accounts payable which remain outstanding at year-end. In November, MG borrows $100,000 on a nonrecourse basis from First Bank. The loan is secured by property with a $200,000 FMV. These are MG's only liabilities at year-end. Basis for the partnership interests at the beginning of the year is $40,000 for Mary and $60,000 for Gary before considering the impact of liabilities. MG has a $200,000 ordinary loss during the current year.
a. How much loss can Mary recognize? Gary?
b. In January of next year, MG plans to distribute $10,000 in cash to Mary. What are the tax implications of the planned distribution?

9-46. *Passive Loss Limitation.* Jill and Rob are equal partners in the JR Partnership, which has operated a department store since Jill and Rob formed the partnership 10 years ago. Jill materially participates in the business but Rob does not. During 1991 the JR Partnership has a $100,000 ordinary loss and a $20,000 capital gain. Each partner has a $40,000 basis immediately before the end of 1991. There is no nonrecourse debt. How much loss and gain must each partner report in 1991?

9-47. *Passive Loss Limitation.* Kate, Chad, and Stan are partners in the KCS Partnership, which operates a manufacturing business. The partnership was formed in 1987 with Kate and Chad each as general partners with a 40% capital and profits interest. Kate materially participates; Chad does not. Stan has a 20% interest as a limited partner. At the end of the current year, the following information was available:

	Kate	Chad	Stan
Basis in partnership (immediately before year-end)	$100,000	$100,000	$50,000
Distributive share of:			
Nonrecourse liability (already included in basis)	50,000	50,000	25,000
Operating losses	(80,000)	(80,000)	(40,000)
Capital gains	20,000	20,000	10,000

a. How much operating loss can each partner deduct in the current year?
b. How much loss could each partner deduct if the KCS Partnership is engaged in rental activities? Assume Kate and Chad both actively participate in the activity but Stan does not.

9-48. *Related Party Transactions.* Susan, Steve and Sandy own 15%, 35% and 50%, respectively, in the SSS Partnership. Susan sells securities for their FMV of $40,000 to the partnership. What are the tax implications of the following independent situations?
a. Susan's basis in the securities is $60,000. The three partners are siblings.
b. Susan's basis in the securities is $50,000. Susan is unrelated to the other partners.
c. Susan's basis in the securities is $30,000. Susan and Sandy are sisters. The partnership will hold the securities as an investment.

9-49. *Related Party Transactions.* Jack, Kyle, and Lynn are equal partners in the JKL Partnership. Jack sells the partnership some land he held as an investment for its $30,000 FMV. What are the tax implications of the sale in the following independent situations?
a. Jack's basis for the land is $40,000, and he is not related to either Kyle or Lynn.
b. Jack's basis for the land is $44,000. Jack and Kyle are brothers but Lynn is unrelated.
c. Jack's basis for the land is $20,000. Jack, Kyle, and Lynn are siblings. The partnership holds the land as investment property.
d. Assume the same facts as in Part c, except that the partnership subdivides the land and sells it as lots.

9-50. *Related Party Transactions.* Beth owns 35% of the BCD Partnership and 52% of the BK Partnership. Cathy owns 40% of the BCD Partnership and 48% of the BK Partnership. Don owns 25% of the BCD Partnership. The BCD Partnership sells TGP Corporation stock that is held as an investment to the BK Partnership for its $110,000 FMV. What are the tax implications of the sale for each of the following independent situations?
   a. BCD's basis for the stock is $164,000.
   b. BCD's basis for the stock is $68,000, and BK holds the stock as an investment.
   c. BCD's basis for the stock is $68,000, and BK holds the stock as inventory for resale to its clients.

9-51. *Guaranteed Payments.* Scott and Dave each invested $100,000 cash when the SD Partnership was formed and they became equal partners. They agreed that the partnership would pay each a 5% guaranteed payment on their $100,000 capital account. Before the two guaranteed payments, current year results were $23,000 of ordinary income and $14,000 of long-term capital gain. What is the amount and character of the income reported by Scott and Dave for the current year from their partnership?

9-52. *Guaranteed Payments.* Allen and Bob are equal partners in the AB Partnership. Bob manages the business and receives a guaranteed payment. What is the amount and character of the income reported by Allen and Bob in each of the following independent situations?
   a. The AB Partnership earns $160,000 of ordinary income before considering Bob's guaranteed payment. Bob is guaranteed a $90,000 payment plus 50% of all income remaining after the guaranteed payment.
   b. Assume the same facts as Part a except that Bob's distributive share is 50% with a guaranteed minimum of $90,000.
   c. The AB Partnership earns only a $140,000 long-term capital gain. Bob is guaranteed $80,000 plus 50% of all amounts remaining after the guaranteed payment.

9-53. *Guaranteed Payments.* Pam and Susan own the PS Partnership. Pam takes care of daily operations and receives a guaranteed payment for her efforts. What are the amount and character of the income each partner reports in each of the following independent situations?
   a. The PS Partnership reports only a $10,000 long-term capital gain. Pam receives a $40,000 guaranteed payment plus a 30% distributive share of all partnership income after deducting the guaranteed payment.
   b. The PS Partnership reports $70,000 of ordinary income and $60,000 of Sec. 1231 gain. Pam receives a $35,000 guaranteed payment plus a 20% distributive share of all partnership income after deducting the guaranteed payment.
   c. The PS Partnership reports $120,000 of ordinary income. Pam receives 40% of partnership income but no less than $60,000.

9-54. *Family Partnership.* Dad gives Son a 20% capital and profits interest in the Family Partnership. Dad holds a 70% interest, and Fred, an unrelated individual, holds a 10% interest. Dad and Fred work in the partnership but Son does not. Fred and Dad receive reasonable compensation for their work. The partnership earns $100,000 ordinary income, and the partners agree to divide this amount based on their relative ownership interests. Fred does not know that Son has a partnership interest.
   a. What income must Father, Son, and Fred report if Family Partnership is an accounting firm?
   b. What income must Father, Son, and Fred report if Family Partnership is a manufacturing firm with substantial inventories?

9-55. *Family Partnership.* Steve wishes to pass his business on to his children, Tracy and Vicki, and gives each a 20% partnership interest to begin getting them involved. Neither daughter is employed by the partnership, which buys and manages real estate. Steve draws only a $40,000 guaranteed payment for his work for the partnership. Reasonable compensation for his services would be $70,000. The partnership reports ordinary income of $120,000 after deducting the guaranteed payment. Distributive shares for the three partners are tentatively reported as: Steve, $72,000; Tracy, $24,000; and Vicki, $24,000. What is the proper distributive share of income for each partner?

TAX FORM/RETURN PREPARATION PROBLEM

9-56. The Dapper-Dons Partnership (employer identification no. 89-3456798) was formed ten years ago as a general partnership to custom tailor men's clothing. Dapper-Dons is located at 123 Flamingo Drive in Miami, Florida 33131. Bob Dapper (social security no. 654-32-1098) manages the business and has a 40% capital and profits interest. His address is 709 Brumby Way, Miami, Florida 33131. Jeremy Dons (social security no. 354-12-6531) owns the remaining 60% interest but is not active in the business. His address is 807 9th Avenue, North Miami, Florida 33134. The partnership values its inventory using the cost method and there was no change in the method used during the current year. The partnership uses the accrual method of accounting. Because of the simplicity of the partnership, it is not subject to the partnership audit procedures. There are no foreign partners, no foreign transactions, no interests in foreign trusts and no foreign financial accounts. This partnership is neither a tax shelter nor a publicly traded partnership. There have been no distributions of property other than cash nor changes in ownership of partnership interests during the current year. The partnership has not acquired a new activity since October 22, 1986. Cash distributions of $155,050 and $232,576 were made to Dapper and Dons, respectively, on December 30 of the current year. Financial statements for Dapper-Dons for the current year are presented in Tables 9-2 and 9-3. Prepare a current year partnership tax return for Dapper-Dons Partnership.

TABLE 9-2 Dapper-Dons Partnership Income Statement for the Year Ended December 31 of the Current Year (Problem 9-56)

Sales		$2,350,000
Returns and allowances		(20,000)
		$2,330,000
Beginning inventory	$ 200,050	
Purchases	624,000	
Labor	600,000	
Supplies	42,000	
Other costs[a]	12,000	
	$1,478,050	
Ending inventory	(146,000)	(1,332,050)
Gross profit		$ 997,950
Salaries for employees other than partners	$51,000	
Guaranteed payment for Dapper	85,000	
Utilities expense	46,428	
Depreciation (MACRS depreciation is $42,311 and ACRS depreciation is $32,000)[b]	49,782	
Automobile expense	12,085	
Office supplies expense	4,420	
Advertising expense	85,000	
Bad debt expense	2,100	
Interest expense (all trade or business related)	45,000	
Rent expense	7,400	
Travel expense (meals cost $4,050 of this amount)	11,020	
Repairs and maintenance expense	68,300	
Accounting and legal expense	3,600	
Charitable contributions[c]	16,400	
Payroll taxes	5,180	
Other taxes (all trade or business related)	1,400	
Total expenses		494,115
Operating profit		$ 503,835
Other income and losses:		
Net long-term capital gain (AB stock)	$18,000	
Net short-term capital loss (CD stock)	(26,075)	
Sec. 1231 gain (sale of storage building)	5,050	

Interest on U.S. treasury bills for entire year ($80,000 face amount)		9,000	
Dividends from 15% owned domestic corporation		11,000	16,975
Net income			$ 520,810

[a] Additional Sec. 263A costs are $7,000 for the current year.
[b] Dapper-Dons acquired and placed into service $40,000 of rehabilitation expenditures for a certified historical property this year. No Sec. 38 property is removed from service before the end of its recovery period during the current year.
[c] All contributions are made in cash to qualifying charities.

TABLE 9-3 Dapper-Dons Partnership Balance Sheet for January 1 and December 31 of the Current Year (Problem 9-56)

	Balance January 1	Balance December 31
Assets:		
Cash	$ 10,000	$ 40,000
Accounts receivable	72,600	150,100
Inventories	200,050	146,000
Marketable securities	220,000	260,000
Building and equipment	374,600	465,000
Minus: Accumulated depreciation	(160,484)	(173,100)
Land	185,000	240,000
Total assets	$901,766	$1,128,000
Liabilities and equities:		
Accounts payable	$ 35,000	$ 46,000
Accrued salaries payable	14,000	18,000
Payroll taxes payable	3,416	7,106
Sales taxes payable	5,200	6,560
Mortgage and notes payable (current maturities)	44,000	52,000
Long-term debt	210,000	275,000
Capital—		
Dapper	236,060	289,334
Dons	354,090	434,000
Total liabilities and equities	$901,766	$1,128,000

CASE STUDY PROBLEM

9-57. Abe and Brenda formed the AB Partnership ten years ago and have been very successful with the business. However, in the current year, economic conditions caused them to lose significant amounts but they expect the economy and their business to return to profitable operations by next year or the year after. Abe manages the partnership business and works in it full-time. Brenda has a full-time job as an accountant for a $39,000 annual salary but she also works in the partnership occasionally. She estimates that she spent about 120 hours working in the partnership this year. Abe has a 40% profits interest, a 50% loss interest and has a basis in his partnership interest on December 31 (before considering this year's operations or outstanding liabilities) of $65,000. Brenda owns a 60% profits interest, a 50% loss interest and has a basis of $80,000 on December 31 (before considering this year's operations or outstanding liabilities). The only liability which is outstanding on December 31 is a recourse debt of $40,000. Neither Abe nor Brenda currently has other investments. The AB Partnership earns the following amounts during the year.

Ordinary loss	$(100,000)
Sec. 1231 gain	10,000
Tax-exempt municipal bond income	14,000

Long-term capital loss	14,000
Short-term capital loss	136,000

Early next year, the AB Partnership is considering borrowing $100,000 from a local bank to be secured by a mortgage on a building which has a $150,000 FMV.

Required: Prepare a memorandum to Abe and Brenda discussing this client matter. Points which should be discussed include: What amounts should Abe and Brenda report on their income tax return for the current year from the AB Partnership? What are their bases in their partnership interests after taking all transactions into effect? What happens to any losses they cannot deduct in the current year? What planning opportunities are presented by the need to borrow money early next year? What planning ideas would you suggest for Brenda?

TAX RESEARCH PROBLEMS

9-58. Robin and Russ are two accountants who have recently become CPAs. They each want to open their own accounting practice but neither can afford to try it alone. The two have agreed to rent adjoining office space from an unrelated third party with Robin paying for her office and Russ paying for his. They will share the cost of a receptionist who will work one-half time for each. Billings will be rendered by the accountant who performed the work, and there will be no sharing of clients or revenues. Are Robin and Russ partners? Do they need to file a partnership return?

A partial list of research sources is

- Sec. 761.
- Reg. Sec. 1.761-1.

9-59. Nancy is a partner in the EAS Partnership. In return for doing the day-to-day management work, Nancy has a distributive share of 40% of profits and losses but not less than a minimum payment of $100,000. In the current year, the partnership has profits before any payment to Nancy of $120,000 made up of $56,000 of ordinary income and $64,000 of long-term capital gains. How much does Nancy receive, and what is the character of her income?

A partial list of research sources is

- Sec. 707(c).
- Reg. Sec. 1.707-1(c), Ex. (2).
- Rev. Rul. 69-180, 1969-1 C.B. 183.

9-60. George is a general partner in the GS Partnership. He has a 40% capital, profits, and loss interest and also has a special allocation of all depreciation deductions on the partnership's office building. If the partnership sells the office building for a gain, George will receive a special allocation of gain up to the amount of depreciation he has claimed (a gain charge-back arrangement). Any loss recognized on the sale of the office building would be allocated based on the usual distributive share arrangement.

All allocations of income, gain, loss, and deductions affect the capital accounts whether they are distributive share items or special allocation items. Liquidation proceeds would be distributed based on capital accounts. George is obligated to repay any negative capital account balance at the time of liquidation.

The $1,100,000 purchase price of the office building was financed by a $1,000,000 recourse loan plus partner contributions. Interest only is paid until the building is sold. On the day the office building is purchased, George has a $100,000 capital account balance and a $500,000 basis for his partnership interest (his capital account plus his 40% share of the $1,000,000 liability). Annual depreciation expenses are calculated using the straight-line Modified ACRS election for the shortest recovery period. The partnership operates at its break-even point (without considering depreciation), but always expects to make a profit. It is likely that the office building will be sold for an amount greater than its purchase price. Does the special allocation of depreciation have substantial economic effect?

A partial list of research sources is

- Sec. 704.
- Reg. Sec. 1.704-1(b)(2) and (5).
- *Stanley C. Orrisch*, 55 T.C. 395 (1971), *aff'd per curiam* in an unpublished opinion (9th Cir., 1973).

10 Special Partnership Issues

CHAPTER OUTLINE

LEARNING OBJECTIVES 10-2
NONLIQUIDATING DISTRIBUTIONS 10-2
- Recognition of Gain 10-3
- Basis Effects of Distributions 10-4
- Holding Period and Character of Distributed Property 10-6

NONLIQUIDATING DISTRIBUTIONS WITH SEC. 751 10-6
- Section 751 Assets Defined 10-6
- Exchange of Sec. 751 Assets and Other Property 10-8

TERMINATING AN INTEREST IN A PARTNERSHIP 10-11
- Liquidating Distributions 10-11
- Sale of a Partnership Interest 10-16
- Retirement or Death of a Partner 10-19
- Exchange of a Partnership Interest 10-2
- Gift of a Partnership Interest 10-23
- Income Recognition and Transfers of a Partnership Interest 10-23
- Termination of a Partnership 10-25
- Mergers and Consolidations 10-28
- Division of a Partnership 10-29

OPTIONAL BASIS ADJUSTMENTS 10-29
- Election to Make Basis Adjustments 10-30
- Optional Adjustments on Transfers 10-30
- Optional Adjustments on Distributions 10-35
- Special Adjustments on Distributions to Transferee Partners 10-38

TAX SHELTER PARTNERSHIPS 10-40
- Tax Shelters and Limited Partnerships 10-40
- Abusive Tax Shelters 10-40
- Publicly Traded Partnerships 10-41

TAX PLANNING CONSIDERATIONS 10-42
- Liquidating Distribution or Sale to Partners 10-42

COMPLIANCE AND PROCEDURAL CONSIDERATIONS 10-42
- Section 754 Election 10-42
- Section 732(d) Election 10-43

PROBLEM MATERIALS 10-45
- Discussion Questions 10-45
- Problems 10-45
- Case Study Problem 10-55
- Tax Research Problems 10-56

LEARNING OBJECTIVES

After studying this chapter, you should be able to

1. Determine the amount and character of the gain or loss recognized by a partner from a nonliquidating partnership distribution
2. Determine the basis of assets received by a partner from a nonliquidating partnership distribution
3. Identify the partnership's Sec. 751 assets
4. Determine the tax implications of a sale or a cash distribution when a partnership has Sec. 751 assets
5. Determine the amount and character of the gain or loss recognized by a partner from a liquidating partnership distribution
6. Determine the basis of assets received by a partner from a liquidating partnership distribution
7. Determine the amount and character of the gain or loss recognized when a partner retires from a partnership or dies
8. Explain the tax implications of a gift of a partnership interest
9. Determine if a partnership has terminated for tax purposes
10. Determine the adjustment required by the sale of a partnership interest or a partnership distribution when the partnership elects to make optional basis adjustments
11. Determine the basis of partnership assets after an optional basis adjustment has been made

Beginning with a discussion of distributions from the partnership to the partner, Chapter 10 continues the discussion of the taxation of partnerships. Simple nonliquidating distributions are first explained, then more complex nonliquidating and liquidating distributions are discussed. Methods of disposing of a partnership interest are explained next. Included in this discussion are sales, the retirement or death of a partner, and gifts of the partnership interest. In addition, transactions that terminate the entire partnership are considered.

One topic unique to the partnership form of doing business is the **optional basis adjustment.** This elective partnership technique causes the basis of partnership assets to be adjusted up or down as a result of (1) distributions from the partnership to partners or (2) sales of partnership interests by existing partners.

The final topic in this chapter is an examination of tax shelters using the limited partnership form. Abusive tax shelter investigations are also discussed.

NONLIQUIDATING DISTRIBUTIONS

There are two categories of distributions from a partnership: liquidating distributions and nonliquidating (or current) distributions. A **liquidating distribution** is a single distribution, or one of a planned series of distributions, that terminates the partner's entire interest in the partnership. All other distributions, including those that substantially reduce a partner's interest in the partnership, are governed by the **nonliquidating (current) distribution** rules.

Nonliquidating Distributions

OBJECTIVE 1
Determine the amount and character of the gain or loss recognized by a partner from a nonliquidating partnership distribution

Although the tax consequences of the two types of distributions are quite similar in many respects, they are sufficiently different to require separate study. First, simple current distributions are discussed. Then complex current distributions involving Sec. 751 property and liquidating distributions are covered.[1]

Recognition of Gain

A current distribution that does not bring Sec. 751 into play cannot result in the recognition of a loss by either the partner who receives the distribution or the partnership. Gain cannot be recognized by the partnership on a current distribution (except for Sec. 751 properties). Partners who receive distributions can only recognize a gain if they receive cash distributions that exceed their basis.[2] Note that a reduction in the partner's ratable share of partnership liabilities is treated as a money distribution and, therefore, causes gain to be recognized if the deemed cash distribution exceeds the partner's basis.

Key Point
Remember that reductions in a partner's share of liabilities are treated as cash distributions (see Example 10-1).

Example 10-1

Self-Study Question
Can gain/loss be recognized in a current distribution?

Answer
Current distributions do not create losses to either the partner or partnership. Ignoring Sec. 751, gains are not recognized by the partnership. However, gains can be recognized by a partner if such partner receives a cash distribution in excess of his basis in his partnership interest.

Melissa is a 30% partner in the ABC Real Estate Partnership until Josh is admitted as a partner in exchange for a cash contribution. After Josh's admission, Melissa holds a 20% interest. Because of large loss deductions, Melissa's basis (before Josh's admission) is $20,000 including her 30% interest in the partnership liabilities of $250,000. She is deemed to receive a cash distribution equal to the $25,000 ([30% − 20%] × $250,000) reduction in her share of partnership liabilities. Since the cash distribution exceeds her basis, Melissa must recognize a $5,000 ($25,000 distribution − $20,000 basis) capital gain.

For property contributed to a partnership after October 3, 1989, which had a deferred precontribution gain or loss, the contributing partner must recognize the precontribution gain or loss when the property is distributed to any other partner within five years of the contribution. The amount of precontribution gain or loss which must be recognized by the contributing partner is determined by the amount of remaining precontribution gain or loss which would have been allocated to the distributing partner if the property had instead been sold for its FMV on the distribution date. The partnership's basis in the property immediately before the distribution and the contributing partner's basis in his partnership interest are both increased for any gain recognized or decreased for any loss recognized.[3]

Example 10-2

Self-Study Question
What type of abuse is this rule designed to eliminate?

Answer
This rule is designed to prohibit a taxpayer from using a partnership to avoid gain/loss recognition on the disposition of property.

Michael contributed land with a basis of $4,000 and FMV of $8,000 to the AB Partnership in 1990. In 1991 the land was distributed to Stephen, another partner in the partnership. At the time of the distribution, the land had a $9,000 FMV. Stephen recognizes no gain on the distribution. Michael must recognize his $4,000 precontribution gain when the property is distributed to Stephen. Michael increases his basis in the partnership by $4,000 and the partnership's basis in the land immediately before the distribution is increased by $4,000. This increase in partnership basis increases the carryover basis to the distributee partner.

---

[1] Section 751 deals with sales of partnership interests and disproportionate distributions from partnerships which have ordinary income assets. The purpose of the section is to prevent partners from turning ordinary income into capital gain.
[2] Secs. 731(a)(1) and (b).
[3] Sec. 704(c).

Basis Effects of Distributions

OBJECTIVE 2
Determine the basis of assets received by a partner from a nonliquidating partnership distribution

In general, the partner's basis for property distributed by the partnership carries over from the partnership. The partner's basis in the partnership interest is reduced by the amount of money received plus the carryover basis claimed for the distributed property.

Example 10-3 ■ Jack has a $25,000 basis for his interest in the MLV Partnership before receiving a current distribution consisting of $4,000 in money, unrealized receivables having a $3,000 basis to the partnership, and land having a $14,000 basis to the partnership. Jack takes a carryover basis in the land and receivables. Following the distribution, his basis in the partnership interest is calculated as follows:

Typical Misconception
In determining the tax consequences of partnership distributions, the basis, not the FMV, of the distributed property is most important. Partners take a carryover basis in the distributed property and a partner's basis in his partnership interest is reduced by the basis of the property distributed.

Predistribution basis in partnership interest	$25,000
Minus: Money received	(4,000)
Carryover basis in receivables	(3,000)
Carryover basis in land	(14,000)
Postdistribution basis in partnership interest	$ 4,000

■

The total bases of all distributed property in the partner's hands is limited to the partner's predistribution basis in his partnership interest.[4] If the partner's predistribution basis is less than the sum of the money received plus the carryover basis of any nonmoney property received, the order in which the basis is allocated is crucial. First, cash and deemed cash distributions reduce the partner's basis in his partnership interest. Next, the remaining basis is allocated to provide a carryover of the partnership's basis for unrealized receivables and inventory. If the partner's predistribution basis is not large enough to allow a carryover of the partnership's basis for these two property categories, the partner's remaining basis is allocated among the unrealized receivables and inventory items based on their relative bases.[5]

Example 10-4 ■ Tracy has a $15,000 basis in her interest in the TP Partnership before receiving a current distribution that consists of $6,000 in money, unrealized receivables with a $4,000 basis to the partnership, and inventory with an $8,000 basis to the partnership. The basis of the distributed property in Tracy's hands is determined as follows:

Key Point
If different types of property are distributed, the partnership distribution rules assume that the property is distributed in the following order: (1) cash, (2) unrealized receivables and inventory, and (3) other property. This ordering can affect both the recognition of gain to the partner and the basis which the partner takes in the distributed property.

Predistribution basis in partnership interest	$15,000
Minus: Money received	(6,000)
Amount to be allocated	$ 9,000

[4] Sec. 732(a)(2).
[5] Sec. 732(c).

$$\text{Basis of unrealized receivables} = \frac{\$4,000}{\$4,000 + \$8,000} \times \$9,000 = \$3,000$$

$$\text{Basis of inventory} = \frac{\$8,000}{\$4,000 + \$8,000} \times \$9,000 = \$6,000$$

If a partner's predistribution basis exceeds the sum of his money distribution plus the carryover basis for any unrealized receivables and inventory, a carryover basis is allocated to the other property received. If there is an insufficient basis for the partnership interest to provide a carryover basis for all the distributed property, the remaining basis for the partnership interest is allocated to the other property based on the relative bases of such properties in the partnership's hands.[6]

Example 10-5 ■ John has a $15,000 basis for his partnership interest before receiving the following property as a current distribution:

Property	Basis to the Partnership
Money	$5,000
Unrealized receivables	4,000
Land parcel 1	4,500
Land parcel 2	3,000

John's basis in his distributed property is calculated as follows:

Predistribution basis	$15,000
Minus: Money received	(5,000)
Basis for nonmoney property	$10,000
Minus: Carryover basis for receivables	(4,000)
Remaining basis to be allocated	$ 6,000

$$\text{Basis of parcel 1} = \frac{\$4,500}{\$4,500 + \$3,000} \times \$6,000 = \$3,600$$

$$\text{Basis of parcel 2} = \frac{\$3,000}{\$4,500 + \$3,000} \times \$6,000 = \$2,400$$

John's basis in his partnership interest is zero after the distribution, since all of its basis is allocated to the money and other property received. ■

Two other points should be noted. First, even when a partner's basis in the partnership interest is reduced to zero by a current distribution, an interest in the partnership is retained. If the partner has no remaining interest in the partnership (as opposed to a zero basis), the distribution would have been a liquidating distribution. Second, the basis of property distributed as a current distribution is always equal to or less than the carryover basis. The basis for the distributed property cannot be increased above the carryover basis amount when it is received as a nonliquidating distribution.

Self-Study Question

Assume the same facts as in Example 10-5 except that the basis in the two parcels of land is only $4,000. What are the tax consequences of the distribution?

Answer

Example 10-5 is a good illustration of the three types of property that can be included in a partnership distribution. If the basis in the two parcels of land were only $4,000 in total, then the partner would take a $4,000 carryover basis in the property and retain a $2,000 basis in his partnership interest.

Typical Misconception

In a partnership distribution, the partner's basis in his partnership interest cannot be less than zero. However, a partner's capital account can be less than zero. One needs to be able to distinguish between references to a partner's basis in his partnership interest and a partner's capital account.

---

[6] Ibid.

Holding Period and Character of Distributed Property

The partner's holding period for property distributed as a current distribution includes the partnership's holding period for such property.[7] The length of time that the partner owns the partnership interest is irrelevant when determining the holding period for the distributed property. Thus, if a new partner receives a distribution of property that was held by the partnership for 2 years preceding his becoming a partner, the new partner's holding period for the distributed property is deemed to begin when the partnership purchased the property (i.e., 2 years ago), rather than on the more recent date when the partnership interest was purchased.

A series of rules regulate the character of the gain or loss recognized when certain property distributed to a partner is subsequently sold or exchanged. These rules are similar to provisions regulating the character of gain or loss on contributed property.

If property that is an unrealized receivable in the partnership's hands is distributed, the income or loss recognized on a subsequent sale of that property by the distributee partner is ordinary income or loss. This ordinary income or loss treatment occurs without regard to the character of the property in the distributee partner's hands or the length of time the property is held by such partner before its disposition.[8]

If property that is inventory in the hands of the partnership is distributed, the income or loss recognized on a subsequent sale by the distributee partner occurring within 5 years of the distribution date is ordinary income or loss.[9] Note that the inventory rule mandates the ordinary income or loss result only for the 5-year period beginning on the distribution date. After 5 years, the character of the gain or loss recognized on the sale of such property is determined by its character in the hands of the distributee partner.

Key Point
Consistent with the discussion in Chapter 9, rules exist so that neither contributions to nor distributions from a partnership can be used to alter the character of certain gains and losses on property held by the partnership or by the individual partners.

NONLIQUIDATING DISTRIBUTIONS WITH SEC. 751

OBJECTIVE 3
Identify the partnership's Sec. 751 assets

So far, the discussion of current distributions has ignored the existence of the Sec. 751 property rules. Now, we must expand our discussion to include them.

Section 751 Assets Defined

Key Point
Section 751 property represents property in a partnership that is likely to produce ordinary income or loss. The application of Sec. 751 in conjunction with partnership distributions or sales of a partnership interest is of greater concern now that capital gains are again subject to a preferential tax rate.

There are two categories of Sec. 751 assets: unrealized receivables and substantially appreciated inventory. These two categories encompass all property that is likely to produce ordinary income when sold or collected. Each of these categories must be carefully defined before any further discussion of Sec. 751.

Unrealized Receivables. Unrealized receivables includes a much broader spectrum of property than the name implies. **Unrealized receivables** are certain rights to payments to be received by the partnership to the extent they are not already included

---

[7] Sec. 735(b).
[8] Sec. 735(a)(1).
[9] Sec. 735(a)(2).

in income under the partnership's accounting methods. They include rights to payments for services performed or to be performed as well as rights to payment for goods delivered or to be delivered (other than capital assets).[10] A common example of unrealized receivables is the accounts receivable of a cash method of accounting partnership.

In addition to rights to receive payments for goods and services, the term *unrealized receivables* includes most potential ordinary income recapture items. A primary example of this type of unrealized receivable is the potential Sec. 1245 or 1250 gain on the partnership's depreciable property. The potential Sec. 1245 or 1250 gain is the amount of depreciation that would be recaptured as ordinary income under Sec. 1245 or 1250 if the partnership property were sold at its fair market value (FMV).[11]

Example 10-6 ■ The LK Partnership has two assets: (1) cash of $10,000 and (2) a machine having a $14,000 basis and a $20,000 FMV. Depreciation of $8,000 has been taken on the machine by the partnership since its purchase. If the machine was sold for its FMV, all $6,000 of the gain would be recaptured under Sec. 1245. Therefore, the LK Partnership has a $6,000 unrealized receivable item. ■

Self-Study Question
What is included in the definition of unrealized receivables?

Answer
Unrealized receivables include not only the obvious cash-method accounts receivable that have yet to be recognized but also most of the potential ordinary income recapture provisions. Therefore, the term unrealized receivables is much broader than it may appear.

The definition of unrealized receivables is not limited to Sec. 1245 and 1250 depreciation recapture. Among the other recapture provisions creating unrealized receivables are Sec. 617(f)(2) (mining property), Sec. 1252 (farmland), and Sec. 1253 (oil, gas, or geothermal property). Assets covered by Sec. 1278 (market discount bonds) and Sec. 1283 (short-term obligations) generate unrealized receivables to the extent the taxpayer would recognize ordinary income if the asset were sold. The unrealized receivable is deemed to have a zero basis. It should be clear that it is truly a rare partnership that totally avoids dealing with the complexities of Sec. 751.

Substantially Appreciated Inventory. **Substantially appreciated inventory** is equally surprising in its breadth. Inventory for purposes of Sec. 751 includes three major types of property:

- Items held for sale in the normal course of partnership business
- Any other property which, if sold by the partnership, would not be considered a capital asset or Sec. 1231 property
- Any other property held by the partnership which, if held by the selling or distributee partner, would be property of the two types listed above[12]

Typical Misconception
The definition of inventory is broadly construed by Sec. 751. In fact, for purposes of determining if inventory is "substantially appreciated," even unrealized receivables are treated as inventory items.

In short, cash, capital assets, and Sec. 1231 assets are the only properties that are not inventory. For purposes of testing whether the inventory is substantially appreciated (but *only* for that purpose), inventory also includes unrealized receivables. The inclusion of unrealized receivables in the definition of inventory makes it more likely that the inventory will be substantially appreciated.

The test to determine whether inventory is substantially appreciated (and therefore taxed under Sec. 751) is purely mechanical. Inventory is substantially appreciated if its FMV exceeds (1) 120% of its adjusted basis to the partnership, and (2) 10% of the FMV of all partnership property other than money.

---

[10] Reg. Sec. 1.751-1(c).
[11] Sec. 751(c).
[12] Sec. 751(d)(2).

Example 10-7 ■ The ABC Partnership owns the following assets on December 31:

	Basis	FMV
Cash	$10,000	$ 10,000
Unrealized receivables	—0—	40,000
Inventory	30,000	34,000
Land (Sec. 1231 property)	40,000	70,000
Total	$80,000	$154,000

For purposes of the substantially appreciated inventory tests, both ABC's unrealized receivables and inventory are included. The inventory's $74,000 FMV exceeds 120% of its adjusted basis ([$30,000 + 0] × 1.20 = $36,000). In addition, the inventory's $74,000 FMV exceeds 10% of the FMV of the nonmoney assets ([$154,000 − $10,000] × 0.10 = $14,400). Therefore, the ABC Partnership has substantially appreciated inventory. ■

Exchange of Sec. 751 Assets and Other Property

OBJECTIVE 4
Determine the tax implications of a sale or cash distribution when the partnership has Sec. 751 assets

A current distribution is partially taxed under Sec. 751 only if (1) the partnership has Sec. 751 assets and (2) there is an exchange of Sec. 751 property for non-Sec. 751 property.[13] Accordingly, if a partnership does not have *both* Sec. 751 property and other property, the rules discussed above for simple current distributions control the taxation of the distribution. Similarly, a distribution that (1) consists of only the partner's share of either Sec. 751 property or non-Sec. 751 property and (2) does not reduce the partner's interest in other property is not affected by the Sec. 751 taxation rules.

Typical Misconception

Even if a partnership has Sec. 751 property, Sec. 751 is not applicable as long as a partner's interest in the ordinary-income type assets is not altered. However, if a distribution of the partnership assets is disproportionate, then Sec. 751 treats that portion of the distribution as a deemed sale between the partnership and the distributee partner, with the corresponding income/loss being recognized.

However, any portion of the distribution representing an exchange of Sec. 751 property for non-Sec. 751 property must be isolated and is not treated as a distribution at all. Instead, it is treated as a sale between the partnership and the partner, and any gain or loss realized on the sale transaction is fully recognized.[14] The character of the recognized gain or loss is determined by the character of the property deemed sold. For the party deemed the seller of the Sec. 751 assets, the gain or loss is ordinary income or loss.

Analyzing the transaction to determine what property was involved in the Sec. 751 transaction is best accomplished by using an orderly, step-by-step approach.

STEP 1: DIVIDE THE ASSETS INTO SEC. 751 ASSETS AND NON-SEC. 751 ASSETS. Inventory must be tested at this time to see if it is substantially appreciated in order to know if it is a Sec. 751 asset.

STEP 2: DEVELOP A SCHEDULE, SUCH AS THE ONE IN TABLE 10-1, TO DETERMINE WHETHER THE PARTNER EXCHANGED SEC. 751 ASSETS FOR NON-SEC. 751 ASSETS OR VICE VERSA. This schedule must be based on the FMV of all the partnership's assets. To make the determination, it is necessary to compare the partner's interest in the partnership's assets before the distribution with his interest in the assets after the distribution. This part of our analysis assumes a fictional nontaxable pro rata distribution equal to the partner's decreased interest in the assets. We can see whether the partner exchanged Sec. 751 assets for non-Sec. 751 assets by comparing the fictional distribution with the actual distribution. Thus, in Table 10-1,

---
[13] Reg. Sec. 1.751-1(b).
[14] Sec. 751(b).

Key Point

Steps 2 and 3 are trying to identify whether or not a disproportionate distribution of Sec. 751 assets has taken place. In Table 10-1, if the column 5 total for Sec. 751 assets is zero, Sec. 751 is not applicable. But as the table illustrates, Anne received $10,000 over and above her share of the partnership cash while not receiving any of her $10,000 share of Sec. 751 assets.

- Column 1 represents the partner's interest (valued at FMV) in each asset before the distribution.
- Column 2 represents the partner's interest (valued at FMV) in each asset after the distribution.
- Column 3 shows the amount of a fictional proportionate distribution which would have occurred if the partner's ownership interest was reduced by taking a pro rata share of each asset. (As such, the proportionate distribution would be nontaxable.)
- Column 4 shows the amounts actually distributed.
- Column 5 shows the difference between the fictional and actual distributions. This column contains the information that must be analyzed to see if a Sec. 751 exchange has occurred.

STEP 3: ANALYZE COLUMN 5 TO DETERMINE WHETHER SEC. 751 ASSETS WERE EXCHANGED FOR NON-SEC. 751 ASSETS. If the column 5 total for the Sec. 751 assets section of Table 10-1 is zero, there is no Sec. 751 exchange. The partner simply received an additional amount of one type of Sec. 751 asset in exchange for relinquishing an interest in some other type of Sec. 751 asset. For example, no Sec. 751 exchange has occurred if a partner exchanged an interest in substantially appreciated inventory for an interest in unrealized receivables. If, however, the column 5 total for the Sec. 751 assets section is an amount other than zero, a Sec. 751 exchange has occurred. One (or more) Sec. 751 properties has been exchanged for one (or more) non-Sec. 751 properties.

Example 10-8 ▪ The ABC Partnership holds the assets listed below on January 1, before making a distribution to Anne.

	Basis	FMV
Cash	$ 75,000	$ 75,000
Unrealized receivables	—0—	15,000
Inventory	30,000	60,000
Total	$105,000	$150,000

TABLE 10-1 Analysis of Sec. 751 Nonliquidating Distribution (Example 10-8)

	Partnership Amount[a]	(1) Anne's Interest before Distribution[a] (1/3)	(2) Anne's Interest after Distribution[a] (1/5)	(3) Fictional Proportionate Distribution (3) = (1) − (2)[a]	(4) Actual Distribution[a]	(5) Difference[b] (5) = (4) − (3)
Sec. 751 Assets:						
Unrealized receivables	$15,000	$ 5,000	$ 3,000	$ 2,000	—0—	$ (2,000)
Inventory	60,000	20,000	12,000	8,000	—0—	(8,000)
Total Sec. 751 Assets	$75,000	$25,000	$15,000	$10,000	—0—	$(10,000)
Non-Sec. 751 Assets:						
Cash	$75,000	$25,000	$10,000[c]	$15,000	$25,000	$ 10,000
Total Non-Sec. 751 Assets	$75,000	$25,000	$10,000	$15,000	$25,000	$ 10,000

[a] Valued at fair market value.
[b] A negative amount means that Anne gave up her interest in a particular property. A positive amount means that she received more than her proportionate interest.
[c] 1/5 interest in remaining cash of $50,000.

On January 1, Anne's partnership interest is reduced from one-third to one-fifth by a $25,000 cash distribution. ABC owes no liabilities on January 1. Prior to the distribution, Anne has a $35,000 basis in this partnership interest. The following steps are needed to determine the tax effects of the distribution:

STEP 1: Determine ABC's Sec. 751 and non-Sec. 751 assets. ABC's Sec. 751 assets include the unrealized receivables and the substantially appreciated inventory. The cash is ABC's only non-Sec. 751 property.

STEP 2: Complete the table used to analyze the Sec. 751 distribution (see Table 10-1).

STEP 3: Analyze column 5 of Table 10-1 to see if a Sec. 751 exchange has occurred. Because Anne's Sec. 751 asset total had declined by $10,000, we know that $10,000 of her proportionate interest in ABC's Sec. 751 assets was given up in exchange for cash. ■

STEP 4: DETERMINE THE GAIN OR LOSS ON THE SEC. 751 DEEMED SALE. It is necessary to assume that the exchange occurring in step 3 above was actually a sale of the exchanged property between the partnership and the partner. This step follows logically from the fact that the partner "bargained" to receive the amounts actually distributed rather than a proportionate distribution. She sold her interest in some assets to receive more than her proportionate share of other assets. This sale is analyzed exactly the same way any other sale is analyzed. The gain (or loss) equals the difference between the FMV of the property received and the adjusted basis of the property given up. Note that up to this point we have been dealing only in terms of the FMV, thus the adjusted basis of property given up must be determined as if that fictional distribution had actually been received.

Example 10-9 ■

Assume the same facts as in Example 10-8. The Sec. 751 sale portion of the distribution is analyzed as Anne receiving $10,000 more cash than her proportionate share and giving up a $2,000 (FMV) interest in the unrealized receivables and an $8,000 (FMV) interest in the inventory. By examining the balance sheet, we can see that the partnership's bases for the unrealized receivables and inventory are $0 and $4,000 ($8,000 × [$30,000 ÷ $60,000]). If Anne received these properties in a current distribution, her basis would be the same as the property's basis in the partnership's hands, or $0 and $4,000, respectively. Therefore, Anne's deemed sale of the Sec. 751 assets is analyzed as follows:

Amount realized	$10,000
Minus: Adjusted basis of property	(4,000)
Realized and recognized gain	$ 6,000

The character of the recognized gain depends on the character of the property sold, in this case, the unrealized receivables and inventory. Therefore, Anne's $6,000 gain is ordinary income. ■

Typical Misconception

Step 4 is crucial if a student is to understand the deemed sale that Sec. 751 creates. In Example 10-9, Anne is treated as if she had exchanged her $10,000 interest in the unrealized receivables and inventory for $10,000 of cash. Thus, Anne has a taxable gain/loss on the deemed sale. To determine Anne's gain/loss on the deemed sale, the adjusted basis of the unrealized receivables and inventory equals whatever her basis would have been if those assets had actually been distributed to her.

STEP 5: DETERMINE THE IMPACT OF THE CURRENT DISTRIBUTION. The last step in analyzing the distribution's effect on the partner is to determine the impact of the portion of the distribution which is not a Sec. 751 exchange. This distribution is treated exactly like any other nonliquidating distribution.

Example 10-10 ■

Assume the same facts as in Examples 10-8 and 10-9. Examining the actual distribution, we see in column 4 of Table 10-1 that only $10,000 of the $25,000 cash

Key Point
After determining the tax effects of the Sec. 751 exchange, the portion of the distribution that was not covered by Sec. 751 must be dealt with. Thus, the regular current distribution rules are applied to the remaining portion of the distribution.

actually distributed is received as part of the Sec. 751 exchange. The remaining $15,000 that is distributed represents a current distribution. Under Sec. 731(a)(1), gain is recognized by a partner on a current distribution only if the cash distributed exceeds their basis in the partnership interest. Anne recognizes no gain because she has a $16,000 basis in the partnership interest immediately after the current distribution. This basis is calculated as follows:

Predistribution basis for partnership interest	$35,000
Minus: Basis of property deemed distributed in Sec. 751 exchange ($0 unrealized receivables + $4,000 inventory)	(4,000)
Basis before current distribution	$31,000
Minus: Cash distributed	(15,000)
Postdistribution basis of partnership interest	$16,000

After the entire distribution is complete, Anne owns a partnership interest with a basis of $16,000 and has $25,000 in money. She has recognized $6,000 in ordinary income.

TERMINATING AN INTEREST IN A PARTNERSHIP

There are numerous ways to terminate an interest in a partnership. The two most common are receiving a liquidating distribution or selling the interest. Other possibilities include giving the interest away, exchanging the interest for corporate stock, and transferring the interest at death. Each of these methods of disposing of a partnership interest is considered.

Liquidating Distributions

OBJECTIVE 5
Determine the amount and character of the gain or loss recognized by a partner from a liquidating partnership distribution

A liquidating distribution is defined as a distribution, or one of a series of distributions, that terminates a partner's interest in the partnership.[15] If the partner's interest is drastically reduced, but not terminated, the distribution is reported as a current distribution. A liquidating distribution can occur when (1) only one member of a partnership terminates his interest, (2) several partners terminate their interests but the partnership continues, or (3) the entire partnership terminates and each partner receives a liquidating distribution. Rules for taxation of a liquidating distribution are the same whether one partner terminates his interest or the entire partnership liquidates.

Key Point
The rules for gain recognition are the same for liquidating and current distributions. However, in a liquidating distribution, the partner recognizes a loss if: (1) the only assets distributed are cash, unrealized receivables, and inventory and (2) the adjusted basis in such assets is less than the partner's basis in

Gain or Loss Recognition by the Partner. The rule for recognizing gain on a liquidating distribution is exactly the same rule used for a current distribution. Gain is recognized only if the money distributed (including money deemed distributed to the partner from a liability reduction) exceeds the partner's predistribution basis in his partnership interest.[16]

While loss can never be recognized from a current distribution, a loss can be recognized from a liquidating distribution. A loss is recognized only if the distribution

---
[15] Sec. 761(d).
[16] Sec. 731(a)(1).

his partnership interest. The loss is necessary because, in a liquidating distribution, the partner does not have a partnership interest afterward.

consists of money (including money deemed distributed), unrealized receivables, and inventory, but no other property.[17] The amount of the loss is the difference between the partner's basis in the partnership interest before the distribution and the sum of money plus the bases of the receivables and inventory (to the partnership immediately before the distribution) that are received.

Example 10-11 ■

Dana's interest in the ABC Partnership is terminated when her basis in the partnership is $35,000. She receives a liquidating distribution of $10,000 cash and inventory with a $12,000 basis to the partnership. Her recognized loss is $13,000 ($35,000 − [$10,000 + $12,000]). ■

OBJECTIVE 6
Determine the basis of assets received by a partner in a liquidating partnership distribution

Basis in Assets Received. The basis of an asset received by the partner in a liquidating distribution is determined using rules similar to those used to determine the basis of an asset received in a current distribution. For both kinds of distributions, the basis in unrealized receivables and inventory is generally the same as the property's basis in the partnership's hands. Under no condition will the basis of these two types of assets be increased. Occasionally, however, the partner's basis in his partnership interest is so small that after making the necessary reduction for money (and deemed money) distributions, the basis in the partnership interest is smaller than the partnership's bases for the unrealized receivables and inventory that are distributed. In such cases, the remaining basis in the partnership interest must be allocated among the unrealized receivables and inventory items based on their relative bases on the partnership's books.[18] This means that the bases for the unrealized receivables and inventory are reduced, and the amount of ordinary income to be recognized on their ultimate sale, exchange, or collection is increased.

Example 10-12 ■

Typical Misconception
The basis to a partner of distributed unrealized receivables or inventory can never be greater than the partnership's basis in those assets. Also, if the partner's basis in his partnership interest is not sufficient, the partner's basis in the distributed unrealized receivables and inventory will be less than the partnership's basis in those assets.

Beth receives a pro rata liquidating distribution from the ABC Partnership when the basis for her partnership interest is $30,000. She receives $20,000 cash, unrealized receivables with a $100 basis to the partnership, and inventory with a $14,000 basis to the partnership. First, Beth's interest in her partnership interest is reduced by the $20,000 of cash received. Next, the remaining $10,000 basis is allocated between the receivables and inventory as follows:

$$\text{Receivables:} \frac{\$100}{\$14,000 + \$100} \times \$10,000 = \$71$$

$$\text{Inventory:} \frac{\$14,000}{\$14,000 + \$100} \times \$10,000 = \$9,929$$
■

Remember that a liquidating distribution of cash, unrealized receivables, and inventory with a total basis on the books of the partnership that is less than the partner's basis in his partnership results in the recognition of a loss. However, no loss is recognized if the distribution includes any property other than cash, unrealized receivables, and inventory. Instead, all of the remaining basis in the partnership interest must be applied to the other property received regardless of that property's basis to the partnership or its FMV. Application of this rule can create strange results.

[17] Sec. 731(a)(2).
[18] Sec. 732(c).

Example 10-13 ■

Typical Misconception

If the partner still has basis in his partnership interest, after a liquidating distribution that includes property other than cash, unrealized receivables, and inventory, this remaining basis is allocated to the "other property" received by the partner. This rule can produce some unusual results. Look to Example 10-13 as an illustration of this point.

Assume the same facts as in Example 10-11, except that Dana's distribution includes an office typewriter having a $50 basis to the partnership and a $100 FMV as part of the distribution. The allocation of basis proceeds as follows:

Predistribution basis for partnership interest	$35,000
Minus: Money received	(10,000)
Basis after money distribution	$25,000
Minus: Basis of inventory to partnership	(12,000)
Remaining basis of partnership interest	$13,000

The entire $13,000 remaining basis of the partnership interest is allocated to the typewriter. ■

The basis allocation procedure illustrated in Example 10-13 delays the loss recognition until the typewriter is either depreciated or sold. However, the allocation procedure may also change the character of the loss since Dana would recognize a capital loss when she receives the liquidating distribution in Example 10-11. In Example 10-13, the character of Dana's loss is determined by the character of the typewriter in her hands (or in some cases by a series of specific rules that are discussed below). Worst of all, if she converts the typewriter into personal-use property, the loss on its sale or exchange is nondeductible.

If two or more assets other than unrealized receivables or inventory are distributed together, the remaining basis in the partnership interest is allocated among them based on their relative bases in the partnership's hands. Note that such an allocation process can lead to either a decrease or increase in the total basis of these assets.[19] This potential for increasing the assets' bases is unique to partnership liquidating distributions.

Example 10-14 ■

Before receiving a liquidating distribution, Craig's basis in his interest in the BCD Partnership is $60,000. The distribution consists of $10,000 in money, unrealized receivables having a $2,000 basis to the partnership, and two tracts of undeveloped land having bases of $6,000 and $18,000 to the partnership. His bases in the assets received are calculated as follows:

Predistribution basis for partnership interest	$60,000
Minus: Money received	(10,000)
Basis of unrealized receivables to the partnership	(2,000)
Basis allocated to two tracts of land	$48,000

$$\text{Basis of tract 1: } \frac{\$6,000}{\$6,000 + \$18,000} \times \$48,000 = \$12,000$$

$$\text{Basis of tract 2: } \frac{\$18,000}{\$6,000 + \$18,000} \times \$48,000 = \$36,000$$

■

Key Point

If neither gain nor loss is recognized in a liquidating distribution, the partner's basis in the distributed assets always equals the partner's former basis in his partnership interest.

In a liquidating distribution, the amount of money received plus the basis of the nonmoney property received in the hands of the distributee partner normally equals the partner's predistribution basis in the partnership interest. The only two exceptions to this rule occur when (1) the money received exceeds the partner's basis in his partnership interest and a gain must be recognized or (2) money, unrealized receiv-

[19] Sec. 732(c)(2).

ables, and inventory are the only assets distributed and a loss must be recognized. In all other liquidating distributions, the distributee partner recognizes no gain or loss. Instead, that partner's predistribution basis in his partnership interest is transferred to the cash and other property received.

HOLDING PERIOD IN DISTRIBUTED ASSETS. The distributee partner's holding period for any assets received in a liquidating distribution includes the partnership's holding period for such property.[20] If the partnership received the property as a contribution from a partner, the partnership's holding period may also include the period of time the contributing partner held the property (see Chapter 9). Therefore, the holding period for property received in a liquidating distribution may include both the time the partnership holds the property and the time a contributing partner holds the property. Note that the distributee partner's holding period for his partnership interest is irrelevant in determining the holding period of the assets received.

Example 10-15 ■ George purchases an interest in the DEF Partnership on June 1, 1991, but he cannot get along with the other partners. On July 1, 1991, he receives a liquidating distribution which terminates his interest in the partnership. George's distribution includes land that the partnership has owned since August 1, 1988. George's holding period for the land commences on August 1, 1988, even though his holding period for the partnership interest begins almost 3 years later. ■

The character of the gain or loss recognized on a subsequent sale of distributed property is determined using the same rules as for a current distribution.

Key Point

The main difference in how the mechanics of the Sec. 751 rules are applied to current versus liquidating distributions is that after a liquidating distribution, the partner always has a zero interest in the partnership assets because he/she is no longer a partner in the partnership.

Effects of Sec. 751. Section 751 has essentially the same impact on both liquidating and current distributions. To the extent that the partner's interest in Sec. 751 assets is exchanged for other assets (or vice versa), that portion of the transaction is removed from the distribution rules. Instead, this portion of the transaction is treated as a sale occurring between the partnership and the partner. There is one notable difference between liquidating distributions and current distributions having Sec. 751 implications; that is, the postdistribution interest in partnership assets is zero for the liquidating distribution since it terminates the partner's interest in the partnership.

Example 10-16 ■ The ABC Partnership holds the following assets on December 31:

	Basis	FMV
Cash	$75,000	$ 75,000
Unrealized receivables	—0—	15,000
Inventory	15,000	60,000
Total	$90,000	$150,000

Al has a one-third interest in the partnership before receiving $50,000 in cash as a liquidating distribution. The partnership has no liabilities, and Al's predistribution basis in his partnership interest is $30,000. The following steps are needed to determine the tax effects of the liquidating distribution:

STEP 1: Determine ABC's Sec. 751 and non-Sec. 751 assets. The Sec. 751 assets include the unrealized receivables and the substantially appreciated inventory. The cash is ABC's only non-Sec. 751 asset.

STEP 2: Complete the table used to analyze the Sec. 751 distributions (see Table 10-2).

[20] Sec. 735(b).

Self-Study Question
What is the deemed Sec. 751 exchange shown in Table 10-2?

Answer
Column 5 shows that Al received $25,000 of excess cash in lieu of $25,000 of Sec. 751 assets. Thus, the Sec. 751 exchange is a deemed sale by Al of $25,000 of unrealized receivables and inventory to the partnership in exchange for $25,000 of cash. If one can create a table similar to Table 10-2, the Sec. 751 computations are much easier to understand.

STEP 3: Analyze column 5 of Table 10-2 to see if a Sec. 751 exchange has occurred. Table 10-2 shows that Al exchanges $5,000 of unrealized receivables and $20,000 of inventory for $25,000 cash.

STEP 4: Determine the gain or loss on the Sec. 751 deemed sale. Al is deemed to have sold unrealized receivables and inventory for cash. Assume Al first got the receivables and inventory in a current distribution. He receives the partnership's bases for the assets of $0 and $5,000, respectively. The deemed sale results in Al recognizing a $20,000 gain.

Amount realized	$25,000
Minus: Adjusted basis of property	(5,000)
Realized and recognized gain	$20,000

Al's gain is ordinary income since it results from his deemed sale of receivables and inventory to the partnership.

STEP 5: Determine the impact of the non-Sec. 751 portion of the distribution. The liquidating distribution is only the $25,000 cash he receives that was *not* a part of the Sec. 751 transaction. To determine its impact, we must first find Al's basis in his partnership interest after the Sec. 751 transaction but before the $25,000 liquidating distribution.

Predistribution basis in the partnership interest	$30,000
Minus: Basis of receivables and inventory received in fictional Sec. 751 transaction	(5,000)
Basis before money distribution	$25,000
Minus: Money distribution	(25,000)
Gain recognized on liquidating distribution	$ —0—

No further gain or loss is recognized from the liquidating distribution portion of the transaction. ■

Effects of Distribution on the Partnership. A partnership recognizes no gain or loss on liquidating distributions to its partners.[21] If a Sec. 751 deemed sale occurs, however, the partnership may be required to recognize gain or loss on assets deemed sold to its partner. A liquidating distribution normally does not itself terminate the

TABLE 10-2 Analysis of Sec. 751 Liquidating Distribution (Example 10-16)

	Partnership Amount[a]	(1) Al's Interest before Distribution[a] (1/3)	(2) Al's Interest after Distribution[a] (0)	(3) Fictional Proportionate Distribution (3) = (1) − (2)[a]	(4) Actual Distribution[a]	(5) Difference[b] (5) = (4) − (3)
Sec. 751 Assets:						
Unrealized receivables	$15,000	$ 5,000	—0—	$ 5,000	—0—	$ (5,000)
Inventory	60,000	20,000	—0—	20,000	—0—	(20,000)
Total Sec.751 Assets	$75,000	$25,000	—0—	$25,000	—0—	$(25,000)
Non-Sec. 751 Assets:						
Cash	$75,000	$25,000	—0—	$25,000	$50,000	$25,000
Total Non-Sec. 751 Assets	$75,000	$25,000	—0—	$25,000	$50,000	$25,000

[a] Valued at fair market value.
[b] A negative amount means that Al gave up his interest in a particular property. A positive amount means that Al received more than his proportionate interest.

[21] Sec. 731(b).

partnership. The partnership terminates if none of the remaining partners continue to operate the business of the partnership in a partnership form.[22] The partnership may also be affected by a liquidating distribution if the partnership has made a Sec. 754 election to make optional basis adjustments.

Topic Review 10-1 presents a summary of the tax consequences of current and liquidating distributions.

Sale of a Partnership Interest

Self-Study Question

What is the character of gain/loss on the sale of a partnership interest?

Answer

Since a partnership interest is generally a capital asset, the sale of a partnership interest usually results in a capital gain/loss being recognized. However, if a partnership has Sec. 751 assets, the partner is deemed to sell his share of the Sec. 751 assets directly with a corresponding ordinary gain/loss being recognized.

When a partner sells a partnership interest, capital gain or loss on the sale is recognized as if corporate stock was sold.[23] However, to the extent Sec. 751 applies, the partner must recognize ordinary income or loss from the sale of his interest in unrealized receivables and substantially appreciated inventory.[24] The sale of a partnership interest may have three other effects: (1) the partner's share of the partnership's liabilities is acquired by the purchaser, (2) an adjustment to the basis of the partnership's assets may be made if an optional basis adjustment election has been made, and (3) the partnership may be terminated. Each of these situations related to the sale of a partnership interest is examined below.

Section 751 Properties. As with distributions, the effects of Sec. 751 should be calculated first so that the remainder of the transaction can be properly analyzed. The first step has two parts: (1) determine the amount realized for the Sec. 751 property and (2) calculate the adjusted basis of such property to the partner. The partner's adjusted basis for the Sec. 751 property equals the basis that the property would have if the partner received the property in a current distribution occurring just prior to the sale of the partnership interest. Next, the buyer and seller can allocate the price paid for the partnership interest among the Sec. 751 and non-Sec. 751 properties in any manner that they choose. If the allocation occurs at arm's length, it is generally acceptable to the IRS.[25] If no allocation is agreed upon, the amount allocated to each Sec. 751 property is based on the relative FMVs of all of the partnership's properties. The difference between the amount realized and adjusted basis for the Sec. 751 properties is the ordinary income or loss that must be recognized by the partner on the sale.

Example 10-17 ■ Troy sells his one-fourth interest in the TV Partnership to Steve for $50,000 cash when the partnership's assets are as follows:

	Basis	FMV
Cash	$ 40,000	$ 40,000
Unrealized receivables	—0—	36,000
Inventory	40,000	92,000
Land	40,000	32,000
Total	$120,000	$200,000

The partnership has no liabilities on the sale date. Troy's basis in his partnership interest is $30,000 on such date. Both the receivables and inventory are Sec. 751 assets. Assuming Troy and Steve do not agree to an allocation of the sales price, Troy's gain or loss for the Sec. 751 deemed sale is calculated as follows:

---

[22] Sec. 708.
[23] Sec. 741.
[24] Sec. 751(a).
[25] Reg. Sec. 1.751-1(a).

Amount realized for Sec. 751 assets ([0.25 × $36,000] + [0.25 × $92,000])	$32,000
Minus: Adjusted basis of Sec. 751 assets ([0.25 × $0] + [0.25 × $40,000])[a]	(10,000)
Sec. 751 ordinary income	$22,000

[a] Troy's basis for the receivables and inventory received in the deemed current distribution equals the partnership's basis for such properties.

After the Sec. 751 portion of the sale is isolated, it is not difficult to analyze the remaining sale. The sales price minus the portion of the proceeds allocated to the Sec. 751 assets is the amount realized for the sale of the remaining partnership interest. For calculating gain or loss on the sale, the partner's basis in his partnership interest equals the predistribution basis for the partnership interest minus the amount of basis allocated to the Sec. 751 assets. Any gain or loss on the sale of the remaining partnership interest is considered to be gain or loss derived from the sale of a capital asset.

Example 10-18 ■ Assume the same facts as in Example 10-17. Analyzing the non-Sec. 751 portion of the sale transaction occurs as follows:

		Sale of	
	Total	Sec. 751 Assets	Remaining Partnership Interest
Amount realized	$50,000	$32,000	$18,000
Minus: Adjusted basis	(30,000)	(10,000)	(20,000)
Recognized gain or loss	$20,000	$22,000	($2,000)
Ordinary income		$22,000	
Capital loss			($2,000)

Key Point

Once the Sec. 751 gain/loss has been determined, the remaining gain/loss is a capital gain/loss. Example 10-18, illustrates that without Sec. 751, these two types of gains/losses would have simply been netted together.

The Sec. 751 portion of the sale remains the same as in Example 10-17. The $18,000 ($50,000 − $32,000) remainder of the purchase price is allocated to the remaining partnership interest along with the $20,000 ($30,000 − $10,000) remainder of the basis for the partnership interest. ■

Typical Misconception

Although the partner's distributive share of liabilities is included in the amount realized, this is somewhat misleading. This same amount is also reflected in the partner's basis in his partnership interest. Thus, since the same amount is in both the amount realized and the adjusted basis, the partner's share of the partnership liabilities really cancels out.

The separation of the sale of a partnership interest into its two components may yield both a gain and a loss as is illustrated by Example 10-18. If the entity theory prevailed instead, no assets would be separated out, and Troy would report a $20,000 capital gain. Because of Sec. 751, Troy must report both ordinary income and a capital loss.

Liabilities. When a partnership has liabilities, each partner's distributive share of the liabilities is part of the basis for the partnership interest. When the partnership interest is sold, the partner is relieved of the liabilities. Accordingly, the amount realized on the sale of a partnership interest is made up of money plus the FMV of nonmoney property received plus the seller's distributive share of partnership liabilities that are assumed or acquired by the purchaser.[26]

---

[26] Sec. 752(d).

TOPIC REVIEW 10-1

Current and Liquidating Distributions

Tax Consequences	Current Distributions	Liquidating Distributions
Impact on Partner:		
Money (or deemed money from liability changes) distributed	Recognize gain only if money distributed exceeds basis in partnership before distribution.	Recognize gain only if money distributed exceeds basis in partnership before distribution.
Unrealized receivable and/or inventory distributed	Carryover basis (limited to basis in partnership before distribution reduced by money distributed).	Carryover basis (limited to basis in partnership before distribution reduced by money distributed).
	No gain or loss is recognized.	Loss recognized if only money, inventory and receivables distributed with bases less than basis in partnership interest before distribution.
Other property distributed	Carryover basis (limited to basis in partnership interest before distribution reduced by money and carryover basis in inventory and receivables).	Basis equal to basis in partnership interest before distribution reduced by money and carryover basis in inventory and receivables.
	No gain or loss is recognized.	No gain or loss is recognized.
Impact on Partnership:	No gain or loss is recognized.	No gain or loss is recognized.
Other tax consequences to the partnership	If a Sec. 751 deemed sale or exchange occurs, gain or loss on the deemed sale may be recognized by the partner and/or the partnership.	If a Sec. 751 deemed sale or exchange occurs, gain or loss on the deemed sale may be recognized by the partner and/or the partnership.

Example 10-19 ■ Andrew is a 30% partner in the ABC Partnership when he sells his entire interest to Michael for $40,000 cash. At the time of the sale, Andrew's basis is $27,000, which includes his $7,000 distributive share of partnership liabilities. The

partnership has no Sec. 751 assets. Andrew's $20,000 gain on the sale is calculated as follows:

Amount realized:		
Cash	$40,000	
Liabilities assumed by purchaser	7,000	$47,000
Minus: Adjusted basis		(27,000)
Gain recognized on sale		$20,000

Impact on the Partnership. When one partner sells his partnership interest, the sale usually has no more impact on the partnership than the sale of corporate stock by one shareholder has on the corporation. Only the partner and the purchaser of the interest are affected. However, if (1) the partnership elects under Sec. 754 to make optional basis adjustments or (2) the partnership interest that is sold is sufficiently large so that under Sec. 708 its sale terminates the partnership for tax purposes, the partnership itself is affected. Both of these effects are discussed later in this chapter.

Retirement or Death of a Partner

OBJECTIVE 7
Determine the amount and character of the gain or loss recognized when a partner retires from a partnership or dies

If a partner dies or retires from a partnership, that partner's interest can be sold either to an outsider or to one or more existing partners.[27] The results of such a sale are outlined above. Frequently, however, a partner or a deceased partner's assignee departs from the partnership in return for payments made by the partnership itself.[28] When the partnership buys out the partner's interest, the analysis of the tax results focuses on two types of payments: (1) payments made in exchange for the partner's interest in partnership property[29] and (2) other payments.

Typical Misconception
The significance of the two different kinds of payments is not readily apparent to some taxpayers. The "payments for partnership property" are not deductible by the partnership and possibly are not income to the retiring partner. On the other hand, payments considered in the second category are deductible by the partnership (or they reduce the distributive shares that must be recognized by other partners) and usually are income to the retiring partner.

Payments for Partnership Property. Generally, the valuation placed on the retiring partner's interest in the partnership properties by the partners in an arm's-length transaction is accepted by the IRS. The payments made for the property interest are largely taxed under the liquidating distribution rules. There are two exceptions to these rules.

1. Payments made for the retiring or deceased partner's interest in unrealized receivables must be separated from payments for other property and are not taxed under the distribution rules.
2. Payments for partnership goodwill are taxed under the distribution rules only to the extent that the partnership agreement provides for a payment for goodwill to a retiring partner or a deceased partner's successor-in-interest.[30]

Both of these payments result in the recognition of ordinary income by the recipient. The remaining property payments are likely to generate capital gain to the

---

[27] Note that retirement from the partnership in this context has nothing to do with reaching a specific age and leaving the employ of the partnership but instead refers to the partner's withdrawal at any age from a continuing partnership.

[28] Sec. 736.

[29] Sec. 736(b).

[30] A deceased partner's successor-in-interest is the party that succeeds to the rights of the deceased partner's partnership interest (e.g., the decedent's estate or an heir or legatee of the deceased partner). A deceased partner's successor-in-interest is treated as a partner by the tax laws until his interest in the partnership has been completely liquidated.

retiring partner (except payments made for substantially appreciated inventory, which are taxed under Sec. 751). Like any liquidating distribution made to a partner, payments made to a retiring partner or a deceased partner's successor-in-interest in exchange for their property interest are not deductible by the partnership.

Other Payments. A second set of rules must be followed if a retiring or a deceased partner's successor-in-interest receives payments other than a payment for an interest in partnership property. Payments taxed under these rules include

- Payments for unrealized receivables
- Payments for goodwill if (1) the partnership agreement is silent as to goodwill or (2) the amount that is paid for goodwill exceeds the amount specified in the partnership agreement

Typical Misconception
The main difference between a payment being taxed as a distributive share or as a guaranteed payment is the character of the income recognized by the recipient partner. If the payment is taxed as a distributive share, the character of the income is determined by the type of income earned by the partnership. The payment is ordinary income if it is treated as a guaranteed payment.

Under these rules, a payment is taxed either as a distributive share or a guaranteed payment. If the excess payment is determined as a function of partnership income (e.g., 10% of the partnership's net income), the income is considered a distributive share of partnership income.[31] Accordingly, the character of the income flows through to the partner, and each of the remaining partners is taxed on a smaller amount of partnership income. The income must be reported in the partner's tax year which includes the partnership year-end from which the distributive share arises regardless of when the distribution is actually received.

If, on the other hand, the amount of the excess payment is determined without regard to the partnership income, the payment is treated as a guaranteed payment.[32] If the payment is a guaranteed payment, the retiring partner recognizes ordinary income, and the partnership generally has an ordinary deduction. Like all guaranteed payments, the income is includible in the recipient's income for his tax year with or within which ends the partnership tax year in which the partnership claims its deduction (see Chapter 9).[33]

Example 10-20 ■ When Bob retires from the ABC Partnership after having been a partner for 5 years, he receives a cash payment of $65,000. At the time of Bob's retirement, his basis for his partnership interest basis is $50,000, and the partnership's balance sheet is as follows:

	Basis	FMV
Assets:		
Cash	$ 75,000	$ 75,000
Receivables	—0—	15,000
Inventory	24,000	45,000
Land	51,000	75,000
Total	$150,000	$210,000
Liabilities and Capital:		
Liabilities	$ 30,000	$ 30,000
Bob's capital	40,000	60,000
Audrey's capital	40,000	60,000
Cathy's capital	40,000	60,000
Total	$150,000	$210,000

---

[31] Sec. 736(a)(1).
[32] Sec. 736(a)(2).
[33] Reg. Sec. 1.736-1(a)(5).

Key Point

Partners are granted great flexibility under Sec. 736 in selecting the method of structuring a transfer. For instance, in Example 10-20 the partners are free to provide, in the partnership agreement, for payments for goodwill. This would not only make the $5,000 payment nondeductible by the partnership, but would also create capital gain income for Bob. However, in this example, the partners did not provide for goodwill payments. Thus, the $5,000 payment is deductible by the partnership and ordinary income to Bob.

The partnership agreement makes no mention of goodwill.

In the absence of a valuation agreement, it is assumed that the partnership pays Bob a ratable share of the FMV of each asset. The $75,000 amount received ($65,000 cash payment + $10,000 release from partnership liabilities) should be divided as follows:

Cash	$25,000
Receivables	5,000
Inventory	15,000
Land	25,000
Excess payment	5,000
Total	$75,000

■

Payments for Partnership Property. The portion of the $75,000 payment considered to be for property equals the sum of the payments for cash, inventory, and land ($65,000). These payments are taxed under the distribution rules (including the Sec. 751 rules for substantially appreciated inventory).

The Sec. 751 transaction must be accounted for first. If Bob received his share of the inventory in a current distribution, the basis for Bob's one-third interest in this asset would be $8,000 (0.333 × $24,000). Instead, he receives $15,000 cash for his share of the inventory and must report $7,000 ($15,000 − $8,000 basis) of ordinary income.

Other Payments. The payments for the unrealized receivables are taxed as guaranteed payments since the amounts are determined without reference to partnership income. Because the partnership agreement makes no provision for a partner receiving payments for goodwill upon retirement from the partnership, the excess payment for goodwill is also treated as a guaranteed payment. Both of the payments that are treated as guaranteed payments are deductible by the partnership and taxed as ordinary income to the recipient. Since they are guaranteed payments, they do not affect the partner's basis.

Basis. We have now accounted for (1) a $15,000 payment for Bob's interest in inventory, (2) a $5,000 payment for unrealized receivables, and (3) a $5,000 excess payment for goodwill. The $50,000 remainder of the payment received by Bob ($75,000 − [$15,000 + $5,000 + $5,000]) is a liquidating distribution. Distributions reduce the partner's basis in the partnership interest, and gain is recognized if a cash distribution exceeds the basis in the partnership interest.

Under the liquidating distribution rules, Bob's basis in his partnership interest is allocated as follows:

Basis in partnership interest before transaction	$50,000
Minus: Basis of inventory deemed distributed under Sec. 751	(8,000)
Basis after Sec. 751 deemed distribution	$42,000
Minus: Cash received as a distribution ($75,000 − [$15,000 + $5,000 + $5,000])	(50,000)
Cash distributed in excess of basis	$ 8,000

The $8,000 cash distribution in excess of basis is taxed as long-term capital gain.

A retiring partner who receives payments from the partnership is considered to be a partner in that partnership until the last payment is received. Likewise, a deceased partner's successor-in-interest is considered to be a member of the partnership until the last payment is received.[34]

Exchange of a Partnership Interest

Exchange for Another Partnership Interest. A partner may also terminate a partnership interest by exchanging it either for an interest in another partnership or a different interest in the same partnership. The Tax Reform Act of 1984 mandated that exchanges involving interests in different partnerships did not qualify for such treatment.[35] Nevertheless, the IRS still allows exchanges of interests within a single partnership.[36]

Example 10-21 ■

Self-Study Question

Can the exchange of a partnership interest qualify for nonrecognition treatment as a like-kind exchange?

Answer

Yes, if the exchange of interests is within a single partnership. However, exchanges of partnership interests in different partnerships are not considered a like-kind exchange.

Pam and Dean are equal partners in the PD General Partnership, which owns and operates a farm. The two partners agree to convert PD into a limited partnership with Pam becoming a limited partner and Dean having both a general and a limited partnership interest in PD. Even though the partners exchange a general partnership interest for a limited partnership interest (plus an exchange of a general partnership interest for a general partnership interest for Dean), no gain or loss is recognized from the exchange. If, however, a partner's interest in the partnership's liabilities is changed, that partner's basis must be adjusted. If liabilities are reduced and a deemed distribution in excess of the basis for the partnership interest occurs, gain must be recognized. ■

Exchange for Corporate Stock. A partnership interest may be exchanged for corporate stock in a transaction that qualifies under the Sec. 351 nonrecognition rules (see Chapter 2). For purposes of Sec. 351, a partnership interest is considered property. If the other requirements of Sec. 351 are met, a single partner's partnership interest can be transferred for stock in a new or an existing corporation in a nontaxable exchange. This exchange is taxed to the partner as if he had exchanged any other property under the Sec. 351 rules. The basis in the corporate stock is determined by the partner's basis in the partnership interest. The holding period for the stock received in the exchange includes the holding period for the partnership interest. As a result of the exchange, one of the corporation's assets is an interest in a partnership, and the corporation (not the transferor) is now the partner of record. As such, the corporation must report its distributive share of partnership income along with all of its other earnings.

Self-Study Question

If a partnership is incorporated, does the form of the transaction make a difference?

Answer

The form of an incorporation involving a partnership can make a difference. For example, if an existing corporation was an S corporation, the S election would be terminated if, as a result of the incorporation transaction, the partnership ends up being a shareholder. Also, if it is desirable to have the newly issued stock qualify as Sec. 1244 stock, then the partnership's partners need to be the original shareholders.

Incorporation. When limited liability is important, the entire partnership may choose to incorporate. Normally such an incorporation can be structured to fall within the Sec. 351 provisions and can be partially or totally tax exempt. When a partnership chooses to incorporate, there are three possible alternatives:

1. The partnership contributes its assets and liabilities to the corporation in exchange for the corporation's stock (and possibly securities). The stocks (and securities) are then distributed to the partners in a liquidating distribution of the partnership.
2. The partnership liquidates by distributing its assets to the partners. The partners then contribute the properties to the new corporation in exchange for its stock (and possibly securities).

---

[34] Reg. Sec. 1.736-1(a)(1)(ii).
[35] Sec. 1031(a)(2)(D).
[36] Rev. Rul. 84-52, 1984-1 C.B. 157.

3. The partners contribute their partnership interests directly to the new corporation in exchange for stock (and possibly securities) of the corporation. The partnership is liquidated, with the corporation receiving all of the partnership's assets and liabilities and the partners receiving a stock (and possibly a security) interest in the corporation.

The tax implications of the incorporation and the impact of partnership liabilities, gain to be recognized, basis in the corporate assets, and the new shareholders' bases in their stock and securities may be different depending upon the form chosen for the transaction.[37]

Gift of a Partnership Interest

OBJECTIVE 8
Explain the tax implications of a gift of a partnership interest

When a partner disposes of a partnership interest by giving away some or all of it, the role of partnership liabilities can lead to unusual results. The donee becomes liable for the distributive share of the partnership's liabilities associated with the gifted partnership interest. Accordingly, for tax purposes, the donor has a partial sale and a partial gift.[38]

Key Point
When a partnership interest is gifted, the partnership liabilities shifted from the donor to the donee are treated as a sale. If the amount of debt relief to the donor is greater than the adjusted basis of the partnership interest being transferred, the donor will recognize a gain.

The donor must recognize a gain on the sale portion of the transfer that is equal to the difference between the amount realized when the donee assumes the distributive share of the partnership liabilities and the donor's basis in the entire partnership interest on the date of transfer. If the basis of the partnership interest exceeds the distributive share of liabilities, no loss is recognized.

The gift tax is levied on the FMV of the entire partnership interest on the date of the gift minus the amount realized on the partial sale resulting from the liability transfer. The donee's basis in the transferred partnership interest is equal to the greater of liabilities assumed or the donor's basis in the partnership interest plus any gift tax paid on the appreciation.[39]

Example 10-22 ▪ Jack owns 40% of the JKL Partnership before giving away a 10% interest in the partnership to son Andrew. Before making the gift, Jack's basis for his entire interest is $240,000, which includes his $200,000 distributive share of liabilities. The FMV of the 10% interest Jack transfers to Andrew is $62,500. Jack's transaction is analyzed as a sale of an amount equal to the $50,000 (0.25 × $200,000) in liabilities assumed by Andrew, with a basis for that 10% interest of $60,000 (0.25 × $240,000). Jack realizes a $10,000 loss, which cannot be recognized. Jack must report a gift of $12,500 ($62,500 FMV − $50,000 liabilities assumed by donee) for gift tax purposes. Andrew's basis in his partnership interest is equal to the greater of the assumed liabilities ($50,000) or Jack's basis for the interest ($60,000) plus any gift tax Jack must pay on the appreciation. Thus, Andrew's basis is the $60,000 amount adjusted for any gift taxes paid. ▪

Topic Review 10-2 summarizes the tax consequences of a number of alternative methods for terminating an investment in a partnership.

Income Recognition and Transfers of a Partnership Interest

The partnership tax year closes with respect to any partner who sells or exchanges his entire interest in a partnership or any partner whose interest in the partnership is liquidated. The partnership tax year closes on the sale or exchange date or the date of

[37] Rev. Rul. 84-111, 1984-2 C.B. 88.
[38] Reg. Sec. 1.1001-1(e).
[39] Reg. Sec. 1.1015-1(a).

TOPIC REVIEW 10-2

Terminating an Investment in a Partnership

Method	Tax Consequences to Partner
Death or retirement:	
Amounts paid for property (excluding unrealized receivables and goodwill which was not mentioned in the partnership agreement)	Liquidating distribution tax consequences apply to the amount paid.
Amounts paid in excess of property values:	
Amounts not determined by partnership income	Ordinary income.
Amounts determined by reference to partnership income	Distributive share of partnership income.
Sale of partnership interest to outsider	Capital gain (loss) except for ordinary income (loss) reported on Sec. 751 assets.
Gift of partnership interest	Sale to extent of liability assumed by donee. Gain recognized equal to liability assumed minus adjusted basis of partnership interest.
Exchange for partnership interest:	
In same partnership	No tax consequences
In different partnership	Capital gain (loss) except for ordinary income (loss) on Sec. 751 assets.
Exchange for corporate stock	No gain or loss generally recognized if qualifies as a Sec. 351 corporate formation. Capital gain (loss) except for ordinary income (loss) on Sec. 751 assets if the exchange does not qualify for Sec. 351 treatment.
Incorporation of partnership	Tax consequences depend on form of transaction used for incorporation.

final payment on a liquidation. As a result, that partner's share of all items earned by the partnership must be reported in the partner's tax year that includes the transaction date.[40]

The partnership tax year does not close with respect to a partner whose interest is transferred by gift. The donor's share of income up to the date of the gift must be reported.[41] When a partner dies, the partnership tax year does not close with respect to the partner. The deceased partner's distributive share of income for the partner-

[40] Sec. 706(c)(2).
[41] Reg. Sec. 1.706-1(c)(5).

ship tax year during which the partner's death occurs must be reported by the deceased partner's estate or successor-in-interest.[42]

Termination of a Partnership

OBJECTIVE 9
Determine if a partnership has terminated for tax purposes

Events Causing a Termination to Occur. Because of the complex relationships among partners and their liability for partnership debts, state partnership laws provide for the termination of a partnership under a wide variety of conditions. Section 708(b) was enacted to avoid the tax complexity created by the wide variety of state laws and the numerous termination conditions. That section provides that only two conditions terminate a partnership.

Typical Misconception
Taxpayers often do not understand the difference between a partnership tax year closing for a specific partner versus a partnership tax year closing for all partners due to a termination of the partnership itself. Obviously, the tax consequences of these two events are drastically different.

- A partnership terminates for tax purposes if no part of any business, financial operation, or venture of the partnership continues to be carried on by any of its partners in a partnership.
- A partnership terminates for tax purposes if within a 12-month period there is a sale or exchange of at least 50% of the total interest in partnership capital and profits.

No Business Operated as a Partnership. If no partner continues to operate any business of the partnership through the same or another partnership, the original partnership terminates. To avoid termination, the partnership must maintain both partners and business activity. For example, if one partner retires from a two-person partnership and the second partner continues the business alone, the partnership terminates. However, if one partner in a two-member partnership dies, the partnership does not terminate as long as the deceased's estate or successor-in-interest continues to share in the profits and losses of the partnership business.[43]

Likewise, a partnership terminates if it ceases to carry on any business or financial venture. The courts have allowed a partnership to continue under this rule even though the partnership sold all its assets and retained only a few installment notes.[44] In spite of the courts' recent flexibility in these circumstances, it is wiser to maintain more than a nominal level of assets if continuation of the partnership is desired.

Key Point
In order for the 50% rule to terminate a partnership, there must be a sale or exchange of 50% or more of the capital and profits interests. Sales or exchanges occurring within a 12-month period are aggregated; however, if the same interest is sold twice within 12 months, it is only counted once.

Sale or Exchange of at Least a 50% Interest. The second condition that leads to the termination of a partnership is the sale or exchange of at least a 50% interest in both partnership capital and profits within a 12-month period. The relevant 12-month period is determined without reference to the tax year of either the partnership or any partner but rather is any 12 consecutive months. To cause termination, the partnership interest must be transferred by sale or exchange. Transactions or occurrences that do not constitute a sale or exchange (e.g., the gifting of a partnership interest or the transferring of a partnership interest at death) cannot cause a partnership to terminate as long as partners continue the partnership business. Likewise, as long as at least two partners remain, the removal of a partner who owns in excess of 50% of the total partnership capital and profits interests can be accomplished without terminating the partnership by making a liquidating distribution.[45]

Measuring the portion of the total partnership capital and profits interest that has been transferred often presents difficulties. Multiple exchanges of the same partner-

---

[42] Reg. Sec. 1.706-1(c)(3).
[43] Reg. Sec. 1.708-1(b)(1)(i)(a).
[44] For example, see *Max R. Ginsburg v. U.S.*, 21 AFTR 2d 1489, 68-1 USTC ¶ 9429 (Ct. Cls., 1968).
[45] Reg. Sec. 1.708-1(b)(1)(ii).

ship interest are counted only once for purposes of determining whether the 50% maximum is exceeded. When several different small interests are transferred within a 12-month period, the partnership's termination occurs on the date of the transfer that first crosses the 50% threshold.[46]

Example 10-23 ■ On August 1, 1990, Michael sells his 30% capital and profits interest in the LMN Partnership to Steve. On June 1, 1991, Steve sells the 30% interest acquired from Michael to Andrew. For purposes of Sec. 708, the two sales are considered to be the transfer of a single partnership interest. Thus, the LMN Partnership does not terminate unless there are other sales of partnership interests totaling at least 20% of LMN's capital and profits interests during any 12-month period that includes either August 1, 1990, or June 1, 1991. ■

Example 10-24 ■ On July 15, 1990, Kelly sells Carlos a 37% capital and profits interest in the KRS Partnership. On November 14, 1990, Rick sells Diana a 10% capital and profits interest in the KRS Partnership. On January 18, 1991, Sherrie sells Evan a 5% capital and profits interest in the KRS Partnership. The KRS Partnership terminates on January 18, 1991, since the cumulative interest sold within the 12-month period that includes January 18, 1991, first exceeds 50% on that date. ■

Effects of Termination.

Key Point
If the year-ends of the partners and the partnership are not the same, a termination of the partnership can result in more than 12 months of partnership income/loss being reported in the tax returns of some partners.

IMPORTANCE OF TIMING. When a partnership terminates, its tax year is closed, requiring the partners to include their share of partnership earnings for the short-period partnership tax year in their tax returns. If the termination is not properly timed, partnership income for a regular 12-month tax year may already be included in the same return that must include the short tax year. As partners and partnerships are increasingly forced to adopt the same tax year, this will be less of a problem.

Example 10-25 ■

Self-Study Question
What are the tax consequences of a partnership termination caused by a 50% change in ownership?

Answer
When a partnership terminates, as a result of a 50% change of ownership, the partnership is first treated as making a liquidating distribution. Since the partnership continues to operate, the partners are likewise treated as making a contribution of the liquidated assets back to the new partnership. This hypothetical distribution/contribution is subject to the regular partnership rules and could possibly result in a gain/loss being recognized and a basis change taking place.

Joy is a calendar-year taxpayer who owns a 40% capital and profits interest in the ATV Partnership. ATV has a natural business year-end of March 31, and with IRS permission uses that date as its tax year-end. For the partnership tax year ending March 31, 1991, Joy has an $80,000 distributive share of ordinary income. Pat, who owns the remaining 60% capital and profits interests, sells his interest to Collin on November 30, 1991. Because more than 50% of the capital and profits interests have changed hands, the ATV Partnership terminates on November 30, 1991, and the partnership's tax year ends on that date.

Joy's tax return for the tax year ending on December 31, 1991, must include (1) the $80,000 distributive share from the partnership tax year for the period April 1, 1990, through March 31, 1991, and (2) the distributive share of partnership income for the short tax year including the period April 1, 1991, through November 30, 1991. ■

LIQUIDATING DISTRIBUTIONS AND CONTRIBUTIONS. When a termination occurs for tax purposes, a pro rata liquidating distribution is deemed to have been made to all partners. Gain or loss must be recognized by the partners under the liquidating distribution rules. An actual liquidating distribution may occur if the termination occurs because of the cessation of business. If, however, the termination occurs because of a greater than 50% change in ownership of the capital and profits interests, an actual distribution usually does not occur. Nevertheless, gain or loss

---

[46] Ibid.

must be recognized, and the bases of assets deemed distributed must be adjusted as they would be in an actual liquidating distribution.

If a termination occurs for tax purposes because of a greater than 50% change in ownership of the capital and profits interests, it is likely that the partnership's actual business activity will continue uninterrupted. If the partnership's business continues, a deemed contribution of property to the new partnership must follow the deemed distribution.[47] Generally, no gain is recognized on the contribution of the assets to the "new" partnership.[48] The partner's bases in these assets carry over to the partnership under Sec. 722.

Example 10-26 ■ The ABC Partnership terminates for tax purposes on July 15, when Anna's 52% capital and profits interest is sold to Diane. Beth, who has a 20% interest in the partnership with a $70,000 basis at the time of the termination, is deemed to receive a pro rata liquidating distribution consisting of 20% of each partnership asset. The partnership's basis in the assets deemed distributed to Beth and her basis in the assets after the deemed distribution are as follows:

	Partnership's Basis	Beth's Basis
Cash	$ 5,000	$ 5,000
Receivables	—0—	—0—
Inventory	5,000	5,000
Building	30,000	45,000
Land	10,000	15,000
Total	$50,000	$70,000

The portion of Beth's total $70,000 basis allocable to the building and the land is determined as follows:

Beth's basis in old partnership interest before the distribution	$70,000
Minus: Cash	(5,000)
Carryover basis for receivables	—0—
Carryover basis for inventory	(5,000)
Basis to allocate to building and land	$60,000

Allocation of the total basis to the building and the land occurs as follows:

$$\text{Basis for building: } \$60,000 \times \frac{\$30,000}{\$30,000 + \$10,000} = \$45,000$$

$$\text{Basis for land: } \$60,000 \times \frac{\$10,000}{\$30,000 + \$10,000} = \$15,000$$

On the deemed contribution to the new partnership, the $70,000 total basis of the assets in Beth's hands carries over to the partnership, and the partnership's basis in her share of the building and land is increased from $40,000 to $60,000 by the termination. ■

CHANGES IN ACCOUNTING METHODS. Not only does a termination result in a change to the basis of some partnership assets, it may cause numerous other changes in the partnership's accounting methods. The termination ends all partnership elections. Thus, all partnership elections concerning its tax year and accounting

---
[47] Reg. Sec. 1.708-1(b)(1)(iv).
[48] Sec. 721.

methods must be made in the new partnership's first tax year. If the partnership has a favorable year-end for its tax year, it is lost unless permission is received from the IRS to continue its prior election or a Sec. 444 election is made.

The election that allows the partnership to make optional basis adjustments (discussed below) is also terminated. A partnership may find this to be a benefit of a termination, since the optional basis adjustment is sometimes troublesome for a partnership and is frequently difficult to revoke.

Mergers and Consolidations

Key Point
The principal concern when two or more partnerships are combined is which partnership's tax year, accounting methods, and elections will survive the merger. This determination is made by examining the capital and profits interests of the partners of the old partnerships.

When two or more partnerships join together to form a new partnership, it is necessary to know which, if any, of the old partnerships are continued and which are terminated. An old partnership, whose partner(s) own more than 50% of the profits and capital interests of the new partnership, is considered to be continued as the new partnership.[49] Accordingly, the new partnership must continue with the tax year and accounting methods and elections of the old partnership which is considered to continue. All of the other old partnerships are considered to have been terminated.[50]

Example 10-27 ■ The AB and CD Partnerships are merged to form the ABCD Partnership. April and Ben each own 30% of ABCD, and Carole and David each own 20% of ABCD. The ABCD Partnership is considered a continuation of the AB Partnership since 60% of ABCD is owned by the former partners of AB. ABCD is bound by the tax year, accounting method, and other elections made by AB. CD is considered to terminate on the date of the merger. ■

It is possible that the partners of two or more of the old partnerships will hold the requisite profits and capital interest in the new partnership. When two or more old partnerships satisfy this requirement, the old partnership that is credited with contributing the greatest dollar value of assets to the new partnership is considered the continuing partnership and all other partnerships are terminated. Sometimes, none of the old partnerships account for more than 50% of the capital and profits of the new partnership. In that case, all of the old partnerships terminate, and the merged partnership is a new entity which can make its own tax year and accounting method elections.

Example 10-28 ■ Three partnerships are merged to form the ABCD Partnership. The AB Partnership (owned by Andy and Bill) contributes assets valued at $140,000 to ABCD, while the BC (owned by Bill and Cathy) and CD (owned by Cathy and Drew) Partnerships contribute assets valued at $180,000 and $120,000, respectively. The capital and profits interests of the partners in the new partnership are Andy, 20%; Bill, 35%; Cathy, 19%; and Drew, 26%. Both the old AB Partnership and the old BC Partnership had partners who now own more than 50% of the new partnership (Andy and Bill own 55%, and Bill and Cathy own 54%). The BC Partnership contributes more assets ($180,000) to the new partnership than the AB Partnership ($140,000). Therefore, the ABCD Partnership is a continuation of the BC Partnership. Both the AB and CD Partnerships terminate on the merger date. ■

---

[49] Sec. 708(b)(2)(A).
[50] Reg. Sec. 1.708-1(b)(2)(i).

Division of a Partnership

Key Point
The principal concern of a partnership division is to determine which of the two or more new partnerships is the continuation of the prior partnership.

When a partnership is divided into two or more new partnerships, any of the new partnerships, whose partners own collectively more than 50% of the profits and capital interests in the old partnerships, are considered a continuation of the old partnership.[51] All partnerships which are continuations of the old partnership are bound by the old partnership's tax year and accounting method elections. Any other partnership that is created by the division is considered a new partnership eligible to make its own tax year and accounting method elections. If no new partnership meets the criteria for continuation of the divided partnership, the divided partnership is terminated on the division date. The interest of any partner of the divided partnership who does not own an interest in a continuing partnership is considered to be liquidated on the division date.[52]

Example 10-29 ▪ The RSTV Partnership is in the real estate and insurance business. Randy owns a 40% interest and Sam, Tom, and Vicki each own 20% of RSTV. The partners agree to split the partnership, with the RS Partnership receiving the real estate operations and the TV Partnership receiving the insurance business. Because Randy and Sam own more than 50% of the RSTV Partnership (40% + 20% = 60%), the RS Partnership is a continuation of the RSTV Partnership and must report its results using the same tax year and accounting method elections that RSTV employed. Tom and Vicki are considered to have terminated their interests in RSTV and to have received a liquidating distribution of the insurance business property. The TV Partnership makes its tax year and accounting method elections following the rules for a new partnership. ▪

OPTIONAL BASIS ADJUSTMENTS

OBJECTIVE 10
Determine the adjustment required by the sale of a partnership interest or a partnership distribution when the partnership elects to make optional basis adjustments

In general, the partnership tax rules provide that no adjustment to the basis of partnership property occurs upon the sale or exchange of a partnership interest, when the partnership interest is transferred upon the death of a partner, or when a distribution is made to a partner. Sometimes, it could benefit the partnership or its partners to be able to adjust the partnership's basis in its assets.

Example 10-30 ▪ Eric purchases from Amy a 25% interest in the ABCD Partnership. Eric pays Amy $60,000 cash and assumes Amy's $20,000 share of partnership liabilities. At the time of Eric's purchase, the ABCD Partnership has the following balance sheet:

---
[51] Sec. 708(b)(2)(B).
[52] Reg. Sec. 1.708-1(b)(2)(ii).

Typical Misconception
The basis that a partnership has in its assets (sometimes referred to as "inside basis") is not necessarily the same as the basis that the partners have in their partnership interests (sometimes referred to as "outside basis"). This difference usually results from (1) a sale or exchange of a partnership interest, (2) a transfer of a partnership interest at the death of a partner, and (3) a distribution to a partner.

	Basis	FMV
Assets:		
Cash	$ 40,000	$ 40,000
Receivables	—0—	20,000
Inventory	30,000	40,000
Building	140,000	180,000
Land	30,000	40,000
Total	$240,000	$320,000
Liabilities and Capital:		
Liabilities	$ 80,000	$ 80,000
Amy's capital	40,000	60,000
Becky's capital	40,000	60,000
Chris's capital	40,000	60,000
Dana's capital	40,000	60,000
Total	$240,000	$320,000

[a]If the building were sold, $40,000 of Sec. 1245 ordinary income would be recognized.

Eric pays an appropriate FMV price for the partnership interest, yet his share of the partnership's basis in its assets is only $60,000 (0.25 × $240,000) compared to his $80,000 basis in his partnership interest. The problem this creates is apparent when it is remembered that under Sec. 751(a) Amy's share of the ordinary income from the receivables and inventory assets is taxed to her when she sells her interest to Eric, while the asset's basis to the partnership is unchanged. Thus, when the partnership disposes of these assets, Eric's distributive share of this ordinary income (which actually has already been taxed to Amy) must be reported. ■

An election is available for a partnership to make an adjustment to the basis of its assets.[53] However, the blessing is a mixed one. Once the optional basis adjustment election is made, the partnership must make the required adjustments for *all* sales, exchanges, transfers on death, and distributions. Some of the required adjustments decrease (rather than increase) the partnership's basis in its assets. In addition, the election can only be revoked with IRS permission, and that permission is not easily granted.

Key Point
A Sec. 754 election allows a partnership to make special basis adjustments for its assets in certain circumstances. This election is a mixed blessing, for the adjustments can result in decreases to basis as well as increases to basis. Once the election is made, it can be revoked only with IRS permission.

Election to Make Basis Adjustments

Since the basis adjustments are optional, the partnership itself must file an election under Sec. 754 to make the adjustments. (See the Compliance and Procedural Considerations section of this chapter for a discussion of the election procedures.) The election applies to (1) all transfers of a partnership interest by sale or exchange or upon the death of a partner under Sec. 743 and (2) all distributions of partnership property under Sec. 734. The election is effective for all transfers and distributions for the year in which the election is made and for all subsequent years until the election is revoked.

Optional Adjustments on Transfers

When a partner's interest is sold to an outsider, the outsider's basis in his partnership interest is the sum of the purchase price and the partner's share of partnership liabilities. The new partner's proportionate share of the partnership's basis in its

[53] Sec. 754.

assets seldom equals his basis in the partnership interest. A new partner is taxed on his share of gains and losses as the partnership recognizes them. Since the partner's distributive share of gains and losses recognized while he is a partner is reflected in his basis in the partnership interest, the difference is largely one of timing. However, if the partnership continues for many years, the timing difference may be quite significant.

Example 10-31 ■ Assume the same facts as in Example 10-30. The ABCD Partnership sells the building for its $180,000 FMV and recognizes a $40,000 ($180,000 − $140,000 basis) gain, which is characterized by Sec. 1245 as ordinary income. Eric recognizes a $10,000 (0.25 × $40,000) share of the ordinary income and also increases his basis for the partnership interest by $10,000. If nothing else changes in the partnership since Eric purchases his interest, he has a $90,000 basis ($80,000 original basis + $10,000 income recognized), but the FMV of the interest remains unchanged at $80,000. Accordingly, Eric would recognize a $10,000 capital loss if he sells his partnership interest for its FMV. Eric recognizes $10,000 ordinary income from partnership operations and a $10,000 loss (which would likely be a capital loss) if he sells his partnership interest. The loss recognition is, of course, delayed until he actually disposes of the partnership interest. ■

The result can be quite different if the partnership has an election to make optional basis adjustments in effect for the year of the transfer. The optional basis adjustment election permits the partnership's bases in its assets to be adjusted so that the new partner's initial basis in his partnership interest and his proportionate share of the partnership's basis for its assets are equal. If the partner's initial basis in his partnership interest exceeds his proportionate share of the partnership's basis for its assets, the partnership's basis for its assets is increased with respect to the transferee partner only. (Conversely, if the partner's basis in the partnership interest is less than his proportionate share of the partnership's basis for its assets, the partnership's basis for its assets is decreased.) Overall, the transferee's total basis in the partnership's assets after the optional basis adjustment is the same as if a direct interest is purchased in each individual asset. However, because Sec. 755 mandates a specific set of allocation rules (discussed below), the partner's basis in an individual asset after the optional basis adjustment may not be the same as when a proportionate interest in that asset is purchased.

Key Point
The partnership will increase/decrease the basis of its assets by the difference in the transferee's basis in the partnership interest and the transferee's share of the basis in the partnership assets. Adjustments are made with respect to the transferee partner only.

Amount of the Adjustment. The amount of the optional basis adjustment equals the difference between the transferee partner's initial basis for his partnership interest and his share of the partnership's adjusted basis for all of its properties.[54] The transferee partner's share of the partnership's basis for its properties equals the sum of the partner's interest in the partnership capital plus the partner's share of the partnership's liabilities. The transferee partner's share of the adjusted basis of partnership property must also reflect any special allocations of gain or loss on contributed partnership property to the other partners. The calculation of the adjustment amount is illustrated in the following example.

Example 10-32 ■ Rose purchases a one-third capital and profits interest in the PDK Partnership from Kyle for $22,000 in cash. At the time of the purchase, an election to make optional basis adjustments is in effect. No special allocations are mentioned in the

---

[54] Sec. 743(b).

partnership agreement. At the time of Rose's purchase, PDK's balance sheet is as follows:

	Basis	FMV
Assets:		
Cash	$ 5,000	$ 5,000
Accounts receivable	10,000	10,000
Inventory	20,000	21,000
Depreciable assets	20,000	40,000
Total	$55,000	$76,000
Liabilities and Capital:		
Liabilities	$10,000	$10,000
Pam's capital	15,000	22,000
Dan's capital	15,000	22,000
Kyle's capital	15,000	22,000
Total	$55,000	$76,000

The $7,000 optional basis adjustment amount is calculated as follows:

Rose's initial basis in partnership interest ($22,000 + [0.333 × $10,000])	$25,333
Minus: Rose's share of partnership basis in assets ($15,000 + [0.333 × $10,000])	(18,333)
Optional basis adjustment	$ 7,000

The calculation of the transferee's interest in the partnership's basis for its assets can be quite complex if there are special allocations among the partners or if the allocation of liabilities is complex, as might occur with a limited partnership interest. While these complexities are beyond the scope of this text, the general idea of equalizing basis for the partner and partnership is retained throughout the more complicated calculations.

OBJECTIVE 11
Determine the basis of partnership assets after an optional basis adjustment has been made

Allocation of Adjustment to Assets. Once the amount of the basis adjustment arising from the transfer is determined, the basis adjustments must be allocated to the various partnership assets under Sec. 755. While it seems logical to allocate to each asset the amount necessary to bring it to its FMV, such a simple approach is not taken. Instead, the Regulations mandate a three-step process to arrive at the proper allocation.

First, the assets are divided into two groups—capital gain assets and ordinary income assets. The capital gain assets group only includes those assets which are capital assets or Sec. 1231 property. All other property is included in the ordinary income assets category.[55]

Second, the FMV and the transferee's proportionate share of the partnership's common basis is determined for both asset groups.[56] The basis adjustment amount (determined in the preceding section) must be allocated between the two classes of assets to reduce the difference between the FMV and the partner's share of the

---
[55] Sec. 755(b).
[56] The partnership's common basis is that portion of basis shared by the partners and does not include any optional basis adjustments relating to a single partner.

partnership's common basis for each group. If one of the classes of assets increases in value while the other class declines in value, a positive basis adjustment is allocated only to the class of property that has increased in value, and a negative basis adjustment is allocated only to the class of property that has declined in value.[57]

Third, the adjustment is allocated to the individual assets within the class so that it proportionately reduces the difference between the FMV and the adjusted basis (to the partnership) for each asset. If the adjustment is positive, any asset in the class having a basis greater than its FMV is excluded from the allocation. If the adjustment is negative, any asset in the class having a basis less than its FMV is excluded from the allocation.

Example 10-33 ■

Key Point
The allocation rules mandate a three-step process: (1) divide the assets into two groups (capital versus ordinary), (2) determine to which group(s) the adjustment is to be allocated, and (3) allocate the actual adjustment to the specific assets within the appropriate group so as to reduce the gap between the FMV and the adjusted basis of those assets.

Tami purchases a one-third interest in the KTY Partnership for $15,000. Her ratable share of the partnership's assets is as follows:

	FMV (1)	Common Basis (2)	Difference (3) = (1) − (2)
Capital gain assets:			
Asset A	$ 5,000	$1,000	$4,000
Asset B	2,000	4,000	(2,000)
Total	$ 7,000	$5,000	$2,000
Ordinary income assets:			
Asset C	$ 4,000	$2,500	$1,500
Asset D	4,000	1,500	2,500
Total	$ 8,000	$4,000	$4,000
Total assets	$15,000	$9,000	$6,000

Tami's share of the partnership's common basis in its assets is $9,000. The amount of her optional basis adjustment is $6,000 ($15,000 − $9,000). The difference between her share of the common basis and her $15,000 purchase price (FMV) for the two classes of assets is $2,000 for the capital gain assets and $4,000 for the ordinary income assets. Within the capital gain assets, only asset A has appreciated. Since the optional basis adjustment is positive, the entire adjustment for capital gain assets must be allocated to asset A. This allocation results in asset A having a $3,000 ($1,000 + $2,000) basis. The $4,000 adjustment for the ordinary income assets is allocated $1,500 to asset C and $2,500 to asset D to bring each asset up to its FMV. ■

Typical Misconception
Even though the optional basis adjustment is really a matter of timing, it can have other tax consequences. For example, the adjustment will affect the amount of depreciation, depletion, or amortization allowed to the transferee partner. In addition, the adjustment could convert what would be a capital gain on the sale of a partnership interest to ordinary income through the increased depreciation deductions.

Effects of the Adjustment. Records of the basis adjustments are kept by the partnership. However, because the basis adjustment only belongs to the transferee partner, the partnership must keep the adjustments separate from the assets' regular accounts.[58] Several different transactions are affected by the basis adjustment, so the burden of recordkeeping for the partnership may become a significant factor.

If the basis adjustment is allocated to a depreciable asset, the positive basis adjustment is depreciated (along with the property's adjusted basis on the partnership's books) and the transferee partner will report this additional depreciation. If a negative basis adjustment is made to a depreciable asset, the transferee partner must include an additional income amount from the partnership interest thereby resulting in a smaller "net" depreciation amount.[59]

---

[57] Reg. Sec. 1.755-1(a).
[58] Sec. 743(b).
[59] Prop. Reg. Secs. 1.168-2(n) and -4(d)(8).

Basis adjustments also have an impact on distributions received from partnerships. If a basis adjustment is made to a property and the property is subsequently distributed to the transferee partner, the transferee partner treats the basis adjustment as part of the partnership's basis for the property and uses it as part of his carryover basis.[60] If an optional basis adjustment is made to a property and the property is later distributed to some other partner without the transferee partner receiving a distribution, the distributee partner does not receive the benefit of the basis adjustment. Instead, the transferee partner must reallocate the amount of the basis adjustment from the distributed property to similar property retained by the partnership.[61] If all of the partners including the transferee partner receive distributions of property that are subject to optional basis adjustments, the transferee partner's basis in the property received includes the optional basis adjustment for the property he receives and for similar property distributed to the other partners.[62]

Example 10-34 ■ ABC Partnership makes a current distribution of land to each of its three partners. Bonnie purchased her partnership interest after the partnership elected under Sec. 754 to make optional basis adjustments. The three pieces of land have the following adjustments applicable only to Bonnie as a result of purchasing the partnership interest.

Land	Common Basis	Basis Adjustment to B
Parcel 1	$20,000	$2,000
Parcel 2	24,000	1,000
Parcel 3	22,000	4,000

Bonnie, whose basis in her partnership interest is $60,000 before the distribution, receives Parcel 2, Andrew receives Parcel 1, and Camille receives Parcel 3. Bonnie's basis in Parcel 2 is a carryover from the partnership's common basis in the parcel ($24,000) plus her basis adjustment for the parcel she receives ($1,000) plus the basis adjustments for the parcels received by Andrew and Camille ($2,000 and $4,000, respectively), for a total basis in Parcel 2 of $31,000. After the distribution, Bonnie's basis in her partnership interest is $29,000 ($60,000 − $31,000). ■

If the partnership sells property for which a special basis adjustment is made, the transferee partner reports a different amount of gain or loss from the other partners. The effect of a positive basis adjustment is to increase the asset's basis for the transferee partner and, accordingly, to reduce the amount of gain (or increase the amount of loss) to be reported by the transferee partner. Conversely, a negative basis adjustment decreases the asset's basis and increases the gain (or decreases the loss) to be reported by that partner.[63]

Example 10-35 ■ Zane has a 25% interest in the XYZ Partnership, which he purchased while a Sec. 754 election was in effect. The partnership has an $8,000 basis in a machine, and Zane has a positive basis adjustment of $1,000 with respect to the machine. If the

---

[60] Reg. Sec. 1.743-1(b)(2)(ii).
[61] Similar property is defined by Reg. Secs. 1.755-1(a)(1)(i) and -1(b) as property of the same class (e.g., capital assets, Sec. 1231 assets, or ordinary income assets).
[62] Reg. Sec. 1.743-1(b)(2)(ii).
[63] Reg. Sec. 1.743-1(b)(2).

partnership sells the machine for $14,000, his distributive share of the $6,000 gain would be $1,500 (0.25 × $6,000) if there were no special basis adjustment. Because Zane has a $1,000 positive basis adjustment for this asset, his gain is decreased to $500 ($1,500 − $1,000). ∎

Optional Adjustments on Distributions

As noted earlier, the general rule for distributions is that no basis adjustment is made at the partnership level even if a distributee partner does not take a carryover basis in the distributed property. The inequities caused by the no adjustment rule can be easily seen by considering an example.

Example 10-36 ∎

Key Point
Inequities can result from partnership distributions as well as from transfers of partnership interests. For example, if gain is recognized in a cash distribution or loss is recognized in a liquidating distribution, neither the gain nor the loss is reflected in the basis of the partnership assets. The optional basis adjustments that are allowed for these distributions affect all partners instead of just the transferee partner.

Jennifer receives $6,000 cash as a liquidating distribution for her one-third interest in the XYZ Partnership. Jennifer's basis in her partnership interest is $4,000. XYZ's balance sheet immediately preceding the distribution is as follows:

	Basis	FMV
Assets:		
Cash	$ 6,000	$ 6,000
Land	6,000	12,000
Total	$12,000	$18,000
Partners' capital:		
Jennifer	$ 4,000	$ 6,000
Rick	4,000	6,000
Suzanne	4,000	6,000
Total	$12,000	$18,000

The XYZ Partnership has $6,000 of unrealized gain immediately preceding the distribution, all of which is attributable to the land. Each partner's share of the gain is $2,000. Because Jennifer receives cash in excess of her basis in the partnership interest, she must report a $2,000 ($6,000 − $4,000) gain. The two remaining partners, Rick and Suzanne, retain the land as their only remaining asset, and the land's basis is not adjusted under the general rules for partnership distributions. The partnership's remaining $6,000 of unrealized gain is divided between Rick and Suzanne. If the land is sold, Rick and Suzanne must each report a $3,000 gain. Jennifer's share of the unrealized gain on the land is shifted to Rick and Suzanne, even though Jennifer already paid a tax on the $2,000 gain inherent in liquidating her partnership interest. An optional basis adjustment will increase the basis of the land by $2,000 and restore each of the two remaining partners to the position of having $2,000 of unrealized gain. ∎

Once a Sec. 754 election is in effect, optional basis adjustments must be made on distributions as well as on transfers of partnership interests. Unlike basis adjustments made relative to the transferee partner when a sale or exchange of a partnership interest occurs, basis adjustments resulting from a partnership distribution apply to the common basis of partnership assets.[64] Accordingly, no special account is

---

[64] Sec. 734(b).

necessary for the basis adjustment, and all partners receive the benefit (or detriment) of the adjustment.[65]

Amount of the Adjustment. An optional basis adjustment is necessary when a distribution is made only if the distributee partner does not take a carryover basis for property that is received. There are four situations in which a carryover basis is not the result of a distribution.

1. Cash in excess of a partner's basis in the partnership interest is distributed as part of a current or liquidating distribution and the distributee partner must recognize gain. The appropriate optional basis adjustment is to increase the basis of the remaining partnership assets by an amount equal to the gain recognized.[66]

Example 10-37 ■ Assume the same facts as in Example 10-36, except that a Sec. 754 election is in effect. The partnership increases the basis of its remaining asset (land) by $2,000. The unrealized gain remaining after the basis adjustment is made is reduced to $4,000, and each of the two remaining partners only recognize a $2,000 gain if the land is sold. ■

2. Cash, unrealized receivables, and inventory are the only assets distributed in a liquidating distribution and the distributee partner must recognize a loss. The appropriate optional basis adjustment is to decrease the basis of the remaining partnership assets by an amount equal to the recognized loss.[67]

Example 10-38 ■ Elena has a $20,000 basis in her EFG Partnership interest before receiving a liquidating distribution of $4,000 cash and inventory with a basis to the partnership of $14,000. The partnership has no Sec. 751 assets. Elena must recognize a $2,000 loss on the distribution. If a Sec. 754 election is in effect, EFG must decrease its basis in the remaining partnership assets by the $2,000 amount of the loss. ■

Key Point
Under the partnership distribution rules, the basis of assets received in a distribution may have to be adjusted due to either (1) a partner's excess basis in his partnership interest or (2) a partner's lack of basis in his partnership interest. These two situations are also reflected in the optional basis adjustments.

3. A partner receives a property distribution where the basis of the distributed asset(s) on the books of the partnership exceeds the partner's basis in his partnership interest. The partner must decrease the basis of the asset(s) received so that its basis equals the predistribution basis of his partnership interest. The optional basis adjustment is an increase to the basis of the remaining partnership assets by an amount equal to the difference between the total basis of the distributed properties in the partnership's hands and the basis of the properties in the hands of the distributee partner.[68]

Example 10-39 ■ Jamal has a $10,000 basis in his JK Partnership interest before receiving a distribution of land having a basis of $12,000 on JK's books. Jamal's basis in the land is limited to $10,000 (Jamal's basis in his partnership interest). If a Sec. 754 election is in effect, JK must increase the basis of its remaining assets by $2,000 ($12,000 − $10,000). ■

---

[65] If the distribution liquidates one partner's interest in the partnership, the adjustment to the partnership's common basis benefits all partners who remain in the partnership.
[66] Sec. 734(b)(1)(A).
[67] Sec. 734(b)(2)(A).
[68] Sec. 734(b)(1)(B).

4. A partner receives a liquidating distribution when the predistribution basis for his partnership interest exceeds the sum of the bases for the distributed properties on the partnership's books. The distributee partner's total basis for the distributed properties are stepped up to an amount in excess of their total basis on the partnership's books. The optional basis adjustment is a decrease to the basis of the remaining partnership assets in an amount equal to the excess of the total basis of the distributed properties in the partner's hands over the total basis of such properties on the partnership's books.[69]

Example 10-40 ■ Karen's basis in the KM Partnership interest is $21,000 before receiving a liquidating distribution of two parcels of land held as an investment by the partnership. The two parcels of land have a basis to the partnership of $4,000 and $8,000, respectively. Karen's bases in the two parcels of land are $7,000 and $14,000, respectively, as follows:

$$\text{Parcel 1:} \frac{\$4,000}{\$4,000 + \$8,000} \times \$21,000 = \$7,000 \text{ basis}$$

$$\text{Parcel 2:} \frac{\$8,000}{\$4,000 + \$8,000} \times \$21,000 = \$14,000 \text{ basis}$$

This $9,000 ($21,000 − $12,000) increase in the total basis of the land requires the KM Partnership to decrease the basis of its remaining assets by $9,000 if a Sec. 754 election is in effect. ■

Allocation of Basis Adjustments. The optional basis adjustments on distributions preserve the amount of unrealized gain or loss in the assets after adjusting for gain or loss recognized on the transaction. This preservation is accomplished by keeping the postdistribution basis of the assets to the distributee partner and the partnership equal to the predistribution basis of the assets to the partnership plus any gain (or minus any loss) recognized by the distributee partner.

The optional basis adjustment is allocated among partnership assets under a set of rules defined by Sec. 755. Like the rules for adjustments occurring when a partnership interest is transferred, the allocation process does not necessarily increase or decrease the asset's basis to its FMV. The allocation of the optional basis adjustment occurring as a result of a distribution begins with a separation of partnership assets into capital gain assets and ordinary income assets.

After the categorization of assets takes place, the determination of the group of assets affected by the adjustment must be made. If the adjustment is caused by an increase or decrease in the bases of assets from one of the two categories, the adjustment is allocated to that same category of assets.[70] If the adjustment is caused because the distributee partner has to recognize a gain or loss, the entire adjustment is allocated to the partnership's capital gain assets.[71]

Example 10-41 ■ Assume the same facts as in Example 10-40. The optional basis adjustment is caused by Karen having to increase the basis of the land held as an investment (a capital gain asset). The $9,000 negative adjustment is, accordingly, allocated to KM's remaining capital gain properties. ■

[69] Sec. 734(b)(2)(B).
[70] Reg. Sec. 1.755-1(b)(1).
[71] Reg. Sec. 1.755-1(b)(1)(ii).

Example 10-42 ■ Assume the same facts as in Example 10-38. The optional basis adjustment is caused by Elena recognizing a $2,000 loss on the liquidating distribution. The entire $2,000 negative adjustment is allocated to EFG's basis in its remaining capital gain assets. ■

Additional Comment

Sec. 755 has a basic flaw in its allocation scheme. The Sec. 755 allocation scheme does not adjust an asset's basis to its FMV; thus, it may leave an unused basis adjustment.

The basis adjustment within an asset category is generally allocated to reduce the difference between the FMV and the adjusted basis of the partnership property. Accordingly, if the adjustment is to increase the basis of the remaining partnership assets, assets that have a basis greater than their FMV are not adjusted. Conversely, if the adjustment is to decrease the basis of the remaining partnership assets, assets having a basis less than their FMV are not adjusted. Remember, assets cannot be adjusted downward to less than a zero basis nor upward to more than their FMV. Problems may arise if the partnership has no assets in the class that must be adjusted or if the mandated adjustment is too large to be absorbed by assets in the appropriate class. If the adjustment cannot be fully utilized, the unused adjustment must be applied to subsequently acquired property in the appropriate class.[72]

Example 10-43 ■ Al recognizes a $5,000 gain on a cash distribution from the ABC Partnership when a Sec. 754 election is in effect. Just prior to the distribution, ABC has the following assets:

Assets	Basis	FMV
Cash	$ 30,000	$ 30,000
Inventory	19,000	20,000
Land-parcel 1	40,000	39,000
Land-parcel 2	26,000	28,000
Total	$115,000	$117,000

A $5,000 positive optional basis adjustment is required in the basis of ABC's capital gain assets (the land). Parcel 1 cannot be adjusted because its basis already exceeds its FMV. Parcel 2 can be adjusted upward only by $2,000, so that its adjusted basis equals its FMV. Any further adjustment to Parcel 2 would increase (rather than decrease) the difference between its basis and FMV. Therefore, the partnership has a $3,000 positive adjustment that cannot be used now. However, this adjustment can be used later when the partnership acquires capital gain assets having a basis less than their FMV (e.g., a contribution of appreciated capital gain property by a new or existing partner). ■

Special Adjustments on Distributions to Transferee Partners

Even though a Sec. 754 election might benefit a transferee partner, the partnership may be reluctant to agree to the election because of the potential detriment at the partnership level. Section 732(d) provides some basis adjustment relief to the transferee partner without the requirement that the Sec. 754 election be made. However, the benefits of Sec. 732(d) are only available to transferee partners who (1)

---

[72] Reg. Sec. 1.755-1(b)(4).

Self-Study Question

When is Sec. 732(d) applicable to a transfer of a partnership interest?

Answer

Section 732(d) applies to a transferee partner if (1) the partnership interest is acquired by sale, exchange, or upon the death of a partner, (2) no Sec. 754 election is in effect, and (3) the transferee partner receives a subsequent distribution of property from the partnership.

acquire a partnership interest by sale or exchange or upon the death of a partner at a time when no Sec. 754 election is in effect *and* (2) receive a subsequent distribution of property (other than money) from the partnership. If both requirements are met, the transferee partner may treat the property as if an optional basis adjustment occurs when the partnership interest is received.[73]

This optional basis adjustment is elective for any distribution of property received within 2 years after the transfer of the partnership interest. In some circumstances, however, the optional basis adjustment is mandatory without regard to the length of time since the transfer. The mandatory application of Sec. 732(d) is rare and is beyond the scope of this introductory text.[74]

Calculating the Adjustment. The basis adjustment under the elective application of Sec. 732(d) is calculated as if a Sec. 754 election was in effect at the time of the transfer. This hypothetical adjustment is not reduced by any depreciation that would have occurred if the Sec. 754 election was in effect on the transfer date, since such hypothetical depreciation is not allowed.[75] In effect, Sec. 732(d) adjusts the partnership's basis for the property just prior to its distribution.

Sections 732(d) and 751. Since Sec. 732(d) only deals with distributions, it might seems to have no relevance to computing gains and losses on deemed sales of Sec. 751 assets in a distribution or on actual sales of a partnership interest where the partnership has Sec. 751 assets. However, deemed or actual sales of Sec. 751 assets involve a hypothetical current distribution of a portion of the partnership's assets to the partner followed by a sale of the Sec. 751 assets. If the hypothetical current distribution in the Sec. 751 transaction occurs within the requisite 2-year time period, the optional basis adjustment can be elected.[76]

Example 10-44 ■ Ken purchases a 25% interest in the YWX Partnership on July 1, 1990, for $40,000. On that date Ken's share of the common basis and FMV of the partnership's assets is as follows:

Assets	Common Basis	FMV
Cash	$ 8,000	$ 8,000
Inventory	12,000	24,000
Land	6,000	8,000
Total	$26,000	$40,000

On May 1, 1991, Ken receives a current distribution from the partnership. Part of the distribution is a Sec. 751(b) transaction, which is considered a sale of inventory by Ken to the partnership for $6,000 cash. The partnership's basis in the inventory is $3,000. Without a Sec. 732(d) election, Ken's basis for the inventory would be $3,000 and $3,000 of ordinary income would be recognized. If he makes a

---

[73] Sec. 732(d).

[74] The mandatory application of Sec. 732(d) can occur only if its application shifts basis away from a depreciable asset to a nondepreciable asset received in a distribution. Its application can occur years after the transfer of the interest. The total lack of litigation related to its use apparently indicates that neither taxpayers nor the IRS often apply this rule.

[75] Reg. Sec. 1.732-1(d)(1).

[76] Reg. Secs. 1.732-1(e) and 1.751-1(b)(2)(iii).

Sec. 732(d) election, the partnership's basis (and Ken's basis after the deemed distribution) for the inventory is $6,000. Such an election permits Ken to report no ordinary income on the Sec. 751(b) transaction. ∎

TAX SHELTER PARTNERSHIPS

Limited partnerships are discussed in the beginning sections of Chapter 9 and in this chapter. Here, we examine tax shelters that are organized as limited partnerships.

Tax Shelters and Limited Partnerships

Tax shelters at their best are good investments that reduce the amount of an investor's tax bill (see Chapter 17 of *Prentice Hall's Federal Taxation: Individuals* text). Traditionally, shelter benefits arise from leverage, income deferral, and tax credits.

Prior to the Tax Reform Act of 1986, limited partnerships were the primary vehicle for tax shelter investments. However, the Tax Reform Act of 1986 greatly reduced the benefits of limited partnerships as tax shelters by invoking the passive activity loss limitations for activity conducted in a limited partnership form. The limited partnership still allows an investor to limit liability while receiving the benefits of the shelter's tax attributes to save taxes on other passive income. Since the Tax Reform Act of 1986, limited partnerships that generate passive income rather than losses have become popular investments for investors who already hold loss-generating limited partnership interests.

Abusive Tax Shelters

Most tax shelters are based on legitimate tax benefits provided by the tax laws as incentives for specific taxpayer behavior. As such, the use of tax shelters can represent good tax planning for investors. However, some tax shelters derive their benefits from overvaluation of assets, a large nonrecourse debt that is never intended to be paid, and other similar questionable manipulations of both the facts and the tax laws. Many of these investment opportunities fall into the category of abusive shelters, which represent a prime target for IRS investigations. The IRS distinguishes between abusive and nonabusive tax shelters as follows: Abusive tax shelters involve transactions with little or no economic reality, inflated appraisals, unrealistic allocations, etc., where the claimed tax benefits are disproportionate to the economic benefits. Such shelters typically seek to evade taxes. Nonabusive tax shelters involve transactions with legitimate economic reality, where the economic benefits outweigh the tax benefits. Such shelters seek to defer or minimize taxes.[77]

Beginning in October 1983, abusive shelters have been the object of active IRS searches. Each district has personnel assigned to search newspapers, magazines, and other IRS investigations as well as federal, state, and local information agencies for tax shelters that seem abusive. A team of IRS personnel with legal, auditing, and criminal experience then studies the facts of the shelter in question and the

Historical Note

Because partnerships are treated as flow-through entities, they have historically been popular for activities designed to produce tax losses (tax shelters). However, since the Tax Reform Act of 1986, profit partnerships are more in demand. This is due, in part, to the fact that many investors are now interested in generating passive income to offset their passive losses.

Historical Note

In recent years, probably no tax policy issue has generated more discussion than "abusive tax shelters." Concern has been widespread that large amounts of capital have been attracted to investments with no real economic substance. Consequently, the IRS has devoted significant resources to investigating, auditing, and litigating any activity it perceives to be an abusive tax shelter.

---

[77] Arthur Andersen & Co., *Tax Shelters—The Basics* (New York: John Wiley, 1985), p. 30.

promoter's history to determine if the shelter warrants further examination. If the team of IRS personnel decides that further action is needed, a revenue agent is assigned to fully investigate the shelter and to suggest a course of additional action for the IRS.

The IRS has several options if it determines that a tax shelter is abusive.

1. A financial penalty may be assessed by the IRS against the promoter and anyone who assists in the tax-shelter project.
2. The IRS can also seek an injunction against the promoter to prevent future sales of the abusive shelter.
3. If the IRS determines that the claimed benefits are not in compliance with the law, it can (a) notify all investors that their tax returns will be examined if tax benefits are claimed from the abusive shelter, and (b) notify the appropriate district to review the investors' returns to ensure that the abusive shelter deductions do not go unchallenged.[78] The IRS's effort to challenge flagrantly abusive shelters is both aggressive and generally successful.[79]

Publicly Traded Partnerships

The Revenue Act of 1987 moved to restrict still further the benefits of tax shelter ownership by changing the taxation of **publicly traded partnerships** (PTPs). A PTP is defined as a partnership whose interests are either traded on an established securities exchange or are traded in a secondary market or the equivalent thereof. A partnership which meets the requirements is taxed as a corporation under Sec. 7704.

There are two exceptions for partnerships which would otherwise be classified as PTPs:

- Partnerships which have 90% or more of their gross income being "qualifying income" continue to be taxed under the partnership rules.
- Partnerships which were in existence on December 17, 1987 and have not added a substantial new line of business since that date are grandfathered. In general, application of the PTP rules for these partnerships is delayed until tax years beginning after December 31, 1997.

For the 90% of gross income test qualifying income is defined in Sec. 7704(d) as including certain interest, dividends, real property rents (but not personal property rents), income and gains from the sale or disposition of a capital asset or Sec. 1231(b) trade or business property that is held for the production of passive income, and gain from the sale or disposition of real property. It also includes gains from certain commodity trading and natural resource activities. It should be noted that any PTP which is not taxed as a corporation because of this 90% exception is subject to separate and more restrictive Sec. 469 passive loss rules than are partnerships which are not publicly traded.

If a partnership is classified as a PTP to be taxed as a corporation during a tax year, there is a deemed contribution of all partnership assets and all partnership liabilities to a corporation in exchange for all the corporate stock. The stock is then deemed distributed to the partners in complete liquidation of the partnership. This transaction is taxed exactly as if it had physically occurred rather than being deemed to have occurred.

---

[78] Rev. Proc. 83-78, 1983-2 C.B. 595, *modified by* Rev. Proc. 84-84, 1984-2 C.B. 782.

[79] Examples of the government's success can be seen in *U.S. v. Gerald J. Landsberger*, 50 AFTR 2d 82-5445, 82-2 USTC ¶ 9497 (8th Cir., 1982); and *U.S. v. Charles D. Shugarman*, 54 AFTR 2d 84-6327, 84-2 USTC ¶ 9871 (D.C. Va., 1984).

TAX PLANNING CONSIDERATIONS

Self-Study Question
What difference does it make if the withdrawal of a partner is structured as a sale of a partnership interest rather than a liquidating distribution?

Answer
Three potential differences are (1) the optional basis adjustments are applied differently, (2) a liquidating distribution of a 50% interest does not terminate the partnership, and (3) payments for goodwill in a liquidating distribution have the flexibility of being taxed as either capital gain (nondeductible by the partnership) or as ordinary income (deductible by the partnership).

Liquidating Distribution or Sale to Partners

An unusual tax planning opportunity exists when one partner withdraws from a partnership and the remaining partners proportionately increase their ownership of the partnership. The partners can structure the ownership change as either a liquidating distribution made by the partnership or as a sale of the partnership interest to the remaining partners. In fact, the substance of the two transactions is the same, and only the form is different. This difference in form can, however, make a substantial difference in the tax consequences in a number of areas.

- If the transferor partner receives payment for his interest in the partnership's Sec. 751 assets, ordinary income must be recognized no matter how the transaction is structured. The partnership's basis in Sec. 751 assets is increased in the case of a liquidating distribution. When a sale transaction takes place, the partnership's basis in Sec. 751 assets is increased only if the partnership has an optional basis adjustment election in effect.

- If the partnership has an optional basis adjustment election in effect, the allocation of the adjustment to the individual partnership assets can be different depending on whether the transaction is structured as a sale or as a liquidating distribution.

- If the interest being transferred exceeds 50% of the profits and capital interests, a sale to the remaining partners terminates the partnership. A liquidating distribution does not cause a termination to occur.

- If the transferor partner receives payment for his interest in partnership goodwill in a sales transaction, a capital gain is reported. A goodwill payment that is received as part of a liquidating distribution can be made either as (1) a property payment taxed as a capital gain under Sec. 736(b) or as (2) a guaranteed payment taxed as ordinary income under Sec. 736(a). In the latter case, the partnership can claim a deduction for the payment and reduce its ordinary income or increase its ordinary loss.

Because the tax implications of the sale transaction and liquidating distribution alternatives are both numerous and complex, the partners should make their choice only after careful consideration.

COMPLIANCE AND PROCEDURAL CONSIDERATIONS

Section 754 Election

The Sec. 754 election brings both the optional basis adjustments of Secs. 734 and 743 into play. Once the decision to file a Sec. 754 election is made, the procedure is simple. The election is filed along with a timely filed partnership return for the year in which a distribution or transfer occurs. If the election is properly filed, the partnership can make optional basis adjustments for distributions or transfers reported on the tax return filed with the election. The Sec. 754 election requires a written statement that must (1) include the name and address of the partnership making the election, (2) be signed by any one of the partners, and (3) contain a declaration that the partnership

Historical Note

If the date for making a Sec. 754 election is missed due to good cause, the IRS, at its discretion, may grant a reasonable extension. For example, the IRS has allowed an extension both when a partner was misled by advice received from his tax accountant and when an executor of an estate failed to mail the paperwork into the IRS.

elects under Sec. 754 to apply the optional basis adjustment provisions found in Secs. 734(b) and 743(b). The election remains in effect until it is revoked or until the partnership is terminated.[80]

Revocation of the Election. The election to make optional basis adjustments is not easily revoked, but it is possible to do so with IRS approval. Approval can be given if there are sufficient grounds. Regulation Sec. 1.754-1(c) cites some examples that may be considered reason for revocation, including the following:

- A change in the nature of the partnership's business
- A substantial increase in the partnership's assets
- A change in the character of the partnership's assets
- An increased frequency of retirements or shifts in partnership interests

These examples represent situations in which the administrative burden of having an election for optional basis adjustments would substantially increase and would make revocation of the election desirable. However, no application for revocation will be approved if its primary purpose is to avoid reducing the basis of partnership assets that would otherwise result from a distribution or transfer.

If the partnership has an acceptable business reason for requesting the revocation, the partnership must file with the appropriate IRS district director an application requesting the revocation of the election. The application must be filed no later than 30 days after the close of the partnership tax year with respect to which the revocation is intended to take effect. The application must describe the conditions which the partners believe warrant the revocation, and one of the partners must sign the application.[81]

Key Point

Since a Sec. 732(d) election may not need to be made for many years after the transfer of the partnership interest, it is critical that the information needed to make the election be obtained on the date of the actual transfer. If such information is not available at the later date, the Sec. 732(d) election may be of no benefit to the partner.

Section 732(d) Election

Under Sec. 732(d), a partner can elect to treat property received in a distribution as if the partnership had an optional basis adjustment election in effect when the partnership interest was purchased. This election must be filed with the tax return for the year in which the distribution occurs if property subject to depreciation, depletion, or amortization is included in the distribution. If no such properties are included in the distribution, the election does not have to be made until the first year in which the basis of the distributed property is pertinent in calculating the partner's income tax liability.[82]

This election may be made many years after the transfer of the partnership interest to the distributee partner. By that time, the partner may have difficulty determining the basis and FMV amounts for the partnership assets which existed at the time the partnership interest was purchased. Thus, the delay between the transfer and the filing of the Sec. 732(d) election makes it very difficult for the average taxpayer to use this provision. Data that allows the election to be made should routinely be gathered at the time that a partnership interest is purchased.

When an election is made to use the Sec. 732(d) optional basis adjustment, the partner must file a statement along with his tax return that an election to make a basis adjustment on the distributed property will be made. The partner must include the computation of the special basis adjustment and the allocation of the adjustment to the individual distributed properties.[83]

---

[80] Reg. Sec. 1.754-1(b).
[81] Reg. Sec. 1.754-1(c).
[82] Reg. Sec. 1.732-1(d)(2).
[83] Reg. Sec. 1.732-1(d)(3).

Ch. 10 / Special Partnership Issues

PROBLEM MATERIALS

DISCUSSION QUESTIONS

10-1. Explain the condition that differentiates a current distribution from one of a series of liquidating distributions.

10-2. What determines the basis of property distributed in a nonliquidating distribution in the distributee partner's hands?

10-3. What determines the basis of property distributed in a liquidating distribution in the distributee partner's hands?

10-4. Cindy has a $4,000 basis in her partnership interest before receiving a nonliquidating distribution of property having a $4,500 basis and a $6,000 FMV from the CDE Partnership. Cindy has a choice of receiving either inventory or a capital asset. She will hold the distributed property as an investment for no more than two years before she sells it. What tax difference (if any) will occur as a result Cindy's selection of one property or the other to be distributed by the partnership?

10-5. What items are included in the definition of unrealized receivables for purposes of Sec. 751? Why are such items given the special Sec. 751 treatment?

10-6. Which of the following items are considered to be inventory for purposes of Sec. 751?
   a. Supplies
   b. Inventory
   c. Notes receivable
   d. Land held for investment purposes
   e. Lots held for resale

10-7. The AB Partnership has inventory items which have a $100,000 FMV. If the inventory is substantially appreciated for Sec. 751 purposes, what do you know about the basis of the partnership's inventory and the FMV of all the partnership's assets?

10-8. Explain the conditions when Sec. 751 has an impact on nonliquidating (current) distributions.

10-9. What conditions are required in order for a partner to recognize a loss when a distribution is received from a partnership?

10-10. Can the basis of unrealized receivables and inventory received in a liquidating distribution be greater to the partner than to the partnership? Can the basis of unrealized receivables and inventory received in a distribution be smaller to the partner than to the partnership? Explain.

10-11. Is it possible for a partner to recognize both a gain and a loss on the sale of a partnership interest? If so, under what conditions?

10-12. Tyra has a zero basis in her partnership interest and a share in partnership liabilities which are quite large. Explain how these facts will affect the taxation of her departure from the partnership using the following methods of terminating her interest in the partnership.
   a. A liquidating distribution of property
   b. A sale of the partnership interest to a current partner for cash
   c. A charitable contribution of the interest
   d. Abandonment of the partnership interest

10-13. Explain the conditions under which the Sec. 736 rules apply to a partner's departure from a partnership.

10-14. A difference exists in the tax treatment for a contribution of a partnership interest to a charity when the partnership has liabilities and a gift of that same interest to an individual. Identify this difference in treatment.

10-15. What are the advantages and disadvantages to the partnership and its partners when a partnership termination is caused by a sale of more than a 50% capital and profits interest?

10-16. What are the advantages of a partnership electing under Sec. 754 to make optional basis adjustments?

10-17. What are the disadvantages of a partnership electing under Sec. 754 to make optional basis adjustments?

10-18. How is the amount of an optional basis adjustment calculated when a partnership interest is sold? When a partner receives a property distribution?

10-19. Do optional basis adjustments normally change the asset bases to make them equal to their FMV? If not, why?

10-20. Section 755 dictates the allocation of an optional basis adjustment amount among the partnership's assets. How does the adjustment process differ for adjustments arising from transfers and those arising from distributions?

10-21. When can a Sec. 732(d) election be used by a partner? How does it differ from the optional basis adjustment election?

10-22. How can a Sec. 732(d) election affect a sale of Sec. 751 assets as part of a sale of the partnership interest since the Sec. 732(d) election deals only with distributed assets?

10-23. Why is the partnership entity the form often chosen for a tax shelter?

10-24. What is an abusive tax shelter?

10-25. What is a publicly traded partnership? Are all publicly traded partnerships taxed as corporations?

10-26. What are the tax and economic differences between a sale of a partnership interest to the remaining partners and the liquidation of the partnership interest by making a distribution of partnership property?

PROBLEMS

10-27 *Current Distributions.* In the following independent situations, determine the amount of gain or loss to be recognized, the basis of any distributed property, and the partner's remaining basis in the partnership interest. Each distribution is a current distribution, and any distributions involving Sec. 751 property are pro rata to all partners.
   a. Anne has a $29,000 basis in her partnership interest before receiving a distribution of $9,000 cash and land having a $17,000 basis to the partnership and a $30,000 FMV.
   b. Bill has a $250,000 basis in his partnership interest before receiving a distribution of land having a $160,000 basis to the partnership and a $147,000 FMV, inventory having a $33,600 basis to the partnership and a $44,000 resale value, and $42,000 cash. On the same day the partnership also pays liabilities of $300,000 in addition to making the distribution. Bill's share of the liabilities is $30,000.
   c. Caitlin has an $18,000 basis in her partnership interest before receiving a distribution of land having a $6,000 basis to the partnership and a $15,000 FMV, inventory having a $5,800 basis to the partnership and a $6,500 FMV, and corporate stock having a $12,000 basis to the partnership and a $15,000 FMV.
   d. Doug has a $20,000 basis in his partnership interest before receiving a distribution of $3,000 cash, receivables having a $4,000 basis to the partnership and a $7,000 FMV, inventory having a $4,000 basis to the partnership and a $6,000 FMV, and land having a $3,500 basis to the partnership and a $2,000 FMV.

10-28. *Current Distributions.* Complete the chart for each of the following independent distributions. Assume that all distributions are nonliquidating, and pro rata to the partners, and no contributed property was distributed.

	Partner's Basis	Property Distributed	Property's Basis to Partnership	Property's FMV	Property's Basis to Partner
a.	Predistribution $20,000	Cash	$ 6,000	$ 6,000	
	Postdistribution $_____	Land	4,000	15,000	$_____
		Machinery	3,000	2,000	$_____
b.	Predistribution $30,000	Cash	$24,000	$24,000	
	Postdistribution $_____	Inventory	6,000	8,000	$_____
		Unrealized receivable	1,000	14,000	$_____
c.	Predistribution $15,000	Land	$ 6,000	$ 4,000	$_____
	Postdistribution $_____	Inventory	7,000	7,500	$_____
		Cash	3,000	3,000	
d.	Predistribution $26,000	Cash	$35,000	$35,000	
	Postdistribution $_____	Land—Parcel 1	6,000	10,000	$_____
		Land—Parcel 2	18,000	18,000	$_____
e.	Predistribution $12,000	Land—Parcel 1	$ 4,000	$ 6,000	$_____
	Postdistribution $_____	Land—Parcel 2	6,000	10,000	$_____
		Land—Parcel 3	4,000	10,000	$_____

10-29. Current Distributions. Susan, Sam, and Steve are equal partners in the SSS Partnership which was formed in 1987. There have been no additional property contributions since its formation. In 1987 the partnership borrowed $90,000 which remained outstanding until it was repaid earlier in the current year. At the beginning of the current year the partner's bases were: Susan, $40,000; Sam, $32,000; and Steve, $28,000. Operations for the current year were exactly at the breakeven point. At year-end, each partner received a distribution of land. The three pieces of land were lots from a large tract of land being developed by the partnership and each lot had a $5,000 basis and a $10,000 FMV. For each partner: what is the amount of gain or loss to be recognized, the basis of the distributed land, and their remaining basis in the partnership interest?

10-30. Current Distribution of Contributed Property. In 1990, Andrew contributed land, having an $18,000 basis and a $22,000 FMV, and $4,000 in money to the ABC Partnership when it was formed. In December 1991, the land that Andrew had contributed was distributed by the partnership to Bob, another partner. At the time of the distribution, the land had a $21,000 FMV and Andrew and Bob's bases in their partnership interests were $21,000 and $30,000, respectively.
a. What gain or loss must be recognized on the distribution and who must recognize it?
b. What are the bases for Andrew and Bob's interests in the partnership after the distribution?
c. What is Bob's basis in the distributed land?

10-31. Current Distribution of Contributed Property. The ABC Partnership made the following current distributions in 1991. (The dollar amounts listed are the amounts before any implications of the distribution are considered.)

Partner	Type of Property	Basis	FMV	Partner's Basis in Partnership Interest
Abner	Land	$ 4,000	$10,000	$19,000
Beth	Inventory	1,000	10,000	5,000
Cathy	Money	10,000	10,000	8,000

The land Abner received has been contributed by Beth during 1990 when its basis was $4,000 ans its FMV was $8,000. The inventory Beth received had been contributed by Cathy in 1990 when its basis was $1,000 and its FMV was $4,000. For each independent situation: What gain or loss must be recognized? What is the basis of distributed property after the distribution? What are the bases of the partnership interests after the distribution? Assume that there are no Sec. 751 implications.

10-32. *Current Distribution With Sec. 751.* The KLM Partnership owns the following assets on March 1 of the current year:

Assets	Basis	FMV
Cash	$ 30,000	$ 30,000
Receivables	—0—	16,000
Inventory	50,000	52,000
Supplies	6,000	6,500
Equipment[a]	9,000	10,500
Land (investment)	40,000	65,000
Total	$135,000	$180,000

[a] Depreciation of $4,000 has been claimed on the equipment.

a. Which partnership items are unrealized receivables?
b. Is the partnership's inventory substantially appreciated?
c. Assume the KLM Partnership has no liabilities and that Kay's basis for her partnership interest is $33,750. On March 1, of the current year, Kay receives a $20,000 current distribution in cash, which reduces her partnership interest from one-third to one-fourth. What are the tax results of the distribution (i.e., the amount and character of any gain, loss or income recognized; Kay's basis in her partnership interest; and the partnership's basis in its remaining assets)?

10-33. *Current Distribution With Sec. 751.* The JAS Partnership owns the following assets on October 1 of the current year:

Assets	Basis	FMV
Cash	$ 48,000	$ 48,000
Receivables	12,000	12,000
Inventory	21,000	24,000
Building[a]	190,000	240,000
Land	36,500	76,000
Total	$307,500	$400,000

[a] Sale of the building for its FMV would result in $50,000 of Sec. 1245 gain being recognized.

a. Which partnership items are unrealized receivables?
b. Is the partnership's inventory substantially appreciated?
c. Assume the JAS Partnership has no liabilities and Jack's basis in his partnership interest is $76,875. On October 1 of the current year, Jack receives a $25,000 current distribution in cash, which reduces his partnership interest from one-fourth to one-fifth. What are the tax results of the distribution (i.e., the amount and character of any gain, loss, or income recognized; Jack's basis in his partnership interest; and the partnership's basis in its remaining assets)?

10-34. *Liquidating Distribution.* Sara receives her proportionate share of each asset held by the SK Partnership as a liquidating distribution at a time when the basis of her partnership interest is $42,000. The partnership has $100,000 in liabilities, and her share of the liabilities is $5,000. She receives the following assets in the liquidating distribution:

Assets	Basis	FMV
Cash	$12,000	$12,000
Receivables	6,000	8,000
Building	21,000	30,000
Land	7,000	15,000
Total	$46,000	$65,000

No depreciation recapture will apply if the building is sold.

a. What are the amount and character of the gain or loss recognized by Sara and the SK Partnership on the liquidating distribution?
b. What is Sara's basis in each asset she receives?

10-35. *Liquidating Distribution.* Marinda is a one-third partner in the MWH Partnership before she receives $100,000 cash as a liquidating distribution. Immediately before Marinda receives the distribution, the partnership has the following assets.

Assets	Basis	FMV
Cash	$100,000	$100,000
Marketable securities	50,000	90,000
Investment land	90,000	140,000
Total assets	$240,000	$330,000

At the time of the distribution, the partnership has $30,000 of outstanding liabilities which the three partners share equally. Marinda's basis in her partnership interest before the distribution was $80,000. What are the amount and character of the gain or loss recognized by Marinda and the MWH Partnership on the liquidating distribution?

10-36. *Liquidating Distributions.* The AB Partnership pays its only liability (a $100,000 mortgage) on April 1 of the current year and terminates that same day. Alison and Bob were equal partners in the partnership but have partnership bases immediately preceding these transactions of $110,000 and $180,000, respectively. The two partners receive identical distributions with each receiving the following assets.

Assets	Partnership's Basis
Cash	$20,000
Inventory	33,000
Receivables	10,000
Building	40,000
Land	15,000
Total	$118,000

There is no recapture potential on the building. What are the tax implications to Alison, Bob, and the AB Partnership of the April 1 transactions (basis of assets to Alison and Bob, amount and character of gain or loss recognized, etc.)?

10-37. *Sale of a Partnership Interest.* April has a $50,000 basis in her one-fourth interest in the ABC Partnership when she sells her partnership interest to Nora for $60,000 cash. At the time of the sale the partnership has the following assets:

Assets	Basis	FMV
Cash	$ 35,000	$ 35,000
Inventory	50,000	82,000
Accounts receivable	40,000	38,000
Land	75,000	125,000
Total	$200,000	$280,000

The partnership had $40,000 of recourse liabilities at the time of the sale which the 4 partners share equally.
a. What are the amount and character of April's gain or loss on the sale?
b. What is Nora's basis in her partnership interest?
c. What impact will this sale have on the partnership and the other partners?

10-38. *Sale of Partnership Interest.* Andrew has a $60,000 basis in his one-third interest in the

JAS Partnership when he sells it to Michael for $80,000. On the sale date, the general partnership reports $30,000 of liabilities and the following assets:

Assets	Basis	FMV
Cash	$ 50,000	$ 50,000
Inventory	60,000	95,000
Land	70,000	125,000
Total	$180,000	$270,000

a. What are the amount and character of Andrew's recognized gain or loss on the sale?
b. What is Michael's basis in his partnership interest?
c. Assuming no Sec. 754 election has been made, what is the partnership's basis in its assets after the sale?
d. If a Sec. 754 election is in effect when Andrew sells his interest, what is the partnership's basis in its assets after the sale?

10-39. Sale of Partnership Interest. Clay owned 60% of the CAP Partnership and sold one-half of his interest (30%) to Steve for $75,000 cash. Prior to the sale, Clay's basis in his entire partnership interest was $96,000 including his $30,000 share of partnership liabilities. Partnership assets on the sale date were:

Assets	Basis	FMV
Cash	$ 50,000	$ 50,000
Inventory	30,000	60,000
Land	80,000	190,000
Total	$160,000	$300,000

a. What are the amount and character of Clay's recognized gain on the sale? What is his remaining basis in his partnership interest?
b. What is Steve's basis in his partnership interest?
c. If no Sec. 754 election is in effect, how will the partnership's basis in its assets be affected? Should Steve make a Sec. 732(d) election if he receives a distribution of inventory one year after his purchase?
d. How would your answers to Parts a and c change if Clay sold his entire interest to Steve for $150,000 cash?

10-40. Retirement of a Partner. Suzanne retires from the BRS Partnership when the basis of her one-third interest is $105,000. The partnership agreement provides that a retiring partner will receive payment for goodwill equal to 10% of the preceding year's income. Last year's partnership income was $150,000. At the time of her retirement, the partnership had the following assets.

Assets	Basis	FMV
Cash	$145,000	$145,000
Receivables	40,000	40,000
Land	130,000	220,000
Total	$315,000	$405,000

The partnership has $60,000 of liabilities at the time Suzanne retires. The partnership will pay Suzanne cash of $130,000—$115,000 for her interest in the net assets and $15,000 goodwill—to retire her partnership interest.
a. What are the amount and character of gain or loss which Suzanne must recognize?
b. Assuming no Sec. 754 election has been made, what is the impact of the retirement on the partnership and the remaining partners?

10-41. Retirement of a Partner. Brian owns 40% of the ABC Partnership before his retirement on April 15 of the current year. On that date his basis in the partnership interest was $40,000. The partnership's balance sheet on that date is as follows:

Assets	Basis	FMV
Cash	$ 60,000	$ 60,000
Receivables	14,000	24,000
Land	26,000	40,000
Total	$100,000	$124,000
Liabilities	$ 20,000	$ 20,000
Capital - Abner	16,000	20,800
- Brian	32,000	41,600
- Charles	32,000	41,600
Total	$100,000	$124,000

What are the amount and character of the gain or loss that Brian and the ABC Partnership must recognize for the following independent retirement payments?

a. Brian receives $41,600 cash on April 15.
b. Brian receives $50,000 cash on April 15. The partnership agreement requires goodwill payments and the partners agree that $8,400 is a payment for goodwill.
c. Brian receives $30,000 cash on April 15 of the current year plus $10,000 on April 15 of each of the next three years.

10-42. Retirement of a Partner. Kim retires from the KLM Partnership on January 1 of the current year. At that time, her basis in the partnership is $75,000, and the partnership reports the following balance sheet:

	Basis	FMV
Assets:		
Cash	$100,000	$100,000
Receivables	—0—	30,000
Inventory	30,000	40,000
Land	95,000	100,000
Total	$225,000	$270,000
Liabilities and Capital:		
Liabilities	$ 75,000	$ 75,000
Kim's Capital	50,000	65,000
Larry's Capital	50,000	65,000
Michael's Capital	50,000	65,000
Total	$225,000	$270,000

Explain the tax consequences (i.e., amount and character of gain or loss recognized and Kim's basis for any assets received) of the partnership making the retirement payments described in the following independent situations.

a. Kim receives $65,000 cash on January 1.
b. Kim receives $75,000 cash on January 1, and the partners agree that $10,000 is to be a payment for her share of the partnership's goodwill. The partnership agreement provides for such goodwill payments.
c. Kim receives $75,000 cash on January 1 and the partnership agreement makes no provision for goodwill payments.
d. Kim receives $65,000 cash on January 1 of the current year and will receive 15% of partnership ordinary income for each of the next 5 years.

10-43. Death of a Partner. When Jerry dies on April 16 of the current year, he owns a 40% interest in the JM Partnership and Michael owns the remaining 60% interest. All of his assets are held in his estate for a two-year period while the estate is being settled. Jerry's estate is his successor-in-interest for the partnership interest. Under a formula contained in the partnership agreement, the partnership must pay Jerry's successor-in-interest $40,000 cash shortly after his/her death plus $90,000 for each of the two years immediately following a partner's death. The partnership agreement does not mention goodwill. It does provide that all payments to a retiring partner will first be payments for the partner's share of assets and then any additional payments will be Sec. 736(a) payments. When Jerry died, the partnership had the following assets:

Assets	Basis	FMV
Cash	$100,000	$100,000
Land	200,000	300,000
Total	$300,000	$400,000

Jerry's basis for the partnership interest on the date of his death was $120,000 including his $30,000 share of partnership liabilites.

a. How will the payments be taxed to Jerry's successor-in-interest?
b. What are the implications of the payments for the partnership?

10-44. *Death of a Partner.* Bruce dies on June 1 of the current year. On the date of his death he holds a one-third interest in the ABC Partnership which has a $100,000 basis. Under the partnership agreement, Bruce's successor-in-interest, his wife, is to receive the following amounts from the partnership: $130,000 cash, the partnership's assumption of Bruce's $20,000 share of partnership liabilities, plus 10% of partnership net income for the next 3 years. The partnership's assets immediately preceding Bruce's death are as follows:

Assets	Basis	FMV
Cash	$200,000	$200,000
Receivables	—0—	90,000
Inventory	20,000	40,000
Land	80,000	120,000
Total	$300,000	$450,000

a. What are the amount and character of the gain or loss that Bruce's wife must recognize when the first year's payment is received?
b. What is the character of the gain recognized from the partnership interest for the following 3 years?
c. When does Bruce's successor-in-interest cease to be a member of the partnership?

10-45. *Liquidation or Sale of a Partnership Interest.* John has a 60% capital and profits interest in the JAS Partnership with a basis of $331,200 when he decides to retire. Andrew and Stephen want to continue the partnership's business. On the date John retires, the partnership's balance sheet is as follows:

	Basis	FMV
Assets:		
Cash	$160,000	$160,000
Receivables	42,000	60,000
Inventory	30,000	36,000
Building[a]	200,000	300,000
Land	120,000	180,000
Total	$552,000	$736,000
Liabilities and Capital:		
Liabilities	$120,000	$120,000
John's Capital	259,200	369,600
Andrew's Capital	86,400	123,200
Stephen's Capital	86,400	123,200
Total	$552,000	$736,000

[a] Sale of the building will result in $80,000 of ACRS depreciation recapture under Sec. 1245.

a. What are the tax implications for John, Andrew, Stephen and the JAS Partnership if

Andrew and Stephen purchase one-half of John's partnership interest for a cash price of $184,800 each? (Include in your answer the amount and character of the recognized gain or loss, basis of the partnership assets and any other relevant tax implications.)

b. What are the tax implications for John, Andrew, Stephen, and the JAS Partnership if the partnership pays John a liquidating distribution made up of 60% of each partnership asset?

10-46. *Liquidation or Sale of a Partnership Interest.* Amy retires from the AJS Partnership on January 1 of the current year when her basis in her partnership interest is $120,000. Amy receives $160,000 in cash from the partnership for her interest. On that date, the partnership balance sheet is as follows:

Assets	Basis	FMV
Cash	$180,000	$180,000
Receivables	—0—	60,000
Land	180,000	300,000
Total	$360,000	$540,000
Liabilities	$ 60,000	$ 60,000
Capital - Amy	100,000	160,000
- Joan	100,000	160,000
- Stephanie	100,000	160,000
Total	$360,000	$540,000

a. What are the amount and character of Amy's recognized gain or loss?
b. What are the bases of the partnership assets after the payment if a Sec. 754 election is in effect at the time of the payment?
c. How would your answers to Parts a and b change if Joan and Stephanie each purchased one-half of Amy's partnership interest for $80,000 cash instead of having the partnership distribute the $160,000 in cash to Amy?

10-47. *Exchange of Partnership Interests.* Josh holds a general partnership interest in the JLK Partnership having a $40,000 basis and a $60,000 FMV. The JLK Partnership is a limited partnership that engages in real estate activities. Diana has an interest in the CDE Partnership having a $20,000 basis and a $60,000 FMV. The CDE Partnership is a general partnership that also engages in real estate activities. Neither partnership has any Sec. 751 assets or liabilities.
a. What are the tax implications if Josh and Diana simply exchange their partnership interests?
b. What are the tax implications if instead Diana exchanges her general partnership interest in the CDE Partnership for a limited partnership interest in the same partnership (and Josh retains his same interest in the JLK Partnership)?

10-48. *Gift of Partnership Interests.* Tracy owns a one-half interest in the TU Real Estate Partnership and has a $90,000 basis in her partnership interest. Her share of partnership liabilities is $100,000. The FMV of the interest is $200,000. The partnership has no Sec. 751 assets. What is the amount and character of any recognized gain or loss and the basis of the partnership interest to the new owner if Tracy gives the interest to her son?

10-49. *Termination of a Partnership.* Juanita, Carrie, and Robert owned 60%, 30%, and 10%, respectively, of the JCR Partnership immediately before Juanita sold her partnership interest to Molly for $54,000 cash. The partnership had the following balance sheet at the time of the sale.

	Basis	FMV
Assets:		
Cash	$10,000	$ 10,000
Inventory	18,000	20,000
Land	42,000	70,000
Total	$70,000	$100,000
Equities		
Liabilities	$10,000	$ 10,000
Capital - Juanita	36,000	54,000
- Carrie	18,000	27,000
- Robert	6,000	9,000
Total	$70,000	$100,000

Juanita had a $42,000 basis in her partnership interest. Carrie and Robert have $23,000 and $7,000 bases in their partnership interests, respectively.

    a. What amount of gain or loss must be recognized by Juanita, Carrie, Robert, and Molly as a result of this sale?

    b. What are the bases of the partnership assets after this sale?

10-50. *Termination of a Partnership.* Individuals, Wendy, Xenia, and Yancy own 40%, 8%, and 52%, respectively, of the WXY Partnership. For each of the following independent situations determine if the WXY Partnership terminates and, if so, the date on which the termination occurs.

    a. Wendy sells her entire interest to Alan on June 1, 1991. Alan sells one-half of the interest to Beth on November 15, 1991.

    b. Yancy receives a series of liquidating distributions totaling $100,000. He receives 4 equal annual payments on January 1 of years 1991 through 1994.

    c. Wendy and Xenia each receive a liquidating distribution on September 14, 1991.

    d. Yancy sells his interest to Karen on June 1, 1991, for $10,000 cash and a $90,000 installment note. The note will be paid in monthly installments of $10,000 principal plus interest (at a rate acceptable to the IRS) beginning on July 1, 1991. Yancy has no applicable installment obligations.

    e. The WXY and ABC Partnerships combine their businesses on December 30, 1991. Ownership of the new, combined partnership is as follows: Wendy, 20%; Xenia, 4%; Yancy, 26.5%; Albert, 20%; Beth, 19.5%; and Carl, 10%.

    f. On January 1, 1991, the WXY Partnership divides its business into two new businesses. The WX Partnership is owned equally by Wendy and Xenia. Yancy continues his share of the business as a sole proprietorship.

10-51. *Termination of a Partnership.* For each of the following independent situations determine which partnership(s) (if any) terminate and which partnership(s) (if any) continue.

    a. The KLMN Partnership is created when the KL Partnership merges with the MN Partnership. The ownership of the new partnership is held 25% by Katie, 30% by Laura, 25% by Michael, and 20% by Neal.

    b. The ABC Partnership, with $150,000 in assets, is owned equally by Amy, Beth, and Chuck. The CD Partnership, with $100,000 in assets, is owned equally by Chuck and Drew. The two partnerships merge and the resulting ABCD Partnership is owned as follows: Amy, 20%; Beth, 20%; Chuck, 40%; and Drew, 20%.

    c. The WXYZ Partnership results when the WX and YZ Partnerships merge. Ownership of WXYZ is held equally by the four partners. WX contributes $140,000 in assets and YZ contributes $160,000 in assets to the new partnership.

    d. The DEFG Partnership is owned 20% by Dawn, 40% by Eve, 30% by Frank, and 10% by Greg. Two new partnerships are formed by the division of DEFG. The two new partnerships, the DE and FG Partnerships, are owned in proportion to their relative interests in the DEFG Partnership by the individuals for whom they are named.

    e. The HIJK Partnership is owned equally by its four partners before its division. Two new partnerships, the HI and JK Partnerships, are formed out of the division with the new partnerships owned equally by the partners for whom they are named.

10-52. Optional Basis Adjustment. Patty pays $100,000 cash for Stan's one-third interest in the STU Partnership. The partnership has a Sec. 754 election in effect. Just prior to the sale of Stan's interest, STU's balance sheet appears as follows:

	Basis	FMV
Assets		
Cash	$ 80,000	$ 80,000
Inventory	55,000	60,000
Land	105,000	160,000
Total	$240,000	$300,000
Partners' capital:		
Stan	$ 80,000	$100,000
Traffic Corporation	80,000	100,000
Union Corporation	80,000	100,000
Total	$240,000	$300,000

a. What is the total amount of the optional basis adjustment to be made?
b. What assets receive an allocation of the optional basis adjustment? What is the new basis for each asset?
c. If STU sells the land for its $160,000 FMV immediately after Patty purchases her interest, how much gain or loss will she report as a result of the land sale?

10-53. Optional Basis Adjustment. Kate sells her one-fifth interest in the KKL Partnership to Rhonda for $20,000 cash on June 1, 1991. The partnership has a Sec. 754 election in effect on that date. KKL reports the following balance sheet immediately preceding the sale:

	Basis	FMV
Assets:		
Cash	$10,000	$10,000
Marketable securities	22,000	30,000
Receivables	15,000	20,000
Equipment	15,000	20,000
Land	30,000	40,000
Total	$92,000	$120,000
Liabilities and Capital:		
Liabilities	$20,000	$ 20,000
Kate's Capital	14,400	20,000
Jim's Capital	28,800	40,000
Laura's Capital	28,800	40,000
Total	$92,000	$120,000

a. What is the total amount of the optional basis adjustment to be made?
b. What assets receive an allocation of the optional basis adjustment? What is the new basis for each asset?
c. If KKL sells the marketable securities for their $30,000 FMV immediately after Rhonda purchases her interest, how much gain or loss will she report as a result of selling the marketable securities?

10-54. Optional Basis Adjustment. Tom receives a current distribution from the TAD Partnership of inventory having a $14,000 basis and a $16,000 FMV. Prior to the distribution Tom has a $10,000 basis in his partnership interest. Assume that Sec. 751 does not apply to the distribution and that a Sec. 754 election is in effect.
a. What is the amount of the optional basis adjustment resulting from the distribution?

b. What assets have their bases affected by the adjustment?

c. How would your answer to Part a change if Tom's basis in his partnership interest is $15,000 immediately preceding the distribution?

10-55. *Optional Basis Adjustment.* Dave receives a distribution from the CDE Partnership. The partnership owns the following assets immediately preceding the distribution:

Assets	Basis	FMV
Cash	$ 40,000	$ 40,000
Inventory	30,000	35,000
Land parcel 1	65,000	60,000
Land parcel 2	40,000	60,000
Total	$175,000	$195,000

Assuming the partnership has a Sec. 754 election in effect, what is the amount of the optional basis adjustment (if any) resulting from the following independent distributions? What assets will have their bases affected by the distributions? Assume Secs. 736 and 751 do not apply.

a. Dave's basis for his interest is $30,000 before he receives $34,000 cash as a current distribution.

b. Dave's basis for his interest is $30,000 before he receives land parcel 2 as a liquidating distribution.

c. Dave's basis for his interest is $25,000 before he receives inventory having a $20,000 basis to the partnership as a liquidating distribution.

10-56. *Disposal of a Tax Shelter.* Maria buys an interest in a real estate tax shelter in 1985 and deducts losses from its operation for several years. The property has been fully depreciated on a straight-line basis. Her basis in her limited partnership interest is zero, but her share of partnership liabilities is $100,000. Explain the tax results for the following independent situations.

a. Maria sells her partnership interest for $5 cash.

b. Maria gives the interest to Fred, who works in the same office with her.

CASE STUDY PROBLEM

10-57. Mark Green and his brother Michael purchased land in Orlando, Florida in 1960. At that time they began their investing as Green Brothers Partnership with capital they obtained from placing second mortgages on their homes. Their investments have flourished both because of the prosperity and growth of the area and because they have shown an ability to select prime real estate for others to develop. Over the years, they have acquired a great amount of land and have sold some to developers.

Their tax year has just closed and the partnership has the following balance sheet.

	Basis	FMV
Assets:		
Cash	$200,000	$ 200,000
Accounts receivable	90,000	90,000
Land held for investment	310,000	1,010,000
Total	$600,000	$1,300,000
Equities:		
Mortgages	$400,000	$ 400,000
Capital - Mark	100,000	450,000
- Michael	100,000	450,000
Total	$600,000	$1,300,000

Mark and Michael each have a basis in their partnership interest of $300,000. Last spring,

Mark had a serious heart attack. On his doctor's advice, Mark wants to retire from all business activity and terminate his interest in the partnership. He is interested in receiving some cash now but is not adverse to receiving part of his payment over time.

You have been asked to advise to provide the brothers with information on how to terminate Mark's interest in the partnership. Several possibilities have occurred to Mark and Michael and they want your advice as to which is best for Mark from a tax standpoint. (Michael understands that the resulting choice may not be the best option for him.) The possibilities they have considered include the following:

1. Michael has substantial amounts of cash and could purchase Mark's interest directly. However, the brothers think that it would probably take almost all the cash Michael could raise and they are concerned about any future cash needs Michael might have. They would prefer to have Mark receive $120,000 now plus $110,000 per year for each of the next three years. Mark would also receive interest at a market rate on the outstanding debt. This would qualify for installment reporting. However, installment sale rules for related parties would apply.
2. The partnership could retire Mark's interest. They have considered the option of paying Mark $150,000 now plus 50% of partnership profits for the next three years. Alternatively, they could arrange for Mark to have a $150,000 payment now and a guaranteed payment of $100,000 per year for the next three years. They expect that the dollar amounts to be received by Mark would be approximately the same for the next three years under these two options.
3. John Watson, a long time friend of the family, has expressed an interest in buying Mark's share for $450,000 cash immediately. Michael and John are comfortable that they could work well together.

Mark has substantial amounts of money in savings accounts and in stocks and bonds which have a ready market. He has invested in no other business directly. He always pays taxes at the highest marginal rates.

Prepare a memorandum summarizing the advice that you would give the two brothers on the options that they have considered.

TAX RESEARCH PROBLEMS

10-58. The ABC Partnership is owned equally by Arnie, Becky, and Clay. The three individuals have bases in their partnership interests of $80,000, $120,000, and $160,000, respectively. For business reasons, the partnership needs to be changed into the ABC Corporation, and all three owners agree to the change. The only question to be resolved is how to best structure the transfer from a tax standpoint. The partnership is expected to have the following assets on the date that the change is to occur:

	Basis	FMV
Cash	$ 50,000	$ 50,000
Accounts receivable	60,000	55,000
Inventory	150,000	200,000
Land	200,000	295,000
Total	$460,000	$600,000

Liabilities of $100,000 are expected to be owed on the exchange date. Two possible structures are being considered for making the change:
a. ABC Partnership makes a liquidating distribution of a one-third interest in each asset to each of the partners. The partners then contribute their share of each asset to the new ABC Corporation in exchange for stock.
b. ABC Partnership transfers all of its assets and liabilities to the new ABC Corporation in exchange for all of its stock. ABC Partnership then liquidates by distributing the ABC stock to Arnie, Becky, and Clay.

Will the difference in the form of these two transactions affect the tax consequences? If so, what will the differences in tax treatment be?

A partial list of resources is

- Sec. 351.
- Rev. Rul. 70-239, 1970-1 C.B. 74.
- Rev. Rul. 84-111, 1984-2 C.B. 88.

10-59. Betsy sells her 20% interest in the BCD Partnership for a cash payment of $10,000 when the basis in her interest is $27,000. At the time of the sale, BCD has nonrecourse liabilities that total $100,000 on a building that has a FMV of only $80,000. The partnership has no other liabilities. What impact will owing liabilities in excess of the building's FMV have on the gain or loss that Betsy must recognize?

A partial list of resources is

- Sec. 752.
- *Beulah B. Crane v. CIR,* 35 AFTR 776, 47-1 USTC ¶ 9217 (USSC, 1947).
- *CIR v. John R. Tufts,* 51 AFTR 2d 83-1132, 83-1 USTC ¶ 9328 (USSC, 1983).

10-60. Della retires from the BCD Partnership when her basis in her partnership interest is $60,000. At the date of her retirement, the partnership's balance sheet is as follows:

Assets	Basis	FMV
Cash	$ 50,000	$ 50,000
Receivables	—0—	30,000
Equipment[a]	40,000	50,000
Land	120,000	140,000
Total	$210,000	$270,000
Liabilities	$ 30,000	$ 30,000
Capital - Bruce	60,000	80,000
- Celia	60,000	80,000
- Della	60,000	80,000
Total	$210,000	$270,000

[a] If the equipment were sold for $50,000, the entire gain would be recaptured as Sec. 1245 ordinary income.

Della will receive payments of $20,000 cash plus 5% of partnership ordinary income for each of the next 5 years. The partnership agreement specifies that goodwill will be paid for when a partner retires. Bruce, Celia and Della agree that the partnership has $30,000 in goodwill when Della retires and she will be paid for her one-third share. What is the amount and character of the income that Della must report for each of the next 5 years? What is the tax impact of the retirement on the partnership for the next 5 years? (Assume the partnership earns $100,000 of ordinary income each year for the next 5 years.)

A partial list of resources is

- Sec. 736.
- Reg. Sec. 1.736-1.

11 S Corporations

CHAPTER OUTLINE

LEARNING OBJECTIVES 11-2
S CORPORATION REQUIREMENTS 11-3
  Shareholder Requirements 11-3
  Corporate Requirements 11-4
ELECTION OF S CORPORATION STATUS 11-5
  Making the Election 11-5
  Termination of the Election 11-7
S CORPORATION OPERATIONS 11-11
  Taxable Year 11-11
  Accounting Method Elections 11-12
  Ordinary Income or Loss 11-12
  Special S Corporation Taxes 11-15
LIFO RECAPTURE TAX 11-18
RECAPTURE OF PREVIOUSLY CLAIMED INVESTMENT TAX CREDITS 11-18
TAXATION OF THE SHAREHOLDER 11-18
  Income Allocation Procedures 11-18
  Family S Corporations 11-20
  Loss and Deduction Pass-through to Shareholders 11-21
BASIS ADJUSTMENTS 11-25
  Basis Adjustments to S Corporation Stock 11-25
  Basis Adjustments to Shareholder Debt 11-26
S CORPORATION DISTRIBUTIONS 11-27
  Corporations Having No Earnings and Profits 11-27
  Corporations Having Accumulated Earnings and Profits 11-29
OTHER RULES 11-32
  Tax Preference Items and Other AMT Adjustments 11-32
  Transactions Involving Shareholders and Other Related Parties 11-33
  Fringe Benefits Paid to a Shareholder-Employee 11-34
CONTROVERSIAL ISSUES 11-35
  Second Class of Stock Requirement 11-35
TAX PLANNING CONSIDERATIONS 11-37
  Advantages of S Corporation Treatment 11-37
  Disadvantages of S Corporation Treatment 11-38
  Election to Allocate Income Based on S Corporation's Accounting Methods 11-39
  Increasing the Benefits from S Corporation Losses 11-39
  Passive Income Requirements 11-40
  Using an S Corporation When Liquidating 11-41
COMPLIANCE AND PROCEDURAL CONSIDERATIONS 11-42
  Making the Election 11-42
  Filing the Corporate Tax Return 11-42
  Estimated Tax Payments 11-43
  Administrative Rules 11-44
  Sample S Corporation Tax Return 11-45
PROBLEM MATERIALS 11-45
  Discussion Questions 11-45
  Problems 11-48
  Tax Form/Return Preparation Problem 11-53
  Case Study Problem 11-55
  Tax Research Problems 11-56

LEARNING OBJECTIVES

After studying this chapter, you should be able to

1. Explain the requirements for being taxed under Subchapter S
2. Explain the procedures for electing to be taxed under Subchapter S
3. Identify the events that will result in termination of the S corporation election
4. Determine the permitted tax years for an S corporation
5. Calculate the amount of any special S corporation tax levies
6. Calculate a shareholder's allocable share of ordinary income or loss and separately stated items
7. Determine the limitations on a shareholder's deduction of S corporation losses
8. Calculate a shareholder's basis in his S corporation's stock and debt
9. Determine the taxability of an S corporation's distributions to its shareholders
10. Explain the procedures for filing an S corporation tax return
11. Determine the estimated tax payments required of an S corporation and its shareholders

Key Point
The S corporation rules are deceptively simple. Although taxed much like a partnership, an S corporation must also adhere to many of the corporate tax rules.

This chapter discusses a special type of corporate entity known as an S corporation. The S corporation rules, located in Subchapter S of the Internal Revenue Code, were enacted in 1958 to permit small corporations to enjoy the nontax advantages of the corporate form of organization without being subject to the possible tax disadvantages of the corporate form (e.g., double taxation when corporate income is paid to shareholders as a dividend). Three purposes were stated for these rules:

1. To permit businesses to select a particular form of business organization without being influenced by tax considerations
2. To provide aid for small businesses by allowing the income of the business to be taxed to shareholders rather than being taxed at the corporate level
3. To permit corporations realizing losses for a period of years to obtain a tax benefit of offsetting the losses against income at the shareholder level[1]

For legal and business purposes, S corporations are treated as a corporation. For federal income tax purposes, however, they are treated similar to a partnership.[2] Like a partnership, the profits and losses of the S corporation are passed through to the shareholders, and the S corporation can make tax-free distributions of its previously taxed earnings. Although generally taxed like a partnership, the S corporation still follows many of the basic Subchapter C tax provisions (e.g., S corporations use the corporate tax rules regarding liquidations and tax-free reorganizations instead of the partnership rules). A comparison of the S corporation, partnership, and C corporation rules is presented in Appendix C.

Key Point
Much of the renewed interest in S corporations stems from the 3 percentage point differential between individual and corporate income tax rates.

The Tax Reform Act of 1986 reduced the top individual tax rate from 50% to 28%. The 31% top individual tax rate is currently 3 percentage points below the top tax rate for C corporations. This change has made the S corporation election more attractive for many closely held corporations. This chapter examines the requirements for making an S corporation election and the tax rules that apply to S corporations.

---

[1] S. Rept. No. 1983, 85th Cong., 2d Sess., p. 87 (1958).
[2] Some states do not recognize an S corporation as a conduit for state income tax purposes. Instead, they are taxed under the state income tax laws in the same manner as a C corporation.

S CORPORATION REQUIREMENTS

OBJECTIVE 1
Explain the requirements for being taxed under Subchapter S

The S corporation requirements are divided into two categories—shareholder requirements and corporate requirements. A corporation that satisfies both the shareholder and corporate requirements is known as a small business corporation. Only small business corporations can elect to be taxed under Subchapter S of the Internal Revenue Code. Each set of requirements is outlined below.

Shareholder Requirements

Three shareholder requirements must be satisfied on each day of the tax year.[3]

1. The corporation must not have more than 35 shareholders.
2. All shareholders must be individuals, estates, or certain kinds of trusts.
3. None of the individual shareholders can be classified as a nonresident alien.

Typical Misconception
To refer to S corporations as small business corporations is misleading. S corporations may be small in the sense that they can have no more than 35 shareholders, but there are no limitations in terms of FMV of assets or gross income.

35-Shareholder Rule. Section 1361(c)(1) treats a husband and wife (and their estates) as a single shareholder for purposes of applying the 35-shareholder limit. When stock is owned jointly by two unmarried individuals (e.g., as tenants in common or as joint tenants), each owner is considered a separate shareholder.

Eligible Shareholders. Corporations and partnerships cannot own S corporation stock. This restriction prevents a corporation or a partnership having a large number of owners from avoiding the 35-shareholder limitation by purchasing S corporation stock and being treated as a single shareholder.

Five types of trusts can own S corporation stock—grantor trusts, voting trusts,[4] testamentary trusts, **qualified Subchapter S trusts** (QSSTs),[5] and beneficiary-controlled trusts (i.e., trusts that distribute all of their income to a single income beneficiary who is treated as the owner of the trust). Grantor trusts and beneficiary-controlled trusts can own S corporation stock only if the grantor or the beneficiary is a qualified shareholder. Each beneficiary of a voting trust must also be an eligible shareholder. A testamentary trust (i.e., a trust created under the terms of a will) that receives S corporation stock is an eligible shareholder for a 60-day period that begins on the transfer date. This period is extended to 2 years for any testamentary grantor-type trust that (1) owned the stock prior to the grantor or deemed owner's death, (2) continues in existence, and (3) has its entire corpus included in the grantor or deemed owner's gross estate.

Example 11-1 ■ Joan, a U.S. citizen, owns 25% of the stock of Waldo Corporation, an electing S corporation. At the time of her death, the Waldo stock passes to Joan's estate. The estate is a qualifying shareholder, and the transfer does not affect the S corporation election. If the stock is subsequently transferred to a trust that is provided for in Joan's will, the testamentary trust can hold the Waldo stock for a 60-day period

---

[3] Secs. 1361(b)(1)(A)-(C).

[4] A **voting trust** is an arrangement whereby the stock owned by a number of shareholders is placed under the control of a trustee for purposes of exercising the voting rights possessed by the stock. One reason for creating a voting trust is to increase the voting power of a group of minority shareholders in the selection of corporate directors or the establishment of corporate policies.

[5] A QSST is a domestic trust that owns stock in one or more S corporations and distributes (or is required to distribute) all of its income to its sole income beneficiary. The income beneficiary must make an irrevocable election to have the QSST rules contained in Sec. 1361(d) apply. These rules cause the beneficiary to be treated as the owner (and, therefore, the shareholder) of the portion of the trust consisting of the S corporation stock. A separate election must be made for each S corporation's stock that is owned by the trust.

before the election is terminated. The 60-day period is extended to 2 years if a trust held the Waldo stock at the time of Joan's death, if Joan was considered the deemed owner of the trust, and if the entire corpus of the trust is included in Joan's estate. ■

The trust in Example 11-1 can hold the S corporation stock for an indefinite period of time only if an election is made by the trust's income beneficiary to have it treated as a QSST. Otherwise, the S corporation election will be terminated at the end of the 60-day or 2-year period, whichever is applicable.

Alien Individuals. Individuals who are not U.S. citizens (i.e., alien individuals) can only own S corporation stock if they are residents of the United States. The election is terminated if S corporation stock is purchased by an alien individual who does not reside in the United States. (See Chapter 15 for a discussion of the taxation of alien individuals.)

Corporate Requirements

Three corporate requirements must be satisfied on each day of the tax year:

1. The corporation must be a domestic corporation.
2. The corporation must not be an "ineligible" corporation.
3. The corporation must have only one class of stock issued and outstanding.[6]

The first requirement precludes foreign corporations and unincorporated entities that do not meet the federal income tax definition of a corporation from making an S corporation election.

A corporation may be an ineligible corporation in one of three ways:

Typical Misconception
While S corporations cannot have corporate shareholders, S corporations can own stock in other corporations, but no more than 79% of another corporation unless the corporation has not begun business and does not have gross income.

1. Corporations that maintain a special federal income tax status are not eligible to make an S corporation election. For example, financial institutions (i.e., banks) and insurance companies are not eligible.
2. Corporations that have elected the special Puerto Rico and U.S. possessions tax credit (Sec. 936) or the special Domestic International Sales Corporation tax exemption are ineligible to make the S corporation election.
3. Corporations that are members of an affiliated group cannot make an S corporation election.[7] This rule permits the S corporation to own stock of a second domestic or foreign corporation, provided that it does not own a sufficient amount of stock to create an affiliated group.

Section 1361(c)(6) permits an S corporation to exceed the 80% stock ownership minimum contained in the affiliated group definition (Sec. 1504) for any period within the tax year, provided it owns the stock of a corporation that has not begun business by the end of the period and does not have gross income for the period.

A corporation that has two classes of stock issued and outstanding cannot be an S corporation. Treasury stock, unissued stock, stock options, warrants, phantom stock plans, stock appreciation rights, and convertible debt issues are not considered "stock" for purposes of this test. In addition, a second class of stock is not created if the only difference between the two classes of stock relates to voting rights.[8] The

---

[6] Sec. 1361(b)(1).
[7] The affiliated group definition used here is the same one used for consolidated tax return purposes (i.e., 80% of total voting power and 80% of total value of outstanding stock) except that it only requires that the stock ownership test be satisfied. This definition does not require that the investee corporation also be an includible corporation, or that a consolidated tax return be filed.
[8] Sec. 1361(c)(4).

exercise of an option or warrant, or the conversion of a debt instrument into stock, may terminate the S corporation's election if the newly issued stock is of a different class and the difference is other than a difference in voting rights. (See the Controversial Issues section of this chapter for a discussion of the second class of stock rules and a set of quite controversial proposed Treasury Regulations.)

Example 11-2 ■ Kelly Corporation has two classes of common stock outstanding. The Class A and Class B common stock give the shareholders identical rights and interests in the profits and assets of the corporation. Class A stock has one vote per share. Class B stock is nonvoting. Kelly Corporation is treated as having only one class of stock outstanding and can make an S corporation election. ■

ELECTION OF S CORPORATION STATUS

OBJECTIVE 2
Explain the procedures for electing to be taxed under Subchapter S

The S corporation election exempts a corporation from all taxes imposed by Chapter 1 of the Internal Revenue Code (Secs. 1-1399) except for the following:

Sec. 1374 capital gains tax
Sec. 1374 built-in gains tax
Sec. 1375 excess net passive income tax
Sec. 1363(d) LIFO reserve recapture tax

This rule exempts the S corporation from the accumulated earnings tax, the personal holding company tax, the corporate alternative minimum tax and the Superfund Environmental tax for (1) the tax year in which the election is first effective and (2) all subsequent tax years until the election is revoked or terminated.

The S corporation election affects the shareholders in three ways:

1. The shareholders must report their pro rata share of the S corporation's ordinary income or loss as well as any separately stated items.
2. Distributions made to the shareholders come under a series of special rules that generally treat most distributions as a tax-free recovery of the shareholders' stock investments.
3. The shareholders' bases in the stock are adjusted for their ratable share of the ordinary income or loss and any separately stated items.

Making the Election

The S corporation election can only be made by small business corporations. In order for a small business corporation to make a valid S corporation election, the election (Form 2553) must be filed in a timely manner and all of the corporation's shareholders must consent to the election. Existing corporations can make a timely S corporation election (1) at any time during the tax year preceding the year for which the election is to be effective or (2) on or before the fifteenth day of the third month of the year for which the election is to be effective.[9]

Example 11-3 ■ Waco Corporation, a calendar-year taxpayer, has been in existence for several years. Waco wants to be taxed as an S corporation for 1991 and subsequent years. The election can be made any time during 1990 or between January 1 and March

---
[9] Sec. 1362(b)(1).

Self-Study Question

Would the answer to Example 11-3 change if it had been a member of an affiliated group through 1/15/91?

Answer

Yes. Since Waco was an ineligible corporation for a portion of the 75-day period of 1991, an S corporation election would not be effective until 1/1/92.

15, 1991. If the election is made after March 15, 1991, it becomes effective in 1992. ∎

For a new corporation, the S corporation election can be made at any time on or before the fifteenth day of the third month of its initial tax year. A new corporation's initial tax year commences with the first day on which the corporation has shareholders, acquires assets, or begins business.

If the S corporation election is made during the first 2½ months of the tax year for which it is first to be effective, the corporation must also meet all of the small business corporation requirements on each day of the tax year that precedes the election date and on the election date. If one of the requirements is not met on any day that precedes the election date, the election becomes effective in the S corporation's next tax year.

Consent of Shareholders. Each person who is a shareholder on the date that the election is made must consent to the election.[10] The consent is binding on the current tax year and all future tax years. No additional consents are required of shareholders who acquire the stock between the election date and its effective date or at any subsequent date.

Section 1362(b)(2) imposes a special rule on the shareholders when an election is made after the beginning of the tax year for which it is to be effective. Each shareholder who owned stock at any time during the portion of the year that precedes the time the election is made, and who is not a shareholder at the time the election is made, must also consent to the election.

Example 11-4 ∎

Sara and Harry own all of the stock of Kraft Corporation. Sara sells all of her Kraft stock to Lisa on February 10, 1991. The next day Kraft Corporation elects to be taxed as an S corporation. For the election to apply in 1991, Sara, Harry, and Lisa must consent to the election. If Sara refuses to consent to the election, the election will not begin until 1992. ∎

Each tenant (whether husband and wife or not) must consent to the S corporation election if the stock is owned as tenants in common, joint tenants, or tenants in the entirety. If the S corporation stock is owned as community property, the consent must be made by each person having a community property interest. If the shareholder is a minor, the consent can be made by the minor or the minor's legal representative (e.g., a natural parent or legal guardian).

Key Point

The procedures for making an S corporation election are very precise. Taxpayers must be very careful to understand and adhere to each requirement so as not to invalidate an S corporation election inadvertently.

All of the appropriate procedures for making the S corporation election and filing the necessary consents must be adhered to. Failure to do so will result in the S corporation election being deferred or declared invalid.

- Make sure the election is filed on or before the fifteenth day of the third month of the tax year. Late elections will prevent the S corporation benefits from being claimed until the next tax year.
- Make sure that all of the small business corporation requirements are met when the election is filed. If the election is filed after the beginning of the tax year, planning is needed to ensure that the small business corporation requirements are met from the first day of the tax year on.
- Make sure that all of the necessary consents are obtained. Failure to obtain the consent of a shareholder (e.g., one spouse of a couple that jointly holds the S corporation stock) will invalidate the S corporation election.

[10] Sec. 1362(a)(2).

Topic Review 11-1 presents a summary of the S corporation requirements and procedures for making the election.

Termination of the Election

OBJECTIVE 3
Identify the events that will result in termination of the S corporation election

The S corporation election is terminated when the corporation either (1) revokes the election or (2) terminates the election because it ceases to meet the small business corporation requirements. Each of these actions is examined below. The requirements for making a new S corporation election following a termination are also discussed.

Self-Study Question
Can the revocation of an S corporation election ever be retroactive? Prospective?

Answer
A revocation can be retroactive to the beginning of the year if made within the first 75 days of that year. A revocation can be prospective to any **subsequent** date.

Revocation of the Election. A corporation can revoke its S corporation election in any tax year as long as it meets the requirements regarding shareholder consent and timeliness. Shareholders owning more than one-half of the corporation's stock (including nonvoting stock) on the day on which the revocation is made must consent to the revocation.[11] A revocation that is made on or before the fifteenth day of the third month of the tax year is effective on the first day of the S corporation's tax year. A revocation that is made after the first 2½ months of the tax year is effective on the first day of the next tax year. An exception is provided that permits the S corporation to select a prospective date for the revocation to be effective. The prospective date can be the date on which the revocation is made or any subsequent date.[12]

TOPIC REVIEW 11-1

S Corporation Requirements and Election Procedures

Requirements

Shareholder:
1. The corporation may have no more than 35 shareholders. Husbands and wives and their estates count as 1 shareholder.
2. All shareholders must be individuals, estates, or certain kinds of trusts. Eligible trusts include: grantor trusts, voting trusts, testamentary trusts, beneficiary-controlled trusts, and qualified Subchapter S trusts.
3. All of the individual shareholders must be U.S. citizens or resident aliens.

Corporate:
1. The corporation must be a domestic corporation or an unincorporated entity that meets the federal income tax definition of a corporation.
2. The corporation must not be an ineligible corporation (e.g., a bank, an insurance company, or a member of an affiliated group, etc.). Affiliated groups are permitted only if the subsidiary is an "inactive" corporation.
3. The corporation must have only one class of stock issued and outstanding. Differences in voting rights are ignored.

Making the Election

1. The S corporation election can be made at anytime during the tax year preceding the year for which the election is effective or on or before the 15th day of the 3rd month of the tax year for which the election is effective. Late elections are effective with the next tax year.
2. Each shareholder who is a shareholder on the date that the election is made must consent to the election. If the election is made after the beginning of the tax year, each person who was a shareholder during the portion of the tax year preceding the election must also consent to the election.

---

[11] Sec. 1362(d)(1)(B).
[12] Secs. 1362(d)(1)(C) and (D).

Example 11-5 ■ Adobe Corporation, a calendar-year taxpayer, has been taxed as an S corporation for several years. However, the corporation has become quite profitable, and management feels that it would be advantageous to make a public stock offering in order to obtain additional capital during 1991. Adobe Corporation can revoke its S corporation election any time before March 16, 1991, and have the election terminated at the close of business on December 31, 1990. If the revocation election is made after March 15, 1991, it does not take effect until January 1, 1992. In either case, the corporation may specify a prospective 1991 revocation date as long as the date specified is on or after the date the revocation is made. ■

Additional Comment
If it is impossible to obtain the majority vote necessary for revocation, several of the terminating events are relatively easy to create if a termination of an S corporation election is desired.

Termination of the Election. The S corporation election is terminated if the corporation fails one or more of the small business corporation requirements on any day after the first day that the election is effective.[13] The termination generally occurs on the date of the terminating event. Events that can terminate the election include:

- Exceeding the 35-shareholder limit
- Having an ineligible shareholder own some of the stock
- Creating a second class of stock
- Acquiring stock of a second corporation that creates an affiliated group
- Retaining a prohibited tax status
- Selecting an improper taxable year
- Failing the passive investment income test for 3 consecutive years.

Merger of an S corporation into another corporation or the liquidation of the S corporation will also terminate the S corporation election.

The passive investment income test is applied annually. It results in a termination of the S corporation election if (1) more than 25% of the corporation's gross receipts are passive investment income for each of 3 consecutive tax years *and* (2) the corporation has Subchapter C earnings and profits (E&P) at the end of each of the 3 consecutive tax years.[14] If the test is failed for 3 consecutive tax years, the election is terminated on the first day of the next (fourth) tax year.

Historical Note
Previously, a termination was deemed to be effective on the first day of the tax year in which the terminating event occurred. To stop this abuse, the rule was changed so that an S corporation election is terminated on the day preceding the date of the terminating event.

Passive investment income includes royalties, rents,[15] dividends, interest, annuities, and gains from the sale or exchange of stocks and securities. Subchapter C E&P include only earnings that have accrued in tax years in which an S corporation election was not in effect (i.e., the corporation was taxed under the C corporation rules).

Example 11-6 ■ Silver Corporation is created in 1991 and elects to be taxed as an S corporation. Silver can earn an unlimited amount of passive income during a tax year without any fear of losing its S corporation status or being subject to the Sec. 1375 penalty tax on excess net passive income because it has never been taxed as a C corporation. (See page 11-15 for a discussion of this tax.) ■

Allocation of Income. If a terminating event occurs sometime other than on the first day of the tax year, an "S termination year" is created. The **S termination year** is divided into an "S short year" and "C short year." The **S short year** commences on the first day of the tax year and ends on the day preceding the day on which the

---

[13] Sec. 1362(d)(2).
[14] Sec. 1362(d)(3).
[15] Proposed Reg. Sec. 1.1362-3(d)(5)(iv) excludes from the rent definition any payments received for the use or occupancy of property if the corporation also performs significant services (i.e., services not customarily rendered in connection with the rental) in return for the payment.

termination is effective. The **C short year** commences on the day on which the termination is effective and continues through the last day of the corporation's tax year.[16]

Example 11-7 ■ Dixon Corporation has been taxed as an S corporation for several years. Paula and Frank each own one-half of Dixon's stock. Paula sells one-half of her Dixon stock to Eagle Corporation on July 1, 1991. The sale terminates the S corporation election effective with the close of business on June 30, 1991 because Eagle Corporation is an ineligible shareholder. Assuming that Dixon is a calendar-year taxpayer, the S short year includes the period January 1 through June 30, 1991. The C short year includes the period July 1 through December 31, 1991. ■

The S short year income is reported by the S corporation's shareholders according to the normal reporting rules described below. The C corporation reports the income earned during the C short year. The C short year income tax liability must be determined on an annualized basis using the Sec. 443 procedures. The S short year return and C short year return are both due on the due date for the corporation's tax return for the tax year had the termination not occurred (including any extensions).[17]

Key Point
Income/loss can be allocated in the termination year under either of two methods. Careful consideration should be given to the possible tax advantages of a daily allocation versus an actual closing of the books.

Two sets of rules can be used to allocate the termination year's income between the S short year and the C short year. The general rule of Sec. 1362(e)(2) allocates the ordinary income or loss and the separately stated items between the S short year and C short year based on the number of days in each year. A special election is available under Sec. 1362(e)(3) that permits the ordinary income or loss and separately stated items to be allocated between the two years according to the corporation's normal tax accounting rules. The second alternative can be used only if all persons who were shareholders at any time during the S short year and all persons who are shareholders on the first day of the C short year consent to the election.[18] (See page 11-39 for further discussion of the Tax Planning Considerations of this election.)

Example 11-8 ■ Assume the same facts as in Example 11-7, except that Dixon Corporation reports the following operating results:

Period	Ordinary Income (Loss)
January 1 through June 30, 1991	($ 60,000)
July 1 through December 31, 1991	240,000
Total	$180,000

Additional Comment
In Example 11-8, in order to use an actual closing of the books to allocate the income/loss of Dixon, Eagle Corporation must consent. Due to the impact of such an election, it should be discussed as part of the negotiation of the stock sale.

Assuming each month has 30 days, the daily allocation method would have $90,000 of ordinary income reported in both the S short year and the C short year. Using the special allocation, the $60,000 of ordinary loss would pass through to Paula and Frank as their share of the loss from the S short year. Dixon Corporation would have $240,000 of taxable income in its C short year, which would be taxed using the C corporation tax rates. ■

Inadvertent Termination. Special rules permit the S corporation election to continue if an inadvertent termination occurs by ceasing to be a small business corporation or by failing the passive investment income test for 3 consecutive years. If

---

[16] Sec. 1362(e)(1).
[17] Sec. 1362(e)(6)(B).
[18] Sec. 1362(e)(3)(B).

such a termination should occur, the S corporation or its shareholders must take the necessary steps, within a reasonable time period after discovering the event creating the termination, to restore its small business corporation status. If the Internal Revenue Service (IRS) determines that the termination was inadvertent, the corporation and all persons owning stock during the termination period must agree to make the adjustments necessary to report the income for this period as if the S corporation election had been in effect continuously.[19]

Example 11-9 ■

Additional Comment
*The IRS also allowed an S corporation election to remain in effect even though the S corporation was momentarily **affiliated** as part of a divisive reorganization [Rev. Rul. 72-320, 1972-1 C.B. 270].*

Frye Corporation is created in 1988 and operates as a C corporation during that year. Frye Corporation elects S corporation treatment in 1989. During 1988, the corporation incorrectly computed its E&P and believed that no Subchapter C E&P existed for its only pre-S corporation tax year. From 1989 through 1991, Frye earns large amounts of passive investment income, but does not pay the Sec. 1375 excess net passive income tax or worry about termination of its election because it thinks that it does not have any accumulated E&P from its C corporation tax year. Upon auditing Frye's tax returns, the IRS finds that Subchapter C E&P did, in fact, exist from 1988, and terminates the S corporation election effective on January 1, 1992. If the Subchapter C E&P is distributed and the shareholders report the dividend income, the IRS will likely treat the occurrence as an inadvertent termination and not revoke the election. ■

New Election Following a Termination. Section 1362(g) requires a corporation that terminates its S corporation election to wait 5 tax years before making a new election.[20] This delay applies unless the IRS consents to an earlier reelection. Proposed Reg. Sec. 1.1362-6(a) indicates that permission for an early reelection can occur when (1) more than 50% of the corporation's stock is owned by persons who did not own stock on the date of termination or (2) the event causing the termination was not reasonably within the control of the corporation or the shareholders having a substantial interest in the corporation *and* was not part of a plan to terminate the election involving the corporation or such shareholders.

Example 11-10 ■

Victor Corporation, a calendar-year taxpayer, is owned by Terri and has been taxed under the S corporation rules for 10 years. In January 1991, Terri sells all of the Victor stock to Michelle. Payments for the Victor stock are to be made by Michelle over a 5-year period. After the second year, Michelle fails to make the necessary payments and Terri repossesses the Victor stock. During the time Michelle holds the stock, Victor Corporation revokes the S corporation election. Victor Corporation should be able to immediately apply for reelection of S corporation status because a more than 50% ownership change has occurred since the date of the termination. ■

Key Point
The most common cause of inadvertent terminations is the sale of an S corporation's stock. Therefore, an S corporation should have a strict buy-sell agreement to guard itself against an ill-advised sale of its stock.

Avoiding the Termination of an S Corporation Election. The termination of an S corporation election generally carries with it substantial negative tax consequences in the form of increased corporate or shareholder taxes. The S corporation's owners, management, and tax advisor need to understand the various events that can cause the termination of the S corporation election. Some of the steps that can be taken to prevent an untimely termination include the following:

---

[19] Sec. 1362(f). Proposed Reg. Sec. 1.1362-5(b) holds that a termination will be inadvertent if the terminating event (1) was not reasonably within the control of the corporation and was not part of a plan to terminate the election or (2) took place without the corporation's knowledge and reasonable safeguards were in place to prevent the event from occurring.

[20] *Termination* is defined here as including both revocation of the S corporation election and loss of the election because one or more of the small business corporation requirements were not met.

1. Monitor all transfers of S corporation stock. Make certain that the purchaser or transferee of the stock is not an ineligible shareholder (e.g., corporation, partnership, or nonresident alien).
2. Establish procedures for the S corporation to purchase the stock of deceased shareholders which could result in the stock being acquired by a trust that is ineligible to be a shareholder.
3. Establish restrictions on the transferability of the S corporation stock by having the shareholders enter into a stock purchase agreement. Such an agreement could provide that the stock cannot be transferred without the prior consent of all other shareholders and, if the necessary consent cannot be obtained, the stock will be repurchased by the corporation at a specified price (e.g., at book value).
4. Monitor all S corporation investment activities. Make sure that the S corporation does not own more than 80% of the stock of another corporation.
5. Monitor the passive income that is earned by an S corporation that has previously been taxed for one or more years as a C corporation. Make certain that the passive income requirement is not failed for 3 consecutive years by taking action to reduce the level of passive income or to distribute the Subchapter C E&P.

S CORPORATION OPERATIONS

S corporations make the same accounting period and accounting method elections that are made by a C corporation. Each year, the S corporation must compute and report to the IRS and to its shareholders its ordinary income or loss and its separately stated items. The special S corporation rules are explained below.

OBJECTIVE 4
Determine the permitted tax years for an S corporation

Taxable Year

Section 1378(a) requires that the S corporation's taxable year be a permitted year. A permitted year is defined as:

- A taxable year ending on December 31st (including a 52-53 week year)
- Any fiscal year for which the corporation establishes a business purpose.[21]

Additional Comment
The requirement that all S corporations adopt calendar years (with March 15th return due dates) caused a hardship for tax return preparers. Sec. 444 is a compromise provision that allows a fiscal year for filing purposes, but requires a Sec. 7519 required payment of the deferred taxes.

Section 1378(b) specifically notes that a deferral of income to shareholders is not considered a necessary business purpose. An S corporation that adopts a fiscal year that coincides with its natural business year is thought to have satisfied the business purpose requirement. The natural business year for an S corporation depends on the type of business that is conducted. When a trade or business has nonpeak and peak periods of business, the natural business year is considered to end at, or soon after, the close of the peak period of business. A business whose income is steady from month to month, year-round, does not have a natural business year. An S corporation's adoption of, or a change to, a fiscal year which is an "ownership" tax year is also permitted. An ownership tax year is the same tax year that is used by shareholders owning more than 50% of the corporation's outstanding stock. The 50% requirement must be met on the first day of the tax year to which the change relates. Failure to meet the 50% "ownership" tax year requirement on the first day of any later tax year,

---

[21] Some S corporations use a "grandfathered" fiscal year: a fiscal year for which IRS approval was obtained after June 30, 1974. Excluded are fiscal years that result in a deferral of income of 3 months or less.

requires a change to a calendar year or other approved fiscal year. S corporations can also adopt, or change to, a fiscal year for which IRS approval is obtained based on the facts and circumstances of the situation.[22]

Section 444 permits an S corporation to elect to use a fiscal year other than a permitted year.[23] The fiscal year elected under Sec. 444 must have a deferral period of 3 months or less (e.g., a September 30th or later fiscal year-end for an S corporation otherwise required to use a calendar year). An S corporation that is changing its tax year can elect to use a new fiscal year under Sec. 444 only if the deferral period is no longer than the shorter of 3 months or the deferral period of the tax year that is being changed. A Sec. 444 election is not required of an S corporation that satisfies the business purpose exception.

S corporations that elect under Sec. 444 to use a fiscal year must make the necessary required payment under Sec. 7519 (see Chapter 9 for an explanation of these payment requirements). When the required payment is computed, the base year net income is the aggregate of all S corporation income, gain, loss, and deduction items that are described in Sec. 1366 (see page 11-13). Revocation or termination of the S corporation election also terminates the Sec. 444 election unless the corporation becomes a personal service corporation. Termination of the Sec. 444 election permits the S corporation to obtain a refund of prior Sec. 7519 payments.

Topic Review 11-2 presents a summary of the alternative tax years that are available to an S corporation.

Accounting Method Elections

The accounting method elections used to compute ordinary income or loss and the separately stated items are made by the S corporation rather than the individual shareholders. As with a partnership, these elections are made independent of the accounting method elections made by its shareholders. Three elections generally reserved for the S corporation's shareholders are as follows:

1. Sec. 617 election relating to deduction and recapture of mining exploration expenditures
2. Sec. 901 election to take a credit (rather than a deduction) for foreign income taxes
3. Sec. 613A election to claim cost or percentage depletion.[24]

Key Point
S corporations are most like partnerships in their method of reporting income/losses. Both are flow-through entities that provide K-1s to their owners with their respective shares of income/loss items.

Ordinary Income or Loss

S corporations do not compute their taxable income in the same manner as C corporations. Because S corporations are taxed similarly to a partnership, they are treated as if they were individual taxpayers. Thus, they report both an ordinary income or loss amount and a series of separately stated items.

The S corporation's separately stated items are the same ones that apply in partnership taxation under Sec. 702(a).[25] The items required to be separately stated by Sec. 702(a) include:

---

[22] Temporary Reg. Sec. 1.1378-1 and Rev. Proc. 87-32, 1987-2 C.B. 396, explain the procedures for an S corporation adopting a fiscal year or changing the tax year of a new or existing S corporation. The tests for a natural business year are found in Sec. 4.04 of Rev. Proc. 83-25, 1983-1 C.B. 689. Rev. Rul. 87-58, 1987-2 C.B. 224, examines 8 situations concerning whether the tax year is a permitted year, or not.

[23] Special transitional rules found in Sec. 444 permitted S corporations to retain their 1986 tax year without having to change to a calendar year for 1987 and later tax years. These transitional rules are explained in the Sec. 444 regulations.

[24] Secs. 1363(c) and 613A(c)(10)(A). Special rules are found in Sec. 613A(c)(13) relating to percentage depletion on properties held by an S corporation. A detailed discussion of the percentage depletion issue is beyond the scope of this book.

[25] Sec. 1366(a).

TOPIC REVIEW 11-2

Alternative S Corporation Tax Years

Type of Tax Year	Requirements
Calendar year (including certain 52-53 week years)	The permitted tax year that is required unless one of the other exceptions applies.
Fiscal year for which business purpose is established	A permitted year includes a tax year for which the corporation establishes a business purpose that is acceptable to the IRS.
Ownership year	IRS approval will be granted if the same tax year is requested that is used by shareholders owning more than one-half of the corporation's outstanding stock. This test must be met on the first day of the year for which approval is requested as well as for each succeeding year.
Natural business year	IRS approval will be granted if 25% or more of the gross receipts for the each of the three most recent 12-month periods are in the last 2 months of the requested tax year.
Facts and circumstances year	Approval for a fiscal year based on business purpose (other than an ownership tax year or natural business year) can be based on the facts and circumstances of the situation.
"Grandfathered" fiscal year	A tax year for which IRS approval was granted after June 30, 1974. A tax year for which a three-month or shorter deferral period was approved does not qualify as a grandfathered tax year.
Nonpermitted fiscal year	A Sec. 444 election permits a nonpermitted tax year to be used if the deferral period is 3 months or less. To maintain the fiscal year as a permitted tax year, the necessary required payments must be made. Transitional rules permitted many S corporations to continue to use their last tax year beginning in 1986.

- Net short-term capital gains and losses
- Net long-term capital gains and losses
- Sec. 1231 gains and losses

- Charitable contributions
- Dividends that are eligible for a dividends-received deduction
- Taxes paid to a foreign country or to a U.S. possession
- Any other item provided by the Regulations.

Regulation Sec. 1.702-1(a)(8) adds for partnerships several other items to the list begun by the Code. The same additions from the Regulations apply to S corporations and include, among others, the following:

- Tax-exempt or partially tax-exempt interest
- Recoveries of bad debts, prior taxes, and delinquency amounts
- Gains and losses from wagering transactions
- Soil and water conservation expenditures
- Intangible drilling and development costs
- Certain mining exploration expenditures

Section 1366(b) requires the character of any separately stated item to be determined as if the item were (1) realized directly by the shareholder from the same source from which it was realized by the corporation or (2) incurred by the shareholder in the same manner as it was incurred by the corporation. Thus, the character of an income, gain, deduction, loss, or credit item does not change merely because the item is passed through and taxed to the shareholders.

Deductions That Cannot Be Claimed. S corporations also have several deductions that cannot be claimed, including

- The 70%, 80% or 100% dividends-received deduction (i.e., because dividends are passed through to the S corporation's shareholders)
- The same deductions that are disallowed to a partnership under Sec. 703(a)(2) (e.g., personal and dependency exemptions, additional itemized deductions for individuals, taxes paid or accrued to a foreign country or to a U.S. possession, charitable contributions, oil and gas depletion, and NOL carrybacks and carryforwards).[26]

Self-Study Question

Since S corporations are conduits, can NOL carryforwards from a C corporation tax year flow through to the S corporation's shareholders?

Answer

No. C corporation NOLs are not a good reason to make an S election, because the NOLs cannot be carried to an S corporation tax year.

Similarity to C Corporation Treatment. S corporations are treated as corporations for certain tax matters. For example, an S corporation can elect to amortize its organizational expenditures under Sec. 248. Also, the 20% reduction in certain tax preference benefits under Sec. 291 applies to an S corporation if the corporation (or a predecessor corporation) was a C corporation in any of its 3 preceding tax years.[27]

Carryforwards and Carrybacks When Status Changes. Some S corporations may operate as a C corporation during a period of years that either precede the making of an S corporation election or follow the termination of an S corporation election. No carryforwards or carrybacks that originate in a C corporation tax year can be carried to an S corporation tax year other than certain carryforwards that can be used to offset the built-in gains tax. Similarly, no carryforwards or carrybacks can be created in an S corporation tax year that can be taken to a C corporation tax year.[28] Losses from an S corporation tax year, of course, are passed through to the

---

[26] Sec. 1363(b)(2).
[27] Secs. 1363(b)(3) and (4).
[28] Sec. 1371(b).

shareholder and, if in excess of the shareholder's income for the year, can create a NOL carryforward or carryback for the shareholder.

Special S Corporation Taxes

OBJECTIVE 5
Calculate the amount of any special S corporation tax levies

The S corporation is subject to three special tax levies—the excess net passive income tax, the built-in gains tax, and the capital gains tax. Each of these is explained below.

Key Point
The excess net passive income tax is of most concern to a former C corporation that has accumulated E&P. A corporation that has always been an S corporation is much less likely to have a passive income problem.

Excess Net Passive Income Tax. The **excess net passive income (or Sec. 1375) tax** is levied when (1) an S corporation has passive investment income for the tax year that exceeds 25% of its gross receipts and (2) at the close of the tax year the S corporation has Subchapter C E&P. The excess net passive income tax equals the S corporation's excess net passive income times the highest corporate tax rate (34% for 1991).[29]

The **excess net passive income** is determined as follows:

$$\text{Excess net passive income} = \text{Net passive income} \times \frac{\text{Passive investment income} - 25\% \text{ of gross receipts}}{\text{Passive investment income}}$$

The excess net passive income is limited to the corporation's taxable income, which is defined as the amount determined under Sec. 63 for a C corporation without any reduction for (1) the NOL deduction or (2) the dividends-received and dividends-paid deductions. Net passive income equals passive investment income minus any deductions that are directly related to its production.[30]

Example 11-11 ■ Paoli Corporation reports the following results for 1991:

Service (nonpassive) income	$35,000
Dividend income	37,000
Interest income	28,000
Passive income-related expenses	10,000
Other expenses	25,000

At the end of 1991, Paoli's E&P for its C corporation tax years amounts to $60,000. Paoli's excess net passive income is determined as follows:

$$\$33,846 = (\$65,000 - \$10,000) \times \frac{\$65,000 - (0.25 \times \$100,000)}{\$65,000}$$

The excess net passive income tax (at 1991 rates) is $11,508 ($33,846 × 0.34). The special tax reduces (on a pro rata basis) the dividend income and interest income items that are passed through to the shareholders. The S corporation election is not terminated at the end of 1991 unless Paoli was also subject to the tax in 1989 and 1990. ■

Built-in Gains Tax. The Tax Reform Act of 1986 added a second corporate level tax on gains that are recognized by an S corporation that was formerly a C corporation. This tax, called the **built-in gains ("new" Sec. 1374) tax**, is imposed on any gain

---

[29] Sec. 1375(a). The passive investment income and Subchapter C E&P terms have the same definition here as when they were defined on page 11-8.

[30] Sec. 1375(b). Regulation Sec. 1.1375-1A(f), Ex. (2) indicates that passive income that is subject to the Sec. 1375 tax includes municipal bond interest that is otherwise exempt from the federal income tax. S corporations should not assume that the tax will not apply because all of its passive investment income is tax-exempt.

> **Key Point**
>
> "New" Sec. 1374 applies to an S corporation that made an S corporation election after 12/31/86. The motivation for this tax was the concern that C corporations would use the S corporation election to avoid the repeal of the General Utilities doctrine.

accruing prior to conversion (known as a **built-in gain**) and which is recognized by the S corporation during the 10-year period commencing on the date that the S corporation election took effect (known as the recognition period). Although this tax was enacted to prevent taxpayers from avoiding the repeal of the *General Utilities* doctrine by making an S corporation election prior to liquidating the corporation or selling its assets, the tax ramifications of the built-in gains tax extends far beyond corporations that are in the process of liquidating.

The built-in gains tax applies to S corporation tax years beginning after December 31, 1986, where (1) the S corporation was formerly a C corporation and (2) the current S corporation election was made after December 31, 1986.[31] Former C corporations that made their current S corporation election before January 1, 1987, are subject to the S corporation capital gains tax described below.

Example 11-12 ■ Tatum Corporation, a calendar-year taxpayer, is incorporated in 1983 and operates as a C corporation through the end of 1986. On February 3, 1987, Tatum Corporation files an S corporation election that is effective for 1987 and later tax years. Because Tatum's S corporation election is filed after January 1, 1987, it is subject to the S corporation built-in gains tax for 10 years. ■

> **Self-Study Question**
>
> Can loss or credit carryforwards from a previous C corporation tax year help reduce the built-in gain tax?
>
> **Answer**
>
> Yes. Both NOL and capital loss carryforwards reduce the amount of recognized built-in gain taxed under "new" Sec. 1374. A general business and minimum tax credit carryforward reduces the actual built-in gains tax.

The Sec. 1374 tax equals the highest tax rate imposed by Sec. 11(b) for the tax year (34% for 1991) times the S corporation's net recognized built-in gain for the tax year. The net recognized built-in gain amount equals the lesser of (1) the net of the corporation's recognized built-in gains and losses or (2) taxable income if it were taxed as a C corporation but was unable to claim any dividends-received deduction or NOL deduction.[32] If the net of the recognized built-in gains and losses exceeds the corporation's taxable income and the S corporation election was made after March 30, 1988, the excess built-in gain amount is carried over to the next tax year where it may be subject to the Sec. 1374 built-in gains tax. NOL and capital loss carryforwards arising in a C corporation tax year, however, can reduce the lesser of the two amounts described in the preceding sentence. No current year credits are permitted to reduce the built-in gains tax except for the nonhighway use of gasoline and other fuels credit. Carryovers of the general business and minimum tax credits that originated in a C corporation tax year also can reduce the built-in gains tax.[33] The built-in gains tax is passed on to the shareholders as if it were a loss. The loss must be allocated proportionately among the recognized built-in gains that resulted in the tax being imposed.

A recognized built-in gain (loss) is any gain (loss) recognized on an asset disposition occurring during the recognition period unless the S corporation can establish that (1) the asset was not held by the S corporation as of the beginning of the first day of the first tax year to which the S corporation election applies, or (2) the recognized gain (loss) exceeds the excess [if any] of the property's FMV (adjusted basis) over its adjusted basis (FMV) on such first day.[34] Dispositions include events

---

[31] Sec. 1374(a). Qualified small business corporations with less than a $10 million valuation that were permitted an additional 2-year waiver of the repeal of the *General Utilities* doctrine when liquidating also were permitted an additional 2 years to make their S corporation election and avoid the built-in gains tax. The built-in gains tax is avoided by these corporations if the S corporation election was made before January 1, 1989. Corporations making such a delayed election are instead subject to the Sec. 1374 capital gains tax described below.

[32] Sec. 1374(d)(2).

[33] Secs. 1374(b)(2) and (3).

[34] Secs. 1374(d)(3) and (4). Income and gains can be taxed under both the excess net passive income (Sec. 1375) and built-in gains (Sec. 1374) taxes. Any such income or gain is fully taxed under the Sec. 1374 rules. The portion of the income or gain that is taxed under the built-in gains tax is excluded from the passive investment income tax (Sec. 1375(b)(4)).

other than sales or exchanges, including, for example, the collection of accounts receivable by a cash-method-of-accounting taxpayer and the completion of a long-term contract by a taxpayer using the completed contract method.[35] Built-in losses also include deductions claimed during the recognition period that are attributable to periods before the first S corporation tax year. The net recognized built-in gain for a tax year cannot exceed the excess of (1) the net unrealized built-in gain (i.e., excess of the FMV of the S corporation's assets at the beginning of its first tax year for which the S corporation election is in effect over their total adjusted basis on such date) over (2) the total net recognized built-in gain for prior taxable years beginning in the recognition period.[36]

Example 11-13 ■ Assume the same facts as in Example 11-12, except that Tatum Corporation makes its S corporation election on August 1, 1990, effective for 1991 and later tax years; its net unrealized built-in gain at the beginning of 1991 is $510,000; its recognized built-in gains in 1991 are $60,000; and its 1991 taxable income is $180,000. By making the election after December 31, 1986, the built-in gains tax applies to Tatum Corporation. Tatum's built-in gains tax is $20,400 ($60,000 × 0.34) for 1991. This tax reduces the pass-through of Tatum's ordinary income or separately stated income items that triggers the imposition of the tax. ■

> **Typical Misconception**
> "Old" Sec. 1374 is applicable only to corporations that made S corporation elections prior to 1/1/87, or 1/1/89 under the special two-year extension for small corporations.

Capital Gains Tax. The **capital gains (or "old" Sec. 1374) tax** was enacted to prevent C corporations that expect to realize a long-term capital gain from avoiding double taxation of the gain by (1) making an S corporation election, (2) recognizing the gain, (3) distributing the gain to its shareholders, and then (4) revoking the election so it could be taxed as a C corporation in future periods. The capital gains tax is imposed on a corporation that made its S corporation election prior to January 1, 1987, and that for the tax year in question has (1) taxable income in excess of $25,000 and (2) a net capital gain that is in excess of (a) $25,000 and (b) 50% of its taxable income. S corporations that meet both requirements are exempt from the capital gains tax if the S corporation election was in effect for the shorter of its 3 immediately preceding tax years or its entire existence.

In 1991 the capital gains tax will apply to only a few former C corporations, since the three-year time period during which such tax is levied will have passed for all but the small number of corporations qualifying for the two year-extension of the January 1, 1987 cutoff (see footnote 31) and those S corporations owning substituted basis property. Special rules apply to an S corporation that makes its S corporation election before the January 1, 1987 or 1989 cutoff date and acquires property having a substituted basis within 3 years of the beginning of the initial S corporation tax year (Sec. 1374(c)(1)) or that is a "successor" corporation (Sec. 1374(c)(2)).

> **Key Point**
> The amount of tax paid on capital gains by an S corporation reduces the amount of capital gains that pass through to the shareholders.

The capital gains tax is the lesser of (1) the alternative tax rate (34% in 1991) times the amount of the net capital gain in excess of $25,000 or (2) the regular corporate tax rate(s) times the corporation's taxable income as would be determined if it were not an S corporation.[37] The amount of the capital gains tax reduces the capital gains passed through to the shareholders. For purposes of the capital gains tax, taxable income is defined by Sec. 1374(d) as being the amount determined under Sec. 63 for a

---

[35] Sec. 1374(d)(5).

[36] Secs. 1374(c)(2) and (d)(1). The recognition period can be extended to beyond 10 years if property having a carryover basis is acquired in a tax-free transaction (e.g., a tax-free reorganization) from a C corporation. For such properties, the 10-year recognition period commences on the date the S Corporation acquired the properties.

[37] Sec. 1374(b).

C corporation without any reduction for (1) the NOL deduction and (2) the dividends-received deductions.

LIFO RECAPTURE TAX

If a C corporation using the LIFO inventory method elects S corporation treatment, Sec. 1363(d)(3) requires the corporation to include its LIFO recapture amount in gross income for its last C corporation tax year. The LIFO recapture amount is the excess of the inventory's basis for tax purposes under the FIFO method over its basis under the LIFO method at the close of the final C corporation tax year. Any tax increase incurred in the final C corporation tax year is payable in four installments; that is, on or before the due date for the final C corporation tax return and on or before the due date for the first three S corporation tax returns. The S corporation's inventory basis is increased by the LIFO recapture amount that is included in gross income.

RECAPTURE OF PREVIOUSLY CLAIMED INVESTMENT TAX CREDITS

Electing S corporation status does not trigger an investment tax credit recapture. The election is considered a mere change in the form of conducting the trade or business. S corporations are liable for the recapture of investment tax credits (e.g., the rehabilitation credit, energy credit, and reforestation credit) claimed while the S election was not in effect. Investment tax credits claimed while an S corporation, and the effects of any recapture, are accounted for at the shareholder level. Termination of the S corporation election does not trigger any credit recapture.

TAXATION OF THE SHAREHOLDER

OBJECTIVE 6
Calculate a shareholder's allocable share of ordinary income or loss and separately stated items

Income Allocation Procedures

An S corporation's shareholders must report their pro rata share of the ordinary income or loss and separately stated items for the S corporation's tax year that ends with or within the shareholder's tax year.[38] Each shareholder's pro rata share of the aforementioned items is determined by

---

[38] Sec. 1366(a). If the shareholder dies during the S corporation's tax year, the income earned during the portion of the tax year preceding death is reported on the shareholder's tax return. The income for the period of time that the estate holds the S corporation stock is reported on its fiduciary tax return.

Typical Misconception
An S corporation's income/loss is allocated basically the same as a partnership's except that a partnership may have the added flexibility of making certain special allocations under Sec. 704.

1. Allocating an equal portion of the item to each day in the tax year (by dividing the amount of the item by the number of days in the S corporation's tax year)
2. Allocating an equal portion of the daily amount for the item to each share of stock that is outstanding on each day (by dividing the daily amount for the item by the number of shares of stock outstanding on a particular day)
3. Totaling the daily allocations for each outstanding share of stock
4. Totaling the amounts allocated for each share of stock held by the shareholder

Special allocations (such as those that are found in Sec. 704 under the partnership tax rules) of the ordinary income or loss and separately stated items are not permitted.

If there is a sale of the S corporation stock during the year, the transferor reports the earnings allocated to the transferred shares through the day preceding the transfer date. The transferee's share of the earnings is reported from the transfer date through the end of the tax year.

Example 11-14 ■ Fox Corporation, an electing S corporation, is owned equally by Arnie and Bonnie during all of 1991. During 1991, Fox reports ordinary income of $146,000 and a long-term capital gain of $36,500. Arnie and Bonnie each report $73,000 (0.50 × $146,000) of ordinary income and $18,250 (0.50 × $36,500) of long-term capital gain. ■

Example 11-15 ■ Assume the same facts as in Example 11-14, except that Bonnie sells one-half of her shares to Clay on April 1, 1991 (the ninety-first day of Fox's tax year). Arnie reports the same ordinary income and long-term capital gain from his investment. Bonnie and Clay report ordinary income and long-term capital gain as follows:

Ordinary Income

Bonnie: $\left(\$146{,}000 \times \dfrac{1}{2} \times \dfrac{90}{365} \right) + \left(\$146{,}000 \times \dfrac{1}{4} \times \dfrac{275}{365} \right) = \$45{,}500$

Clay: $\$146{,}000 \times \dfrac{1}{4} \times \dfrac{275}{365} = \$27{,}500$

Total $\$73{,}000$

Long-Term Capital Gain

Bonnie: $\left(\$36{,}500 \times \dfrac{1}{2} \times \dfrac{90}{365} \right) + \left(\$36{,}500 \times \dfrac{1}{4} \times \dfrac{275}{365} \right) = \$11{,}375$

Clay: $\$36{,}500 \times \dfrac{1}{4} \times \dfrac{275}{365} = 6{,}875$

Total $\$18{,}250$ ■

A special election is available for allocating the ordinary income or loss and separately stated items when the shareholder's interest in the S corporation is terminated during the tax year. If the election is made, the income is allocated according to the accounting methods employed by the S corporation (instead of on a daily basis). The election divides the S corporation's tax year into two parts ending on

Key Point

Shareholders of an S corporation need to be aware that when they sell all their stock, they have the option of having income/loss determined by an actual closing of the books rather than an allocation on a daily basis.

1. The day the shareholder's interest in the corporation is terminated
2. The last day of the S corporation's tax year

This election can only be made if all persons who are shareholders during the tax year agree to the election.[39] This election is explored in greater detail in the Tax Planning Considerations section of this chapter.

Family S Corporations

Family S corporations have been an important tax planning device. This type of tax planning quite often involves a high-tax-bracket taxpayer gifting stock to a minor child who generally has little other income. This results in income splitting among family members.

The IRS has the power to ignore such transfers when they appear to be primarily tax motiviated. Regulation Sec. 1.1373-1(a)(2) indicates that "a donee or purchaser of stock in the corporation is not considered a shareholder unless such stock is acquired in a bona fide transaction and the donee or purchaser is the real owner of the stock." The IRS has enjoyed success in litigating cases dealing with intrafamily transfers of S corporation stock when the transferor (usually a parent) retains the economic benefits and control over the stock transferred to the transferee (usually a child).[40] The IRS has enjoyed less success when one family member purchases the stock from another family member at its market value.

The IRS also has the statutory authority under Sec. 1366(e) to adjust the income, loss, deduction, or credit items allocated to a family member to reflect the value of services rendered or capital provided to the corporation. Section 1366(e) defines family as including spouse, ancestors, lineal descendants, and trusts created for such individuals. This provision (1) permits the reallocation of income to provide for full compensation of a shareholder or nonshareholder for services and capital provided to the corporation and (2) reduces the residual income that is reported by the S corporation and which is allocated to the shareholders according to their stock ownership. Such a reallocation prevents both the shifting of income from the family member providing the services or capital to other family members, but also the avoidance of employment taxes. Alternatively, the IRS can determine that too much compensation is paid to a shareholder and reduce that shareholder's salary and increase the residual income that is allocated based on stock ownership.

Example 11-16 ■ Harvey Corporation, an electing S corporation, reports ordinary income of $200,000 after a deduction of $20,000 is claimed for Harvey's salary. The Harvey stock is owned equally by Harvey and his three children. None of Harvey's three children are employed by Harvey Corporation. It is subsequently determined that reasonable compensation for Harvey is $80,000. This adjustment increases Harvey's salary income and Harvey Corporation's compensation deduction by $60,000 ($80,000 − $20,000) and reduces Harvey Corporation's ordinary income to $140,000 ($200,000 − $60,000). Each shareholder's ratable share of ordinary income is reduced from $50,000 ($200,000 ÷ 4) to $35,000 ($140,000 ÷ 4).

---

[39] Sec. 1377(a)(2).
[40] See, for example, *Gino A. Speca v. CIR*, 47 AFTR 2d 81-468, 80-2 USTC ¶ 9692 (7th Cir., 1980) and *Henry D. Duarte*, 44 T.C. 193 (1965), where the IRS's position prevailed. See, also *Gavin S. Millar*, 1975 PH T.C. Memo ¶ 75,113, 34 TCM 554 (1975), and *Donald O. Kirkpatrick*, 1977 PH T.C. Memo ¶ 77,281, 36 TCM 1122 (1977), where the taxpayers prevailed.

Taxation of the Shareholder • 11-21

Key Point
The advantages of family S corporations have been somewhat curtailed. For example, income from stock of an S corporation gifted to a child under age 14 is subject to the "kiddie tax."

Alternatively, if the IRS can prove that the stock transfer to the three children is not a bona fide transfer, all $220,000 of Harvey Corporation's income is taxed to Harvey—$80,000 as salary and $140,000 as an allocation of ordinary income. ■

The use of family S corporations as a tax planning device has been curtailed by the 1986 Tax Act. As mentioned earlier, gifts of S corporation stock have been used to enable part of the S corporation's income to be reported in the tax returns of minor children. Children under age 14 now must pay tax on their unearned income in excess of $1,100 at the top marginal tax rate of their parents, reducing the attractiveness of many gifts of S corporation stock from a tax planning perspective.[41]

OBJECTIVE 7
Determine the limitations on a shareholder's deduction of S corporation losses

Loss and Deduction Pass-through to Shareholders

The S corporation's ordinary loss and separately stated loss and deduction items pass through to the shareholders at the end of the corporation's tax year. These items are reported in the shareholder's tax year in which the S corporation's tax year ends.

Allocation of the Loss. Using the rules outlined above, allocation of the loss occurs on a daily basis. Thus, shareholders receive an allocation of the ordinary loss and separately stated items even if the stock is owned for only a portion of the year. If the ordinary loss and other separately stated loss and deduction pass-throughs exceed the shareholder's income, the excess may create a NOL for the shareholder and result in a carry back or carry over to the shareholder's other tax years.

Example 11-17 ■ Kauai Corporation, an electing S corporation, reports a $70,000 ordinary loss during 1991. At the beginning of 1991, Elvis and Frank own equally all of Kauai's stock. On July 1, 1991 (the 182nd day of Kauai's tax year), Frank gives one-fourth of his stock to his son George. Elvis is allocated $35,000 of ordinary loss. Frank and George are allocated ordinary losses as follows:

Frank: $\left(\$70{,}000 \times \dfrac{1}{2} \times \dfrac{181}{365} \right) + \left(\$70{,}000 \times \dfrac{3}{8} \times \dfrac{184}{365} \right) = \$30{,}589$

George: $\$70{,}000 \times \dfrac{1}{8} \times \dfrac{184}{365}$ = $\underline{\$ \ 4{,}411}$

Total $\underline{\underline{\$35{,}000}}$

All three shareholders can deduct these losses on their individual tax returns subject to the loss limitations described below. ■

Shareholder Loss Limitations. Each shareholder's deduction for his share of the ordinary loss and the separately stated loss and deduction items is limited to the sum of the adjusted basis for his S corporation stock plus the adjusted basis of any indebtedness owed directly by the S corporation to the shareholder. Unlike the

---
[41] Sec. 1(g)(l).

Typical Misconception

The amount of losses that can be deducted by a shareholder of an S corporation, unlike a partnership, is not increased by the S corporation's general liabilities unless the creditor is that same shareholder.

partnership taxation rules, a shareholder cannot increase his basis in the stock for purposes of determining the loss deduction limitation by a ratable share of the general S corporation liabilities. However, a positive basis adjustment is made for any ordinary income or separately stated income or gain items reported in the "loss" year before the shareholder's loss limitation is determined.[42]

Many S corporations are basically nothing more than incorporated forms of sole proprietorships or partnerships. As a result, banks and other lending institutions often require one or more of the shareholders to personally guarantee any loans made to the S corporation. The IRS and the courts have, in general, held that this form of indirect borrowing by the S corporation does not create a corporate indebtedness to the shareholder. As a result, the shareholder's loss limitation is not increased as a result of his acting as a guarantor until the shareholder makes a payment of part or all of the corporation's liability or the shareholder executes a note at the bank in full satisfaction of the corporation's liability. Such an action on the part of the shareholder converts the guarantee into an indebtedness of the corporation to the shareholder which increases the shareholder's loss limitation.[43]

The adjusted basis of the S corporation stock and debt is generally determined as of the last day of the S corporation's tax year. If the S corporation stock is disposed of before that date, the adjusted basis of the stock and debt is instead determined on the day preceding the disposition date.

Example 11-18 ■ Tillis Corporation, an electing S corporation, is owned equally by Pat and Bill. During 1991 Tillis reports an ordinary loss of $100,000. Tillis's liabilities at the end of 1991 include $100,000 of accounts payable, $150,000 of mortgage payable, and a $20,000 note owed to Bill. Pat and Bill each had a $40,000 adjusted basis for their Tillis stock on January 1, 1991. The ordinary loss is allocated equally to Pat and Bill. Pat's $50,000 loss allocation is only partially deductible in 1991 (i.e., up to $40,000) since his $40,000 basis for the Tillis stock is exceeded. Bill's $50,000 loss allocation is fully deductible in 1991 since his loss limitation is $60,000 ($40,000 + $20,000). ■

The loss and deduction pass-through is allocated to each share of stock. If the pass-through for an individual share of stock exceeds that share's basis, the "excess" amount is allocated to all of the shareholder's remaining shares. Once the losses and deductions have reduced the basis of all shares of stock to zero, they are applied against the basis of any amount owed by the S corporation to the shareholder.

Any loss or deduction pass-through that is not currently deductible is carried over to succeeding tax years until the shareholder has a basis in his stock or in an amount owed to him by the S corporation. The shareholder is permitted an unlimited carryover for the loss or deduction item.[44] The additional adjusted basis amount can originate from a number of sources, including (1) subsequent profits earned by the S

---

[42] Sec. 1366(d)(1). Amounts owed by an S corporation to a conduit entity that has the shareholder as an owner or beneficiary will not increase the shareholder's loss limitation. See, for example, *E. J. Frankel*, 61 T.C. 343 (1973), *aff'd.* in unpublished opinion by Third Circuit Court of Appeals in 1974 (partnership); *Ruth M. Prashker*, 59 T.C. 172 (1972) [estate]; and *James Y. Robertson*, 32 AFTR 2d 73-5556, 73-2 USTC ¶ 9645 (D.C. Nev., 1973) [trust].

[43] Rev. Rul. 70-50, 1970-1 C.B. 178; 71-288, 1971-2 C.B. 319; and 75-144, 1975-1 C.B. 277. See also *Estate of Daniel Leavitt v. CIR*, 63 AFTR 2d 89-1437 (4th Cir., 1989) *aff'g.* 90 T.C. 206 (1988) among a series of decisions which uphold the IRS's position. However, see *Edward M. Selfe v. U.S.*, 57 AFTR 2d 86-464, 86-1 USTC ¶ 9115 (11th Cir., 1986) for a transaction where a guarantee was held to increase the shareholder's loss limitation because the transaction was structured as a borrowing of monies followed by a capital contribution to the corporation.

[44] Sec. 1366(d)(2). If more than one type of loss or deduction item is passed through to the shareholder, the carryover amount is allocated to each of the passed-through items based on their relative amounts.

corporation, (2) additional capital contributions or loans made by the shareholder to the corporation, or (3) purchases of additional stock from other shareholders.

Example 11-19 ▪ Assume the same facts as in Example 11-18, except that Tillis Corporation reports ordinary income of $20,000 in 1992. Pat and Bill are each allocated $10,000 of ordinary income in 1992. This income provides Pat with the necessary $10,000 basis for his Tillis stock to deduct the $10,000 loss carryover from 1991. ▪

Special Shareholder Loss and Deduction Limitations. The S corporation's shareholders are subject to four special loss and deduction limitations. These limitations may prevent the S corporation's shareholder from using losses or deductions that are passed through by the S corporation, even though the general loss limitation described above does not otherwise apply. Application of the special loss limitations to S corporations and their shareholders occurs as follows:

1. *At-Risk Rules:* The Sec. 465 at-risk rules are applied at the shareholder level. The loss from a particular S corporation activity is deductible only to the extent of the aggregate amount for which the taxpayer is at risk in the activity at the close of the S corporation's tax year.
2. *Passive Activity Loss and Credit Limitation Rules:* Losses and credits from a passive activity can be applied against income from that passive activity or other passive activities earned in the same or a subsequent tax year. An S corporation shareholder must personally meet the Sec. 469(h)(1) material participation standard for an activity in order to avoid the passive activity limitation. Material participation by the S corporation in an activity does not permit a passive investor to deduct the portion of the S corporation's loss against his salary and other "active" income.
3. *Hobby Loss Rules:* Losses incurred by an S corporation are subject to the Sec. 183 hobby loss rules. Deductions incurred by the S corporation are limited to the activity's gross income unless the taxpayer can establish that the activity is engaged in a profit-making activity.
4. *Investment Interest Limitation Rules:* Investment interest deductions are limited to the taxpayer's net investment income. Investment income earned by, and investment interest expense incurred by, an S corporation are passed through to its shareholders and enter into the calculation of their individual investment interest limitations.

Extended discussions of each of the four limitations are contained in *Prentice Hall's Federal Taxation: Individuals* text.

Post-termination Loss Carryovers. Loss and deduction carryovers that are incurred in S corporation tax years can be carried over even though the S corporation election has been terminated. These carryovers can only be deducted in the **post-termination transition period.**[45] The length of the post-termination transition period depends upon the event causing the termination of the S corporation election. The general rule is that the period commences on the day after the last day of the corporation's final S corporation tax year and ends on the later of (1) 1 year after the last day or (2) the due date for the final S corporation tax return (including any extensions). If the S corporation election is terminated for a prior tax year as a result of a determination, the period runs for 120 days beginning on the determination date. Section 1377(b)(2) defines a determination as a court decision that becomes final, a

---

[45] Sec. 1366(d)(3).

closing agreement, or an agreement between the corporation and the IRS that the corporation failed to qualify as an S corporation.

The loss and deduction carryovers can be deducted only up to the adjusted basis of the shareholder's stock at the end of the post-termination transition period.[46] Losses that cannot be deducted because of the basis limitation are lost forever. Losses that are deducted reduce the basis of the shareholder's stock.

Topic Review 11-3 presents a summary of the rules governing deductibility of S corporation losses and deductions that are passed through to the shareholders.

TOPIC REVIEW 11-3

Deductibility of S Corporation Losses and Deductions That Are Passed Through to the Shareholders

Allocation Process

1. Losses and deductions are allocated based on the number of shares of stock owned by each shareholder on each day to the tax year. Special allocations of losses and deductions are not permitted.
2. Termination of the S corporation election or termination of the shareholder's interest in the S corporation during the tax yeqr requires the tax year to be divided into two parts. An election can be made to allocate the loss or deduction according to the accounting methods used by the corporation.

General Loss Limitation

1. The loss or deduction pass-through is done on a per-share basis and is limited to the shareholder's basis in the S corporation stock. Once the basis for all the S corporation stock is reduced to zero, the losses reduce the basis of any S corporation indebtedness to the shareholder.
2. Losses and deductions that are not able to be deducted receive an unlimited carryover to a tax year in which the shareholder again has basis in his stock or S corporation debt.

Special S Corporation Loss Limitations

1. *At-risk limitation.* Losses from an activity conducted by an S corporation are deductible by a shareholder only up to the amount that the shareholder is at risk in the activity at the close of the tax year.
2. *Passive activity loss and credit limitation.* Losses and credits from a passive activity conducted by an S corporation are deductible only against passive income earned or taxes owed with respect to passive activities. Whether the material participation and active participation exceptions can apply is based on the shareholder's participation in the activity.
3. *Hobby loss rules.* Losses incurred by an S corporation are subject to the hobby loss rules if the activity conducted by the S corporation is not a profit-making activity. As such, losses are deductible to the extent of gross income.
4. *Investment interest limitation rules.* Investment interest income and deductions pass-through from the S corporation to the shareholder. These amounts enter into determining the deductible investment interest expense at the shareholder level.
5. *Separately stated items.* Various separately stated loss and deduction items are subject to limits at the shareholder level (e.g., charitable contributions, long-term capital losses) even though they are not subject to corporate-level limits. Some separately stated items are subject to corporate level limits and not shareholder limits (e.g., the 20% nondeductible portion of travel and entertainment expenses).

---

[46] Sec. 1366(d)(3)(B).

Example 11-20 ■ Pearson Corporation has been an electing S corporation for several years. On July 1, 1991, its S corporation election is terminated when part of its stock is acquired by an ineligible shareholder. For the period ended June 30, 1991, Helen is allocated $60,000 of Pearson's ordinary loss. Only $45,000 of this loss can be deducted by Helen because the basis of her Pearson stock is reduced to zero by the loss. The $15,000 unused loss is carried over to the post-termination transition period, which ends on June 30, 1992 (assuming that Pearson does not extend the March 15, 1992, due date for the S short year tax return). Helen must have an adjusted basis for the Pearson stock of at least $15,000 at the close of business on June 30, 1992, in order to use the loss. Helen should consider making additional capital contributions of at least $15,000 between July 1, 1991, and June 30, 1992, to utilize the loss that is otherwise lost forever. ■

BASIS ADJUSTMENTS

OBJECTIVE 8
Calculate a shareholder's basis in his S corporation's stock and debt

Adjustments must be made annually to the basis of the shareholder's S corporation stock. If the S corporation is indebted to the shareholder, the basis of the debt may need to be adjusted downward for loss or deduction pass-throughs and upward to reflect restoration of the basis when subsequent profits are earned. Each of these adjustments is described below.

Basis Adjustments to S Corporation Stock

Self-Study Question

Why is the determination of stock basis in an S corporation important?

Answer

Some of the more important reasons: (a) To determine gain/loss on the sale of the stock, (b) to determine the amount of losses that can be deducted, and (c) to determine the amount of distributions that are tax-free.

The basis of the shareholder's stock is determined as follows:[47]

Initial investment (or basis at beginning of tax year)
Plus: Additional capital contributions made during the year
         Allocable share of ordinary income
         Allocable share of separately stated income and gain items
         Excess of depletion claimed by the corporation over its basis
            in the depletable property
         Recapture of investment credits
Minus: Allocable share of ordinary loss
         Allocable share of separately stated loss and deduction items
         Allocable share of any expense that is not deductible in
            determining ordinary income (loss) and that cannot be
            charged to the capital account
         Allowance for investment tax credit
         Distributions excluded from the shareholder's gross income

Adjusted basis for stock (but not less than zero)

The initial basis for the S corporation stock depends on the method by which it is acquired. Stock purchased from the corporation or another shareholder will take a cost basis. Stock received as part of a Sec. 351 corporate formation transaction

---

[47] Sec. 1367(a). Special adjustment rules apply to S corporations claiming a deduction for percentage depletion with respect to oil and gas wells under Sec. 613A because the depletion deduction is claimed at the shareholder level (and not the corporate level).

generally takes a carryover basis from the assets transferred. Stock acquired by gift will take the donee's basis (adjusted for gift taxes paid) or FMV (if lower). Stock acquired at death will take the decedent's basis. No basis adjustment occurs when the initial S corporation election is made, nor does the basis include any portion of the entity's liabilities as is the case with a partnership.

The basis adjustments made to the S corporation stock parallel those made to a partnership interest. The ordinary income and separately stated income and gain items increase the shareholder's basis whether they are taxable, tax-exempt, or receive preferential tax treatment. If the S corporation is audited and a series of adjustments are made to its operating results, both the original allocations and any adjustments that are required must be reflected in the basis of the stock. The investment tax credit adjustment equals the basis reduction made when the energy credit and rehabilitation credit are claimed, or when the credits are recaptured.

Example 11-21 ■ Marlo Corporation, an electing S corporation, is owned by Cathy. At the beginning of 1991, Cathy's adjusted basis for the Marlo stock is $105,000. During 1991, Marlo reports the following operating results:

Ordinary income	$70,000
Municipal bond interest income	15,000
Dividends from domestic corporations	6,000
Long-term capital gain	8,000
Short-term capital loss	17,000

Cathy's adjusted basis for the Marlo stock at the end of 1991 is $187,000 ($105,000 + $70,000 + $15,000 + $6,000 + $8,000 − $17,000). ■

The basis adjustment is made at the end of the S corporation's tax year when the results for the entire period are known. Because the profits and losses are allocated ratably on a daily basis to all shares held on each day of the tax year by the shareholder, a gain or loss realized on the sale of the stock of an S corporation during the tax year is not determinable until the ordinary income or loss and separately stated items allocable to the shares sold are known. Similarly, when the S corporation stock becomes worthless during a tax year, the shareholder must make the necessary positive and negative basis adjustments before the amount of the worthless security loss can be determined.

Example 11-22 ■ Diaz Corporation, an electing S corporation, is owned equally by Mike, Carlos, and Juan. Mike's 100 shares of Diaz stock have a $25,000 adjusted basis at the beginning of 1991. During 1991, Diaz Corporation reports ordinary income of $36,500 and municipal bond interest income of $14,600. After 30 days of 1991, Mike sells all of the Diaz stock for $30,000. Assuming the daily method is used to allocate the income items, Mike's basis for the Diaz stock is determined as follows:

$$\$26{,}400 = \$25{,}000 + \left(\$36{,}500 \times \frac{30}{365} \times \frac{1}{3}\right) + \left(\$14{,}600 \times \frac{30}{365} \times \frac{1}{3}\right)$$

Mike must report a $3,600 ($30,000 − $26,400) gain on the sale. ■

Basis Adjustments to Shareholder Debt

After the shareholder's basis in the S corporation stock is reduced to zero, the basis of any S corporation indebtedness to the shareholder still outstanding at the end of the S corporation's tax year is reduced by the remainder of the available loss and deduction

S Corporation Distributions • 11-27

Key Point
Losses first reduce the basis in the stock and then any amount of debt owed to the shareholder by the S corporation. Subsequent increases in basis are added first to the debt and then to the stock.

items (but not below zero).[48] If a shareholder has more than one loan outstanding at year-end, the basis reduction is applied to all of the indebtednesses based upon the relative adjusted basis for each loan. Any ordinary income or separately stated gain or income items allocated to the shareholder in subsequent tax years first restores the basis of any S corporation indebtedness to the shareholder that is outstanding at the end of its tax year. Once all previous decreases to the basis of an S corporation's debt are restored, any additional positive basis adjustments increase the basis of the shareholder's S corporation stock.[49]

Repayment of a shareholder indebtedness results in gain being recognized by the shareholder if the payment amount exceeds the debt's adjusted basis. If the indebtedness is secured by a note, the difference is a gain that results from the exchange of the note. Ordinarily, such gain is characterized as a capital gain because it arises from the exchange of a capital asset. Generally, if the indebtedness is not secured by a note or other evidence of the indebtedness, the repayment is ordinary income.[50]

Example 11-23 ■

Self-Study Question
What happens when a debt owed to the shareholder is paid off after the basis of the debt has been reduced by previous losses?

Answer
The shareholder will recognize income to the extent of the excess of the debt payment over his basis in the debt.

At the beginning of 1989, Betty owns one-half of the stock of Trailer Corporation, an electing S corporation. Betty's basis for the Trailer stock is $40,000. Trailer Corporation owes Betty $20,000 on January 1, 1989. During 1989 and 1990, Trailer Corporation reports an ordinary loss of $100,000 and ordinary income of $10,000, respectively. Betty's $50,000 loss pass-through from 1989 first reduces the basis of her Trailer stock from $40,000 to 0. Next, the $10,000 remainder of the loss pass-through reduces the basis of Trailer's note from $20,000 to $10,000. Betty's $5,000 allocation of 1990's ordinary income increases the basis for the Trailer note from $10,000 to $15,000. If the note is repaid before the end of 1991, Betty reports a $5,000 ($20,000 − $15,000) long-term capital gain resulting from the repayment plus any ordinary income or separately stated items resulting from Trailer's 1991 operations. If the debt was instead unsecured (i.e., an advance from the shareholder that is not secured by a note), the gain would instead be ordinary income. ■

S CORPORATION DISTRIBUTIONS

OBJECTIVE 9
Determine the taxability of an S corporation's distributions to its shareholders

Two sets of rules apply to S corporation distributions. One applies to S corporations having accumulated E&P. Accumulated E&P may exist if an S corporation was subject to tax as a C corporation in a pre-S corporation tax year or if the S corporation has accumulated E&P under the Subchapter S rules in existence during pre-1983 years. Another set of distribution rules applies to S corporations that do not have E&P (e.g., a corporation that is formed after 1982 and elects to be taxed as an S corporation in its initial tax year). These rules are explained below.

Key Point
Two separate sets of rules exist for distributions depending on whether or not the S corporation has accumulated E&P.

Corporations Having No Earnings and Profits

Corporations no longer must determine their E&P for any year in which they are taxed as an S corporation. For S corporations with no accumulated E&P, a two-tier rule applies. Distributions are initially tax-free and reduce the shareholder's adjusted basis in the stock (but not below zero). If the distribution exceeds the basis of the

---
[48] No basis adjustments are made to debt repaid before the end of the tax year.
[49] Sec. 1367(b)(2)(B).
[50] Rev. Ruls. 64-162, 1964-1 (Part I) C.B. 304 and 68-537, 1968-2 C.B. 372.

shareholder's stock, the "excess" is treated as a gain from the sale or exchange of the stock.[51]

All income, gain, loss, or deduction pass-throughs for the year must be reflected in the shareholder's basis before the taxability of the distribution can be determined. Thus, the sequencing of the income recognition and distribution steps permits the S corporation to make tax-free distributions throughout the tax year in anticipation of earning a specific profit amount by year-end.

Example 11-24

Self-Study Question

Can distributions in excess of stock basis be tax-free to the extent of debts owed to the shareholder?

Answer

No. While the amount of deductible losses can be increased by the amount of shareholder debts, tax-free distributions are strictly limited to stock basis.

Liberty Corporation, an electing S corporation, is owned entirely by Sandy. At the beginning of 1991, Sandy's adjusted basis in the Liberty stock is $20,000. During 1991, Liberty reports ordinary income of $30,000 and a long-term capital loss of $5,000. Liberty makes a $35,000 cash distribution to Sandy on June 15. Sandy's basis for the Liberty stock must be adjusted for the ordinary income and capital loss before determining the taxability of the distribution. Because the $45,000 ($20,000 + $30,000 − $5,000) adjusted basis for the Liberty stock exceeds the $35,000 distribution amount, the entire distribution is excluded from Sandy's gross income. The distribution reduces the Liberty stock's basis to $10,000 ($45,000 − $35,000). If Liberty instead reports only $5,000 of ordinary income and no capital loss, $10,000 of the distribution is taxable. The ordinary income increases the Liberty stock's basis to $25,000 ($20,000 + $5,000). Because the distribution exceeds the Liberty stock's adjusted basis by $10,000 ($35,000 − $25,000), the excess distribution is taxable to Sandy as a capital gain. The basis of the Liberty stock is zero at year-end. ∎

If an S corporation makes a nonliquidating distribution to its shareholders, the S corporation must recognize gain when appreciated property is distributed.[52] No loss is recognized when property that has declined in value is distributed. The gain recognized on the distribution may be taxed at the corporate level as part of the S corporation's capital gains, built-in gains, or the excess net passive income tax levy. The gain also becomes part of the S corporation's ordinary income or loss, or is passed through as a separately stated item depending upon the type of property distributed and the character of the gain recognized. After this adjustment is made, the property can be distributed tax-free provided the sum of the money plus the FMV of the nonmoney property distributed does not exceed the shareholder's basis for his stock. The basis for the S corporation stock is reduced by the amount of the distribution.

Example 11-25

Additional Comment

The distribution of the appreciated stock in Example 11-25 produced income only to Echo. A similar distribution by a C corporation would result in a double tax by producing income at both the corporate and shareholder levels.

Echo Corporation is owned entirely by Tad and has always been an S corporation. Tad's adjusted basis in the Echo stock at the beginning of 1991 is $50,000. Echo reports $30,000 of ordinary income for 1991 (exclusive of the effects of a property distribution made to Tad). On December 1, 1991, Echo distributes some Cable Corporation stock to Tad. The stock, which cost $40,000 and is worth $100,000, was held as an investment for 3 years. Echo must report $60,000 ($100,000 − $40,000) of capital gain from distributing the stock. Tad must report $30,000 of ordinary income and $60,000 of long-term capital gain from Echo's 1991 activities. Tad's adjusted basis for the Echo stock is increased to $140,000 ($50,000 + $30,000 + $60,000). The distribution is tax-free since the $140,000 basis for the Echo stock exceeds the $100,000 distribution amount. The basis of the Echo stock is $40,000 ($140,000 − $100,000) at year-end. ∎

[51] Sec. 1368(b).
[52] Sec. 311(b).

Corporations Having Accumulated Earnings and Profits

Prior Rules. Under the pre-1983 rules, an S corporation accumulated up to three E&P balances each year. Undistributed taxable income (UTI) that was constructively taxed to the S corporation's shareholders on the last day of its tax year became a separate earnings classification that could be distributed tax-free only during the first 2½ months of the next tax year. After this 2½-month period had passed, the UTI became part of the S corporation's previously taxed income (PTI) balance. The PTI amount could be distributed tax-free only after the S corporation distributed its current year's earnings. E&P in excess of PTI became part of the corporation's accumulated E&P account.

> **Key Point**
> The AAA represents the cumulative income/loss recognized in post-1982 S corporation years. To the extent the AAA is positive and sufficient basis exists in the stock, distributions from an S corporation are tax-free.

Current Rules. Under current rules, some S corporations still have PTI and accumulated E&P balances from which part or all of a distribution may be treated as having been made. The current rules require S corporations that have accumulated E&P balances to maintain an **Accumulated Adjustments Account** (AAA) and an Other Adjustments account from which most of their distributions are made. The existence of the PTI, accumulated E&P, Other Adjustments, and AAA earnings balances makes the tax treatment of cash and property distributions somewhat more complicated than the rules explained in the preceding section.

Money Distributions. For corporations having an accumulated E&P balance, cash distributions come from the five tiers of earnings illustrated in Table 11-1. Distributions are made from the first tier until it is exhausted. The distributions are then made from the second tier until that tier is used up, and so on. Amounts distributed after the five tiers are exhausted are taxed as a gain recognized on the sale of the S corporation stock. Each of these 5 tiers is usually maintained as a working paper account and not as a general ledger account.

The AAA is the cumulative total of the ordinary income or loss and separately stated items accumulated for the S period. The S period is the most recent continuous

> **Key Point**
> Distributions that come out of the AAA, previously taxed income, and other adjustments also reduce the basis of the S corporation stock.

TABLE 11-1 Source of Distributions Made by S Corporations Having Accumulated Earnings and Profits

		Types of Distributions Coming from Tier		
Tier	Classification	Money Distributions?	Property (Nonmoney) Distributions?	Taxable or Tax-Free Distributions?
1	Accumulated Adjustments Account	Yes	Yes	Tax-free[a]
2	Previously Taxed Income	Yes	No	Tax-free[a]
3	Accumulated E&P[b]	Yes	Yes	Taxable
4	Other Adjustments	Yes	Yes	Tax-free[a]
5	Basis of S corporation stock	Yes	Yes	Tax-free[a]

[a] This type of distribution is taxable, as a capital gain in most cases, if the amount of money plus the FMV of the nonmoney property distributed exceeds the adjusted basis of the S corporation stock.

[b] This account includes primarily earnings accruing in C corporation tax years and limited amounts of earnings from pre-1983 S corporation tax years. In general no additions are made to this account while an S corporation election is in effect. This account is adjusted downward for dividend distributions, stock redemptions, partial or complete liquidations, tax-free reorganizations, or investment tax credit recapture amounts for which the corporation is liable.

period during which the corporation has been an S corporation. No tax years beginning before January 1, 1983, are included in this period.[53]

The year-end AAA balance is determined as follows:[54]

	AAA balance at the beginning of the year
Plus:	Ordinary income
	Separately-stated income or gain items (except for tax-exempt income)
	Excess of depletion claimed by the corporation over its basis in the depletable property
Minus:	Ordinary loss
	Separately stated loss or deduction items (except for expenses or losses related to the production of tax-exempt income)
	Expenses that are not deductible in determining ordinary income (loss) and that cannot be charged to the capital account
	Distributions excluded from the shareholder's gross income
	AAA balance at the end of the year

Three differences exist between the positive and negative adjustments required for the AAA and the basis calculation for the S corporation stock:

1. Tax-exempt income does not increase the AAA, but increases the basis of the S corporation stock.
2. Nondeductible expenses that reduce the basis of the S corporation stock also reduce the AAA, except for those expenses related to the production of tax-exempt income.
3. The AAA balance can be negative (e.g., when the cumulative losses exceed the cumulative profits), but the shareholder's basis in the S corporation stock cannot be less than zero.

Typical Misconception

Even though the basis of S corporation stock cannot be less than zero, the AAA can be negative. This result can occur if cumulative losses exceed cumulative profits.

An Other Adjustments account is maintained only by corporations having accumulated E&P at year-end. This account is increased for tax-exempt income earned and decreased by the expenses incurred in earning the tax-exempt income, distributions out of the Other Adjustments account, and federal taxes paid by the S corporation that are attributable to C corporation tax years.

Example 11-26 ■ Smith Corporation, an electing S corporation, reports the following results during 1991:

Ordinary income	$30,000
Long-term capital gain	15,000
Municipal bond interest income	5,000
Dividend from domestic corporation	3,000
Charitable contribution	8,000

Smith's AAA and accumulated E&P balances at the beginning of 1991 are $40,000 and $25,000, respectively. The AAA balance at the end of 1991 is $80,000

---

[53] Sec. 1368(e). If there is no accumulated E&P at year-end, an AAA is still required for reporting the S corporation's balance sheet on its tax return. The AAA includes all items of income, gain, loss, and deduction for the tax year, including tax-exempt income and nondeductible losses and expenses related to the tax-exempt income. No Other Adjustments account is maintained.

[54] Special AAA adjustment rules are found in Sec. 1368 that apply to S corporations claiming a deduction for percentage depletion with respect to oil and gas wells under Sec. 613A. These rules are beyond the scope of this text.

($40,000 + $30,000 + $15,000 + $3,000 − $8,000). The Other Adjustments balance at the end of 1991 is $5,000. The accumulated E&P balance does not change. ∎

Example 11-27 ∎ Assume the same facts as in Example 11-26, except that Smith makes $50,000 cash distributions to Silvia, its sole shareholder, on June 1 and December 1. Silvia's basis for her Smith stock on January 1, 1991, is $60,000. The basis of Silvia's stock is increased to $105,000 ($60,000 + $30,000 + $15,000 + $5,000 + $3,000 − $8,000) by Smith's 1991 operations. The $80,000 AAA balance is allocated ratably to each of the distributions. The AAA allocation occurs as follows:

$$\$40{,}000 = \$50{,}000 \times \frac{\$80{,}000}{\$50{,}000 + \$50{,}000}$$

Typical Misconception

If S corporation stock is sold, the AAA account remains with the S corporation. But if an S election terminates, other than for the post-termination transition period, the AAA is extinguished.

Accordingly, $40,000 of each distribution comes out of Smith's AAA. This portion of the distribution is tax-free since the distributions in total are less than the basis of the Smith stock. The remaining $10,000 ($50,000 − $40,000) of each distribution comes out of Smith's accumulated E&P (tier 3) and is taxable as dividend income because the corporation does not have any PTI. Smith's accumulated E&P is reduced to $5,000 ($25,000 − $20,000) at year-end. The Other Adjustments balance is not affected by the distribution since the accumulated E&P has not been exhausted. The basis of the Smith stock is $25,000 ($105,000 − $80,000) at year-end because a dividend distribution does not reduce the basis of the S corporation's stock. ∎

Example 11-28 ∎ Assume the same facts as in Example 11-27, except that on January 1, 1991, Smith also has a $15,000 PTI balance and Silvia's basis for the Smith stock is instead $75,000. The first $80,000 of the distributions still come from the AAA (tier 1). The next $15,000 of the distributions now comes from PTI (tier 2). Both of these amounts are excluded from gross income since they do not exceed the $120,000 ($75,000 + $45,000 adjustment for 1991's operations) basis of the Smith stock. The remaining $5,000 of the distribution is a dividend paid out of accumulated E&P (tier 3). The basis of the Smith stock is $25,000 ($120,000 − $80,000 − $15,000) at year-end. ∎

Key Point

If an S corporation wants to distribute its PTI balance tax-free, the distribution must be of money and not property.

Property Distributions. Property distributions (other than money) made by an S corporation having accumulated E&P require the recognition of gain according to the general rules outlined on page 11-28 for an S corporation not having accumulated E&P. Property distributions affect the earnings tiers differently than money distributions since the former can only come out of the AAA, accumulated E&P, Other Adjustments, and S corporation stock basis tiers. Distributions of PTI must be made in money. An S corporation's shareholders may find a money distribution more advantageous than a property distribution because money can be distributed tax-free if the corporation has a PTI balance, whereas a similar property distribution might be taxed as a dividend.

Special Distribution Elections. Two special elections are available to change the distribution order. Separate elections are available to the S corporation to treat none of its distributions as having come from the Accumulated Adjustments Account (AAA) or the Previously Taxed Income (PTI) account. If either election is made, distributions will normally come from accumulated E&P. These elections permit Subchapter C E&P to be distributed so as to avoid the excess net passive income tax and termination of the S corporation election. Further discussion of this election is contained in the Tax Planning Considerations section of the chapter.

Post-Termination Transition Period. Distributions of money made during the S corporation's post-termination transition period can be made tax-free. These distributions come first from the former S corporation's AAA balance and then from current and accumulated E&P. The amounts from the AAA are tax-free and reduce the shareholder's basis for the stock.[55] The AAA balance disappears when the end of the post-termination period is reached. Even though the profits earned during the S corporation election period can no longer be distributed tax-free from the AAA after the post-termination transition period ends, they can still be distributed tax-free from the shareholder's basis in his stock once the corporation's current and accumulated E&P has been distributed. Any distributions made from current or accumulated E&P and nonmoney distributions made from the AAA during the post-termination transition period are taxable.

Topic Review 11-4 presents a summary of the taxation of S corporation income and gains that are passed through to the shareholders and S corporation distributions.

OTHER RULES

In addition to the differences discussed above, S corporations are treated differently than C corporations in a number of other ways. Some of these differences are examined below. They include tax preference items and other alternative minimum tax (AMT) adjustments, expenses owed by the S corporation to a shareholder, related party sales and exchanges, and fringe benefits paid by the S corporation to a shareholder-employee.

Key Point
An S corporation is not subject to the AMT, but instead the AMT adjustments flow through to the S corporation's shareholders. Circumstances determine if this is an advantage.

Tax Preference Items and Other AMT Adjustments

The S corporation is not subject to the corporate AMT. Instead, the S corporation passes through all of its tax preference items contained in Sec. 57(a) to its shareholders. These tax preference items are then included in the shareholders' AMT calculations. Allocation of the tax preference items occurs on a daily basis, unless one of the two special elections is made to allocate the items based upon the corporation's tax accounting methods.

Code Sec. 56(a) prescribes a number of adjustments to the tax reporting of certain transactions and occurrences for AMT purposes from that which is used for income tax purposes. The amount of these special AMT adjustments is also passed through to the S corporation's shareholders and included in their individual AMT calculations.

S corporations do not have to make an adjustment for the difference between adjusted current earnings and alternative minimum taxable income that is required of a C corporation in calculating its AMT liability. For certain corporations, this difference may make an S corporation election attractive.[56]

[55] Sec. 1371(e).
[56] Sec. 56(g)(6).

TOPIC REVIEW 11-4

Taxation of S Corporation Income and Distributions
Taxation of Income to the Corporation

1. Unlike with a partnership, special corporate tax levies are imposed on an S corporation:
   a. Built-in gains tax—applicable to the net recognized built-in gain of an S corporation that has a history as a C corporation and which makes its S corporation election after December 31, 1986 (or after December 31, 1988 for qualified S corporations valued at $10 million or less).
   b. Capital gains tax—applicable to certain capital gains of corporations who make their S corporation election prior to January 1, 1987 (or January 1, 1989 if a qualified corporation) and who have been an S corporation for less than the shorter of 3 years or its entire existence.
   c. Excess net passive income tax—applicable to S corporations that have accumulated Subchapter C E&P at the close of the tax year and who earn passive investment income in excess of 25% of gross receipts during the tax year.
   d. LIFO recapture tax—a LIFO recapture tax is imposed when a C corporation that uses the LIFO inventory method in its final C corporation tax year makes an S corporation election.
   e. Recapture of investment tax credits—the corporation remains liable for investment tax credits claimed when it was a C corporation and which are recaptured when it holds S corporation status.

Allocation of Income to the Shareholders
1. Income and gains are allocated based on the number of shares of stock owned by each shareholder on each day of the tax year. Special allocations of income and gain are not permitted. 2. Termination of the S corporation election or termination of the shareholder's interest in the S corporation during the tax year requires the tax year to be divided into two parts. An election can be made to allocate the income or gain according to the accounting methods used by the corporation.
Shareholder Distributions
1. Income and gain allocated to the shareholder increases the basis of the S corporation stock. For any S corporation that does not have an E&P balance, the amount of money plus the FMV of any nonmoney property distributed is tax-free provided it does not exceed the shareholder's basis in the S corporation stock. Gain (but not loss) is recognized at the corporate level when nonmoney property is distributed. 2. If the S corporation has accumulated E&P, as many as four E&P tiers must be maintained. These are: Accumulated Adjustments Account; Previously Taxed Income (pre-1983 E&P), Accumulated Earnings and Profits, and Other Adjustments Account. Distributions come from each tier in succeeding order until the tier is exhausted (see Table 11-1). Only distributions out of accumulated E&P are taxable to the shareholder, unless the stock basis is fully exhausted and capital gain must be recognized.

Transactions Involving Shareholders and Other Related Parties

The Sec. 267(a)(2) related party transaction rules deny a payor a deduction for an expense paid to a related payee when a mismatching of the expense and income items occurs as a result of differences in accounting methods. Two related party situations directly involve S corporations. These include transactions involving two S corpora-

Key Point

An S corporation and any shareholder who owns stock directly or indirectly in the S corporation is considered a related party for purposes of deferring deductions under Sec. 267(a)(2).

tions or an S corporation and a C corporation where more than 50% of the value of each corporation's stock is directly or indirectly owned by the same persons.[57] Section 267(a)(2) would, for example, prevent an S corporation using the accrual method of accounting from currently deducting a year-end expense accrued for an item that is owed to an S corporation using the cash method of accounting when both corporations are owned by the same shareholders. The expense can be deducted by the first S corporation on the day that the income is includible in the second S corporation's gross income.

The S corporation is considered to be a pass-through entity and is subject to the special Sec. 267(e) rules that extend the general related party transaction rules described above to any payment made by the S corporation to *any* person who directly or indirectly owns S corporation stock. This prevents the S corporation from deducting a payment to be made to one of its shareholders or to someone who indirectly owns such stock until the payee reports the income. Payments made to the S corporation by a person who directly or indirectly owns S corporation stock are also similarly restricted.

Example 11-29 ■ Vassar Corporation, an electing S corporation, uses the accrual method of accounting. On September 1, 1991, Vassar borrows $50,000 from Joan, who owns 10% of the Vassar stock. Interest is charged at a 12% annual rate. Joan uses the cash method of accounting. At year-end, Vassar accrues $2,000 of interest expense on the loan. Six months of interest (including the $2,000 of accrued interest) is paid to Joan on March 1, 1992. Vassar Corporation cannot deduct the 1991 interest accrual when determining its ordinary income or loss until it is paid in 1992. ■

Section 267(a)(1) denies a deduction for losses incurred on the sale or exchange of property directly or indirectly between related parties. The same definition of a related party is used for this purpose as is used in applying Sec. 267(a)(2) to expense transactions involving an S corporation. Any loss that is disallowed to the seller on the related party sale or exchange can be used to offset gains realized by the purchaser on a subsequent sale or exchange.

Fringe Benefits Paid to a Shareholder-Employee

Typical Misconception

The cost of many fringe benefits provided by a C corporation is deductible to the corporation and nontaxable to the employee. However, fringe benefits paid to a 2% shareholder-employee of an S corporation are nondeductible unless taxable to the shareholder-employee as compensation.

The S corporation is not treated as a corporate taxpayer with respect to fringe benefits paid to any 2% shareholder.[58] Instead, the S corporation is treated the same as a partnership, and the 2% shareholder is treated as a partner of such partnership. Because of this restriction, many fringe benefits paid to a 2% shareholder-employee of an S corporation are not deductible in arriving at the amount of its ordinary income

---

[57] Section 267(b) includes in the definition of related parties the following additional relationships that may involve an S corporation:
- An individual and a corporation where more than 50% of the value of its outstanding stock is owned directly or indirectly by the individual
- A fiduciary of a trust and a corporation where more than 50% of the value of its outstanding stock is owned directly or indirectly by the trust or its grantor
- A corporation and a partnership where more than 50% of each entity is owned by the same person

The Sec. 267(c) constructive ownership rules are applied to determine if the stock ownership threshold has been exceeded.

[58] Section 1372(b) defines a 2% shareholder as any person who directly or indirectly owns on any day of the S corporation's tax year more than 2% of its outstanding stock or stock possessing more than 2% of its voting power. The Sec. 318 stock attribution rules are used to determine if the 2% threshold has been exceeded.

or loss and generally are treated as a distribution of the corporation's earnings.[59] Any owner-employee may deduct the fringe benefit item on his or her individual tax return if it otherwise qualifies as an itemized deduction. An alternative to treating the fringe benefit as a distribution is to treat it as taxable compensation and deductible by the corporation.

The 25% deduction for health insurance costs incurred by self-employed taxpayers is available to an S corporation shareholder, whether such shareholder owns more than 2% of the S corporation's stock or not. The earned income limit for claiming such a deduction is determined exclusively by referencing the shareholder's wages from the S corporation as his earned income.

Example 11-30 ■ Edison Corporation, an electing S corporation, is owned equally by Billy and Cathy. Billy and 10 other individuals are employed by Edison Corporation. All employees receive group term life insurance benefits based on their annual salaries. All of the employees except for Billy can qualify for the Sec. 79 group term life insurance premium exclusion. Billy is treated as a partner and, therefore, does not qualify as an employee. Edison Corporation can deduct the premiums paid on the policies for all employees except for Billy. The premium paid on Billy's policy is treated as a distribution and is taxable or nontaxable according to the S corporation distribution rules described above. Billy cannot deduct the premiums because they do not qualify as itemized deductions. ■

CONTROVERSIAL ISSUES

Key Point
A second class of stock does not exist if the only difference between the two classes of stock relates to voting rights.

Second Class of Stock Requirement

The question of whether a second class of stock exists has caused problems for the IRS and taxpayers for more than 30 years. It appeared that this problem had been lessened once the Congress mandated in 1982 that a second class of stock does not exist if the only difference between the two classes of stock relates to voting rights.[60] This is far from the truth since today a major controversy has developed about a new set of Proposed Treasury Regulations that may withdraw S corporation status for corporations on a prospective basis.[61]

Corporations wishing to elect or maintain S corporation status must avoid having the IRS find that a second class of stock exists. This is a particular problem for S corporations that represent little more than incorporated proprietorships or closely held partnerships. In such situations, debt instruments often resemble equity interests. If the debt instrument is recharacterized as an equity interest, there is automatic concern with whether the new equity issue represents a second class of stock. If it does, the S corporation election is involuntarily terminated.

The original Treasury Regulations issued in 1959 took the position that the new equity issue was automatically a second class of stock.[62] In 1966, the Tax Court held that such a recharacterization did not automatically create a second class of stock.[63]

---

[59] Sec. 1372(a). Fringe benefits that are subject to these rules include the $5,000 employee death benefit exclusion (Sec. 101(b)); accident and health benefit plan premiums (Secs. 105 and 106); group term life insurance premiums (Sec. 79); and meals and lodging furnished for the convenience of the employer (Sec. 119).
[60] Sec. 1361(c)(4).
[61] Published in *Federal Register* on October 5, 1990.
[62] Reg. Sec. 1.1371-1(g), T.D. 6432 (December 29, 1959).
[63] *W. C. Gamman*, 46 T.C. 1 (1966).

The Regulations were amended in 1966 to indicate that an additional capital contribution would not create a second class of stock if (1) the debt obligations and stock were held in the same proportion and (2) ownership of the debt instruments and the stock remained the same.[64] However, subsequent changes in the relative amounts of the debt instruments and the stock created by sales, exchanges, redemptions, gifts, or repayments could reopen the question. As a result, in 1972 these regulations were held invalid by the Tax Court and a number of appeals courts as tending to discourage the use of debt financing by small business corporations and exceeding the original Congressional intent.[65]

The IRS indicated in 1973 that it would not litigate the question of a second class of stock in cases involving debt obligations that were factually similar to those cases that held the regulations in question to be invalid.[66] It deleted the invalid regulations in 1980, but did not offer a replacement.

> **Key Point**
>
> *If debt instruments satisfy the safe-harbor rules, such instruments cannot be construed to be equity. However, such debt needs to have been issued in an S corporation tax year.*

This problem discouraged some S corporations from using debt financing until the following set of safe-harbor rules for straight debt instruments was issued in 1982:

- The debt must represent an unconditional promise to pay a sum certain of money on a specified date or on demand.
- The interest rate and interest payment dates must not be contingent on profits, the borrower's discretion, or similar factor.
- The debt must not be convertible directly or indirectly into stock.
- The creditor must be an individual, estate, or trust eligible to be an S corporation shareholder.[67]

The committee reports accompanying this legislation indicate that the regulations are to treat the debt instrument in such a way so as to prevent tax avoidance as well as unfair, harsh results to the taxpayer. The debt instruments may not have any ordinary income or loss or separately stated items allocated to them. Interest paid on the obligations is deductible by the S corporation and taxable to the holder.

Debt instruments that do not fall within the safe-harbor rules are classified as debt or equity according to the tax law classification rules that otherwise apply to this question (e.g., Sec. 385 or the body of judicial decisions). (See Chapter 2 of this volume for a discussion of the general debt-equity classification rules.)

There are two reasons that will generally cause the safe-harbor rules to be inapplicable. The first reason is that the debt instrument was issued when the S corporation was a C corporation and is not covered by the safe-harbor rules. The second reason is that the debt instrument fails one or more of the four safe-harbor tests outlined above. In both of these situations one must look to case law and the Treasury Regulations for guidance.

The new proposed second-class-of-stock Treasury Regulations apply to both "safe harbor" debt and other debt. These Regulations contain a number of provisions that are particularly troublesome to tax practitioners. For example, when outstanding shares of stock do not have identical rights to current distributions and liquidation proceeds, for any reason, the corporation is considered to have more than one class of stock. Distributions cannot differ in timing or amount with respect to any share of stock (other than some limited exceptions) without causing a corporation to lose its S election. In addition, many kinds of actual or deemed distributions often made by

---

[64] T.D. 6904 (December 27, 1966).

[65] See, for example, *Shores Realty Co., Inc.* v. *U.S.*, 30 AFTR 2d 72-5672, 72-2 USTC ¶ 9715 (5th Cir., 1972), and *Portage Plastics Co., Inc.* v. *U.S.*, 31 AFTR 2d 73-864, 73-1 USTC ¶ 9261 (7th Cir., 1973).

[66] T.I.R. 1248 (July 27, 1973).

[67] Sec. 1361(c)(5). The fact that the interest rate is dependent upon the prime rate or a similar factor not related to the debtor corporation will not disqualify the instrument from coming under the safe-harbor rules.

closely-held corporations (e.g., non pro-rata distributions made to shareholders, based on their differing income tax brackets, to help them pay the income taxes on their S corporation income, interest-free loans, and unreasonable compensation) would be found to convey differing rights to distributions and liquidation proceeds. As a result, a loss of the S election would occur. Tax practitioners also have been severely critical of the fact that when any obligation is found to be equity it is automatically considered to be a second class of stock, without regard to the proportionality of the holdings of the purported debt and other stock that is outstanding. Straight debt that is found to be equity, however, is not automatically considered to be a second class of stock. Finally, the Regulations (if adopted) were to apply retroactively to tax years beginning after 1982. This means that an S corporation could retroactively lose its election for as many as 9 calendar years.

According to a recent statement made by the IRS Commissioner, it appears that these Regulations will be modified in two ways. First, the Regulations would be prospective in their application. Second, changes will be made to the disproportionate distribution rules. The revised Regulations, however, have not yet been issued.

TAX PLANNING CONSIDERATIONS

Key Point
Of all the advantages of an S election, possibly the most significant is that an S election generally avoids the double taxation which is inherent in our corporate tax system.

Advantages of S Corporation Treatment

A number of advantages are available to a corporation that elects S corporation treatment. Some of them are

1. The corporation's income is exempt from the corporate income tax. An S corporation's income is taxed only to its shareholders who may be in a lower tax bracket than the corporation.
2. The corporation's losses are passed through to the shareholders and can be used to reduce the taxes owed on other types of income. This feature can be especially important for new businesses. An S corporation election can be made, the start-up losses passed through to the owners, and the election terminated once it becomes advantageous to be taxed as a C corporation.
3. Undistributed income that was taxed to the shareholder is not taxed when subsequently distributed unless the distribution exceeds the shareholder's basis for his stock.
4. Capital gains, dividend income, and tax-exempt income are separately stated and pass through to the shareholders. Such amounts when earned by a C corporation receive preferential tax treatment only at the corporation level. These items become commingled with other earnings and are taxed as dividends when distributed by the C corporation.
5. Deductions, losses, and tax credits are separately stated and passed through to the shareholders. These amounts are subject to the various ceilings for the tax attribute at the shareholder level. This treatment can permit a tax benefit to be claimed by a shareholder when it would otherwise be denied to the corporation (e.g., a shareholder can claim the general business credit benefit even though the S corporation reports a substantial loss for the year).
6. S corporations are not subject to the corporate alternative minimum tax. Their tax preference items and other adjustments are passed through to their shareholders. S corporations do not have to make the adjusted current earnings adjustment that is required of C corporations in computing their alternative minimum tax liability.

7. S corporations are not subject to the personal holding company tax. Corporations can generally earn an unlimited amount of passive income without being subject to a special tax levy provided they have not retained E&P earned while a C corporation.
8. S corporations are not subject to the accumulated earnings tax. Therefore, investments or transactions that are indicative of an unreasonable accumulation of earnings do not cause problems for the S corporation.
9. Splitting the S corporation's income between family members is possible. However, income splitting is restricted by the requirement that reasonable compensation be provided to family members who provide capital and services to the S corporation.
10. Section 448 restricts the use of the cash method of accounting by certain C corporations, partnerships, and tax shelters. This prohibition on the use of the cash method of accounting does not apply to an S corporation unless it falls within the tax shelter definition.

Disadvantages of S Corporation Treatment

A number of disadvantages also exist for a corporation that elects S corporation treatment. Some of these include

1. A C corporation is treated as a separate tax entity from its shareholders. Although the corporate tax rates are in general higher than the individual tax rates, the 15% and 28% corporate tax rates that apply to a C corporation may be lower than the marginal tax rates of the S corporation's shareholders. These lower tax rates may reduce the total tax burden if the earnings are to be retained in the business.
2. The S corporation's earnings are taxed to the shareholders even though they are not distributed. This may require the corporation to make dividend or salary payments to permit the shareholder to pay the taxes owed on the S corporation's earnings in order to prevent the shareholder from having to withdraw funds from other investments. The S corporation election may reduce the after-tax earnings that can be retained in the business because of the need to distribute earnings to the shareholders.
3. S corporations are subject to an excess net passive income tax, a capital gains tax, and a built-in gains tax. Partnerships are not subject to any of these taxes.
4. Dividends received by the S corporation are not eligible for the dividends-received deduction as is the case for a C corporation.
5. Allocation of ordinary income or loss and the separately stated items is based on the stock owned on each day of the tax year. Special allocations of particular items are not permitted as they are in a partnership.
6. The loss limitation for an S corporation shareholder is smaller than for a partner in a partnership. Shareholders can increase their loss limitation by the basis of any debt that they are owed by the S corporation. Partners, on the other hand, can increase their loss limitation by their ratable share of all partnership liabilities.
7. S corporations are subject to the at-risk, passive activity limitation, hobby loss, and investment interest rules. C corporations are not generally subject to these rules.
8. An S corporation is restricted in the type and number of shareholders it can have, the capital structure it can use, and the investment that it can make in a second corporation. Partnerships and C corporations are not so restricted.
9. S corporations are restricted to using a calendar year as their tax year, unless they can establish a business purpose for a fiscal year or they have made a special election under Sec. 444. Similar restrictions are also applicable to

Typical Misconception
The structure of an S corporation can create a real hardship for a shareholder if large amounts of income are flowing through without any compensation payments or distributions of cash to help pay the tax on the income.

partnerships. The Sec. 444 election requires a special payment to be made by the S corporation or partnership. C corporations (other than personal service corporations) can generally adopt any tax year without regard to these restrictions or special payment rules.

Election to Allocate Income Based on S Corporation's Accounting Methods

As a general rule, the S corporation's ordinary income or loss and separately stated items are allocated based on the amount of stock owned by each shareholder on each day of the S corporation's tax year. A special election is available to allocate the income based on the S corporation's accounting methods when (1) the S corporation election is terminated or (2) an S corporation shareholder terminates his interest in the corporation.[68] The use of the S corporation's tax accounting method to allocate the year's profit or loss can permit the S corporation to shift income between shareholders.

Example 11-31 ■

Key Point
Shareholders of an S corporation should not overlook the planning possibilities available in the allocation of income/loss when an S corporation election terminates or an S corporation shareholder terminates his interest.

July Corporation, an electing S corporation, is owned equally by Rod and Dana at the beginning of 1991. During 1991, July reports ordinary income of $146,000. On April 1, 1991, Dana sells all of his July stock to Randy. July Corporation earns $125,000 of its ordinary income after April 1, 1991. Rod is allocated $73,000 ($146,000 × 0.50) of ordinary income. His income allocation is the same whether the daily allocation method or the special allocation election is used. In total, Dana and Randy are allocated $73,000 of ordinary income. Dana and Randy can allocate the ordinary income amount in the following ways:

Daily Allocation	Special Election
Dana: $146,000 \times \dfrac{1}{2} \times \dfrac{90}{365} = \$18,000$	$(\$146,000 - \$125,000) \times \dfrac{1}{2} = \$10,500$
Randy: $146,000 \times \dfrac{1}{2} \times \dfrac{275}{365} = \$55,000$	$\$125,000 \times \dfrac{1}{2} = \$62,500$

The shifting of the $7,500 in income from Dana to Randy when the special election is made will also reduce Dana's adjusted basis for his July stock when determining his gain or loss on the sale. The $7,500 difference between the income allocations under the two methods may be a point for negotiation between Dana and Randy, particularly if their marginal tax rates were markedly different. ■

Increasing the Benefits from S Corporation Losses

At the shareholder level, the deduction that can be claimed for S corporation losses is restricted to the basis of the S corporation stock plus the basis of any amounts owed by the S corporation to the shareholder. Losses that are passed through in excess of this limitation are carried over to a subsequent tax year when the shareholder again has a basis for the stock investment or debt obligation. If the shareholder's marginal tax rate is expected to be the same or lower in a future tax year when the loss carryover can be used, the shareholder should consider either increasing the basis of his stock investment or loaning additional funds to the corporation before the end of the

---

[68] Sections 1362(e) and 1377(a) prevent the daily allocation method from applying to any items resulting from making a Sec. 338 (deemed liquidation) election or when there is a sale or exchange of 50% or more of the S corporation's stock during an S termination year.

current tax year. Conversely, if the loans are never expected to be repaid, he should not lend the S corporation additional amounts just to secure an additional tax deduction, which is worth at most 31 cents (at 1991 rates) for each dollar that is loaned. If the shareholder's marginal tax rate is expected to be higher in future tax years, deferring additional capital contributions or loans until after the end of the current tax year should be considered.

Example 11-32 ■

Key Point

If an S corporation shareholder has losses that have been suspended due to lack of basis, either contributions to capital or bona fide loans to the corporation will create the necessary basis to obtain the loss deduction.

Bailey Corporation, a qualifying S corporation, is owned entirely by Nancy. Bailey Corporation expects large losses in 1991 that will result in a $100,000 ordinary loss. Nancy's basis for the Bailey stock (before any adjustment for the current loss) is $35,000. Bailey Corporation also owes Nancy $25,000. Nancy's 1991 marginal tax rate is 31%. This marginal tax rate is expected to decline to 15% in 1992. Nancy should consider making $40,000 ($100,000 loss − [$35,000 stock basis + $25,000 loan basis]) of additional capital contributions or loans to Bailey Corporation before the end of 1991 in order to obtain an additional $6,400 ([0.31 − 0.15] × $40,000) of tax benefits from deducting the anticipated loss carryover in the current year. If Nancy's 1991 and 1992 marginal tax rates are expected to be 15% and 31%, respectively, the $6,400 tax benefit (less the time value of money for 1 year) can be obtained by having Nancy merely defer her capital contributions or loans to Bailey Corporation until 1992. Alternatively, Nancy could use the loss carryover to offset profits reported by Bailey Corporation in 1992. These profits would restore part or all of the basis of Bailey Corporation's debt to Nancy (and possibly increase the basis of Nancy's Bailey stock). The basis would then be partially or fully offset by the $40,000 loss carryover. ■

The S corporation loss carryover is only available to the shareholder who held the stock when the loss was incurred. A shareholder should consider increasing the basis of the stock in order to take advantage of the carryover before the stock is sold. The purchasing shareholder does not acquire the carryover.

Passive Income Requirements

The S corporation can earn an unlimited amount of passive income each year without incurring any penalty provided it does not have any E&P accumulated in a C corporation tax year (known as Subchapter C E&P) at the end of its tax year. An S corporation election thus can permit a corporation to avoid the personal holding company penalty surtax.

Potentially, S corporations that have operated as a C corporation and have accumulated Subchapter C E&P are liable for the excess net passive income tax. In addition, their S corporation election may be terminated if the passive investment income exceeds 25% of gross receipts for 3 consecutive tax years. The S corporation can avoid both of these possible problems by making a special election under Sec. 1368(e)(3) to distribute its entire Subchapter C E&P balance to its shareholders. The distribution results in a tax cost for the shareholders by paying tax on the dividend income that results. To the shareholders, the cost of the election can be small if (1) the accumulated E&P balance is insignificant or (2) the shareholder has a current year NOL (excluding the distribution) or a NOL carryover. The ultimate long-run benefit, however, may be great because it permits the S corporation to earn an unlimited amount of passive investment income tax-free in subsequent tax years.

Example 11-33 ■

Hawaii Corporation is incorporated in 1985. It operates for a number of years as a C corporation, during which time it accumulates $30,000 of E&P. Most of Hawaii's gross income now comes from rentals and interest, constituting passive investment

Tax Planning Considerations • **11-41**

income. Hawaii makes an election to be taxed under Subchapter S starting in 1991. The excess net passive income tax will apply in 1991 if Hawaii's rentals and interest exceed 25% of its gross receipts, for the year, unless (1) an election to distribute the accumulated E&P is made and (2) the earnings are distributed by the end of Hawaii's first tax year as an S corporation. ∎

S corporations that earn rental income can also avoid the passive income tax and the possibility of having its election terminated if significant services are rendered to the occupant of the space. Significant services are defined by Prop. Reg. Sec. 1.1362-3(d)(5)(iv) as being primarily for the occupant's convenience and "are other than those usually or customarily rendered in connection with the rental of rooms or other space for occupancy only." Thus, maid service constitutes significant services, but the providing of heat and light and the cleaning of public spaces do not constitute significant services.

Example 11-34 ∎ Assume the same facts as in Example 11-33, except that Hawaii Corporation provides significant services to its tenants in connection with its rental activities. Because the services are significant, Hawaii Corporation only has a passive income problem if its interest income exceeds 25% of its gross receipts. If the 25% threshold is not exceeded. Hawaii can avoid having to distribute its Subchapter C E&P in 1991. ∎

Key Point

Since the existence of E&P in an S corporation can not only create a tax at the corporate level but can also cause the S corporation election to be terminated, consideration should be given to having the S corporation elect to distribute its E&P.

Corporations that experience a passive income problem in 2 consecutive tax years should carefully monitor their passive income in the next year. If they see that their passive income for the third year will exceed the 25% threshold, they should make certain that they elect to distribute their accumulated Subchapter C E&P before year-end. This will not only prevent loss of the S corporation election, but also avoid having to pay the Sec. 1375 tax.

Using an S Corporation When Liquidating

The Sec. 336(a) rules requiring recognition of gain or loss when liquidating distributions are made apply to both C corporations and S corporations. When property that has declined in value is distributed, the shareholders of a C corporation may recognize losses and other deductions related to the liquidation that exceed the amount of its income for the tax year of liquidation. This NOL may be able to be carried back in order to obtain a refund of taxes paid in prior years. An S corporation election, and its inherent passthrough of income and losses, might prove to be an advantage for the shareholders of a liquidating corporation incurring such losses and deductions in two situations:

- If the C corporation was taxed at low marginal rates in the preceding three years, the losses and deductions may provide a greater tax savings by being passed through and reported on the shareholders' tax returns.
- If the C corporation paid no taxes in the preceding three years, the losses and deductions will provide a tax benefit only if they are passed through and reported on the shareholders' tax returns. If no S corporation election is made, the losses and deductions are lost when the liquidation is completed.

Key Point

An S election may prove advantageous if a regular C corporation is in danger of being classified as a personal holding company. An S corporation cannot be a personal holding company.

An S corporation election may also prove advantageous if the corporation may be classified as a personal holding company for any of its tax years during the liquidation period. A closely held C corporation may be classified as a personal holding company whenever it earns predominantly passive income during a tax year. Such a situation might occur when the corporation discontinues its operating activities, sells its assets in an installment sale, and then holds the installment obligations for a period of time prior to liquidating. The interest income would constitute personal holding company income and may cause the closely held C corporation to be subject to the personal holding company tax. By making an S corporation election, the liquidating corporation will be exempt from the personal holding company tax. Liquidating corporations, that make an S corporation election after having been a C corporation for a number of years, should carefully examine the tax consequences of the built-in gains tax which will apply to the liquidating distributions. Further discussion of the personal holding company tax rules is found in Chapter 5.

COMPLIANCE AND PROCEDURAL CONSIDERATIONS

Making the Election

The S corporation election is made by filing Form 2553 (Election by Small Business Corporation to Tax Corporation Income Directly to Shareholders). The election form can be signed by any person who is authorized to sign the S corporation's tax return under Sec. 6037. Form 2553 is filed with the IRS Service Center designated in the instructions. No extensions of time to file the S corporation election are granted.[69]

Shareholder consents to the S corporation election can be made either on Form 2553 or on a separate consent statement signed by the shareholder and attached to the corporation's election form. Proposed Reg. Sec. 18.1362-2(a) outlines the other information that must be provided with a separate consent. Extensions of time for filing shareholder consents to the S corporation election can be granted by the IRS.[70]

A Sec. 444 election to use a fiscal year is made on Form 8716 which must be filed by the earlier of (1) the 15th day of the fifth month following the month that includes the first day of the tax year for which the election will be first effective or (2) the due date for the income tax return resulting from the election.[71] A copy of the Form 8716 must be attached to the Form 1120S for the first tax year for which the Sec. 444 election is effective. A corporation desiring to make a Sec. 444 election must also state its intention in a statement attached to its S corporation election form (Form 2553).[72]

Filing the Corporate Tax Return

OBJECTIVE 10
Explain the procedures for filing an S corporation tax return

All S corporations, whether they owe any taxes under Secs. 1374 or 1375 or not, must file a tax return if they are in existence for part or all of the tax year. An S corporation must file its corporate tax return not later than the fifteenth day of the third month following the end of the tax year.[73] The S corporation reports its results on Form 1120S (U.S. Income Tax Return for an S Corporation). A completed S corporation tax return is illustrated in Appendix B. An S corporation is allowed an automatic 6-month extension of time for filing its tax return by filing Form 7004 (Application for Automatic Extension of Time to File U.S. Corporation Income Tax Return).[74]

---

[69] Rev. Rul. 60-183, 1960-1 C.B. 625.
[70] Prop. Reg. Sec. 18.1362-2(c).
[71] Temp. Reg. Sec. 1.444-3T(b)(1).
[72] Temp. Reg. Sec. 1.444-3T(b)(3).
[73] Sec. 6072(b).
[74] Reg. Sec. 1.6081-3.

Example 11-35 ■ Simpson Corporation, an electing S corporation, uses the calendar year as its tax year. Its tax return is generally due on March 15. An automatic extension of 6 months is permitted for the return, thus extending its due date until September 15. ■

All S corporations that must file a tax return must furnish each person that is a shareholder at any time during the tax year with a copy of the tax return. The return must be made available to the shareholder not later than the day on which it is filed.[75] The S Corporation's ordinary income or loss and certain passive income or loss items are reported on an individual shareholder's Form 1040, Schedule E. Most separately stated items are reported on other supporting schedules to Form 1040, as illustrated on the Form 1120S, Schedule K-1 presented in Appendix B.

An S corporation is subject to the same basic 3-year statute of limitations that applies to other taxpayers. This 3-year period applies for purposes of determining the time period during which

1. The corporation remains liable for assessments of the excess net passive income tax, the capital gains tax, and the built-in gains tax.
2. The IRS can question the correctness of an S corporation election that was made for a particular tax year.[76]

Determination of the Sec. 7519 required payment is made on a computation worksheet provided in the instructions for the Form 1120S. A required payment does not have to be made if the total of such payments for the current year and all preceding years is $500 or less. Amounts less than the $500 threshold are carried over to succeeding years. The required payment amount is due on or before May 15th regardless of the fiscal year that is used. The required payment and the computation worksheet must accompany a Form 8752 which is also used to secure a refund of prior Sec. 7519 payments.[77]

Estimated Tax Payments

OBJECTIVE 11
Determine the estimated tax payments required of an S corporation and its shareholders

S corporations are required to make estimated tax payments for tax years beginning after 1989 if their estimated tax liability is reasonably expected to be $500 or more. Estimated tax payments are required for the corporate level liability attributable to the built-in gains tax (new Sec. 1374), the capital gains tax (old Sec. 1374), the excess net passive income tax (Sec. 1375), and recapture of investment tax credits claimed in tax years in which the corporation was taxed as a C corporation (Sec. 1371(d)(2)).[78] In addition, the S corporation's shareholders must include their income, gain, loss, deduction, and credit passthroughs in their own estimated tax calculations.

The corporate estimated tax payment requirements described for a C corporation in Chapter 3 also apply to an S corporation with respect to these three liabilities. The required quarterly installment is 25% of the lesser of (1) 90% of the tax shown on the return for the tax year, or (2) the sum of 90% of the built-in gains tax, capital gains tax, and investment tax credit recapture amounts plus 100% of the excess net passive income tax reported for the preceding tax year.[79]

An S corporation cannot use the prior year tax liability exception of Sec. 6655(d)(1)(B)(ii) when determining the required payment to be made with respect to

---

[75] Sec. 6037(b).
[76] Sec. 6233.
[77] Temp. Reg. Sec. 1.7519-2T.
[78] Sec. 6655(g)(4)(A).
[79] Sec. 6655(g)(4)(C).

Self-Study Question

Is an S corporation required to make estimated tax payments?

Answer

Yes. For years beginning after 12/31/89, an S corporation is responsible to pay estimated taxes if the corporation is subject to capital gains, built-in gains, passive income, or ITC recapture taxes. Also, shareholders are required to include their S corporation income/loss and credit passthroughs in determining their estimated tax payments.

the built-in gains tax, capital gains tax, and investment tax credit recapture amounts. This exception is available with respect to the excess net passive income tax portion of the required payment without regard to whether any tax was owed in the prior year or not.[80] All corporations can use the prior year tax liability exception for the excess net passive income tax whether they are "large" corporations under Sec. 6655(d)(2) or not. The annualization election of Sec. 6655(e) is also available when determining the quarterly estimated tax payment amounts.[81] An S corporation's failure to make timely estimated tax payments, or a timely final payment when the tax return is filed, will cause it to be subject to interest and penalties like other taxpayers.

The S corporation's shareholders must include their ratable share of the ordinary income or loss and separately stated items in determining their estimated tax liability. Such amounts are treated as having been received concurrently by the shareholders throughout the S corporation's tax year. Thus, ordinary income or loss and separately stated items for an S corporation tax year that ends with or within the shareholder's tax year are included in the estimated tax calculation to the extent they are attributable to months in the S corporation tax year that precede the month in which the installment is due.

Example 11-36 ■ Amigo Corporation, an electing S corporation, is 50% owned by Jorge. Both Amigo and Jorge use the calendar year as their tax year. Amigo Corporation reports the following results for 1991:

Time Period	Ordinary Income
January 1, 1991 through March 31, 1991	$ 40,000
January 1, 1991 through May 31, 1991	60,000
January 1, 1991 through August 31, 1991	150,000
January 1, 1991 through December 31, 1991	180,000

Jorge includes his ratable share of Amigo's ordinary income in his estimated tax calculation, as follows:

Installment Due Date	Interim Period	Ordinary Income
April 15	January 1, 1991 through March 31, 1991	$20,000 (0.50 × $40,000)
June 15	January 1, 1991 through May 31, 1991	30,000 (0.50 × $60,000)
September 15	January 1, 1991 through August 31, 1991	75,000 (0.50 × $150,000)
January 15	January 1, 1991 through December 31, 1991	90,000 (0.50 × $180,000)

■

Key Point

If the IRS is conducting an audit of an S corporation, the audit is conducted in a unified proceeding at the corporate level rather than in separate audits of each S corporation shareholder.

Administrative Rules

As with a partnership, Sec. 6241 requires that the tax treatment of any Subchapter S item—that is, generally any income, loss, deduction, or credit item of an S corporation—be determined at the corporate level. Section 6242 requires each S corporation shareholder to report each Subchapter S item in a manner that is consistent with the treatment that the item received on the corporate tax return. An item can receive inconsistent treatment only if the shareholder notifies the IRS of the

---

[80] Sec. 6655(g)(4)(B).
[81] Sec. 6655(g)(4)(E).

difference. The method of making such a notification will parallel the procedural rules for partnerships found in the Temporary Regulations for Secs. 6221 and 6222.

Because of the similarity of S corporations and partnerships, the rules governing administrative and judicial proceedings for a partnership also apply to most S corporation matters. Section 6241 requires that administrative and judicial proceedings relating to the tax treatment of Subchapter S items take place in a unified proceeding at the corporate level. Section 6243 requires that an S corporation's shareholders be given notice of the administrative or judicial proceedings involving the determination of any Subchapter S item at the corporate level. The procedures to be employed in these proceedings will parallel the procedural rules for partnerships found in the Temporary Regulations for Secs. 6223 through 6231.

Sample S Corporation Tax Return

A sample S corporation Form 1120S and supporting Schedules D and K-1 are presented in Appendix B to this book. The other supporting information has been omitted. Two differences should be noted between the S corporation tax return and a partnership tax return. First, the S corporation tax return provides for the determination of a corporate tax liability and the payment of the three special taxes that can be levied on the S corporation. No such items are shown on the partnership return. Second, the S corporation return does not require a reconciliation of the shareholders' basis adjustments as occurs on a partnership tax return. Commencing with the 1990 tax year, Schedule M-1 and M-2 reconciliations similar to that required of a C corporation are required of an S corporation. The Schedule M-1 requires a reconciliation of book income with the reported ordinary income (loss). The Schedule M-2 requires a reconciliation of the Accumulated Adjustments, Other Adjustments, and Previously Taxed Income accounts. The AAA reconciliation is required of all shareholders, even though the corporation may not have accumulated E&P in prior years. The Other Adjustments account is maintained only by corporations that have an accumulated E&P balance at year-end. The account is adjusted for tax-exempt income and the related nondeductible expenses for the year. Note that if there is no accumulated E&P at the end of the tax year, the AAA includes all income, gain, loss, and deduction items for the tax year, including tax-exempt income and nondeductible losses and expenses related to such income. If there is accumulated E&P at the end of the tax year, the AAA is determined by taking into account only the taxable portion of the S corporation's income and any expenses and losses other than those related to the production of the tax-exempt income. The effect of this difference is to place municipal bond interest income (net of any related expenses) behind accumulated E&P when determining the order of distribution. A company having an accumulated E&P balance might consider having the municipal bonds owned at the shareholder level rather than at the corporate level, or distributing the accumulated E&P balance.

PROBLEM MATERIALS

DISCUSSION QUESTIONS

11-1. Which of the following classifications make a shareholder ineligible to own the stock of an S corporation?
  a. U.S. citizen
  b. Domestic corporation
  c. Partnership where all the partners are U.S citizens
  d. Estate of a deceased U.S. citizen

e. Grantor trust created by a U.S. citizen
f. Nonresident alien individual

11-2. Which of the following taxes do not apply to an S corporation?
a. Accumulated earnings tax
b. 31% maximum tax rate on capital gains
c. Corporate alternative minimum tax
d. Built-in gains tax
e. Personal holding company tax
f. Excess net passive income tax

11-3. What is the format for making an S corporation election? Who must consent to the S corporation election?

11-4. What events will cause an S corporation election to be terminated?

11-5. Which of the following events will cause an S corporation election to be terminated?
a. The S corporation earning 100% of its gross receipts in its first tax year from passive sources.
b. The S corporation issuing nonvoting stock that has a dividend preference.
c. The S corporation purchasing 100% of the single class of stock of a second domestic corporation that has conducted business activities for four years.
d. A new, individual shareholder purchasing 10% of the S corporation's stock and not consenting to the election within 30 days of the purchase date.
e. The S corporation earning tax-exempt interest income.

11-6. What is an inadvertent termination? What actions on the part of the S corporation and its shareholders are needed to correct an inadvertent termination?

11-7. What is the format for revoking an S corporation election? Who must consent to the revocation? When can a revocation be filed that is effective on the first day of the tax year?

11-8. An S corporation has revoked its S corporation election. How long must the corporation wait in order to make a new election? What circumstances permit an early reelection?

11-9. What tax years can be adopted by a newly created corporation that makes an S corporation election for its first tax year? If a fiscal year is permitted, does it require IRS approval?

11-10. At the time Cable Corporation makes its S corporation election it elects to use a fiscal year based upon a Sec. 444 election. What other requirement(s) must be satisfied in order for Cable Corporation to continue to use its fiscal year election for future tax years?

11-11. Explain how the amount of the required payment is determined when a fiscal year election is made under Sec. 444.

11-12. What events will result in a refund of required payments that have been paid in prior tax years?

11-13. What are Subchapter C earnings and profits? How does the existence of such earnings affect the S corporation's ability to earn passive income?

11-14. Explain the legislative purpose behind the enactment of the S corporation built-in gains tax.

11-15. Which of the following items are included in an S corporation's ordinary income or loss?
a. Long-term capital gains
b. Sec. 1231 losses
c. Sec. 1245 gains
d. Dividend income received from a domestic corporation
e. Interest income from corporate bonds
f. Interest income from state bonds
g. Charitable contributions

h. Salary expense paid to a shareholder-employee
i. Investment interest expense
j. Straight-line depreciation on real property

11-16. Explain the procedures for allocating an S corporation's ordinary income or loss. What special allocation elections are available?

11-17. What is the limitation on the amount of the loss pass-through that can be deducted by an S corporation shareholder? What happens to any losses in excess of this limitation?

11-18. What actions can be taken by an S corporation shareholder to increase the amount of the S corporation's losses that can be deducted in the year that they are incurred?

11-19. What is a post-termination transition period? What loss carryovers can be deducted by an S corporation's shareholder during this period?

11-20. Which of the following deduction or loss provisions may apply to an S corporation or its shareholders?
a. Dividends-received deduction
b. Amortization of organizational expenditures
c. Sec. 291 restriction on tax preferences
d. Hobby loss rules
e. At-risk rules
f. Investment interest limitation
g. Passive activity limitation

11-21. Explain the positive and negative adjustments that are made to (1) the basis of an S corporation shareholder's stock investment and (2) the basis of an S corporation debt that is owed to the shareholder.

11-22. Explain the differences between the tax treatment accorded nonliquidating property distributions made by S corporations and partnerships.

11-23. What nonliquidating distributions made by an S corporation are taxable to its shareholders? tax-free to its shareholders?

11-24. What is an Accumulated Adjustments Account? What income, gain, loss, and deduction items *do not* affect this account?

11-25. List five advantages and five disadvantages of making an S corporation election.

11-26. Explain the differences between the way the following items are reported by an S corporation and a C corporation.
a. Ordinary income or loss
b. Capital gains and losses
c. Tax-exempt interest income
d. Charitable contributions
e. Nonliquidating property distributions
f. Fringe benefits paid to a shareholder-employee

11-27. When is the S corporation's tax return due? What extensions of time are available for filing the return?

11-28. What S corporation tax levies must be prepaid by having the corporation make "quarterly" estimated tax payments? Can a shareholder owning S corporation stock use the corporation's estimated tax payments to reduce the amount of his/her individual estimated tax payments? Explain.

11-29. Review the completed C corporation, partnership, and S corporation tax returns presented in Appendix B. What major similarities and differences in content and format do you find between the three tax returns?

PROBLEMS

11-30. Making the Election. Voyles Corporation, a calendar-year taxpayer formed in 1989, desires to make an election to be taxed as an S corporation commencing with 1991. Sue and Andrea each own one-half of the Voyles stock.
  a. How does Voyles Corporation make the S corporation election?
  b. When can Voyles Corporation file its election form?
  c. If the election in Part b is not filed in a timely manner, when will it first take effect?

11-31. Termination of the Election. Orlando Corporation, a calendar-year taxpayer, has been taxed as an S corporation for several years. On July 10, 1991, Orlando Corporation authorizes a second class of nonvoting preferred stock that pays a 10% annual dividend. The stock is sold to Sid on September 15, 1991, to raise additional equity capital. Sid owns no other Orlando stock.
  a. Does Orlando Corporation's election terminate? If so, when is the termination first effective?
  b. What tax returns must be filed by Orlando Corporation for 1991? When are they due?
  c. How would your answer to Parts a and b change if the second class of stock was nonvoting Class B common stock?

11-32. Revocation of the Election. Tango Corporation, a calendar-year taxpayer, has been taxed as an S corporation for several years. Tango's business activities have become very profitable in recent years. On June 15, 1991, its sole shareholder desires to revoke the S corporation election.
  a. How does Tango revoke its S corporation election? When does the revocation take effect?
  b. Assume the revocation is effective July 1, 1991. What tax returns are required of Tango for 1991? for 1992? When are these returns due?
  c. If a new S corporation election is made after the revocation, when does it first take effect?

11-33. Sale of S Corporation Interest. Peter and his wife, Alice, own all of the stock of Galleon Corporation. Galleon Corporation elected to be taxed under Subchapter S in 1985. Peter and Alice sold one-half of their Galleon stock to a partnership owned by Rob and Susan (not husband and wife) at the close of business on December 31, 1990 for a $75,000 profit. What are the tax consequences of the sale transaction for Peter and Alice? for the corporation? As Peter and Alice's CPA do you have any advice for them?

11-34. Selecting a Tax Year. Indicate in each of the following situations, if the taxpayer can accomplish what is proposed. Provide adequate authority for your answer including any special elections that are needed or requirements that must be satisfied. Assume that all individuals use the calendar year as their tax year unless otherwise indicated.
  a. Will and Carol form the Classic Corporation. They desire that the corporation adopt a fiscal year ending January 31 as its tax year to provide a maximum deferral for their income. An S corporation election is made for its initial tax year ending January 31, 1992.
  b. Mark and Dennis have owned and operated the Plastic Corporation for several years. Plastic Corporation has used a fiscal year ending June 30 since its organization as a C corporation because it conforms to the corporation's natural business year. An S corporation election is made for its tax year beginning July 1, 1991.
  c. Edith owns all the stock of Elite Corporation, an electing S corporation. Elite Corporation uses a fiscal year ending September 30 as its tax year. The IRS approved Elite Corporation's use of the fiscal year in 1980 because it provided the corporation with an income deferral of only 3 months.

11-35. Passive Income Tax Levy. North Corporation was organized in 1984 by Oliver. An S corporation election is made by North Corporation for 1989 after it accumulates $60,000 of E&P as a C corporation. In 1991 North Corporation reports the following results:

Dividends from domestic corporations	$ 60,000
Rental income	100,000
Services income	50,000
Expenses related to rental income	30,000
Other expenses	20,000

Significant services are not provided in connection with earning the rental income.

a. Is North Corporation subject to the excess net passive income tax? If so, what is its tax liability?
b. What is the effect of the excess net passive income tax levy on North's pass-throughs of ordinary income and separately stated items?
c. What advice would you give North Corporation regarding its activities?

11-36. *Built-in Gains Tax.* Tad Corporation was created in 1983. In its first year, it elected to use the cash method of accounting and adopted a tax year ending December 31. An S corporation election was made on August 15, 1990, effective for Tad's 1991 tax year. At the beginning of 1991, Tad has assets with a $600,000 FMV and a $180,000 adjusted basis. During 1991 Tad reports taxable income of $250,000 excluding the following transactions:

- Collects accounts receivables outstanding on January 1, 1991, in the amount of $200,000. The receivables have a zero adjusted basis. Receivables in the amount of $250,000 are outstanding at year-end.
- Sells an automobile on February 1, 1991, for $3,500. The automobile has a $2,000 adjusted basis and a $3,000 FMV on January 1, 1991.
- Sells land for $60,000 that it held 3 years in anticipation of building its own office building. The land has a $45,000 FMV and a $25,000 adjusted basis on January 1, 1991.
- Paid accounts payable outstanding on January 1, 1991, of $125,000. $110,000 of the payables are deductible expenses.

a. What is the amount of Tad's built-in gains tax liability? (Assume Tad is not eligible for the special 2-year extension for making its S corporation election and avoiding the built-in gains tax liability.)
b. What is the effect of the built-in gains tax liability on Tad's pass-throughs of ordinary income and separately stated items?

11-37. *Built-in Gains Tax.* Bender Corporation was created in 1986 and adopted a calendar year as its tax year. In December 1989 Bender Corporation made a valid S corporation election after accumulating $125,000 of Subchapter C E&P. At the beginning of its first S corporation tax year (1990) Bender's net unrealized built-in gain was $600,000, after a $200,000 reduction for unrealized built-in losses. During 1990 it reported recognized built-in gains of $125,000, recognized built-in losses of $40,000, and taxable income of $50,000. During 1991 Bender reported recognized built-in gains of $180,000, recognized built-in losses of $60,000, and taxable income of $200,000. One-third of 1991's built-in gains are capital gains. The remainder of the 1990 and 1991 built-in gains and losses are ordinary income or loss.
a. What is Bender's built-in gains tax for 1990? for 1991?
b. What is the effect of the built-in gains tax liability on Bender's pass-throughs of ordinary income and separately stated items?

11-38. *Determination of Pass-throughs.* West End Corporation, an S corporation using an accrual method of accounting, is owned by Amelia. Amelia uses the cash method of accounting. West End reports the following results for 1991:

Operating profit:	
(excluding the items indicated below)	$275,000
Dividend income:	
From a domestic corporation 25% owned by West End	12,000
From a foreign corporation 1% owned by West End	6,000
Interest income:	
Installment sales of merchandise	9,000
Municipal bonds	7,000
Corporate bonds	3,000
Gains and losses on property sales:	
Sec. 1231 gain	9,000
Long-term capital gain	11,000
Long-term capital loss	6,000
Short-term capital gain	8,000
Sec. 1245 gain	10,000

MACRS depreciation on plant, equipment, and panels	46,000
Charitable contributions	25,000
Salary expense (all paid to A in 1991)	60,000
Rental expense on building leased from A ($6,000 of the rentals remained unpaid at year-end)	36,000
Repairs expense	36,000
State and local taxes	6,000
Interest on loans taken out to acquire stock investments	10,000
Capital expenditure for solar heating panels	18,000

    a. What is West End's ordinary income?
    b. What are West End's separately stated items?

11-39. *Allocation of Income to Shareholders.* John owns all of the stock of Lucas Corporation, an electing S corporation. John's basis for the 1,000 shares is $125,000. On June 11, 1991, John gifts 100 shares of stock to his younger brother Michael who has been working in the business for one year. Lucas Corporation reports $80,000 of ordinary income and $10,000 of investment interest for 1991. What amount of income is allocated to John? to Michael?

11-40. *Sale of S Corporation Interest.* Al and Ruth each own one-half of the stock of Chemical Corporation, an electing S corporation. During 1991 Chemical Corporation earns $15,000 per month of ordinary income. On April 5 Ruth sells her entire stock interest to Patty. A business asset is sold on August 18 and a $75,000 Sec. 1231 gain is recognized. What alternatives (if any) exist for allocating Chemical Corporation's 1991 income?

11-41. *Allocation of Income to Shareholders.* Toyland Corporation, an electing S corporation, uses the calendar year as its tax year. Bob, Alice, and Carter own 60, 30, and 10 shares, respectively, of the Toyland stock. No other stock is outstanding. Carter's basis for his stock is $26,000 on January 1, 1991. On July 1, 1991, Alice gifted one-half of her stock to Mike. On December 1, 1991, Carter sold his stock to Mike for $45,000. Toyland reports the following results for 1991:

Ordinary income	$120,000
Long-term capital loss	10,000
Charitable contributions	6,000

    a. What amounts of income, loss, or deduction are reported by the four shareholders (assuming that no special elections are made)?
    b. What gain or loss is recognized by Carter when the Toyland stock is sold?

11-42. *Allocation of Income to Shareholders.* Redfern Corporation, a calendar-year taxpayer, has been an S corporation for several years. The Redfern stock is owned equally by Rod and Ken. On July 1, 1991, Redfern Corporation issues additional common stock that is purchased by Blackfoot Corporation. Rod, Ken, and Blackfoot Corporation each end up owning one-third of the Redfern stock. During 1991, Redfern Corporation reports ordinary income of $125,000 and a short-term capital loss of $15,000. Eighty percent of the ordinary income and all of the capital loss are accrued after Blackfoot Corporation purchases its stock. Redfern makes no distributions to its shareholders during 1991. What income and losses are reported by Redfern and Blackfoot Corporations and Rod and Ken as a result of the 1991 activities (assume all months have 30 days)?

11-43. *Allocation of Losses to Shareholders.* Raider Corporation, an electing S corporation, is owned equally by Monte and Allie. Both individuals actively participate in Raider's activities. On January 1, 1991, Monte and Allie have adjusted bases for their Raider stock of $80,000 and $90,000, respectively. During 1991, Raider Corporation reports the following results:

Ordinary loss	$175,000
Tax-exempt interest income	20,000
Long-term capital loss	32,000

Raider's balance sheet at year-end shows the following liabilities: accounts payable, $90,000; mortgage payable, $30,000; and note payable to Allie, $10,000.

a. What income and deductions will Monte and Allie report from Raider's 1991 activities?
b. What basis does Monte have for his stock investment on December 31, 1991?
c. What basis does Allie have for her stock investment and note on December 31, 1991?
d. What loss carryovers are available for Monte and Allie to 1992?

11-44. *Use of Loss Carryovers.* Assume the same facts as in the preceding example except that Raider Corporation reports $75,000 of ordinary income, $20,000 of tax-exempt income, and a $25,000 long-term capital gain in 1992.
a. What income and deductions will Monte and Allie report from Raider's 1992 activities?
b. What basis does Monte have in his stock investment on December 31, 1992?
c. What basis does Allie have in her stock investment and note on December 31, 1992?
d. What loss carryovers (if any) are available to Monte and Allie to 1993?

11-45. *Allocation of Losses to Shareholders.* Hammer Corporation, an electing S corporation, is owned by Tommy, who has a $100,000 basis for his investment on January 1, 1990. Tommy actively participates in Hammer's activities. The Hammer Corporation operating results were not good in 1990, with an ordinary loss of $175,000 being reported. The size of the loss required Tommy to lend Hammer Corporation $50,000 on August 10, 1990, to provide funds needed for operations. The loan is secured by a Hammer Corporation note. Hammer Corporation rebounds during 1991 and reports ordinary income of $60,000. The $50,000 note is repaid on December 15, 1991.
a. What amount of Hammer's 1990 loss can Tommy report on his 1990 income tax return?
b. What is Tommy's basis for the Hammer stock and note on December 31, 1990?
c. What income and deductions will Tommy report from Hammer's 1991 activities and the loan repayment?
d. What tax planning advice can you offer Tommy about the timing of the loan repayment?

11-46. *Post-Termination Loss Utilization.* Stein Corporation, an electing S corporation, has 400 shares of stock outstanding. The shares are owned equally by Chuck and Linda. Both individuals actively participate in Stein's activities. Each shareholder contributed $60,000 when Stein was organized on September 10, 1990. Start-up losses during 1990 result in Stein reporting a $210,000 ordinary loss. Stein's activities have since become profitable, and the S corporation election is voluntarily revoked on March 1, 1991, with no prospective revocation date being specified. In 1991, Stein reports $360,000 of taxable income ($30,000 per month). Stein makes no distributions to its shareholders in either 1990 or 1991.
a. What amount of loss is deductible by Chuck and Linda in 1990?
b. What amount of loss must be carried over by Chuck and Linda to 1991?
c. If Chuck reported only $5,000 of other business income in 1990, what happens to the "excess" S corporation losses that are deducted?
d. What portion of the loss carryover from Part b can be deducted in 1991? What happens to any unused portion of the loss?
e. What advice can you offer to Chuck and Linda to enhance their utilization of the Stein loss?

11-47. *Utilization of Loss Passthroughs by Shareholders.* Rocket Corporation, an electing S corporation, is owned by Tina, who has an $80,000 basis for her investment on January 1, 1990. During the first 11 months of 1990, Rocket Corporation reports an ordinary loss of $100,000. An additional $20,000 loss is expected for December 1990. Tina earns $250,000 of ordinary income from her other activities in 1990. Her other income is expected to decline to $75,000 in 1991 and continue at that level in future years. The 1991 losses for Rocket Corporation are expected to be only $20,000. Rocket Corporation projects a $50,000 profit for 1992 and each of the next 4 years. What advice can you offer Tina about using her Rocket Corporation losses and retaining S corporation status in future years? How would your answer change if Tina's income from her other activities had instead been $75,000 in 1990 and $250,000 in 1991.

11-48. *Stock Basis Adjustment.* For each of the following items, indicate whether they will increase, decrease, or cause no change in the S corporation's ordinary income (loss), accumulated adjustments account and in the shareholder's stock basis. The corporation in question has always been an S corporation.
a. Operating profit

b. Dividend income received from domestic corporation
c. Interest income earned on corporate bond held as an investment
d. Life insurance proceeds paid on death of corporate officer
e. Long-term capital gain
f. Sec. 1231 loss
g. Sec. 1245 gain
h. Charitable contributions
i. Fines paid for having overweight trucks
j. Depreciation
k. Pension plan contributions for employees
l. Salary paid to owner
m. Premiums paid on life insurance policy in Part d
n. Distribution of money (but not in excess of current year's earnings)
o. Distribution out of accumulated E&P

11-49. Stock Basis Adjustment. Assume the same facts as in Problem 11-48 except that the S Corporation was formed in 1988 and made its S corporation election in 1990. During its time period it was a C corporation, $30,000 of E&P was accumulated. How would your answers for Parts a through o change?

11-50. Taxability of Distributions. Sweets Corporation is organized in January 1991 and immediately elects to be taxed as an S corporation. All of the Sweets stock is owned by Tammy, who contributes $40,000 in cash to start the business. Sweets' 1991 results are reported below:

Ordinary income	$36,000
Short-term capital loss	4,000
Charitable contributions	1,000

On July 10, 1991, Sweets Corporation makes a $10,000 cash distribution to Tammy.
a. What income is recognized as a result of the distribution?
b. What is the basis for the Sweets stock following the distribution?
c. How would your answers to Parts a and b change if Sweets' distribution is instead $75,000?

11-51. Taxability of Distributions. Vogel Corporation is incorporated on January 15, 1991 by Curt who makes a $60,000 capital contribution. Vogel makes a timely S corporation election for 1991. During 1991 Vogel reports $60,000 of ordinary income, $40,000 of Sec. 1231 gain, $5,000 of tax-exempt interest income and $3,000 of charitable contributions. On December 1, 1991 Vogel distributes $5,000 cash and land contributed by Curt that is no longer needed in the business. The land which had a $10,000 basis and a $12,000 FMV when contributed to the corporation in January has an $18,000 FMV when distributed.
a. What income is reported by Vogel Corporation and Curt as a result of the distribution?
b. What is the basis for the Vogel stock following the distribution?
c. What are Vogel's earnings balances on December 31, 1991?

11-52. Taxability of Distributions. Stable Corporation is organized in 1980 by Hal, who has continued to own all of its stock. An S corporation election is made in 1984. At the beginning of 1991, Stable Corporation reports the following earnings accumulations:

Accumulated Adjustments Account	$60,000
Previously Taxed Income	25,000
Accumulated E&P	20,000

Hal's basis for his Stable stock on January 1, 1991, is $120,000. During 1991 Stable reports the following results from its operations:

Ordinary income	$30,000
Tax-exempt interest income	15,000
Long-term capital loss	20,000

Stable Corporation makes a $65,000 cash dividend to Hal on August 8, 1991.
a. What income, gain or loss is recognized as a result of the distribution?

b. What is the basis of the Stable stock on December 31, 1991?
c. What are Stable's earnings balances on December 31, 1991?
d. How would your answers to Parts a through c change if Stable instead distributes $115,000?

11-53. *Taxability of Distributions.* Tampa Corporation is organized in 1982, with Jeff and John each purchasing one-half of its initial stock offering. No change in the stock ownership occurs. An S corporation election is made in 1983. At the beginning of 1991, Tampa Corporation reports the following earnings accumulations:

Accumulated Adjustments Account	$100,000
Previously Taxed Income	40,000
Accumulated E&P	30,000

The bases for Jeff and John's stock investments on January 1, 1991, are $100,000 and $80,000, respectively. Tampa reports ordinary income of $30,000 during 1991. Tampa makes property distributions to Jeff and John on April 5, 1991. It distributes $100,000 in money to Jeff and land held as an investment having an FMV of $100,000 (and an adjusted basis of $70,000) to John.
a. What income is recognized by Tampa, Jeff, and John as a result of the distributions?
b. What are the bases of the Tampa stock for Jeff and John following the distributions?
c. What are Tampa's earnings balances on December 31, 1991?

11-54. *Utilization of Loss Pass-throughs by Shareholders.* Morning Corporation is being formed by Alice, a single taxpayer, in 1991. Alice is planning to purchase all of Morning's common stock for $100,000. Morning will obtain additional capital by borrowing $75,000 from a local bank. Morning will conduct a variety of service activities with little need to retain its capital in the business. Start-up losses of $90,000 are expected during Morning's first year of operation. Pretax operating profits of $250,000 (before reduction for Alice's salary) are expected to be earned each year starting in 1992. Alice expects to withdraw $100,000 of Morning's profits as a salary. Her other income consists primarily of dividends and interest and is expected to amount to $100,000 annually. What advice can you provide Alice about the advisability of making an S corporation election in the initial tax year? in a later tax year? How would your answers change if the Morning Corporation's expected annual income is instead $350,000? $500,000? (Hint: A comparison of the total tax liability for Alice and Morning Corporation as both an S and C corporation might be helpful.)

11-55. *Allocation of Income Between Family Members.* Bright Corporation, an electing S corporation, has been 100% owned by Betty since it was created in 1984. The corporation has been quite profitable in recent years, and in 1991 it reports ordinary income of $240,000 after paying Betty a $60,000 salary. On January 1, 1991, Betty gifts 15% of the Bright stock to each of her three sons, John, Andrew, and Stephen, in the hope that they will work in the family business. Gift taxes are paid on the transfers. The sons are ages 16, 9, and 2 at the present time and are not currently active in the business. Bright distributes $10,000 in cash to each son and $36,667 in cash to Betty in 1991.
a. What income is reported by Betty, John, Andrew, and Stephen for 1991 as a result of Bright's activities? How will the income be taxed to the children?
b. Assuming that the IRS determines a reasonable salary for Betty to be $120,000, how would your answer to Part a change?

TAX FORM/RETURN PREPARATION PROBLEM

11-56. Bottle-Up, Inc., was organized on January 8, 1983, and elected to be taxed as an S corporation on January 24, 1983. The necessary consents to the election were filed in a timely manner. Its federal tax identification number is 38-1507869. Their address is 1234 Hill Street, Gainesville, FL 32607. Bottle-Up, Inc., uses the calendar year as its year, the accrual method of accounting, and the first-in, first-out (FIFO) inventory method. Bottle-Up manufactures ornamental glass bottles. No changes to its inventory costing methods were made this year. The specific identification method is used for bad debts for book and tax purposes. Herman Hiebert (S/S No. 123-45-6789) and Melvin Jones (S/S No. 100-67-2000) own 500 shares each. Both individuals materially participate in Bottle-Up's single activity. Herman Hiebert is the tax matters person. Financial statements for Bottle-Up for the current year are shown in Tables

11-2 through 11-4. Prepare a current-year S corporation tax return for Bottle-Up, showing yourself as the paid preparer.

TABLE 11-2 BOTTLE-UP, INC., Income Statement, for the Year Ended December 31st of the Current Year (Problem 11-56)

Sales		$2,500,000
Returns and allowances		(15,000)
		$2,485,000
Beginning inventory	$ 102,000	
Purchases	900,000	
Labor	200,000	
Supplies	80,000	
Utilities	100,000	
Other manufacturing costs	188,000[a]	
	$1,570,000	
Ending inventory	(96,000)	1,474,000[b]
Gross profit		$1,011,000
Salaries[c]	$ 451,020	
Utilities expense	54,000	
Depreciation (MACRS and ACRS depreciation is $36,311)	11,782	
Automobile and truck expense	26,000	
Office supplies expense	9,602	
Advertising expense	105,000	
Bad debts expense	620	
Rent expense	30,000	
Interest expense[d]	1,500	
Meals and entertainment expense	21,000	
Selling expenses	100,000	
Repairs and maintenance expense	38,000	
Accounting and legal expense	4,500	
Charitable contributions[e]	9,000	
Insurance expense[f]	24,500	
Hourly employees' fringe benefits	11,000	
Payroll taxes	36,980	
Other taxes	2,500	
Penalties (fines for overweight trucks)	1,000	($ 938,004)
Operating profit		$ 72,996
Other income and losses:		
Long-term gain on sale of capital assets	$ 48,666	
Sec. 1231 loss	(1,100)	
Interest on U.S. Treasury bills	1,200	
Interest on state bonds	600	
Dividends from domestic corporations	11,600	
Investment expenses	(600)	60,366
Net income		$ 133,362

[a] $38,000 of book and tax depreciation is allocable to cost of sales. The accelerated depreciation preference on real estate placed in service before 1987 is $2,500. The depreciation adjustment on property placed in service after 1986 is $9,000.
[b] The cost of goods sold amount reflects the Uniform Capitalization Rules of Sec. 263A. The appropriate restatements have been made in prior years.
[c] Officer salaries of $120,000 are included in the total.
[d] Investment interest expense is $500. All other interest expense is trade-or business-related.
[e] All contributions were made in cash to qualifying charities.
[f] Includes $3,000 of premiums paid for policies on lives of corporate officers. Bottle-Up is the beneficiary for both policies.

TABLE 11-3 BOTTLE-UP, INC., Balance Sheet, for January 1st and December 31st of the Current Year (Problem 11-56)

	January 1	December 31
Assets:		
Cash	$ 15,000	$116,948
Accounts receivable	41,500	45,180
Inventories	102,000	96,000
Stocks	103,000	74,000
Treasury bills	15,000	16,000
Municipal bonds	10,000	10,000
Building and equipment	374,600	375,000
Minus: Accumulated depreciation	(160,484)	(173,100)
Land	160,000	190,000
Total	$660,616	$750,028
Liabilities and equities:		
Accounts payable	$ 36,000	$ 10,000
Accrued salaries payable	12,000	6,000
Payroll taxes payable	3,416	7,106
Sales taxes payable	5,200	6,560
Due to Mr. Hiebert	10,000	5,000
Mortgage and notes payable (current maturities)	44,000	52,000
Long-term debt	210,000	260,000
Capital stock	10,000	10,000
Retained earnings	330,000	393,362
Total	$660,616	$750,028

TABLE 11-4 BOTTLE-UP, INC., Statement of Change in Retained Earnings, for the Year Ended December 31st of the Current Year (Problem 11-56)

Balance, January 1st		$330,000[a]
Plus: Net income	$133,362	
Minus: Dividends	(70,000)	63,362
Balance, December 31st		$393,362

[a]The January 1 Accumulated Adjustments Account balance is $274,300.

CASE STUDY PROBLEM

11-57. Debra has operated a family counseling practice for a number of years as a sole proprietor. She owns the condominium office space that she occupies in addition to her professional library and office furniture. She has a limited amount of working capital and little need to accumulate additional business assets. Her total business assets are about $150,000 with an $80,000 mortgage on the office space being her only liability. Typically she has withdrawn any unneeded assets at the end of the year. Debra has used her personal car for business travel and charged the business for the mileage at the appropriate mileage rate provided by the IRS. Over the last three years Debra's practice has grown so that she now forecasts $80,000 of income being earned in 1991. Debra has contributed small amounts to an Individual Retirement Annuity each year, but has never reached the $2,000 annual limit. Although she has never been sued, Debra has recently become more concerned about legal liability. An attorney friend of hers has suggested that she incorporate her business in order to protect herself against being sued and to save taxes.

Required: Being a good friend of Debra's and a CPA, she asks your opinion on incorporating her business. You are to meet with Debra tomorrow for lunch. Prepare a draft of the points you feel should be discussed over lunch about incorporating the family counseling practice.

TAX RESEARCH PROBLEMS

11-58. Cato Corporation is incorporated on July 1, 1988, in California with Tim and Elesa, husband and wife, owning all of the Cato stock. On August 15, 1988, Cato Corporation makes an S corporation election effective for tax year 1988. Tim and Elesa file the necessary consents to the election. On March 10, 1991, Tim and Elesa transfer 15% of the Cato stock to the Reid and Susan Trust, an irrevocable trust created 3 years earlier for the benefit of their two minor children. In early 1992, Tim and Elesa's tax accountant learns about the transfer and advises the couple that the transfer of the stock to the trust may have terminated Cato's S corporation election. Is there any action that can be taken by Tim and Elesa that will permit Cato Corporation to retain its S corporation election?

A partial list of research sources is

- Secs. 1361(c)(2), 1362(d)(2), and 1362(f).
- Prop. Reg. Secs. 18.1361-1A(h) and 1.1362-5.
- Rev. Rul. 86-110, 1986-2 C.B. 151.

11-59. One of your wealthy clients, Cecil, invests $100,000 in the stock of an electing S corporation. The corporation, which is solely owned by Cecil, is in the process of developing a new food product. It is anticipated that the new business will need approximately $200,000 in capital (other than trade payables) during the first 2 years of its operations before it starts to earn sufficient profits to pay a return on the shareholder's investment. The first $100,000 of this total is to come from Cecil's contributed capital. The remaining $100,000 of funds will come from one of the following three sources:

1. Have the corporation borrow the $100,000 from a local bank. Cecil is required to act as a guarantor for the loan.
2. Have the corporation borrow $100,000 from the estate of Cecil's late husband. Cecil is the sole beneficiary of the estate.
3. Have Cecil lend $100,000 to the corporation from her personal funds.

Interest at a rate acceptable to the IRS is to be paid by the S corporation. During the first 2 years of operations, the corporation anticipates losing $125,000 before it begins to earn a profit. Evaluate the tax ramifications of each of the three financing alternatives.

A partial list of research sources is

- Sec. 1366(d)(1).
- *Edward M. Selfe* v. *U.S.*, 57 AFTR 2d 86-464, 86-1 USTC ¶ 9115 (11th Cir., 1985).
- *Milton T. Raynor,* 50 T.C. 762 (1968).
- *Ruth M. Prashker,* 59 T.C. 172 (1972).

11-60. Hi-Tech Corporation was incorporated in 1988 with Andy and Steve each contributing $250,000 in cash to acquire one-half of the Hi-Tech stock. A timely S corporation election was made by Hi-Tech Corporation for calendar year 1988. On January 1, 1991, Hi-Tech Corporation acquired all of the assets and liabilities of Software Corporation in a Type C tax-free reorganization. Software Corporation, an accrual method of accounting taxpayer, was liquidated as part of the reorganization. At the time of the acquisition, Software Corporation's assets had a $600,000 FMV and a $350,000 adjusted basis. Included as part of the assets was a parcel of land having a $70,000 FMV and a $20,000 adjusted basis that had been held by Software Corporation for seven years. Hi-Tech Corporation sold the land for cash on June 1, 1991. Hi-Tech Corporation collected all $90,000 of Software Corporation's accounts receivable at their face amount. In addition, Hi-Tech Corporation paid all $60,000 of Software Corporation's accounts payable which represented unpaid deductible expenses. Is Hi-Tech Corporation subject to the built-in gains tax for 1991? If so, which of the above transactions will result in a built-in gain being recognized?

A partial list of research sources is

- Sec. 1374.
- Announcement 86-128, I.R.B. 1986-51, 22.
- P.L. 100-647, Sec. 1006(f)(5)(A) [1988].

12 The Gift Tax

CHAPTER OUTLINE

LEARNING OBJECTIVES 12-2
CONCEPT OF TRANSFER TAXES 12-2
   History and Purpose of Transfer Taxes 12-2
THE UNIFIED TRANSFER TAX SYSTEM 12-3
   Unified Rate Schedule 12-3
   Impact of Taxable Gifts on Death Tax Base 12-4
   Unified Credit 12-4
GIFT TAX FORMULA 12-4
   Determination of Gifts 12-5
   Exclusions and Deductions 12-6
   Gift-Splitting Election 12-6
   Cumulative Nature of Gift Tax 12-6
   Unified Credit 12-7
TRANSFERS SUBJECT TO THE GIFT TAX 12-8
   Transfers for Inadequate Consideration 12-8
   Statutory Exemptions from the Gift Tax 12-9
   Cessation of Donor's Dominion and Control 12-11
   Valuation of Gifts 12-13
   Gift Tax Consequences of Certain Transfers 12-15
EXCLUSIONS 12-18
   Amount of the Exclusion 12-18
   Present Interest Requirement 12-19
GIFT TAX DEDUCTIONS 12-20
   Marital Deduction 12-21
   Charitable Contribution Deduction 12-24
THE GIFT-SPLITTING ELECTION 12-25
COMPUTATION OF THE GIFT TAX LIABILITY 12-26
   Effect of Previous Taxable Gifts 12-26
   Unified Credit Available 12-27
COMPREHENSIVE ILLUSTRATION 12-27
   Background Data 12-28
   Calculation of Tax Liability 12-28
BASIS CONSIDERATIONS FOR A LIFETIME GIVING PLAN 12-28
   Property Received by Gift 12-29
   Property Received at Death 12-30
CONTROVERSIAL ISSUES 12-30
   Below Market Loans: Gift and Income Tax Consequences 12-30
   De Minimis Rules 12-31
TAX PLANNING CONSIDERATIONS 12-32
   Tax-Saving Features of *Inter Vivos* Gifts 12-32
   Negative Aspects of Gifts 12-33
COMPLIANCE AND PROCEDURAL CONSIDERATIONS 12-34
   Filing Requirements 12-34
   Due Date 12-34
   Gift-Splitting Election 12-35
   Short-Form Gift Tax Return 12-35
   Liability for Tax 12-35
   Determination of Value 12-35
   Statute of Limitations 12-36
PROBLEM MATERIALS 12-37
   Discussion Questions 12-37
   Problems 12-39
   Tax Form/Return Preparation Problems 12-42
   Case Study Problem 12-42
   Tax Research Problems 12-43

LEARNING OBJECTIVES

After studying this chapter, you should be able to

1. Understand the concept of a unified transfer tax system
2. Explain the gift tax formula
3. Identify a number of transfers subject to the gift tax
4. Determine whether an annual gift tax exclusion is available
5. Identify deductions available for gift tax purposes
6. Apply the gift-splitting rules
7. Calculate the gift tax liability
8. Understand how basis affects the overall tax consequences
9. Recognize the filing requirements for gift tax returns

The **gift tax** is a wealth transfer tax that applies if the property transfer occurs during a person's lifetime. It is similar to the estate tax which applies to transfers associated with death. Both the gift tax and the estate tax are part of the unified transfer tax system under which gratuitous transfers of property between persons are subject to taxation. The vast majority of all property transfers are exempt from these transfer taxes as a result of the annual exclusion and the various deductions and credits. However, planning for reducing these transfer taxes is a significant matter for wealthy or moderately wealthy individuals.

This chapter discusses both the structure of the gift tax (including the exclusion, deduction, and credit provisions) and exactly which property transfers fall within its purview. The income tax basis rules (discussed in Chapter 5 of the *Prentice Hall's Federal Taxation: Individuals* volume) are reviewed in the context of their implications for choosing properties to transfer by gift instead of at death.

CONCEPT OF TRANSFER TAXES

OBJECTIVE 1
Understand the concept of a unified transfer tax system

Code Section 102 explicitly excludes gifts and inheritances from the recipient's gross income.[1] Thus, the recipient of a gift incurs no income tax liability. The donor, however, is primarily obligated to pay the gift tax, a type of excise tax. The gift tax applies to the act of transferring property to another person who pays either no consideration or consideration with a value lower than that of the property received. The gift tax is levied on the donor, that is, the person transferring the property.

Key Point
The person liable for the gift tax is the person who makes the gift—the DONOR.

History and Purpose of Transfer Taxes

The United States has had an estate tax since 1916 and a gift tax since 1932.[2] Over the years the structure of the gift and estate taxes has remained fairly constant. However, details, such as the amount of the exclusion and the rate schedules, have

---

[1] The income earned from property received as a gift or an inheritance, however, is not exempt from the income tax.
[2] A gift tax was also in existence from 1924 to 1926.

Key Point
Reasons for the gift tax are: (a) to raise revenues; (b) to prevent the avoidance of estate taxes; (c) to make up for the fact that income produced from gifted property is often taxed at a lower marginal income tax rate to the donee than to the donor, and; (d) to redistribute wealth.

changed numerous times. Very significant changes were made by the Tax Reform Act of 1976 (the 1976 Act), which adopted a unified rate schedule for gift and estate tax purposes. The Economic Recovery Tax Act of 1981 (the 1981 Act) increased the amount of the exclusion and removed the ceiling on the amount deductible for gifts or bequests to one's spouse.

There are several purposes for the gift tax, one of the most important of which is to raise revenue. However, because of the fairly generous exclusion and credit legislated by Congress, the gift tax yields only a small fraction of the federal government's total revenues. Only those donors making relatively large gifts owe any gift taxes. Another purpose of the gift tax is to serve as a backstop to the estate tax and to prevent individuals from avoiding a significant amount of—if not all—estate taxes by disposing of property prior to death. For example. without the gift tax, persons knowing they are terminally ill could dispose of their property "on their death bed" and escape the transfer tax. In addition, the gift tax increases the government's revenues to make up for some of the income tax revenue that is lost because income produced by the gifted property sometimes is taxed to a person in a lower tax bracket. Another purpose for levying gift and estate taxes is the redistribution of wealth.

There is no way to know what the distribution of wealth would have been if Congress had not enacted transfer taxes. One research study, however, estimates that more than 41% of this nation's net wealth is concentrated in the hands of the top 1% of the population.[3] Such concentration has remained relatively constant since the 1950s.

THE UNIFIED TRANSFER TAX SYSTEM

The 1976 Act greatly revamped the transfer tax system by combining the separate estate and gift tax systems into one unified transfer tax system. While Chapters 12 and 13 use the terminology *gift tax* and *estate tax,* these taxes are actually components of the same unified transfer tax system. The system also includes the generation-skipping transfer tax, a topic discussed in Chapter 13. The unification of the transfer tax system removes the previous law's bias toward favorable tax treatment of lifetime gifts in comparison with transfers at death. The three most significant elements of the unified system—the unified rate schedule, the inclusion of taxable gifts in the death tax base, and the unified credit—are discussed below.

Key Point
The purpose of the 5% surtax is to phase-out the benefits of both the progressive rate structure and the unified credit (to be discussed later in this chapter).

Unified Rate Schedule

Before the 1976 Act mandated a **unified rate schedule** applicable to both lifetime transfers and transfers at death, the gift tax rates were only 75% of the estate tax rates on a transfer of the same size. The unified rate schedule is effective for gifts made after 1976 and deaths occurring after 1976. The rates are progressive. For gifts and deaths through 1992, the rate schedule goes as high as 55%; after 1992 the rate schedule reaches a peak of 50%. Beginning with transfers made after 1987, the transfer tax rate schedule contains a phase-out provision. For large estates, the benefit

---

[3] U.S. Congress, Joint Economic Committee, *The Concentration of Wealth in the United States* (Washington, D.C.: U.S. Government Printing Office, July 1986), p. 24. The following assets were not included in the estimates of net wealth: pension benefits, automobiles, and household durables.

Self-Study Question

Use the rate schedule in Code Sec. 2001 to determine the amount of gift tax (before credits) on 1991 taxable gifts of: (a) $4,000,000. The tax is: On the first $3,000,000—$1,290,800; Plus 55% of the $1,000,000 excess—$550,000; Gross tax equals $1,840,800. (b) $30,000,000. The tax is: On the first $3,000,000—$1,290,800; Plus 55% of $27,000,000—$14,850,000; Plus 5% of excess over $10,000,000 but not in excess of $21,040,000, $11,040,000—$552,000; Gross tax equals $16,692,800.

of the rates below 55% (50% after 1992) is phased out, as is the benefit of the unified credit. The phase-out is accomplished by imposing an additional 5% tax on tax bases in excess of $10,000,000 but not in excess of $21,040,000 ($18,340,000 after 1992). Thus, if in 1991 a donor makes a taxable gift of $30,000,000, such gift will, in effect, be taxed at a 55% flat rate even if this is the first gift the donor makes.

Impact of Taxable Gifts on Death Tax Base

Prior to 1977, lifetime gifts were viewed separately from dispositions at death. By making gifts, an individual could shift the taxation of properties from the top of the estate tax rate schedule to the bottom of the gift tax rate schedule. Few taxpayers could take advantage of this shifting, however, because only persons with a relatively large amount of property could afford to part with sizable amounts of their assets while alive.

Under today's unified system, taxable gifts affect the size of the tax base at death. Any taxable gifts (other than gifts included in the gross estate) made after 1976 are called **adjusted taxable gifts,** and such gifts are included in the donor's death tax base. They are valued at their fair market value (FMV) on the date of the gift. The addition of such taxable gifts to the tax base at death can result in the donor-decedent's estate being taxed at a higher marginal tax rate. However, such gifts are not taxed for a second time upon the donor's death because gift taxes (computed at current rates) on these gifts are subtracted in determining the estate tax liability.

Example 12-1 ■

Key Point

At the taxpayer's death, the unified tax is computed on the sum of: (1) the taxable estate, plus (2) the adjusted taxable gifts. The tax on this sum is reduced by the tax that would have been payable (at current rates) on the adjusted taxable gifts made after December 31, 1976.

In 1982, Dan makes taxable gifts totaling $500,000. When Dan dies in the current year, the value of the gifted property has tripled. Dan's death tax base includes the $500,000 of post-1976 taxable gifts. They are valued for estate tax purposes at their fair market value on the date of the gift; the post-gift appreciation escapes the transfer tax system. Thus, the transfer tax value is fixed or "frozen" at the date-of-gift value. ■

Note that unification (including taxable gifts that become part of the tax base at death) extends only to gifts made after 1976. Congress exempts gifts made prior to 1977 from unification because it did not want to retroactively change the two separate transfer tax systems that previously existed.

Unified Credit

The **unified credit** reduces dollar for dollar a certain amount of the tax computed on the taxable gifts or the taxable estate. The amount of the credit varies, depending upon the year of the transfer. With respect to the gift and estate tax formulas, the full credit is available for lifetime transfers and again in determining the tax payable at death. In concept, however, an individual's estate does not receive the benefit of this unified credit amount at death to the extent the credit has already been used against lifetime transfers (as explained in Chapter 13). The gift tax formula, including the unified credit, is discussed below.

GIFT TAX FORMULA

The formula described in this section is used to calculate a donor's gift tax liability for the year of the transfer. As with income taxes, gift tax reporting is done on an annual

OBJECTIVE 2
Explain the gift tax formula

Key Point
The gift tax applies to cumulative lifetime gifts made since the enactment of the gift tax in 1932. The unified gift and estate tax, enacted in 1976, applies only to cumulative lifetime gifts made after 1976. This means that a taxable gift of $75,000 made in 1970 would not be included in the unified tax base of a decedent whose death occurred in 1991.

basis. Figure 12-1 illustrates the formula for determining the donor's annual gift tax liability. This formula is discussed in detail later in the chapter.

Determination of Gifts

The starting point in the process is to determine which, if any, of the taxpayer's transfers constitute gifts. The next section discusses the various types of transfers that the statute views as gifts. All gifts are valued at their FMVs on the date of the gift. Next, the aggregate amount of gifts for the period is determined. The aggregate gifts are then reduced by any exclusions and deductions. Finally, the tax is computed according to the formula illustrated in Figure 12-1.

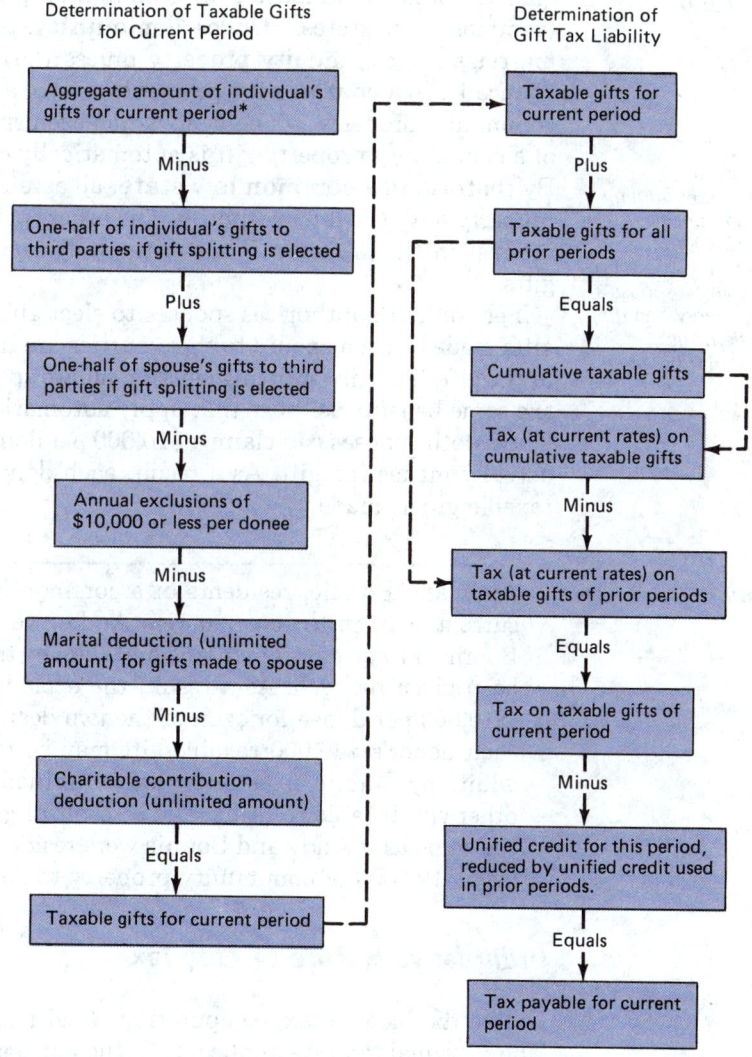

*Valued at fair market value on date of gift.

FIGURE 12-1 The Gift Tax Formula

Exclusions and Deductions

The maximum amount that is excludible annually is $10,000 per donee.[4] If the gifts made to a donee do not equal at least $10,000, the amount excludible is limited to the amount of the gift made to such donee. Exclusions may be claimed for transfers to an unlimited number of donees.

Two types of deductions are available for reducing the amount of the taxable gifts. Most transfers to one's spouse generate a marital deduction; there is no ceiling on the amount of this deduction. Similarly, most transfers to charitable organizations are canceled out by the charitable contribution deduction.

Gift-Splitting Election

Congress authorized gift-splitting provisions to achieve more comparable tax consequences between taxpayers of community property and noncommunity property (common law) states.[5] Under **community property law,** assets acquired after marriage are community property unless they are acquired by gift or inheritance. Typically, in a **community property state,** a large portion of the spouses' assets is community property, property in which each spouse has a one-half interest. One-half of a community property gift is automatically considered to be given by each spouse. By contrast, in a **common law state,** all assets acquired during the marriage are the property of the acquiring spouse. The other spouse does not automatically acquire an interest in the property. Thus, often only one spouse owns enough assets to make gifts.

Section 2513 authorizes spouses to elect gift splitting. As a result of this election, gifts made by each spouse to third parties are treated as if each spouse made one-half of the gift. The gift-splitting election allows spouses in common law states to achieve the same benefits as those that apply automatically for gifts of community property. Thus, both spouses can claim a $10,000 per donee exclusion although only one spouse actually makes the gift. As a result, each donee may receive up to $20,000 before a taxable gift is made.

Key Point
The gift tax return is due annually on April 15 for both fiscal-year and calendar-year taxpayers.

Typical Misconception
Individuals often think they can only make up to $10,000 in gifts each year that would not be subject to the gift tax. Actually, the $10,000 exclusion applies to each donee per year; therefore, the total amount of tax-free gifts in a given year can be much greater than $10,000.

Key Point
Some advantages of gift-splitting are: (a) doubling the excluded amount per donee (up to $20,000); (b) using a spouse's lower gift tax rate, and; (c) using a spouse's unified credit, even when the spouse has little or no property that could be gifted.

Example 12-2 ■ Andy and Bonnie, residents of a common law state, are married throughout the current year. In the current year Andy gives his brother $100,000 cash. Andy and Bonnie may elect gift splitting and thereby treat the $100,000 gift as if $50,000 had been given by each. As a result, the excludible portion of the gift totals $20,000 ($10,000 per donee for each of the two deemed donors). By electing gift splitting, each donor's $40,000 taxable gift may be taxed at a lower marginal tax rate. In addition, Bonnie is able to use a unified credit amount that she might not otherwise be able to utilize. As a result of gift splitting, the tax consequences are the same as if Andy and Bonnie were residents of a community property state and gave $100,000 of community property to Andy's brother. ■

Cumulative Nature of Gift Tax

Unlike the income tax, computations of gift tax liabilities are cumulative in nature. The marginal tax rate applicable to the current period's taxable gifts is a function of

---

[4] Sec. 2503(b).
[5] The eight traditional community property states are Louisiana, Texas, New Mexico, Arizona, California, Washington, Idaho, and Nevada. Wisconsin has adopted a new state marital property law that is basically the same as community property.

both the taxable gifts for the current period and the aggregate taxable gifts for all earlier periods.

Example 12-3 ■ Sandy and Jack each make taxable gifts in the current year totaling $200,000. However, for previous periods Sandy's taxable gifts total $100,000, while Jack's total $1,500,000. Because Jack's cumulative total taxable gifts are larger than Sandy's, Jack's current year gifts are taxed at a higher marginal tax rate. ■

Self-Study Question

Al and Beth, husband and wife, live in a common law state. In 1991 Al makes a gift of $620,000 to each of two children by a previous spouse. Al and Beth agree to split the gift. Neither Al nor Beth has made taxable gifts in any prior year. What are Al's and Beth's taxable gifts in 1991?

Answer

One-half of each gift, a total of $620,000, is reported on each taxpayer's gift tax return. Neither Al nor Beth has any gift tax liability for 1991 due to the annual exemptions and the unified credit. Al has effectively used Beth's unified credit without Beth ever having ownership or control over Al's property.

Unified Credit

Prior to 1977, the Code allowed a $30,000 specific exemption. Donors could deduct this exemption whenever they desired. Typically, donors claimed it as early as they needed to in order to reduce the amount of gifts that would otherwise be taxable. The 1976 Act repealed this exemption and replaced it with the unified credit.[6] Consequently, the gift tax computed for gifts made in 1977 and later years is reduced dollar for dollar by the unified credit. The unified credit has the effect of allowing donors to make a certain amount of taxable gifts (known as the **exemption equivalent**) without incurring a gift tax liability. The maximum amount of the credit increased progressively as follows:

Year of Gift	Amount of Credit	Exemption Equivalent
January through June, 1977	$ 6,000	$ 30,000
July through December, 1977	30,000	120,666
1978	34,000	134,000
1979	38,000	147,333
1980	42,500	161,563
1981	47,000	175,625
1982	62,800	225,000
1983	79,300	275,000
1984	96,300	325,000
1985	121,800	400,000
1986	155,800	500,000
1987 and later years	192,800	600,000

The amount creditable for a particular year is the excess of (1) the credit amount for that year over (2) the credit that could have been claimed for the taxable gifts made by the individual in earlier years. Recall that no credit is allowed for gifts made before 1977.

Example 12-4 ■ Gina makes her first taxable gift,[7] $200,000 in amount, in 1978. Gina used the $34,000 unified credit available for 1978 to reduce her $54,800 gift tax liability. Gina's next taxable gift is made in 1984. The taxable amount is $500,000. Gina's 1984 gift tax liability of $175,000 ($229,800 − $54,800) was reduced by a unified credit of $62,300 ($96,300 − $34,000). If she makes taxable gifts in either 1991 or 1992, the maximum credit she can claim against her current tax is $96,500 ($192,800 − $96,300). ■

---

[6] Sec. 2505.
[7] No credit is used for a gift that is completely nontaxable.

Key Point
The gift tax on a $30 million gift made in 1991 is $16,500,000, net of the $192,800 unified credit. This $16,500,000 is a flat 55% of the $30 million gift. At this level, all gifts made by the taxpayer have been taxed at 55%, and the taxpayer has not been given the advantage of either the progressive rate structure or the unified credit.

As mentioned earlier, the benefit of the unified credit is phased out for taxable amounts between $10,000,000 and $21,040,000 ($18,340,000 after 1992) by the imposition of an additional 5% tax.

After the passage of the 1976 Act, prospective donors quickly realized the advantages of making gifts in 1976 to avoid the unification provisions. Some prospective donors had made such small gifts in the past that they had used none or only part of their specific exemption. Congress adopted a special rule that affects donors who used any portion of their specific exemption between September 9, 1976 and December 31, 1976.[8] The amount of unified credit otherwise available to such donors is reduced by 20% of the amount of the specific exemption they claimed between September 9 and December 31, 1976. The maximum reduction in the unified credit as a result of this provision is $6,000 (0.20 × $30,000).

Example 12-5 ■ In November 1976 Maria makes a large taxable gift, her first gift. Maria uses her $30,000 specific exemption to reduce the taxable gift amount. As a result, the unified credit that Maria could otherwise claim after 1976 is reduced by $6,000 (0.20 × $30,000). Moreover, her 1976 taxable gifts are not includible in her death tax base. ■

TRANSFERS SUBJECT TO THE GIFT TAX

OBJECTIVE 3
Identify a number of transfers subject to the gift tax

In general, property transferred for less than adequate consideration in money or money's worth is deemed to be a gift within the gift tax context. The gift occurs when the donor gives up all control over the transferred property. Congress has legislated several provisions that exempt various property transfers that might otherwise be viewed as gifts from the scope of the gift tax. These exemptions include direct payments of medical expenses and tuition, transfers to political organizations, property settlements in conjunction with a divorce, and qualified disclaimers.

Transfers for Inadequate Consideration

Self-Study Question
Consider two points: (a) The gift tax is a tax on cumulative lifetime gifts, and (b) The unified credit is reduced by 20% of the pre-1977 specific exemption used on gifts made between September 9 and December 31, 1976. What implications do these two points have for record keeping?

Answer
Taxpayers must keep track of all gifts previously made, since amounts for previous gifts are part of the calculation for current gift tax due.

In addition, taxpayers must keep a record of how much of the specific exemption they used between September 9 and December 31, 1976, in order to determine how much of the unified credit is available to them.

As mentioned earlier, the initial step in determining the donor's gift tax liability is deciding which transfers constitute gifts for gift tax purposes. Section 2501(a) states that a gift tax is imposed on "the transfer of property by gift." Thus, if *property* is transferred *by gift,* the transferor potentially incurs a gift tax liability. Perhaps surprisingly, the Code does not define the term *gift.* Section 2511(a) expands on Sec. 2501(a) by indicating that the tax is applicable "whether the transfer is in trust or otherwise, whether the gift is direct or indirect, and whether the property is real or personal, tangible or intangible."

A transaction is subject to the gift tax even though not entirely gratuitous if "the value of the property transferred by the donor exceeds the value in money or money's worth of the consideration given therefor."[9] In such circumstances the amount of the gift is the difference between the value of the property the donor gives up and the value of the consideration in money or money's worth received. The following

---
[8] Sec. 2505(c).
[9] Reg. Sec. 25.2512-8.

Key Point
The amount of the gift made is the FMV of property gifted reduced by the FMV of any consideration received by the donor.

discussion examines in more depth the scope of the rule regarding transfers for less than adequate consideration.

Bargain Sales. Often an individual wants to sell an asset to a family member, but the prospective buyer cannot afford to pay the full FMV of the property. If the buyer pays consideration of less than the FMV of the transferred property, the seller makes a gift to the buyer. The amount of the gift is the bargain element of the transaction; that is, the excess of the property's FMV over its sales price.

Example 12-6 ■   Martha sells her ranch, having a $1,000,000 FMV, to her son Stan. Stan can afford to pay only $300,000 of consideration. In the year of the sale, Martha makes a gift to Stan of $700,000—the excess of the ranch's FMV over the consideration received.   ■

Transfers in Normal Course of Business. There is an exception to the general rule that a transfer for inadequate consideration triggers a gift. According to the Regulations, a transaction arising "in the ordinary course of business (a transaction which is bona fide, at arm's length, and free from any donative intent)" is considered to have been made for adequate consideration.[10] Thus, no gift arises when a buyer acquires property for less than its FMV if the acquisition is in the ordinary course of business.

Example 12-7 ■   John, a merchant, has a clearance sale and sells a diamond bracelet valued at $30,000 to Bess. Bess pays $12,000, the "clearance price." Because the clearance sale arose in the ordinary course of John's business, the bargain element ($18,000) does not constitute a gift to Bess.   ■

Self-Study Question
Ben's adult son Clarence, who is not Ben's dependent, is in need of a liver transplant. Since Clarence does not have the financial ability to pay the cost of the surgical procedure, Ben pays the $100,000 medical fee directly to the hospital. Is the payment for Clarence's benefit a taxable gift?

Answer
The payment is not a taxable gift because of Sec. 2503(e).

Statutory Exemptions from the Gift Tax

For various reasons, including simplifying the administration of the gift tax, Congress has enacted several provisions that exempt certain transactions from the purview of the gift tax. In the absence of these statutory rules, some of these transactions could constitute gifts.

Payment of Medical Expenses or Tuition. Section 2503(e) states that a "qualified transfer" is not treated as a transfer of property by gift. The term *qualified transfer* is defined as an amount paid on behalf of an individual to (1) an educational organization for tuition or (2) any person who provides medical care as payment for such medical care. Such payments are exempt from gift treatment only if made *directly* to the educational organization or to the person providing the medical care. *Educational organization* has the same definition as for charitable contribution purposes,[11] and *medical care* has the same definition as for medical expense deduction purposes.[12] Note that only tuition—and not room, board, and books—is addressed by this rule. Note also that the identity of the person whose expenses are paid is not important. The special exemption applies even if the payments are made on behalf of an individual who is not a relative.

---

[10] Ibid.
[11] Section 170(b)(1)(A)(ii) defines educational organization in the context of the charitable contribution deduction.
[12] Section 213(d) defines medical care in the context of the medical expense deduction.

If one makes payments on behalf of another and the expenditures constitute support which the payor must furnish under state law, such payments are support and not gifts. State law determines the definition of support. Generally, payments of medical expenses for one's minor child would be categorized as support and not a gift, even in the absence of Sec. 2503(e). On the other hand, state law does not generally require parents to pay medical expenses or tuition for an adult child. Thus, the enactment of Sec. 2503(e) removed such payments from the gift tax.

According to the Staff of the Joint Committee on Taxation, special rules concerning tuition and medical expense payments were enacted because

> Congress was concerned that certain payments of tuition made on behalf of children who have attained their majority, and of special medical expenses on behalf of elderly relatives, technically could be considered gifts under prior law. The Congress believed such payments should be exempt from gift taxes.[13]

Example 12-8 ■ Gary pays $9,000 for his adult grandson's tuition at medical school and $11,000 for the grandson's room and board in the medical school's dormitory. All payments are made directly to the educational organization. The direct payment of the tuition to the medical school is exempted by Sec. 2503(e) from being treated as a gift. Gary is not required under state law to pay for room and board for an adult grandson. Thus, such payments are not support. Gary has made an $11,000 gift to the grandson. ■

Example 12-9 ■ Assume the same facts as in Example 12-8, except that Gary pays the money to his grandson, who in turn pays the money to the medical school. The amount of Gary's gift is $20,000. Because Gary does not pay the tuition directly to the school, Gary does not meet all of the conditions for exempting the tuition payments from gift tax treatment. ■

Transfers to Political Organizations. Congress adopted a provision specifically exempting transfers to a political organization from being deemed to be a transfer of property by gift.[14] In the absence of this special rule, these transfers would generally be subjected to gift tax treatment.

Example 12-10 ■ Ann transfers $2,000 to a political organization founded to promote the campaign of Thomas for governor. Ann's $2,000 transfer does not fall within the statutory definition of a gift. ■

Key Point
Property transfers as a result of a divorce agreement are generally not considered to be gifts.

Property Settlements in Conjunction with Divorce. Congress enacted special rules addressing property transfers in the context of a divorce in order to reduce litigation. Earlier, the courts were often called upon to resolve the issue of whether the transferee gave up consideration in money or money's worth in exchange for receiving property as part of a divorce settlement. Section 2516 specifies circumstances in which property settlements in connection with a divorce are automatically exempted from being treated as gifts. Thus, for qualifying transfers it is not necessary to deliberate whether the transferee furnished consideration in money or money's worth.

For Sec. 2516 to be applicable, the spouses must adopt a written agreement concerning their marital and property rights and the divorce must occur during a 3-year period beginning 1 year before the agreement is made. No gift arises from any

---

[13] U.S., Congress, Staff of the Joint Committee on Taxation, *General Explanation of the Economic Recovery Tax Act of 1981* (Washington, D.C.: U.S. Government Printing Office, 1981), p. 273.
[14] Sec. 2501(a)(5).

transfer made in accordance with such agreement if property is transferred (1) to either spouse in settlement of marital or property rights or (2) to provide reasonable support for the children while they are minors.

Example 12-11 ■

Self-Study Question

Harry dies, willing his entire estate equally to his three children. Angela, one of the children, has accumulated a substantial estate herself due to a successful writing career and wishes to have her share of Harry's estate go to her "poorer" siblings. Can Angela's share go to one of her siblings without Angela's making a taxable gift?

Answer

By making a qualified disclaimer under Code Sec. 2518, Angela can refuse to accept the property, and the property will pass under another clause of the will or under state law to someone else, perhaps a sibling. Angela will not be considered as having made a taxable gift.

In June 1990, Hal and Wanda sign a property agreement whereby Hal is to transfer $750,000 to Wanda in settlement of her property rights. Hal makes the transfer in May 1991. Hal and Wanda receive a divorce decree in July 1991. Hal is not deemed to have made a gift to Wanda by making the transfer. ■

Qualified Disclaimers. Sometimes a person who is named to receive property under a decedent's will prefers not to receive such property and would like to disclaim (not accept) it. Typically, the person is quite ill, elderly, or is very wealthy. State disclaimer statutes allow individuals to say "no thank you" to the property willed to them. State law also addresses how to determine who will receive the property after the original beneficiary declines to accept it.

Section 2518(a) states that persons making a qualified disclaimer are to be treated as if the disclaimed property was never transferred to them. Thus, the person making the disclaimer is not deemed to have made a gift to the person who receives the asset as a result of the disclaimer.

A **qualified disclaimer** is defined as meeting the following four tests:

1. It is an irrevocable, unqualified, written refusal to accept property.
2. The transferor or his legal representative receives the refusal no later than 9 months after the later of (a) the day the transfer is made or (b) the day the person named to receive the property becomes age 21.
3. The person disclaiming has not accepted the property interest or any of its benefits.
4. As a result of the disclaimer, the property passes to (a) the decedent's spouse or (b) a person other than the one disclaiming it. In addition, the person disclaiming the property cannot direct who is to receive the property.[15]

Example 12-12 ■

Doug dies on February 1, 1991, and wills 500 acres of land to Joan. If Joan disclaims the property in a manner that meets all of the tests for a qualified disclaimer, Joan will not be treated as making a gift to the person who receives the property as a result of his disclaimer. ■

Example 12-13 ■

Assume the same facts as in Example 12-12, except that Joan instead disclaims the property on January 2, 1992. Joan's action arose too late to meet the second qualified disclaimer test above. Joan makes a gift to the person who receives the property as a result of his disclaimer. ■

Cessation of Donor's Dominion and Control

A gift does not occur until a transfer becomes complete. The gift is valued as of the date the transfer becomes complete. Thus, the time when a transfer becomes complete is important in two contexts—determination of whether a gift has arisen and, if so, the amount of its value. According to the Regulations, a gift becomes complete—and is thus deemed made and valued—when the donor "has so parted with dominion and control as to leave in him no power to change its disposition, whether for his own benefit or for the benefit of another."[16] A gift is not necessarily complete just because

---

[15] Sec. 2518(b).
[16] Reg. Sec. 25.2511-2(b).

the transferor is not entitled to any further personal benefits from the property. If the transferor still has influence over the benefits others may receive from the transferred property, the transfer is incomplete with respect to the portion of the property over which control has been retained.

Revocable Trusts. A transferor who conveys property to a revocable trust has made an incomplete transfer. The creator of a revocable trust can change the trust provisions, including the identity of the beneficiaries. Moreover, the creator may demand the return of the trust property. Because the transferor does not give up any control over property conveyed to a revocable trust, the individual does not make a gift when funding the trust. Once trust income is distributed by the trustee to a beneficiary, however, the creator of the trust loses control over the distributed funds. The creator then makes a completed gift of the distributed income amounts.

Example 12-14 ■ On May 1, 1991, Ted transfers $500,000 to a revocable trust with First National Bank as trustee. The trustee must pay out all the income to Ed during Ed's lifetime. At Ed's death, the property is to be paid over to Ed, Jr. On December 31, 1991, the trustee distributes $35,000 of income to Ed. The May 1 transfer is incomplete; thus, no gift arises upon the funding of the trust. A $35,000 gift to Ed occurs on December 31, 1991, because Ted no longer has control over the distributed income. ■

Example 12-15 ■ Assume the same facts as in Example 12-14, except that Ted amends the trust instrument on July 7, 1992, to make the trust irrevocable. By this date, the trust property has appreciated to $612,000. Ted makes a completed gift of $612,000 on July 7, 1992. ■

Key Point

If the donor of property retains control over any portion of such property, then no gift is considered to have been made with respect to that portion of the property which the donor still controls.

Other Retained Powers. Even transfers to an irrevocable trust can be deemed incomplete with respect to the portion of the trust over which the creator kept control. The Regulations state that if "the donor reserves any power over its [the property's] disposition, the gift may be wholly incomplete, or may be partially complete and partially incomplete, depending upon all the facts in the particular case."[17] They add that one must examine the terms of the power to determine the scope of the donor's retention of control. The Regulations elaborate by indicating that "[a] gift is . . . incomplete if and to the extent that a reserved power gives the donor the power to name new beneficiaries or to change the interests of the beneficiaries."[18]

Example 12-16 ■ On May 3, 1991, Art transfers $300,000 of property in trust with First National Bank as trustee. Art names Bob and/or Sue to receive the trust income for 15 years and Karl to receive the trust property at the end of 15 years. Art reserves the power to determine how the income is to be divided between Bob and Sue each year. Because Art reserves the power over payment of the income for the 15-year period, this portion of the transfer is incomplete on May 3. The valuation of the completed gift to Karl is determined from actuarial tables discussed in the next section of the chapter. ■

Example 12-17 ■ Assume the same facts as in Example 12-16, except that on December 31, 1991, Art instructs the trustee to distribute the trust's $30,000 of income as follows: $18,000 to Bob and $12,000 to Sue. Once the income is paid out, Art loses control over it.

[17] Ibid.
[18] Reg. Sec. 25.2511-2(c).

Thus, on December 31, Art makes an $18,000 gift to Bob and a $12,000 gift to Sue. ∎

Example 12-18 ■ Assume the same facts as in Example 12-16, except that on May 3, 1992, when the trust assets are valued at $360,000, Art relinquishes his powers over payment of income and gives this power to the trustee. Art's transfer of the income interest (with a remaining term of 14 years) becomes complete on May 3, 1992. The valuation of the gift of a 14-year income interest is determined from actuarial tables. ∎

A summary of various complete, incomplete, and partially complete transfers can be found in Topic Review 12-1.

Valuation of Gifts

General Rules. All gifts are valued at their FMV as of the date of the gift (i.e., the date the transfer becomes complete). The Regulations state that a property's value is "the price at which such property would change hands between a willing buyer and a willing seller, neither being under any compulsion to buy or to sell, and both having reasonable knowledge of relevant facts."[19] According to the Regulations, stocks and bonds traded on a stock exchange or over the counter are valued at the mean of the highest and lowest selling price on the date of the gift.[20] In general, the guidelines for valuing properties are the same, regardless of whether the property is conveyed during life or at death. However, valuation of life insurance policies depends upon when the transfer occurs—during life or at death. This topic is discussed in a later section of this chapter, as well as in Chapter 13's coverage of the estate tax.

Life Estates and Remainder Interests. Often one may transfer less than his entire interest in a property. For example, an individual may transfer property in trust and reserve the right to the trust's income for life. Another individual will be named to receive the property upon the transferor's death. In such a situation, the transferor is said to have retained a **life estate** and given a **remainder interest.** Only the remainder interest is subject to the gift tax unless the gift is to a family member, as

TOPIC REVIEW 12-1

Examples of Complete and Incomplete Transfers

Complete Transfers—Subject to Gift Tax:
   Property transferred outright to donee
   Property transferred in trust with donor retaining
     no powers over the trust
Incomplete Transfers—Not Subject to Gift Tax:
   Property transferred to a revocable trust
   Property transferred to an irrevocable trust for which
     the donor has discretionary powers over income and
     the remainder interest
Partially Complete Transfers—Only a Portion Subject to Gift Tax:
   Property transferred to an irrevocable trust for which the
     donor has discretionary powers over income but not
     the remainder interest[a]

[a]The gift of the remainder interest constitutes a completed transfer.

[19] Reg. Sec. 25.2512-1.
[20] Reg. Sec. 25.2512-2.

discussed in the estate freeze section below. If the transferor keeps an annuity (a fixed amount) for life and names another person to the receive the remainder at the transferor's death, the gift is of just the remainder.

A grantor may also transfer property in trust with the promise that (1) another person is to receive the income for a certain number of years and (2) at the end of that time period the property will revert to the grantor. In this case, the donor retains a reversionary interest while the other party receives a term certain interest.[21] Only the term certain interest is subject to the gift tax. Trusts whereby the grantor retains a reversionary interest have disadvantageous income tax consequences to the grantor if they are created after March 1, 1986. Chapter 14 discusses the income tax treatment of such trusts.

Life estates, annuity interests, remainders, and term certain interests are valued from actuarial tables. These tables must be used regardless of the actual earnings rate of the transferred assets. The tables appear in Appendix E. Table R(1) is used for valuing life estates and remainders and Table B for term certain interests. Code Sec. 7520 calls for the actuarial tables to be revised every month. These tables incorporate an interest rate, rounded to the nearest 0.2%, that is 120% of the Federal midterm rate applicable for the month of the transfer.[22] In addition, the tables were revised to take into account the most recent mortality experience. Additional revisions to reflect mortality experience are to be made at least once every 10 years. Use of the actuarial tables is illustrated with the following examples.

Example 12-19 ■   On May 3, 1991, Amy transfers $300,000 of property in trust with First National Bank as trustee, Amy names Joe and/or Lou to receive the trust income for 15 years but reserves the power to determine how the income is to be divided between Joe and Lou each year. Amy specifies that Ray is to receive the trust property at the end of the fifteenth year. Only the gift of the remainder interest is a completed transfer because Amy reserves the right to determine how the income is to be divided. The gift is valued from Table B. If the interest rate is 10%, the amount of the gift is $71,818 (0.239392 × $300,000). ■

Example 12-20 ■   Assume the same facts as in Example 12-19, except that on May 3, 1994, when the trust assets are valued at $360,000, Amy transfers her power over the payment of trust income to the trustee. The income interest has a remaining term of 12 years. The gift of the 12-year income interest is valued from Table B by subtracting the factor for a remainder interest (0.318631 if the interest rate is 10%) from 1.0. Thus, the amount of the gift is $245,293 (0.681369 × $360,000). ■

Example 12-21 ■   On July 5, 1991, Don transfers $100,000 of property in trust and names Larry (age 60) to receive all of the income for the rest of Larry's life and Ruth (age 25) to receive the trust assets upon Larry's death. Don names a bank as the trustee. The amount of each donee's gift is determined from Table R(1). If the interest rate is 10% and Larry is age 60, the value of the gift to Ruth, as calculated from the single life remainder factors column of Table R(1), is $22,674 (0.22674 × $100,000). The remaining portion of the $100,000 that was transferred, $77,326 ($100,000 − $22,674), is the value of the life estate transferred to Larry. ■

---

[21] **Term certain interest** means that a particular person has an interest in the property held in trust for a specified period of time. The person having such interest does not own or hold title to the property, but has a right to receive the income from such property for a specified period of time. At the end of the period of time, the property reverts to the grantor.

[22] The applicable rate for determining the present value of an annuity, an interest for life or a term of years, or a remainder or reversionary interest for March 1991 is 9.4% (Rev. Rul. 91-15, I.R.B. 1991-9, 6).

Key Point

In estate freeze transfers, Congress has shifted its emphasis from including the FMV of the transferred stock in the donor's (decedent's) estate to enacting new valuation rules that will generally increase the amount which is a taxable gift at the time of the actual transfer.

Special Valuation Rules—Estate Freezes. In recent years Congress became concerned that individuals were able to shift wealth to other individuals, usually in a younger generation, without paying their "fair share" of transfer taxes. An approach they commonly used was to recapitalize a corporation (by exchanging common stock for both common and preferred shares) and then to give the common stock to individuals in the younger generation. This technique was one of a variety of transactions known as "estate freezes." In 1987 Congress first changed the tax treatment for estate freezes by providing that generally the transferor's gross estate would include both the preferred shares owned at death and the common shares gifted earlier.

In 1990 Congress repealed retroactively the provisions it had enacted in 1987 and decided to address the "problem" of estate freezes by writing new valuation rules that apply at the time a gift occurs. The thrust of these rules—new Chapter 14 (Sections 2701 through 2704) of the Code—is to ensure that gifts are not undervalued. A couple of the more common situations governed by the new rules are described below, but the rules are too complicated to warrant a complete discussion. If a parent owns 100% of the stock of a corporation and then gives the common stock to his children and retains the preferred, the value of the right to the preferred dividends will be deemed to be zero unless the stock is cumulative preferred. If the donor creates a trust in which he retains an interest and in which he gives an interest to a family member, the value of the transferor's interest is treated as zero unless the retained interest is an annuity interest or a unitrust interest calling for distributions equal to a specified percentage of the current FMV of the trust. The effect of these rules is to increase the amount of the gift unless the transferor structures the transaction to avoid having a value of zero assigned to his/her retained interest.

Gift Tax Consequences of Certain Transfers

Self-Study Question

Madge deposits $50,000 in a joint bank account in her name and her niece Susan's name. During the current year, the bank credited the account with interest earned of $4,000. No withdrawals are made during the year. Has Madge made a gift to Susan?

Answer

Madge has not made a gift to Susan because Susan has not withdrawn anything from the account. The interest earned by the account will be reported by Madge on her personal income tax return, since none of the money in the account is owned by Susan.

Some transactions that cause the transferor to have made a gift are straightforward. It is easy to see that the disposition is within the scope of the gift tax if, for example, an individual places the title to stock or real estate solely in another person's name and receives less than adequate consideration in return. The Regulations include the following examples of transactions that may be subject to the gift tax: forgiving of a debt; assignment of the benefits of a life insurance policy; transfer of cash; and transfer of federal, state, or municipal bonds.[23] The gratuitous transfer of state and local bonds falls within the scope of the gift tax, even though interest on such bonds is exempt from federal income taxation. The following discussion concerns the gift tax rules for several transfers that are more complicated than putting the title to realty or stock solely in the name of another person.

Creation of Joint Bank Accounts. There are gift tax consequences for parties maintaining a bank account that is jointly owned. Funding a joint bank account is an incomplete transfer because the depositor is free to withdraw the amount deposited into the account. A gift occurs when one party withdraws an amount in excess of the amount he deposited.[24] The transfer is complete at that time because the withdrawn money is subject to only the withdrawing person's control.

Example 12-22 ■ On May 1, 1991, Connie deposits $100,000 into a joint bank account in the names of Connie and Ben. Ben makes no deposits. On March 1, 1992, Ben withdraws $20,000 from the joint account and purchases an auto. No gift arises upon the

---

[23] Reg. Sec. 25.2511-1(a).
[24] Reg. Sec. 25.2511-1(h)(4).

creation of the bank account. However, on March 1, 1992, Connie makes a gift to Ben in the amount of $20,000—the excess of Ben's withdrawal over Ben's deposit. ∎

Creation of Other Joint Tenancies. A completed gift arises when the transferor titles real estate or other properties in the names of himself and another (e.g., a spouse, a sibling, or a child) as joint tenants. **Joint tenancy** is a popular form for the ownership of property from a convenience standpoint. This form of ownership serves as a substitute for a will. Each joint tenant is deemed to have an equal interest in the property. The person furnishing the consideration to acquire the property is deemed to have made a gift to the other joint tenant in an amount equal to the value of his pro rata interest in the property.[25]

Example 12-23 ∎ Karol purchases land for $250,000 and immediately has it titled in the names of Karol and Lee, as joint tenants with right of survivorship. Karol and Lee are not husband and wife. As a result, Karol is making a gift to Lee of $125,000, or one-half the value of the property. ∎

Transfer of Life Insurance Policies. The mere naming of another as the beneficiary of a life insurance policy is an incomplete transfer. The owner of the policy can change the beneficiary designation at any time. However, if an individual irrevocably assigns all ownership rights in an insurance policy to another party, this transaction constitutes a gift of the policy to the new owner.[26] Ownership rights include the ability to change the beneficiary, borrow against the policy, and cash the policy in for its cash surrender value.

The payment of a premium on an insurance policy owned by another is considered a gift to the policy's owner. The amount of the gift is the amount of the premium paid. The tax result is the same as if cash is transferred to the policy owner and used by the owner to pay the annual premium.

Regulation Sec. 25.2512-6 describes the technique for valuing gifts of life insurance policies. The transferred policy is valued at the amount that it would cost to purchase a comparable policy on the gift date. The Regulations point out, however, that if the policy is several years old, the cost of a comparable policy is not readily ascertainable. In such a situation the policy is valued at its interpolated terminal reserve (i.e., an amount similar to the policy's cash surrender value) plus the amount of any unexpired premiums. The insurance company will furnish information concerning the interpolated terminal reserve.

Example 12-24 ∎ On September 1, 1991, Bill transfers all of his ownership rights in a $300,000 life insurance policy on his own life to Susan. The policy's interpolated terminal reserve is $24,000 as of September 1. On July 1, 1991, Bill paid the policy's $4,800 annual premium. Bill makes a gift to Susan on September 1, 1991, in the amount of $28,000 ($24,000 + [10/12 × $4,800]). ∎

Example 12-25 ∎ Assume the same facts as in Example 12-24, and that on July 1, 1992, Bill pays the $4,800 annual premium on the policy now owned by Susan. As a result of the premium payment, Bill makes a $4,800 gift to Susan. ∎

---

[25] Reg. Sec. 25.2511-1(h)(5). If the two joint tenants are husband and wife, no taxable gift will arise because of the unlimited marital deduction.
[26] Reg. Sec. 25.2511-1(h)(8).

Example 12-26 ■ Assume the same facts as in Examples 12-24 and 12-25, except that Susan, who now owns the policy, changes the beneficiary of the policy from Frank to John. This transaction is not a gift because Susan has not given up control; she can change the beneficiary again in the future. ■

Exercise of a General Power of Appointment. Section 2514 provides the rules concerning powers of appointment. A **power of appointment** exists when a person transfers property (perhaps in trust) and grants someone else the power to specify who eventually will receive the property. Thus, possession of a power of appointment has some of the same benefits as ownership of the property. Powers can be general or special. *Potential* gift tax consequences are associated with the powerholder's exercise of a **general power of appointment.** A person possesses a general power of appointment if he has the power to appoint the property (have the property paid) to himself, his creditors, his estate, or the creditors of his estate. The words "his estate" mean that there are no restrictions concerning to whom the individual may bequeath the property.

A gift occurs when a person exercises a general power of appointment and names some other person to receive the property.[27] The gift is made to the person named to receive the property. The exercise of a general power of appointment in favor of the holder of the power is not a gift (i.e., one cannot make a gift to himself).

Example 12-27 ■

Additional Comment

As a general rule, substantially appreciated property should not be transferred by gift. It should be transferred at death to take advantage of the "step-up" in basis to the estate tax value (usually FMV at date of death). If Mary in Example 12-28 were elderly, it might be better to transfer an asset other than the land so as to obtain the basis increase.

Additional Comment

Assume in Example 12-28 that Mary has made previous taxable gifts to the extent that any additional gifts she makes will be subject to the 55% gift tax rate. If G represents the amount of the gift and T is the amount of the tax, then

$G = \$3,000,000 - T$ *and*
$T = .55G$

Substituting .55G for T in the first equation and solving for G, we get G = $1,935,484, the amount of the gift. The tax is 55% of this amount, or $1,064,516. The calculation becomes more difficult when more than one marginal gift tax rate applies. Mary's gain equals the $1,064,516 gift tax paid by Sam over the $15,000 basis she has in the property, or $1,049,516.

In 1991, Tina creates an irrevocable trust and names Van to receive the income for life. In addition, Tina gives Van a general power of appointment exercisable during his life as well as at his death. Assume that Tina made a gift to Van at the time that the property was transferred to the trust in 1991. In addition, in 1992 Van instructs the bank trustee to distribute $50,000 of trust property to Kay. Through the exercise of his general power of appointment in favor of Kay, Van makes a $50,000 gift to Kay in 1992. ■

Net Gifts. A **net gift** occurs when an individual makes a gift to a donee who agrees to pay the gift tax as a condition to receiving the gift. The amount of the gift is the excess of the value of the transferred property over the amount of the gift tax paid by the donee. The donee's payment of the gift tax is treated as consideration paid to the donor. Because the amount of the gift is dependent upon the amount of gift tax payable, which in turn is a function of the amount of the gift, the calculations require the use of simultaneous equations.[28]

The net gift strategy is especially attractive for persons who would like to remove a rapidly appreciating asset from their estate but are unable to pay the gift tax because of liquidity problems. However, there is one potential disadvantage to a net gift: The Supreme Court has ruled that the donor must recognize as a gain the excess of the gift tax payable over his adjusted basis in the property.[29] The Court's rationale is that the donee's payment of the donor's gift tax liability constitutes an "amount realized" for purposes of determining the gain or loss realized on a sale, exchange, or other disposition. From a practical standpoint, this decision only affects donors who

---

[27] In general, the exercise of a special power of appointment is free of gift tax consequences. In the case of special powers of appointment, the holder of the power does not have an unrestricted ability to name the persons to receive the property. For example, he may be able to appoint to only his descendants.

[28] In Rev. Rul. 75-72 (1975-1 C.B. 310), the IRS explained how to calculate the amount of the net gift and the gift tax. In Ltr. Rul. 7842068 (July 20, 1978), the IRS stated that the donor's available unified credit, and not the donee's, must be used to calculate the gift tax payable.

[29] *Victor P. Diedrich v. CIR*, 50 AFTR 2d 82-5054, 82-1 USTC ¶ 9419 (USSC, 1982).

12-18 • Ch. 12 / The Gift Tax

transfer property that is so highly appreciated that its adjusted basis is less than the amount of gift tax liability triggered by its disposition.

Example 12-28 ■ Mary transfers land with a $3,000,000 FMV to her son, Sam, who agrees to pay the gift tax liability. Mary's adjusted basis in the land is $15,000. The amount of the gift is $3,000,000 less the gift tax paid by Sam. Simultaneous equations are used to calculate the amount of the gift and the gift tax liability. Mary must recognize gain equal to the excess of the gift tax liability paid by Sam over Mary's $15,000 basis in the property. ■

EXCLUSIONS

OBJECTIVE 4
Determine whether an annual gift tax exclusion is available

In many instances a portion or all of a transfer by gift is tax-free because of the annual exclusion authorized by Sec. 2503(b). The purpose of the **annual exclusion** was explained by the Senate Finance Committee in 1932 as follows:

> Such exemption . . . is to obviate the necessity of keeping an account of and reporting numerous small gifts, and . . . to fix the amount sufficiently large to cover in most cases wedding and Christmas gifts and occasional gifts of relatively small amount.[30]

As a result of the availability of the annual exclusion, most gift transactions result in the donor's making no taxable gift. Consequently, administration of the gift tax provisions is a much simpler task than it would otherwise be.

Amount of the Exclusion

The amount of this exclusion, which is analogous to an exclusion from gross income for income tax purposes, is currently $10,000.[31] It is available each year for an unlimited number of donees. For transfers made in trust, each beneficiary is deemed to be a separate donee. Any number of donors may make a gift to the same donee, and each is eligible to claim the exclusion. The only limitations on the annual exclusion are the donor's wealth, generosity, and imagination in identifying donees.

Example 12-29 ■ In 1991, Ann and Bob each give $10,000 cash to each of Tad and Liz. Ann and Bob again make gifts of $10,000 cash to Tad and Liz in 1992. For both 1991 and 1992, Ann receives $20,000 of exclusions ($10,000 for the gift to Tad and $10,000 for the gift to Liz). The same result applies to Bob. ■

Key Point
The income that would have been received by the donor on the property given away goes to the donee of the property. This also helps, over time, to reduce the estate of the donor. It might also reduce the total income taxes paid by the economic (family) unit.

The annual exclusion is a significant tax planning device. There is no comparable estate tax provision. So long as a donor's gifts to a particular donee do not exceed the excludible amount, the donor will never make any taxable gifts or have any gift tax liability. Because taxable gifts will be zero, the donor's estate tax base will not include any adjusted taxable gifts. A donor who each year for 10 years gives $10,000 per donee to each of 10 donees removes $1 million (10 × $10,000 × 10) from being taxed in his estate. The donor does this without making any taxable gifts or paying any gift tax. The $1 million would have been taxed in the donor's estate, at perhaps a 55% rate,

---
[30] S. Rept. No. 665, 72nd Cong., 1st Sess. (1932), reprinted in 1939-1 C.B. (Part 2), pp. 525-26.
[31] On January 1, 1982, the annual exclusion was increased from $3,000 to $10,000.

unless either (1) the gifts were made to or (2) the property was willed to the donor's surviving spouse.

Present Interest Requirement

While we generally speak of the annual exclusion as if it were available automatically for all gifts, in actuality, it is not. A donor receives an exclusion for only those gifts that constitute a present interest.

Definition of Present Interest. A **present interest** is defined as "an unrestricted right to the immediate use, possession, or enjoyment of property or the income from property (such as a life estate or term certain)."[32] Only such interests qualify for the annual exclusion. If only a portion of a transfer constitutes a present interest, the excluded portion of the gift may not exceed the value of the present interest.

Key Point
It is extremely important to distinguish between gifts that are present interests and those that are future interests, since the $10,000 exclusion per donee applies only to gifts that are present interests.

Definition of Future Interest. A future interest is the opposite of a present interest. Gifts of future interests are ineligible for the annual exclusion. A definition of a future interest follows. A **future interest** "is a legal term, and includes reversions, remainders, and other interests . . . which are limited to commence in use, possession, or enjoyment at some future date or time."[33] The following examples help demonstrate the attributes of present and future interests.

Example 12-30 ■ Nancy transfers $500,000 of property to an irrevocable trust with a bank serving as trustee. Nancy names Norm (age 55) to receive all of the trust income quarterly for the rest of Norm's life. At Norm's death, the property is to pass to Ellen (age 25) or Ellen's estate. Norm has an unrestricted right to immediate enjoyment of the income. Norm, thus, has a present interest. Ellen, however, has a future interest because Ellen cannot enjoy the property or any of the income until Norm dies. ■

Example 12-31 ■

Self-Study Question
Betty, age 79, deeds her house to her son Mark, who lives with her. Mark orally agrees to let Betty live in the home until her death. Has Betty made a gift of a present interest to Mark?

Answer
Possibly. Even though Betty's intent may have been to create a life estate for herself and a remainder (future) interest for Mark, she may have made a gift of a present interest if the oral contract is unenforceable under local law.

Greg transfers $800,000 of property to an irrevocable trust with a bank serving as trustee and instructs the trustee to distribute all of the trust income semiannually to Greg's three adult children, Jill, Katy, and Laura. The trustee is to use its discretion in deciding how much to distribute to each individual. Moreover, it is authorized to distribute nothing to a particular beneficiary if it deems such action to be in the beneficiary's best interest. Although all of the income must be paid out, the trustee has complete discretion to determine how much to pay to a particular beneficiary. None of the beneficiaries have the assurance that they will receive a trust distribution. Thus, no present interests are created. ■

Special Rule for Trusts for Minors. Congress realized that many parents would not find it desirable for trusts created for minor children to distribute all of their income to the young children. It enacted Sec. 2503(c), which contains provisions that authorize special trusts for minors, to address parents' concerns about the distribution of trust income to minors. Section 2503(c) allows parents (and other donors) to create trusts for children under age 21 that need not distribute all of their income annually. Such trusts, known as **2503(c) trusts,** allow donors to claim the annual exclusion if the following two conditions are met:

1. Until the beneficiary becomes age 21, the trustee may pay the income and/or the underlying assets to the beneficiary.

---
[32] Reg. Sec. 25.2503-3(b).
[33] Reg. Sec. 25.2503-3(a).

2. Any income and underlying assets that are not paid to the beneficiary will pass to that beneficiary when he or she reaches age 21. If the beneficiary should die before becoming age 21, the income and underlying assets are either payable to the beneficiary's estate or to any person the minor may appoint if the minor possesses a general power of appointment over the property.

If the trust instrument contains the provisions listed above, no part of the trust is considered to be a gift of a future interest. Therefore, the entire transfer is eligible for the annual exclusion.

As a result of Sec. 2503(c), donors creating trusts for donees under age 21 can get an exclusion, even though the trustee has discretion over paying out the trust income. The trustee must, however, distribute the assets and accumulated income to the beneficiary when he reaches age 21.

Key Point
The holder of a Crummey power must be given notice of a contribution to the trust to which the power relates and must be given a reasonable time period within which to exercise the power.

Crummey Trust. The **Crummey trust** is yet another technique that allows the donor to obtain an annual exclusion upon setting up a discretionary trust. The trust can terminate at whatever age the donor specifies and can be created for a beneficiary of any age. Thus, the *Crummey* trust is a much more flexible arrangement than the 2503(c) trust.

The *Crummey* trust is named for a Ninth Circuit Court of Appeals case holding that the trust beneficiaries had a present interest as a result of certain language in the trust instrument.[34] That language, which is referred to interchangeably as a "*Crummey* power," "*Crummey* demand power," or "*Crummey* withdrawal power," entitled each beneficiary to demand a distribution of the lesser of $4,000 or the amount transferred to the trust that year. If such power was not exercised by a specified date, it expired. The reason for the "lesser of" language with respect to the demand power is as follows: The largest present interest needed by the donor is equal to the annual exclusion amount. In years in which the gift is smaller than the annual exclusion amount, the donor simply needs to be able to exclude the amount of that year's gift. In addition, the donor wants to restrict the amount to which the beneficiary can have access. Today, the maximum amount that the beneficiary can withdraw is likely to be set at $10,000 (the amount of the annual exclusion) or $20,000 if gift splitting is anticipated.

The court held that the demand power gave each beneficiary a present interest; the amount of the present interest was the maximum amount that the beneficiary could require the trustee to pay over to him that year. Use of the *Crummey* trust technique entitles the donor to receive the annual exclusion while creating a discretionary trust that terminates at whatever age the donor deems appropriate. The donor thereby avoids the more restrictive rules of Sec. 2503(c). Generally, the donor hopes the beneficiary will not exercise the demand right.

GIFT TAX DEDUCTIONS

OBJECTIVE 5
Identify deductions available for gift tax purposes

The formula for determining taxable gifts allows two types of deductions—marital and charitable contribution. The **marital deduction** is for transfers to one's spouse. The **charitable contribution deduction** is for gifts to charitable organizations. Section 2524 states that the deductible amount in either case may not exceed the amount of the "includible gift," that is, the amount of the gift in excess of the annual exclusion.

---

[34] *D. Clifford Crummey v. CIR*, 22 AFTR 2d 6023, 68-2 USTC ¶ 12,541 (9th Cir., 1968).

Marital Deduction

Key Point
The marital deduction is allowed because a taxpayer who transfers property to his spouse has not, in effect, made a transfer—that is, the property has not left the economic (husband/wife) unit.

Generally, the marital deduction results in tax-free interspousal transfers. There is an exception, however, for gifts of certain terminable interests. This exception is discussed below. Congress first enacted the marital deduction in 1948. The rationale for this deduction is to provide more uniform treatment of community property and noncommunity property donors. To recap, in community property states, most property acquired after marriage is owned equally by each spouse. In noncommunity property states, however, the spouses' wealth is often divided unequally. Such spouses can equalize each individual's share of the wealth only by engaging in a gift-giving program. As a result of the marital deduction, spouses can shift wealth between themselves completely free of any gift tax consequences.

Unlimited Amount. Over the years, the amount of the marital deduction has varied. For gifts made after 1981, the rules are very favorable; there is an unlimited marital deduction. One spouse may deduct up to 100% of the amount of gifts made to the other spouse. The amount of the marital deduction, however, is limited to the amount of the gift that is in excess of the excluded portion.[35] For gifts made after 1981, transfers of community property are eligible for the marital deduction; earlier such gifts did not qualify for the deduction.

Example 12-32 ■ A wife gives her husband stock valued at $450,000. She excludes $10,000 of this transfer using her annual exclusion and claims a $440,000 marital deduction. Thus, no taxable gift arises from her gift to her husband. ■

Gifts of Terminable Interests—General Rule.

NONDEDUCTIBLE TERMINABLE INTERESTS. A **terminable interest** is an interest that ends or is terminated when (1) some event occurs (or fails to occur) or (2) a specified amount of time passes. Some, but not all, terminable interests are ineligible for the marital deduction.[36] A marital deduction is denied only when the transfer is of a nondeductible terminable interest. A nondeductible terminable interest has one of the following characteristics:

- The donor keeps an interest or conveys an interest to a third party who does not pay adequate consideration. The donee-spouse's interest ceases at a set time (such as at death), and the property then passes to either the donor or a third party; or
- Immediately after making the gift, the donor has the power to name someone else to receive an interest in the property, and the person named may possess the property upon the termination of the donee-spouse's interest.[37]

The following three examples illustrate some of the subtleties of the definition of nondeductible terminable interests. In the first example, a marital deduction is available because the interest transferred is not a nondeductible terminable interest.

Example 12-33 ■ A patent is a terminable interest because the property interest terminates at the end of the patent's legal life. Nevertheless, the patent does not constitute a nondeductible terminable interest; when the patent's legal life expires, a third party will not possess an interest in the patent. Thus, a donor will receive a marital deduction for a patent transferred to a spouse. ■

---

[35] Sec. 2524.
[36] Sec. 2523(b).
[37] Ibid.

In the second example, a marital deduction is denied because the first of the two alternative requirements for a nondeductible terminable interest has been met.

Example 12-34 ■ A donor transfers property in trust and (1) names his spouse to receive trust income, at the trustee's discretion, annually for the next 15 years and (2) states that at the end of the 15-year period the trust's assets are to be distributed to their child. The donor has given his spouse a nondeductible terminable interest. When the spouse's interest ceases, the property passes to their child, a recipient who did not pay adequate consideration. Thus, the donor receives no marital deduction. ■

In the third example, a marital deduction is available. In this case, the donee-spouse has a general power of appointment over the trust's assets in addition to having a lifetime income interest. The donee-spouse determines the persons to eventually receive the property.

Example 12-35 ■ The donor gives his spouse the right to all the income from a trust for life plus a general power of appointment over the trust's assets. He has transferred an interest eligible for the marital deduction. The general power of appointment may be exercisable during life, at death, or at both times. In addition, the donee-spouse must be entitled to receive the income annually or more frequently. ■

Additional Comment

In 1978 Brad, desiring to provide his wife, Sonia, with income for her life, transferred property to a trust, income to be distributed annually to his wife until her death, with a general power of appointment in Sonia over the remainder. The general power of appointment in Sonia was necessary so the property in the trust would be nonterminable interest property and would be eligible for the gift tax marital deduction.

The rationale behind the nondeductible terminable interest rule is that a donor should obtain a marital deduction only if an interest that will have transfer tax significance to the donee-spouse is conveyed. In other words, when the donee-spouse makes a lifetime gift of a property that was received as a result of an interspousal transfer, a transfer subject to the gift tax occurs. If the donee-spouse retains the property until death, the item is included in the donee-spouse's estate.

QTIP Provisions. Commencing in 1982, a major change was made to the nondeductible terminable interest rule. Under the new rule, transfers of qualified terminable interest property are eligible for the marital deduction.[38] Such transfers are commonly referred to as *QTIP transfers*. **Qualified terminable interest property** is property

- Which is transferred by the donor spouse,
- In which the donee has a "qualifying income interest for life," and
- For which a special election has been made.

A spouse has the necessary "qualifying income interest for life" if

- The spouse is entitled to all of the income from the property annually or more often; and
- No person has a power to appoint any part of the property to any person other than the donee-spouse unless the power cannot be exercised while the spouse is alive.

The QTIP rule enhances the attractiveness of making transfers to one's spouse. Donors can now receive a marital deduction—and thereby make a nontaxable transfer—without having to grant their spouse full control over the gifted property. The QTIP rule is especially attractive for donors who want to ensure that their

[38] Sec. 2523(f).

children by a previous marriage will receive the property upon the donee-spouse's death.

The donor does not have to claim a marital deduction even though the transfer otherwise qualifies as a QTIP transfer. Claiming the deduction on such transfers is elective.[39] If the donor elects to claim a marital deduction, the donee-spouse must include the QTIP trust property in his or her estate. The amount included in the estate is the value of the QTIP trust property as of the donee-spouse's date of death. Thus, as with other transfers qualifying for the marital deduction, the interspousal transfer is tax-free. The taxable event is postponed until the donee-spouse transfers the property.

Example 12-36

Additional Comment

Assume the same facts as in the previous comment except that Brad has been married twice. He had two children by his first wife and three children with Sonia. Brad could not be sure his first two children would ever receive anything from the trust because Sonia could exercise her general power of appointment in favor of her three children (or someone else). If this transfer were to occur after the enactment of the QTIP provisions, Brad would not have to give Sonia a general power of appointment over the corpus; the trust instrument could specify that the remainder, on Sonia's death, would go equally to all five children. Brad could thus control the ultimate disposition of the remainder.

A wife (Jo) transfers $1 million of property in trust with First National Bank acting as trustee. All of the trust income is payable to Jo's husband (Ed) quarterly for the rest of his life. Ed is age 64 at the time of the transfer. Upon Ed's death, the property will pass to Jo's nieces. This gift is eligible for a marital deduction. If Jo elects to claim the marital deduction, she will receive a $990,000 ($1,000,000 − $10,000) marital deduction. The deduction is limited to the amount of the includible gift.

Note that Jo's marital deduction in the preceding example is for $990,000 and not for the value of Ed's life estate. If Jo elects to claim the marital deduction, Ed's gross estate will include the value of the entire trust. The trust is valued as of the date of Ed's death. The QTIP provision permits Jo to receive a marital deduction while still being able to specify who will receive the property upon her husband's death.

A summary of the eligibility of a transfer for the marital deduction and the amount of the marital deduction that can be claimed is presented in Topic Review 12-2.

TOPIC REVIEW 12-2

Marital Deduction

Examples of Transfers Eligible for the Marital Deduction:
  Property transferred to spouse as sole owner
  Property transferred in trust with all of the income
    payable to the spouse for life and over which the
    donee-spouse has a general power of appointment
  Property transferred in trust with all of the income
    payable to the spouse for life and for which the
    donor-spouse named the remainderman—marital
    deduction available if elected under QTIP rule
Examples of Transfers Ineligible for the Marital Deduction:
  Property transferred in trust with the income payable
    to the spouse for life, but in the trustee's discretion,
    and for which the donor-spouse named the remainderman
  Property transferred in trust with all of the income
    payable to the spouse for a specified number of years
    and for which the donor-spouse named the remainderman
Amount of the Marital Deduction:
  The amount of the transfer minus the portion eligible
    for the annual exclusion

---

[39] The donor might decide not to claim the marital deduction if the donee-spouse has substantial assets already or a short life expectancy, especially if the gifted property's value is expected to appreciate at a high annual rate.

Charitable Contribution Deduction

Charitable contributions in excess of $10,000 per recipient organization must be reported on a gift tax return. Such transfers will not create taxable gifts, however, if they meet the requirements for a charitable contribution deduction. Claiming an income tax deduction for a charitable contribution does not preclude the donor from also obtaining a gift tax deduction. In contrast with the income tax provisions, there is no percentage limitation for the gift tax charitable contribution deduction. The only ceiling on the deduction is imposed by Sec. 2524, which limits the deduction to the amount of the gift that is in excess of the excluded portion.

Example 12-37 ■

An Additional Comment

A charitably minded taxpayer could avoid the gift (and the estate) tax entirely by giving all of his or her property to a qualified charitable organization. Actually, the taxpayer could give (or will) up to $600,000 to noncharitable donees as long as the balance of his or her property was given (or willed) to charity and still pay no gift (or estate) tax.

Fred gives stock valued at $75,000 to State University. Fred receives a $10,000 annual exclusion and a $65,000 charitable contribution deduction when computing his taxable gifts. ■

Transfers Eligible for the Deduction. To be deductible, the gift must be made to a charitable organization. The rules defining charitable organizations are quite similar for income, gift, and estate tax purposes.[40] According to Sec. 2522, a gift tax deduction is available for contributions to the following:

- The United States or any subordinate level of government within the United States as long as the transfer is solely for public purposes
- A corporation, trust fund, etc., that is organized exclusively for religious, charitable, scientific, literary, or educational purposes, or to foster amateur sports competition, including the encouragement of art and the prevention of cruelty to children or animals
- A fraternal society or similar organization operating under the lodge system if the gifts are to be used in the United States only for religious, charitable, scientific, literary, or educational purposes
- A war veterans' post or organization organized in the United States or one of its possessions if no part of their net earnings accrues to the benefit of private shareholders or individuals

Self-Study Question

Assume in Example 12-38 that Al was age 60 at the time of the gifts and that the appropriate interest rate was 10%. What is the amount of Al's charitable contribution?

Answer

The value of the remainder interest gifted to charity through the trust, from actuarial tables, is 0.22674. The charitable deduction on the gift tax return is $181,392 ($800,000 × 0.22674). The same amount is also allowable as a charitable contribution deduction on Al's income tax return for that year.

Split-Interest Transfers. Specialized rules apply when a donor makes a transfer for both private (i.e., an individual) and public (i.e., a charitable organization) purposes. Such arrangements are known as **split-interest transfers.** An example of a split-interest transfer is the gift of a residence to one's sister for life and the gift of a remainder interest to a college or university. If a donor gives a charitable organization a remainder interest, the charitable contribution deduction is forfeited unless the remainder interest is in either a personal residence (not necessarily the donor's principal residence), a farm, a charitable remainder annuity trust or unitrust, or a pooled income fund.[41] A split-interest gift of a present interest that is made to a

---

[40] In contrast to the income tax rules, a charitable contribution deduction is available under the gift tax rules for transfers made to foreign charitable organizations. No deduction is available, however, for gifts made to foreign governments.

[41] In a **charitable remainder annuity trust,** an individual receives trust distributions for a certain time period or for life. The annual distributions are a uniform percentage (5% or higher) of the value of the trust property, valued on the date of the transfer. For a **charitable remainder unitrust,** the distributions are similar, except that they are a uniform percentage (5% or higher) of the value of the trust property, revalued at least annually. Thus, the annual distributions from a unitrust, but not an annuity trust, vary from one year to the next. A **pooled income fund** is similar in concept to a mutual fund. The various individual beneficiaries receive annual distributions of their proportionate shares of the fund's total income.

charity qualifies for a charitable contribution deduction only if the charity receives a guaranteed annuity interest or a unitrust interest.

Example 12-38 ■ Al transfers $800,000 of property to a charitable remainder annuity trust. He reserves an annuity of $56,000 per year for his remaining life and specifies that upon his death the trust property will pass to the American Red Cross. In the same year, Al gives a museum a remainder interest in his antique furniture collection and reserves a life estate for himself.

Each of these is a split-interest transfer. Unfortunately for the donor, only the remainder interest in the charitable remainder annuity trust is eligible for a charitable contribution deduction. Consequently, Al makes a taxable gift in an amount equal to the value of the remainder interest in the antique furniture. Even though the furniture is not an income-producing property, the value of the remainder interest is determined from the actuarial tables found in Appendix E. ■

THE GIFT-SPLITTING ELECTION

OBJECTIVE 6
Apply the gift-splitting rules

The gift-splitting provisions of Sec. 2513 allow spouses to treat a gift that is actually made by one of them to a third party as if each spouse had made one-half of the gift. This election offers several advantages, as follows:

- If only one spouse makes a gift to a particular donee, the election enables $20,000 (instead of $10,000) to be given to the donee before a taxable gift arises.
- If per-donee transfers exceed $20,000 and taxable gifts occur, the election may lower the applicable marginal gift tax rate.
- Each spouse's unified credit may be used to reduce the gift tax payable.

In order to take advantage of the gift-splitting election, the spouses must meet certain requirements at the time of the transfer. These conditions include

- The spouses must be U.S. citizens or residents.
- At the time of the gift(s) for which the election is made, the donor-spouse must be married to the person who consents to gift splitting. In addition, the donor-spouse must not remarry before the end of the year.

Key Point
A wife makes a gift of $40,000 to a child in March 1991 and a gift of $60,000 to another child in November of the same year. If her husband elects to gift split, the election will apply to both gifts (the election is all or none for each year). If her husband so elects, he will report one-half of each gift on his own gift tax return.

The gift-splitting election is effective for all transfers to third parties made during that portion of the year that the spouses were married to each other.

If a spouse living in a community property state makes a gift of separate property (e.g., an asset received by inheritance), gift splitting may be desired. If this is the case, the election automatically extends to gifts of community property. Of course, splitting each spouse's gifts of community property has no impact on the amount of the taxable gifts.

Note that gift splitting is an all-or-nothing proposition. Spouses electing it for one gift must elect it for all gifts to third parties for that year. Each year's election stands alone, however, and is not binding on future years.[42] The procedural aspects of the gift-splitting election are discussed in the Compliance and Procedural Considerations section of this chapter.

---

[42] If the nondonor-spouse has made substantial taxable gifts relative to those made by the donor-spouse, the gift tax liability for the period in question may be lower if the spouses do not elect gift splitting.

12-26 • Ch. 12 / The Gift Tax

Example 12-39 ■ Eli and Joy are married on April 1, 1991. They are still married to each other at the end of the year. In March 1991, Eli gives Amy $60,000. In July 1991, Eli gives Barb $48,000 and Joy gives Claire $20,000. If the couple elects gift splitting, the election is only effective for the July gifts. Each spouse is treated as giving $24,000 and $10,000 to Barb and Claire, respectively. Because they may not elect gift splitting for the gift Eli makes prior to their marriage, Eli is treated as giving $60,000—the amount he actually transfers—to Amy. Under gift splitting, both Eli and Joy exclude $10,000 of gifts to both Barb and Claire, or a total of $40,000. Eli also excludes $10,000 of his gift to Amy. ■

Key Point
The gift-splitting election is a year-by-year election. For example, a husband and wife could elect to gift split in 1988, 1990, and 1992, but elect not to gift split in 1989, 1991, and 1993.

Upon the death of the actual donor or the spouse who consented to gift splitting, the amount of such decedent's adjusted taxable gifts must be included in the estate tax base. By electing gift splitting, the amount of the taxable gifts the donor-decedent is deemed to have made is reduced. Under gift splitting, the adjusted taxable gifts include only the portions of the gifts that are taxable on the gift tax returns filed by the donor-decedent. Of course, a portion is also reported by the nondonor-spouse's estate.

COMPUTATION OF THE GIFT TAX LIABILITY

Effect of Previous Taxable Gifts

OBJECTIVE 7
Calculate the gift tax liability

Additional Comment
Taxpayers need to be certain to retain a permanent file of copies of gift tax returns.

The gift tax computation involves a cumulative process. All of the donor's previous taxable gifts (i.e., those made in 1932 or later years) plus the donor's taxable gifts for the current year affect the marginal tax rate at which current gifts are taxed. Thus, two donors making the same taxable gifts in the current period may owe very different gift tax liabilities because one may have made substantially larger taxable gifts in earlier periods than the other donor. The process outlined below must be used to compute the gross tax levied on the current period's taxable gifts.

1. Determine the gift tax liability (at current rates) on the donor's cumulative taxable gifts (taxable gifts of current period plus aggregate taxable gifts of previous periods).
2. Determine the gift tax liability (at current rates) on the donor's cumulative taxable gifts made through the end of the preceding period.
3. Subtract the gift tax determined in step 2 from the gift tax determined in step 1. The difference equals the gross gift tax on the current period's taxable gifts.

This process is needed in order to tax the gifts on a progressive basis over the donor's lifetime.

Note that, although the gift tax rates have varied over the years, the current rate schedules are used in the calculation. This rule holds even when some or all of the gifts are made when different rates are in effect. This process ensures that the taxable gifts of the current period are taxed at the appropriate rate, given the donor's earlier gift history.

Example 12-40 ■ In 1975, Tony makes $2 million in taxable gifts. These gifts are the first Tony ever made. The tax imposed under the 1975 rate schedule is $564,900. Tony's next taxable gifts are made in 1991. The taxable amount of these gifts is $400,000. The tax on Tony's 1991 taxable gifts is calculated as follows:

Tax on $2,400,000 cumulative taxable gifts	$976,800
Minus: Tax on $2,000,000 of taxable gifts from previous periods	(780,800)
Tax on $400,000 of taxable gifts made in the current period	$196,000

This cumulative process results in the $400,000 gift in Example 12-40 being taxed at a 49% rate—the marginal gift tax rate applicable to taxable transfers ranging between $2,000,000 and $2,500,000. If the gift tax computations were not cumulative, the tax on the $400,000 of gifts would be determined by using the lowest marginal rates and would have been only $121,800. Because the tax on taxable transfers made in previous periods is determined by reference to the current rate schedule, Tony's 1975 gift tax liability, incurred when the gift tax rates were lower, is not relevant to the determination of his current gift tax.

Unified Credit Available

Congress enacted a unified credit for both gift and estate tax purposes commencing in 1977. The **unified credit** reduces the amount of the gross gift tax that is owed on current period gifts. The amount of the credit increased over the years (see page 12-7 or inside back cover), until it reached a maximum of $192,800 for 1987 and later years. Donors who have already made taxable gifts in the post-1976 period have already used some of their credit. In such situations, the amount of the credit available for the current year is reduced by the aggregate amount allowable as a credit in all preceding years. If after 1987 the donor's cumulative taxable transfers exceed $10,000,000, the benefit of the unified credit begins to be phased out.

Example 12-41 ■ Debbie makes her first taxable gift in 1978. The taxable amount of the 1978 gift is $100,000, which results in a gross gift tax of $23,800. Debbie claims $23,800 (of the $34,000 available credit) on her 1978 return to reduce her net gift tax liability to zero. Debbie makes her next taxable gift in 1984. The taxable amount of the gift is $400,000. The tax on the $400,000 gift equals (1) the tax on $500,000 of total gifts (at 1984 gift tax rates) of $155,800 minus (2) the tax on $100,000 of previous gifts (at 1984 gift tax rates) of $23,800, or $132,000. The credit amount for 1984 is $96,300. Debbie's gift tax is reduced by a credit of only $72,500 ($96,300 − $23,800), because $23,800 was allowable as a credit against her 1978 gift tax liability. If Debbie is planning to make additional taxable gifts, $96,500 ($192,800 − [$23,800 + $72,500]) of unified credit will be available to reduce the gift tax liability in the future. ■

COMPREHENSIVE ILLUSTRATION

The following comprehensive illustration demonstrates the computation of one donor's gift tax liability for the situation where the donors elect gift splitting. Computation of the wife's gift tax liability is shown.

Background Data

Hugh and Wilma Brown are married to each other throughout 1990. Hugh makes no taxable gifts in earlier periods. Wilma's previous taxable gifts are $300,000 in 1975 and $200,000 in 1978. In 1990 Wilma makes the following gratuitous transfers:

- $80,000 in cash to son Billy
- $24,000 in jewelry to daughter Betsy
- $30,000 in medical expense payments to Downtown Infirmary for medical care of grandson Tim
- Remainder interest in vacation cabin to friend Ruth Cain. Wilma (age 60) retains a life estate. The vacation cabin is valued at $100,000.
- $600,000 of stocks to First National Bank in trust with all of the income payable semiannually to husband Hugh (age 62) for life and remainder payable at Hugh's death to Jeff Bass, Wilma's son by an earlier marriage, or Jeff's estate. Wilma wants to elect the marital deduction.

In 1990 Hugh's only gifts were

- $80,000 of stock to State University
- $600,000 of land to daughter Betsy

Assume the applicable interest rate for valuing life estates and remainders is 10%.

Calculation of Tax Liability

The medical expense payments are exempt from the gift tax under Sec. 2503(e). The vacation cabin is valued at $100,000, and the remainder interest therein at $22,674 (0.22674 ×$100,000) (see Table R(1), age 60 in Appendix E) for gift tax purposes. The stock is transferred to a QTIP trust, and election of the marital deduction makes the entire interest treated as having been given to Hugh Brown.

Table 12-1 shows the computation of Wilma's gift tax liability for 1990. These same facts are used for the sample United States Gift Tax Return, Form 709, in Appendix B.

BASIS CONSIDERATIONS FOR A LIFETIME GIVING PLAN

OBJECTIVE 8
Understand how basis affects the overall tax consequences

Prospective donors should consider the tax-saving features of making a series of lifetime gifts (discussed in the Tax Planning Considerations section of this chapter). Lifetime giving plans can remove income from the donor's income tax return and transfer it to the donee's income tax return, where it may be taxed at a lower marginal tax rate. A series of gifts may permit property to be transferred to a donee without incurring a gift tax liability and thus enable the donor to eliminate part or all of his estate tax liability. These two advantages must be weighed against the unattractive basis rules applicable for such transfers.[43]

---

[43] Chapter 5 of *Prentice Hall's Federal Taxation: Individuals* text presents the basis rules in detail.

Self-Study Question

Barkley purchased a tract of land in 1955 for $90,000. In 1974, when the FMV of the land was $300,000, he made a gift of the land to his son Tracy. He paid gift tax of $23,000 on the gift. What is Tracy's basis in the land? What if the gift had been made after December 31, 1976?

Answer

Assuming the gift was made in 1974, Tracy's basis is $90,000 plus the $23,000 gift tax, or $113,000. Had Barkley made the gift after 1976 and the other factors remained the same, Tracy's basis would be $90,000 plus ($210,000/$300,000 × $23,000), or $106,100.

TABLE 12-1 *Comprehensive Gift Tax Illustration*

Wilma's actual 1990 gifts:		
Billy, cash		$ 80,000
Betsy, jewelry		24,000
Ruth, remainder interest in vacation cabin (future interest)		22,674
Husband Hugh and son Jeff, transfer to QTIP trust		600,000
Total gifts made by Wilma		$726,674
Minus:	One-half of Wilma's gifts made to third parties that are deemed made by Hugh (0.50 × $126,674)	(63,337)
Plus:	One-half of Hugh's gifts made to third parties (State University and Betsy), that are deemed made by Wilma (0.50 × $680,000)	340,000
Minus:	Annual exclusions for gifts of present interests ($10,000 each for gifts made to Billy, Betsy, Hugh, and State University)	(40,000)
Minus:	Marital deduction ($600,000 − $10,000)	(590,000)
Minus:	Charitable contribution deduction ($40,000 − $10,000)	(30,000)
Taxable gifts for current period		$343,337
Tax on cumulative taxable gifts of $843,337[a]		$284,701
Minus:	Tax on previous taxable gifts of $500,000 (current rate schedule)	(155,800)
Tax on taxable gifts of $343,337 for the current period		$128,901
Minus: Unified credit:		
Credit for 1990	$192,800	
Minus: Credit allowable for prior periods	(34,000)[b]	(158,800)
Tax payable for 1990		$—0—

[a] $300,000 (in 1975) + $200,000 (in 1978) + $343,337 (in 1990).
[b] 0 (for 1975) + $34,000 (for 1978).

Self-Study Question

Betty gave property to Mary when the FMV of the property was $75,000. Betty's basis in the property was $100,000, and Betty paid gift taxes of $16,000 on the gift. What is Mary's basis in the gifted property?

Answer

Mary's basis for determining gain is $100,000; her basis for determining loss is $75,000. None of the gift taxes paid can be used to increase the basis of the property.

Property Received by Gift

The carryover basis rules apply to property received by gift. Provided the property's FMV on the date of the gift exceeds its adjusted basis, the donee's basis in such property is the same as the donor's basis. In addition, the donee's basis may be increased by some or all of the gift tax that is paid by the donor. In the case of pre-1977 gifts, all of the gift tax paid by the donor may be added to the donor's adjusted basis. For post-1976 transfers, however, only that portion of the gift tax represented by the following fraction may increase the donor's adjusted basis:

$$\frac{\text{Amount of property's appreciation from acquisition date through date of gift}}{\text{FMV of property on the date of the gift}}$$

In no event, however, can the gift tax adjustment increase the donee's basis above the property's FMV on the date of the gift.

If the gifted property's FMV on the date of the gift is less than the donor's adjusted basis, the basis rules are more complicated. For purposes of determining gain, the donee's basis is the same as the donor's adjusted basis. For purposes of determining loss, the donee's basis is the property's FMV on the date of the gift. If the donee sells the property for an amount between its FMV as of the date of the gift and the donor's adjusted basis, the donee recognizes no gain or loss. The property's basis cannot be

Additional Comment

Phil owns investment property worth $350,000 in which his adjusted basis is $500,000. Unless there are overriding reasons why the property should be kept in the family, Phil should sell the property before his death to realize an income tax-deductible loss. If he gives the property to his child, the loss basis in the child's hands is $350,000, and no income tax deduction for the $150,000 decline in market value would ever be taken. If he dies holding the loss property, his heirs will take the estate tax return value (FMV) as their basis, and the income tax deduction for the $150,000 loss is lost.

increased by any gift tax paid in circumstances where the donor's adjusted basis exceeds the property's FMV as of the date of the gift. Prospective donors should dispose of property that has declined in value by selling it instead of gifting it.

Property Received at Death

In general, the basis rules that apply to property received as a result of another's death call for a step-up or step-down to the property's FMV as of the decedent's date of death. The recipient's basis is the same as the amount at which the property is valued on the estate tax return. On that return, properties are valued at either their FMV on the decedent's date of death or on the alternate valuation date. Generally the alternate valuation date is 6 months after the date of death. While these rules are generally thought of as providing for a step-up in basis, if the property has declined in value prior to the transferor's death, the basis is stepped-down to its date of death or alternate valuation date value.

In certain circumstances there is no step-up in basis for appreciated property transferred at death.[44] This exception applies if the following two statements are true:

- The decedent receives the appreciated property as a gift during the one-year period preceding his or her death.
- The property passes to the donor or to the donor's spouse as a result of the donee-decedent's death.

Prior to the enactment of the rule, a widely publicized planning technique was the transfer of appreciated property to an ill spouse who, in turn, could will the property back to the donor-spouse, who would receive the property at a stepped-up basis. The interspousal transfers by gift and at death are tax-free because of the unlimited marital deduction that is available under both the gift tax and estate tax rules. Consequently, prior to the change in the statute the property received a step-up in basis at no transfer tax cost.

Example 12-42 ■ In June 1990, Sarah makes a gift of property valued at $700,000 to Tom, her spouse. Sarah's adjusted basis in the property is $120,000. Tom dies in March 1991. At this time, the property is worth $740,000. If the property passes back to Sarah upon Tom's death, Sarah's basis will be $120,000. However, if the property passes to someone other than Sarah at Tom's death, its basis will be stepped-up to $740,000. If Tom lives for more than 1 year after receiving the gift, the basis is stepped-up whether the property passes to Sarah or someone else at Tom's death. ■

CONTROVERSIAL ISSUES

Below Market Loans: Gift and Income Tax Consequences

Section 7872 provides definitive rules concerning both the gift and income tax consequences of below-market loans. In general, it treats the lender as making a gift to the borrower and receiving interest income. The borrower is treated as paying interest expense. Congress enacted Sec. 7872 in response to a Supreme Court case[45] that held

---

[44] Sec. 1014(e).
[45] *Esther C. Dickman v. CIR*, 53 AFTR 2d 84-1608, 84-1 USTC ¶ 9240 (USSC, 1984).

Additional Comment
If the lender and borrower keep double-entry books, the lender would debit Gifts Made (a reduction in equity) and credit Interest Income (taxable income). The borrower would debit Interest Expense (which may or may not be tax deductible) and would credit Gifts Received (an economic income concept).

that the transfer of the right to use money without paying sufficient interest is a transfer of property for purposes of the gift tax.

In the case of a demand loan, the lender is treated as having made a gift in each year in which the loan is outstanding.[46] The amount of the gift equals the foregone interest income with respect to the portion of the year that the loan is outstanding. The foregone interest income is calculated by referring to the difference between the interest rate the lender charged and the federal short-term rate of Sec. 1274(d), for the period in question.[47]

For income tax purposes, the foregone interest is treated as being retransferred from the borrower to the lender on the last day of each calendar year in which the loan is outstanding. The amount of the foregone interest is the same as for gift tax purposes. The lender reports the foregone interest as income for the year in question. The borrower gets an interest expense deduction for the same amount unless one of the rules limiting the interest deduction applies.[48]

Example 12-43 ■ On July 1 Frank loans $500,000 to Susan, who signs an interest-free demand note. The loan is still outstanding on December 31. Assume that 10% is the applicable interest rate. Frank is deemed to have made a gift to Susan on December 31, of $25,000 (0.10 × $500,000 × 6/12). Frank must report $25,000 of interest income. Susan deducts $25,000 of interest expense provided the deduction is not otherwise limited or disallowed. ■

De Minimis *Rules*

Under one of the *de minimis* rules of Sec. 7872, neither the income nor the gift tax rules apply to any gift loan made directly between individuals for any day on which the aggregate loans outstanding between the borrower and the lender are $10,000 or less. All loans are counted in determining if the $10,000 amount has been exceeded, irrespective of their interest rate. The *de minimis* exception cannot be used to exempt any loan directly attributable to the purchase or carrying of income-producing assets.

A second *de minimis* exception potentially permits loans of $100,000 or less to receive more favorable income tax treatment. The exception is not applicable for gift tax purposes, however. This *de minimis* exception treats the amount retransferred to the lender as not exceeding the borrower's net investment income (as defined in Sec. 163(d)(3)) for the year. Moreover, if the borrower's net investment income for the year is $1,000 or less, such amount is treated as being zero. Thus, the lender would not have to report any interest income.

The provisions just discussed are inapplicable when the interest arrangements of any loan have the avoidance of any federal tax as one of their principal purposes. Should such a purpose be present, the general income tax rules of Sec. 7872 apply to such loans. The provisions do not apply to any day on which the total outstanding loans between the borrower and the lender exceed $100,000. In determining whether the taxpayer meets the $100,000 or $10,000 loan limitations, a husband and wife are treated as one person.

Example 12-44 ■ On August 1 of the current year, Mike loans $100,000 to Don. No other loans are outstanding between the parties. Avoidance of federal taxes is not a principal purpose of the loan. Don signs a demand note providing for the payment of simple

---

[46] Sec. 7872(a).
[47] For March 1991, the short-term federal rate, compounded semiannually, is 6.74%.
[48] Limitations on the deductibility of interest expense are discussed in Chapter 6 of the *Prentice Hall's Federal Taxation: Individuals* text.

interest at a 6% annual rate. Assume 10% is the applicable interest rate. The loan is still outstanding on December 31. Mike is treated as having made a gift to Don on December 31, in the amount of $1,667 ($100,000 × [0.10 − 0.06] × 5/12). This gift is not reported unless Mike's aggregate gifts to Don in the current year exceed $10,000.

If Don's net investment income for the current year exceeds $1,667, Mike reports both the $1,667 of imputed interest income under Sec. 7872 and the interest actually received. In turn, subject to rules that may disallow some or all of the interest expense deduction, Don deducts both the $1,667 interest expense under Sec. 7872 and the interest he actually paid. If Don's net investment income is between $1,001 and $1,667, each party reports interest income or expense under Sec. 7872 equal to Don's net investment income. Mike and Don report no interest income or expense under Sec. 7872 if Don's net investment income is $1,000 or less. ∎

TAX PLANNING CONSIDERATIONS

Additional Comment

Laura, who is always in the 28% marginal income tax bracket, makes a gift of $10,000 to each of her six grandchildren each year for eight years. At the inception of the gift program, all of the grandchildren are under age 6. The gift monies are invested at 10%. The grandchildren have no income during the eight-year period except the investment return on the gift monies. Assume Laura's estate will be taxed in the 39% marginal estate tax rate. The parents of the grandchildren are always in the 28% marginal income tax bracket. Given these facts, the after-tax amount retained by the family unit through Laura's eight-year gift program exceeds by $271,937 the amount the family unit would retain in the absence of the gift program.

Although the tax law's bias in favor of lifetime transfers was reduced by the 1976 tax law changes that introduced the unification concept, lifetime gifts still provide many more advantages than disadvantages. The pros and cons of lifetime gifts from an estate planning perspective are discussed below.

Tax-Saving Features of Inter Vivos Gifts

Use of Annual Exclusion. The annual exclusion offers the opportunity for donors who start making gifts to several donees per year relatively early in their lifetime to keep substantial amounts of property off the transfer tax rolls. The tax-free amount can be doubled if a husband and wife make use of the gift-splitting election.

There is no estate tax counterpart to the annual gift tax exclusion. Consequently, a terminally ill person whose will includes bequests of approximately $10,000 to each of several individuals would realize substantial transfer tax savings if gifts—instead of bequests—were made to these individuals.

Removal of Post-gift Appreciation from Tax Base. Another very important advantage of lifetime gifts is that their value is "frozen" at their date of gift value. That is, any post-gift appreciation escapes the transfer tax rolls. Consequently, transfer tax savings are maximized if the donor gives away the assets that appreciate the most.

Removal of Gift Tax Amount from Transfer Tax Base. With one exception, gift taxes paid by the donor are removed from the transfer tax base. The lone exception applies to gift taxes paid on gifts the donor makes within 3 years of dying. Under the gross-up rule (discussed in Chapter 13), the donor's gross estate includes gift taxes paid on gifts made within 3 years of the donor's death.

Income Splitting. Originally, one of the most favorable consequences of lifetime gifts was income splitting. The compression of the income tax rate schedules beginning in 1987 has lessened the benefits of income shifting. As a result of the gift, the income produced by the gifted property is taxed to the donee, who may have a lower marginal income tax rate. If income tax savings do arise, they accrue each year during the post-gift period. Thus, the income tax savings can be quite sizable over a span of several years.

Additional Comment

If a terminally ill spouse, Sam, has no property, an election to gift split can be made to effectively use up Sam's unified credit. Another method of utilizing Sam's unified credit is to make Sam a gift of property in trust which meets the following requirements: (a) income from the trust must go to Sam for life, (b) remainder is subject to a general power of appointment in Sam, and (c) if the general power of appointment is not exercised during Sam's lifetime (or by will on Sam's death), the remainder must pass to specified beneficiaries other than the donor.

Gift in Contemplation of Donee-Spouse's Death. At times, a terminally ill spouse may have very few assets. If such a spouse died, a sizable portion of his or her unified credit would be "wasted" because the decedent's estate would be well below the amount of the exemption equivalent provided by the unified credit. If the healthier spouse is relatively wealthy, he or she could make a gift to the ill spouse to create an estate in an amount equal to the estate tax exemption equivalent. Because of the unlimited marital deduction, the gift would be tax-free. Upon the death of the donee-spouse, no estate tax would be payable because the estate tax liability would not exceed the unified credit. The donee-spouse should not transfer his or her property back to the donor-spouse at death. Otherwise, the donee-spouse's unified credit would be wasted, and the original tax planning would be negated. Moreover, the "returned property" would be included in the surviving spouse's estate.

A gift of appreciated property in contemplation of the donee-spouse's death provides an additional advantage. If the property does not pass back to the donor-spouse, its basis is increased to its value on the donee's date of death. In the event the property is willed to the donor-spouse, a step-up in basis still occurs if the date of the gift precedes the donee's date of death by more than 1 year.

Lessening State Transfer Tax Costs. All states levy a death tax. Only 7 states impose a gift tax.[49] Therefore, in most states the tax cost of lifetime transfers is lower than that for transfers at death.

Key Point

A charitable gift prior to death removes the property from the estate of the donor AND provides an income tax deduction. A charitable gift on death reduces the estate but does not provide an income tax deduction to the decedent.

Income Tax Savings from Charitable Gifts. Some individuals are inclined to dispose of a portion of their property by transferring it to charitable organizations. Assuming the disposition is of a type eligible for a charitable contribution deduction, the transfer tax implications are the same—no taxable transfer—irrespective of whether the transfer occurs *inter vivos* or at death. From an income tax standpoint, however, a lifetime transfer is preferable because only lifetime transfers produce an income tax deduction for charitable contributions.

Negative Aspects of Gifts

Loss of Step-up in Basis. Persons deliberating about whether to make gifts or not or which properties to give should keep in mind that the donee receives no step-up in basis for property acquired by gift. From a practical standpoint, sacrifice of the step-up in basis is insignificant if the donee does not plan to sell the property and/or if the property is not of a character subject to an allowance for depreciation.

Prepayment of Estate Tax. A donor who makes taxable gifts in an amount in excess of the exemption equivalent must pay a gift tax. Upon such a donor's death, the taxable gift is included in his estate tax base as an adjusted taxable gift. The gift tax

---

[49] The states that impose a gift tax are Delaware, Louisiana, New York, North Carolina, South Carolina (until July 1, 1991), Tennessee, and Wisconsin (effective through 1991).

paid during the donor's lifetime reduces the donor's estate tax liability. In a sense, the donor's payment of the gift tax results in prepayment of a portion of the estate tax.

COMPLIANCE AND PROCEDURAL CONSIDERATIONS

Filing Requirements

OBJECTIVE 9
Recognize the filing requirements for gift tax returns

Section 6019 specifies the circumstances in which a gift tax return should be filed. In general, the donor will file Form 709 (United States Gift Tax Return). In certain circumstances, however, the donor may file a simpler return, Form 709A (United States Short Form Gift Tax Return). A completed Form 709 appears in Appendix B. The facts used in the preparation of the completed Form 709 are the same as the facts of the comprehensive illustration.

As is the case with respect to income tax returns, a return is often required even though the taxable amount and the tax payable are both zero. A donor must file a gift tax return for any calendar year in which gifts are made other than:

- Gifts to one's spouse that qualify for the marital deduction
- Gifts that are fully shielded from taxation because they do not exceed the annual exclusion amount

However, if the gift to the spouse is of qualified terminable interest property (QTIP), the gift must be reported on the gift tax return. The marital deduction is not available for these transfers unless the donor makes the necessary election. Such an election must be made on a gift tax return.

Key Point
Normally a gift tax return is due April 15th of the following year. However, if a donor dies during the year, the gift tax return is due not later than the due date of the donor's estate tax return.

Due Date

All gift tax returns must be filed on a calendar-year basis. Under the general rule, all gift tax returns are due no later than on April 15 following the close of the year of the gift.[50] An extension of time granted for filing an individual income tax return is deemed to automatically extend the filing date for the individual's gift tax return for that year. At present, such extensions are until August 15.

If the donor dies early in the year in which a gift is made, the due date for the donor's final gift tax return may be earlier than April 15. Because information concerning the decedent's taxable gifts is necessary in order to complete the estate tax return, the gift tax return for the year of death is due no later than the due date (including extensions) for the donor's estate tax return.[51] Estate tax returns are due 9 months after the date of death.

Receipt of an extension for filing a gift tax return does not postpone the due date for payment of the tax. Interest is imposed on any gift tax that is not paid by April 15. Unlike with the income tax, estimated payments of gift taxes throughout the reporting period are not required.

---

[50] Sec. 6075(b).
[51] The decedent's post-1976 taxable gifts affect the size of his estate tax base, as discussed in Chapter 13.

Gift-Splitting Election

In order for taxable gifts to be computed under the gift-splitting technique, both spouses must indicate their consent to gift splitting in one of the following ways:[52]

1. Each spouse signifies his or her consent on the other spouse's gift tax return.
2. Each spouse signifies his or her consent on his or her own gift tax return.
3. Both spouses signify their consent on one of the gift tax returns.

The Regulations state that the first approach listed above is the preferred manner for designating consent.

Short-Form Gift Tax Return

A gift tax return is necessary in order to elect gift splitting, even if no gift tax is due. Thus, if one spouse makes a gift to a third party of an amount between $10,001 and $20,000, the spouse must still file a gift tax return. In such situations, the donors can file a simpler gift tax form, Form 709A (United States Short Form Gift Tax Return). This form cannot be filed, however, if the donor gives something other than tangible personal property, cash, or stocks and bonds listed on an exchange.

Liability for Tax

Key Point
As when a husband and wife file a joint income tax return, if gift splitting is elected, the husband and wife have joint and several liability for the entire gift tax liability regardless of who made the actual gifts.

The gift tax is to be paid by the donor,[53] and if the spouses consent to gift splitting, the entire gift tax liability is a joint and several liability of the spouses.[54] Thus, if spouses do not pay the tax voluntarily, the IRS may attempt to collect whatever amount it deems appropriate from either spouse, irrespective of the size of the gift the spouse actually made.

In the rare event that the donor does not pay the gift tax, the donee becomes personally liable for the gift tax.[55] A donee's liability is, however, limited to the value of the gift.

Key Point
It is possible, though rare, that a donee could be liable for gift taxes.

Determination of Value

One of the most difficult problems encountered by donors and their tax advisors is the determination of the FMV of the gifted property. This task is especially difficult if the gifted property is stock in a closely held business, an oil and gas property, or land in an area where few sales occur.

If the transfer involves a sale, the IRS can argue that the asset's value exceeds its sales price and, thus, there is a gift to the extent of the bargain element. This problem is especially common with sales to family members. In situations where the donor is giving a property whose value is not readily determinable, it is advisable for the donor to have the property appraised before filing the gift tax return.

Penalty for Undervaluation. Penalties potentially apply for undervaluations of properties for gift and estate tax purposes. Section 6662 imposes a penalty, at 1 of 2

---

[52] Reg. Sec. 25.2513-2(a)(1).
[53] Sec. 2502(c).
[54] Sec. 2513(d).
[55] Reg. Sec. 301.6324-1.

rates, on underpayments of gift or estate taxes resulting from a "valuation understatement." The amount on which the penalty is imposed is the underpayment of the transfer tax attributable to the valuation understatement.

No penalty applies if the valuation shown on the return exceeds 50% of the amount determined to be the correct value. If the value reported on the return is 50% or less of the correct value, the penalty rate is as shown below.

Ratio of Value Per Return to Correct Value	Penalty Rate
More than 25% but 50% or less	20%
25% or less	40%

Section 6662(g)(2) exempts a taxpayer from paying the penalty if the underpayment is less than $5,000. In addition, the statute empowers the Secretary of the Treasury to waive the penalty if the taxpayer shows good faith and a reasonable cause for the valuation claimed.

Example 12-45 ■ Donna has already used her available unified credit. She gives land to her son and reports its value at $400,000 on her gift tax return. Donna's return is audited, and she agrees that $900,000 was the correct value of the property. Because the value stated on the return is only 44.44% ([$400,000 ÷ $900,000] × 100) of the correct value, a 20% penalty is levied on the underpayment attributable to the valuation understatement. If Donna is in the 50% marginal gift tax bracket, the gift tax underpayment is $250,000 (0.50 × [$900,000 − $400,000]). Thus, the penalty is $50,000 (0.20 × $250,000) unless the Secretary waives it. ■

Additional Comment

Even if a taxpayer questions whether a gift was made, it is probably a good idea to file a gift tax return. The filing of the return causes the statute of limitations to start and limits the amount of time during which the IRS may question the valuation of the gift.

Statute of Limitations

In general, the statute of limitations for gift tax purposes is 3 years after the later of the date the return was filed or the return's due date.[56] The statute of limitations is extended from 3 to 6 years if the donor omits from the gift tax return gifts whose value in total is more than 25% of the gifts reported on the return. If the donor files no return because, for example, he is unaware that he made any gifts, the tax may be assessed at any time.

The cumulative nature of the gift tax causes the taxable gifts of earlier years to affect the gift tax owed in subsequent periods. Once the statute of limitations has expired, the IRS cannot argue that taxable gifts of prior periods were undervalued (and thus the current period's gifts should be taxed at a higher rate than that used by the donor) as long as a gift tax was paid on the earlier gifts. In such circumstances, for purposes of the cumulative computations of the gift tax, the value of a gift made in the prior period is "the value of such gift which was used in computing the tax for the last preceding calendar period for which a tax was assessed or paid."[57]

Because of the unified credit, many donors do not owe any gift tax, even though they make taxable gifts. While the IRS cannot collect additional tax on such gifts after the expiration of the statute of limitations, it can increase the value of such gifts for purposes of calculating the cumulative taxable gifts and the tax thereon. As a result, the marginal tax rate applicable to the gifts of the current period may be increased.[58]

---

[56] Sec. 6501.
[57] Sec. 2504(c).
[58] Reg. Sec. 25.2504-2.

Example 12-46 ■ Andy files a gift tax return in 1985, reporting taxable gifts of $250,000. The unified credit reduces Andy's gift tax payable to zero. In 1993, Andy files a gift tax return to report gifts made in 1992. The IRS examines Andy's 1992 return, and in the process reviews the values reported on Andy's 1985 return. The IRS may not collect any additional tax with respect to the 1985 gifts. Because no tax is paid on such gifts, the IRS can, however, contend that for purposes of calculating the tax on the 1992 taxable gifts, the 1985 taxable gifts exceed $250,000. ■

PROBLEM MATERIALS

DISCUSSION QUESTIONS

12-1. Describe two ways in which the transfer tax (estate and gift tax) system is a unified system.

12-2. Determine whether the following statement is true or false: Every donor who makes a taxable gift incurs a gift tax liability. Explain your answer.

12-3. What was the Congressional intent for enacting the gift-splitting provisions?

12-4. Under what circumstances must the unified credit that is usually available be reduced (by a maximum amount of $6,000), even though the donor has never claimed any unified credit?

12-5. Is a grandparent's payment of his grandchild's college tuition treated differently for gift tax purposes than his payment of a neighbor's medical expenses? Explain.

12-6. Is a gratuitous transfer to a political organization treated as a gift for gift tax purposes?

12-7. Which of the following events involving Steve constitute gifts for gift tax purposes?
  a. Transferring all of his ownership rights in a life insurance policy to another person
  b. Depositing funds into a joint bank account in the names of Steve and another party (who deposits nothing)
  c. Paying for land and having it titled in the names of Steve and his son as joint tenants with right of survivorship
  d. Steve's paying a hospital for the medical expenses of a neighbor
  e. Steve's making a $1,000,000 demand loan to an adult child and charging no interest

12-8. What does a person have to do in order to make a gift of a life insurance policy?

12-9. What is a net gift?

12-10. When might a potential donor be interested in making a net gift? Explain the potential income tax problem with making a net gift.

12-11. What is the purpose of the gift tax annual exclusion?

12-12. Determine the accuracy of the following statement. All gifts are eligible for the annual exclusion.

12-13. Compare and contrast a 2503(c) trust and a *Crummey* trust.

12-14. From a nontax standpoint, which technique would a parent likely prefer for making transfers to a minor child—a 2503(c) trust or a *Crummey* trust?

12-15. Explain the requirements for qualifying a property transfer as a transfer of a qualified terminable interest property.

12-16. Why do some donors find the qualified terminable interest property transfer an especially attractive arrangement for making transfers to their spouses?

12-17. Evaluate the accuracy of the following statement: A donor cannot incur a gift tax liability if his only gifts are gifts to a U.S. charitable organization. Explain.

12-18. List three advantages to spouses of electing to use the gift-splitting election.

12-19. Both Tom and Virginia make taxable gifts of $250,000 in 1991. Will their 1991 gift tax liabilities necessarily be identical? Explain.

12-20. A donor made his first taxable gift a number of years ago and his second taxable gift in the current year. In the intervening years, the gift tax rates increased. In working with the part of the gift tax formula dealing with the tax on taxable gifts of previous periods, which rate schedule is used—the one applicable in the year in which the first taxable gift was made or the one for the current period?

12-21. A mother is trying to decide which of the two assets listed below to give to her adult daughter.

Asset	FMV	Adjusted Basis	Annual Net Income from the Asset
Apartment	$2,400,000	$1,500,000	($10,000)
Stock	2,400,000	2,200,000	240,000

The mother has a higher marginal income tax rate than her daughter. Describe the pros and cons of giving each of the two properties.

12-22. Phil and Marcy have been married for a number of years. Marcy is very wealthy, but Phil is not. In fact, Phil has only $10,000 of property. Phil has been very ill recently, and his doctor feels it is likely that he will die within the next year. Do you have any tax planning suggestions for the couple?

12-23. Assume that the facts remain the same as in Problem 12-22, except that Marcy has decided to give Phil property valued at $590,000. Phil will likely leave the gifted property to their children under his will.
  a. What are the gift tax consequences to Marcy and the estate tax consequences to Phil of the transfer (assuming the property does not appreciate prior to his death)?
  b. Assume Marcy is trying to decide whether to give Phil stock with an adjusted basis of $10,000 or land with an adjusted basis of $500,000. Each asset is valued at $590,000. Which asset would you recommend she give and why?

12-24. How do the below-market loan rules affect lenders?

12-25. Explain how a lifetime gift of property fixes or "freezes" the gifted property's value for transfer tax purposes.

12-26. List five advantages and two disadvantages of disposing of property by gift instead of at death.

12-27. Dick wants to transfer property with a $400,000 FMV to an irrevocable trust with a bank as the trustee. Dick will name his cousin Earl to receive all of the trust income annually for the next 13 years. Then the property will revert to Dick. In the last few years, the income return (yield) on the property has been 7%. Assume this yield is not likely to increase and that the rate for the actuarial tables is 10%.
  a. What will be the amount of Dick's gift to Earl?
  b. Would you recommend that Dick transfer the property yielding 7% to this type of a trust? Explain. If not, what type of property would you recommend that Dick transfer to the trust?

12-28. In general, what is the due date for the gift tax return? What circumstances permit a donor either more or less time to file the return?

12-29. In 1987, Frank sells realty to Stu, his son, for $400,000. Frank does not report this transaction as a gift. In 1996, the IRS audits Frank's 1994 income tax return and somehow finds out about the sale. The IRS then contends that the property sold was worth $700,000 in 1987, and that Frank made a $300,000 gift to Stu in 1987.
  a. Can the IRS collect the gift tax on the 1987 gift? If not, will the 1987 gift affect the tax due on later gifts that may be made by Frank?
  b. Assume instead that the IRS conducts its audit in 1990. Will Frank be subject to any penalty? Explain.

PROBLEMS

12-30. *Calculation of Gift Tax.* In the current year Amelia makes taxable gifts aggregating $5 million. Her only other taxable gifts amount to $1 million, all of which were made in 1985.
  a. What is Amelia's current gift tax liability?
  b. What is her current gift tax liability under the assumption that she made the $1 million of taxable gifts in 1974 instead of in 1985?

12-31. *Calculation of Gift Tax.* Cecil made taxable gifts as follows: $100,000 in 1974, $650,000 in 1978, and $200,000 in the current year. What is Cecil's current year gift tax liability?

12-32. *Determination of Taxable Gifts.* In the current year, Beth, who is single, sells stock valued at $40,000 to Linda for $18,000. Later that year, Beth gives Linda $12,000 in cash.
  a. What is the amount of Beth's taxable gifts?
  b. How would your answer to Part a change if Beth instead gives the cash to Patrick?

12-33. *Determination of Taxable Gifts.* In the current year, Clay gives $30,000 cash to each of his eight grandchildren. His wife makes no gifts during the current year.
  a. What are Clay's taxable gifts assuming Clay and his wife do *not* elect gift splitting?
  b. How would your answer to Part a change if gift splitting is elected?

12-34. *Determination of Taxable Gifts.* In the current year, Diane gives $50,000 of stock to Mel and $120,000 of bonds to Nan. In the current year, Diane's husband gives $150,000 of land to Opal. Assume the couple elects gift splitting for the current year.
  a. What are the couple's taxable gifts?
  b. How would your answer to Part a change if Diane gives the $50,000 of stock to Opal (instead of to Mel)?

12-35. *Recognition of Transactions Treated As Gifts.* In the current year, Emily, a widow, engages in the following transactions. Determine the amount of the completed gift, if any, arising from each of the following occurrences.
  a. Emily names Lauren the beneficiary of a $100,000 life insurance policy on Emily's life. The beneficiary designation is not irrevocable.
  b. Emily deposits $50,000 cash into a checking account in the joint names of herself and Matt, who deposits nothing to the account. Later that year, Matt withdraws $12,000 from the account.
  c. Emily pays $22,000 of Noah's medical expenses directly to County Hospital.
  d. Emily transfers the title to land valued at $60,000 to Olive.

12-36. *Calculation of Gift Tax.* Assume the same facts as in Problem 12-35. Emily's history of prior gifts is as follows:

Year	Amount of Taxable Gifts
1974	$500,000
1984	2,000,000

What is the gift tax liability with respect to Emily's current gifts?

12-37. *Recognition of Transactions Treated as Gifts.* In the current year Marge (age 67) engages in the following transactions. Determine the amount of the completed gift, if any, arising from each of the following events. Assume 10% is the applicable interest rate.
  a. Marge transfers $100,000 of property in trust and irrevocably names herself to receive $8,000 per year for life and Joy (age 37) to receive the remainder.
  b. Marge pays her grandson's $15,000 tuition to a university.
  c. Marge gives the same grandson stock valued at $72,000.
  d. Marge deposits $150,000 into a revocable trust. Later in the year the bank trustee distributes $18,000 of income to the named beneficiary, Gail.

12-38. *Recognition of Transactions Treated as Gifts.* Determine the amount of the completed gift, if any, arising from each of the following occurrences.
  a. A parent sells real estate valued at $1.8 million to an adult child who pays $1 million in consideration.

b. Prior to marriage, Al transfers $800,000 of stocks to Barb, his future wife. Barb signs an agreement waiving her future marital rights in Al's property. Such rights are estimated to be worth $800,000.
c. A furniture store holds a clearance sale and sells a customer a $5,000 living room suite for $1,500.
d. A parent purchases food and clothing costing $8,500 for his minor child.
e. A citizen contributes $1,500 cash to a political organization.
f. Zeke loans $600,000 interest free to Henry, who signs a demand note on August 1st. Assume 10% is the applicable interest rate.

12-39. *Determination of Unified Credit.* In November 1976, Mike makes a taxable gift of $100,000. In arriving at the amount of his taxable gift, Mike elects to deduct his $30,000 specific exemption. In the current year Mike makes his next gift; the taxable amount is $600,000.
  a. What unified credit may Mike claim on his current year's return?
  b. What unified credit can be claimed on Mike's current year return if the 1976 gift is made in May instead of November?

12-40. *Valuation of Gifts.* On September 1 of the current year, Norm transfers a $100,000 whole life insurance policy on his life to Norm, Jr. as owner. On September 1, the policy's interpolated terminal reserve is $30,000. Norm paid the most recent annual premium ($1,800) on June 1. What is the amount of the gift Norm made in the current year?

12-41. *Gift Tax Deductions.* Tina makes cash gifts of $400,000 to her spouse and $60,000 to the City Art Museum. What are the amounts of the deductions available for these gifts when calculating Tina's income tax and gift tax liabilities?

12-42. *Annual Exclusion.* For each of the following situations, determine the amount of the annual exclusion that is available. Explain your answer.
  a. Tracy creates a trust in the amount of $300,000 for the benefit of her 8-year-old daughter, May. She names Third National Bank as trustee. Before May reaches age 21, the trustee in its discretion is to pay income or corpus (trust assets) to May or for her benefit. When May reaches age 21, she will receive the unexpended portion of the trust income and corpus. If May dies before reaching age 21, the unexpended income and corpus will be paid to her estate or a party (or parties) she appoints under a general power of appointment.
  b. Assume the same facts as in Part a, except Tracy's daughter is age 28 when Tracy creates the trust and that the trust agreement contains age 41 wherever age 21 appears in Part a.

12-43. *Annual Exclusion.* During the current year Will gives $40,000 cash to Will, Jr. and a remainder interest in a few acres of land to Suzy. The remainder interest is valued at $32,000. Will and his wife Helen elect gift splitting, and during the current year Helen gives Joyce $8,000 of stock. What is the total amount of the annual gift tax exclusions available to Will and Helen?

12-44. *Annual Exclusion.* Bonnie, a widow, transfers $1 million of property to a trust with a bank named as trustee. For as long as Bonnie's daughter Carol is alive, Carol is to receive all of the trust income annually. Upon Carol's death, the property is to be distributed to Carol's children. Presently Carol is age 32 and has three children. How many gift tax exclusions does Bonnie receive for the transfer?

12-45. *Calculation of Gift Tax.* Before 1991 neither Hugo nor Wanda, his wife, made any gifts. In 1991 Hugo gives $10,000 cash to each of his 30 nieces, nephews, and grandchildren. In 1992 Wanda gives $30,000 of stock to each of the same persons. What is the *minimum* legal gift tax liability (before reduction for the unified credit) for each spouse for each year?

12-46. *Marital Deduction.* Hugh makes the gifts listed below to Winnie, his wife (age 37). What is the amount of the marital deduction, if any, that is attributable to each?
  a. $500,000 is transferred to a trust with a bank named as trustee. All of the income must be paid to Winnie monthly for life. At Winnie's death the property passes to Hugh's sisters or their estates.
  b. $300,000 is transferred to a trust with a bank named as trustee. Income is payable at the trustee's discretion to Winnie annually until the earlier of her death or her remarriage.

When payments to Winnie cease, the property is to be distributed to Hugh's children by a previous marriage or their estates.

12-47. *Calculation of the Marital Deduction.* In the current year Meg makes the transfers described below to Pete, her spouse, age 47. What is the amount of her marital deduction, if any, attributable to each transfer?
   a. In June she gives him land valued at $45,000.
   b. In October she gives him a 15-year income interest in a trust with a bank as trustee. She names their daughter to receive the remainder interest. The irrevocable trust is funded with $400,000, and 10% is the applicable interest rate.

12-48. *Charitable Contribution Deduction.* Velma (age 67) transfers a remainder interest in a vacation cabin (with a total value of $100,000) to a charitable organization. She retains a life estate in the cabin for herself.
   a. What is the amount of the charitable contribution deduction, if any, attributable to this transfer? Assume the rate for the actuarial tables is 10%.
   b. How will your answer to Part a change if Velma instead gives a remainder interest in a valuable oil painting (worth $100,000) to the organization?

12-49. *Calculation of Gift Tax.* In the current year Homer and his wife Wilma make the gifts listed below. Homer's previous taxable gifts consist of $200,000 made in 1970 and $800,000 made in 1984. Wilma has made no previous taxable gifts.

Wilma's current year gifts were	
to Art	$500,000
to Bart	8,000
Homer's current year gifts were	
to Linda	$700,000
to a charitable organization	60,000
to Norma (future interest)	460,000

   a. What are the gift tax liabilities of Homer and Wilma for the current year, assuming gift splitting is elected?
   b. How would the gift tax liabilities for each spouse in Part a change if gift splitting is not elected?

12-50. *Calculation of Gift Tax.* In the current year Henry and his wife Winnie made the gifts shown below. All gifts are of present interests. What is Winnie's gift tax payable for the current year if the couple elects gift splitting and Winnie's previous taxable gifts (made in 1985) total $1,000,000?

Winnie's current gifts were	
to Janet	$80,000
to Cindy	70,000
to Henry	40,000
Henry's current gifts were	
to Janet	30,000

12-51. *Basis Rules.* In June 1990, Karen transfers property with a $75,000 FMV and a $20,000 adjusted basis to Hal, her husband. Hal dies in March 1991; the property has appreciated to $85,000 in value by then.
   a. What is the amount of Karen's taxable gift?
   b. If Hal wills the property to Dot, his daughter, what would be Dot's basis for the property?
   c. How would your answer to Part b change if Hal instead wills the property to Karen?
   d. How would your answer to Part c change if Hal does not die until August 1991?
   e. What gain would Hal recognize if he sells the property for $95,000 in July 1990?

12-52. *Basis Rules.* Martha is considering giving away stock in Ace Corporation or Gold Corporation. Each has a current FMV of $500,000, and each has the same estimated appreciation rate. Martha's basis in the Ace stock is $100,000, and her basis in the Gold stock is $450,000. Which stock would you suggest that she give away and why, or does it make any difference?

12-53. *Below-Market Loans.* On October 1, 1991, Sam loans Tom $10 million. Tom signs an interest-free demand note. The loan is still outstanding on December 31, 1991. Explain the income tax and gift tax consequences of the loan to both Sam and Tom. Assume that the federal short-term rate is 9%.

12-54. *Below-Market Loans.* Assume the same facts as in Problem 12-53, except the amount of the loan is $42,000. This is the only loan between Sam and Tom. Tom's 1991 net investment income is $600.

12-55. *Filing Requirements.* In 1991 Jane gives $15,000 cash to Ann and $12,000 cash to Bob. Hank, her husband, makes identical gifts in 1991. May Jane file Form 709A (the short form) instead of Form 709?

TAX FORM/RETURN PREPARATION PROBLEMS

12-56. Dave and Sara Moore of Chicago, Illinois, engage in the transactions described below in the current year. Use this information to prepare a gift tax return (Form 709) for Dave. He and Sara want to use gift splitting. Assume the rate for the actuarial tables used is 10%. Dave's transactions are summarized below.

		Amount
1.	Tuition paid to Harvard University for son-in-law, Jim Smith	$ 12,000
2.	Room and board paid to Harvard University for Jim Smith	11,000
3.	Sports car purchased for Jim Smith	18,000
4.	Premium paid on life insurance policy on Dave's life. The policy was transferred to Dave's sister, Amy Lane, as owner in 1979	11,000
5.	Land given to daughter, Glenda Moore	68,000
6.	Remainder interest in personal residence given to State University. Dave (age 70) retains a life estate. The total value of the residence is $80,000.	
7.	Stocks transferred to trust with First National Bank named as trustee. The trust income is payable to Sara (age 60) semiannually for life. The remainder is payable at Sara's death to daughter, Amanda Webb, or her estate.	350,000

Sara's only gift was $42,000 of cash paid to Dave's sister, Amy Lane. Dave's gift history includes a $600,000 taxable gift made in 1975 and a $400,000 taxable gift made in 1982.

12-57. Alice Arnold, a widow, engages in the transactions listed below in the current year. Use this information to prepare a gift tax return (Form 709) for Alice.

		Amount
1.	Cash paid to daughter, Brenda Bell	$ 70,000
2.	Stock transferred to son, Al Arnold	300,000
3.	$400,000 interest-free demand loan made to Brenda Bell on July 1 (the loan is still outstanding on December 31)	

Assume 8% is the applicable interest rate. Alice has made only one previous taxable gift—$100,000 (taxable amount) in 1983.

CASE STUDY PROBLEM

12-58. Your client, Karen Kross recently married Larry Kross; she is age 72 and quite wealthy and in reasonably good health. To date, Karen has not made any taxable gifts, but Larry made taxable gifts totaling $700,000 in 1988. Karen is considering giving each of her five college-age grandchildren approximately $22,000 of cash for them to use to pay their college expenses of tuition and room and board for the year. In addition, she is considering giving her three younger grandchildren $3,000 each to use for orthodontic bills. Karen wants to give her daughter property valued at $400,000. She is trying to choose between a gift of cash and a gift of stock with a basis of $125,000. As for her son, she would like to give him $400,000 of property also, but would like for the property to be kept in a discretionary trust with a bank as trustee for at least 15 years. Karen has been approached by an agricultural museum about making a contribution to it and, as a result, is contemplating deeding her family farm to the museum but retaining a life estate in the farm.

Required: Prepare a memorandum to the tax partner of your firm that discusses the transfer tax and income tax consequences of the proposed transactions described above. Also, make any recommendations that you deem appropriate.

TAX RESEARCH PROBLEMS

12-59. Steve's employer provides group term life insurance for all of its employees, and the employer pays the annual premium on May 5 of each year. In 1983 Steve irrevocably transferred all of his ownership rights in the $40,000 policy on his life to his son Theo as owner. Steve is age 56 on May 5, 1991. Steve is not a "key employee." The corporation has thousands of employees, and it would be extremely difficult to determine the actual cost of the premium allocable to the insurance on Steve's life. Determine the gift tax consequences, if any, of the employer's payment of the annual premium on May 5, 1991. Be sure to denote the amount of the gift, if any.

A partial list of research sources is

- Reg. Sec. 25.2512-6.
- Rev. Rul. 76-490, 1976-2 C.B. 300.
- Rev. Rul. 84-147, 1984-2 C.B. 201.

12-60. On January 1, 1986, Amy makes an interest-free demand loan in the amount of $300,000 to her son Ben. On January 1, 1991, the state statute of limitations with respect to enforcing payment of this loan expires. As a result, Amy can no longer enforce payment. What are the gift tax consequences in 1991 with respect to the expiration of the statute of limitations? (You need not address any other tax matters.)

A partial list of research sources is

- *Estate of Grace E. Lang,* 64 T.C. 404 (1975), *aff'd.* and *rev'g.* 45 AFTR 2d 80-1756, 80-1 USTC ¶ 13,340 (9th Cir., 1980).

12-61. Wendy owns two $100,000 life insurance policies on the life of her husband, Harold. The beneficiary of each policy is the couple's adult child, Jenny. On May 1, 1991, Harold and Wendy are killed in a private plane crash. Their deaths are deemed to be simultaneous. Under their state's law concerning simultaneous deaths, Wendy is deemed to survive Harold. What gift tax consequences, if any, arise from the payment of the policy proceeds to the beneficiary, Jenny?

A partial list of research sources is

- Reg. Sec. 25.2511-1(h)(8).
- *Estate of Lillian Goldstone,* 78 T.C. 1143 (1982).

13 The Estate Tax

CHAPTER OUTLINE

LEARNING OBJECTIVES 13-2
ESTATE TAX FORMULA 13-2
- Gross Estate 13-2
- Deductions 13-4
- Adjusted Taxable Gifts and Tax Base 13-4
- Tentative Tax on Estate Tax Base 13-5
- Reduction for Post-1976 Gift Taxes 13-5
- Unified Credit 13-6
- Other Credits 13-6

THE GROSS ESTATE—VALUATION 13-6
- Date-of-Death Valuation 13-6
- Alternate Valuation Date 13-9

THE GROSS ESTATE—INCLUSIONS 13-10
- Comparison of Gross Estate with Probate Estate 13-10
- Property in Which Decedent Had an Interest 13-10
- Dower or Curtesy Rights 13-11
- Transferor Provisions 13-11
- Annuities and Other Retirement Benefits 13-15
- Jointly Owned Property 13-16
- General Powers of Appointment 13-17
- Life Insurance 13-18
- Consideration Offset 13-19
- Recipient Spouse's Interest in QTIP Trust 13-20

DEDUCTIONS 13-21
- Debts and Funeral and Administration Expenses 13-21
- Losses 13-22
- Charitable Contribution Deduction 13-23
- Marital Deduction 13-24

COMPUTATION OF TAX LIABILITY 13-27
- Taxable Estate and Tax Base 13-27
- Tentative Tax and Reduction for Post-1976 Gift Taxes 13-27
- Unified Credit 13-28
- Other Credits 13-28

COMPREHENSIVE ILLUSTRATION 13-30
- Background Data 13-30
- Calculation of Tax Liability 13-31

LIQUIDITY CONCERNS 13-33
- Deferral of Payment of Estate Tax 13-33
- Stock Redemptions to Pay Death Taxes 13-34
- Special Use Valuation of Farm Realty 13-35

GENERATION-SKIPPING TRANSFER TAX 13-35

TAX PLANNING CONSIDERATIONS 13-36
- Use of *Inter Vivos* Gifts 13-37
- Use of Exemption Equivalent 13-37
- What Size Marital Deduction Is Best? 13-37
- Use of Disclaimers 13-38
- Role of Life Insurance 13-39
- Qualifying the Estate for Installment Payments 13-39
- Where to Deduct Administration Expenses 13-40
- Flower Bonds 13-40

COMPLIANCE AND PROCEDURAL CONSIDERATIONS 13-40
- Filing Requirements 13-40
- Due Date 13-41
- Valuation 13-41
- Election of Alternate Valuation Date 13-41
- Documents to Be Included with Return 13-41

PROBLEM MATERIALS 13-42
- Discussion Questions 13-42
- Problems 13-43
- Comprehensive Problems 13-47
- Tax Form/Return Preparation Problems 13-48
- Case Study Problem 13-49
- Tax Research Problems 13-50

LEARNING OBJECTIVES

After studying this chapter, you should be able to

1. Explain the formula for the estate tax
2. Describe the methods for valuing interests
3. Determine which interests are includible in the gross estate
4. Identify deductions available for estate tax purposes
5. Calculate the estate tax liability
6. Identify tax provisions that alleviate liquidity problems
7. Recognize the filing requirements for estate tax returns

Gift taxes and estate taxes are wealth transfer taxes that are part of the unified transfer tax system. Both the gift tax and the estate tax account for only a small portion of the federal government's collections from taxation. Their history and purposes were discussed in Chapter 12.

As previously noted, the term *gift taxes* applies to lifetime transfers and the term *estate taxes* applies to dispositions of property that occur as a result of the transferor's death. This chapter discusses the structure of the estate tax. It examines in detail the types of interests and transactions that result in inclusions in the decedent's gross estate. The various deductions and credits affecting the estate tax liability and the rules concerning the taxable gifts that impact on the estate tax base are also discussed.

It is essential for the reader to keep in mind that the estate tax is a wealth transfer tax, not a property or an income tax. This point will make it easier to understand the rules surrounding the estate tax.

ESTATE TAX FORMULA

OBJECTIVE 1
Explain the formula for the estate tax

The tax base for the federal estate tax is the total of the decedent's (1) taxable estate (i.e., the gross estate less the deductions discussed below) and (2) adjusted taxable gifts (post-1976 taxable gifts). After the gross tax liability on the tax base is determined, various credits—including the unified credit—are subtracted to arrive at the net estate tax payable. The estate tax formula appears in Figure 13-1.

Gross Estate

Self-Study Question
Barb transfers $500,000 in trust, income for life to herself, remainder interest to her daughter Joan. Is there a taxable gift?

Answer
Yes, the value of the remainder interest is a completed gift and is not eligible for the annual $10,000 gift tax exclusion.

As illustrated in Figure 13-1, the process of arriving at the decedent's estate tax liability begins with determining which items are included in the gross estate. Items included in the gross estate are valued at either the decedent's date of death or the alternate valuation date.[1] As a transfer tax, the estate tax is levied on dispositions that are essentially testamentary in nature. Transactions are viewed as being essentially **testamentary** in nature if the transferor's control or enjoyment of the property in question ceases at death, not before death.[2]

---

[1] The alternate valuation date is the earlier of (1) 6 months after the date of death or (2) the date the property is disposed of.

[2] An example of a transaction that is essentially **testamentary** in nature is a situation where the donor transfers property in trust but reserves a lifetime right to receive the trust income.

Estate Tax Formula • 13-3

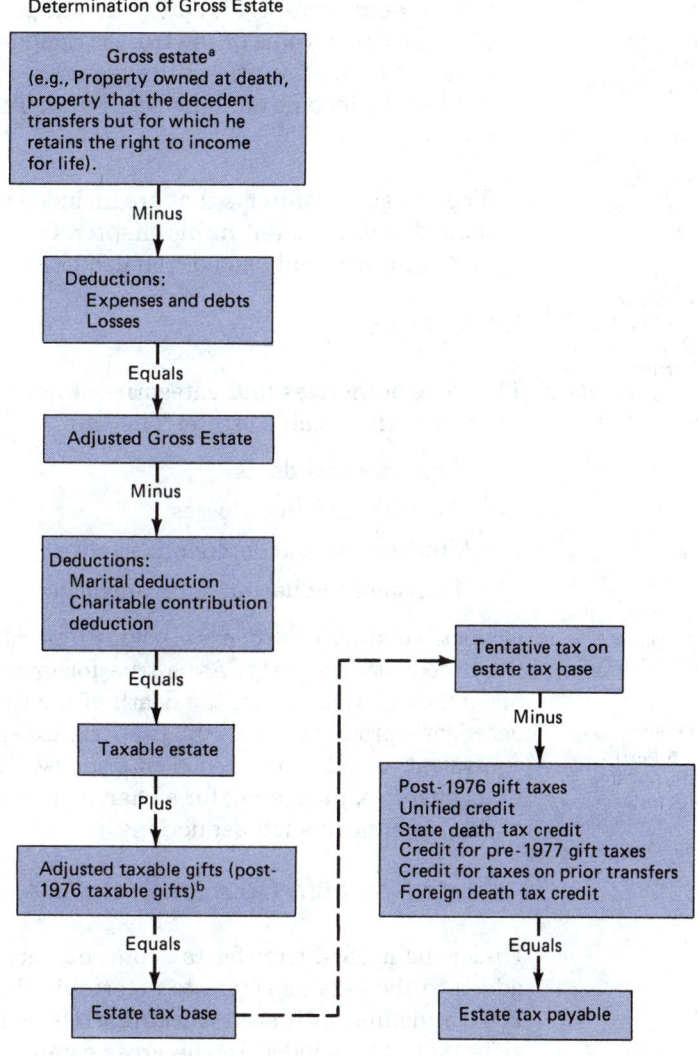

FIGURE 13-1 Estate Tax Formula

Self-Study Question

What part, if any, of the value of the trust assets will be included in Barb's estate?

Answer

The value of the entire trust will be included in Barb's estate, since she retained the income from the trust until her death.

Inclusions in the gross estate extend to a much broader set of properties than merely those to which the decedent holds title at the time of death. The fact that the decedent makes a lifetime transfer that generates a taxable gift does not guarantee that the transferred property will be removed from the decedent's gross estate. Although generally an individual removes property from his gross estate by giving it to another prior to death, the donor's gross estate must include the gifted property if either (1) the right to receive the income generated by such property or (2) control over the property is retained during the donor's lifetime.

Example 13-1 ■ In the current year, Ted transfers stocks to an irrevocable trust with a bank named as trustee. Under the terms of the trust agreement, Ted is to receive the trust income annually for the rest of his life. In the current year, Ted makes a taxable gift of the remainder interest (but not the income interest) in the trust. If the value of

13-4 • Ch. 13 / The Estate Tax

Self-Study Question

Suppose that Barb (in the previous Self-Study Question) names a qualified charitable organization the remainderman and reserves to herself a life annuity of 7% each year, based on the original $500,000 transfer. Is there a taxable gift?

Answer

The value of the remainder interest is a completed gift. However, the gift qualifies for the charitable contribution deduction and, consequently, Barb is not liable for any gift tax.

the remainder interest is sufficiently large, Ted incurs a gift tax liability. When Ted dies, the entire value of the trust is included in Ted's gross estate, even though Ted does not have legal title to the property. Because the shift in the enjoyment of the right to the income does not occur until Ted's death, the transfer is testamentary in nature. ■

The categories of items that are included in the gross estate and their valuation are examined in detail later in this chapter. Once the components of the gross estate have been determined and valued, the deductions from the gross estate are calculated.

Deductions

The Code authorizes four categories of items that may be deducted in arriving at the amount of the taxable estate. They are

- Expenses and debts
- Casualty and theft losses
- Transfers to the decedent's spouse
- Transfers to charitable organizations

Self-Study Question

What part, if any, of the value of the trust assets will be included in Barb's estate?

Answer

The value of the entire trust will be included in Barb's estate for the reason stated above. Her estate, however, will be allowed a charitable contribution deduction for the same amount.

Deductible kinds of expenses include funeral expenses and expenses of administering the decedent's property. As is true for gift tax purposes, there is no ceiling on the marital deduction. Thus, the death of the first spouse is free of estate taxes if all the decedent's property, or all the property except for an amount equal to the exemption equivalent, is left to the decedent's spouse.[3] Property passing to charitable organizations qualifies, in general, for a charitable contribution deduction. There is no ceiling on the amount of such deductions.

Adjusted Taxable Gifts and Tax Base

Under the unified transfer tax concept, certain gifts (i.e., adjusted taxable gifts) are added to the taxable estate to determine the amount of the estate tax base. Section 2001(b) defines **adjusted taxable gifts** as taxable gifts made after 1976 other than gifts that are included in the gross estate. Very few gifts are included in the gross estate; thus almost every post-1976 taxable gift is classified as an adjusted taxable gift.

Key Point

If a decedent leaves all of his property to his spouse, the decedent's exemption equivalent is lost. In addition, the estate of the survivor is increased and may be pushed into higher unified tax brackets.

Adjusted taxable gifts are valued at their date-of-gift values; therefore, any post-gift appreciation escapes both the gift tax and estate tax. Allowable deductions and exclusions are subtracted in determining the adjusted taxable gifts amount. The potential effect of having to increase the taxable estate by adjusted taxable gifts is to force the estate into a higher marginal tax rate.

Example 13-2 ■

Key Point

Income earned by gifted property is the donee's, and is not included in the donor's estate.

In 1982, Amy makes $5,000,000 of taxable gifts. In 1991, Amy dies with a taxable estate of $4,000,000. The property Amy gives away in 1982 appreciates to $7,000,000 in value by 1991. Amy's estate tax base is calculated as follows:

Taxable estate	$4,000,000
Plus: Adjusted taxable gifts (valued at date-of-gift values)	5,000,000
Estate tax base	$9,000,000

---

[3] The exemption equivalent, as explained in Chapter 12, is the size of the tax base for which the gift tax or estate tax liability will be exactly cancelled by the unified credit.

The $2,000,000 of post-gift appreciation escapes transfer taxation. The decedent's $9,000,000 tax base includes the gifted property, as valued on the date of the gift. ∎

Key Point

If a taxpayer dies in 1991 leaving a taxable estate of $21,040,000, the estate tax is a flat 55% of the estate, or $11,572,000. The unified credit has been completely phased-out.

Tentative Tax on Estate Tax Base

Once the amount of the tax base has been determined, the next step is to calculate the tax on this base. Section 2001(c) contains the unified tax rates; they are reproduced on the inside back cover. For tax bases in excess of $2.5 million, Congress approved a gradual lowering of the tax rates beginning in 1982. For estates of persons dying through 1992, the top marginal tax rate is 55%. The top rate declines to 50% for estates where the decedent dies after 1992. The benefits of the marginal tax rates below 55% (or 50% after 1992) and the unified credit are phased-out for larger estates when the date of death is after 1987. This phase-out is accomplished by imposing an additional 5% tax on tax bases in excess of $10,000,000 but not in excess of $21,040,000 ($18,340,000 after 1992). As described below, the tax determined from the rate schedules is reduced by the decedent's post-1976 gift taxes.

Example 13-3 ∎

Additional Comment

Example 13-3 refers to the 55% marginal tax rate as the highest marginal tax rate in 1991. The 55% rate does not include the 5% surcharge to phase-out the unified tax credit. One might argue that the marginal tax rate for taxable estates between $10,000,000 and $21,040,000 in 1991 and 1992 is 60%.

Assume the same facts as in Example 13-2. The tax on Amy's $9,000,000 tax base is $4,590,800. The estate is taxed at a 55% marginal rate, the highest rate applicable in 1991. ∎

Reduction for Post-1976 Gift Taxes

Adjusted taxable gifts, in effect, are not taxed twice because Sec. 2001(b)(2) allows a reduction to the estate tax for gift taxes imposed on post-1976 taxable gifts. If the rate schedule for the year of death differs from the schedule applicable for the year of the gift, the tax on post-1976 taxable gifts is determined by using the rate schedule in effect for the year of death. This rule works to the disadvantage of decedents who make taxable gifts and pay taxes at a higher rate than the rate in effect on the date of death. The rationale for this rule is to ensure that the estate pays a transfer tax at the current marginal tax rate for a decedent with a particular size taxable estate and adjusted taxable gifts.

Example 13-4 ∎

Assume the same facts as in Examples 13-2 and 13-3. Recall that in 1982 Amy made $5,000,000 of taxable gifts. The tax on $5,000,000 of 1982 taxable gifts is $2,530,800. Amy is entitled to a $62,800 unified credit and pays $2,468,000 of gift taxes. Amy's 1982 gifts are taxed at a 65% marginal rate. For the year of Amy's death (1991), the marginal rate for $5,000,000 of transfers is 55%. Consequently, the reduction for gift taxes on post-1976 taxable gifts is limited to the amount of gift taxes that would be payable if the 1991 rate schedule was in effect in the year of the gift. This amount is calculated as follows:

Tax on $5,000,000 at 1991 rates	$2,390,800
Minus: Unified credit for 1982 (the year of the gift)	(62,800)
Tax that would have been payable on $5,000,000 if 1991 rates were in effect	$2,328,000

Note that the only part of the gift tax computation that is changed is that the 1991 transfer tax rates are used. The actual credit applicable for the year of the gift (and not the credit for the year of death) is subtracted. ∎

Example 13-5

Self-Study Question

Taxpayer made net taxable gifts in 1987 of $3,000,000, on which she paid gift taxes of $1,098,000 (Gross tax of $1,290,800 minus the unified credit of $192,800). Taxpayer died in 1991, leaving a taxable estate of $100,000. Determine the amount of her estate tax liability.

Answer

The unified tax base is $3,100,000, the sum of the 1987 taxable gifts and the $100,000 estate. The 1991 tax on $3,100,000 is $1,345,800. The unified credit of $192,800 and the credit for gift taxes paid of $1,098,000 reduces the tax liability to $55,000. The tax due equals the additional tax base of $100,000 times the 55% marginal estate tax rate.

Self-Study Question

Calculate the 1991 tax on a $600,000 estate. Assume the decedent has a unified tax base of $600,000.

Answer

The unified tax on a $600,000 tax base is: Tax on first $500,000—$155,800; Tax on next $100,000 at 37%—$37,000; Tax on $600,000 equals $192,800. Note: the unified credit of $192,800 reduces the liability to zero.

From Examples 13-3 and 13-4, Amy's estate tax, before reduction for any credits, is calculated as follows:

Tax on $9,000,000 tax base (Example 13-3)		$4,590,800
Minus:	Tax on $5,000,000 of post-1976 taxable gifts, at 1991 rates (Example 13-4)	(2,328,000)
Estate tax, before reduction for credits		$2,262,800

Unified Credit

The unified credit of Sec. 2010 enables a tax base of a certain size, referred to as the exemption equivalent, to be completely free of transfer taxes. Like the situation for gift tax purposes, the unified credit has increased over the years. For decedents dying in 1987 and later years, the unified credit is $192,800, which is equivalent to a $600,000 exemption. The amount of the unified credit by year is reproduced on the inside back cover.

The estate tax computation permits an estate to subtract the entire unified credit applicable to the year of death (reduced by any phase-out for certain pre-1977 gifts) regardless of the amount of the unified credit that the decedent claimed for gift tax purposes. As a conceptual matter, however, only one unified credit is available. Under the unification concept, the estate tax is computed on a tax base consisting of the taxable estate plus the adjusted taxable gifts. The reduction to the tentative tax on the tax base amount for post-1976 gift taxes is not for the amount of the "gross" tax on the adjusted taxable gifts but, rather, for the "gross" tax on such gifts minus the unified credit. This computation achieves the same result as allowing the unified credit amount to be subtracted only once against all of a person's transfers.

Other Credits

In addition to the unified credit—the only credit available for gift tax purposes—the Code authorizes four credits for estate tax purposes. These additional credits are discussed in more detail on pages 13-28 through 13-30.

THE GROSS ESTATE—VALUATION

Date-of-Death Valuation

OBJECTIVE 2
Describe the methods for valuing interests

All property included in the gross estate is valued at either its fair market value (FMV) as of the date of death or the alternate valuation date. The valuation date election is an all-or-nothing proposition. Each item included in the gross estate must be valued as of the same date (i.e., the executor may not value some items at what they are worth on the date of death and others at what they are worth on the alternate valuation date).

Typical Misconception
The basis of inherited property is the value of the property on the estate tax return. Because fair market value is used in the estate tax return, the basis of property to an heir could be higher or lower than the decedent's basis. This change is referred to as a "step-up" or a "step-down" in basis. Many taxpayers hear so much about "step-up" that they sometimes forget that "step-down" may also occur.

Fair market value is defined as "the price at which the property would change hands between a willing buyer and a willing seller, neither being under any compulsion to buy or to sell and both having reasonable knowledge of relevant facts."[4] In general, the FMV of a particular asset on a certain date is the same regardless of whether the property is being valued for gift or estate tax purposes. Life insurance on the life of the transferor is an exception to this rule. Upon the death of the insured, the policy is valued at its face value, whereas it is valued at a lesser amount while the insured is alive. Generally, this lesser amount is either the cost of a comparable contract or the policy's interpolated terminal reserve plus the unexpired portion of the premium.

With respect to certain types of properties, the Regulations contain detailed descriptions of the valuation approach. However, the valuation of interests in closely held businesses is described in only very general terms. More detailed rules can often be found in supplementary sources (e.g., revenue rulings and judicial decisions). Valuation rules for several interests are discussed below. For purposes of this discussion, it is assumed that date-of-death valuation is elected.

Listed Stocks. Stocks traded on a stock exchange are valued at the average of their highest and lowest selling prices on the date of death.[5] If no sales occur on the date of death, but sales do take place within a few days before and after such date, the estate tax value is a weighted average of the high and low sales prices on the nearest trade dates before and after the date of death. The average is weighted inversely in relation to the number of days separating the sales dates and the date of death.

Example 13-6 ■ Bob, who dies on November 15, owns 100 shares of Jet Corporation stock that is traded on the New York Stock Exchange. Jet stock trades at a high of $120 and a low of $114 on November 15. On Bob's estate tax return the stock is valued at $117 per share, the average of $120 and $114. ■

Example 13-7 ■ Susan, who dies on May 7, owns 100 shares of Top Corporation stock that is traded on the New York Stock Exchange. On May 7 there are no sales of Top stock. The sales occurring closest to May 7 take place 2 business days before May 7 and 3 business days after May 7. On the earlier date, the stock trades at a high of $500 and a low of $490, with an average of $495. On the later date, the high is $492 and the low is $490, for an average of $491. The date-of-death per-share valuation of the stock is computed under the inverse weighted average approach, as follows:

$$\frac{[3 \times \$495] + [2 \times \$491]}{5} = \$493.40$$

■

The total value of the block of Top stock is $49,340 (100 × $493.40).

In certain circumstances, the decedent may own such a large block of stock that the price at which the stock is traded in the market may not represent the FMV per share for the decedent's number of shares. A departure from the traditional valuation rule for stocks is allowed in such circumstances. These regulations, referred to as the blockage regulations, state,

> In certain exceptional cases, the size of the block of stock to be valued in relation to the number of shares changing hands in sales may be relevant in determining whether selling prices reflect the fair market value of the block of stock to be valued. If the executor can

[4] Reg. Sec. 20.2031-1(b).
[5] Reg. Sec. 20.2031-2(b).

show that the block of stock to be valued is so large in relation to the actual sales on the existing market that it could not be liquidated in a reasonable time without depressing the market, the price at which the block could be sold as such outside the usual market, as through an underwriter, may be a more accurate indication of value than market quotations.[6]

Interests in Firms Whose Stock Is Not Publicly Traded. Often the decedent owns stock in a firm whose shares are not publicly traded. No regulations specifically address the valuation rules for this type of an interest. Rather detailed guidelines are found in Rev. Rul. 59-60, however.[7] The ruling lists the following items, among others, as factors to be considered in valuing such stock:

- Nature and history of the business
- General economic outlook and the outlook for this specific industry
- Book value of the stock and the business's financial condition
- Firm's earning capacity
- Firm's dividend-paying capacity
- Market values of actively traded stocks of companies engaged in the same business or a similar one

Real Estate. Perhaps surprisingly, the Regulations do not specifically address the question of the valuation approach for real estate. Thus, the general valuation principles concerning a price that would be acceptable to a willing buyer and a willing seller must be implemented without the benefit of more specific guidance. Appraisal literature discusses three techniques for valuing realty: comparable sales, reproduction cost, and capitalization of earnings.[8] Unfortunately, it may be difficult to locate a comparable real estate sale. The reproduction cost, of course, is not applicable to valuing land. Capitalization of earnings is often used in valuing commercial realty. At times, all three approaches may be used.

Annuities, Interests for Life or a Term of Years, Reversions, Remainders. Actuarial tables are used to value annuities, interests for life or a term of years, reversions, and remainders that are included in the gross estate.[9] The same tables apply for both estate and gift tax purposes. (See Chapter 12 for a discussion of the use of these tables.) The following example illustrates a situation when the actuarial tables have to be used to value an inclusion in the decedent's estate.

Key Point
Larry's father created a trust and named Larry the income beneficiary for 30 years. At the time of Larry's death, he was entitled to receive the income from the trust for 12 additional years. The present value of the right to receive income from the trust for 12 additional years will be included in Larry's gross estate. Actuarial tables will be used to value the income interest.

Example 13-8 ■

In 1987 Tony gives property to a trust with a bank named as trustee and his daughter named to receive all of the trust income for the next 15 years (i.e., a term certain interest). At the end of the fifteenth year, the property reverts to Tony or his estate. Tony dies exactly 4 years after creating the trust; the trust property is valued at $100,000 at Tony's death. At Tony's death, the trust has 11 years to

---

[6] Reg. Sec. 20.2031-2(e). As examples of cases dealing with the blockage discount, see *Horace Havemeyer v. U.S.*, 33 AFTR 1069, 45-1 USTC ¶ 10,194 (Ct. Cls., 1945); *Estate of Charles M. Prell*, 48 T.C. 67 (1967); and *Estate of David Smith*, 57 T.C. 650 (1972). The *Smith* case extended the blockage concept to large holdings of works of art.

[7] 1959-1 C.B. 237.

[8] For a discussion of techniques for appraising real estate, see: Byrl N. Boyce and William N. Kinnard, Jr., *Appraising Real Property* (Lexington, MA: Lexington Books, 1984).

[9] Section 7520 provides that the interest rate potentially changes every month. Notice 89-60, 1989-1 C.B. 700, provides the tables. A segment of these tables is included in Appendix E.

continue until the property reverts to Tony's estate. The inclusion in Tony's estate is the value of a reversionary interest following a term certain interest with 11 remaining years. If 10% is the applicable rate for the actuarial tables, the reversionary interest is valued at $35,049 (0.350494 × $100,000) by using the excerpt from Table B of the actuarial tables included in Appendix E. ∎

Alternate Valuation Date

Section 2032 authorizes the executor to elect to value all property included in the gross estate at its FMV on the alternate valuation date. Congress authorized the alternate valuation date in response to the stock market crash of 1929. Its purpose was to make sure an entire estate could not be confiscated for taxes because of a sudden, substantial drop in values.

In general, the **alternate valuation date** is 6 months after the date of death. In situations where the property is distributed, sold, exchanged, or otherwise disposed of within 6 months of the date of death, the alternate valuation date is the date of sale or other disposition.

Example 13-9 ∎

Self-Study Question

Elwood's estate consisted of cash of $60,000, life insurance of $150,000, NYSE stocks valued at $90,000, and a lot and building. The real estate was appraised by two independent real estate appraisers. One valued the property at $150,000 and the second valued the property at $200,000. Which value should the estate report?

Answer

The higher value, $200,000. Since the gross estate is less than the equivalent exemption, no estate tax will be due. Therefore, valuing the property at $200,000 will not increase the tax. In addition, the heirs receive a higher basis that decreases (increases) the gain (loss) recognized when they dispose of the property in the future.

Key Point

The alternate valuation date cannot be elected unless both the gross estate and the estate tax are reduced by the election.

Ron dies on March 3 of the current year. Ron's estate includes two items—stock and land. The stock is still owned by the estate on September 3, but the land is sold on August 20. If Ron's executor elects the alternate valuation date, the stock is valued as of September 3. The land, however, is valued as of August 20, because it is disposed of prior to the end of the 6-month period. Of course, the value of land generally would change very little, if any, between August 20 and September 3. ∎

If the executor elects the alternate valuation date, generally any changes in value that occur *solely* because of a "mere lapse of time" are to be ignored in determining the property's value.[10] In a limited number of situations, one must consider this rule concerning the "mere passage of time." One example of such a situation involves valuing patents. If the executor elects the alternate valuation date, he must ignore any change in value that is attributable to the fact that the patent's remaining life is 6 months shorter on the alternate valuation date than it was on the date of death.

The basis of property received as the result of another's death is the property's FMV as of either the decedent's date of death or an alternate valuation date.[11] The alternate valuation date formerly offered a substantial tax planning advantage in situations when no estate tax was owed because the decedent took advantage of the unlimited marital deduction. If the property appreciated between the date of death and the alternate valuation date, the recipient could receive an increased basis by having the executor elect the alternate valuation date. If the estate took advantage of the unlimited marital deduction, it could achieve an additional step-up in basis without increasing the estate tax liability.

For estates of decedents dying after July 18, 1984, however, such a tax planning strategy does not exist. Now the alternate valuation date can be elected only if such election decreases (1) the value of the gross estate, and (2) the estate tax liability (after reduction for credits).[12] As a result of this new provision, electing the alternate valuation date cannot result in achieving a higher step-up in basis.

[10] Reg. Sec. 20.2032-1(f).
[11] Sec. 1014(a).
[12] Sec. 2032(c).

TOPIC REVIEW 13-1

Valuation

All property included in the gross estate is valued at its fair market value.

In general, property included in the gross estate is valued as of the decedent's date of death.

In certain circumstances the executor may elect to value the property at its alternate valuation date, which is usually six months after the date of death.

The alternate valuation date may not be elected unless the election reduces the value of the gross estate and the estate tax liability (after reduction for credits).

Adjusted taxable gifts (which are included in the estate tax base but not in the gross estate) are valued at their date-of-gift values.

Topic Review 13-1 summarizes the valuation rules.

THE GROSS ESTATE—INCLUSIONS

OBJECTIVE 3
Determine which interests are includible in the gross estate

As Figure 13-1 illustrates, the process of calculating the decedent's estate tax liability commences with determining the components of the gross estate. The **gross estate** is analogous to gross income. Once the components of the gross estate have been identified, they must be valued. As previously mentioned, the gross estate encompasses a much wider array of items than merely those to which the decedent held title at death. For example, under certain statutory provisions, referred to as the *transferor sections*, the gross estate includes items previously transferred by the decedent. For decedents other than nonresident aliens, the fact that property is located in a foreign country does not preclude it from being included in the gross estate.

Comparison of Gross Estate with Probate Estate

Self-Study Question
Which of the following properties will be included in (a) the probate estate, (b) the gross estate, (c) both the probate and gross estate, or (d) neither estate?
1. Realty held in joint tenancy with the decedent's spouse. (The answer is b.)
2. Realty held as a tenant in common with the decedent's spouse. (The answer is c.)
3. A life insurance policy owned by the decedent in which the decedent's spouse is named the beneficiary. (The answer is b.)
4. A life insurance policy always owned by the decedent's spouse in which the decedent's children are named the beneficiaries. (The answer is d.)

The gross estate is a federal tax law concept. The probate estate is a state law concept. To oversimplify, the **probate estate** can be defined as encompassing those properties that (1) pass subject to the will (or under an intestacy statute) and (2) are subject to court administration. Often, a decedent's gross estate is substantially larger than his probate estate. For example, suppose that at the time of death, the decedent owns a life insurance policy on his own life. The decedent's daughter is the beneficiary. The policy is not a part of the decedent's probate estate because it is payable directly to the daughter, but it is included in the gross estate.

Property in Which the Decedent Had an Interest

Section 2033, which is sometimes referred to as the *generic section*, provides that the gross estate includes the value of all property the decedent beneficially owned at the time of death. Its broad language taxes such items as a personal residence, automobile, stocks, and any other asset titled in the decedent's name. Because the rule refers to "beneficial ownership," however, its scope extends beyond assets to which the decedent held title. For example, such items as remainder interests are also included in the gross estate.

Example 13-10 ■ Ken's will names Ann to receive trust income for life and Bill or Bill's estate to receive the trust remainder upon Ann's death. Bill's gross estate, therefore, includes the value of the remainder interest even if Bill predeceases Ann. If Bill does not outlive Ann, the passage of the remainder is controlled by Bill's will. The transfer is associated with Bill's death, and, hence, is subject to the estate tax. ■

Example 13-11 ■ At the time of his death, the following assets are in Mark's name: personal residence, mountain cabin, Zero Corporation stock, checking account, and savings account. Mark beneficially owns each of these items when he dies. Under Sec. 2033, each item is included in Mark's gross estate. ■

Self-Study Question

Dorothy died on April 10. At that time she owned Z Corporation bonds which paid interest on April and October 1. Dorothy also owned stock in X and Y Corporations. X Corporation had declared a dividend on March 15 payable to stockholders of record on April 1. Y Corporation had declared a dividend on March 31 payable to stockholders of record on April 15. Dorothy's estate received Dorothy's interest and dividend payments on the payment dates. Should any of the interest or dividends be included in Dorothy's gross estate?

Dower or Curtesy Rights

Certain state laws provide surviving spouses with dower or curtesy rights.

- **Dower** is a widow's interest in her deceased husband's property.
- **Curtesy** is a widower's interest in his deceased wife's property.

Because of dower and curtesy provisions, married individuals may not have absolute control over the disposition of all of their properties. State law entitles the surviving spouse to a certain portion of the decedent spouse's estate, even though the decedent may have willed a smaller portion to the surviving spouse. The decedent's gross estate is not reduced for the value of the property in which the surviving spouse has a dower or curtesy interest or some other statutory interest.[13]

Example 13-12 ■ The laws of a certain state provide that widows are entitled to receive one-third of their decedent husband's property. The husband's gross estate is not reduced by his widow's dower rights (one-third interest) in his property. ■

Answer

The X Corporation dividend must be included in the gross estate since the date of record occurred prior to Dorothy's death. The Y Corporation dividend will not be included in the estate because the date of record was after Dorothy's death. The Z Corporation bond interest that must be included in the estate is the interest which accrued between the April 1 payment date and the decedent's April 10 date of death.

Transferor Provisions

Sections 2035 through 2038 are referred to as the transferor provisions. They apply if (1) the decedent earlier made a transfer of a type specified in the Code section in question, *and* (2) the decedent did not receive adequate consideration in money or money's worth for the transferred interest. If one of the transferor provisions applies, the transferred property is included in the gross estate at its date-of-death or alternate valuation date value.

Gifts Made Within 3 Years of Death. Section 2035(d) specifies the circumstances in which a gift that a decedent makes within 3 years of death triggers an inclusion in the gross estate. The scope of this provision, which is relatively narrow, encompasses the following two types of transfers made by the donor-decedent within 3 years prior to death:

- A life insurance policy on the decedent's life that would have been taxed in the gross estate under Sec. 2042 had it not been given away

[13] Sec. 2034.

Key Point

Any property which passes outright to the decedent's spouse, due to dower or curtesy rights in the state law, is eligible for the marital deduction and will not be included in the unified tax base.

- An interest in property that would have been taxed under Sec. 2036 (transfers with a retained life estate), 2037 (transfers taking effect at death), or 2038 (revocable transfers) had it not been transferred

Of these situations, the most common involves the insured's gifting a life insurance policy on his own life and dying within 3 years of the transfer. In the case of new insurance policies, the potential for an inclusion can be avoided if the decedent never owned the new policy. In other words, instead of the insured purchasing a new policy and then giving it to a transferee as owner, the other party should be the one who buys the new policy.

Example 13-13 ■ On April 1, 1988, Roy transfers to Sally ownership of a $400,000 life insurance policy on his own life purchased in 1984. Sally is the policy's beneficiary. Roy dies on February 3, 1991. Because Roy dies within 3 years of giving away the policy, the policy is included in Roy's gross estate. The estate tax value of the policy is its $400,000 face value. If Roy had lived until at least April 2, 1991, the policy transfer would have fallen outside the 3-year rule, and the policy would not have been included in Roy's gross estate. ■

Example 13-14 ■ Roy makes a gift of stock to Troy on May 1, 1990. Roy dies on February 3, 1991. The stock is worth $80,000 on the gift date and $125,000 at the time of Roy's death. The stock is not included in Roy's gross estate. The gifted property is not life insurance on Roy's life, nor is it property that would have been taxed in Roy's estate under Secs. 2036 through 2038 had he kept such property. ■

Self-Study Question

Why is Sec. 2035(d) so narrow in scope?

Answer

Taxable gifts made after 1976 are now part of the unified tax base. In years prior to 1977, a gift of property was subject to the gift tax but was not subject to the estate tax on the death of the donor. To combat "death-bed" gifts, prior law caused gifts that were made "in contemplation of death" to be included in the gross estate.

Gross-Up Rule. The donor-decedent's gross estate is increased by any gift tax that he or his estate pays on any gift that he or his spouse makes during the 3-year period ending with the decedent's death.[14] This provision, known as the gross-up rule, applies with respect to the gift tax triggered by a gift of any type of property during the 3-year look-back period.

Only gift taxes paid on post-1976 gifts are affected by this rule. The purpose of the rule is to foreclose the opportunity that existed under pre-1977 law to reduce one's gross estate (and thereby one's taxable estate) by removing the gift tax on "deathbed" gifts from the gross estate. The donor's estate received a credit for some or all of the gift tax paid. Consequently, under the pre-1977 rules a person on his deathbed could prepay a portion of his estate tax and at the same time reduce his gross estate by the amount of the gift tax.

The effect of this rule, as illustrated in the two examples below, is to reinstate the estate to the position it would be in if no gift tax liability were incurred.

Example 13-15 ■ In late 1988 Joan makes a $1,000,000 taxable gift of stock and pays a gift tax of $153,000 ($345,800 gross tax − $192,800 unified credit). Joan dies in early 1991. Joan's gross estate does not include the stock, but it does include the $153,000 gift tax paid because the gift is made within 3 years of her death. ■

Example 13-16 ■ In late 1988 Hal makes a gift of stock having a $2,020,000 FMV, and he and Wanda, his wife, elect gift splitting. Each is deemed to have made a $1,000,000 taxable gift, and each pays $153,000 ($345,800 gross tax − $192,800 unified credit)

---

[14] Sec. 2035(c).

The Gross Estate—Inclusions • 13-13

Self-Study Question

Refer to Example 13-16. Assume that Hal, the spouse who actually made the gift, paid Wanda's $153,000 gift tax as well as his own $153,000 gift tax. Would Wanda's $153,000 gift tax be included in her gross estate?

Answer

No, it would not be included since it did not reduce her estate when it was paid.

of gift tax. Wanda dies in early 1990. Wanda's gross estate includes the $153,000 in gift tax she paid on the portion of her husband's gift that she is deemed to have made within 3 years of her death. ∎

Transfers with Retained Life Estate. Section 2036, although entitled "Transfers with Retained Life Estate," extends beyond taxing solely those lifetime transfers made by the decedent in which he retained a life estate. The two primary types of transfers that are taxed under Sec. 2036 are those for which the decedent

- Kept possession or enjoyment of the property or the right to its income
- Retained the power to designate the person who is to possess or enjoy the property or to receive its income

Thus, Sec. 2036 applies when the transferor kept (1) the income or enjoyment or (2) the right to control other individuals' income or enjoyment.

The retention, directly or indirectly, of voting rights in stock of a controlled corporation that has been transferred can also cause the stock to be included in the transferor's gross estate.[15] A controlled corporation is one in which the decedent owned (directly, indirectly, or constructively), or had the right to vote, stock that possessed at least 20% of the voting power.[16]

The retention of income, control, or voting rights for one of three retention periods listed below causes the transferred property to be included in the transferor's gross estate. The three periods are

Self-Study Question

Mary owns a $500,000 face amount life insurance policy on her life. Dick is the named beneficiary. The cash value of the policy is $70,000. How can Mary make a gift of the policy to Dick and keep the amount of the gift within the $10,000 annual gift tax exemption amount?

Answer

One way is to borrow $60,000 from the insurance company against the value of the policy, thus reducing the value of the policy to $10,000. If Mary continues to pay the premiums on the policy and wishes to pay off the policy loan, the total amount of premiums and loan paid by Mary in each year following the year of the gift should not exceed $10,000. A second way to keep the gift amount below $10,000 is to have the insurance company rewrite the policy into separate policies, each having a value of less than $10,000. She could then gift one policy each year for several years.

- The transferor's lifetime
- A period that cannot be determined without referring to the transferor's death (e.g., the transferor retained the right to quarterly payments of income, but payments ceased with the last quarterly payment prior to the transferor's death)
- A period that in fact does not end before the transferor's death

An implied agreement or understanding is sufficient to trigger taxation. For example, if a mother gives a residence to her daughter and continues to occupy the residence alone and rent free, the residence will likely be included in the mother's estate. The rationale is that there was an implied understanding that the mother could occupy the residence for life.

If Sec. 2036 applies to a transfer, and the decedent's retention of enjoyment or control extends to all of the transferred property, 100% of the value of the transferred property is included in the transferor's gross estate.[17] However, if the transferor keeps the right to only one-third of the income for life and retains no control over the remaining two-thirds, his estate includes just one-third of the date-of-death value of the property. The following three examples illustrate some of the transactions that cause Sec. 2036 to apply.

Example 13-17 ∎ In 1986 David (age 30) transfers an office building to Ellen but retains the right to collect all of the income from the building for life. David dies in 1991. Because David retained the income right for life, there is a Sec. 2036 inclusion. The amount included is 100% of the building's date-of-death value. ∎

---

[15] Sec. 2036(b)(1).
[16] Sec. 2036(b)(2).
[17] Reg. Sec. 20.2036-1(a).

Example 13-18 ■ Assume the same facts as in Example 13-17, except that David retains the right to income for only 15 years. David dies 5 years after the transfer; therefore, David has the right to receive the income for the remaining 10-year period. Because the retention period does not *in fact* end before David's death, his gross estate includes 100% of the property's date-of-death value. ■

Example 13-19 ■ Tracy creates a trust and names Alice, Brad, and Carol to receive the trust income for their joint lives and Dick to receive the remainder upon the death of the first among Alice, Brad, and Carol to die. Tracy reserves the right to designate the portion of the income to be paid to each income beneficiary each year. Tracy dies before any of the other parties. Because the control over the flow of income does not end before Tracy's death, the date-of-death value of the trust assets is included in Tracy's estate. If Tracy had instead "cut the string" and not kept control over the income flow, she could have removed the trust property from her estate. ■

Self-Study Question

Refer to Example 13-19. Assume the same facts except that the trust is directed to distribute its annual income equally to Alice, Brad, and Carol for the duration of their joint lives. Also assume that Tracy names Dick and Eva the remaindermen. Will the value of the trust be included in Tracy's gross estate?

Answer

No, since Tracy retained no power to alter the enjoyment of the property.

Reversionary Interests. Under Sec. 2037 the transferor's gross estate includes earlier transferred property if (1) the decedent stipulates that another person must survive him in order to own the property and (2) the value of the decedent's reversionary interest exceeds 5% of the value of the transferred property. If there is the chance that the property will pass back to the transferor under the terms of the transfer, the transferor has a reversionary interest. Actuarial techniques are used to value the reversionary interest.[18] Section 2037 does not apply if the value of the reversionary interest does not exceed the 5% *de minimis* amount.

Example 13-20 ■ Beth transfers an asset to Tammy for life and then to Doug for life. The asset is to revert to Beth, if Beth is still alive, upon the death of either Tammy or Doug, whoever dies second. If Beth is not alive upon the death of the survivor of Tammy and Doug, the asset is to pass to Don or to a charitable organization if Don is not alive. Thus, Don must live longer than Beth in order to receive the property. The property is included in Beth's estate if the value of Beth's reversionary interest exceeds 5% of the property's value. The amount that is included is not the value of Beth's reversionary interest, but rather the date-of-death value of the gifted property less the value of Tammy's and Doug's intervening life estates. ■

Revocable Transfers. Section 2038 covers the rules for revocable transfers. However, this provision also taxes all transfers over which the decedent has, at the time of his death, the power to change the enjoyment by altering, amending, revoking, or terminating an interest. Section 2038 can apply even though the decedent does not originally have powers over the property. The crucial factor is that the transferor possesses the powers at the time of death regardless of whether they were retained originally.

The estate must include only the value of the interest that is subject to change by the decedent. Sections 2038 and 2036 overlap greatly. If one amount is taxable under one section and a different amount is taxable under the other section, the gross estate includes the larger amount. Two types of transfers taxed by Sec. 2038 are illustrated in the following examples.

---

[18] The **reversionary interest** is the interest that will return to the transferor; often it will return only if certain contingencies occur. The value of Beth's reversionary interest in Example 13-20 is a function of the present value of the interest Beth would receive after the deaths of Tammy and Doug, valued as from actuarial tables (see Appendix E) and coupled with the probability that Tammy and Doug would die before Beth.

Example 13-21 ■ Joe creates and funds a revocable trust. Joe names his son to receive the income for life and his grandson to receive the property upon the son's death. Because the trust is revocable, Joe may change the terms of the trust or take back the trust property during his lifetime. Joe's power to revoke the transfer extends to the entire amount of the trust. Thus, Joe's gross estate includes the date-of-death value of the entire trust. ■

Example 13-22 ■ Vicki creates a trust and names Gina to receive the income for life and Matt to receive the remainder. Vicki, however, retains the right to substitute Liz (for Matt) as remainderman. When Vicki dies, she has the authority to change the enjoyment of the remainder. Thus, the value of the trust's remainder interest is includible in Vicki's estate. ■

Annuities and Other Retirement Benefits

Self-Study Question

Reggie purchased a 15-year term certain annuity. If Reggie dies before the end of the 15-year term of the annuity, his estate will be entitled to the remaining payments. Reggie died after receiving nine of the fifteen payments. Will the value of the remaining six payments be included in Reggie's estate?

Answer

Yes, Sec. 2039 requires that the present value of the six payments be included in his gross estate.

Section 2039 explicitly addresses the estate tax treatment of annuities. Even if this section had not been enacted, some annuities would probably have been taxable under the more general language of Sec. 2033, because the decedent would have been viewed as having an interest in the property. For an annuity to be included in the gross estate, it must involve payments made under a contract or an agreement. In addition, the decedent (1) must be receiving such payments at the time of his death or (2) must have the right to collect such payments alone or with another person. For the payments to be included in the decedent's estate, they must be paid for the decedent's life, a period that may not be determined without referring to the decedent's date of death or for a period that does not actually end before the decedent's death.

Annuities Not Related to Employment. The purchase of an annuity designed to pay benefits to the purchaser and then to a named survivor upon the purchaser's death, or to both parties simultaneously and then to the survivor, is a form of wealth shifting. The other party receives wealth that originates with the purchaser. This type of transfer is different from most other wealth transfers because it involves a series of annuity payments instead of a transfer of a tangible property.

The amount included in the gross estate with respect to annuities or other retirement benefits is a fraction (described below) of the value of the annuity or lump-sum payment to be received by the surviving beneficiary. If the annuity simply ceases with the death of the decedent in question, nothing is to be received by another party and nothing is included in the gross estate. Annuities are valued at the cost of a comparable contract.[19] To determine the figure to be included in the gross estate, this cost is multiplied by a fraction that represents the portion of the purchase price that the decedent has contributed.

Example 13-23 ■ In 1983 Jim purchases a joint and survivor annuity to pay benefits to himself and his son and then to the survivor. Jim and his son start collecting payments in 1989. In 1991, Jim dies. Jim is survived by his son. At the time of Jim's death, the cost of a comparable contract providing the same benefits to the son is $180,000. Because Jim has provided all of the consideration to purchase the annuity, his gross estate

---

[19] Reg. Sec. 20.2031-8(a).

includes 100% of the $180,000 cost of a comparable contract. This annuity arrangement represents a shifting of wealth from Jim to his son upon Jim's death. ■

Employment-Related Retirement Benefits. Recall that the cost of a comparable contract is multiplied by a fraction representing the portion of the purchase price contributed by the decedent to determine the amount of an annuity that is includible in the decedent's gross estate. Section 2039(b) states that contributions from the decedent's employer (or former employer) are treated as contributions made by the decedent, provided such payments are made as a result of the employment relationship.[20] Thus, 100% of the benefits from an employment-related annuity are included in the gross estate.[21]

Example 13-24 ■

Self-Study Question

On his retirement at age 65, Winslow elected to take a joint and survivor annuity from his qualified pension plan, which had been entirely financed by Winslow's employer. The plan provided Winslow and his wife, Alma, with a monthly pension payment of $2,500. Winslow died seven years later. What amount, if any, must be included in Winslow's gross estate with respect to the pension annuity?

Answer

The value of the payments, $2,500 per month for Alma's remaining expected life, will be included in Winslow's gross estate. Actuarial methods will be used to value the annuity.

Pat was employed by Wheel Corporation at the time of his death. Wheel Corporation maintains a qualified retirement plan to which it makes 60% of the contributions and its employees contribute 40%. Pat's spouse is to receive an annuity valued at $350,000 from the retirement plan. Because the employer's contributions are considered to have been made by the employee, Pat is deemed to have provided all of the consideration for the retirement benefits. Consequently, Pat's gross estate includes 100% of the annuity's $350,000 date of death value. ■

Jointly Owned Property

Section 2040 addresses the estate tax treatment of jointly owned property (i.e., property owned in a joint tenancy with right of survivorship or tenancy by the entirety arrangement).[22] An important characteristic of such a form of ownership is that, upon the death of one joint owner, the decedent's interest passes automatically (by right of survivorship) to the surviving joint owner(s). Section 2040 contains two sets of rules, one for property jointly owned by spouses and one for all other jointly owned properties.

Ownership Involving Persons Other Than Spouses. When persons other than spouses or persons in addition to spouses own property as joint owners, a test to determine the amount of consideration furnished is used to ascertain the amount

---

[20] Section 2039(c) [prior to its repeal] allowed an exclusion for a portion of the retirement benefits payable from qualified plans for the estates of decedents dying prior to 1985.

[21] Section 4980A imposes a 15% tax on "excess accumulations" attributable to a qualified retirement plan as of an employee's death. This tax, which is an addition to the regular estate tax, may not be reduced by the unified credit. "Excess accumulations" equal the excess of (1) the value of the decedent's interest in the retirement benefits over (2) the present value of an annuity of $150,000.

[22] The following definitions are from Henry Campbell Black, *Black's Law Dictionary*, Rev. 5th ed., Ed. by Joseph R. Nolan, Michael J. Connolly, et al. (St. Paul, Minn.: West Publishing Co., 1979).

Joint tenancy with right of survivorship—An estate in fee-simple, fee-tail, for life, for years, or at will, arising by purchase or grant to two or more persons. Joint tenants have one and the same interest, accruing by one and the same conveyance, commencing at one and the same time, and held by one and the same undivided possession. The primary incident of joint tenancy is survivorship, by which the entire tenancy on the decease of any joint tenant remains to the survivors, and at length to the last survivor.

Tenancy by the entirety—is created by a conveyance to husband and wife, whereupon each becomes seized and possessed of the entire estate and after the death of one the survivor takes the whole. And is available only to husband and wife. The grand characteristic which distinguishes it from a joint tenancy is that it can be terminated only by joint action of husband and wife during their lives, while "joint tenancy" may be terminated by one tenant's conveyance of his interest.

Both joint tenancies with right of survivorship and tenancies by the entirety have the feature of survivorship. When one joint owner dies, his interest passes by right of survivorship to the remaining joint owner(s). Only spouses may use the tenancy by the entirety arrangement. A joint tenancy with right of survivorship may be severed by the action of any joint owner, whereas a tenancy by the entirety arrangement continues unless severed by the joint action of both joint owners.

includible.[23] Under this test, property is included in a joint owner's gross estate in accordance with the portion of the consideration he furnished to acquire the property. Obviously, this portion can range between 0% and 100%.

Example 13-25 ■

Key Point

Property held in joint tenancy at time of death will not be included in the probate estate. Joint tenancies are sometimes referred to as the "poor man's" will.

In 1987 Fred and Jack provide $10,000 and $30,000 of consideration, respectively, to purchase realty titled in the names of Fred and Jack as joint tenants with right of survivorship. Fred dies in 1991 and is survived by Jack. In 1991 the realty is valued at $60,000. Fred's gross estate includes $15,000 (0.25 × $60,000) because Fred furnished 25% of the consideration to acquire the property. If Jack instead predeceases Fred in 1991, his estate would include $45,000 (0.75 × $60,000). ■

If part of the consideration furnished by one joint tenant is originally received gratuitously from another joint tenant, the consideration is attributable to the joint tenant who made the gift. If all joint owners acquire their interests by gift, devise, bequest, or inheritance, the decedent joint owner's estate includes his proportionate share of the date-of-death value of the jointly owned property.

Example 13-26 ■

Typical Misconception

The tracing rule is easy to understand, but difficult to implement. Suppose, for example, that a joint tenancy between a parent and a child was created in a parcel of real estate thirty years ago. The child has just died of a heart attack and the parent, due to the onset of old age, has no memory. What goes into the child's gross estate? Perhaps one-half the value of the property, but the burden of proof to keep a portion of the property out of the estate is on the estate, not the IRS.

Ray gives stock valued at $50,000 to Sandy. Three years later Sandy uses this stock (now valued at $60,000) as partial consideration to acquire realty costing $120,000. Ray furnishes the remaining $60,000 of consideration. The realty is titled in the names of Ray and Sandy as joint tenants with right of survivorship. Because Sandy received the asset that he used as consideration as a gift from Ray (the other joint tenant), Sandy is treated as having furnished no consideration. If Sandy dies before Ray, Sandy's estate will include none of the realty's value. But if Ray predeceases Sandy, Ray's estate will include the entire date-of-death value. ■

Ownership Involving Only Spouses. If spouses are the only joint owners, the property is classified as a **qualified joint interest.** Section 2040(b)(1) provides that in the case of qualified joint interests, the decedent's gross estate includes one-half the value of the qualified joint interest. The 50% inclusion rule applies automatically regardless of the relative amount of consideration provided by either spouse.

Example 13-27 ■

Self-Study Question

Fred and Myrtle, husband and wife, hold title to their home in joint tenancy with right of survivorship. They have three children. Fred is killed in an airplane crash. What part of the value of the residence will be included in Fred's estate? Who will own the residence if Fred wills his property to the children?

Answer

One-half the value of the residence would be included in Fred's gross estate. Myrtle will own the residence after Fred's death because it passes to her by right of survivorship.

Wilma provides all of the consideration to purchase stock costing $80,000. She has the stock registered in her name and her husband's name as joint tenants with right of survivorship. The estate of the first spouse to die, regardless of which spouse it is, will include 50% of the value of the jointly owned stock. Of course, upon the second spouse's death, all of the property will be included in the gross estate because it will no longer be jointly owned property. ■

General Powers of Appointment

Section 2041 requires certain property interests that the decedent never owns in a legal sense to be included in the gross estate. This occurs because the decedent had the power to designate who would eventually own the property. The authority to designate the owner—a significant power—is referred to as a power of appointment. There are both general and special (i.e., more restricted) powers of appointment.

Only a general power of appointment results in an addition to the gross estate. If a general power was created before October 22, 1942, however, there is no inclusion unless the decedent exercised the power. For a post-1942 general power of appointment, there is an inclusion regardless of whether the power is exercised. A general

---

[23] Sec. 2040(a).

power of appointment exists if the holder can exercise the power in favor of himself, his estate, his creditors, or the creditors of his estate. Being exercisable in favor of the decedent's estate means that there are no restrictions on the powerholder's ability to name the person(s) to receive the property. The power may be exercisable during the decedent's life, by his will, or both.

If the appointment power is limited by an ascertainable standard, it is not a general power. Appointment powers are governed by an ascertainable standard and are free of estate tax consequences if they may be exercised solely for purposes of the decedent's health, support, maintenance, or education.

Example 13-28 ■ When Kathy dies in 1950, her will creates a trust from which Doris is to receive the income for life. In addition, Doris is granted the power to designate by will the person or persons to receive the trust's assets. Doris has a testamentary general power of appointment. The trust's assets are included in Doris's gross estate regardless of whether Doris exercises the power. If Kathy had instead died in 1940, Doris would have had a pre-1942 power of appointment. Such powers are taxed only if exercised. ■

Example 13-29 ■ Assume the same facts as in Example 13-28, except that Kathy's will merely empowers Doris to name which of her descendants would receive the trust assets. Doris now has only a special power of appointment because she does not have the power to leave the property to whomever she desires (e.g., the power to appoint the property to her estate). Because Doris's power of appointment is only a special power, the value of the trust is not included in Doris's gross estate. ■

Typical Misconception
Many taxpayers who own life insurance policies on their own lives believe that their estates will not owe estate taxes on the life insurance proceeds if they name someone other than themselves as the beneficiary. At the time of death, life insurance will be included in the gross estate of the decedent if the decedent held any (one) of the incidents of ownership in the policy.

Life Insurance

Section 2042 addresses the estate tax treatment of life insurance policies on the life of the decedent. Life insurance policies owned by the decedent on the lives of others are taxed under the more general language of Sec. 2033. According to Sec. 2042, a decedent's gross estate includes the value of policies on his own life if (1) the proceeds are receivable by the executor or for the benefit of the estate, or (2) the decedent had any "incidents of ownership" in the policy at the time of death. The Regulations list the following powers as a partial inventory of the incidents of ownership:

- To change the beneficiary
- To surrender or cancel the policy
- To borrow against the policy
- To pledge the policy for a loan
- To revoke an assignment of the policy[24]

The examples in the Regulations of incidents of ownership involve economic rights over the insurance policies. Judicial decisions have also been important in defining what constitutes incidents of ownership. In some jurisdictions, the phrase has been interpreted to be broader than simply relating to economic powers.[25]

---

[24] Reg. Sec. 20.2042-1(c)(2).
[25] See, for example, *Estate of James H. Lumpkin, Jr., v. CIR*, 31 AFTR 2d 73-1381, 73-1 USTC ¶ 12,909 (5th Cir., 1973), wherein the court held that the right to choose how the proceeds were to be paid—in a lump sum or in installments—was an incident of ownership.

If the decedent could have exercised the incidents of ownership only in conjunction with another party, the policy is nevertheless included in the gross estate. Moreover, it is the legal power to exercise ownership rights, compared with the practical ability to do so, that leads to an inclusion. The Supreme Court in the *Estate of Marshal L. Noel* emphasized the decedent-insured's legal powers in a situation where the insured was killed in a plane crash and the policies he owned on his life were in his spouse's possession on the ground. The Court held that the decedent possessed incidents of ownership and thus the policies were includible in his gross estate.[26]

Example 13-30 ■ Tracy purchases an insurance policy on her life in 1980. In 1984 she transfers all of her incidents of ownership in the policy to her daughter. Seven years after the transfer, Tracy dies. Tracy's niece has always been the policy's beneficiary. The policy is not included in Tracy's gross estate because Tracy did not have any incidents of ownership in the policy at the time of her death, nor is her estate the beneficiary. ■

Example 13-31 ■ Assume the same facts as in Example 13-30, except that Tracy's estate is instead designated as the policy's beneficiary. Because Tracy's estate is designated as the beneficiary, the policy is included in her gross estate. The policy is valued at its face value. ■

It is not sufficient to consider only Sec. 2042 in determining whether a life insurance policy on the decedent's life is includible in their gross estate. Recall from the discussion on page 13-12 that a life insurance policy is includible in a decedent's gross estate if the individual makes a gift of a life insurance policy on his own life within 3 years of dying.[27]

Example 13-32 ■ In 1989 Ken gives all of his incidents of ownership in a life insurance policy on his own life to his son, Jeff. The face value of the policy is $400,000. Jeff has always been the beneficiary. Ken dies in 1991. Because Ken dies within 3 years of giving Jeff the policy, Ken's gross estate includes the policy. The policy is valued at its date-of-death value of $400,000. The potential problem of making a transfer of a life insurance policy within 3 years of death could have been avoided if Jeff had been the one who originally owned the policy. In that case, Ken would not have made a transfer and need not have been concerned with the 3-year rule. ■

Self-Study Question
In reviewing his estate tax plan, Farmer Brown is concerned the estate will not have sufficient cash to pay its estate taxes. Farmer Brown could buy life insurance so his estate will have cash to pay the estate taxes. However, if Farmer Brown owns the policy or if he names his estate the beneficiary of the policy, the proceeds of the policy will also be taxed in his gross estate. What should he do to remove the life insurance from his gross estate?

Answer
Farmer Brown should have his children (or an irrevocable life insurance trust) buy the life insurance and name themselves the beneficiaries, even if Farmer Brown has to provide the funds for the premiums (by making gifts).

Consideration Offset

Section 2043 allows an offset against inclusions in the gross estate for consideration that was received with respect to certain transactions.[28] This offset is allowed only if the decedent received some, but less than adequate, consideration with respect to an earlier transaction. The gross estate is reduced by an offset for the partial consideration received. The consideration is valued as of the transfer date. This offset, called the consideration offset, serves the same function as a deduction in that it reduces the

---

[26] *CIR v. Estate of Marshal L. Noel*, 15 AFTR 2d 1397, 65-1 USTC ¶ 12,311 (USSC, 1965).
[27] The gifted insurance policy is included under the rules of Sec. 2035(d)(2).
[28] Section 2043 provides a consideration offset for items included in the gross estate under Secs. 2035 through 2038 and 2041.

taxable estate. If the decedent receives consideration equal to the value of the property transferred, the property in question is not included in the gross estate. No offset is permitted if the property is not included in the decedent's gross estate.

The consideration offset is designed to prevent a double counting of property in the decedent's estate. For example, if an individual makes a transfer that is includible in the gross estate and receives partial consideration in return, the consideration received is part of the gross estate unless it has been consumed. Sections 2035 through 2038 also require the transferred property to be included in the gross estate, even though it is not owned on the date of death.

Example 13-33 ■ In 1989, Steve transfers a $300,000 life insurance policy on his life to Earl. The policy is worth $75,000 at the time of transfer, and Earl pays $48,000 cash for the policy. Steve dies in 1991 with the $48,000 cash still in his savings account. Steve's gross estate includes both the amount in the savings account and the $300,000 face value of the insurance policy. Under Sec. 2043, Steve's gross estate is reduced by the $48,000 consideration received on the transfer of the insurance policy. The insurance policy on Steve's life would be excluded from Steve's estate if Steve survived the transfer by more than 3 years. No consideration offset is permitted in this situation because the property for which the consideration is received is not included in the gross estate. ■

Recipient Spouse's Interest in QTIP Trust

Key Point
A widow or widower should attempt, during her or his lifetime, to reduce her or his estate by gifts, charitable or otherwise, so that her or his estate is no more than the $600,000 exemption equivalent. If the person is the beneficiary of a QTIP trust, all income must be distributed at least annually. It is important that this unconsumed income be gifted away so as to not increase the estate of the survivor.

Chapter 12 contains a discussion of the gift tax consequences of transferring qualified terminable interest property (QTIP) to one's spouse. The estate tax rules for QTIP interests are explained at pages 13-26 and 13-27. Claiming a marital deduction with respect to QTIP interests is voluntary. Should the donor or the executor elect to claim a marital deduction for QTIP interests transferred to the spouse during life or at death, the transferred property is generally included in the recipient spouse's gross estate.[29] A QTIP interest included in the gross estate, like other property included in the gross estate, is valued at its date-of-death or alternate valuation date value.

The QTIP interest is excluded from the gross estate of the surviving spouse if the transferor spouse does not elect to claim a martial deduction and if the recipient spouse has a life estate, has no general power of appointment, and was not the transferor. Therefore, no Code sections act to cause the property to be includible in the gross estate.

There is no inclusion in the gross estate for QTIP interests for which a marital deduction is elected if the recipient spouse disposes of all or a portion of his or her income interest during his or her lifetime. Dispositions of all or a portion of one's income interest in a QTIP are treated under Sec. 2519 as a transfer of all interests in the QTIP other than the qualifying income interest.

Example 13-34 ■ Henry dies in 1986. His will creates a $600,000 QTIP trust for his widow, Wendy, age 75. Henry's executor elects to claim a marital deduction for the QTIP trust. Wendy dies in 1991. By then, the assets in the QTIP trust have appreciated to $850,000. Wendy's gross estate includes the QTIP trust, which is valued at $850,000. If Henry's executor did not claim a marital deduction for the QTIP trust, the value of the trust would be excluded from Wendy's estate. ■

---

[29] Sec. 2044.

TOPIC REVIEW 13-2

Inclusions in the Gross Estate

Code Section	Type of Property or Transaction Included
2033	Property in which the decedent had an interest
2035	Gift taxes on property given away within 3 years of death plus certain property (primarily life insurance) given away within 3 years of death
2036	Property which the decedent transferred but in which the decedent retained economic benefits or the power to control enjoyment
2037	Property which the decedent transferred but for which the decedent has too large a reversionary interest
2038	Property which the decedent transferred but over which the decedent held the power to alter, amend, revoke or terminate an interest
2039	Annuities
2040	Jointly owned property
2041	Property over which the decedent possessed a general power of appointment
2042	Life insurance on the decedent's life
2044	QTIP trust for which a marital deduction was claimed by the decedent's spouse

Topic Review 13-2 summarizes the inclusions in the gross estate.

DEDUCTIONS

OBJECTIVE 4
Identify deductions available for estate tax purposes

As mentioned earlier in this chapter, there are four categories of deductions from the gross estate. Two of these deduction categories (debts and funeral and administration expenses and casualty and theft losses) cause the tax base to refect the net wealth passed to the decedent's heirs, legatees, or devisees. The two remaining deduction categories provide the estate with a reduction in the tax base for transfers to one's spouse (the marital deduction) or to charitable organizations (the charitable contribution deduction). There is no deduction, however, for the amount of wealth that is diverted to the government in the form of estate taxes. Each deduction category is examined below.

Debts and Funeral and Administration Expenses

Section 2053 authorizes deductions for mortgages and other debts owed by the decedent, as well as for the decedent's funeral and administration expenses. Mortgages and all other debts of the decedent are deductible provided they represent bona fide contracts for an adequate and full consideration in money or money's worth. Even

Typical Misconception

Most taxpayers are so used to dealing with the fact that expenses for income tax purposes must be paid or accrued in order to be deductible that they do not recognize that the expenses of administering an estate can be estimated at the time the estate tax return is due. This is necessary because the administration of the estate can go on long after the estate tax return is filed.

debts relating to an expenditure for which no income tax deduction would be allowable are deductible. Interest, state and local taxes, and trade or business expenses that are accrued at the date of death are deductible on both the estate tax return (as a debt of the decedent) and on the estate's income tax return (as an expense known as a deduction in respect of a decedent) when they are paid. (See Chapter 14 for a discussion of the income tax implications.)

Examples of administration expenses include executor's commissions, attorneys' fees, court costs, accountants' fees, appraisers' fees, and expenses of preserving and distributing the estate. The executor must decide whether to deduct administration expenses on the estate tax return or the estate's income tax return. Such expenses cannot be deducted twice, although some may be deducted on the estate tax return and others on the estate's income tax return.

An estate that does not owe any estate tax (e.g., due to the unlimited marital deduction or the unified credit) should deduct administration expenses on its income tax return because no tax savings will result if they are deducted on the estate tax return. If an estate owes estate taxes, its marginal estate tax rate will be at least 37% because the tax base will exceed the $600,000 exemption equivalent. Consequently, the administration expenses should be deducted on the estate tax return because the highest income tax rate for an estate in 1991 is 31%.

Funeral expenses are deductible only on the estate tax return. The estate may deduct any funeral expenses that are allowable under local law including "[a] reasonable expenditure for a tombstone, monument, or mausoleum, or for a burial lot, either for the decedent or his family, including a reasonable expenditure for its future care."[30] The transportation costs of the person bringing the body to the burial place also are deductible as funeral expenses.

Example 13-35 ■ At Ed's date of death, Ed owes a $75,000 mortgage on his residence, plus $280 of interest accrued thereon, and $320 of personal expenditures charged to a department store charge card. The estate's administration expenses are estimated to be $32,000. His funeral expenses total $12,000. Under Sec. 2053, Ed's estate can deduct $75,600 ($75,000 + $280 + $320) for debts and $12,000 for funeral expenses. The $32,000 of administration expenses are deductible on the estate tax return, on the estate's income tax return for the year in which they are paid, or some on each return. Ed's estate will get an income tax deduction for the accrued interest whenever it is paid. ■

Losses

Key Point

The executor should elect to deduct any casualty or theft loss, when such loss is allowable, from the estate tax return if the estate will be liable for any estate tax liability. Since the highest marginal income tax rate is 31% and the lowest estate tax rate is 37% when a tax is owed, the deduction should be taken on the return with the highest marginal tax rate.

Section 2054 authorizes a deduction for losses incurred from theft or casualty while the estate is being settled. Just as in the context of the income tax, examples of casualties include fires, storms, and earthquakes. The amount of the loss takes into consideration the amount of any insurance compensation received. If the alternate valuation date is elected, the loss may not be used to reduce the alternate value and then used again as a loss deduction. As with administration expenses, the executor must decide whether to deduct the loss on the estate tax return or the estate's income tax return. There is no double deduction for these losses.

Example 13-36 ■ Sam dies on May 3 of the current year. One of the items included in Sam's gross estate is a mountain cabin valued at $35,000. The uninsured cabin is totally destroyed in a landslide on August 18 of the current year. If the date-of-death

---

[30] Reg. Sec. 20.2053-2.

valuation is chosen, the cabin is included in the gross estate at $35,000. The executor must choose between claiming a Sec. 2054 deduction on the estate tax return or a casualty loss deduction on the estate's income tax return. ■

Example 13-37 ■ Assume the same facts as in Example 13-36, except that Sam's executor elects the alternate valuation date. The cabin is valued at zero when determining the value of the gross estate. No loss deduction is available for the casualty on the estate tax return. The estate cannot claim an income tax deduction for the casualty loss either, because the property's adjusted basis in its hands is zero. ■

Additional Comment
Persons who have a desire to leave property to a charity at the time of their death should be encouraged to give the property prior to death. If they do so, they can obtain an income tax deduction for the gift and at the same time reduce their estate by the amount of the gift.

Charitable Contribution Deduction

Section 2055 authorizes a deduction for transfers to charitable organizations. The rules concerning eligible donee organizations are the same as for gift tax purposes.

Because there is no ceiling on the amount of the estate tax charitable contribution deduction, a decedent could eliminate his estate tax liability by willing all of his property (or all of his property except for an amount equal to the exemption equivalent) to a charitable organization. Similarly, an estate tax liability could be eliminated if an amount equal to the exemption equivalent is willed to the decedent's children and the rest of the estate is willed to the surviving spouse and a charitable organization (e.g., in equal shares).[31]

Computing the Deduction. Computation of the estate tax charitable contribution deduction can be somewhat complicated in certain circumstances. Suppose the decedent (a widow) has a $5 million gross estate and no Sec. 2053 or 2054 deductions. The decedent's will specifies that her son is to receive $3 million and a charitable organization is to receive the residue (the rest not explicitly disposed of). Assume that state law specifies that death taxes are payable from the residue. Because $3 million of property passes to the decedent's child, the estate will definitely owe some estate taxes. The charitable organization will receive $2 million, less the estate taxes payable therefrom. The estate tax liability depends upon the amount of the charitable contribution deduction, which in turn depends upon the amount of the estate tax liability. Simultaneous equations are required in order to calculate the amount of the charitable contribution deduction.[32]

Example 13-38 ■ Don (a widower) dies with a gross estate of $6,000,000. Don wills State University $1,000,000 and the residue of his estate to his children. Under state law, death taxes are payable from the residue. Don's estate receives a charitable contribution deduction for $1,000,000. ■

Split-Interest Transfers. If the decedent's will provides for a split-interest transfer (i.e., a transfer of interests to both an individual and a charitable organization), the rules concerning whether a charitable contribution deduction is available are very technical. Basically, the rules are the same as for gift tax purposes.

Example 13-39 ■ Jane dies in 1991 with a gross estate of $2,500,000. Under Sec. 2036, one of the items included in Jane's gross estate is her personal residence, valued at $350,000. She gave City Art Museum a remainder interest in the residence in 1986 but

---

[31] Another way the estate could owe no taxes is if all of the property, or all of the property except for the exemption equivalent, is shielded from taxation by the marital deduction.

[32] The simultaneous equation problem does not generally occur if a charity is willed a specific dollar amount.

retained the right to live there rent free for the rest of her life. Upon Jane's death, no other individuals have an interest in the residence. Jane received an income tax deduction in 1986 for the transfer of the remainder interest. Her estate receives a $350,000 charitable contribution deduction.

There is no added estate tax cost attributable to her lifetime transfer. The residence is included in her gross estate, but the inclusion is a wash because of the charitable contribution deduction claimed for the amount of the inclusion. ■

Marital Deduction

The fourth category of deduction is the marital deduction for certain properties passing to the decedent's surviving spouse.[33] For estates of decedents dying after 1981, there is no ceiling on the marital deduction. Thus, the decedent's estate does not owe any federal estate taxes if all of the items includible in the decedent's gross estate (or all items except an amount equal to the exemption equivalent) pass to the surviving spouse.[34] If the surviving spouse is not a U.S. citizen, however, a marital deduction is not available unless the decedent's property passes to a special trust called a qualified domestic trust.

The marital deduction is intended to provide equal treatment for decedents of common law and community property states. As mentioned in Chapter 12, marital property is treated differently under each type of state law. In community property states, for example, a large portion of the assets acquired after a couple is married constitutes community property (i.e., property owned equally by each spouse). On the other hand, in common law states, one spouse may own the majority of the assets acquired after marriage. Thus, if there were no marital deduction, the progressive estate tax rates could cause the combined estate tax liability to be higher for a couple living in a noncommunity property state. Nevertheless, a marital deduction is even available to a decedent dying after 1981 who owns nothing but community property.

Only certain transfers to the surviving spouse are eligible for the marital deduction. The estate does not receive a marital deduction unless the interest conveyed to the surviving spouse will be subject to either the estate tax in the recipient spouse's estate or to the gift tax if transferred while the surviving spouse is alive. In other words, the surviving spouse can generally escape transfer taxation on the transferred property only by consuming it.

The following three tests must be met before an interest qualifies for the marital deduction:

1. The property must be included in the decedent's gross estate.
2. The property must pass to the recipient spouse in a qualifying manner.
3. The interest conveyed must not be a nondeductible terminable interest.

Test 1: Property Must Be in Gross Estate. No property passing to the surviving spouse is eligible for the marital deduction unless the property is included in the decedent's gross estate. The reason for this rule is obvious: Something that is excluded from the gross estate cannot generate a deduction.

Example 13-40 ■ At the time of Gail's death there is a life insurance policy on her life for which her spouse, Al, is the beneficiary. Gail's sister always had the incidents of ownership in the policy. Gail also had the title to the personal residence in which she and Al lived. The residence is willed to Al. The residence qualifies for the marital

---

[33] Sec. 2056.
[34] Some states have not adopted an unlimited marital deduction; therefore, some estates may owe state death taxes, even though no federal liability exists.

deduction. Even though the insurance proceeds are payable to Al, Gail's estate receives no marital deduction for the insurance. The policy is excluded from Gail's gross estate because she had no incidents of ownership, her estate was not the beneficiary, and the policy was not transferred within 3 years of her death. ■

Test 2: The Passing Requirement. Property is not eligible for the marital deduction unless it passes to the decedent's spouse in a qualifying manner. According to Sec. 2056(c), property is deemed to pass from one spouse to the other if the recipient-spouse receives the property as a result of the following:

- A bequest or devise under the decedent's will
- An inheritance resulting from the decedent's dying intestate
- Dower or curtesy rights
- An earlier transfer from the decedent
- Right of survivorship
- An appointment by the decedent under a general power of appointment or in default of appointment
- A designation as the beneficiary of a life insurance policy on the decedent's life

In addition, a surviving spouse's interest in a retirement benefit plan is considered to have passed from the decedent to the survivor to the extent the retirement benefits are included in the gross estate.[35]

Test 3: The Terminable Interest Rule. The last test requires that the recipient-spouse's interest not be classified as a nondeductible terminable interest.[36] A terminable interest is one that ceases upon the passage of time or the occurrence of some event. Some terminable interests qualify for the marital deduction, however, because only nondeductible terminable interests fail to generate a marital deduction. Nondeductible terminable interests have the following features:

- An interest in the property must pass or have passed from the decedent to a person other than the surviving spouse, and such person must have paid less than adequate consideration in money or money's worth
- The other person may possess or enjoy any part of the property after the termination of the surviving spouse's interest.

Thus, if the decedent makes a transfer whereby the surviving spouse receives the right to receive all of the income annually for life and a general power of appointment over the property, the property is eligible for the marital deduction. As discussed below, as a result of the QTIP provisions a marital deduction is available for certain transfers that would otherwise be disqualified.

Example 13-41 ■ At the time of Louis's death he wills a copyright with a 10-year remaining life to his spouse, Tina, age 42. His will also sets up a trust for the benefit of Tina, whom he entitles to receive all of the income semiannually until the earlier of her remarriage or her death. Upon Tina's remarriage or death, the trust property is to be

---

[35] Reg. Sec. 20.2056(e)-1(a)(6).
[36] Nondeductible terminable interests are also precluded from eligibility for the marital deduction for gift tax purposes.

Self-Study Question

A decedent, by will, creates a trust with income to the surviving spouse for 25 years, remainder to children. The surviving spouse's life expectancy is 16 years. Does the property qualify for the marital deduction?

Answer

The property does not qualify because the surviving spouse's interest terminates at the end of 25 years. The fact that his or her life expectancy is less than the term of the income interest is immaterial.

Self-Study Question

How does the donor spouse or decedent spouse who establishes a QTIP trust control the disposition of the trust corpus?

Answer

The donor or decedent spouse states in the trust instrument or in his will who the remainder interest will go to on the death of the surviving spouse. This allows the donor or decedent spouse to control the ultimate disposition of the property.

distributed to the couple's children or their estates. Both the copyright and the trust are terminable interests. The copyright is eligible for the marital deduction because it is not a nondeductible terminable interest. No person other than Tina receives an interest in the copyright. No marital deduction is available for the trust because it is a nondeductible terminable interest. Upon the termination of Tina's interest, the children will possess the property, and they receive their interests from Louis without paying adequate consideration. ∎

QTIP Transfers. For the estates of persons dying after 1981, Sec. 2056(b)(7) authorizes a marital deduction for transfers that were previously ineligible for the deduction. The eligible transfers are of qualified terminable interest property (called QTIP transfers). The QTIP provisions are somewhat revolutionary because they allow a marital deduction in situations where the recipient spouse is not entitled to control which parties eventually receive the property.

Qualified terminable interest property is defined as property which passes from the decedent in which the surviving spouse has a qualifying income interest for life, and to which an election applies. A spouse has a qualifying income interest for life if the following are true:

- He or she is entitled to all of the income from the property payable at least annually.
- No person has a power to appoint any portion of the property to anyone other than the surviving spouse, unless the power cannot be exercised during the spouse's lifetime (e.g., exercisable only at or after the death of the surviving spouse).

Claiming the marital deduction with respect to QTIP transfers is not mandatory. In the event the executor elects to claim a marital deduction for the QTIP transfer, the marital deduction is for the entire amount of the QTIP transfer. In other words, the deduction is not limited to the value of the surviving spouse's life estate.

If the marital deduction is elected in the first spouse's estate, the property is taxed in the surviving spouse's estate under Sec. 2044 or is subject to the gift tax in such spouse's hands if disposed of during the spouse's lifetime.[37] Thus, as with other interspousal transfers, the QTIP provisions allow a postponement of the taxable event until the second spouse dies or disposes of the interest by gift. If the taxable event is postponed, the property is valued at its FMV as of the date of the second spouse's transfer by gift or at death.

Example 13-42 ∎

Key Point

Refer to Example 13-42. The executor may elect QTIP status for less than the entire property in the trust. For example, the executor in the example might elect QTIP treatment for only 60% of the $1,000,000 placed in the trust. If this is done, on Mary's death, 60% of $1,300,000, or $780,000 is included in her estate.

Tom dies in 1987. He is survived by his spouse, Mary, who lives until 1991. Tom's will calls for setting up a $1,000,000 trust from which Mary would receive all of the income quarterly for the rest of her life. Upon Mary's death, the property is to be distributed to Tom's children by a previous marriage. At Mary's death, the trust assets are valued at $1,300,000. If Tom's executor elects to claim a marital deduction, Tom's estate receives a $1,000,000 marital deduction. Section 2044 includes $1,300,000 in Mary's gross estate. If Tom's executor forgoes electing the marital deduction, Mary's gross estate excludes the value of the trust. The trust assets will be taxed in the estate of one of the spouses. ∎

---

[37] Section 2519 states that if a recipient spouse disposes of a qualifying income interest for life for which the donor or the executor elected a marital deduction under the QTIP rules, the recipient spouse is treated as having made a gift of everything except the qualifying income interest. Under the generic gift rules of Sec. 2511, the gift of the income interest is treated as a gift.

TOPIC REVIEW 13-3

Estate Tax Deductions	
Code Section	Type of Deduction
2053	Funeral and administration[a] expenses and debts
2054	Casualty and theft losses[a]
2055	Charitable contributions[b]
2056	Marital deduction[b]

[a] Deductible on the estate tax return or on the estate's income tax return.
[b] No limit on deductible amount.

The aggregate amount of the four categories of deductions is subtracted from the gross estate amount to determine the taxable estate. Topic Review 13-3 summarizes the estate tax deductions.

COMPUTATION OF TAX LIABILITY

OBJECTIVE 5
Calculate the estate tax liability

As mentioned earlier, the estate tax base is the aggregate of the decedent's taxable estate and his adjusted taxable gifts. Figure 13-1 illustrates how these two concepts are combined in the estate tax formula.

Taxable Estate and Tax Base

The gross estate's value is reduced by the deductions to arrive at the amount of the taxable estate. Before 1977, the taxable estate was the tax base for the estate tax. Under the unification provisions effective after 1976, however, the estate tax base consists of the taxable estate plus the adjusted taxable gifts. Adjusted taxable gifts are defined as all taxable gifts made after 1976 other than gifts included in the gross estate. The addition of the adjusted taxable gifts to the estate tax base may cause an estate to be taxed at a higher marginal tax rate. If the decedent elects gift splitting, the decedent's adjusted taxable gifts equal the amount of the taxable gifts the individual is deemed to have made after applying the gift-splitting provisions. Adjusted taxable gifts can arise from consenting to gift splitting, even though the decedent never actually gives away any property.

Adjusted taxable gifts are valued at date-of-gift values; therefore, any post-gift appreciation is exempt from the transfer taxes. The estate tax computations for decedents who never made any gifts in excess of the excludable amount reflect no adjusted taxable gifts.

Tentative Tax and Reduction for Post-1976 Gift Taxes

The tentative tax is computed on the estate tax base, which is the sum of the taxable estate and the adjusted taxable gifts, if any.[38] The unified transfer tax rates are found

Self-Study Question
Verda died penniless. During her lifetime Verda had agreed to split gifts with her husband Phil. As a result, she had lifetime taxable gifts made after 1976 of $750,000. What is the amount of her unified tax base?

Answer
Her unified tax base is $750,000, the amount of her lifetime taxable gifts.

[38] Sec. 2001(b).

Self-Study Question

Refer to the previous self-study question. What is the amount of the unified tax, before credits? After credits?

Answer

The unified tax before credits is $248,300. This tax is reduced by the unified credit of $192,800 and by a gift tax credit of $55,500, which leaves zero tax due.

in Sec. 2001(c) and are reproduced on the inside back cover. The tentative tax is reduced by the decedent's post-1976 gift taxes. In determining the tax on post-1976 taxable gifts, the effect of gift splitting is taken into consideration. That is, the amount of the post-1976 gift taxes is usually the levy imposed on the taxable gifts that the decedent is deemed to have made after applying any gift-splitting election.

If the tax rates change between the time of the gift and the time of death, the gift tax reduction equals the amount of gift taxes that would have been payable on post-1976 gifts if the rate schedule applicable to the year of death had been in effect in the year of the gift. The only "as if" computation is for the gross tax amount; the unified credit actually used on the gift tax return is subtracted to determine the amount of gift tax that would have been payable.

Unified Credit

Self-Study Question

David made gifts in 1976 and properly filed a gift tax return for the year. Lifetime taxable gifts consist only of taxable gifts made after 1976. Why should David retain a copy of the 1976 gift tax return?

Answer

If any of David's pre-1977 lifetime gift tax exemption was used after September 8, 1976 and before January 1, 1977, 20% of the amount used permanently reduces David's post-1976 unified tax credit.

The excess of the tentative tax over the post-1976 gift taxes is reduced by the unified credit of Sec. 2010. The amount of this credit has changed over the years. For 1987 and later tax years the amount is $192,800 (see inside back cover). With a credit of $192,800, the tax on a $600,000 tax base is completely eliminated. The unified credit never generates a refund; the most relief it can provide is to eliminate an estate's federal estate tax liability. For decedents who have died after 1987, the credit begins to phase out if the tax base exceeds $10,000,000.

Section 2010(c) provides that the unified credit otherwise available for estate tax purposes must be reduced because of certain pre-1977 gifts. Prior to 1977, a $30,000 lifetime exemption was available for the gift tax. Donors could claim some or all of this exemption whenever they so desired. The exemption was repealed and replaced with the unified credit for 1977 and later years. If the decedent claimed any portion of the $30,000 exemption with respect to gifts made after September 8, 1976, and before January 1, 1977, the unified credit is reduced by 20% of the amount of the exemption claimed.

Example 13-43 ■ Carl dies in 1991 with a tax base of $2,000,000. In October 1976, Carl made his first taxable gift. Carl claimed the $30,000 exemption in order to reduce the amount of his taxable gifts. Thus, Carl's $192,800 unified credit for 1991 must be reduced by $6,000 (0.20 × $30,000). If Carl claims the exemption by making a gift on or before September 8, 1976, his estate would be entitled to the full $192,800 credit. ■

Other Credits

The Code authorizes four additional credits—a state death tax credit, a gift tax credit on pre-1977 gifts, a credit on estate taxes paid on prior transfers, and a credit on foreign death taxes. The last three credits apply less frequently than the unified credit and the state death tax credit. These credits, like the unified credit, cannot exceed the amount of the estate tax actually owed.

State Death Tax Credit. All states levy some form of death tax—an inheritance tax, an estate tax, or both. Many states have enacted a simple system whereby the state death tax equals the credit for state death taxes allowed on the federal estate tax return.

The maximum credit allowable on the federal return is calculated in accordance with the schedule contained in Sec. 2011(b). Appendix D contains the schedule. In order to claim this maximum credit, the estate must have paid state death taxes equal to or in excess of the credit calculated using the schedule.

To use the Sec. 2011(b) schedule, one must first determine the size of the decedent's adjusted taxable estate. The "adjusted taxable estate" terminology appears only in Sec. 2011 and is defined as the taxable estate reduced by $60,000. Thus, adjusted taxable gifts have no impact on the state death credit.

Section 2011(f) limits the state death tax credit to the amount of the estate tax (after reduction for the unified credit). Some states have not adopted an unlimited marital deduction. If decedents in such states take advantage of the unlimited marital deduction on their federal estate tax return, the estate will owe no federal taxes but may owe some state death taxes. Its federal credit for state death taxes is nevertheless zero because its federal estate tax after the unified credit is zero.

Example 13-44 ■ John dies in 1991 with a taxable estate of $3,600,000 and adjusted taxable gifts of $1,000,000. John's estate pays $250,000 of state death taxes. John's adjusted taxable estate is $3,540,000 ($3,600,000 − $60,000), and John's maximum state death tax credit (from the Sec. 2011(b) schedule in Appendix D) is $238,800. ■

Example 13-45 ■ Assume the same facts as in Example 13-44, except that John's estate pays state death taxes of $230,000. The credit for state death taxes is limited to the smaller of the state death tax credit from Appendix D($238,800) or the actual death taxes that were paid ($230,000), or $230,000. ■

Credit for Pre-1977 Gift Taxes. Section 2012(a) authorizes a credit for gift taxes paid by the decedent on pre-1977 gifts that must be included in the gross estate. Remember that Sec. 2001(b)(2) allows a reduction for gift taxes paid on post-1976 gifts. The following transaction involves a situation in which the credit for pre-1977 gift taxes is applicable.

Example 13-46 ■ In 1975 Tom creates a trust from which he is to receive the income for life and his son, Tom, Jr., is to receive the remainder. Tom pays a gift tax on the gift of the remainder. Upon Tom's death in the current year, the date-of-death value of the trust's assets is included in his estate under Sec. 2036. Tom's estate receives a credit for some or all of his 1975 gift taxes. ■

In general, the credit for pre-1977 gift taxes equals the amount of gift taxes paid with respect to transfers included in the gross estate. Because of a ceiling rule, however, the amount of the credit is sometimes lower than the amount of gift taxes paid. A discussion of the credit ceiling computation is beyond the scope of this text.

Credit for Tax on Prior Transfers. The credit available under Sec. 2013 for the estate taxes paid on prior transfers reduces the tax impact of property being taxed in more than one estate in quick succession. Without this credit, the overall tax cost could be quite severe if the legatee dies soon after the original decedent. The credit applies if the person who transfers the property (i.e., the transferor-decedent) to the decedent in question (i.e., the transferee-decedent) dies no more than 10 years before, or within 2 years after, the date of the transferee-decedent's death. The potential credit is the smaller of: (1) the federal estate tax of the transferor-decedent that is attributable to the transferred interest or (2) the federal estate tax of the transferee-decedent that is attributable to the transferred interest.

To determine the final credit, the potential credit is multiplied by a percentage that varies inversely with the period of time separating the two dates of death. If the transferor dies no more than 2 years before or after the transferee, the credit percentage is 100%. As specified in Sec. 2013(a), the other percentages are as follows:

Number of Years by Which Transferor's Death Precedes the Transferee's Death	Credit Percentage
More than 2, but not more than 4	80
More than 4, but not more than 6	60
More than 6, but not more than 8	40
More than 8, but not more than 10	20

The following two examples illustrate situations in which the credit for the taxes paid on prior transfers is applicable.

Example 13-47 ■ Mary dies on March 1, 1986. All of Mary's property passes to Debra, her daughter. Debra dies on June 1, 1991. All of Debra's property passes to her son. Both Mary's and Debra's estates pay federal estate taxes. Debra's estate is entitled to a credit for a percentage of some, or all, of the taxes paid by Mary's estate. Because Mary's death precedes Debra's death by 5 years and 3 months, the credit for the tax paid on prior transfers is 60% of the potential credit. ■

Example 13-48 ■ Ed dies on May 7, 1990. One of the items included in Ed's estate is a life insurance policy on Sam's life. Sam had given Ed all of his incidents of ownership in this policy on December 13, 1989. Sam dies on June 15, 1991, or within 3 years of making a gift of the insurance policy on his own life. The policy is included in Sam's gross estate under Sec. 2035. Because Sam dies within 2 years of Ed's death, (1) Ed's estate is entitled to a credit for 100% of the potential credit and (2) an amended return must be filed to claim this credit. ■

Self-Study Question

What is the result of the maximum credit provision with respect to the foreign death tax credit?

Answer

The result is to tax the property located in the foreign country at the U.S. estate tax rate or the foreign country's tax rate, whichever is the higher.

Foreign Death Tax Credit. Under Sec. 2014, the estate is entitled to a credit for some or all of the death taxes paid to a foreign country for property located in that foreign country and included in the gross estate. The maximum credit is the smaller of (1) the foreign death tax attributable to the property situated in the foreign country that imposed the tax or (2) the federal estate tax attributable to the property situated in the foreign country and taxed by such country.

COMPREHENSIVE ILLUSTRATION

The following comprehensive illustration demonstrates the computation of the estate tax liability.

Background Data

Herman Estes dies on October 13, 1990. Herman, an Ohio resident, is survived by his widow, Ann, and several adult children. During his lifetime, Herman makes three gifts, as follows:

- In 1974, he gives his son, Billy, $103,000 cash. Herman claims the $30,000 exemption (then available) and a $3,000 annual exclusion. The taxable gift is thus $70,000.
- In 1978, he gives his daughter, Dotty, $203,000 cash. He claims a $3,000 annual exclusion and makes a $200,000 taxable gift on which he pays a $28,000 gift tax.

- In December 1988, he gives his son, Johnny, land then worth $490,000. Herman claims a $10,000 annual exclusion and makes a $480,000 taxable gift on which he claims the available unified credit and he pays an $11,900 gift tax. On October 13, 1990, the land is worth $550,000.

Properties discovered after Herman's death appear below. All amounts represent date-of-death values.

- Checking account containing $10,000.
- Savings account containing $75,000.
- Land worth $400,000 held in the names of "Herman and Ann, joint tenants with right of survivorship." Herman provided all of the consideration to buy the land in January 1982.
- Life insurance policy 123-A with a face value of $200,000. Herman had incidents of ownership; Johnny is the beneficiary.
- A personal residence worth $325,000.
- Stock in Ajax Corporation worth $600,000.
- Qualified pension plan to which Herman's employer made 60% of the contributions and Herman made 40%. Ann is to receive a lump-sum distribution of $240,000.
- A trust created under the will of Herman's mother, Amelia, who died in 1970. Herman was entitled to receive all of the income quarterly for life. In his will, Herman could appoint the trust assets to "such of his descendants as he desired." The trust assets are valued at $375,000.

At his death, Herman owes a $25,200 bank loan, including accrued interest. Balances due on his various charge cards total $6,500. Herman's funeral expenses are $15,000, and his administration expenses are estimated to be $70,000. Assume that tax savings will be maximized if the administration expenses are deducted on the estate tax return.

Herman's will contains the following provisions:

- "To my wife, Ann, I leave my residence and my checking and savings accounts."
- "I leave $200,000 of property in trust with First Bank as trustee. My wife, Ann, is to receive all of the income from this trust fund quarterly for the rest of her life. Upon Ann's death, the trust property is to be divided equally among our three children."
- "To the American Cancer Society I leave $10,000."
- "I appoint the property in the trust created by my mother, Amelia Estes, to my daughter, Dotty."
- "The residue of my estate is to be divided equally between my two sons, Johnny and Billy."

Calculation of Tax Liability

The computation of Herman's estate tax liability is illustrated in Table 13-1. These same facts are used for the sample Estate Tax Return (Form 706) included in Appendix B. For illustration purposes, it is assumed that (1) the executor elects to claim the marital deduction on the QTIP trust and (2) Herman's state death taxes equal the federal credit for state death taxes.

Note that the computation set out in Table 13-1 is affected by several factors:

- Herman had only a special power of appointment over the assets in the trust created by his mother. Therefore, the trust property is not included in his estate.
- Assets that pass to the surviving spouse outside the will, such as by survivorship, can qualify for the marital deduction.
- Only post-1976 taxable gifts are added to the taxable estate as adjusted taxable gifts.
- The estate tax payable is not reduced by pre-1977 gift taxes unless the gifted property is included in the gross estate.
- Because the highest marginal income tax rate for the estate is less than the 41% marginal estate tax rate and an estate tax liability is owed (even with the

TABLE 13-1 *Comprehensive Estate Tax Illustration*

Gross estate:	
Checking account	$ 10,000
Savings account	75,000
Land held in joint tenancy with wife (0.50 × $400,000)	200,000
Life insurance	200,000
Personal residence	325,000
Stock	600,000
Qualified pension plan	240,000
Gross-up for gift tax paid on 1988 gift	11,900
Total gross estate	$1,661,900
Minus:	
Debts:	
Bank loan, including accrued interest	(25,200)
Charge cards	(6,500)
Funeral expenses	(15,000)
Administration expenses	(70,000)
Marital deductions:	
Residence	(325,000)
Checking account	(10,000)
Savings account	(75,000)
QTIP trust	(200,000)
Land	(200,000)
Qualified pension plan	(240,000)
Charitable contribution deduction	(10,000)
Total reductions to gross estate	($1,176,700)
Taxable estate	$ 485,200
Plus adjusted taxable gifts:	
1978	200,000
1988	480,000
Estate tax base	$1,165,200
Tentative tax on tax base	$ 413,532
Minus:	
Reduction for post-1976 gift taxes	(39,900)[a]
Unified credit	(192,800)
State death tax credit	(9,526)[b]
Estate tax payable	$ 171,306

[a]$28,000 (for 1978) + $11,900 (for 1988) = $39,900.
[b]This figure is calculated based on the table reproduced in Appendix D and a $425,200 adjusted taxable estate.

available credits), administration expenses should be deducted on the estate tax return.

LIQUIDITY CONCERNS

OBJECTIVE 6
Identify tax provisions that alleviate liquidity problems

Liquidity is one of the major problems facing persons planning their estates and eventually executors that are managing the estates. Life insurance is one source often used to help address this problem. In general, the entire amount of the estate tax liability is due 9 months after the decedent's death. Certain provisions, however, allow the executor to pay some or all of the estate tax liability at a later date. Deferral of the payment of part or all of the estate taxes and three other provisions aimed at alleviating a liquidity problem are discussed below.

Deferral of Payment of Estate Taxes

Reasonable Cause. Section 6161(a)(1) authorizes the Secretary of the Treasury to extend the payment date for the estate taxes for a reasonable period. The term *reasonable period* is defined as a period of not longer than 12 months. Moreover, the IRS may extend the payment date for a maximum period of 10 years if the executor shows "reasonable cause" for not being able to pay some, or all, of the estate tax liability on the regular date.[39]

Whenever the executor pays a portion of the estate tax subsequent to the regular due date, the estate owes interest on the portion of the tax for which payment is postponed. In general, the interest rate, which is governed by Sec. 6621, is the same as that applicable to underpayments. The interest rate on underpayments potentially fluctuates quarterly with changes in the rate paid on short-term U.S. Treasury obligations.[40]

Remainder or Reversionary Interests. If the gross estate includes a relatively large remainder or reversionary interest, liquidity problems could result if the estate has to pay the entire estate tax liability soon after the decedent's death. The estate might not gain possession of the assets until many years after the decedent's death. For example, the estate might include a remainder interest in an asset in which a healthy, 30-year-old person has a life estate. Section 6163 permits the executor to elect to postpone payment of the tax attributable to a remainder or reversionary interest until 6 months after the other interests terminate. This postponement is available even in the absence of liquidity problems. In addition, upon being convinced of reasonable cause, the Secretary of the Treasury may grant an additional extension of not more than 3 years.

Self-Study Question
Why might a person who owns a substantial interest in a small business choose to gift during their life property other than the business interest?

Answer
If this person is aware of the 5 year deferral, 10 installment option of Sec. 6166, he may want to retain the business interest in his estate so that his estate will qualify for Sec. 6166 treatment.

Interests in Closely Held Businesses. Section 6166 authorizes the executor to pay a portion of the estate tax in as many as 10 annual installments in certain situations. Executors may elect to apply Sec. 6166 if

- The gross estate includes an interest in a closely held business.
- The value of the closely held business exceeds 35% of the value of the adjusted gross estate.

---

[39] Sec. 6161(a)(2).
[40] Sec. 6621. The interest rate is discussed in Chapter 16. For the first quarter of 1991, the interest rate is 11%.

Closely held businesses are defined as proprietorships and partnerships or corporations having no more than 15 owners.[41] If a corporation or partnership has more than 15 owners, it can be classified as closely held if the decedent's gross estate includes 20% or more of the capital interest (in the partnership) or the voting stock (in the corporation).[42]

The adjusted gross estate is defined as the gross estate less *allowable* Sec. 2053 and 2054 deductions. Consequently, in determining whether the estate meets the 35% requirement, all administration expenses and casualty and theft losses must be subtracted, regardless of whether the executor elects to deduct them on the estate tax return or the estate's income tax return.

Once the election is chosen, certain restrictions regarding its use must be met, including

- The portion of the estate tax that can be paid in installments is the ratio of the value of the closely held business interest to the value of the adjusted gross estate.
- The first of the 10 allowable installments is generally not due until 5 years after the due date for the return. (This defers the last payment for as many as 15 years.)
- Interest on the tax due is payable annually, even during the first 5 years.

Some or all of the installment payments may accrue interest at a rate of only 4%. The maximum amount of deferred tax to which the 4% rate applies is $345,800 minus the amount of the unified credit available for the year of death.[43] The interest rate on any additional deferred tax amounts is the same as the rate applicable to underpayments (discussed in footnote 40).

Example 13-49 ■ Frank dies on March 1, 1991. Frank's gross estate, which includes a proprietorship interest valued at $1,000,000, is $2,600,000. The executor deducts all $100,000 of the potential Sec. 2053 and 2054 deductions on the estate tax return. Frank has no marital or charitable contribution deductions and makes no taxable gifts. Frank's adjusted gross estate, taxable estate, and tax base are $2,500,000. His estate tax payable is $833,000 ($1,025,800 − $192,800). Frank's closely held business interest comprises 40% ($1,000,000 ÷ $2,500,000) of his adjusted gross estate.

Thus, $333,200 (0.40 × $833,000) may be paid in 10 equal annual installments. The first installment payment is due on December 1, 1996. The 4% interest rate applies to $153,000 ($345,800 − $192,800) of Frank's deferred tax liability. Interest accrues on the remaining $180,200 ($333,200 − $153,000) at the rate for underpayments. ■

Stock Redemptions to Pay Death Taxes

It is difficult for a shareholder to receive cash or other property in his role as a shareholder and avoid reporting dividend income equal to the amount of the cash or the FMV of the other property received. (Chapter 4 provides more details concerning this topic.) At a shareholder's death, however, Sec. 303 provides a chance for the estate to treat a stock redemption as a sale or exchange of the property. Thus, the amount of income recognized is limited to the excess of the redemption price over the adjusted basis of the stock surrendered. Generally, this excess is minimal because of the step-up in basis that occurs at the time of the decedent's death.

---

[41] Sec. 6166(b)(1).
[42] Ibid.
[43] Sec. 6601(j).

To qualify for Sec. 303 treatment, the stock in the corporation that is redeeming the shares must make up more than 35% of the value of the decedent's gross estate, less any *allowable* Sec. 2053 and 2054 deductions. The maximum amount of redemption proceeds eligible for exchange treatment is the total of the estate's death taxes and funeral and administration expenses, regardless of whether they are deducted on the estate tax return or the estate's income tax return.

Special Use Valuation of Farm Realty

Self-Study Question

Why might an heir of farmland not want an estate to use the special valuation method of Sec. 2032A when filing the estate tax return?

Answer

The heir may prefer the higher basis he would get for the farmland if FMV is used rather than the special farmland value, especially if the estate taxes are payable out of the residual estate and the heir does not share in that residual.

In 1976 Congress became concerned that farms sometimes had to be sold to generate the funds needed to pay estate taxes. This situation was attributable, in part, to the fact that the FMV of the farm land in many areas was relatively high, perhaps because suburban housing was being built nearby. Congress enacted Sec. 2032A, which allows a property to be valued using a formula approach that attempts to value the property at what it is worth for farming purposes. The lowest valuation that is permitted is $750,000 less than the property's FMV.

A number of requirements must be met before the executor can elect the special valuation rules.[44] An additional tax is levied if during the 10-year period after the decedent's death the new owner of the property (1) disposes of it or (2) no longer uses it as a farm. In general, the amount of the additional tax equals the estate tax savings that arose from the lower Sec. 2032A valuation.

GENERATION-SKIPPING TRANSFER TAX

The Tax Reform Act of 1976 enacted a third transfer tax—the generation-skipping transfer tax (GSTT)—to fill a void in the gift and estate tax structure. In 1986 Congress repealed the original GSTT retroactive to its original effective date and replaced it with a revised GSTT. The new GSTT is generally applicable to inter vivos transfers made after September 25, 1985, and transfers at death made after October 22, 1986.

For years, a popular estate planning technique, especially among the very wealthy, involved giving persons in different generations an interest in the same property. For example, a decedent might set up a testamentary trust in which successive life estates were created for a child and a grandchild and a remainder interest was set up for a great grandchild. Under this arrangement, an estate tax would be imposed at the death of the person establishing the trust but not again until the great grandchild's death. The GSTT's purpose is to ensure that some form of transfer taxation is imposed one time a generation. It accomplishes its purpose by subjecting transfers that escape gift or estate taxation for one or more generations to the GSTT.

The GSTT is levied at a flat rate—the highest rate under the estate and gift tax rate schedule, which is 55% through 1992 and 50% thereafter.[45] The tax applies to taxable terminations of and taxable distributions from generation-skipping transfers. A **generation-skipping transfer** involves a disposition that

- Provides interests for more than one generation of beneficiaries who are in a younger generation than the transferor, or

---

[44] For example, the farm real and personal property must make up at least 50% of the adjusted value of the gross estate, and the farm real property must comprise 25% or more of the adjusted value of the gross estate.

[45] Sec. 2641.

- Provides an interest solely for a person two or more generations younger than the transferor.[46]

For family members, generation assignments are made according to the family tree. The second type of arrangement listed above is known as a direct skip, because it skips one or more generations.

Example 13-50 ■ Tom creates a trust with income payable to Tom, Jr., for life and a remainder interest distributable to Tom, III, upon the death of Tom, Jr. (his father). This is a generation-skipping transfer because Tom, Jr., and Tom, III, are one and two generations younger, respectively, than the transferor (Tom). ■

Example 13-51 ■ Tom transfers an asset directly to Tom, III, his grandson. This is a direct skip type of generation-skipping transfer because the transferee (Tom, III) is two generations younger than the transferor (Tom). ■

The termination of an interest in a generation-skipping arrangement is known as a taxable termination.[47] This event triggers imposition of the GSTT. The tax is levied on the before-tax amount transferred. The trustee pays the tax.

Example 13-52 ■ In 1991 a taxable termination occurs with respect to a generation-skipping trust valued at $2,000,000. The tax is $1,100,000 (0.55 × $2,000,000). The trustee pays the tax and distributes the $900,000 of remaining assets to the beneficiary. ■

In the case of a direct skip, the amount subject to the GSTT is the value of the property received by the transferee.[48] The transferor is liable for the tax. If the direct skip occurs *inter vivos,* the GSTT paid by the transferor is treated as an additional transfer subject to the gift tax.[49] As a result, the total transfer tax liability (GSTT plus gift tax) can exceed the value of the property received by the donee.

Example 13-53 ■ In 1991 Susan gives $1,000,000 to her granddaughter. Assume that Susan has used all of her unified credit and is in the 55% marginal gift tax bracket. The GSTT is $550,000 (0.55 × $1,000,000). The amount subject to the gift tax is the value of the property transferred ($1,000,000) plus the GSTT paid ($550,000). Thus, the gift tax is $852,500 (0.55 × $1,550,000). ■

Every grantor is entitled to a $1 million exemption from the GSTT.[50] The grantor elects when, and against which transfers, to apply this exemption. Appreciation on the property for which the exemption is elected is also exempt from the GSTT.

TAX PLANNING CONSIDERATIONS

The effectiveness of many of the pre-1977 transfer tax-saving strategies has been diluted. This reduced effectiveness is attributable to the unification of the transfer tax system in general, the adoption of a unified rate schedule, and the concept of

---

[46] Sec. 2611.
[47] Sec. 2612(a).
[48] Sec. 2623.
[49] Sec. 2515.
[50] Sec. 2631(a).

adjusted taxable gifts in particular. To some extent, the enactment of provisions that (1) allow a higher tax base to be free of estate taxes and (2) permit most interspousal transfers to be devoid of transfer tax consequences counterbalances unification. Various tax planning considerations which need to be explored in the process of trying to reduce the transfer taxes applicable to a family unit are discussed below.

Use of Inter Vivos Gifts

Key Point
Gifting of income producing property transfers the future income on such property to the donee. The removal of this future income from the donor's possession can be important in reducing the degree to which a taxpayer's estate grows over time.

One of the most significant strategies for reducing transfer taxes is a well-designed, long-term gift program. As long as the gifts to each donee do not exceed the $10,000 per donee annual exclusion, there will be no additions to the gross estate and no adjusted taxable gifts. Thousands of dollars of property may be passed to others free of any transfer tax consequences if (1) enough donees are selected and (2) gifts are made over a substantial number of years. If taxable gifts do occur, the post-gift appreciation is removed from the estate tax base. Moreover, if the donor lives more than 3 years after the date of the gift, the gift tax paid is removed from the gross estate.

The opportunities for reducing transfer taxes through the use of lifetime gifts should be weighed against the income tax disadvantage of forgoing the step-up in basis that would occur if the property is retained until death. However, unless the donee is the donor's spouse, income taxes on the income produced by the gifted property may be reduced, although not as significantly as was possible prior to the compression of the income tax rates that apply to 1987 and later tax years.

Use of Exemption Equivalent

Self-Study Question
What types of property should one consider gifting?

Answer
Gift property which either (a) is expected to substantially appreciate in future years, (b) produces substantial amounts of income, or (c) represents family heirlooms which will probably be passed from the donee to the donee's heirs.

As a result of the exemption equivalent, a certain amount of property—$600,000 currently—may pass to persons other than the decedent's spouse without any estate taxes being extracted therefrom. There is no limit on the amount of property that can be transferred to the spouse tax-free. Thus, because the spouse presumably will die before any children or grandchildren (i.e., individuals to whom people who are creating wills often will property), wealthy persons should contemplate leaving at least an amount equal to the exemption equivalent to persons other than their spouse. Otherwise, they will waste some or all of their exemption equivalent, and the property will be taxed when the surviving spouse dies.

Making full use of the exemption equivalent enables a husband and wife to transfer to third parties an aggregate of $1,200,000 currently without incurring any estate taxes. The strategy of making gifts to an ill spouse, who is not wealthy, to keep the donee-spouse's exemption equivalent from being wasted was discussed earlier (see Chapter 12). Under this technique the wealthier spouse makes gifts to the other spouse free of gift taxes because of the marital deduction. The recipient spouse then has an estate that can be passed tax-free to children, grandchildren, or other individuals because of the exemption equivalent.

What Size Marital Deduction Is Best?

To reiterate, there is no ceiling on the amount of property eligible for the marital deduction. Even so, the availability of an unlimited marital deduction does not necessarily mean that it should be used. From a tax perspective wealthier persons should leave an amount equal to the exemption equivalent to someone other than the spouse. Alternatively, they could leave the spouse an income interest in the exemption equivalent amount of property along with the power to invade such property for reasons of health, support, maintenance, or education.

In certain circumstances, it may be preferable for an amount in excess of the exemption equivalent to pass directly to third parties. It might be beneficial for the first spouse's estate to pay some estate taxes if the surviving spouse already has substantial property and has a relatively short life expectancy, especially if the decedent spouse's assets are expected to rapidly increase in value.

Example 13-54 ■ Paul dies in 1991 with a $3,000,000 gross estate and no deductions other than the marital deduction. At the time of Paul's death, his wife has a life expectancy of 2 years. The assets she owns in 1991 are estimated to be worth $6,000,000 in 1993. Paul's property is expected to increase in value by 25% during the 2-year period following his death. Paul wills his spouse, Jill, $1,000,000 and his children the rest. The estate tax payable for each spouse's estate is as follows:

	Paul	Jill
Gross estate	$3,000,000	$7,250,000[a]
Minus: Marital deduction	(1,000,000)	—0—
Taxable estate and tax base	$2,000,000	$7,250,000
Estate tax, after unified credit	$ 588,000	$3,435,500
Combined estate tax		$4,023,500

[a] $6,000,000 + (1.25 × $1,000,000) = $7,250,000. ■

Example 13-55 ■ Assume the same facts as in Example 13-54 except that Paul wills everything except $600,000 to Jill. The estate tax payable for each spouse's estate is as follows:

Self-Study Question
Given the facts of Examples 13-54 and 13-55, which of the two estate plans would you advise Paul and Jill to adopt?

Answer
For any after (income) tax rate of return of up to 27.94%, Paul and Jill should select the plan in Example 13-54. This outcome assumes that Jill will live only two years longer than Paul.

	Paul	Jill
Gross estate	$3,000,000	$9,000,000[a]
Minus: Marital deduction	(2,400,000)	—0—
Taxable estate and tax base	$ 600,000	$9,000,000
Estate tax, after unified credit	—0—	$4,398,000
Combined estate tax		$4,398,000

[a] $6,000,000 + (1.25 × $2,400,000) = $9,000,000. ■

The combined estate tax liability is $374,500 higher in Example 13-55 than in Example 13-54. However, in Example 13-55, no tax is owed upon the first spouse's death. Because the estate taxes for the second spouse's estate are not payable until some later date, their present value should also be considered.

Use of Disclaimers

Because a qualified disclaimer is not treated as a gift, disclaimers can be valuable estate planning tools (see Chapter 12). If, for example, all of a decedent's property is willed to the surviving spouse, such spouse could disclaim an amount at least equal in size to the exemption equivalent. This act would enable the decedent's estate to take full advantage of the unified credit. Alternatively, a decedent's children or grandchildren might disclaim some bequests, if, as a result of their disclaimer, the property would pass instead to the surviving spouse. This approach might be desirable if the estate otherwise would receive a relatively small marital deduction. Bear in mind, however, that one of the conditions for having a qualified disclaimer is that the person making the disclaimer has no input with respect to which persons receive the disclaimed property.

Role of Life Insurance

Life insurance is an important asset with respect to estate planning for the following reasons:

- It can help provide the liquidity for paying estate taxes and other costs associated with death.
- It has the potential for large appreciation. If the insured gives away his incidents of ownership and survives the gift by more than 3 years, his estate benefits by keeping the appreciation out of his estate.

Assume an individual is contemplating purchasing a new insurance policy on his life and transferring it to another individual as a gift. The insured must live for more than 3 years after making the gift in order to exclude the face amount of the policy from his gross estate. Should the insured die within 3 years of gifting the policy, the policy's face amount is included in his gross estate. Should the donee instead purchase the policy, the insured will not make a gift and the three-year rule will not be a factor.

Qualifying the Estate for Installment Payments

It can be quite beneficial for an estate owning an interest in a closely held business to qualify for installment payment of estate taxes under Sec. 6166. In a sense, the estate can borrow a certain amount of dollars from the government at 4% and the rest at a higher, but still favorable, rate.

Judicious selection of the properties that are disposed of by lifetime gifts can raise the odds that the estate will qualify for such treatment. Retaining closely held business interests and gifting other assets will increase the likelihood of being able to elect the installment payments. However, closely held business interests often have a potential for great appreciation and, consequently, from the standpoint of reducing the size of the estate are good candidates for gifts.

It is not possible for persons to make gifts to restructure their estates and qualify for Sec. 6166 if they wait until soon before their death to do so. If the decedent makes gifts within 3 years of dying, the closely held business interest must make up more than 35% of the adjusted gross estate as determined by both of the following computations:

1. Calculate the ratio of the closely held business to the actual adjusted gross estate.
2. Redo the calculations after revising the ratio to include (at date of death values) any property given away within 3 years of death.

Example 13-56 ■ Joe dies in 1991. Joe's estate includes a closely held business interest valued at $400,000 and other property valued at $650,000. Joe's allowable Sec. 2053 and 2054 deductions total $50,000. In 1989, partly in hopes of qualifying his estate for

Sec. 6166 treatment, Joe makes gifts of listed securities of $300,000 (at 1991 valuations). He pays no gift tax on the gift. The two tests for determining whether Joe's estate is eligible for Sec. 6166 are as follows.

$$\text{Excluding gifts: } \$400,000 \div \$1,000,000 = 40\%$$
$$\text{Including gifts: } \$400,000 \div \$1,300,000 = 30.77\%$$

The estate may not elect Sec. 6166 treatment because it meets the more than 35% test in only one of the two computations. ■

Where to Deduct Administration Expenses

Another tax planning opportunity concerns the choice of where to deduct administration expenses—on the estate tax return, on the estate's income tax return, or some in each place. The decision should be made based upon where the deduction will yield the greatest tax savings. Thus, if the marginal estate tax rate exceeds the estate's marginal income tax rate, which it will if the estate owes an estate tax, the executor should deduct the expenses on the estate tax return. If no estate taxes are owed because of the exemption equivalent or the marital deduction, administration expenses should be deducted on the estate's income tax return.

Flower Bonds

Certain U.S. bonds that typically sell at a discount because of their relatively low interest rate are eligible to be redeemed at face value in payment of federal estate taxes. Such bonds are often referred to as **flower bonds.** To the extent such bonds do not exceed the federal estate tax liability, they must be valued in the gross estate at their face value, even though their selling price is lower. Persons who are terminally ill should seriously consider purchasing flower bonds. Because such bonds are worth their face value when used to pay federal estate taxes, an investment, for example, of $90,000 (measured at market value) can be used to satisfy $100,000 of federal estate tax liability.

COMPLIANCE AND PROCEDURAL CONSIDERATIONS

Filing Requirements

OBJECTIVE 7
Recognize the filing requirements for estate tax returns

Section 6018 indicates the circumstances in which estate tax returns are necessary. In general, no return is necessary unless the value of the gross estate exceeds the amount of the exemption equivalent—$600,000 currently. An exception applies, however, if the decedent makes any post-1976 taxable gifts or claims any portion of the $30,000 specific exemption after September 8, 1976 and before January 1, 1977. In such circumstances, a return need not be filed unless the value of the gross estate exceeds the amount of the exemption equivalent minus the total of the decedent's adjusted taxable gifts and the amount of the specific exemption claimed against gifts made after September 8, 1976 and before January 1, 1977.

A completed sample Estate Tax Return (Form 706) appears in Appendix B. The facts on which the preparation of the return is premised are the same as for the comprehensive illustration appearing on pages 13-30 through 13-33.

Due Date

Estate tax returns generally must be filed within 9 months after the decedent's date of death.[51] The Secretary of the Treasury is authorized to grant a "reasonable" extension of time for filing.[52] The maximum extension period is 6 months. Obtaining an extension does not extend the time for paying the estate tax. Section 6601 requires interest to be paid on any portion of the tax that is not paid by the due date of the return, determined without regard to the extension period. Thus, to avoid interest, the tax must be paid by the original due date.

Valuation

One of the most difficult tasks of preparing estate tax returns is valuing the items included in the gross estate. Some items (e.g., one-of-a-kind art objects) may truly be unique. For many properties the executor should arrange for appraisals by experts.

If the value of any property reported on the return is 50% or less of the amount determined to be the proper value, an undervaluation penalty is imposed.[53] Under certain conditions, however, the Secretary of the Treasury can waive this penalty. A waiver is possible only with proof that (1) there is a reasonable cause for the valuation claimed and (2) the claim is made in good faith. This penalty is increased if a gross valuation misstatement occurs; that is the estate tax valuation as 25% or less than the amount determined to be the proper value.[54] These penalties are discussed in more detail in Chapter 12.

Election of Alternate Valuation Date

The executor may elect to value the gross estate on the alternate valuation date instead of on the date of death. The executor must make this irrevocable election on the estate tax return. The election does not necessarily have to be made on a timely return, but no election is possible if the return is filed more than a year after the due date (including extensions).

Documents to Be Included with Return

The instructions for the Estate Tax Return (Form 706) indicate that numerous documents and other papers must be filed with the return. Some of the more important items that should accompany the form include

- A certified copy of the will if the decedent died testate (i.e., having made and left a valid will)
- A schedule describing the qualified terminable interest property and its value if the executor makes the QTIP election
- Copies of appraisals for real estate
- A Form 712 (obtained from the insurance companies) for each life insurance policy on the decedent's life
- Copies of written trust and other instruments with respect to lifetime transfers made by the decedent

---

[51] Sec. 6075(a).
[52] Sec. 6081(a).
[53] Sec. 6662(g).
[54] Sec. 6662(h).

- Certified or verified copies of instruments granting the decedent a power of appointment, even if the power is not a general one
- A certified copy of the order admitting the will to probate if the will makes bequests for which a marital deduction or charitable contribution deduction are claimed.

In addition, the executor should submit at the time of filing the return (or as soon thereafter as possible) a certificate from the proper officer of the taxing state that denotes the amount of the state death taxes and the payment date.

PROBLEM MATERIALS

DISCUSSION QUESTIONS

13-1. In general, at what amount are items includible in the gross estate valued? (Answer in words.) Indicate one exception to the general valuation rules and the reason for this exception.

13-2. Compare the valuation rules used for gift tax and estate tax purposes.

13-3. Compare the valuation for gift and estate tax purposes of a $150,000 group term life insurance policy on the transferor's life.

13-4. Explain how shares of stock traded on a stock exchange are valued. What is the blockage rule?

13-5. Assume that the properties included in the gross estate have appreciated during the 6-month period immediately after death. May the executor elect the alternate valuation date and thereby achieve a larger step-up in basis? Explain.

13-6. List an advantage and a disadvantage of electing the alternate valuation date.

13-7. Explain the Congressional intent for enacting Sec. 2034.

13-8. Is stock transferred by gift two weeks prior to death included in the decedent's gross estate? In the estate tax base?

13-9. From a tax standpoint, which of the following alternatives is preferable:
   a. Buying a new insurance policy on your life and soon thereafter giving it to another person, or
   b. Encouraging the other person to buy the policy with funds previously accumulated?
   Explain your answer.

13-10. Explain the difference between the estate tax treatment for gift taxes paid on gifts made two years prior to death and on gifts made ten years prior to death.

13-11. In what circumstances is the gross-up rule applicable?

13-12. Can the gross-up rule ever apply to a spouse who is not the actual donor but who consents to gift splitting? Explain.

13-13. A widow owns a valuable eighteenth-century residence that she would like the state historical society to have someday. Explain the estate tax consequences of the following two alternatives:
   a. She deeds the state historical society a remainder interest in the residence and reserves the right to live there for the rest of her life.
   b. She gifts her entire interest in the house to the society and moves to another home for the rest of her life.

13-14. List three retention periods that can cause Sec. 2036 (transfers with retained life estate) to apply to a transferor's estate.

13-15. What characteristics do Secs. 2035-2037 have in common?

13-16. When does the consideration furnished rule apply to property that is held as joint tenants with right of survivorship?

13-17. What are the two circumstances in which life insurance on the decedent's life is includible in the gross estate under Sec. 2042? If insurance policies on the decedent's life escape being included under Sec. 2042, are they definitely excluded from the gross estate? Explain.

13-18. Is the right to borrow against a life insurance policy an incident of ownership? Explain.

13-19. Indicate two situations in which property that has previously been subject, at least in part, to gift taxation is nevertheless included in the donor-decedent's gross estate.

13-20. Al dies in the current year. Under Al's will, property is put in trust with a bank named as trustee. Al's will names Pam to receive the trust income annually for life and empowers Pam to will the property to whichever of her brothers, sisters, or descendants she so desires. When Pam dies she wills the property to two of her children in equal shares. Is the trust included in Pam's estate? Explain.

13-21. Determine the accuracy of the following statement. The gross estate includes a general power of appointment possessed by the decedent only if the decedent exercised the power.

13-22. Carl dies in 1985. His will calls for the creation of a trust to be funded with $1,000,000 of property. The bank trustee must distribute all of the trust income semiannually to Carl's widow for the rest of her life. Upon the widow's death, the trust assets are to be distributed to the couple's grandchildren. The widow dies in the current year; by then the trust assets have appreciated to $1,300,000. Are the trust assets included in the widow's gross estate? Explain.

13-23. List the various categories of estate tax deductions, and compare them with the categories of gift tax deductions. What differences exist?

13-24. Is a double deduction available for administration expenses? Explain.

13-25. Mona is survived by her husband, Matt, who receives the following interests as a result of his wife's death. Does Mona's estate receive a marital deduction for them? Explain.
   a. $400,000 of life insurance proceeds; Matt is the beneficiary; their son Sam has held the incidents of ownership for 10 years.
   b. $700,000 trust fund with income payable to Matt until the earlier of his death or remarriage. When Matt's income interest ceases, the property passes to their daughter.

13-26. Compare the credits available for estate tax purposes with the credits available for gift tax purposes. What differences exist?

13-27. What is the tax policy reason for the installment payment rules for estate taxes owed with respect to closely held business interests?

13-28. Assume that Larry is wealthier than Jane, his wife, and that he is likely to die before her. From an overall tax standpoint (considering transfer taxes and income taxes), is it preferable for Larry to transfer property to Jane *inter vivos* or at death, or does it matter? Explain.

13-29. Roger desires to "freeze" the value of his estate. Which of the following assets would you recommend that Roger transfer during his lifetime (more than one asset may be suggested):
   a. Life insurance on his life
   b. Cash
   c. Corporate bonds (assume interest rates are expected to rise)
   d. Stock in a closely held business with a bright future
   e. Land in a boom town

13-30. Refer to Problem 13-29. Explain the negative considerations, if any, with respect to Roger's making gifts of the assets that you recommended.

13-31. From a tax standpoint, why is it advisable for a married person to dispose of an amount equal to the exemption equivalent to persons other than his spouse?

13-32. When is the estate tax return due? In general, when is the estate tax due?

PROBLEMS

13-33. *Valuation.* Kay dies on May 5 of the current year. Her executor elects date-of-death valuation. Kay's gross estate includes the items listed below. What is the estate tax value of each item?

a. 1,000 shares of M Corporation stock, traded on a stock exchange on May 5 at a high of 47, a low of 40, and a close of 46.
b. Life insurance policy on the life of Kay having a face value of $500,000. The cost of a comparable policy immediately before Kay's death is $125,250.
c. Life insurance policy on the life of Kay's son having a face value of $100,000. The cost of a comparable policy immediately before Kay's death is $27,230.
d. Personal residence appraised at a FMV of $175,000 and valued for property tax purposes at $135,000.

13-34. Valuation. Mary dies on April 3 of the current year. As of this date, Mary's gross estate is valued at $2,800,000. On October 3, Mary's gross estate is valued at $2,500,000. No assets are distributed or sold prior to October 3. Mary's estate has no deductions or adjusted taxable gifts. What is Mary's *lowest* possible estate tax liability?

13-35. Estate Tax Formula. Sue dies on May 3, 1991. On March 1, 1990, Sue gives Tom some land valued at $810,000. Sue applies a unified credit of $192,800 against the tax due on this transfer. On Sue's date of death the land is valued at $600,000.
a. What is the amount included in Sue's gross estate?
b. What is the amount of Sue's adjusted taxable gifts as a result of making the 1990 gift?

13-36. Transferor Provisions. Val dies on May 13, 1991. On October 3, 1990, she gives a $400,000 life insurance policy on her own life to Ray. Because the value of the policy is relatively low, the transfer does *not* cause any gift tax to be payable. What is the amount included in Val's gross estate as a result of the 1990 gift?

13-37. Transferor Provisions. Refer to Problem 13-36. What amount is included in Val's gross estate if the property given is land instead of a life insurance policy?

13-38. Transferor Provisions. Refer to Problem 13-36. What amount would be included in Val's gross estate if Val instead dies on May 14, 1995?

13-39. Transferor Provisions. What amount, if any, is included in Doug's gross estate in each of the following situations:
a. In 1982 Doug creates a trust and funds it with $400,000 of assets. He names a bank as trustee. The trust instrument provides that the income is payable to Doug annually for life. Upon Doug's death, the assets are to be divided equally among Doug's descendants. Doug dies in 1991 at the age of 72. The trust assets are then worth $560,000.
b. In 1983 Doug transfers title to his personal residence to his daughter. The residence is worth $50,000 on the transfer date. Doug continues to live alone in the residence until his death. He does not pay any rent. At Doug's death in 1991, the residence is worth $85,000.
c. In 1983 Doug creates a trust and funds it with $200,000 of assets. Doug names himself trustee. According to the trust agreement, all the trust income is to be paid out annually for 25 years. The trustee, however, is to decide how much income to pay each year to each of the three beneficiaries—Doug's children. Upon termination of the trust, the assets are to be distributed equally among Doug's three children or their estates. The trust's assets are worth $310,000 when Doug dies in 1991.
d. Assume the same facts as in Part c, except that the trustee is a bank.
e. In 1984 Doug creates a revocable trust with a bank named as trustee. He names his grandchild Joe as the beneficiary for life. Upon Joe's death, the property is to be distributed equally among Joe's descendants. The trust assets are worth $400,000 when Doug dies in 1991.

13-40. Transferor Provisions. Lou transfers property to an irrevocable trust in 1987 with a bank named as trustee. Lou names Al to receive the trust income annually for life and Pat or Pat's estate to receive the remainder upon Al's death. Lou reserves the power to designate Mike or Mike's estate (instead of Pat or Pat's estate) to receive the remainder. Upon Lou's death, the trust assets are valued at $200,000, and Al is age 50; Mike, age 27; and Pat, age 32. Assume a 10% rate for the actuarial tables.
a. How much, if any, is included in Lou's gross estate?

b. How much would have been included in Lou's gross estate if Lou had *not* retained any powers over the trust? (Assume that Lou survives for more than 3 years after the transfer.)

13-41. *Annuities.* Maria dies in the current year, 2 years after her retirement. At the time of her death, she is covered by the two annuities listed below.

1. An annuity purchased by Maria's father providing benefits to Maria upon her reaching age 65. Upon Maria's death, survivor benefits are payable to her sister. The sister's benefits are valued at $45,000.
2. An annuity purchased by Maria's former employer under a qualified plan to which only the employer contributes. Benefits are payable to Maria upon her retirement. Upon Maria's death an annuity valued at $110,000 is payable to her son.

a. What is the amount of the inclusion in Maria's gross estate with respect to each annuity?
b. How would your answer for the first annuity change if Maria's husband had instead purchased the annuity?
c. How would your answer for the second annuity change if the employer had instead made 70% of the contributions to the qualified plan and Maria had made the remaining 30%?

13-42. *Jointly Owned Property.* In 1983 Art purchases land for $60,000 and immediately titles it in the names of Art and Bart, joint tenants with right of survivorship. Bart pays no consideration. In 1991 Art dies and is survived by Bart. The land's value has appreciated to $300,000.
a. What is the amount of the inclusion in Art's gross estate?
b. If Bart died before Art, what amount would be included in Bart's gross estate?
c. Assume that Art dies in 1991 and Bart dies in 1993 when the land is worth $320,000. What amount is included in Bart's gross estate?

13-43. *Jointly Owned Property.* In 1983 Fred and Gail pool their resources and purchase a mountain cabin. Fred provides $10,000 of consideration, and Gail furnishes $30,000. In 1991 Gail dies and is survived by Fred. The property, which they had titled in the names of Fred and Gail, joint tenants with right of survivorship, is valued at $90,000 in 1991. What amount is included in Gail's gross estate?

13-44. *Jointly Owned Property.* Mrs. Cobb buys land costing $80,000 in 1983. She has the land titled in the names of Mr. and Mrs. Cobb, joint tenants with right of survivorship. Mrs. Cobb dies in 1991 and is survived by Mr. Cobb. In 1991 the land's value is $200,000.
a. What amount is included in Mrs. Cobb's gross estate?
b. What is the amount, if any, of the marital deduction that Mrs. Cobb's estate can claim with respect to the land?
c. Assume Mr. Cobb dies in 1995 when the land is worth $240,000. What amount is included in his gross estate?

13-45. *Powers of Appointment.* Scott dies in 1991. He is the income beneficiary for life of each of the trusts described below. For each trust indicate whether it is includible in Scott's gross estate.
a. A trust created under the will of Scott's mother, who died in 1968. Upon Scott's death, the trust assets are to pass to those of Scott's descendants whom Scott directs by his will. Should Scott fail to appoint the trust property, the trust assets are to be distributed to the Smithsonian Institution. Scott wills the property to his twin daughters in equal shares.
b. An *inter vivos* trust created in 1960 by Scott's father. The trust agreement authorizes Scott to appoint the property to "whomever he so desires." The appointment could be made only by his will. Scott appoints the property to an elderly neighbor.
c. A trust created by Scott in 1963. Upon Scott's death, the property is to pass to his children.
d. A trust created under the will of Scott's grandmother, who died in 1937. Her will authorizes Scott to appoint the property by his will to "whomever he so desires." In default of appointment, the property is to pass to Scott's descendants in equal shares. Scott's will does not mention this trust.
e. Assume the same facts as in Part b, except that Scott's will does not mention the trust property.

13-46. *Life Insurance.* Joy dies on November 5, 1991. Soon after Joy's death, the following insurance policies on Joy's life are discovered. With respect to each policy, indicate the amount includible in Joy's gross estate.

Policy Number	Owner	Beneficiary	Face Value
123	Joy	Joy's husband	$400,000
757	Joy's son	Joy's estate	225,000
848	Joy's son	Joy's son	300,000
414	Joy's daughter	Joy's husband	175,000

Joy transferred policies 757 and 848 to her son in 1986. She transferred policy 414 to her daughter in 1990.

13-47. *Life Insurance.* Refer to Problem 13-46. What is the net addition to Joy's taxable estate with respect to the insurance policies listed above if the property passing under Joy's will goes to Joy's son?

13-48. *Deductions.* When Brad dies in 1991, his gross estate is valued at $3,400,000. He owes debts totaling $500,000. Funeral and administration expenses are estimated at $15,000 and $50,000, respectively. It is estimated that the marginal estate tax rate will exceed his estate's marginal income tax rate. Brad wills his church $30,000. What is Brad's adjusted gross estate?

13-49. *Marital Deduction.* Assume the same facts as in Problem 13-48 and that Brad wills to his wife his stock and cash (total value of $800,000). His will also provides for setting up a trust to be funded with $400,000 of property with a bank named as trustee. His wife is to receive all of the trust income semiannually for life, and upon her death the trust assets are to be distributed equally among Brad's children and grandchildren.
a. What is the amount of Brad's taxable estate? List two possible answers.
b. Assume Brad's widow dies in 1997. With respect to Brad's former assets, which items will be included in the widow's gross estate? List two possible answers.

13-50. *Marital Deduction.* Assume the same facts as in Problems 13-48 and 13-49 and that prior to Brad's death his wife already owns property valued at $300,000. Assume that each asset owned by each spouse increases 20% in value by 1997 and that Brad's executor elects to claim the maximum marital deduction possible. From a tax standpoint, was the executor's strategy of electing the marital deduction on the QTIP trust a wise decision? Support your answer with computations.

13-51. *Adjusted Taxable Gifts.* Will dies in 1991. He never married. At the time he dies, his sole asset is cash of $1,000,000. Assume no debts or funeral and administration expenses. His gift history is as follows:

Date	Amount of Taxable Gifts	FMV of Gift Property at Date of Death
October 1977	$270,000	$290,000
October 1981	90,000	85,000

a. What is Will's estate tax base?
b. How would your answer to Part a change if the first gift is made in 1974 (instead of 1977)?

13-52. *Estate Tax Base.* Bess dies in 1991. Her gross estate totals $3,000,000. Included in her gross estate is a $100,000 life insurance policy on her life that she gave away in 1990. The taxable gift that arose from giving away the policy was $15,000. In 1989 Bess made a $40,000 taxable gift of stock whose value increased to $75,000 by the time Bess died. Assume her estate tax deductions total $80,000.
a. What is her estate tax base?
b. What unified credit will her estate claim?

13-53. *Installment Payments.* Claire dies on May 1, 1991. Her gross estate consists of the following items:

Cash	$ 40,000
Stocks traded on a stock exchange	200,000
Personal residence	175,000
25% capital interest in 6-person partnership	325,000

Claire's Sec. 2053 deductions total $30,000. She has no other deductions.

a. What fraction of Claire's federal estate taxes may be paid in installments under Sec. 6166? When is the first installment payment due?

b. May Claire's estate elect Sec. 6166 treatment if the stocks are valued at $2,000,000 instead of $200,000? If not, does Claire's estate necessarily have to pay the entire estate tax in February 1992? Explain.

13-54. *State Death Tax Credit*. Dale dies with a taxable estate of $680,000 and a tax base of $710,000. Dale's estate pays state death taxes of $20,000. What is the credit for state death taxes?

COMPREHENSIVE PROBLEMS

13-55. Bonnie dies on June 1, 1991. Bonnie is survived by her husband, Abner, and two sons, Carl and Doug. Bonnie's only lifetime taxable gift is made in October 1987 in the taxable amount of $700,000. She does not elect gift splitting. By the time of her death, the value of the gifted property (stock) has risen to $820,000.

Bonnie's executor discovers the items shown below. Amounts shown are the FMVs of the items as of June 1, 1991.

Cash in checking account in her name	$100,000
Cash in savings account in her name	430,000
Stock in names of Bonnie and Doug, joint tenants with right of survivorship. Bonnie provided all the consideration ($3,000) to purchase the stock.	25,000
Land in names of Bonnie and Abner, joint tenants with right of survivorship. Abner provided all the consideration to purchase the land.	360,000
Personal residence in Bonnie's name	250,000
Life insurance on Bonnie's life; Bonnie is owner and Bonnie's estate is beneficiary (face value)	210,000
Trust created by will of Bonnie's mother (who died in 1965). Bonnie is entitled to all the trust income for life, and she could will the trust property to whomever she desired. She wills it to her sons in equal amounts.	700,000

Bonnie's debts, as of her date of death, are $60,000. Her funeral and administration expenses total $80,000. The executor deducts the administration expenses on the estate tax return.

Bonnie's will includes the following:

"I leave my residence to my husband Abner."

"$250,000 of property is to be transferred to a trust with First Bank named as trustee. All of the income is to be paid to my husband, Abner, semiannually for the rest of his life. Upon his death the property is to be divided equally between my two sons or their estates."

"I leave $10,000 to the American Cancer Society."

Assume that the executor elects to claim the maximum marital deduction possible.
Compute the following with respect to Bonnie's estate:
a. Gross estate
b. Adjusted gross estate
c. Taxable estate
d. Adjusted taxable gifts
e. Estate tax base
f. Tentative tax on estate tax base

g. Federal estate tax payable (assume her state death taxes exactly equal the amount of the credit for state death taxes)

13-56. Assume the same facts as in Problem 13-55, except (1) the joint tenancy land is held in the names of Bonnie and Doug, joint tenants with right of survivorship, and Bonnie provided 55% of the consideration to buy the land; (2) Bonnie's executor does not elect to claim the marital deduction on the QTIP trust; and (3) the administration expenses ($65,000) are deducted on the estate's income tax return. (Assume that there is no taxable gift on the purchase of the joint tenancy land.)

TAX FORM/RETURN PREPARATION PROBLEMS

13-57. Prepare an Estate Tax Return (Form 706) for Judy Griffin (464-55-3434), who dies on June 30, 1990. Judy is survived by her husband, Greg, and her daughter, Candy. Judy was a resident of 17 Fiddlers Way, Nashville, Tennessee 37205. She was employed as a corporate executive with Sounds of Country, Inc., a recording company, at the time of her death. The assets discovered at Judy's death are listed below. Amounts shown are date-of-death values.

Savings account in Judy's name	$190,000
Checking account in Judy's name	10,000
Personal residence (having a $200,000 mortgage)	500,000
Household furnishings	75,000
400 shares of stock in XYZ Corporation (quotes on June 30, 1990, are high of 70, low of 60, close of 67)	?
Land in New York (inherited from her mother in 1970)	140,000
Porsche purchased by Greg in 1982 as an anniversary gift to Judy	45,000

Other items include the following:
1. Life insurance policy 1: Judy purchased a $200,000 life insurance policy on her life on August 1, 1987, and paid the first annual premium of $2,500. The next day, she transferred the policy to her brother, Todd, who is also the beneficiary. Judy paid the premium on August 1, 1988, and 1989.
2. Life insurance policy 2: A $150,000 whole life policy on Greg's life. Judy purchased the policy in 1977 and has always paid the $1,200 semiannual premium due on March 30 and September 30. Interpolated terminal reserve is $25,000. The beneficiary is Judy or her estate. Judy is the owner of the policy.
3. Employer annuity: Judy's employer established a qualified pension plan in 1979. The employer contributes 60% and the employee pays 40% of the required annual contributions. Judy chose a settlement option that provides for annual payments to Greg until his death. The annuity receivable by Greg is valued at $600,000.

Other information includes the following:
1. In October 1988, Judy transferred to her brother, Todd, $1,520,000 of stock that she received as a gift. Judy and Greg elected gift splitting. This was the first taxable gift for each spouse, and they paid their own portion of the gift tax from their own funds. When Judy dies, the stocks have appreciated to $1,600,000.
2. Unpaid bills at death include $2,500 owed on a bank credit card.
3. The cost of Judy's funeral and tombstone totals $25,000.
4. Judy's administration expenses are estimated at $55,000. Her estate's marginal transfer tax rate will be higher than the estate's marginal income tax rate.
5. Judy's will includes the following dispositions of property:

"I leave $60,000 of property in trust with Fourth Bank named as trustee. All income is to be paid semiannually to my husband, Greg, for life or until he remarries, whichever occurs first. At the termination of Greg's interest, the property will pass to my daughter, Candy, or her estate."

"To my beloved husband, Greg, I leave my XYZ stock. The rest of my property I leave to my daughter, Candy, except that I leave $10,000 to the University of Tennessee."

6. Assume the state estate tax payable equals the maximum credit available on the federal return for state death taxes.

7. Claim the QTIP election if possible.

13-58. Prepare an Estate Tax Return (Form 706) for Joe Blough (177-47-3217) of 1412 Robin Lane, Birmingham, Alabama 35208. Joe died on November 12, 1990; he was survived by his spouse Joan and their daughter Katy. Joe was a bank vice president. Date-of-death values of the assets discovered at Joe's death are listed below.

Checking and savings accounts in names of Joe and Joan, joint tenants with right of survivorship	$800,000
Second home, in Joe's name	450,000
Life insurance policy on Joe's life; his estate is the beneficiary and Joan is the owner	250,000

Other pertinent information is as follows:

1. In 1985 Joe gave his sister land then valued at $220,000. He and Joan elected gift splitting. This was Joe's first taxable gift. The land was worth $350,000 when Joe died.
2. Joan owns the house that had been the couple's principal residence. Its value is $750,000.
3. Joe willed all of his property to their daughter Katy.
4. For simplicity, assume there are no administration expenses and that funeral expenses are $11,000.
5. Assume that state death taxes are equal to the federal credit for state death taxes.

CASE STUDY PROBLEM

13-59. Your clients, Matt and Mindy Mason, have come to you for estate planning advice. Each is age 66 and in reasonably good health. Mr. and Mrs. Mason have no children by their marriage, but each was previously married and Mrs. Mason has two children (Brett and Becky) by her previous marriage. Mr. and Mrs. Mason, residents of a non-community property state, own the assets with the FMVs listed below:

	Mr. Mason	Mrs. Mason
Cash	$1,000,000	$1,500,000
Life insurance on self	1,300,000	-0-
Stocks in public companies	2,000,000	800,000
Residence	-0-	400,000
Stock in solely-owned company	125,000	-0-

In addition, Mrs. Mason is the beneficiary of a trust created under the will of her mother, who died in 1975. The trust is currently valued at $350,000. Under the trust instrument, Mrs. Mason is entitled to receive all of the trust income for life and may specify in her will the person(s) to receive the remainder interest. Mr. Mason's nephew (Norman) is the beneficiary of the insurance policy on Mr. Mason's life.

Fortunately, both Mr. and Mrs. Mason are free of debt.

Mr. Mason's will includes the following provisions at present:

> I leave all of my property to my spouse, Mindy Mason, if she survives me. If she does not survive me, I leave all of my property to my favorite charitable organization, the Humane Society of Louisville.

Mrs. Mason's will includes the following provisions at present:

> I leave each of my grandchildren [five persons are named] and each of my nieces and nephews [twenty-five persons are named] $15,000 each.

> I leave assets valued at $600,000 to my son and daughter (Brett and Becky) in equal shares.

> I appoint the property of the trust created under my mother's will to my sister, Helen Adams, or her descendants.

> The rest of my estate I leave to a trust with First Bank as trustee. My spouse, Matt, is to receive all of the trust income annually until the earlier of his death or remarriage. The

remainder is to pass in equal shares to my son and daughter, or their descendants. Should my spouse predecease me, all of the rest of my estate is to be divided equally between my son and daughter, or their descendants.

Assume that there will be no funeral or administration expenses for either spouse. Assume also that no death taxes are payable from property eligible for the marital or charitable contribution deductions. Assume that state death taxes are equal to the credit for state death taxes available on the federal estate tax return.

Required: Prepare a memorandum to the tax partner of your firm that:
- **a.** Calculates the total estate taxes payable by the two estates under the situations listed below. Ignore further appreciation. Assume that:
  1. Matt dies first.
  2. Mindy dies first.
- **b.** Makes estate planning recommendations that would reduce the couple's estate tax liability. Assume that Matt will die first.
- **c.** In making your suggestions to the clients, what factors besides tax consequences should you consider?

TAX RESEARCH PROBLEMS

13-60. Roy, a Texas resident, dies in 1991, at the age of 80, survived by his bachelor son, Ted. At the time of his death, Roy is living in a residence that he purchased in 1970 and that he and Ted occupy as their personal residence. In 1975, Roy deeded the residence to Ted, but until his death Roy continues to live in the house with Ted without paying rent. After deeding the house to Ted, Roy never has any visitors unless he first receives Ted's permission. On many occasions, Roy mentions to his friends that he fears Ted will commit him to a nursing home. After the transfer, Ted pays all of the property taxes on the residence. The residence is valued at $150,000 at Roy's death. What amount, if any, is included in Roy's gross estate with respect to the residence?

A partial list of research sources is

- Reg. Sec. 20.2036-1.
- *Estate of Allen D. Gutchess,* 46 T.C. 554 (1966).
- *Estate of Emil Linderme, Sr.,* 52 T.C. 305 (1969).
- *Estate of Sylvia H. Roemer,* 1983 PH T.C. Memo ¶ 83,509, 46 TCM 1176.
- Rev. Rul. 70-155, 1970-1 C.B. 189.

13-61. Val, a resident of Illinois, dies on May 12, 1991. Seven days before she dies (May 5), she writes four checks for $10,000 each, payable to each of her four grandchildren. Val mails the checks on May 6, and each donee receives the check on or before May 9. None of the donees deposit their check until after Val's death. As of Val's date of death, the balance in her checking account is $52,127. This balance includes the $40,000 of outstanding checks issued to her grandchildren.

What amount should be reported on Val's estate tax return with respect to the checking account? Assume the executor elects date-of-death valuation.

A partial list of research sources is

- Sec. 2031(a).
- Reg. Secs. 20.2031-5 and 25.2511-2(b).
- *Estate of Ella M. Belcher,* 83 T.C. 227 (1984).
- *Daniel F. McCarthy, et al., Trustees v. U.S.,* 57 AFTR 2d 86-1515, 85-2 USTC ¶ 13,648 (D.C. Ill., 1985).

13-62. Randy died on June 10, 1991. His will created a trust from which his surviving spouse is entitled to receive all of the trust income quarterly for life; however, any income accumulated between the last quarterly payment date and his spouse's date of death is to be paid to the remainderman, Randy, Jr. Is the trust eligible for the marital deduction under the QTIP rules?

A partial list of research sources is

- Prop. Reg. Sec. 20.2056(b)-7(c).
- *Estate of Rose D. Howard,* 91 T.C. 329 (1988).

14 Income Taxation of Trusts and Estates

CHAPTER OUTLINE

LEARNING OBJECTIVES 14-2
BASIC CONCEPTS 14-2
   Inception of Trusts 14-2
   Inception of Estates 14-3
   Reasons for Creating Trusts 14-3
   Basic Principles of Fiduciary Taxation 14-4
PRINCIPLES OF FIDUCIARY ACCOUNTING 14-5
   The Importance of Identifying Income and Principal 14-5
   Effects of State Law or Terms of Trust Instrument 14-6
   Principal and Income—The Uniform Act 14-6
   Categorization of Depreciation 14-7
FORMULA FOR TAXABLE INCOME AND TAX LIABILITY 14-8
   Gross Income 14-9
   Deductions for Expenses 14-9
   Distribution Deduction 14-10
   Personal Exemption 14-11
   Credits 14-12
DISTRIBUTABLE NET INCOME 14-12
   Significance of DNI 14-12
   Definition of DNI 14-13
   Manner of Computing DNI 14-14
DETERMINING A SIMPLE TRUST'S TAXABLE INCOME 14-15
   Allocation of Expenses to Tax-Exempt Income 14-16
   Determination of DNI and the Distribution Deduction 14-17
   Tax Treatment for Beneficiary 14-17
   Short-Cut Approach to Proving Correctness of Taxable Income 14-18
   Effect of a Net Operating Loss 14-19
   Effect of a Net Capital Loss 14-19
COMPREHENSIVE ILLUSTRATION—DETERMINING A SIMPLE TRUST'S TAXABLE INCOME 14-20
   Background Data 14-20
   Trustee's Fee 14-20
   Distribution Deduction and DNI 14-21
   Trust's Taxable Income 14-22
   Categorizing a Beneficiary's Income 14-22
DETERMINING TAXABLE INCOME FOR COMPLEX TRUSTS AND ESTATES 14-22
   Determination of DNI and the Distribution Deduction 14-23
   Tax Treatment for Beneficiary 14-24
   Effect of a Net Operating Loss 14-28
   Effect of a Net Capital Loss 14-28
COMPREHENSIVE ILLUSTRATION—DETERMINING A COMPLEX TRUST'S TAXABLE INCOME 14-29
   Background Data 14-29
   Trustee's Fee 14-29
   Distribution Deduction and DNI 14-30
   Trust's Taxable Income 14-31
   Additional Observations 14-32
ACCUMULATION DISTRIBUTION RULES 14-32
   Purpose 14-32
   When Applicable 14-33
SECTION 644 TAX 14-34
   Purpose 14-34
   When Applicable 14-34
   Computation of the Tax 14-34
INCOME IN RESPECT OF A DECEDENT 14-35
   Definition and Common Examples 14-35
   Significance of IRD 14-36
GRANTOR TRUST PROVISIONS 14-38
   Purpose and Effect 14-38
   Revocable Trusts 14-39
   Clifford Trusts 14-39
   Post-1986 Reversionary Interest Trusts 14-40
   Retention of Administrative Powers 14-41
   Retention of Economic Benefits 14-41
   Control of Others' Enjoyment 14-42
TAX PLANNING CONSIDERATIONS 14-42
   Ability to Shift Income 14-43
   Timing of Distributions 14-43
   65-Day Rule 14-44
   Property Distributions 14-44
   Choice of Year-End for Estates 14-44
   Deduction of Administration Expenses 14-45
COMPLIANCE AND PROCEDURAL CONSIDERATIONS 14-45
   Filing Requirements 14-45
   Due Date for Return and Tax 14-46
   Section 644 Tax—Information about Grantor's Income 14-46
   Documents to Be Furnished to IRS 14-46
   Sample Simple and Complex Trust Returns 14-47
PROBLEM MATERIALS 14-47
   Discussion Questions 14-47
   Problems 14-48
   Tax Form/Return Preparation Problems 14-51
   Case Study Problem 14-52
   Tax Research Problems 14-53

LEARNING OBJECTIVES

After studying this chapter, you should be able to

1. Understand the basic concepts concerning trusts and estates
2. Distinguish between principal and income
3. Explain how to calculate the tax liability of a trust or estate
4. Understand the significance of distributable net income
5. Determine the taxable income of a simple trust
6. Determine the taxable income of a complex trust
7. Recognize the significance of income in respect of a decedent
8. Explain the effect of the grantor trust provisions
9. Recognize the filing requirements for fiduciary returns

Chapters 12 and 13 examined two components of the transfer tax system—the gift tax and the estate tax. We return to income taxation by exploring the basic rules for the taxation of trusts and estates, two special tax entities. Income generated by property owned by an estate or a trust is reported on an income tax return for that entity. In general, the tax rules governing estates and trusts are identical. Unless the text states that a rule applies to only one of these entities, the discussion concerns both estates and trusts. Subchapter J (Secs. 641 through 692) contains the special tax rules applicable to estates and trusts. These entities are often referred to as **fiduciaries,** and their taxation as **fiduciary taxation.** This chapter describes the basic provisions of Subchapter J.

This chapter discusses principles of fiduciary accounting, a concept that influences the tax consequences. The major focus of the chapter is on the determination of the taxable income of the fiduciary and the amount taxable to beneficiaries. Comprehensive examples concerning the computations are included, and Appendix B includes completed tax returns (Form 1041) for both a simple and a complex trust. The chapter also explores the circumstances that cause the grantor (transferor) to be taxed on the trust's income.

BASIC CONCEPTS

OBJECTIVE 1
Understand the basic concepts concerning trusts and estates

Inception of Trusts

Often a relatively wealthy person (one for whom gift and estate taxes are relevant) will create trusts for tax and other reasons (e.g., conserving assets). **Trusts** may be created at any point in time by transferring property to the trusts. The property in the trust is administered by a **trustee** for the benefit of the beneficiary. The transferor names the trustee. The trustee may be either an individual or an institution, such as a bank, and there can be more than one trustee.

If the transfer occurs during the transferor's lifetime, the trust is called an **inter vivos trust.** The transferor is known as the **grantor** or the **trustor.** A trust created under the direction of a decedent's will is referred to as a **testamentary trust.** The

Key Point

A trust is a contract between two parties, the grantor, and the trustee. The grantor gives the trustee legal title to property which the trustee then holds for the benefit of a third party(ies), called the beneficiary(ies). The trustee, acting in a fiduciary capacity, manages the property for the duration of the trust. Beneficiaries of a trust may have an income interest, which means that they receive part or all of the trust's income, or they may have a remainder interest, which means that they will receive the property held by the trust at some specified time. A beneficiary may hold both an income interest and a remainder interest. The grantor may be a beneficiary and the grantor can also be the trustee.

assets used to fund a testamentary trust are those that were formerly held by the decedent's estate. A trust may continue to exist for whatever time is specified in the trust instrument or the will, subject to the constraints of the **Rule Against Perpetuities**.[1]

Inception of Estates

Estates come into being only upon the death of the person whose assets are being administered. The estate continues in existence until the duties of the executor (i.e., the person(s) named in the will to manage the property and distribute the assets) have been completed. An executor's duties include collecting the assets, paying the debts and taxes, and distributing the properties. The time to perform the duties may vary from a year or two to over a decade, depending upon many factors (e.g., whether anyone contests the will).

Sometimes the decedent's survivors can reduce their personal income taxes by preserving the estate's existence. The estate is a separate tax entity. Thus, continuing the estate's existence achieves the advantage of having some income taxed to yet another taxpayer, but the estate's tax rates are very compressed. The Regulations provide, however, that if the IRS considers the administration of an estate to have been "unreasonably prolonged," it will view the estate as having been terminated for federal tax purposes after the expiration of a "reasonable period" for performance of the administrative duties.[2] In such a situation, the income is taxed directly to the individuals entitled to receive the assets of the estate. These persons may have a higher marginal tax rate than the estate.

Reasons for Creating Trusts

A myriad of reasons—both tax and nontax—exist for creating trusts. Some of these reasons are discussed here.

Tax Saving Aspects of Trusts. If the trust is irrevocable, meaning the grantor cannot require the trustee to return the assets, one of the primary tax purposes for establishing the trust has traditionally been to achieve income splitting. With income splitting, the income from the trust assets is taxed to at least one taxpayer (i.e., the trust or the beneficiary) at a lower marginal tax rate than the grantor. Because of the compression of the rate schedules after 1986, trusts do not offer the same potential for income shifting now that they originally did. Sometimes the trust instrument authorizes the trustee to use his discretion in "sprinkling" the income among several beneficiaries or accumulating it within the trust. In such circumstances, the trustee must consider the tax effects of (1) making a distribution of income to one beneficiary rather than another or (2) retaining income in the trust.

Individuals may also create trusts in order to minimize their estate taxes. As discussed in Chapter 13, in order for the transferor to exclude the property conveyed to the trust from the gross estate, the transferor must not (1) retain the right to receive the trust income or the power to control which other persons receive the

---

[1] The Rule against Perpetuities is the "[p]rinciple that no interest in property is good unless it must vest, if at all, not later than 21 years, plus period of gestation, after some life or lives in being at time of creation of interest." Henry C. Black, *Black's Law Dictionary*, Rev. 5th ed., Ed. by Joseph R. Nolan, Michael J. Connolly, et al. (St. Paul, Minn.: West Publishing Co., 1979), p. 1,195.

[2] Reg. Sec. 1.641(b)-3(a).

income[3] or (2) have, at the time of death, the power to alter the identity of any persons named earlier to receive such assets.[4]

Nontax Aspects of Trusts. Reduction of taxes is not always the foremost reason for establishing trusts. Trusts, including Sec. 2503(c) trusts and *Crummey* trusts, are often used when minors are the donees so that a trustee can manage the assets. (See Chapter 12 for a discussion of such trusts.) Even when the donee is an adult, donors may sometimes prefer that the assets be managed by a trustee deemed to have better management skills than the donee. Other donors may want to avoid conveying assets directly to a donee if they fear the donee would soon consume most of them.

The creation of a **revocable trust** (i.e., one in which the grantor may demand that the assets be returned) does not yield any income or estate tax savings for the grantor. Nevertheless, revocable trusts, including ones in which the grantor is also the beneficiary, are frequently created for nontax purposes. The grantor may desire to have his properties managed by an individual or an institution with superior management skills. In states in which the probate costs for administering a decedent's estate are relatively high, use of a revocable trust reduces probate costs because assets in a revocable trust avoid probate. In this text, a trust is deemed to be irrevocable unless it is explicitly denoted as being revocable.

Basic Principles of Fiduciary Taxation

Key Point

Essentially, an estate or a trust is taxed only on income which it retains. Taxable income which it passes on (distributes) to the income beneficiaries is taxable to those beneficiaries.

Throughout the rest of this chapter several basic principles of fiduciary taxation should be kept in mind. These features are discussed below. They apply to all trusts other than grantor trusts. (See pages 14-38 through 14-42 for a description of the tax treatment of grantor trusts.)

Trusts and Estates as Separate Taxpayers. An estate or a trust is a separate taxpaying entity. If the estate or trust has any taxable income, it pays an income tax. Such tax is calculated by using Form 1041. The 1991 tax rates applicable to estates and trusts are reproduced on the inside back cover. These rates became indexed for inflation beginning in 1989. The rates are very compressed in comparison with the rates for individuals.

Example 14-1 ■ For calendar year 1991 a trust reports taxable income of $10,000. Its tax liability is $2,351.50. An unmarried individual not qualifying as a head of household would owe taxes of $1,500 on $10,000 of taxable income. ■

No Double Taxation. Unlike the situation for corporations, there is no double taxation of the income earned by an estate or trust. The estate or trust receives a deduction for the income it distributes to its beneficiaries. The beneficiaries, in turn, report the amount of their receipts as income on their individual returns. Thus, the current income is taxed once, to the fiduciary or to the beneficiary or some to each, depending upon whether it is distributed or not. In total, all of the estate or trust's current income is taxed, perhaps some to the fiduciary and the remaining amount to the beneficiary. One of the primary purposes of the Subchapter J rules is to determine exactly where the estate or trust's current income is taxed.

---

[3] Sec. 2036.
[4] Sec. 2038.

Example 14-2 ■ For 1991, the Hill Trust has total dividend income of $25,000, of which $15,000 is distributed at the trustee's discretion to Beth. Beth is taxed on $15,000, the amount of the distribution. The trust is taxed on the income it retains or accumulates, $10,000 in this case, less a $100 personal exemption (discussed on page 14-11). ■

Conduit Approach. A conduit approach governs for fiduciary income taxation. Under this approach, the distributed income has the same character in the hands of the beneficiary as it has to the trust. Thus, if the trust distributes tax-free interest income on state and local bonds, such income retains its tax-free character at the beneficiary level.

Example 14-3 ■ For 1991, the Hill Trust receives $15,000 of dividends and $10,000 of tax-free interest. It distributes all of its receipts to its beneficiary. The beneficiary is deemed to receive $15,000 of dividend income and $10,000 of tax-free interest. ■

Self-Study Question

King Trust receives interest on a bank savings account. All of the income of the trust is distributed to Anne. Since the trust is treated as a conduit, the interest is reported by Anne as ordinary interest income. Why might this be important?

Answer

For purposes of the limitation on the deduction Anne may be allowed for investment interest expenses, the interest from the trust is part of Anne's investment income. For purposes of the passive loss limitations, the interest is classified as portfolio income.

Similarity to Rules for Individuals. Section 641(b) states "[T]he taxable income of an estate or trust shall be computed in the same manner as in the case of an individual, except as otherwise provided in this part." Sections 641-683 appear in "this part" (Part I) of Subchapter J. Thus, the tax effect for fiduciaries is the same as for individuals if the provisions of Secs. 641-683 do not specify tax treatment different from that applicable for individual taxpayers. Sections 641-683 do not contain any special treatment for interest income from state and local bonds or for state and local tax payments. Consequently, an estate or trust is entitled to an exclusion for state and local bond interest and the same deductions for state and local taxes that individuals receive. On the other hand, Sec. 642(b) specifies the amount of the personal exemption to which fiduciaries are entitled. Thus, this portion of Subchapter J preempts the Sec. 151 rule concerning the amount of the personal exemption for individuals.

PRINCIPLES OF FIDUCIARY ACCOUNTING

OBJECTIVE 2
Distinguish between principal and income

Key Point

The trust is allowed a deduction for a personal exemption, but the deduction amount is substantially lower than the personal exemption amount allowed an individual.

For a better understanding of the special tax treatment of fiduciary income, especially the determination of to whom the estate's or trust's current income is taxed, one needs to have a general knowledge of the principles of fiduciary accounting. In a sense, fiduciary accounting is similar to fund accounting for governmental entities. All receipts and disbursements are classified as either income or principal (or corpus).

The Importance of Identifying Income and Principal

When computing taxable income, we are generally concerned with whether a particular item is included in or deducted from gross income. When answering fiduciary tax questions, however, we also need to consider whether an item is classified as principal (or corpus) or income for fiduciary accounting purposes. For example, certain items (e.g., interest on state bonds) may constitute fiduciary accounting income but are not included in the gross income calculation. Other items (e.g., capital gains) may be included in gross income but may be classified as principal for fiduciary accounting purposes.

Typical Misconception

The distribution of an amount that exceeds the fiduciary accounting income to an income beneficiary is an unauthorized invasion of corpus, or principal. Such a distribution reduces the amount the remainderman will eventually receive from the trust, and the trustee may be violating his fiduciary responsibility to the remainderman if the distribution is made.

One of the most difficult aspects of feeling comfortable with the fiduciary taxation rules is to appreciate the difference between fiduciary accounting income and income in the general tax sense. In understanding and applying the Code, one has to know in which context the word *income* is used. Section 643(b) provides guidance for this matter. It states, "[F]or purposes of this subpart and subparts B, C and D [Secs. 641-668], the term 'income' when not preceded by the words 'taxable,' 'distributable net,' 'undistributed net,' or 'gross,' means the amount of income of the estate or trust for the taxable year determined under the terms of the governing instrument and applicable local law." In other words, within most of Subchapter J, the word *income* refers to income in the fiduciary accounting context unless other words modify the word *income*. In this text, the terminology *net accounting income* is used to refer to the excess of accounting gross income over expenses charged to accounting income.

The categorization of a receipt or disbursement as principal or income generally affects whether the fiduciary or the beneficiary pays tax on the income. For example, if a gain is classified as principal and the trustee can distribute only income, the trust is taxed on the gain. Even though an item may constitute income for tax purposes, it cannot be distributed to a beneficiary if it constitutes principal under the fiduciary accounting rules unless the trustee is authorized to distribute principal. If the trust instrument stipulates that the trustee can distribute only income prior to the termination of the trust, the amount of fiduciary accounting income sets the ceiling on the current distribution that the trustee can make to a beneficiary.

Example 14-4 ■

Self-Study Question

A trust agreement provides that all trust income is to be distributed to Janet until Joe's 35th birthday, at which time the trust is to terminate and distribute all of its corpus to Joe. MNO stock is the only property owned by the trust. The stock was purchased for $15,000 by the trust 15 years ago. The stock is worth $100,000. Suppose that the trust sells the stock before it terminates. Is Janet entitled to the $85,000 profit and Joe to the $15,000 difference?

Answer

This question stresses the reason why income and principal must be differentiated. Joe and Janet will likely have differences of opinion over who should get what. The trustee, in his fiduciary capacity, must follow the definitions of income and corpus as stated in the trust agreement, or if not there, in the state law. He may even have to go to court to get direction.

In 1991, the Bell Trust has net accounting income of $18,000. In addition, it sells stock for a $40,000 capital gain. Under state law the gain is allocated to the principal. The trust instrument requires the trustee to distribute all of the trust's income to Beth annually until she reaches age 45. The trust assets are to be paid to Beth on her forty-fifth birthday (five years from now). In 1991, the trustee must distribute $18,000 to Beth. The capital gain cannot be distributed currently because it is allocated to principal, and the trustee is not empowered to make distributions of principal.

■

Effects of State Law or Terms of Trust Instrument

Recall that for purposes of Subchapter J, *income* generally refers to income as determined under the governing instrument and applicable local law. Grantors can influence the tax consequences to trusts and their beneficiaries because they can define income and principal in the trust instrument in whatever manner they desire. For example, they can specify that gains are to be included in income. Under state law, the definitions in the trust instrument preempt any definitions contained in state statutes. In the absence of definitions in the trust instrument, the applicable state statute controls for classifying items as principal or income. For purposes of defining principal and income, many states have adopted the *Revised Uniform Principal and Income Act* (hereafter referred to as the *Uniform Act*) in its entirety or with minor modifications.[5]

Principal and Income—The Uniform Act

Income Receipts. The Uniform Act defines *income* as "the return in money or property derived from the use of principal."[6] It lists income as including the following: rent, interest, corporate distributions of dividends, distributions by a regulated

---

[5] The *Revised Uniform Principal and Income Act* is a model set of rules proposed by the Uniform Commission on State Laws. States can voluntarily adopt such provisions verbatim or in amended form.

[6] *Revised Uniform Principal and Income Act*, Sec. 3(a).

investment company from ordinary income, and the net profits of a business.[7] The rules are more detailed for receipts from the disposition of natural resources. A portion (27½%) of the receipts from royalties is added to principal as a depletion allowance.[8] The remainder of the royalties constitutes income.

Principal Receipts. **Principal** is defined in the Uniform Act as "the property which has been set aside by the owner or the person legally empowered so that it is held in trust eventually to be delivered to the **remainderman** while the return or use of the principal is in the meantime taken or received by or held for accumulation for an **income beneficiary**."[9] Among the categories of receipts included in principal are the following: consideration received on the sale or other transfer of principal or on repayment of a loan, stock dividends, receipts from disposition of corporate securities, and 27.5% of royalties received from natural resources.[10]

Expenditures. The Uniform Act provides guidance for expenditures also. Among the important charges for which income is to be reduced are the following:

1. Ordinary expenses, including regularly recurring property taxes, insurance premiums, interest, and ordinary repairs
2. A reasonable allowance for depreciation
3. Tax payable by the trustee if it is levied on receipts classified as income[11]

Some of the more significant expenditures chargeable to principal are:

1. Principal payment on an indebtedness
2. Extraordinary repairs or expenses incurred in making a capital improvement
3. Any tax levied upon gain or other receipts allocated to principal even if the tax is described as an income tax[12]

Generally, the agreement with the trustee specifies the respective portions of the trustee's fee that are chargeable to income and corpus.

Example 14-5 ■

The governing instrument for the Smith Trust contains no definitions of income and principal. The state in question has adopted the Uniform Act. For 1991 the trust has the following receipts and disbursements:

Dividends	$12,000
Proceeds from sale of stock, including $20,000 of gain	70,000
Trustee's fee, all charged to income	1,000
CPA's fee for preparation of tax return	500

The trust's net accounting income is $10,500 ($12,000 − $1,000 − $500). The gain on the sale of stock and the rest of the sales proceeds constitute corpus. ■

Categorization of Depreciation

As mentioned above, depreciation is charged to income under the Uniform Act; it thereby reduces net accounting income and the maximum amount that can be distributed to a beneficiary when the trust instrument does not authorize the

---

[7] Ibid., Secs. 3(a), 6(c) and (d), and 8(a).
[8] Ibid., Sec. 9(a).
[9] Ibid., Sec. 3(b).
[10] Ibid.
[11] Ibid., Sec. 13(a).
[12] Ibid., Sec. 13(c).

Ch. 14 / Income Taxation of Trusts and Estates

income, the distribution to the income beneficiary will be $14,000 and $11,000 of the income will be set aside for the remainderman. What is the impact if depreciation is chargeable to principal?

distribution of corpus. Many states have departed from the Uniform Act's treatment of depreciation by providing that depreciation is a charge against principal (instead of against income). If depreciation is charged against principal, the maximum amount that can be distributed to the income beneficiaries is not reduced by the depreciation deduction. This result is advantageous to the income beneficiary. (See page 14-9 for a discussion of the tax treatment of depreciation.)

A statement in the trust instrument concerning the accounting treatment for depreciation overrides a provision of state law. Some trust instruments specify that the trustee set aside (and not distribute) a certain amount of income as a "reserve" for depreciation.

Example 14-6 ■

Answer

The income distribution will be $25,000. If the trust holds the building to the end of its useful life, the building will theoretically "turn to dust" overnight and the remainderman would receive nothing (as far as the building is concerned).

Park Trust, whose trust instrument is silent with respect to depreciation, collects rental income of $17,000 and pays property taxes of $1,000. Its depreciation expense is $4,000. Under state law, all depreciation is charged to principal. Therefore, the trust's net accounting income is $16,000 ($17,000 − $1,000). If the trust instrument mandates current distribution of all the income, the beneficiary receives $16,000. If the trust instrument states that depreciation is charged against income, the income distribution is limited to $12,000. ■

Topic Review 14-1 summarizes the treatment under the Uniform Act of the major receipts and expenditures of fiduciaries.

FORMULA FOR TAXABLE INCOME AND TAX LIABILITY

OBJECTIVE 3
Explain how to calculate the tax liability of a trust or estate

The formula for determining a fiduciary's taxable income and income tax liability is very similar to the formula applicable to individuals. There are three major differences, though. A fiduciary's deductions are not divided between deductions *for*

TOPIC REVIEW 14-1

Classification as Principal or Income under the Uniform Act

Income Account	Principal Account
Income:	Receipts:
Rent	Consideration (including gains)
Interest	received upon disposition
Dividends	of property
Net profits of a business	Stock dividends
72½% of royalties	27½% of royalties
Expenses:	Expenditures:
Ordinary expenses (e.g., property	Principal payments on debt
taxes, insurance, interest,	Extraordinary repairs and
and ordinary repairs)	capital improvements
Taxes levied on accounting income	Taxes levied on gains and
Depreciation[a]	other items of principal

[a] Many state laws depart from the Uniform Act and characterize depreciation as a charge to principal.

and *from* adjusted gross income (AGI). Instead, a fiduciary's deductions are simply deductible in arriving at taxable income. A fiduciary receives no standard deduction. A type of deduction inapplicable to individuals—the distribution deduction—is available in computing a fiduciary's taxable income. Figure 14-1 illustrates the formula for computing a fiduciary's taxable income and tax liability.

Gross Income

The items included in a trust's or estate's gross income are the same as those included in an individual's gross income. However, the categorization of income is not identical for tax and accounting purposes. For example, a gain usually constitutes principal for accounting purposes, but it is part of gross income for tax purposes.

Example 14-7 ■ For 1991, Duke Trust receives $8,000 interest on corporate bonds, $20,000 interest on state bonds, and a $50,000 capital gain. The trust reports gross income of $58,000 ($8,000 + $50,000). Its accounting income is $28,000 ($8,000 + $20,000). ■

Deductions for Expenses

Fiduciaries incur numerous deductible expenses for its expenditures. These expenses, which parallel those of individuals, include interest, taxes (e.g., state and local income taxes and property taxes), fees for investment advice, fees for tax return preparation, expenses associated with producing income, and trade or business expenses. In

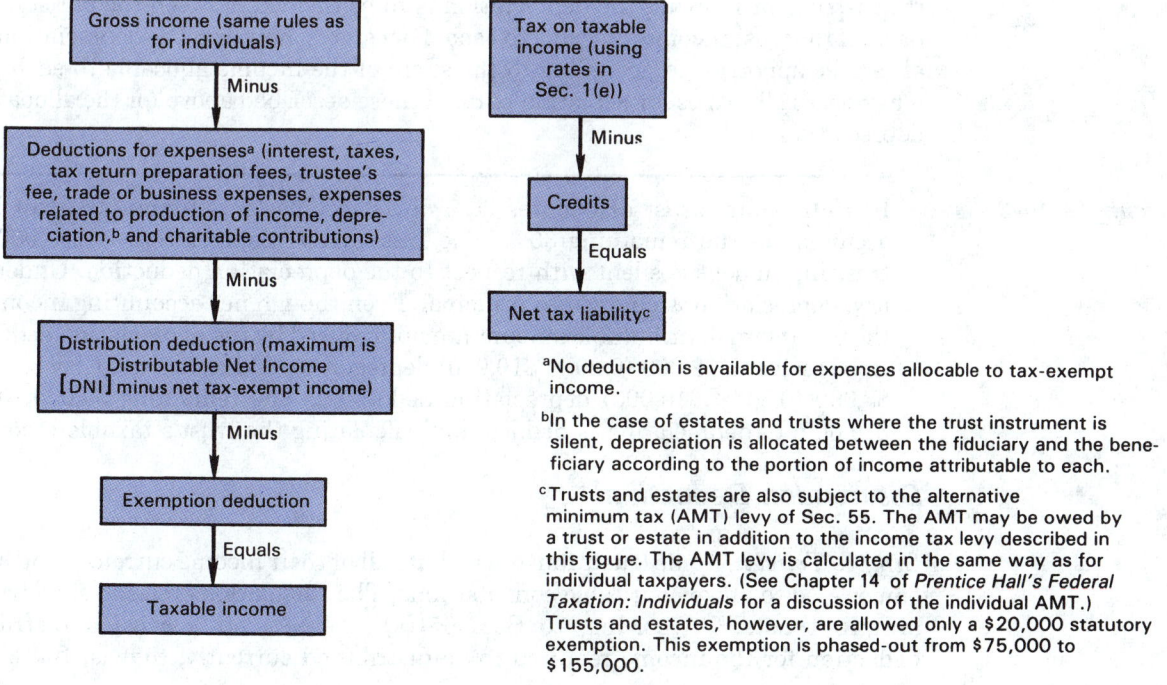

FIGURE 14-1 Formula for Determining the Taxable Income and Tax Liability of a Fiduciary

Key Point

Trustees' and executors' fees and tax return preparation fees are not subject to the 2% miscellaneous itemized deduction floor.

addition, fiduciaries may deduct the trustee's fee. This fee, which is similar to a property management fee incurred by an individual, is deductible under Sec. 212 as an expense incurred for the management of property held for the production of income.

Miscellaneous itemized deductions reduce taxable income only to the extent the aggregate amount of such deductions exceeds 2% of the taxpayer's AGI. Although estates and trusts do not literally have AGI, according to Sec. 67(e), a hypothetical AGI amount for an estate or trust is determined in the same fashion as for an individual except that the deductions for costs which are paid or incurred in connection with the administration of the estate or trust and would not have been incurred if the property were not held in such trust or estate, and the deductions allowable for the personal exemption and the distribution deduction are not to be treated as itemized deductions. Costs incurred for trustees' and executors' fees are incremental costs attributable to the holding of the property by a trust or estate as are the costs of having income tax returns prepared for estates and trusts. Thus, trustees' and executors' fees and tax return preparation fees are not categorized as miscellaneous itemized deductions. It might be argued that fees paid to an investment advisor are not additional costs attributable to the use of the trust or estate form. If this argument is correct, such fees are subject to the 2% nondeductible floor. Forthcoming Treasury Regulations should address this uncertainty.

An executor can deduct administration expenses on the estate's income tax return if such items are not also deducted on the estate tax return. Unlike the situation for individuals, there is no limit on a fiduciary's charitable contribution deduction. A deduction is not allowed, however, unless a charitable contribution is authorized in the trust instrument.[13]

A depreciation or depletion deduction is available to an estate or trust only to the extent it is not allowable to beneficiaries under Secs. 167(h) or 611(b).[14] According to Sec. 167(h), the depreciation deduction for trusts is to be apportioned between the income beneficiaries and the trust pursuant to the terms of the trust instrument. If the instrument is silent, the depreciation is to be divided between the parties on the basis of the trust income allocable to each. For estates, however, the depreciation must always be apportioned according to the share of the income allocable to each party. The Sec. 611(b) rules for depletion parallel those described above for the allocation of depreciation.

Example 14-8 ■ In 1991 Nunn Trust distributes 20% of its income to Bob and 50% to Clay. It accumulates the remaining 30%. The trust's 1991 depreciation is $10,000. The trust instrument is silent with respect to the depreciation deduction. Under state law, depreciation is charged to principal. Even though net accounting income and the maximum distributable amount are not reduced by the depreciation deduction, Bob receives a $2,000 (0.20 × $10,000) depreciation deduction and Clay receives a $5,000 (0.50 × $10,000) depreciation deduction. The remaining $3,000 (0.30 × $10,000) of depreciation is deducted in calculating the trust's taxable income. ■

Distribution Deduction

Simple Trusts. Some trusts must distribute all of their income currently and are not empowered to make charitable contributions. The Regulations refer to such trusts as **simple trusts**.[15] According to Sec. 651(a), these trusts receive a distribution deduction for the income required to be distributed currently; that is, 100% of the

---

[13] Sec. 642(c)(1).
[14] Sec. 642(e).
[15] Reg. Sec. 1.651(a)-1.

Formula for Taxable Income and Tax Liability • 14-11

Typical Misconception
The definition of a simple trust is commonly misunderstood. A trust which must distribute all of its income currently, which is not, under the trust agreement, a beneficiary, and does not distribute corpus during the year, is a simple trust for that year. Income, as used here, is fiduciary accounting income.

trust income. No words modify the word *income;* therefore, *income* means accounting income. If the accounting income that must be distributed exceeds the trust's distributable net income (see page 14-13), the distribution deduction may not exceed the distributable net income. As used in this context, the distributable net income amount does not include any tax-free income (net of related deductions) that may have been earned by the trust.[16] Whatever amount is deductible at the trust level is taxed to the beneficiaries receiving the distributions.

Complex Trusts. Trusts that are not required to distribute all of their income currently are referred to as **complex trusts**.[17] The distribution deduction for complex trusts and all estates is the sum of (1) the income required to be distributed currently and (2) any other amounts (such as discretionary payments) properly paid, credited, or required to be distributed for the year. As is the case for simple trusts, the distribution deduction may not exceed the trust's or estate's distributable net income (reduced by its tax-exempt income net of any related deductions).[18] The complex trust's or estate's beneficiaries report gross income totalling the amount of the distribution deduction.[19]

Example 14-9 ■ Green Trust must distribute 25% of its income annually to Amy. In addition, the trustee in its discretion may distribute income to Amy or Brad. In 1991 the trust has accounting income and distributable net income of $100,000. None of the income is from tax-exempt sources. The trust makes a $25,000 mandatory distribution to Amy and $10,000 discretionary distributions each to Amy and Brad. The trust's distribution deduction is $45,000 ($25,000 + $10,000 + $10,000). Amy and Brad report trust income of $35,000 and $10,000, respectively, on their individual returns. ■

Personal Exemption

One of the differences between the rules for individuals and the rules for fiduciaries is the amount of the personal exemption. Under Sec. 151, individuals are allowed personal exemptions. Section 642(b) authorizes an exemption for fiduciaries that applies in lieu of the amount for individuals. There is no exemption for a trust or estate in the year of termination.

Key Point
A trust, whether it is a simple trust or a complex trust, is eligible for the $300 personal exemption if it is required to distribute all of its income.

Estates are entitled to a $600 exemption. The exemption amount for trusts differs, depending upon the terms of the trust. If the trust instrument requires that the trustee distribute all of the income annually, the trust receives a $300 exemption. Otherwise, $100 is the exemption amount. In certain years some trusts may be required to make current distributions of all their income, while in other years they may be directed to accumulate the income or to make distributions at the trustee's discretion. For such trusts the exemption amount is $300 in some years and $100 in other years.

Example 14-10 ■ Gold Trust is established in 1991 with Jack as the beneficiary. The trust instrument instructs the trustee to make discretionary distributions of income to Jack during the years 1991 through 1995. Beginning in 1996, the trustee is to pay all of the trust income to Jack currently. For 1991 through 1995, the trust's exemption is $100. Beginning in 1996, it rises to $300. ■

[16] Sec. 651(b).
[17] Reg. Sec. 1.661(a)-1.
[18] Secs. 661(a) and (c).
[19] Sec. 662(a).

Recall that a trust receives a distribution deduction for income currently distributed to its beneficiaries. At first blush, it appears that (1) the distribution deduction balances out the income of trusts that must distribute currently all of their income, and (2) such trusts receive no tax benefits from their exemption deduction. True, the exemption produces no tax savings for such trusts if they have no income from gains credited to principal. Tax savings result from the personal exemption, however, if the trust has gains and the gains are not distributed. The exemption reduces the amount of gain otherwise taxed at the trust level.

Example 14-11 ■ Cook Trust is required to distribute all of its income currently. Capital gains are characterized as principal. In 1991, Cook Trust has $25,000 of interest income from corporate bonds and a $10,000 capital gain. It has no expenses. It receives a distribution deduction of $25,000 and a $300 personal exemption. Its taxable income is $9,700 ($25,000 + $10,000 − $25,000 − $300). ■

The personal exemption amount for individuals is adjusted annually for changes in the consumer price index. No comparable provision exists for the personal exemption for fiduciaries. The Committee Reports do not discuss why indexing of the exemption for fiduciaries was not proposed. The rate schedules for fiduciaries and individuals became indexed for inflation beginning in 1989.

Credits

In general, the rules for tax credits for fiduciaries are the same as those for individuals. A fiduciary does not, generally, incur expenditures of the type that trigger some of the personal credits, such as the credit for household and dependent care expenses. Trusts and estates are allowed a foreign tax credit determined in the same manner as for individual taxpayers, except that the credit is limited to the amount of foreign taxes not allocable to the beneficiaries.[20]

DISTRIBUTABLE NET INCOME

OBJECTIVE 4
Understand the significance of distributable net income

As stated earlier in this chapter, the primary function of Subchapter J is to determine to whom—the fiduciary, the beneficiary, or some to each—the estate's or the trust's current income is to be taxed. **Distributable net income** (DNI) plays a key role in determining the amount taxed to each party. In fact, DNI has been referred to as "the pie to be cut for tax purposes."[21]

Significance of DNI

DNI sets the ceiling on the amount of distributions taxed to the beneficiaries. As mentioned earlier, beneficiaries are taxed on the lesser of (1) the amount of their distributions or (2) their share of the amount of DNI (reduced by net tax-exempt

---

[20] Sec. 642(a)(1).
[21] M. Carr Ferguson, James L. Freeland, and Richard B. Stephens, *Federal Income Taxation of Estates and Beneficiaries* (Boston: Little, Brown, 1970), p. 1x.

Self-Study Question
What functions does distributable net income (DNI) serve?

Answer
1. Establishes the maximum amount on which the beneficiaries may be taxed, 2. Establishes the maximum amount which the trust or estate may deduct as a distribution deduction, and 3. Establishes the character of the income or expense in DNI that flows to the beneficiaries—income flows to the beneficiaries in proportion to the part each different type of income or expense has in DNI.

income). These statements assume that the trust makes no distributions of income accumulated in a prior period; therefore, the accumulation distribution rules of Secs. 665 through 668 are inapplicable (see pages 14-32 through 14-34).

Just as the total amount taxed to the beneficiaries equals the fiduciary's distribution deduction, DNI represents not only the maximum that can be taxed to the beneficiaries but also the maximum that can be deducted at the fiduciary level. Recall from the preceding section that the distribution deduction is the smaller of (1) the amount distributed or (2) the fiduciary's DNI. The distribution deduction may not, however, include any portion of tax-exempt income (net of any related deductions) that is deemed to have been distributed.

DNI also determines the character of the beneficiaries' income. Under the conduit approach, each beneficiary's distribution is deemed to consist of various categories of income (net of deductions) in the same proportion as the total of each class of income bears to the total DNI. For example, if 40% of the trust's income consists of dividends, 40% of each beneficiary's distribution is deemed to consist of dividends.

An exception applies, however, if the governing instrument or local law specifically allocates particular types of income to certain beneficiaries. Allocations prescribed in the trust instrument are honored for tax purposes only to the extent that they have an economic effect independent of the tax results.[22] For example, an allocation of all of a trust's dividend income to Amy, irrespective of the total amount of income earned, and an allocation of the remainder of the trust's income to Bob would have economic implications independent of the tax consequences.

Example 14-12 ■ Sun Trust has $30,000 of DNI for 1991; its DNI includes $10,000 of rental income and $20,000 of corporate bond interest. The trust instrument requires that each year the trustee distribute 30% of the trust's income to Joe and 70% to Paula. The trust instrument does not require an allocation of the different types of income to the two beneficiaries. Because the trust has no tax-exempt income and must distribute all of its income, it receives a distribution deduction of $30,000.

Joe reports $9,000 (0.30 × $30,000) of trust income, and Paula reports $21,000 (0.70 × $30,000) of trust income. Because rents comprise one-third ($10,000 ÷ $30,000) of DNI, the composition of the income reported by Joe and Paula is one-third rental income and two-thirds corporate bond interest. ■

Definition of DNI

Section 643(a) defines *DNI*, as the fiduciary's taxable income, adjusted as follows:

- No distribution deduction is subtracted.
- No personal exemption is subtracted.
- Capital gains are not included and capital losses are not subtracted unless such gains and losses are allocated to accounting income instead of principal.
- Extraordinary dividends and taxable stock dividends are not included if they are allocable to principal.
- An addition is made for tax-exempt interest (minus the expenses allocable thereto).

---

[22] Reg. Secs. 1.652(b)-2(b) and 1.662(b)-1.

Key Point
The difference between net accounting income and DNI is that DNI is reduced by certain expenses that are charged to principal. These expenses do not decrease net accounting income nor do they decrease the amount of money that can be distributed.

Because one purpose of DNI is to set a ceiling on the distribution deduction, the distribution deduction is not subtracted from taxable income in determining DNI. If capital gains and extraordinary dividends are allocated to corpus, they are excluded from DNI because they cannot be distributed. Tax-exempt interest is part of accounting income and can be distributed even though it is excluded from gross income. Consequently, DNI includes tax-exempt income (net of the nondeductible expenses allocable to such income). Even though net tax-exempt income is included in DNI, no distribution deduction is available for the portion of the distribution that is deemed to consist of tax-exempt income.

In general, net accounting income and DNI are the same, with one exception. If some expenses (e.g., trustee's fees) are charged to principal, such expenses reduce DNI even though they do not lessen net accounting income. The trustee's fees are deductible in arriving at taxable income. But taxable income is not adjusted upward for such expenses to arrive at DNI. Reduction of DNI by the expenses charged to principal provides a tax advantage for the income beneficiary because these fees lessen the amount that is taxable to the beneficiary. However, they do not decrease the money that can be distributed to the beneficiary.

Manner of Computing DNI

The amount of taxable income is in large measure a function of the distribution deduction, and the distribution deduction depends upon the amount of DNI. The distribution deduction cannot exceed DNI. Thus, the Sec. 643(a) definition of DNI, which involves making adjustments to a fiduciary's taxable income, does not translate to a workable definition from a practical standpoint. Under the definition, the computation is circular because the distribution deduction must be computed in order to know the amount of income taxable to the fiduciary.

There are, however, two alternate, practical means of determining DNI. Under the first approach you begin with taxable income exclusive of the distribution deduction and make the adjustments to taxable income that the Code specifies. Of course, an adjustment for the distribution deduction is not necessary.

Example 14-13 ■ For 1991 Derby Trust reports the following results. The trust must distribute all of its income annually.

	Amounts Allocable to	
	Income	Principal
Corporate bond interest	$20,000	
Rental income	30,000	
Gain on sale of investment land		$40,000
Property taxes	5,000	
Trustee's fee charged to corpus		2,000
Distribution to beneficiary	45,000	

The trust's taxable income exclusive of the distribution deduction is computed as follows:

Corporate bond interest		$20,000
Rental income		30,000
Capital gain		40,000
Minus:	Property taxes	(5,000)
	Trustee's fee	(2,000)
	Personal exemption	(300)
Taxable income exclusive of distribution deduction		$82,700

Now that taxable income exclusive of the distribution deduction has been determined, DNI can be computed in the following manner:

Taxable income exclusive of distribution deduction	$82,700
Plus: Personal exemption	300
Minus: Capital gain	(40,000)
DNI	$43,000

The second method for determining DNI is to calculate the amount of net accounting income and reduce such amount by any expenses charged to corpus. In a few situations DNI is a larger amount than the amount arrived at under this approach, but the discussion of such situations is beyond the scope of this book.

Example 14-14 ■ Assume the same facts as in Example 14-13. The following steps illustrate the second approach to calculating the DNI amount.

Corporate bond interest	$20,000
Rental income	30,000
Minus: Property taxes	(5,000)
Net accounting income	$45,000
Minus: Trustee's fee charged to corpus	(2,000)
DNI	$43,000

Note that although the beneficiary receives a $45,000 cash distribution (net accounting income), only $43,000 (DNI) is reported as income. The beneficiary receives $2,000 tax-free. Thus, an income beneficiary benefits from trustee's fees being charged to principal. The trust's distribution deduction is limited to $43,000 (DNI), even though the amount paid to the beneficiary is higher.

DETERMINING A SIMPLE TRUST'S TAXABLE INCOME

OBJECTIVE 5
Determine the taxable income of a simple trust

The term *simple trust* does not appear in the Code. The Regulations interpreting Secs. 651 and 652—the statutory rules for trusts that distribute current income only—use the term *simple trust*. The provisions of these two Code sections are applicable only to trusts whose trust agreements (1) require that all income be distributed currently and (2) do not authorize charitable contributions. Moreover, such provisions are inapplicable if the trust makes distributions of principal. Congress's purpose for formulating one set of rules for simple trusts and another for

14-16 • Ch. 14 / Income Taxation of Trusts and Estates

Self-Study Question

A trust, although not required to do so, distributes all of its income for the year. In the same year, it has a long term capital gain on the sale of NYSE stocks. Under the trust agreement, the gain is allocated to principal. The trust does not distribute corpus and none of its beneficiaries are charities. Is the trust a simple or a complex trust? What is the amount of its personal exemption?

Answer

It is a complex trust, since it is not required to distribute all of its income. It would be a simple trust if it was required to distribute all of its income. The exemption is $100, since distributions are discretionary.

estates and all other trusts is not known. Possibly, Congress simply wanted to reduce the amount of words tax advisors need to read to determine the taxable income of a simple trust.

Some trusts may be required to pay out all of their income currently in certain years and may be permitted to retain a portion of their income in other years. In some of the years in which they must distribute all of their income, they may also make mandatory or discretionary distributions of principal. These trusts are simple trusts in some years and complex trusts in others. The amount of the personal exemption, however, turns not on whether the trust is simple or complex but on whether it must pay out all of its income currently. Suppose, for example, a trust must pay out all of its current income and one-fourth of its principal. Because the trust distributes principal, it is a complex trust. It claims a $300 personal exemption because of the mandate to distribute all of its income. Table 14-1 highlights the trust classification rules and the $300 or $100 exemption dichotomy.

Allocation of Expenses to Tax-Exempt Income

Recall that expenses related to producing tax-exempt income are not deductible.[23] Thus, if a trust has income from both taxable and tax-exempt sources and it incurs expenses that are not directly attributable to the production of taxable income, a portion of such expenses may not be deducted. Regulation Secs. 1.652(b)-3 and 1.652(c)-4(e) address the issue of the allocation of deductions. An expense that is directly attributable to one type of income, such as a repair expense for rental property, is allocated thereto. Expenses not directly related to any item of income, such as a trustee's fee for administering the trust's assets, may be allocated to any type of income that is included in computing DNI, provided that a portion of the expense is allocated to nontaxable income. Regulation Sec. 1.652(b)-3 sets forth the following formula for determining the amount of indirect expenses allocable to nontaxable income:

TABLE 14-1 *Trust Classification Rules and the Size of the Exemption*

Situation	Classification	Exemption Amount
1. Required to pay out all of its income, makes no charitable contributions, distributes no principal	Simple	$300
2. Required to pay out all of its income, makes no charitable contributions, distributes principal	Complex	$300
3. Required to pay out all of its income, authorized to make charitable contributions, distributes no principal	Complex	$300
4. Authorized to make discretionary distributions of income, makes no charitable contributions, distributes no principal	Complex	$100
5. Authorized to make discretionary distributions of income and principal, makes no charitable contributions	Complex	$100

---

[23] Sec. 265(1).

Determining a Simple Trust's Taxable Income • 14-17

$$\frac{\text{Tax-exempt income (net of expenses directly attributable thereto)}}{\text{Accounting income (net of all direct expenses)}} \times \begin{array}{c}\text{Expenses not directly}\\\text{attributable to any}\\\text{item of income}\end{array} = \begin{array}{c}\text{Indirect}\\\text{expenses}\\\text{allocable to}\\\text{nontaxable}\\\text{income}\end{array}$$

Example 14-15 ■

Self-Study Question

A trust can allocate indirect expenses arbitrarily (after the appropriate allocation is made to tax-exempt income). Hill Trust has rental income, taxable interest income, and dividend income this year. To which income would you suggest allocating the trustee's fee?

Answer

If possible the trust should take into consideration the tax status of its beneficiaries. In a situation where the sole beneficiary has nondeductible rental losses of his own, it would be beneficial to charge the fee to interest or dividend income, thus reducing the beneficiaries' portfolio income.

For 1991, the Mason Trust reports the following results:

Dividends	$12,000
Interest from corporate bonds	6,000
Tax-exempt interest from state bonds	18,000
Capital gain (allocated to corpus)	20,000
Trustee's fee	4,000

Accounting gross income is $36,000 ($12,000 + $6,000 + $18,000). The trustee's fee is an indirect expense that must be allocated to the tax-exempt income as follows:

$$\frac{\$18,000}{\$36,000} \times \$4,000 = \$2,000$$

Thus, the Mason Trust cannot deduct $2,000 of its trustee's fee. The remaining $2,000 may be allocated to dividends or corporate bond interest in whatever amounts the return preparer desires. ■

Determination of DNI and the Distribution Deduction

As mentioned above, DNI is defined as taxable income with several adjustments, including a subtraction for capital gains credited to principal. According to the methods described above, a practical technique for determining DNI involves beginning with taxable income exclusive of the distribution deduction. Once DNI has been determined, the distribution deduction and the trust's taxable income can both be calculated.

A simple trust must distribute all of its income currently. Thus, a simple trust generally receives a distribution deduction equal to the amount of its net accounting income.[24] There are two exceptions to this general rule:

1. The distribution deduction may not exceed DNI. Therefore, if a trust has expenses that are charged to corpus (as in Example 14-14), the distribution deduction is limited to the DNI amount because DNI is smaller than net accounting income.
2. Because tax-exempt income is not included in the trust's gross income, no distribution deduction is available with respect to that income (net of the expenses allocable thereto) included in DNI.[25]

Tax Treatment for Beneficiary

The aggregate gross income reported by the beneficiaries is equal to the trust's net accounting income, subject to the constraint that the aggregate of their gross income does not exceed the trust's DNI. If DNI is lower than net accounting income and there

---

[24] Sec. 651(a).
[25] Sec. 651(b).

is more than one beneficiary, each beneficiary's share of gross income is the following fraction of total DNI:[26]

$$\frac{\text{Amount of income required to be distributed to such beneficiary}}{\text{Amount of income required to be distributed to } all \text{ beneficiaries}}$$

The income received by the beneficiaries retains the character that it had at the trust level. Thus, if the trust receives tax-exempt interest, the beneficiaries are deemed to have received tax-exempt interest. Unless the trust instrument specifically allocates particular types of income to certain beneficiaries, the income of each beneficiary is viewed as consisting of the same fraction of each category of income as the total of such category bears to total DNI.

Example 14-16 ■ For 1991, Crane Trust's DNI is $80,000—$20,000 of net tax-exempt interest and $60,000 of net dividends. Net accounting income for 1991 is $88,000 ($22,000 + $66,000) because $8,000 of trustee's fees are charged to corpus. The trust instrument requires that one-eighth of the income be distributed annually to Matt and the remaining seven-eighths of the income to Pat. The distributions to Matt and Pat are $11,000 and $77,000, respectively. The distribution deduction and the aggregate gross income of the beneficiaries are limited to $60,000 ($80,000 DNI − $20,000 net tax-exempt interest). Matt and Pat will report gross income of $7,500 (0.125 × $60,000) and $52,500 (0.875 × $60,000), respectively. Dividends make up 75% ($60,000 ÷ $80,000) of DNI and 100% ($60,000 ÷ $60,000) of taxable DNI; therefore, all of Matt's and Pat's *gross* income is deemed to consist of dividends. Matt and Pat are also viewed as having received $2,500 (0.125 × $20,000) and $17,500 (0.875 × $20,000), respectively, of tax-exempt interest. ■

Key Point

The beneficiaries of a simple trust are taxed on their distributable share of their trust's income—whether or not it is distributed.

Because a simple trust must distribute all of its income currently, trustees cannot defer the taxation of trust income to the beneficiaries by postponing distributions until the beginning of the next year. Beneficiaries of simple trusts are taxed currently on their pro rata share of taxable DNI regardless of the actual amount distributed to them during the year.[27]

Short-Cut Approach to Proving Correctness of Taxable Income

A short-cut approach may be used to verify the correctness of the amount calculated as a simple trust's taxable income. Because a simple trust must distribute all of its income currently, the only item taxable at the trust level should be the amount of gains (net of losses) credited to principal, reduced by the personal exemption. The taxable income calculated under the short-cut approach should equal the taxable income determined under the formula illustrated in Figure 14-1. The steps of the short-cut approach are as follows:

- Start with the excess of gains over losses credited to principal.
- Subtract the $300 personal exemption.

---

[26] Sec. 652(a).
[27] Reg. Sec. 1.652(a)-1.

Example 14-17 ■ For 1991 West Trust, which must distribute all of its income currently, has $25,000 of corporate bond interest, a $44,000 long-term capital gain, and a $4,000 long-term capital loss. Under the short-cut approach, its taxable income is calculated as $39,700 ([$44,000 − $4,000] − $300 personal exemption). ■

Effect of a Net Operating Loss

Self-Study Question

In its first year, Bell Trust has $800 taxable interest income and $2,000 trustee's fees and other expenses. As a result, it has a NOL of $1,200. For tax purposes, the loss is carried forward. Is the loss deductible in the second year in determining the fiduciary accounting income?

If a trust incurs a net operating loss (NOL), the loss is not passed through currently to the beneficiaries unless the loss arises in the year the trust terminates. Trusts are allowed to carry an NOL back and forward. In determining the amount of the NOL, deductions are not allowed for either charitable contributions or the distribution deduction.[28] In the year a trust terminates, any loss that would otherwise qualify for a loss carryover at the trust level may be reported on the individual return of the beneficiary(ies) succeeding to the trust's property.[29]

Example 14-18 ■

Answer

One would have to rely on the state law or the trust agreement for such an interpretation. It may be necessary for the trustee to file a court action to determine the correct answer. If the loss is not deductible from future income, the remainderman is the eventual loser. The NOL can pass through to the remainderman if the trust terminates.

In 1991, the year it terminates, New Trust incurs a $10,000 NOL. In addition, it has a $40,000 NOL carryover from 1989 and 1990. At termination, New Trust distributes 30% of its assets to Kay and 70% to Liz. Because 1991 is the termination year, Kay may report a $15,000 (0.30 × $50,000) NOL on her 1991 return, and Liz may report a $35,000 (0.70 × $50,000) NOL on her 1991 return. Prior to 1991, the beneficiaries are ineligible to report any of the trust's NOLs on their returns. ■

Effect of a Net Capital Loss

Self-Study Question

Why do the regulations (see footnotes 29 and 31) allow unused NOLs and capital losses to be used by the remainderman on the termination of a trust?

The maximum capital loss that a trust can deduct is the lesser of $3,000 or the excess of its capital losses over capital gains.[30] Because simple trusts must distribute all of their accounting income currently and the distribution deduction reduces their taxable income to zero, they receive no tax benefit from capital losses that are in excess of capital gains. Nevertheless, the trust's taxable income for the year of the loss is reduced by its net capital loss, up to a maximum of $3,000. In determining the capital loss carryover, capital losses that produced no tax benefit are deemed to be available as a carryover to offset capital gains realized by the trust in subsequent years. In addition, if all of the capital loss carryovers have not been absorbed by capital gains by the trust's termination date, the remaining capital loss is passed through in the termination year to the beneficiaries succeeding to the trust's property.[31]

Example 14-19 ■

Answer

Losses that cannot be offset against future gains (either income or corpus) have, in effect, depleted the corpus of the trust. Since the remainderman's interest has been depleted by these losses, it seems reasonable to allow a "pass-through" entity to pass these losses through to the final taxpayer at the end of the entity's life.

Old Trust, which is required to distribute all of its income currently, has two sales of capital assets during its existence. In 1989 it sells an asset at a $20,000 loss. In 1990 it sells an asset for a $6,000 gain. In 1991 it terminates and distributes its assets equally between its two beneficiaries, Joy and Tim. The trust is not a simple trust in 1991 because it distributes principal that year. In its 1989 return the trust

---

[28] Reg. Sec. 1.642(d)-1(b).
[29] Reg. Sec. 1.642(h)-1. A trust is never categorized as a simple trust in the year it terminates because in its final year it always makes distributions of principal.
[30] Sec. 1211(b).
[31] Reg. Sec. 1.642(h)-1.

deducts a $3,000 capital loss. Because the loss provided no benefit on the 1989 return, the carryover to 1990 is $20,000, and $6,000 of it is offset against 1990's $6,000 capital gain. The remaining $14,000 is carried forward to 1991. Because 1991 is the termination year, a $7,000 (0.50 × $14,000) capital loss is passed through to both Joy's and Tim's individual returns for 1991. Joy experiences a $12,000 capital gain by selling assets in 1991. Joy offsets the $7,000 trust loss against her own gain. Tim sells no assets in 1991. Therefore, Tim may deduct $3,000 of the loss from the trust against his other income. ■

Topic Review 14-2 describes how to calculate the taxable income of a trust.

COMPREHENSIVE ILLUSTRATION— DETERMINING A SIMPLE TRUST'S TAXABLE INCOME

A number of the points discussed previously are reviewed by the comprehensive illustration that follows. The facts for this illustration are used to complete the Form 1041 for a simple trust, which appears in Appendix B.

Background Data

The Bob Adams Trust was established by a gift from Zed Brown in 1982. Its trust instrument requires that the trustee (First Bank) distribute all of the trust income at least annually to Bob Adams for life. Capital gains are credited to principal. The 1990 results of the trust are as follows:

	Amounts Allocable	
	Income	Principal
Dividends	$30,000	
Rental income from land	5,000	
Tax-exempt interest	15,000	
Rental expenses	1,000	
Trustee's fee		$ 1,200
Fee for preparation of tax return	500	
Long-term capital gain on sale of stock		12,000
Distribution of net accounting income to Bob	48,500	
Payments of estimated tax		2,600

Trustee's Fee

As mentioned earlier, a portion of the trustee's fee is nondeductible because it must be allocated to tax-exempt income. The trust receives $50,000 ($30,000 + $5,000 + $15,000) of gross accounting income, of which $15,000 is tax-exempt. Therefore, $360 ([$15,000 ÷ $50,000] × $1,200) of the trustee's fee is allocated to tax-exempt income

TOPIC REVIEW 14-2

Calculation of Trust Taxable Income

Gross income[a]
 Minus: Deductions for expenses[a]
           Distribution deduction
           Personal exemption
 Taxable income

[a] Rules for calculating these amounts are generally the same as for individual taxpayers.

and is nondeductible.[32] All of the return preparation fee is deductible because no such fee would have been incurred if the trust's income had been entirely from tax-exempt sources.

Distribution Deduction and DNI

One of the key amounts affecting taxable income is the distribution deduction. Taxable income exclusive of the distribution deduction can be the starting point for determining the amount of DNI, a number crucial in quantifying the distribution deduction. The trust's taxable income, exclusive of the distribution deduction, is calculated as follows:

Dividends		$30,000
Rental income		5,000
Long-term capital gain		12,000
Minus:	Rental expenses	(1,000)
	Deductible portion of trustee's fee	(840)
	Fee for tax return preparation	(500)
	Personal exemption	(300)
Taxable income, exclusive of distribution deduction		$44,360

Distributable net income can now be calculated by making the adjustments shown below to taxable income, exclusive of the distribution deduction.[33]

Taxable income, exclusive of distribution deduction		$44,360
Plus:	Personal exemption	300
Minus:	Long-term capital gain	(12,000)
Plus:	Tax-exempt interest, net of $360 of allocable expenses	14,640
DNI		$47,300

Recall that the distribution deduction cannot exceed the DNI, as reduced by tax-exempt income (net of any allocable expenses). The distribution deduction may be computed as follows:

---

[32] A discrepancy exists in the Regulations with respect to how to allocate expenses to tax-exempt income. According to Reg. Sec. 1.652(b)-3(b), the denominator is accounting income net of direct expenses. Regulation Sec. 1.652(c)-4(e) makes computations where accounting income is not reduced by direct expenses to arrive at the denominator. The latter approach is used in the text.

[33] Another way of determining the amount of DNI is to reduce the net accounting income of $48,500 by the $1,200 of expenses charged to principal. The resulting amount is $47,300.

Smaller of:	Net accounting income ($48,500) or DNI ($47,300)		$47,300
Minus:	Tax-exempt interest	$15,000	
	Minus: Allocable expenses	(360)	(14,640)
Distribution deduction			$32,660

Trust's Taxable Income

Once the amount of the distribution deduction has been determined, the trust's taxable income can be calculated. Table 14-2 illustrates this calculation.

Categorizing a Beneficiary's Income

In addition to taxable income, the amount of each category of income received by the beneficiary must be determined. Income reported by the beneficiary retains the same character that it had at the trust level. Thus, Bob is deemed to have received dividends, rents, and tax-exempt interest. Rental expenses are, of course, charged against rental income. The deductible portion of the trustee's fee and the tax return preparation fee can be allocated in full to rents or dividends, or some to each. If they are allocated to rental income, the character of Bob's income is determined as follows:

	Dividends	Rents	Tax-exempt Interest	Total
Accounting income	$30,000	$ 5,000	$15,000	$50,000
Minus: Expenses:				
Trustee's fee		(840)	(360)	(1,200)
Rental expenses		(1,000)		(1,000)
Tax return preparation fee		(500)		(500)
DNI	$30,000	$ 2,660	$14,640	$47,300

Bob reports $30,000 of dividend income and $2,660 of rental income on his individual return.

DETERMINING TAXABLE INCOME FOR COMPLEX TRUSTS AND ESTATES

OBJECTIVE 6
Determine the taxable income of a complex trust

The caption to Subpart C of Part I of Subchapter J (Secs. 661 through 664) is entitled "Distribution for Estates and Trusts Accumulating or Distributing Corpus." In general, the rules applicable to estates and these trusts (complex trusts) are the same. The Code does not contain the term *complex trust*. According to the Regulations, "A

Key Point

The short cut approach to computing taxable income used in Table 14-2 consists of all of the income allocated to corpus minus the personal exemption.

TABLE 14-2 *Comprehensive Illustration—Determining a Simple Trust's Taxable Income*

Gross income:	
Dividends	$30,000
Rental income	5,000
Long-term capital gain	12,000
Minus: expense deductions:	
Rental expenses	(1,000)
Deductible portion of trustee's fee	(840)
Fee for tax return preparation	(500)
Minus: Distribution deduction	(32,660)
Minus: Personal exemption	(300)
Taxable income	$11,700[a]

[a] The short-cut approach to verifying taxable income is as follows:

Long-term capital gain	$12,000
Minus: Personal exemption	(300)
Taxable income	$11,700

trust to which subpart C is applicable is referred to as a 'complex' trust."[34] Recall from the discussion about simple trusts that a trust that must distribute all of its income currently can be classified as a complex trust for a particular year if it also pays out some principal during the year. Trusts that can accumulate income are categorized as complex trusts, even in years in which they make discretionary distributions of all of their income. A trust is also a complex trust if the trust instrument provides for amounts to be paid to, or set aside for, charitable organizations (see Table 14-1).

Many of the rules are the same for simple and complex trusts, but some differences exist. Different rules are used to determine the distribution deduction for the two types of trusts. The rules for determining an estate's distribution deduction are the same as those applicable to complex trusts. The personal exemption differs, however; it is $600 for an estate and $300 or $100 for a complex trust. The $300 amount applies for years in which a trust must pay out all of its income; otherwise, the exemption is $100.

Determination of DNI and the Distribution Deduction

Section 661(a) defines the distribution deduction for complex trusts and estates as being the sum of (1) the total current income *required* to be paid out currently plus (2) any other amounts "properly paid or credited or required to be distributed" (i.e., discretionary distributions) to the beneficiary during the year. If the fiduciary has the option of making mandatory distributions from either income or principal, such a distribution is counted as "current income required to be paid" if it is paid out of the trust's income. Just as in the case of simple trusts, the amount of the trust's DNI acts as a ceiling on the amount of the distribution deduction.

Example 14-20 ■ For 1991, Able Trust has net accounting income and DNI of $30,000, all from taxable sources. It makes a $15,000 mandatory distribution of income to Sam and a $4,000 discretionary distribution to Ted. Its distribution deduction is computed as follows:

[34] Reg. Sec. 1.661(a)-1.

14-24 • Ch. 14 / Income Taxation of Trusts and Estates

Income required to be distributed currently	$15,000
Plus: Other amounts "properly paid," etc.	4,000
Tentative distribution deduction	$19,000
DNI	$30,000
Distribution deduction (lesser of tentative distribution deduction or DNI)	$19,000

DNI is not reduced by the charitable contribution deduction when comparing DNI with the mandatory current distributions in order to determine the amount of the distribution deduction. DNI is, however, reduced by the charitable contribution deduction when calculating the deductible discretionary distributions.

Example 14-21 ■ Assume the same facts as in Example 14-20, except that net accounting income and DNI (exclusive of the charitable contribution deduction) are both $15,000. In addition, the trust, in accordance with its trust instrument, pays $3,000 to a charitable organization.

Tentative distribution deduction (see calculation in Example 14-20)	$19,000
DNI (excluding charitable contribution deduction)	$15,000
Distribution deduction (lesser of tentative distribution deduction or DNI)	$15,000

If the distributions to Sam and Ted instead were both discretionary, DNI is reduced to $12,000 by the charitable contribution, thereby causing a similar reduction in the amount of the distribution deduction. ■

As is the situation for simple trusts, there is an additional constraint on the amount of the distribution deduction. No distribution deduction is allowed with respect to tax-exempt income (net of allocable expenses).

Example 14-22 ■ Assume the same facts as in Example 14-20, except that net accounting income and DNI consist of $20,000 of corporate bond interest and $10,000 of tax-exempt interest. Because one-third ($10,000 ÷ $30,000) of the DNI is from tax-exempt sources, tax-exempt income is deemed to make up one-third of the distributions. Thus, the distribution deduction is only $12,667 (0.667 × $19,000). ■

The DNI concept is summarized in Topic Review 14-3.

Key Point

Distributions to beneficiaries retain the same character as the income has at the fiduciary level; for example, the character of rents, interest, dividends, or tax-exempt income flow through to the beneficiary.

Tax Treatment for Beneficiary

General Rules. In general, the amount of any distributions from estates or complex trusts includible in a beneficiary's gross income equals the sum of (1) the amount of current income required to be distributed currently to the beneficiary, plus (2) any other amounts "properly paid or credited, or required to be distributed" (i.e., discretionary distributions) to the beneficiary during the year.[35] There are three

---

[35] Sec. 662(a).

exceptions to this general rule. Exceptions are authorized for the tier system and separate share rules of trusts and for specific bequests of estates.

Because income retains the character it has at the fiduciary level, beneficiaries do not include distributions of tax-exempt income in their gross income. Each beneficiary's distribution is deemed to consist of tax-exempt income in the proportion that total tax-exempt income bears to total DNI.[36] Thus, if 30% of DNI is from tax-exempt income, 30% of each beneficiary's distribution is deemed to consist of tax-free income.

Even in the absence of distributions of principal, mandatory payments to beneficiaries can exceed DNI because at times accounting income may exceed DNI. When the total income required to be distributed currently exceeds DNI (before reduction for the charitable contribution deduction), each beneficiary reports as gross income the following ratio of DNI attributable to taxable sources:

$$\frac{\text{Income required to be distributed currently to the beneficiary}}{\text{Aggregate income required to be distributed to all beneficiaries currently}}[37]$$

In calculating the portion of DNI includible in the gross income of each beneficiary receiving mandatory distributions, DNI is not reduced for the charitable contribution deduction.

Example 14-23 ■

Self-Study Question

In calculating the portion of DNI to be included in each beneficiary's gross income is DNI reduced for the charitable contribution deduction?

Answer

DNI is not reduced for charitable contributions in determining the DNI to be included in the gross income of mandatory beneficiaries, but it is reduced in arriving at the DNI to be included in the gross income of discretionary beneficiaries.

For 1991, York Trust has net accounting income of $125,000 but DNI of only $100,000 because certain expenses are charged to principal. The trust is required to distribute $100,000 of income to Jean and $10,000 to Mary. It makes no discretionary distributions or charitable contributions. Because the trust's mandatory distributions exceed its DNI, the amount each beneficiary reports as gross income is as follows:

Beneficiary	Gross Income
Jean	$90,909 = ($100,000 ÷ $110,000) × $100,000
Mary	$9,091 = ($10,000 ÷ $110,000) × $100,000

■

The Tier System. If both principal and income are distributed, distributions will exceed income even if net accounting income and DNI are equal. For years in which the sum of (1) current income required to be distributed currently and (2) all other amounts properly paid or required to be distributed (e.g., discretionary payments of income or any payments of corpus) exceed DNI, the amount taxable to each beneficiary is calculated under a tier system. Beneficiaries to whom income distributions must be made are commonly referred to as *tier-1 beneficiaries*.[38] All other beneficiaries are known as *tier-2 beneficiaries*. An individual can be both a tier-1 and a tier-2 beneficiary if both mandatory and discretionary payments are received in the same year.

Under the tier system, tier-1 beneficiaries are the first to absorb income. The total income taxed to this group is the lesser of (1) aggregate mandatory distributions or (2) DNI. DNI is determined without reduction for charitable contributions. If required income distributions plus all other payments exceed DNI, each tier-2 beneficiary includes in income a fraction of the excess of (1) DNI over (2) the income required to be distributed currently. Section 662(a)(2) states that the fraction is as follows:

---

[36] Sec. 662(b).
[37] Sec. 662(a)(1).
[38] The terms tier-1 and tier-2 do not appear in the Code or Regulations.

TOPIC REVIEW 14-3

The Distributable Net Income (DNI) Concept

Calculation of DNI:
Taxable income, exclusive of distribution deduction[a]
Plus: Personal exemption
Minus: Capital gains (or plus deductible capital losses)
Plus: Tax-exempt interest (net of allocable expenses)
DNI[b]

[a] Gross income (dividends, taxable interest, rents, capital gains) minus deductible expenses and minus personal exemption.
[b] In general, DNI is the same amount as net accounting income minus trustee's fees charged to corpus.

Significance of DNI:
1. DNI, exclusive of net tax-exempt income included therein, sets the ceiling on the distribution deduction.
2. DNI, exclusive of net tax-exempt income included therein, sets the ceiling on the aggregate amount of gross income reportable by the beneficiaries.

$$\frac{\text{Other amounts properly paid or required to be distributed to such beneficiary}}{\text{Aggregate of amounts properly paid or required to be distributed to } all \text{ beneficiaries}}$$

Example 14-24 ■ For 1991, Eagle Trust has net accounting income and DNI of $80,000, all from taxable sources. The trustee is required to distribute $30,000 of income to Holly currently. In addition, the trustee makes discretionary distributions of $60,000, $15,000 to Holly and $45,000 to Irene. $10,000 of the discretionary distributions are from corpus. The gross income to be reported by each beneficiary is determined as follows.

Gross income from mandatory distributions:
Lesser of:
  1. Amount required to be distributed $30,000
                   or
  2. DNI $80,000
Amount reportable by Holly $30,000
Gross income from other amounts paid:
Lesser of:
  1. All other amounts paid $60,000
                   or
  2. DNI minus amount required to be $50,000
     distributed ($80,000 − $30,000)
Amount reportable by Holly and Irene $50,000

The portions of the $50,000 to be reported by each beneficiary are calculated as follows:

      Holly's: $50,000 × ($15,000 ÷ $60,000) = $12,500
      Irene's: $50,000 × ($45,000 ÷ $60,000) = $37,500

Recapitulation of gross income is calculated as follows:

	Amount Reported by	
	Holly	Irene
Mandatory distributions	$30,000	$—0—
Discretionary distributions	12,500	37,500
Total	$42,500	$37,500

Tier-2 beneficiaries can receive more favorable tax treatment than tier-1 beneficiaries. Tier-1 beneficiaries are generally taxed on their total distributions, whereas tier-2 beneficiaries are more likely to receive a portion of their distributions tax-free.

Self-Study Question

What is the ultimate effect of the separate share rule?

Answer

It has the effect of treating the trust as two or more separate trusts, each with its own DNI. This "separate" DNI is allocated only to the specific beneficiary of each share of the trust.

Separate Share Rule. Some trusts with more than one beneficiary can be treated as consisting of separate trusts for purposes of determining the amount of the trust's distribution deduction and the beneficiaries' gross income.[39] In calculating the trust's income tax liability, however, these trusts are treated as a single taxpaying entity. Trusts eligible for this treatment, known as the **separate share rule,** must have governing instruments that require that distributions be made in "substantially the same manner as if separate trusts had been created."[40] If the separate share rule is applicable, the amount of the income taxable to a beneficiary for a particular year can differ from the amount that would be taxable to such beneficiary in the absence of this rule. Beneficiaries generally receive favorable tax treatment from the separate share rule.

Example 14-25 ■ Berry Trust is created for the benefit of Dale and John. According to the trust instrument, no income is to be distributed until a beneficiary reaches age 21. Moreover, income is to be divided into two equal shares. Once a beneficiary reaches age 21, the trustee may make discretionary distributions of income and corpus to such beneficiary, but distributions may not exceed a beneficiary's share. Each beneficiary is to receive his remaining share of the trust assets on his thirtieth birthday. To the extent he has received distributions of income and principal, such earlier distributions will be taken into account in determining his final distribution.

On January 1, 1991, Dale reaches age 21; John is age 16. In 1991, the trust has DNI and net accounting income of $50,000, all from taxable sources. During 1991, the trustee distributes $25,000 of income (Dale's 50% share) and $80,000 of principal to Dale. No distribution of income or corpus is made to John. Under the separate share rule, the trust's distribution deduction and Dale's gross income inclusion are limited to his share of DNI, or $25,000. Dale receives the remaining $80,000 distribution tax-free. Berry Trust is taxed on John's separate share of the income (all accumulated), or $25,000. In the absence of the separate share rule, Dale would be taxed on $50,000 (the lesser of DNI or his total distributions). ■

Specific Bequests. Recall that a beneficiary is taxed on "other amounts properly paid, credited, or required to be distributed,"[41] subject to the constraint that the maximum amount taxed to all beneficiaries is the fiduciary's DNI. Thus, a beneficiary

---

[39] Sec. 663(c).
[40] Reg. Sec. 1.663(c)-3(a).
[41] Sec. 662(a)(2).

can be required to report gross income, even though a distribution is received from the principal account. Such a result may surprise a beneficiary who receives a noncash distribution of principal from an estate.

Example 14-26 ■

Key Point

The executor of an estate should carefully consider the timing of property distributions where the property being distributed is not the subject of a specific bequest. If possible, property (other than specific bequests) should be distributed in a year when there is little or no DNI.

Doug dies in 1990, leaving a will that bequeaths all of his property (whatever it might be) to his sister Tina. During 1991, Doug's estate has $50,000 of DNI, all from taxable sources. During 1991, the executor distributes no cash, but he does distribute Doug's coin collection, valued at $22,000, to Tina. The adjusted basis of the coin collection is $22,000, its value at the date of death. The distribution of the coin collection is classified as an "other amount properly paid" because it is a distribution. Even though the executor distributes no income, Tina reports $22,000 of gross income. If the coin collection's adjusted basis and FMV exceed $50,000 (DNI), Tina's gross income would be limited to the amount of DNI, $50,000. ■

Properties that are distributed do not trigger a distribution deduction at the estate level or the recognition of gross income at the beneficiary level, however, if such properties constitute a "bequest of a specific sum of money or of specific property" to be paid at one time or in not more than three installments.[42] If Doug's will in Example 14-26 includes specific bequest language (e.g., "I bequeath my coin collection to Tina"), Tina would not report any gross income as a result of receiving the coin collection.

More income is generally taxed at the estate level (and less at the beneficiary level) if the decedent's will includes numerous specific bequests. If the estate has a lower marginal tax rate than its beneficiaries' marginal tax rates, the optimal tax result is to have the income taxed to the estate because the tax liability is lower.

Example 14-27 ■

Dick dies in 1990. Dick bequeaths $100,000 cash to Fred. Dick's residence, valued at $300,000, is devised to Gary. The executor distributes the cash and the residence in 1991, when the estate has $475,000 of DNI, all from taxable sources. Because the cash and residence constitute specific bequests, the estate gets no distribution deduction and the beneficiaries report no gross income. ■

Key Point

Generally, the tax consequences of both NOLs and net capital losses are the same for estates and complex trusts as for simple trusts.

Effect of a Net Operating Loss

The tax consequences of an NOL are the same for estates and complex trusts as for simple trusts. An NOL can be carried back and carried forward. In the year the trust or estate terminates, any remaining NOL is passed through to the beneficiaries who succeed to the assets. If the estate incurs NOLs over a series of years, a tax incentive exists for terminating the estate as early as possible so that the beneficiaries can "reap the benefit" of the loss deductions.

Effect of a Net Capital Loss

The tax effect of having capital losses in excess of capital gains is generally the same for estates and complex trusts as for simple trusts. In the case of simple trusts, however, there is no immediate tax benefit when capital losses exceed capital gains. Estates and complex trusts often do not distribute all of their income and, thus, have taxable income. As in the case of an individual taxpayer, the maximum capital loss deduction is the lesser of (1) $3,000 or (2) the excess of its capital losses over capital gains.[43]

---

[42] Sec. 663(a)(1).
[43] Sec. 1211(b).

Example 14-28 ■ For 1990, Gold Trust has $30,000 of net accounting income and DNI, all from taxable sources. It makes discretionary distributions totalling $7,000 to Amy. Its one sale of a capital asset results in an $8,000 long-term capital loss. The trust can deduct $3,000 of capital losses in arriving at its taxable income. The trust can carry over the remaining $5,000 of capital loss to 1992. Suppose that in 1991, Gold Trust sells a capital asset for a $5,000 long-term capital gain. It will offset the $5,000 loss carryover against the $5,000 capital gain. ■

COMPREHENSIVE ILLUSTRATION—DETERMINING A COMPLEX TRUST'S TAXABLE INCOME

The comprehensive illustration below enables us to review a number of points discussed earlier. A sample Form 1041 for a complex trust appears in Appendix B; it is prepared on the basis of the facts in this illustration.

Background Data

The Cathy and Karen Stevens Trust was established by Ted Tims in 1982. Its trust instrument empowers the trustee (Merchants Bank) to distribute income in its discretion to Cathy and Karen for the next 15 years. The trust will then be terminated, and the trust assets will be divided equally between Cathy and Karen, irrespective of the amount of distributions each has previously received. In other words, separate shares are not to be maintained. Under state law, capital gains are part of principal.

The 1990 income and expenses of the trust are reported below. With the exception of the information concerning distributions and payments of estimated tax, the amounts are the same as in the comprehensive illustration for a simple trust discussed previously in the chapter.

	Amounts Allocable to	
	Income	Principal
Dividends	$30,000	
Rental income from land	5,000	
Tax-exempt interest	15,000	
Rental expenses	1,000	
Trustee's fee		$ 1,200
Fee for preparation of tax return	500	
Long-term capital gain on sale of stock		12,000
Distribution of net accounting income to:		
Cathy	14,000	
Karen	7,000	
Payments of estimated tax	5,240	3,360

Trustee's Fee

Recall that a portion of the trustee's fee must be allocated to tax-exempt income. The expenses so allocated are nondeductible. Of the trust's $50,000 ($30,000 + $5,000 +

$15,000) gross accounting income, $15,000 is from tax-exempt sources. Consequently, the nondeductible trustee's fee is $360 ([$15,000 ÷ $50,000] × $1,200). The remaining $840 of the fee is deductible.

Distribution Deduction and DNI

The primary function of the Subchapter J rules is to provide guidance for calculating the amounts taxable to the beneficiaries and to the fiduciary. One of the crucial numbers in the process is the distribution deduction. The amount of DNI must be known in order to arrive at the amount of the distribution deduction. Taxable income, exclusive of the distribution deduction, is the starting point for calculating DNI, and is computed as follows:

Dividends		$30,000
Rental income		5,000
Long-term capital gain		12,000
Minus:	Rental expenses	(1,000)
	Deductible portion of trustee's fee	(840)
	Fee for tax return preparation	(500)
	Personal exemption	(100)
Taxable income, exclusive of distribution deduction		$44,560

DNI is calculated by adjusting taxable income, exclusive of the distribution deduction, as follows:

Taxable income, exclusive of distribution deduction		$44,560
Plus:	Personal exemption	100
Minus:	Long-term capital gain	(12,000)
Plus:	Tax-exempt interest (net of $360 of allocable expenses)	14,640
DNI		$47,300

The distribution deduction is the lesser of (1) amounts required to be distributed, plus other amounts properly paid or credited, or required to be distributed, or (2) DNI. This amount must be reduced by tax-exempt income (net of allocable expenses). DNI, exclusive of net tax-exempt income, is calculated as follows:

DNI	$47,300
Minus: Tax-exempt income (net of $360 of allocable expenses)	(14,640)
DNI, exclusive of net tax-exempt income	$32,660

In no event may the distribution deduction exceed $32,660, the DNI, exclusive of net tax-exempt income. The DNI ceiling is of no practical significance in this example, however, because the total income distributed is only $21,000.

Because a portion of the payments received by each beneficiary is deemed to consist of tax-exempt income, the distribution deduction is less than the $21,000 distributed. The actual amount of each beneficiary's tax-exempt income is determined by dividing DNI into categories of income. In this categorization process, rental expenses must be charged against rental income, and $360 of trustee's fees must be charged against tax-exempt income. In this example the deductible trustee's fee and the tax return preparation fee are charged against rental income. They could, however, be charged against dividend income or against both income categories. Total DNI of $47,300 is categorized as follows:

	Dividends	Rents	Tax-exempt Interest	Total
Accounting income	$30,000	$5,000	$15,000	$50,000
Minus: Expenses:				
Trustee's fee		(840)	(360)	(1,200)
Rental expenses		(1,000)		(1,000)
Fee for tax return preparation		(500)		(500)
DNI	$30,000	$2,660	$14,640	$47,300

Because the complex trust illustration involves two beneficiaries and three categories of income, we must calculate the amount of each distribution that comes from each income category. These steps were not needed in the simple trust illustration because it involved only one beneficiary.

Category of Income	Proportion of DNI
Dividends	63.4249% = $30,000 ÷ $47,300
Rental income	5.6237% = $ 2,660 ÷ $47,300
Tax-exempt income	30.9514% = $14,640 ÷ $47,300
Total	100.0000%

As a result, 30.9514% of each beneficiary's distribution represents tax-exempt interest. This amount is ineligible for a distribution deduction. The amount of the distribution deduction, which cannot exceed the $32,660 DNI, exclusive of net tax-exempt income, is determined as follows:

Amount distributed	$21,000
Minus: Net tax-exempt income deemed distributed (0.309514 × $21,000)	(6,500)
Distribution deduction	$14,500

The distributions received by the beneficiaries are deemed to consist of three categories of income in the amounts shown below.

Components of Distributions	Cathy	Karen	Total
Dividends (63.4249%)	$8,879	$4,440	$13,319
Plus: Rental income (5.6237%)	788	393	1,181
Gross income (69.0486%)	$9,667	$4,833	$14,500
Plus: Tax-exempt interest (30.9514%)	4,333	2,167	6,500
Total income (100.0000%)	$14,000	$7,000	$21,000

Trust's Taxable Income

Once the amount of the taxable and tax-exempt distributions has been quantified, the trust's taxable income can be calculated. Table 14-3 illustrates this calculation.

Unlike the simple trust situation, there is no short-cut approach to verifying taxable income for complex trusts and estates except in the years when such entities distribute all of their income. If all their income is distributed, the short-cut approach applicable to simple trusts can be used to verify taxable income.

Additional Observations

A few additional observations are in order concerning the Stevens Trust:

- If the entity is an estate instead of a trust, all amounts except the personal exemption are the same. The estate's personal exemption would be $600, instead of $100.
- Assume that (1) the trust incurs $2,000 of depreciation expense, chargeable against principal under state law, and (2) the trust instrument does not require a reserve for depreciation. Because approximately 56% of the trust's income is accumulated (i.e., $26,300 of its $47,300 DNI), $1,120 (0.56 × $2,000) of the depreciation is deductible by the trust. Its taxable income is $1,120 lower. The remaining $880 (0.44 × $2,000) is deductible on the beneficiaries' returns. The $880 of depreciation is then divided between the two beneficiaries in accordance with their pro rata share of the total distributions. Cathy deducts, therefore, $587 ($880 × [$14,000 ÷ $21,000]), and Karen deducts $293 ($880 × [$7,000 ÷ $21,000]). In summary, the depreciation is deductible as follows:

Trust	$1,120
Cathy	587
Karen	293
Total	$2,000

ACCUMULATION DISTRIBUTION RULES

Purpose

The **accumulation distribution** rules, also known as the throwback rules, are an exception to the general rule that DNI serves as a ceiling on the amount taxable to a beneficiary. Under the general rule, the beneficiary excludes from his gross income that portion of any distribution that exceeds DNI. If there were no exceptions to the general rule, great opportunities would have existed prior to 1987 for reducing taxes through the timing of distributions from complex trusts.[44] For example, assume that

- A beneficiary, Jeff, is in the top marginal tax bracket for many years prior to 1987.
- The discretionary trust accumulates $10,000 of its income each year from 1979 through 1986; the accumulated income totals $80,000, net of taxes. After 1986 the trust no longer accumulates income.
- In 1991 the trust has DNI and net accounting income of $12,000, all from taxable sources.
- In 1991 the trust distributes $92,000 ($12,000 + $80,000).

[44] Because of the compression of the tax rate schedules for fiduciary taxpayers beginning in 1987, there is less incentive for trustees to accumulate income in order to reduce income taxes.

TABLE 14-3 *Comprehensive Illustration—Determining a Complex Trust's Taxable Income*

Gross income:	
Dividends	$30,000
Rental income	5,000
Long-term capital gain	12,000
Minus: expense deductions:	
Rental expenses	(1,000)
Deductible portion of trustee's fee	(840)
Fee for tax return preparation	(500)
Minus: Distribution deduction	(14,500)
Minus: Personal exemption	(100)
Taxable income	$30,060

If the accumulation distribution rules did not exist, the beneficiary in our example would receive a $92,000 distribution and pay taxes on only $12,000. Considerable savings would have arisen from having the income for the earlier years accumulated and taxed at the trust's lower rates. In the post-1986 era, trusts reach the top tax bracket very quickly. The tax incentive for trusts to accumulate income is lessened. Nontax reasons (e.g., the need to reinvest monies in additional business assets for a trade or business conducted by a trust) will continue to apply, however.

The accumulation distribution rules preclude the beneficiary in the example from being taxed on only $12,000 in 1991. Under the *concept* of these rules, Jeff would pay a tax in 1991 on the $80,000 of accumulated income and $12,000 of current income that he received. The amount of the tax would equal the additional tax he would have paid for 1979 through 1986 had the trust distributed all of its income currently. The statutory provisions governing throwbacks adopted a somewhat simplified approach that does not completely mesh with the concept for taxing throwbacks. The statute does, however, ensure that the beneficiary is taxed on more than the current period's DNI.

> **Key Point**
>
> The theory behind the throwback rules is to put the trust beneficiary in the same after-tax position he would have been in had the accumulated income been distributed in the year it was received by the trust. Note that estates are exempt from the throwback rules.

When Applicable

The accumulation distribution rules appear in Secs. 665 through 668, Subpart D of Part I of Subchapter J. Subpart D is entitled "Treatment of Excess Distributions by Trusts."Consequently, estates are exempt from the throwback rules. As a result, a beneficiary of an estate is never taxed on more than the estate's current DNI. If a trust has never accumulated income, it is also exempt from the throwback rules. Any distribution in excess of DNI that such a trust makes is classified as a tax-free distribution of principal. At times, a trust's net accounting income will exceed its DNI because of expenses that are charged against principal. In such situations, the trust is exempt from the throwback rules if it distributes all of its net accounting income, but no more, even though the distribution exceeds DNI.[45]

Distributions of income accumulated prior to the birth of the distributee/beneficiary, or prior to such beneficiary's reaching age 21, are exempt from the throwback rules. At the time this provision was enacted, the Code did not contain the rule taxing unearned income of children under age 14 at their parents' top tax rate. (Comprehensive coverage of this topic is included in Chapter 2 of the *Prentice Hall's Federal Taxation: Individuals* companion text.) The probable reason for this exemption is that at the time of enactment beneficiaries younger than 21 generally had a low marginal tax rate and the opportunity for saving taxes was probably not the

> **Key Point**
>
> The throwback rules do not apply to distributions made out of a Sec. 2503(c) minor's trust. This rule allows the trust to accumulate the trust income up to the time the minor child reaches 21 years of age. At age 21, the trust income must be distributed to the child. Thus, the child does not have to be given dominion over the trust income prior to reaching age 21.

---

[45] Sec. 665(b).

motivating factor in accumulating the income. Subsequent to 1986, this exception can present an opportunity for saving taxes by accumulating income within a trust; if such income were instead distributed to children under age 14, any income received in excess of $1,000 would be taxed at the parents' rates.

Example 14-29 ∎ Bell Trust is formed in 1987 for the benefit of Brenda, then age 17. The trustee in its discretion accumulates all of the income until 1991, when it distributes the accumulated income to Brenda on her twenty-first birthday. It also distributes the current income for 1991. Because the income is accumulated while the beneficiary was under age 21, it is exempt from the throwback rules. Otherwise, such rules would apply. ∎

SECTION 644 TAX

Purpose

Section 644 was enacted to eliminate a tax-planning opportunity for trusts. Prior to its enactment, taxpayers were able to convey highly appreciated assets to trusts, let the trusts sell the assets shortly after receiving them, and have the gains taxed to a new taxpayer (the trust) in a lower tax bracket. Under Sec. 644, if a trustee sells appreciated property "soon" (not more than 2 years) after receiving it, the tax on the gain is the same as if the donor had sold the asset.

When Applicable

Section 644 is applicable if the following two conditions are present:

1. The trust sells property at a gain within 2 years of the transfer of the property in trust.
2. The FMV of the property at the time of the transfer exceeds the property's adjusted basis immediately after the transfer.[46]

The adjusted basis immediately after the transfer is the donor's adjusted basis, increased by a portion of the gift taxes paid by the donor. Note that sales will fall outside the purview of Sec. 644 if they occur more than 2 years after the date of transfer. Section 644 does not apply if the trust acquires property as the result of a death or if the trust is one of several types of charitable trusts.[47]

Computation of the Tax

The Sec. 644 tax is imposed on the trust's *includible gain*, which is the lesser of (1) the gain recognized by the trust or (2) the excess of the property's FMV at the time it is transferred to the trust over the property's adjusted basis immediately after the

---

[46] Sec. 644(a)(1).
[47] Sec. 644(e). The types of charitable trusts exempted from the scope of Sec. 644 are pooled income funds and charitable remainder annuity trusts and unitrusts.

transfer.[48] Thus, post-transfer appreciation is not taxed under Sec. 644. If the trust and the transferor have the same tax year, the Sec. 644 tax is the additional tax (including any alternative minimum tax) the transferor would have owed had the includible gain been included in his own income for the year of the sale.[49] Because trusts must now use a calendar year, most trusts and transferors will have the same tax year.

Although the amount of the Sec. 644 tax is a function of the transferor's income, the trust pays the tax. The amount of the includible gain (net of any allocable deductions) is not included in the fiduciary's taxable income.[50] Thus, the includible gain is subject to the Sec. 644 tax, but not the regular income tax.

Example 14-30 ■ In 1990, Dana forms York Trust and transfers to it, among other items, Major Corporation stock valued at $100,000. Dana purchased the stock for $20,000 several years earlier. Dana paid no gift tax on the transfer. The trust instrument allocates gains to principal and requires all income to be distributed currently. In 1991, the trustee sells the Major stock for $110,000, or a $90,000 ($110,000 − $20,000) capital gain. The trust's only other income for 1991 is $45,000 of dividends. There are no expenses. Both the trust and Dana are calendar-year taxpayers. Dana's marginal tax rate for 1991 is 31%.

The Sec. 644 tax owed by the trust is computed as follows. To simplify the analysis, it is assumed that Dana does not owe any alternative minimum tax for 1991.

Includible gain (lesser of $90,000 realized gain or $80,000 [$100,000 − $20,000] pre-transfer gain)	$80,000
Times: Transferor's marginal tax rate (limited to 28%)	× 0.28
Sec. 644 tax liability	$22,400

The trust's taxable income is determined in the computations below.

Dividends	$45,000
Long-term capital gain (in excess of portion taxed under Sec. 644)	10,000
Minus: Distribution deduction	(45,000)
Personal exemption	(300)
Taxable income	$ 9,700

The $9,700 of taxable income is taxed at the Sec. 1(e) fiduciary rates. ■

INCOME IN RESPECT OF A DECEDENT

Definition and Common Examples

OBJECTIVE 7
Recognize the significance of income in respect of a decedent

Section 691 specifies the tax treatment for specific types of income known as "income in respect of a decedent." **Income in respect of a decedent (IRD)** is defined as "those amounts to which a decedent was entitled to as gross income but which were not properly includible in computing his taxable income for the tax year ending with

[48] Sec. 644(b).
[49] Sec. 644(a)(2).
[50] Sec. 641(c)(1).

Self-Study Question

Roger, a cash method taxpayer, is a medical doctor. At the time of Roger's death, he has $150,000 due him from patients for his services. These accounts receivable are "property" in which Roger has an interest at the time of his death and are therefore included in his gross estate. Why are the accounts receivable income in respect of a decedent?

Answer

Since the accounts receivable also represent income which Roger earned while alive, but did not report as income due to his accounting method, they also constitute income to his estate (or his heirs) when they are collected. The accounts receivable are therefore income in respect of a decedent (IRD).

the date of his death or for a previous tax year under the method of accounting employed by the decedent."[51] Because most individuals use the cash method of accounting, IRD generally consists of income earned, but not actually or constructively received, prior to death. Common examples of IRD include the following:

- Interest earned, but not received, prior to death
- Salary, commission, or bonus earned, but not received, prior to death
- Dividend collected after the date of death, for which the record date precedes the date of death
- Gain portion of collections on an installment sale that takes place before the date of death

Significance of IRD

Double Taxation. Recall from Chapter 13 that a decedent's gross estate includes properties to the extent of his interest therein. The decedent has an interest in any income earned but not actually or constructively received prior to death. Thus, the decedent's gross estate includes income accrued as of the date of death. Assuming the decedent used the cash method of accounting, this accrued income is not included in gross income until the period in which it is collected. The income is taxed to the party (i.e., the estate or a named individual) entitled to receive it. Thus, IRD is taxed under both the transfer tax system and the income tax system. The income is also taxed twice if the decedent collects a dividend check, deposits it into his or her bank account, and dies before consuming the cash. In this case, the dividend must be included in the decedent's individual income tax return, and the cash (from the dividend check) must be included in the decedent's gross estate.

Example 14-31 ■ Doug dies July 1, 1991. Included in Doug's gross estate is an 8%, $1,000 corporate bond that pays interest each September 1 and March 1. Doug's gross estate also includes accrued interest for the period March 2 through July 1 of $27 ($1,000 × 0.08 × 4/12). On September 1, 1991, Doug's estate collects $40 of interest, of which $27 constitutes IRD. The income tax return for Doug's estate includes $40 of interest income. ■

Section 691(c) Deduction. Some relief for the double taxation of IRD is provided in the form of the Sec. 691(c) deduction. This deduction equals the federal estate taxes attributable to the IRD included in the gross estate. The total Sec. 691(c) deduction is the excess of (1) the decedent's actual federal estate tax over (2) the federal estate tax that would be payable if the IRD was excluded from the decedent's gross estate. If the IRD is collected in more than one tax year, the Sec. 691(c) deduction for a particular tax year is determined by the following formula:[52]

$$\text{Sec. 691(c) deduction for the year} = \text{Total Sec. 691(c) deduction} \times \frac{\text{IRD included in gross income for the year}}{\text{Total IRD}}$$

Example 14-32 ■ Pam dies in 1990 with a taxable estate and estate tax base of $1,000,000. Pam's estate owes no state death taxes. Pam's gross estate includes $250,000 of IRD, none of which is received by her surviving spouse. The estate collects $200,000 of the

---

[51] Reg. Sec. 1.691(a)-1(b).
[52] Sec. 691(c)(1).

IRD during its 1991 tax year. The Sec. 691(c) deduction for Pam's estate for 1991 is calculated as shown below.

Actual federal estate tax liability (on base of $1,000,000)	$153,000
Minus: Federal estate tax on base ($750,000) determined by excluding IRD from gross estate	(55,500)
Total Sec. 691(c) deduction	$ 97,500
Sec. 691(d) deduction available in 1991: ($200,000 ÷ $250,000) × $97,500 =	$ 78,000

■

Self-Study Question

Karl receives his regular monthly paycheck on May 1. He opens a savings account and deposits the paycheck in the savings account. He dies on May 10. He did not make any withdrawals from the savings account prior to his death. On June 1, Karl's employer pays Karl's estate 1/3 of Karl's monthly salary (the amount Karl had earned prior to his death on May 10). What are the tax consequences?

Deductions in Respect of a Decedent. Section 691(b) authorizes **deductions in respect of a decedent (DRD).** Such deductions include trade or business expenses, expenses for the production of income, interest, taxes, depletion, etc. that are accrued prior to death but are not deductible on the decedent's final income tax return because the decedent used the cash method of accounting. Because some of these accrued expenses have not been paid prior to death, they may also be deductible as debts on the estate tax return. The accrued expenses are also deductible on the estate's income tax return when paid by the estate. Thus, a double benefit can be obtained for DRD.

Example 14-33 ■

Answer

Karl's gross estate will include his savings account. Karl's final income tax return will include his salary through April 30 (i.e., his May 1 check is subject to both the income and the estate tax). Karl's estate gets no relief under Sec. 691(c) from this double taxation on his April salary, but the income taxes owed on this salary (and the May salary) are deductible as a debt on his estate tax return.

Karl's gross estate will include 1/3 of his May salary. His estate will also report this amount as income. This is income in respect of a decedent, so the estate will get some relief under Sec. 691(c) from the double tax.

Dan dies on September 20, 1991. At the time of his death, Dan owes $18,000 of salaries to the employees of his proprietorship. The executor pays the total September payroll of $29,000 on September 30, 1991. The $18,000 of accrued salaries is deductible as a debt on the estate tax return. As a trade or business (Sec. 162) expense, the salaries also constitute DRD. The $18,000 of DRD, plus any other amounts paid, are deductible on the estate's income tax return for the period of payment.

■

No Step-up in Basis. Most property received as the result of a decedent's death acquires a basis equal to its FMV on the date of death or the alternate valuation date. Not so, however, for properties classified as IRD. Items of IRD retain the same basis that they had in the decedent's hands.[53]

This carryover basis rule for IRD items is especially unfavorable when the decedent sold a highly appreciated asset soon before death, collected a relatively small portion of the sales price before death, and reported the sale under the installment method of accounting. If, for example, the gain was 80% of the sales price, 80% of each principal payment in the postdeath period will continue to be characterized as gain. If the sale was instead postponed until after the date of death, the gain would have been restricted to the postdeath appreciation (if any) because the step-up in basis rules would have applied to the asset.

Example 14-34 ■

On June 3, 1991, Joel sells a parcel of investment land for $40,000. The land has a $10,000 adjusted basis in Joel's hands. The buyer pays $8,000 down and signs a $32,000 note at an interest rate acceptable to the IRS. The note is payable June 3, 1992. Joel chooses to use the installment method for reporting the $30,000 ($40,000 − $10,000) gain. The gross profit ratio is 75% ($30,000 gain ÷ $40,000

---

[53] Sec. 1014(c).

Self-Study Question
Roger died leaving $150,000 of zero basis accounts receivable uncollected. What basis does his estate have in these accounts receivable?

Answer
Zero. The accounts receivable constitute IRD.

contract price). Joel dies accidentally on June 4, 1991. A gain of $6,000 (0.75 × $8,000) is reported on Joel's final individual income tax return. The estate reports a gain of $24,000 (0.75 × $32,000 collections) on its 1992 tax return when it collects the $32,000 balance due on June 3, 1992. Had the contract for sale been entered into a few days after Joel's death, the gain would have been zero because the land's basis would have been its $40,000 FMV at the date of death. ∎

GRANTOR TRUST PROVISIONS

OBJECTIVE 8
Explain the effect of the grantor trust provisions

This portion of the chapter examines the provisions affecting a special type of trust known as a **grantor trust.** Grantor trusts are governed by Secs. 671 through 679, a self-contained unit of the Code. As discussed previously, income of a regular (or nongrantor) trust or an estate is taxed to the beneficiary or the fiduciary in accordance with the portion that is distributed or accumulated. In the case of a grantor trust, however, the trust's grantor (creator) is taxed on some or all of the trust's income even though such income may have been distributed to the beneficiary. In certain circumstances, a person other than the grantor or the beneficiary (e.g., a person with powers over the trust) must pay tax on the trust's income.

Purpose and Effect

Key Point
The purpose of the grantor trust rules is to prevent tax avoidance through the use of transfers in trust where the grantor has not given up enough control of the transferred assets. This is done by making the grantor report all or part of the trusts's income on his individual tax return.

The grantor trust rules are intended to make those grantors who do not give up enough control or economic benefits when they create a trust pay a price by being taxed on part or all of the trust's income. A grantor must report some or all of a trust's income on his individual tax return if he does not (1) part with enough control over the trust assets or (2) give up the right to income produced by the assets for a sufficiently long time period. For transfers after March 1, 1986, the grantor is generally taxed on the trust's income if the trust property will return to the grantor or the grantor's spouse at any time. According to the Tax Court, the grantor trust rules have the following purpose and result:

> This subpart [Secs. 671 through 679] enunciates the rules to be applied where, in described circumstances, a grantor has transferred property to a trust but has not parted with complete dominion and control over the property or the income which it produces.... [W] here the grantor makes a formal but incomplete transfer of that property in trust, retaining the enjoyment of the fruits of ownership through the power to control or receive the income or reacquire the corpus, subpart E provides, in substance that the transfer of legal title is to be disregarded insofar as such enjoyment has been retained.... The obvious purpose is to prevent the use of a temporary or incomplete transfer in trust as a means of tax avoidance.[54]

Sections 671 through 679 use the terminology "treated as owner." Section 671 specifies that when a grantor or other party (such as a person with control over distributions) is "treated as owner," the income, deductions, and credits attributable to the portion of the trust with respect to which the grantor is treated as owner are reported directly on the grantor's (or other party's) tax return and not on the trust's

---

[54] *William Scheft,* 59 T.C. 428, at 430-431 (1972).

return. The fiduciary return contains only those items attributable to the portion of the trust for which the grantor (or other party) is not treated as the owner.[55]

Unfortunately, the rules governing when a transfer is complete for income tax purposes (meaning the grantor avoids being taxed on the trust's income) do not agree completely with the rules concerning whether (1) the transfer is complete for gift tax purposes or (2) the transferred property is removed from the donor's gross estate. In certain circumstances, a donor can make a taxable gift and still be taxed on the income from the transferred property. For example, assume a donor makes a transfer to a trust with the income payable annually to the donor's sister for 6 years and a reversion of the property to the donor occurring at the end of the sixth year. The donor makes a gift, subject to the gift tax, of the value of an income interest for 6 years. Under the grantor trust rules, however, the donor continues to be taxed on the trust's income.

Retention of certain powers over property conveyed in trust can cause the trust assets to be included in the donor's gross estate even though these powers do not cause the donor to be taxed on the trust income. Assume that a donor has the discretionary power to pay out or accumulate trust income until the beneficiary reaches age 21. The trust assets, including any accumulated income, are distributed to the beneficiary on her twenty-first birthday. The donor is not taxed on the trust income, but if the donor dies before the beneficiary attains age 21, the donor's gross estate will include the trust property because of Sec. 2036 (see Chapter 13).

Additional Comment
A common use of the revocable trust is to avoid probate for the property held by the trust. On the death of the grantor, the trustee of the revocable trust distributes the trust property in accordance with the trust agreement. Since the trustee holds legal title to the property, he can distribute the property without going through the probate process.

Revocable Trusts

The grantor of a revocable trust is able to control the assets conveyed to the trust by altering the terms of the trust (including changing the identity of the beneficiaries) and/or withdrawing assets from the trust. Not surprisingly, the trust is ignored as a separate entity for tax purposes. Section 676 provides that the grantor is taxed on the income generated by a revocable trust. As Chapter 12 points out, a transfer of assets to a revocable trust is an incomplete transfer and thereby a transaction not subject to the gift tax.

Example 14-35 ■ In 1991, Tom transfers property to a revocable trust. Tom names Ann to receive the income for life and Beth to receive the remainder. The trust's income for 1991 consists of $15,000 of dividends and an $8,000 long-term capital gain. The dividends are distributed to Ann. The gain is credited to principal and not distributed. Because the trust is revocable, the dividend and capital gain income are taxed directly to Tom on his 1991 individual return. Nothing is taxed to the trust or its beneficiaries. ■

Clifford Trusts

Not all trusts subject to the grantor trust rules are revocable trusts. Certain irrevocable trusts are also subject to the grantor trust rules if, for example, the grantor has a reversionary interest that reverts (passes back) too soon or holds certain administrative powers. Prior to its amendment in 1986, Sec. 673(a) provided that the grantor is taxed on the trust's accounting income if the trust assets revert to the grantor within 10 years of the transfer date. If, however, the reversion date is more

---

[55] For trusts created before March 2, 1986, the grantor may be treated as the owner with respect to the trust's capital gains but not its ordinary income because the property returns to the grantor after a period of more than 10 years. In such a situation the grantor is taxed on the capital gains and the trust and/or the beneficiary on the ordinary income.

than 10 years from the transfer date, the grantor is not taxed on the accounting income. If the grantor specifies that the trust will exist until the death of the beneficiary (at which time the assets will revert to the grantor), the grantor will not be taxed on the trust's accounting income, even though the beneficiary's life expectancy may not exceed 10 years.[56] Regardless of when the trust terminates, the grantor is always taxed on capital gains credited to principal because such gains are being held for distribution to the grantor upon termination of the trust.[57] The gains are taxed in the year realized and not at the termination of the trust.

If the trust period is long enough for the grantor to escape being taxed on the trust's accounting income, the trust is often referred to as a **Clifford** or **short-term trust.** The phrase *Clifford trust* relates to the *Clifford* case, a case decided prior to the adoption of the statutory rules concerning reversionary interest trusts.[58] In *Clifford*, however, the Supreme Court concluded that the grantor was taxable on the trust income because the reversion would occur too soon after the transfer.

Example 14-36 involves a trust for which the grantor successfully shifts the taxability of the accounting income.

Example 14-36 ▪ In June 1984, Ted transferred property to a trust whose trust instrument specifies that all of its income is payable annually to Amy for the next 12 years. At the end of 12 years, the property reverts to Ted. Amy is taxed on the trust's accounting income. Ted is taxed on any capital gains. ▪

The next example concerns a reversion within 10 years.

Example 14-37 ▪ Assume the same facts as in Example 14-36, except the term of the trust is instead 8 years. Ted is taxed on the accounting income because the assets revert to Ted in 10 years or less. Ted is also taxed on any capital gains. ▪

In the next example, the property reverts upon the death of the income beneficiary.

Example 14-38 ▪ Assume the same facts as in Example 14-36, except the trust is to exist for the life of Ted's elderly father, Fred, who is the income beneficiary. According to actuarial tables, Fred's life expectancy is 8 years. Because the term of the trust is for Fred's life, Fred is taxed on the accounting income. The capital gains are again taxed currently on Ted's tax return. ▪

Typical Misconception
The Clifford, or short-term, trust cannot be used as an income shifting device any longer. The reversion of corpus to the grantor at the end of the term of the trust now causes the trust to be treated as a grantor trust.

Post-1986 Reversionary Interest Trusts

The 1986 Tax Reform Act sounded the death knell for *Clifford* trusts. It amended Sec. 673(a) with respect to transfers made after March 1, 1986, to provide that the grantor is taxed on the accounting income of the trust if he has a reversionary interest in either income or principal. Under Sec. 672(e), a grantor is now treated as holding any interest held by his spouse. Thus, the spousal remainder trust, wherein an interest passes to the spouse (instead of reverting to the grantor) at the end of a specified time period, is no longer a viable income-shifting device.

There are two exceptions to the provision taxing the grantor holding a reversionary interest or whose spouse holds a remainder interest. The grantor trust rules do not apply if, as of the inception of the trust, the value of the reversionary interest does not

Key Point
Exceptions to the reversionary interest rules apply when (1) the reversion does not exceed 5% of the value of the trust, and (2) the reversion would occur only if the beneficiary should die before reaching age 21 and the beneficiary is a lineal descendent of the grantor.

---
[56] Sec. 673(c). This rule applies to transfers made prior to March 2, 1986.
[57] Sec. 677(a).
[58] *Helvering v. George B. Clifford, Jr.,* 23 AFTR 1077, 40-1 USTC ¶ 9265 (USSC, 1940).

exceed 5% of the value of the trust. The second exception applies when the reversion would occur only if the beneficiary should die before reaching age 21 and the beneficiary is a lineal descendant of the grantor.

Example 14-39 ■ In 1991, Paul establishes a trust with income payable to his elderly parent for 15 years. The assets of the trust will then revert to Paul. The value of Paul's reversionary interest exceeds 5%. Because Paul has a reversionary interest valued at above 5% and the transfer arises after March 1, 1986, Paul is taxed currently on the trust's accounting income. ■

The next example illustrates the application of one of the exceptions.

Example 14-40 ■ In 1991 Paul transfers property to a trust with income payable to his daughter Ruth until Ruth reaches age 21. On Ruth's twenty-first birthday, she is to receive the trust property outright. In the event Ruth should die before reaching age 21, the trust assets will revert to Paul. Paul is not taxed on the accounting income because his reversion is contingent on the death of the beneficiary (a lineal descendant) prior to age 21. ■

Retention of Administrative Powers

Under the rules of Sec. 675, the grantor is taxed on the accounting income and gains if he or his spouse hold certain administrative powers. Such powers include, but are not limited to, the following:

- The power to purchase or exchange trust property for less than adequate consideration in money or money's worth
- The power to borrow from the trust without adequate interest or security except where the trustee (who is someone other than the grantor) is empowered under a general lending power to make loans irrespective of interest or security
- The power exercisable in a nontrustee capacity to (a) vote stock of a corporation in which the holdings of the grantor and the trust are significant from the standpoint of voting control and (b) reacquire the trust property by substituting other property of equal value

Retention of Economic Benefits

Under the rules of Sec. 677, the grantor is taxed on the portion of the trust with respect to which the income may be

- Distributed to the grantor or his spouse
- Held or accumulated for future distribution to the grantor or his spouse
- Used to pay premiums on life insurance policies on the life of the grantor or his spouse

Typical Misconception
Keep in mind that this discussion covers trusts created by the grantor, who is the insured. If the trust was created by a person other than the grantor, say a parent or relative other than the grantor's spouse, the income required to be used for the payment of life insurance would not be taxed to the insured since the insured is not the grantor.

Use of trust income to provide support for a child whom the grantor is legally obligated to support also yields obvious economic benefits to the grantor. A grantor is treated as receiving and is thereby taxed on any trust income that is distributed by the trustee and used to support persons that the grantor is legally obligated to support (e.g., children). However, the mere existence of the discretionary power to use trust income for support purposes does not cause the grantor to be taxed on the trust income. Taxation turns on whether the trust income is actually used to meet the support obligation.

The first example deals with the payment of premiums on an insurance policy on the grantor's life.

Example 14-41 ▪ One of the assets of Gold Trust is a life insurance policy on the life of Maria, the trust's grantor. The trust instrument requires that $1,000 of trust income be used to pay the insurance premiums and that the rest be distributed to Wayne. Section 677 requires Maria to be taxed on $1,000 of accounting income. The remaining income is taxed to Wayne under the general trust rules. ▪

The rule concerning income held for eventual distribution to the grantor is illustrated in the next example.

Example 14-42 ▪ Judy created a trust in 1985 with all the income payable to Eric for 15 years. The trust assets will then revert to Judy. Section 677 taxes Judy on the capital gains provided they are credited to corpus. Eric is taxed on the accounting income. ▪

The next example concerns use of trust income to support the grantor's minor child.

Example 14-43 ▪ Hal creates a trust and empowers the bank trustee to distribute income to his minor son, Louis, until the son reaches age 21. When Louis reaches age 21, the trust assets including accumulated income are paid over to the child. In 1991, when Louis is age 15, the trustee distributes $5,000 that is used to support the child and $8,000 that is deposited into the child's savings account. The remaining $12,000 of income is accumulated. Hal is taxed on the $5,000 used to support his son. Louis includes $8,000 in his gross income, and the trust pays tax on $12,000 less its $100 exemption. ▪

Control of Others' Enjoyment

Section 674 requires the grantor to be taxed on trust income if he, his spouse, or someone not having an interest in the trust (e.g., a trustee) has the power to control others' beneficial enjoyment. A situation within the scope of Sec. 674 would occur, for example, if the grantor is the trustee of a trust over which the trustee has complete discretion to pay out the income or corpus in any amount he deems appropriate to some or all of its three beneficiaries. There are many exceptions, including, for example, exceptions for independent trustees, to Sec. 674's general rule of taxing the grantor.

Under Sec. 678, an individual other than the trust's grantor or beneficiary can be required to report the trust income. The other individual is taxed on the trust income if he has the power under the trust instrument to vest the trust principal or the income in himself, provided such power is exercisable solely by such individual.

Topic Review 14-4 summarizes the grantor trust rules.

TAX PLANNING CONSIDERATIONS

Many tax planning opportunities exist with respect to estates and trusts, including (1) the ability to shift income to the fiduciary and/or the beneficiaries and (2) the opportunity for executors or trustees of discretionary trusts to consider the tax

TOPIC REVIEW 14-4

Grantor Trust Rules

Factual Situation	Tax Treatment
1. Trust is revocable.	Ordinary income and capital gains are taxed to grantor.
2. Irrevocable trust (funded prior to March 2, 1986) pays income to third party beneficiary for more than 10 years and property then reverts to grantor.	Ordinary income is taxed to beneficiary, and capital gains are taxed to grantor.
3. Same as number 2, except trust is funded on or after March 2, 1986, and the value of the reversionary interest exceeds 5% of the value of the trust.	Ordinary income and capital gains are taxed to grantor.
4. The grantor of an irrevocable trust retains administrative powers described in the Code.	Ordinary income and capital gains are taxed to grantor.
5. The income of an irrevocable trust is disbursed to meet the grantor's obligation of supporting his children.	Ordinary income and capital gains are taxed to grantor.
6. The income of an irrevocable trust is disbursed to pay the premium on a life insurance policy on the life of the grantor or the grantor's spouse.	Ordinary income and capital gains are taxed to grantor.

Additional Comment

In 1991 the first $3,450 of trust income is taxed at 15%. If the trust is a complex trust, it is entitled to a personal deduction of $100. In other words, a trust pays no tax on $100 of income and only 15% on the next $3,450 of income. If the trust distributes dividend and/or interest income to a child under age 14 who is a dependent and has no other unearned income, the child pays no tax on the first $1,100 of that income. If the child's parents are continually in the 28% or 31% income tax bracket, some income tax savings can still be achieved under the current law by using a trust to spread income over different entities. For the situation described here, a Sec. 2503(c) trust is commonly used.

consequences of the timing of distributions. These and other tax planning considerations are discussed below.

Ability to Shift Income

Prior to 1987, one of the primary tax advantages of using trusts was the ability to shift income from the grantor to the trust or the beneficiary. Two changes that took effect in 1987 have reduced the tax advantages of shifting income. First, the tax rate schedules for all taxpayers—but especially for fiduciaries—are very compressed. Second, unearned income in excess of $1,100 of children under age 14 is taxed at the higher of the parents' or the child's tax rate, even if distributed from a trust or estate. Depending upon whether the income is distributed or retained, it is taxed to the trust or the beneficiary or a portion to each. Because the trust is a separate taxpayer, any income taxed to it is taxed under the trust's rate schedule. If the beneficiary already has income from other sources, the income shifted to the beneficiary may not be taxed at the lowest rates. An income tax savings can nevertheless occur whenever a portion of the shifted income is taxed at a rate lower than the rate the grantor would pay on that income.

Timing of Distributions

Persons managing estates and discretionary trusts can reduce taxes through carefully planning the timing of distributions. From a tax standpoint, the executor or trustee should consider the beneficiary's income from other sources and make distributions in

Additional Comment
Tax considerations are only one of many things that must be examined, and may be of little importance when compared to many of the other considerations. Since we are dealing solely with tax, we need to remember that tax really is just one factor to consider in any decision making process.

amounts that equalize the marginal tax rates of the beneficiary and the fiduciary. If the trust is a **sprinkling trust** (a discretionary trust with several beneficiaries), the trustee can accomplish tax savings for the beneficiaries by making distributions to the beneficiaries who have the lowest marginal tax rate that year. Of course, nontax reasons might require a trustee to distribute income to other beneficiaries also.

65-Day Rule

The 65-day rule of Sec. 663(b) allows trustees of complex trusts to treat distributions made during the first 65 days of the trust's tax year as if they had been made on the last day of the preceding tax year. If the trustee does not make the election, the distributed income is deducted by the trust and taxed to the beneficiary in the year the actual distribution is made. This rule creates some tax planning flexibility as illustrated below.

Example 14-44 ■

Key Point
When you consider the fact that one frequently cannot determine the exact amount of income a trust (or any other entity) has earned until after the end of the tax year, you can see that the 65-day rule is extremely helpful with respect to distribution planning.

In 1990 Edison Trust distributes no income to Heidi, its beneficiary. Heidi anticipates having a higher marginal tax rate than the trust in 1990. In February 1991 Heidi projects her 1990 taxable income and determines that an unanticipated loss will lower her marginal tax rate below the trust's 1990 marginal tax rate. No later than March 6, 1991, the trustee may make a distribution to Heidi and elect to treat such distribution as if it were made in 1990. This distribution can equalize the marginal tax rates of the trust and the beneficiary. ■

Property Distributions

A special tax saving election is available for trusts that make nonmoney (or property) distributions. Under the general rule affecting property distributions, the trust gets a distribution deduction equal to the lesser of (1) the fiduciary's adjusted basis in the property or (2) the property's FMV.[59] If the trust distributes appreciated property, the trustee can elect to recognize a gain on the distribution. The gain is the excess of the property's FMV over its adjusted basis on the distribution date. If the election is not made, the trust recognizes no gain as a result of distributing the property.

If the trustee elects to recognize the gain, the distribution deduction equals the property's FMV. The beneficiary, in turn, takes a basis equal to the property's adjusted basis to the trust plus the gain recognized by the trust on the distribution. In the case of property that will likely be sold soon after distribution, the election provision allows the trustee to choose where the appreciation will be taxed; that is, at the trust level or the beneficiary level. If the distribution involves appreciated capital gain property, the capital gain that is recognized may offset capital loss carryovers from prior tax years.

Choice of Year-End for Estates

Prior to 1987, a fiduciary taxpayer had complete freedom in choosing its original tax year as long as it made the choice on a timely filed return. Proper timing of the estate's or trust's year-end deferred the reporting of income by a beneficiary from one tax year to the next because distributions from an estate or trust are taxed to the beneficiaries in their tax year in which the fiduciary's year ends.[60]

Because of the ability to defer the taxation of trust distributions to beneficiaries by choosing a noncalendar year, Congress in 1986 required all trusts other than

---
[59] Sec. 643(d).
[60] Secs. 652(c) and 662(c).

Key Point
Generally, a trust must now use the calendar year as its tax year.

tax-exempt and wholly charitable trusts to use a calendar year as its tax year.[61] The rule applies to tax years beginning after December 31, 1986. Because the rule affects existing trusts in addition to new trusts, some trusts had to change their tax year. Estates, however, are completely free to choose a year-end, probably because death is a high price to pay to achieve favorable tax treatment for a beneficiary.

Example 14-45 ■ Madison Estate adopts a fiscal year ending on January 31. During the period February 1, 1990, through January 31, 1991, Madison Estate distributes $30,000 to Bob, a calendar-year beneficiary. The estate's DNI exceeds $30,000. Bob reports $30,000 of estate income on his individual return for 1991, Bob's tax year during which the estate's tax year ended. By choosing the January 31 year-end (instead of a calendar year-end), the executor postpones the taxation of income to Bob from 1990 to 1991. ■

Deduction of Administration Expenses

Chapter 13 points out that the executor must elect where to deduct administration expenses—on the estate tax return, the estate's income tax return, or some on each return. Unlike the situation for deductions in respect of a decedent, Sec. 642(g) provides there is no double deduction for administration expenses. Such expenses should be deducted where they will yield the greatest tax savings. Of course, if the surviving spouse receives all of the decedent's property or all except for an amount equal to the exemption equivalent, the deduction of administration expenses on the estate tax return will produce no tax savings because the estate will owe no estate taxes.

COMPLIANCE AND PROCEDURAL CONSIDERATIONS

OBJECTIVE 9
Recognize the filing requirements for fiduciary returns

Filing Requirements

General Rule. Every estate that has gross income of at least $600 for the tax year must file an income tax return (Form 1041). A trust income tax return (also generally Form 1041) is required for every trust that (1) has taxable income or (2) has gross income of $600 or more.[62] In addition, every estate or trust that has a nonresident alien as a beneficiary must file a return.[63] A simplified trust form, Form 1041S, is available for use by simple trusts with no taxable income. This form may be prepared for simple trusts that (1) have no capital gains or losses and (2) have an income distribution deduction equal to the amount of income that must be distributed currently.

Special Grantor Trust Rule. In certain circumstances, a fiduciary return need not be filed for grantor trusts created in a tax year beginning in 1981 or later. This

---

[61] Sec. 645.
[62] Secs. 6012(a)(3) and (4).
[63] Sec. 6012(a)(5).

exemption applies to a revocable trust where the grantor serves as trustee or a cotrustee. Here, the grantor is taxed on all of the trust income because the trust is revocable. The exemption is also available for revocable trusts in which (1) a husband and wife are the only grantors; (2) at least one of the spouses is a trustee or cotrustee; (3) at least one of the spouses is taxed on all of the trust income; and (4) the husband and wife file a joint return.[64] Trusts created prior to 1981 may take advantage of these exemptions in future years by preparing a current year's return that states, "Pursuant to Sec. 1.671-4(b), this is the final return for this grantor trust."

Fiduciary returns are necessary for all other grantor trusts, provided the trusts meet the general filing requirements. Income taxable to the grantor is not reported on the fiduciary return, but rather is disclosed on a separate attachment to the return.

Due Date for Return and Tax

The due date for fiduciary returns (Form 1041) is the same as for individuals; they are due on the fifteenth day of the fourth month following the end of the tax year.[65] If an extension is desired, Form 2758 must be filed. The extension period is for 4 months, but an additional extension for 2 months may be requested.

Both trusts and estates must generally make estimated tax payments.[66] Estates, however, are exempted from making estimated tax payments for their first 2 tax years. If the tax liability exceeds the estimated tax payments, the balance of the tax is due on or before the due date for the return.[67] Estimated tax payments for a trust or an estate are made by using Form 1041-ES. The amount of any estimated tax installment required to be paid by the trust or estate by a particular due date in order to avoid an underpayment penalty is the appropriate percentage times the lowest of the following annual amounts:

1. 90% of the tax shown on the return for the current year
2. 100% of the tax shown on the return for the prior year
3. 100% of the annualized income installment for the current year.[68]

Section 644 Tax—Information about Grantor's Income

If a portion of the gain realized by a trust is taxed under Sec. 644, the trustee or the person preparing the trust's tax return must obtain information concerning the grantor's income tax results for the applicable period. If the grantor does not file his return by the due date for the trust return, the trust must request an extension within which to file its return.

Documents to Be Furnished to IRS

The executor or the trustee need not file a copy of the will or the trust instrument with the return. However, at times the IRS may request a copy of such documents. If the IRS makes such a request, the executor or the trustee should also transmit the following:

1. A statement signed under penalty of perjury that the copy is true and complete
2. A statement naming the provisions of the will or trust agreement that the

---

[64] Reg. Sec. 1.671-4(b).
[65] Sec. 6072(a).
[66] Sec. 6654(1).
[67] Sec. 6151(a).
[68] Sec. 6654(d) and Ann. 87-32, I.R.B. 1987-16, 12.

executor or the trustee believes control how the income is to be divided among the fiduciary, the beneficiaries, and the grantor (if applicable).

Sample Simple and Complex Trust Returns

Appendix B contains samples of simple and complex trust returns (Form 1041s), respectively. They also illustrate the completion of Schedule K-1 for the reporting of income, etc. to the beneficiary. One copy of Schedule K-1 for each beneficiary is filed with Form 1041. In addition, each beneficiary receives a copy of his Schedule K-1, so that he knows the amount and type of gross income to report with respect to the distributions he receives. If the beneficiary is entitled to a deduction for depreciation, information concerning the amount appears on lines 4(b)(1), (2), and (3) of Schedule K-1.

The Sec. 644 tax is not owed in the two sets of facts illustrated in the sample returns. When such tax is owed, the amount should be entered on line 1b of Schedule G of Form 1041. In addition, a schedule should be attached for disclosing the computation of the tax. Moreover, only the gain in excess of the Sec. 644 gain should be included in the trust's taxable income and taxed at the trust's tax rates.

PROBLEM MATERIALS

DISCUSSION QUESTIONS

14-1. Is the income of an estate or trust subject to double taxation? Explain.

14-2. Compare the rate schedule for estates and trusts with the rate schedule for unmarried individuals.

14-3. Given the changes made by the 1986 Tax Act to the tax rate schedules, do any reasons exist today for creating a trust?

14-4. Are the benefits of the personal exemption deduction phased-out for trusts and estates with sufficiently high income?

14-5. What is the significance of the income and principal categorization scheme used for fiduciary accounting purposes?

14-6. List some common examples of principal and income items.

14-7. A trust owns some properties on which depreciation is claimed. The trust distributes all its income to its one income beneficiary. By whom is the trust's depreciation deductible?

14-8. What is the relevance of state law with respect to the classification of items as principal or income?

14-9. A trust from which Irene is entitled to receive only distributions of income and for which Beth will receive the remainder interest sells property at a gain. Income and corpus are classified in accordance with the Uniform Act. Will Irene receive a distribution of an amount equal to the gain? Explain.

14-10. Refer to Question 14-9. Which taxpayer (the Trust, Irene, or Beth) pays the tax on the gain?

14-11. Is there any limitation on a trust's charitable contribution deduction?

14-12. What is the amount of the personal exemption for trusts and estates?

14-13. Is the taxable income of estates and trusts determined by referring to most of the same tax provisions that affect individuals?

14-14. What is the significance of distributable net income (DNI)?

14-15. a. Are net accounting income and DNI always the same amount?
b. If not, explain why a difference may develop.
c. Are capital gains usually included in DNI?

14-16. a. Describe the short-cut approach for verifying the correctness of the amount calculated earlier as a simple trust's taxable income.
b. Can a short-cut verification process be applied with respect to trusts and estates that accumulate some of their income? Explain.

14-17. Explain how to determine the allowable deduction for trustee's fees.

14-18. Assume that a trust collects rental income and interest income on tax-exempt bonds. Will a portion of the rental expenses be nondeductible because of having to be allocated to tax-exempt income? Explain.

14-19. When does the NOL of a trust or estate produce tax deductions for the beneficiaries?

14-20. The Mary Morgan Trust is a simple trust that engages in one sale of a capital asset in the current year. The sale results in a loss.
a. When will the capital loss produce a tax benefit for the trust or its beneficiary? Explain.
b. Would the result necessarily be the same for a complex trust? Explain.

14-21. Determine the accuracy of the following statement: Complex trusts always receive a $100 personal exemption.

14-22. Describe the tier system.

14-23. Determine the accuracy of the following statement: Under the tier system, beneficiaries who receive mandatory distributions of income are more likely to be taxed on the distributions they receive than are beneficiaries who receive discretionary distributions.

14-24. a. What is the purpose of the accumulation distribution rules?
b. Are the accumulation distribution rules an exception to the general rule that DNI sets the ceiling on the amount taxable to the beneficiary? If so, explain.
c. List two situations in which the accumulation distribution rules do not apply even though (1) the fiduciary earlier accumulated income and (2) the current year's distributions exceed the current year's DNI.

14-25. Answer the following questions relating to the Sec. 644 tax.
a. What does the term "includible gain" mean?
b. Who pays the tax on a trust's includible gain?

14-26. Indicate whether, and why, you agree with the following statement: If today's tax rate structure had always existed, there would not be much of a policy reason for imposing the Sec. 644 tax.

14-27. a. What is income in respect of a decedent (IRD)?
b. Describe one tax disadvantage and one tax advantage that occur as a result of a receipt having been classified as IRD.

14-28. Describe three situations that cause trusts to be subject to the grantor trust rules.

14-29. Determine the accuracy of the following statement: The tax treatment is the same for all trusts that involve reversionary interests to the grantor.

14-30. Determine the accuracy of the following statement: If the grantor trust rules apply to a trust, the grantor is always taxed on both the trust's ordinary income and its gains.

14-31. Explain the 65-day rule and the tax planning opportunity it provides.

14-32. a. What is the due date for fiduciary returns?
b. Must estates and trusts make payments of estimated taxes?

PROBLEMS

14-33. *Calculation of the Tax Liability.* A trust has taxable income of $18,000 in the current year. What is its income tax liability?

14-34. Determination of Taxable Income. A simple trust has the following receipts and expenditures for the current year. The long-term capital gain and trustee's fees are part of principal.

Dividends	$30,000
Long-term capital gain	12,000
Trustee's fees	1,500
Distribution to beneficiary	30,000

a. What is the trust's taxable income under the formula approach of Figure 14-1?
b. What is the trust's taxable income under the short-cut approach?

14-35. Determination of Taxable Income. Refer to Problem 14-34. How would your answer to Part a change if the trust also receives $10,000 interest from tax-exempt bonds, and it distributes $40,000 instead of $30,000?

14-36. Determination of Taxable Income and Tax Liability. A simple trust has the following receipts and expenditures for the current year. Assume the trust instrument is silent with respect to capital gains and that state law concerning trust accounting income follows the Uniform Act. Assume the trustee's fee is charged to principal.

Corporate bond interest	$30,000
Tax-exempt interest	20,000
Long-term capital gain	8,000
Trustee's fee	2,000
Distribution to beneficiary	50,000

a. What is the trust's taxable income under the formula approach of Figure 14-1?
b. What is the trust's tax liability?
c. How, if at all, would the tax and nontax consequences differ if the trustee's fee is charged to income instead of principal?

14-37. Determination of Taxable Income. During the current year a simple trust has the following receipts and expenditures. Assume that trustee's fees are charged to income and that the Uniform Act governs for classification of income items.

Dividends	$40,000
Long-term capital gain	15,000
Trustee's fees	2,000

a. How much must be distributed to the beneficiary?
b. What is the trust's taxable income under the short-cut approach?

14-38. Determination of Distribution Deduction. A trust has net accounting income of $18,000 and DNI of $16,000. What is its distribution deduction under the following situations:
a. It distributes $18,000, and all of its income is from taxable sources.
b. It distributes $18,000, and it has tax-exempt income (net of allocable expenses) of $2,000.
c. It distributes $6,000, and all of its income is from taxable sources.

14-39. Determination of Beneficiary's Income. A trust is authorized to make discretionary distributions of income and principal to its two beneficiaries, Roy and Sandy. For the current year it has DNI and net accounting income of $36,000, all from taxable sources. It distributes $20,000 to Roy and $40,000 to Sandy. How much gross income does each beneficiary report, assuming that the accumulation distribution rules do not apply?

14-40. Determination of Beneficiary's Income. Refer to Problem 14-39. How would your answer change if the trust instrument requires that $10,000 per year be distributed to Sandy and if the trustee also makes discretionary distributions of $20,000 to Roy and $30,000 to Sandy?

14-41. Determination of Accounting Income and Distribution. A trust has the receipts and expenditures listed below for the current year. Assume the Revised Uniform Principal and Income Act governs an item's classification as principal or income. What is the trust's net accounting income and the maximum distribution possible? Assume the trust cannot pay out principal.

Dividends	$12,000
Interest on tax-exempt bonds	5,000
Gain on sale of capital asset	20,000
Rental income from land	3,000
Property taxes on rental property	200
Trustee's fee charged to principal in accordance with agreement with trustees	1,200

14-42. *Determination of Taxable Income.* Refer to Problem 14-41. Assume the trustee must pay out all of its income currently to its beneficiary, Ralph.
  a. What is the deductible portion of the trustee's fee?
  b. What is the trust's taxable inome exclusive of the distribution deduction?
  c. What is the trust's DNI?
  d. What is the trust's taxable income using the formula approach of Figure 14-1?

14-43. *Determination of Taxable Income.* Refer to Problem 14-42. How would your answers change if the trust is a discretionary trust that distributes $8,000 to its beneficiary, Ralph?

14-44. *Calculation of Deductible Expenses.* The Ellen Edison Trust reports the receipts and expenditures listed below. What are the trust's *deductible* expenses?

Dividends	$15,000
Rental income	6,000
Interest from tax-exempt bonds	7,000
Property taxes on rental property	500
Maintenance of rental property	1,300
CPA's fee for tax return preparation	700
Trustee's fee	1,800

14-45. *Tax Treatment of Capital Losses.* A simple trust had a long-term capital loss of $10,000 for 1990 and a long-term capital gain of $15,000 for 1991. Explain the tax treatment for the 1990 capital loss assuming the trust is in existence at the end of 1992.

14-46. *Tax Treatment of Capital Losses.* Refer to Problem 14-45. How would your answer change if the trust is instead a complex trust that makes no distributions in 1990 and 1991? Assume the trust earns $8,000 of corporate bond interest income each year.

14-47. *Section 644 Tax.* Last year Chris transferred stock valued at $60,000 to a trust. The stock's adjusted basis is $10,000. Chris pays no gift tax on the transfer. The trust sells the stock in the current year for $150,000. Both Chris and the trust report on a calendar-year basis. Chris, who is single, claims the standard deduction and has $300,000 of taxable income in the current year.
  a. What is the Sec. 644 tax? (Ignore any alternative minimum tax implications.)
  b. What gain (if any) is included in the trust's taxable income?

14-48. *Section 644 Tax.* Refer to Problem 14-47. Explain how your answer would change for each of the two independent situations indicated below:
  a. Chris instead makes the transfer four years prior to the sale.
  b. Chris's adjusted basis for the property is instead $80,000.

14-49. *Revocable Trusts.* A revocable trust created by Brad, realizes $12,000 of dividend income and a $40,000 capital gain. It distributes $12,000 to Karen, its beneficiary. How much income is taxed to the trust, the grantor, and the beneficiary?

14-50. *Reversionary Interest Trusts.* Holly Todd Trust is created by Holly in 1985. For 12 years the trust income is payable to her son, Jack (age 17 in 1985). At the end of the twelfth year, the trust assets are to revert to Holly. In the current year, the trust realizes $20,000 of dividend income and an $18,000 long-term capital gain. How much income is taxed to the trust, the grantor, and the beneficiary in the current year?

14-51. *Reversionary Interest Trusts.* Refer to Problem 14-50. Explain how your answers would change for each independent situation indicated below:
  a. The term of the trust is 7 years (instead of 12).

b. The trust is for the life of Holly's father, Allen (the beneficiary), who has a life expectancy of 8 years.
c. Holly creates the trust in October 1991 for a term of 13 years.

14-52. *Income in Respect of Decedent.* The following items are reported on the first income tax return for the Ken Kimble Estate. Mr. Kimble died on July 1, 1991.

Dividends	$10,000
Interest on corporate bonds	18,000
Collection on installment note from sale of investment land	24,000

The record date was June 14 for $6,000 of the dividends and October 31, for the remaining $4,000 of dividends. The bond interest is payable annually on October 1. Mr. Kimble's basis in the land is $8,000. He sells it in 1990 for a total sales price of $48,000 and reports his gain under the installment method. What is the amount of IRD reported on the estate's income tax return?

14-53. *Income in Respect of Decedent.* Julie Brown died on May 29 of the current year. She was employed prior to her death, and her gross salary was $2,000 per month. She was paid on the last day of each month. She owned stock that paid quarterly dividends of $800 per quarter each March 31, June 30, September 30, and December 31. Assume her estate chooses a calendar year as its tax year. What is the amount of gross income to be reported on the estate's first income tax return?

14-54. *Income Recognition by Beneficiary.* Joan died April 17, 1990. Joan's executor chose a tax year for the estate that ends on March 31. The estate's only beneficiary, Kathy, reports on a calendar year. The executor of Joan's estate makes the following distributions to Kathy:

June 1990	$ 5,000
August 1990	10,000
March 1991	12,000
August 1991	14,000

The 1990 and 1991 distributions do not exceed DNI. How much income does Kathy report on her 1990 return as a result of the distributions from the estate? On her 1991 return?

TAX FORM/RETURN PREPARATION PROBLEMS

14-55. Marion Mosley creates the Jenny Justice Trust in 1975 with First Bank named as trustee. For 20 years the trust is to pay out all of its income semi-annually to the beneficiary, Jenny Justice. At the end of the twentieth year, the trust assets are to be distributed to Jenny's descendants. Capital gains are credited to principal, and depreciation is charged to principal. For the current year the trust reports the following results:

	Amounts Allocable to	
	Income	Principal
Rental income	$15,000	
Dividend income	27,000	
Interest on tax-exempt bonds	8,000	
Long-term capital gain on sale of stock		30,000[a]
Maintenance and repairs of rental property	1,500	
Property taxes on rental property	700	
Fee for tax return preparation	500	
Trustee's fee		2,000
Depreciation		2,400

[a] The sales price and adjusted basis are $110,000 and $80,000, respectively. Mr. Mosley acquired the stock in 1970.

Prepare a Form 1041, including any needed Schedule K-1s, for the Jenny Justice Trust. The trustee's address is P.O. Box 100, Dallas, TX. 75202. The identification number of the trust is

74-6224343. Jenny, whose Social Security number is 252-37-1492, resides at 2 Mountain View, Birmingham, AL 35205.

14-56. Mark Wilson created an irrevocable trust in 1984 by transferring to it appreciated assets. Because of the unified credit, he owed no gift tax on the transfer. The trustee in its discretion is to pay out income and/or corpus to Doug Weldon (017-22-1344) until Doug becomes age 33. Then the property is to be distributed to Doug or his estate. The trustee is First Bank, 20 State St., Boston, MA 02111. Doug resides at 38 Walden Ln., Boston, MA 02115.

During 1990 the following events occurred with respect to the trust:

Dividends received	$ 9,000
Rent received on raw land	1,200
Interest received from City of Salem bonds	13,000
Accountant's fee paid for 1989 return	275
Trustee's fee paid:	
Charged to income	250
Charged to corpus	400
Property taxes paid on land	140
Proceeds received from sale of stock	18,000

The stock was valued at $7,000 when transferred to the trust in 1984. Mark Wilson had paid $9,200 for the stock in 1982. The trustee distributed $5,100 to Doug during 1990 and paid $800 of estimated income taxes on behalf of the trust. Prepare a Form 1041 and accompanying Schedule K-1 for the Mark Wilson Trust (74-9871234).

14-57. Mark Meadows creates a trust in 1980 with Merchants Bank named as trustee. The trustee in its discretion is to pay out income to Mark's children, Angela and Barry, for 15 years. Then the trust will terminate, and its assets, including accumulated income, will be paid to Angela and Barry in equal amounts. (Separate shares are *not* to be maintained.) In the current year the trustee distributes $3,000 to Angela and $9,000 to Barry. The trust reports the following results for the current year.

	Amounts Allocable to	
	Income	Principal
Dividends	$50,000	
Interest on corporate bonds	4,000	
Interest on City of Cleveland bonds	9,000	
Long-term capital loss on sale of stock		$12,000[a]
Trustee's fee		2,400
CPA's fee for tax return preparation	400	

[a] Mr. Meadows purchased the stock for $30,000 in 1970. It is valued at $44,000 when he transfers it to the trust in 1980. The trust sells the stock for $18,000.

Prepare a Form 1041, including any needed Schedule K-1s, for the trust established by Mr. Meadows. The trustee's address is 201 Fifth Ave., New York, NY 10017. The trust's identification number is 74-5271322. Angela (127-14-1732) and Barry (127-14-1733) reside at 3 East 246th St., Huntington, NY 11743.

CASE STUDY PROBLEM

14-58. Arthur Rich, a widower, is considering setting up a trust (or trusts) for each of his three minor children. The trust will be funded at $900,000 (or $300,000 in the case of three trusts). He will name a bank as trustee. A friend suggested that he might want to consider a year-end of January 31 for the trusts. The friend also suggested that Arthur might want to make each trust a complex discretionary trust. Arthur is a little apprehensive about the idea of a trust that would be complex. Arthur's friend warned him that the trust income should not be spent on providing support for Arthur's children. The friend also said, "In 1985 I set up a trust for my minor child for 15 years and specified that at the end of the 15th year the property would pass back to me. Why don't you do the same? You might need the income from the $900,000 of property in your golden years?"

Required: Prepare a memorandum to the tax partner of your firm concerning the above client matter. As part of your analysis, consider the following:

a. What tax reasons, if any, can you think of for having three trusts instead of one?
b. What is the reason the friend suggested a year-end of January 31?
c. What is your reaction to the friend's suggestion about the year-end?
d. What is the tax treatment of a discretionary trust?
e. To what extent do trusts serve as income shifting arrangements?
f. What can you say to Arthur about his apprehension about a complex trust?
g. Why did the friend warn against spending income for support?
h. What is your opinion about the friend's suggestion for a 15-year trust?

TAX RESEARCH PROBLEMS

14-59. A simple trust incurs a trustee's fee of $3,000 for the current year. Its receipts during the current year are as follows:

	Amounts Allocable to	
	Income	Principal
Dividends from listed stocks	$22,000	
Interest on tax-exempt bonds	5,000	
Corporate distribution from a closely held firm; amount is not treated as a dividend because the firm has no earnings and profits	12,000	
Long-term capital gain on sale of land		32,000

What is the *deductible* portion of the trustee's fee?
A partial list of research sources is

- Reg. Secs. 1.652(b)-3(b) and 1.652(c)-4(e).
- Rev. Rul. 77-355, 1977-2 C.B. 82.
- Rev. Rul. 80-165, 1980-1 C.B. 134.

14-60. In 1990 Bill Ames dies at the age of 48. One of the items included in his gross estate is the principal residence where he and his widow, Lynn (age 46), lived for 20 years. In accordance with Bill's will, the residence and numerous other assets pass to a trust. Lynn is entitled to all of the trust income for the rest of her life.

In 1991 the trust sells the residence for $300,000. Its FMV in 1990 was $200,000. The trust pays $310,000 for a "replacement" house that Lynn moves into as her principal residence. May the trust use the nonrecognition rules of Sec. 1034?

A partial list of research sources is

- Secs. 1034 and 57.
- Rev. Rul. 54-583, 1954-2 C.B. 158.
- *Blanche F. Davies,* 54 T.C. 170 (1970).

14-61. A trust makes charitable contributions authorized by the trust instrument from principal, but not from income. What deduction is available on the trust's income tax return for the charitable contributions?

A partial list of research sources is

- Secs. 642(c)(1) and 661.
- Reg. Sec. 1.663(a)-2.
- *Estate of A. Lindsay O'Connor,* 69 T.C. 165 (1977).
- *U.S. Trust Co. v. U.S.,* 58 AFTR 2d 86-6152, 86-2 USTC ¶9777 (5th Cir., 1986).

15 U.S. Taxation of Foreign-Related Transactions

CHAPTER OUTLINE

LEARNING OBJECTIVES 15-2
JURISDICTION TO TAX 15-2
TAXATION OF U.S. CITIZENS AND RESIDENT ALIENS 15-4
   Foreign Tax Credit 15-4
   Foreign-Earned Income Exclusion 15-8
   U.S. Citizens and Resident Aliens Employed in Puerto Rico and U.S. Possessions 15-14
TAXATION OF NONRESIDENT ALIENS 15-15
   Definition of Nonresident Alien 15-16
   Investment Income 15-16
   Trade or Business Income 15-18
TAXATION OF U.S. PERSONS DOING BUSINESS ABROAD 15-20
   Domestic Subsidiary Corporations 15-21
   Foreign Branches 15-21
   Foreign Corporations 15-21
   Controlled Foreign Corporations 15-25
   Special Foreign Corporation Forms 15-34
   Foreign Sales Corporations 15-34
   Domestic International Sales Corporations 15-39
   Possessions Corporations 15-40
TAX PLANNING CONSIDERATIONS 15-42
   Deduction Versus Credit for Foreign Taxes 15-42
   Election to Accrue Foreign Taxes 15-42
   Special Earned Income Elections 15-44
   Tax Treaties 15-45
   Special Resident Alien Elections 15-45
COMPLIANCE AND PROCEDURAL CONSIDERATIONS 15-46
   Reporting the Foreign Tax Credit 15-46
   Reporting the Earned Income Exclusion 15-47
   Filing Requirements for Aliens and Foreign Corporations 15-47
   FSC and DISC Filing Requirements 15-48
PROBLEM MATERIALS 15-48
   Discussion Questions 15-48
   Problems 15-50
   Tax Form/Return Preparation Problems 15-55
   Case Study Problem 15-55
   Tax Research Problems 15-56

LEARNING OBJECTIVES

After studying this chapter, you should be able to

1. Understand the characteristics used to determine the U.S. taxes owed on a foreign-related transaction
2. Determine the foreign tax credit available to a U.S. taxpayer
3. Calculate the earned income exclusion available to U.S. taxpayers employed abroad
4. Determine whether a foreign individual is a resident or nonresident alien
5. Determine the U.S. tax liability for a nonresident alien or foreign corporation
6. Calculate the deemed paid tax credit available for an investor in a foreign corporation
7. Determine whether a foreign corporation is a CFC or not
8. Explain the special tax provisions applying to a controlled foreign corporation
9. Explain the special tax benefits accruing to a foreign sales corporation
10. Calculate the annual interest charge resulting from a domestic international sales corporation's deferred tax liability

Taxes imposed by the U.S. government on international transactions must be considered when making many kinds of business decisions. For example, U.S. income tax considerations affect whether a foreign business should be conducted directly by a U.S. corporation or indirectly through a foreign subsidiary corporation. The placement and compensation of U.S. employees in businesses operated outside the United States also requires careful consideration because, in many cases, such individuals can exempt part or all of their foreign salaries and allowances from U.S. taxation.

This chapter is intended to provide a general awareness of the U.S. tax laws in an international setting. The discussion is limited to coverage of the U.S. taxation of international operations because of the impracticality of examining the laws of individual foreign countries in the space provided.

JURISDICTION TO TAX

OBJECTIVE 1
Understand the characteristics used to determine the U.S. taxes owed on a foreign-related transaction

The U.S. income tax laws use the following four characteristics to determine the tax treatment accorded foreign-related transactions:

- The taxpayer's country of citizenship
- The taxpayer's country of residence
- The type of income earned
- The location where the income is earned

Table 15-1 illustrates that changing these four characteristics can substantially alter the taxpayer's U.S. tax treatment. The discussion examines how these characteristics interact.

Typical Misconception

Many people believe that income earned outside the United States is not subject to taxation by the United States. This is incorrect. U.S. citizens, residents, and domestic corporations are taxable by the United States on their worldwide income.

TABLE 15-1 *U.S. Jurisdiction for Taxation*

Taxpayer Classification	Income Subject to U.S. Taxation
U.S. citizen	Worldwide income
Domestic corporation	Worldwide income
Resident alien	Worldwide income
Nonresident alien	1. U.S. source investment income 2. U.S. source and some foreign source income that is effectively connected with the conduct of a U.S. trade or business
Foreign corporation	1. U.S. source investment income 2. U.S. source and some foreign source income that is effectively connected with the conduct of a U.S. trade or business

The U.S. tax laws provide different tax treatments according to the taxpayer's country of citizenship or country of organization. U.S. citizens and domestic corporations[1] are taxed by the United States on their worldwide income. Individuals who are not U.S. citizens and foreign corporations are taxed according to their country of residence.

Individuals who are not U.S. citizens are called **aliens.** The U.S. income tax laws divide aliens into two classes: resident aliens and nonresident aliens. A **resident alien** is an individual whose residence is the United States *but* who is not a U.S. citizen. Such individuals are taxed on their worldwide income in the same manner as a U.S. citizen. A **nonresident alien** is an individual whose residence is not the United States *and* who is not a U.S. citizen. These individuals are taxed only on their U.S. source investment income and their income that is effectively connected with a U.S. trade or business.

A foreign corporation is a U.S. resident if it conducts trade or business activities in the United States during the year. A resident foreign corporation is taxed on its U.S. source investment income and its income that is effectively connected with a U.S. trade or business. A nonresident foreign corporation is taxed only on its U.S. investment income.

U.S. citizens, resident aliens, and domestic corporations generally receive the same tax treatment for the various kinds of income that they earn. They are taxed on their worldwide income. In general, the same rules apply whether the income is earned in the United States, in a foreign country, or a U.S. possession. Some special treatments are available for income earned in foreign countries or in U.S. possessions.

1. Compensation received by a U.S. citizen or resident alien who works in a foreign country or countries for an extended period of time is eligible for a special exclusion of up to $70,000.
2. The income taxes paid to a foreign country or a U.S. possession can be credited against the U.S. tax liability. This tax credit is limited to the portion of the taxpayer's U.S. tax liability that is attributable to non-U.S. income.

The tax treatment accorded nonresident aliens and foreign corporations depends upon whether they conducted a trade or business in the United States at some time during the year. If no such activities are conducted, the nonresident aliens and foreign corporations are taxed only on their U.S. source investment income. If they conduct a trade or business in the United States at some time during the year, the nonresident

Key Point

The place where income is earned or sourced (either U.S. or foreign) is determined under a complex set of rules, depending upon the type of income. For example, with certain exceptions, interest income is sourced in the country of residence of the obligor.

---

[1] Sections 7701(a)(3) and (4) define a domestic corporation as a corporation created or organized under federal law or the laws of one of the 50 states or the District of Columbia. All other corporations are foreign corporations.

aliens and foreign corporations are taxed on both their U.S. source investment income and their income that is effectively connected with the conduct of the U.S. trade or business. Trade or business and investment income earned by aliens and foreign corporations in foreign countries is generally exempt from U.S. taxation.

TAXATION OF U.S. CITIZENS AND RESIDENT ALIENS

This portion of the chapter examines the two most often encountered foreign tax provisions applicable to U.S. citizens and resident aliens—the foreign tax credit and the foreign-earned income exclusion. Both provisions reduce the burden of having income taxed both in the foreign country in which it is earned and in the United States.

Foreign Tax Credit

OBJECTIVE 2
Determine the foreign tax credit available to a U.S. taxpayer

The **foreign tax credit** permits U.S. taxpayers to avoid double taxation by crediting income taxes paid or accrued to (1) a foreign country (including political subdivisions like provinces and cities) or (2) a U.S. possession against the U.S. income tax liability. The foreign tax credit reduces a U.S. taxpayer's total worldwide tax liability on income earned in foreign countries or U.S. possessions to the higher of the U.S. or the foreign tax rate.

Key Point
This double taxation is caused by two different jurisdictions taxing the same income, rather than one jurisdiction taxing the same income twice (such as dividends from a C corporation). The foreign-earned income exclusion and income tax treaties, as well as the foreign tax credit, are all ways of mitigating the double tax.

Creditable Taxes. The foreign tax credit benefits are available only for income taxes paid or accrued to a foreign country or a U.S. possession. Other foreign taxes are deductible according to the rules of Code Sec. 164 that are explained in Chapter 14 of the companion volume—*Prentice Hall's Federal Taxation: Individuals.*

The IRS regularly promulgates information as to the creditability of specific foreign tax levies.[2] These notices save time and effort in determining whether a specific tax levy is creditable. Some foreign tax levies have been the subject of litigation. Summaries of these promulgations and judicial decisions can be found in the major tax services.

Additional Comment
Recognize that foreign income taxes are also deductible under Sec. 164. However, taxpayers may not both deduct and credit the same foreign income taxes. Whether a taxpayer credits or deducts the foreign income taxes is an annual election.

Eligibility for the Credit. Section 901(a) permits U.S. citizens and resident aliens to claim a foreign tax credit for income taxes paid or accrued to a foreign country or a U.S. possession. This type of tax credit is known as a *direct credit.*

Taxpayers who use the accrual method of accounting must claim the foreign tax credit in the year in which the tax levy accrues. A taxpayer who uses the cash method of accounting claims the foreign tax credit in the year in which the tax is paid unless a special election is made to accrue the taxes (the advantages of this election are discussed in the Tax Planning Considerations section of this chapter).

Translation of the Foreign Tax Payments. Determining the amount of the credit necessitates translating the tax payment made in a foreign currency into U.S. dollars.

---

[2] Reg. Sec. 1.901-2. See, for example, Rev. Rul. 89-44, 1989-1 C.B. 237, relating to taxes levied by South Africa. Many additional private letter rulings have been issued in recent years that examine the creditability of foreign taxes for particular taxpayers.

Cash-basis taxpayers use the exchange rate on the payment date to do this. Accrual-basis taxpayers use the exchange rate on the date the foreign tax accrues to calculate a tentative foreign tax credit amount. Generally, this is the last day of the tax year that is used for foreign tax purposes. If the exchange rate changes between the accrual date and the payment date, an accrual-basis taxpayer must make an adjustment to the amount of the credit for the increase or decrease in the translated tax amount.[3]

Example 15-1 ■ U.S. citizen Bill is a resident of Country A during 1990. Country A permits its residents to make a single tax payment on the first day of the third month following the close of the taxpayer's tax year. Bill's tax year for both U.S. and Country A taxing purposes is the calendar year. Bill remits a 60,000 pirog payment for 1990's Country A taxes on March 1, 1991. The exchange rate between the pirog and the U.S. dollar on December 31, 1990, is 1 pirog = $0.50 (U.S.). The exchange rate on the March 1, 1991, payment date is 1 pirog = $0.60 (U.S.). If Bill uses the cash method of accounting, a $36,000 (60,000 pirogs × $0.60) foreign tax credit can be claimed. If Bill uses the accrual method of accounting, the year-end foreign tax credit amount is $30,000 (60,000 pirogs × $0.50). This amount increases to $36,000 (60,000 pirogs × $0.60) because of the exchange rate change that takes place between the accrual and payment dates. ■

Foreign Tax Credit Limitation

Additional Comment

The numerator of the limiting fraction is U.S. taxable income from foreign sources. The foreign taxes actually paid or accrued are computed using the tax laws of the foreign jurisdiction. Since these tax laws may differ significantly, determining whether the limitation is a limiting factor cannot necessarily be determined by simply comparing the stated tax rates of the two countries.

CALCULATION OF THE GENERAL LIMITATION. The foreign tax credit limitation was instituted to prevent the credit from being used to reduce taxes levied on income earned in the United States. This limit, which sets the maximum foreign tax credit as that portion of the gross U.S. tax liability originating from foreign source taxable income, is calculated as follows:

$$\text{Overall foreign tax credit limitation} = \text{U.S. tax liability} \times \frac{\text{Taxable income from all foreign countries}}{\text{Total worldwide taxable income}}$$

The foreign tax credit equals the lesser of (1) the creditable taxes paid or accrued to all foreign countries and U.S. possessions or (2) the overall foreign tax credit limitation. The overall limitation permits taxpayers to offset "excess" foreign taxes paid in one country against "excess" limitation amounts that result from activities in other countries during the same tax year. The only caveat is that the total foreign taxes paid or accrued on foreign source taxable income may not exceed the total U.S. tax due on such income.[4]

Example 15-2 ■ U.S. citizen Theresa has $10,000 of taxable income from U.S. sources and $10,000 of taxable income (wages) from Country B in 1991. Theresa pays $3,200 of taxes to Country B in 1991. Assuming a 28% U.S. tax rate, Theresa's gross U.S. tax liability can be determined as follows:

---

[3] Sec. 986(a) and Rev. Ruls. 73-491, 1973-2 C.B. 267 and 73-506, 1973-2 C.B. 268. If the taxpayer has filed his U.S. tax return by the date the foreign tax is paid, an amended tax return must be filed to report the amount of the increase or decrease in the credit.

[4] Sec. 904(a). The "excess" foreign tax amount equals the excess of the foreign taxes paid or accrued over the foreign tax credit limitation. The "excess" limitation amount equals the excess of the foreign tax credit limitation over the foreign taxes paid or accrued.

Self-Study Question

Richards Corporation, a U.S. corporation, earns $100,000 in Country X, $200,000 in Country Z, and $200,000 in the U.S. It pays $10,000 in taxes to X and $90,000 in taxes to Z. Assume a flat U.S. tax rate of 34%. Compute Richards's post-credit U.S. tax liability.

Answer

Pre-credit U.S. tax = $170,000 ($500,000 × 0.34). The credit is the lesser of $100,000 ($10,000 + $90,000) or $102,000 ($170,000 × 300/500). Note that although Richards pays taxes to Country Z at a much higher rate than the U.S. rate, all of the foreign taxes are creditable because the limit is computed on an overall basis and the Country X tax rate is so low.

Source of Income	Taxable Income	U.S. Tax Liability
United States	$10,000	$2,800
Country B	10,000	2,800
Total	$20,000	$5,600

Theresa's foreign tax credit limitation is determined as follows:

$$\$2,800 = \$5,600 \times \frac{\$10,000}{\$20,000}$$

Without any limit on the foreign tax credit, Theresa could take a $3,200 credit for foreign taxes paid, which would reduce the tax on U.S. income to $2,400 ($5,600 − $3,200). The foreign tax credit limitation reduces the foreign tax credit to the amount of U.S. taxes owed on the Country B income, or $2,800. This limit ensures that full U.S. tax is paid on the U.S. income. As will be discussed below, the excess credit amount can be carried back and over to other tax years. ■

DETERMINING THE INCOME AMOUNTS. The income amounts used in the credit limitation calculation are determined according to the source of income rules found in Secs. 861 through 865. These rules can be summarized as follows:

- Personal service income—compensation for personal services is earned in the location where the personal services are performed.

- Sales of personal property (other than inventory property)—income from this category of property sales involving a U.S. resident is earned in the United States. Income from such sales earned by a nonresident is earned outside the United States.[5]

- Sales of inventory property—income derived from inventory property that is purchased and sold is earned in the country where the sale occurs. Income from inventory property that is produced and sold is earned partially in the country where the production occurs and partially where the sale occurs.[6]

- Rents and royalties—rental or royalty income is earned in the place where the tangible and intangible property is located or used. For intangible properties (e.g., patents, copyrights, trademarks, and goodwill) this rule applies if the income is contingent on the productivity, use, or disposition of the intangible property.

- Sales of real property—income derived from the sale of real property is earned in the country where the property is located.

- Interest—interest income is generally earned in the obligor's country of residence. For this purpose, a U.S. resident includes U.S. citizens, resident aliens, domestic corporations, and foreign partnerships and foreign corporations that conduct a U.S. trade or business during the tax year.

- Dividends—dividend income is generally earned in the distributing corporation's country of incorporation.

---

[5] Sec. 865(a). Income from sales of personal property (including inventory) by a nonresident that is attributable to an office or place of business located in the United States is considered to have been earned in the United States. Section 865(g) defines the terms resident and nonresident for personal property sales. The definition used is generally based on the individual's domicile.

[6] Sec. 865(b) and Reg. Secs. 1.863-3(b) and (c). For tax purposes an inventory sale generally takes place in the location where the title passes from the buyer to the seller. The IRS may depart from this general rule where the sale is arranged in a particular manner for tax-avoidance purposes.

Additional Comment

In general, deductions follow the income associated with them. Deductions not associated with a specific type of income (such as charitable contributions and standard deductions) are allocated to all classes of income.

Deductions and losses are allocated to the foreign source gross income according to the rules outlined in Treas. Reg. Sec. 1.861-8 and reduce the foreign source taxable income amount. For individual taxpayers, taxable income is computed without any deduction being claimed for personal exemptions. Itemized deductions are allocated between U.S. and foreign source income. These rules are beyond the scope of this text.

FOREIGN TAX CREDIT CARRYBACKS AND CARRYOVERS. Excess foreign tax credits can be carried back 2 years and forward 5 years to a tax year in which the taxpayer has an excess foreign tax credit limitation. The total of the foreign taxes paid or accrued in a tax year, plus any carryback or carryover of excess credits to the tax year, cannot exceed the taxpayer's foreign tax credit limitation. When a taxpayer reports excess credits in more than one year, the excess credits are used in a first-in, first-out (FIFO) manner.[7]

Example 15-3 ■

Additional Comment

Since 1988, U.S. tax rates tend to be lower than the tax rates of many foreign jurisdictions. This fact, coupled with the imposition of separate limitation baskets, has caused many taxpayers to remain in an excess foreign tax credit position.

U.S. citizen Kathy accrues $125,000 of creditable foreign taxes in 1991. Kathy's 1991 foreign tax credit limitation is $80,000. The $45,000 of 1991 excess credits can be carried back to 1989 and 1990 and forward to 1992 through 1996. The use of the credit carryback is illustrated below.

	1989	1990	1991
Foreign tax accrual	$80,000	$ 90,000	$125,000
Foreign tax credit limitation	85,000	100,000	80,000
Excess credits			45,000
Excess limitation	5,000	10,000	

The excess credits are first carried back to 1989 and then to 1990. Amended tax returns must be filed for both 1989 and 1990 to claim the $15,000 of credit carryback that can be used in those two years. The remaining $30,000 ($45,000 − $15,000) of excess credits can be carried forward and are lost if not used by the end of 1996. ■

SPECIAL FOREIGN TAX CREDIT LIMITATIONS. For many taxpayers, more than one foreign tax credit calculation is required. The Sec. 904 foreign tax credit limitations create a number of "baskets" of income, for which separate foreign tax credit limitation calculations must be made.[8] These baskets include

Typical Misconception

A separate limitation applies to the dividends received from each, separate noncontrolled foreign corporation.

- Passive income: Income classified as foreign personal holding company income. This basket generally includes dividends, interest, annuities, rents, and royalties.
- High withholding tax interest: Interest income that is subject to a withholding tax (or similar gross-basis tax) of a foreign country or U.S. possession where the tax rate is at least 5%.
- Financial services income: Income that is (1) derived from the active conduct of banking, financing, or a similar business, or the investment activities of an insurance company, or (2) derived from insurance under the Subpart F income rules.
- Shipping income: Income classified as foreign base company shipping income under the Subpart F income rules.
- Noncontrolled foreign corporation (Sec. 902) dividends: Dividend income received by a corporate shareholder owning at least 10% of the stock of each noncontrolled (up to 50% U.S.-owned) foreign corporation.

[7] Sec. 904(c).
[8] Sec. 904(d)(1).

- Foreign oil and gas income.
- Dividends from a domestic international sales corporation (DISC) or former DISC.
- Taxable income attributable to the foreign trade income of a foreign sales corporation (FSC).
- Distributions from a FSC or a former FSC.
- Income other than the income included in any of the items listed above.

For some taxpayers, their income will fall only into the last, "other income" category. These taxpayers must make only one calculation of their foreign tax credit limitation. Other taxpayers may be required to make only two or three calculations of foreign tax credit limitations. Many of the large multinational corporations, of course, are required to make each of the calculations.

Excess foreign taxes paid or accrued within a particular foreign tax credit basket cannot be used to offset excess limitation amounts within another basket. By separating the calculation of the foreign tax credit limitation into separate pools, taxpayers are prevented from using excess credits arising from foreign taxes paid or accrued on income taxable at a high rate in a foreign country (e.g., salary or business profits) to offset U.S. taxes owed on income taxed at a low tax rate in a foreign country or not taxed at all (e.g., interest, dividends, or shipping income).

Example 15-4 ■ Assume the same facts as in Example 15-2, except that Theresa also earns $10,000 of interest income in Country C that is not subject to local taxation. The additional U.S. tax liability resulting from this interest income is $2,800 ($10,000 × 0.28). Two foreign tax credit limitations must be calculated for Theresa:

$$\text{Interest Income} \quad \$2,800 = \$8,400 \times \frac{\$10,000}{\$30,000}$$

$$\text{Wages Income} \quad \$2,800 = \$8,400 \times \frac{\$10,000}{\$30,000}$$

Theresa can claim a $2,800 foreign tax credit—the lesser of the $2,800 foreign tax credit limitation or the $3,200 tax accrual—with respect to the Country B wages. No foreign tax credit can be claimed with respect to the Country C interest income since no foreign taxes were paid on this income. Even though the interest income is foreign source income and the worldwide method of calculating the foreign tax credit limitation is used by the United States, the $400 of excess taxes paid with respect to the Country B wages cannot be used to offset the U.S. taxes owed on the Country C interest income. This inability to offset the two amounts occurs because the interest income is included in the separate, passive income basket and the salary income is included in the "other income" basket. Theresa must still carry the excess foreign taxes back to the second preceding tax year. ■

Topic Review 15-1 presents a summary of the foreign tax credit provisions.

OBJECTIVE 3
Calculate the earned income exclusion available to U.S. taxpayers employed abroad

Foreign-Earned Income Exclusion

Special earned income exclusions exist for individuals working in foreign countries, Puerto Rico, and certain U.S. possessions. These exclusions are examined in the next two sections of this chapter.

TOPIC REVIEW 15-1

Foreign Tax Credit

1. Foreign income taxes paid or accrued to a foreign country or a U.S. possession are able to be deducted or credited by U.S. taxpayers.
2. The election to deduct or credit foreign taxes is made annually. Generally a taxpayer will elect to credit their foreign taxes.
3. Cash method of accounting taxpayers can elect to accrue their foreign taxes. This election generally accelerates by one year the time for claiming the credit and may reduce the need to carry back or carry over excess credits.
4. A direct credit is available for foreign taxes paid or accrued by the taxpayer as well as for foreign taxes withheld by a foreign payor.
5. Foreign taxes are translated at the exchange rate for the date on which they are accrued or paid depending on the taxpayer's accounting method. If the exchange rate changes between the accrual date and the payment date, an adjustment must be made by an accrual method taxpayer for the difference in the two amounts. This difference may increase or decrease the foreign tax credit that is claimed.
6. The foreign tax credit limitation prevents foreign taxes from offsetting the U.S. tax liability on U.S. source income. The foreign tax credit that can be claimed is the lesser of (1) the creditable taxes paid or accrued to all foreign countries and U.S. possessions, or (2) the overall foreign tax credit limitation. Excess credits can be carried back 2 years and forward 5 years. A series of special foreign tax credit limitations apply to many taxpayers (e.g., passive income limitation, foreign oil and gas income, etc.). An excess credit amount from one special limitation cannot be used claimed against an excess limitation amount available with another special limitation.

U.S. Citizens and Resident Aliens Employed Abroad. U.S. citizens and resident aliens employed abroad are taxed by the United States on their worldwide income. The individuals may incur additional costs when living abroad in order to maintain the same standard of living they had in the United States. In addition, overseas employment may involve inconveniences, substandard living conditions, and hazardous duty. These individuals are generally paid special allowances to compensate for the higher foreign living costs and the inconveniences encountered. These special allowances may be taxed by both the United States and the country of residence. The U.S. employer generally compensates U.S. employees for these additional tax costs so individuals do not bear any increased tax burden. All of these costs can make hiring a U.S. national more expensive than hiring a non-U.S. national who has the same skills.

To help U.S. firms compete abroad, the U.S. government established a policy of reducing the U.S. tax burden on U.S. citizens and resident aliens living abroad for an extended period of time. Taxpayers who are bona fide residents of a foreign country (or countries) for an entire tax year, or who are physically present in a foreign country (or countries) for 330 full days[9] out of a 12-month period, can exclude $70,000 of foreign-earned income in 1987 and later tax years. This benefit, which is known as the *foreign-earned income exclusion,* is available to taxpayers who meet the bona fide resident test or the physical presence test.

Bona Fide Resident Test. A U.S. citizen (but not a resident alien) satisfies the bona fide resident test of Sec. 911(d)(1)(A) if that individual (1) has been a resident of

---
[9] A "full" day is a continuous 24-hour period beginning with midnight and ending with the following midnight.

a foreign country (or countries) for an uninterrupted period which includes an entire tax year and (2) has maintained a tax home in a foreign country (or countries) during the period of residence.

For Sec. 911 purposes, an individual's tax home is defined in the same way it is for determining the deductibility of travel expenses incurred while away from home.[10] In other words, an individual's tax home is his or her regular or principal place of business. Temporary absences from the foreign country for trips back to the United States or to other foreign countries normally do not interrupt an individual's foreign residency period.

An individual is not a bona fide resident of a foreign country if that person (1) submits a statement to the taxing authorities of that country claiming to be a nonresident *and* (2) receives a tax exemption for earned income from that country's taxing authorities based upon being a nonresident.[11]

An individual does not qualify for the earned income exclusion until he or she has been a foreign resident for an *entire tax year*. At the end of that time, the individual can retroactively claim the Sec. 911 benefits from the date that he or she became a foreign resident.

> **Key Point**
> Whether a U.S. citizen has established foreign residency is based on all the pertinent facts and circumstances. This is different from the determination of whether a foreign citizen has established U.S. residency. The latter is based upon either the (1) green card test or (2) the substantial physical presence test (discussed later in this chapter).

Example 15-5

> **Self-Study Question**
> During a 12-month period, U.S. citizen Robert's work requires him to be physically present in a foreign country for 317 days. If Robert delays his return to the U.S. by vacationing overseas for 13 more days, will he qualify for the foreign-earned income exclusion?
>
> **Answer**
> Yes. The foreign physical presence can be for any reason.

U.S. citizen Mark, who uses the calendar year as his tax year, is transferred by his employer to Country P. Mark becomes a Country P resident upon his arrival at noon on July 15, 1988. At that time Mark's tax home is established in P's capital city. Mark's residency in P is maintained until his return to the United States at 2 p.m. on January 10, 1991. Mark first qualifies for the Sec. 911 benefits as a bona fide resident of a foreign country on December 31, 1989. This permits Mark to claim the earned income exclusion starting with July 15, 1988. Mark can continue to claim the exclusion through January 10, 1991. ∎

Physical Presence Test. A taxpayer who cannot satisfy the bona fide resident requirements can still qualify for the Sec. 911 benefits by satisfying the physical presence test of Sec. 911(d)(1)(B). To qualify, the taxpayer must meet two requirements.

1. Be physically present in a foreign country (or countries) for at least 330 *full* days during a 12-month period.
2. Maintain a tax home in a foreign country (or countries) during the period of presence.

> **Typical Misconception**
> A day is not just any 24-hour period. In order to count a day, the taxpayer must be in a foreign country for a period of 24 hours beginning and ending at midnight.

The 330 days do not need to be consecutive, nor does the taxpayer need to be in the same country at all times. The 12-month period may begin on any day of the calendar year. The period ends on the day before the corresponding calendar day in the twelfth succeeding month.

Example 15-6

Assume the same facts as in Example 15-5. The 330 days of physical presence commence with the first full day Mark is present in Country P (July 16, 1988) and includes a total of 169 days through the end of 1988. The 161 additional days needed to reach 330 days include January 1, 1989, through June 10, 1989. One possible 12-month period for Mark thus commences on July 16, 1988, and runs through July 15, 1989. An alternative 12-month period could include, for example, June 11, 1988, through June 10, 1989, whereby the 330 days of physical presence are at the end of the time period. ∎

---

[10] Sec. 911(d)(3).
[11] Sec. 911(d)(5).

Foreign-Earned Income Defined. Earned income means wages, salaries, professional fees, and other amounts received as compensation for personal services actually rendered.[12] Earned income is excludable only if it is foreign source income. The source of income rules described above are used to determine whether income is earned in the United States or a foreign country. In general income is allocated to the location where the services are performed. If services are performed in more than one location during the tax year, allocation between the two or more locations is based on the number of days worked in each location.[13]

Fringe benefits that are excluded from gross income under a Code provision other than Sec. 911 (e.g., meals and lodging furnished for the convenience of the employer and excluded under Sec. 119) do not diminish the annual dollar ceiling for the exclusion. Items that generally are taxable to the recipient, but which are excluded from the definition of earned income for Sec. 911 purposes, include pensions and annuities, amounts paid by the United States or one of its agencies to an employee,[14] and amounts received more than one tax year after the tax year in which the services are performed.

Additional Comment

Note that in Example 15-6, Mark would prefer to use the 12-month period of June 11, 1988, through June 10, 1989, when computing the exclusion for 1988 in order to have more days of the year in the qualifying period and, hence, a larger exclusion.

Amount of the Exclusion. The earned income exclusion is available only for the number of days in the tax year during which the taxpayer meets either the bona fide resident requirement or the physical presence requirement. Section 911(b)(2)(A) limits the earned income exclusion to the lesser of the following:

- The individual's foreign-earned income
- The amount of the daily exclusion times the number of days during the tax year that the individual qualifies for the exclusion

The annual and daily limits are $70,000 and $191.78 ($191.26 in leap years), respectively.

Example 15-7 ■ U.S. citizen Lee, who uses the calendar year as his tax year, establishes a tax home and residency in Country A on November 1, 1989 (the 305th day of the year). Lee maintains his tax home and residency there until March 31, 1991 (the 90th day), when Lee returns to the United States. Lee earns salary and allowances at a $15,000 monthly rate while employed abroad. The amount of Lee's available exclusion is determined as follows:

Taxable Year	Foreign-Earned Income	Qualifying Days (1)	Daily Exclusion Amount (2)	Amount Excluded (3) = (1) × (2)
1989	$ 30,000	61	191.78	$11,699
1990	180,000	365	191.78	70,000
1991	45,000	90	191.78	17,260

Individuals satisfying the residency requirement can claim the exclusion for each day they are a resident of the foreign country whether or not they are physically

---

[12] Sec. 911(d)(2).
[13] Sec. 911(b)(1)(A).
[14] Civilian officers and employees of the U.S. government who are employed abroad can exclude from gross income certain foreign area allowances and cost-of-living allowances under Sec. 912. No further coverage of these rules is presented because of their limited applicability. Enlisted personnel serving in Operation Desert Storm can exclude compensation received for active service for any month during any part of which they served in a combat zone or were hospitalized as a result of injuries sustained in a combat zone. Commissioned officers can exclude up to $500 of combat pay per month.

present in a foreign country on that day. Individuals satisfying the physical presence requirement can claim the exclusion for each day of a 12-month period that falls within the tax year whether they are physically present in a foreign country on that day or not. Because an individual only needs to be physically present in a foreign country for 330 days out of the 12-month period (365 days), it is possible that an individual might qualify for the exclusion for as many as 35 days prior to arrival in the foreign country, or for as many as 35 days subsequent to departure from the foreign country. Such an extension of the qualifying period in the year of arrival and/or departure may be a reason for calculating the exclusion using the physical presence requirement in these years.[15]

Example 15-8 ■ Assume the same facts as in Example 15-7, except that it is also known that Lee was physically present in Country A at all times from his arrival in 1989 to his departure in 1991. Lee's first 330 full days in Country A run from November 2, 1989, through September 27, 1990. Lee's last 330 full days in Country A run from May 5, 1990, through March 30, 1991. Lee's two corresponding 12-month periods run from September 28, 1989 (the 271st day of 1989), through September 27, 1990, and from May 5, 1990, through May 4, 1991 (the 124th day of 1991). The amount of Lee's available exclusion is determined below:

Taxable Year	Foreign-Earned Income	Qualifying Days (1)	Daily Exclusion Amount (2)	Amount Excluded (3) = (1) × (2)
1989	$ 30,000	95	$191.78	$18,219
1990	180,000	365	191.78	70,000
1991	45,000	124	191.78	23,781

Lee obtains a larger exclusion in 1989 and 1991 under the physical presence test. The additional benefits of using this tax planning device are diminished to the extent that Lee is physically present in the United States during his period of foreign residence. ■

Key Point

A taxpayer may elect to use or not use the foreign-earned income exclusion and the housing cost exclusion. A choice between excluding or deducting the housing cost amount, however, is not generally available (see below). Once an election to take an exclusion is made, it is effective for that year and all subsequent years.

Housing Cost Exclusion or Deduction. Section 911(a)(2) permits an individual taxpayer who is eligible for the foreign-earned income exclusion to exclude or deduct a **housing cost amount,** which is determined as follows:

$$\text{Housing cost amount} = \text{Housing expenses incurred} - \text{Base housing amount}$$

$$\text{Base Housing Amount} = 0.16 \times \text{Salary of a federal employee compensated at Step 1, GS-14 rate} \times \frac{\text{Number of qualifying days in the tax year}}{\text{Number of days in the tax year}}$$

The annual rate of pay for an individual having the federal government Step 1, GS-14 pay classification is determined as of January 1 of the year in which the taxpayer's tax year begins. For 1990 and 1991 these amounts are $48,592 and $50,342, respectively. This makes the base housing amount equal to $7,775 for 1990 and $8,055 for 1991 for taxpayers qualifying for the Sec. 911 benefits for the entire tax year. The daily base housing amount is $21.30 in 1990 and $22.07 in 1991.

---

[15] Reg. Sec. 1.911-3(d).

Housing expenses include any reasonable expenses paid or incurred for housing in a foreign country for the taxpayer, his spouse, and any dependents during the portion of the year that the taxpayer qualifies for the Sec. 911 benefits. Housing expenses also include expenses incurred for a second home if the taxpayer must maintain a separate home outside the United States for his spouse and dependents at a location other than their tax home because of adverse living conditions.[16]

The exclusion is limited to the lesser of the employer-provided amount or the individual's foreign-earned income. Any amount excluded as a housing cost amount reduces the taxpayer's foreign-earned income for purposes of computing the basic exclusion. Employer-provided amounts include any amounts which are foreign earned income and included in the employee's gross income for the tax year (without regard to Sec. 911). Such amounts include, but are not limited to, salary or allowances paid by the employer (including allowances other than housing allowances), reimbursements made for housing, in-kind housing (other than that excluded under Sec. 119), and reimbursements made to third parties on behalf of the employee.

Example 15-9 ■ U.S. citizen John is a bona fide resident of Country M for all of 1991. John, who uses the calendar year as his tax year, receives $120,000 in salary and allowances from his employer. Included in this total is $15,000 in housing allowances. Eligible housing expenses incurred by John in 1991 are $18,000. John's housing cost amount is $9,945 ($18,000 − $8,055). Since John's employer-provided amount is $120,000, all of the housing cost amount can be excluded. In addition, John can exclude the lesser of his foreign-earned income exclusion ceiling ($70,000, since he qualified for all of 1991) or his foreign-earned income (after a reduction for the housing cost amount exclusion) [$110,055 = $120,000 − $9,945]. Therefore, his total exclusion is $80,225 ($10,225 + $70,000). Only $39,775 of John's total compensation is subject to U.S. taxation. ■

Additional Comment
Employer-provided amounts include all compensation amounts provided by the employer (salary, bonus, allowances, etc.), not just the amount identified as the housing allowance.

Any portion of the housing cost amount that is not attributable to employer-provided amounts is a *for* AGI deduction.[17] Thus, if an individual has only self-employment income, the entire housing cost amount is deducted. Such would be the case in Example 15-9 if John were self-employed and the $120,000 represented commission income. His $9,945 housing cost amount could only be claimed as a *for* AGI deduction.

The housing cost deduction is limited to the taxpayer's foreign-earned income minus the sum of the foreign-earned income and housing cost amount exclusions. If the deduction for housing costs exceeds its limitation, the excess amount can be carried forward to the next year and deducted (subject to that year's limitation).

Key Point
If an individual has only W-2 income (no self-employment income), he is eligible for only the housing cost exclusion since the entire housing cost amount is attributable to employer-provided amounts. The housing cost exclusion and deduction can both be taken only in those situations where an individual has both W-2 income and self-employment income. Proration of the housing cost amount between a deduction and an exclusion is based on the relative amounts of W-2 income and self-employment income that the taxpayer has.

Disallowance of Deductions and Credits. Section 911(d)(6) prohibits taxpayers from claiming deductions or credits with respect to their excluded income. The rules used to determine the nondeductible portion of an individual's employment-related expenses and the noncreditable portion of an individual's foreign taxes are presented below.

EMPLOYMENT-RELATED EXPENSES. Any employment-related expenses that are allocated to a taxpayer's excluded foreign-earned income are nondeductible. Expenses that are related to other forms of income are deductible in full. Although housing

[16] Sec. 911(c)(2).
[17] Sec. 911(c)(3)(A).

expenses are related to overseas employment, no restriction is placed on deducting the housing cost amount.[18]

Example 15-10 ■ Don reports $150,000 of foreign-earned income and $15,000 of employment-related expenses in 1991. Don also incurs $12,000 of itemized deductions that are not directly related to foreign-earned income and that are not subject to the 2% of AGI floor. Don may exclude $70,000 of his foreign-earned income. The exclusion prevents Don from deducting $7,000 of employment-related expenses. All of the itemized deductions can be deducted.

$$\$7{,}000 \text{ (nondeductible expenses)} = \$15{,}000 \text{ (Expenses directly attributable to foreign-earned income)} \times \frac{\$70{,}000 \text{ (Excluded foreign-earned income)}}{\$150{,}000 \text{ (Total foreign-earned income)}} \blacksquare$$

FOREIGN INCOME TAXES. Foreign income taxes that are paid or accrued with respect to excluded foreign-earned income cannot be credited or deducted. The disallowed foreign taxes are determined by using the following formula.[19]

$$\text{Disallowed taxes} = \text{Foreign income taxes paid or accrued} \times \frac{\text{Excluded foreign-earned income (less expenses related to excluded income)}}{\text{Total foreign-earned income (less expenses related to foreign-earned income) subject to tax in the foreign country}}$$

If a taxpayer's income taxes are paid or accrued on earned income and other income and the taxes owed on the two amounts cannot be separated, the denominator of the fraction must include the total of all income amounts subject to tax in the foreign country (minus all related expenses).

Example 15-11 ■ Assume the same facts as in Example 15-10, except that Don also incurs $33,750 of Country F income taxes on his earned income. Don's $15,750 of noncreditable foreign taxes are computed as follows:

$$\$15{,}750 = \$33{,}750 \times \frac{\$70{,}000 - \$7{,}000}{\$150{,}000 - \$15{,}000}$$

Thus, Don can credit only $18,000 ($33,750 − $15,750) of his foreign taxes. ■

U.S. Citizens and Resident Aliens Employed in Puerto Rico and U.S. Possessions

Sections 931 and 933 provide special income exclusions for U.S. citizens or residents who earn income either in a U.S. possession (i.e., American Samoa, Guam, and the Northern Mariana Islands)[20] or in Puerto Rico. Under Secs. 931 and 933, a U.S.

---

[18] Sec. 911(d)(6) and Reg. Sec. 1.911-6(a). Miscellaneous itemized expenses are subject to the 2% nondeductible floor whether the taxpayer is eligible for the Sec. 911 exclusion or not.

[19] Reg. Sec. 1.911-6(c).

[20] Sec. 931(c). Special rules for residents of the Virgin Islands are found in Sec. 932. The rules presented here were enacted in the Tax Reform Act of 1986. Prior law applies until the implementing agreements are effective. To date such agreements have not been entered into.

TOPIC REVIEW 15-2

Foreign Earned Income and Housing Cost Amount Exclusions

1. U.S. citizens can qualify under the bona fide resident test; that is, they must have been a resident of a foreign country(ies) for an uninterrupted period including an entire tax year and have maintained a tax home in a foreign country(ies) during the residence period.
2. U.S. citizens and resident aliens are permitted to qualify under the physical presence test. They must (a) be physically present in a foreign country(ies) for at least 330 full days during a 12-month period and (b) maintain a tax home in a foreign country(ies) during the period of presence.
3. The earned income exclusion equals the lesser of (a) the taxpayer's foreign earned income or (b) the $191.78 daily exlusion ($191.26 in leap years) times the number of days in the tax year that the taxpayer qualifies for the exclusion.
4. For the residence test, qualifying days includes the number of days during the tax year that the taxpayer met the residency and tax home tests. For the physical presence test, the taxpayer can claim the exclusion for the number of days in any 12-month period that falls within the tax year whether the taxpayer is physically present in the foreign country(ies) on that day or not.
5. Employees can exclude a housing cost amount in addition to the basic earned income exclusion. Self-employed individuals can deduct the housing cost amount. The housing cost amount equals the housing expenses incurred minus the base housing amount ($8,055 for 1991) for the portion of the tax year for which the taxpayer qualifies for the earned income exclusion.
6. Taxpayers qualifying for the earned income exclusion are unable to claim deductions or credits with respect to their excluded income. The disallowed expenses equal the employee expenses directly attributable to the foreign earned income times the portion of the foreign earned income that is excluded. A similar rule applies to the foreign tax credit. The disallowed taxes equals the foreign income taxes paid or accrued times the portion of the foreign earned income (net of expenses related to such income) that is excluded.
7. Eligible taxpayers make the foreign earned income exclusion election by filing Form 2555. This form is also used for the housing cost exclusion or deduction. A taxpayer may revoke the earned income or housing cost exclusions with IRS consent. A 5-year waiting period is required before a new election can be made unless the IRS consents to an earlier re-election.

citizen or resident alien who has been a bona fide resident of Puerto Rico or a specified possession for an entire tax year can exclude any income that is derived from Puerto Rican sources, from sources within the specified possession, or from the conduct of a trade or business within any possession.

Topic Review 15-2 presents a summary of the foreign earned income and housing cost amount exclusions.

TAXATION OF NONRESIDENT ALIENS

Whether an alien individual is a U.S. resident or not determines the U.S. tax treatment of that person's income. Under Sec. 871, U.S. taxation of nonresident aliens is limited to (1) their U.S. source investment income and (2) any U.S. income (and limited foreign income) that is effectively connected with the conduct of a U.S. trade or business.

Definition of Nonresident Alien

OBJECTIVE 4
Determine whether a foreign individual is a resident or nonresident alien

Additional Comment
This weighted average counts each day in the current year as 1, each day in the immediately preceding year as 1/3, and each day in the year before that as 1/6.

With certain specific exceptions,[21] aliens who do not satisfy the Sec. 7701(b) definition of resident aliens are considered nonresident aliens. Aliens are U.S. residents if they meet one of the following tests:

1. *Lawful resident test:* They are lawful permanent residents of the United States at any time during the tax year. An alien having a "green card" visa status for immigration purposes is considered a permanent resident.
2. *Substantial presence test:* They are present in the United States for 31 or more days during the current calendar year *and* present in the United States for a total of 183 days during the current tax year and the two preceding tax years when using the weighted-average calculation described in Sec. 7701(b)(3)(A).

Example 15-12 ▪

Key Point
A citizen of another country generally is considered a U.S. resident if one of two tests are met: (1) The "green card" test (the individual is granted legal permission to reside permanently in the U.S.) or (2) a "substantial physical presence" test (the individual is physically present in the U.S. for at least (a) 31 days during the current year and (b) the sum of 183 days during the current tax year and the two preceding years [counting current-year days as 1, last-year days as 1/3, and the preceding-year days as 1/6]).

Marco, an alien individual, is present in the United States for 122 days in 1991 and 122 days each in 1989 and 1990. In determining his alien status, Marco counts all 122 days from 1991, one-third of the 122 days from 1990 (40.67 = 0.6667 × 122), and one-sixth of the 122 days from 1989 (20.33 = 0.1667 × 122), or a total 183 days (122 + 40.67 + 20.33). He satisfies both the 31-day and 183-day requirements.■

Aliens typically maintain a dual status in their first and last years in which they maintain residency. This dual status means that their tax computation is based on nonresident alien status for part of the tax year and resident alien status for the remainder of the tax year. An individual who is in his first year and who satisfies the lawful permanent resident test commences his residency period on the first day of the first year that he is physically present in the United States as a lawful permanent resident. An individual who satisfies the substantial presence test commencing with his first year becomes a resident on the first day of the first year that he is physically present in the United States.

Aliens terminate their residence on the last day of the last year that they are lawful residents in the United States. Aliens who satisfy the physical presence test for a particular year maintain residency through the last day of that year that they are physically present in the United States (ignoring periods of nominal U.S. presence).

Investment Income

OBJECTIVE 5
Determine the U.S. tax liability for a nonresident alien or foreign corporation

Typical Misconception
Alien individuals who are U.S. residents are taxable on their worldwide income, just as U.S. citizens are. They file a regular Form 1040. Nonresident aliens subject to U.S. taxation file Form 1040NR.

Passive or investment income is taxed to a nonresident alien only when it is U.S. source income. Section 871(a)(1)(A) includes the following types of income in this classification—interest; dividends; rents; salaries;[22] premiums; annuities; compensation; and other fixed or determinable annual or periodical gains, profits, or income. Capital gains earned in the United States (other than in the conduct of a U.S. trade or business) are only taxed to nonresident aliens if they are physcially present in the

---

[21] A nonresident alien can also become a resident alien by being married to a U.S. citizen or resident alien and electing to be treated as a resident alien under Sec. 6013(g). (See the Tax Planning Considerations section of this chapter.)

[22] Income earned from the performance of personal services is ordinarily trade or business income. Salary income is trade or business income even if the alien does not conduct a U.S. trade or business in the tax year in which the income is reported for tax purposes (e.g., no services are performed in the United States in the year in which a final paycheck is collected by a cash method of accounting taxpayer) if it is attributable to an earlier tax year and would have been treated as effectively connected with the conduct of a U.S. trade or business in that year.

United States for at least 183 days during the tax year.[23] Some exceptions to this general rule reduce the nonresident alien's U.S. tax burden:

- Interest income earned by a nonresident alien from deposits maintained with a U.S. or foreign office of a U.S. bank or other financial institution is exempt from U.S. taxation provided it is not effectively connected with the alien's conduct of a U.S. trade or business.
- Portfolio interest, that is, interest paid on registered and unregistered obligations issued by U.S. taxpayers and that are held by a nonresident alien as a portfolio investment, is exempt from U.S. taxation.[24]
- Income derived from the sale of personal property in the United States is not fixed or determinable annual or periodic income. As a result, casual sales of inventory that are not extensive enough to constitute a trade or business are not taxed in the United States.
- Gain from the sale of intangible assets (e.g., patents, copyrights, trademarks, etc.) is taxed as ordinary income to the extent that the payments are contingent on the productivity, use, or diposition of the intangible asset. Income that is not a contingent payment is a capital gain that is sourced inside the United States if it is sold by a U.S. resident and is sourced outside the United States if sold by a nonresident.

Example 15-13 ■ Paula is a citizen and resident of Country A. Paula licenses a patent to a U.S. corporation in return for a $2 per unit fee for each unit produced. During 1991, Paula receives $18,000 from the U.S. corporation as a licensing fee. Paula is not physically present in the United States during 1991. The $18,000 is a contingent payment and is taxed as ordinary income. If a single $18,000 payment is received in exchange for all rights to the patent, a sale of the patent would be deemed to have occurred outside the United States and is therefore exempt from U.S. taxation.■

Key Point
Many tax treaties reduce this flat 30% rate for specific types of income.

Ordinary investment income and capital gains earned by a nonresident alien are taxed at a 30% rate.[25] The rate is applied to the gross income amount. No deductions or losses can reduce the income that is taxed. Collection of the tax levy is accomplished by having the last U.S. payor withhold the tax levy from the amount that is paid to the alien. If the U.S. payor fails to withhold the proper amount of U.S. taxes, the payor becomes liable for the taxes if the alien does not pay them as well as any penalties and additions to tax that are otherwise attributable to failure to withhold.[26]

Example 15-14 ■ First State Bank issues the dividend checks for a domestic corporation. One of the corporation's shareholders is Kelly, a nonresident alien, who is to receive a $30,000 dividend. If the dividend is investment income to Kelly, First State Bank must withhold $9,000 ($30,000 × 0.30) in U.S. taxes from Kelly's payment. It must then remit these taxes to the U.S. government. Kelly need not make any other tax payments with respect to the dividend. The 30% rate that is applied to investment income is reduced by the terms of many tax treaties that the United States has

---

[23] Sec. 871(a)(2). The capital gains can be reduced by U.S. capital losses, and only the net gain is taxed.

[24] Portfolio obligations might include, for example, obligations issued by a domestic corporation in the Eurobond market.

[25] Sec. 871(a). The 30% tax rate applies to capital gains of a nonresident alien only if they are present in the United States for at least 183 days during a tax year. In most cases such a time period means that the individual is not a nonresident alien at all, but a resident alien.

[26] Secs. 1441(a) and 1461.

Trade or Business Income

A nonresident alien who owns or operates a business in the United States involving the sale of services, products, merchandise, and so on is considered to be engaged in the conduct of a U.S. trade or business. A partner in a partnership or a beneficiary of a trust or estate is considered to be conducting a U.S. trade or business if the partnership, trust, or estate is engaged in the conduct of a U.S. trade or business.

Nonresident aliens who (1) are in the United States for less than 90 days in a year; (2) are employed by a nonresident alien, a foreign partnership, or a foreign corporation that does not engage in the conduct of a U.S. trade or business or by a foreign place of business maintained by a U.S. party; and (3) do not earn more than $3,000 for their services are considered not to have engaged in the conduct of a U.S. trade or business. Their wages are exempt from U.S. taxation because such wages are classified as foreign source income.

Nonresident aliens who invest in stocks, securities, and so on through a broker are also considered not to have conducted a U.S. trade or business. As a result, their capital gains are exempt from U.S. taxation unless they are present in the United States for more than 183 days during the tax year which in most cases means that the individual is not a nonresident alien at all, but a resident alien.

Special Election for Real Estate Investors. A special election is available for investors in U.S. real estate. This election permits an alien's real estate activities to be considered a trade or business even though they would not otherwise meet the trade or business requirements (e.g., a passive investment in real estate). This election permits the taxpayer to claim all deductions and losses associated with the activities. If the election is not made and the activity does not constitute a trade or business, the rental income is taxed at a 30% rate (without any reduction for deductions and losses).[27] Gains from the sale of U.S. real property interests (whether capital or ordinary in nature) are taxed as effectively connected with the conduct of a U.S. trade or business. A U.S. real property interest is either a direct or indirect (e.g., an investment in a corporation or a partnership) interest in real property that is located in the United States.[28]

Effectively Connected Test. Income is "effectively connected" with the conduct of a U.S. trade or business if either an asset-use or business-activities test is satisfied. The asset-use test is satisfied if an asset is held or used in the conduct of a U.S. trade or business. The income that is generated by the asset is thus effectively connected with the conduct of a U.S. trade or business. For example, interest income earned by an alien from a certificate of deposit (CD) can be either investment income or trade or business income depending upon the relationship between the funds used to purchase the CD and the taxpayer's U.S. trade or business. The business-activities test is met if the activities of the U.S. trade or business are a material factor in the realization of the income. Capital gain income that is effectively connected with the conduct of a U.S. trade or business is taxable without regard to the number of days that the individual is physically present in the United States.

Income from the sale of inventory and other personal property by a nonresident alien is U.S. source and, therefore, taxable if the alien has a U.S. office and the sale is

---

[27] Sec. 871(d).
[28] Secs. 897(a) and (c).

attributable to that office. This rule does not apply, however, and the income is exempt from U.S. taxation as foreign source income if the property is for foreign use or disposition and if a non-U.S. office participated materially in the sale. When personal property is produced in the United States and then sold abroad by an alien, a portion of the income is allocated to the U.S. production and subject to taxation. The remainder is allocated to the location where the sale occurred and may or may not be taxed in the United States.

Calculating the Tax. An alien who conducts a U.S. trade or business may have to make two separate tax calculations. Investment income that is unrelated to the U.S. trade or business activities is taxed at a 30% rate (unless the rate is reduced by a tax treaty). This tax is collected through the withholding process. Trade or business income is reduced by all related expenses and losses. Nonresident aliens cannot use the standard deduction otherwise available for individual taxpayers. They must itemize their deductions. In addition, nonresident aliens are generally limited to a single personal exemption.[29]

The trade or business income for an unmarried nonresident alien is taxed using the tax rate schedules for a single taxpayer. A married nonresident alien uses the tax rate schedule for married individuals filing separately unless an election to file a joint return is made under Sec. 6013(g) (see the Tax Planning Considerations section of this chapter). The taxes that are owed on the trade or business income can be offset by any available tax credits. The net U.S. tax liability is then paid through estimated tax payments or a remittance that is made when the return is filed.

Example 15-15 ■

Self-Study Question

In Example 15-15, assume Maria also receives $10,000 interest income from a note she received upon the sale of some investment property she had owned in the U.S. How would this change Maria's total U.S. tax liability?

Answer

Maria's U.S. tax liability would increase by $3,000 ($10,000 × 0.30).

Maria is single and a citizen and resident of Country D. In 1991 Maria reports (1) $40,000 of dividend income from a U.S. corporation that is unrelated to Maria's U.S. trade or business and (2) $1,000 of itemized deductions. Maria's U.S. trade or business reports $300,000 of gross income from sales activities; $20,000 of interest income; $225,000 of expenses; and $4,000 of tax credits. Maria's tax liability on her dividend income is $12,000 ($40,000 × 0.30). The taxes owed on Maria's trade or business income are determined as follows:

Gross income:	
Sales	$300,000
Interest	20,000
Total gross income	$320,000
Minus: Trade or business expenses	(225,000)
Adjusted gross income	$ 95,000
Minus: Personal exemption	(2,150)
Itemized deductions	(1,000)
Taxable income	$91,850
Gross tax liability (single rate schedule)	$ 24,349
Minus: Tax credits	(4,000)
Net tax liability	$ 20,349

Maria's total U.S. tax liability is $32,349 ($12,000 + $20,349). ■

Topic Review 15-3 presents a summary of the tax rules applicable to nonresident alien individuals and foreign corporations.

---

[29] Section 873(b) permits certain personal deductions not directly related to trade or business activities to reduce the trade or business income.

TOPIC REVIEW 15-3

Taxation of Nonresident Aliens and Foreign Corporations

1. Nonresident aliens are alien individuals that do not maintain U.S. residency. Resident alien status can be obtained by satisfying either the lawful resident test or the substantial presence test.
2. Aliens will generally maintain a dual status in their first and last years of U.S. residency. The alien is taxed as a resident alien for part of each year and as a nonresident alien for the remainder of the year. Two different tax computations are required of the alien in these years.
3. Passive or investment income (e.g., dividends, interest, etc.) is taxed to a nonresident alien or foreign corporation only when it is U.S. source income. The income is taxed at a 30% rate with no deductions or exemptions permitted. A lower tax rate is permitted the passive or investment income under many of the tax treaties involving the United States and a foreign country.
4. Capital gains earned in the United States (other than those related to the conduct of a U.S. trade or business) are taxed at the 30% rate only if the alien is physically present in the United States for 183 or more days during the tax year. Foreign corporations are taxed only on the capital gains that are effectively connected with the conduct of a U.S. trade or business.
5. The U.S. income tax on the passive or investment income and capital gains is collected by means of withholding at the basic 30% tax rate or at the lower rate specified in a tax treaty. The U.S. tax liability is withheld by the U.S. payor who makes the payment to the nonresident alien or foreign corporation.
6. Ordinary income and capital gains earned by a nonresident alien or foreign corporation are taxed in the United States if they are "effectively connected with the conduct of a U.S. trade or business." The "effectively connected" concept requires satisfaction of the asset-use or business-activities test. Regular business expenses and losses are deductible against the "effectively connected" income. Individuals are permitted only a single personal exemption, and are not permitted to claim a standard deduction. The regular individual and corporate tax rates apply to taxable income. The individual and corporate alternative minimum taxes apply to nonresident aliens and foreign corporations on their U.S. activities. The tax owed on the effectively connected income is paid by means of estimated tax payments.
7. A special election is available to nonresident aliens to file a joint return with their U.S. citizen or resident alien spouse. This election requires the nonresident alien to be subject to worldwide taxation as if a resident alien.

TAXATION OF U.S. PERSONS DOING BUSINESS ABROAD

This section examines the tax laws that apply to U.S. persons that engage in overseas business activities. These activities can involve the exportation of U.S.-produced products, the performance of services overseas, or even the establishment of manufacturing or selling activities in one or more foreign countries. These overseas activities receive a number of favorable tax breaks, including the following:

- Foreign subsidiary corporations are generally exempt from U.S. taxation unless they conduct a U.S. trade or business or make U.S. investments. This tax

Taxation of U.S. Persons Doing Business Abroad • 15-21

Key Point
Note that the first two types (foreign subsidiary corporations and FSCs) of U.S. persons doing business abroad are foreign corporations, while the last two types (DISCs and possessions corporations) are U.S. corporations.

exemption extends to the foreign corporation's U.S. owners, who generally are not taxed on their share of the earnings until they are received as a dividend.

- Qualifying foreign sales corporations (FSCs) are partially exempt from the U.S. corporate income tax, and their shareholders can claim a dividends-received deduction that exempts part or all of their distributions from U.S. taxation.
- Qualifying domestic international sales corporations (DISCs) are exempt from the corporate income tax, and their shareholders are taxed on actual or deemed distributions of the DISC's taxable income. An interest charge is levied on the portion of the DISC's taxable income that is not actually or deemed distributed to its shareholders.
- Corporations conducting a trade or business in Puerto Rico or a U.S. possession can qualify for a special tax credit that can exempt part or all of their non-U.S. income from U.S. taxation.

The remainder of this chapter looks at the alternative ways in which overseas business activities can be conducted and the special tax privileges that apply to them.

Domestic Subsidiary Corporations

Domestic subsidiary corporations provide two nontax advantages for making sales to foreign purchasers. First, the foreign sales activities can be operationally separate from any domestic activities. Second, the subsidiary corporation's liabilities are separate from those of its parent corporation. Thus, the parent corporation's assets are protected from foreign creditors if there are large overseas losses.

Profits from the overseas sales activities are taxed when they are earned. Losses are deductible when they are incurred. Because the overseas sales activities are conducted by a domestic corporation, the foreign activities can be reported as part of a consolidated tax return. Thus, foreign losses can be used to reduce the tax liability on domestic profits and vice versa.

Foreign Branches

A domestic corporation may elect to conduct its overseas sales or manufacturing activities through a foreign branch. A **foreign branch** is an office or other establishment (e.g., a manufacturing plant) of a domestic entity that operates in a foreign country. A branch is treated as an extension of the domestic corporation. Profits from the overseas activities are reported by the domestic corporation in the year they are earned. It does not matter whether they have been remitted to the United States or not. Foreign income taxes paid or accrued on these profits are creditable under the Sec. 901 direct credit rules.

Losses from overseas activities are reported in the year they are incurred. Losses can reduce the taxes due on domestic profits. The deductibility of these losses is a major advantage of using a foreign branch to establish the initial overseas activities. By using a branch activity, a domestic corporation can deduct start-up losses when they are incurred. Once the overseas activities become profitable, the domestic corporation can incorporate the foreign branch and defer any U.S. income taxes owed on the profits until they are remitted to the United States.

Foreign Corporations

There are four advantages to conducting overseas business activities through a foreign corporation:

1. The foreign corporation's liabilities are separated from those of the parent corporation, thus limiting the domestic corporation's losses to its capital investment.
2. The U.S. income tax levy on the domestic corporation's ratable share of the foreign corporation's earnings is postponed until the earnings are remitted to the United States.
3. A domestic corporation receiving a dividend from a foreign corporation in which it has at least a 10% stock interest can claim a special deemed paid tax credit for a ratable share of the foreign income taxes paid by the foreign corporation.
4. A domestic corporation receiving a dividend from a foreign corporation in which it has at least a 10% stock interest can claim a dividends-received deduction with respect to the portion of the dividend made from the corporation's undistributed profits that are effectively connected with the conduct of a U.S. trade or business.

The last three of these advantages are explored below along with the tax treatment accorded the foreign corporation's U.S. activities.

Additional Comment
This deferral privilege is eliminated for certain types of income of controlled foreign corporations, discussed later in this chapter.

Deferral Privilege. For tax purposes, foreign corporations are considered as separate entities from their shareholders. A tax exemption known as the **deferral privilege** is provided by the U.S. government for the foreign corporation's earnings. The corporation's earnings are taxed as dividend income when they are remitted to the United States.

Example 15-16 ■ Adobe Corporation, a U.S. corporation, owns all of the stock of Delta Corporation, a foreign corporation. In 1987, Delta Corporation reports $300,000 in after-tax profits. These profits are remitted to the United States as a dividend in 1991. No U.S. income taxes are due on Delta Corporation's profits until 1991. This result can be contrasted to a foreign branch activity where the earnings would be taxed to Adobe Corporation in 1987. The value of the tax deferral equals the amount of U.S. taxes that are deferred times the time value of money for 4 years. ■

Losses incurred by a foreign corporation cannot be deducted by any of its shareholders. Instead, the losses are carried back or forward and reduce the profits reported by the foreign corporation in other years that can be distributed to its shareholders.

Example 15-17 ■ Boston Corporation, a U.S. corporation, owns all of the stock of Gulf Corporation, a foreign corporation. In 1991 Gulf Corporation reports $125,000 in losses. None of Gulf Corporation's losses can be used to reduce Boston's taxable income. Had the $125,000 of losses instead been reported by a foreign branch activity established by Boston, the loss could have been used by Boston to offset the profits earned on its U.S. operations in 1991. ■

Foreign Tax Credit. A U.S. corporation that uses a foreign branch to operate overseas and incurs a foreign tax liability can claim a direct foreign tax credit to offset the U.S. taxes that are due on its profits. If the U.S. corporation conducts its foreign operations indirectly through a foreign subsidiary corporation, the foreign subsidiary incurs the foreign tax liability and the U.S. corporation can only claim a direct foreign tax credit for the income taxes that are withheld from the foreign corporation's dividend remittances. Since most foreign countries impose higher income tax levies on a foreign corporation's profits than on its dividend remittances, the foreign tax credit rules could discourage the use of foreign subsidiary corporations by denying a tax credit for most of the foreign income taxes incurred. To remedy this inequity, Congress enacted the Sec. 902 **deemed paid foreign tax credit** for non-U.S. income taxes paid or accrued by a foreign corporation.

In order to claim a deemed paid foreign tax credit, two conditions must be met:

Key Point
The foreign corporation's earnings and profits must be calculated using U.S. tax concepts.

1. The foreign corporation must make a dividend payment to the domestic corporation out of its earnings and profits (E&P).
2. The domestic corporation must own at least 10% of the foreign corporation's voting stock on the date of the distribution.[30]

OBJECTIVE 6
Calculate the deemed paid tax credit available for an investor in a foreign corporation

CALCULATING THE DEEMED PAID CREDIT. The deemed paid credit for post-1986 tax years of a domestic corporate distributee is calculated by using the following formula.[31]

$$\begin{matrix} \text{Deemed} \\ \text{paid} \\ \text{foreign tax} \\ \text{credit} \end{matrix} = \frac{\begin{matrix}\text{Dividend paid to} \\ \text{domestic corporation} \\ \text{out of post-1986} \\ \text{undistributed earnings}\end{matrix}}{\begin{matrix}\text{Undistributed earnings} \\ \text{accumulated in post-} \\ \text{1986 tax years}\end{matrix}} \times \begin{matrix}\text{Creditable taxes} \\ \text{paid or accrued by the} \\ \text{foreign corporation in} \\ \text{post-1986 tax years}\end{matrix}$$

Typical Misconception
The deemed paid foreign tax credit is available from first-, second-, and third-tier foreign corporations (but not lower-tier corporations). The credit becomes available only as an actual dividend is paid from each subsidiary to its parent. The U.S. corporation actually takes the credit when the first-tier foreign corporation pays a dividend to the U.S. corporation.

The undistributed earnings amounts are based on the foreign corporation's E&P for its post-1986 tax years. The dividend definition used in calculating the numerator is the same one that is used for domestic corporations (see Chapter 4).

Both the deemed paid tax credit and the amount of the actual dividend that is paid to the domestic corporation are included in gross income.[32] Such a step prevents the domestic corporation from benefiting from both a tax deduction and a tax credit for the income taxes that are paid or accrued by the foreign corporation.

Example 15-18

Key Point
The deemed paid foreign tax credit is available only to corporate U.S. shareholders. Individual U.S. shareholders are not eligible.

Coastal Corporation, a U.S. corporation, owns 40% of the stock of Bay Corporation, a foreign corporation. During 1991, Bay Corporation reports $200,000 of E&P, pays $50,000 in foreign income taxes, and remits $60,000 in dividends to Coastal Corporation. Foreign country M withholds $6,000 in foreign income taxes from the dividend payment. In prior post-1986 tax years, Bay Corporation reported $100,000 of E&P, paid $40,000 in foreign income taxes, and paid no dividends. Coastal's calculation for the deemed paid foreign tax credit for the 1991 dividend is as follows:

$$\$18,000 = \frac{\$60,000}{\$200,000 + \$100,000} \times (\$50,000 + \$40,000)$$

The $18,000 deemed paid credit is included in Coastal Corporation's gross income and enters into the calculation of its U.S. tax liability.

---

[30] Secs. 902(a) and 902(b)(1)–(3). The deemed paid credit benefits are also available for foreign taxes paid by subsidiary corporations of the foreign corporation.
[31] Sec. 902(a).
[32] Sec. 78.

Dividend	$60,000
Plus: Deemed paid credit	18,000
Gross income	$78,000
Times: Corporate tax rate	× 0.34
Gross U.S. tax liability	$26,520
Minus: Deemed paid credit	(18,000)
Direct credit	(6,000)
Net U.S. tax liability	$ 2,520

TRANSLATING THE DIVIDEND AND FOREIGN TAXES INTO U.S. DOLLARS. Normally the foreign corporation's books and records are maintained in the local currency. To report the remittance to the U.S. taxing authorities, the dividend must be translated into U.S. dollars. If the distributee is a domestic corporation eligible for the deemed paid credit, the foreign corporation's E&P and foreign taxes must also be translated into U.S. dollars. The current exchange rate for the date that the dividend distribution is taken into income is used to translate a dividend paid by a noncontrolled foreign corporation and the related E&P.[33] Translation of foreign taxes for purposes of the deemed paid credit takes place using the exchange rate in effect for the date the taxes are paid.[34]

Example 15-19 ■ Houston Corporation, a U.S. corporation, owns 40% of the stock of Far East Corporation, a foreign corporation. At the end of 1991, Far East Corporation pays a 150,000 pira dividend to Houston Corporation. In 1990 and 1991, Far East earns a total of 200,000 pira in pretax profits. It pays 30,000 and 20,000 pira, respectively, in taxes in 1990 and 1991. The exchange rate between the pira and the dollar is 1 pira = $0.22 (U.S.) on the dividend payment date. The 1990 and 1991 foreign taxes were paid when the exchange rates were 1 pira = $0.20 (U.S.) and 1 pira = $0.25 (U.S.), respectively. The translated dividend amount is 150,000 pira × $0.22 = $33,000. The translated foreign taxes amount is $11,000 ([30,000 pira × $0.20] + [20,000 pira × $0.25]). ■

Taxation of a Foreign Corporation's U.S. Activities

REGULAR AND ALTERNATIVE MINIMUM TAXES. A foreign corporation that (1) earns investment income in the United States or (2) conducts a U.S. trade or business is taxed by the U.S. government. In general the rules governing U.S. taxation of a foreign corporation's income parallel those for nonresident aliens described earlier.

Section 881(a) taxes the U.S. source investment income of a foreign corporation at a 30% rate. Capital gains that are not effectively connected with the conduct of a U.S. trade or business are exempt from taxation. The U.S. taxes on the investment income are collected through the withholding process.[35]

Section 882(a) taxes the portion of the foreign corporation's income that is effectively connected with the conduct of a U.S. trade or business. The 15% to 39% corporate tax rates of Sec. 11(b) and the 20% corporate alternative minimum tax rate of Sec. 55(b) are used to determine the corporate tax liability. The earnings from the conduct of a U.S. trade or business are not taxed to the foreign corporation's U.S. shareholders until they are distributed.

Additional Comment
Dividends received from a foreign corporation that come from E&P earned in the U.S. are eligible for a dividends-received deduction.

---

[33] Reg. Secs. 1.301-1(b) and 1.902-1(g) and *The Bon Ami Co.*, 39 BTA 825 (1939).
[34] Sec. 986(b).
[35] Sec. 1442.

Section 245(a) permits a domestic corporation receiving a dividend from a foreign corporation in which it has at least a 10% stock interest to claim a 70%, 80%, or 100% dividends-received deduction with respect to the portion of the dividend made from the corporation's undistributed profits that are effectively connected with the conduct of a U.S. trade or business. This deduction is available because these earnings were already subject to the U.S. corporate income tax.

BRANCH PROFITS TAX. Foreign corporations that conduct their U.S. activities by using a U.S. subsidiary corporation are subject to a second level of taxation when the subsidiary corporation's profits are distributed in the form of a dividend. This additional levy is in the form of a withholding tax at a 30% rate or at a lower rate that is specified in a tax treaty. U.S. branches of foreign corporations are subject to a second type of tax levy, the branch profits tax, that is similar to the withholding described for distributions made by a U.S. subsidiary of a foreign corporation.[36] U.S. branches are taxed on their dividend equivalent amount and their allocable interest under the branch profits tax rules.

The dividend equivalent portion of the tax equals 30% (or a lower rate specified in a tax treaty) times the dividend equivalent amount. The dividend equivalent amount equals the foreign corporation's E&P for the tax year that are effectively connected with the conduct of its U.S. trade or business increased by the decrease (or decreased by the increase) in the foreign corporation's net equity in its branch assets during the year. Thus, the branch profits tax base is increased by earnings remitted to the foreign corporation during the year that reduce the branch's U.S. trade or business assets and is decreased by earnings that are reinvested in the branch's U.S. trade or business assets during the year. The allocable interest portion of the branch tax provides that certain interest paid by the U.S. branch is taxed as if it were paid by a U.S. corporation. Hence, the interest is U.S. source income and subject to a U.S. withholding tax of 30% (or a lower rate specified in a treaty).

Controlled Foreign Corporations

Prior to the Subpart F Rules. Prior to the enactment of the controlled foreign corporation (CFC) provisions (known as the Subpart F rules) in 1962, U.S. corporations used foreign subsidiaries located in "tax-haven" nations to minimize their tax liability on overseas operations. The usual scenario worked this way:

1. A U.S. manufacturing corporation formed a sales subsidiary in a foreign country that imposed either no corporate income tax or a low corporate tax rate.
2. The goods and services were shipped directly by the U.S. corporation to the foreign purchasers.
3. The tax haven sales subsidiary was billed for the goods by the U.S. corporation.
4. The tax haven sales subsidiary, in turn, billed the foreign purchasers at a higher price.
5. The tax haven sales subsidiary's profits largely escaped U.S. and local taxation.

Example 15-20 ■ Under pre-CFC rules, Chicago Corporation, a U.S. corporation forms Island Corporation, a foreign corporation, to handle its foreign widget sales. The foreign country in which Island Corporation is incorporated imposes no corporate income tax. Assume that Chicago's overseas widget sales annually result in a $1,000,000 profit and a $340,000 ($1,000,000 × 0.34) U.S. tax liability. If the same profit

---

[36] Sec. 884(a).

is divided equally between Chicago and Island, their worldwide tax cost is reduced substantially. Chicago's $500,000 share of the profit results in a $170,000 ($500,000 × 0.34) U.S. tax liability. Island owes no U.S. or local income tax liability on its share of the profit. Chicago owes no tax on Island's share of the profits since they have not been distributed as a dividend. Figure 15-1 illustrates this. Even under these rules, however, an attempt by Chicago to maximize its tax deferral by selling its widgets to Island at cost would probably be challenged by the IRS under Sec. 482. These rules would limit Island's profit to the portion of the $1,000,000 that it had earned based upon the services it had provided. ∎

Under the Subpart F Rules. The Subpart F rules short-circuit this scenario by accelerating U.S. taxation of certain forms of "tainted" income (see Figure 15-2 for a summary of the Subpart F "tainted" income categories).

Example 15-21 ∎

Key Point
The income is taxable to Chicago (the CFC's U.S. parent) as a deemed dividend, rather than being taxed directly to the CFC.

Assume the same facts as in Example 15-20, except that Island Corporation is a CFC. Under the U.S. tax laws, Island's profit on sales of widgets to both related and unrelated parties located outside of Island's country of incorporation is considered "tainted" or Subpart F income and is constructively distributed to Chicago Corporation on the last day of Island Corporation's tax year. Only the portion of Island Corporation's profits attributable to widget sales in Island's country of incorporation is exempt from current U.S. taxation. If all of Island Corporation's sales are made outside its country of incorporation, its $1,000,000 of profits would be taxed to Chicago Corporation under the Subpart F rules. ∎

Because of the increased tax cost incurred when the Subpart F rules are triggered, one of the major tax planning objectives of U.S. investors is structuring overseas

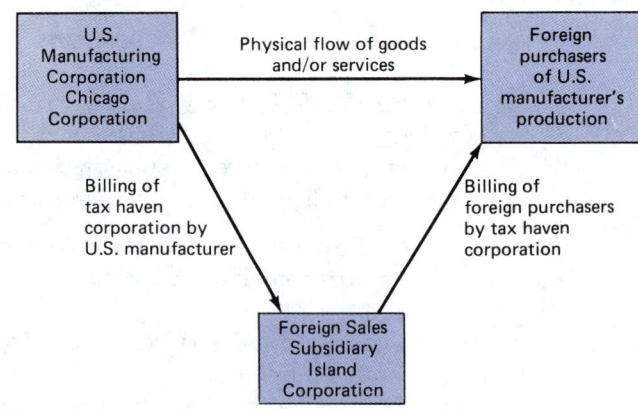

Direct sale by Chicago:
    $1,000,000 profit x 0.34 = $340,000 U.S. tax liability for Chicago

Indirect sale by Chicago and Island with profit divided equally:
    Chicago: $500,000 profit x 0.34 = $170,000 U.S. tax liability
    Island: $500,000 profit x 0 = 0 Local country tax liability (and no U.S. tax
        liability for Chicago until remitted to the U.S.)

Subpart F rules:

Chicago: $1,000,000 constructive distribution x 0.34 U.S. tax liability = $340,000 U.S. tax
    liability
Island: $1,000,000 profit x 0 = 0 Local country tax liability (and no U.S. tax
    liability for Chicago when remitted to the U.S.)

FIGURE 15-1 Illustration of Use of Tax-haven Sales Subsidiary (Example 15-20)

activities to avoid these rules by avoiding CFC status, or structuring the transaction to avoid reporting "tainted" Subpart F income.

OBJECTIVE 7
Determine whether a foreign corporation is a CFC or not

CFC Defined. A **CFC** is a foreign corporation having more than 50% of its voting stock or more than 50% of the value of its outstanding stock owned by "U.S. shareholders" on any day of the foreign corporation's tax year.[37] A **U.S. shareholder** is a U.S. person who owns at least 10% of the foreign corporation's voting stock.[38] An individual is treated as owning all of the stock that he owns directly, indirectly, or constructively. Constructive ownership is determined by applying the stock attribution rules of Sec. 318 (see Chapter 4) with some technical modifications that are found in Sec. 958(b).

Example 15-22

Europa Corporation, a foreign corporation, is owned by five unrelated individuals. Al, Bill, and Cass are U.S. citizens who own 24%, 20%, and 9%, respectively, of Europa Corporation's single class of stock. Duane and Elaine are nonresident aliens who own 40% and 7%, respectively, of Europa's stock. Only Al and Bill are "U.S. shareholders" because they are the only U.S. persons who own at least 10% of Europa's stock. Europa Corporation is not a CFC since Al and Bill together only own 44% of its stock. If Al were instead the father of Bill and Cass, Cass would now be a U.S. shareholder since he would own 53% (9% directly + 44% constructively from Al and Bill) of Europa's stock after applying the family attribution rules. Europa then is a CFC because its three U.S. shareholders own in total 53% (24% + 20% + 9%) of its stock.

OBJECTIVE 8
Explain the special tax provisions applying to a controlled foreign corporation

Typical Misconception
This election allows the individual to take the deemed paid foreign tax credit. However, the election is seldom made because the income is taxed again when it is actually distributed rather than being distributed tax free.

Constructive Distributions of Subpart F Income. U.S. shareholders must report their ratable shares of the CFC's Subpart F income each year. A U.S. shareholder is taxed on the Subpart F income items only when the foreign corporation is a CFC for at least 30 days during its tax year. If this requirement is met, each U.S. shareholder's ratable share of the Subpart F income items must be reported as a deemed dividend that is distributed on either the last day of the CFC's tax year or the last day on which CFC status is retained.[39]

The constructive distribution is included in the U.S. shareholder's gross income and increases the shareholder's basis in the CFC stock. If the U.S. shareholder is a domestic corporation, a deemed paid foreign tax credit is available under Sec. 960 for a ratable share of the CFC's foreign income taxes. An individual shareholder may elect under Sec. 962 to have the constructive distribution taxed as if they were a domestic corporation, or be taxed as an individual taxpayer.

Subpart F income includes five categories of income: income from the insurance of U.S. and foreign risks that originate outside the country of organization; foreign base company income; boycott-related income; income equal to the amount of any bribes or other illegal payments paid by or on behalf of the CFC; and income from countries where for political or other reasons the deferral privilege is denied. These items are discussed below.

INSURANCE OF U.S. AND FOREIGN RISKS. Income derived by the CFC from the insurance of certain U.S. and foreign risks is Subpart F income. Included in this category are premiums for property insurance on property located in, a liability

---

[37] Sec. 957(a). A CFC must adopt the same tax year as their majority U.S. shareholder if on the first day of the CFC's tax year (or other days as prescribed by the IRS) 50% or more of the voting power or value of all classes of the CFC's stock is directly, indirectly, or constructively owned by a single U.S. shareholder.

[38] Sec. 951(b). A U.S. person includes individual citizens or resident aliens of the United States, a domestic corporation, a domestic partnership, or a domestic trust or estate.

[39] Sec. 951(a).

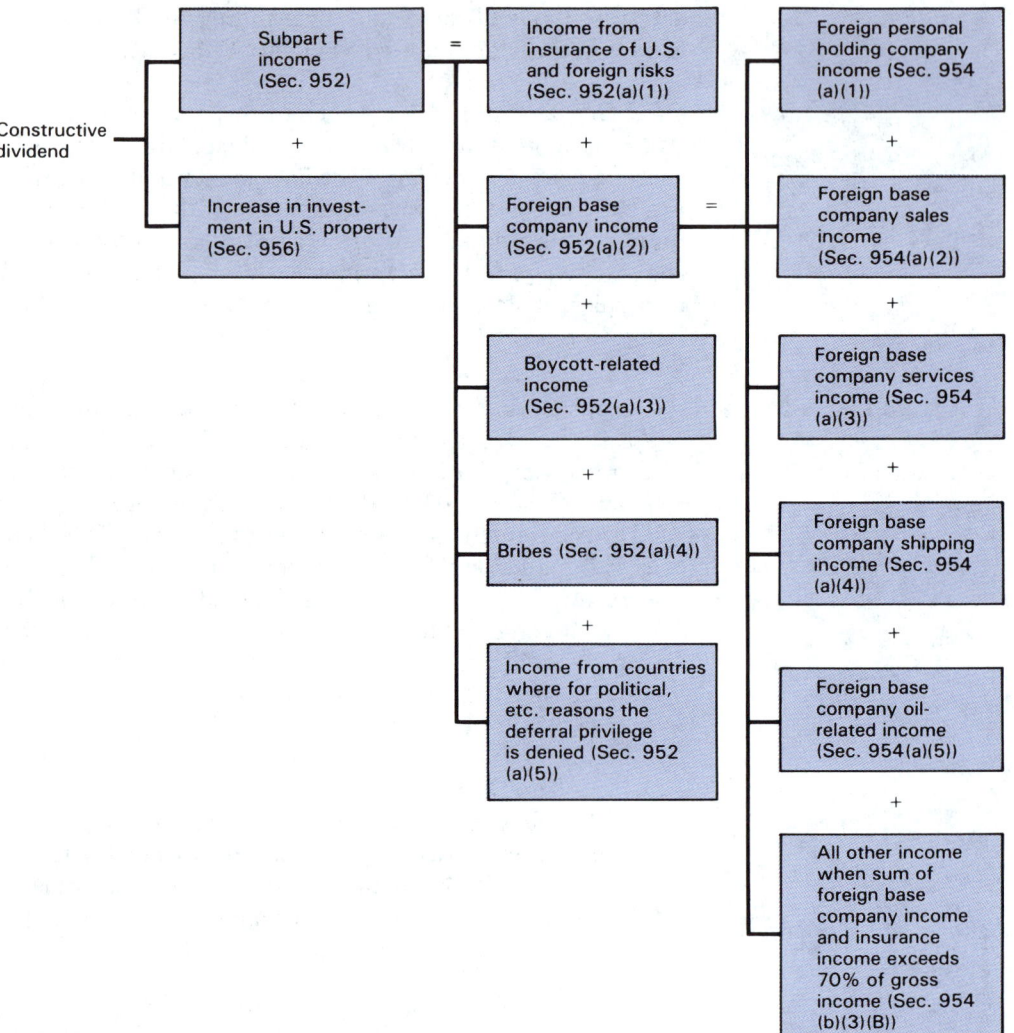

FIGURE 15-2 Amount of Income of Controlled Foreign Corporation Ordinarily Included in Gross Income of U.S. Shareholders

arising out of an activity in, or in connection with the lives or health of residents of, a country other than the country in which the CFC is organized. Such premiums must be of a type that would be taxed under the U.S. tax laws if they were instead earned by a domestic (U.S.) insurance company.

FOREIGN BASE COMPANY INCOME. This income category is the largest of all of the Subpart F income categories. It is composed of the following five subcategories of income.

1. *Foreign personal holding company income* (FPHCI) includes passive income such as dividends, interest, royalties, annuities, rents, and gains from the sale of a property producing one of the previously mentioned passive income forms; gain from the sale of a property that does not produce income; gain from commodities transactions; and foreign exchange gains. It excludes rents and royalties received from (a) a corporation that is a related person for the use of property within the CFC's country of incorporation, or (b) an unrelated person if such payments are connected with the CFC's active conduct of a trade or business. Dividends and interest are not

FPHCI if received from a related person that is a corporation created or organized in the CFC's country of incorporation if the related person has a substantial part of its assets involved in a trade or business in that country.[40]

Example 15-23 ■ Time Corporation is a CFC incorporated in Country X. Time receives interest and dividends from two foreign subsidiary corporations, East Corporation and West Corporation. East Corporation is incorporated in Country V. West Corporation is incorporated in Country X and conducts all of its activities in that country. Only the interest and dividend payments received from East Corporation represent FPHCI. ■

Key Point

The goods must be both manufactured and sold for use outside the CFC's country of incorporation. If the goods are manufactured or sold within the CFC's country of incorporation, the assumption is that a good business reason exists for having set up the CFC in that country. Thus, the CFC has no foreign base company sales income.

2. *Foreign base company sales income* includes any fees and profits earned from the sale or purchase of personal property when (a) a related party is involved in the transaction *and* (b) the property is manufactured and sold outside the CFC's country of incorporation. The related party transactions that result in foreign base company sales income are[41]

- The purchase of personal property from a related person and its sale to any person
- The sale of personal property to any person on behalf of a related person
- The purchase of personal property from any person and its sale to a related person
- The purchase of personal property from any person on behalf of a related person

Foreign base company sales income excludes the profit earned when the product is (a) manufactured in the CFC's country of incorporation, (b) sold for use in the CFC's country of incorporation, or (c) manufactured by the CFC itself in its country of incorporation.[42]

Example 15-24 ■ Dublin Corporation is a CFC incorporated in Country F that purchases machine tools from its U.S. parent corporation for sale to unrelated parties. Dublin sells 70% of the tools in Country E and 30% in Country F. Only the profit earned from the tools sold in Country E constitutes foreign base company sales income. If Dublin Corporation manufactured the machine tools itself, none of its profit from the Country E or Country F sales would be foreign base company sales income. ■

Additional Comment

Goods are deemed to have been manufactured by the CFC if it substantially transforms the product (such as making screws and bolts from steel rods) or if its direct labor and factory overhead account for 20% or more of the total cost of goods sold.

3. *Foreign base company services income* includes compensation earned from performing service activities for or on behalf of a related person outside of the country in which the CFC is created or organized. In general, compensation for personal services is earned at the location where the services are performed.[43]

Example 15-25 ■ Andes Corporation, incorporated in Country A, is 100% owned by Hi-Tech Corporation, a domestic corporation. Hi-Tech sells industrial machines to Amazon Corporation for use in Country B. The portion of the sales contract covering

---

[40] Sec. 954(c). Section 954(d)(3) defines a related person for Subpart F purposes as (a) any individual, corporation, partnership, trust, or estate that controls, or is controlled by, the CFC, or (b) any corporation, partnership, trust, or estate controlled by the same persons who control the CFC. Control is defined for this purpose as direct, indirect, or constructive ownership of 50% or more of the total voting power or total value of the CFC's stock.

[41] Sec. 954(d)(1).

[42] Sec. 954(d).

[43] Sec. 954(e).

installation and maintenance of the machines is assigned by Hi-Tech to Andes. Andes is to be paid for these services by Hi-Tech. The installation and maintenance service performed by Andes is foreign base company services income since it is performed for a related party (Hi-Tech) and it is performed outside of Country A. ∎

4. *Foreign base company shipping income* includes compensation earned from (a) the use of any aircraft or vessel in foreign commerce and (b) the hiring or leasing of such a vessel for use in foreign commerce by another person.[44] Foreign base company shipping income excludes income earned from the use of an aircraft or vessel in commerce between two points within the foreign country in which the CFC is created or organized and in which the aircraft or vessel is registered.

5. *Foreign base company oil-related income* includes amounts earned from oil- and gas-related activities (other than any activities involving the extraction of oil and gas) located in a foreign country. Activities producing this type of income include the transportation, shipping, processing, and distribution of oil and gas and any related service activities. These types of income are not taxed under Subpart F if they are earned in the foreign country in which the oil and gas were extracted.[45]

Exceptions to the definition of foreign base company income reduce the burden of Subpart F. Subpart F income excludes

- Income earned by the CFC in its conduct of a U.S. trade or business which is taxed by the United States[46]
- Foreign base company income or insurance income that is subject to an effective foreign tax rate that is greater than 90% of the maximum rate specified in Sec. 11[47]
- Foreign base company income and insurance income that in total is less than the smaller of 5% of the CFC's gross income or $1 million[48]
- Income earned by the CFC that cannot be repatriated to the United States because of currency or other restrictions[49]

When foreign base company income and insurance income exceed 70% of the CFC's gross income, all of the CFC's gross income is foreign base company income or insurance income as appropriate.[50]

The Subpart F income is reduced by any related deductions. Allocation of the deductions to the Subpart F income takes place using the rules found in Reg. Sec. 1.861-8.[51] These regulations are beyond the scope of an introductory chapter.

BOYCOTT-RELATED INCOME. This category includes any income derived by the CFC from the participation in, or cooperation with, an international boycott against a particular nation (or group of nations). The portion of the CFC's profits that are

---

[44] Secs. 951(a)(1)(A)(iii) and 954(f). Prior to 1987, a CFC's foreign base company shipping income was not taxed to the U.S. shareholder if the CFC used these earnings to increase its investment in "qualified foreign base company shipping operations." Although this exemption has been repealed for current earnings, it continues for pre-1987 earnings until the qualified investment is decreased. At that time, the amount of the decrease in the CFC's earnings invested in the qualified shipping operations is taxed to the U.S. shareholder.

[45] Sec. 954(h).
[46] Sec. 952(b).
[47] Sec. 954(b)(4).
[48] Sec. 954(b)(3)(A).
[49] Sec. 964(b).
[50] Sec. 954(b)(3)(B).
[51] Sec. 954(b)(5).

boycott-related is determined by a rather detailed set of rules found in Sec. 999, which are beyond the scope of an introductory chapter.

BRIBES, KICKBACKS, AND OTHER ILLEGAL PAYMENTS. Payments made by or for the CFC of bribes, kickbacks, and other illegal payments result in a loss of the CFC's deferral privilege for a portion of the CFC's earnings equal to the sum of all such payments.

EARNINGS DERIVED IN CERTAIN FOREIGN COUNTRIES. For political reasons certain tax benefits are denied to taxpayers doing business in a selected group of countries. U.S. shareholders of a CFC are denied the deferral privilege on earnings derived in these countries. These countries include those the U.S. government does not recognize, those with whom the U.S. government has severed diplomatic relations, those the U.S. government believes support international terrorism, and South Africa.

Investments in U.S. Property. Under the pre-CFC rules, the foreign subsidiary's profits were often lent to the U.S. parent corporation to avoid the U.S. income tax laws and the foreign income tax withholding rules. Special rules were enacted to prevent CFCs from avoiding U.S. taxation by either investing funds directly in assets located in the United States or making loans to a U.S. shareholder instead of paying dividends. Under these rules, each U.S. shareholder receives a constructive distribution of their pro rata share of the increase in the foreign corporation's earnings that are invested in U.S. property to the extent that such earnings would have been taxed as a dividend if distributed.[52]

The U.S. property investment is measured on the last day of the CFC's tax year and includes only the property's adjusted basis (minus any liability to which it is subject). U.S. property includes any tangible property located in the United States; stock of domestic corporations; obligations of U.S. persons; or any patents, copyrights, and so on that are developed by the CFC for use in the United States.[53] Exceptions to the U.S. property definition include U.S. government obligations, U.S. bank deposits, stock of domestic corporations that are not (1) a U.S. shareholder of the CFC or (2) more than 25% owned by one of the CFC's U.S. shareholders.

Additional Comment

If the CFC guarantees an obligation of a U.S. person, it is deemed to hold that obligation. Thus, if a CFC guarantees a loan of its U.S. parent, the guarantee constitutes the acquisition of U.S. property. This has been a tax trap for taxpayers in the past.

Example 15-26 ■

Forco, a foreign corporation, is a CFC that is in its initial year of operation. Forco reports $1,000,000 of earnings during 1991, none of which is taxed as Subpart F income. On December 31, 1991, Forco has an aggregate U.S. property investment of $400,000. By making this investment, Forco loses its tax deferral for these earnings and causes the $400,000 to be taxed ratably to its U.S. shareholders. ■

Self-Study Question

If $500,000 of the $1,000,000 in Example 15-26 had been Subpart F income (and thus currently taxed to the CFC's U.S. shareholders), would the acquisition of the U.S. property also be taxed currently?

Answer

The E&P invested in U.S. property comes first out of the E&P that has previously been taxed. Therefore, no additional tax levy would be incurred as a result of the investment.

Distributions from a CFC. Distributions made by a CFC are deemed to be paid first from (1) its earnings invested in U.S. property and (2) its most recently accumulated Subpart F income. Distributions of any tax-deferred earnings are not deemed to have been made until after these two forms of previously taxed income have been distributed. Distributions of previously taxed income (i.e., earnings invested in U.S. property and Subpart F income) are tax-free to the U.S. shareholder and reduce the basis of his CFC stock investment.[54]

---

[52] Sec. 951(a)(2). Earnings that have been taxed as Subpart F income may be invested in U.S. property without incurring any additional tax liability. Such amounts, if distributed, would not constitute a dividend.

[53] Secs. 956(a)(3) and (b).

[54] Secs. 959(c) and 961(b).

Example 15-27 ■ Bulldog Corporation, a domestic corporation, owns all of the stock of Marine Corporation, a CFC. Bulldog's cost basis for the Marine stock is $600,000. Marine reports $400,000 of E&P since Bulldog made its investment, of which $175,000 is taxed to Bulldog under the Subpart F rules. Marine makes a $200,000 cash distribution to Bulldog. Of this distribution, $175,000 is tax-free as a distribution of previously taxed Subpart F income. The remaining $25,000 is taxable as a dividend since it represents a distribution of earnings that were not previously taxed under Subpart F. Bulldog's basis for the Marine stock is $600,000 ($600,000 + $175,000 − $175,000) immediately after the distribution. ■

Disposition of CFC Stock. Section 1248 prevents the stock of a CFC from being sold or exchanged at capital gains rates. These rules apply only to a U.S. person who owns at least 10% of the foreign corporation's voting stock when the foreign corporation retained CFC status within 5 years of the disposition date. The gain recognized on the sale or exchange of a CFC's stock is taxed as a dividend to the extent that the gain is attributable to E&P accumulated (1) in a tax year beginning after December 31, 1962 (the effective date of the Subpart F rules), (2) during a time period that the stock sold or exchanged was held by the U.S. person, and (3) while the foreign corporation was a CFC.[55] Any gain exceeding this amount is taxed as a capital gain. The dividend portion of the gain reported by a corporate shareholder qualifies for the deemed paid foreign tax credit.

Example 15-28 ■ Texas Corporation, a domestic corporation, purchases 200 of the 500 outstanding shares of Le Chien Corporation's stock on October 30, 1989. Texas holds the shares continuously until March 31, 1991, when it sells the stock for a $60,000 gain. Le Chien is a CFC at all times while the stock is owned. Le Chien's E&P amounts are as follows: 1989, $60,000; 1990, $30,000; and 1991, $70,000. The E&P attributable to the stock sold or exchanged is determined by using the following formula:

$$\text{E\&P for tax year} \times \frac{\text{Number of shares sold or exchanged}}{\text{Number of shares outstanding}} \times \frac{\text{Number of days shares are owned and corporation is a CFC}}{\text{Number of days in CFC's tax year}} = \text{E\&P attributable to shares sold or exchanged}$$

$$1989: \$60{,}000 \times \frac{200}{500} \times \frac{61}{365} = \$\ 4{,}011$$

$$1990: \$30{,}000 \times \frac{200}{500} \times \frac{365}{365} = 12{,}000$$

$$1991: \$70{,}000 \times \frac{200}{500} \times \frac{90}{365} = \underline{6{,}904}$$

$$\text{Total} \qquad \qquad \underline{\underline{\$22{,}915}}$$

Thus, $22,915 of the gain is dividend income and $37,085 ($60,000 − $22,915) is capital gain. ■

---

[55] Sec. 1248(a).

Typical Misconception
Section 482 applies to transactions involving two U.S. entities as well as to transactions involving a U.S. entity and a foreign entity.

Section 482 Rules. Transactions involving a domestic corporation and a foreign subsidiary present an increased opportunity for tax avoidance. One method of tax avoidance is to have the domestic corporation sell goods and services to the subsidiary at a price that is less than the price that would be arrived at in arm's-length dealings (see Figure 15-1 and related text). Another method is to have the foreign subsidiary pay a less than arm's-length charge for the use of intangibles (such as patents or trademarks). Both situations cause an increased amount of profits to be earned by the foreign subsidiary that are exempt from U.S. taxation.

Example 15-29 ■ Taylor Corporation, a domestic corporation, sells widgets to its wholly owned foreign subsidiary Wheeler. Wheeler Corporation is incorporated in and pays taxes to Country Z. Taylor Corporation normally sells widgets to a U.S. wholesaler providing services similar to those provided by Wheeler at a price of $10. If Taylor Corporation sells the widgets to Wheeler for $8 per unit, Wheeler's profits are increased by an additional $2 per unit. Unless the additional profit is Subpart F income, it is not taxed by the United States until Wheeler remits it to Taylor as a dividend. ■

Example 15-30 ■ Assume the same facts as in Example 15-29, except that Taylor Corporation instead licenses Wheeler to manufacture the widgets and charges a $1 per-unit royalty for each unit produced and sold. A royalty arrangement with an unrelated foreign producer of widgets provides for a $3 per-unit royalty to be paid to Taylor Corporation. The reduced royalty payment increases Wheeler's profits by an additional $2 per unit. Since the profit is derived from manufacturing performed by the CFC, it is unlikely that the additional profit will be taxed as Subpart F income. It is thus exempt from U.S. taxation until Wheeler remits it to Taylor as a dividend. ■

Under Code Sec. 482, the IRS has the power to distribute; apportion; or allocate gross income, deductions, credits, allowances, or any items affecting taxable income between or among controlled entities to prevent tax evasion and to clearly reflect the income of the entities. For Sec. 482 to be used, the following conditions must exist:

1. There must be two or more organizations, trades, or businesses.
2. These entities must be owned or controlled by the same parties.
3. A transaction taking place between the entities must clearly reflect the income that would have been reported had an arm's-length standard been used.

The Sec. 482 rules can apply to transactions taking place between two unincorporated entities, two incorporated entities, or one incorporated entity and one unincorporated entity. The related parties can be either domestic or foreign and do not have to be part of an affiliated group of corporations that files a consolidated tax return.

The Sec. 482 regulations provide rules for determining an arm's-length standard for a number of types of transactions, including

- Loans or advances
- Performance of services
- Sales of intangible properties
- Use of intangible properties
- Sales of tangible properties
- Use of tangible properties[56]

---

[56] Reg. Sec. 1.482-2.

> **Additional Comment**
>
> *Under the current regulations, a special priority order exists for the methods used for the sale of tangible property: (1) comparable uncontrolled price method, (2) resale method, and (3) cost plus method.*

These rules provide a safe haven for the related parties' transactions. If the price charged for the property meets one of the acceptable standards found in the Sec. 482 regulations, it will not be subject to challenge by the IRS.

For the transfer pricing situation illustrated in Example 15-29, the IRS would likely attempt to require the use of a comparable price determined in an uncontrolled situation. If such a price could not be determined, either the resale price method (i.e., sale price minus an appropriate margin) or the cost plus price method is used. For the royalty situation illustrated in Example 15-30, Reg. Sec. 1.482-2(d)(2) provides an indication of the factors which should be considered in attempting to arrive at the price that would be determined in a similar uncontrolled situation. A "super royalty" concept was added by the Tax Reform Act of 1986 that permits the IRS to adjust the payments made for the use of an intangible over time and not have the question of appropriateness of the royalty only be determined at the time of the initial transfer. Thus, the actual profit experience, including changes in the income attributed to the intangible, of the parties must be considered in determining the royalty rate.[57]

Special Foreign Corporation Forms

Foreign corporations have been used by individuals to conduct investment-related activities while avoiding both the U.S. and foreign tax laws. The foreign tax exemption occurs because the companies are formed in foreign countries that have no corporate income tax or that impose a low-rate corporate income tax. The U.S. tax exemption occurs because the U.S. tax laws do not ordinarily tax the U.S. investor's ratable share of a foreign corporation's earnings until paid as a dividend. The shareholders of two foreign corporation investment vehicles, however, do not receive the tax deferral that is normally available for their share of a foreign corporation's earnings. U.S. citizens and resident aliens owning stock in a **foreign personal holding company (FPHC)** must report their share of the entity's undistributed FPHC income annually. A foreign corporation is a FPHC if (1) at least 60% of its income is passive income and (2) at some time during the corporation's tax year more than 50% of the value of its outstanding stock is owned by 5 or fewer individuals who are U.S. citizens or residents.[58] A U.S. person must pay U.S. tax and an interest charge based on the value of the tax deferral received on accumulated foreign earnings when he disposes of the stock of a **passive foreign investment company (PFIC)** or receives an excess distribution from the PFIC.[59] A foreign corporation is a PFIC if 75% or more of its gross income for the tax year is passive income, or at least 50% of the average value of its assets during the tax year produce or are held for producing passive income.

Foreign Sales Corporations

The **foreign sales corporation (FSC)** provisions represent the U.S. government's reaction to a determination by an international tribunal that the portion of the U.S. tax laws regarding the domestic international sales corporation (DISC) violated the General Agreement on Tariffs and Trade (GATT). FSCs were created to rebut these

---

[57] Sec. 482.
[58] Sec. 551(a).
[59] Sec. 1296(a).

arguments and to satisfy the GATT requirements that tax benefits for export activities be permitted only if the income is earned through economic activity outside the home country.

Key Point
As opposed to a DISC, a FSC must be a foreign corporation.

FSC Requirements. A FSC must satisfy each of the following requirements:

- Be a corporation created or organized in (1) a foreign country that is a party to either an exchange of information agreement or a tax treaty with the United States[60] or (2) a qualified U.S. possession
- Have 25 or fewer shareholders at all times during the tax year
- Have only common stock outstanding at all times during the tax year
- Maintain an office located in a foreign country that meets the FSC organization requirements outlined above
- Maintain a set of permanent books of account (including invoices) outside the United States
- Maintain its tax records at a location in the United States
- Have a board of directors that includes at least one individual (either a U.S. citizen or an alien) who is not a U.S. resident
- Not be a member of a controlled group of corporations that includes a DISC as a member
- Have made the necessary election to be taxed as a FSC[61]

OBJECTIVE 9
Explain the special tax benefits accruing to a foreign sales corporation

Advantages of a FSC. FSCs provide exporters with three major tax incentives:

- Exemption of a portion of the FSC's foreign trade income from the U.S. corporate income tax
- Special transfer pricing rules that permit the FSC to use other than arm's-length pricing methods
- Dividend distributions that are eligible for a 70%, 80%, or 100% dividends-received deduction

Each of these advantages is explained below.

Taxation of a FSC's Activities. A FSC's income is divided into two major categories: foreign trade income and other income. Foreign trade income is again subdivided into exempt and nonexempt foreign trade income. Exempt foreign trade income is exempt from the U.S. corporate income tax. The percentage of foreign trade income that is exempt depends upon the transfer pricing method used and whether the FSC has corporate shareholders. (A summary of the exemption percentages is provided in Table 15-2.) Nonexempt foreign trade income is taxed differently depending upon the transfer pricing method used to price the goods or services purchased by the FSC.

FOREIGN TRADE INCOME. If one of the two sets of administrative pricing rules is used, the nonexempt foreign trade income is U.S. source income that is effectively

---

[60] Eligible countries include Australia, Austria, Belgium, Canada, Denmark, Finland, France, Germany, Netherlands, and Sweden. In total, more than 35 countries or possessions meet the requirements.
[61] Secs. 922(a) and 927(f).

TABLE 15-2 *Percentage of Exempt and Nonexempt Foreign Trade Income*

Transfer Pricing Method Used	One or More FSC Corporate Shareholders	
	Portion of foreign trade income that is:	
	Exempt Foreign Trade Income	Nonexempt Foreign Trade Income
Administrative pricing rule—Combined Taxable Income or Gross Receipts Methods	15/23[a]	8/23
Arm's-length pricing rule—with or without Sec. 482	30%	Exemption based on the facts surrounding the transaction

[a] The exempt foreign trade income is different if none of the FSC's stock is owned by a C corporation. In such a case, the exempt foreign trade income is 16/23rds under an administrative pricing rule and 32% under the arm's-length pricing rule. These percentages must be adjusted when both C corporations and individuals own the FSC stock during the year.

connected with the conduct of a U.S. trade or business. If the arm's-length transfer pricing rules are used, the nonexempt foreign trade income is either (1) taxed as being effectively connected with the conduct of a U.S. trade or business, (2) tax exempt as unrelated to a U.S. trade or business or (3) taxed to the FSC's shareholders as Subpart F income. This determination is made by using the same inventory property rules that apply to a foreign corporation that is not a FSC (see page 15-6). The FSC must allocate and apportion its deductions to the exempt foreign trade income on a proportionate basis.

INVESTMENT INCOME. Investment income (e.g., interest, dividends, royalties, annuities, rentals, and gains on the sale of stocks or securities) and carrying charges are taxed as U.S. source income. Such income is considered to be effectively connected with the conduct of a U.S. trade or business.

FOREIGN TAX CREDIT. The FSC generally cannot claim a foreign tax credit. An exception is provided for foreign taxes paid with respect to nonexempt foreign trade income that is calculated by using the arm's-length pricing rules. A second exception is provided with respect to investment income, carrying charges, and non-foreign trade income that is effectively connected with the conduct of a U.S. trade or business. Taxes that are withheld on a FSC's dividend distribution can be credited by its shareholders to the extent they are attributable to one of the two exceptions that are described above.

Key Point

Note that these requirements are all in line with the basic purpose of the FSC legislation: to stimulate U.S. exports of goods and services.

Determination of Foreign Trade Income. **Foreign trade income** is defined by Sec. 923(b) as being the FSC's gross income that is attributable to foreign trading gross receipts. Section 924(a) defines foreign trading gross receipts as including receipts from

- The sale, exchange, or other disposition of export property
- The lease or rental of export property for use by the lessee outside the United States
- Services related to the sale or lease of export property

- Engineering or architectural services performed for non-U.S. construction projects
- Managerial services performed for an unrelated FSC or DISC

The FSC's foreign trading gross receipts do not include receipts (1) from the sale or lease of export property, or from the performance of services, that are to be used in the United States or by the U.S. government or (2) for receipts that are received from another member of the FSC's controlled group.

A FSC's gross receipts are foreign trading gross receipts only if it performs outside the United States (1) the necessary management activities (i.e., location for directors' meetings; location of principal bank account; and payment of dividends, directors' fees and certain other expenses) during the tax year, (2) the necessary economic activities (i.e., solicitation, negotiation, or making of the sales contract) related to a particular transaction, and (3) the non-U.S. direct costs attributable to the transaction must be at least 50% of the total direct costs attributable to the transaction. The management and economic activities requirements do not apply to a "small FSC." The "small FSC" exemption must be elected by a FSC. It applies to a maximum of $5 million of gross receipts during a tax year.

Export property is defined by Sec. 927(a)(1) as property that

- Is manufactured, produced, grown, or extracted in the United States by a person other than the FSC
- Is held primarily for sale, lease, or rental in the ordinary course of a trade or business by, or to, a FSC for use or consumption outside the United States
- Has no more than 50% of its value attributable to articles imported into the United States

Additional Comment

According to a leading authority, most FSCs are commission FSCs (see Rhoades & Langer, Income Taxation of Foreign Related Transactions, *Matthew Bender, p. 4A-9).*

Transfer Pricing Rules. Two types of FSCs are commonly encountered when export propery is being sold. The first type, the *sales FSC,* generally involves the FSC stocking the export property and performing the various services (e.g., warehousing, delivery, extending of credit) that are associated with a wholesaler or distributor. The second type, the *commission FSC,* generally involves the FSC selling the export property for a related or unrelated producer company and earning a sales commission.

With either type of FSC, its taxable income is determined by using either the arm's-length or administrative (non-arm's-length) transfer pricing rules. In the case of the sales FSC, the transfer pricing rules are used to determine the minimum price that the FSC can be charged for the export property. In the case of the commission FSC, the transfer pricing rules are used to determine the maximum commission that can be earned by the FSC when it sells the export property.

ADMINISTRATIVE TRANSFER PRICING RULES. The administrative rules permit the taxable income attributable to a transaction (or a group of transactions) to be any amount that does not exceed the particular ceiling for the pricing method used. The taxable income that can be earned by a FSC from a transaction (or a group of transactions) is an amount not exceeding the largest of

- 1.83% of the foreign trading gross receipts derived by the FSC from the sale
- 23% of the combined taxable income of the FSC and the related supplier attributable to the foreign trading gross receipts derived by the FSC from the sale

The taxable income determined under the gross receipts method cannot exceed two times the taxable income determined under the combined taxable income method.

The administrative transfer pricing rules are used only for sales of export property by a FSC that are acquired from a related person (usually the producer of the export property). A related person is an organization that is owned or controlled (directly or indirectly generally at a 50% level) by the same parties that control the FSC.[62]

ARM'S-LENGTH TRANSFER PRICING RULES. Transactions involving a sale by a FSC of export property acquired from a related person can also be based upon the sales price actually charged the FSC by the related person (or commission paid the FSC by the related person) if the amount satisfies the arm's-length transaction requirements of Sec. 482. Transactions involving export property produced by an unrelated party are always based upon the price that the FSC actually pays for the export property, or the commission the FSC actually is paid.

The transfer price for export property acquired by the FSC from related persons can be determined after the end of the FSC's tax year in order to maximize the taxable income that the FSC can earn for an individual transaction (or a group of transactions). The following formula is used to determine the minimum transfer price that can be charged once a determination is made of the maximum taxable income amount that can be earned by the FSC:

$$\begin{pmatrix}\text{Transfer price} \\ \text{from related} \\ \text{party to the FSC}\end{pmatrix} = \begin{pmatrix}\text{Price actually} \\ \text{charged by} \\ \text{the FSC}\end{pmatrix} - \begin{pmatrix}\text{Maximum} \\ \text{FSC taxable} \\ \text{income}\end{pmatrix} + \begin{pmatrix}\text{FSC} \\ \text{expenses}\end{pmatrix}$$

Example 15-31 ■ Mobile Corporation is a domestic corporation that owns all of the single class of Sales Corporation stock. Sales Corporation is a foreign corporation for which a FSC election is made. During 1991, Sales Corporation acting as a sales FSC incurs $225 in expenses related to a particular sale. Sales Corporation elects to use the gross receipts method to determine its taxable income and is permitted to earn $18.30 in taxable income on its $1,000 in foreign trading gross receipts from the transaction. The minimum transfer price that Mobile Corporation is permitted to charge Sales Corporation is $756.70 ($1,000 − [$18.30 + $225]). If Mobile Corporation charges less than this amount, Sales Corporation's taxable income will exceed the maximum permitted under the gross receipts method. Because the FSC stock is owned by a corporate shareholder, the FSC profit that is exempt from U.S. taxation if the minimum transfer price is charged is $11.93 ($15/23 × $18.30). The FSC profit taxed by the United States is $6.37 ($18.30 − $11.93). ■

The maximum commission that can be earned by a commission FSC equals the amount of the FSC's maximum taxable income plus any FSC expenses that are incurred with respect to the transaction (or group of transactions).

Example 15-32 ■ Assume the same facts as in Example 15-31, except that Sales Corporation is instead a commission FSC. The maximum commission that Sales Corporation can earn with respect to the transaction is $243.30 ($18.30 + $225). Since the FSC's $18.30 of taxable income ($243.30 − $225) does not change from the preceding example, the taxable income and tax-exempt portions of Sales Corporation's taxable income do not change. ■

EXEMPTION OF FSC DIVIDENDS FROM TAXATION. The FSC's earnings are divided into two E&P balances—E&P attributable to foreign trade income and E&P attributable to other income (e.g., investment income and carrying charges). Distri-

[62] Sec. 925(a).

Self-Study Question

How is exempt foreign trade income never subject to U.S. income tax?

Answer

At the FSC, it is foreign source income earned by a foreign corporation—thus, no tax. Then, when the FSC pays dividends to its U.S. corporate shareholders, the dividend is subject to a 100% dividends-received deduction. The U.S. tax exemption may or may not extend to the nonexempt foreign trade income depending on which pricing method is used.

butions from foreign trade income made by the FSC to a U.S. corporation that are determined by using the administrative pricing rules are eligible for the 100% dividends-received deduction. As a result, the exempt foreign trade income is never subject to the U.S. corporate income tax. The nonexempt foreign trade income is taxed only to the FSC. Only the exempt portion of the foreign trade income determined by using the arm's-length pricing rules is eligible for the 100% dividends-received deduction. A 70% or 80% dividends-received deduction is available for dividends paid out of investment income or carrying charges earned by the FSC. No dividends-received deduction is available for the nonexempt foreign trade income determined by using the arm's-length pricing rules unless the income is effectively connected or for distributions made from E&P attributable to other income.[63]

Domestic International Sales Corporations

The special **domestic international sales corporation (DISC)** tax laws were created in 1971 to encourage U.S. companies to engage in export activities. The DISC rules originally provided four special tax advantages:

1. The DISC was exempt from the corporate income tax.
2. The DISC's shareholders could defer up to one-half of the DISC's profits from taxation until they were distributed, the DISC stock was sold or exchanged, or the DISC election was terminated.
3. Special pricing rules could be used to determine the DISC's taxable income.
4. The DISC could loan money to a related producer (known as a *producer's loan*) without the transaction being considered a dividend.

Key Point

A domestic corporation can no longer elect to be a DISC. Most interest-charge DISCs that still exist made their elections prior to 1985, although it is still possible to elect to be an interest-charge DISC.

The 1984 Tax Act reduced the tax advantage of a DISC by (1) eliminating the tax deferral for DISC receipts in excess of $10 million, (2) levying an interest charge on the amount of each shareholder's portion of the DISC's post-1984 tax-deferred earnings, (3) eliminating the ability to make new DISC elections after December 31, 1984 except where the DISC's shareholders agree to pay the appropriate interest charge, and (4) revoking an existing DISC election whenever a FSC election is made by a corporation in the DISC's controlled group. In spite of these restrictions, a number of small "interest-charge" DISC's remain active today.

DISC Requirements and Taxable Income. Because of the reduced importance that DISCs have today, only a brief summary of their tax characteristics will be presented. Like a FSC, a DISC must satisfy a series of organizational requirements (i.e., domestic corporation, one class of stock outstanding, par or stated value of stock of at least $2,500 on each day, not a member of a controlled group that includes a FSC, and a timely election with the consent of all shareholders). In addition, at least 95% of the DISC's assets must be qualified export assets, and at least 95% of the DISC's receipts must be qualified export receipts.

A DISC can elect one of three ways to compute its taxable income. The three alternative methods are: the Section 482 (or arm's length) method; the gross receipts method; and the combined taxable income method. Application of these rules to DISC sales or commission transactions parallels the FSC rules explained above.

Taxation of DISC Distributions. DISCs are exempt from the U.S. corporate income tax. DISC shareholders are taxed on both actual and constructive distributions made by the DISC. DISC shareholders are taxed on the following types of constructive distributions: gross interest income derived from producer's loans,

---

[63] Sec. 245(c).

taxable income attributable to qualified export receipts in excess of $10 million in a tax year, and 1/17 of the DISC's remaining taxable income.[64]

Example 15-33 ■ Alpha Corporation, which has been a DISC for a number of years, is owned entirely by Total Corporation, a domestic corporation taxed at a 34% rate. Both corporations use the calendar year as their tax years. During 1990, Alpha Corporation reports taxable income of $267,000. Included in this total is $12,000 of producer's loan interest. Total Corporation receives a constructive distribution of $27,000 ($12,000 + 1/17 [$267,000 − $12,000]) from Alpha Corporation on December 31, 1990. Total Corporation must pay an interest charge on the $240,000 of tax-deferred DISC profits that are not actually or constructively distributed by Alpha Corporation. ■

OBJECTIVE 10
Calculate the annual interest charge resulting from a domestic international sales corporation's deferred tax liability

All DISC shareholders must pay an interest charge on their DISC-related deferred tax liability. The interest charge that is owed for a particular tax year is based on the cumulative DISC's taxable income earned through the end of the preceding tax year. The DISC-related deferred tax liability equals the additional amount of tax that would be owed by a shareholder whose gross income includes his ratable share of the DISC's tax-deferred profits that were earned in tax years beginning after December 31, 1984. The interest charge is based on the T-Bill rate published annually by the IRS.[65]

Example 15-34 ■ Assume the same facts as in Example 15-33, except that the DISC-related deferred tax liability for pre-1990 tax years is $100,000 and the base period T-Bill rate used for 1991 is 7.50%. Total Corporation's 1991 interest charge is based on the pre-1990 DISC-related deferred tax liability of $100,000 plus the 1990 DISC-related deferred tax liability of $81,600 ($240,000 × 0.34), or $181,600. (No interest charge is owed on 1991's DISC-related deferred tax liability until 1992.) The interest charge owed for 1991 is $13,620 ($181,600 × 0.075). The interest charge must be paid at the time Total Corporation pays its 1991 tax liability. ■

Actual DISC distributions are treated as having been made after the shareholder's share of the DISC's taxable income is constructively received. A DISC's distributions are tax-free if they come out of its previously taxed income. A DISC's previously taxed income is the total of its constructive distributions for the current and preceding tax years that have not been distributed to its shareholders. As part of the enactment of the FSC provisions, the DISC's tax-deferred income balance on December 31, 1984, was frozen and can be distributed tax-free to its shareholders. Tax-deferred DISC income accumulated after December 31, 1984, is taxed when distributed.[66]

The tax-deferred DISC income does not receive a permanent tax exemption. Shareholders who sell or exchange part or all of their DISC stock may have to recognize some or all of the gain as ordinary income.[67]

Possessions Corporations

The **possessions corporation** rules attempt to encourage businesses to expand activities conducted in Puerto Rico or a U.S. possession.[68] A domestic corporation qualifying as a possessions corporation is still taxed by the United States on its

---

[64] Sec. 995(b).
[65] Sec. 995(f).
[66] Sec. 996(a)(1).
[67] Sec. 996(d).
[68] U.S. possessions for Sec. 936 purposes generally includes only Puerto Rico and the Virgin Islands.

worldwide income. Section 936 permits these corporations to claim a special tax credit that has the effect of making tax-exempt certain non-U.S. income. The following four requirements must be satisfied to claim this credit.[69]

- The corporation must make a timely Sec. 936 credit election.
- At least 80% of the corporation's gross income for the 3-year (or shorter) period of time preceding the close of the tax year must be earned in a U.S. possession.
- At least 75% of the corporation's gross income for the 3-year (or shorter) period must be derived from the active conduct of a trade or business in a U.S. possession.
- The corporation must not be a DISC or former DISC, or own stock in a DISC, former DISC, FSC, or former FSC during the tax year.

The Sec. 936 credit reduces the U.S. income tax levied on (1) non-U.S. source taxable income derived by the taxpayer from the active conduct of a trade or business in a U.S. possession, (2) the gain from the sale or exchange of substantially all the assets of a trade or business conducted in a U.S. possession, and (3) qualified possessions source invesment income. Qualified possessions source investment income is defined by Sec. 936(d)(2) as income earned from within a possession where a trade or business is conducted and which can be attributed to funds derived from the active conduct of a trade or business or an investment in that possession. The Sec. 936 credit cannot reduce the tax owed on any qualifying income that is received from a related person in the United States.

The amount of the Sec. 936 credit is determined as follows:[70]

$$\text{Sec. 936 credit} = \text{U.S. income tax liability} \times \frac{\text{Taxable income from qualifying types of income}}{\text{Worldwide taxable income}}$$

Foreign income taxes paid with respect to qualifying types of income cannot be credited. Dividends paid by a possessions corporation are eligible for the appropriate 70%, 80%, or 100% dividends-received deduction.

Example 15-35 ■ Tyson Corporation, a domestic corporation, was organized in early 1991. Tyson operates extensively in Puerto Rico in 1991. Tyson Corporation reports gross income of $600,000, $520,000 of which is from a Puerto Rican trade or business; $40,000 from U.S. activities; and $40,000 from Puerto Rican investments. Tyson Corporation's taxable income is $200,000, $130,000 of which is from the Puerto Rican trade or business; $30,000 from U.S. activities and $40,000 from qualified Puerto Rican investments. The Sec. 936 requirements are met since 93.33% of Tyson's gross income (0.9333 = $560,000 ÷ $600,000) is earned in a U.S. possession and 86.67% of Tyson's gross income (0.8667 = $520,000 ÷ $600,000) is earned from the active conduct of a trade or business in a U.S. possession. Assuming a 34% corporate tax rate, the Sec. 936 credit is

$$\$68,000 \times \frac{\$130,000 + \$40,000}{\$200,000} = \$57,800$$

The net U.S. tax is $10,200 ($68,000 − $57,800), which represents the 34% tax rate times the $30,000 of taxable income derived from the U.S. activities. ■

---

[69] Secs. 936(a)(2), (e), and (f).
[70] Sec. 936(a)(1).

Topic Review 15-4 presents a summary of the tax treatment accorded the various means for doing business abroad.

TAX PLANNING CONSIDERATIONS

Deduction Versus Credit for Foreign Taxes

An election to deduct or credit any paid or accrued foreign income taxes is available to taxpayers annually.[71] Nearly all taxpayers who pay foreign taxes claim them as a credit. This advantage is illustrated in the following example.

Example 15-36 ■ Phil, a U.S. citizen, earns $100 of foreign income. Phil pays $25 in foreign income taxes. Two separate calculations comparing Phil's U.S. tax liability when the foreign taxes are deducted and credited are presented in the following table:

	Deduction	Credit
Gross income	$100	$100
Minus: Foreign income tax deduction	(25)	
Taxable income	$75	$100
Times: Marginal tax rate	× 0.31	× 0.31
Gross U.S. tax liability	$23	$31
Minus: Foreign tax credit		(25)
Net U.S. tax liability	$23	$6

If the foreign income taxes are deducted, Phil's total U.S. and foreign tax liability is $48 ($25 + $23). By claiming the credit, Phil's total U.S. and foreign tax liability is reduced to $31 ($25 + $6). ■

Some taxpayers deduct their foreign income taxes when they have incurred foreign losses, and they feel that the foreign tax payment will not be used as a credit either in the current year or in the 7-year carryback or carryover period. The deduction election provides a taxpayer with current tax benefits if he has U.S. profits in excess of his foreign losses. If such U.S. profits have not been earned, the foreign taxes will increase the taxpayer's NOLs.

Election to Accrue Foreign Taxes

Cash method of accounting taxpayers can elect to claim their foreign tax credit by using either the cash or accrual method of accounting. This election is not available if the foreign taxes are deducted. The election is binding on all tax years and can be revoked only with IRS consent.[72]

This election permits a cash method of accounting taxpayer to credit foreign income taxes that have been accrued but not yet paid. The election does not affect the application of the cash method of accounting to other income or expense items. Two advantages result from this election.

---
[71] Sec. 901(a).
[72] Sec. 905(a).

TOPIC REVIEW 15-4

Taxation of U.S. Persons Doing Business Abroad	
Type of Entity Used	Tax Treatment
Domestic subsidiary corporation	Profits are taxed in the year earned. A direct foreign tax credit is available for foreign taxes paid or accrued. Losses are deducted in the year they are incurred.
Foreign branch	Foreign branches are unincorporated extensions of the domestic taxpayer. Tax rules similar to those for a domestic corporation are used.
Foreign corporation (less than 50% U.S. owned)	A tax deferral is available for a foreign corporation's earnings until remitted to the United States. A domestic corporation can claim a deemed paid credit with respect to dividends received from foreign corporations that are 10% owned.
Foreign corporation (more than 50% U.S. owned)	Same rules as for previous entry. Some income forms of the CFC are taxed in the year in which they are earned. Tax-deferred earnings can be taxed under Subpart F when invested in U.S. property. Previously taxed income is distributed tax-free. Special rules apply to sale or exchange of CFC stock.
Foreign sales corporation	Special export entity that must meet certain mandated administrative and economic activity requirements. Part or all of the FSC's foreign trade income is exempt from U.S. taxation based upon the transfer pricing method used. Administrative transfer pricing methods permit the FSC to use other than arm's length pricing. Dividend distributions may be eligible for a 100% dividends-received deduction. Foreign tax credit is also available for taxes withheld on dividends.
Domestic international sales corporation (DISC)	DISCs are exempt from the U.S. corporate income tax if they meet certain procedural requirements. Constructive distributions are required annually. U.S. shareholders can be taxed on actual and constructive distributions. An interest charge is levied on the U.S. shareholder's portion of the tax deferred earnings. Administrative transfer pricing rules can be used to determine DISC taxable income. DISCs can lend money to a related producer (usually a member of its controlled group).
Possessions corporation	Domestic corporations that earn most of their income from the conduct of a trade or business in a U.S. possession and that make a timely election. The possessions credit eliminates U.S. taxation on non-U.S. income earned from the conduct of a possessions trade or business and qualified possessions source investment income. A 100% dividends-received deduction can eliminate U.S. taxation of dividends paid to a U.S. parent.

1. The election accelerates the time that the foreign tax credit is claimed by one or more tax years from the time the credit would otherwise be claimed.
2. The election eliminates the problem of matching income and foreign taxes for foreign tax credit limitation purposes and obviates the need for a carryback or carryover of excess credits.

Example 15-37 ■ Tulsa Corporation, a domestic corporation, commenced to conduct foreign activities in Country Z in 1988. Tulsa has used the cash method of accounting for several years. Z's tax laws require the use of a calendar year as the reporting period. Taxes that are owed on income earned in a year must be paid by the first day of the third month following the year-end. Tulsa operates overseas in 1988-1990 before closing its business on December 31, 1990. Its results are as follows:

	1988	1989	1990	1991
Foreign source taxable income	$1,000	$1,000	$1,000	$-0-
Foreign taxes accrued	300	300	300	-0-
Foreign taxes paid	-0-	300	300	300
Foreign tax credit limitation (34% corporate tax rate)	340	340	340	-0-
Foreign tax credit:				
Cash method of accounting	-0-	300	300	300
Accrual method of accounting	300	300	300	-0-

Under the cash method of accounting, Tulsa pays its 1988 U.S. taxes without the benefit of any foreign tax credit. Excess credits of $300 are reported in 1991 because of the mismatching of the reporting of the income and the making of the tax payments. $40 of the 1991 tax payment can be carried back to each 1989 and 1990, but $220 ($300 − [$40 + $40]) of the foreign tax credit would be lost since Tulsa has discontinued its foreign activities. If such activities had not been discontinued, they could be carried over and used in later years when the foreign tax credit limitation exceeds the foreign taxes paid. No mismatching occurs if the accrual method of accounting is elected for reporting the foreign tax credit. ■

Special Earned Income Elections

Taxpayers may choose to either break a previously made election to exclude foreign-earned income or not make the initial election, if they find themselves in one of the following two situations:

1. Employed in a foreign country where the foreign tax rate exceeds the U.S. tax rate (e.g., Canada or West Germany)
2. A loss is incurred from overseas employment or trade or business activities

In the first situation, the available foreign tax credits exceed the taxpayer's gross U.S. tax liability. The foreign-earned income exclusion causes part of the excess credits to be lost. By not electing to use Sec. 911, the entire amount of excess credits can be used as a carryback or carryover to another tax year (subject, of course, to the separate pool concepts). These excess credits might prove beneficial if, for example, income was earned in another year in a country where the local tax rate is lower than the U.S. tax rate.

In the second situation, taxpayers who incur losses have an excess of deductions over gross income. By excluding part or all of their foreign-earned income, a similar proportion of the related expenses will be disallowed. Such an action reduces the amount of any available NOL carryback or carryover. A decision not to elect Sec. 911 preserves the full amount of the excess deductions.

Taxpayers do not have an election to either exclude or deduct the housing cost amount. A qualifying taxpayer who earns entirely employer-provided amounts (W-2 income) must exclude the housing cost amount. If only self-employment income is earned, then the housing cost amount can only be deducted. If a combination of the two types of income is earned, then the housing cost amount is divided up between an exclusion and a deduction based upon the relative amounts of the two types of income that were earned.

An election not to use the Sec. 911 benefits is made on the taxpayer's tax return or on an amended tax return. Taxpayers should be cautious when revoking this election because a new election to claim the Sec. 911 benefits cannot be made until 5 years have passed or until the IRS consents to an earlier reelection.[73] Thus, a taxpayer who revokes an election while residing in a country that has a tax rate higher than the United States may not be able to elect to exclude earned income if he moves to a country that has a low tax rate.

Tax Treaties

> **Key Point**
> With certain exceptions, whenever a treaty and the Internal Revenue Code are in conflict, the treaty takes precedence.

A treaty is an agreement negotiated between two sovereign nations. The United States has entered into 34 income tax treaties covering about 50 nations. Income tax treaties have two primary objectives:

1. To reduce or eliminate the burden of double taxation
2. To establish cooperation between the taxing authorities of the two nations

In addition to income tax treaties, the U.S. has entered into estate and gift tax treaties and totalization agreements for social security taxes.

> **Additional Comment**
> The tax treaties do this by designating a "competent authority" to represent each country. The U.S. competent authority is the Assistant Commissioner (International) of the IRS.

The first objective represents the major use of an income tax treaty in tax planning. An income tax treaty involving the United States, however, cannot be used by a U.S. citizen or domestic corporation to reduce their U.S. income tax liability. U.S. citizens and domestic corporations are still taxed on their worldwide income at the regular U.S. tax rates. The treaty can, however, reduce the income taxes paid to the foreign country and may reduce or eliminate any problem that U.S. taxpayers have with excess foreign tax credits. Nonresident aliens and foreign corporations generally can avail themselves of the treaty provisions to reduce the U.S. withholding rate on most forms of investment income. For some types of investment income, the U.S. tax is eliminated.

The second objective is achieved by providing for an exchange of information between the taxing authorities of the two nations to prevent tax evasion and by establishing a mechanism by which taxpayers of one nation can settle tax disputes with the taxing authorities of the second nation.

A taxpayer who takes a position based on a treaty to which the U.S. is a party that overrules an internal revenue law (for example, the Internal Revenue Code) is required by Code Sec. 6114 to disclose such a position on his tax return or on a statement attaching to his return.

Special Resident Alien Elections

> **Additional Comment**
> The special resident alien election is made by attaching to a joint return a statement to the effect that the Sec. 6013(g) election is being made. This election must be made within the time period designated for filing a claim for credit or refund.

Two special elections are available to nonresident alien individuals which permit them to be classified as resident aliens. The first election permits them to be treated as a resident alien in situations where they move to the United States too late in the year to qualify for that year under the substantial presence test (see page 15-16).

This election is available if the alien

1. Does not qualify as a resident alien for the calendar year preceding the year for which the election is being made

---

[73] Sec. 911(e)(2).

2. Qualifies as a resident alien under the substantial presence test in the calendar year immediately following the election year, and
3. a. Was present in the United States for at least 31 consecutive days in the election year and
    b. Was present in the United States for at least 75% of the days in the period beginning with the first day of the 31-consecutive-day period and ending with the last day of the election year.

The election is irrevocable (except with the IRS's consent) and is made on the alien's tax return for the election year, but cannot be made prior to the alien satisfying the substantial presence test for the calendar year following the election year.[74]

Code Sec. 6013(g) permits nonresident aliens who are married to U.S. citizens or resident aliens to elect to be taxed as a resident alien. Such an election requires both individuals to agree to be taxed on their worldwide income and to provide all necessary books, records, and information necessary to ascertain either spouse's tax liability. This election permits nonresident aliens to file a joint tax return with their spouses. By filing the joint return, the couple can take advantage of the lower tax rates for married couples filing jointly.

The special election is available for a tax year only if the nonresident alien is married to a U.S. citizen or resident alien on the last day of the tax year and if both spouses consent to the election. The election applies to the tax year for which the election is made and all subsequent tax years until the election is revoked for one of the following reasons: neither spouse is a U.S. citizen or resident, either spouse dies, the couple separates under a decree of divorce or separate maintenance, or the election is terminated by the IRS. Termination of the election by the IRS generally occurs when either spouse fails to produce the books, records, or information necessary to properly determine the tax liability. If the election is terminated for a reason other than neither spouse being a U.S. citizen or resident alien, a new election cannot be made for a subsequent tax year.

A special election is available under Sec. 6013(h) for the tax year that a nonresident alien becomes a resident alien. This election permits the alien to be treated as a resident alien for income tax and withholding (on wages only) purposes. This election is available if (1) an individual is a nonresident alien at the beginning of the tax year and a resident alien at the end of the year, (2) the individual is married to a U.S. citizen or resident alien at the end of the tax year, and (3) both individuals make a timely election. This election permits the same tax benefits as a Sec. 6013(g) election and eliminates the need to be taxed as a nonresident alien for part of the year and a resident alien for the remainder of the year.

COMPLIANCE AND PROCEDURAL CONSIDERATIONS

Reporting the Foreign Tax Credit

The foreign tax credit is claimed on the taxpayer's income tax return by filing Form 1116 (for noncorporate taxpayers) or Form 1118 (for corporations). Separate forms are filed for each of the separate foreign tax credit limitations for which the taxpayer

---

[74] Sec. 7701(b)(4).

Compliance and Procedural Considerations • **15-47**

must make a foreign tax credit calculation. A completed Form 1116 is illustrated in Appendix B. The form is based upon the following example:

Example 15-38 ■ Andrew Roberts, a U.S. resident having social security number 123-45-6789, reports $30,000 of dividend income from France, on which 35,775 FF (French francs) in French income taxes are withheld on December 31, 1990. Roberts owns 3% of the distributing foreign corporation's outstanding stock. The entire $5,996 foreign tax amount can be claimed as a foreign tax credit since it is less than the applicable foreign tax credit limit for passive income. ■

Reporting the Earned Income Exclusion

The elections for the foreign earned income and housing cost amount exclusions are made separately on Form 2555. Each election must be filed with the income tax return (or an amended tax return) for the first tax year for which the election is made. Once an election is made, it remains in effect for that year and all subsequent tax years unless the IRS consents to revoke the election. Thus, a new election is not required when an individual either moves from one foreign country to another or moves to the United States and then returns to a foreign country some years later. No election is required if the taxpayer desires to deduct the housing cost amount.[75]

Taxpayers whose tax homes are outside the United States and Puerto Rico may request a special 2-month extension of time to file the return.[76] Any return filed before the end of the Sec. 911 qualifying period must be filed without claiming its benefits. If a taxpayer subsequently qualifies for the Sec. 911 benefits, an amended return or refund claim can be filed to recover any overpaid taxes. A taxpayer can avoid having to file an amended return or refund claim by obtaining an additional extension of time for filing the return until after the Sec. 911 qualifying period ends.[77]

A completed Form 2555 is illustrated in Appendix B based on the following example.

Example 15-39 ■ Lawrence Smith, a U.S. citizen, social security number 234-56-7890, is employed in 1990 by the Very Public Corporation in Paris, France. Smith is eligible for the Sec. 911 earned income exclusion for all of 1990 even though he spent 2 business days in the United States. For 1990, Smith is able to exclude $70,000 under the basic earned income exclusion and an additional $2,525 under the housing cost amount exclusion. This amount is reduced by $4,396 for disallowed deductions, leaving a net exclusion of $68,129. ■

Filing Requirements for Aliens and Foreign Corporations

A nonresident alien is required to file his income tax return on or before the fifteenth day of the sixth month following the close of the tax year. A nonresident alien files a Form 1040-NR. If the nonresident alien has wages that are subject to the withholding of income taxes, then Form 1040-NR must be filed on or before the fifteenth day of the fourth month following the close of the tax year.[78]

---

[75] Reg. Sec. 1.911-7(a)(3).
[76] Reg. Sec. 1.6081-5(c). Special extensions are available for armed forces personnel serving in combat zones in connection with Operation Desert Storm.
[77] Reg. Sec. 1.911-7(c). See IR 88-58 for some restrictions on this automatic extension.
[78] Reg. Sec. 1.6072-1(c).

The due date for a foreign corporation's income tax return depends upon whether the corporation has an office or place of business in the United States. If the foreign corporation has an office or place of business in the United States, its due date is the same as for a domestic corporation; that is, on or before the fifteenth day of the third month following the close of its tax year. If the foreign corporation does not have an office or place of business in the United States, its due date is extended two months to the fifteenth day of the sixth month following the close of its tax year. A foreign corporation files Form 1120-F.[79]

FSC and DISC Filing Requirements

The U.S. income tax return of an FSC is due by the 15th day of the third month following the close of its tax year. The FSC files a Form 1120-FSC.[80] An interest-charge DISC's income tax return is due by the fifteenth day of the ninth month following the close of its tax year. An interest-charge DISC files a Form 1120-IC-DISC.[81]

PROBLEM MATERIALS

DISCUSSION QUESTIONS

15-1. What four primary characteristics have been used by the drafters of the U.S. tax laws to determine the taxability of foreign-related transactions? Explain the importance of each characteristic.

15-2. Why is it important for an alien taxpayer to determine whether or not he is a resident of the United States?

15-3. Explain the alternatives available to individual taxpayers for reporting foreign income taxes that have been paid or accrued.

15-4. What types of foreign taxes are eligible to be credited?

15-5. Why did Congress feel that it was necessary to enact the foreign tax credit limitation rules?

15-6. What disadvantages has the separate basket approach to determining the foreign tax credit limitation created for U.S. taxpayers?

15-7. What advantages accrue to a cash method of accounting taxpayer who elects to accrue his foreign taxes for foreign tax credit purposes?

15-8. Determine whether the following statement is true or false: A taxpayer desiring to maximize his foreign tax credit limitation should attempt to minimize the amount of expenses that are allocated to his foreign source income.

15-9. What requirements must be satisfied in order for a U.S. citizen or resident alien living abroad to qualify for the foreign-earned income exclusion?

15-10. Tony, a U.S. citizen, uses the calendar year as his tax year. Tony is transferred to foreign country C on June 15, 1989, and he immediately becomes a resident of that country. His

---
[79] Reg. Secs. 1.6072-2(a) and (b).
[80] Ibid.
[81] Reg. Sec. 1.6072-2(e).

employer transfers him back to the United States on March 10, 1991. Does Tony qualify for the foreign-earned income exclusion as a bona fide resident? If not, is there any other way he can qualify?

15-11. Explain the reasons why a taxpayer might prefer to calculate his foreign-earned income exclusion by using the physical presence rules instead of the bona fide foreign resident rules?

15-12. Why might a taxpayer desire not to elect to use the foreign-earned income exclusion benefits? If such a decision is made in the current tax year, what negative consequences might it have on future tax years?

15-13. Compare the U.S. tax treatment of a nonresident alien and a resident alien, both of whom earn U.S. trade or business and U.S. investment income.

15-14. Explain how a nonresident alien is taxed in the year of arrival and departure if she arrives in the United States on July 1, 1989, and immediately establishes U.S. residency and departs from the United States on October 1, 1991, thereby terminating her U.S. residency.

15-15. How is a nonresident alien's U.S. source investment income taxed? What means are used to collect the tax?

15-16. Why is the "effectively connected" concept important to the taxation of a nonresident alien's trade or business income?

15-17. Manuel, a nonresident alien, conducts a trade or business in the United States during the current year. He earns $25,000 of interest income in the United States during the current year. What factors or tests are used to determine whether the interest income is taxed as investment income or trade or business income by the U.S. taxing authorities?

15-18. What are the advantages of a U.S. corporation conducting foreign business activities through a foreign branch? Through a foreign subsidiary?

15-19. What is the deferral privilege? What tax provisions can produce current U.S. taxation for part or all of a foreign corporation's earnings?

15-20. Why did Congress feel that it was necessary to enact the deemed paid foreign tax credit provisions?

15-21. Kilarney Corporation, a foreign corporation, is incorporated in Country J and is 100% owned by Maine Corporation, a domestic corporation. During the current year Kilarney Corporation earns $500,000 from its Country J operations and $100,000 from its U.S. operations. None of the Country J income is Subpart F income. $50,000 of Kilarney Corporation's after-tax profits are distributed as a dividend to Maine Corporation. Explain how Kilarney Corporation is taxed by the U.S. taxing authorities and whether or not any of Kilarney Corporation's income is taxed to Maine Corporation.

15-22. What is the branch profits tax? Explain the Congressional intent behind its enactment.

15-23. What is a controlled foreign corporation (CFC)?

15-24. Explain the concept of Subpart F income. What are the five major income forms that are taxed under the Subpart F income rules?

15-25. One of the purposes of enacting Subpart F was to prevent the use of holding companies created in tax haven nations to shelter foreign profits from U.S. taxation. Explain how the following income concepts accomplish this purpose.
  a. Foreign personal holding company income.
  b. Foreign base company sales income.
  c. Foreign base company services income.

15-26. What are investments in U.S. property? Explain why Congress made the amount of such investments taxable to U.S. shareholders.

15-27. Explain the tax consequences of a U.S. shareholder receiving a distribution of previously taxed Subpart F income from a CFC.

15-28. How does the taxation of the gain recognized when the stock of a CFC is sold differ from when the stock of a non-CFC is sold?

15-29. Explain how the Sec. 482 and CFC rules work together to reduce tax avoidance in a domestic corporation's use of a foreign sales subsidiary.

15-30. List the major advantages of using a foreign sales corporation (FSC) to conduct export activities.

15-31. Explain the advantages of the administrative pricing methods for a FSC.

15-32. What restrictions have been placed on domestic international sales corporations (DISCs) that reduce their tax incentives?

15-33. What tax incentives does the United States provide in order to induce businesses to expand the activities they conduct in Puerto Rico or a U.S. possession?

PROBLEMS

15-34. *Translation of Foreign Tax Payments.* Arnie, a U.S. citizen who uses the calendar year as his tax year, operates a proprietorship in Country Z. Arnie uses the cash method of accounting. During 1990 he reports 500,000 dubles of pretax profits. Country Z income taxes for calendar year 1990 in the amount of 150,000 dubles are paid on June 1, 1991. Exchange rates between the duble and the U.S. dollar at various times in 1990 and 1991 are as follows:

December 31, 1990	4.00 dubles = $1 (U.S.)
1990 average	3.75 dubles = $1 (U.S.)
June 1, 1991	4.25 dubles = $1 (U.S.)

a. What is the amount of Arnie's translated foreign tax credit? In what year can the credit be claimed?
b. How would your answer to Part a change if Arnie elects to accrue his foreign income taxes and files his U.S. income tax return on April 15, 1991?
c. What type of adjustment to the credit claimed in Part b would be required when Arnie pays his Country Z taxes on June 1, 1991?

15-35. *Foreign Tax Credit Limitation.* Jackson Corporation, a domestic corporation, engages in both U.S. and foreign activities during 1991. All of its overseas activities are conducted by a branch office in Country S. Jackson Corporation uses the cash method of accounting. The results of Jackson's 1991 operations are as follows:

U.S. source taxable income	$2,000,000
Foreign source taxable income	1,500,000
Country S income taxes paid	600,000

a. What is Jackson Corporation's foreign tax credit amount (assuming that the corporate tax rate is 34%)?
b. Are any foreign tax credit carrybacks or carryovers available to be used in other years? If so, in what years can they be used?

15-36. *Foreign Earned Income Exclusion.* Julia, a U.S. citizen, leaves the United States at noon on August 1, 1989, and arrives in Country P at 8:00 a.m. the next day. She immediately establishes a permanent residence in Country P, which she maintains until her return to the United States at 3:00 p.m. on April 5, 1991. Her only trips outside Country P are related to temporary employment in Country B from November 1, 1989, through December 10, 1989, and a U.S. vacation commencing at 5:00 p.m. on June 1, 1990, and ending at 10:00 p.m. on June 30, 1990. Can Julia qualify for the Sec. 911 benefits? If so, what is the amount of her foreign earned income exclusion for the years 1989 through 1991?

15-37. *Foreign Earned Income Exclusion.* Fred, a U.S. citizen, arrives in Country K on July 15, 1989, and proceeds to a construction site in the oil fields where he takes up residence in employer-provided housing where he is required to reside. He remains at the site until his departure on December 1, 1991, except for local travel and the months of July and August, 1990, when he is on vacation in the United States. No services are provided while in the United

States. Fred earns $10,000 per month in salary and allowances while employed overseas. In addition he receives meals and lodging valued at $1,750 per month while in Country K. What is the amount of Fred's earned income exclusions for the years 1989 through 1991?

15-38. *Foreign Earned Income Exclusion.* Dillon, a U.S. citizen, resides overseas in Country K for all of 1991. Dillon is married, files a joint return with his wife, and claims two exemptions. He reports the following information about his 1991 activities:

Salary and allowances (other than for housing)[a]	$175,000
Housing allowance	28,000
Employment-related expenses	7,500
Housing costs	30,000
Itemized deductions	4,000
Country K income taxes	12,000

[a] All Dillon's salary and allowances are attributable to services performed in Country K.

What is Dillon's net U.S. tax liability for 1991 (assume that Dillon elects to exclude his earned income and housing cost amount)?

15-39. *Tax Calculation for a Nonresident Alien.* Mark is a citizen of Country C. During the current year, while he is a nonresident alien for U.S. tax purposes, Mark earns the following amounts:

Dividend paid by a U.S. corporation	$ 2,500
Rentals from a U.S. building	10,000
Interest paid by a foreign corporation	5,000

Mark does not conduct a U.S. trade or business during the current year. His interest and depreciation expenses from leasing the building under a net lease arrangement are $7,000. What is Mark's U.S. tax liability? How is the tax collected?

15-40. *Taxation of a Nonresident Alien.* Joe, a single nonresident alien, is in the United States for 80 days in the current year engaging in the conduct of a U.S. trade or business. Joe reports the following income from his U.S. activities. Indicate how each of the following independent items will be taxed and how the tax will be collected.
  a. $25,000 of dividend income paid by a U.S. corporation on a portfolio stock invesment that is unrelated to Joe's trade or business.
  b. $75,000 of sales commissions earned by Joe. $50,000 is earned on sales made while in the United States, and $25,000 is earned on non-U.S. sales while outside the United States.
  c. A $10,000 capital gain earned on the sale of stock in a U.S. corporation while Joe was in the United States.
  d. $3,000 of interest income earned on a bank account in Joe's home country.

15-41. *Deemed Paid Foreign Tax Credit.* Paper Corporation, a domestic corporation, owns 60% of the stock of Sud Corporation, a foreign corporation. Sud Corporation reports earnings and profits of $200,000 for its post-1986 tax years. Its post-1986 foreign income taxes are $50,000. Sud pays a $90,000 dividend in the current year to its shareholders. A 15% income tax levied by Country T on nonresident shareholders is withheld by Sud Corporation from the dividend payment.
  a. What amount of gross income does Paper Corporation report as a result of receiving the dividend?
  b. What is Paper Corporation's net increase in its U.S. tax liability as a result of receiving the dividend (assume a 34% U.S. corporate tax rate)?
  c. How would your answer to Parts a and b change if the post-1986 foreign income taxes had instead been $80,000?

15-42. *Deemed Paid Foreign Tax Credit.* Duke Corporation, a domestic corporation, owns all of the stock of Taiwan Corporation, a foreign corporation. Taiwan Corporation pays an $80,000 dividend in the current year to Duke Corporation. Taiwan Corporation's post-1986 operating results show $200,000 of earnings and profits and $60,000 of foreign income taxes. Foreign income taxes of $8,000 are withheld on the dividend.

a. What is the amount of Duke Corporation's deemed paid foreign tax credit?
b. What is Duke Corporation's net increase in its U.S. tax liability as a result of receiving the dividend (assume a 34% U.S. corporate income tax rate)?
c. How would your answers to Parts a and b change if the $80,000 dividend were instead paid to U.S. citizen Donna (instead of to Duke Corporation)?

15-43. *Translation of a Dividend.* Dayton Corporation, a domestic corporation, owns all of the stock of Fiero Corporation, a foreign corporation. Fiero Corporation is formed in early 1991. During 1991, Fiero Corporation earns 400,000 pirogs of pretax profits and pays 100,000 pirogs in Country Z income taxes. On August 25, 1991, Fiero Corporation pays a 150,000 pirog dividend to Dayton Corporation. Country Z income taxes are paid by Fiero Corporation on March 1, 1992. The exchange rates between the pirog and the U.S. dollar at various times during 1991 and 1992 are as follows:

January 1, 1991	9.0 pirogs = $1 (U.S.)
August 25, 1991	10.0 pirogs = $1 (U.S.)
1991 average	9.5 pirogs = $1 (U.S.)
March 1, 1992	10.5 pirogs = $1 (U.S.)

a. What are the translated amounts of Dayton Corporation's dividend and deemed paid credit?
b. What is Dayton Corporation's net U.S. tax liability as a result of receiving the dividend (assume a 34% U.S. corporate tax rate)?

15-44. *Foreign Tax Credit Limitation.* Tucson Corporation, a domestic corporation organized in 1989, reports the following information about its activities for the period 1989-1991.

	1989	1990	1991
Foreign tax accrual	$100,000	$120,000	$140,000
Foreign source taxable income	400,000	300,000	500,000
Worldwide taxable income	1,000,000	1,000,000	1,000,000

The foreign source and worldwide taxable income amounts are determined under U.S. law.
a. What is Tucson Corporation's foreign tax credit limitation for the years 1989–1991 (assume a 34% U.S. corporate tax rate)?
b. What happens to Tucson's excess foreign tax credits (if any) during this period? Do any carryovers remain after 1991?
c. How would your answers to Parts a and b change if as part of an IRS audit $100,000 of expenses thought to be "U.S. source" when determining taxable income were required to be reported as "foreign source"?

15-45. *Foreign Tax Credit Carrybacks and Carryovers.* Hamilton Corporation, a domestic corporation, reports the following results from its current year activities:

U.S. source taxable income	$1,000,000
Foreign source taxable income from branch activity in Country M	1,000,000
Foreign taxes accrued on branch income	280,000
Cash dividend payment from India Corporation, a foreign corporation	212,500
Foreign taxes withheld by India Corporation and remitted to Country X government	37,500

India Corporation is 15% owned by Hamilton and pays its dividend on April 20. Its pretax profits from post-1986 tax years are $6,000,000, and its Country X taxes from post-1986 tax years are $1,500,000. Hamilton Corporation has excess foreign tax credit limitations of $20,000 and $40,000 from its two preceding tax years, respectively.
a. What is Hamilton Corporation's foreign tax credit (assuming a 34% U.S. corporate tax rate)?
b. Are any foreign tax credit carrybacks or carryovers available to be used? If so, in what years can they be used?

15-46. *Definition of a CFC.* In the following independent situations, determine whether or not a foreign corporation, having a single class of stock outstanding, is characterized as a controlled foreign corporation.

    a. The foreign corporation's stock is equally owned by Alpha Corporation, a domestic corporation, and Bart, a U.S. citizen. Bart owns none of the Alpha Corporation stock.

    b. Assume the same facts as in Part a, except Bart is instead a nonresident alien.

    c. The foreign corporation's stock is owned 14% by Art, 49% by Bob, 28% by Colleen, and 9% by Danielle. Art, Colleen, and Danielle are U.S. citizens and Bob is a nonresident alien. All four individuals are unrelated.

    d. Assume the same facts as in Part c, except that Danielle is instead Art's daughter.

15-47. *Definition of Foreign Base Company Income.* Manila Corporation, a foreign corporation, is incorporated in Country J. All of Manila Corporation's stock is owned by Simpson Corporation, a domestic corporation. Determine which of the following transactions produce Subpart F income.

    a. Manila Corporation purchases a product from Simpson Corporation and sells it to unrelated parties in Countries J and X.

    b. Manila Corporation receives a dividend from foreign corporation Manila-Sub. All of Manila-Sub's stock is owned by Manila Corporation. Manila-Sub is incorporated and operates exclusively in Country J.

    c. Manila Corporation manufactures a product in Country J and sells it to Simpson Corporation for use in Country Z.

    d. Manila Corporation services machinery manufactured by an unrelated, Country J corporation. Service activities conducted outside of Country J on this machinery constitute 80% of Manila Corporation's gross income.

    e. Manila Corporation purchases a product from an unrelated U.S. corporation and sells it to unrelated persons in Country J.

15-48. *Definition of Foreign Base Company Income.* Apache Corporation, a domestic corporation, owns 80% of the stock of Burrito Corporation, a foreign corporation. Burrito Corporation is incorporated in Country Y. Burrito Corporation's results for the current year are as follows:

Foreign base company sales income	$300,000
Foreign base company services income	150,000
Dividend from Kane Corporation, a 70%-owned Country Y corporation	70,000
Other income	280,000

Kane Corporation performs substantially all of its activities in Country Y.

    a. What amount of income does Apache Corporation have to recognize as a result of Burrito's activities?

    b. How would your answer to Part a change if the dividend is instead from a Country M corporation?

    c. How would your answer to Part b change if the foreign base company sales income is instead $500,000?

15-49. *Transfer Pricing Rules.* Arrow Corporation, a domestic corporation, annually sells 1,000,000 starter motors to Bentley Corporation, a foreign corporation. Bentley is organized in Country K, 100% owned by Arrow, and sells the starters as replacement equipment through auto dealers in Country K. The statutory Country K tax rate is 20%.

    a. What is the value of the annual U.S. tax deferral available to Arrow Corporation if the starters are sold to Bentley for $40, cost $30 to produce, and are sold for $60? Assume Bentley's operating expenses are $4,000,000.

    b. What additional value would accrue to Arrow annually if it were able to charge Bentley $50 for each starter? What mechanisms are likely to be used by U.S. tax authorities to prevent the $50 amount from being charged?

    c. How would your answer to Part a change if the starters were sold by Bentley for use in Country M?

15-50. *Sale of CFC Stock.* Irvan Corporation, a domestic corporation, acquires all of the stock of DeLeon Corporation, a foreign corporation on April 1, 1988, for $300,000. Irvan Corporation sells the DeLeon stock on October 15, 1991, for $825,000. No Subpart F income has been reported by Irvan as a result of DeLeon's activities. DeLeon Corporation reports E&P balances during the period 1988 through 1991 as follows (assume all months have 30 days):

Year	E&P
1988	$120,000
1989	80,000
1990	110,000
1991	144,000

What are the amount and character of Irvan Corporation's gain on the sale of the DeLeon stock?

15-51. *FSC Requirements.* Which of the following events would prevent a corporation from qualifying as a FSC for a tax year?
  a. The FSC has both common and preferred stock outstanding during the second half of the tax year.
  b. The FSC is incorporated in the United States.
  c. The FSC's primary bank account is located in New York.
  d. Part of the FSC's export property sales are to the U.S. government.
  e. The FSC's foreign trading gross receipts exceed $5,000,000.

15-52. *FSC Tax Liability Calculation.* Santiago Corporation elected to be taxed as a FSC last year. Santiago Corporation is 100% owned by a U.S. corporation. During the current year, Santiago sells 60,000 widgets at a price of $100 each. All receipts are foreign trading gross receipts. Santiago's promotion and sales expenses are $16 per unit, and its general and administrative expenses are $4 per unit. Interest income from investments of excess working capital in the current year amount to $3,500. Santiago's accountant has determined that the gross receipts method will maximize its profits.
  a. What are the amount and tax treatment for Santiago's foreign trade income and interest income (assume a 34% U.S. corporate tax rate)?
  b. How would a $20,000 dividend paid to Santiago's parent corporation be taxed?

15-53. *Calculation of DISC Interest-Charge.* Yale Corporation, a domestic corporation, is an interest-charge DISC that is wholly owned by Princeton Corporation, also a domestic corporation. During 1990, Yale Corporation reports $500,000 of taxable income. All of Yale Corporation's $6,000,000 in receipts are qualified export receipts. Included in the receipts is $30,000 of interest income on producer's loans. Princeton Corporation's pre-1990, DISC-related, tax-deferred liability is $268,000.
  a. What amount of Yale Corporation's 1990 taxable income is constructively distributed to Princeton Corporation?
  b. What is the amount of Princeton Corporation's 1991 interest charge on Yale Corporation's DISC-related tax liability (assume a 34% corporate tax rate and a 7.50% T-Bill rate)? When is the interest charge paid by Princeton Corporation?

15-54. *Sec. 936 Credit Calculation.* Travis Corporation, a domestic corporation, commences the conduct of Puerto Rican operations during the current year with the following results:

	Gross Income	Taxable Income
Trade or business income	$1,250,000	$325,000
Qualified possessions source investment income	150,000	150,000
Total	$1,400,000	$475,000

Travis Corporation earns $100,000 of its trade or business gross income in Venezuela. The remainder of the gross income is earned in Puerto Rico. Travis Corporation earns $75,000 of its trade or business gross income from sales to an unrelated person that are collected in the United States.
  a. Is Travis Corporation eligible for the Sec. 936 credit?
  b. What is the amount of Travis Corporation's Sec. 936 credit, if any?

TAX FORM/RETURN PREPARATION PROBLEMS

15-55. Stephen R. and Rachel K. Bates, both U.S. citizens, lived in Country K for all of the current year except when Stephen was temporarily assigned to his employer's home office in the United States. They file a joint return and use the calendar year as their tax year. Their taxpayer identification number is 123-45-6789. The Bateses report the following current-year income and expense items:

Salary:	United States	$ 10,000
	Country K	150,000
Dividends:	From U.S. corporation	2,000
	From Country K corporation	5,000
Foreign business expenses (directly allocable to Country K-earned income)		5,000
Itemized deductions (not directly allocable to any income)		1,800
Country K income taxes paid on April 1 of current year		12,500
Personal and dependency exemptions		3

Last year the Bateses elected to accrue their foreign income taxes for foreign tax credit purposes. No foreign tax credit carryovers are available to the current year. The Bateses estimate that they will owe 75,000 tesos in Country K income taxes for this year on the Country K salary and dividends. On December 31 of the current year, 4 tesos equal $1 (U.S.). The exchange rate between the teso and the dollar does not change between year-end and the date the Country K taxes are paid. No Country K taxes are withheld on the foreign corporation dividend.

Complete the two Form 1116s which the Bateses must file with their current year return in order to claim a foreign tax credit. Ignore the implications of the Sec. 911 earned income exclusion, itemized deduction reduction, personal exemption phase-out, and alternative minimum tax provisions.

15-56. John Lawrence Bailey (social security number 234-56-7890) is employed by American Conglomerate Corporation in Country T. Bailey has resided in Country T with his wife and three children for 7 years. He made one five-day business trip back to the United States in the current year. $1,500 of salary is allocable to Bailey's U.S. business trip. Bailey reports the following tax information about the current year:

Income:	
Base salary	$75,000
Overseas premium	9,000
Cost-of-living allowance	37,500
Housing allowance	30,000
Education allowance	12,750
Home leave travel allowance	11,000
Income tax reimbursement from employer for preceding tax year	18,000
Expenditures:	
Tuition at U.S. school	12,000
Housing expenses (rental of home)	32,500
Itemized deductions	6,000
Foreign income taxes	9,000

Complete a Form 2555 for the Baileys. Assume that all prior tax returns are filed claiming that Mr. Bailey is a bona fide foreign resident and the housing cost amount is claimed as an exclusion.

CASE STUDY PROBLEM

15-57. Mark Pruett, a U.S. citizen, is being transferred abroad by his employer. You have done his tax work for a number of years. His 1991 salary and allowances in Country M will be $175,000 which is substantially above his 1990 salary. This increase is due to the higher cost of living in Country M and his added responsibilities. $30,000 of the allowances are housing allowances. His housing costs are expected to run $36,000 for 1991. The statutory Country M income tax rate is 40%. His employer has a second location in Country T where Mark probably will be transferred in three or four years. The statutory Country T income tax rate is 20%.

Required: Draft a memorandum to Mark explaining the tax consequences of his relocation and whether he should elect to use the foreign earned income exclusion. Note: Do not consider the moving costs involved in relocating Mark.

TAX RESEARCH PROBLEMS

15-58. Spike "Spitball" Weaver was a hard-throwing pitcher who was reaching the end of his major league baseball career. After becoming a "free agent," he signed a rather lucrative 3-year contract (which included a substantial signing bonus) to play for the Tokyo Bombers in the fledgling World Baseball League. This league included 12 teams, only 4 of which were located in the United States. Although Spike's salary is paid over a 12-month period, he resides in Japan only for the 7-month regular season, the preseason training period, and the postseason playoffs. The remainder of his time is spent at his home in Fitzgerald, Georgia. What factors should be considered in allocating Spike's bonus and salary between the U.S. and non-U.S. locations?

A partial list of research sources is

- Reg. Sec. 1.861-4.
- Rev. Rul. 76-66, 1976-1 C.B. 189.
- Rev. Rul. 87-38, 1987-1 C.B. 176.
- *Peter Stemkowski v. CIR,* 50 AFTR 2d 82-5739, 82-2 USTC ¶ 9589 (2nd Cir., 1982).

15-59. Determine whether the taxes levied under each of the Acts listed below are creditable under Sec. 901.

a. West German corporation tax law
b. Canadian Branch Tax Act (imposed on Canadian branches of foreign companies)
c. Ontario (Canada) Corporations Tax Act
d. Ontario (Canada) Mining Tax Act

A partial list of research sources is

- Prentice-Hall, *Federal Taxes,* ¶ 9015.03.
- Commerce Clearing House, *Standard Federal Tax Reporter,* ¶ 28466.318.
- *Texasgulf, Inc. v. U.S.,* 64 AFTR 2d 89-5105, 89-1 USTC ¶ 9385 (Cls. Ct., 1989).

15-60. Kiwi Corporation, a sales FSC, is created on January 1 of the current year. Kiwi Corporation meets all of the FSC requirements for the current year. It sells a product that is produced by its U.S. parent corporation. During 1991, Kiwi sells 20,000 units of the product at a $10.00 per-unit price. All of the sales produced foreign trading gross receipts. The per-unit costs incurred by Kiwi and its U.S. parent corporation are: parent's manufacturing costs, $2.50; FSC's promotion and sales expenses, $3.00; and FSC's general and administrative expenses, $2.00. An arm's-length transfer price for the product would have been $4.60.

a. What is Kiwi's maximum per-unit profit under all three transfer pricing alternatives?
b. Give the amount and tax treatment for Kiwi's exempt foreign trade income and nonexempt foreign trade income under each of the alternative pricing methods.

A partial list of research sources is

- Sec. 925.
- Temp. Reg. Sec. 1.925(a)-1T.

16 Administrative Procedures

CHAPTER OUTLINE
LEARNING OBJECTIVES 16-2
ROLE OF THE INTERNAL
   REVENUE SERVICE 16-2
  Enforcement and
    Collection 16-2
  Interpretation of the
    Statute 16-3
  Organization of the IRS 16-3
AUDITS OF TAX
   RETURNS 16-3
  Percentage of Returns
    Audited 16-5
  Selection of Returns for
    Audit 16-5
  Alternatives for a Taxpayer
    Whose Return Is
    Audited 16-7
  Ninety-Day Letter 16-10
  Litigation 16-11
REQUESTS FOR
   RULINGS 16-12
  Information to Be Included in
    Taxpayer's Request 16-12
  Will the IRS Rule? 16-13
  When Rulings Are
    Desirable 16-14

DUE DATES 16-14
  Due Dates for Returns 16-14
  Extensions 16-15
  Due Dates for Payment of the
    Tax 16-15
  Interest on Tax Not Timely
    Paid 16-16
  Penalties 16-17
ESTIMATED TAXES 16-20
  Payment Requirements 16-20
  Penalty for Underpaying
    Estimated Taxes 16-21
  Exceptions to the Penalty 16-22
OTHER MORE SEVERE
   PENALTIES 16-23
  Negligence 16-23
  Substantial
    Understatement 16-24
  Civil Fraud 16-26
  Criminal Fraud 16-27
STATUTE OF
   LIMITATIONS 16-28
  General 3-Year Rule 16-29
  Six-Year Rule for "Substantial"
    Omissions 16-30
  When No Return Is Filed 16-31

  Other Exceptions to 3-Year
    Rule 16-31
  Refund Claims 16-32
LIABILITY FOR TAX 16-33
  Joint Returns 16-33
  Transferee Liability 16-35
TAX PRACTICE ISSUES 16-35
  Statements on Responsibilities in
    Tax Practice 16-35
  Statutory Provisions Concerning
    Tax Return Preparers 16-38
  Rules of *Circular 230* 16-39
CONTROVERSIAL ISSUE 16-40
  Concept of "Substantial
    Authority" 16-40
PROBLEM MATERIALS 16-41
  Discussion Questions 16-41
  Problems 16-43
  Tax Research Problems 16-45

LEARNING OBJECTIVES

After studying this chapter, you should be able to

1. Understand the role of the IRS in our tax system
2. Discuss how returns are selected for audit and the alternatives available to persons whose returns are audited
3. Describe the IRS's ruling process
4. Recognize the due dates for tax returns and penalties associated with not abiding by such dates
5. Explain the penalty for not paying estimated taxes
6. Describe more severe penalties, including the fraud penalty
7. Understand the statute of limitations
8. Explain which taxpayers are liable for unpaid taxes
9. Recognize the standards to which tax advisors should adhere

This chapter provides an overview of the administrative and procedural aspects of tax practice, an area with which all tax advisors should have some familiarity. The specific matters discussed include the role of the Internal Revenue Service (IRS), the manner in which tax returns are chosen for audit, taxpayers' alternatives to immediately agreeing to pay a proposed deficiency, due dates for returns, penalties potentially affecting taxpayers, and the statute of limitations. Tax practice topics related to CPAs are also explored, including the *Statements on Responsibilities in Tax Practice* of the American Institute of Certified Public Accountants (AICPA), and penalty provisions in the Internal Revenue Code that affect tax advisors and tax return preparers.

ROLE OF THE INTERNAL REVENUE SERVICE

OBJECTIVE 1
Understand the role of the IRS in our tax system

The IRS is a part of the Treasury Department. The top IRS official is called the commissioner. The IRS employs almost 100,000 persons in civil service (as opposed to political) positions. The responsibilities of the IRS include the enforcement of and interpretation of tax laws.

Enforcement and Collection

Key Point
The U.S. tax structure is based on a self-assessment system. While the level of voluntary compliance is actually quite high, one of the principal purposes of the IRS is to enforce compliance with the federal tax laws by those taxpayers who may willfully or inadvertently fail to pay their fair share of the tax burden.

One of the most significant functions of the IRS is the enforcement of the tax laws.[1] The IRS is responsible for ensuring that taxpayers file returns, report their tax liabilities correctly, and pay any tax due.

The United States enjoys a high level of voluntary compliance with its tax laws. However, because some persons do not comply voluntarily, it is necessary for the IRS to perform audits on selected taxpayers' returns and investigate certain nonfilers. In

---

[1] The IRS does not have enforcement duties, however, with respect to the taxes on guns and alcohol.

addition, because a number of ambiguities (grey areas) exist with respect to the proper interpretation of the tax laws, taxpayers and the IRS may not agree on the tax treatment of certain transactions. As part of its enforcement duties, the IRS must attempt to discover situations where taxpayers report these ambiguous transactions in their tax returns differently from the manner in which the IRS would have treated them. As a later discussion points out, taxpayers may litigate these differences if they do not agree with the position that the IRS takes in auditing their returns.

Not only must the IRS try to ensure that taxpayers report the correct tax liability, it must also make sure that taxpayers pay their taxes. For various reasons, some taxpayers file returns without paying any or all of the tax owed. The IRS's collection personnel are responsible for collecting as much as possible from such persons or entities.

Interpretation of the Statute

Self-Study Question
How are letter rulings different from other IRS administrative interpretations (i.e., revenue rulings, revenue procedures, notices, and information releases)?

Answer
Letter rulings are written for specific taxpayers (not the general public) and have no precedential value.

As noted in Chapter 1, generally the statutory language is of such a general nature that administrative and judicial interpretations are necessary. The IRS is charged with making some of the administrative interpretations. Its most important administrative interpretations are revenue rulings, revenue procedures, notices, and information releases. Each of these interpretations is available to the general public. In addition, the IRS also issues interpretations to specific taxpayers in the form of letter rulings. Letter rulings, however, have no precedential value. These interpretations are discussed in detail in Chapter 1.

Organization of the IRS

The IRS must perform its responsibilities on a nationwide basis. For purposes of easier administration, the IRS is divided into seven geographic regions, each headed by a regional commissioner. The regions are further subdivided into 63 districts, for whom the chief administrative officer is the district director. Each state has at least one district, and large states (e.g., New York, California, and Texas) consist of more than one district. The IRS also operates ten service centers throughout the nation that are responsible for receiving and processing tax returns.[2] An organizational chart of the IRS appears in Figure 16-1. At the national level, besides the commissioner, other top officials include the senior deputy commissioner, an assistant commissioner (for inspection), a series of assistants to the commissioner, and the chief counsel. The chief counsel's office prepares regulations and represents the government in Tax Court cases.

AUDITS OF TAX RETURNS

One of the IRS's most significant enforcement activities is auditing tax returns. All returns are subject to some verification. For example, one job the service centers

---

[2] IRS Service Centers are located in Andover, Massachusetts; Chamblee, Georgia; Austin, Texas; Holtsville, New York; Covington, Kentucky; Fresno, California; Kansas City, Missouri; Memphis, Tennessee; Ogden, Utah; and Philadelphia, Pennsylvania.

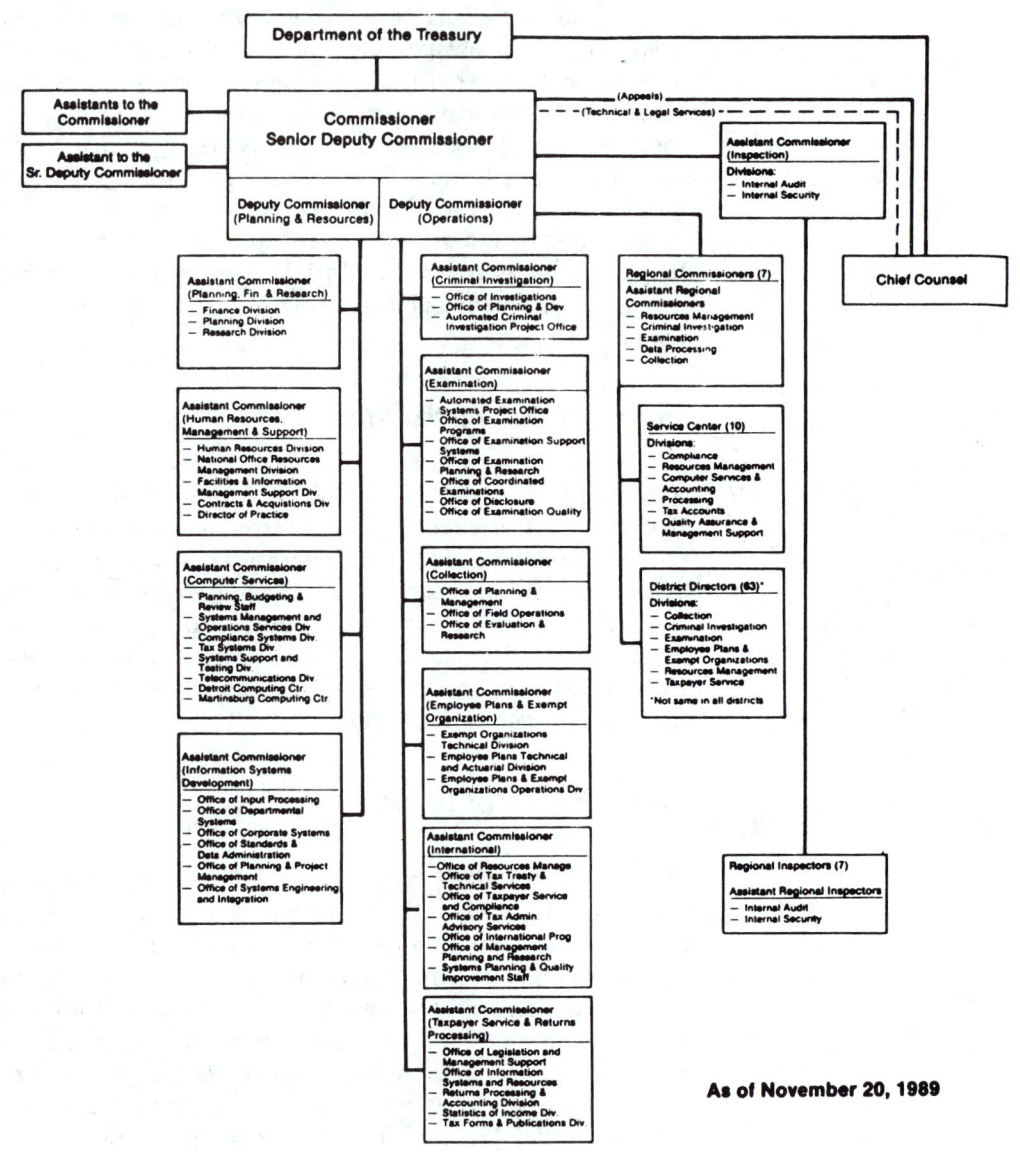

FIGURE 16-1 Internal Revenue Service—Organizational Chart

Note: On December 19, 1990 the Treasury Department announced the retitling of the following positions:

From	To
Senior Deputy Commissioner	Deputy Commissioner
Deputy Commissioner (Operations)	Chief Operations Officer
Deputy Commissioner (Planning and Operations)	Chief Financial Officer

Two Assistant Chief Information Officers (not shown) are retitled as Assistant Commissioners for Information Systems Development and Assistant Commissioner for Information Systems Management. These changes are not shown on the diagram.

Source: Prentice Hall Information Services, *Federal Taxes 2d* (Englewood Cliffs, N.J.: Maxwell Macmillan, Inc., 1990), ¶ 76,559.86.

OBJECTIVE 2

Discuss how returns are selected for audit and the alternatives available to persons whose returns are audited

perform is verifying the arithmetic and checking whether amounts are properly carried from one line to another on each return. Also, a check is made to determine whether any items, such as signatures and social security numbers, are missing. Computers also compare (or "match") by social security number the amounts reported on a taxpayer's return with employer- or payor-filed documents (Forms W-2 and 1099) filed with the service center.[3] To date, however, a 100% matching of these documents with tax return information has not been possible.

If the service center detects an error in the tax liability that has been reported on the return, the center transmits to the taxpayer a notice outlining the additional tax or refund due. If the information reported on a return does not agree with Forms W-2 or 1099 submitted by an employer or payor that contain the taxpayer's social security number, the taxpayer will be requested to provide a written explanation of the discrepancy or pay some additional tax.

Percentage of Returns Audited

Only a small fraction of all returns are audited. For example, for fiscal 1989, the IRS audited only 0.92% of all individual returns, 2.02% of all corporate returns, 0.72% of all partnership returns, and 0.12% of all fiduciary returns. For individuals with "total positive income" (i.e., gross income before losses and other deductions) of $50,000 or more, the audit rate was 6.47%, and corporations with assets of at least $250 million had a 64.24% rate. As a result of its audit process, the IRS recommended additional taxes and penalties totaling $21.28 billion in that year.[4]

The audit percentages described above may be misleading because over half of the returns filed are subjected to a computerized "instant audit" in which the IRS compares the tax return information with documents (Forms 1099 and W-2) submitted by payors and employers. According to a former commissioner of the IRS, "[M]ore than half of the individual returns filed are simple enough so that a matching with forms filed by employers and interest payors is sufficient to insure compliance."[5]

Selection of Returns for Audit

Returns are chosen for audit in a variety of ways. Most returns, however, are selected under the *discriminant function (DIF)* process described below. The IRS's objective in using the DIF process is to make the audit process as productive as possible by minimizing the number of audits resulting in the collection of no additional taxes. The DIF process has improved the IRS's ability to select returns for audit. In 1989 the IRS failed to collect additional taxes on only about 14% of the individual returns it audited.[6] By comparison, in the late 1960s, prior to the advent of the DIF program, the IRS failed to collect additional taxes in 40% of its audits.[7]

Discriminant Function (DIF) Program. Two-thirds of the individual returns audited in 1982 were chosen under the DIF program.[8] The IRS began laying the groundwork for the DIF program in the mid-1960s in an effort to

Typical Misconception

Arithmetic checks and the matching of figures reported by taxpayers with those reported by employers and other payors is sufficient to ensure proper compliance by most taxpayers. Since these procedures are not considered audits, the low percentage of returns actually audited is somewhat misleading.

---

[3] Form W-2 reports employees' salaries and withholding tax, and Form 1099 reports income such as interest and dividends.

[4] *1989 Annual Report of the Commissioner of the IRS* (Washington, D.C.: U.S. Government Printing Office, 1990), pp. 14, 46, 50.

[5] Bureau of National Affairs, *BNA Daily Tax Reports,* June 20, 1984, p. G-1.

[6] *1989 Annual Report of the Commissioner of the IRS* (Washington, D.C.: U.S. Government Printing Office, 1990), p. 49.

[7] Bureau of National Affairs, *BNA Daily Tax Reports,* November 26, 1984, p. G-2.

[8] J. L. Wedick, Jr., "Looking for a Needle in a Haystack—How the IRS Selects Returns for Audit," *The Tax Adviser,* November 1983, p. 673.

Historical Note

Several attempts have been made by taxpayers to make the actual DIF program public information. However, so far the courts have refused to require the IRS to provide such detailed information. The basic thrust of the DIF program is that a return will be flagged if enough items on the return are out of the norm for a taxpayer in that particular income bracket.

- Reduce the staff and computer time necessary to screen returns
- Identify the returns most likely to contain errors
- Reduce the number of audited returns for which an examination results in little or no additional tax[9]

An assistant commissioner described the DIF selection process in the following manner:

> DIF is a type of statistical analysis, using multiple variables or criteria to differentiate between two populations. For the IRS, those populations are tax returns needing examination versus those returns not needing examination. DIF essentially identifies items on tax returns having predictive power; that is, the selected items on returns in the "need to examine" group show up differently than those in the "no need to examine" group. DIF takes several items on a tax return and reduces them to a single score, which is then used as a major determinant as to whether a particular return will be examined.[10]

Returns with a relatively high DIF score have characteristics in common with returns for which the IRS earlier assessed a deficiency upon audit (e.g., the return may have reported a relatively high casualty loss or charitable contribution deduction). Because the IRS does not have the resources to audit all returns with a relatively high DIF score, IRS managers choose which of the higher scored returns should be given top priority for an audit.

The IRS develops its DIF formulas based upon information from the Taxpayer Compliance Measurement Program (TCMP), discussed below. As part of its TCMP examination, the IRS divides returns into two groups: returns with significant tax changes and returns with, at most, small tax changes. The only items on the tax returns that are used in the DIF program are those that are most valuable in distinguishing between the returns with a significant change in taxes and those with little or no change.

Key Point

The TCMP generates the information that the IRS uses to build its DIF program. Thus, taxpayers from all income levels are randomly selected for a TCMP audit. In a TCMP audit, the IRS is more interested in the information it gathers than the additional taxes it might collect.

Taxpayer Compliance Measurement Program. A small fraction of audited returns are selected at random under the **Taxpayer Compliance Measurement Program.** As discussed above, the purpose of the TCMP is to improve the selection process of the DIF program. Under TCMP, every 3 years about 50,000 individual returns are audited. TCMP audits are also conducted for other entities such as corporations.

In a TCMP audit, the IRS agent audits every item on the tax return. Taxpayers undergoing this type of examination should realize, however, that their returns were chosen completely at random and not because it appeared that an assessment of additional taxes would result. The probability of undergoing a TCMP audit has been compared to the likelihood of being "hit by a bus" and the experience of such an audit as being "about as comforting if it happens."[11]

Other Methods. In addition to DIF and TCMP, several other methods exist for selecting returns for audit. The percentage of returns chosen under these other methods is relatively small. Some returns are chosen because the taxpayer filed a claim for refund of taxes paid previously, and the IRS decides to audit the tax return

---

[9] Ibid., pp. 673-4.
[10] Ibid., p. 674.
[11] P. N. Strassels and R. Wood, *All You Need to Know About the IRS* (New York: Random House, 1979), p. 11.

before issuing a refund of the requested amount. A few returns are audited because the IRS receives a tip from one taxpayer (perhaps a disgruntled former employee) that another taxpayer did not correctly handle some items on a return. If the IRS does collect additional taxes as a result of such an audit, it is empowered to pay a reward to the individual furnishing the tip. The reward is completely discretionary, although it cannot exceed 10% of the additional tax and penalties found due.[12] Sometimes the process of examining the return of an entity (e.g., a corporation) will suggest an audit of a related party's return (e.g., a major stockholder).

From time to time, the IRS carries on special investigatory projects to gain some indication of the degree of tax compliance with respect to certain transactions. Some returns are chosen for audit as a result of these pilot programs. For example, during 1989 the IRS sampled 3,000 to 4,000 individual returns to determine whether certain expenses were misclassified in order to avoid the 2% floor applicable to miscellaneous itemized deductions. Another study investigated whether taxpayers attempted to circumvent the passive loss rules by reporting their rental activities on Schedule C as active business activities.[13]

Key Point
Depending on the expected complexity of an audit, a correspondence audit, an office audit, or a field audit will be performed.

Alternatives for a Taxpayer Whose Return Is Audited

When a taxpayer is notified of an impending audit, such notice will indicate whether the audit is a correspondence audit, an office audit, or a field audit. In correspondence audits, all of the communication, such as providing documentation or indicating why certain income was not reported, can be handled through the mail. An office audit results in the taxpayer and/or his tax advisor meeting with an IRS employee at a nearby IRS office. The notice informing the taxpayer about the audit indicates which items will be examined and what information should be brought to the audit. Field examinations are common for business returns and more complex individual returns. The IRS employee conducts these audits either at the taxpayer's place of business or residence or at his tax advisor's office.

Additional Comment
This special rule was designed to reduce the likelihood that the IRS could harass a taxpayer by continually auditing that taxpayer over the identical issue.

Special Relief Rule. A special relief rule exists for repetitive audit examinations for the same item. A taxpayer who receives an audit notice can request that the examination be suspended while a review is conducted to determine whether the audit should proceed if (1) his return was audited for the same item in at least one of the two previous years and (2) the earlier audit did not result in a change to his tax liability. To request the suspension, the taxpayer should call the person whose name and telephone number appears on the audit notice.

Example 16-1 ■ In October 1991, Tony receives notice that the IRS will audit the medical expense deduction claimed on his 1989 return. Tony's 1987 return was audited with respect to medical expenses, but the IRS did not assess any additional tax. Tony may request that the audit of his 1989 return be suspended pending a review of whether the audit should continue. ■

Example 16-2 ■ Assume the same facts as in Example 16-1, except that Tony's 1987 return was audited for employee business expenses. Because that audit dealt with a different item, Tony may not ask for a suspension of the audit. ■

---

[12] Reg. Sec. 301.7623-1(c).
[13] "Tax Report," *Wall Street Journal*, November 30, 1988, p. 1.

16-8 • Ch. 16 / Administrative Procedures

The next few pages discuss taxpayers' rights during an examination of their return. Various alternatives exist. Such alternatives are illustrated in Figure 16-2.

Meeting with a Revenue Agent. Generally, the first step in the audit process involves a meeting of the IRS agent and the taxpayer and/or the taxpayer's advisor. If the taxpayer is fortunate, the agent will agree that the return was correct as filed or, even better, that the taxpayer is entitled to a refund. In most instances, however, the agent contends that the taxpayer owes additional taxes. Taxpayers who do not agree with the outcome of their meeting with the IRS agent may ask to meet with the agent's supervisor. A meeting with the supervisor may or may not lead to an agreement concerning the additional tax due.

Should the taxpayer agree and the agent's supervisor concur in the amount owed, the taxpayer must sign Form 870 (Waiver of Statutory Notice). This indicates the taxpayer's (1) agreement to waive any restrictions on the IRS's ability to assess tax and (2) consent to the IRS's collecting the tax. Signing Form 870 does not, however, preclude the taxpayer from filing a refund suit later.

If the taxpayer agrees that additional tax is owed and pays the tax upon signing the Form 870, interest is due on the tax deficiency from the due date of the return through the payment date. The taxpayer can wait to pay the extra tax. In such a situation, interest ceases to accrue 30 days after Form 870 was signed, and no additional interest is charged if the taxpayer pays the tax due within 10 days of the billing date.

Technical Advice Memoranda. From time to time, the issue in question may be a complex, highly technical one with which the IRS employee has little or no experience. Regardless of the level of the audit, an IRS employee may request advice from the IRS's National Office. Sometimes, the taxpayer may urge the IRS employee to seek such advice. The advice, in the form of Technical Advice Memoranda, is made public in the form of letter rulings. If the advice is favorable to the taxpayer, the agent or appeals officer must follow it. Even if the advice is pro-IRS, the appeals officer may still consider the hazards of litigation in deciding whether to compromise.

Appeal to Appeals Division. If the taxpayer does not sign Form 870, the IRS will send the taxpayer a report, known as a **30-day letter,** detailing the proposed changes and advising the taxpayer of his right to pursue the matter with the Appeals Office. The taxpayer has 30 days in which to request a conference with an appeals officer.

If the audit was a field audit and the amount of additional tax plus penalties and interest in question is more than $10,000, the taxpayer must submit a **protest letter** within the 30-day period. Only a brief written statement is necessary if the amount is between $2,501 and $10,000. Only an oral request is required for office audits, regardless of the amount of the additional tax, penalties, and interest. If the taxpayer does not respond to the 30-day letter, the IRS will follow up with a 90-day letter, which is discussed below.

Protest letters must be submitted to the district director. A protest letter should include the following information:

- The taxpayer's name and address
- A statement that the taxpayer wishes to appeal the findings of the IRS agent to the Appeals Office
- The date and symbols from the letter showing the proposed adjustments
- The tax years involved
- An itemized schedule of the proposed changes with which the taxpayer disagrees

---

Additional Comment

From the perspective of the tax practitioner, clients should be encouraged to allow the tax practitioner to handle the audit. Because taxpayers usually have a limited understanding of the complexities of the tax law and its administration, having the taxpayer physically present at the actual audit generally is not a good idea.

Typical Misconception

Taxpayers should be cautioned about signing Form 870 too quickly. Once this form is properly executed, the taxpayer is no longer permitted to administratively pursue the items under audit within the IRS.

Self-Study Question

When should a taxpayer urge the agent to seek advice in the form of Technical Advice Memoranda (TAM)?

Answer

When the taxpayer has a complicated tax issue that would benefit from the scrutiny of a more technically qualified reviewer. If the TAM is in favor of the taxpayer, the agent is required to follow the decision of the IRS National Office.

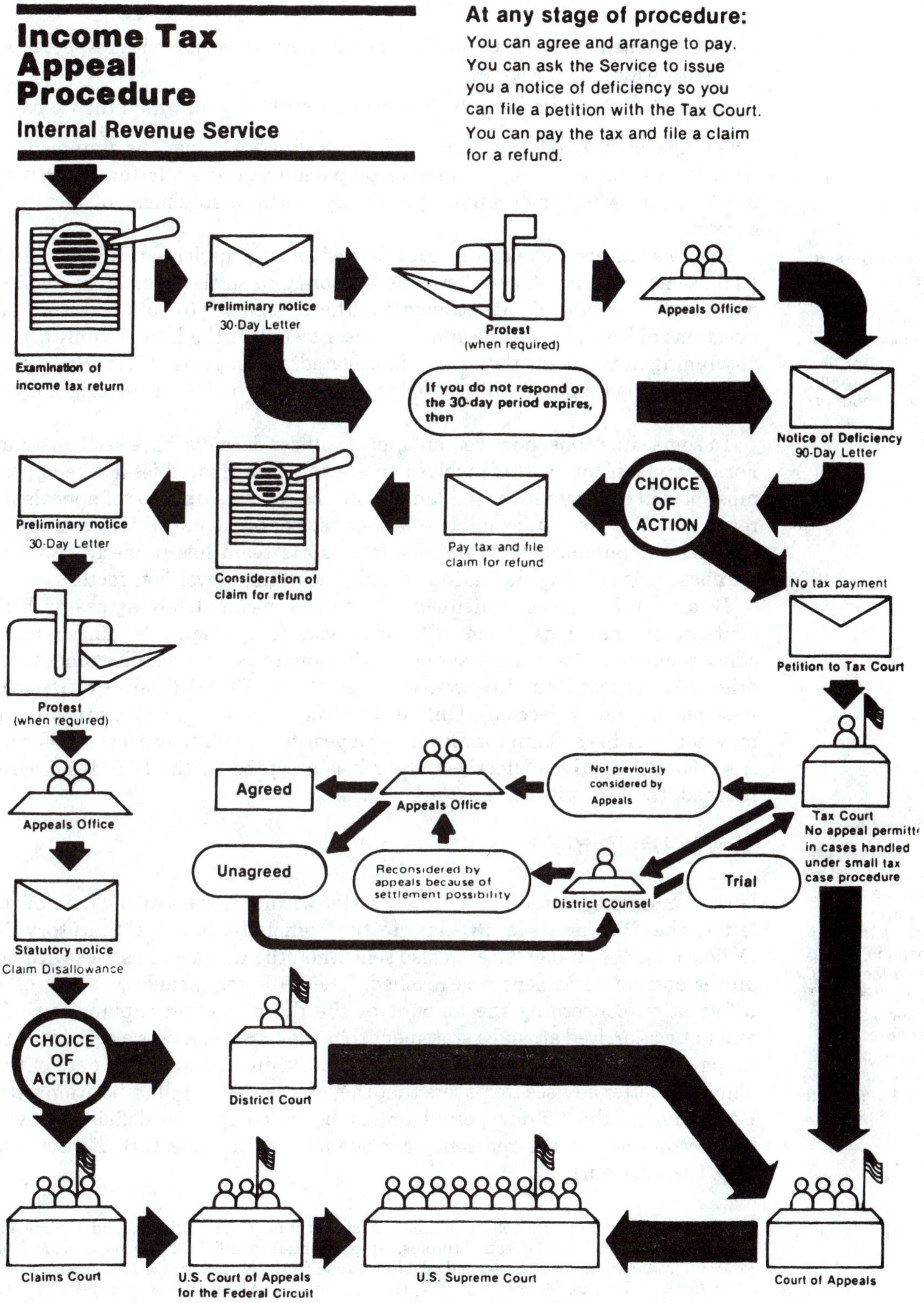

FIGURE 16-2 Alternatives Available to Taxpayers for Whom IRS Proposes a Deficiency

Source: IRS, *Publication No. 556* [Examination of Returns, Appeal Rights, and Claims for Refund] (Washington, D.C.: U.S. Government Printing Office, 1989), p. 9.

- A statement of facts supporting the taxpayer's position with respect to any issues with which he disagrees
- A statement indicating the law or other authority on which the taxpayer relied[14]

The taxpayer must declare, under penalties of perjury, that the statement of facts is true. If the taxpayer's representative prepares the protest letter, the representative must declare whether he knows personally that the statement of facts is true and correct.

Key Point

The appeals officer presently has the authority to settle or compromise issues with the taxpayer. To help alleviate some of the workload and to make the audit process more efficient, the IRS is currently considering giving more of this settlement authority to revenue agents.

Appeals officers are relatively experienced and sophisticated IRS personnel. Unlike IRS agents, appeals officers have the authority to settle cases after considering the hazards of litigation. Their settlement authority extends to both questions of fact and questions of law. Thus, if the appeals officer feels that the IRS has only a 40% chance of winning in the event the matter is litigated, the appeals officer may agree to close the case if the taxpayer will pay an amount equal to 40% of the originally proposed deficiency.

In some situations, however, an appeals officer does not have settlement authority. For example, if the matter involves an appeals coordinated issue, the appeals officer must obtain concurrence or guidance from the regional director of appeals in order to reach a settlement. An example of an **appeals coordinated issue** is the matter of whether the purchaser of a professional sports team has properly apportioned the purchase price among the various assets, including player contracts.[15]

If, after the appeals conference, the taxpayer completely agrees with the IRS's contentions, he signs Form 870. However, if the appeals officer makes some concessions and the parties agree to additional tax of a smaller amount than that originally proposed, the taxpayer will sign Form 870-AD (Waiver of Restrictions on Assessment and Collection). Unlike the situation for Form 870, taxpayers generally may not later file a claim for refund for a year for which they executed Form 870-AD. Also, Form 870-AD is effective only if it is accepted by the IRS. If no agreement is reached, the IRS will issue a 90-day letter.

Ninety-Day Letter

Typical Misconception

If a taxpayer fails to respond to a 30-day letter or make an agreement with the appeals officer, the taxpayer will receive a 90-day letter and will have to petition the Tax Court or agree to be billed for the deficiency by the IRS. This 90-day time limit is strictly enforced. Therefore, if a taxpayer desires to pursue the issue in the Tax Court, he should take the 90-day letter very seriously.

If the taxpayer does not file a protest letter within 30 days of the date of the 30-day letter, the IRS issues a **90-day letter** (officially called a Statutory Notice of Deficiency).[16] A 90-day letter is also sent when the taxpayer has met with an appeals officer and no agreement was reached. The 90-letter includes, among other items, information concerning the amount of the deficiency, an explanation of how the amount was arrived at, and a statement that the IRS will assess a deficiency unless the taxpayer files a petition with the Tax Court within 90 days of the date of the letter.[17] Thus, the letter advises taxpayers that they may either (1) file a petition with the Tax Court during the 90-day period or (2) be billed for the deficiency by the IRS. Taxpayers who pay the deficiency can sue for a refund in a U.S. district court or the U.S. Claims Court.

---

[14] IRS, *Publication No. 556* [Examination of Returns, Appeal Rights, and Claims for Refund], December, 1989, pp. 3 and 4. A sample protest letter is contained in F. W. Norwood, *et al.*, *Federal Taxation: Research, Planning & Procedures,* 2nd ed. (Englewood Cliffs, N.J.: Prentice-Hall, 1979), Appendix G.

[15] *Internal Revenue Manual,* Ch. 8(24)31. An appeals coordinated issue is a specially-designated tax matter for which the IRS desires consistent treatment of the appeals across its regions. Therefore, these appeals are generally coordinated by the Director of Appeals for a particular region that has been so designated by the national Director of the IRS Appeals Division. Guidance is provided to the local region in the handling of the matter by the regional Director of Appeals in accordance with Rev. Proc. 79-34 (1979-2 C.B. 498).

[16] Upon request, the IRS may grant an extension of time for filing a protest letter.

[17] Sec. 6213(a). If the notice is addressed to a person outside the United States, the time period is 150 days instead of 90.

The 90-day time limit is strictly enforced. The Tax Court cannot consider a case if a taxpayer's petition is filed late. During the 90-day period, the IRS is precluded from assessing a deficiency and attempting to make any collections. If the taxpayer petitions the Tax Court, the IRS may not assess a deficiency and try to collect until the court decision becomes final.

Litigation

Taxpayers who disagree with the deficiency proposed by the IRS can, of course, litigate. As discussed in Chapter 1, litigation can begin in one of the three trial courts: the Tax Court, a U.S. district court, or the U.S. Claims Court. After considering the time and expense of litigation, however, some taxpayers may pay the deficiency, even though they strongly believe that their position is correct. If a taxpayer does decide to litigate, the precedents, if any, of the various courts should be considered before deciding where to litigate. Chapter 1 explores the topic of which cases each court must follow.

Key Point

Litigating in the Tax Court has the advantages of: (1) not having to pay the deficiency beforehand and (2) the option of the more informal small tax case procedures if the amount in question does not exceed $10,000 for the year. The disadvantage: the small tax case procedure does not offer an opportunity for appeal.

Tax Court. Taxpayers desiring to litigate in the Tax Court must file their petition with the Tax Court within 90 days of the date of the Statutory Notice of Deficiency. Prior to the scheduled trial date, however, taxpayers may still reach an agreement with the IRS. There are some advantages of going the Tax Court route. The taxpayer does not have to pay the deficiency as a prelude in filing suit. If the amount in question does not exceed $10,000 for a year, the taxpayer may use the more informal small tax case procedures. This alternative is not available in other courts. The small tax case procedures can have a potential disadvantage for the taxpayer, however, because there is no chance for an appeal.

In general, the taxpayer has the burden of proof in Tax Court cases. The IRS, however, bears the burden of proof with respect to any new issues that it raises subsequent to the issuance of the Statutory Notice of Deficiency (90-day letter).[18] The burden of proof also lies with the IRS in fraud cases. Generally, the taxpayer and the IRS have stipulated a number of tax treatment items before going to trial. Because agreement was reached on these stipulated matters, such issues may not be reopened in court.

Taxpayers must pay the additional tax, plus any interest, if they lose in Tax Court and choose not to appeal their case. In some situations, the Tax Court leaves the computation of the additional tax up to the litigating parties. When this happens, the phrase "Entered under Rule 155" appears at the end of the Tax Court's opinion.

Key Point

In order to litigate in a district court or in the U.S. Claims Court, the taxpayer must first pay the deficiency and then file a claim for a refund. After filing the claim for refund, the taxpayer can initiate a suit for refund after the earlier of: (1) six months or (2) the date on which the IRS denies the claim for refund.

District Court or U.S. Claims Court. As a condition of going to either a federal district court or the U.S. Claims Court, the taxpayer must pay the deficiency and file a claim for refund. The refund claim is denied because the IRS just finished arguing that such an amount of additional tax was due. After the notice of denial is received, the taxpayer may file a refund suit. If a denial is not received within 6 months of filing a refund claim, the taxpayer may go ahead and file a suit. The latest possible time for filing suit is 2 years after the IRS disallows the claim.

Appeal of a Lower Court's Decision. Whichever party loses—the taxpayer or the government—may appeal the lower court's decision to an appellate court. If the case began in the Tax Court or a federal district court, the case is appealable to the circuit court of appeals for the taxpayer's geographical jurisdiction. For individuals, the taxpayer's place of residence generally controls which court of appeals has jurisdic-

---

[18] Tax Court Rule No. 142.

tion. In the case of corporations, the firm's principal place of business or office determines which court has jurisdiction. Cases originating in the U.S. Claims Court are appealable to the Circuit Court of Appeals for the Federal Circuit. That is, all cases are heard by the same circuit, irrespective of the taxpayer's residence or principal place of business.

Either the taxpayer or the government can request that the Supreme Court review an appellate court's decision. If the Supreme Court decides to hear a case, it will grant **certiorari.** In any given year, however, the Supreme Court hears only a few cases dealing with tax matters.

REQUESTS FOR RULINGS

OBJECTIVE 3
Describe the IRS's ruling process

As discussed in Chapter 1, the taxpayer can learn how the IRS characterizes the tax effects of a transaction by requesting that it rule on the transaction. The IRS answers the taxpayer's request in the form of a **letter ruling** (sometimes referred to as a private letter ruling) addressed to the taxpayer. A ruling is "a written statement issued to a taxpayer by the Service's National Office that interprets and applies the tax laws to that taxpayer's specific set of facts."[19] Letter rulings are also a matter of public record, but all confidential information is eliminated before they are made public. Legislation enacted in 1987 allows the IRS to charge a user fee for issuing rulings. Revenue Procedure 90-17 describes the user fee system, where the fees range from a low of $50 for computation of an exclusion for an annuitant under Sec. 72, to $5,600 for certain pension plan opinion letters.[20]

Additional Comment
The information requirements for requesting a letter ruling are very precise. In general, a tax professional experienced in dealing with the National Office of the IRS should be consulted. Also, a good blueprint of what should be included in a ruling request can often be found by locating an already published letter ruling and examining its format.

Information to Be Included in Taxpayer's Request

Early each calendar year, the IRS issues a revenue procedure that details how to request a ruling and the information to be contained in the ruling request. Taxpayers or tax advisors should consult the appropriate revenue procedure before requesting a ruling. Appendix A of this ruling contains a checklist that may be used to ensure that the taxpayer's request is in order. The IRS has also issued detailed guidelines about the data to be included in the request for a ruling. For example, the IRS has specified the information to be included in a ruling request concerning the tax effects of transfers to a controlled corporation under Sec. 351. Each ruling request must contain a statement of all the relevant facts, including the following:

- Names, addresses, telephone numbers, and taxpayer identification numbers of all interested parties
- Location of the IRS district director for the taxpayer's geographical area
- A complete, precise statement of the business reasons for the transaction
- A detailed description of the transaction[21]

The taxpayer should also submit copies of the contracts, agreements, deeds, wills, instruments, and other documents that have an impact on the transaction. The

---

[19] Rev. Proc. 91-1, I.R.B. 1991-1, 9, Sec. 2.01.
[20] 1990-1 C.B. 479.
[21] Rev. Proc. 91-1, I.R.B. 1991-1, 9, Sec. 8.01. Certain revenue procedures provide a checklist of information to be included for frequently occurring transactions. See, for example, Rev. Proc. 83-59, 1983-2 C.B. 575, which includes guidelines for requesting rulings under Sec. 351.

taxpayer must include an explicit statement of all the relevant facts and not merely incorporate the language from the documents by reference. The taxpayer should also include a deletions statement indicating what confidential data should be deleted from the ruling prior to its release to the public.

If the taxpayer advocates that the IRS reach a particular conclusion, the basis of this assertion and the authorities relied on must be indicated. Even if the taxpayer is not arguing for any particular tax treatment, an opinion about the tax results must be furnished along with a statement of authorities in support of this position. Moreover, the taxpayer is urged to disclose and discuss any authorities to the contrary. The IRS also indicates that if there are no authorities to the contrary, it would be helpful if the taxpayer made a statement to this effect.

The person on whose behalf a ruling is requested should sign the following declaration: "Under penalties of perjury, I declare that I have examined this request, including accompanying documents, and to the best of my knowledge and belief, the facts presented in support of the requested ruling ... are true, correct, and complete."[22]

Will the IRS Rule?

With respect to income tax and gift tax matters, the IRS will rule only on proposed transactions and on completed transactions for which a return has not yet been filed. For estate tax matters, a ruling will not be issued if the estate tax return has been filed. The IRS will issue rulings with respect to the estate tax consequences of a living person.[23] If no temporary or final regulations have been issued for a particular statutory provision, the following policies govern the issuance of a ruling:

- If the answer seems clear by applying the statute, a ruling will be issued under the usual procedures.
- If the answer seems reasonably certain by applying the statute but not entirely free from doubt, the IRS will rule.
- If the issue cannot be readily resolved in the absence of regulations, a ruling will not be issued.[24]

The IRS has announced, however, that it will entertain ruling requests for all Code Sections added or revised by the Tax Reform Act of 1986 or subsequent Acts even though the interpretation may not seem reasonably clear.[25]

The IRS will not rule on a set of alternative ways of designing a proposed transaction or on the tax consequences of hypothetical transactions. Generally, the IRS will not rule on certain issues because of the factual nature of the problem involved or for other reasons.[26]

From time to time, the IRS discloses, by means of a revenue procedure, a list of the topical areas in which it definitely will not rule. The list is not all-inclusive; the IRS may refuse to issue a ruling in additional areas whenever, in its opinion, the facts and circumstances justify its refusal to rule.

According to Rev. Proc. 91-3, the matters on which the IRS will not rule include the following:

- Whether property qualifies as the taxpayer's principal residence

> **Typical Misconception**
> It is easy to be confused about the difference between letter rulings, which pertain to either prospective transactions or completed transactions for which a return has not yet been filed, and Technical Advice Memoranda, which pertain to completed transactions for which the return has been filed and is under audit.

> **Key Point**
> To conserve some of its resources, the IRS is considering no longer issuing rulings on issues that are clearly and adequately addressed by published authorities.

---

[22] Ibid., Sec. 8.01.
[23] Ibid., Secs. 3.01 and 3.03.
[24] Ibid., Sec. 5.09.
[25] Ibid.
[26] Ibid., Sec. 7.02.

- Whether compensation is reasonable in amount
- Whether a capital expenditure for an item ordinarily used for personal purposes (e.g., a swimming pool) has medical care as its primary purpose
- The determination of the amount of a corporation's earnings and profits[27]

In addition, the revenue procedure lists a number of issues on which rulings will not "ordinarily" be issued. The revenue procedure also enumerates topics on which the IRS will not rule until it resolves the issue through publishing regulations or a revenue ruling, a revenue procedure, or otherwise.

Recently, the IRS announced that it would discontinue issuing letter rulings addressing "issues that are clearly and adequately addressed by published authorities."[28] The reason for restricting the scope of its rulings policy was to allow the IRS to use its resources to address more issues of concern to the general public and to be able to issue letter rulings on a more timely basis. Tax practitioners did not react favorably to the "no comfort rulings" policy, and the IRS decided not to implement the policy. Instead, it will specify certain no-rule areas, design model documents, and publish ruling checklists.[29]

Key Point
Requesting a letter ruling makes most sense relative to transactions that would not be undertaken without certain tax consequences being assured. For example, many corporate mergers and acquisitions are structured so that they qualify as one of the tax-free reorganizations defined in Sec. 368. To ensure this result in large corporate acquisitions, taxpayers often request a ruling from the IRS stating that the acquisition will be tax free.

When Rulings Are Desirable

In certain circumstances it is especially helpful to gain insight into the IRS's assessment of the tax effects of a transaction. In other circumstances, however, the taxpayer might prefer not to request a ruling. If the state of the law is unclear and there is a possibility that the tax results could be disastrous, obtaining a ruling would be desirable, especially if the transaction in question has not been finalized. If the IRS has earlier ruled favorably in a practically identical set of facts, the taxpayer might want to get his own letter ruling as an "insurance policy" with respect to how the IRS interprets the tax results.

A taxpayer would not want to request a ruling if the IRS's position, as expressed in letter rulings or revenue rulings, is unfavorable to taxpayers. At times, taxpayers have no flexibility concerning how to structure a transaction. Because of the possibility that the IRS would rule unfavorably to the taxpayer, it would not be in the taxpayer's best interest to request a ruling. Similarly, a ruling generally should not be sought for an issue if the IRS might also issue an unrequested ruling on related matters. This contingency is especially significant if the taxpayer feels vulnerable on the related matters.

DUE DATES

Due Dates for Returns

OBJECTIVE 4
Recognize the due dates for tax returns and penalties associated with not abiding by such dates

Returns for individuals, fiduciaries, and partnerships are due on or before the fifteenth day of the fourth month following the year-end of the individual or the entity.[30] C corporation and S corporation tax returns, however, are due no later than the fifteenth day of the third month after the firm's year-end. While individuals and

---
[27] Rev. Proc. 91-3, I.R.B. 1991-1, 52.
[28] Rev. Proc. 89-34, 1989-1 C.B. 917.
[29] Ann. 90-65, I.R.B. 1990-20, 23.
[30] Sec. 6072(a). Section 6072(c), however, extends the due date for returns of nonresident alien individuals to the fifteenth day of the sixth month after the end of their tax year.

fiduciaries must have a certain level of income during a year before a return must be filed, all corporations subject to tax under Subtitle A (income taxes) and all partnerships must file a return each year.[31]

Extensions

Congress realized that in some instances it would be difficult or impossible for taxpayers to gather their information and complete the return by the designated due date for filing the return. Thus, it authorized extensions of time for filing returns. Extensions may be granted for a reasonable period of time. Unless the taxpayer is abroad, the extension period cannot exceed 6 months.[32]

Key Point
Normally, filing Form 4868 for the automatic 4-month extension must be properly executed by the due date of the return, that is, on or before the fifteenth day of the fourth month following the year-end of the individual.

Individuals. Individuals may request an automatic extension, that is, the IRS need not be given a reason for the extension, until 4 months after the original due date by filing Form 4868. An extension is not available, however, unless the taxpayer executes Form 4868.

If a taxpayer still needs additional time as the end of the 4-month extension period draws near, an additional extension of up to 2 months may be requested by filing Form 2688. The taxpayer must state detailed reasons for needing more time. This additional extension is not automatic. However, even if the IRS denies the request, it often grants the taxpayer a brief grace period for filing.

Example 16-3 ■ Bob and Alice, his wife, are calendar-year taxpayers. They may automatically get an extension for filing their 1991 return until August 15, 1992, by executing Form 4868. Suppose that both have been quite ill throughout 1992. As August 15 draws near, they may submit Form 2688 and request an additional extension until no later than October 15, 1992. They must explain their reasons when requesting an additional extension. ■

Corporations. Corporations request an automatic extension for filing by submitting Form 7004 by the original due date of the return. Although the Code states that 3 months is the automatic extension period, the Regulations and Form 7004 instructions state that the automatic extension period is for 6 months.[33] Because the automatic extension period is for 6 months, no further discretionary extensions are available.

Example 16-4 ■ Able Corporation reports on a fiscal year ending March 31. The regular due date for its return is June 15. It may file Form 7004 and request an automatic 6-month extension that postpones the due date for the return until December 15. ■

Due Dates for Payment of the Tax

It is important to understand that obtaining an extension merely postpones the due date for the return. It does not extend the time for paying the tax. In general, the due date for the tax payment is the same as the due date for the return (determined

---

[31] Secs. 6012(a)(2) and 6031(a).
[32] Sec. 6081(a).
[33] Sec. 6081(b) and Reg. Sec. 1.6081-3(a).

16-16 • Ch. 16 / Administrative Procedures

Typical Misconception
Obtaining an extension defers the date on which the return must be filed, but it does not defer payment of the tax liability. Therefore, an extension for filing must be accompanied by a payment of an estimate of the taxpayer's eventual tax liability. Computing this estimated tax liability can be difficult since much of the information necessary to complete the return may be incomplete or not yet available.

without regard to extensions).[34] The first estimated tax installment for an individual taxpayer is due on the due date for the preceding year's return, and the additional payments are due 2, 5, and 9 months later. Taxpayers who elect to let the IRS compute their tax must pay within 30 days of the date the IRS mails a notice stating the amount of tax payable.[35]

Interest is imposed on any tax that is not paid by the return's due date, as determined without regard to extensions. When individuals request an automatic extension, they should project their tax liability to the best of their ability. Any tax owed, after all withholding tax and estimated tax payments are subtracted from the calculated amount, should be remitted along with the extension request. In addition, if an extension for filing a gift tax return is also requested (on the same form), the estimated amount of gift tax liability should be remitted. Similarly, corporations should remit the amount of the tax liability they anticipate, reduced by any estimated tax already paid, with their automatic extension request.

Interest on Tax Not Timely Paid

Any tax not paid by the original due date for the return is subject to an interest charge.[36] Basically, taxpayers incur interest expense in three contexts.

- They request an extension for filing but inaccurately estimate their tax liability and, thus, must pay some additional tax when they file their return.
- They file on time but are not financially able to pay some, or all, of their tax liability.
- Their return is audited, and it is determined that they owe additional taxes.

Self-Study Question
What is the theoretical justification for charging taxpayers a percentage point more interest than the government must pay?

Answer
There is no reasonable justification. This is simply another example of how tax policy decisions are "revenue driven."

Determination of Rate. The IRS's interest rate is determined under the rules of Sec. 6621. The rate varies with fluctuations in the federal short-term rates; potentially the interest rate changes at the beginning of each calendar quarter. In general, the interest rate for underpayments of tax is three percentage points higher than the federal short-term rate, and the rate for overpayments is two percentage points higher. For corporate underpayments exceeding $100,000, the rate for underpayments is five percentage points above the federal short-term rate if the deficiency is not paid before a certain date. Rates are rounded to the nearest full percent. Interest rates recently applicable are as follows:

Period	General Rate for Underpayments	Rate for Overpayments
January 1 through March 31, 1991	11%	10%
January 1 through December 31, 1990	11%	10%

Example 16-5 ■ Ann's 1989 individual return is audited in March 1991. Ann is a calendar-year taxpayer. The IRS contends that Ann owes $2,700 of additional taxes. Ann pays the additional taxes on March 31, 1991. Ann must also pay interest on the $2,700

---

[34] Sec. 6151(a).
[35] Sec. 6151(b)(1). The special estimated tax payment rules for C corporations, S corporations, and trusts and estates are described in Chapters 3, 11, and 14, respectively, of this volume.
[36] Secs. 6601(a) and (b)(1).

deficiency for the period April 16, 1990, through March 31, 1991. The interest rate is 11% for this entire period. The interest rate is compounded daily (see discussion below). ■

Historical Note
Probably two of the most significant changes in tax administration have been: (1) that interest is now compounded daily and (2) that the rate charged is tied to the prime rate, which has resulted in a much higher rate than in years past. Prior to these two changes, taxpayers who played the "audit lottery" by always taking the most aggressive positions incurred very little risk.

Daily Compounding. Daily compounding of interest applies to both the interest that taxpayers owe the government and interest that the government owes taxpayers who have overpaid their taxes. The task of computing interest under daily compounding rules has been facilitated greatly because the IRS has issued Rev. Proc. 83-7 containing tables to be used for calculating the interest.[37] These tables are reproduced in the major tax services.

Period for Which Interest Is Imposed. Interest is usually imposed from the original due date of the return until the date of payment. In certain instances, however, an exception applies with respect to the interest levied on a deficiency. If the IRS does not issue a notice and demand for payment within 30 days after the taxpayer signs a Form 870 (Waiver of Statutory Notice), no interest can be charged for the period between the end of the 30-day period and the date the IRS issues its notice and demand.[38]

Example 16-6 ■ Cindy receives an automatic extension for filing her 1991 return. She submits her return, along with the $700 balance she owes on her 1991 tax, on June 24, 1992. She owes interest on $700 for the period April 16 through June 24, 1992. Interest is compounded daily using the interest rate for underpayments determined under Sec. 6621. ■

Example 16-7 ■ Ron files his 1988 individual return on March 17, 1989. The return is audited in 1991, and on January 24, 1991, Ron signs a Form 870, on which he agrees that he owes a $780 deficiency. The IRS does not issue a notice and demand for payment until March 19, 1991. Ron pays the deficiency 2 days later. Ron owes interest, compounded daily at the Sec. 6621 underpayment rate, for the period April 16, 1989, through February 23, 1991. No interest can be levied for the period February 24 through March 19, 1991, because the IRS does not issue its notice and demand for payment until more than 30 days after Ron signs Form 870. ■

Penalties

Penalties for failure to file on time and failure to pay by the due date are two commonly encountered penalties for income, estate, and gift tax purposes. These penalties are assessed in addition to the interest charged on taxes paid after the due date. Penalty charges—as opposed to interest—are not deductible in calculating taxable income. Interest is treated as personal interest and is totally nondeductible after 1990.

Failure to File. Taxpayers who do not file a return by the due date generally are liable for a penalty of 5% per month (or fraction thereof) of the amount of the net tax

---

[37] Rev. Proc. 83-7, 1983-1 C.B. 583.
[38] Sec. 6601(c).

due.[39] A fraction of a month, even just a day, counts as a full month. In general, the maximum penalty for failing to file is 25%. If the taxpayer receives an extension, the extended due date counts as the due date. In determining the amount of the net tax due (i.e., the amount subject to the penalty), the taxpayer's tax is reduced by any taxes paid by the return's due date (e.g., withholding and estimated tax payments) and tax credits claimed on the return.[40] If any failure to file is fraudulent, the penalty rate is 15% per month with a maximum penalty of 75%.[41]

Penalties are not levied if a taxpayer can prove that he did not file a timely return because of a "reasonable cause"(as opposed to "willful neglect"). According to the Regulations, reasonable cause exists if "the taxpayer exercised ordinary business care and prudence and was nevertheless unable to file the return within the prescribed time."[42] It is not surprising that much litigation deals with the issue of reasonable cause.

Note that the penalty imposed for not filing on time is generally a function of the net tax due. However, with respect to some income tax returns a minimum penalty applies.[43] The minimum penalty was enacted because of the cost to the IRS of identifying nonfilers. If an income tax return is not filed within 60 days of the due date (including any extensions), the penalty will be no less than the smaller of (1) $100 or (2) 100% of the tax due on the return. Taxpayers who owe no tax are not subject to the failure-to-file penalty. The penalty is waived if the taxpayer shows reasonable cause for not filing.

Additional Comment

The most common reason given to support "reasonable cause" for failing to file a timely tax return is reliance on one's tax advisor. Other possible arguments include severe illness or serious accident.

Example 16-8 ■

Earl files his 1991 individual income tax return on July 4, 1992. No extension was requested, and Earl did not have reasonable cause for his late filing but fraud did not occur. Earl's 1991 return shows a balance due of $400. Under the regular rules, the late filing penalty would be $60 (0.05 × 3 months × $400). Because of the minimum penalty provisions invoked by the failure to file the return within 60 days of the due date, Earl's penalty is $100. ■

In general, interest is not imposed on any penalty that is paid within 10 days of the date that notification is given of the penalty. Interest is levied under Sec. 6601(e)(2)(B) on the failure-to-file penalty, however, from the due date of the return (including any extensions) until the payment date.

Self-Study Question

If a taxpayer does not have sufficient funds to pay his tax liability by the filing date, should the taxpayer wait until the funds are available before filing the actual tax return?

Answer

No. He should file the return on a timely basis. This avoids the 5% per month failure-to-file penalty. The taxpayer will still be liable for the failure-to-pay penalty, but at least this is only 0.5% per month.

Failure to Pay. The **failure-to-pay penalty** is imposed at a rate of 0.5% per month (or fraction thereof).[44] The maximum penalty is 25%. The penalty is imposed on the amount of tax shown on the return less any tax payments (e.g., withholding, estimated tax, other payments, and credits) made before the beginning of the month for which the penalty is being calculated.[45] The term *other payments* is relevant when computing the penalty for months subsequent to months in which the taxpayer makes payments of part of the tax liability. As with the failure-to-file penalty, the failure-to-pay penalty is waived if the taxpayer shows reasonable cause for not paying.

[39] Sec. 6651(a).
[40] Sec. 6651(b)(1).
[41] Sec. 6651(f).
[42] Reg. Sec. 301.6651-1(c)(1).
[43] Sec. 6651(a).
[44] Sec. 6651(a)(2).
[45] Sec. 6651(b)(2).

Because the tax is due on the original due date for the return, taxpayers who request an extension without paying 100% of their tax liability generally owe a failure-to-pay penalty. The Regulations provide some relief by exempting a taxpayer from the penalty if the additional tax due with the filing of the extended return does not exceed 10% of the tax owed for the year.[46]

Example 16-9 ■ Gary requests an extension for filing his 1991 individual income tax return. His 1991 tax payments include withholding of $4,500, estimated tax payments of $2,000, and $1,000 sent with his request for an automatic extension. He files his return on June 7, 1992, showing a total tax of $8,000 and a balance due of $500. Gary is exempt from the failure-to-pay penalty because the $500 balance due does not exceed 10% of his 1991 liability (0.10 × $8,000 = $800). Had Gary's 1991 tax instead been $9,000, he would have owed an additional tax of $1,500 and a failure-to-pay penalty of $15 (0.005 × 2 months × $1,500). ■

The 0.5% penalty rises to 1% a month, or fraction thereof, in certain circumstances. The rate is 1% for any month beginning after the earlier of

- 10 days after the date the IRS gives the taxpayer notice that it plans to make a levy on the taxpayer's salary or property, or
- The day the IRS gives notice and demand for immediate payment because it believes that collection is in jeopardy

Example 16-10 ■ Ginny files her 1988 individual income tax return on April 11, 1989. Ginny, however, does not pay her tax liability. On October 5, 1991, the IRS notifies Ginny of its plans to levy on her property. The failure-to-pay penalty is 0.5% per month for the period April 15, 1989, through October 15, 1991. Beginning on October 16, 1991, the penalty rises to 1% per month, or fraction thereof. ■

In many instances, both the failure-to-file and the failure-to-pay penalties are owed. Taxpayers who do not file a timely return are likely to owe additional taxes. Some taxpayers file on time to avoid the failure-to-file penalty, even though they cannot pay the balance due on their taxes. Barring a showing of reasonable cause, such taxpayers will still incur the failure-to-pay penalty.

The statute contains a special rule for calculating the 5% per month failure-to-file penalty for periods in which both penalties are applicable. The 5% per month failure-to-file penalty is reduced by the failure-to-pay penalty.[47] Thus, the total penalties for a given month will not exceed 5%; for months when both penalties are incurred, the failure-to-file penalty generally becomes a 4½% effective rate (0.05 − 0.005). Note, however, that there is no reduction if the minimum penalty for failure to file is applicable.

Example 16-11 ■ Pam files her 1991 individual income tax return on August 5, 1992, without having requested an extension. Her total tax is $20,000. Pam pays $15,000 in a timely manner and the $5,000 balance when the return is filed. No reasonable cause can be shown for Pam's late filing and late payment, but she did not engage in fraud. Pam's penalties are computed as follows:

[46] Reg. Sec. 301.6651-1(c)(3) and (4).
[47] Sec. 6651(c)(1).

Failure-to-pay penalty:
$5,000 × 0.005 × 4 months $ 100
Failure-to-file penalty:
$5,000 × 0.05 × 4 months $1,000
Minus: Reduction for failure-to-pay penalty
imposed for same period   (100)   900
Total penalties $1,000

Example 16-12 ■ Assume the same facts as in Example 16-11 except that Pam instead pays the $5,000 balance on November 17, 1992. The penalties are as follows:

Failure-to-pay penalty:
$5,000 × 0.005 × 8 months (April 16 through
November 17, 1992) $ 200
Failure-to-file penalty:
$5,000 × 0.05 × 4 months (April 16 through
August 5, 1992) $1,000
Minus: Reduction for failure-to-pay penalty levied
for April 16 through August 5 ($5,000 ×
0.005 × 4 months)   (100)   900
Total penalties $1,100

ESTIMATED TAXES

OBJECTIVE 5
Explain the penalty for not paying estimated taxes

In general, individuals having income from sources other than salaries and wages should pay quarterly estimated tax installments. As a result, the balance due with the filing of their return is usually relatively small. C corporations, S corporations and trusts also have to pay estimated taxes. Estates, however, are exempt from paying estimated taxes for their first two tax years. S corporations pay estimated taxes only on their corporate tax levies—the built-in gains tax, capital gains tax, excess net passive income tax—and any investment tax credit recapture amount. The C corporation, S corporation, and fiduciary estimated tax payment requirements are discussed in Chapters 3, 11, and 14, respectively.

Key Point

In general, those individuals who are self-employed or have sources of substantial income other than salaries or wages (i.e., interest, dividends, K-1 income from partnerships, S corporations, estates, or trusts) are the taxpayers who should be most concerned about making timely estimated tax payments.

Payment Requirements

In general, individuals should make quarterly estimated tax payments if they have more than a relatively small amount of income from sources other than salary and wages. Assuming an individual's income other than from salary and wages is earned fairly uniformly throughout the year, four equal quarterly payments of estimated taxes should be made. To avoid imposition of a penalty, the estimated payments should be calculated as follows:

Step 1: Determine the lesser of
   a. 90% of the taxpayer's regular tax, alternative minimum tax (if any), and the self-employment tax for the current year, or
   b. 100% of the taxpayer's prior year regular tax, alternative minimum tax (if any), and self-employment tax if a return was filed for the prior year

Step 2: Calculate the total of
  a. Tax credits for the current year
  b. Taxes withheld on the current year's wages
  c. Overpayments of the prior year's tax liability that the taxpayer requests be credited against the current year's tax
Step 3: Multiply the excess of the amount from Step 1 over the amount from Step 2 by 25%.[48]

For calendar-year individual taxpayers, the quarterly payments are due April 15, June 15, September 15, and January 15.

Example 16-13 ■

Mike's regular tax on his 1991 taxable income is $35,000. Mike also owes $2,000 of self-employment tax but no alternative minimum tax. Mike's 1990 total tax liability, for both income and self-employment taxes, is $24,000. Taxes withheld from Mike's wages in 1991 are $8,000. Mike does not have an overpayment of his 1990 tax or any 1991 credits. Mike should have made quarterly estimated tax payments of $4,000, as calculated below.

Lesser of:	(a) 90% of current year's tax (0.90 × $37,000 = $33,300) or	
	(b) 100% of prior year's tax ($24,000)	$24,000
Minus:		
	Taxes withheld from 1991 wages	(8,000)
Minimum estimated tax payment—to avoid penalty (under general rule)		$16,000
Quarterly estimated tax payments (0.25 × $16,000)		$ 4,000

■

Additional Comment
Although it is simpler to use the amount of tax paid in the preceding year as a safe harbor, the estimate of the current year's tax liability is clearly preferable if the current year's tax liability is expected to be significantly less than the preceding year's tax liability.

The ability to make estimated tax payments based on the preceding year's income is especially significant for taxpayers with rapidly rising levels of income. To protect themselves against a penalty, these taxpayers need only pay in an amount equal to the prior year's tax liability. Using the exception to the estimated tax rules eliminates the need for a high degree of accuracy in estimating the current year's tax liability.

Penalty for Underpaying Estimated Taxes

Additional Comment
If a taxpayer is having taxes withheld as well as making estimated tax payments, a certain amount of tax planning is possible. Withholdings are deemed to have been withheld equally throughout the year. Thus, larger amounts could be withheld in the last quarter and the taxpayer could still avoid any underpayment of estimated tax penalties.

With the exceptions discussed in the next section, taxpayers who do not pay in the requisite amount of estimated tax by the appropriate date are generally subject to a penalty for underpayment of estimated taxes. The penalty is at the same rate as the interest rate applicable under Sec. 6621 to late payments of tax.[49] The penalty for each quarter is calculated separately.

The amount subject to the penalty is the excess of (1) the total tax that should have been paid during the quarter (e.g., $6,000 [$24,000 prior year's tax liability ÷ 4] in Example 16-13) over (2) the sum of the estimated tax actually paid during that quarter on or before the installment date plus the withholding that is attributable to that quarter. Unless the taxpayer proves otherwise, the withholding is deemed to take place equally during each quarter. This rule creates a planning opportunity. Persons who have not paid sufficient amounts of estimated tax in the first three quarters can foreclose the imposition of the penalty by having large amounts of tax withheld during the last quarter.

---

[48] Secs. 6654(d), (f), and (g).
[49] Daily compounding is not applicable in calculating the penalty.

Example 16-14 ■

The penalty is assessed for the time period beginning with the due date for the quarterly installment and ending on the earlier of (1) the date the underpayment is actually paid or (2) the due date for the return (April 15 assuming a calendar-year taxpayer). The next example illustrates the computation of the underpayment penalty.

Assume the same facts as in Example 16-13, except that Mike pays only $3,000 of estimated tax payments on April 15, June 15, and September 15 of 1991, and January 15 of 1992, and that 10% is the Sec. 6621 underpayment rate for the entire time period. Mike files his 1991 return on March 30, 1992, and pays the $17,000 ($37,000 − $8,000 withholding − $12,000 estimated taxes) balance due at that time. Mike's underpayment penalty is determined as follows:

	Quarter			
	First	Second	Third	Fourth
Amount that should have been paid ($24,000 ÷ 4)	$6,000	$6,000	$6,000	$6,000
Minus: Withholding	(2,000)	(2,000)	(2,000)	(2,000)
Estimated tax payment	(3,000)	(3,000)	(3,000)	(3,000)
Underpayment	$1,000	$1,000	$1,000	$1,000
Number of days of underpayment; ends with earlier of March 30 or April 15, 1992	350	289	197	75
Penalty at 10% annual rate for number of days of underpayment	$ 96	$ 79	$ 54	$ 20

The total penalty equals $249 ($96 + $79 + $54 + $20). The $249 penalty is not deductible. ■

Interest is not assessed on underpayments of estimated tax.[50] But if the entire tax is not paid by the due date for the return, interest and perhaps a failure-to-pay penalty will be levied on the unpaid amount.

Exceptions to the Penalty

In certain circumstances, individuals who have not paid in the requisite amount of estimated tax will nevertheless be exempted from the underpayment penalty. No penalty is imposed if the taxpayer's tax exceeds the taxes withheld from wages for the year in question by less than $500. Similarly, the taxpayer will not owe a penalty, regardless of the size of the underpayment, if the taxpayer owed no taxes for the prior year, if the prior year consisted of 12 months, and if the taxpayer was a U.S. citizen or resident alien for the entire preceding year. The Secretary of the Treasury is empowered to waive the penalty otherwise due in the case of "casualty, disaster, or other unusual circumstances" or for newly retired or disabled individuals.[51]

Typical Misconception
Many self-employed taxpayers assume they are not liable for estimated taxes if they have sufficient itemized deductions and dependency exemptions to create zero taxable income or a taxable loss. However, a self-employment tax liability may exist even if there is no taxable income. Thus, many taxpayers in this situation end up with an overall tax liability with an accompanying estimated tax penalty.

[50] Sec. 6601(h).
[51] Sec. 6654(e).

Example 16-15 ■ Paul's 1991 tax is $2,200, the same amount as his 1990 tax. His withholding tax is $1,730, and Paul does not pay any estimated taxes. Paul pays the $470 balance due on March 17, 1992. Under the general rules, Paul is subject to the underpayment penalty because he does not meet either the 90% of 1991 tax or 100% of 1990 tax minimums. However, because Paul's tax exceeds the withholding from his wages by less than $500, he does not owe any penalty for underpaying his estimated tax. ■

In certain circumstances, taxpayers may be exempt from the underpayment penalty in some quarters but not in others. These additional exceptions to the underpayment penalty are beyond the scope of this text.[52] (Additional coverage on the other exceptions (e.g., the annualization of income exception) is contained in Chapter 14 of *Prentice Hall's Federal Taxation: Individuals* text.)

OTHER MORE SEVERE PENALTIES

OBJECTIVE 6
Describe more severe penalties, including the fraud penalty

In addition to the penalties for failure to file, failure to pay, and underpayment of estimated tax, taxpayers can be subject to other more severe penalties. These include the so-called accuracy-related penalty and the fraud penalty. Each of these penalties is discussed below.[53] An accuracy-related penalty of 20% applies to the portion of any underpayment that is attributable to negligence, any substantial understatement of income tax, and several other errors beyond the scope of this text. An accuracy-related penalty is not levied, however, if the fraud penalty is imposed on the underpayment or if no return was filed.

Negligence

The accuracy-related **negligence** penalty applies whenever the IRS determines that taxpayers have underpaid any part of their taxes as a result of negligence or disregard of the rules or regulations (but without intending to defraud).[54] The penalty amount is 20% of the underpayment attributable to negligence. Interest is levied on the negligence penalty at the rates applicable to underpayments.[55]

Example 16-16 ■ Ted's 1990 individual return is audited. Ted agrees to the assessment of a $7,500 deficiency, of which $2,500 is attributable to negligence. Ted pays the $7,500 of additional tax on October 13, 1993. Ted incurs a negligence penalty of $500 (0.20 × $2,500). ■

The Code defines **negligence** as "any failure to make a reasonable attempt to comply with the provisions" of the Code. Disregard of the rules or regulations is defined as "any careless, reckless, or intentional disregard".[56] One leading tax authority describes the situations in which the negligence penalty has generally been imposed as having the following characteristics:

---

[52] Section 6654(d)(2) allows for computation of the underpayments, if any, by annualizing income. Relief from the underpayment penalty may result from applying the annualization rules. Corporations but not individuals, are permitted a seasonal adjustment to the annualization rules.
[53] Secs. 6662(a) and (b).
[54] Secs. 6662(b) and (c).
[55] Sec. 6601(e)(2)(B).
[56] Sec. 6662(c).

[They] usually involve failures to keep proper records, substantial omissions, or exaggerated or unwarranted deductions that cannot be attributed to mistake or the taxpayer's resolution of reasonable doubts in his own favor but that do not entail destruction of records, concealment, barefaced lies, and other hallmarks of tax fraud.[57]

This authority also points out that the "disregard of rules and regulations" portion of the penalty is rarely levied when the taxpayer fails to follow regulations that he or his tax advisor think are invalid.[58] The Code now provides that the penalty will not be imposed with respect to any portion of an underpayment for which the taxpayer had reasonable cause for his position and acted in good faith.[59]

Example 16-17 ■

Additional Comment

Theoretically, penalties are used to deter taxpayers from willfully disregarding federal tax laws. Some taxpayers have been concerned that the IRS has used the multitude of tax penalties primarily as a source of revenue. This is accomplished by "stacking" penalties (i.e., applying several penalties to a single underpayment), which can result in the assessed penalties being greater than the actual tax owed. Recent legislation has attempted to alleviate some of this concern.

Gary's 1991 individual return is audited, and he agrees to the assessment of a $4,000 deficiency. Assume that Gary had reasonable cause for adopting his tax return positions and acted in good faith. Gary will not be liable for a penalty for negligence. ■

Substantial Understatement

Taxpayers who substantially understate their income tax liability will be liable for an accuracy-related penalty for their substantial understatements. The Code defines a substantial understatement as an understatement of tax exceeding the greater of (1) 10% of the tax required to be shown on the return or (2) $5,000 (or $10,000 in the case of a C corporation).[60] Thus, this penalty cannot apply unless the taxpayer's tax is understated by more than $5,000 (or $10,000 if a C corporation). If the penalty applies, it is equal to 20% of the amount of the underpayment of tax that is attributable to the substantial understatement. Some or all of the penalty may be waived if the taxpayer shows reasonable cause and good faith for his position.

Self-Study Question

How is an understatement different from an underpayment?

Answer

Understatements do not include those underpayments for which there was either substantial authority or adequate disclosure.

Understatement versus Underpayment. The amount of tax classified as attributable to the substantial understatement may be less than the amount of the underpayment. In general, the amount of the understatement is calculated as the amount by which (1) the amount of tax required to be shown (e.g., the correct tax) exceeds (2) the amount of tax shown on the return. However, because the amount of tax attributable to certain items is not treated as an understatement, the additional tax attributed to such items is not subject to the penalty. An underpayment for a transaction other than a tax shelter item is *not* treated as an understatement if either of the following is true:

- There is or was substantial authority for the tax treatment the taxpayer adopted, or
- The taxpayer discloses, either on the return or in a statement attached to the return, the relevant facts affecting the tax treatment for the transaction.

Example 16-18 ■

Val's 1991 individual income tax return is examined, and Val agrees to the assessment of a $9,000 deficiency, which increases her 1991 taxes from $25,000 to $34,000. Val neither made adequate disclosure with respect to the transactions for

---

[57] Boris I. Bittker, *Federal Taxation of Income, Estates, and Gifts* (Boston: Warren, Gorham & Lamont, 1981), vol. 4, pp. 114-15.
[58] Ibid., pp. 114-17.
[59] Sec. 6664(c).
[60] Sec. 6662(d)(1).

which the deficiency is assessed nor had substantial authority for the tax treatment used. Thus, Val's understatement is also $9,000. This deficiency is a substantial understatement because it exceeds both 10% of her correct tax ($3,400 = 0.10 × $34,000) and the $5,000 minimum. She incurs a substantial understatement penalty of $1,800 (0.20 × $9,000). ∎

Example 16-19 ∎

Additional Comment
Even though the substantial understatement penalty is a taxpayer penalty, tax preparers must make their clients aware of the issues and the potential risks. In some situations, failure to do so has resulted in the client attempting to collect from the preparer the amount of the substantial understatement penalty.

Assume the same facts as in Example 16-18 except that Val has substantial authority for the tax treatment adopted for a transaction that results in a $1,000 additional assessment. In addition, she makes adequate disclosure for a second transaction on which the IRS assesses additional taxes of $1,500. Although Val's total deficiency is $9,000, her understatement is $6,500 ($9,000 − [$1,000 + $1,500]). This amount still constitutes a substantial understatement (more than 10% of V's tax and $5,000). Because of the substantial authority and adequate disclosure, the penalty is only $1,300 (0.20 × $6,500). ∎

As in the case of the negligence penalty, the substantial understatement penalty bears interest. The interest rate is that applicable to underpayments, and the interest is incurred for the period beginning with the due date of the return.

Substantial Authority. Recall that except for tax-shelter items, the penalties are not imposed for transactions where the taxpayer has substantial authority for the tax treatment adopted. Defining *substantial authority,* however, is quite difficult. According to the Committee Reports, Congress adopted this standard, in part, because it was new. The Committee Reports elaborate on this concept in the following manner:

> [T]he courts will be free to look at the purpose of this new provision in determining whether substantial authority existed . . . such a standard should be less stringent than a "more likely than not" standard and more stringent than a "reasonable basis" standard. Thus, it is anticipated that this new standard will require that a taxpayer have stronger support for a position than a mere "reasonable basis" (a "reasonable basis" being one that is arguable, but fairly unlikely to prevail in court . . .) . . . the weight of the authorities that support the taxpayer's position should be substantial when compared with those supporting other positions.[61]

The Committee Reports also give the following guidance concerning the process for evaluating whether substantial authority exists in a particular situation.

> It will be necessary to weigh court opinions, Treasury regulations and official administrative pronouncements (such as revenue rulings and revenue procedures) that involve the same or similar circumstances and are otherwise pertinent, as well as the Congressional intent reflected in the committee reports, to determine whether the position is supported by present law and may be taken with the good faith expectation that it reflects the proper treatment of the item.[62]

No doubt, it will take years for the meaning of the term *substantial authority* to be clarified through the judicial system. In the meantime, taxpayers need to realize that adopting a protaxpayer position with respect to a relatively sizable grey-area transaction can result in incurring a 20% penalty. If their return involves a nontax-shelter item and it is audited, they will owe a 20% penalty unless (1) they had substantial authority for their tax treatment or (2) they disclosed adequate informa-

---

[61] Conf. Rept. 97-760, 97th Cong., 2d Sess., p. 575 (1982).
[62] Ibid. Regulations addressing the meaning of substantial authority are discussed on pages 16-40 and 16-41.

tion concerning the transaction. However, making a disclosure on a tax return may create a red flag that increases the probability of an audit.

Tax Shelters. Different rules apply to transactions that constitute tax shelters in determining whether there is an understatement. If a deficiency is assessed for a tax-shelter transaction, adequate disclosure cannot prevent the deficiency from being classified as an understatement. Instead of the taxpayer needing substantial authority, the taxpayer must meet a more stringent test to prevent a deficiency from being classified as an understatement. Here, the taxpayer must "reasonably believe" that the tax treatment used was "more likely than not" the proper tax treatment. "More likely than not" means a greater than 50% probability.[63] A *tax shelter* is defined as an arrangement for which the principal purpose is the avoidance or evasion of federal income tax.[64]

Example 16-20 ■ Assume the same facts as in Example 16-19, except that (1) Val's entire deficiency is related to tax-shelter items and (2) Val does not reasonably believe that the tax treatment used is more likely than not the proper tax treatment for the transaction in question. Val's understatement is the full $9,000 because the disclosure provides no relief for tax-shelter items and Val does not "reasonably believe" that the tax treatment used was more likely than not correct. Val's penalty is $1,800 (0.20 × $9,000). ■

Civil Fraud

The IRS may contend that errors on a taxpayer's return are attributable to fraudulent acts. At times criminal charges may also be filed against a taxpayer; taxpayers found guilty of such charges may receive a prison sentence. At other times the IRS may not press the criminal charges but will only attempt to have the taxpayer held liable for taxes, interest, and a civil fraud penalty. In both civil and the criminal cases, the IRS has the burden of proof when it charges fraud. However, in civil cases, proof consists of "clear and convincing evidence," whereas for criminal purposes, the standard is "beyond a reasonable doubt."

Fraud differs from simple, honest mistakes and negligence: It involves a deliberate attempt to deceive. Because the IRS cannot establish intent per se, it attempts to prove intent in an indirect fashion by emphasizing some of the taxpayer's actions. One leading authority describes fraud cases as having some of the following elements:

> Fraud cases ordinarily involve systematic omissions from gross income or fictitious deductions or dependency claims, accompanied by the falsification or destruction of records or false or inconsistent statements to the investigating agents, especially where records are not kept by the taxpayer. The taxpayer's education and business experience are also relevant.[65]

If part of a tax underpayment is the result of fraud, a fraud penalty equal to 75% of the portion of the underpayment attributable to fraud will be levied under Sec. 6663.

---

[63] Reg. Sec. 1.6661-5(d)(1).
[64] Sec. 6662(d)(2)(C)(ii).
[65] Boris I. Bittker, *Federal Taxation of Income, Estates, and Gifts* (Boston: Warren, Gorham & Lamont, 1981), vol. 4, pp. 114-19.

If, however, the IRS establishes that any portion of the underpayment is due to fraud, the entire underpayment is treated as resulting from fraud unless the taxpayer establishes by a preponderance of the evidence the portion that is not attributable to fraud. Like the negligence penalty, the fraud penalty bears interest.[66]

Example 16-21 ■

Typical Misconception
The amount of the civil fraud penalty is 75% of the portion of the underpayment attributable to fraud. Once any portion of the underpayment is held to be due to fraud, the entire underpayment is treated as resulting from fraud, unless the taxpayer establishes otherwise.

Ned's 1991 individual return is audited in 1993, and the IRS establishes that Ned's underpayment is due to fraud. Ned agrees to the IRS's assessing a $40,000 deficiency and establishes that only $32,000 of the deficiency is attributable to fraudulent acts. The rest results from mistakes that the IRS did not feel were due to negligence. Ned's civil fraud penalty is $24,000 (0.75 × $32,000). ■

The fraud penalty can be assessed with respect to income, gift, and estate tax returns. However, if the fraud penalty is imposed, the negligence and substantial understatement penalties are not levied on the portion of the underpayment resulting from fraud.[67]

No fraud penalty can be collected on a joint return from a spouse who has not committed a fraudulent act.[68] In other words, one spouse is not liable for the other spouse's fraudulent acts.

Key Point
Few taxpayers are charged with criminal fraud. But for those taxpayers who are accused of criminal fraud, the government's conviction rate is high, with penalties being assessed of up to $100,000 and 5 years in prison.

Criminal Fraud

Few taxpayers are charged with fraud under the criminal provisions in any one year. No distinct lines separate the activities that trigger criminal fraud charges from those that bring only civil fraud charges.

The Department of Justice must agree with the IRS's contention that criminal tax fraud charges should be filed against the taxpayer in question. The government's conviction rate in criminal fraud cases is high, and the government wants to keep it that way so the public will feel that such charges are only brought when the outcome is fairly certain. Thus, in fiscal 1989, the IRS completed 5,253 criminal investigations, and it recommended prosecution in 3,242 of them. During fiscal 1989, there were 2,282 convictions. Prison sentences were handed down in 1,574 of those cases.[69]

Burden of Proof. As mentioned earlier, the government must prove beyond a reasonable doubt that the taxpayer actually committed the crime of which he is accused. The proof standard is quite stringent. In fact, it is the same standard the plaintiff must meet in any other type of criminal case (e.g., a murder case).

Criminal Fraud Investigations. Criminal fraud investigations are carried out by the Criminal Investigation Division of the IRS. The agents responsible for the investigation are referred to as **special agents.** Under IRS policy, at the first meeting between the special agent and the taxpayer, the special agent must

- Identify himself as such
- Advise the taxpayer that he is the subject of a criminal investigation

---

[66] Sec. 6601(e)(2)(B).
[67] Sec. 6662(b).
[68] Sec. 6663(c).
[69] *1989 Annual Report of the Commissioner of the IRS* (Washington, D.C.: U.S. Government Printing Office, 1990), p. xx.

16-28 • Ch. 16 / Administrative Procedures

• Advise the taxpayer of his rights to remain silent and consult legal counsel

Additional Comment

Any time a tax professional learns a client has been engaged in activities that may constitute tax fraud, such client should be immediately referred to a qualified tax lawyer. Taxpayers are usually granted privileged communication only within an attorney-client relationship.

Penalty Provisions. Provisions concerning the penalties associated with various tax crimes are contained in Chapter 75, Subchapter A, of the Code (Secs. 7201 through 7216). Some of the more important penalties are discussed below.

SECTION 7201. Section 7201 provides for the assessment of a penalty against any person who "willfully attempts . . . to evade or defeat any tax." The maximum penalty is $100,000 ($500,000 for corporations), a prison sentence of up to 5 years, or both. In order to obtain a conviction under this section, the IRS must prove that the taxpayer paid less tax than was actually owed. Because this is so difficult to prove, the government may decide to file charges under another Code section. It is easier for the government to prove beyond a reasonable doubt that a taxpayer willfully failed to pay tax or file a return or willfully filed a false return than it is to prove that the taxpayer paid less than the correct amount of taxes.

SECTION 7203. Section 7203 imposes a penalty on persons who "willfully" fail to pay tax or file a return. The maximum fine is $25,000 ($100,000 for corporations), a prison sentence of no more than one year, or both. If the government charges the taxpayer with willfully failing to prepare a return, it need not prove that the taxpayer owes additional tax in order to impose the penalty.

SECTION 7206. Persons other than the taxpayer can be charged under Sec. 7206. This section addresses any person who "willfully" makes and subscribes any return "which he does not believe to be true and correct as to *every material matter*" (emphasis added). Litigation has arisen over what constitutes a material matter.[70] The scope of Sec. 7206 extends beyond just the taxpayer because it applies to any person who

> [W]illfully aids or assists in, or procures, counsels, or advises the preparation or presentation under, or in connection with any matter arising under the internal revenue laws, of a return, affidavit, claim, or other document, which is fraudulent or is false as to any material matter, whether or not such falsity or fraud is with the knowledge or consent of the person authorized or required to present such return, affidavit, claim, or document.[71]

The maximum penalty under Sec. 7206 is $100,000 ($500,000 for corporations), a prison sentence of up to 3 years, or both. The government need not prove that more tax is owed.

Topic Review 16-1 summarizes the penalty provisions that potentially affect taxpayers.

STATUTE OF LIMITATIONS

OBJECTIVE 7
Understand the statute of limitations

The statute of limitations has the same practical implications in the tax area as in other contexts. It stipulates a time limit during which the government must assess tax

---

[70] See, for example, *U.S. v. Joseph DiVarco*, 32 AFTR 2d 73-5605, 73-2 USTC ¶ 9607 (7th Cir., 1973), wherein the court held that the source of the taxpayer's income as stated on the tax return is a material matter.

[71] Sec. 7206(2).

TOPIC REVIEW 16-1

Penalties Levied on Taxpayers	
Penalty	Code Section
Failure to File:	
General rule—	
5% per month or fraction thereof; 25% maximum[a]	6651(a)
Minimum penalty if late more than 60 days—	
Smaller of $100 or 100% of tax due	6651(a)
Fraudulent reason for not filing—	
15% per month or fraction thereof; 75% maximum	6651(f)
Failure to Pay:	
0.5% per month or fraction thereof; 25% maximum[a]	6651(a)
Failure to Pay Estimated Tax—	
Penalty at same rate as interest rate for deficiency; imposed for period between due date for estimated tax payments and earlier of date paid or due date for return	6654
Accuracy Related Penalties:	
Negligence—	
20% of underpayment due to negligence	6662(c)
Substantial Understatement of Income Tax—	
20% of underpayment attributable to substantial understatement (portion for which no substantial authority and no disclosure exists)	6662(d)
Civil Fraud:	
75% of portion of underpayment attributable to fraud	6663
Criminal Fraud:	
Willful attempt to evade tax—	
$100,000 ($500,000 for corporations) and/or up to 5 years in prison	7201
Willful failure to pay tax or file return—	
$25,000 ($100,000 for corporations) and/or up to 1 year in prison	7203
Willful making of false return—	
$100,000 ($500,000 for corporations) and/or up to 3 years in prison	7206

[a] If the taxpayer owes both the failure-to-file and the failure-to-pay penalties for a given month, the total penalty for such month is limited to 5%.

or be barred from either assessing such tax or filing a court proceeding to collect the tax. The statute of limitations also limits the time during which a taxpayer may claim a refund of an overpayment of tax.

General 3-Year Rule

Under the general rule of Sec. 6501(a), the statute of limitations is 3 years after the return is filed, regardless of whether the return is timely filed. A return that is filed prior to its due date is treated as if it was filed on the due date.[72]

---

[72] Sec. 6501(b)(1).

Example 16-22 ■ Tom files his 1991 individual return on March 3, 1992. The government may not assess additional taxes for 1991 after April 15, 1995. ■

Example 16-23 ■ Bob files his 1991 individual return on November 4, 1992. The statute of limitations for this return expires on November 4, 1995. ■

Key Point
It is interesting to note that a 25% omission of gross income extends the basic statute to 6 years, whereas a 25% overstatement of deductions is still subject to the basic 3-year statute. However, if fraud can be shown, there is no statute of limitations.

Six-Year Rule for "Substantial" Omissions

Income Tax Returns. In the case of "substantial" omissions from returns, the statute of limitations is 6 years after the later of the date the return is filed or the return's due date. For income tax purposes, the 6-year statute is applicable if the taxpayer omits from gross income an amount exceeding 25% of the gross income shown on the return. If an item is disclosed either on the return or in a statement attached to the return, it is not treated as an omission if the disclosure is "adequate to apprise the Secretary of the nature and amount of such item."[73] In the case of taxpayers operating a trade or business, gross income for purposes of the 25% omission test means the taxpayer's sales revenues (and not the taxpayer's gross profit).[74] Taxpayers benefit from this special meaning of gross income because it allows the 25% test to be applied to a larger number.

Example 16-24 ■ Peg files her 1991 return on March 31, 1992. Her return shows $6,000 of interest from corporate bonds and $30,000 of salary. Peg attaches a statement to her return which indicates why she thinks a $2,000 receipt is nontaxable. However, as a result of an oversight, she does not report an $8,000 capital gain. Instead of the $10,000 literally omitted from the return, Peg is deemed to have omitted only $8,000, because the $2,000 receipt is disclosed. Because the $8,000 omission does not exceed $9,000 (0.25 × $36,000 gross income stated in the return), the statute of limitations expires on April 15, 1995. ■

Observe also that claiming excessive deductions will not result in a 6-year statute of limitations. However, if fraud can be shown with the omission in Example 16-24, there will be an unlimited statute of limitations.

Example 16-25 ■ Assume the same facts as in Example 16-24, except that Peg does not make adequate disclosure concerning the $2,000 receipt. Thus, $10,000 is considered to have been omitted from gross income. Because $10,000 is more than 25% of the gross income shown on Peg's return, the 6-year statute of limitations applies. ■

Example 16-26 ■ Rita operates a sole proprietorship. Rita's 1991 return, filed on March 17, 1992, shows sales of $100,000 and cost of goods sold of $70,000. Rita inadvertently fails to report $9,000 of interest income received on a loan made to a relative. For purposes of the 25% omission test, her gross income is deemed to be $100,000, not $30,000. Thus, because the omitted interest ($9,000) does not exceed 25% of the gross income shown on her return ($25,000 = 0.25 × $100,000), the statute of limitations expires on April 15, 1995. ■

Gift and Estate Tax Returns. A similar 6-year statute of limitations applies for gift and estate tax purposes. If items that exceed 25% of the gross estate or the total

---

[73] Sec. 6501(e).
[74] Generally, *gross income* is defined by Reg. Sec. 1.61-3(a) as sales less cost of goods sold.

amount of gifts stated on the return are omitted from the gross estate or the total amount of gifts, the statute of limitations expires 6 years after the later of the date the return is filed or the due date. Items disclosed on the return or in a statement attached to the return "in a manner adequate to apprise the Secretary of the nature and amount of such item" do not count as omissions.[75] Understatements of the value of assets disclosed on the return are not treated as omissions.

Example 16-27 ■ John files a gift tax return for 1991 on April 1, 1992. The return reports one gift of $600,000. In 1991, John sells land to his son for $700,000. At the time, John thinks that the land's FMV is $700,000 and does not disclose the sale on the gift tax return. Upon audit, it is determined that the FMV of the land on the sale date is $900,000. Thus, a $200,000 gift to the son arose. The omission ($200,000) exceeds 25% of the amount of gifts stated on the return ($150,000 = 0.25 × $600,000). The 6-year statute of limitations applies. ■

When No Return Is Filed

There is no statute of limitations if the taxpayer does not file a return.[76] That is, the government may assess tax or initiate a court proceeding for collection at any point in time.

Example 16-28 ■ Jill does not file a tax return for 1991. The statute of limitations never expires with respect to 1991. Consequently, if the government discovers 20 years later that the return was not filed, it is able to assess a 1991 tax against Jill. ■

Other Exceptions to 3-Year Rule

Typical Misconception
Why would a taxpayer ever agree to extend the statute of limitations? When an audit is already in progress, if a taxpayer refuses to extend the statute, the agent will simply assert a deficiency for each item in question. Had the taxpayer given the agent more time, chances are that many of the items in question would never have been included in the revenue agent's report.

Extension of the 3-Year Period. There are many other exceptions to the general 3-year statute of limitations, some of which are discussed here. The taxpayer and the IRS can mutually agree in writing to extend the statute of limitations for taxes other than the estate tax.[77] In such situations, the statute of limitations is extended until the date agreed upon by the two parties. Such agreements are usually executed when a return is being audited near the time the general statute of limitations is set to expire. Taxpayers may agree to extend the statute of limitations because they think that if they do not agree, the IRS will assess a higher deficiency than it would if it had a longer time to spend on the audit.

Carrybacks. In the case of a year to which net operating losses are carried back, the statute of limitations is open until the statute expires with respect to the year in which the net operating loss arises.[78]

When Fraud Is Proven.

DEFICIENCY AND CIVIL FRAUD PENALTY. If the government is successful in proving that a taxpayer's return was "false or fraudulent . . . with the intent to evade tax" or that the taxpayer engaged in a "willful attempt . . . to defeat or evade tax," there is no statute of limitations.[79] In other words, the government may assess the tax or begin a court proceeding to collect the tax and the interest thereon at any time. In

---

[75] Sec. 6501(e)(2).
[76] Sec. 6501(c)(3).
[77] Sec. 6501(c)(4).
[78] Sec. 6501(h).
[79] Secs. 6501(c)(1) and (2).

addition, if fraud is proven, the government can also collect the civil fraud penalty. If fraud is not proven, and the regular 3-year statute and the special 6-year statute for 25% omissions have expired, no additional taxes can be assessed. Frequently the fraud issue is very significant in litigated matters because the government must prove fraud to be able to assess a deficiency.

Example 16-29 ■ The IRS audits Trey's 1996 return in 1998. It also looks at some prior years' returns and contends that Trey has willfully attempted to evade tax on his 1991 return. Trey's litigation in the Tax Court on the fraud issue is successful. Because the IRS does not prove fraud, additional taxes may not be assessed for 1991. However, if the IRS had proven fraud, the statute of limitations for the 1991 return would have still been open and the additional taxes could be assessed. ■

Key Point
Even though a taxpayer is "home free" after 6 years with respect to being prosecuted under the criminal provision, he or she is still subject to possible civil fraud penalties if fraud is proven at any time after the 6-year period.

CRIMINAL PROVISIONS. Taxpayers must be indicted for criminal violations of the tax law within a certain period or they are "home free." For most criminal offenses in the tax area, the maximum time period for indictment is 6 years after the commission of the offense.[80] Taxpayers cannot be prosecuted, tried, or punished unless an indictment is made during that time period. Note that the 6-year period refers to the date of the commission of the offense, not to the date the return is filed. Persons who file fraudulent returns can commit offenses related to the returns at a subsequent date. An example of an offense that is often committed after the filing of a return is depositing money into a bank account under a fictitious name.

Example 16-30 ■ In March 1992, Tony files a fraudulent 1991 return in which he attempts to evade tax. Prior to filing, Tony keeps a double set of books. In 1991 Tony deposits some funds into a bank account under a fictitious name. In 1993 he moves to another state, and, on May 3, 1993, he transfers these funds to a new bank account under a different fictitious name. Depositing money into the new account is an offense relating to the fraudulent return. Provided Tony engages in no additional offenses, the statute of limitations for indictment expires on May 3, 1999. ■

Self-Study Question
Suppose a taxpayer incorrectly includes an item in a tax return and then, after the statute of limitations has run for that year, he correctly includes the item in a subsequent return. Is it equitable that the taxpayer should have to pay tax on the same item twice?

Answer
No. A complicated set of provisions [Secs. 1311-1314] exists that allows, in specific situations, otherwise closed years to be opened if a position taken in an open year is inconsistent with a position taken in a closed year.

Refund Claims

After a certain amount of time has expired, taxpayers are precluded from obtaining a refund. Taxpayers are generally not entitled to a refund of overpayments of tax unless they file a claim for refund by the later of (1) 3 years from the date the return is filed or (2) 2 years from the date the tax is paid.[81] A return filed prior to the due date is deemed to have been filed on the due date. The due date is determined without regard to extensions. In most cases taxpayers pay the tax concurrently with filing the return. Generally, when the later of the two dates is 2 years after the payment of the tax, it means that the taxpayer's return has been audited, a deficiency proposed, and additional taxes assessed and paid. The additional taxes may have been paid, for example, 2 years after the due date for the return. In such a situation the taxpayer may file for a refund of these taxes at any time within 2 years after making the additional payment (or a total of 4 years after the filing date). If the taxpayer does not file a claim until more than 3 years after the date of filing the return, the maximum refund the taxpayer can receive is the amount of tax paid during the 2-year period immediately preceding the date the claim for refund is filed.

---

[80] Sec. 6531.
[81] Sec. 6511(a).

Example 16-31 ◼ Pat files his 1991 return on March 11, 1992. The return shows taxes of $5,000, and Pat pays this entire amount when he files his return. No additional tax is paid. Pat must file a claim for refund by April 15, 1995. The maximum refundable amount is $5,000. ◼

Example 16-32 ◼ Assume the same facts as in Example 16-31, except that Pat's 1991 return is audited, and Pat pays a $1,200 deficiency on October 3, 1994. Pat may file a claim for refund as late as October 3, 1996. If Pat's claim is filed later than April 15, 1995, however, the refund may not exceed $1,200 (the amount of tax paid during the 2-year period immediately preceding the filing of the claim). ◼

LIABILITY FOR TAX

OBJECTIVE 8
Explain which taxpayers are liable for unpaid taxes

Taxpayers have the primary liability for payment of their tax. Transferees, however, can also be liable for the tax, as discussed below.

Joint Returns

If spouses file a joint income tax return, the liability for taxes is joint and several, even if only one of the spouses had income.[82] Consequently, the government may collect a deficiency from either spouse, regardless of whether the underpayment relates to that spouse's income or deductions. This rule perhaps has its most practical significance when the spouse to whom the deficiency is attributable has "left the country" and the IRS can more easily locate the other spouse.

If spouses originally file a joint return, they cannot amend their return and file separate returns after the due date for the return.[83] This rule is intended to prevent a spouse from escaping the joint and several liability aspect of having filed a joint return. In other words, a married individual may not substitute a separate return for the joint return if she learns after the due date that they omitted gross income from their return.

Validity of Joint Return. In general, a joint return must include the signatures of both spouses in order to be recognized as valid. If one spouse cannot sign because of a disability, the return is viewed as valid if that spouse orally consents to the other spouse's signing for him.[84] A joint return is deemed to be invalid if one spouse forces the other to file jointly under duress.

Key Point
Spouses filing joint returns have joint and several liability. However, the innocent spouse provisions provide equitable relief in certain situations.

Innocent Spouse Provision. Congress enacted the **innocent spouse provision** in order to provide relief from liability for additional taxes in certain circumstances.[85] In order for a spouse to be relieved of liability for certain additional taxes, the following four conditions must be met:

- A joint return must have been filed.
- The return must have included "a substantial understatement of tax attributable to grossly erroneous items of one spouse."

---
[82] Sec. 6013(d)(3).
[83] Reg. Sec. 1.6013-1(a)(1).
[84] Reg. Sec. 1.6012-1(a)(5).
[85] Sec. 6013(e).

- The spouse contending for relief must establish that he or she did not know about, and "had no reason to know" about, the substantial understatement.
- Based upon all the facts and circumstances, it must be "inequitable" for the other spouse to be liable for the deficiency attributable to the substantial understatement.

TEST FOR SUBSTANTIAL UNDERSTATEMENT OF TAX. Relief from liability first involves the objective test of a substantial understatement of tax. The Code defines a substantial understatement as an understatement in excess of $500.[86]

For relief to be granted, such understatement must be attributed to a grossly erroneous item of the other spouse. The following two situations each meet the definition of a grossly erroneous item:

- An item of gross income attributable to the other spouse is omitted from gross income.
- The other spouse makes any claim for a deduction, credit, or basis in an amount for which there is "no basis in fact or law."

The would-be innocent spouse must also meet the subjective tests of proving that he had no reason to know about the understatement and that it would be inequitable for him to have to pay the tax resulting from the understatement.

Example 16-33 ∎ For 1991, Bill omitted $4,500 of his income from the joint return he filed with May, his spouse. The IRS audited the return, discovered the omitted income, and assessed $1,395 in additional tax. The understatement, which exceeds the $500 minimum, is a result of an omission of Bill's gross income. The IRS cannot collect the $1,395 of tax from May, provided she did not know about, and had no reason to know about the omission, and it would be inequitable to hold her liable. ∎

"NO BASIS IN FACT OR LAW." Originally innocent spouse relief was available only if the other spouse omitted gross income. The 1984 law extended relief for certain situations involving improper deductions, credits, or basis. Thus, the "no basis in fact or law" requirement is new terminology. In many instances, the courts must also decide whether there is a "basis in fact or law" for an item (e.g., deduction, etc.) claimed.

The understatement attributable to deductions, and so on for which there is no basis in fact or law must exceed a certain percentage of the would-be innocent spouse's adjusted gross income (AGI) in order for the innocent spouse provisions to apply. (There is no comparable minimum threshold for gross income omissions.) If the would-be innocent spouse's AGI for the preadjustment year is $20,000 or less, the understatement must be more than 10% of such spouse's AGI. If the would-be innocent spouse has preadjustment year AGI in excess of $20,000, the understatement must exceed 25% of that spouse's AGI. **Preadjustment year** is defined as the most recent tax year of the spouse ending before the date the deficiency notice is mailed.

Example 16-34 ∎ Jim and Joy file a joint return for 1991. Jim claims tax deductions of $8,000 for items that clearly constitute personal expenses. The IRS mails a deficiency notice for $2,480 of additional tax in 1993. The understatement is attributable to deductions that had no basis in fact or law. Joy's AGI for 1992 (the preadjustment

---

[86] Sec. 6013(e)(3).

year) is $19,000. Because the understatement exceeds $1,900 (0.10 × $19,000), Joy potentially qualifies for relief from the $2,480 additional tax liability if she also has no reason to know about the understatement and it is considered inequitable for her to be liable. ∎

Example 16-35 ∎ Assume the same facts as in Example 16-34, except that Joy's AGI for 1992 is $28,000. Joy is ineligible for innocent spouse relief because the understatement ($2,480) does not exceed 25% of the preadjustment year AGI ($7,000 = 0.25 × $28,000). ∎

THE EFFECT OF COMMUNITY PROPERTY LAWS. Community property laws are ignored in determining to whom income (other than income from property) is attributable. Thus, if one spouse living in a community property state wins money by gambling, the gambling earnings are not viewed as community property for purposes of the innocent spouse provisions. If the gambling winnings are omitted from a joint return, they are deemed to be solely the income of the spouse who gambled. Thus, if the conditions discussed above are met, the other spouse qualifies as an innocent spouse.

Typical Misconception
A taxpayer cannot escape payment of taxes by transferring assets to a transferee (donees, heirs, legatees, etc.) or a fiduciary (estate of the taxpayer, decedent, donor, etc.).

Transferee Liability

Section 6901 indicates that the IRS may collect taxes from persons other than the taxpayer. The two categories of persons from whom the taxes may be collected are transferees and fiduciaries. Transferees include donees, heirs, legatees, devisees, shareholders of dissolved corporations, parties to a reorganization, and other distributees.[87] Fiduciaries include the estate of a taxpayer, decedent, or donor as the case may be. In general, the statute of limitations with respect to a transferee expires 1 year after the statute of limitations would have run out with respect to (1) the taxpayer in the case of income taxes, (2) the executor for estate taxes, and (3) the donor for gift taxes.

Example 16-36 ∎ Lake Corporation is liquidated in 1991 and all of its assets are distributed to its sole shareholder, Leo. If the IRS audits Lake's return and assesses a deficiency, Leo (the distributee) is responsible for paying the deficiency. ∎

TAX PRACTICE ISSUES

OBJECTIVE 9
Recognize the standards to which tax advisors should adhere

A number of statutes and guidelines govern what constitutes proper behavior of CPAs and others engaged in tax practice. The tax laws also provide for the assessment of penalties against tax return preparers and tax advisors in certain circumstances.

Statements on Responsibilities in Tax Practice

The standards set by professional organizations are not legally enforceable, although they have a great deal of moral clout. The most comprehensive guidelines for CPAs in tax practice were set forth by the Tax Division of the American Institute of Certified

---

[87] Reg. Sec. 301.6901-1(b).

Public Accountants (AICPA) in their advisory ***Statements on Responsibilities in Tax Practice*** **(SRTP).**[88] The Tax Division articulated the following objectives for the SRTPs:

- To recommend appropriate standards of responsibilities... and to promote their uniform application by CPAs
- To encourage the development of increased understanding of the responsibilities of the CPA by the Treasury Department and Internal Revenue Service
- To foster increased public understanding of, compliance with, and confidence in our tax system through awareness of the recommended standards of responsibilities of CPAs[89]

> **Key Point**
> According to the AICPA's *SRTP*, a CPA should: (1) use client's estimates, when reasonable; (2) inform the client of errors; and (3) except where required by law, not inform the IRS of errors without the permission of the client.

Some of the more important guidelines contained in the SRTP are highlighted below. Statement No. 4 discusses the use of estimates in the following manner:

- A CPA may prepare tax returns involving the use of the taxpayer's estimates if it is impracticable to obtain exact data, and the estimated amounts are reasonable under the facts and circumstances known to the CPA. When the taxpayer's estimates are used, they should be presented in such a manner as to avoid the implication of greater accuracy than exists.

Keep in mind, however, that with respect to certain expenses, no deduction is available unless the taxpayer has the proper documentation.[90] Thus, a CPA cannot use estimates for such amounts.

Statement No. 6 contains guidelines concerning what CPAs should do when they have knowledge of errors made by clients or earlier return preparers. The recommendations are as follows:

- The CPA should inform the client promptly upon becoming aware of an error in a previously filed return or upon becoming aware of a client's failure to file a required return. The CPA should recommend the measures to be taken. Such recommendation may be given orally. The CPA is not obligated to inform the Internal Revenue Service, and the CPA may not do so without the client's permission, except where required by law.

In Statement No. 7, the CPA's responsibilities in an administrative proceeding (e.g., an audit) are described.

- When the CPA is representing a client in an administrative proceeding with respect to a return that contains an error of which the CPA is aware, the CPA should inform the client promptly upon becoming aware of the error. The CPA should recommend the measures to be taken. Such recommendation may be given orally. The CPA is neither obligated to inform the Internal Revenue Service nor is he or she permitted to do so without the client's permission, except where required by law.
- The CPA should request the client's agreement to disclose the error to the Internal Revenue Service.

Statement No. 8 makes the following comments about the form—oral or written—of the advice given by CPAs.

---

[88] AICPA, *Statements on Responsibilities in Tax Practice, 1988 Revision,* Introduction, ¶ .03.
[89] Ibid.
[90] Section 274(d) precludes deductions for certain expenditures (e.g., travel expenses including meals and lodging) unless the taxpayer can substantiate them by "adequate records or sufficient" corroborating evidence.

- Although oral advice may serve a client's needs appropriately in routine matters or in well-defined areas, written communications are recommended in important, unusual, or complicated transactions.

With respect to the procedural aspects of return preparation, Statement No. 3 furnishes the guidance shown below.

- In preparing or signing a return, the CPA may in good faith rely without verification upon information furnished by the client or by third parties. Yet, the CPA should not ignore the implications of information furnished and should make reasonable inquiries if the information furnished appears to be incorrect, incomplete, or inconsistent either on its face or on the basis of other facts known to the CPA. In this connection, the CPA should refer to the client's returns for prior years whenever feasible.
- Where the Internal Revenue Code or income tax regulations impose a condition with respect to deductibility or other tax treatment of an item (such as taxpayer maintenance of books and records or substantiating documentation to support the reported deduction or tax treatment), the CPA should make appropriate inquiries to determine to his or her satisfaction whether such condition has been met.
- The individual CPA who is required to sign the return should consider information actually known to that CPA from the tax return of another client when preparing a tax return if the information is relevant to that tax return, its consideration is necessary to properly prepare that tax return, and use of such information does not violate any law or rule relating to confidentiality.

Statement No. 1 provides standards with which a CPA should comply in taking positions on a tax return or in recommending such positions. The following guidance is given.

- A CPA should not recommend to a client that a position be taken with respect to the tax treatment of any item on a return unless the CPA has a good faith belief that the position, if challenged, has a realistic possibility of being sustained administratively or judicially on its merits.
- A CPA should not prepare or sign a return as an income tax return preparer if the CPA knows that the return takes a position that the CPA could not recommend under the standard expressed [above].
- Notwithstanding [the above], a CPA may recommend a position that the CPA concludes is not frivolous as long as the position is adequately disclosed on the return or claim for refund.
- In recommending certain tax return positions and in signing a return on which a tax return position is taken, a CPA should, where relevant, advise the client as to the potential penalty consequences of the recommended tax return position and the opportunity, if any, to avoid such penalties through disclosure.

Statement No. 1 elaborates on the "good faith" belief requirement as follows:

- The standards suggested herein require that a CPA in good faith believe that the position is warranted in existing law or can be supported by a good faith argument for an extension, modification, or reversal of existing law. For example, the CPA may reach such a conclusion on the basis of well-reasoned articles, treatises, IRS General Counsel Memoranda, a General Explanation of a Revenue Act prepared by the staff of the Joint Committee on Taxation, and Internal

Key Point

*According to the AICPA's **STRP**, a CPA should: (1) rely on reasonable information from the client without verification; (2) not recommend a position that would not have a realistic possibility of being sustained administratively or judicially, nor sign a return that takes such a position; and (3) advise a client of potential penalties for any recommended tax positions.*

Key Point

As evidenced by the formidable list of possible penalties, an individual considering becoming a tax return preparer needs to be aware of certain procedures that are required by the IRS.

Revenue Service written determinations (for example, private letter rulings), whether or not such sources are treated as "authority" under section 6661.

Statutory Provisions Concerning Tax Return Preparers

Sections 6694 through 6696 regulate tax return preparers by imposing penalties on them in certain circumstances. Section 7701(a)(36) defines an income tax return preparer as a "person who prepares for compensation, or who employs one or more persons to prepare for compensation, any return of tax imposed by subtitle A [income tax] or any claim for refund of tax imposed by subtitle A." Preparation of a substantial portion of a return or refund claim is treated as preparation of such return or claim. Note that estate and gift tax returns and claims for refund of such taxes are not affected by these statutory provisions.

Section 6695 imposes penalties for

- Failure to furnish the taxpayer with a copy of the return or claim ($50 per failure)
- Failure to sign a return or claim ($50 per failure)
- Failure to furnish one's identification number ($50 per failure)
- Failure to keep a copy of a return or claim or, in lieu thereof, to maintain a list of taxpayers for whom returns or claims were prepared ($50 per failure, up to a maximum of $25,000 for a return period)
- Failure to file the return disclosing the names, identification numbers, and places of work of each income tax return preparer employed ($50 per return plus $50 for each failure to set forth an item in the return)
- Endorsement or other negotiation of an income tax refund check made payable to anyone other than the preparer ($500 per check)

The first five penalties described above will not be levied if the preparer shows that the failure is due to "reasonable cause."[91]

The penalties just described relate to procedural matters. However, in certain circumstances a preparer will owe a penalty under Sec. 6694 as a result of understating the taxpayer's tax liability. The preparer must pay a $250 penalty if any of the understatement is due to a position which does not have a realistic possibility of being sustained on its merits provided the preparer knew, or reasonably should have known of, the position and the position either was frivolous or was not disclosed. If any of the understatement results from the preparer's willful attempt to understate taxes or reckless or intentional disregard of rules or regulations, the penalty is $1,000.

Regulation Sec. 1.6694-1(a), which interprets a slightly different version of Sec. 6694, contains additional guidance with respect to disregard of rules or regulations. It states that the term *rules and regulations* includes provisions of the Code, the Regulations, and revenue rulings. According to Notice 90-20, the IRS "will treat a position as having a realistic possibility of being sustained on 'its merits' if a reasonable and well-informed analysis by a person knowledgeable in the tax law would lead such a person to conclude that the position has approximately a one in three, or greater, likelihood of being sustained on its merits."[92]

Regulation Sec. 1.6694-1(b) addresses the willful understatement penalty. It states that preparers are considered to have willfully understated taxes if they have attempted to wrongfully reduce taxes by disregarding pertinent information. The

---

[91] Regulation Sec. 1.6695-1(b)(5) states that reasonable cause is "a cause which arises despite ordinary care and prudence exercised by the individual preparer."
[92] Notice 90-20, 1990-1 C.B. 328.

Regulation provides that generally the preparer may rely on information furnished by the taxpayer. (This is similar to the SRTP guidelines.) Preparers should, however, make reasonable inquiries if the taxpayer's information appears incorrect or incomplete. Preparers must also make appropriate inquiries of the taxpayer to determine whether the taxpayer meets the statutory or regulatory requirements (e.g., documentation) necessary to claim a deduction.

Topic Review 16-2 summarizes the penalty provisions applicable to tax return preparers.

> **Key Point**
>
> In addition to the standards imposed on most tax practitioners by their respective professional organizations, the IRS has promulgated a set of practice requirements that must be adhered to by those practicing before the IRS.

Rules of Circular 230

Treasury Department Circular 230 (or *Circular 230*) regulates the practice of attorneys, CPAs, enrolled agents, and enrolled actuaries before the IRS. Practice before the IRS includes representing taxpayers in meetings with IRS agents and appeals officers. Persons who do not comply with the rules and regulations of *Circular 230* can be barred from practicing before the IRS. Such persons are entitled to an administrative hearing, however.

The following are among the duties and restrictions applicable to persons practicing before the IRS.[93]

- If the practitioner knows that a client has not complied with federal tax laws or has made an error in or omissions from any return, the practitioner should promptly advise the client of the error or omission.
- Each person practicing before the IRS is expected to exercise due diligence in

TOPIC REVIEW 16-2

Penalties Levied on Tax Return Preparers

Penalty	Amount	Code Section
Procedural matters:		
Failure to provide copy to taxpayer	$ 50	6695(a)
Failure to sign	50	6695(b)
Failure to furnish identification number	50	6695(c)
Failure to keep copy of return or list of taxpayers	50	6695(d)
Failure to file return regarding preparers employed	50	6695(e)
Endorsement of another's tax refund check	500	6695(f)
Understatement of tax because of position without realistic possibility of being sustained	250	6694(a)
Willful attempt to understate taxes and reckless or intentional disregard of rules or regulations	1,000	6694(b)

Note: The amounts shown above are per item or per return; most of the penalties provide for a maximum that can be imposed in the event of numerous violations.

---

[93] *Treasury Department Circular 230* (1985), Secs. 10.21 and 10.22.

preparing returns, determining the correctness of representations made to the Treasury Department, and determining the correctness of representations made to clients about tax matters.

Circular 230 also contains a detailed discussion of practices persons must follow in conjunction with issuing tax-shelter opinions.[94]

CONTROVERSIAL ISSUE

Concept of "Substantial Authority"

As noted earlier, a penalty can be levied against taxpayers who substantially understate their tax liability. Recall that this penalty is not always imposed with respect to additional taxes that are assessed. For example, the penalty does not apply if the taxpayer (1) has "substantial authority" for the position adopted on the tax return or (2) makes adequate disclosure about the transaction that triggered the additional tax. Rev. Proc. 91-19[95] describes circumstances in which the adequate disclosure exception will be that.

The concept of substantial authority comes into play as one of the exceptions to the penalty for substantial understatement of one's tax liability. Regulations issued in 1985 offer some guidance with respect to interpreting the term *substantial authority*, stating that "substantial authority"

Typical Misconception

The fact that proposed regulations do not constitute substantial authority is beneficial to the taxpayer. If the proposed regulations are contrary to a taxpayer's position, they do not have to be considered in determining substantial authority. However, if proposed regulations are consistent with a taxpayer's position, since such regulations represent the Treasury's current position, the IRS is not likely to litigate the issue.

- Is a less stringent standard than the "more likely than not" test applicable to tax-shelter items but a stronger test than the "reasonable basis" standard that the taxpayer must meet to avoid the negligence penalty
- Only exists if "the weight of authorities supporting the treatment is substantial in relation to the weight of authorities supporting contrary positions"
- Involves a situation where the taxpayer's position is stronger than one that is arguable but fairly unlikely to prevail in court[96]

According to the Regulations, the following are considered authority: statutory provisions, temporary and final regulations, court cases, revenue rulings, revenue procedures, tax treaties, and Congressional intent as reflected in committee reports and floor statements of a bill's managers. The Ways and Means Committee Report for the *Revenue Reconciliation Act of 1989* expands the list of authorities to include "proposed regulations, private letter rulings, technical advice memoranda, information or press releases, notices, and any other similar documents published by the IRS in the *Internal Revenue Bulletin*" as well as the *General Explanation of the Joint Committee on Taxation* (also known as the "Blue Book"). The 1989 legislation also mandates that at least once a year the IRS publish a list of positions that, in its opinion, lack substantial authority and affect a significant number of taxpayers.[97] The time for assessing substantial authority is the date the return is filed or the last day of the tax year covered by the return.

In general, the Regulations do not allow decisions of the taxpayer's geographical jurisdiction to be awarded additional weight in assessing whether substantial

---

[94] Ibid., Sec. 10.33.
[95] I.R.B. 1991-10, 24.
[96] Reg. Sec. 1.6661-3.
[97] Sec. 6662(d)(2)(D).

authority exists. They do, however, give special emphasis to the decisions of the Court of Appeals for the taxpayer's circuit. According to the Regulations

> The applicability of court cases to the taxpayer by reason of the taxpayer's residence in a particular jurisdiction is not taken into account in determining whether there is substantial authority for the tax treatment of an item. Notwithstanding the preceding sentence, however, there is substantial authority for the tax treatment of an item if the treatment is supported by controlling precedent of a United States Court of Appeals to which the taxpayer has a right of appeal with respect to the item.[98]

Example 16-37 ■ Authorities addressing a particular issue are as follows:
— For the government—Tax Court and Fourth Circuit Court of Appeals
— For taxpayers—U.S. District Court for Rhode Island and First Circuit Court of Appeals

The taxpayer (Tina) is a resident of Rhode Island, which is in the First Circuit. Tina would be deemed to have "substantial authority" for a protaxpayer position because such an interpretation is supported by the Circuit Court of Appeals for Tina's geographical jurisdiction. ■

PROBLEM MATERIALS

DISCUSSION QUESTIONS

16-1. What are the duties and responsibilities of the IRS Service Centers?

16-2. Name some of the administrative interpretations that the IRS is responsible for issuing.

16-3. a. Describe three ways in which the IRS selects returns for audit.
b. Explain the difference between how returns are selected for audit and the scope of the audit for returns selected under both the DIF and the TCMP procedures.

16-4. What is the purpose of the TCMP program?

16-5. For fiscal year 1989 what percentage of individual returns was chosen for audit?

16-6. In addition to the DIF and the TCMP procedures, what is one other method for choosing returns for audit?

16-7. Al's individual return shows salary income and an exemption for himself; he has no itemized deductions. On the other hand, Ben's individual return reports self-employment income, a large loss from a limited partnership, a casualty loss deduction equal to 25% of his AGI, charitable contribution deductions equal to 30% of his AGI, and an exemption for himself. Al's return shows higher taxable income than Ben's. Which return is more likely to be selected for audit under the DIF program? Under the TCMP program? Explain your answers.

16-8. Tom receives a notice that the IRS has decided to audit his 1991 return with respect to his deduction for interest expense. His 1989 return was audited for his charitable contribution deduction. The IRS did not, however, assess a deficiency with respect to Tom's 1989 return. Is any potential "relief" available to Tom with respect to the audit of his 1991 return?

16-9. Brad's 1991 return is chosen for audit on the employee business expense issue. Brad has just finished meeting with a revenue agent; the agent contends that he owes $775 of additional taxes. Discuss briefly the alternatives available to Brad.

16-10. What is the difference between a 30-day letter and a 90-day letter?

[98] Reg. Sec. 1.6661-3(b)(4)(ii).

16-11. Explain when technical advice might be sought regarding a tax matter.

16-12. List the trial courts in which a taxpayer can begin litigation concerning a tax matter.

16-13. Why is the Tax Court so popular as a forum for beginning litigation?

16-14. In what situations is a protest letter necessary?

16-15. What general types of information should be included in a request for a ruling?

16-16. In what circumstances will the IRS rule on estate tax issues?

16-17. Describe the recent changes in the IRS's policy concerning letter rulings.

16-18. Tracy wants to take advantage of a "terrific business deal" by entering into a transaction with Homer. Homer, quite domineering and impatient, wants Tracy to finalize the transaction within 2 weeks and under the exact terms proposed by Homer. Otherwise, Homer will offer the "deal" to another party. Tracy is unsure about the tax consequences of the proposed transaction. Would you advise Tracy to request a ruling? Explain.

16-19. For individuals and corporations, when are the following?
  a. Due date for the income tax return, assuming no extension is requested
  b. Due date for return assuming an automatic extension request is filed
  c. Latest possible due date for the return

16-20. Must a taxpayer execute any paperwork in order to take advantage of the automatic extension provision? Explain.

16-21. Evaluate the following statement. Obtaining an extension for filing an income tax return gives the taxpayer an additional amount of time to pay the tax at no interest cost.

16-22. Briefly explain the rules that determine what interest rate will be charged for tax underpayments. Is the rate the same for overpayments as for underpayments? In which months does the interest rate for underpayments potentially change?

16-23. Stan does not have sufficient assets in April 1991 to pay his 1990 tax liability. However, he does anticipate paying the tax by August 1991. He wonders if he should request an extension of time for filing instead of simply filing his return and paying the tax in August. What is your response?

16-24. What is the rate at which the payment for underpaying estimated taxes is imposed? How is the amount of the penalty calculated?

16-25. Distinguish between the burden of proof the government must meet for imposition of the civil fraud and criminal fraud penalties.

16-26. Assume that a taxpayer owes substantial additional taxes as a result of an audit. Nevertheless, the IRS may decide not to argue for applying the substantial understatement penalty. Explain two reasons why the IRS might not argue for imposing such a penalty.

16-27. Maria's correct tax liability is determined to be $40,000 upon audit. She agrees that she owes a $7,000 deficiency. Will she necessarily have to pay the substantial understatement penalty? Explain.

16-28. Distinguish between the circumstances that would lead to the imposition of the civil fraud penalty as opposed to the negligence penalty.

16-29. Tony's return was audited, and Tony agreed that he owed additional taxes plus the negligence penalty. Is the negligence penalty necessarily imposed on the total additional taxes that Tony owes? Explain.

16-30. In general, when does the statute of limitations expire? List four exceptions to the general rule.

16-31. What is the purpose of the innocent spouse provisions?

16-32. When should a CPA sign a tax return as a preparer for purposes of the tax return preparer provisions of the Code? Can a CPA be penalized for failing to follow the *Statements on Responsibilities in Tax Practice (SRTP)*?

16-33. List five penalties that can be assessed against tax return preparers under the Code. For purposes of the SRTP and the Code, must a CPA audit the information a client furnishes?

16-34. According to the SRTP, what standard should be met in order for a CPA to take a position on a tax return?

16-35. Explain why the government might bring criminal tax fraud charges against a taxpayer under Sec. 7206 instead of Sec. 7201. How do the maximum penalties under Secs. 7201, 7203, and 7206 compare?

PROBLEMS

16-36. *Calculation of Penalties.* Amy files her 1991 calendar-year return and pays the balance due on August 13, 1992, without having requested an extension. The tax shown on her return is $20,000. Her 1991 withholding tax is $12,000. Amy pays no estimated taxes and does not claim any tax credits on her 1991 return.
  a. What penalties will Amy owe (ignoring the penalty for underpayment of estimated taxes)? Assume there is no fraud.
  b. On what dollar amount, and for how many days, will Amy owe interest?

16-37. *Calculation of Penalties.* Refer to Problem 16-36. How will your answers change if Amy instead files her return on June 18 and pays the balance of her taxes on September 8, 1992, and her withholding tax is
  a. $19,000?
  b. $20,500?
  c. How will your answer to Part a change if Amy requests an automatic extension?

16-38. *Calculation of Penalties.* The tax shown on Cindy's tax returns for 1990 and 1991 were $5,000 and $8,000, respectively. Cindy's withholding tax for 1991 was $5,200, and she paid no estimated taxes. Cindy filed her 1991 return on March 17, 1992, but she did not have sufficient funds to pay any taxes at the time she filed her return. She paid the $2,800 balance due on June 19, 1993. What is the amount of any penalties that Cindy owes?

16-39. *Calculation of Penalties.* Ted's 1991 return reported tax of $1,800. Ted's withholding for 1991 was $2,200. Because of his poor memory, Ted did not file his 1991 return until May 28, 1992. What is the amount of any penalties that Ted owes?

16-40. *Calculation of Penalties.* Bob, a calendar year taxpayer, files his 1991 individual return on July 17, 1992, without having requested an extension. His return shows a balance due of $4,000. Bob pays the balance due on November 3, 1992. What are Bob's penalties for his failure to file and his failure to pay his tax on time? Assume there is no fraud.

16-41. *Calculation of Penalties.* Carl, a calendar year taxpayer, requests an automatic extension for filing his 1991 return. By April 15, 1992, he has paid $20,000 of taxes in the form of withholding and estimated taxes. He does not pay any additional tax with his extension request. Carl files his return and pays the balance of the taxes due on June 19, 1992. What penalties will Carl owe if his 1991 tax is $23,000? $20,800?

16-42. *Determination of Interest.* Refer to Problem 16-41.
  a. Will Carl owe any interest? If so, on what amount and for how many days?
  b. Assume the applicable interest rate is 11%. Compute Carl's interest payable if his 1991 tax is $23,000. (See Rev. Proc. 83-7, 1983-1 C.B. 583, or a major tax service, for the compounding tables.)

16-43. *Penalty for Underpayment of Estimated Taxes.* Ed's tax liability for 1990 was $24,000. Ed projects that his tax for 1991 will be $38,000. Ed is self-employed and, thus, will have no withholding. How much estimated taxes should he pay for 1991?

16-44. *Penalty for Underpayment of Estimated Taxes.* Refer to Problem 16-43. Assume that Ed expects that his income for 1991 will decline and that his tax liability for 1991 will be only $15,000. How much estimated taxes, at a minimum, should Ed pay for 1991? What is a potential problem that Ed could encounter if he pays in just this amount of estimated taxes?

16-45. *Penalty for Underpayment of Estimated Taxes.* Pam's 1990 income tax liability is

$23,000. Pam, a calendar year taxpayer, files her 1991 individual return showing a $30,000 income tax liability (before reduction for withholding) on April 1, 1992. In addition, Pam owes self-employment taxes of $2,600. Taxes withheld from Pam's salary total $5,000; she has paid no estimated taxes.

  a. Will Pam owe a penalty for not paying estimated taxes? Explain.
  b. How many dollars, if any, per quarter are subject to the penalty? For what period will the penalty be imposed for each quarter's underpayment?
  c. How would your answers to Parts a and b change if Pam's 1990 tax liability is instead $17,000?

16-46. Penalty for Underpayment of Estimated Taxes. Hugh's 1991 projected tax liability is $20,000. Although Hugh has substantial dividend and interest income, he does not pay any estimated taxes. Hugh's withholding for January through November 1991 is $1,300 per month. For December 1991 he wants to increase the amount of his withholding to avoid the penalty for underpaying estimated taxes. Hugh's 1990 liability (exclusive of his withholding) is $19,000. What amount should be withheld from Hugh's December check? Explain.

16-47. Substantial Understatement Penalty. Kay's 1991 individual return shows a $6,000 deduction for a questionable item. The item is not a tax-shelter item. Kay does not make a disclosure regarding this item. Kay's return is audited, and she concedes to the assessment of a deficiency. As a result, her tax liability increases from $20,000 to $21,680. Assume Kay lacks substantial authority for claiming the deduction.

  a. What is the substantial understatement penalty (if any) that will be levied?
  b. Will the penalty bear interest?
  c. How would your answer to Parts a and b change if the deduction is instead for $20,000, and her tax liability increases by $5,600 to $25,600?

16-48. Substantial Understatement Penalty. Refer to Part c of Problem 16-47. Assume that Kay has substantial authority and discloses the transaction. How would your original answer change if

  a. The transaction does not involve a tax-shelter item?
  b. The transaction does involve a tax-shelter item?

16-49. Negligence Penalty. Matt's 1991 individual return is audited, and the IRS assesses a $9,000 deficiency, $3,000 of which results from Matt's negligence. What is Matt's negligence penalty? Does the penalty bear interest?

16-50. Negligence Penalty. Pearl's current year individual return is audited. It is determined that, among other errors, she negligently did not report dividend income of $8,000 on her return. The deficiency with respect to the dividends is $2,240. The IRS argues for an additional $12,000 deficiency for various other errors that do not involve negligence. What is Pearl's negligence penalty with respect to the $14,240 of deficiencies?

16-51. Fraud Penalty. Hank, a bachelor, owes $60,000 of additional taxes, all because of fraudulent acts.

  a. What is the amount of the civil fraud penalty?
  b. What criminal fraud penalty might be levied under Sec. 7201?

16-52. Fraud Penalty. Hal and Wanda, his wife, are in the 28% marginal tax bracket for the current year. Wanda fraudulently omits $50,000 of gross income from their joint return. Hal does not participate in or know about her fraudulent acts. Hal, however, overstates his deductions by $10,000 because of an oversight.

  a. If the government is successful in proving fraud in a civil case, what fines and/or penalties will Wanda owe? If Hal and Wanda establish that the overstatement of deductions is not attributable to fraud, can the government collect the civil fraud penalty from Hal?
  b. If the government is successful in proving fraud in a criminal case, what fines and/or penalties will Wanda owe? Can she or Hal receive a prison sentence?

16-53. Claim for Refund. Mimi, a calendar year taxpayer, files her 1991 individual return on March 17, 1992, and pays the balance of her taxes on that date. She later discovers that she overlooked some deductions that she should have claimed on the return. By what date must she file a claim for refund?

16-54. *Statute of Limitations.* Frank, a calendar year taxpayer, reports $100,000 of gross income and $60,000 of taxable income on his 1991 return, which he files on March 10, 1992. He omits a $52,000 long-term capital gain and a $10,000 short-term capital loss from his return. When does the statute of limitations concerning the government's ability to collect the taxes expire if
  a. His omission results from an oversight?
  b. His omission of the gain arose because of an attempt to evade tax?

16-55. *Statute of Limitations.* Refer to Problem 16-54. Assume Frank commits fraudulent acts with respect to his 1991 return as late as November 4, 1993. When does the statute of limitations for indicting Frank for criminal tax fraud expire?

16-56. *Innocent Spouse Provisions.* Wilma has no income for 1991, but she files a joint return with her husband, Hank. Their 1991 return shows $40,000 of gross income and AGI and $24,000 of taxable income. Hank has $12,000 of gambling winnings (no losses) in 1991, but he omits them from the return. Wilma does not know about Hank's gambling activities, much less his winnings. The IRS audits their 1991 return and assesses additional taxes.
  a. Does Wilma satisfy the objective tests for relief under the innocent spouse provisions?
  b. What subjective tests must Wilma also meet in order to qualify as an innocent spouse?

16-57. *Innocent Spouse Provisions.* Joe and Joan filed a joint return for 1991. They are in the 28% marginal tax bracket. Joan omitted from the return a prize valued at $8,000 that she had won. Does Joe meet the objective test for relief under the innocent spouse provisions?

TAX RESEARCH PROBLEMS

16-58. Art is named executor of the Estate of Stu Stone, his father, who dies on February 3, 1991. Art engages Larry to serve as the estate's attorney. Larry advises Art that the estate must file an estate tax return. He does not, however, mention the due date. Art, a pharmacist, has no experience with tax matters other than the preparation of his own income tax return. Art provides Larry with all the necessary information by June 15, 1991. On six occasions Art contacts Larry to check on the progress on the estate tax return. Each time, Larry assures Art that "everything is under control." On November 15, 1991, Art contacts Larry for the seventh time. He learns that because of a clerical oversight the return—due on November 2, 1991—has not been filed. Larry apologizes and says he will make sure that an associate finishes the return promptly. The return, showing an estate tax liability of $75,200, is filed on December 7, 1991. Will the estate owe the failure-to-file penalty?

A partial list of research sources is

- Sec. 6151(a).
- *U.S. v. Robert W. Boyle,* 55 AFTR 2d 85-1535, 85-1 USTC ¶ 13,602 (USSC, 1985).

16-59. Mel, a physician, brought legal action against a television station in the city in which he practiced medicine because the station had reported that 6 years ago Mel had filed fraudulent Medicare claims. The basis of Mel's suit was that his medical reputation had been damaged as a result of the television report. Mel's fee income did, in fact, decline after the television report, which he alleged was incorrect. The case was settled out of court 2 years ago, and Mel received a $50,000 settlement for compensatory damages. Mel excluded the damages from his gross income. His return for the year of receipt has been audited, and the IRS contends that the damages are gross income. Mel would like to meet with an appeals officer. Prepare a protest letter and assume that Mel is a resident of the 11th Circuit.

A partial list of resources is

- Sec. 104.
- *Paul F. Roemer, Jr. v. CIR,* 52 AFTR 2d 83-5994, 83-2 USTC ¶ 9600 (9th Cir., 1983).
- *James E. Threlkeld,* 87 T.C. 1294 (1987).

16-60. Gene employs his attorney to draft identical trust instruments for trusts for each of his three minor children. Before he signs the instruments, Gene wishes to receive a ruling from the IRS concerning whether the trusts will qualify for the gift tax annual exclusion. Your task is to prepare a request for a letter ruling. Each trust instrument names the Fourth City Bank as trustee and states the trust is irrevocable. It further provides that until the beneficiary reaches age 21, the trustee in its discretion is to pay income and/or principal (corpus) to the beneficiary.

Upon reaching age 21, the beneficiary has 60 days in which to request that the trust assets be paid over to him. Otherwise, the assets will stay in the trust until the beneficiary reaches age 35. The beneficiary is also granted a general testamentary power of appointment over the trust assets. If the beneficiary dies before the trust terminates and does not exercise his power of appointment (because, for example, he dies without a will), the trust property will be distributed to family members in accordance with state intestacy laws. The three beneficiaries are Judy (age 5), Terry (age 7), and Grady (age 11). Each trust will be funded with property valued at $100,000.

A partial list of research sources is

- Secs. 2503(b) and (c).
- Reg. Sec. 25.2503-4.
- Rev. Rul. 67-270, 1967-2 C.B. 349.
- Rev. Rul. 74-43, 1974-1 C.B. 285.
- Rev. Rul. 81-7, 1981-1 C.B. 474.

APPENDIX

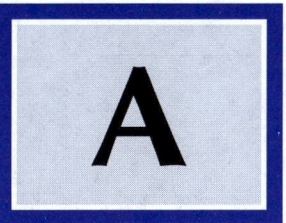

Tax Research Working Paper File

George Dunn

Tax File

December 1991

INDEX TO WORKING PAPERS

Item	Page Reference
Draft of Client Letter	A-1
Memo to File, Patsy Partner	B-1
Summary of Questions and Conclusions	C-1
Detailed Questions and Conclusions	D-1

CARTER, PARKER, & ADAMS, CPAs
1011 Sunshine Blvd.
Tampa, Florida 33602

December 20, 1991

Mr. George Dunn
15 Coral Court
Tampa, Florida 33611

We are pleased to report the results of our research concerning whether you will have to report any gain on the sale of your former residence. Before discussing our conclusions, I would like to restate briefly the facts that you related to me in our phone conversation of December 15. Please review these facts carefully because our conclusions depend upon an accurate understanding of all the relevant facts.

- - - (Summary of facts goes here.) - - -

Assuming that the preceding paragraphs constitute an accurate statement of all the relevant facts, we conclude that authority exists for viewing 105 Orange St. as your principal residence as of the date of sale. Accordingly, because the cost of your new residence exceeded the sales price (net of expenses) of your former residence, you may defer all of the gain. Deferral of the gain will reduce the basis of your new property. Whether a property constitutes your principal residence depends on all the facts and circumstances and your failure to occupy a house at the sale date does not automatically disqualify the house from being classified as your principal residence. We have a good faith belief that classification of 105 Orange St. as your principal residence on the sale date has a realistic possibility of being sustained administratively or judicially if challenged.

However, if your return is audited, the Internal Revenue Service may argue that you are ineligible for deferral because, in their opinion, you had abandoned 105 Orange St. as your principal residence by the sale date. We will be happy to discuss this matter with you in more detail.

Thank you for consulting us. It is important that this letter be kept confidential. If you have any questions concerning our conclusions, please call.

Sincerely,

Patsy Partner

D-R-A-F-T

December 15, 1991

MEMO TO FILE

FROM: Patsy Partner

SUBJECT: George Dunn-Tax Engagement

Today George Dunn called to inquire about the tax results of the sale of his former residence, 105 Orange St., Tampa, Florida. Basically, he wants to know whether he will have to report any gain on the sale.

Dunn purchased the house in 1963 at a cost of $75,000. He made no improvements to the house. In 1965 he married Linda Graves, but the house continued to be held solely in his name. This is the first house that Dunn has owned. George and Linda occupied the house as their only residence until February 14, 1991, when they decided to get a divorce. Mr. Dunn moved into an apartment on February 14, 1991, and Mrs. Dunn continued to live in the house while she contemplated relocating to her hometown of Ponca City, Oklahoma. Dunn thought that if Mrs. Dunn did move back to Oklahoma, he would move back into the house after the divorce, provided Mrs. Dunn did not receive the house as part of her property settlement with respect to the divorce.

The divorce became final on September 13, 1991. Mrs. Dunn received stocks and bonds, but not the house, as her property settlement. She moved backed to Oklahoma on September 15, 1991, and Mr. Dunn started making plans to move back into the house. Time pressures from business kept him too busy to move immediately. On September 25, 1991, George decided to spend some of his free time touring model homes in a new development in Tampa. One of the homes, 15 Coral Court, turned out to be the house he had always dreamed of owning. He anticipated he could sell 105 Orange St. for almost as much as the asking price of 15 Coral Court.

Dunn thought about the new house for several days, and on October 4 he contracted to buy 15 Coral Court for $250,000. That same day he listed 105 Orange St. with the realtor who sold him his new house. On December 13, 1991, Dunn sold his Orange St. house for $235,000 cash. There was no debt on his property. He incurred no fixing-up expenses. His selling expenses totaled $15,000. Dunn will move to Coral Court by the end of this month. Subsequent to the move, he anticipates that this property will be his only residence.

Dunn hopes that his sale will be eligible for rollover of the gain under Sec. 1034. He is not 55 years old; consequently, he will not be eligible for the special rules affecting "older persons" who sell their homes.

We need to determine whether 105 Orange St. still qualifies as Dunn's principal residence, given that he did not live there for the period (approximately 10 months) between the date of the couple's decision to get a divorce and the sale date. I told Dunn we'd try to finish our research within a week. I have assigned Steve Staff the responsibility of researching this matter and drafting a client letter. Steve is to finish this assignment within 5 days. (He already has several other projects on which he is working.)

George Dunn

Summary of Questions and Conclusions

	Work Paper Reference

1. Does Dunn's sale qualify for a deferral of his realized gain?

    <u>Conclusion</u>: It qualifies for deferral <u>provided</u> the house meets the principal residence test as of the sale date.   D-1

2. Did the house constitute Dunn's principal residence as of the sale date?

    <u>Conclusion</u>: We have a good faith belief that classification of the house as his principal residence on the sale date, even though he did not occupy it on the date, is a position warranted in existing law. The IRS may, however, contend that he had abandoned this house as his principal residence. We should advise Dunn of the IRS's possible position and determine whether he wants us to file his return on the basis that he qualifies for deferral.   D-4

George Dunn

Work Papers

1. Does Dunn's sale qualify for deferral of recognition of the gain?

   Conclusion: Yes, provided 105 Orange St. meets the test of being Dunn's principal residence as of the sale date. Section 1034 is the controlling authority. It reads as follows:

SEC. 1034. ROLLOVER OF GAIN ON SALE OF PRINCIPAL RESIDENCE.

Last amendment.—The heading of Sec. 1034 appears above as amended by Sec. 405(c)(1) of Public Law 95-600, Nov. 6, 1978, effective (Sec. 405(d) of P.L. 95-600) for sales and exchanges of residences after July 26, 1978, in taxable years ending after such date.

(a) **Nonrecognition of Gain.**—If property (in this section called "old residence") used by the taxpayer as his principal residence is sold by him, and, within a period beginning 2 years before the date of such sale and ending 2 years after such date, property (in this section called "new residence") is purchased and used by the taxpayer as his principal residence, gain (if any) from such sale shall be recognized only to the extent that the taxpayer's adjusted sales price (as defined in subsection (b)) of the old residence exceeds the taxpayer's cost of purchasing the new residence. } See ques. 2 } See ques. 1(a)

(b) **Adjusted Sales Price Defined.**—

   (1) *In general.*—For purposes of this section, the term "adjusted sales price" means the amount realized, reduced by the aggregate of the expenses for work performed on the old residence in order to assist in its sale. } See ques. 1(b)

   (2) *Limitations.*—The reduction provided in paragraph (1) applies only to expenses—

   (A) for work performed during the 90-day period ending on the day on which the contract to sell the old residence is entered into;
   (B) which are paid on or before the 30th day after the date of the sale of the old residence; and
   (C) which are—
      (i) not allowable as deductions in computing taxable income under section 63 (defining taxable income), and
      (ii) not taken into account in computing the amount realized from the sale of the old residence.

   } Not Applicable

(c) **Rules for Application of Section.**—For purposes of this section:

(d) **Limitation.**—

} Not Applicable

D-1

(e) **Basis of New Residence.**—Where the purchase of a new residence results, under subsection (a) or under section 112(n) of the Internal Revenue Code of 1939, in the nonrecognition of gain on the sale of an old residence, in determining the adjusted basis of the new residence as of any time following the sale of the old residence, the adjustments to basis shall include a reduction by an amount equal to the amount of the gain not so recognized on the sale of the old residence. For this purpose, the amount of the gain not so recognized on the sale of the old residence includes only so much of such gain as is not recognized by reason of the cost, up to such time, or purchasing the new residence.

} *If gain is deferred, the basis of the "new" house is affected.*

(f) **Tenant-Stockholder in a Cooperative Housing Corporation.**

(g) **Husband and Wife.**—If the taxpayer and his spouse, in accordance with regula-

(h) **Members of Armed Forces.**—

(i) **Special Rule for Condemnation.**—In the case of the seizure, requisition, or con-

} *Not Applicable*

(j) **Statute of Limitations.**—If the taxpayer during a taxable year sells at a gain property used by him as his principal residence, then—
  (1) the statutory period for the assessment of any deficiency attributable to any part of such gain shall not expire before the expiration of 3 years from the date the Secretary is notified by the taxpayer (in such manner as the Secretary may by regulations prescribe) of—
    (A) the taxpayer's cost of purchasing the new residence which the taxpayer claims results in nonrecognition of any part of such gain,
    (B) the taxpayer's intention not to purchase a new residence within the period specified in subsection (a), or
    (C) a failure to make such purchase within such period; and
  (2) such deficiency may be assessed before the expiration of such 3-year period notwithstanding the provisions of any other law or rule of law which would otherwise prevent such assessment.

} *Cost will be reported on 1991 return.*

(k) **Individual Whose Tax Home Is Outside the United States.**—The running of any

(*l*) **Cross Reference.**—

} *Not Applicable*

D-2

Tax Research Working Paper File • A-11

1 (a) What gain is recognized if 105 Orange St. constitutes his principal residence?

Conclusion: No gain is recognized if the old house is still his principal residence because the cost of the replacement residence exceeds the adjusted sales price of the old residence.

Adjusted sales price	$220,000	See ques. 1(b)
Minus: Cost of replacement residence	(250,000)	
Recognized gain (but not less than 0)	$ -0-	

1 (b) What is the adjusted sales price of the old residence?

Conclusion: The adjusted sales price is $220,000.

Amount realized	$220,000	See ques. 1(c)
Minus: Expenses for work performed to assist with sale	(-0-)	
Adjusted sales price	$220,000	

1 (c) What is the amount realized:

Conclusion: The amount realized is $220,000.

Section 1001(b) defines amount realized as follows:

> **(b) Amount Realized.**—The amount realized from the sale or other disposition of property shall be the <u>sum of any money received plus the fair market value of the property (other than money) received</u>. In determining the amount realized—
> (1) there shall not be taken into account any amount received as reimbursement for real property taxes which are treated under section 164(d) as imposed on the purchaser, and
> (2) there shall be taken into account amounts representing real property taxes which are treated under section 164(d) as imposed on the taxpayer if such taxes are to be paid by the purchaser.

Money received ($235,000 - $15,000)	$220,000	See ques. 1(d)
Plus: FMV of other property received	-0-	
Amount realized	$220,000	

D-3

1 (d) How do the selling expenses affect the amount realized?

Conclusion: The selling expenses are subtracted from the sale price to compute the amount realized. Regulation Sec. 1.1034-1(b)(4) states that items that "are properly an offset against the considerations received upon the sale (such as commissions and expenses of advertising the property for sale, of preparing the deed, and of other legal services in connection with the sale)" are to be subtracted from the consideration received to arrive at the amount realized.

2 Did 105 Orange St. constitute Dunn's principal residence as of the date of disposition?

Conclusion: Reasonable authority exists to treat 105 Orange St. as his principal residence on the disposition date. However, because Dunn had not occupied the house for the approximate 10 month period immediately preceding its sale, the IRS may contend that he had abandoned the house as his principal residence.

2 (a) What is the definition of "principal residence"? Section 1034 does not define "principal residence." Regulation Sec. 1.1034-1(c)(3) provides some guidance concerning the definition.

> **(3) Property used by the taxpayer as his principal residence.**—(i) Whether or not property is used by the taxpayer as his residence, and whether or not property is used by the taxpayer as his principal residence (in the case of a taxpayer using more than one property as a residence), depends upon all the facts and circumstances in each case, including the good faith of the taxpayer. The mere fact that property is, or has been, rented is not determinative that such property is not used by the taxpayer as his principal residence. For example, if the taxpayer purchases his new residence before he sells his old residence, the fact that he temporarily rents out the new residence during the period before he vacates the old residence may not, in the light of all the facts and circumstances in the case, prevent the new residence from being considered as property used by the taxpayer as his principal residence. Property used by the taxpayer as his principal residence may include a houseboat, a house trailer, or stock held by a tenant-stockholder in a cooperative housing corporation (as those terms are defined in section 216(b)(1) and (2)), if the dwelling which the taxpayer is entitled to occupy as such stockholder is used by him as his principal residence (section 1034(f)). Property used by the taxpayer as his principal residence does not include personal property such as a piece of furniture, a radio, etc., which, in accordance with the applicable local law, is not a fixture.

D-4

(ii) Where part of a property is used by the taxpayer as his principal residence and part is used for other purposes, an allocation must be made to determine the application of this section. If the old residence is used only partially for residential purposes, only that part of the gain allocable to the residential portion is not to be recognized under this section and only an amount allocable to the selling price of such portion need be invested in the new residence in order to have the gain allocable to such portion not recognized under this section. If the new residence is used only partially for residential purposes only so much of its cost as is allocable to the residential portion may be counted as the cost of purchasing the new residence.

Thus, whether a property constitutes one's principal residence is a factual issue, and property can be rented to another without its automatically being disqualified from principal residence status. The statement concerning renting property indicates that a property may still be a taxpayer's principal residence even though he does not live in such property as of the date of the sale.

According to the Committee Reports (H. Rept. No. 586, 82d Cong., 1st Sess., 109 (1951); S. Rept. No. 781 (Pt. 2), 82d Cong., 1st Sess., 32 (1951), accompanying the legislation that added the predecessor of Sec. 1034 to the Code, the word "residence" is used "in contradistinction to property used in trade or business and property held for the production of income." The Committee Reports also state that renting out either the old or the new residence will <u>not necessarily</u> prevent deferral of the gain.

Dunn did not hold 105 Orange St. for the production of income or use it in his trade or business, Thus, the argument can be made that treating 105 Orange St. as his principal residence is within the spirit of the legislation that authorized deferral of gain in certain situations.

2 (b) Do any judicial or administrative authorities address the availability of deferral under Sec. 1034 to taxpayers not occupying the property on the date of sale? If so, what result do such authorities reach?

<u>Conclusion</u>: There are numerous authorities, several of which are summarized below, that address the issue.

The holdings differ, based upon the applicable facts. An analysis of such authorities leads to the conclusion that we have a good faith belief for adopting the position that the 105 Orange St. house was still his principal residence on the date of sale. Special emphasis is placed on <u>Clapham</u> and <u>Barry</u> (decided for the taxpayer) and <u>Young</u> (decided for the IRS).

<u>Cases in Favor of Principal Residence Status:</u>

<u>Ralph L. Trisko</u>, 29 T.C. 515 (1957), <u>acq.</u> 1959-1 C.B. 5. The taxpayer (T) leased his residence while working abroad. He intended to reoccupy the house upon his return but could not because of rent controls and a lease obligation. He later sold the house to generate funds to use for buying a replacement house. The court allowed deferral of the gain even though T had moved from the house several years earlier. The IRS stated it will follow <u>Trisko</u> only in cases which are "factually similar."

<u>Robert W. Aagaard</u>, 56 T.C. 191 (1971), <u>acq.</u> 1971-2 C.B. 1. Here the Tax Court held that Sec. 1034 was applicable, even though the taxpayer did not occupy the old residence at the time of sale <u>or intend to return</u> to the house.

<u>Robert G. Clapham</u>, 63 T.C. 505 (1975), <u>acq.</u> 1979-2 C.B. 1. Here the taxpayers (T) offered their old house for sale about 4 months prior to moving to rental property located in another city. T rented the old house (with an option to buy) for a year because of lack of offers. T leased it again for a short time and then let it stay vacant. T bought and moved into the new house about 9 months before finally selling the old one. T did not plan to return to the old house.

The Tax Court held that Sec. 1034 was available. It placed emphasis on the fact that T's <u>only desire</u>

D-6

with respect to the old house was to sell it as soon
as possible and that he accepted his first offer.
The court stressed that T rented the old house because
of "the exigencies of the real estate market."

Arthur R. Barry, 1971 PH T.C. Memo ¶ 71,179, 30 TCM
757. In this case taxpayer (T), a military officer,
occupied a house in Maryland from August 1955 through
July 1960. Then he was stationed in Germany and
Colorado. At the time he moved from Maryland he
planned to return to his home there upon his retirement
from the military. He rented the home on a yearly
basis until September 1965, when he listed it for sale
because he had decided to live in Colorado after his
retirement from the military in November 1965. He
sold the Maryland house in August 1966 and in November
1966 occupied the house he had purchased in Colorado.

The Tax Court concluded that the Maryland house
retained its status as T's principal residence until
the sale date. It emphasized that T at all times intended to occupy this home and that he did not offer it
for sale prior to his changing his principal residence
to Colorado. It characterized the change in his principal residence in 1966 as resulting from "an unexpected
change of plans." It added that he could not have
adopted his temporary military quarters as "new" principal residence because his scheduled retirement time
was in the near future.

Lee D. Andrews, 1981 PH T.C. Memo ¶ 81,247, 41 TCM 1533
(aff'd. by Fourth Circuit in unpublished opinion 7/6/82).
In Andrews the taxpayers (T) lived in Washington D.C.,
during 1973 and the first half of 1974.
In July 1974 they moved to North Carolina. In June 1974,
in anticipation of their move, they listed their D.C.
home for rent. In August 1974 they purchased

a home in North Carolina. They sold their D.C. home in April 1975.

In allowing Sec. 1034 treatment, the Tax Court stressed that deferral is not automatically precluded just because the seller does not occupy the property on the date of the sale. In deciding that T had not abandoned the D.C. house as his principal residence, the Tax Court was influenced by the fact that when T moved to North Carolina, he was <u>uncertain whether he would stay</u> there or return to D.C. Because of the uncertainty of his plans, it was appropriate for him to keep the D.C. house.

Cases Denying Principal Residence Status:

<u>William C. Stolk</u>, 40 T.C. 345 (1963), <u>acq.</u> 1964-2 C.B. 7. In this case, Mr. Stolk (T) moved out of his old house located outside New York City in June 1953. Having no intention to return to the house, he had all of his furniture moved from it. T moved to an apartment in Manhattan. His old house stood vacant until its sale in July 1955. In September 1955 he purchased a house in Virginia. T then began spending his weekends in Virginia.

The Tax Court held that from about May 1953 until July 1955, at least, T's principal residence was his Manhattan apartment. It concluded that he had <u>abandoned</u> the old house as his principal residence. Although in <u>Trisko</u> the seller received deferral of gain with respect to a house he did not occupy at the time of sale, the court found <u>Stolk</u> to be distinguishable from <u>Trisko</u>. It stated that <u>Trisko</u> does not stand for the broad proposition that the taxpayer does not have to live in the property as of its sale date.

<u>Richard T. Houlette</u>, 48 T.C. 350 (1967). In <u>Houlette</u>, the taxpayer (T) was a Coast Guard Officer. In July 1955 he was transferred from Oregon to Alaska. For a

few months prior to moving he tried to sell his house but could not do so without incurring a loss. Thus, he rented the property under a 2-year lease that he later extended for another year. Upon the expiration of the second lease, T again tried to sell. Having no success in selling, T rented the property again. In September, 1960, T purchased a new home. In the interim period he had lived in rental property. In May, 1961 T finally sold his old home.

The Tax Court denied Sec. 1034 treatment because it decided the old house no longer constituted T's principal residence. It recognized that actual occupancy on the sale date is not a universal requirement for qualifying for Sec. 1034. In its opinion, "however, the facts and circumstances must be exceptional and unusual to permit the conclusion that a principal residence is being used by the taxpayer at the time of sale if he is not in possession thereof and occupying same at that time." The court placed importance on the fact that T had **not occupied** the old house for almost **6 years**, that it **was rented** during the entire period, that T **persistently tried to sell it**, and that he had **no** intentions to reoccupy the house.

Claud R. Young, 1985 PH T.C. Memo ¶ 85,122, 49 TCM 981. Here Mr. Young (T) was divorced in October 1975. In the divorce proceedings he was awarded 25% interest in the house that he and his ex-wife had occupied. On the day of the divorce he moved into an apartment, and his ex-wife and child continued to live in the house. In November 1976 T and his ex-wife entered into an agreement whereby he conveyed to her his 25% interest in the house in exchange for being released from the obligation to pay alimony and the mortgage and other fees related to the house. In November 1977 T bought a new house.

The Tax Court declined to allow a deferral of the gain. It concluded that the old house ceased to be T's principal residence after he ceased to live there and the court awarded exclusive use to his ex-wife and child. It stated, "generally, cases in which taxpayers have been allowed the benefits of section 1034(a) even though they were not in possession of the old residence at the time of sale involve either the temporary rental of the property or . . . exceptional and unusual facts and circumstances over which the taxpayer had no control." It added that, "a divorce while often unpleasant and unwanted, is uniquely personal and is not the type of external objective circumstances that allows a taxpayer not in possession of a home to be deemed a resident therein for purposes of section 1034(a)." *[See page D-11]*

Application of the Cases to Dunn's Facts:

Dunn thought that he would move back to his old house unless his ex-wife received it as a property settlement. He did not place the home on the market until he had contracted to buy a new home. His purchase of a new home was a spur-of-the-moment decision. He sold his old home about 10 months after moving out of it and about 3 months after it was determined who would receive the house in the property settlement. It was not possible, from an emotional standpoint, for him to occupy the house with his ex-wife after their final decision to seek a divorce.

A taxpayer is not unconditionally required to live in a property on the sale date in order for it to receive principal residence status. Whether a house is the taxpayer's principal residence depends on all the facts and circumstances. Dunn's move from his old house was a result of the "exigencies" (Clapham) of his pending divorce. Unlike Stolk, he never abandoned the old house; rather, like Barry his decision to sell resulted from an "unexpected change of plans." Dunn's facts meet the "exceptional and unusual circumstances" test described in Houlette as being a precondition to getting Sec. 1034 treatment for a property not occupied at the sale date.

If Dunn's return is audited, the IRS may argue that he had abandoned his old house. In fact, it may cite Young as holding that a divorce situation never meets the "exceptional and unusual" facts and circumstances test for qualifying a house that the taxpayer does not live in for nonrecognition under Sec. 1034. Our counter-argument is that the language concerning divorce situations (page D-10) is not a holding to be applied across the board but, rather, is restricted to factual situations similar to those in Young. Unlike Dunn, Young knew when he moved from the house that he could not reoccupy it. His sale occurred 2 years after he moved in contrast with 10 months for Dunn's sale. Furthermore, Dunn sold his property about 2 months after his decision not to reoccupy it.

We have a good faith belief for classifying 105 Orange St. as Dunn's principal residence on the sale date that is warranted in existing law. We should, however, advise Dunn of the position the IRS might take if it audits his return and inquire concerning what position he wants us to take.

APPENDIX B

Completed Tax Forms

Form No.	Form Title	Page No.
1120	U.S. Corporation Income Tax Return	B-2
1120-A	U.S. Corporation Short-Form Income Tax Return	B-6
4626	Alternative Minimum Tax—Corporation	B-8
1120	Consolidated U.S. Corporation Income Tax Return	B-9
1065	U.S. Partnership Return of Income	B-12
1120S	U.S. Income Tax Return for an S Corporation	B-17
709	U.S. Gift (and Generation-Skipping Transfer) Tax Return	B-24
706	U.S. Estate (and Generation-Skipping Transfer) Tax Return	B-28
1041	U.S. Fiduciary Income Tax Return (Simple Trust)	B-55
1041	U.S. Fiduciary Income Tax Return (Complex Trust)	B-60
1116	Computation of Foreign Tax Credit	B-66
2555	Foreign Earned Income	B-68

B-2 • App. B / Completed Tax Forms

Form 1120 — U.S. Corporation Income Tax Return

Department of the Treasury / Internal Revenue Service
For calendar year 1990 or tax year beginning _____, 1990, ending _____, 19____
▶ Instructions are separate. See page 1 for Paperwork Reduction Act Notice.
OMB No. 1545-0123
1990

Check if a—
- A Consolidated return ☐
- B Personal holding co. ☐
- C Personal service corp. (as defined in Temp. Regs. sec. 1.441-4T—see Instructions) ☐

Use IRS label. Otherwise, please print or type.

Name: American Manufacturing Corporation
Number, street, and room or suite no.: 4910 N.E. 53rd Avenue
City or town, state, and ZIP code: Gainsville, FL 32611

D Employer identification number: 38-7654321
E Date incorporated: 2-1-82
F Total assets: $3,229,665

G Check applicable boxes: (1) ☐ Initial return (2) ☐ Final return (3) ☐ Change in address

Income

1a	Gross receipts or sales 7,850,000 b Less returns and allowances 61,450 c Bal ▶	1c	7,788,550
2	Cost of goods sold (Schedule A, line 7)	2	4,084,000
3	Gross profit (line 1c less line 2)	3	3,704,550
4	Dividends (Schedule C, line 19)	4	750
5	Interest	5	18,550
6	Gross rents	6	
7	Gross royalties	7	
8	Capital gain net income (attach Schedule D (Form 1120))	8	
9	Net gain or (loss) from Form 4797, Part II, line 18 (attach Form 4797)	9	(1,047)
10	Other income (see Instructions—attach schedule)	10	
11	**Total income**—Add lines 3 through 10 ▶	11	3,722,753

Deductions (See Instructions for limitations on deductions.)

12	Compensation of officers (Schedule E, line 4)	12	225,000
13a	Salaries and wages 550,000 b Less jobs credit -0- c Balance ▶	13c	550,000
14	Repairs	14	49,650
15	Bad debts	15	3,274
16	Rents	16	5,000
17	Taxes	17	88,775
18	Interest	18	78,333
19	Contributions (see Instructions for 10% limitation)	19	31,875
20	Depreciation (attach Form 4562) 20 209,534		
21	Less depreciation claimed on Schedule A and elsewhere on return 21a 69,500	21b	140,034
22	Depletion	22	742,734
23	Advertising	23	
24	Pension, profit-sharing, etc., plans	24	
25	Employee benefit programs	25	45,900
26	Other deductions (attach schedule)	26	1,076,350
27	**Total deductions**—Add lines 12 through 26 ▶	27	3,036,925
28	Taxable income before net operating loss deduction and special deductions (line 11 less line 27)	28	685,828
29	Less: a Net operating loss deduction (see Instructions) 29a		
	b Special deductions (Schedule C, line 20) 29b 600	29c	600
30	Taxable income—Line 28 less line 29c	30	685,228
31	Total tax (Schedule J, line 10)	31	

Tax and Payments

32	Payments: a 1989 overpayment credited to 1990 32a		
	b 1990 estimated tax payments 32b 260,000		
	c Less 1990 refund applied for on Form 4466 32c ( ) d Bal ▶ 32d 260,000		
	e Tax deposited with Form 7004 32e		
	f Credit from regulated investment companies (attach Form 2439) 32f		
	g Credit for Federal tax on fuels (attach Form 4136). See Instructions 32g	32h	260,000
33	Enter any penalty for underpayment of estimated tax—Check ▶ ☐ if Form 2220 is attached	33	
34	Tax due—If the total of lines 31 and 33 is larger than line 32h, enter amount owed	34	
35	Overpayment—If line 32h is larger than the total of lines 31 and 33, enter amount overpaid	35	51,275
36	Enter amount of line 35 you want: Credited to 1991 estimated tax ▶ 51,275 Refunded ▶	36	-0-

Please Sign Here
Under penalties of perjury, I declare that I have examined this return, including accompanying schedules and statements, and to the best of my knowledge and belief, it is true, correct, and complete. Declaration of preparer (other than taxpayer) is based on all information of which preparer has any knowledge.

▶ Signature of officer: William A. Brown   William A. Brown   Date: 3/15/91   ▶ Title: President

Paid Preparer's Use Only

Preparer's signature ▶	Andrew D. Kramer	Date 3/12/91	Check if self-employed ☐ Preparer's social security number 123:45:6589
Firm's name (or yours if self-employed) and address ▶	Kramer + Associates, P.A. 2250 N.W. 24th Ave, Gainsville, FL		E.I. No. ▶ 01:000 0001 ZIP code ▶ 32601

Form 1120 (1990) Page **2**

Schedule A — Cost of Goods Sold (See Instructions for line 2, page 1.)

1	Inventory at beginning of year	98,000
2	Purchases	1,901,000
3	Cost of labor	1,533,000
4a	Additional section 263A costs (see Instructions—attach schedule)	92,000
b	Other costs (attach schedule)	967,000
5	Total—Add lines 1 through 4b	4,591,000
6	Inventory at end of year	507,000
7	Cost of goods sold—Line 5 less line 6. Enter here and on line 2, page 1.	4,084,000

8a Check all methods used for valuing closing inventory:
  (i) ☒ Cost (ii) ☐ Lower of cost or market as described in Regulations section 1.471-4 (see Instructions)
  (iii) ☐ Writedown of "subnormal" goods as described in Regulations section 1.471-2(c) (see Instructions)
  (iv) ☐ Other (Specify method used and attach explanation.) ▶ _____
 b Check if the LIFO inventory method was adopted this tax year for any goods (if checked, attach Form 970) . . . . ☐
 c If the LIFO inventory method was used for this tax year, enter percentage (or amounts) of closing inventory computed under LIFO . . . . **8c** | 100%
 d Do the rules of section 263A (with respect to property produced or acquired for resale) apply to the corporation? . . ☒ Yes ☐ No
 e Was there any change in determining quantities, cost, or valuations between opening and closing inventory? If "Yes," attach explanation . . . . ☐ Yes ☒ No

Schedule C — Dividends and Special Deductions (See Instructions.)

	(a) Dividends received	(b) %	(c) Special deductions: (a) × (b)
1 Dividends from less-than-20%-owned domestic corporations that are subject to the 70% deduction (other than debt-financed stock)		70	
2 Dividends from 20%-or-more-owned domestic corporations that are subject to the 80% deduction (other than debt-financed stock)	750	80	600
3 Dividends on debt-financed stock of domestic and foreign corporations (section 246A)		see Instructions	
4 Dividends on certain preferred stock of less-than-20%-owned public utilities		41.176	
5 Dividends on certain preferred stock of 20%-or-more-owned public utilities		47.059	
6 Dividends from less-than-20%-owned foreign corporations and certain FSCs that are subject to the 70% deduction		70	
7 Dividends from 20%-or-more-owned foreign corporations and certain FSCs that are subject to the 80% deduction		80	
8 Dividends from wholly owned foreign subsidiaries subject to the 100% deduction (section 245(b))		100	
9 Total—Add lines 1 through 8. See Instructions for limitation			600
10 Dividends from domestic corporations received by a small business investment company operating under the Small Business Investment Act of 1958		100	
11 Dividends from certain FSCs that are subject to the 100% deduction (section 245(c)(1))		100	
12 Dividends from affiliated group members subject to the 100% deduction (section 243(a)(3))		100	
13 Other dividends from foreign corporations not included on lines 3, 6, 7, 8, or 11			
14 Income from controlled foreign corporations under subpart F (attach Forms 5471)			
15 Foreign dividend gross-up (section 78)			
16 IC-DISC and former DISC dividends not included on lines 1, 2, or 3 (section 246(d))			
17 Other dividends			
18 Deduction for dividends paid on certain preferred stock of public utilities (see Instructions)			
19 Total dividends—Add lines 1 through 17. Enter here and on line 4, page 1. ▶	750		
20 Total deductions—Add lines 9, 10, 11, 12, and 18. Enter here and on line 29b, page 1 ▶			600

Schedule E — Compensation of Officers (See Instructions for line 12, page 1.)

Complete Schedule E only if total receipts (line 1a, plus lines 4 through 10, of page 1, Form 1120) are $500,000 or more.

(a) Name of officer	(b) Social security number	(c) Percent of time devoted to business	Percent of corporation stock owned (d) Common	(e) Preferred	(f) Amount of compensation
1 William A. Brown	841-39-7176	100 %	50 %	%	170,000
Scott A. Veil	311-48-1248	100 %	5 %	%	80,000
Hank M. Lewis	267-39-1501	100 %	5 %	%	50,000
		%	%	%	
		%	%	%	

2 Total compensation of officers	300,000
3 Less: Compensation of officers claimed on Schedule A and elsewhere on return	(75,000)
4 Compensation of officers deducted on line 12, page 1	225,000

Form 1120 (1990) Page 3

Schedule J — Tax Computation

1. Check if you are a member of a controlled group (see sections 1561 and 1563) . . . . . . ▶ ☐
2. If the box on line 1 is checked:
   a. Enter your share of the $50,000 and $25,000 taxable income bracket amounts (in that order):
      (i) $_____ (ii) $_____
   b. Enter your share of the additional 5% tax (not to exceed $11,750) ▶ $_____
3. Income tax (see Instructions to figure the tax). Check this box if the corporation is a qualified personal service corporation (see Instructions on page 12). ▶ ☐ . . . . **3** | **232,978**
4. a. Foreign tax credit (attach Form 1118) **4a**
   b. Possessions tax credit (attach Form 5735) **4b**
   c. Orphan drug credit (attach Form 6765) **4c**
   d. Credit for fuel produced from a nonconventional source (see Instructions) **4d**
   e. General business credit. Enter here and check which forms are attached:
      ☒ Form 3800 ☐ Form 3468 ☐ Form 5884
      ☐ Form 6478 ☐ Form 6765 ☐ Form 8586 . . . **4e** | **24,733**
   f. Credit for prior year minimum tax (attach Form 8801) . . . **4f**
5. **Total**—Add lines 4a through 4f . . . . **5** | **24,733**
6. Line 3 less line 5 . . . . **6** | **208,245**
7. Personal holding company tax (attach Schedule PH (Form 1120)) **7**
8. Recapture taxes. Check if from: ☒ Form 4255 ☐ Form 8611 . . . . . . **8** | **480**
9. a. Alternative minimum tax (attach Form 4626). See Instructions **9a**
   b. Environmental tax (attach Form 4626) **9b**
10. **Total tax**—Add lines 6 through 9b. Enter here and on line 31, page 1 . . . . . **10** | **208,725**

Additional Information (See General Instruction F.)

H Refer to the list in the Instructions and state the principal:
  (1) Business activity code no. ▶ 3998
  (2) Business activity ▶ Manufacturing
  (3) Product or service ▶ Machinery

I (1) Did the corporation at the end of the tax year own, directly or indirectly, 50% or more of the voting stock of a domestic corporation? (For rules of attribution, see section 267(c).) . . . **No: X**
  If "Yes," attach a schedule showing: (a) name, address, and identifying number; (b) percentage owned; and (c) taxable income or (loss) before NOL and special deductions of such corporation for the tax year ending with or within your tax year.

  (2) Did any individual, partnership, corporation, estate, or trust at the end of the tax year own, directly or indirectly, 50% or more of the corporation's voting stock? (For rules of attribution, see section 267(c).) If "Yes," complete (a) through (c) . . . **Yes: X**
    (a) Attach a schedule showing name, address, and identifying number.
    (b) Enter percentage owned ▶ 50%
    (c) Was the owner of such voting stock a foreign person? (See Instructions.) **Note:** If "Yes," the corporation may have to file Form 5472 . . . **No: X**
    If "Yes," enter owner's country ▶ _____

J Was the corporation a U.S. shareholder of any controlled foreign corporation? (See sections 951 and 957.) . . . **No: X**
  If "Yes," attach Form 5471 for each such corporation.

K At any time during the tax year, did the corporation have an interest in or a signature or other authority over a financial account in a foreign country (such as a bank account, securities account, or other financial account)? . . . **No: X**
  (See General Instruction F and filing requirements for form TD F 90-22.1.)
  If "Yes," enter name of foreign country ▶ _____

L Was the corporation the grantor of, or transferor to, a foreign trust that existed during the current tax year, whether or not the corporation has any beneficial interest in it? . . . **No: X**
  If "Yes," the corporation may have to file Forms 3520, 3520-A, or 926.

M During this tax year, did the corporation pay dividends (other than stock dividends and distributions in exchange for stock) in excess of the corporation's current and accumulated earnings and profits? (See sections 301 and 316.) . . . **No: X**
  If "Yes," file Form 5452. If this is a consolidated return, answer here for parent corporation and on **Form 851**, Affiliations Schedule, for each subsidiary.

N During this tax year, did the corporation maintain any part of its accounting/tax records on a computerized system? . . . **No: X**

O Check method of accounting:
  (1) ☐ Cash
  (2) ☒ Accrual
  (3) ☐ Other (specify) ▶ _____

P Check this box if the corporation issued publicly offered debt instruments with original issue discount . . . ☐
  If so, the corporation may have to file Form 8281.

Q Enter the amount of tax-exempt interest received or accrued during the tax year ▶ $ —0—

R Enter the number of shareholders at the end of the tax year if there were 35 or fewer shareholders ▶ 10

Completed Tax Forms • B-5

Form 1120 (1990) Page **4**

Schedule L — Balance Sheets

Assets	Beginning of tax year (a)	Beginning of tax year (b)	End of tax year (c)	End of tax year (d)
1 Cash		137,500		146,000
2a Trade notes and accounts receivable	212,000		692,825	
b Less allowance for bad debts	(16,100)	195,900	(32,400)	660,425
3 Inventories		98,000		507,000
4 U.S. government obligations				223,650
5 Tax-exempt securities (see Instructions)				
6 Other current assets (attach schedule)		4,200		6,300
7 Loans to stockholders		12,000		10,000
8 Mortgage and real estate loans				105,491
9 Other investments (attach schedule)		25,000		30,000
10a Buildings and other depreciable assets	492,400		1,557,400	
b Less accumulated depreciation	(109,920)	382,480	(191,610)	1,365,790
11a Depletable assets				
b Less accumulated depletion	( )		( )	
12 Land (net of any amortization)		35,000		167,500
13a Intangible assets (amortizable only)	12,000		12,000	
b Less accumulated amortization	(3,500)	8,500	(4,700)	7,300
14 Other assets (attach schedule)				
15 Total assets		898,580		3,229,665
Liabilities and Stockholders' Equity				
16 Accounts payable		306,850		84,319
17 Mortgages, notes, bonds payable in less than 1 year				
18 Other current liabilities (attach schedule)		142,100		238,333
19 Loans from stockholders				
20 Mortgages, notes, bonds payable in 1 year or more				1,250,000
21 Other liabilities (attach schedule)		110,630		158,000
22 Capital stock: a Preferred stock				
b Common stock	250,000	250,000	500,000	500,000
23 Paid-in or capital surplus				450,000
24 Retained earnings—Appropriated (attach schedule)				
25 Retained earnings—Unappropriated		89,000		548,383
26 Less cost of treasury stock		( )		( )
27 Total liabilities and stockholders' equity		898,580		3,229,665

Schedule M-1 — Reconciliation of Income per Books With Income per Return
(This schedule does not have to be completed if the total assets on line 15, column (d), of Schedule L are less than $25,000.)

1 Net income per books	584,383	7 Income recorded on books this year not included on this return (itemize):		
2 Federal income tax	265,210	a Tax-exempt interest $		4,754
3 Excess of capital losses over capital gains	4,500	Deferred gain—land sales,		65,000
4 Income subject to tax not recorded on books this year (itemize):		gain—building sale		86,000
Gain on auto sale	4,833	8 Deductions on this return not charged against book income this year (itemize):		
5 Expenses recorded on books this year not deducted on this return (itemize):		a Depreciation . . . $27,244		
a Depreciation $		b Contributions carryover $		
b Contributions carryover $		Amortization 1,200		
c Travel and entertainment $ 6,500				
Political contribution 600				28,444
Penalty on overweight truck 4,000	11,100	9 Total of lines 7 and 8		184,198
6 Total of lines 1 through 5	870,026	10 Income (line 28, page 1)—line 6 less line 9		685,828

Schedule M-2 — Analysis of Unappropriated Retained Earnings per Books (line 25, Schedule L)
(This schedule does not have to be completed if the total assets on line 15, column (d), of Schedule L are less than $25,000.)

1 Balance at beginning of year	89,000	5 Distributions: a Cash	125,000
2 Net income per books	584,383	b Stock	
3 Other increases (itemize):		c Property	
		6 Other decreases (itemize):	
		7 Total of lines 5 and 6	125,000
4 Total of lines 1, 2, and 3	673,383	8 Balance at end of year (line 4 less line 7)	548,383

B-6 • *App. B / Completed Tax Forms*

Form 1120-A — U.S. Corporation Short-Form Income Tax Return

Department of the Treasury / Internal Revenue Service

Instructions are separate. See them to make sure you qualify to file Form 1120-A.
For calendar year 1990 or tax year beginning _____, 1990, ending _____, 19 ___

1990 OMB No. 1545-0890

A Check this box if corp. is a personal service corp. (as defined in Temp. Regs. sec. 1.441-4T—see Instructions) ▶ ☒

Use IRS label. Otherwise, please print or type.

Name: A Kid's Space
Number, street, and room or suite no.: 3296 N.W. 24th Avenue
City or town, state, and ZIP code: Gainsville, Florida 32605

B Employer identification number: 38-0000002
C Date incorporated: 4-5-83
D Total assets: $ 68,775

E Check applicable boxes: (1) ☐ Initial return (2) ☐ Change in address
F Check method of accounting: (1) ☒ Cash (2) ☐ Accrual (3) ☐ Other (specify) ▶

Income

1a	Gross receipts or sales 185,400 b Less returns and allowances —0— c Balance ▶	1c	185,400
2	Cost of goods sold	2	
3	Gross profit (line 1c less line 2)	3	185,400
4	Domestic corporation dividends subject to the 70% deduction	4	
5	Interest	5	1,960
6	Gross rents	6	
7	Gross royalties	7	
8	Capital gain net income (attach Schedule D (Form 1120))	8	1,040
9	Net gain or (loss) from Form 4797, Part II, line 18 (attach Form 4797)	9	
10	Other income	10	
11	**Total income**—Add lines 3 through 10 ▶	11	188,400

Deductions

12	Compensation of officers	12	44,000
13a	Salaries and wages 50,400 b Less jobs credit —0— c Balance ▶	13c	50,400
14	Repairs	14	2,320
15	Bad debts	15	
16	Rents	16	18,000
17	Taxes	17	6,740
18	Interest	18	5,625
19	Contributions (see Instructions for 10% limitation)	19	700
20	Depreciation (attach Form 4562) 20 6,580		
21	Less depreciation claimed elsewhere on return 21a	21b	6,580
22	Other deductions (attach schedule)	22	26,471
23	**Total deductions**—Add lines 12 through 22 ▶	23	160,836
24	Taxable income before net operating loss deduction and special deductions (line 11 less line 23)	24	27,564
25	Less: a Net operating loss deduction 25a		
	b Special deductions 25b	25c	—0—
26	**Taxable income**—Line 24 less line 25c	26	27,564
27	Total tax (Part I, line 7)	27	9,372

Tax and Payments

28	Payments:		
a	1989 overpayment credited to 1990 28a		
b	1990 estimated tax payments 28b 8,900		
c	Less 1990 refund applied for on Form 4466 28c ( ) Bal ▶ 28d 8,900		
e	Tax deposited with Form 7004 28e		
f	Credit from regulated investment companies (attach Form 2439) 28f		
g	Credit for Federal tax on fuels (attach Form 4136) 28g		
h	**Total payments**—Add lines 28d through 28g	28h	8,900
29	Enter any penalty for underpayment of estimated tax—Check ▶ ☒ if Form 2220 is attached	29	
30	**Tax due**—If the total of lines 27 and 29 is larger than line 28h, enter amount owed	30	472
31	**Overpayment**—If line 28h is larger than the total of lines 27 and 29, enter amount overpaid	31	
32	Enter amount of line 31 you want: Credited to 1991 estimated tax ▶ _____ Refunded ▶	32	

Please Sign Here

Under penalties of perjury, I declare that I have examined this return, including accompanying schedules and statements, and to the best of my knowledge and belief, it is true, correct, and complete. Declaration of preparer (other than taxpayer) is based on all information of which preparer has any knowledge.

Signature of officer: A. Teacher — Date: 3/15/91 — Title: President

Paid Preparer's Use Only

Preparer's signature	Stephen R. Kramer	Date 3/12/91	Check if self-employed ▶ ☐ Preparer's social security number 987:65:4321
Firm's name (or yours if self-employed) and address	Kramer and Associates, P.A. 2250 N.W. 24th Ave, Gainsville, Fla.		E.I. No. ▶ 01:0000001 ZIP code ▶ 32605

For Paperwork Reduction Act Notice, see page 1 of the Instructions.

Form **1120-A** (1990)

Form 1120-A (1990) Page **2**

Part I — Tax Computation

1	Income tax (see Instructions to figure the tax). Check this box if the corp. is a qualified personal service corp. (see Instructions). ▶ ☐	9,372
2a	General business credit. Check if from: ☐ Form 3800 ☐ Form 3468 ☐ Form 5884 ☐ Form 6478 ☐ Form 6765 ☐ Form 8586	
b	Credit for prior year minimum tax (attach Form 8801)	
3	**Total credits**—Add lines 2a and 2b	-0-
4	Line 1 less line 3	9,372
5	Recapture taxes. Check if from: ☐ Form 4255 ☐ Form 8611	
6	Alternative minimum tax (attach Form 4626). See Instructions	
7	**Total tax**—Add lines 4 through 6. Enter here and on line 27, page 1.	9,372

Additional Information (See General Instruction F.)

G Refer to the list in the Instructions and state the principal:

(1) Business activity code no. ▶ **8200**

(2) Business activity ▶ **Services**

(3) Product or service ▶ **Educational**

H Did any individual, partnership, estate, or trust at the end of the tax year own, directly or indirectly, 50% or more of the corporation's voting stock? (For rules of attribution, see section 267(c).) Yes ☒ No ☐
If "Yes," attach schedule showing name, address, and identifying number.

I Enter the amount of tax-exempt interest received or accrued during the tax year . ▶ $ -0-

J (1) If an amount for cost of goods sold is entered on line 2, page 1, complete (a) through (c):
(a) Purchases (see Instructions)
(b) Additional sec. 263A costs (see Instructions—attach schedule)
(c) Other costs (attach schedule) . . -0-

(2) Do the rules of section 263A (with respect to property produced or acquired for resale) apply to the corporation? . . . Yes ☐ No ☒

K At any time during the tax year, did you have an interest in or a signature or other authority over a financial account in a foreign country (such as a bank account, securities account, or other financial account)? (See General Instruction F for filing requirements for form TD F 90-22.1.) . . . . . Yes ☐ No ☒
If "Yes," enter the name of the foreign country ▶

L Enter amount of cash distributions and the book value of property (other than cash) distributions made in this tax year ▶ $ -0-

Part II — Balance Sheets

		(a) Beginning of tax year	(b) End of tax year
Assets			
1	Cash	3,175	8,544
2a	Trade notes and accounts receivable	12,320	10,240
b	Less allowance for bad debts	( )	( )
3	Inventories		
4	U.S. government obligations		
5	Tax-exempt securities (see Instructions)		
6	Other current assets (attach schedule)		
7	Loans to stockholders		
8	Mortgage and real estate loans		
9a	Depreciable, depletable, and intangible assets	51,769	66,120
b	Less accumulated depreciation, depletion, and amortization	(12,812)	(18,746)
10	Land (net of any amortization)	9,800	9,800
11	Other assets (attach schedule)	1,400	1,200
12	Total assets	65,652	77,158
Liabilities and Stockholders' Equity			
13	Accounts payable	3,179	3,104
14	Other current liabilities (attach schedule)	7,600	4,000
15	Loans from stockholders	7,000	
16	Mortgages, notes, bonds payable	19,510	17,210
17	Other liabilities (attach schedule)		
18	Capital stock (preferred and common stock)	20,000	20,000
19	Paid-in or capital surplus		
20	Retained earnings	8,363	32,000
21	Less cost of treasury stock	( )	( )
22	Total liabilities and stockholders' equity	65,652	77,158

Part III — Reconciliation of Income per Books With Income per Return (Must be completed by all filers.)

1	Net income per books	24,481			
2	Federal income tax	4,173	6	Income recorded on books this year not included on this return (itemize)	
3	Excess of capital losses over capital gains				
4	Income subject to tax not recorded on books this year (itemize)		7	Deductions on this return not charged against book income this year (itemize)	2,490
5	Expenses recorded on books this year not deducted on this return (itemize)	1,400	8	Income (line 24, page 1). Enter the sum of lines 1 through 5 less the sum of lines 6 and 7	27,564

B-8 • App. B / Completed Tax Forms

Form 4626
Department of the Treasury
Internal Revenue Service

Alternative Minimum Tax—Corporations
(including environmental tax)
▶ See separate instructions.
▶ Attach to your tax return.

OMB No. 1545-0175

1990

Name	Employer identification number
Miami Corporation	38-1507869

1	Taxable income or (loss) before net operating loss deduction. (**Important:** See instructions if you are subject to the environmental tax.)		**1**	350,000
2	**Adjustments:**			
a	Depreciation of tangible property placed in service after 1986	**2a** 17,500		
b	Amortization of certified pollution control facilities placed in service after 1986	**2b**		
c	Amortization of mining exploration and development costs paid or incurred after 1986	**2c**		
d	Amortization of circulation expenditures paid or incurred after 1986 (personal holding companies only)	**2d**		
e	Basis adjustments in determining gain or loss from sale or exchange of property	**2e** (16,500)		
f	Long-term contracts entered into after February 28, 1986	**2f**		
g	Installment sales of certain property	**2g**		
h	Merchant marine capital construction funds	**2h**		
i	Section 833(b) deduction (Blue Cross, Blue Shield, and similar type organizations only)	**2i**		
j	Tax shelter farm activities (personal service corporations only)	**2j**		
k	Passive activities (closely held corporations and personal service corporations only)	**2k**		
l	Certain loss limitations	**2l**		
m	Other adjustments	**2m**		
n	Combine lines 2a through 2m		**2n**	1,000
3	**Tax preference items:**			
a	Depletion	**3a**		
b	Tax-exempt interest from private activity bonds issued after August 7, 1986	**3b**		
c	Appreciated property charitable deduction	**3c**		
d	Intangible drilling costs	**3d**		
e	Reserves for losses on bad debts of financial institutions	**3e**		
f	Accelerated depreciation of real property placed in service before 1987	**3f** 10,000		
g	Accelerated depreciation of leased personal property placed in service before 1987 (personal holding companies only)	**3g**		
h	Amortization of certified pollution control facilities placed in service before 1987	**3h**		
i	Add lines 3a through 3h		**3i**	10,000
4	Pre-adjustment AMTI. Combine lines 1, 2n, and 3i		**4**	361,000
5	**Adjusted current earnings adjustment:**			
a	Enter your adjusted current earnings	**5a** 900,000		
b	Subtract line 4 from line 5a (even if one or both of these figures is a negative number). Enter zero if the result is zero or less (see instructions for examples)	**5b** 539,000		
c	Multiply line 5b by 75%		**5c**	404,250
6	Combine lines 4 and 5c. If zero or less, stop here (you are not subject to the alternative minimum tax)		**6**	765,250
7	Alternative tax net operating loss deduction. (Do not enter more than 90% of line 6.)		**7**	
8	Alternative minimum taxable income (subtract line 7 from line 6)		**8**	765,250
9	**Exemption phase-out computation** (members of a controlled group, see instructions for lines 9a through 9c):			
a	Tentative exemption amount. Enter $40,000	**9a**		
b	Enter $150,000	**9b**		
c	Subtract line 9b from line 8. If zero or less, enter zero	**9c**		
d	Multiply line 9c by 25%	**9d**		
e	Exemption. Subtract line 9d from line 9a. If zero or less, enter zero		**9e**	0
10	Subtract line 9e from line 8. If zero or less, enter zero		**10**	765,250
11	Multiply line 10 by 20%		**11**	153,050
12	Alternative minimum tax foreign tax credit (see instructions for limitation)		**12**	
13	Tentative minimum tax (subtract line 12 from line 11)		**13**	153,050
14	Regular tax liability before all credits except the foreign tax credit and possessions tax credit		**14**	119,000
15	**Alternative minimum tax**—Subtract line 14 from line 13. If the result is zero or less, enter zero. Also enter the result on line 9a, Schedule J, Form 1120, or on the comparable line of other income tax returns		**15**	34,050
16	**Environmental tax**—Subtract $2,000,000 from line 6 (computed without regard to your environmental tax deduction), and multiply the result, if any, by 0.12% (.0012). Enter on line 9b, Schedule J, Form 1120, or on the comparable line of other income tax returns (members of a controlled group, see instructions)		**16**	0

For Paperwork Reduction Act Notice, see separate instructions.

Form **4626** (1990)

Completed Tax Forms • B-9

Form 1120 — U.S. Corporation Income Tax Return

Department of the Treasury — Internal Revenue Service

For calendar year 1990 or tax year beginning _____, 1990, ending _____, 19 ____

► Instructions are separate. See page 1 for Paperwork Reduction Act Notice.

OMB No. 1545-0123

1990

Check if a—
- A Consolidated return ☒
- B Personal holding co. ☐
- C Personal service corp. (as defined in Temp. Regs. sec. 1.441-4T—see Instructions) ☐

Use IRS label. Otherwise, please print or type.

Name: Alpha Manufacturing Corp. and Subsidiaries
Number, street, and room or suite no.: 820 N.W. First Place
City or town, state, and ZIP code: Gainsville, Florida 32670

- D Employer identification number: 38-0000001
- E Date incorporated: 9-15-72
- F Total assets (see Specific Instructions): $

G Check applicable boxes: (1) ☐ Initial return (2) ☐ Final return (3) ☐ Change in address

Income

1a	Gross receipts or sales	6,147,000	
1b	Less returns and allowances	-0-	
1c	Bal ►		6,147,000
2	Cost of goods sold (Schedule A, line 7)		2,301,000
3	Gross profit (line 1c less line 2)		3,846,000
4	Dividends (Schedule C, line 19)		40,000
5	Interest		156,000
6	Gross rents		195,000
7	Gross royalties		
8	Capital gain net income (attach Schedule D (Form 1120))		67,939
9	Net gain or (loss) from Form 4797, Part II, line 18 (attach Form 4797)		39,172
10	Other income (see Instructions—attach schedule)		10,000
11	**Total income**—Add lines 3 through 10 ►		4,354,111

Deductions (See Instructions for limitations on deductions.)

12	Compensation of officers (Schedule E, line 4)		165,000
13a	Salaries and wages 1,356,000 b Less jobs credit -0- c Balance ►		1,356,000
14	Repairs		83,000
15	Bad debts		48,500
16	Rents		179,000
17	Taxes		138,000
18	Interest		58,000
19	Contributions (see Instructions for 10% limitation)		15,000
20	Depreciation (attach Form 4562)	246,093	
21a	Less depreciation claimed on Schedule A and elsewhere on return	77,400	
21b			168,693
22	Depletion		
23	Advertising		269,140
24	Pension, profit-sharing, etc., plans		140,000
25	Employee benefit programs		105,000
26	Other deductions (attach schedule)		1,284,000
27	**Total deductions**—Add lines 12 through 26 ►		4,009,333
28	Taxable income before net operating loss deduction and special deductions (line 11 less line 27)		344,778
29	Less: a Net operating loss deduction (see Instructions) 29a		
	b Special deductions (Schedule C, line 20) 29b 32,000		
29c			32,000
30	Taxable income—Line 28 less line 29c		312,778
31	Total tax (Schedule J, line 10)		105,234

Tax and Payments

32	Payments: a 1989 overpayment credited to 1990 32a		
	b 1990 estimated tax payments 32b		
	c Less 1990 refund applied for on Form 4466 32c ( ) d Bal ► 32d 146,000		
	e Tax deposited with Form 7004 32e		
	f Credit from regulated investment companies (attach Form 2439) 32f		
	g Credit for Federal tax on fuels (attach Form 4136). See Instructions 32g		
32h			146,000
33	Enter any **penalty** for underpayment of estimated tax—Check ► ☐ if Form 2220 is attached		
34	Tax due—If the total of lines 31 and 33 is larger than line 32h, enter amount owed		
35	Overpayment—If line 32h is larger than the total of lines 31 and 33, enter amount overpaid		40,766
36	Enter amount of line 35 you want: Credited to 1991 estimated tax ► _____ Refunded ►		

Please Sign Here

Under penalties of perjury, I declare that I have examined this return, including accompanying schedules and statements, and to the best of my knowledge and belief, it is true, correct, and complete. Declaration of preparer (other than taxpayer) is based on all information of which preparer has any knowledge.

Signature of officer: U. R. Stuck Date: 3/15/91 Title: President

Paid Preparer's Use Only

Preparer's signature: John A. Kramer	Date: 3/12/91	Check if self-employed ☐
Preparer's social security number: 241:69:3967		
Firm's name (or yours if self-employed) and address: Kramer and Associates, P.A. 2250 N.W. 24th Ave. Gainsville, FL	E.I. No. ► 01:0000001	ZIP code ► 32605

B-10 • App. B / Completed Tax Forms

Form 1120—Consolidated Taxable Income Computation

Line	Title	Consolidated	Eliminations	1 Alpha Mfg. Corp.	2 Beta Corp.	3 Charlie Corp.	4 Delta Corp.	5 Echo Corp.
1	Gross Receipts Returns/Allowances	$6,147,000	($109,000)[1] 85,000[2]	$1,566,000	$2,680,000	$676,000		$1,249,000
	Cost Goods/Operations	(2,301,000)		(783,000)	(1,390,000)	(128,000)		—0—
3	Gross Profit	$3,846,000	($24,000)	$ 783,000	$1,290,000	$548,000	—0—	$1,249,000
4	Dividends (Sch. C)	40,000	(170,000)[3]	210,000				
5	Interest	156,000		46,000	89,000			21,000
6	Gross Rents	195,000		195,000			$195,000	
7	Gross Royalties							
8	Capital Gain Net Income (Sch. D)	67,939		67,939				
9	Net Gain or Loss from Form 4797	39,172	(11,358)	52,760	(4,000)			
10	Other Income	10,000[4]	1,770[5]	10,000				
11	Total Income	$4,354,111	($203,588)	$1,169,699	$1,375,000	$548,000	$195,000	$1,270,000
12	Compensation of Officers	$ 165,000		$ 165,000				
13	Salaries and Wages	1,356,000		138,000	$ 240,000	$377,000	$ 36,000	565,000
14	Repairs	83,000		19,000	18,000	7,000	18,000	21,000
15	Bad Debts	48,500			36,500	4,000		8,000
16	Rents	179,000		93,000	39,000	11,000		36,000
17	Taxes	138,000[4]		36,000	27,000	10,000	16,000	49,000
18	Interest	58,000		27,000			29,000	2,000
19	Contributions	15,000[4]		9,000	4,000			2,000
20	Depreciation	246,093		101,900	62,930	24,370	24,043	32,850
21a	Depreciation shown elsewhere on return	(77,400)		(77,400)				
21b	Depreciation	168,693		24,500	62,930	24,370	24,043	32,850
22	Depletion	—0—						
23	Advertising	269,140			233,140	27,000		19,000
24	Pension, Profit Sharing, etc. plans	140,000		39,000	21,000	35,000		45,000
25	Employee Benefit Programs	105,000		26,000	16,000	29,000		34,000
26	Other Deductions	1,284,000[4]		409,000	401,000	72,000	49,000	353,000
27	Total Deductions	$4,009,333	—0—	$ 985,500	$1,088,570	$596,370	$172,043	$1,166,850

Line	Title	Consolidated	Eliminations	1 Alpha Mfg. Corp.	2 Beta Corp.	3 Charlie Corp.	4 Delta Corp.	5 Echo Corp.
28	Taxable Income Before NOL Dedn. and Special Deductions	$ 344,778	($203,588)	$ 184,199	$ 286,430	($48,370)	$ 22,957	$ 103,150
29a	NOL Deduction	(32,000)						
29b	Special Deductions	(32,000)						
30	Taxable Income	$ 312,778	($203,588)	$ 152,199	$ 286,430	($48,370)	$ 22,957	$ 103,150

Explanatory Notes

[1] Increase in deferred intercompany profits on the sale of inventory items from Alpha to Beta during 1990 are eliminated from the revenues. The amount will be restored when Beta sells the inventory outside the affiliated group or some other restoration occurs.

[2] Restoration of deferred intercompany profits arising from the sale of inventory items from Alpha to Beta in 1990 and prior years. These goods were sold outside the affiliated group in 1990.

[3] Intragroup dividends paid by Beta and Echo to Alpha are eliminated. All remaining dividends are from unaffiliated domestic corporations.

[4] The supporting schedule of component items is not reproduced here.

[5] Alpha sold a truck to Beta on May 27, 1990. The truck originally cost $26,000 and depreciation of $12,358 ($26,000 × [.1429 + .2449 + .0875]) had been claimed. The sales price was $25,000. The truck (a seven-year property) was acquired on June 1, 1988. The entire $11,358 gain ($25,000 − [$26,000 − $12,358]) on the intercompany transaction was deferred. Because Beta continued depreciating the property (seven-year recovery period) in 1990, $1,770 of the deferred gain was restored by Alpha.

$$\$11{,}358 \text{ (deferred gain)} \times \frac{\$3{,}895 \text{ (depreciation)}}{\$25{,}000 \text{ (sales price)}} = \$1{,}770 \text{ (restored gain)}$$

B-12 • App. B / Completed Tax Forms

Form 1065 — U.S. Partnership Return of Income

Department of the Treasury / Internal Revenue Service

For calendar year 1990, or tax year beginning _____, 1990, and ending _____, 19___.
▶ See separate instructions.

OMB No. 1545-0099 — 1990

A Principal business activity: Manufacturing
B Principal product or service: Furniture
C Business code number: 2500

Use IRS label. Otherwise, please print or type.
Name: Johns and Lawrence
Number, street, and room or suite no.: 1234 University Ave.
City or town, state, and ZIP code: Gainsville, Florida 32611

D Employer identification number: 76-3456789
E Date business started: 6/1/80
F Total assets: $302,200

G Check applicable boxes: (1) ☐ Initial return (2) ☐ Final return (3) ☐ Change in address (4) ☐ Amended return
H Check accounting method: (1) ☐ Cash (2) ☒ Accrual (3) ☐ Other (specify) ▶ _____
I Number of partners in this partnership ▶ 2

		Yes	No
J	Is this partnership a limited partnership?		X
K	Are any partners in this partnership also partnerships?		X
L	Is this partnership a partner in another partnership?		X
M	Is this partnership subject to the consolidated audit procedures of sections 6221 through 6233? If "Yes," see "Designation of Tax Matters Partner" on page 2		X
N	Does this partnership meet all the requirements shown in the instructions for Question N?	X	
O	Does this partnership have any foreign partners?		X
P	Is this partnership a publicly traded partnership as defined in section 469(k)(2)?		X
Q	Has this partnership filed, or is it required to file, Form 8264, Application for Registration of a Tax Shelter?		X
R	Was there a distribution of property or a transfer (for example, by sale or death) of a partnership interest during the tax year? If "Yes," see the instructions concerning an election to adjust the basis of the partnership's assets under section 754.		X
S	At any time during the tax year, did the partnership have an interest in or a signature or other authority over a financial account in a foreign country (such as a bank account, securities account, or other financial account)? (See the instructions for exceptions and filing requirements for form TD F 90-22.1.) If "Yes," enter the name of the foreign country. ▶		X
T	Was the partnership the grantor of, or transferor to, a foreign trust which existed during the current tax year, whether or not the partnership or any partner has any beneficial interest in it? If "Yes," you may have to file Forms 3520, 3520-A, or 926		X

Caution: Include only trade or business income and expenses on lines 1a through 21 below. See the instructions for more information.

Income

1a	Gross receipts or sales	434829	
b	Less returns and allowances	14621	1c 420,208
2	Cost of goods sold (Schedule A, line 7)		270,102
3	Gross profit—Subtract line 2 from line 1c		150,106
4	Ordinary income (loss) from other partnerships and fiduciaries (attach schedule)		
5	Net farm profit (loss) (attach Schedule F (Form 1040))		
6	Net gain (loss) from Form 4797, Part II, line 18		
7	Other income (loss) (see instructions) (attach schedule)		
8	Total income (loss)—Combine lines 3 through 7		150,106

Deductions (see instructions for limitations)

9a	Salaries and wages (other than to partners)	26,000	
b	Less jobs credit		9c 26,000
10	Guaranteed payments to partners		18,000
11	Rent		20,000
12	Interest		4,000
13	Taxes		8,000
14	Bad debts		
15	Repairs		2,400
16a	Depreciation (see instructions)	9,976	
b	Less depreciation reported on Schedule A and elsewhere on return	1,000	16c 8,976
17	Depletion (Do not deduct oil and gas depletion.)		
18a	Retirement plans, etc.		
b	Employee benefit programs		18b 24,200
19	Other deductions (attach schedule)		
20	Total deductions—Add lines 9c through 19		111,576
21	Ordinary income (loss) from trade or business activities—Subtract line 20 from line 8		38,530

Please Sign Here: Under penalties of perjury, I declare that I have examined this return, including accompanying schedules and statements, and to the best of my knowledge and belief, it is true, correct, and complete. Declaration of preparer (other than general partner) is based on all information of which preparer has any knowledge.

Signature of general partner: Andrew S. Lawrence   Date: 3/14/90

Paid Preparer's Use Only
Preparer's signature: I. M. Busy Date: 3/10/91 Check if self-employed ☒ Preparer's social security no.: 987:65:4231
Firm's name (or yours if self-employed) and address: I.M. Busy, 395 S. Medical Complex, Gainsville, Fl. 32607
ZIP code: 32607

For Paperwork Reduction Act Notice, see page 1 of separate instructions.

Form **1065** (1990)

Form 1065 (1990) Page 2

Schedule A — Cost of Goods Sold

1	Inventory at beginning of year	32,000
2	Purchases less cost of items withdrawn for personal use	170,400
3	Cost of labor	75,102
4a	Additional section 263A costs (see instructions) (attach schedule)	10,000
b	Other costs (attach schedule)	35,000
5	Total—Add lines 1 through 4b	322,502
6	Inventory at end of year	52,400
7	Cost of goods sold—Subtract line 6 from line 5. Enter here and on page 1, line 2	270,102

8a Check all methods used for valuing closing inventory:
   (i) ☒ Cost   (ii) ☐ Lower of cost or market as described in Regulations section 1.471-4
   (iii) ☐ Writedown of "subnormal" goods as described in Regulations section 1.471-2(c)
   (iv) ☐ Other (specify method used and attach explanation) ▶ ....
  b Check this box if the LIFO inventory method was adopted this tax year for any goods (if checked, attach Form 970) . . . ▶ ☐
  c Do the rules of section 263A (with respect to property produced or acquired for resale) apply to the partnership? . . . ☒ Yes ☐ No
  d Was there any change in determining quantities, cost, or valuations between opening and closing inventory? . . . ☐ Yes ☒ No
    If "Yes," attach explanation.

Schedule L — Balance Sheets

Caution: Read the instructions for Question N on page 9 of the instructions before completing Schedules L and M.

	Assets	Beginning of tax year (a)	(b)	End of tax year (c)	(d)
1	Cash		60,000		62,000
2a	Trade notes and accounts receivable	24,000		23,000	
b	Less allowance for bad debts	-0-	24,000	-0-	23,000
3	Inventories		32,000		52,400
4	U.S. government obligations				
5	Tax-exempt securities				
6	Other current assets (attach schedule)		7,000		
7	Mortgage and real estate loans				
8	Other investments (attach schedule)				
9a	Buildings and other depreciable assets	211,600		211,600	
b	Less accumulated depreciation	105,200	106,400	115,176	96,424
10a	Depletable assets				
b	Less accumulated depletion				
11	Land (net of any amortization)		92,000		92,000
12a	Intangible assets (amortizable only)				
b	Less accumulated amortization				
13	Other assets (attach schedule)				
14	Total assets		321,400		325,824
	Liabilities and Capital				
15	Accounts payable		26,000		25,000
16	Mortgages, notes, bonds payable in less than 1 year		4,000		3,600
17	Other current liabilities (attach schedule)		3,600		4,200
18	All nonrecourse loans				
19	Mortgages, notes, bonds payable in 1 year or more		30,000		30,000
20	Other liabilities (attach schedule)				
21	Partners' capital accounts		257,800		263,024
22	Total liabilities and capital		321,400		325,824

Schedule M — Reconciliation of Partners' Capital Accounts

(Show reconciliation of each partner's capital account on Schedule K-1 (Form 1065), Item K.)

(a) Partners' capital accounts at beginning of year	(b) Capital contributed during year	(c) Income (loss) from lines 1, 2, 3c, and 4 of Schedule K	(d) Income not included in column (c), plus nontaxable income	(e) Losses not included in column (c), plus unallowable deductions	(f) Withdrawals and distributions	(g) Partners' capital accounts at end of year (combine columns (a) through (f))
257,800		41,930	5,500	(8,100)	(34,106)	263,024

Designation of Tax Matters Partner (See instructions.)
Enter below the general partner designated as the tax matters partner (TMP) for the tax year of this return:

Name of designated TMP ▶ Andrew S. Lawrence   Identifying number of TMP ▶ 297-63-2110

Address of designated TMP ▶ 436 N.W. 24th Ave., Gainsville, FL. 32607

Form 1065 (1990) — Page 3

Schedule K — Partners' Shares of Income, Credits, Deductions, Etc.

	(a) Distributive share items		(b) Total amount
Income (Loss)			
1	Ordinary income (loss) from trade or business activities (page 1, line 21)	1	38,530
2	Net income (loss) from rental real estate activities (attach Form 8825)	2	
3a	Gross income from other rental activities — 3a		
b	Less expenses (attach schedule) — 3b		
c	Net income (loss) from other rental activities	3c	
4	Portfolio income (loss) (see instructions):		
a	Interest income	4a	
b	Dividend income	4b	2,000
c	Royalty income	4c	
d	Net short-term capital gain (loss) (attach Schedule D (Form 1065))	4d	3,500
e	Net long-term capital gain (loss) (attach Schedule D (Form 1065))	4e	(2,100)
f	Other portfolio income (loss) (attach schedule)	4f	
5	Guaranteed payments to partners	5	18,000
6	Net gain (loss) under section 1231 (other than due to casualty or theft) (attach Form 4797)	6	
7	Other income (loss) (attach schedule)	7	
Deductions			
8	Charitable contributions (see instructions) (attach list)	8	6,000
9	Section 179 expense deduction (attach Form 4562)	9	
10	Deductions related to portfolio income (see instructions) (itemize)	10	
11	Other deductions (attach schedule)	11	
Investment Interest			
12a	Interest expense on investment debts	12a	
b (1)	Investment income included on lines 4a through 4f above	12b(1)	
(2)	Investment expenses included on line 10 above	12b(2)	
Credits			
13a	Credit for income tax withheld	13a	
b	Low-income housing credit (see instructions):		
(1)	From partnerships to which section 42(j)(5) applies for property placed in service before 1990	13b(1)	
(2)	Other than on line 13b(1) for property placed in service before 1990	13b(2)	
(3)	From partnerships to which section 42(j)(5) applies for property placed in service after 1989	13b(3)	
(4)	Other than on line 13b(3) for property placed in service after 1989	13b(4)	
c	Qualified rehabilitation expenditures related to rental real estate activities (attach Form 3468)	13c	
d	Credits (other than credits shown on lines 13b and 13c) related to rental real estate activities (see instructions)	13d	
e	Credits related to other rental activities (see instructions)	13e	
14	Other credits (see instructions)	14	
Self-Employment			
15a	Net earnings (loss) from self-employment	15a	56,530
b	Gross farming or fishing income	15b	
c	Gross nonfarm income	15c	
Adjustments and Tax Preference Items			
16a	Accelerated depreciation of real property placed in service before 1987	16a	4,514
b	Accelerated depreciation of leased personal property placed in service before 1987	16b	
c	Depreciation adjustment on property placed in service after 1986	16c	
d	Depletion (other than oil and gas)	16d	
e (1)	Gross income from oil, gas, and geothermal properties	16e(1)	
(2)	Deductions allocable to oil, gas, and geothermal properties	16e(2)	
f	Other adjustments and tax preference items (attach schedule)	16f	
Foreign Taxes			
17a	Type of income ▶		
b	Foreign country or U.S. possession ▶		
c	Total gross income from sources outside the U.S. (attach schedule)	17c	
d	Total applicable deductions and losses (attach schedule)	17d	
e	Total foreign taxes (check one): ▶ ☐ Paid ☐ Accrued	17e	
f	Reduction in taxes available for credit (attach schedule)	17f	
g	Other foreign tax information (attach schedule)	17g	
Other			
18a	Total expenditures to which a section 59(e) election may apply	18a	
b	Type of expenditures ▶		
19	Other items and amounts required to be reported separately to partners (see instructions) (attach schedule)		
Analysis			
20a	Total distributive income/payment items—Combine lines 1 through 7 above	20a	

b Analysis by type of partner:

	(a) Corporate	(b) Individual i. Active	(b) Individual ii. Passive	(c) Partnership	(d) Exempt organization	(e) Nominee/Other
(1) General partners		59,930				
(2) Limited partners						

B-14 • App. B / Completed Tax Forms

Completed Tax Forms • B-15

SCHEDULE K-1 (Form 1065)
Department of the Treasury
Internal Revenue Service

Partner's Share of Income, Credits, Deductions, Etc.
▶ See separate instructions.
For calendar year 1990 or tax year beginning _____, 1990, and ending _____, 19___

OMB No. 1545-0099

1990

Partner's identifying number ▶ 297-63-2110
Partnership's identifying number ▶ 76-3456789

Partner's name, address, and ZIP code:
Andrew S. Lawrence
436 N.W. 24th Avenue
Gainsville, FL 32607

Partnership's name, address, and ZIP code:
Johns and Lawrence
1234 University Avenue
Gainesville, FL 32611

A Is this partner a general partner? ☒ Yes ☐ No

B Partner's share of liabilities (see instructions):
- Nonrecourse . . . . $ 0
- Qualified nonrecourse financing . $ 0
- Other . . . . $ 31,400

C What type of entity is this partner? ▶ Individual

D Is this partner a ☐ domestic or a ☐ foreign partner?

E Enter partner's percentage of:
	(i) Before change or termination	(ii) End of year
Profit sharing	_____%	50%
Loss sharing	_____%	50%
Ownership of capital	_____%	50%

F IRS Center where partnership filed return ▶ Atlanta, Ga.

G(1) Tax shelter registration number ▶ _____
(2) Type of tax shelter ▶ _____

H(1) Did the partner's ownership interest in the partnership change after Oct. 22, 1986? . . . . ☐ Yes ☒ No
If "Yes," attach statement. (See Form 1065 Instructions.)

(2) Did the partnership start or acquire a new activity after Oct. 22, 1986? . . . . ☐ Yes ☒ No
If "Yes," attach statement. (See Form 1065 Instructions.)

I Check here if this partnership is a publicly traded partnership as defined in section 469(k)(2) ☒

J Check applicable boxes: (1) ☐ Final K-1 (2) ☐ Amended K-1

K Reconciliation of partner's capital account:

(a) Capital account at beginning of year	(b) Capital contributed during year	(c) Income (loss) from lines 1, 2, 3, and 4 below	(d) Income not included in column (c), plus nontaxable income	(e) Losses not included in column (c), plus unallowable deductions	(f) Withdrawals and distributions	(g) Capital account at end of year (combine columns (a) through (f))
128,900	—	20,965	2,750	(4050)	(17,053)	131,512

	(a) Distributive share item		(b) Amount	(c) 1040 filers enter the amount in column (b) on:
Income (Loss)	1	Ordinary income (loss) from trade or business activities	1	19,265	See Partner's Instructions for Schedule K-1 (Form 1065)
	2	Net income (loss) from rental real estate activities	2		
	3	Net income (loss) from other rental activities	3		
	4	Portfolio income (loss):			
	a	Interest	4a		Sch. B, Part I, line 1
	b	Dividends	4b	1,000	Sch. B, Part II, line 5
	c	Royalties	4c		Sch. E, Part I, line 4
	d	Net short-term capital gain (loss)	4d	1,750	Sch. D, line 5, col. (f) or (g)
	e	Net long-term capital gain (loss)	4e	(1,050)	Sch. D, line 12, col. (f) or (g)
	f	Other portfolio income (loss) (attach schedule)	4f		(Enter on applicable line of your return)
	5	Guaranteed payments to partner	5	9,000	See Partner's Instructions for Schedule K-1 (Form 1065)
	6	Net gain (loss) under section 1231 (other than due to casualty or theft)	6		
	7	Other income (loss) (attach schedule)	7		(Enter on applicable line of your return)
Deductions	8	Charitable contributions	8	3,000	Sch. A, line 14 or 15
	9	Section 179 expense deduction (attach schedule)	9		
	10	Deductions related to portfolio income (attach schedule)	10		See Partner's Instructions for Schedule K-1 (Form 1065)
	11	Other deductions (attach schedule)	11		
Investment Interest	12a	Interest expense on investment debts	12a		Form 4952, line 1
	b	(1) Investment income included on lines 4a through 4f above	b(1)		See Partner's Instructions for Schedule K-1 (Form 1065)
		(2) Investment expenses included on line 10 above	b(2)		
Credits	13a	Credit for income tax withheld	13a		See Partner's Instructions for Schedule K-1 (Form 1065)
	b	Low-income housing credit:			
		(1) From section 42(j)(5) partnerships for property placed in service before 1990	b(1)		Form 8586, line 5
		(2) Other than on line 13b(1) for property placed in service before 1990	b(2)		
		(3) From section 42(j)(5) partnerships for property placed in service after 1989	b(3)		
		(4) Other than on line 13b(3) for property placed in service after 1989	b(4)		
	c	Qualified rehabilitation expenditures related to rental real estate activities (see instructions)	13c		
	d	Credits (other than credits shown on lines 13b and 13c) related to rental real estate activities (see instructions)	13d		See Partner's Instructions for Schedule K-1 (Form 1065)
	e	Credits related to other rental activities (see instructions)	13e		
	14	Other credits (see instructions)	14		

For Paperwork Reduction Act Notice, see Form 1065 Instructions.

Schedule K-1 (Form 1065) 1990

*The second Schedule K-1 for the other 50% partner is not reproduced here, but contains a similar distributive share of partnership income and loss.

Schedule K-1 (Form 1065) 1990 — Page 2

		(a) Distributive share item		(b) Amount	(c) 1040 filers enter the amount in column (b) on:
Self-employment	15a	Net earnings (loss) from self-employment	15a	28,265	Sch. SE, Section A or B
	b	Gross farming or fishing income	15b		⎫ (See Partner's Instructions for
	c	Gross nonfarm income	15c		⎭ Schedule K-1 (Form 1065))
Adjustments and Tax Preference Items	16a	Accelerated depreciation of real property placed in service before 1987	16a	2,257	(See Partner's Instructions for Schedule K-1 (Form 1065) and Form 6251 Instructions)
	b	Accelerated depreciation of leased personal property placed in service before 1987	16b		
	c	Depreciation adjustment on property placed in service after 1986	16c		
	d	Depletion (other than oil and gas)	16d		
	e	(1) Gross income from oil, gas, and geothermal properties	e(1)		
		(2) Deductions allocable to oil, gas, and geothermal properties	e(2)		
	f	Other adjustments and tax preference items (attach schedule)	16f		
Foreign Taxes	17a	Type of income ▶			Form 1116, Check boxes
	b	Name of foreign country or U.S. possession ▶			Form 1116, Part I
	c	Total gross income from sources outside the U.S. (attach schedule)	17c		Form 1116, Part I
	d	Total applicable deductions and losses (attach schedule)	17d		Form 1116, Part I
	e	Total foreign taxes (check one): ▶ ☐ Paid ☐ Accrued	17e		Form 1116, Part II
	f	Reduction in taxes available for credit (attach schedule)	17f		Form 1116, Part III
	g	Other foreign tax information (attach schedule)	17g		See Form 1116 Instructions
Other	18a	Total expenditures to which a section 59(e) election may apply	18a		(See Partner's Instructions for Schedule K-1 (Form 1065))
	b	Type of expenditures ▶			
Recapture of Tax Credits	19	Recapture of low-income housing credit:			
	a	From section 42(j)(5) partnerships	19a		⎫ Form 8611, line 8
	b	Other than on line 19a	19b		⎭

	20	Investment credit properties:	A	B	C	
	a	Description of property (State whether recovery or nonrecovery property. If recovery property, state whether regular percentage method or section 48(q) election used.)				Form 4255, top
	b	Date placed in service				Form 4255, line 2
	c	Cost or other basis				Form 4255, line 3
	d	Class of recovery property or original estimated useful life				Form 4255, line 4
	e	Date item ceased to be investment credit property				Form 4255, line 8

Supplemental Information

21 Supplemental information required to be reported separately to each partner (attach additional schedules if more space is needed):

Completed Tax Forms • **B-17**

Form 1120S — U.S. Income Tax Return for an S Corporation

Department of the Treasury / Internal Revenue Service

For calendar year 1990, or tax year beginning _____, 1990, and ending _____, 19___.
► See separate instructions.

OMB No. 1545-0130
1990

A Date of election as an S corporation: **1-10-1983**

B Business code no.: **3490**

Name: **Supreme Metal Fabricating Co.**
Number, street, and room or suite no.: **1120 Pasa Way**
City or town, state, and ZIP code: **Austin, Tx. 78701**

C Employer identification number: **74-1234567**
D Date incorporated: **1-1-1983**
E Total assets: **$ 668,950**

F Check applicable boxes: (1) ☐ Initial return (2) ☐ Final return (3) ☐ Change in address (4) ☐ Amended return

G Check this box if this is an S corporation subject to the consolidated audit procedures of sections 6241 through 6245 ► ☐

H Enter number of shareholders in the corporation at end of the tax year ► **2**

Caution: Include *only* trade or business income and expenses on lines 1a through 21. See the instructions for more information.

Income

1a	Gross receipts or sales **3,525,000** b Less returns and allowances **7,500** c Bal ►	1c	3,517,000
2	Cost of goods sold (Schedule A, line 7)	2	1,915,000
3	Gross profit (subtract line 2 from line 1c)	3	1,602,500
4	Net gain (loss) from Form 4797, Part II, line 18	4	91,800
5	Other income (see instructions) (attach schedule)	5	
6	**Total** income (loss)—Combine lines 3 through 5 ►	6	1,694,300

Deductions (See instructions for limitations.)

7	Compensation of officers	7	110,000
8a	Salaries and wages **585,000** b Less jobs credit **10,500** c Bal ►	8c	574,500
9	Repairs	9	46,000
10	Bad debts	10	1,700
11	Rents	11	225,750
12	Taxes	12	45,000
13	Interest	13	40,000
14a	Depreciation (see instructions) **42,300**		
14b	Depreciation reported on Schedule A and elsewhere on return **36,800**		
14c	Subtract line 14b from line 14a	14c	5,500
15	Depletion (**Do not deduct oil and gas depletion.** See instructions.)	15	
16	Advertising	16	75,000
17	Pension, profit-sharing, etc., plans	17	
18	Employee benefit programs	18	25,000
19	Other deductions (attach schedule)	19	434,750
20	**Total** deductions—Add lines 7 through 19 ►	20	1,583,200
21	Ordinary income (loss) from trade or business activities—Subtract line 20 from line 6	21	111,100

Tax and Payments

22	**Tax:**		
a	Excess net passive income tax (attach schedule) — 22a		
b	Tax from Schedule D (Form 1120S) — 22b		
c	Add lines 22a and 22b	22c	-0-
23	**Payments:**		
a	1990 estimated tax payments — 23a		
b	Tax deposited with Form 7004 — 23b		
c	Credit for Federal tax on fuels (attach Form 4136) — 23c		
d	Add lines 23a through 23c	23d	-0-
24	Enter any **penalty** for underpayment of estimated tax—Check ► ☐ if Form 2220 is attached	24	
25	**Tax due**—If the total of lines 22c and 24 is larger than line 23d, enter amount owed ►	25	None
26	**Overpayment**—If line 23d is larger than the total of lines 22c and 24, enter amount overpaid ►	26	
27	Enter amount of line 26 you want: Credited to 1991 estimated tax ► _____ Refunded ►	27	

Please Sign Here
Signature of officer: *Able Moses* Date: **3/15/91** Title: **President**

Paid Preparer's Use Only
Preparer's signature: *I.M. Certified* Date: **3/10/91** Check if self-employed ► ☒ Preparer's social security number: **987:65:4321**
Firm's name (or yours if self-employed) and address: **I.M. Certified, 145 River Road, Gainsville, Fl.** E.I. No. ► _____ ZIP code ► **32601**

For Paperwork Reduction Act Notice, see page 1 of separate instructions. Form **1120S** (1990)

B-18 • App. B / Completed Tax Forms

Form 1120S (1990) Page **2**

Schedule A — Cost of Goods Sold (See instructions.)

1	Inventory at beginning of year	97,500
2	Purchases	1,185,000
3	Cost of labor	517,500
4a	Additional section 263A costs (see instructions) *(attach schedule)*	87,500
b	Other costs *(attach schedule)*	177,500
5	Total—Add lines 1 through 4b	2,065,000
6	Inventory at end of year	150,000
7	Cost of goods sold—Subtract line 6 from line 5. Enter here and on line 2, page 1	1,915,000

8a Check all methods used for valuing closing inventory:
  (i) ☒ Cost
  (ii) ☐ Lower of cost or market as described in Regulations section 1.471-4
  (iii) ☐ Writedown of "subnormal" goods as described in Regulations section 1.471-2(c)
  (iv) ☐ Other (specify method used and attach explanation) ▶ _____

  b Check this box if the LIFO inventory method was adopted this tax year for any goods *(if checked, attach Form 970)* . . . ▶ ☐
  c If the LIFO inventory method was used for this tax year, enter percentage (or amounts) of closing inventory computed under LIFO . . . **8c** 100%
  d Do the rules of section 263A (with respect to property produced or acquired for resale) apply to the corporation? . . . ☒ Yes ☐ No
  e Was there any change in determining quantities, cost, or valuations between opening and closing inventory? . . . ☐ Yes ☒ No
  If "Yes," attach explanation.

Additional Information Required (continued from page 1)

		Yes	No
I	Did you at the end of the tax year own, directly or indirectly, 50% or more of the voting stock of a domestic corporation? For rules of attribution, see section 267(c). If "Yes," attach a schedule showing: **(1)** name, address, and employer identification number; and **(2)** percentage owned.		X
J	Refer to the list in the instructions and state your principal: **(1)** Business activity ▶ Manufacturing **(2)** Product or service ▶ Winches		
K	Were you a member of a controlled group subject to the provisions of section 1561?		X
L	At any time during the tax year, did you have an interest in or a signature or other authority over a financial account in a foreign country (such as a bank account, securities account, or other financial account)? (See instructions for exceptions and filing requirements for form TD F 90-22.1.) If "Yes," enter the name of the foreign country ▶ _____		X
M	Were you the grantor of, or transferor to, a foreign trust that existed during the current tax year, whether or not you have any beneficial interest in it? If "Yes," you may have to file **Forms 3520, 3520-A, or 926**		X
N	During this tax year did you maintain any part of your accounting/tax records on a computerized system?	X	
O	Check method of accounting: **(1)** ☐ Cash **(2)** ☒ Accrual **(3)** ☐ Other (specify) ▶ _____		
P	Check this box if the S corporation has filed or is required to file **Form 8264,** Application for Registration of a Tax Shelter . . . ▶ ☐		
Q	Check this box if the corporation issued publicly offered debt instruments with original issue discount . . . ▶ ☐ If so, the corporation may have to file **Form 8281,** Information Return for Publicly Offered Original Issue Discount Instruments.		
R	If the corporation: **(1)** filed its election to be an S corporation after 1986, **(2)** was a C corporation before it elected to be an S corporation **or** the corporation acquired an asset with a basis determined by reference to its basis (or the basis of any other property) in the hands of a C corporation, and **(3)** has net unrealized built-in gain (defined in section 1374(d)(1)) in excess of the net recognized built-in gain from prior years, enter the net unrealized built-in gain reduced by net recognized built-in gain from prior years (see instructions) . . . ▶ $ _____		
S	Check this box if the corporation had subchapter C earnings and profits at the close of the tax year (see instructions) ▶ ☐		

Designation of Tax Matters Person (See instructions.)

Enter below the shareholder designated as the tax matters person (TMP) for the tax year of this return:

Name of designated TMP ▶ Able Moses   Identifying number of TMP ▶ 263-63-6363

Address of designated TMP ▶ 1710 Lauaca, Austin, TX 78707

Form 1120S (1990) Page **3**

Schedule K — Shareholders' Shares of Income, Credits, Deductions, Etc.

		(a) Pro rata share items			(b) Total amount
Income (Loss)	1	Ordinary income (loss) from trade or business activities (page 1, line 21)		1	111,100
	2	Net income (loss) from rental real estate activities (attach Form 8825)		2	
	3a	Gross income from other rental activities — 3a	71,000		
	b	Less expenses (attach schedule) — 3b	28,400		
	c	Net income (loss) from other rental activities		3c	42,600
	4	Portfolio income (loss):			
	a	Interest income		4a	1,800
	b	Dividend income		4b	12,500
	c	Royalty income		4c	
	d	Net short-term capital gain (loss) (attach Schedule D (Form 1120S))		4d	7,500
	e	Net long-term capital gain (loss) (attach Schedule D (Form 1120S))		4e	26,000
	f	Other portfolio income (loss) (attach schedule)		4f	
	5	Net gain (loss) under section 1231 (other than due to casualty or theft) (attach Form 4797)		5	
	6	Other income (loss) (attach schedule)		6	
Deductions	7	Charitable contributions (see instructions) (attach list)		7	6,210
	8	Section 179 expense deduction (attach Form 4562)		8	10,000
	9	Deductions related to portfolio income (loss) (see instructions) (itemize)		9	1,760
	10	Other deductions (attach schedule)		10	
Investment Interest	11a	Interest expense on investment debts		11a	
	b	(1) Investment income included on lines 4a through 4f above		11b(1)	
		(2) Investment expenses included on line 9 above		11b(2)	
Credits	12a	Credit for alcohol used as a fuel (attach Form 6478)		12a	
	b	Low-income housing credit (see instructions):			
		(1) From partnerships to which section 42(j)(5) applies for property placed in service before 1990		12b(1)	
		(2) Other than on line 12b(1) for property placed in service before 1990		12b(2)	
		(3) From partnerships to which section 42(j)(5) applies for property placed in service after 1989		12b(3)	
		(4) Other than on line 12b(3) for property placed in service after 1989		12b(4)	
	c	Qualified rehabilitation expenditures related to rental real estate activities (attach Form 3468)		12c	
	d	Credits (other than credits shown on lines 12b and 12c) related to rental real estate activities (see instructions)		12d	
	e	Credits related to other rental activities (see instructions)		12e	
	13	Other credits (see instructions)		13	
Adjustments and Tax Preference Items	14a	Accelerated depreciation of real property placed in service before 1987		14a	2,710
	b	Accelerated depreciation of leased personal property placed in service before 1987		14b	
	c	Depreciation adjustment on property placed in service after 1986		14c	13,650
	d	Depletion (other than oil and gas)		14d	
	e	(1) Gross income from oil, gas, or geothermal properties		14e(1)	
		(2) Deductions allocable to oil, gas, or geothermal properties		14e(2)	
	f	Other adjustments and tax preference items (attach schedule)		14f	
Foreign Taxes	15a	Type of income ▶			
	b	Name of foreign country or U.S. possession ▶			
	c	Total gross income from sources outside the U.S. (attach schedule)		15c	
	d	Total applicable deductions and losses (attach schedule)		15d	
	e	Total foreign taxes (check one): ▶ ☐ Paid ☐ Accrued		15e	
	f	Reduction in taxes available for credit (attach schedule)		15f	
	g	Other foreign tax information (attach schedule)		15g	
Other Items	16a	Total expenditures to which a section 59(e) election may apply		16a	
	b	Type of expenditures ▶			
	17	Total property distributions (including cash) other than dividends reported on line 19 below		17	31,000
	18	Other items and amounts required to be reported separately to shareholders (see instructions) (attach schedule) Tax exempt interest			
	19	Total dividend distributions paid from accumulated earnings and profits		19	4,000
	20	Income (loss) (Required only if Schedule M-1 must be completed.)—Combine lines 1 through 6 in column (b). From the result subtract the sum of lines 7 through 11a, 15e, and 16a		20	187,530

Form 1120S (1990) Page 4

Schedule L — Balance Sheets

Assets	Beginning of tax year (a)	(b)	End of tax year (c)	(d)
1 Cash		38,325		159,000
2a Trade notes and accounts receivable	47,500		33,500	
b Less allowance for bad debts	2,500	45,000	2,000	31,000
3 Inventories		97,500		150,000
4 U.S. government obligations		30,000		30,000
5 Tax-exempt securities				
6 Other current assets (attach schedule)		127,500		
7 Loans to shareholders		750		3,750
8 Mortgage and real estate loans				
9 Other investments (attach schedule)				
10a Buildings and other depreciable assets	600,000		390,000	
b Less accumulated depreciation	292,500	307,500	96,000	294,000
11a Depletable assets				
b Less accumulated depletion				
12 Land (net of any amortization)		75,000		
13a Intangible assets (amortizable only)				
b Less accumulated amortization				
14 Other assets (attach schedule)		800		700
15 Total assets		722,375		668,950
Liabilities and Shareholders' Equity				
16 Accounts payable		42,000		75,000
17 Mortgages, notes, bonds payable in less than 1 year		165,275		103,295
18 Other current liabilities (attach schedule)		67,500		38,325
19 Loans from shareholders		5,100		10,800
20 Mortgages, notes, bonds payable in 1 year or more				
21 Other liabilities (attach schedule)		177,500		20,000
22 Capital stock		75,000		75,000
23 Paid-in or capital surplus				
24 Retained earnings		190,000		346,530
25 Less cost of treasury stock		( )		( )
26 Total liabilities and shareholders' equity		722,375		668,950

Schedule M-1 — Reconciliation of Income per Books With Income per Return

(You are not required to complete this schedule if the total assets on line 15, column (d), of Schedule L are less than $25,000.)

1 Net income per books	164,230	5 Income recorded on books this year not included on Schedule K, lines 1 through 6 (itemize):		
2 Income included on Schedule K, lines 1 through 6, not recorded on books this year (itemize):		a Tax-exempt interest $ 4,000		
Gain on sale of dep. property	36,000	Prepaid rent 5,000		9,000
3 Expenses recorded on books this year not included on Schedule K, lines 1 through 11a, 15e, and 16a (itemize):		6 Deductions included on Schedule K, lines 1 through 11a, 15e, and 16a, not charged against book income this year (itemize):		
a Depreciation $		a Depreciation $ 6,200		
b Travel and entertainment $ 2,500				6,500
	2,500	7 Total of lines 5 and 6		15,200
4 Total of lines 1 through 3	202,730	8 Income (loss) (Schedule K, line 20)—Line 4 less line 7		187,530

Schedule M-2 — Analysis of Accumulated Adjustments Account, Other Adjustments Account, and Shareholders' Undistributed Taxable Income Previously Taxed (See instructions.)

	(a) Accumulated adjustments account	(b) Other adjustments account	(c) Shareholders' undistributed taxable income previously taxed
1 Balance at beginning of tax year	136,400	xxx	xxx
2 Ordinary income from page 1, line 21	111,100		
3 Other additions	94,400		
4 Loss from page 1, line 21	(xxx)		
5 Other reductions	(17,970)	( )	
6 Combine lines 1 through 5	323,930		
7 Distributions other than dividend distributions	31,000		
8 Balance at end of tax year—subtract line 7 from line 6	292,930	xxx	xxx

SCHEDULE D (Form 1120S)
Department of the Treasury
Internal Revenue Service

Capital Gains and Losses and Built-In Gains

▶ Attach to Form 1120S.
▶ See separate instructions.

OMB No. 1545-0130

1990

Name: Supreme Metal Fabricators
Employer identification number: 74-1234567

Part I — Short-Term Capital Gains and Losses—Assets Held One Year or Less

(a) Kind of property and description (Example, 100 shares of "Z" Co.)	(b) Date acquired (mo., day, yr.)	(c) Date sold (mo., day, yr.)	(d) Gross sales price	(e) Cost or other basis, plus expense of sale	(f) Gain or (loss) ((d) less (e))
1 100 sh. Trick Titanium stock	2/1/90	11/25/90	56,000	48,500	7,500

2 Short-term capital gain from installment sales from Form 6252, line 22 or 30 . . . . **2**
3 Net short-term capital gain or (loss)—Combine lines 1 and 2 and enter here. Also enter this amount on Form 1120S, Schedule K, line 4d or line 6 (but first reduce it by any tax shown on line 23 below) **3** 7,500

Part II — Long-Term Capital Gains and Losses—Assets Held More Than One Year

(a)	(b)	(c)	(d)	(e)	(f)
4 40 Austin Ind. School Dist. Bonds	4/5/84	10/17/90	42,100	37,600	4,500
1000 sh. Casa Grande Truck Sales	10/16/86	12/4/90	111,400	89,900	21,500

5 Long-term capital gain from installment sales from Form 6252, line 22 or 30 . . . . **5**
6 Net long-term capital gain or (loss)—Combine lines 4 and 5 and enter here. Also enter this amount on Form 1120S, Schedule K, line 4e or line 6 (but first reduce it by any tax shown on lines 15 and 23 below) . **6** 26,000

Part III — Capital Gains Tax (See instructions before completing this part.)

7 Enter section 1231 gain from line 9, Form 4797 . . . . **7**
8 Net long-term capital gain or (loss)—Combine lines 6 and 7 . . . . **8**

Note: If the corporation is liable for the excess net passive income tax (Form 1120S, page 1, line 22a) or the built-in gains tax (Part IV below), see the line 9 instructions before completing line 9.

9 Net capital gain—Enter excess of net long-term capital gain (line 8) over net short-term capital loss (line 3) **9**
10 Statutory minimum **10** $25,000
11 Subtract line 10 from line 9 . . . . **11**
12 Enter 34% of line 11 . . . . **12**
13 Taxable income (see instructions and attach computation schedule) **13**
14 Enter tax on line 13 amount (see instructions and attach computation schedule) **14**
15 Tax—Enter smaller of line 12 or line 14 here and on Form 1120S, page 1, line 22b **15**

Part IV — Built-In Gains Tax (See instructions before completing this part.)

16 Excess of recognized built-in gains over recognized built-in losses (see instructions and attach computation schedule) **16**
17 Taxable income (see instructions and attach computation schedule) **17**
18 Net recognized built-in gain—Enter smaller of line 16 or line 17 (see instructions) **18**
19 Section 1374(b)(2) deduction **19**
20 Subtract line 19 from line 18. (If zero or less, enter zero here and on line 23.) **20**
21 Enter 34% of line 20 . . . . **21**
22 Business credit and minimum tax credit carryforwards under section 1374(b)(3) from C corporation years . **22**
23 Tax—Subtract line 22 from line 21 (if zero or less, enter zero). Enter here and on Form 1120S, page 1, line 22b . **23**

For Paperwork Reduction Act Notice, see page 1 of Instructions for Form 1120S.

Schedule D (Form 1120S) 1990

B-22 • App. B / Completed Tax Forms

SCHEDULE K-1 (Form 1120S) Department of the Treasury Internal Revenue Service	Shareholder's Share of Income, Credits, Deductions, Etc. ▶ See separate instructions. For calendar year 1990 or tax year beginning , 1990, and ending , 19	OMB No. 1545-0130 1990
Shareholder's identifying number ▶ 263-63-6363		Corporation's identifying number ▶ 74-1234567
Shareholder's name, address, and ZIP code Able Moses 1710 Lavaca Austin, Tx. 78707		Corporation's name, address, and ZIP code Supreme Metal Fabricating Co. 1120 Pasa Way Austin, Tx. 78701

A Shareholder's percentage of stock ownership for tax year (see Instructions for Schedule K-1) . . . . ▶ 50 %
B Internal Revenue Service Center where corporation filed its return ▶ Austin, Tx.
C (1) Tax shelter registration number (see Instructions for Schedule K-1) . . . . ▶ N/A
  (2) Type of tax shelter ▶
D If the shareholder acquired corporate stock after 10/22/86, check here ▶ ☐ and enter the shareholder's weighted percentage increase in stock ownership for 1990 (see Instructions for Schedule K-1) . . . . ▶ %
E If any activity for which income or loss is reported on line 1, 2, or 3, was started or acquired by the corporation after 10/22/86, check here ▶ ☐ and enter the date of start up or acquisition in the date space on line 1, 2, or 3 **below**.
F Check applicable boxes: **(1)** ☐ Final K-1   **(2)** ☐ Amended K-1

		(a) Pro rata share items		(b) Amount	(c) Form 1040 filers enter the amount in column (b) on:
Income (Loss)	1	Ordinary income (loss) from trade or business activities. If applicable, enter date asked for in item E . . . . ▶	1	55,550	See Shareholder's Instructions for Schedule K-1 (Form 1120S).
	2	Net income (loss) from rental real estate activities. If applicable, enter date asked for in item E . . . . ▶	2		
	3	Net income (loss) from other rental activities. If applicable, enter date asked for in item E . . . . ▶	3	21,300	
	4	Portfolio income (loss):			
	a	Interest	4a	900	Sch. B, Part I, line 1
	b	Dividends	4b	6,250	Sch. B, Part II, line 5
	c	Royalties	4c		Sch. E, Part I, line 4
	d	Net short-term capital gain (loss)	4d	3,750	Sch. D, line 5, col. (f) or (g)
	e	Net long-term capital gain (loss)	4e	13,000	Sch. D, line 12, col. (f) or (g)
	f	Other portfolio income (loss) (attach schedule)	4f		(Enter on applicable line of your return.)
	5	Net gain (loss) under section 1231 (other than due to casualty or theft)	5		See Shareholder's Instructions for Schedule K-1 (Form 1120S)
	6	Other income (loss) (attach schedule)	6		(Enter on applicable line of your return.)
Deductions	7	Charitable contributions	7	3,105	Sch. A, line 14 or 15
	8	Section 179 expense deduction (attach schedule)	8	5,000	See Shareholder's Instructions for Schedule K-1 (Form 1120S).
	9	Deductions related to portfolio income (loss) (attach schedule) .	9	880	
	10	Other deductions (attach schedule)	10		
Investment Interest	11a	Interest expense on investment debts	11a		Form 4952, line 1
	b	(1) Investment income included on lines 4a through 4f above .	b(1)		See Shareholder's Instructions for Schedule K-1 (Form 1120S).
		(2) Investment expenses included on line 9 above	b(2)		
Credits	12a	Credit for alcohol used as fuel	12a		Form 6478, line 10
	b	Low-income housing credit:			
		(1) From section 42(j)(5) partnerships for property placed in service before 1990	b(1)		
		(2) Other than on line 12b(1) for property placed in service before 1990	b(2)		Form 8586, line 5
		(3) From section 42(j)(5) partnerships for property placed in service after 1989	b(3)		
		(4) Other than on line 12b(3) for property placed in service after 1989	b(4)		
	c	Qualified rehabilitation expenditures related to rental real estate activities (see instructions)	12c		See Shareholder's Instructions for Schedule K-1 (Form 1120S).
	d	Credits (other than credits shown on lines 12b and 12c) related to rental real estate activities (see instructions)	12d		
	e	Credits related to other rental activities (see instructions) . .	12e		
	13	Other credits (see instructions)	13		

For Paperwork Reduction Act Notice, see Form 1120S Instructions.   Schedule K-1 (Form 1120S) 1990

*A second Schedule K-1 for the other 50% Shareholder is not reproduced here to save space. The allocations for the other shareholder are the same as for Able Moses.

Schedule K-1 (Form 1120S) (1990) — Page 2

	(a) Pro rata share items		(b) Amount	(c) Form 1040 filers enter the amount in column (b) on:
Adjustments and Tax Preference Items	14a Accelerated depreciation of real property placed in service before 1987	14a	1,355	See Shareholder's Instructions for Schedule K-1 (Form 1120S) and Form 6251 Instructions.
	b Accelerated depreciation of leased personal property placed in service before 1987.	14b		
	c Depreciation adjustment on property placed in service after 1986	14c	6,825	
	d Depletion (other than oil and gas)	14d		
	e (1) Gross income from oil, gas, or geothermal properties	e(1)		
	(2) Deductions allocable to oil, gas, or geothermal properties	e(2)		
	f Other adjustments and tax preference items *(attach schedule)*	14f		
Foreign Taxes	15a Type of income ▶			Form 1116, Check boxes
	b Name of foreign country or U.S. possession ▶			Form 1116, Part I
	c Total gross income from sources outside the U.S. *(attach schedule)*	15c		Form 1116, Part I
	d Total applicable deductions and losses *(attach schedule)*	15d		Form 1116, Part I
	e Total foreign taxes (check one): ▶ ☐ Paid ☐ Accrued	15e		Form 1116, Part II
	f Reduction in taxes available for credit *(attach schedule)*	15f		Form 1116, Part III
	g Other foreign tax information *(attach schedule)*	15g		See Form 1116 Instructions
Other Items	16a Total expenditures to which a section 59(e) election may apply	16a		See Shareholder's Instructions for Schedule K-1 (Form 1120S).
	b Type of expenditures ▶			
	17 Property distributions (including cash) other than dividend distributions reported to you on Form 1099-DIV.	17	15,500	
	18 Amount of loan repayments for "Loans from Shareholders"	18		
Recapture of Tax Credits	19 Recapture of low-income housing credit:			
	a From section 42(j)(5) partnerships	19a		} Form 8611, line 8
	b Other than on line 19a	19b		

		A	B	C	
	20 Investment credit properties:				
	a Description of property (State whether recovery or non-recovery property. If recovery property, state whether regular percentage method or section 48(q) election is used.)				Form 4255, top
	b Date placed in service				Form 4255, line 2
	c Cost or other basis				Form 4255, line 3
	d Class of recovery property or original estimated useful life				Form 4255, line 4
	e Date item ceased to be investment credit property				Form 4255, line 8

21 Supplemental information required to be reported separately to each shareholder *(attach additional schedules if more space is needed):*

Supplemental Information

Tax-exempt bond interest $2000

B-24 • App. B / Completed Tax Forms

Form 709 (Rev. December 1989)
Department of the Treasury
Internal Revenue Service

United States Gift (and Generation-Skipping Transfer) Tax Return
(Section 6019 of the Internal Revenue Code) (For gifts made after December 31, 1988, and before January 1, 1990)
Calendar year 19 **90**
▶ See separate instructions. For Privacy Act Notice, see the Instructions for Form 1040.

OMB No. 1545-0020
Expires 11-30-92

Part 1.—General Information

1 Donor's first name and middle initial **Wilma**	2 Donor's last name **Brown**	3 Social security number **123 45 6789**
4 Address (number and street) **2 Main Street**		5 Domicile **U.S.A.**
6 City, state, and ZIP code **Dalton, Georgia 35901**		7 Citizenship **U.S.A.**

		Yes	No
8	If the donor died during the year, check here ▶ ☐ and enter date of death _____, 19 ___		
9	If you received an extension of time to file this Form 709, check here ▶ ☐ and attach the Form 4868, 2688, 2350, or extension letter.		
10	If you (the donor) filed a previous Form 709 (or 709-A), has your address changed since the last Form 709 (or 709-A) was filed?		X
11	Gifts by husband or wife to third parties.—Do you consent to have the gifts (including generation-skipping transfers) made by you and by your spouse to third parties during the calendar year considered as made one-half by each of you? (See instructions.) (If the answer is "Yes," the following information must be furnished and your spouse is to sign the consent shown below. If the answer is "No," skip lines 12–17 and go to Schedule A.).	X	
12	Name of consenting spouse **Hugh Brown**	13 SSN **987-65-4321**	
14	Were you married to one another during the entire calendar year? (See instructions.)	X	
15	If the answer to 14 is "No," check whether ☐ married ☐ divorced or ☐ widowed, and give date (see instructions) ▶		
16	Will a gift tax return for this calendar year be filed by your spouse?		X

17 **Consent of Spouse**—I consent to have the gifts (and generation-skipping transfers) made by me and by my spouse to third parties during the calendar year considered as made one-half by each of us. We are both aware of the joint and several liability for tax created by the execution of this consent.

Consenting spouse's signature ▶ **Hugh Brown**   Date ▶ **3-2-91**

Part 2.—Tax Computation

1	Enter the amount from Schedule A, Part 3, line 15	**343,337**
2	Enter the amount from Schedule B, line 3	**500,000**
3	Total taxable gifts (add lines 1 and 2)	**843,337**
4	Tax computed on amount on line 3 (see Table for Computing Tax in separate instructions)	**284,701**
5a	Enter the lesser of line 3 or $21,040,000 . . . 5a **843,337**	
b	Subtract $10,000,000 from line 5a (do not enter less than zero) 5b **0**	
c	Enter 5% (.05) of line 5b	5c **0**
6	Total tentative tax on the amount on line 3 (add lines 4 and 5c)	**284,701**
7	Tax computed on amount on line 2 (see Table for Computing Tax in separate instructions)	**155,800**
8a	Enter the lesser of line 2 or $21,040,000 . . . 8a **500,000**	
b	Subtract $10,000,000 from line 8a (do not enter less than zero) 8b **0**	
c	Enter 5% (.05) of line 8b	8c **0**
9	Total tentative tax on the amount on line 2 (add lines 7 and 8c)	**155,800**
10	Balance (subtract line 9 from line 6)	**128,901**
11	Maximum unified credit (nonresident aliens, see instructions)	192,800 00
12	Enter the unified credit against tax allowable for all prior periods (from Sch. B, line 1, col. C)	**34,000**
13	Balance (subtract line 12 from line 11)	**158,800**
14	Enter 20% (.20) of the amount allowed as a specific exemption for gifts made after September 8, 1976, and before January 1, 1977 (see instructions)	**0**
15	Balance (subtract line 14 from line 13)	**158,800**
16	Unified credit (enter the smaller of line 10 or line 15)	**128,901**
17	Credit for foreign gift taxes (see instructions)	
18	Total credits (add lines 16 and 17)	**128,901**
19	Balance (subtract line 18 from line 10) (do not enter less than zero)	**0**
20	Generation-skipping transfer taxes (from Schedule C, Part 4, col. H, total)	
21	Total tax (add lines 19 and 20)	**0**
22	Gift and generation-skipping transfer taxes prepaid with extension of time to file	
23	If line 22 is less than line 21, enter BALANCE DUE (see instructions)	**none**
24	If line 22 is greater than line 21, enter AMOUNT TO BE REFUNDED	

Under penalties of perjury, I declare that I have examined this return, including any accompanying schedules and statements, and to the best of my knowledge and belief it is true, correct, and complete. Declaration of preparer (other than donor) is based on all information of which preparer has any knowledge.

Donor's signature ▶ **Wilma Brown**   Date ▶ **3-2-91**

Preparer's signature (other than donor) ▶ **Sally Preparer** Sally Preparer   Date ▶ **3-2-91**

Preparer's address (other than donor) ▶ **110 Last Bank Tower, Gainsville, Fl. 32601**

For Paperwork Reduction Act Notice, see page 1 of the separate instructions for this form.   Form **709** (Rev. 12-89)

Form 709 (Rev. 12-89) Page 2

SCHEDULE A — Computation of Taxable Gifts

Part 1.—Gifts Subject Only to Gift Tax. *Gifts less political organization, medical, and educational exclusions—see instructions*

A Item number	B Donee's name, relationship to donor (if any), and address and description of gift. If the gift was made by means of a trust, enter trust's identifying number below and attach a copy of the trust instrument. If the gift was securities, enter the CUSIP number(s), if available.	C Donor's adjusted basis of gift	D Date of gift	E Value at date of gift
1	Billy Brown — Cash	80,000	1990	80,000
2	Betsy Brown — Jewelry	18,000	1990	24,000
3	Ruth Cain — Remainder interest — vacation cabin (.22674 × $100,000)	15,000	1990	22,674
4	Trust at First Bank, income to Hugh Brown for life. Remainder to Jeff Brown. (QTIP Trust)	480,000	1990	600,000

Part 2.—Gifts Which are Direct Skips and are Subject to Both Gift Tax and Generation-Skipping Transfer Tax. You must list the gifts in chronological order. *Gifts less political organization, medical, and educational exclusions—see instructions*   N/A

A Item number	B Donee's name, relationship to donor (if any), and address and description of gift. If the gift was made by means of a trust, enter trust's identifying number below and attach a copy of the trust instrument. If the gift was securities, enter the CUSIP number(s), if available.	C Donor's adjusted basis of gift	D Date of gift	E Value at date of gift
1				

Part 3.—Gift Tax Reconciliation

1	Total value of gifts of donor (add column E of Parts 1 and 2)	1	726,674
2	One-half of items __1–3__ attributable to spouse (see instructions)	2	63,337
3	Balance (subtract line 2 from line 1)	3	663,337
4	Gifts of spouse to be included (from Schedule A, Part 3, line 2 of spouse's return—see instructions)	4	340,000
	If any of the gifts included on this line are also subject to the generation-skipping transfer tax, check here ▶ ☐ and enter those gifts also on Schedule C, Part 1.		
5	Total gifts (add lines 3 and 4)	5	1,003,337
6	Total annual exclusions for gifts listed on Schedule A (including line 4, above) (see instructions)	6	40,000
7	Total included amount of gifts (subtract line 6 from line 5)	7	963,337

Deductions (see instructions)

8	Gifts of interests to spouse for which a marital deduction will be claimed, based on items __4__ of Schedule A	8	600,000	
9	Exclusions attributable to gifts on line 8	9	10,000	
10	Marital deduction—subtract line 9 from line 8	10	590,000	
11	Charitable deduction, based on items __gifts of spouse__ less exclusions	11	30,000	
12	Total deductions—add lines 10 and 11			12	620,000
13	Subtract line 12 from line 7			13	343,337
14	Generation-skipping transfer taxes payable with this Form 709 (from Schedule C, Part 4, col. H, Total)			14	
15	Taxable gifts (add lines 13 and 14). Enter here and on line 1 of the Tax Computation on page 1			15	343,337

(If more space is needed, attach additional sheets of same size.)

Form 709 (Rev. 12-89) Page **3**

SCHEDULE A — Computation of Taxable Gifts (continued)

16 Terminable Interest (QTIP) Marital Deduction. (See instructions.)

☒ ◄ Check here if you elected, under the rules of section 2523(f), to include gifts of qualified terminable interest property on line 8, on page 2. Enter the item numbers (from Schedule A) of the gifts for which you made this election ▶ 4

SCHEDULE B — Gifts From Prior Periods

Did you (the donor) file gift tax returns for prior periods? (If "Yes," see instructions for completing Schedule B below.) ☐ Yes ☐ No

A Calendar year or calendar quarter (see instructions)	B Internal Revenue office where prior return was filed	C Amount of unified credit against gift tax for periods after December 31, 1976	D Amount of specific exemption for prior periods ending before January 1, 1977	E Amount of taxable gifts
1975	Atlanta, Georgia	-0-	-0-	300,000
1978	Atlanta, Georgia	34,000		200,000

1 Totals for prior periods (without adjustment for reduced specific exemption)	**1**	34,000	-0-	500,000
2 Amount, if any, by which total specific exemption, line 1, column D, is more than $30,000			**2**	-0-
3 Total amount of taxable gifts for prior periods (add amount, column E, line 1, and amount, if any, on line 2) (Enter here and on line 2 of the Tax Computation on page 1.)			**3**	500,000

SCHEDULE C — Computation of Generation-Skipping Transfer Tax N/A

Note: *Inter vivos direct skips which are completely excluded by the grandchild exclusion and/or the GST exemption must still be fully reported (including value and exclusions and exemptions claimed) on Schedule C.*

Part 1.—Generation-Skipping Transfers

A Item No. (from Schedule A, Part 2, col. A)	B Value (from Schedule A, Part 2, col. E)	C Split Gifts (enter ½ of col. B) (see instructions)	D Subtract col. C from col. B	E Annual Exclusion Claimed	F Subtract col. E from col. D	G Grandchild Exclusion Claimed	H Net Transfer (subtract col. G from col. F)
1							
2							
3							
4							
5							
6							
7							
8							

If you elected gift splitting and your spouse was required to file a separate Form 709 (see the instructions for "Split Gifts"), you must enter all of the gifts shown on Schedule A, Part 2, of your spouse's Form 709 here.

In column C, enter the item number of each gift in the order it appears in column A of your spouse's Schedule A, Part 2. We have preprinted the prefix "S-" to distinguish your spouse's item numbers from your own when you complete column A of Schedule C, Part 4.

In column D, for each gift, enter the amount reported in column C, Schedule C, Part 1, of your spouse's Form 709.

Split gifts from spouse's Form 709 (enter item number)	Value included from spouse's Form 709
S-	
S-	
S-	
S-	
S-	
S-	
S-	
S-	

Total grandchild exclusions claimed on this return. Must equal total of column D, Schedule C, Part 2.

(If more space is needed, attach additional sheets of same size.)

Form 709 (Rev. 12-89) Page 4

SCHEDULE C — Computation of Generation-Skipping Transfer Tax (continued) N/A

Part 2.—Grandchild Exclusion Reconciliation

Name of Grandchild	A Maximum Allowable Exclusion	B Total of Exclusions Claimed on Previous Returns	C Exclusion Available for This Return (subtract col. B from col. A)	D Exclusion Claimed on this Return	E Exclusion Available for Future Returns (subtract col. D from col. C)
	$2,000,000				
	$2,000,000				
	$2,000,000				
	$2,000,000				
	$2,000,000				
	$2,000,000				
	$2,000,000				
	$2,000,000				

Total grandchild exclusions claimed on this return. Must equal total of column G, Part 1

Part 3.—GST Exemption Reconciliation (Code section 2631) and Section 2652(a)(3) Election

Check box ▶ ☐ if you are making a section 2652(a)(3) (special QTIP) election (see instructions)
Enter the item numbers (from Schedule A) of the gifts for which you are making this election ▶ _____

1	Maximum allowable exemption	1	$1,000,000
2	Total exemption used for periods before filing this return	2	
3	Exemption available for this return (subtract line 2 from line 1)	3	
4	Exemption claimed on this return (from Part 4, col. C total, below)	4	
5	Exemption allocated to transfers not shown on Part 4, below. You must attach a Notice of Allocation. (See instructions.)	5	
6	Add lines 4 and 5	6	
7	Exemption available for future transfers (subtract line 6 from line 3)	7	

Part 4.—Tax Computation

A Item No. (from Schedule C, Part 1)	B Net transfer (from Schedule C, Part 1, col. H)	C GST Exemption Allocated	D Divide col. C by col. B	E Inclusion Ratio (subtract col. D from 1.000)	F Maximum Gift Tax Rate	G Applicable Rate (multiply col. E by col. F)	H Generation-Skipping Transfer Tax (multiply col. B by col. G)
1					55% (.55)		
2					55% (.55)		
3					55% (.55)		
4					55% (.55)		
5					55% (.55)		
6					55% (.55)		
7					55% (.55)		
8					55% (.55)		
					55% (.55)		
					55% (.55)		
					55% (.55)		
					55% (.55)		
					55% (.55)		
					55% (.55)		
					55% (.55)		
Total exemption claimed. Enter here and on line 4, Part 3, above. May not exceed line 3, Part 3, above			**Total generation-skipping transfer tax.** Enter here, on line 14 of Schedule A, Part 3, and on line 20 of the Tax Computation on page 1				

(If more space is needed, attach additional sheets of same size.)

B-28 • App. B / Completed Tax Forms

Form **706** (Rev. July 1990) Department of the Treasury Internal Revenue Service	**United States Estate (and Generation-Skipping Transfer) Tax Return** Estate of a citizen or resident of the United States (see separate instructions). To be filed for decedents dying after December 31, 1989, and before January 1, 1993. For Paperwork Reduction Act Notice, see page 1 of the Instructions.	OMB No. 1545-0015 Expires 6-30-93

Part 1.—Decedent and Executor

1a Decedent's first name and middle initial (and maiden name, if any) **Herman**	1b Decedent's last name **Estes**	2 Decedent's social security no. **999 : 11 : 4444**
3a Domicile at time of death (county and state) **Ohio**	3b Year domicile established **1934**	4 Date of birth **1917**	5 Date of death **10-13-90**

6a Name of executor (see instructions) **John Johnson**

6b Executor's address: **10 Main Place, Dayton, Ohio 45347**

6c Executor's social security number: **998 : 12 : 5732**

7a Name and location of court where will was probated or estate administered

7b Case number

8 If decedent died testate, check here ▶ [X] and attach a certified copy of the will.
9 If Form 4768 is attached, check here ▶ ☐
10 If Schedule R-1 is attached, check here ▶ ☐

Part 2.—Tax Computation

1	Total gross estate (from Part 5, Recapitulation, page 3, item 10)	1	1,661,900
2	Total allowable deductions (from Part 5, Recapitulation, page 3, item 20)	2	1,176,700
3	Taxable estate (subtract line 2 from line 1)	3	485,200
4	Adjusted taxable gifts (total taxable gifts (within the meaning of section 2503) made by the decedent after December 31, 1976, other than gifts that are includible in decedent's gross estate (section 2001(b))	4	680,000
5	Add lines 3 and 4	5	1,165,200
6	Tentative tax on the amount on line 5 from Table A in the instructions	6	413,532
7a	If line 5 exceeds $10,000,000, enter the lesser of line 5 or $21,040,000. If line 5 is $10,000,000 or less, skip lines 7a and 7b and enter zero on line 7c	7a	
b	Subtract $10,000,000 from line 7a	7b	
c	Enter 5% (.05) of line 7b	7c	0
8	Total tentative tax (add lines 6 and 7c)	8	413,532
9	Total gift tax payable with respect to gifts made by the decedent after December 31, 1976. Include gift taxes paid by the decedent's spouse for such spouse's share of split gifts (section 2513) only if the decedent was the donor of these gifts and they are includible in the decedent's gross estate (see instructions)	9	39,900
10	Gross estate tax (subtract line 9 from line 8)	10	373,632
11	Unified credit against estate tax from Table B in the instructions	11	192,800
12	Adjustment to unified credit. (This adjustment may not exceed $6,000. See instructions.)	12	
13	Allowable unified credit (subtract line 12 from line 11)	13	192,800
14	Subtract line 13 from line 10 (but do not enter less than zero)	14	180,832
15	Credit for state death taxes. Do not enter more than line 14. Compute credit by using amount on line 3 less $60,000. See Table C in the instructions and **attach credit evidence** (see instructions)	15	9,526
16	Subtract line 15 from line 14	16	171,306
17	Credit for Federal gift taxes on pre-1977 gifts (section 2012)(attach computation)	17	
18	Credit for foreign death taxes (from Schedule(s) P). (Attach Form(s) 706CE)	18	
19	Credit for tax on prior transfers (from Schedule Q)	19	
20	Total (add lines 17, 18, and 19)	20	
21	Net estate tax (subtract line 20 from line 16)	21	171,306
22	Generation-skipping transfer taxes (from Schedule R, Part 2, line 10)	22	
23	Section 4980A increased estate tax (from Schedule S, Part I, line 17) (see instructions)	23	
24	Total transfer taxes (add lines 21, 22, and 23)	24	171,306
25	Prior payments. Explain in an attached statement	25	
26	United States Treasury bonds redeemed in payment of estate tax	26	
27	Total (add lines 25 and 26)	27	
28	Balance due (or overpayment) (subtract line 27 from line 24)	28	171,306

Under penalties of perjury, I declare that I have examined this return, including accompanying schedules and statements, and to the best of my knowledge and belief, it is true, correct, and complete. Declaration of preparer other than the executor is based on all information of which preparer has any knowledge.

Signature(s) of executor(s): **John Johnson**   Date: **2-14-91**

Signature of preparer other than executor: **Mary Mason**   Address (and ZIP code): **100 Tower Avenue, Austin, Texas 78703**   Date: **2-14-91**

Note: Instruction pages omitted: 5, 9, 13, 15, 17, 21, 32.

Form 706 (Rev. 7-90)

Estate of: Herman Estes

Part 3.—Elections by the Executor

Please check the "Yes" or "No" box for each question.	Yes	No
1 Do you elect alternate valuation?		X
2 Do you elect special use valuation? If "Yes," you must complete and attach Schedule A–1		X
3 Do you elect to pay the taxes in installments as described in section 6166? If "Yes," you must attach the additional information described in the instructions.		X
4 Do you elect to postpone the part of the taxes attributable to a reversionary or remainder interest as described in section 6163?		X

Part 4.—General Information (Note: Please attach the necessary supplemental documents. You must attach the death certificate.)

Authorization to receive confidential tax information under Regulations section 601.502(c)(3)(ii), to act as the estate's representative before the Internal Revenue Service, and to make written or oral presentations on behalf of the estate if return prepared by an attorney, accountant, or enrolled agent for the executor:

Name of representative (print or type)	State	Address (number, street, and room or suite no., city, state, and ZIP code)
John Johnson	Ohio	10 Main Place, Dayton, Ohio 45347

I declare that I am the ☐ attorney ☐ accountant ☐ enrolled agent (you must check the applicable box) for the executor and prepared this return for the executor. I am not under suspension or disbarment from practice before the Internal Revenue Service and am qualified to practice in the state shown above.

Signature	CAF number	Date	Telephone number
	111-2222	2-14-90	512-444-4444

1 Death certificate number and issuing authority (attach a copy of the death certificate to this return).
   1246, County Coroner

2 Decedent's business or occupation. If retired, check here ▶ ☒ and state decedent's former business or occupation.
   Executive

3 Marital status of the decedent at time of death:
   ☒ Married
   ☐ Widow or widower—Name, SSN and date of death of deceased spouse ▶
   ☐ Single
   ☐ Legally separated
   ☐ Divorced—Date divorce decree became final ▶

4a Surviving spouse's name	4b Social security number	4c Amount received (see instructions)
Ann Estes	555 77 9999	1,050,0000

5 Individuals (other than the surviving spouse), trusts, or other estates who receive benefits from the estate (do not include charitable beneficiaries shown in Schedule O) (see instructions). For Privacy Act Notice (applicable to individual beneficiaries only), see the Instructions for Form 1040.

Name of individual, trust, or estate receiving $5,000 or more	Identifying number	Relationship to decedent	Amount (see instructions)
Johnny Estes	555-61-4107	Son	342,600*
Billy Estes	556-63-4437	Son	142,600

* The daughter, Dorothy Estes, receives the trust corpus of trust set up by Amelia Estes.

All unascertainable beneficiaries and those who receive less than $5,000 ▶

Total 485,200

(Continued on next page)

Form 706 (Rev. 7-90)

Part 4.—General Information (continued)

		Yes	No
	Please check the "Yes" or "No" box for each question.		
6	Does the gross estate contain any section 2044 property (qualified terminable interest property (QTIP) from a prior gift or estate)(see instructions)?		X
7a	Have Federal gift tax returns ever been filed?	X	
	If "Yes," please attach copies of the returns, if available, and furnish the following information:		
7b	Period(s) covered 1974, 1978, 1988 7c Internal Revenue office(s) where filed Cincinnati, Ohio		
	If you answer "Yes" to any of questions 8–16, you must attach additional information as described in the instructions.		
8a	Was there any insurance on the decedent's life that is not included on the return as part of the gross estate?		X
b	Did the decedent own any insurance on the life of another that is not included in the gross estate?		X
9	Did the decedent at the time of death own any property as a joint tenant with right of survivorship in which (1) one or more of the other joint tenants was someone other than the decedent's spouse, and (2) less than the full value of the property is included on the return as part of the gross estate? If "Yes," you must complete and attach Schedule E		X
10	Did the decedent, at the time of death, own any interest in a partnership or unincorporated business or any stock in an inactive or closely held corporation?		X
11a	Did the decedent make any transfer described in section 2035, 2036, 2037, or 2038 (see the instructions for Schedule G)? If "Yes," you must complete and attach Schedule G	X	
b	If "Yes," was it a valuation freeze subject to section 2036(c)?		X
12	Were there in existence at the time of the decedent's death:		
a	Any trusts created by the decedent during his or her lifetime?		X
b	Any trusts not created by the decedent under which the decedent possessed any power, beneficial interest, or trusteeship?	X	
13	Did the decedent ever possess, exercise, or release any general power of appointment? If "Yes," you must complete and attach Schedule H.		X
14	Was the marital deduction computed under the transitional rule of Public Law 97-34, section 403(e)(3) (Economic Recovery Tax Act of 1981)?		X
	If "Yes," attach a separate computation of the marital deduction, enter the amount on item 18 of the Recapitulation, and note on item 18 "computation attached."		
15	Was the decedent, immediately before death, receiving an annuity described in the "General" paragraph of the instructions for Schedule I? If "Yes," you must complete and attach Schedule I.	X	
16	Did the decedent have a total "excess retirement accumulation" (as defined in section 4980A(d)) in qualified employer plans and individual retirement plans? If "Yes," you must complete and attach Schedule S.		X

Part 5.—Recapitulation

Item number	Gross estate	Alternate value	Value at date of death
1	Schedule A—Real Estate		325,000
2	Schedule B—Stocks and Bonds		600,000
3	Schedule C—Mortgages, Notes, and Cash		85,000
4	Schedule D—Insurance on the Decedent's Life (attach Form(s) 712)		200,000
5	Schedule E—Jointly Owned Property (attach Form(s) 712 for life insurance)		200,000
6	Schedule F—Other Miscellaneous Property (attach Form(s) 712 for life insurance)		
7	Schedule G—Transfers During Decedent's Life (attach Form(s) 712 for life insurance)		11,900
8	Schedule H—Powers of Appointment		
9	Schedule I—Annuities		240,000
10	Total gross estate (add items 1 through 9). Enter here and on line 1 of the Tax Computation.		1,661,900

Item number	Deductions	Amount
11	Schedule J—Funeral Expenses and Expenses Incurred in Administering Property Subject to Claims	85,000
12	Schedule K—Debts of the Decedent	31,700
13	Schedule K—Mortgages and Liens	
14	Total of items 11 through 13	116,700
15	Allowable amount of deductions from item 14 (see the instructions for item 15 of the Recapitulation)	116,700
16	Schedule L—Net Losses During Administration	
17	Schedule L—Expenses Incurred in Administering Property Not Subject to Claims	
18	Schedule M—Bequests, etc., to Surviving Spouse	1,050,000
19	Schedule O—Charitable, Public, and Similar Gifts and Bequests	10,000
20	Total allowable deductions (add items 15 through 19). Enter here and on line 2 of the Tax Computation.	1,176,700

Form 706 (Rev. 7-90)

Estate of: Herman Estes

SCHEDULE A—Real Estate

(For jointly owned property that must be disclosed on Schedule E, see the Instructions for Schedule E.)

(Real estate that is part of a sole proprietorship should be shown on Schedule F. Real estate that is included in the gross estate under section 2035, 2036, 2037, or 2038 should be shown on Schedule G. Real estate that is included in the gross estate under section 2041 should be shown on Schedule H.)

(If you elect section 2032A valuation, you must complete Schedule A and Schedule A-1.)

Item number	Description	Alternate valuation date	Alternate value	Value at date of death
1	Personal residence, house and lot located at 105 Elm Court, Dayton, Ohio			325,000
	Total from continuation schedule(s) (or additional sheet(s)) attached to this schedule			
	TOTAL. (Also enter on Part 5, Recapitulation, page 3, at item 1.)			325,000

(If more space is needed, attach the continuation schedule from the end of this package or additional sheets of the same size.)

Schedule A—Page 4

Form 706 (Rev. 7-90)

Estate of:	**Decedent's Social Security Number**

SCHEDULE A-1—Section 2032A Valuation

Part 1.—Type of Election:

☐ **Protective election (Regulations section 20.2032A-8(b)).**—Complete Part 2, line 1, and column A of lines 3 and 4. (See instructions.)

☐ **Regular election.**—Complete all of Part 2 (including line 11, if applicable) and Part 3. (See instructions.)

Part 2.—Notice of Election (Regulations section 20.2032A-8(a)(3))

Note: *All real property entered on lines 2 and 3 must also be entered on Schedules A, E, F, G, or H, as applicable.*

1 Qualified use—check one ▶ ☐ Farm used for farming, *or*
▶ ☐ Trade or business other than farming

2 Real property used in a qualified use, passing to qualified heirs, and to be specially valued on this Form 706.

A Schedule and item number from Form 706	B Full value (without section 2032A(b)(3)(B) adjustment)	C Adjusted value (with section 2032A(b)(3)(B) adjustment)	D Value based on qualified use (without section 2032A(b)(3)(B) adjustment)

Totals . . . .

Attach a legal description of all property listed on line 2.
Attach copies of appraisals showing the column B values for all property listed on line 2.

3 Real property used in a qualified use, passing to qualified heirs, but not specially valued on this Form 706.

A Schedule and item number from Form 706	B Full value (without section 2032A(b)(3)(B) adjustment)	C Adjusted value (with section 2032A(b)(3)(B) adjustment)	D Value based on qualified use (without section 2032A(b)(3)(B) adjustment)

Totals . . . .

If you checked "Regular election," you must attach copies of appraisals showing the column B values for all property listed on line 3.

(Continued on next page)

Schedule A-1—Page 6

Form 706 (Rev. 7-90)

4 Personal property used in a qualified use and passing to qualified heirs.

A Schedule and item number from Form 706	B Adjusted value (with section 2032A(b)(3)(B) adjustment)	A (continued) Schedule and item number from Form 706	B (continued) Adjusted value (with section 2032A(b)(3)(B) adjustment)
		"Subtotal" from Col. B, below left	....

Subtotal . . . . _____   **Total adjusted value** . . . . _____

5 Enter the value of the total gross estate as adjusted under section 2032A(b)(3)(A). ▶ _____

6 Attach a description of the method used to determine the special value based on qualified use.

7 Did the decedent and/or a member of his or her family own all property listed on line 2 for at least 5 of the 8 years immediately preceding the date of the decedent's death? . . . . ☐ Yes ☐ No

8 Were there any periods during the 8-year period preceding the date of the decedent's death during which the decedent or a member of his or her family:

	Yes	No
a Did not own the property listed on line 2 above?		
b Did not use the property listed on line 2 above in a qualified use?		
c Did not materially participate in the operation of the farm or other business within the meaning of section 2032A(e)(6)?		

If "Yes" to any of the above, you must attach a statement listing the periods. If applicable, describe whether the exceptions of sections 2032A(b)(4) or (5) are met.

9 Attach affidavits describing the activities constituting material participation and the identity and relationship to the decedent of the material participants.

10 Persons holding interests. Enter the requested information for each party who received any interest in the specially valued property.

	Name	Address
A		
B		
C		
D		
E		
F		
G		
H		

	Identifying number	Relationship to decedent	Fair market value	Special use value
A				
B				
C				
D				
E				
F				
G				
H				

You must attach a computation of the GST tax savings attributable to direct skips for each person listed above who is a skip person. (See Instructions.)

11 Woodlands election.—Check here ▶ ☐ if you wish to make a woodlands election as described in section 2032A(e)(13). Enter the Schedule and item numbers from Form 706 of the property for which you are making this election ▶ ....

You must attach a statement explaining why you are entitled to make this election. The IRS may issue regulations that require more information to substantiate this election. You will be notified by IRS if you must supply further information.

Schedule A-1—Page 7

Form 706 (Rev. 7-90)

Part 3.—Agreement to Special Valuation Under Section 2032A

Estate of: _____ | **Date of Death** _____ | **Decedent's Social Security Number** _____

We (list all qualified heirs and other persons having an interest in the property required to sign this agreement)
_____
_____,

being all the qualified heirs and _____
_____,

being all other parties having interests in the property which is qualified real property and which is valued under section 2032A of the Internal Revenue Code, do hereby approve of the election made by _____,
Executor/Administrator of the estate of _____,
pursuant to section 2032A to value said property on the basis of the qualified use to which the property is devoted and do hereby enter into this agreement pursuant to section 2032A(d).

The undersigned agree and consent to the application of subsection (c) of section 2032A of the Code with respect to all the property described on line 2 of Part 2 of Schedule A-1 of Form 706, attached to this agreement. More specifically, the undersigned heirs expressly agree and consent to personal liability under subsection (c) of 2032A for the additional estate and GST taxes imposed by that subsection with respect to their respective interests in the above-described property in the event of certain early dispositions of the property or early cessation of the qualified use of the property. It is understood that if a qualified heir disposes of any interest in qualified real property to any member of his or her family, such member may thereafter be treated as the qualified heir with respect to such interest upon filing a Form 706-A and a new agreement.

The undersigned interested parties who are not qualified heirs consent to the collection of any additional estate and GST taxes imposed under section 2032A(c) of the Code from the specially valued property.

If there is a disposition of any interest which passes or has passed to him or her or if there is a cessation of the qualified use of any specially valued property which passes or passed to him or her, each of the undersigned heirs agrees to file a **Form 706-A,** United States Additional Estate Tax Return, and pay any additional estate and GST taxes due within 6 months of the disposition or cessation.

It is understood by all interested parties that this agreement is a condition precedent to the election of special use valuation under section 2032A of the Code and must be executed by every interested party even though that person may not have received the estate (or GST) tax benefits or be in possession of such property.

Each of the undersigned understands that by making this election, a lien will be created and recorded pursuant to section 6324B of the Code on the property referred to in this agreement for the adjusted tax differences with respect to the estate as defined in section 2032A(c)(2)(C).

As the interested parties, the undersigned designate the following individual as their agent for all dealings with the Internal Revenue Service concerning the continued qualification of the specially valued property under section 2032A of the Code and on all issues regarding the special lien under section 6324B. The agent is authorized to act for the parties with respect to all dealings with the Service on matters affecting the qualified real property described earlier. This authority includes the following:

- To receive confidential information on all matters relating to continued qualification under section 2032A of the specially valued real property and on all matters relating to the special lien arising under section 6324B.
- To furnish the Service with any requested information concerning the property.
- To notify the Service of any disposition or cessation of qualified use of any part of the property.
- To receive, but not to endorse and collect, checks in payment of any refund of Internal Revenue taxes, penalties, or interest.
- To execute waivers (including offers of waivers) of restrictions on assessment or collection of deficiencies in tax and waivers of notice of disallowance of a claim for credit or refund.
- To execute closing agreements under section 7121.
- Other acts (specify) ▶ _____

By signing this agreement, the agent agrees to provide the Service with any requested information concerning this property and to notify the Service of any disposition or cessation of the qualified use of any part of this property.

Name of Agent	Signature	Address

The property to which this agreement relates is listed in Form 706, United States Estate (and Generation-Skipping Transfer) Tax Return, and in the Notice of Election, along with its fair market value according to section 2031 of the Code and its special use value according to section 2032A. The name, address, social security number, and interest (including the value) of each of the undersigned in this property are as set forth in the attached Notice of Election.

IN WITNESS WHEREOF, the undersigned have hereunto set their hands at _____,
this _____ day of _____.

Qualified Heirs _____

Other Interested Parties

Schedule A-1—Page 8

Form 706 (Rev. 7-90)

Estate of: Herman Estes

SCHEDULE B—Stocks and Bonds

(For jointly owned property that must be disclosed on Schedule E, see the Instructions for Schedule E.)

Item number	Description including face amount of bonds or number of shares and par value where needed for identification. Give CUSIP number if available.	Unit value	Alternate valuation date	Alternate value	Value at date of death
1	Stock in A corporation, 1000 shares, $10 par value	600.			600,000
	Total from continuation schedule(s) (or additional sheet(s)) attached to this schedule . . .				
	TOTAL. (Also enter on Part 5, Recapitulation, page 3, at item 2.)				600,000

(If more space is needed, attach the continuation schedule from the end of this package or additional sheets of the same size.)
(The instructions to Schedule B are in the separate instructions.)

Form 706 (Rev. 7-90)

Estate of: Herman Estes

SCHEDULE C—Mortgages, Notes, and Cash
(For jointly owned property that must be disclosed on Schedule E, see the Instructions for Schedule E.)

Item number	Description	Alternate valuation date	Alternate value	Value at date of death
1	Checking account			10,000
2	Savings account (includes accrued interest through date of death)			75,000
	Total from continuation schedule(s) (or additional sheet(s)) attached to this schedule . . .			
	TOTAL. (Also enter on Part 5, Recapitulation, page 3, at item 3.)			85,000

(If more space is needed, attach the continuation schedule from the end of this package or additional sheets of the same size.)

Schedule C—Page 11

Form 706 (Rev. 7-90)

Estate of: Herman Estes

SCHEDULE D—Insurance on the Decedent's Life
You must attach a Form 712 for each policy.

Item number	Description	Alternate valuation date	Alternate value	Value at date of death
1	Life insurance policy 123-A, Life Insurance Company of Ohio. Beneficiary: Johnny Estes			200,000
	Total from continuation schedule(s) (or additional sheet(s)) attached to this schedule . . .			
	TOTAL. (Also enter on Part 5, Recapitulation, page 3, at item 4.)			200,000

(If more space is needed, attach the continuation schedule from the end of this package or additional sheets of the same size.)

Schedule D—Page 12

Form 706 (Rev. 7-90)

Estate of: Herman Estes

SCHEDULE E—Jointly Owned Property
(If you elect section 2032A valuation, you must complete Schedule E and Schedule A-1.)

PART 1.— Qualified Joint Interests—Interests Held by the Decedent and His or Her Spouse as the Only Joint Tenants (Section 2040(b)(2))

Item number	Description For securities, give CUSIP number, if available.	Alternate valuation date	Alternate value	Value at date of death
1.	Land			400,000

	Total from continuation schedule(s) (or additional sheet(s)) attached to this schedule			
1a	Totals 1a			400,000
1b	Amounts included in gross estate (one-half of line 1a) 1b			200,000

PART 2.—All Other Joint Interests

2a State the name and address of each surviving co-tenant. If there are more than three surviving co-tenants, list the additional co-tenants on an attached sheet.

	Name	Address (number and street, city, state, and ZIP code)
A.		
B.		
C.		

Item number	Enter letter for co-tenant	Description (including alternate valuation date if any) For securities, give CUSIP number, if available.	Percentage includible	Includible alternate value	Includible value at date of death

	Total from continuation schedule(s) (or additional sheet(s)) attached to this schedule			
2b	Total other joint interests 2b			

3 Total includible joint interests (add lines 1b and 2b). Also enter on Part 5, Recapitulation, page 3, at item 5

(If more space is needed, attach the continuation schedule from the end of this package or additional sheets of the same size.)

Form 706 (Rev. 7-90)

Estate of: *Herman Estes*

SCHEDULE F—Other Miscellaneous Property Not Reportable Under Any Other Schedule
(For jointly owned property that must be disclosed on Schedule E, see the Instructions for Schedule E.)
(If you elect section 2032A valuation, you must complete Schedule F and Schedule A-1.)

		Yes	No
1	Did the decedent at the time of death own any articles of artistic or collectible value in excess of $3,000 or any collections whose artistic or collectible value combined at date of death exceeded $10,000? . . . . If "Yes," full details must be submitted on this schedule.		X
2	Has the decedent's estate, spouse, or any other person, received (or will receive) any bonus or award as a result of the decedent's employment or death? . . . . If "Yes," full details must be submitted on this schedule.		X
3	Did the decedent at the time of death have, or have access to, a safe deposit box? . . . . If "Yes," state location, and if held in joint names of decedent and another, state name and relationship of joint depositor.		X

If any of the contents of the safe deposit box are omitted from the schedules in this return, explain fully why omitted.

Item number	Description For securities, give CUSIP number, if available.	Alternate valuation date	Alternate value	Value at date of death
1				
	Total from continuation schedule(s) (or additional sheet(s)) attached to this schedule . . .			
	TOTAL. (Also enter on Part 5, Recapitulation, page 3, at item 6.)			

(If more space is needed, attach the continuation schedule from the end of this package or additional sheets of the same size.)

Schedule F—Page 16

Form 706 (Rev. 7-90)

Estate of: *Herman Estes*

SCHEDULE G—Transfers During Decedent's Life
(If you elect section 2032A valuation, you must complete Schedule G and Schedule A-1.)

Item number	Description For securities, give CUSIP number, if available.	Alternate valuation date	Alternate value	Value at date of death
A.	Gift tax paid by the decedent or the estate for all gifts made by the decedent or his or her spouse within 3 years before the decedent's death (section 2035(c))	X X X X X		11,900
B.	Transfers includible under section 2035(a), 2036, 2037, or 2038:			
1				
	Total from continuation schedule(s) (or additional sheet(s)) attached to this schedule			
	TOTAL. (Also enter on Part 5, Recapitulation, page 3, at item 7.)			11,900

SCHEDULE H—Powers of Appointment
(If you elect section 2032A valuation, you must complete Schedule H and Schedule A-1.)

Item number	Description	Alternate valuation date	Alternate value	Value at date of death
1				
	Total from continuation schedule(s) (or additional sheet(s)) attached to this schedule			
	TOTAL. (Also enter on Part 5, Recapitulation, page 3, at item 8.)			

(If more space is needed, attach the continuation schedule from the end of this package or additional sheets of the same size.)
(The instructions to Schedules G and H are in the separate instructions.)

Form 706 (Rev. 7-90)

Estate of: Herman Estes

SCHEDULE I—Annuities

Note: *Generally, no exclusion is allowed for the estates of decedents dying after December 31, 1984 (see instructions).*

A Are you excluding from the decedent's gross estate the value of a lump-sum distribution described in section 2039(f)(2)? If "Yes," you must attach the information required by the instructions.

			Yes	No
				X

Item number	Description Show the entire value of the annuity before any exclusions.	Alternate valuation date	Includible alternate value	Includible value at date of death
1	Qualified pension plan, Buckeye Corporation Beneficiary - Ann Estes, spouse			240,000
	Total from continuation schedule(s) (or additional sheet(s)) attached to this schedule . .			
	TOTAL. (Also enter on Part 5, Recapitulation, page 3, at item 9.)			240,000

(If more space is needed, attach the continuation schedule from the end of this package or additional sheets of the same size.)
(The instructions to Schedule I are in the separate instructions.)

Form 706 (Rev. 7-90)

Estate of: Herman Estes

SCHEDULE J—Funeral Expenses and Expenses Incurred in Administering Property Subject to Claims

Note: *Do not list on this schedule expenses of administering property not subject to claims. For those expenses, see the Instructions for Schedule L.*

If executors' commissions, attorney fees, etc., are claimed and allowed as a deduction for estate tax purposes, they are not allowable as a deduction in computing the taxable income of the estate for Federal income tax purposes. They are allowable as an income tax deduction on Form 1041 if a waiver is filed to waive the deduction on Form 706 (see the Form 1041 instructions).

Item number	Description	Expense amount	Total Amount
1	A. Funeral expenses:	15,000	
	Total funeral expenses		15,000
	B. Administration expenses:		
1	Executors' commissions—amount estimated/agreed upon/paid. (Strike out the words that do not apply.)		
2	Attorney fees—amount estimated/agreed upon/paid. (Strike out the words that do not apply.)		70,000
3	Accountant fees—amount estimated/agreed upon/paid. (Strike out the words that do not apply.)		
4	Miscellaneous expenses:	Expense amount	
	Total miscellaneous expenses from continuation schedule(s) (or additional sheet(s)) attached to this schedule		
	Total miscellaneous expenses		
	TOTAL. (Also enter on Part 5, Recapitulation, page 3, at item 11.)		85,000

(If more space is needed, attach the continuation schedule from the end of this package or additional sheets of the same size.)

Form 706 (Rev. 7-90)

Estate of: Herman Estes

SCHEDULE K—Debts of the Decedent, and Mortgages and Liens

Item number	Debts of the Decedent—Creditor and nature of claim, and allowable death taxes	Amount unpaid to date	Amount in contest	Amount claimed as a deduction
1	Bank loan (including accrued interest through DOD)	25,200		25,200
2	American Express, Visa and Master Card	6,500		6,500

Total from continuation schedule(s) (or additional sheet(s)) attached to this schedule . . . .

TOTAL. (Also enter on Part 5, Recapitulation, page 3, at item 12.) **31,700**

Item number	Mortgages and Liens—Description	Amount
1		

Total from continuation schedule(s) (or additional sheet(s)) attached to this schedule . . . .

TOTAL. (Also enter on Part 5, Recapitulation, page 3, at item 13.) . . . .

(If more space is needed, attach the continuation schedule from the end of this package or additional sheets of the same size.)
(The instructions to Schedule K are in the separate instructions.)

Schedule K —Page 22

Form 706 (Rev. 7-90)

Estate of:

SCHEDULE L—Net Losses During Administration and Expenses Incurred in Administering Property Not Subject to Claims

Item number	Net losses during administration (**Note:** *Do not deduct losses claimed on a Federal income tax return.*)	Amount
1		
	Total from continuation schedule(s) (or additional sheet(s)) attached to this schedule	
	TOTAL. (Also enter on Part 5, Recapitulation, page 3, at item 16.)	

Item number	Expenses incurred in administering property not subject to claims (Indicate whether estimated, agreed upon, or paid.)	Amount
1		
	Total from continuation schedule(s) (or additional sheet(s)) attached to this schedule	
	TOTAL. (Also enter on Part 5, Recapitulation, page 3, at item 17.)	

(If more space is needed, attach the continuation schedule from the end of this package or additional sheets of the same size.)
(The instructions to Schedule L are in the separate instructions.)

Schedule L —Page 23

Form 706 (Rev. 7-90)

Estate of: Herman Estes

SCHEDULE M—Bequests, etc., to Surviving Spouse

Terminable Interest (QTIP) Marital Deduction.—If you elect to claim a marital deduction for qualified terminable interest property (QTIP) under section 2056(b)(7), you MUST list on Part 2 of Schedule M all of the property for which you are making the election. Listing property on Part 2 constitutes the making of the QTIP election. No marital deduction will be allowed for any terminable interest property that is listed on Part 1 of Schedule M.

		Yes	No
1	Did any property pass to the surviving spouse as a result of a qualified disclaimer? If "Yes," attach a copy of the written disclaimer required by section 2518(b).		X
2	Is the surviving spouse a U.S. citizen?	X	
3	**Qualified Domestic Trust.**—Do you elect under section 2056A(d) to treat any trusts reported on Schedule M as qualified domestic trusts? (see instructions)		X
4	**Election out of QTIP Treatment of Annuities.**—Do you elect under section 2056(b)(7)(C)(ii) to not treat as qualified terminable interest property any joint and survivor annuities that are included in the gross estate and would otherwise be treated as qualified terminable interest property under section 2056(b)(7)(C)? (see instructions)		X

Part 1.—Property Interests Which Are Not Subject to a QTIP Election

(**Note:** A marital deduction will NOT be allowed for any terminable interest property (QTIP) that is listed on Part 1 of Schedule M.)

Item number	Description of property interests passing to surviving spouse	Value
1	Residence	325,000
2.	Checking Account	10,000
3.	Savings Account	75,000
4.	Land, held in joint tenancy	200,000
5.	Qualified pension plan	240,000

Total from continuation schedule(s) (or additional sheet(s)) attached to this schedule . . . .

Total value of property interests not subject to a QTIP election (enter here and on line 1 of Part 3 on the next page) **850,000**

(If more space is needed, attach the continuation schedule from the end of this package or additional sheets of the same size.)
(The instructions to Schedule M are in the separate instructions.)

Schedule M—Page 24

Form 706 (Rev. 7-90)

Part 2.—Property Interests Which Are Subject to a QTIP Election
(**Note:** *Listing terminable interest property on Part 2 of Schedule M constitutes the making of a QTIP election for that property under section 2056(b)(7). A marital deduction will not be allowed for any terminable interest property that is not listed on Part 2. If you use a continuation page for Part 2, be sure that it is clearly labeled as Schedule M, Part 2.*)

Item number	Description of property interests passing to surviving spouse (Describe portion of trust for which allocation is made.)	Value
1	Trust with First Bank as Trustee	200,000

Total from continuation schedule(s) (or additional sheet(s)) attached to this schedule . . . .

A. Total value of property interests subject to a QTIP election . . . . **A** 200,000

Part 3.—Reconciliation

1 Enter the total from part 1 . . . . **1** 850,000

2 Total interests passing to surviving spouse (add lines A and 1, above) **2** 1,050,000

3a Federal estate taxes (including section 4980A taxes) payable out of property interests listed on Parts 1 and 2 **3a**
 b Other death taxes payable out of property interests listed on Parts 1 and 2 . . . . **3b**
 c Federal and state GST taxes payable out of property interests listed on Parts 1 and 2 . . . . . **3c**
 d Add items a, b, and c . . . . **3d** —0—

4 Net value of property interests listed on Schedule M (subtract 3d from 2). Also enter on Part 5, Recapitulation, page 3, at item 18 **4** 1,050,000

(If more space is needed, attach the continuation schedule from the end of this package or additional sheets of the same size.)

Schedule M—Page 25

Form 706 (Rev. 7-90)

Estate of:

SCHEDULE O—Charitable, Public, and Similar Gifts and Bequests

			Yes	No
1a	If the transfer was made by will, has any action been instituted to have interpreted or to contest the will or any of its provisions affecting the charitable deductions claimed in this schedule? . . . . If "Yes," full details must be submitted with this schedule.			
b	According to the information and belief of the person or persons filing the return, is any such action planned? . . . . If "Yes," full details must be submitted with this schedule.			
2	Did any property pass to charity as the result of a qualified disclaimer? . . . . If "Yes," attach a copy of the written disclaimer required by section 2518(b).			

Item number	Name and address of beneficiary	Character of institution	Amount
1	American Cancer Society	Charity	10,000

Total from continuation schedule(s) (or additional sheet(s)) attached to this schedule. . . . .

3	Total	3	10,000
4a	Federal estate tax (including section 4980A taxes) payable out of property interests listed above 4a		
b	Other death taxes payable out of property interests listed above 4b		
c	Federal and state GST taxes payable out of property interests listed above 4c		
d	Add items a, b, and c	4d	
5	Net value of property interests listed above (subtract 4d from 3). Also enter on Part 5, Recapitulation, page 3, at item 19	5	10,000

(If more space is needed, attach the continuation schedule from the end of this package or additional sheets of the same size.)
(The instructions to Schedule O are in the separate instructions.)

Form 706 (Rev. 7-90)

Estate of:

SCHEDULE P—Credit for Foreign Death Taxes

List all foreign countries to which death taxes have been paid and for which a credit is claimed on this return.

If a credit is claimed for death taxes paid to more than one foreign country, compute the credit for taxes paid to one country on this sheet and attach a separate copy of Schedule P for each of the other countries.

The credit computed on this sheet is for the _____
(Name of death tax or taxes)

_____ imposed in _____
(Name of country)

Credit is computed under the _____
(Insert title of treaty or "statute")

Citizenship (nationality) of decedent at time of death

(All amounts and values must be entered in United States money)

1. Total of estate, inheritance, legacy, and succession taxes imposed in the country named above attributable to property situated in that country, subjected to these taxes, and included in the gross estate (as defined by statute) . . . .

2. Value of the gross estate (adjusted, if necessary, according to the instructions for item 2) . . . .

3. Value of property situated in that country, subjected to death taxes imposed in that country, and included in the gross estate (adjusted, if necessary, according to the instructions for item 3) . . . .

4. Tax imposed by section 2001 reduced by the total credits claimed under sections 2010, 2011, and 2012 (see instructions)

5. Amount of Federal estate tax attributable to property specified at item 3. (Divide item 3 by item 2 and multiply the result by item 4.)

6. Credit for death taxes imposed in the country named above (the smaller of item 1 or item 5). Also enter on line 18 of Part 2, Tax Computation . . . .

SCHEDULE Q—Credit for Tax on Prior Transfers

Part 1.—Transferor Information

	Name of transferor	Social security number	IRS office where estate tax return was filed	Date of death
A				
B				
C				

Check here ▶ ☐ if section 2013(f) (special valuation of farm, etc., real property) adjustments to the computation of the credit were made (see instructions).

Part 2.—Computation of Credit (see instructions)

Item	Transferor A	Transferor B	Transferor C	Total A, B, & C
1 Transferee's tax as apportioned (from worksheet, (line 7 + line 8) × line 35 for each column) . . .				
2 Transferor's tax (from each column of worksheet, line 20)				
3 Maximum amount before percentage requirement (for each column, enter amount from line 1 or 2, whichever is smaller)				
4 Percentage allowed (each column) (see instructions)	%	%	%	
5 Credit allowable (line 3 × line 4 for each column)				
6 TOTAL credit allowable (add columns A, B, and C of line 5). Enter here and on line 19 of Part 2, Tax Computation				

(The instructions to Schedules P and Q are in the separate instructions.)

Schedules P and Q—Page 27

Form 706 (Rev. 7-90)

Schedule R.—Generation-Skipping Transfer Tax

Note: *To avoid application of the deemed allocation rules, Form 706 and Schedule R should be filed to allocate the GST exemption to trusts which may later have taxable terminations or distributions under section 2612 even if the form is not required to be filed to report estate or GST tax.*

Part 1.— GST Exemption Reconciliation (Section 2631) and Section 2652(a)(3) (Special QTIP) Election

Check box ▶ ☐ if you are making a section 2652(a)(3) (special QTIP) election (see instructions)

1	Maximum allowable GST exemption	$1,000,000
2	Total GST exemption allocated by the decedent against decedent's lifetime transfers	
3	Total GST exemption allocated by the executor, using Form 709, against decedent's lifetime transfers	
4	GST exemption allocated on line 6 of Schedule R, Part 2	
5	GST exemption allocated on line 6 of Schedule R, Part 3	
6	Total GST exemption allocated on line 4 of Schedule(s) R-1	
7	Total GST exemption allocated to intervivos transfers and direct skips (add lines 2–6)	
8	GST exemption available to allocate to trusts and section 2032A interests (subtract line 7 from line 1)	

9 Allocation of GST exemption to trusts (as defined for GST tax purposes):

A Name of trust	B Trust's EIN (if any)	C GST exemption allocated on lines 2–6, above (see instructions)	D Additional GST exemption allocated (see instructions)	E Trust's inclusion ratio (optional—see instructions)

9D	Total. May not exceed line 8, above	
10	GST exemption available to allocate to section 2032A interests received by individual beneficiaries (subtract line 9D from line 8). You must attach special use allocation schedule (see instructions)	

(The instructions to Schedule R are in the separate instructions.)

Schedule R—Page 28

Form 706 (Rev. 7-90)

Estate of:

Part 2.—Direct Skips Where the Property Interests Transferred Bear the GST Tax on the Direct Skips

Name of skip person	Description of property interest transferred	Estate tax value

1 Total estate tax values of all property interests listed above	1	
2 Estate taxes, state death taxes, and other charges borne by the property interests listed above	2	
3 GST taxes borne by the property interests listed above but imposed on direct skips other than those shown on this Part 2. (See instructions.)	3	
4 Total fixed taxes and other charges. (Add lines 2 and 3.)	4	
5 Total tentative maximum direct skips. (Subtract line 4 from line 1.)	5	
6 GST exemption allocated	6	
7 Subtract line 6 from line 5	7	
8 GST tax due (divide line 7 by 2.818182)	8	
9 Enter the amount from line 8 of Schedule R, Part 3	9	
10 **Total GST taxes payable by the estate.** (Add lines 8 and 9.) Enter here and on line 22 of the Tax Computation on page 1	10	

Schedule R—Page 29

Form 706 (Rev. 7-90)

Estate of:

Part 3.—Direct Skips Where the Property Interests Transferred Do Not Bear the GST Tax on the Direct Skips

Name of skip person	Description of property interest transferred	Estate tax value

1 Total estate tax values of all property interests listed above	1	
2 Estate taxes, state death taxes, and other charges borne by the property interests listed above	2	
3 GST taxes borne by the property interests listed above but imposed on direct skips other than those shown on this Part 3. (See instructions.)	3	
4 Total fixed taxes and other charges. (Add lines 2 and 3.)	4	
5 Total tentative maximum direct skips. (Subtract line 4 from line 1.)	5	
6 GST exemption allocated	6	
7 Subtract line 6 from line 5	7	
8 GST tax due (multiply line 7 by .55). Enter here and on Schedule R, Part 2, line 9	8	

Schedule R—Page 30

SCHEDULE R-1 (Form 706)
(July 1990)
Department of the Treasury
Internal Revenue Service

Generation-Skipping Transfer Tax
Direct Skips From a Trust
Payment Voucher

OMB No. 1545-0015
Expires 6-30-93

Executor: File one copy with Form 706 and send two copies to the fiduciary. Do not pay the tax shown. See the separate instructions.
Fiduciary: See instructions on following page. Pay the tax shown on line 6.

Name of trust	Trust's EIN
Name and title of fiduciary	Name of decedent
Address of fiduciary (number and street)	Decedent's SSN	Service Center where Form 706 was filed
City, state, and ZIP code	Name of executor
Address of executor (number and street)	City, state, and ZIP code
Date of decedent's death	Filing due date of Schedule R, Form 706 (with extensions)

Part 1.—Computation of the GST Tax on the Direct Skip

Description of property interests subject to the direct skip	Estate tax value

1	Total estate tax value of all property interests listed above.	1
2	Estate taxes, state death taxes, and other charges borne by the property interests listed above	2
3	Tentative maximum direct skip from trust. (Subtract line 2 from line 1.)	3
4	GST exemption allocated	4
5	Subtract line 4 from line 3.	5
6	**GST tax due from fiduciary (divide line 5 by 2.818182) (See instructions if property will not bear the GST tax.)**	6

Under penalties of perjury, I declare that I have examined this return, including accompanying schedules and statements, and to the best of my knowledge and belief, it is true, correct, and complete.

Signature(s) of executor(s) _____ Date _____

Signature of fiduciary or officer representing fiduciary _____ Date _____

Form 706 (Rev. 7-90)

Estate of:

SCHEDULE S—Increased Estate Tax on Excess Retirement Accumulations
(Under section 4980A(d) of the Internal Revenue Code)

Part I   **Tax Computation**

1. Check this box if a section 4980A(d)(5) spousal election is being made . . . . ▶ ☐
You must attach the statement described in the instructions.
2. Enter the name and employer identification number (EIN) of each qualified employer plan and individual retirement account in which the decedent had an interest at the time of death:

	Name	EIN
Plan #1		
Plan #2		
Plan #3		
IRA #1		
IRA #2		
IRA #3		

	A Plan #1	B Plan #2	C Plan #3	D All IRAs
3 Value of decedent's interest				
4 Amounts rolled over after death	▓▓▓	▓▓▓	▓▓▓	
5 Total value (add lines 3 and 4)				▓▓▓
6 Amounts payable to certain alternate payees (see instructions)				
7 Decedent's investment in the contract under section 72(f) .				▓▓▓
8 Excess life insurance amount				
9 Decedent's interest as a beneficiary				
10 Total reductions in value (add lines 6, 7, 8, and 9) . . .				
11 Net value of decedent's interest (subtract line 10 from line 5)				

12 Decedent's aggregate interest in all plans and IRAs (add columns A–D of line 11) . . . . ▶	12	
13 Present value of hypothetical life annuity (from Part III, line 4)	13	▓▓▓
14 Remaining unused grandfather amount (from Part II, line 4)	14	
15 Enter the greater of line 13 or line 14	15	
16 Excess retirement accumulation (subtract line 15 from line 12)	16	
17 Increased estate tax (multiply line 16 by 15%). Enter here and on line 23 of the Tax Computation on page 1.	17	

(The instructions to Schedule S are in the separate instructions.)

Form 706 (Rev. 7-90)

Part II — Grandfather Election

1. Was a grandfather election made on a previously filed Form 5329? . . . . ▶ ☐ Yes ☐ No
   If "Yes," complete lines 2–4 below. **You may not make or revoke the grandfather election after the due date (with extensions) for filing the decedent's 1988 income tax return.** If "No," enter "-0-" on line 4 and skip to Part III.

2. Initial grandfather amount . . . . | 2 |
3. Total amount previously recovered . . . . | 3 |
4. Remaining unused grandfather amount (subtract line 3 from line 2). Enter here and on Part I, line 14, on page 33 . . . . | 4 |

Part III — Computation of Hypothetical Life Annuity

1. Decedent's attained age at date of death (in whole years, rounded down) . . . . | 1 |
2. Applicable annual annuity amount (see instructions) . . . . | 2 |
3. Present value multiplier (see instructions) . . . . | 3 |
4. Present value of hypothetical life annuity (multiply line 2 by line 3). Enter here and on Part I, line 13, on page 33 . . . . | 4 |

Schedule S — Page 34

Form 706 (Rev. 7-90) (Make copies of this schedule before completing it if you will need more than one schedule.)

Estate of: _____

CONTINUATION SCHEDULE

Continuation of Schedule _____
(Enter letter of schedule you are continuing.)

Item number	Description For securities, give CUSIP number, if available.	Unit value (Sch B or E only)	Alternate valuation date	Alternate value	Value at date of death or amount deductible
1					
	TOTAL. (Carry forward to main schedule.).				

See instructions on next page.   **Continuation Schedule—Page 35**

Completed Tax Forms • B-55

Form 1041 — U.S. Fiduciary Income Tax Return 1990

Department of the Treasury—Internal Revenue Service

For the calendar year 1990 or fiscal year beginning _____, 1990, and ending _____, 19 ___ OMB No. 1545-0092

Check applicable boxes:
- ☐ Decedent's estate
- ☐ Simple trust
- ☐ Complex trust
- ☐ Grantor type trust
- ☐ Bankruptcy estate
- ☐ Family estate trust
- ☐ Pooled income fund

Name of estate or trust (grantor type trust, see instructions): **Bob Adams Trust (Simple Trust)**
Name and title of fiduciary: **First Bank**
Number, street, and room or suite no.: **Post Office Box 100**
City, state, and ZIP code: **Nashville, Tennessee**

Employer identification number: **74-1237211**
Date entity created: **1982**

Nonexempt charitable and split-interest trusts, check applicable boxes:
- ☐ Described in section 4947(a)(1)
- ☐ Not a private foundation
- ☐ Described in section 4947(a)(2)

Number of Schedules K-1 attached: ____

Check applicable boxes: ☐ First return ☐ Final return ☐ Amended return Change in Fiduciary's ☐ Name or ☐ Address

Income
Line	Description	Amount
1	Interest income	30,000
2	Dividends	
3	Income (or losses) from partnerships, other estates, or other trusts	
4	Net rental and royalty income (or loss) (attach Schedule E (Form 1040)) (see below)	4,000
5	Net business and farm income (or loss) (attach Schedules C and F (Form 1040))	
6	Capital gain (or loss) (attach Schedule D (Form 1041))	12,000
7	Ordinary gain (or loss) (attach Form 4797)	
8	Other income (state nature of income)	
9	**Total** income (combine lines 1 through 8)	46,000

Deductions
Line	Description		Amount
10	Interest	10	
11	Taxes	11	
12	Fiduciary fees ($1,200 − $360)	12	840
13	Charitable deduction (from Schedule A, line 6)	13	
14	Attorney, accountant, and return preparer fees	14	500
15a	Other deductions NOT subject to the 2% floor (attach schedule)	15a	
15b	Allowable miscellaneous itemized deductions subject to the 2% floor	15b	
15c	Add lines 15a and 15b	15c	
16	**Total** (add lines 10 through 15c)	16	1,340
17	Adjusted total income (or loss) (subtract line 16 from line 9). Enter here and on Schedule B, line 1	17	44,660
18	Income distribution deduction (from Schedule B, line 17) (attach Schedules K-1 (Form 1041))	18	32,660
19	Estate tax deduction (including certain generation-skipping transfer taxes) (attach computation)	19	
20	Exemption	20	300
21	**Total** deductions (add lines 18 through 20)	21	32,960
22	Taxable income of fiduciary (subtract line 21 from line 17)	22	11,700
23	**Total** tax (from Schedule G, line 7)	23	2,567 50
24a	Payments: 1990 estimated tax payments and amount applied from 1989 return	24a	2,600 00
24b	Treated as credited to beneficiaries	24b	
24c	Subtract line 24b from line 24a	24c	
24d	Tax paid with extension of time to file: ☐ Form 2758 ☐ Form 8736 ☐ Form 8800	24d	
24e	Federal income tax withheld	24e	
24i	Credits: f Form 2439 ____ ; g Form 4136 ____ ; h Other ____ ; Total	24i	
25	**Total** payments (add lines 24c through 24e, and 24i)	25	2,600 00
26	**Penalty** for underpayment of estimated tax	26	
27	If the total of lines 23 and 26 is larger than line 25, enter **TAX DUE**	27	
28	If line 25 is larger than the total of lines 23 and 26, enter **OVERPAYMENT**	28	32 50
29	Amount of line 28 to be: a Credited to 1991 estimated tax ▶ 32.50 ; b Refunded ▶	29	-0-

Please Sign Here
Signature of fiduciary or officer representing fiduciary: **Tom Trusty** Date: **3/16/91** EIN of fiduciary: **38 1505087**

Paid Preparer's Use Only
Preparer's signature: **Karen Certified** Date: **3/16/91** Check if self-employed: ☒ Preparer's social security no.: **444 17 1313**
Firm's name: **Karen Certified, One Opry Place, Nashville, TN** ZIP code: **47617**

For Paperwork Reduction Act Notice, see page 1 of the separate Instructions. Form **1041** (1990)

Line 4 - Net Rental Income:
Rental Income $5,000 − Rental Expenses $1,000 = Net Rental Income: $4,000

Form 1041 (1990) Page **2**

Schedule A — Charitable Deduction—Do not complete for a simple trust or a pooled income fund.

1	Amounts paid or permanently set aside for charitable purposes from current year's gross income	1
2	Tax-exempt interest allocable to charitable distribution (see instructions)	2
3	Subtract line 2 from line 1	3
4	Enter the net short-term capital gain and the net long-term capital gain of the current tax year allocable to corpus paid or permanently set aside for charitable purposes (see instructions)	4
5	Amounts paid or permanently set aside for charitable purposes from gross income of a prior year (see instructions)	5
6	**Total** (add lines 3 through 5). Enter here and on page 1, line 13	6

Schedule B — Income Distribution Deduction (see instructions)

1	Adjusted total income (from page 1, line 17) (see instructions)	1	44,660
2	Adjusted tax-exempt interest (see instructions)	2	14,640
3	Net gain shown on Schedule D (Form 1041), line 17, column (a). (If net loss, enter zero.)	3	
4	Enter amount from Schedule A, line 4	4	
5	Long-term capital gain included on Schedule A, line 1	5	
6	Short-term capital gain included on Schedule A, line 1	6	
7	If the amount on page 1, line 6, is a capital loss, enter here as a positive figure	7	
8	If the amount on page 1, line 6, is a capital gain, enter here as a negative figure	8	(12,000)
9	Distributable net income (combine lines 1 through 8)	9	47,300
10	Amount of income for the tax year determined under the governing instrument (accounting income) **10** 48,500		
11	Amount of income required to be distributed currently (see instructions)	11	48,500
12	Other amounts paid, credited, or otherwise required to be distributed (see instructions)	12	
13	Total distributions (add lines 11 and 12). (If greater than line 10, see instructions.)	13	48,500
14	Enter the amount of tax-exempt income included on line 13	14	14,640
15	Tentative income distribution deduction (subtract line 14 from line 13)	15	33,860
16	Tentative income distribution deduction (subtract line 2 from line 9)	16	32,660
17	Income distribution deduction. Enter the smaller of line 15 or line 16 here and on page 1, line 18	17	32,660

Schedule G — Tax Computation (see instructions)

1	Tax: **a** Tax rate schedule 2,567.50 ; **b** Other taxes .... ; Total ▶		1c	2,567 50
2a	Foreign tax credit (attach Form 1116)	2a		
b	Credit for fuel produced from a nonconventional source	2b		
c	General business credit. Check if from: ☐ Form 3800 or ☐ Form (specify) ▶	2c		
d	Credit for prior year minimum tax (attach Form 8801)	2d		
3	**Total** credits (add lines 2a through 2d) ▶		3	
4	Subtract line 3 from line 1c		4	2,567 50
5	Recapture taxes. Check if from: ☐ Form 4255 ☐ Form 8611		5	
6	Alternative minimum tax (attach Form 8656)		6	
7	**Total** tax (add lines 4 through 6). Enter here and on page 1, line 23 ▶		7	2,567 50

Other Information (see instructions)

		Yes	No
1	Did the estate or trust receive tax-exempt income? (If "Yes," attach a computation of the allocation of expenses.) Enter the amount of tax-exempt interest income and exempt-interest dividends ▶ $ 15,000 (see below)	X	
2	Did the estate or trust have any passive activity losses? (If "Yes," enter these losses on **Form 8582**, Passive Activity Loss Limitations, to figure the allowable loss.)		X
3	Did the estate or trust receive all or any part of the earnings (salary, wages, and other compensation) of any individual by reason of a contract assignment or similar arrangement?		X
4	At any time during the tax year, did the estate or trust have an interest in or a signature or other authority over a financial account in a foreign country (such as a bank account, securities account, or other financial account)? (See the instructions for exceptions and filing requirements for Form TD F 90-22.1.) If "Yes," enter the name of the foreign country ▶		X
5	Was the estate or trust the grantor of, or transferor to, a foreign trust which existed during the current tax year, whether or not the estate or trust has any beneficial interest in it? (If "Yes," you may have to file Form 3520, 3520-A, or 926.)		X
6	Check this box if this entity has filed or is required to file **Form 8264**, Application for Registration of a Tax Shelter . ▶ ☐		
7	Check this box if this entity is a complex trust making the section 663(b) election	▶ ☐	
8	Check this box to make a section 643(e)(3) election (attach Schedule D (Form 1041))	▶ ☐	
9	Check this box if the decedent's estate has been open for more than 2 years	▶ ☐	
10	Check this box if the trust is a participant in a Common Trust Fund that was required to adopt a calendar year	▶ ☐	

Line 1 – Allocation of expenses: $15,000 / $50,000 × $1,200 = $360 of trustee fee allocated to tax-exempt income.

Completed Tax Forms • B-57

SCHEDULE D (Form 1041)
Department of the Treasury
Internal Revenue Service

Capital Gains and Losses
▶ File with Form 1041. See the separate Form 1041 instructions.

OMB No. 1545-0092

1990

Name of estate or trust: **Bob Adams Trust**

Employer identification number: **74-123111**

Do not report section 644 gains on Schedule D (See Form 1041 instructions for line 1b, Schedule G.)

Part I — Short-Term Capital Gains and Losses—Assets Held One Year or Less

(a) Description of property (Example, 100 shares 7% preferred of "Z" Co.)	(b) Date acquired (mo., day, yr.)	(c) Date sold (mo., day, yr.)	(d) Gross sales price	(e) Cost or other basis, as adjusted, plus expense of sale (see instructions)	(f) Gain (or loss) (col. (d) less col. (e))
1					

2 Short-term capital gain from installment sales from Form 6252	2	
3 Net short-term gain (or loss) from partnerships, S corporations, and other fiduciaries	3	
4 Net gain (or loss) (combine lines 1 through 3)	4	
5 Short-term capital loss carryover (see instructions)	5	( )
6 Net short-term gain (or loss) (combine lines 4 and 5). Enter here and on line 15 below ▶	6	

Part II — Long-Term Capital Gains and Losses—Assets Held More Than One Year

(a) Description of property	(b) Date acquired	(c) Date sold	(d) Gross sales price	(e) Cost or other basis	(f) Gain (or loss)
7 1,000 shares of ABC Corporation stock	1-2-1941	6-9-1990	15,000	3,000	12,000

8 Long-term capital gain from installment sales from Form 6252	8	
9 Net long-term gain (or loss) from partnerships, S corporations, and other fiduciaries	9	
10 Capital gain distributions	10	
11 Enter gain, if applicable, from Form 4797	11	
12 Net gain (or loss) (combine lines 7 through 11)	12	12,000
13 Long-term capital loss carryover (see instructions)	13	( )
14 Net long-term gain (or loss) (combine lines 12 and 13). Enter here and on line 16 below ▶	14	12,000

Part III — Summary of Parts I and II

	(a) Beneficiaries	(b) Fiduciary	(c) Total
15 Net short-term gain (or loss) from line 6, above			
16 Net long-term gain (or loss) from line 14, above		12,000	12,000
17 Total net gain (or loss) (combine lines 15 and 16) ▶		12,000	12,000

If line 17, column (c), is a net gain, enter the gain on Form 1041, line 6, and DO NOT complete Parts IV and V. If line 17, column (c), is a net loss, complete Parts IV and V, as necessary.

For Paperwork Reduction Act Notice, see page 1 of the Instructions for Form 1041.   Schedule D (Form 1041) 1990

Schedule D (Form 1041) 1990

Part IV — Computation of Capital Loss Limitation

18 Enter here and enter as a (loss) on Form 1041, line 6, the smaller of:
(i) The net loss on line 17, column (c); **or**
(ii) $3,000 . . . . 18 (   )

If the net loss on line 17, column (c) is more than $3,000, OR if the taxable income on line 22, page 1, of Form 1041 is zero or less, complete Part V to determine your capital loss carryover.

Part V — Computation of Capital Loss Carryovers From 1990 to 1991

Section A.—Computation of Carryover Limit

19 Enter taxable income (or loss) for 1990 from Form 1041, line 22 19

20 Enter loss from line 18, above, as a positive amount 20

21 Enter amount from Form 1041, line 20 21

22 Adjusted taxable income (Combine lines 19, 20, and 21, but do not enter less than zero) . . . 22

23 Enter the lesser of lines 20 or 22 23

Section B.—Short-Term Capital Loss Carryover
(Complete this part only if there is a loss on line 6, Schedule D, Part I, and line 17, column (c).)

24 Enter loss shown on line 6, Schedule D, Part I, as a positive amount 24

25 Enter gain, if any, from line 14. (If that line is blank or shows a loss, enter zero) 25

26 Enter amount from line 23, above 26

27 Add lines 25 and 26 27

28 Subtract line 27 from line 24. If zero or less, enter zero. This is the fiduciary's short-term capital loss carryover from 1990 to 1991. If this is the final return of the estate or trust, also enter on line 12c, Schedule K-1 (Form 1041) 28

Section C.—Long-Term Capital Loss Carryover
(Complete this part only if there is a loss on line 14 and line 17, column (c).)

29 Enter loss from line 14 as a positive amount 29

30 Enter gain, if any, from line 6, Schedule D, Part I. (If that line is blank or shows a loss, enter zero) . . 30

31 Enter amount from line 23, above 31

32 Enter amount, if any, from line 24, above 32

33 Subtract line 32 from line 31. If zero or less, enter zero 33

34 Add lines 30 and 33 34

35 Subtract line 34 from line 29. If zero or less, enter zero. This is the fiduciary's long-term capital loss carryover from 1990 to 1991. If this is the final return of the estate or trust, also enter on line 12d, Schedule K-1 (Form 1041) 35

*U.S. Government Printing Office: 1990 — 265-218

Completed Tax Forms • B-59

SCHEDULE K-1
(Form 1041)
Department of the Treasury
Internal Revenue Service

Beneficiary's Share of Income, Deductions, Credits, Etc.—1990
for the calendar year 1990, or fiscal year
beginning ...., 1990, ending ...., 19 .....
Complete a separate Schedule K-1 for each beneficiary.

OMB No. 1545-0092

1990

☐ Amended K-1
☐ Final K-1

Name of estate or trust
Bob Adams Trust

Beneficiary's identifying number ▶ 323-15-1417

Estate's or trust's employer identification number ▶ 74-1237211

Beneficiary's name, address, and ZIP code
Bob Adams
#3 Andy Jackson Highway
Nashville, Tennessee 47629

Fiduciary's name, address, and ZIP code
First Bank
Post Office Box 100
Nashville, Tennessee 47617

Reminder: *If you received a short year 1987 Schedule K-1 that was from a trust required to adopt a calendar year, be sure to include one-fourth of those amounts reported as income, in addition to the items reported on this Schedule K-1, on the appropriate lines of your 1990 Form 1040 and related schedules.*

(a) Allocable share item	(b) Amount	(c) Calendar year 1990 Form 1040 filers enter the amounts in column (b) on:
1 Interest	30,000	Schedule B, Part I, line 1
2 Dividends		Schedule B, Part II, line 5
3a Net short-term capital gain		Schedule D, line 5, column (g)
b Net long-term capital gain		Schedule D, line 12, column (g)
4a Other taxable income: (itemize)	2,660	Schedule E, Part III
(1) Rental, rental real estate, and business income from activities acquired before 10/23/86	2,660	
(2) Rental, rental real estate, and business income from activities acquired after 10/22/86		
(3) Other passive income		
b Depreciation, including cost recovery (itemize):		
(1) Attributable to line 4a(1)		
(2) Attributable to line 4a(2)		
(3) Attributable to line 4a(3)		
c Depletion (itemize):		
(1) Attributable to line 4a(1)		
(2) Attributable to line 4a(2)		
(3) Attributable to line 4a(3)		
d Amortization (itemize):		
(1) Attributable to line 4a(1)		
(2) Attributable to line 4a(2)		
(3) Attributable to line 4a(3)		
5 Income for minimum tax purposes	32,660	
6 Income for regular tax purposes (add lines 1 through 4a)	32,660	
7 Adjustment for minimum tax purposes (subtract line 6 from line 5)		Form 6251, line 4t
8 Estate tax deduction (including certain generation-skipping transfer taxes) (attach computation)		Schedule A, line 26
9 Excess deductions on termination (attach computation)		Schedule A, line 21
10 Foreign taxes (list on a separate sheet)		Form 1116 or Schedule A (Form 1040), line 7
11 Tax preference items (itemize):		
a Accelerated depreciation		(Include on the applicable
b Depletion		line of Form 6251)
c Amortization		
12 Other (itemize):		
a Trust payments of estimated taxes credited to you		Form 1040, line 56
b Tax-exempt interest	14,640	Form 1040, line 8b
c Short-term capital loss carryover		Schedule D, line 6, column (f)
d Long-term capital loss carryover		Schedule D, line 15, column (f)
e		(Include on the applicable line
f		of appropriate tax form)
g		

For Paperwork Reduction Act Notice, see page 1 of the Instructions for Form 1041.

Schedule K-1 (Form 1041) 1990

B-60 • App. B / Completed Tax Forms

Form 1041 — U.S. Fiduciary Income Tax Return 1990

Department of the Treasury—Internal Revenue Service

For the calendar year 1990 or fiscal year beginning _____, 1990, and ending _____, 19___

OMB No. 1545-0092

Check applicable boxes:
- ☐ Decedent's estate
- ☐ Simple trust
- ☐ Complex trust
- ☐ Grantor type trust
- ☐ Bankruptcy estate
- ☐ Family estate trust
- ☐ Pooled income fund

Name of estate or trust (grantor type trust, see instructions): **Cathy and Karen Stephens Trust**

Name and title of fiduciary: **Merchants Bank**

Number, street, and room or suite no.: **Sun Plaza I**

City, state, and ZIP code: **Tampa, Florida 32843**

Employer identification number: **74-5727422**

Date entity created: **1982**

Nonexempt charitable and split-interest trusts, check applicable boxes (see instructions):
- ☐ Described in section 4947(a)(1)
- ☐ Not a private foundation
- ☐ Described in section 4947(a)(2)

Number of Schedules K-1 attached ▶ **2**

Check applicable boxes:
- ☐ First return
- ☐ Final return
- ☐ Amended return
- Change in Fiduciary's ☐ Name or ☐ Address

Income

Line	Description	Amount
1	Interest income	30,000
2	Dividends	
3	Income (or losses) from partnerships, other estates, or other trusts	
4	Net rental and royalty income (or loss) (attach Schedule E (Form 1040)) (see below)	4,000
5	Net business and farm income (or loss) (attach Schedules C and F (Form 1040))	
6	Capital gain (or loss) (attach Schedule D (Form 1041))	12,000
7	Ordinary gain (or loss) (attach Form 4797)	
8	Other income (state nature of income)	
9	**Total** income (combine lines 1 through 8)	46,000

Deductions

Line	Description	Amount
10	Interest	
11	Taxes	
12	Fiduciary fees	840
13	Charitable deduction (from Schedule A, line 6)	
14	Attorney, accountant, and return preparer fees	500
15a	Other deductions NOT subject to the 2% floor (attach schedule)	
15b	Allowable miscellaneous itemized deductions subject to the 2% floor	
15c	Add lines 15a and 15b	
16	**Total** (add lines 10 through 15c)	1,340
17	Adjusted total income (or loss) (subtract line 16 from line 9). Enter here and on Schedule B, line 1	44,660
18	Income distribution deduction (from Schedule B, line 17) (attach Schedules K-1 (Form 1041))	14,500
19	Estate tax deduction (including certain generation-skipping transfer taxes) (attach computation)	
20	Exemption	100
21	**Total** deductions (add lines 18 through 20)	14,600
22	Taxable income of fiduciary (subtract line 21 from line 17)	30,060
23	**Total** tax (from Schedule G, line 7)	8,417

Tax and Payments

24a	Payments: 1990 estimated tax payments and amount applied from 1989 return	8,600
24b	Treated as credited to beneficiaries	
24c	Subtract line 24b from line 24a	8,600
24d	Tax paid with extension of time to file: ☐ Form 2758 ☐ Form 8736 ☐ Form 8800	
24e	Federal income tax withheld	
	Credits: f Form 2439 _____; g Form 4136 _____; h Other _____; Total ▶ 24i	
25	**Total** payments (add lines 24c through 24e, and 24i)	8,600
26	**Penalty** for underpayment of estimated tax (see instructions)	
27	If the total of lines 23 and 26 is larger than line 25, enter **TAX DUE**	183
28	If line 25 is larger than the total of lines 23 and 26, enter **OVERPAYMENT**	
29	Amount of line 28 to be: a Credited to 1991 estimated tax ▶ 183; b Refunded ▶	-0-

Please Sign Here

Signature of fiduciary or officer representing fiduciary: **Fred Fiduo** Date: **3/20/91** EIN of fiduciary ▶ **38-4371419**

Paid Preparer's Use Only

- Preparer's signature: **Sarah Public** Date: **3/15/91** Check if self-employed ▶ ☒ Preparer's social security no.: **127-84-3978**
- Firm's name: **Sarah Public** E.I. No. ▶
- Address: **Sun Plaza III, Tampa, Florida** ZIP code ▶ **32843**

For Paperwork Reduction Act Notice, see page 1 of the separate Instructions. Form **1041** (1990)

Line 4 — Net Rental Income:
Rental Income $5,000 − Rental Expenses ($1,000) = Net Rental Income $4,000

Form 1041 (1990) Page **2**

Schedule A — Charitable Deduction—Do not complete for a simple trust or a pooled income fund.

1	Amounts paid or permanently set aside for charitable purposes from current year's gross income	1	
2	Tax-exempt interest allocable to charitable distribution (see instructions)	2	
3	Subtract line 2 from line 1	3	
4	Enter the net short-term capital gain and the net long-term capital gain of the current tax year allocable to corpus paid or permanently set aside for charitable purposes (see instructions)	4	
5	Amounts paid or permanently set aside for charitable purposes from gross income of a prior year (see instructions)	5	
6	**Total** (add lines 3 through 5). Enter here and on page 1, line 13	6	-0-

Schedule B — Income Distribution Deduction (see instructions)

1	Adjusted total income (from page 1, line 17) (see instructions)	1	44,660
2	Adjusted tax-exempt interest (see instructions)	2	14,640
3	Net gain shown on Schedule D (Form 1041), line 17, column (a). (If net loss, enter zero.)	3	
4	Enter amount from Schedule A, line 4	4	
5	Long-term capital gain included on Schedule A, line 1	5	
6	Short-term capital gain included on Schedule A, line 1	6	
7	If the amount on page 1, line 6, is a capital loss, enter here as a positive figure	7	
8	If the amount on page 1, line 6, is a capital gain, enter here as a negative figure	8	(12,000)
9	Distributable net income (combine lines 1 through 8)	9	47,300
10	Amount of income for the tax year determined under the governing instrument (accounting income) 10	48,500	
11	Amount of income required to be distributed currently (see instructions)	11	—
12	Other amounts paid, credited, or otherwise required to be distributed (see instructions)	12	21,000
13	Total distributions (add lines 11 and 12). (If greater than line 10, see instructions.)	13	21,000
14	Enter the amount of tax-exempt income included on line 13	14	6,500
15	Tentative income distribution deduction (subtract line 14 from line 13)	15	14,500
16	Tentative income distribution deduction (subtract line 2 from line 9)	16	32,660
17	Income distribution deduction. Enter the smaller of line 15 or line 16 here and on page 1, line 18	17	14,500

Schedule G — Tax Computation (see instructions)

1	Tax: **a** Tax rate schedule 8,417 ; **b** Other taxes ____ ; Total ▶		1c	8,417
2a	Foreign tax credit (attach Form 1116)	2a		
b	Credit for fuel produced from a nonconventional source	2b		
c	General business credit. Check if from: ☐ Form 3800 or ☐ Form (specify) ▶ ____	2c		
d	Credit for prior year minimum tax (attach Form 8801)	2d		
3	**Total** credits (add lines 2a through 2d) ▶		3	
4	Subtract line 3 from line 1c		4	8,417
5	Recapture taxes. Check if from: ☐ Form 4255 ☐ Form 8611		5	
6	Alternative minimum tax (attach Form 8656)		6	
7	**Total tax** (add lines 4 through 6). Enter here and on page 1, line 23 ▶		7	8,417

Other Information (see instructions)

		Yes	No
1	Did the estate or trust receive tax-exempt income? (If "Yes," attach a computation of the allocation of expenses.) Enter the amount of tax-exempt interest income and exempt-interest dividends ▶ $ 15,000 (see below)	X	
2	Did the estate or trust have any passive activity losses? (If "Yes," enter these losses on **Form 8582**, Passive Activity Loss Limitations, to figure the allowable loss.)		X
3	Did the estate or trust receive all or any part of the earnings (salary, wages, and other compensation) of any individual by reason of a contract assignment or similar arrangement?		X
4	At any time during the tax year, did the estate or trust have an interest in or a signature or other authority over a financial account in a foreign country (such as a bank account, securities account, or other financial account)? (See the instructions for exceptions and filing requirements for Form TD F 90-22.1.) If "Yes," enter the name of the foreign country ▶		X
5	Was the estate or trust the grantor of, or transferor to, a foreign trust which existed during the current tax year, whether or not the estate or trust has any beneficial interest in it? (If "Yes," you may have to file Form 3520, 3520-A, or 926.)		X
6	Check this box if this entity has filed or is required to file **Form 8264**, Application for Registration of a Tax Shelter ▶ ☐		
7	Check this box if this entity is a complex trust making the section 663(b) election ▶ ☐		
8	Check this box to make a section 643(e)(3) election (attach Schedule D (Form 1041)) ▶ ☐		
9	Check this box if the decedent's estate has been open for more than 2 years ▶ ☐		
10	Check this box if the trust is a participant in a Common Trust Fund that was required to adopt a calendar year ▶ ☐		

Line 1 — Allocation of expenses — $15,000 / $50,000 × $1,200 = $360 of trustee fees allocated to tax-exempt income.

SCHEDULE D (Form 1041)
Department of the Treasury
Internal Revenue Service

Capital Gains and Losses

▶ File with Form 1041. See the separate Form 1041 instructions.

OMB No. 1545-0092

1990

Name of estate or trust: Cathy and Karen Stephens Trust

Employer identification number: 74-5727422

Do not report section 644 gains on Schedule D (See Form 1041 instructions for line 1b, Schedule G.)

Part I — Short-Term Capital Gains and Losses—Assets Held One Year or Less

(a) Description of property (Example, 100 shares 7% preferred of "Z" Co.)	(b) Date acquired (mo., day, yr.)	(c) Date sold (mo., day, yr.)	(d) Gross sales price	(e) Cost or other basis, as adjusted, plus expense of sale (see instructions)	(f) Gain (or loss) (col. (d) less col. (e))
1					

2 Short-term capital gain from installment sales from Form 6252 . . . . **2**
3 Net short-term gain (or loss) from partnerships, S corporations, and other fiduciaries **3**
4 Net gain (or loss) (combine lines 1 through 3) **4**
5 Short-term capital loss carryover (see instructions) . . . . **5** (   )
6 Net short-term gain (or loss) (combine lines 4 and 5). Enter here and on line 15 below . . . . . ▶ **6**

Part II — Long-Term Capital Gains and Losses—Assets Held More Than One Year

(a)	(b)	(c)	(d)	(e)	(f)
7 1,000 shares TST Corporation stock	10/1/77	3/6/90	32,000	20,000	12,000

8   Long-term capital gain from installment sales from Form 6252 . . . . **8**
9   Net long-term gain (or loss) from partnerships, S corporations, and other fiduciaries **9**
10 Capital gain distributions **10**
11 Enter gain, if applicable, from Form 4797 . . . . **11**
12 Net gain (or loss) (combine lines 7 through 11) **12** 12,000
13 Long-term capital loss carryover (see instructions) . . . . **13** (   )
14 Net long-term gain (or loss) (combine lines 12 and 13). Enter here and on line 16 below . . . . ▶ **14** 12,000

Part III — Summary of Parts I and II

	(a) Beneficiaries	(b) Fiduciary	(c) Total
15 Net short-term gain (or loss) from line 6, above			
16 Net long-term gain (or loss) from line 14, above		12,000	12,000
17 Total net gain (or loss) (combine lines 15 and 16) ▶		12,000	12,000

If line 17, column (c), is a net gain, enter the gain on Form 1041, line 6, and DO NOT complete Parts IV and V. If line 17, column (c), is a net loss, complete Parts IV and V, as necessary.

For Paperwork Reduction Act Notice, see page 1 of the Instructions for Form 1041.

Schedule D (Form 1041) 1990

Schedule D (Form 1041) 1990 Page 2

Part IV — Computation of Capital Loss Limitation

18 Enter here and enter as a (loss) on Form 1041, line 6, the smaller of:
   (i) The net loss on line 17, column (c); or
   (ii) $3,000 . . . . 18 (   )

If the net loss on line 17, column (c) is more than $3,000, OR if the taxable income on line 22, page 1, of Form 1041 is zero or less, complete Part V to determine your capital loss carryover.

Part V — Computation of Capital Loss Carryovers From 1990 to 1991

Section A.—Computation of Carryover Limit

19 Enter taxable income (or loss) for 1990 from Form 1041, line 22 19

20 Enter loss from line 18, above, as a positive amount 20

21 Enter amount from Form 1041, line 20 21

22 Adjusted taxable income (Combine lines 19, 20, and 21, but do not enter less than zero) 22

23 Enter the lesser of lines 20 or 22 23

Section B.—Short-Term Capital Loss Carryover
(Complete this part only if there is a loss on line 6, Schedule D, Part I, and line 17, column (c).)

24 Enter loss shown on line 6, Schedule D, Part I, as a positive amount 24

25 Enter gain, if any, from line 14. (If that line is blank or shows a loss, enter zero) 25

26 Enter amount from line 23, above 26

27 Add lines 25 and 26 27

28 Subtract line 27 from line 24. If zero or less, enter zero. This is the fiduciary's short-term capital loss carryover from 1990 to 1991. If this is the final return of the estate or trust, also enter on line 12c, Schedule K-1 (Form 1041) 28

Section C.—Long-Term Capital Loss Carryover
(Complete this part only if there is a loss on line 14 and line 17, column (c).)

29 Enter loss from line 14 as a positive amount 29

30 Enter gain, if any, from line 6, Schedule D, Part I. (If that line is blank or shows a loss, enter zero) . . 30

31 Enter amount from line 23, above 31

32 Enter amount, if any, from line 24, above 32

33 Subtract line 32 from line 31. If zero or less, enter zero 33

34 Add lines 30 and 33 34

35 Subtract line 34 from line 29. If zero or less, enter zero. This is the fiduciary's long-term capital loss carryover from 1990 to 1991. If this is the final return of the estate or trust, also enter on line 12d, Schedule K-1 (Form 1041) 35

*U.S. Government Printing Office: 1990 — 265-218

SCHEDULE K-1 (Form 1041)
Beneficiary's Share of Income, Deductions, Credits, Etc.—1990

Department of the Treasury
Internal Revenue Service

for the calendar year 1990, or fiscal year
beginning ...., 1990, ending ...., 19 .....

Complete a separate Schedule K-1 for each beneficiary.

OMB No. 1545-0092

1990

Name of estate or trust: Cathy and Karen Stephens Trust

☐ Amended K-1
☐ Final K-1

Beneficiary's identifying number ▶ 411-36-4761

Estate's or trust's employer identification number ▶ 74-5727422

Beneficiary's name, address, and ZIP code:
Cathy Stephens
13 Sunny Shores
Miami, Florida 33131

Fiduciary's name, address, and ZIP code:
Merchant's Bank
Sun Plaza I
Tampa, Florida 32843

Reminder: If you received a short year 1987 Schedule K-1 that was from a trust required to adopt a calendar year, be sure to include one-fourth of those amounts reported as income, in addition to the items reported on this Schedule K-1, on the appropriate lines of your 1990 Form 1040 and related schedules.

(a) Allocable share item	(b) Amount	(c) Calendar year 1990 Form 1040 filers enter the amounts in column (b) on:
1 Interest		Schedule B, Part I, line 1
2 Dividends	8,879	Schedule B, Part II, line 5
3a Net short-term capital gain		Schedule D, line 5, column (g)
b Net long-term capital gain		Schedule D, line 12, column (g)
4a Other taxable income: (itemize)	788	Schedule E, Part III
(1) Rental, rental real estate, and business income from activities acquired before 10/23/86	788	
(2) Rental, rental real estate, and business income from activities acquired after 10/22/86		
(3) Other passive income		
b Depreciation, including cost recovery (itemize):		
(1) Attributable to line 4a(1)		
(2) Attributable to line 4a(2)		
(3) Attributable to line 4a(3)		
c Depletion (itemize):		
(1) Attributable to line 4a(1)		
(2) Attributable to line 4a(2)		
(3) Attributable to line 4a(3)		
d Amortization (itemize):		
(1) Attributable to line 4a(1)		
(2) Attributable to line 4a(2)		
(3) Attributable to line 4a(3)		
5 Income for minimum tax purposes	9,667	
6 Income for regular tax purposes (add lines 1 through 4a)	9,667	
7 Adjustment for minimum tax purposes (subtract line 6 from line 5)		Form 6251, line 4t
8 Estate tax deduction (including certain generation-skipping transfer taxes) (attach computation)		Schedule A, line 26
9 Excess deductions on termination (attach computation)		Schedule A, line 21
10 Foreign taxes (list on a separate sheet)		Form 1116 or Schedule A (Form 1040), line 7
11 Tax preference items (itemize):		
a Accelerated depreciation		(Include on the applicable)
b Depletion		(line of Form 6251)
c Amortization		
12 Other (itemize):		
a Trust payments of estimated taxes credited to you		Form 1040, line 56
b Tax-exempt interest	4,333	Form 1040, line 8b
c Short-term capital loss carryover		Schedule D, line 6, column (f)
d Long-term capital loss carryover		Schedule D, line 15, column (f)
e		(Include on the applicable line)
f		(of appropriate tax form)
g		

For Paperwork Reduction Act Notice, see page 1 of the Instructions for Form 1041.

Schedule K-1 (Form 1041) 1990

Completed Tax Forms • B-65

SCHEDULE K-1 (Form 1041)	Beneficiary's Share of Income, Deductions, Credits, Etc.—1990	OMB No. 1545-0092
Department of the Treasury Internal Revenue Service	for the calendar year 1990, or fiscal year beginning ...., 1990, ending ...., 19..... Complete a separate Schedule K-1 for each beneficiary.	1990

Complete a separate Schedule K-1 for each beneficiary.

☐ Amended K-1
☐ Final K-1

Name of estate or trust: Cathy and Karen Stevens Trust

Beneficiary's identifying number ▶ 456-78-1230

Estate's or trust's employer identification number ▶ 74-5727422

Beneficiary's name, address, and ZIP code:
Karen Stevens
1472 Ski Run
Vail, Colorado 74820

Fiduciary's name, address, and ZIP code:
Merchant's Bank
Sun Plaza I
Tampa, Florida 32843

Reminder: *If you received a short year 1987 Schedule K-1 that was from a trust required to adopt a calendar year, be sure to include one-fourth of those amounts reported as income, in addition to the items reported on this Schedule K-1, on the appropriate lines of your 1990 Form 1040 and related schedules.*

(a) Allocable share item	(b) Amount	(c) Calendar year 1990 Form 1040 filers enter the amounts in column (b) on:
1 Interest		Schedule B, Part I, line 1
2 Dividends	4,440	Schedule B, Part II, line 5
3a Net short-term capital gain		Schedule D, line 5, column (g)
b Net long-term capital gain		Schedule D, line 12, column (g)
4a Other taxable income: (itemize)	393	Schedule E, Part III
(1) Rental, rental real estate, and business income from activities acquired before 10/23/86	393	
(2) Rental, rental real estate, and business income from activities acquired after 10/22/86		
(3) Other passive income		
b Depreciation, including cost recovery (itemize):		
(1) Attributable to line 4a(1)		
(2) Attributable to line 4a(2)		
(3) Attributable to line 4a(3)		
c Depletion (itemize):		
(1) Attributable to line 4a(1)		
(2) Attributable to line 4a(2)		
(3) Attributable to line 4a(3)		
d Amortization (itemize):		
(1) Attributable to line 4a(1)		
(2) Attributable to line 4a(2)		
(3) Attributable to line 4a(3)		
5 Income for minimum tax purposes	4,833	
6 Income for regular tax purposes (add lines 1 through 4a)	4,833	
7 Adjustment for minimum tax purposes (subtract line 6 from line 5)		Form 6251, line 4t
8 Estate tax deduction (including certain generation-skipping transfer taxes) (attach computation)		Schedule A, line 26
9 Excess deductions on termination (attach computation)		Schedule A, line 21
10 Foreign taxes (list on a separate sheet)		Form 1116 or Schedule A (Form 1040), line 7
11 Tax preference items (itemize):		
a Accelerated depreciation		(Include on the applicable)
b Depletion		(line of Form 6251)
c Amortization		
12 Other (itemize):		
a Trust payments of estimated taxes credited to you		Form 1040, line 56
b Tax-exempt interest	2,167	Form 1040, line 8b
c Short-term capital loss carryover		Schedule D, line 6, column (f)
d Long-term capital loss carryover		Schedule D, line 15, column (f)
e		(Include on the applicable line)
f		(of appropriate tax form)
g		

For Paperwork Reduction Act Notice, see page 1 of the Instructions for Form 1041. Schedule K-1 (Form 1041) 1990

Form 1116
Department of the Treasury
Internal Revenue Service

Foreign Tax Credit
Individual, Fiduciary, or Nonresident Alien Individual
▶ Attach to Form 1040, 1040NR, 1041, or 990-T.
▶ See separate Instructions.

OMB No. 1545-0121
1990
Attachment Sequence No. **19**

Name: Andrew Roberts

Identifying number as shown on page 1 of your tax return: 123-45-6789

Use a separate Form 1116 for each category of income listed below. Check only **one** box. Before you check a box, read **Categories of Income** on page 2 of the Instructions. This form is being completed for credit for taxes on:

- ☒ Passive income
- ☐ High withholding tax interest
- ☐ Financial services income
- ☐ Shipping income
- ☐ Dividends from a DISC or former DISC
- ☐ Certain distributions from a foreign sales corporation (FSC) or former FSC
- ☐ Lump-sum distributions (see Instructions before completing form)
- ☐ General limitation income—all other income from sources outside the United States (including income from sources within U.S. possessions)

Resident of (name of country) ▶ United States

Note: If you paid taxes to one foreign country or U.S. possession, use column A in Part I and line A in Part II. If you paid taxes to **more than one** foreign country or U.S. possession, use a separate column and line for each country or possession.

Part I — Taxable Income or Loss From Sources Outside the United States for Separate Category Checked Above

	Foreign Country or U.S. Possession			Total
	A	B	C	(Add Cols. A, B, and C)
Enter the name of the foreign country or U.S. possession ▶	France			
1 Gross income from sources within country shown above and of the type checked above. (See Instructions.): Dividends	30,000			**1** 30,000
Applicable deductions and losses (See Instructions.):				
2 Expenses directly allocable to the income on line 1 (attach schedule)				
3 Pro rata share of other deductions not directly allocable:				
a Certain itemized deductions or standard deduction. (See Instructions.)	12,000			
b Other deductions (attach schedule)	—			
c Add lines 3a and 3b	12,000			
d Total foreign source income. (See Instructions.)	30,000			
e Gross income from all sources. (See Instructions.)	210,000			
f Divide line 3d by line 3e	.1428571			
g Multiply line 3c by line 3f	1,714			
4 Pro rata share of interest expense. (See Instructions.):				
a Home mortgage and personal interest from line 7 of the worksheet on page 3 of the Instructions				
b Other interest				
5 Losses from foreign sources				
6 Add lines 2, 3g, 4a, 4b, and 5	1,714			**6** 1,714
7 Subtract line 6 from line 1. Enter the result here and on line 14 ▶				**7** 28,286

Part II — Foreign Taxes Paid or Accrued (See Instructions.)

Country	Credit is claimed for taxes (you must check one):	Foreign taxes paid or accrued							
		In foreign currency				In U.S. dollars			
	☒ Paid ☐ Accrued	Taxes withheld at source on:			(d) Other foreign taxes paid or accrued	Taxes withheld at source on:			(h) Other foreign taxes paid or accrued	(i) Total foreign taxes paid or accrued (add cols. (e) through (h))
	Date paid or accrued	(a) Dividends	(b) Rents and royalties	(c) Interest		(e) Dividends	(f) Rents and royalties	(g) Interest		
A	12-31-90	35,775 FF				5,996			None	5,996
B										
C										

8 Add lines A through C, column (i). Enter the total here and on line 9 ▶ **8**

For Paperwork Reduction Act Notice, see page 1 of separate Instructions.

Form **1116** (1990)

Form 1116 (1990) Page **2**

Part III Figuring the Credit

9	Enter amount from line 8. This is the total foreign taxes paid or accrued for the category of income checked above Part I	9	5,996
10	Carryback or carryover (attach detailed computation)	10	
11	Add lines 9 and 10	11	5,996
12	Reduction in foreign taxes. (See Instructions.)	12	
13	Subtract line 12 from line 11. This is the total amount of foreign taxes available for credit	13	5,996
14	Enter amount from line 7. This is your taxable income or (loss) from sources outside the United States (before adjustments) for the category of income checked above Part I. (See Instructions.) . . .	14	28,286
15	Adjustments to line 14. (See Instructions.)	15	
16	Combine the amounts on lines 14 and 15. This is your net foreign source taxable income. (If the result is zero or less, you have no foreign tax credit for the type of income you checked on page 1. Skip lines 17 through 21.)	16	28,286
17	**Individuals:** Enter amount from Form 1040, line 35. If you are a nonresident alien, enter amount from Form 1040NR, line 33. **Estates and trusts:** Enter your taxable income without the deduction for your exemption	17	159,000
18	Divide line 16 by line 17. (If line 16 is more than line 17, enter the figure "1.")	18	.177899371
19	**Individuals:** Enter amount from Form 1040, line 40, **less** any amounts on Form 1040, lines 41 and 42. If you are a nonresident alien, enter amount from Form 1040NR, line 38, **less** any amount on Form 1040NR, line 39. **Estates and trusts:** Enter amount from Form 1041, Schedule G, line 1c, or Form 990-T, line 8	19	44,520
20	Multiply line 19 by line 18. (Maximum amount of credit)	20	7,920
21	Enter the amount from line 13 or line 20, whichever is smaller. (If this is the only Form 1116 you are completing, skip lines 22 through 29 and enter this amount on line 30. Otherwise, complete the appropriate lines in Part IV.) . . . . ▶	21	5,996

Part IV Summary of Credits From Separate Parts III (See Instructions.)

22	Credit for taxes on passive income	22	5,996
23	Credit for taxes on high withholding tax interest	23	
24	Credit for taxes on financial services income	24	
25	Credit for taxes on shipping income	25	
26	Credit for taxes on dividends from a DISC or former DISC	26	
27	Credit for taxes on certain distributions from a FSC or former FSC . .	27	
28	Credit for taxes on lump-sum distributions	28	
29	Credit for taxes on general limitation income (all other income from sources outside the U.S.)	29	
30	Add lines 22 through 29	30	5,996
31	Reduction of credit for international boycott operations. (See "Reduction of Credit for International Boycott Operations" in instructions for line 12.)	31	
32	Subtract line 31 from line 30. This is your foreign tax credit. Enter here and on Form 1040, line 43; Form 1040NR, line 40; Form 1041, Schedule G, line 2a; or Form 990-T, line 9a . . . . . ▶	32	5,996

B-68 • App. B / Completed Tax Forms

Form 2555
Department of the Treasury
Internal Revenue Service

Foreign Earned Income
▶ See separate Instructions. ▶ Attach to front of Form 1040.

OMB No. 1545-0067

1990
Attachment Sequence No. 34

For Use by United States Citizens and Resident Aliens Only

Your name: Lawrence Smith
Your social security number: 234:56:7890

Foreign address (including country): 123 Rue de Havre 75011 Paris, France
Your occupation: Financial Vice-President

Name of employer ▶ Very Public Corporation

Employer's address:
- U.S. ▶ 50 Park Ave, New York, N.Y. 10016
- Foreign ▶ 11 Rue de Nanettes/5e 'Etage, 75011 Paris, France

Employer is (check any that apply) ▶
- ☐ A foreign entity
- ☐ A foreign affiliate of a U.S. company
- ☒ A U.S. company
- ☐ Self
- ☐ Other (specify) ▶

Enter earlier years (after 1981) that you filed Form 2555 to claim either of the exclusions ▶ 1986 – 1989

If you chose to claim an exclusion in an earlier year (after 1981), have you revoked your choice? . . . . ☐ Yes ☒ No
If "Yes," give the type of exclusion and the tax year for which the revocation was effective ▶

Test under which you qualify to claim the exclusion(s) and/or deduction ▶
- ☐ Bona fide residence test (Part I)
- ☐ Physical presence test (Part II)

Are you a U.S. citizen? . . . . ☒ Yes ☐ No

Did you maintain a separate foreign residence for your family because of adverse living conditions at your tax home? (See **Second Foreign Household** on page 3 of the Instructions.) . . . . . . ☐ Yes ☐ No

If "Yes," give city and country of the separate foreign residence. Also show the number of days during your tax year that you maintained a second household at that address

List your tax home(s) during your tax year and date(s) established: 123 Rue de Havre, 75011 Paris, France July 10, 1986

Complete either Part I or Part II. If an item does not apply, write "NA." If you do not provide the information asked for, any exclusion or deduction you claim may be disallowed.

Part I — Taxpayers Qualifying Under Bona Fide Residence Test (See Instructions.)

1. Date bona fide residence began July 10, 1986, ended Present
2. Kind of living quarters in foreign country ▶ ☐ Purchased house ☒ Rented house or apartment ☐ Rented room ☐ Quarters furnished by employer
3. Did any of your family live with you abroad during any part of the tax year? . . . . ☒ Yes ☐ No
   If "Yes," who and for what period? ▶ Wife and two children – entire period
4. a Have you submitted a statement to the authorities of the foreign country where you claim bona fide residence that you are not a resident of that country? (See Instructions.) . . . . ☐ Yes ☒ No
   b Are you required to pay income tax to the country where you claim bona fide residence? (See Instructions.) . . . . ☒ Yes ☐ No
   If "Yes" to 4a and "No" to 4b, you do not qualify as a bona fide resident. Do not complete the rest of Part I.
5. Complete the following for days present in the United States or its possessions during the tax year. (**Do not** include the income from column (d) below in Part III, but report it on Form 1040.)

(a) Date arrived in U.S.	(b) Date left U.S.	(c) Number of days in U.S. on business	(d) Income earned in U.S. on business (attach computation)	(a) Date arrived in U.S.	(b) Date left U.S.	(c) Number of days in U.S. on business	(d) Income earned in U.S. on business (attach computation)
2-16-90	2-19-90	2	$1,200 (See schedule attached)				

6. a State any contractual terms or other conditions relating to the length of your employment abroad Indefinite time period
   b State the type of visa under which you entered the foreign country Resident
   c Did your visa limit the length of your stay or employment in a foreign country? . . . . ☐ Yes ☒ No
      If "Yes," attach explanation.
   d Did you maintain a home in the United States while living abroad? . . . . ☒ Yes ☐ No
      If "Yes," show address of your home, whether it was rented, and the names and relationships of the occupants
      4710 N.W. 68th Terrace, Gainsville, Florida 32601 (Rented to unrelated party)

For Paperwork Reduction Act Notice, see page 1 of separate Instructions.

Form **2555** (1990)

Form 2555 (1990) Page **2**

Part II — Taxpayers Qualifying Under Physical Presence Test (See Instructions.)

7 The physical presence test is based on the 12-month period from _____ through _____
8 Enter your principal country of employment during your tax year ▶ _____
9 Enter all travel abroad during the 12-month period shown on line 7. Exclude travel between foreign countries that did not involve travel on, or over, international waters, or in, or over, the United States, for 24 hours or more. If the last entry is an arrival in a foreign country, enter the number of full days to the end of the 12-month period. If you have no travel to report during the period, write in the schedule below that you were physically present in a foreign country or countries during the entire 12-month period. (**Do not** include the income from column **(f)** below in Part III, but report it on Form 1040.)

(a) Name of country (including U.S.)	(b) Date arrived	(c) Date left	(d) Full days present in country	(e) Number of days in U.S. on business	(f) Income earned in U.S. on business (attach computation)

Part III — All Taxpayers

Note: *On lines 10 through 14 enter all income, including noncash income, that you earned and actually or constructively received during your 1990 tax year for services you performed in a foreign country. If any of the foreign earned income received this tax year was earned in a prior tax year, or will be earned in a later tax year (such as a bonus), see the Instructions. Do not include income from line 5, column (d), or line 9, column (f). Report amounts in U.S. dollars, using the exchange rates in effect when you actually or constructively received the income.*

If you are a cash basis taxpayer, report on Form 1040 all income you received during 1990, no matter when you performed the service.

1990 Foreign Earned Income		Amount (in U.S. dollars)
10 Total wages, salaries, bonuses, commissions, etc.	10	60,000
11 Allowable share of income for personal services performed (see Instructions):		
a In a business (including farming) or profession	11a	
b In a partnership (give name, address, and nature of income) _____	11b	7,600
12 Noncash income (market value of property or facilities furnished by employer—attach statement showing how it was determined):		
a Home (lodging)	12a	
b Meals	12b	
c Car	12c	
d Other property or facilities (specify) _____	12d	
13 Allowances, reimbursements, or expenses paid on your behalf for services you performed:		
a Cost of living and overseas differential	13a 27,000	
b Family	13b	
c Education	13c 8,000	
d Home leave	13d 6,400	
e Quarters	13e	
f For any other purpose (specify) *less U.S. source income*	13f (1,200)	
g Add lines 13a through 13f and enter the total	13g	40,200
14 Other foreign earned income (specify) _____	14	
15 Add lines 10 through 12d, line 13g, and line 14 and enter the total	15	107,800
16 Total amount of meals and lodging included on line 15 that is excludable. (See Instructions.)	16	
17 Subtract line 16 from line 15 and enter the result. This is your **foreign earned income** ▶	17	107,800

Go to page 3. Complete Part IV next if you choose to claim the housing exclusion or are claiming the housing deduction. Otherwise, skip to Part V.

Form 2555 (1990)

Part IV — For Taxpayers Claiming Housing Exclusion AND/OR Deduction

#	Description		Amount
18	Qualified housing expenses for the tax year. (See Instructions.)		10,300
19	Number of days in your qualifying period that fall within your 1990 tax year. (See Instructions.)	19 365	
20	Multiply $21.30 by the number of days on line 19. Enter the result, but do not enter more than $7,775.00		7,775
21	Subtract line 20 from line 18. (If the result is zero or less, do not complete the rest of Part IV or any of Part VII.)		2,525
22	Enter employer-provided amounts. (See Instructions.)	22 107,800	
23	Enter the amount from line 17	23 107,800	
24	Divide the amount on line 22 by the amount on line 23 and enter the result as a decimal (to two places). (Limited to 1.00.)		×1.00
25	**Housing exclusion.** Multiply the amount on line 21 by the decimal amount on line 24. Enter the result, but do not enter more than the amount on line 22. Also enter this amount on line 35 ▶		2,525

Note: If the amount on line 21 is **more than** the amount on line 25, complete line 26. Otherwise, skip to Part V if you choose to claim the foreign earned income exclusion.

| 26 | Subtract line 25 from line 21. Enter the result here and on line 40. (Complete Parts V and VI before Part VII if you choose to claim the foreign earned income exclusion.) ▶ | | –0– |

Part V — For Taxpayers Claiming Foreign Earned Income Exclusion

27	Maximum foreign earned income exclusion		$70,000	00
28	Number of days in your qualifying period that fall within your 1990 tax year. (See Instructions for line 19.)	28 365		
29	Divide the number of days on line 28 by the number of days in your 1990 tax year (usually 365) and enter the result as a decimal (to two places)		×1.00	
30	Multiply the amount on line 27 by the decimal amount on line 29		70,000	
31	Enter the amount from line 17	31 107,800		
32	Enter the amount from line 25	32 2,525		
33	Subtract line 32 from line 31. Enter the result		105,275	
34	**Foreign earned income exclusion.** Compare the amounts on lines 30 and 33. Enter the **smaller** of the two amounts here and on line 36 ▶		70,000	

Part VI — For Taxpayers Claiming Housing Exclusion, Foreign Earned Income Exclusion, or Both

35	Housing exclusion from line 25	35 2,525	
36	Foreign earned income exclusion from line 34	36 70,000	
37	Add lines 35 and 36 and enter the total		72,525
38	Deductions allowed in figuring your adjusted gross income (Form 1040, line 31) that are allocable to the excluded income. (See Instructions and attach computation.)		4,396
39	Subtract line 38 from line 37. Enter the result here and in parentheses on Form 1040, line 22. Next to the amount write "Exclusion(s) from Form 2555." On Form 1040 subtract the amount from your income to arrive at total income on Form 1040, line 23 ▶		68,129

Part VII — For Taxpayers Claiming Housing Deduction

Note: Complete this part only if: (1) you entered an amount on line 26, and (2) the amount on line 17 is more than the amount on line 37.

40	Enter the amount from line 26		40	
41	Enter the amount from line 17	41		
42	Enter the amount from line 37	42		
43	Subtract line 42 from line 41 and enter the result		43	
44	Compare the amounts on lines 40 and 43. Enter the **smaller** of the two amounts here		44	–0–

Note: If the amount on line 43 is **more than** the amount on line 44 and you could not deduct all of your 1989 housing deduction because of the 1989 limitation, complete the worksheet on page 4 of the Instructions to figure how much of your 1989 housing deduction may be carried over to 1990. Otherwise, enter –0– on line 45.

45	Housing deduction carryover from 1989 (from worksheet on page 4 of the Instructions)		45	None
46	Add lines 44 and 45. Enter the total here and on Form 1040 to the left of line 30. Next to the amount on Form 1040 write "Deduction from Form 2555." Add it to the total adjustments reported on that line ▶		46	–0–

APPENDIX C

Comparison of Tax Attributes for C Corporations, Partnerships, and S Corporations

Appendix C: Comparison of Tax Attributes for C Corporations, Partnerships, and S Corporations

Tax Attribute	C Corporation	Partnership	S Corporation
I. General Characteristics			
Application of the separate entity versus conduit (flow through) concept.	*Entity:* The corporation is treated as a separate tax-paying entity. If income is distributed to shareholders in the form of dividends, the shareholders are subject to a second tax levy on such amounts.	*Modified conduit:* The partners report their distributive share of partnership ordinary income and separately stated items on their individual returns. Most elections, such as depreciation methods, accounting period and methods, are made at the partnership level.	*Modified conduit:* Similar to the partnership form of organization. However, the S Corporation may be subject to tax at the corporate level on excess net passive income, or built-in gains under special circumstances.
Period of Existence.	Continues until dissolution; not effected by sales of stock by shareholders.	Termination can occur by agreement, or by death, retirement, or disaffiliation of a partner.	Same as for C Corporation.
Transferability of Interest.	Stock can be easily transferred; corporation may retain right to buy back shares.	Addition of new partner or transfer of partner's interest generally requires approval of other partners.	Same as for C Corporation.
Liability Exposure.	Shareholders generally only liable for capital contributions.	General partners are personally, jointly, and severally liable for partnership obligations. Limited partner usually liable only for capital contributions.	Same as for C Corporation.
Management Responsibility.	Shareholders may be part of management or may hire outside management.	All general partners participate in management. Limited partners generally do not participate.	Because of limited number of shareholders, shareholders are usually part of management.
II. Election and Restrictions			
1. Restrictions on: a. Type of owners.	No restriction.	No restriction.	Limited to individuals, estates, and certain kinds of trusts.

Appendix C: Comparison of Tax Attributes for C Corporations, Partnerships, and S Corporations

Tax Attribute	C Corporation	Partnership	S Corporation
b. Number of owners.	No restriction.	No restriction.	Limited to 35 shareholders.
c. Type of entity.	Includes domestic or foreign corporations, unincorporated entities known as associations, and certain kinds of trusts. A publicly traded partnership is taxed as a corporation unless more than 90% of its income is qualifying income.	Includes a variety of unincorporated entities. Certain joint undertakings are excluded from partnership status.	Domestic corporations and unincorporated entities (e.g., associations) are eligible.
d. Special tax classifications.	No restriction.	No restriction.	Domestic corporation cannot be a financial institution, insurance company, Domestic International Sales Corporation, or have elected the special Puerto Rico & U.S. Possessions tax credit.
e. Investments made by entity.	No restriction.	No restriction.	S Corporation must own less than 80% of the voting power and 80% of the value of a second corporation.
f. Capital structure.	No restriction.	No restriction.	Limited to a single class of stock that is outstanding. Differences in voting rights are disregarded. Special "safe harbor" rules are available.
g. Passive interest income.	No restriction.	No restriction.	Passive investment income cannot exceed 25% of gross receipts for three consecutive tax years when the corporation also has Subchapter C E&P at the end of the year.
2. Election and shareholder consent.	No election required.	No election required.	Election can be made during the preceding tax year or first 2½ months of the tax year. Shareholders must consent to the election.

Appendix C: Comparison of Tax Attributes for C Corporations, Partnerships, and S Corporations

Tax Attribute	C Corporation	Partnership	S Corporation
3. Termination of election.	Not applicable.	The partnership can terminate if it does not carry on any business, financial operation, or venture or if a sale or exchange of at least 50% of the profits or capital interests occurs within a 12-month period.	Occurs if one of the requirements is failed after the election is first effective or if the passive investment income text is failed for three consecutive tax years.
4. Revocation of election.	Not applicable.	Not applicable.	Election may be revoked only by shareholders owning more than one-half of the stock. Must be made in first 2½ months of tax year or on a prospective basis.
5. New election.	Not applicable.	Not applicable.	Not permitted for 5-year period without IRS consent to early reelection.

III. Accounting Periods and Elections

Tax Attribute	C Corporation	Partnership	S Corporation
1. Taxable year.	Calendar year or fiscal year is permitted. Personal service corporations are restricted to using a calendar year unless approval is obtained to use a fiscal year. A special election is available to use a fiscal year resulting in a 3-month or less income deferral if a series of minimum distribution requirements are met.	Generally use tax year of majority or principal partners. Otherwise a calendar year is required. Can use a fiscal year that has a business purpose for which IRS approval is obtained. An electing partnership may elect to use a fiscal year resulting in a 3-month or less income deferral if an additional required payment is made.	Same as for a partnership except that majority or principal partner rules do not apply.
2. Accounting methods.	Elected by the corporation. Use of cash method of accounting is restricted for certain personal service corporations and C Corporations having $5,000,000 or more gross receipts.	Elected by the partnership. Restrictions on the use of the cash method of accounting apply to partnerships having a C Corporation as a partner or that are tax shelters.	Elected by the S Corporation. Restrictions on the use of the cash method of accounting apply to S corporations that are tax shelters.

Appendix C: Comparison of Tax Attributes for C Corporations, Partnerships, and S Corporations

IV. Taxability of Profits

Tax Attribute	C Corporation	Partnership	S Corporation
1. Taxability of profits.	Ordinary income and capital gains are taxed to the corporation. Profits are taxed a second time when distributed.	Ordinary income and separately stated income and gain items are passed through to the partners at the end of the partnership's tax year whether or not distributed.	Same as partnership.
2. Allocation of profits.	Not applicable.	Based on partnership agreement. Special allocations are permitted.	Based on stock ownership on each day of the tax year. Special allocations are not permitted.
3. Character of income.	Profits that are distributed (including tax-exempt income) are dividends to extent of earnings and profits (E&P).	Items receiving special treatment (e.g., capital gains or tax-exempt income) are passed through separately to the partner and retain same character as when earned by the partnership.	Same as partnership.
4. Maximum tax rate for earnings.	15% on the first $50,000; 25% from $50,000 to $75,000; 34% above $75,000. A 5% surtax applies to taxable income from $100,000 to $335,000. Special rules apply to controlled groups. Personal service corporations are taxed at a flat 34% rate.	Rates of tax applicable to individual partners from 15% through 31% are levied on the income from the business. C Corporation rates apply to corporate partners.	Same as partnership except for certain special situations where a special corporate tax applies to the S Corporation.
5. Special tax levies.	Can be subject to accumulated earnings tax, personal holding company tax, corporate alternative minimum tax, and Superfund environmental tax.	Not applicable.	Can be subject to built-in gains tax and excess net passive income tax.
6. Income splitting between family members.	Only possible when earnings are distributed to shareholder. Dividends received by shareholder under age 14 are taxed at parents' marginal tax rate.	Transfer of partnership interest by gift will permit income splitting. Subject to special rules for transactions involving family members requiring payment of reasonable compensation for capital and services. Income received by partner under age 14 is taxed at parents' marginal tax rate.	Transfer of S Corporation interest by gift will permit income splitting. Special rules apply to transactions involving family members requiring payment of reasonable compensation for capital and services. Income received by partner under age 14 is taxed at parents' marginal tax rate.

Appendix C: Comparison of Tax Attributes for C Corporations, Partnerships, and S Corporations

V. Treatment of Special Income, Gain, Loss, Deduction and Credit Items

Tax Attribute	C Corporation	Partnership	S Corporation
1. Capital gains and losses.	Long-term capital gains are taxed at regular tax rates. Capital losses offset capital gains; excess losses carried back 3 years and forward 5 years.	Passed through to partners (according to partnership agreement).	Passed through to shareholders (on a daily basis according to stock ownership).
2. Section 1231 gains and losses.	Eligible for long-term capital gain or ordinary loss treatment. Loss recapture occurs at the corporate level.	Passed through to partners. Loss recapture occurs at the partner level.	Same as partnership.
3. Dividends received from domestic corporation.	Eligible for 70%, 80%, or 100% dividends-received deduction.	Passed through to partners.	Same as partnership.
4. Organizational expenditures.	Amortize over 60 or more months.	Same as C Corporation.	Same as partnership.
5. Charitable contributions.	Limited to 10% of taxable income.	Passed through to partners. Limitations apply at partner level.	Same as partnership.
6. Expensing of asset acquisition costs.	Limited to $10,000 annually.	Limited to $10,000 annually for the partnership and for each partner.	Same as partnership.
7. Expenses owed to related parties	Regular Sec. 267 rules apply to payments and sales or exchanges made to or by the corporation and certain other related parties.	Regular Sec. 267 rules can apply. Special Sec. 267 rules for passthrough entities apply to payments made by the partnership to a partner.	Same as partnership.

Appendix C: Comparison of Tax Attributes for C Corporations, Partnerships, and S Corporations

Tax Attribute	C Corporation	Partnership	S Corporation
8. Employment-related tax considerations.	An owner-employee may be treated as an employee for Social Security tax and corporate fringe benefit purposes. The corporate qualified pension and profit-sharing benefits available to owner-employees are comparable to the plan benefits for self-employed individuals (partners and sole proprietors).	A partner is not considered an employee of the business. Therefore, the partner must pay self-employment tax on the net income from the business. Corporate fringe benefits such as group term life insurance are not available (i.e., the premiums are not deductible by the business and are not excludable from the partner's income). Self-employed persons may deduct 25% of health insurance premiums for AGI for themselves, their spouses, and dependents if health insurance is also provided for employees of the business.	Corporate fringe benefits are generally not available to S Corporation shareholders. S Corporation shareholders may be treated as employees, however, for Social Security tax payments and qualified pension and profit sharing plan rules. Special deduction for 25% of health insurance premiums is also available to S corporation shareholders.
9. Tax preference items.	Subject to the corporate alternative minimum tax at the corporate level.	Passed through to partners and taxed under the individual alternative minimum tax rules.	Same as partnership.

VI. Deductibility of Losses and Special Items

Tax Attribute	C Corporation	Partnership	S Corporation
1. Deductibility of losses.	Losses create net operating loss (NOL) which can be carried back 3 years or forward 15 years or capital loss which can be carried back 3 years or forward 5 years.	Ordinary losses and separately stated loss and deduction items are passed through to the partners at the end of the partnership tax year. May create a personal NOL.	Same as partnership.
2. Allocation of losses.	Not applicable.	Based on partnership agreement. Special allocations are permitted.	Based on stock ownership on each day of the tax year. Special allocations are not permitted.
3. Shareholder and entity loss limitations.	Passive losses may be restricted under the passive activity limitation if the C Corporation is either closely-held or a personal service corporation.	Limited to partner's basis for the partnership interest. Ratable share of all partnership liabilities are included in basis of partnership interest. Excess losses are carried over indefinitely until partnership interest again has a basis. Subject to at risk, passive activity, and hobby loss restrictions.	Limited to shareholder's basis for the stock interest plus basis of S Corporation debts to the shareholder. Excess losses are carried over indefinitely until shareholder again has basis for stock or debt. Subject to the at risk, passive activity, and hobby loss restrictions.

Appendix C: Comparison of Tax Attributes for C Corporations, Partnerships, and S Corporations

Tax Attribute	C Corporation	Partnership	S Corporation
4. Basis adjustments for debt and equity interests.	Not applicable.	Basis in partnership interest reduced by loss and deduction passthrough. Subsequent profits will increase basis of partnership interest.	Basis in S Corporation stock reduced by loss and deduction passthrough. Once basis of stock has been reduced to zero, any other losses and deductions reduce basis of debt (but not below zero). Subsequent profits will restore basis reductions to debt before increasing basis of stock.
5. Investment interest deduction limitation.	Not applicable.	Investment interest expenses and income are passed through to the partners. Limitation applies at partner level.	Same as partnership.

VII. Distributions

Tax Attribute	C Corporation	Partnership	S Corporation
1. Taxability of nonliquidating distributions to shareholder.	Taxable as dividends if made from current or accumulated E & P. Additional distributions reduce shareholder's basis for stock, or cause capital gain to be recognized.	Tax-free unless the money or money equivalents that are received by the partner exceeds their basis for the partnership interest.	Tax-free if made from the Accumulated Adjustment Account, PTI, or shareholder's basis for his stock. Taxable if made out of accumulated E & P or after stock basis has been reduced to zero.
2. Taxability of nonliquidating distributions to distributing entity.	Gain (but not loss) recognized as if the property had been sold immediately before the distribution.	No gain or loss recognized by the partnership except when a disproportionate distribution of Sec. 751 property occurs.	Gain (but not loss) recognized and passed through to the shareholders as if the property had been sold immediately before the distribution. Gain may be taxed to the S Corporation under one of the special tax levies.

Appendix C: Comparison of Tax Attributes for C Corporations, Partnerships, and S Corporations

Tax Attribute	C Corporation	Partnership	S Corporation
3. Basis adjustment to owner's investment for distribution.	None unless the distribution is in excess of E & P.	Amount of money or adjusted basis of distributed property reduces basis in partnership interest.	Amount of money or FMV of distributed property reduces basis of stock except when distribution is made out of accumulated E & P.

VIII. Other Items

	C Corporation	Partnership	S Corporation
1. Tax return.	Form 1120 or 1120A	Form 1065 (Information Return).	Form 1120S (Information Return).
2. Due date.	March 15 for calendar-year C Corporation.	April 15 for calendar-year partnership.	March 15 for calendar-year S Corporation.
3. Extensions of time permitted.	6 months.	4 months.	6 months.
4. Estimated tax payments required.	Yes—April 15, June 15, September 15, and December 15 for calendar-year C Corporation.	No—estimated taxes are required of the partners for passed through income, etc.	Yes—for 1990 and later tax years. Applies only to built in gains tax, excess net passive income tax, and investment tax credit recapture amount.
5. Audit rules.	Corporation is audited independently of its shareholders.	Special audit rules apply requiring audit of partnership and requiring partners to take a position consistent with the partnership tax return.	Same as partnership.

APPENDIX D

Credit for State Death Taxes

If the Adjusted Taxable Estate[a] Is:	The Maximum Tax Credit Shall Be:
Not over $90,000	8/10ths of 1% of the amount by which the adjusted taxable estate exceeds $40,000.
Over $90,000 but not over $140,000	$400 plus 1.6% of the excess over $90,000.
Over $140,000 but not over $240,000	$1,200 plus 2.4% of the excess over $140,000.
Over $240,000 but not over $440,000	$3,600 plus 3.2% of the excess over $240,000.
Over $440,000 but not over $640,000	$10,000 plus 4% of the excess over $440,000.
Over $640,000 but not over $840,000	$18,000 plus 4.8% of the excess over $640,000.
Over $840,000 but not over $1,040,000	$27,600 plus 5.6% of the excess over $840,000.
Over $1,040,000 but not over $1,540,000	$38,800 plus 6.4% of the excess over $1,040,000.
Over $1,540,000 but not over $2,040,000	$70,800 plus 7.2% of the excess over $1,540,000.
Over $2,040,000 but not over $2,540,000	$106,800 plus 8% of the excess over $2,040,000.
Over $2,540,000 but not over $3,040,000	$146,800 plus 8.8% of the excess over $2,540,000.
Over $3,040,000 but not over $3,540,000	$190,800 plus 9.6% of the excess over $3,040,000.
Over $3,540,000 but not over $4,040,000	$238,800 plus 10.4% of the excess over $3,540,000.
Over $4,040,000 but not over $5,040,000	$290,800 plus 11.2% of the excess over $4,040,000.
Over $5,040,000 but not over $6,040,000	$402,800 plus 12% of the excess over $5,040,000.
Over $6,040,000 but not over $7,040,000	$522,800 plus 12.8% of the excess over $6,040,000.
Over $7,040,000 but not over $8,040,000	$650,800 plus 13.6% of the excess over $7,040,000.
Over $8,040,000 but not over $9,040,000	$786,800 plus 14.4% of the excess over $8,040,000.
Over $9,040,000 but not over $10,040,000	$930,800 plus 15.2% of the excess over $9,040,000.
Over $10,040,000	$1,082,800 plus 16% of the excess over $10,040,000.

[a]Taxable estate minus $60,000.
Source: IRC, Sec. 2011(b).

APPENDIX E

Actuarial Tables

TRANSFERS MADE AFTER APRIL 30, 1989
EXCERPT FROM TABLE R(1)
SINGLE LIFE REMAINDER FACTORS

	Interest Rate						
AGE	9.4%	9.6%	9.8%	10.0%	10.2%	10.4%	10.6%
25	.03164	.03029	.02902	.02784	.02673	.02569	.02472
26	.03328	.03186	.03052	.02928	.02811	.02701	.02598
27	.03509	.03360	.03219	.03088	.02965	.02849	.02741
28	.03708	.03550	.03403	.03264	.03134	.03013	.02898
29	.03925	.03760	.03604	.03458	.03322	.03193	.03072
30	.04162	.03988	.03825	.03671	.03527	.03391	.03264
31	.04421	.04238	.04067	.03905	.03753	.03610	.03475
32	.04702	.04510	.04329	.04160	.04000	.03849	.03707
33	.05007	.04806	.04616	.04438	.04269	.04111	.03961
34	.05336	.05125	.04926	.04738	.04561	.04394	.04236
35	.05690	.05469	.05260	.05063	.04877	.04702	.04535
36	.06068	.05836	.05617	.05411	.05215	.05031	.04856
37	.06470	.06228	.05999	.05783	.05578	.05384	.05200
38	.06899	.06646	.06407	.06180	.05965	.05761	.05568
39	.07356	.07092	.06841	.06604	.06379	.06165	.05962
40	.07841	.07565	.07303	.07055	.06820	.06596	.06383
41	.08355	.08067	.07794	.07535	.07288	.07054	.06832
42	.08896	.08596	.08312	.08041	.07784	.07539	.07306
43	.09466	.09154	.08858	.08576	.08308	.08052	.07808
44	.10067	.09743	.09434	.09141	.08861	.08594	.08340
45	.10699	.10362	.10042	.09736	.09445	.09167	.08901
46	.11362	.11013	.10680	.10363	.10060	.09770	.09494
47	.12059	.11697	.11352	.11022	.10707	.10406	.10119
48	.12787	.12412	.12055	.11713	.11386	.11073	.10774
49	.13544	.13157	.12787	.12433	.12094	.11769	.11458
50	.14331	.13931	.13548	.13182	.12831	.12494	.12172
51	.15150	.14737	.14342	.13963	.13600	.13251	.12917
52	.16004	.15579	.15172	.14780	.14405	.14044	.13698
53	.16896	.16458	.16038	.15635	.15247	.14875	.14517
54	.17822	.17372	.16940	.16524	.16124	.15740	.15370
55	.18785	.18322	.17878	.17450	.17039	.16642	.16261

EXCERPT FROM TABLE R(1)
SINGLE LIFE REMAINDER FACTORS

	Interest Rate						
AGE	9.4%	9.6%	9.8%	10.0%	10.2%	10.4%	10.6%
56	.19785	.19310	.18854	.18414	.17991	.17583	.17190
57	.20824	.20338	.19870	.19419	.18984	.18564	.18160
58	.21904	.21407	.20927	.20464	.20018	.19587	.19172
59	.23023	.22515	.22024	.21551	.21093	.20652	.20225
60	.24178	.23659	.23158	.22674	.22206	.21753	.21316
61	.25366	.24837	.24325	.23831	.23353	.22890	.22442
62	.26584	.26045	.25524	.25020	.24532	.24059	.23601
63	.27832	.27284	.26754	.26240	.25742	.25260	.24793
64	.29111	.28555	.28016	.27493	.26987	.26495	.26019
65	.30429	.29865	.29317	.28787	.28271	.27771	.27286
66	.31788	.31217	.30663	.30124	.29601	.29093	.28600
67	.33191	.32614	.32053	.31508	.30978	.30462	.29961
68	.34638	.34055	.33488	.32937	.32401	.31879	.31371
69	.36120	.35533	.34961	.34405	.33863	.33336	.32822
70	.37634	.37043	.36468	.35907	.35361	.34829	.34310
71	.39171	.38578	.38000	.37436	.36886	.36349	.35826
72	.40733	.40138	.39558	.38991	.38439	.37899	.37373
73	.42321	.41725	.41143	.40575	.40021	.39479	.38950
74	.43940	.43345	.42763	.42195	.41639	.41096	.40565
75	.45598	.45004	.44424	.43856	.43301	.42758	.42226
76	.47297	.46706	.46129	.45563	.45009	.44467	.43937
77	.49033	.48447	.47873	.47311	.46761	.46221	.45693
78	.50800	.50220	.49652	.49094	.48548	.48013	.47488
79	.52582	.52009	.51448	.50897	.50356	.49826	.49306
80	.54366	.53802	.53248	.52705	.52171	.51647	.51133
81	.56134	.55579	.55035	.54499	.53974	.53457	.52950
82	.57875	.57331	.56796	.56270	.55753	.55245	.54745
83	.59581	.59047	.58523	.58007	.57500	.57001	.56510
84	.61253	.60731	.60218	.59713	.59216	.58726	.58245
85	.62896	.62387	.61886	.61392	.60906	.60428	.59956
86	.64496	.64000	.63511	.63030	.62555	.62088	.61627
87	.66031	.65548	.65071	.64602	.64139	.63683	.63233
88	.67507	.67037	.66574	.66117	.65666	.65221	.64783
89	.68952	.68495	.68045	.67601	.67163	.66730	.66304

Source: Notice 89-60, I.R.B. 1989-22, 16.

EXCERPT FROM TABLE B
TERM CERTAIN REMAINDER FACTORS

	Interest Rate						
YEARS	9.4%	9.6%	9.8%	10.0%	10.2%	10.4%	10.6%
1	.914077	.912409	.910747	.909091	.907441	.905797	.904159
2	.835536	.832490	.829460	.826446	.823449	.820468	.817504
3	.763744	.759571	.755428	.751315	.747232	.743178	.739153
4	.698121	.693039	.688003	.683013	.678069	.673168	.668312
5	.638136	.632335	.626597	.620921	.615307	.609754	.604261
6	.583305	.576948	.570671	.564474	.558355	.552313	.546348
7	.533186	.526412	.519737	.513158	.506674	.500284	.493985
8	.487373	.480303	.473349	.466507	.459777	.453156	.446641
9	.445496	.438233	.431101	.424098	.417221	.410467	.403835
10	.407218	.399848	.392624	.385543	.378603	.371800	.365131
11	.372228	.364824	.357581	.350494	.343560	.336775	.330137
12	.340245	.332869	.325666	.318631	.311760	.305050	.298496
13	.311010	.303713	.296599	.289664	.282904	.276313	.269888
14	.284287	.277110	.270127	.263331	.256719	.250284	.244022
15	.259860	.252838	.246017	.239392	.232957	.226706	.220634
16	.237532	.230691	.224059	.217629	.211395	.205350	.199489
17	.217123	.210485	.204061	.197845	.191828	.186005	.180369
18	.198467	.192048	.185848	.179859	.174073	.168483	.163083
19	.181414	.175226	.169260	.163508	.157961	.152612	.147453
20	.165826	.159878	.154153	.148644	.143340	.138235	.133321
21	.151578	.145874	.140395	.135131	.130073	.125213	.120543
22	.138554	.133097	.127864	.122846	.118033	.113418	.108990
23	.126649	.121439	.116452	.111678	.107108	.102733	.098544
24	.115767	.110802	.106058	.101526	.097195	.093056	.089100
25	.105820	.101097	.096592	.092296	.088198	.084289	.080560

Source: Notice 89-60, I.R.B. 1989-22, 16.

APPENDIX F

Glossary

Accounting method The method used to determine the tax year in which income and expenses are reported for tax purposes. Generally, the same method must be used for tax purposes as is used for keeping books and records. The accounting treatment used for any item of income or expense and for specific items (e.g., installment sales and contracts) is included in this term.

Accounting period See Tax year.

Accumulated Adjustments Account (AAA) Account that must be kept by S corporations. The cumulative total of the ordinary income or loss and separately stated items for the most recent S corporation election period.

Accumulated earnings and profits The sum of the undistributed current earnings and profits balances (and deficits) from previous years reduced by any distributions that have been made out of accumulated earnings and profits.

Accumulated earnings credit Deduction that reduces the accumulated taxable income amount. It does not offset the accumulated earnings tax on a dollar-for-dollar basis. Different rules apply for operating companies, service companies, and holding or investment companies.

Accumulated earnings tax Penalty tax on corporations other than those subject to the personal holding company tax among others. It is levied on a corporation's current year addition to its accumulated earnings balance in excess of the amount needed for reasonable business purposes and not distributed to the shareholders. This tax is intended to discourage companies from retaining excessive amounts of earnings if the funds are invested in activities that are unrelated to the business's needs. The tax is 28% of accumulated taxable income.

Accumulation distribution rules (throwback rules) Exception to the general rule that distributable net income (DNI) serves as a ceiling on the amount taxable to a beneficiary. Under the general rule, the beneficiary excludes the portion of any distribution in excess of DNI from his gross income. Accumulation distributions made by a trust are taxable to the beneficiaries in the year received.

Acquiescence policy IRS policy of announcing whether it agrees or disagrees with a Tax Court regular decision. Such statements are not issued for every case.

Acquisitive reorganization A transaction in which the acquiring corporation obtains all or part of the stock or assets of a target corporation.

Adjusted current earnings Alternative minimum taxable income for the tax year plus or minus a series of special adjusted current earnings adjustments specified in Sec. 56(g)(4) (e.g., special depreciation calculation, special E&P rules, etc.).

Adjusted current earnings adjustment 75% of the excess (if any) of the adjusted current earnings of the corporation over the alternative minimum taxable income (determined without regard to this adjustment and the alternative tax NOL deduction). A downward adjustment is provided for 75% of the excess (if any) of alternative minimum taxable income (determined without regard to this adjustment and the alternative tax NOL deduction) over the adjusted current earnings of the corporation.

Adjusted grossed-up basis For Sec. 338 purposes, the sum of (1) the basis of a purchasing corporation's stock interest in a target corporation plus (2) an adjustment for the target corporation's liabilities on the day following the acquisition date plus or minus (3) other relevant items.

Adjusted income from rents (AIR) This amount is equal to the corporation's gross income from rents reduced by the deductions claimed for amortization or depreciation, property taxes, interest, and rent.

Adjusted net book income (ANBI) For alternative minimum tax purposes, the corporation's net income or loss before federal taxes as set forth in the applicable financial statement.

Adjusted ordinary gross income (AOGI) A corporation's adjusted ordinary gross income is its ordinary gross income reduced by (1) certain expenses incurred in connection with gross income from rents, mineral, oil and gas royalties, and working interests in oil or gas wells, (2) interest received by dealers on certain U.S.

F-1

obligations, (3) interest received from condemnation awards, judgments, or tax refunds, and (4) rents from certain tangible personal property manufactured or produced by the corporation.

Adjusted taxable gift Taxable gifts made after 1976 that are valued at their date-of-gift value. These gifts affect the size of the transfer tax base at death.

Administrative interpretation Treasury Department interpretation of a provision of the Code. Such interpretations may be in the form of Treasury Regulations, revenue rulings, or revenue procedures.

Advance ruling See letter ruling.

Affiliated corporations A group consisting of a parent corporation and at least one subsidiary corporation.

AIR See Adjusted income from rents.

Alien Individuals who are not U.S. citizens.

Alternate valuation date The alternate valuation date is the earlier of 6 months after the date of death or the date the property is sold, exchanged, distributed, etc. by the estate. Unless this option is elected, the gross estate is valued at its fair market value on the date of the decedent's death.

Alternative minimum tax (AMT) Tax which applies to individuals, corporations, and estates and trusts if it exceeds the taxpayer's regular tax liability. Most taxpayers are not subject to this tax. This tax equals the amount by which the tentative minimum tax exceeds the regular tax.

Alternative minimum taxable income (AMTI) The taxpayer's taxable income (1) increased by tax preference items and (2) adjusted for income, gain, deduction, and loss items that have to be recomputed under the alternative minimum tax system.

ANBI See Adjusted net book income.

AMT See Alternative minimum tax.

AMTI See Alternative minimum taxable income.

Announcement Information release issued by the IRS to provide a technical explanation of a current tax issue. Announcements are aimed at tax practitioners rather than the general public.

Annual exclusion An exemption that is intended to relieve a donor from keeping an account of and reporting the numerous small gifts (e.g., wedding and Christmas gifts) made throughout the year. This exclusion is currently $10,000 per donee.

AOGI See Adjusted ordinary gross income.

Appeals coordinated issue Issue over which the appeals officer must obtain a concurrence of guidance from the regional director of appeals in order to render a decision.

Assignment of income doctrine A judicial requirement that income be taxed to the person that earns it.

Association A business trust, partnership, or other unincorporated entity that is made up of associates and is taxed as a corporation because it has a joint profit motive, continuity of life, centralized management, limited liability, or free transferability of interests.

At-risk basis Essentially the same amount as the regular partnership basis with the exception that liabilities increase the at-risk basis only if the partner is at-risk for such an amount.

At-risk rules These rules limit the partner's loss deductions to his at-risk basis.

Bardahl formula Mathematical formula for determining the amount of working capital that a business reasonably needs for accumulated earnings tax purposes. For a manufacturing company, the formula is based on the business's operating cycle.

Boot Property that may not be received tax-free in certain tax-free transactions (i.e., any money, short-term debt, and so on).

Bootstrap acquisition An acquisition where an investor purchases part of a corporation's stock and then has the corporation redeem the remainder of the seller's stock.

Branch profits tax Special tax levied by the U.S. government on the branch activities of a foreign corporation doing business in the United States.

Brother-sister controlled group This type of controlled group exists if (1) 5 or fewer individuals, estates, or trusts own at least 80% of the voting stock or 80% of the value of each corporation and (2) there is common ownership of more than 50% of the voting power or 50% of the value of all classes of stock.

Built-in deduction A deduction that accrues in a separate return limitation year but which is recognized for tax purposes in a consolidated return year.

Built-in gain A gain that accrued prior to the conversion of a C corporation to an S corporation.

Built-in gains tax Tax on built-in gains that are recognized by the S corporation during the 10-year period commencing on the date that the S corporation election took effect.

Capital gain property For charitable contribution deduction purposes, property upon which a long-term capital gain would be recognized if that property was sold at its fair market value.

Capital gains tax Tax levied on an S corporation that realizes a high proportion of its income as capital gains. The tax is the lesser of (1) 34% times the amount of the net capital gain in excess of $25,000 or (2) the regular corporate tax rate(s) times the corporation's taxable income. This tax is intended to prevent corporations from avoiding double taxation of the gain by making an

S corporation election and then revoking it after realizing the gain and distributing it to the shareholders.

Capital interest The amount a partner would receive if the partnership liquidated on the day the partnership interest was received.

C corporation Form of business entity that is taxed as a separate tax-paying entity. Its income is subject to an initial tax at the corporate level. Its shareholders are subject to a second tax if dividends are paid from the corporation's earnings and profits. This type of corporation is sometimes referred to as a regular corporation.

Certiorari An appeal from a lower court (i.e., a federal court of appeals) which the U.S. Supreme Court agrees to hear. Such appeals, which are made as a writ of certiorari, are generally not granted unless (1) a constitutional issue needs to be decided or (2) there is a conflict among the lower court decisions that must be clarified.

Charitable contribution deduction Contributions of money or property made to qualified organizations (i.e., public charities and private nonoperating foundations). The amount of the deduction depends upon (1) the type of charity receiving the contribution, (2) the type of property contributed, and (3) other limitations mandated by the tax law.

Charitable remainder annuity trust This type of trust makes distributions to individuals for a certain time period or for life. The annual distributions are a uniform percentage (5% or higher) of the value of the trust property as valued on the date of transfer.

Charitable remainder unitrust This type of trust makes annual distributions for either a specified time period or for life. The distributions are a uniform percentage (5% or higher) of the value of the property as revalued annually.

Clifford trust A trust that is normally held for a 10-year period after which the principal reverts to the grantor. The trust accounting income is not generally taxed to the grantor.

Closed-fact situation Situation or transaction that has already occurred.

Closed transaction Situation where the property in question (e.g., property distributed in a corporate liquidation) can be valued with reasonable certainty. The gain or loss reported on the transaction is determinable at the time the transaction occurs. See open transaction doctrine.

Closely held corporation A corporation that is owned by either a single individual or a small group of individuals who may or may not be family members.

Closely held C corporation For purposes of the at-risk rules, a C corporation in which more than 50% of the stock is owned by 5 or fewer individuals at any time during the last half of the corporation's tax year.

Collapsible corporation Corporation formed or availed of principally for the manufacturing, construction, or production of property or for the purchase of Sec. 341 assets with the intention of either (1) selling or exchanging the stock of the corporation or (2) distributing the property to its shareholders before the corporation has realized a substantial portion of the taxable income to be derived from the property.

Combined controlled group A group of three or more corporations which are members of a parent-subsidiary or brother-sister controlled group. In addition, at least one of the corporations must be the parent corporation of the parent-subsidiary controlled group and a member of a brother-sister controlled group.

Combined taxable income The total amount of the separate taxable incomes of the individual group members of an affiliated group that is filing a consolidated tax return.

Common law state All states other than the community property states are common law states. In such states, all assets acquired during the marriage are the property of the acquiring spouse.

Community property law Law in community property states mandating that all property acquired after marriage is generally community property unless acquired by gift or inheritance. Each spouse owns a one-half interest in community property.

Community property state The eight traditional community property states (Louisiana, Texas, New Mexico, Arizona, California, Washington, Idaho, and Nevada) and Wisconsin (which adopted a similar law). These states do not follow the common law concept of property ownership.

Complex trust Trust that is not required to distribute all of its income currently.

Consent dividend Hypothetical dividend generally deemed paid to a personal holding company's shareholders on the last day of the corporation's tax year. May also be paid so as to avoid the accumulated earnings tax.

Consistency period The 12-month period preceding the acquisition period, the 12-month or shorter acquisition period, and the 12-month period that follows the acquisition period.

Consolidated return change of ownership (CRCO) rules These rules affect affiliated groups who have (1) incurred net operating losses and (2) had a major change in the parent corporation's stock ownership and (3) acquired a profitable corporation. They restrict the affiliated group's ability to use its net operating loss carryforwards to the extent its old members contribute to consolidated taxable income.

Consolidated return year A tax year for which a consolidated return is filed or is required to be filed by an affiliated group.

Consolidated taxable income The taxable income amount reported on a consolidated return filed by a group of affiliated corporations. The calculation of this amount is determined by establishing each member's separate taxable income and then following a series of steps that result in a consolidated amount.

Consolidated tax return A single tax return filed by a group of related corporations (i.e., affiliated group).

Consolidation A form of tax-free reorganization involving two or more corporations whose assets are acquired by a new corporation. The stock, securities, and other consideration transferred by the acquiring corporation is then distributed by each target corporation to its shareholders and security holders in exchange for their stock and securities.

Constructive dividend An indirect payment, or undeclared dividend, made to a shareholder without the benefit of a formal declaration usually resulting from a reclassification of a transaction by the IRS. Transactions that can produce constructive dividends include the payment of unreasonable compensation or the making of loans to shareholders.

Continuity of interest doctrine The judicial requirement that shareholders who transfer property to a transferee corporation continue their ownership in the property through holding the transferee corporation's stock in order to defer recognition of their gains.

Controlled foreign corporation Foreign corporation that is (1) directly or indirectly controlled by U.S. shareholders at any time during the taxable year provided that (2) such U.S. shareholders control more than 50% of its voting power or more than 50% of the value of the outstanding stock.

Controlled group A controlled group is two or more separately incorporated businesses owned by a related group of individuals or entities. Such groups include parent-subsidiary groups, brother-sister groups, or combined groups.

Corporation A separate taxpaying entity (such as an association, joint stock company, or insurance company) that must file a tax return every year, even when it had no income or loss for the year.

Crummey trust Technique that allows a donor to set up a discretionary trust and obtain an annual exclusion. Such a trust arrangement allows the beneficiary to demand an annual distribution of the lesser of $10,000 or the amount transferred to the trust that year.

C short year That portion of an S termination year that commences on the day on which the termination is effective and continues through to the last day of the corporation's tax year.

Current distribution See Nonliquidating distribution.

Current earnings and profits Earnings and profits calculated annually by (1) adjusting the corporation's taxable income (or net operating loss) for items that must be recomputed, (2) adding back any excluded income items, income deferrals, and deductions not allowed in computing earnings and profits, and (3) subtracting any expenses and losses not deductible in computing the corporation's taxable income.

Curtesy A widower's interest in his deceased wife's property.

Deductions in respect of a decedent (DRD) Deduction accrued prior to death but not includible on decedent's final tax return because of the decedent's method of accounting.

Deemed liquidation election Election under Sec. 338 permitting an acquiring corporation that acquires a controlling interest in a target corporation's stock to step-up or step-down the basis of the target corporation's assets to their adjusted grossed-up basis by having the target corporation be liquidated for tax purposes only.

Deemed paid foreign tax credit An indirect foreign tax credit that is available to a domestic corporation owning at least 10% of the voting stock of a foreign corporation when the foreign corporation pays or accrues creditable foreign taxes.

Deferral privilege A tax exemption provided U.S. taxpayers who own stock of a foreign corporation. The foreign corporation's earnings are generally not taxed in the United States until repatriated unless an exception such as the Subpart F rules applies.

Deferred intercompany transaction Intercompany transaction involving (1) the sale or exchange of property; (2) the performance of services in which the acquiring party capitalizes the amount of the expenditure for the services; or (3) any other transaction involving an expenditure that is capitalized by the acquiring party.

Deficiency dividend This type of dividend substitutes an income tax levy on the dividend payment at the shareholder level for the payment of the personal holding company tax.

DIF See Discriminant Function Program.

Discriminant Function Program Program used by the IRS to select individual returns for audit. This system is intended to identify those tax returns which are most likely to contain errors.

Dissolution A legal term implying that a corporation has surrendered the charter that it originally received from the state.

Distributable net income (DNI) Maximum amount of distributions taxed to the beneficiaries and deducted by a trust or estate.

Distributive share The portion of partnership taxable and nontaxable income, losses, credits, and so on that the partner must report for tax purposes.

Dividend A distribution of property made by a corporation out of its earnings and profits.

Dividends-paid deduction Distributions made out of a corporation's earnings and profits are eligible for this deduction for personal holding company tax and accumulated earnings tax purposes. The deduction is equal to the amount of money plus the adjusted basis of the nonmoney property distributed.

Dividends-received deduction This deduction attempts to mitigate the triple taxation that would occur if one corporation paid dividends to a corporate shareholder who, in turn, distributed such amounts to its individual shareholders. Certain restrictions and limitations apply to this deduction.

Divisive reorganization Transaction in which part of a transferor corporation's assets are transferred to a second, newly created corporation that is controlled by either the transferee or its shareholders.

DISC See Domestic International Sales Corporation.

DNI See Distributable net income.

Domestic corporation Corporation that is incorporated in one of the 50 states or under federal law.

Domestic International Sales Corporation (DISC) A domestic corporation that earns most of its income from exports.

Dower A widow's interest in her deceased husband's property.

DRD See Deductions in respect of a decedent.

E & P See Earnings and profits.

Earnings and profits A measure of the corporation's ability to pay a dividend from its current and accumulated earnings without an impairment of capital.

Estate A legal entity which comes into being only upon the death of the person whose assets are being administered. The estate continues in existence until the duties of the executor have been completed.

Excess loss account A negative investment account of a member of an affiliated group that files a consolidated tax return which attaches to an investment in a lower-tier corporation.

Excess net passive income An amount equal to the S corporation's net passive income multiplied by the fraction consisting of its passive investment income less 25% of its gross receipts divided by its passive investment income. It is limited to the corporation's taxable income.

Excess net passive income tax Tax levied when (1) an S corporation has passive investment income for the taxable year that exceeds 25% of its gross receipts and (2) at the close of the tax year the S corporation has earnings and profits from C corporation tax years.

Exemption equivalent That portion of the tax base that is completely free of transfer taxes as a result of the unified credit.

Failure-to-file-penalty Penalty imposed for the failure to timely file a return. The penalty is assessed in the amount of 5% per month (or fraction thereof) on the amount of the net tax due. The maximum penalty for failing to file is 25%.

Failure-to-pay penalty Penalty imposed at the rate of 0.5% per month (or fraction thereof) on the amount of tax shown on the return less any tax payments made before the beginning of the month for which the penalty is being calculated. The maximum penalty is 25%.

Fair market value (FMV) The amount that would be realized from the sale of a property at a price that is agreeable to both the buyer and the seller when neither party is obligated to participate in the transaction.

Fiduciary A person or other entity (e.g., a guardian, executor, trustee, or administrator) who holds and manages property for someone else.

Fiduciary taxation The special tax rules that apply to fiduciaries (e.g., trusts and estates).

Flower bonds Bonds that sell at a discount because of their relatively low interest rate and are eligible to be redeemed at face value in payment of federal estate taxes.

FMV See Fair market value.

Foreign branch An office or other establishment of a domestic entity that operates in a foreign country.

Foreign corporation A corporation that is incorporated under the laws of a country other than the United States.

Foreign personal holding company (FPHC) A foreign corporation that (1) is more than 50% owned by no more than 5 U.S. citizens or residents at any time during the taxable year and (2) earns at least 50% of its gross income from foreign personal holding company income. The gross income amount increases to 60% if the company did not have foreign personal holding company status in the previous taxable year.

Foreign Sales Corporation (FSC) Corporation that is created or organized under the laws of certain foreign countries or U.S. possessions (other than Puerto Rico) and which earns most of its income from export activities.

Foreign tax credit Tax credit given to mitigate the possibility of double taxation faced by U.S. citizens, residents, and corporations earning foreign income.

Foreign trade income Income earned by a foreign sales corporation that is attributable to foreign trading gross receipts.

Forum shopping The ability to consider differing precedents in choosing the forum for litigation.

FPHC See Foreign Personal Holding Company.

FSC See Foreign sales corporation.

Future interest Such interests include reversions, remainders, and other interests that may not be used, owned, or enjoyed until some future date.

General partner Partner or partners with (1) the authority to make management decisions and commitments for the partnership and (2) unlimited liability for all partnership debts.

General partnership A partnership where the two or more partners do not provide that one or more of the partners is a limited partner.

General power of appointment Power of appointment under which the holder can appoint the property to himself, his estate, his creditors, or the creditors of his estate. Such power may be exercisable during the decedent's life, by his will, or both.

Generation-skipping transfer A disposition that (1) provides interests for more than one generation of beneficiaries who are in a younger generation than the transferor or (2) provides an interest solely for a person two or more generations younger than the transferor.

Gift tax A wealth transfer tax that applies if the property transfer occurs during a person's lifetime.

Grantor The transferor who creates a trust.

Grantor trust Trust governed by Secs. 671 through 679. The income from such trusts is taxed to the grantor even if some or all of the income has been distributed.

Gross estate The gross estate includes items to which the decedent held title at death as well as certain incomplete transfers made by the decedent prior to death.

Guaranteed minimum Minimum amount of payment guaranteed to a partner. This amount is important if the partner's distributive share is less than his guaranteed minimum. See also Guaranteed payment.

Guaranteed payment Minimum amount of payment guaranteed to a partner in the form of a salary-like payment made for services provided to the partnership and interest-like payments for the use of invested capital. Guaranteed payments, which may be in the form of a guaranteed minimum amount or a set amount, are taxed as ordinary income. See also Guaranteed minimum.

Hedge agreement This is an obligation on the part of a shareholder-employee to repay to the corporation any portion of salary that is disallowed by the IRS as a deduction. It is also used in connection with other corporate payments to shareholder-employees (e.g., travel and entertainment expenses).

Housing cost amount A special deduction or exclusion equal to the housing expenses incurred by a taxpayer eligible for the Sec. 911 earned income exclusion minus the base housing amount.

Income beneficiary Entity or individual that receives the income from a trust.

Income in respect of a decedent (IRD) Amount to which the decedent was entitled as gross income but which were not properly includible in computing his taxable income for the tax year ending with his date of death or for a previous tax year under the method of accounting employed by the decedent.

Information release An administrative pronouncement concerning an issue that the IRS thinks the general public will be interested in. Such releases are issued in lay terms and widely published.

Innocent spouse provision This provision exempts a spouse from penalty and liability for tax if such spouse had no knowledge of nor reason to know about an item of taxable income that is in dispute.

Intercompany transaction Transaction that takes place during a consolidated return year between corporations that are members of the same group immediately after the transaction.

Interpretative Regulations Treasury Regulations that serve to interpret the provisions of the Internal Revenue Code.

Inter vivos trust Transfer to a trust that is made during the grantor's lifetime.

IRD See Income in respect of a decedent.

Irrevocable trust Trust under which the grantor cannot require the trustee to return the trust's assets.

Joint tenancy A popular form of property ownership that serves as a substitute for a will. Each joint tenant is deemed to have an equal interest in the property.

Judicial decisions Decision rendered by a court deciding the case that is presented to it by a plaintiff and defendant. These decisions are important sources of the tax law and can come from trial courts and appellate courts.

Legislative reenactment doctrine Rule holding that Congress's failure to change the wording in the Code over an extended period signifies that Congress has approved the treatment provided in the regulations.

Letter ruling Letter rulings originate from the IRS at the taxpayer's request. They describe how the IRS will treat a proposed transaction. It is only binding on the person requesting the ruling provided the transaction is completed as proposed in the ruling. Letter rulings that are of general interest are published as Revenue rulings.

Life estate A property transfer in trust that results in the transferor reserving the right to income for life. Another individual is named to receive the property upon the transferor's death.

Limited partner Partner who has no right to be active in the management of the partnership and whose liability is limited to his original investment plus any additional amounts that he is obligated to contribute.

Limited partnership A partnership where one or more of the partners is designated as a limited partner.

Liquidating distribution A distribution that (1) liquidates a partner's entire partnership interest due to retirement, death, or other business reason or (2) partially or totally liquidates a shareholder's stock interest in a corporation following the adoption of a plan at liquidation.

Loss corporation A corporation entitled to use a net operating loss carryover or having a net operating loss for the taxable year in which an ownership change occurs.

Majority partners The one or more partners in a partnership who have an aggregate interest in partnership profits and capital in excess of 50%.

Marital deduction Deduction allowed for tax-free interspousal transfers other than those for gifts of certain terminable interests.

Memorandum (memo) decision Decision issued by the Tax Court dealing with a factual variation on a matter where the law has already been decided in an earlier case.

Merger A form of tax-free reorganization in which the acquiring corporation transfers its stock, securities, and other consideration to the target corporation in exchange for its assets and liabilities. The target corporation then distributes these items to its shareholders and security holders in exchange for their stock and securities.

Minimum tax credit (MTC) A tax credit allowed for the amount of alternative minimum tax that arose because of deferral and permanent adjustments and preference items. This credit may be carried over and used to offset regular tax liabilities in subsequent years.

MTC See Minimum tax credit.

Negligence The Code defines negligence as (1) any failure to reasonably attempt to comply with the Code and (2) "careless, reckless, or intentional disregard" of the rules and regulations.

Negligence penalty Penalty assessed if the IRS finds that the taxpayer has filed an incorrect return because of negligence. Generally this penalty is 20% of the underpayment attributable to negligence.

Net gift A gift upon which the donee pays the gift tax as a condition to receiving the gift.

Net operating loss (NOL) A net operating loss occurs when business expenses exceed business income for any taxable year. Such losses may be carried back 3 years or carried forward 15 years to a year in which the taxpayer has taxable income. The loss is carried back first and must be deducted from years in chronological order unless a special election is made to forgo the carryback.

Net Sec. 1231 gain The excess of Sec. 1231 gains over Sec. 1231 losses.

Net Sec. 1231 loss The excess of Sec. 1231 losses over Sec. 1231 gains.

New loss corporation Any corporation permitted to use a net operating loss carryover after a stock ownership change occurs.

Ninety-day letter Officially called a Statutory Notice of Deficiency, this letter is sent when (1) the taxpayer does not file a protest letter within 30 days of receipt of the 30-day letter or (2) the taxpayer has met with an appeals officer but no agreement was reached. The letter notifies the taxpayer of the amount of the deficiency, how that amount was determined, and that a deficiency will be assessed if a petition is not filed with the Tax Court within 90 days. The taxpayer is also advised of the alternatives available to him.

NOL See Net operating loss.

Nonliquidating (current) distribution Distribution that reduces, but does not eliminate, a partner's partnership interest or that is made by a corporation without first adopting a plan of liquidation.

Nonrecourse loan Loan for which the borrower has no liability.

Nonresident alien Individual whose residence is not the United States and who is not a U.S. citizen.

OGI See Ordinary gross income.

Old loss corporation Any corporation that is allowed to use a net operating loss carryover, or which has a net operating loss for the tax year in which an ownership change occurs, and which undergoes the requisite stock ownership change.

Open-fact or tax-planning situation A situation that is pending but has not yet occurred. That is, the facts and events surrounding the transaction are still controllable.

Open transaction doctrine Valuation technique for property that can only be valued on the basis of uncertain future payments. This doctrine determines the shareholder's gain or loss when the asset is sold, collected, or able to be valued. Assets that cannot be valued are assigned a value of zero.

Optional basis adjustment An elective technique that adjusts the basis for the partnership interest and the underlying assets up or down as a result of (1) distributions from the partnership to its partners, (2) sales of partnership interests by existing partners, or (3) transfers of the interest following the death of a partner.

Ordinary gross income (OGI) A corporation's ordinary gross income is its gross income reduced by (1) capital gains and (2) Sec. 1231 gains.

Ordinary income property For charitable contribution deduction purposes, any property that would result in the recognition of ordinary income if it was sold. Such property includes inventory, works of art or manuscripts created by the taxpayer, capital assets that have been held for one year or less, and Sec. 1231 property that results in ordinary income due to depreciation recapture.

Parent-subsidiary controlled group To qualify as such, a common parent must own at least 80% of the

Partial liquidation This occurs when a corporation discontinues one line of business, distributes the assets related to that business to the shareholders, and continues in at least one other line of business.

Partner A member of a partnership. The member may be an individual, trust, estate, or corporation. See also General partner and Limited partner.

Partnership Syndicate, group, pool, joint venture, or other unincorporated organization which carries on a business or financial operation or venture and which has at least two partners.

Partnership agreement Agreement that governs the relationship between the partners and the partnership.

Partnership item Virtually all items reported by the partnership for the taxable year, including tax preference items, credit recapture items, guaranteed payments, and at-risk amounts.

Partnership ordinary income The positive sum of all partnership items of income, gain, loss, or deduction that do not have to be separately stated.

Partnership ordinary loss The negative sum of all partnership items of income, gain, loss, or deduction that do not have to be separately stated.

Partnership taxable income The sum of all taxable items among the separately stated items plus the partnership ordinary income or ordinary loss.

Party to a reorganization Such parties include (1) corporations that result from a reorganization and (2) the corporations involved in a reorganization where one corporation acquires the stock or assets of the other corporation.

Passive activity limitation Separate limitation on the amount of losses and credits that can be claimed with respect to a passive activity.

Passive foreign investment company (PFIC) A foreign corporation having passive income as 75% or more of its gross income for the tax year, or at least 50% of the average value of its assets during the tax year producing or held for producing passive income.

Passive income Income from an activity that does not require the taxpayer's material involvement or participation. Thus, income from tax shelters and rental activities generally fall into this category.

Passive loss Loss generated from a passive activity. Such losses are computed separately. They may be used to offset income from other passive activities, but may not be used to offset either active income or portfolio income.

Permanent difference Items that are reported in taxable income but not book income or vice versa. Such differences include book income items that are nontaxable in the current year and will never be taxable and book expense items that are nondeductible in computing taxable income for the current year and will never be deductible.

Personal holding company (PHC) A closely held corporation (1) that is owned by 5 or fewer shareholders who own more than 50% of the corporation's outstanding stock at any time during the last half of its tax year and (2) whose PHC income equals at least 60% of the corporation's adjusted ordinary gross income for the tax year. Certain corporations (e.g., S corporations) are exempt from this definition.

Personal holding company income (PHCI) Twelve categories of income including the following: dividends; interest; annuities; royalties (other than minerals, oil and gas, computer software, and copyright royalties); adjusted income from rents; adjusted income from mineral, oil and gas royalties or working interests in oil and gas wells; computer software royalties; copyright royalties; produced film rents; income from personal service contracts involving a 25% or more shareholder; rental income from corporate property used by a 25% or more shareholder; and distributions from estates and trusts.

Personal holding company tax This tax is equal to 28% of the undistributed personal holding company income. It is intended to prevent closely held companies from converting an operating company into a nonoperating company. Thus, it is assessed in addition to the regular corporate income tax.

Personal service corporation Corporation whose principal activity is the performance of personal services.

PHC See Personal holding company.

PHCI See Personal holding company income.

Plan of liquidation. A written document detailing the steps to be undertaken while carrying out the complete liquidation of a corporation.

Plan of reorganization A consummated transaction that is specifically defined as a reorganization.

Pooled income fund A fund in which individuals receive an income interest for life and a charitable contribution deduction equal to the remainder interest for amounts contributed to the fund. The various individual beneficiaries receive annual distributions of income based upon their proportionate share of the fund's earnings.

Possessions corporation A domestic corporation that earns over a 3-year period (1) at least 80% of its gross income from within a U.S. possession and (2) at least 75% of its gross income from the active conduct of a trade or a business within a U.S. possession. Such a corporation can elect a special tax credit under Sec. 936 which eliminates its U.S. tax liability on certain forms of income.

Post-termination transition period The period of time following the termination of the S corporation election during which (1) loss and deduction carryovers can be deducted or (2) distributions of S corporation earnings can be made tax-free.

Power of appointment The power to designate the eventual owner of a property. Such appointments may be general or specific. See also General power of appointment.

Pre-adjustment AMTI Alternative minimum taxable income determined without the adjusted current earnings adjustment and the alternative tax NOL deduction.

Pre-adjustment year For purposes of the innocent spouse provisions, the most recent tax year of the spouse ending before the date the deficiency is mailed.

Preferential dividend Dividends are preferential if (1) the amount distributed to a shareholder exceeds his ratable share of the distribution as determined by the number of shares that are owned or (2) the distribution amount for a class of stock is more or less than its rightful amount.

Preferred stock bailout A provision mandated by Sec. 306 which prevents shareholders who receive nontaxable preferred stock dividends from receiving capital gain treatment upon the sale or redemption of the preferred stock.

Present interest An unrestricted right to the immediate use, possession, or enjoyment of property or the income from property (e.g., a life estate or term certain).

Primary cite The highest level official reporter which reports a particular case is called the primary cite.

Principal partner Partner who owns at least a 5% interest in the partnership's capital or profits.

Private Letter Ruling See Letter Ruling.

Probate estate Those properties that (1) pass subject to the will or under an intestacy statute and (2) are subject to court administration are part of the probate estate.

Profits interest Interest in the partnership's future earnings.

Property Cash, tangible property (e.g., buildings and land) and intangible property (e.g., franchise rights, trademarks, and leases).

Protest letter If the additional tax in question is more than $10,000 and the IRS audit was a field audit, the taxpayer must file a protest letter within 30 days. If no such letter is sent, then the IRS will follow-up with a 90-day letter. See also Ninety-day letter.

Publicly traded partnership A partnership that is actively traded on an established securities exchange or is traded in a secondary market or the equivalent thereof. Such partnerships which are formed after December 17, 1987 are taxed as corporations unless they earn predominantly passive income; publicly traded partnerships that existed before that date will be treated as partnerships until their first tax year beginning after 1997 except when they add a new line of business.

QTIP See Qualified terminable interest property.

Qualified disclaimer Disclaimer made by a person named to receive property under a decedent's will who wishes to renounce the property and any of its benefits. Such a disclaimer must be in written form and be irrevocable. In addition, it must be made no later than 9 months after the later of the day the transfer is made or the day the recipient becomes 21 years old. The property must pass to either the decedent's spouse or another person not named by the person making the disclaimer.

Qualified joint interest If spouses are the only joint owners of a property, that property is classified as a qualified joint interest.

Qualified Subchapter S trusts (QSSTs) A domestic trust that owns stock in one or more S corporations and distributes (or is required to distribute) all of its income to its sole income beneficiary. The beneficiary must make an irrevocable election to be treated as the owner of the trust consisting of the S corporation stock. A separate election must be made for each corporation's stock that is owned by the trust.

Qualified terminable interest property (QTIP) QTIP property is property for which a special election has been made that makes it eligible for the marital deduction. Such property must be transferred by the donor spouse to a donee spouse who has a qualifying interest for life. In other words, the donor does not have to grant full control over the property to his spouse.

Reasonable business needs For accumulated earnings tax purposes, the amount that a prudent businessman would consider appropriate for the business's bona fide present and future needs, Sec. 303 (death tax) redemption needs, and excess business holding redemption needs.

Recapitalization A tax-free change in the capital structure of an existing corporation for a bona fide business purpose.

Recourse loan Loan for which the borrower remains liable until repayment is complete. If the loan is secured, the lender can be repaid by selling the security. Any difference in the sale amount and the loan amount must be paid by the borrower.

Regular corporation See C corporation.

Regular decision Tax Court decision that is issued on a particular issue for the first time.

Regular tax A corporation's tax liability for income tax purposes reduced by foreign tax credits allowable for income tax purposes.

Remainder interest The portion of an interest in the property retained by a transferor who is not transferring his entire interest in a property.

Remainderman The person entitled to the remainder interest.

Resident alien An individual whose residence is the United States, but who is not a U.S. citizen.

Revenue procedure Issued by the national office of the IRS, revenue procedures reflect the IRS's position on procedural aspects of tax practice issues. Revenue procedures are published in the Cumulative Bulletin.

Revenue ruling Issued by the national office of the IRS, revenue rulings reflect the IRS's interpretation of a narrow tax issue. Revenue rulings, which are published in the Cumulative Bulletin, have less weight than the Treasury Regulations.

Reverse triangular merger Type of tax-free transaction in which a subsidiary corporation is merged into a target corporation and the target corporation stays alive as a subsidiary of the parent corporation.

Reversionary interest The interest in a property that might revert back to the transferor under the terms of the transfer. If the amount of reversionary interest is 5% or less, it is not included in the gross estate.

Revocable trust Trust under which the grantor may demand that the assets be returned.

Rule against perpetuities The requirement that no property interet vest more than 21 years, plus the gestation period, after some life or lives in being at the time the interest is created.

S corporation Election that can be made by small business corporations that allows them to be taxed like partnerships rather than like C corporations. Small business corporations are those that meet the 35-shareholder limitation, the type of shareholder restrictions, and the one class of stock restriction.

Secondary cite Citation to a secondary source (i.e., an unofficial reporter) for a particular case.

Section 341 assets For collapsible corporation purposes, inventory, property held primarily for sale to customers in the ordinary course of business, unrealized receivables or fees, and Sec. 1231 property (e.g., depreciable or real property used in a trade or business) that is held for less than 3 years.

Section 382 loss limitation rules Limitation which principally prevents trafficking in NOLs. Applies to corporate acquisitions, stock redemptions, and reorganizations when a more than 50 percentage point change in ownership occurs. The NOL that can be used in a tax year is limited to the value of the loss corporation's stock times a long-term tax exempt federal rate.

Section 2503(c) trust Trust created for children under age 21 that need not distribute all of its income annually. The undistributed interest passes to the beneficiary when age 21 is attained or his estate should he die before age 21.

Security A long-term (i.e., generally 10 years or more) debt obligation.

Security holder Person who owns an indebtedness that is considered to be a security.

Separate return limitation year Any separate return year except (1) a separate return year of the group member that is designated as the parent corporation for the consolidated return year to which the tax attribute is carried or (2) a separate return year of any corporation that was a group member for every day of the loss year.

Separate return limitation year (SRLY) rules Limitation on the amount of net operating loss and other deduction and loss amounts from a separate return year that can be used by an affiliated group in a consolidated return year to the member's contribution to consolidated taxable income.

Separate return year A tax year for which a corporation (1) files a separate return or (2) joins in the filing of a consolidated return with a different affiliated group.

Separate share rule Rule permitting a trust with several beneficiaries to treat each beneficiary as having a separate trust interest for purposes of determining (1) the amount of the distribution deduction and (2) the beneficiary's gross income.

Separate taxable income The taxable income of an individual corporate member of an affiliated group filing a consolidated tax return. This amount is used to calculate the group's combined taxable income.

Short-period tax return A tax return covering a period of less than 12 months. Short period returns are commonly filed in the first or final tax year or when a change in tax year is made.

Short-term trust Trust whose period is long enough for the grantor to escape being taxed on the trust's accounting income. A *Clifford* trust is a short-term trust.

Simple trust Trust that must distribute all of its income currently and is not empowered to make a charitable contribution.

Small cases procedure When $10,000 or less is in question for a particular year, a taxpayer may opt to have the case heard by a special commissioner rather than the regular Tax Court. The commissioner's opinion cannot be appealed and has no precedential value.

Sole proprietorship Form of business entity owned by an individual who reports all items of income and expense on Schedule C of his individual return.

Special agents The IRS agents responsible for criminal fraud investigations.

Spinoff A tax-free distribution in which a parent corporation distributes the stock and securities of a subsidiary to its shareholders without receiving anything in exchange.

Split-interest transfer A transfer made for both private (i.e., an individual) and public (i.e., a charitable organization) purposes.

Split-off Tax-free distribution in which a parent corporation distributes a subsidiary's stock and securities to some of its shareholders in exchange for part or all of their stock and securities in the parent corporation.

Split-up Tax-free distribution in which a parent corporation distributes the stock or securities of two or more subsidiaries to its shareholders in exchange for all of their stock and securities in the parent corporation. The parent corporation then goes out of existence.

Sprinkling trust A discretionary trust with several beneficiaries.

SRTP See Statements on Responsibilities in Tax Practice.

S short year That portion of an S termination year that commences on the first day of the tax year and ends on the day preceding the day on which the termination is effective.

Statements on Responsibilities in Tax Practice (SRTP) Ethical standards of practice and compliance set by the Tax Division of the American Institute of Certified Public Accountants. These statements, which are not legally binding, have a great deal of influence over ethics in tax practice.

Statutory regulations Treasury Regulations that are treated as law. Such regulations may be over-turned by the courts on the grounds that they (1) exceed the scope of the delegated authority or (2) are unreasonable.

Step transaction doctrine A judicial doctrine which the IRS can use to collapse a multistep transaction into a single transaction (either taxable or tax-free) in order to prevent the taxpayers from arranging a series of business transactions to obtain a tax result that is not available if only a single transaction is used.

S termination year A tax year in which a termination event occurs on any day other than the first day of the tax year. It is divided into an S short year and a C short year.

Stock redemption The acquisition by a corporation of its own stock in exchange for property. Such stock may be cancelled, retired, or held as treasury stock.

Subpart F income A series of income categories that are deemed distributed to the U.S. shareholders of a controlled foreign corporation on the last day of its tax year. Subpart F income includes: income from insurance of U.S. and foreign risks, foreign base company income, boycott-related income, bribes, and income from countries where for political reasons, etc. the deferral privilege is denied.

Substantially appreciated inventory This type of inventory includes (1) items held for sale in the normal course of partnership business, (2) other property which would not be considered a capital asset or Sec. 1231 property if it was sold by the partnership, and (3) any other property held by the partnership which would fall into the above classification if it was held by the selling or distributee partner.

Target corporation The corporation that transfers its assets as part of a taxable or tax-free acquisition transaction. May also be known as the acquired or transferor company.

Tax matters partner (1) Partner who is designated by the partnership or (2) the gerneral partner having the largest profits interests at the close of the partnership's tax year.

Taxpayer Compliance Measurement Program (TCMP) A stratified random sample used to select tax returns for audit. The program is intended to test the extent to which taxpayers are in compliance with the law.

Tax research The process of solving a specific tax-related question on the basis of both tax law sources and the specific circumstances surrounding the particular situation.

Tax services Multivolume commentaries on the tax law. Generally these commentaries contain copies of the Internal Revenue Code and the Treasury Regulations. Also included are editorial comments prepared by the publisher of the tax service, current matters, and a cross-reference to various government promulgations and judicial decisions.

Tax year The period of time (usually 12 months) selected by a taxpayer to compute their taxable income. The tax year may be a calendar year or a fiscal year. The election is made on the taxpayer's first return and cannot be changed without IRS approval. The tax year may be less than 12 months if it is the taxpayer's first or final return or if the taxpayer is changing accounting periods.

TCMP See Taxpayer Compliance Measurement Program.

Technical advice memorandum Such memoranda are administrative interpretations issued by the national office of the IRS in the form of a letter ruling. Taxpayers may request them if they need guidance about the tax treatment of complicated technical matters which are being audited.

Temporary differences Items which are included in book income in the current year but which were included in taxable income in the past or will be included in the future. Book income items that are nontaxable in the current year even though they were taxed in the past or will be taxed in the future and book expenses that are not currently deductible even though that status was different in the past or will be different in the future are categorized as temporary differences.

Temporary Regulations Regulations issued to provide guidance for taxpayers pending the issuance of the final

regulations. Temporary Regulations are binding upon taxpayers.

Tentative minimum tax (TMT) Tax calculated by (1) multiplying 20% times the corporation's alternative minimum taxable income less a statutory exemption amount and (2) deducting allowable foreign tax credits.

Term certain interest A person holding such an interest has a right to receive income from property for a specified term, but does not own or hold title to such property. The property reverts to the grantor at the end of the term.

Terminable interest A property interest that ends when (1) some event occurs (or fails to occur) or (2) a specified amount of time passes.

Testamentary Of, pertaining to, or of the nature of a testament or will.

Testamentary transfers A transferor's control or enjoyment of a property ceases at death.

Testamentary trust Trust created under the direction of a decedent's will and funded by the decedent's estate.

Thirty-day letter A report sent to the taxpayer if the taxpayer does not sign Form 870 (Waiver of Statutory Notice) concerning any additional taxes assessed. The letter details the proposed changes and advises the taxpayer of his right to pursue the matter with the Appeals Office. The taxpayer then has 30 days in which to request a conference.

Throwback dividends For accumulated earnings tax and personal holding company tax purposes, these are distributions made out of current or accumulated earnings and profits in the first two and one-half months after the close of the tax year.

Tier-1 beneficiary Beneficiary to whom a distribution must be made.

Tier-2 beneficiary Beneficiary who receives a discretionary distribution.

TMT See Tentative minimum tax.

Transferor corporation The corporation that transfers its assets as part of a reorganization. May also be known as acquired or target corporation.

Triangular merger A type of merger transaction where the parent corporation uses a subsidiary corporation to serve as the acquiring corporation.

Triangular reorganization A type of reorganization (i.e., Type A, B, or C) where the parent corporation uses a subsidiary corporation to serve as the acquiring corporation.

Trust An arrangement created either by will or by an inter vivos declaration whereby trustees take title to property for the purpose of protecting it or conserving it for the beneficiaries.

Trustee An individual or institution which administers a trust for the benefit of a beneficiary.

Trust income Return in money or property derived from the use of the trust's principal.

Trustor The grantor or transferor of a trust.

Type A reorganization Type of corporate reorganization that meets the requirements of state or federal law, may take the form of a consolidation, a merger, a triangular merger, or a reverse triangular merger.

Type B reorganization Reorganization characterized by a stock-for-stock exchange. The target corporation remains in existence as a subsidiary of the acquiring corporation.

Type C reorganization A transaction that requires the acquiring corporation to obtain substantially all of the target corporation's assets in exchange for its voting stock and a limited amount of other consideration. The target corporation is generally liquidated.

Type D reorganization This type of reorganization may be either acquisitive or divisive. In the former, substantially all of the transferor corporation's assets (and possibly some or all of its liabilities) are acquired by a controlled corporation. The target corporation is liquidated. The latter involves the acquisition of the part or all of the transferor corporation's assets (and liabilities) by a controlled subsidiary corporation(s). The transferor corporation may either remain in existence or be liquidated.

Type E reorganization This type of reorganization changes the capital structure of a corporation. The corporation remains in existence.

Type F reorganization The old corporation's assets or stock are transferred to a single newly formed corporation in this type of transaction. The "old" corporation is liquidated.

Type G reorganization This type of reorganization may be either acquisitive or divisive. In either case, part or all of the target or transferor corporation's assets (and possibly some or all of its liabilities) are transferred to another corporation as part of a bankruptcy proceeding. The target or transferor corporation may either remain in existence or be liquidated.

Unified credit The unified credit enables a tax base of a certain size (i.e., the exemption equivalent) to be completely free of transfer taxes. This credit is phased out for tax bases in excess of $10,500,000 if the decedent dies after 1987. It may only be subtracted once against all of a person's transfers—throughout one's lifetime and at death.

Unified rate schedule Progressive rate schedule for estate and gift taxes. These rates are effective for gifts made after 1976 and deaths occurring after 1976.

Unrealized receivable Right to payment for goods and services that has not been included in the partnership's income because of its method of accounting.

Unreported decisions District court decisions that are not reported in official reporters. Such decisions may be reported in secondary reporters that report only tax-related cases.

U.S. shareholder For controlled foreign corporation purposes, a U.S. person who owns at least 10% of the foreign corporation's voting stock.

Voting trust An arrangement whereby the stock owned by a number of shareholders is placed under the control of a trustee for purposes of exercising the voting rights possessed by the stock. This practice increases the voting power of the minority shareholders.

Wealth transfer taxes Estate taxes (i.e., the tax on dispositions of property that occur as a result of the transferor's death) and gift taxes (i.e., the tax on lifetime transfers) are wealth transfer taxes.

Writ of certiorari See Certiorari.

APPENDIX

Index of Code Sections

1, 1-30, 9-18–9-19
1-1399, 11-5
1(e), 14-35
1(g)(1), 11-21 n
11, 8-7, 8-25, 15-30
11(b), 3-25 n, 3-31–3-32, 8-5, 8-32, 11-16, 15-24
21-29, 5-13, 8-35
26(b), 5-3
27, 3-24 (Table 3-3), 5-3
28, 3-24 (Table 3-3)
29, 3-24 (Table 3-3)
34, 3-24 (Table 3-3)
38, 3-24 (Table 3-3), 7-6
38(c), 5-13, 8-34 n
38(c)(3)(B), 3-32 n
39, 5-13 n
39(a), 8-34
53, 3-24 (Table 3-3), 5-12 n
55, 5-3 n
56(a), 5-5 n, 11-32
56, 5-36, 8-33
56-58, 8-33
   56(a)(1), 5-5 n
56(g), 8-33
56(g)(1), 5-8 n
56(g)(2), 5-8 n
56(g)(4)(A), 5-9 n
56(g)(4)(B)(i), 5-9 n
56(g)(4)(B)(ii), 5-9 n
56(g)(4)(C)(i), 5-9 n
56(g)(4)(C)(ii), 5-9 n
56(g)(4)(D)(i), 5-10 n
56(g)(4)(D)(ii), 5-10 n
56(g)(4)(D)(iii), 5-10 n
56(g)(4)(D)(iv), 5-9 n
56(g)(4)(G), 5-10 n
56(g)(4)(I), 5-9 n
56(g)(6), 5-8 n, 5-37 n, 11-32 n
57, 5-36, 8-33
57(a), 5-3 n, 11-32
59(a)(2), 5-14 n
59(e), 5-36
59(e)(4)(A), 5-36 n
59(e)(4)(B), 5-36 n
59(e)(6), 5-36
59A(a), 5-14
59A(b), 5-14
61, 2-13 n, 9-13
61(a)(12), 6-17 n
63, 11-15, 11-17
67(e), 14-10
72, 16-12

78, 15-23 n
79, 11-35 n, 11-35
83, 9-12
101(b), 11-35 n
102, 12-2
105, 11-35 n
106, 11-35 n
108, 5-9
108(b)(5), 9-20
118(a), 2-32 n
119, 11-35 n, 15-11, 15-13
151, 14-5, 14-11
152(a), 1-5 n
162, 1-39, 3-6, 3-10 n, 3-12, 4-46, 5-17, 9-36, 14-37
162(a), 4-13, 5-43
162(a)(2), 1-7, 1-9–1-10
162(l), 2-3
163(a), 2-30 n
163(d), 3-6
163(d)(3), 12-31
163(e), 2-30 n, 2-30
164, 15-4
164(a)(5), 5-14
165, 1-17, 2-36 n
165(g), 1-17
165(g)(1), 2-34 n
165(g)(2), 2-34 n
165(g)(3), 2-34 n, 6-7, 6-11, 6-29
166, 2-36 n, 2-36
166(d), 2-35
167(h), 14-10
168(b)(2), 5-37 n
168(b)(5), 5-37 n
168(i)(7), 2-26 n, 8-13–8-14
168(i)(7)(A), 9-11 n
168(g), 4-5–4-6, 5-5–5-6, 5-8
170, 3-21
170(a)(1), 3-12 n
170(a)(2), 3-12 n
170(b)(1)(A)(ii), 12-9 n
170(b)(2), 3-15 n
170(d)(2), 3-15 n
170(e)(1)(A), 3-13 n
170(e)(1)(B), 3-14 n
170(e)(3), 3-13 n
170(e)(4), 3-14 n
170(e)(5), 3-14 n
171, 2-30
172, 8-21
172(b)(3)(C), 3-20 n, 8-41 n
172(c), 3-19 n
173, 5-10, 5-36

174, 5-36
179, 3-40–3-41, 4-5–4-6, 9-21
179(d)(6), 3-32 n
183, 3-6, 11-23
195, 3-12
195(b), 3-12 n
195(c)(1), 3-12 n
212, 3-6, 14-10
212-221, 9-20 n
213(d), 12-9 n
243, 3-8
243(a), 3-16 n
243(a)(3), 3-18 n
243(b)(5), 3-18 n
244, 3-8
245, 3-8, 3-18 n
245(a), 15-25
245(c), 15-39 n
246(b)(1), 3-16 n
246(b)(2), 3-16 n
246(c)(1), 3-18 n
246A, 3-19 n
248, 3-8, 3-10, 5-10, 9-15, 11-14
248(b), 3-11
248(c), 3-10 n
262, 1-7
263, 5-36
263A, 5-10, 8-11
265(1), 14-16 n
267, 2-19, 2-37, 3-32, 4-7, 9-34 n, 9-34
267(a)(1), 2-37, 3-22–3-23, 3-32, 11-34
267(a)(2), 3-22–3-23, 3-32, 8-16, 8-17 (Topic Review 8-2), 11-33–11-34
267(b), 6-15, 11-34 n
267(b)(2), 3-22 n
267(b)(3), 3-32 n, 8-16
267(c), 11-34 n
267(c)(4), 1-5
267(d), 3-23 n
267(e), 11-34
267(e)(3), 3-22 n
267(f), 8-37
267(f)(2), 8-12 n
269, 7-37–7-38, 7-41
269(b), 6-26–6-27
274(d), 16-36 n
279, 2-31 (Table 2-1)
280A, 1-4, 1-30
280H, 3-4 n, 3-4
291, 3-9–3-10, 6-14, 11-14
301, 4-2, 4-13, 4-19, 4-32–4-35, 4-40, 4-45 (Topic Review 4-3), 6-32
301(b), 4-9 n

G-1

301(b)(1), 7-12
301(d), 4-10 *n*
301(e), 4-6 *n*
302, 2-31 (Table 2-2), 4-38, 4-41, 6-6, 7-34
302(a), 4-30
302(b), 4-33–4-34, 4-41, 4-45 (Topic Review 4-3), 7-11 *n*, 7-11, 7-13, 7-33
302(b)(1), 4-24–4-26, 4-35–4-36 (Topic Review 4-2), 7-19
302(b)(2), 4-21, 4-23, 4-26, 4-36 (Topic Review 4-2), 4-41, 7-12 *n*, 7-33
302(b)(3), 1-14–1-15, 4-23, 4-30, 4-36 (Topic Review 4-2), 4-47
302(b)(4), 4-25, 4-32, 4-36 (Topic Review 4-2)
302(c), 4-20 *n*
302(c)(1)(A), 4-26 *n*
302(c)(2), 4-23 *n*, 4-44
302(c)(2)(A), 1-15, 4-23 *n*, 4-49 *n*
302(c)(2)(C), 4-24 *n*
302(c)(2)(C)(i), 1-15
302(d), 4-19 *n*
302(e)(2), 4-26
303, 2-31 (Table 2-2), 4-26–4-30, 4-33–4-34, 4-36 (Topic Review 4-2), 4-38, 5-27, 5-32, 13-34–13-35
303(b)(1), 4-28 *n*
303(b)(2)(A), 4-27 *n*
303(b)(2)(B), 4-28 *n*
303(b)(3), 4-28 *n*
304, 4-2, 4-33–4-34, 4-34 *n*, 4-36 (Topic Review 4-2)
304(b)(2), 4-34 *n*
305, 4-15–4-16
305(a), 4-14–4-15
305(b), 2-31 (Table 2-1), 4-14, 4-16
306, 1-14, 2-31 (Table 2-2), 4-30–4-33, 4-36 (Topic Review 4-2), 6-27
306(a)(1), 4-31 *n*
306(a)(2), 4-32 *n*
306(b), 4-32
306(c), 4-31
306(c)(2), 4-31 *n*
307(a), 4-15 *n*
307(b)(1), 4-16 *n*
311, 4-29, 4-43, 4-45 (Topic Review 4-3), 7-9, 8-18
311(a), 4-10 *n*, 4-17 *n*
311(b), 8-18, 11-28 *n*
311(b)(2), 4-10 *n*
312, 4-4 *n*, 5-8
312(a), 4-11 *n*
312(a)(2), 4-11 *n*
312(b), 4-11 *n*
312(c), 4-11 *n*
312(d), 4-17 *n*
312(k), 4-6 *n*
312(k)(3), 4-6 *n*
312(n), 4-6 *n*
312(n)(2), 4-6 *n*
312(n)(4), 5-10
312(n)(5), 4-5 *n*
312(n)(6), 4-5 *n*
312(n)(7), 4-30 *n*
316(a), 4-2
317, 4-17 *n*
317(a), 4-2, 4-9
318, 2-13 *n*, 4-20, 4-24–4-25, 4-27, 4-35, 6-10, 11-34, 15-27

318(a), 4-20, 4-22, 4-25, 4-32 *n*, 4-34, 4-34 *n*
318(a)(1), 1-15, 4-20 *n*, 4-23 *n*, 4-49, 5-48
318(a)(1), 6-21
318(a)(2), 4-21 *n*, 6-21
318(a)(3), 4-21 *n*, 6-21
318(a)(4), 4-21 *n*
318(a)(5)(B), 4-20 *n*
331, 6-3 (Table 6-1), 6-5–6-6, 6-9, 6-11–6-12, 6-32
331(a), 6-6
332, 6-2, 6-3 (Table 6-1), 6-4 (Table 6-2), 6-5, 6-10 *n*, 6-9–6-12, 6-14, 6-14 *n*, 6-18, 6-20, 6-20 *n*, 6-26, 6-28–6-32
332(a), 6-9 6-11–6-12, 6-29
332(b)(1), 6-10 *n*
332(b)(2), 6-10 *n*
332(b)(3), 6-11 *n*
334(a), 6-3 (Table 6-1), 6-7
334(b), 6-3 (Table 6-1), 6-26 *n*
334(b)(1), 6-12, 6-17
336, 6-13, 7-9
336(a), 6-4 (Table 6-2), 6-13–6-14, 11-41
336(b), 6-13
336(d)(1)(A), 6-15
336(d)(1)(B), 6-15
336(d)(2), 6-15– 6-16
336(d)(3), 6-14
336(e), 6-14 *n*
337, 6-20, 6-30, 7-9
337(a), 6-4 (Table 6-2), 6-14 *n*, 6-14–6-15, 6-26 *n* 6-29
337(b), 6-17
337(b)(2)(B), 6-14 *n*
337(c), 6-14
338, 6-2, 6-4, 6-20, 6-20 *n*, 6-21–6-22, 6-25–6-27, 6-27 (Topic Review 6-2), 6-31, 7-6, 7-42–7-44, 11-39 *n*
338(b)(1), 6-22 *n*
338(b)(2), 6-22 *n*, 6-24 *n*
338(b)(4), 6-23 *n*
338(b)(6), 6-23 *n*
338(e), 6-21 *n*
338(g), 6-21 *n*, 6-31
338(h)(2), 6-21 *n*
341(b), 6-7 *n*
346(a), 6-6
351, 1-14, 2-12–2-20, 2-20 *n*, 2-21, 2-21 (Topic Review 2-2), 2-22–2-26 (Topic Review 2-3), 2-27–2-28, 2-30, 2-31 (Table 2-1), 2-35, 2-37–2-41, 4-31, 6-4 (Table 6-2), 6-15, 6-21, 7-37, 9-8, 10-22, 10-24 (Topic Review 10-2), 11-25, 16-12, 16-12 *n*
351(a), 2-11–2-13
351(b), 2-12, 2-18, 2-18 *n*, 2-25
351(d)(1), 2-13 *n*
351(d)(2), 2-13 *n*
351(d)(3), 2-13 *n*
351(e)(1), 2-12 *n*
351(e)(2), 2-12 *n*
351(f), 2-22 *n*
354, 6-21, 7-29, 7-44
354(a), 7-10, 7-33
354(a)(2), 7-10 *n*
354(a)(2)(B), 7-33 *n*
354(b)(1), 7-24 *n*
355, 4-2, 4-26, 4-36, 4-38, 4-40–4-45 (Topic Review 4-3), 4-45, 6-21, 7-29–7-30
355(a), 4-38

355(a)(1)(D), 4-39
355(a)(3), 4-40 *n*
355(b)(2), 4-39 *n*
355(c), 4-43
355(c)(1), 4-43 *n*
355(c)(2), 4-43
356, 4-40, 4-42, 4-43, 6-21, 7-11, 7-29
356(a), 7-10
356(a)(2), 4-41 *n*, 7-11
356(b), 4-40 *n*
356(c), 4-41 *n*
356(d)(2)(B), 7-10 *n*, 7-34 *n*
357, 2-23, 2-25
357(a), 2-23, 2-26 (Topic Review 2-3)
357(b), 2-26 (Topic Review 2-3), 2-38
357(c), 2-24–2-26 (Topic Review), 2-38, 7-9, 7-13 (Topic Review 7-2), 7-25
357(c)(1)(B), 7-30 *n*
357(c)(3), 2-24 *n*, 2-26 (Topic Review 2-3)
357(c)(3)(A), 2-25 *n*
358, 2-25, 4-42, 7-12
358(a)(1), 2-19 *n*
358(a)(2), 2-19 *n*
358(b)(1), 2-20 *n*
358(d)(2), 2-25 *n*
361, 7-8, 7-44
361(a), 7-8
361(b), 7-8
361(c), 7-9 *n*
361(c)(1), 7-9 *n*, 7-30 *n*
361(c)(2), 7-9 *n*
361(c)(2)(C), 7-9 *n*
361(c)(3), 7-9 *n*
361(c)(4), 7-9 *n*
362, 2-22 *n*
362(a), 2-32 *n*
362(b), 7-10
362(c)(1), 2-33 *n*
362(c)(2), 2-33 *n*
368, 2-31 (Table 2-1)
368(a)(1), 7-7
368(a)(1)(A), 7-7, 7-14 *n*
368(a)(1)(B), 7-26
368(a)(1)(C), 7-21 *n*, 7-22, 7-24
368(a)(1)(D), 7-24 *n*, 7-25, 7-29
368(a)(1)(E), 7-32
368(a)(1)(F), 7-33 *n*, 7-34
368(a)(1)(G), 7-28 *n*, 7-29
368(a)(2)(A), 7-25
368(a)(2)(B), 7-22, 7-24
368(a)(2)(C), 7-19 *n*
368(a)(2)(D), 7-19
368(a)(2)(E), 7-21
368(a)(2)(G), 7-21 *n*
368(a)(2)(H), 7-24
368(b), 7-44
368(c), 2-13, 4-38 *n*, 7-19 *n*, 7-27, 7-29 *n*
381, 8-13
381(a), 6-4 (Table 6-2), 6-18 *n*, 7-37
381(a)(1), 6-26 *n*
381(c), 7-37–7-38
382, 7-28 *n*, 7-37–7-41, 8-24, 8-24 *n*, 8-25, 8-26 *n*, 8-27–8-29 (Topic Review 8-3), 8-31, 8-35
382-384, 8-20, 8-26 *n*
382(b)(1), 7-40 *n*
382(b)(2), 7-40 *n*
382(b)(3), 7-41 *n*
382(c), 7-40 *n*
382(f), 7-40 *n* 382(g), 7-39 *n*

382(k)(1), 7-39 n
382(k)(2), 7-39 n
382(k)(3), 7-39 n
383, 7-37–7-38, 7-41, 8-31
384, 7-37–7-38, 7-41
385, 2-29, 11-36
404(b), 3-22 n
441, 2-6 n, 3-3 n, 6-26
441(i), 3-3 n
443, 11-9
443(a)(2), 3-3 n
444, 3-3–3-4, 3-7 (Topic Review 3-1), 9-4 n, 9-17–9-20 (Topic Review 9-2), 9-41–9-42, 10-28, 11-12 n, 11-12–11-13 (Topic Review 11-2), 11-38–11-39, 11-42
446, 3-4 n, 6-26
447, 3-4 n
448, 3-5 n, 8-9, 11-38
448(d), 3-26
453, 2-38, 7-5 n, 8-13
453(A), 5-9
453(f)(6)(C), 7-12
453(h), 6-5
453(h)(1)(A), 6-12 n
453(h)(1)(B), 6-12 n
453(h)(1)(C), 6-12 n
465, 3-8, 5-16 n, 11-23
465(a), 3-23, 9-32 n
465(b)(6), 9-32 n
465(e), 9-32 n
469, 3-4, 5-16 n, 9-32, 10-41
469(a)(2)(B), 3-24 n
469(a)(2)(C), 3-24 n
469(e)(2), 3-24 n
469(h)(1), 11-23
469(h)(2), 9-34 n
482, 15-26, 15-33–15-34 n, 15-34, 15-36 (Table 15-2), 15-38–15-39
501, 5-35, 8-4
501-504, 5-15, 5-25
511(a), 5-35
512(b), 5-35
512(b)(12), 5-36
513(a), 5-35
532(a), 5-25
532(b), 5-26 n
532(c), 5-26 n
533(a), 5-26
533(b), 5-26
534, 5-26
535(b)(1), 5-32 n
535(b)(2), 5-32 n
535(b)(3), 5-32 n
535(b)(4), 5-32 n
535(b)(5), 5-32 n
535(b)(6), 5-32
535(b)(7), 5-32
535(c), 5-33 n
537, 5-27, 5-31
537(a), 5-31
542(a), 5-15 n
542(a)(2), 5-15
542(c), 5-15 n
543(a)(2), 5-18 n
543(a)(6), 5-15
543(a)(7), 5-20 n
543(a)(8), 5-18 n
543(b)(1), 5-16 n
543(b)(2), 5-16 n

543(b)(3), 5-17 n
543(c)(5), 5-15 n
543(c)(7), 5-15 n
543(c)(10), 5-15 n
544, 5-16, 5-20
544(a)(4)(A), 5-16 n
545(b)(1), 5-21 n
545(b)(2), 5-21 n
545(b)(3), 5-21 n
545(b)(4), 5-21 n
545(b)(5), 5-21 n
547, 5-23
547(c), 5-23 n
547(d), 5-23 n
547(e), 5-23 n
551(a), 15-34 n
561(a), 5-22 n
561(a)(3), 5-23 n
562(a), 5-22 n
562(b), 5-23 n
562(b)(1)(B), 5-33 n
562(b)(2), 5-23
562(c), 5-22 n, 5-32 n
563(a), 5-33 n
563(b), 5-22 n
564, 5-23
565, 5-22 n
582(a), 2-35 n
611(b), 14-10
613A, 8-8 (Table 8-1), 11-12, 11-25 n, 11-30 n
613A(c)(7)(D), 9-19 n
613A(c)(10)(A), 11-12 n
613A(c)(13), 11-12 n
616, 5-36
617, 5-36, 9-12, 9-20, 11-12
617(f)(2), 10-7
641-668, 14-6
641-683, 14-5–14-6
641-692, 14-2
641(b), 14-5
641(c)(1), 14-35 n
642(a)(1), 14-12 n
642(b), 14-5, 14-11
642(c)(1), 14-10 n
642(e), 14-10 n
642(g), 14-45
643(a), 14-13–14-14
643(b), 14-6
643(d), 14-44 n
644, 14-34 n, 14-34–14-35, 14-46–14-47
644(a)(1), 14-34 n
644(a)(2), 14-35 n
644(b), 14-35 n
644(c)(1), 14-35 n
644(e), 14-34 n
645, 14-45 n
651, 14-15
651(a), 14-10, 14-17 n
651(b), 14-11 n, 14-17 n
652, 14-15
652(a), 14-18 n
652(c), 14-44 n
661-664, 14-22
661(a), 14-11 n, 14-23
661(c), 14-11 n
662(a), 14-11 n, 14-24
662(a)(1), 14-25 n
662(a)(2), 14-25, 14-27 n
662(b), 14-25

662(c), 14-44 n
663(a)(1), 14-28 n
663(b), 14-44
663(c), 14-27 n
665-668, 14-13, 14-33
665(b), 14-33 n
671, 14-38
671-679, 14-38
672(e), 14-40
673(a), 14-39–14-40
673(c), 14-40 n
674, 14-42
675, 14-41
676, 14-39
677, 14-41–14-42
677(a), 14-40 n
678, 14-42
691, 14-35
691(b), 14-37
691(c), 14-36–14-37
691(c)(1), 14-36 n
701, 9-4 n
701-761, 9-2
702, 9-21
702(a), 9-5 n, 9-18, 9-21, 11-12
702(a)(8), 9-22
702(b), 9-22
703(a), 9-20
703(a)(2), 11-14
703(a)(2)(F), 9-19 n
703(b), 9-19
704, 9-24–9-25, 9-40, 11-19
704(a), 9-37
704(b), 9-23 n, 9-22
704(c), 9-24, 10-3 n
704(d), 9-30–9-32, 9-34
704(e)(2), 9-38 n
705, 9-29, 9-32–9-33
705(a), 9-5 n
705(b), 9-26 n
706, 9-15, 9-18, 9-20 (Topic Review 9-2)
706(a), 9-15
706(b), 9-4 n
706(b)(3), 9-17 n
706(c)(2), 10-24 n
706(c)(2)(B), 9-23 n, 9-39
706(d), 9-39
707(b), 9-34
707(b)(1), 9-34
707(b)(2), 9-35 n, 9-35
707(c), 9-34, 9-36 n, 9-35
708, 10-16 n, 10-19, 10-26
708(b), 10-25
708(b)(2)(A), 10-28 n
708(b)(2)(B), 10-29 n
709(b), 9-15 n
721, 9-6, 9-7, 9-11 n, 10-27 n
721(a), 9-7
721(b), 9-7
722, 9-5 n, 9-6 n, 9-9 n, 10-27
723, 9-6 n, 9-9
724, 9-10 n, 9-10
724(d)(1), 9-10 n
731(a), 9-9 n
731(a)(1), 9-6 n, 10-3 n, 10-11, 10-11 n
731(a)(2), 9-6 n, 10-12 n
731(b), 10-3 n, 10-15 n
732(a)(2), 10-4 n
732(c), 10-4 n, 10-12 n
732(c)(2), 10-13 n

732(d), 10-38, 10-39 *n*, 10-39–10-40, 10-43
733, 9-6 *n*
734, 10-30, 10-42
734(b), 10-35 *n*, 10-43
734(b)(1)(A), 10-36 *n*
734(b)(1)(B), 10-36 *n*
734(b)(2)(A), 10-36 *n*
734(b)(2)(B), 10-37 *n*
735(a)(1), 10-6 *n*
735(a)(2), 10-6 *n*
735(b), 10-6 *n*, 10-14 *n*
736, 10-19 *n*
736(a), 2-25, 10-42
736(a)(1), 10-20 *n*
736(a)(2), 10-20 *n*
736(b), 10-19 *n*, 10-42
741, 10-16 *n*
742, 9-5 *n*
743, 10-30, 10-42
743(b), 10-31 *n*, 10-33 *n*, 10-43
751, 10-2, 10-3 *n*, 10-3, 10-6–10-9 (Table 10-1), 10-9–10-11, 10-14–10-15 (Table 10-2), 10-15–10-18 (Topic Review 10-1), 10-20–10-21, 10-24 (Topic Review 10-2), 10-36, 10-39, 10-42
751(a), 10-16 *n*, 10-30
751(b), 10-8 *n*, 10-39–10-40
751(c), 9-10 *n*, 10-7 *n*
751(d)(2), 10-7 *n*
752, 9-7
752(a), 9-5 *n*, 9-27 *n*
752(b), 9-5 *n*, 9-11, 9-27 *n*
752(d), 10-17 *n*
754, 10-16, 10-19, 10-30 *n*, 10-30, 10-34–10-39, 10-42–10-43
755, 10-31–10-32, 10-37
755(b), 10-32 *n*
761(a), 9-3 *n*
761(d), 10-11 *n*
801, 8-4 *n*, 8-4
861-865, 15-6
865(a), 15-6 *n*
865(b), 15-6 *n*
865(g), 15-6
871, 15-15
871(a), 15-17 *n*
871(a)(1)(A), 15-16
871(a)(2), 15-17 *n*
871(d), 15-18 *n*
873(b), 15-19 *n*
881(a), 15-24
882(a), 15-24
884(a), 15-25 *n*
897(a), 15-18 *n*
897(c), 15-18 *n*
901, 9-20, 11-12, 15-21
901(a), 15-4, 15-42 *n*
902, 15-7, 15-23
902(a), 15-23 *n*
902(b)(1), 15-23 *n*
902(b)(2), 15-23 *n*
902(b)(3), 15-23 *n*
904, 15-7
904(a), 15-5 *n*
904(c), 15-7 *n*
904(d)(1), 15-7 *n*
905(a), 15-42 *n*
911, 15-10–15-14 *n*, 15-44–15-45, 15-47
911(a)(2), 15-12

911(b)(1)(A), 15-11 *n*
911(b)(2)(A), 15-11
911(c)(2), 15-13 *n*
911(c)(3)(A), 15-13 *n*
911(d)(1)(A), 15-9
911(d)(1)(B), 15-10
911(d)(2), 15-11 *n*
911(d)(3), 15-10 *n*
911(d)(5), 15-10 *n*
911(d)(6), 15-3–15-14 n
911(e)(2), 15-45 *n*
912, 15-11 *n*
922(a), 15-35 *n*
923(b), 15-36
924(a), 15-36
925(a), 15-38 *n*
927(a)(1), 15-37
927(f), 15-35 *n*
931, 15-14
931(c), 15-14 *n*
932, 15-14 *n*
933, 15-14
936, 3-24 (Table 3-3), 8-4, 8-40, 11-4, 15-40 *n*, 15-41
936(a)(1), 15-41 *n*
936(a)(2), 15-41 *n*
936(d)(2), 15-41
936(e), 15-41 *n*
936(f), 15-41 *n*
951(a), 15-27 *n*
951(a)(1)(A)(iii), 15-30 *n*
951(a)(2), 15-31 *n*
951(b), 15-27 *n*
952(a)(1), 15-28 (Fig. 15-2)
952(a)(2), 15-28 (Fig. 15-2)
952(a)(3), 15-28 (Fig. 15-2)
952(a)(4), 15-28 (Fig. 15-2)
952(a)(5), 15-28 (Fig. 15-2)
952(b), 15-30 *n*
954(a)(1), 15-28 (Fig. 15-2)
954(a)(2), 15-28 (Fig. 15-2)
954(a)(3), 15-28 (Fig. 15-2)
954(a)(4), 15-28 (Fig. 15-2)
954(a)(5), 15-28 (Fig. 15-2)
954(b)(3)(A), 15-30 *n*
954(b)(3)(B), 15-28 (Fig. 15-2), 15-30 *n*
954(b)(4), 15-30 *n*
954(b)(5), 15-30 *n*
954(c), 15-29 *n*
954(d), 15-29 *n*
954(d)(1), 15-29 *n*
954(d)(3), 15-29 *n*
954(e), 15-29 *n*
954(f), 15-30 *n*
954(h), 15-30 *n*
956(a)(3), 15-31 *n*
956(b), 15-31 *n*
957(a), 15-27 *n*
958(b), 15-27
959(c), 15-31 *n*
960, 15-27
961(b), 15-31 *n*
962, 15-27
964(b), 15-30 *n*
986(a), 15-5
986(b), 15-24
995(b), 15-40 *n*
995(f), 15-40 *n*
996(a)(1), 15-40 *n*
996(d), 15-40 *n*

999, 15-31
1001, 2-11 *n*
1001(c), 6-12 *n*, 7-3
1012, 7-5 *n*
1014(a), 6-21, 13-9 *n*
1014(c), 14-37 *n*
1014(e), 12-30 *n*
1031(a)(2)(D), 10-22 *n*
1032, 2-21 *n*, 7-9
1034(b)(1), 1-31
1036, 7-32
1211(b), 14-19 *n*, 14-28 *n*
1212(a)(1)(A)(ii), 8-32
1222, 6-3 (Table 6-1), 10-22 *n*
1223(1), 2-20 *n*, 4-43 *n*, 6-3 (Table 6-1), 7-10 *n*, 7-13 *n*, 9-9 *n*
1223(2), 2-20 *n*, 2-22 *n*, 4-10 *n*, 6-3 (Table 6-1), 9-11
1223(5), 4-15 *n*, 4-16 *n*
1223(6), 4-16 *n*
1231, 1-14, 2-18–2-20, 2-20 *n*, 2-21, 2-21 (Topic Review 2-2), 2-26, 3-10, 3-23, 5-16, 5-17 (Fig. 5-1), 6-13, 6-25, 8-8 (Table 8-1), 8-12–8-13, 8-21, 8-22 *n*, 8-28–8-30,8-30 *n*, 8-31, 9-9–9-10, 9-21, 9-23, 9-40, 10-7, 10-32, 10-34 *n*, 11-13
1231(b), 10-41
1231(c), 8-30
1231(c)(3), 8-30 *n*
1231(c)(4), 8-30 *n*
1239, 2-18 *n*, 2-26, 3-22–3-23, 3-32, 8-14 *n*
1239(a), 3-23
1239(b), 6-12 *n*, 8-14 *n*
1242, 2-35 *n*
1243, 2-35 *n*
1244, 2-31 (Table 2-1), 2-33–2-35, 2-39, 2-39 *n*, 6-3 (Table 6-1), 6-7, 6-28
1244(a), 2-34 *n*
1245, 2-18, 2-26, 3-10, 3-13, 6-14, 6-25, 7-4 (Topic Review 7-1), 7-6, 7-8, 8-14–8-15, 8-36, 9-11–9-12, 9-22, 9-40, 10-7, 10-30–10-31
1245(b)(3), 2-18 *n*, 2-25 *n*, 6-14 *n*, 7-8 *n*, 9-11 *n*
1248, 15-32
1248(a), 15-32 *n*
1250, 2-18, 2-28, 3-9–3-10, 3-13, 6-14, 7-4 (Topic Review 7-1), 7-6, 7-8, 8-36, 9-11–9-12, 9-22, 9-40, 10-7
1250(c)(3), 2-18 *n*
1250(d)(3), 2-25 *n*, 6-14 *n*, 7-8 *n*, 9-11 *n*
1252, 9-12, 10-7
1253, 10-7
1254, 9-12
1271(a), 2-30
1272-1275, 2-30
1274(d), 12-31
1278, 10-7
1283, 10-7
1296(a), 15-34 *n*
1361(b)(1), 11-4 *n*
1361(b)(1)(A)-(C), 11-3 *n*
1361(b)(2)(A), 8-4 *n*
1361(c)(1), 11-3
1361(c)(4), 11-4 *n*, 11-35 *n*
1361(c)(5), 11-36
1361(c)(6), 11-4
1361(d), 11-3 *n*
1362(a)(2), 11-6 *n*

Index of Code Sections • G-5

1362(b)(1), 11-5 *n*
1362(b)(2), 11-6
1362(d)(1)(B), 11-7 *n*
1362(d)(1)(C), 11-7 *n*
1362(d)(1)(D), 11-7 *n*
1362(d)(2), 11-8 *n*
1362(d)(3), 11-8 *n*
1362(e), 11-39 *n*
1362(e)(1), 11-9 *n*
1362(e)(2), 11-9
1362(e)(3), 11-9
1362(e)(3)(B), 11-9 *n*
1362(e)(6)(B), 11-9 *n*
1362(f), 11-10it *n*
1362(g), 11-10
1363(a), 5-26 *n*
1363(b)(2), 11-14 *n*
1363(b)(3), 11-14 *n*
1363(b)(4), 11-14 *n*
1363(c), 11-12 *n*
1363(d), 11-5, 11-31
1363(d)(3), 11-18
1366, 11-12
1366(a), 11-12 *n*, 11-18 *n*
1366(b), 11-14
1366(d)(1), 11-22 *n*
1366(d)(2), 11-22 *n*
1366(d)(3)(B), 11-24 *n*
1366(d)(3), 11-23 *n*
1366(e), 11-20
1367(a), 11-25 *n*
1367(b)(2)(B), 11-27 *n*
1368, 11-30 *n*
1368(b), 11-28 *n*
1368(e), 11-30 *n*
1368(e)(3), 11-40
1371(b), 11-14 *n*
1371(d)(2), 11-43
1371(e), 11-32 *n*
1372(a), 11-35 *n*
1372(b), 11-34 *n*
1374, 11-5, 11-15, 11-16 *n*, 11-16–11-17, 11-39–11-40, 11-42–11-43
1374(a), 11-16 *n*
1374(b), 11-17 *n*
1374(b)(2), 11-16 *n*
1374(b)(3), 11-16 *n*
1374(c)(1), 11-17
1374(c)(2), 11-17 *n*, 11-17
1374(d), 11-17
1374(d)(1), 11-17 *n*
1374(d)(2), 11-16 *n*
1374(d)(3), 11-16 *n*
1374(d)(4), 11-16 *n*
1374(d)(5), 11-17 *n*
1375, 11-5, 11-8, 11-10, 11-15, 11-15 *n*, 11-16 *n*, 11-41–11-43
1375(a), 11-15 *n*
1375(b), 11-15 *n*
1375(b)(4), 11-16 *n*
1377(a), 11-39 *n*
1377(a)(2), 11-20
1377(b)(2), 11-23
1378(a), 11-11
1378(b), 11-11
1441(a), 15-17 *n*
1442, 15-24 *n*
1461, 15-17
1501, 1-16 *n*, 8-3
1501-1504, 8-3

1502, 1-16, 8-3
1504, 3-18 *n*, 8-3, 8-5, 11-4
1504(a), 3-33 *n*, 8-3
1504(b), 3-32 *n*, 8-4
1504(c)(2)(A), 8-4 *n*
1561, 3-26 *n*, 8-5
1561(a), 3-32 *n*, 3-36 *n*, 8-32–8-33
1561(a)(2), 3-32 *n*, 5-33
1561(a)(3), 3-32 *n*
1563, 3-26 *n*, 8-5
1563(a)(1), 3-27 *n*
1563(a)(2), 3-28 *n*
1563(a)(3), 3-30 *n*
1563(c), 3-27 *n*
1563(d)(1), 3-27 *n*
1563(d)(2), 3-28 *n*
2001(b), 13-4, 13-27 *n*
2001(b)(2), 13-5, 13-29
2001(c), 13-5, 13-28
2010, 13-6, 13-28
2010(c), 13-28 *n*
2011, 13-29
2011(b), 13-28–13-29
2011(f), 13-29
2012(a), 13-29
2013, 13-29
2013(a), 13-29
2014, 13-30
2032, 13-9
2032(c), 13-9 *n*
2032A, 13-35
2033, 13-10–13-11, 13-15, 13-18, 13-21 (Topic Review 13-2)
2034, 13-11 *n*
2035, 13-21 (Topic Review 13-2), 13-30
2035-2038, 13-11, 13-19 *n*, 13-20
2035(c), 13-12 *n*
2035(d), 13-11
2035(d)(2), 13-19 *n*
2036, 13-12–13-14, 13-21 (Topic Review 13-2), 13-23, 13-29, 14-4–n, 14-39
2036-2038, 13-12
2036(b)(1), 13-13 *n*
2036(b)(2), 13-13 *n*
2037, 13-12, 13-14, 13-21 (Topic Review 13-2)
2038, 13-12, 13-14, 13-21 (Topic Review 13-2), 14-4 *n*
2039, 13-15, 13-21 (Topic Review 13-2)
2039(b), 13-16
2039(c), 13-16 *n*
2040, 13-16, 13-21 (Topic Review 13-2)
2040(a), 13-17 *n*
2040(b)(1), 13-17
2041, 13-17, 13-19 *n*, 13-21 (Topic Review 13-2)
2042, 13-11, 13-18, 13-19, 13-21 (Topic Review 13-2)
2043, 13-19 *n*, 13-19–13-20
2044, 13-20 *n*, 13-21 (Topic Review 13-2), 13-26
2053, 13-21–13-23, 13-27 (Topic Review 13-3), 13-34–13-35, 13-39
2054, 13-22–13-23, 13-27 (Topic Review 13-3), 13-34–13-35, 13-39
2055, 13-23, 13-27 (Topic Review 13-3)
2056, 13-24 *n*, 13-27 (Topic Review 13-3)
2056(b)(7), 13-26
2056(c), 13-25

2501(a), 12-8
2501(a)(5), 12-10 *n*
2502(c), 12-35 *n*
2503(b), 12-6 *n*, 12-18
2503(c), 12-19–12-20, 14-4
2503(e), 12-9–12-10, 12-28
2504(c), 12-36 *n*
2505, 12-7 *n*
2505(c), 12-8 *n*
2511, 13-26 *n*
2511(a), 12-8
2513, 12-6, 12-25
2513(d), 12-35 *n*
2514, 12-17
2515, 13-36
2516, 12-10
2518(a), 12-11
2518(b), 12-11 *n*
2519, 13-20, 13-26 *n*
2522, 12-24
2523(b), 12-21 *n*
2523(f), 12-22 *n*
2524, 12-20 *n*, 12-21 *n*, 12-24
2611, 13-36 *n*
2612(a), 13-36 *n*
2623, 13-36 *n*
2631(a), 13-36 *n*
2641, 13-35 *n*
2701-2704, 7-33, 12-15
4943, 5-31
4980A, 13-16 *n*
6012(a)(2), 3-38 *n*, 16-15 *n*
6012(a)(3), 14-45 *n*
6012(a)(4), 14-45 *n*
6012(a)(5), 14-45 *n*
6013(d)(3), 16-33 *n*
6013(e), 16-33 *n*
6013(e)(3), 16-34 *n*
6013(g), 15-16 *n*, 15-19, 15-46
6013(h), 15-46
6018, 13-40
6019, 12-34
6031(a), 16-15 *n*
6037, 11-42
6037(b), 11-42 *n*
6043, 6-30
6043(a), 6-30
6043(c), 7-45
6072(a), 14-46 *n*, 16-14 *n*
6072(b), 3-39 *n*, 11-42 *n*
6072(c), 16-14 *n*
6075(a), 13-41 *n*
6075(b), 12-34
6081(a), 13-41 *n*, 16-15 *n*
6081(b), 16-15 *n*
6110, 1-27
6114, 15-45
6151(a), 14-46 *n*, 16-16 *n*
6151(b)(1), 16-16 *n*
6154(c), 8-33
6161(a)(1), 13-33
6161(a)(2), 13-33 *n*
6163, 13-33
6166, 4-28, 13-33, 13-39–13-40
6166(b)(1), 13-34 *n*
6213(a), 16-10 *n*
6221, 9-42 *n*, 11-45
6222, 9-42 *n*, 11-45
6223-6231, 11-45
6231(a)(1)(B), 9-42 *n*

6231(a)(3), 9-42
6231(a)(7), 9-42 n
6233, 11-43 n
6241, 11-44, 11-45
6242, 11-44
6243, 11-45
6501, 12-36 n
6501(a), 16-29
6501(b)(1), 16-29 n
6501(c)(1), 16-31 n
6501(c)(2), 16-31 n
6501(c)(3), 16-31 n
6501(c)(4), 16-31 n
6501(e), 16-30 n
6501(e)(2), 16-31 n
6501(h), 16-31 n
6511(a), 16-32 n
6531, 16-32 n
6601, 13-41
6601(a), 16-16 n
6601(b), 5-40
6601(b)(1), 16-16 n
6601(c), 16-17 n
6601(e)(2)(B), 16-18, 16-23 n, 16-27 n
6601(h), 16-22 n
6601(j), 13-34 n
6621, 3-44 n, 3-45–3-46, 13-33 n, 13-33, 16-16–16-17, 16-21–16-22
6651(a), 16-18 n, 16-29 (Topic Review 16-1)
6651(a)(2), 16-18 n
6651(b)(1), 16-18 n
6651(b)(2), 16-18 n
6651(c)(1), 16-19 n
6651(f), 16-18, 16-29 (Topic Review 16-1)
6653, 5-40
6654, 16-29 (Topic Review 16-1)
6654(d), 14-46 n, 16-21 n

6654(d)(2), 16-23 n
6654(e), 16-22 n
6654(f), 16-21 n
6654(g), 16-21 n
6654(l), 14-46 n
6655, 5-39
6655(c)(1), 3-43 n
6655(c)(2), 3-43 n
6655(d)(1), 8-38
6655(d)(1)(B)(ii), 11-43
6655(d)(2), 8-38, 11-44
6655(d)(2)(A), 3-44 n
6655(d)(2)(B), 3-44 n
6655(e), 11-44
6655(e)(1), 3-45 n
6655(e)(2), 3-45 n
6655(e)(3), 3-46 n
6655(g)(1), 3-43 n
6655(g)(2)(A), 3-44 n
6655(g)(2)(B)(ii), 3-44 n
6655(g)(4)(A), 11-43 n
6655(g)(4)(B), 11-44 n
6655(g)(4)(C), 11-43 n
6655(g)(4)(E), 11-44 n
6655(i)(1), 3-43 n
6661, 16-38
6662, 12-35
6662(a), 16-23 n
6662(b), 16-23 n, 16-27 n
6662(c), 16-23 n, 16-29 n (Topic Review 16-1)
6662(d), 16-29 (Topic Review 16-1)
6662(d)(1), 16-24 n
6662(d)(2)(C)(ii), 16-26 n
6662(d)(2)(D), 16-40 n
6662(g), 13-41 n
6662(g)(2), 12-36
6662(h), 13-41 n

6663, 16-26, 16-29 (Topic Review 16-1)
6663(c), 16-27 n
6664(c), 16-24 n
6694, 16-38
6694-6696, 16-38
6694(a), 16-39 (Topic Review 16-2)
6694(b), 16-39 (Topic Review 16-2)
6695, 16-38
6695(a), 16-39 (Topic Review 16-2)
6695(b), 16-39 (Topic Review 16-2)
6695(c), 16-39 (Topic Review 16-2)
6695(d), 16-39 (Topic Review 16-2)
6695(e), 16-39 (Topic Review 16-2)
6695(f), 16-39 (Topic Review 16-2)
6696, 16-38
6901, 16-35
7201, 16-28, 16-29 (Topic Review 16-1)
7201-7216, 16-28
7203, 16-28, 16-29 (Topic Review 16-1)
7206, 16-28
7206(2), 16-28 n, 16-29 (Topic Review 16-1)
7463, 1-20
7519, 9-4 n, 9-18–9-19, 9-42, 11-12, 11-43
7519(c), 9-19
7520, 12-14, 13-8
7701, 1-14
7701(a)(3), 2-8 n, 15-3 n
7701(a)(4), 3-2 n, 15-3 n
7701(a)(36), 16-38
7701(b), 15-16
7701(b)(3)(A), 15-16
7701(b)(4), 15-46 n
7704, 10-41
7704(d), 10-41
7805, 1-16
7872, 1-13, 12-30–12-32
7872(a), 12-31 n
7872(f)(3), 1-13

APPENDIX H

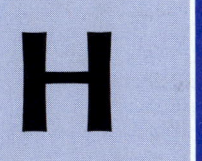

Index of Treasury Regulations

1.56-1, 5-8 n
1.56(g)-1(a)(3), 5-8 n
1.56(g)-1(a)(5), 5-10 n
1.56(g)-1(d)(3), 5-9
1.56(g)-1(d)(4), 5-9
1.56(g)-1(e), 5-10 n
1.56(g)-1(n)(1), 8-33 n
1.56(g)-1(n)(2), 8-33 n
1.56(g)-1(n)(3), 8-34 n
1.61-3(a), 16-30 n
1.61-12(c)(2), 2-30 n
1.83-6(a)(1), 9-13 n
1.83-6(a)(4), 9-13 n
1.83-6(b), 9-13 n
1.118-1, 2-32 n
1.162-7(a), 3-34
1.163-7(f), 2-30 n
1.165-5, 1-17
1.165-5(i), 1-17
1.166-5(b), 2-36
1.166-8(a), 2-35 n
1.168-2(n), 10-33 n
1.168-4(d)(8), 10-33 n
1.168-5(b)(2)(i)(B), 2-26 n
1.168-5(b)(4)(i), 2-26 n
1.168-5(b)(7), 2-27 n
1.170A-11(b)(2), 3-13 n
1.172-1(c), 3-20
1.248-1(a)(2), 3-11 n
1.248-1(a)(3), 3-11 n
1.248-1(b)(2), 3-11 n
1.248-1(b)(3), 6-18 n
1.267(f)-2T, 8-12 n
1.267(g)-2T(c), 8-37
1.301-1(b), 15-24 n
1.301-1(h)(2)(i), 4-17 n
1.301-1(m), 5-42 n
1.302-2(a), 4-25 n
1.302-2(b), 4-24
1.302-2(c), 4-19 n
1.302-3(a), 4-22 n
1.302-4(a), 4-49
1.302-4(d), 4-44
1.306-3(e), 4-31 n
1.307-1, 4-15 n
1.307-1(b), 4-16 n
1.307-2, 4-15 n
1.312-6(c)(1), 4-6 n
1.312-10, 4-44, 7-37 n
1.312-11, 4-44
1.316-2, 4-7 n
1.331-1(e), 6-6
1.332-2(b), 6-11

1.332-2(c), 6-5, 6-10
1.332-3, 6-10 n
1.332-4, 6-11 n
1.332-4(a)(2), 6-31 n
1.332-6, 6-31
1.337-2(b), 6-32 n
1.338(b)-1T(f)(1), 6-24 n
1.338(b)-1T(f)(2), 6-24 n
1.338(b)-1T(g), 6-24 n
1.338(b)-2T(a), 6-24 n
1.338(b)-2T(b)(2), 6-24 n
1.338(b)-3T(a)(1), 6-24
1.338-1T(d), 6-31
1.338-1T(e), 6-31
1.338-1T(e)(1), 6-31
1.338-4T(f)(6), 6-22
1.338-4T(1)(2), 6-26 n
1.346-1, 4-26 n
1.351-1(a)(1), 2-16 n
1.351-1(a)(1)(ii), 2-15 n, 2-16 n, 2-17 n
1.351-1(a)(2), 2-14 n
1.351-1(b)(1), 2-16 n
1.351-1(c)(1), 9-7 n
1.351-3(a), 2-39 n
1.351-3(b), 2-40 n
1.355-2(b), 4-39 n
1.355-2(b)(5), 4-39 n
1.355-2(c), 4-38 n, 4-40 n
1.355-2(d), 4-38 n
1.355-3(b)(2)(ii), 4-46
1.358-2(a)(2), 7-12 n
1.358-2(a)(3), 7-12 n
1.358-2(a)(4), 7-12 n
1.358-2(b)(2), 2-20 n
1.368-1(b), 7-35
1.368-1(c), 7-36
1.368-1(d)(2), 7-35 n
1.368-1(d)(3), 7-36 n
1.368-1(d)(4), 7-36 n
1.368-1(d)(5), 7-36 n
1.368-2(b)(1), 7-14 n
1.368-2(c), 7-27
1.368-2(g), 7-44 n
1.404(b)-1T, 3-22 n
1.442-1(b)(1), 3-4 n
1.442-1(c), 3-4 n
1.444-3T(b)(1), 11-42
1.444-3T(b)(3), 11-42
1.482-2, 15-33 n
1.482-2(d)(2), 15-34
1.533-1(a)(2), 5-26
1.533-1(c), 5-26 n
1.537-1(a), 5-27

1.537-1(b)(2), 5-28
1.537-2(c), 5-27 n
1.543-1(b)(1), 5-17 n
1.543-1(b)(2), 5-18 n
1.543-1(b)(3), 5-18 n
1.543-1(b)(4), 5-18 n
1.543-1(b)(8)(B)(ii), 5-20 n
1.641(b)-3(a), 14-3 n
1.642(d)-1(b), 14-19 n
1.642(h)-1, 14-19 n
1.651(a)-1, 14-10 n
1.652(a)-1, 14-18 n
1.652(b)-2(b), 14-13 n
1.652(b)-3, 14-16
1.652(b)-3(b), 14-21 n
1.652(c)-4(e), 14-16, 14-21 n
1.661(a)-1, 14-11 n, 14-23 n
1.662(b)-1, 14-13 n
1.663(c)-3(a), 14-27 n
1.671-4(b), 14-46 n, 14-46
1.691(a)-1(b), 14-36 n
1.702-1(a)(8), 9-21, 11-14
1.702-1(a)(8)(ii), 9-21 n
1.704-1(b)(2)(ii), 9-25 n
1.704-1(b)(2)(iii)(a), 9-26 n
1.704-1(d)(1), 9-30 n
1.704-1(d)(2), 9-30 n
1.704-1(e)(1)(iv), 9-37 n
1.704-1(e)(1)(v), 9-12 n
1.704-1(e)(2)(ii), 9-38 n
1.706-1(a), 9-36 n
1.706-1(c)(3), 10-25 n
1.706-1(c)(5), 10-24 n
1.707-1(a), 9-7
1.707-1(c), 9-36 n, 9-37 n
1.708-1(b)(1)(i)(a), 10-25 n
1.708-1(b)(1)(ii), 10-25 n
1.708-1(b)(1)(iv), 10-27 n
1.708-1(b)(2)(i), 10-28 n
1.708-1(b)(2)(ii), 10-29 n
1.709-2(a), 9-15 n
1.732-1(d)(1), 10-39 n
1.732-1(d)(2), 10-43 n
1.732-1(d)(3), 10-45 n
1.732-1(e), 10-39 n
1.736-1(a)(1)(ii), 10-22 n
1.736-1(a)(5), 10-20 n
1.743-1(b)(2), 10-34 n
1.743-1(b)(2)(ii), 10-34 n
1.751-1(a), 10-16 n
1.751-1(b), 10-8 n
1.751-1(b)(2)(iii), 10-39 n
1.751-1(c), 10-7 n

H-1

1.752-1(e), 9-28 *n*
1.754-1(c), 10-43 *n*, 10-43
1.754-1(b), 10-43 *n*
1.755-1(a), 10-33 *n*
1.755-1(a)(1)(i), 10-34 *n*
1.755-1(b)(1), 10-37 *n*
1.755-1(b)(1)(ii), 10-37 *n*
1.755-1(b), 10-34 *n*
1.755-1(b)(4), 10-38 *n*
1.761-2(a)(1), 9-4 *n*
1.861-8, 15-7, 15-30
1.863-3(b), 15-6 *n*
1.863-3(c), 15-6 *n*
1.901-2, 15-4
1.902-1(g), 15-24 *n*
1.911-3(d), 15-12 *n*
1.911-6(a), 15-14 *n*
1.911-6(c), 15-14 *n*
1.911-7(a)(3), 15-47 *n*
1.911-7(c), 15-47 *n*
1.1001-1(e), 10-23 *n*
1.1015-1(a), 10-23 *n*
1.1223-1(a), 9-9 *n*
1.1244(c)-2, 2-39 *n*
1.1245-4(c), 7-9 *n*
1.1250-3(c), 7-9 *n*
1.1362-3(d)(5)(iv), 11-8 *n* 11-41
1.1362-5(b), 11-10 *n*
1.1362-6(a), 11-10
1.1371-1(g), 11-35 *n*
1.1373-1(a)(2), 11-20
1.1375-1A(f), 11-15 *n*
1.1378-1, 11-12 *n*
1.1502-1(d), 8-7 *n*
1.1502-1(e), 8-7 *n*
1.1502-3(f), 8-12 *n*
1.1502-4, 8-35
1.1502-5(a), 8-37 *n*
1.1502-6(a), 8-40 *n*
1.1502-12, 8-7 *n*, 8-20 *n*
1.1502-13(a)(1), 8-11 *n*
1.1502-13(b)(1), 8-16 *n*
1.1502-13(c)(1), 8-11 *n*
1.1502-13(c)(2), 8-11 *n*
1.1502-13(c)(3), 8-37 *n*
1.1502-13(c)(4), 8-14 *n*
1.1502-13(d), 8-12 *n*, 8-13 *n*
1.1502-13(e), 8-12 *n*, 8-13 *n*
1.1502-13(f), 8-12 *n*, 8-13 *n*
1.1502-13(f)(1), 8-15 *n*
1.1502-13T(1)(1), 8-14
1.1502-14(a)(1), 8-18 *n*

1.1502-14(a)(2), 8-18 *n*
1.1502-14(a)(3), 8-18 *n*
1.1502-14(c), 8-18
1.1502-15, 8-26 *n*
1.1502-17(a), 8-9 *n*
1.1502-21, 8-24 *n*
1.1502-21(a)(2), 8-22
1.1502-21(a)(2)(i), 8-24 *n*
1.1502-21(a)(2)(ii), 8-24 *n*
1.1502-21(b)(1), 8-25 *n*
1.1502-21(b)(2)(iv), 8-22 *n*
1.1502-21(b)(3), 8-41 *n*
1.1502-21(b)(3)(i), 8-21 *n*
1.1502-21(c)(2), 8-26 *n*
1.1502-21(e), 8-21 *n*
1.1502-21(e)(1), 8-25 *n*
1.1502-21A(c)(5), 8-25 *n*
1.1502-22(a)(1), 8-29 *n*
1.1502-22(a)(2), 8-29 *n*
1.1502-22(a)(3), 8-29 *n*
1.1502-22(b), 8-31 *n*
1.1502-24(a), 8-19 *n*
1.1502-26(a)(1), 8-18 *n*
1.1502-75(a)(1), 8-39 *n*
1.1502-76(a), 8-9 *n*
1.1502-76(b)(2), 8-7 *n*
1.1502-76(b)(5)(i), 8-7 *n*
1.1502-76(b)(5)(ii), 8-8 *n*
1.1502-76(c), 8-39
1.1502-77(a), 8-39 *n*
1.1502-78(a), 8-41 *n*
1.1502-79(a)(3), 8-22 *n*
1.1502-91(a), 8-27 *n*
1.1502-91(c), 8-27 *n*
1.1502-92(b)(1)(i), 8-27 *n*
1.1502-92(b)(1)(ii), 8-27 *n*
1.1502-93(a), 8-28 *n*
1.1502-93(d), 8-28 *n*
1.1502-94(a), 8-28 *n*
1.1502-95(a), 8-28 *n*
1.1502-99, 8-28 *n*
1.1563-1(a)(3), 3-30 *n*
1.6012-1(a)(5), 16-33 *n*
1.6012-2(a)(2), 3-38 *n*, 6-31
1.6013-1(a)(1), 16-33 *n*
1.6031-1(e)(2), 9-4 *n*
1.6043-1(b), 6-30
1.6043-2(a), 6-30–6-31
1.6043-2(b), 6-31
1.6072-1(c), 15-47 *n*
1.6072-2(a), 15-48 *n*
1.6072-2(b), 15-48 *n*

1.6072-2(e), 15-48 *n*
1.6081-3, 3-39 *n*, 11-42 *n*
1.6081-3(a), 16-15 *n*
1.6081-4T, 15-47 *n*
1.6081-5(c), 15-47 *n*
1.6655-3, 8-38
1.6655-4(e)(3), 8-38 *n*
1.6661-3, 16-40 *n*
1.6661-3(b)(4)(ii), 16-41 *n*
1.6661-5(d)(1), 16-26 *n*
1.6694-1(a), 16-38
1.6694-1(b), 16-38
1.6695-1(b)(5), 16-38 *n*
1.7519-2T, 11-43
18.1362-2(a), 11-42
18.1362-2(c), 11-42
20.2031-1(b), 13-7 *n*
20.2031-2(b), 13-7 *n*
20.2031-2(e), 13-8 *n*
20.2031-8(a), 13-15 *n*
20.2032-1(f), 13-9 *n*
20.2036-1(a), 13-13 *n*
20.2042-1(c)(2), 13-18 *n*
20.2053-2, 13-22 *n*
20.2056(e)-1(a)(6), 13-25 *n*
25.2503-3(a), 12-19 *n*
25.2503-3(b), 12-19 *n*
25.2504-2, 12-36 *n*
25.2511-1(a), 12-15 *n*
25.2511-1(h)(4), 12-15 *n*
25.2511-1(h)(5), 12-15 *n*
25.2511-1(h)(8), 12-15 *n*
25.2511-2(b), 12-11 *n*
25.2511-2(c), 12-12 *n*
25.2512-1, 12-13 *n*
25.2512-2, 12-13 *n*
25.2512-6, 12-15
25.2512-8, 12-8 *n*
25.2513-2(a)(1), 12-35 *n*
301.6031-1(e)(2), 9-41 *n*
301.6324-1, 12-35 *n*
301.6501(f)-1, 5-39
301.6651-1(c)(1), 16-18 *n*
301.6651-1(c)(3), 16-19 *n*
301.6651-1(c)(4), 3-46 *n*, 16-19 *n*
301.6901-1(b), 16-35 *n*
301.7623-1(c), 16-7 *n*
301.7701-2, 2-8 *n*
301.7701-2(a)(2), 2-9 *n*
301.7701-2(a)(3), 2-9

APPENDIX

Index of Government Promulgations

Announcements

86-128, 1-25 (Table 1-2), 1-28
87-32, 14-46 n
90-65, 16-14 n

Information Releases

86-70, 1-25 (Table 1-2), 1-28
88-58, 15-47 n

Letter Rulings

7842068, 12-17 n
8511075, 1-25 (Table 1-2), 1-27

Notice

89-60, 13-8
90-20, 16-38, 16-38 n

Revenue Procedures

65-19, 1-25 (Table 1-2), 1-27
74-33, 9-17
77-37, 2-15 n, 2-16 n, 7-14 n, 7-20 n, 7-21 n, 7-24 n, 7-25 n, 7-35 n, 7-44 n
79-34, 16-10 n
82-36, 8-37 n
83-7, 16-17 n, 16-17
83-25, 11-17 n
83-59, 2-40, 16-12 n
83-78, 10-41 n
84-35, 9-42
84-58, 1-18 n
84-84, 10-41 n
87-32, 3-3 n, 9-17, 11-12 n
89-12, 9-4 n
89-34, 16-14 n
89-50, 7-22
90-16, 16-40
90-17, 16-12
90-53, 8-10 n
91-1, 16-12 n, 16-13 n
91-3, 2-40 n, 7-45 n, 16-13, 16-14 n
91-11, 8-10 n

Revenue Rulings

56-613, 2-13 n
59-60, 13-8
59-259, 2-14 n
60-183, 11-42
64-162, 11-27 n
65-235, 6-32 n
66-365, 7-27 n
67-274, 7-26 n
68-55, 2-18–2-19
68-285, 7-27 n
68-348, 6-6
68-537, 11-27 n
69-6, 7-14 n
69-115, 4-46 n
69-608, 4-47, 4-47 n
70-50, 11-22
70-104, 4-44 n
70-106, 6-29 n
70-140, 7-37 n
71-426, 4-44 n
72-380, 4-44 n
73-54, 7-27 n
73-484, 8-37 n
73-491, 15-5 n
73-506, 15-5 n
74-269, 7-33 n
74-296, 4-26 n
74-516, 4-41 n
75-3, 4-26 n
75-67, 5-20 n
75-72, 12-17 n
75-249, 5-20 n
75-250, 5-20 n
75-330, 5-40 n
75-502, 4-25 n
75-521, 6-29 n
76-317, 6-10 n
76-364, 4-25 n, 4-25
77-415, 7-34 n
77-467, 4-44 n
78-94, 2-34 n
79-10, 6-6
79-59, 5-21 n
79-70, 2-17 n
79-106, 2-9 n
79-334, 4-44 n
80-177, 6-6
80-189, 4-35 n
80-198, 2-27 n
80-234, 9-36 n
80-265, 1-25 (Table 1-2), 1-27
81-25, 7-35 n
81-233, 4-44 n
83-82, 1-11 n
83-120, 7-33 n
84-15, 9-19 n
84-52, 10-22 n
84-111, 10-23 n
85-48, 6-6
85-164, 2-20 n
87-54, 5-40 n
87-57, 9-17 n
87-58, 11-12 n
90-99, 1-25 (Table 1-2), 1-27, 12-14 n
89-44, 15-4 n
91-9, 7-40 n

Treasury Decision (T.D.)

6904, 11-36

Treasury Information Release (T.I.R.)

1248, 11-36 n

APPENDIX J

Index of Court Cases

Aqualane Shores, Inc. v. CIR, 2-29, 2-38
Arrowsmith, F. Donald v. CIR, 6-8
Atlas Tool Co., Inc. v. CIR, 5-28

Badias & Seijas, Inc., 6-32
Bardahl International Corp., 5-29
Bardahl Manufacturing Corp., 5-29
Bazley, J. Robert v. CIR, 7-34
Bell Fibre Products Corp., 2-34
Berger, Ernest H., 4-46
Bochner v. Commissioner, 1-7
Bongiovanni, John P., 2-27, 2-31
Bonner v. City of Prichard, 1-23
Burnet v. Edith A. Logan, 6-8
Byrum, Marian A., U.S. v., 1-24

Campbell, William G., 9-13
Carey, Gerald, U.S. v., 4-47
Cartwright, Douglas B., Executor, U.S. v., 1-16
Chapman, Eldon S. et al. v. CIR, 7-27
Chertkof, Jack O., 4-44
Chicago Stock Yards Co., Helvering v., 5-25
CIR v. ———, See opposing party
Clark, Donald E. v. CIR 6-42, 7-11
Clifford, George B. Jr., Helvering v., 14-40
Cox, David L., 1-6–1-8, 1-11–1-12
Crummey, D. Clifford v. CIR, 12-20

Davis, Maclin P., U.S. v., 1-24, 1-25 (Table 1-2), 4-25
Day & Zimmerman, Inc., CIR v., 6-30
Dean, J. Simpson, 1-21, 1-25 (Table 1-2)
Diamond, Sol, 9-12
Diaz, Alfonso, 1-34–1-36
Diaz, Leonarda C., 1-34–1-36, 1-39
Dibs, Albert N., 1-34
Dickman, Esther C. v. CIR 12-30
Diedrich, Victor P. v. CIR, 12-17
DiVarco, Joseph, U.S. v., 16-28
The Donruss Company, U.S. v., 5-26
Doug-Long, Inc., 5-29
Duarte, Henry D., 11-20

Eisner v. Myrtle H. Macomber, 4-14
Evans, A. T., 7-44

Fehrs, Edward J. v. U.S., 4-49
First National Bank of Altoona, CIR v., 7-21
Frankel, E. J., 11-22

Gamman, W. C., 11-35
Gardin, Ronald L., 1-8–1-12
Generes, Edna, U.S. v., 2-36
George L. Riggs, Inc., 6-29
Ginsburg, Max R. v. U.S., 10-25
Golsen, Jack E., 1-11, 1-24
Gregory, Evelyn F. v. Helvering, 7-34, 7-36

Haft, Robin, Trust, 4-49
Hart Metal Products Corp. v. U.S., 5-40
Havemeyer, Horace v. U.S., 13-8
Hawaiian Trust Co. Ltd. v. U.S., 6-27
Helvering v. ———, See opposing party
Hewitt, William, 7-44
Holsey, Joseph R. v. CIR, 4-48

James Armour, Inc., 7-21
John A. Nelson Co. v. Helvering, 7-35
Joseph Weidenhoff, Inc., 1-16
J. W. Wells Lumber Co. Trust A, 1-21, 1-25 (Table 1-2)

King Enterprises, Inc. v. U.S., 7-12
Kintner, Arthur R., U.S. v., 2-8
Kirkpatrick, Donald O., 11-20
Klein, Frederick S., 9-11
Koppers Co., Inc. v. U.S., 6-18

Landsberger, Gerald J., U.S. v., 10-41
Leavitt, Daniel, Estate of v. CIR, 11-22
Lennard, Milton S., Estate of, 4-45
LeTulle, V. L. v. Scofield, 7-35
Lucas v. Guy C. Earl, 2-27
Lucky Stores, Inc., 1-21
Lumpkin, James H. Jr., Estate of v. CIR, 13-18
Lynch, William M. v. CIR, 4-45

McKinney, Edith G., 1-22, 1-25 (Table 1-2)
Malta Temple Association, 3-12
Mayson Manufacturing Co. v. CIR, 4-13
M. E. Blatt Co. v. U.S., 1-16
Millar, Gavin S., 11-20
Morrissey, T. A. v. CIR, 2-8
Moss, John A., Estate, 1-21
Myron's Enterprises v. U.S., 5-28

Noel, Marshall L., Estate of, CIR v., 13-19

Ogden, Mary K. S., 9-39
O. H. Kruse Grain & Milling v. CIR, 2-29
Oswald, Vincent E., 4-46
Ourisman, Florenz R., 2-10

Pahl, John G., 4-46
Panama Refining Co. v. U.S., 1-16
Paparo, Jack, 4-25
Portage Plastics Co., Inc. v. U.S., 11-36
Prashker, Ruth M., 11-22
Prell, Charles M., Estate of, 13-8
Pridemark, Inc. v. CIR, 6-17

Raphan, Benjamin v. U.S., 1-23, 1-25 (Table 1-2)
Richardson, Cecil R., 9-39
Rickey, Jr., Horace B. v. U.S., 1-23, 1-25 (Table 1-2)
Robertson, James Y., 11-22
Russell, Edward H. v. CIR, 7-15

Scheft, William, 14-38
Selfe, Edward M. v. U.S., 11-22
Shores Realty Co., Inc. v. U.S., 11-36
Shugarman, Charles D., U.S. v., 10-41
Simons-Eastern Co. v. U.S., 5-31
Smith, David, Estate of, 13-8
South Texas Lumber Co., CIR v., 1-16
Southwest Consolidated Corp., Helvering v., 7-32
Speca, Gino A. v. CIR, 11-20
Stafford, D. N. v. U.S., 2-13, 9-7
State Office Supply, Inc., 5-30
Stewart, J. T. III, Trust, 6-17
Sun Properties, Inc. v. U.S., 2-29, 2-38

Thatcher, Wilford E. v. CIR, 2-27
The Bon Ami Co., 15-24
Thompson, Margie J., v. U.S., 1-22, 1-25 (Table 1-2)

U.S. v. ———, See opposing party

Vogel Fertilizer Co. v. U.S., 1-24

Wall, H. F. v. U.S., 4-47
Warren Jones Co., 1-21
Weyerhaeuser, R. M., 4-6
W. W. Windle Co., 2-34

Subject Index

Abusive tax shelters
attempts to curtail, 10-40–10-41
compared to nonabusive tax shelters, 10-40–10-41
ACCESS legal data base, 1-39
Accountants, See Certified public accountants(CPAs)
Accounting for acquisitions, 7-5
Accounting methods
accrual method, 3-5
affiliated groups, 8-9
cash method, 3-5
corporation/controlling shareholder using different methods, 3-23
hybrid method, 3-5
liquidating distributions, 6-6
partnerships, 7-15
S corporations, 11-12
Accounting periods
affiliated groups, 8-8–8-9
C corporations, 3-2–3-4
changes in, 3-4
estates, 14-44–14-45
partnerships, 9-15, 9-17–9-19, 9-41–9-42
S corporations, 11-11–11-12, 11-42
trusts, 14-44–14-45
Accrual method of accounting, 3-5, 3-12–3-13, 3-22, 8-9
accrual basis corporations, pledges made by, 3-12–3-13
accrued compensation deductions, limitations on, 3-22
Accumulated Adjustments Account (AAA), 11-29–11-32
Accumulated earnings and profits (E&P), 4-3
compared to current earnings and profits (E&P), 4-7–4-9
Accumulated earnings credit, 5-33–5-34
Accumulated earnings tax, 5-25–5-35, 5-38
accumulated taxable income, 5-32–5-34
accumulated earnings credit, 5-33–5-34
dividends-paid deduction, 5-32–5-33
negative adjustments, 5-32
positive adjustments, 5-32
avoidance of, 5-38
calculation of, 4-34–4-35
corporations subject to, 4-23
determination of tax liability, 5-31–5-34
filing requirements, 5-40
reasonable business needs, evidence of, 5-27–5-31
tax-avoidance motive, evidence of, 5-27

tax-avoidance purpose, proving of, 5-26
tax liability, determination of, 5-31–5-34
Accumulation distribution rules, 14-32–14-34
purpose, 14-32–14-33
when applicable, 14-33–14-34
Acquiescence policy, U.S. Tax Court, 1-20
Acquisitions, 7-1–7-45
accounting for, 7-5
basis, 7-10
bootstrap acquisitions, 4-47–4-48
categories of, 7-5
asset acquisitions, 7-6–7-7
stock acquisitions, 7-5–7-6
holding period, 7-10
recognition of gain/loss, 7-10
stock acquisitions, 6-6, 7-5–7-6, 7-10–7-13
basis of stock/securities received, 7-12
holding period, 7-13
liquidating distributions and, 6-6
recognition of gain/loss, 7-10
taxable acquisitions
tax consequences of, 7-5–7-8
taxable versus tax-free transactions, 7-3–7-5
tax consequences of, 7-3–7-5
tax attributes, 7-37–7-41
assumption of, 7-37–7-38
limitation on use of, 7-38–7-41
tax consequences of, 7-3–7-13
for acquiring corporation, 7-3, 7-9–7-10
for target corporation, 7-3, 7-8–7-9
for target corporation's shareholders, 7-3–7-5, 7-10–7-13
tax-free reorganization
tax consequences of, 7-8–7-13
types of, 7-7–7-8
Acquisitive reorganizations, 7-7, 7-14–7-29
Type A reorganizations, 7-14–7-21
consolidations, 7-14–7-21
mergers, 7-14–7-21
Type B reorganizations, 7-26–7-29
advantages of, 7-28
disadvantages of, 7-28–7-29
solely-for-voting-stock requirement, 7-26–7-27
tax consequences of, 7-28
triangular Type B reorganizations, 7-29
Type C reorganizations, 7-21–7-24
advantages of, 7-23

consideration used to effect reorganization, 7-22–7-23
disadvantages of, 7-23
stock distribution, 7-21–7-22
substantially all requirement, 7-21
tax consequences of, 7-23–7-24
Type D reorganizations, 7-24–7-25
control requirements, 7-24–7-25
tax consequences of, 7-25
Type G reorganization, 7-29
See also Divisive reorganizations; Reorganizations
Active conduct of a trade or business
definition of, 4-45–4-46
Sec. 355, 4-39
Adjusted current earnings, 5-7–5-12
Adjusted grossed-up basis, definition of, 6-23
Adjusted income from rents (AIR), 5-17, 5-18–5-20
Adjusted net book income (ANBI), 5-8 fn
Adjusted ordinary gross income (AOGI), 5-16–5-17
definition of, 5-16–5-17
rental income expenses, reduction by, 5-17
Adjusted taxable gifts, 12-4, 13-4–13-5
valuation of, 13-4–13-5
Adjustments, alternative minimum tax (AMT), 5-5–5-7
Administration expenses
as estate tax deduction, 13-21–13-22
where to deduct, 13-41–13-42
Administrative interpretations, 1-13–1-15, 1-25–1-28
announcements, 1-28
citations of, 1-25
information releases, 1-28
letter rulings, 1-27
revenue procedures, 1-27
revenue rulings, 1-26–1-27
technical advice memoranda, 1-28
Administrative powers, grantor trusts, retention of, 14-41
Administrative procedures, 16-1–16-41
audits of tax returns, 16-3–16-12
Circular 230, 16-39–16-40
civil fraud penalty, 16-26–16-27
criminal fraud penalties, 16-27–16-28
due dates, 16-14–16-20
estimated taxes, 16-20–16-23
Internal Revenue Service, role of, 16-2–16-3
negligence penalty, 16-23–16-24

K-1

Administrative procedures (*continued*)
  rulings, requests for, 16-12–16-14
  statute of limitations, 16-28–16-33
  substantial authority, concept of, 16-25–16-26, 16-40–16-41
  substantial understatement penalty, 16-24–16-26
  tax liability, 16-33–16-35
  tax practice issues, 16-35–16-40
  See also Internal Revenue Service; Statute of limitations; Tax law
Administrative rules, S corporations, 11-44–11-45
Administrative transfer pricing rules, foreign sales corporations (FSCs), 15-37–15-38
Advances, ordinary loss deduction for, 2-36–2-38
Affiliated corporations, worthless securities, 2-34
Affiliated groups, 8-2–8-41
  compared to controlled groups, 8-4–8-5
    differences between definitions, 8-5
  definition of, 8-3–8-5
  elections, 8-8–8-9
    accounting methods, 8-9
    tax years, 8-8–8-9
  filing requirements, 8-2
  requirements for, 8-3–8-4
    includible corporation requirement, 8-4
    stock ownership requirements, 8-3–8-4
  tax liability
    computation of, 8-32–8-34
    alternative minimum tax liability, 8-33–8-34
    regular tax liability, 8-32–8-33
  termination of, 8-9–8-10
    effect on former members, 8-10
    good cause request to discontinue status, 8-10
Aliens
  definition of, 15-3
  filing requirements for, 15-47–15-48
  S corporations and, 11-4
Allocation of basis
  deemed liquidation election, 6-20–6-27
    liquidation of target corporation, 6-26–6-27
    to individual assets, 6-24–6-25
    total basis for allocation, 6-22–6-24
All You Need to Know About the IRS (Strassels/Wood), 16-6 *fn*
Alternate valuation date, 13-9–13-10
  definition of, 13-9
  estate taxes, election of, 13-41
Alternative minimum tax (AMT)
  adjusted current earnings, 5-7–5-12
  adjustments for, 5-5–5-7
  affiliated corporations, 8-33–8-34
  alternative minimum taxable income, 5-3–5-12
  computation of, 5-2–5-14
    foreign tax credit, 5-13–5-14
    general business credit, 5-13
    minimum tax credit, 5-12
  foreign corporations, 15-24–15-25
  S corporations, 11-32
  tax credits and, 5-12–5-13
  trusts and estates, 14-9

Alternative minimum taxable income (AMTI)
  adjusted current earnings, 5-7–5-12
  basis adjustments, 5-5–5-6
  book income adjustment, 5-8n
  definition of, 5-3
  disallowed losses, 5-7
  tax preference items, 5-3–5-5
American Federal Tax Reports (AFTR), 1-23
Announcements, tax law, 1-28
Annual accounting period
  affiliated groups, 8-8–8-9
  C corporations, 3-2–3-4
  partnerships, 9-15, 9-17–9-19, 9-41–9-42
  S corporations, 11-11–11-13, 11-42
  trusts and estates, 14-44–14-45
Annual exclusion
  amount of, 12-18–12-19
  inter vivos gifts, 12-32
  present interest requirement, 12-19–12-20
    Crummey trust, 12-20
    special rule for trusts for minors, 12-19–12-20
  purpose of, 12-18
  result of availability of, 12-18
Annualized income, exception, estimated taxes, 3-45
Annuities
  date-of-death valuation, 13-8–13-9
  estate tax and, 13-15–13-16
    annuities not related to employment, 13-15–13-16
    gross estate, 13-15–13-16
  personal holding company income (PHCI) and, 5-17–5-18
Antichurning rules
  Sec. 338 deemed liquidation, 6-26
  Sec. 351 corporate formation, 2-26
Appeals coordinated issue
  definition of, 16-10
  example of, 16-10
Appeals Court procedures, 1-23–1-24
Appeals Office
  appeals coordinated issue, 16-10
  appeal to, 16-8–16-10
  protest letter, 16-8–16-10
  30-day letter, 16-8
Appraising Real Property (Boyce/Kinnard), 13-8 *fn*
Arm's-length transfer pricing rules, foreign sales corporations (FSCs), 15-38
Asset-for-stock reorganization, Type C reorganization, 7-21–7-25
Assets
  corporations
    formation, 2-22
    taxable acquisition, 7-6–7-7
    tax-free reorganization, 7-8, 7-30
      divisive Type D reorganizations, 7-30
      general rule, 7-10
      recognition of gain or loss on transfer, 7-8
    See also Acquisitions
  partnerships
    formation, 9-9–9-11
    optional basis adjustments, 10-29–10-40

Assignment of income doctrine, 2-27
Associations
  compared to trusts, 2-9
  corporate characteristics, 2-8
  definition of, 2-8
At-risk rules
  C corporations, 3-23–3-24, 5-7
  partnerships, 9-31–9-33
  S corporations, 11-13
Attribution rules
  controlled foreign corporations, 15-27
  related party transactions, 3-22
  reorganizations, 7-37–7-41
  stock redemptions, 4-20–4-21
    attribution from entity, 4-21
    attribution to entity, 4-21
    family attribution, 4-20–4-21
    option attribution, 4-21
Audits, 16-3–16-12
  alternatives for taxpayers, 16-7–16-10
  appeal to Appeals Office, 16-8–16-10
  correspondence audit, 16-7
  field audit, 16-7
  litigation, 16-11–16-12
    appeal of lower court's decision, 16-11–16-12
    district court, 16-11–16-12
    Tax Court, 16-11
    U.S. Claims Court, 16-11
  meeting with revenue agent, 16-8
  office audit, 16-7
  percentage of returns audited, 16-5
  selection of returns for, 16-5–16-7
    discriminant function (DIF) program, 16-5–16-6
    special investigatory projects, 16-7
    Taxpayer Compliance Measurement Program, 16-6
  special relief rule, 16-7–16-8
  technical advice memoranda, 16-8

Bardahl formula, 5-28–5-31
  service companies and, 5-30–5-31
Bargain purchase, of corporate property, 4-14
Bargain sales, gift tax and, 12-9
Basis
  corporate formation, 2-22
  corporate assets, 2-22
  stock, 2-19–2-20
  partnership formation
    partnership assets, 9-9–9-11
    partnership interest 9-9
  partnership liquidating distribution, assets received, 10-12–10-14
  restoration of stock/debt, S corporation, 11-25–11-27
Basis adjustments
  alternative minimum taxable income, 5-5–5-6
  corporate formations, 2-22
  partnerships
    partnership interest, operations, 9-26–9-30
    on distributions, 10-35–10-38
      to transferee partners, 10-38–10-40
    Sec. 754 election, 10-30
    on transfers, 10-30–10-35

S corporations, 11-25–11-27
   to S corporation stock, 11-25–11-26
   to shareholder debt, 11-26–11-27
tax-free reorganization, 7-10
transfers
   at death, 12-30
   by gift, 12-29–12-30
"Baskets" of income, foreign tax credit limitations, 15-5–15-8
Beneficiary
   accumulation distribution rules, 14-32–14-34
     purpose, 14-32–14-33
     when applicable, 14-33–14-33
   complex trusts
     separate share rule, 14-27
     specific bequests, 14-27–14-28
     tax treatment, 14-24–14-28
     tier system, 14-25–14-27
   simple trusts, tax treatment, 4-17–14-18
Bona fide loans, to shareholders, 4-12–4-13
Bona fide resident test, 15-9–15-10
Bond-for-bond exchange, Type E reorganizations, 7-33
Bond-for-stock exchange, Type E reorganizations, 7-33
Book income adjustment, alternative minimum taxable income (AMTI), 5-8
Book income
   reconciliation to taxable income items, 3-40–3-42
Boot
   corporate distribution, stock of controlled subsidiary, 5-38
   corporate formation
     definition of, 2-18
     receipt of, 2-18
     shareholder's basis, 2-19
   tax-free reorganization, 7-8–7-12
     shareholder, 7-10–7-12
     target corporation, 7-8
Bootstrap acquisitions, 4-47–4-48
Boycott-related income, foreign base company, 15-30–15-31
Branch profits tax, foreign corporations, 15-25
Bribes, as foreign base company income, 15-31
Brother-sister corporations
   controlled groups, 3-28–3-30
   stock redemptions, 4-33–4-35
     definition of, 4-33
     treated as distributions, 4-34
     treated as sales, 4-34–4-35
Built-in gains tax, as special S corporation tax, 11-15–11-17
Burden of proof, criminal fraud penalties, 16-27
Business contingencies, as reasonable business need, 5-28
Business enterprise acquisition, as reasonable businessneed, 5-28
Business expansion, as reasonable business need, 5-28
Business purpose requirement, Sec. 355, 4-38

C corporations
   accrual method of accounting and, 3-5

definition, 2-5–2-7
fringe benefits, 2-6
tax advantages, 2-6
tax attributes, 6-18–6-19, 7-37–7-38
tax disadvantages, 2-6–2-7
tax formula, 3-7–3-8
tax rates 3-24–3-26
tax year, 3-2–3-4
See also Closely-held C corporation, Corporations; S corporations
C short year, definition of, 11-8
Calendar year
   C corporation
     versus fiscal year, 3-2–3-4
     short tax period, 3-3
   requirement
     partnerships, 9-15–9-19, 9-41–9-42
     S corporations, 11-11–11-12, 11-42
   See also Tax year
Capital contributions, corporations, 2-32–2-34
   by nonshareholders, 2-32–2-34
   by shareholders, 2-32
Capital gain property, deducting contributions of, 3-14
Capital gains/losses
   affiliated group members, 8-30–8-32
     carrybacks/carryforwards, 8-31–8-32
     departing member's losses, 8-32
     Sec. 382 limitations, 8-31
     Sec. 1231 gains/losses, 8-30
     SRLY rules, 8-31
   corporations, 3-9
     capital loss limitation, 3-9
     determining amount of gain/loss, 8-30
Capital gains tax, as special S corporation tax, 11-17–11-18
Capital interest, 9-12
Capital loss property, partnerships, basis, 9-10–9-11
Capital ownership
   family partnerships, 9-37–9-38
   donor retained control, 9-38
   minor donees, 9-38
Capital structure
   characterization of obligations, 2-29
   choice of, 2-28–2-34
     debt capital, 2-29–2-30
     equity capital, 2-31–2-32
   See also Debt capital; Equity capital
Carrybacks/carryovers
   capital losses, 3-9
   charitable contributions, 3-15
   consolidated capital losses
     departing group member's losses, 8-32
     SRLY rules, 8-31
     taxable income limitation, 8-32
   consolidated NOLs
     special rule for new members, 8-22–8-23
     to separate return year, 8-24
   foreign tax credit, 15-7
   general business credit, 5-12–5-14
   minimum tax credit, 5-12
   net operating losses, 3-19–3-20
     election to forego carryback, 3-20
Cash receipts and disbursements method of accounting, 3-5
   C corporations and, 3-5
   transferor liabilities using, 2-24–2-25

CCH Tax Court Memorandum Decisions, 1-22
Certificates of deposit (CDs), interest income earned by alien from, 15-18
Certified public accountants (CPAs)
   "good faith" belief requirement, 16-37–16-38
   knowledge of errors, 16-36
   positions on tax returns, 16-37
   procedural aspects of return preparation, 16-37
   proper behavior of, 16-35–16-40
   responsibilities, 16-35–16-38
   use of taxpayer estimates, 16-36
Charitable contributions
   affiliated groups, 8-19–8-20
     computed on consolidated basis, 8-19–8-20
   alternative minimum tax, 5-5
   C corporations, 3-12–3-15
     capital gain property contributions, 3-14
     donations of inventory, 3-13–3-14
     limitation, 3-15–3-16
     ordinary income property contributions, 3-13–3-14
     pledges made by accrual-basis corporation, 3-12–3-13
     sequencing of deduction calculation, 3-20–3-22
   estate tax
     computation of, 13-23
     split-interest transfers, 13-23–13-24
   gift tax, 12-24–12-25
     income tax savings from, 12-33
     split-interest transfers, 12-24–12-25
     transfers eligible for deduction, 12-24
Charitable remainder annuity trusts, definition of, 12-24 *fn*
Charitable remainder unitrust, definition of, 12-24 *fn*
Circuit court of appeals, precedential value of decisions, 1-26
Circular 230, 16-39–16-40
Citations
   administrative interpretations, 1-26–1-28
   Internal Revenue Code, 1-14
   judicial decisions, 1-20–1-24
   Treasury Regulations, 1-16
   summary, 1-25
Citators, 1-33–1-39
   Commerce Clearing House Citator (CCH citator), 1-34, 1-35
   Prentice Hall citator, 1-34–1-39
Civil fraud penalty, 16-26–16-27
   when fraud is proven, 16-31–16-32
Claims Court Reporter, 1-23
Client letter, 1-40
Client-oriented tax research, 1-2–1-3
   contexts, 1-2–1-3
     closed-fact situations, 1-2–1-3
     open-fact situations, 1-3
Clifford trusts
   grantor trust rules, 14-39–14-40
   Tax Reform Act (1986) and, 14-40
Closed-fact situations, client-oriented tax research and, 1-2–1-3
Closed transaction doctrine, 6-9
Closed transactions, liquidating distributions, 6-9

Subject Index

Closely held businesses, interests in, and deferral of estate tax payments, 13-33–13-34
Closely held C corporations
  alternative minimum tax adjustments, 5-5–5-7
  at-risk rules and, 3-23–3-24
  passive activity limitation rules, 3-24
  special tax accounting rules for, 3-2–3-5
Closely held corporations
  accumulated earnings tax, 5-25–5-35, 5-38
  advances, ordinary loss deduction for, 2-36–2-37
  alternative minimum tax (AMT), 5-2–5-14
  at risk rules and, 3-23–3-24, 11-23
  capital structure, 2-28–2-34
    characterization of obligations, 2-29
    choice of, 2-28–2-34
    debt capital, 2-29–2-30
    equity capital, 2-31–2-32
  collapsible corporations, 6-7 *fn*
  compensation planning for shareholder-employees, 3-34–3-35
  debt/equity regulations, 2-29
  hobby loss rules, 11-23
    investment interest expense limitations, 11-23
  passive activity limitations, 3-24, 11-23
  personal holding company (PHC) tax, 5-15–5-25, 5-37–5-38
  personal service corporation tax rates, 3-25
  special tax accounting provisions, 3-2–3-5
    cash method of accounting, 3-5
    taxable year, 3-2–3-5, 11-11–11-12, 11-42
  stock losses, ordinary loss deduction for, 2-34–2-35, 2-39
  unreasonable compensation, avoidance of, 4-46–4-47
  worthlessness of stock/debt obligations, 2-34–2-35
  See also Collapsible corporations
The Code, *See* Internal Revenue Code
Collapsible corporations, 6-7
Collection of tax, Internal Revenue Service, role of, 16-2–16-3
Combined controlled groups, 3-30–3-31
Combined taxable income, 8-7
Commerce Clearing House Citator (CCH citator), 1-34
  excerpt from, 1-35
Common law state, 12-5
Community property laws, 12-5
  innocent spouse provision, effect of, 16-33–16-35
  See also Divorce; Innocent spouse provision
Compensation planning
  closely held corporations, 3-34–3-35
    fringe benefits, 3-35
    salary payments, 3-34–3-35
    for shareholder-employees, of closely held corporations, 3-35–3-39
  unreasonable compensation, avoidance of, 4-46–4-47

Complete liquidation
  definition of, 6-5
  tax treatment, 6-1–6-19
Complete termination of interest
  definition of, 4-44–4-45
  family attribution rules and, 4-23–4-24, 4-44–4-45
  stock redemptions, 4-23–4-24, 4-44–4-45
Complex trusts/estates
  distributable net income (DNI), determination of, 14-23–14-24
  distribution deduction, 14-30–14-31
  net capital loss effect, 14-28–14-29
  net operating loss effect, 14-28
  taxable income, 14-22–14-29
    comprehensive illustration, 14-29–14-32
  tax treatment for beneficiary, 14-24–14-28
  See also Simple trusts; Trusts
Computers, as tax research tool, 1-39–1-40
Concentration of Wealth in the United States, The (U.S. Congress), 12-3 *fn*
Conduit approach
  to fiduciary taxation, 14-5
  to partnership taxation, 9-4
Conference Committee, tax law and, 1-13
Consent dividends, 5-22–5-23
Consideration offset, gross estate, 13-19–13-20
Consolidated capital losses, 8-28–8-32
  carrybacks/carryforwards, 8-31–8-32
    departing group member's losses, 8-32
    Sec. 382 limitations, 8-31
    Sec. 1231 gains/losses, 8-31
    SRLY rules, 8-31
    taxable income limitation, 8-31
  determining amount of gain/loss, 8-30
Consolidated net operating losses (NOLs), 8-20–8-28
  carrybacks/carryforwards, 8-21–8-24
    carryback to separate return year, 8-22–8-23
    carryforward to separate return year, 8-24
  Sec. 382 limitation, 8-26–8-28
Consolidated return year, definition of, 8-7 *fn*
Consolidated taxable income, 8-6–8-10
  affiliated group elections, 8-8–8-9
    accounting methods, 8-9
    tax years, 8-8–8-9
  calculation of, 8-6–8-7
  thirty-day rules, 8-7–8-8
Consolidated tax returns, 3-33–3-34, 8-1–8-41
  advantages of filing, 8-36
  affiliated groups
    definition of, 8-3–8-5
    tax liability, 8-22–8-34
  alternative minimum tax, 8-33–8-34
  capital gains/losses, 8-28–8-32
    Sec. 1231 gains/losses, 8-30
  charitable contributions deduction, 8-19–8-20
  disadvantages of filing, 8-36–8-37
  dividends, 8-16–8-19
    consolidated dividends-received deduction, 8-18–8-19

elimination procedure, 8-16–8-18
100% dividends-received deduction election, 8-37
election, 8-39
estimated tax payments, 8-37–8-38
filing for NOL or credit refund, 8-40–8-41
importance of consolidated return election, 8-2
intercompany transactions, 8-11–8-16
  deferred intercompany transactions, 8-11–8-15
  election not to defer gains/losses, 8-37
  other intercompany transactions, 8-16
liability for taxes due, 8-40
net operating losses (NOLs), 8-20–8-28
  carrybacks/carryforwards of, 8-21
  carryback to separate return year, 8-22–8-23
  carryforward to separate return year, 8-24
  current year NOLs, 8-20–8-21
  election to forego carryback, 8-41
  special loss limitations, 8-24–8-28
parent corporation as agent for affiliated groups, 8-39–8-40
rules, source of, 8-3
taxable income, 8-6–8-10
  affiliated group elections, 8-8–8-9
  income included in, 8-7–8-8
  termination of affiliated groups, 8-9–8-10
tax credits, 8-34–8-35
  foreign tax credit, 8-35
  general business credit, 8-34–8-35
Consolidations
  partnerships and, 10-28
  Type A reorganization, 7-14–7-21
    definition of, 7-14
    requirements for, 7-14–7-15
Constructive dividends, 4-12–4-14
  corporate payments for shareholder's benefit, 4-14
  corporate property
    bargain purchase of, 4-14
    shareholder use of, 4-14
  definition of, 4-12
  intentional avoidance of dividend treatment, 4-12
  loans to shareholders, 4-12–4-13
  shareholder property, excessive compensation paid for, 4-13
  shareholders-employees, excessive compensation to, 3-35, 4-13
  unintentional constructive dividends, 4-12
Continuity of business enterprise doctrine, 7-35–7-36
Continuity of interest doctrine
  reorganizations, 7-35
  Sec. 355 distributions, 4-40
Contribution deductions *See also* Charitable contribution deduction
Contribution of services
  corporate formation, 2-14–2-15
  partnerships, 9-12–9-14
    allocating the expense deduction, 9-13
    basis adjustments, 9-13–9-14
    consequences to partnership, 9-13–9-16

Contributions, *See also* Charitable contribution deduction
Controlled corporations, distribution of stock of
  requirements, 4-38–4-40
  types of distributions, 4-36–4-38
  tax consequences
    distributing corporation, 4-43–4-44
    shareholders and security holders, 4-40–4-43
Controlled foreign corporation (CFC), 15-25–15-34
  constructive distribution of income, 15-27–15-32
  definition of, 15-27
    attribution rules, 15-27
    U.S. shareholder defined, 15-27
  disposition of stock, 15-32–15-33
  investments in U.S. property, 15-31
  prior to Subpart F rules, 15-25–15-26
  Sec. 482 rules, 15-33–15-34
  Subpart F income, 15-26–15-32
    boycott-related income, 15-30–15-31
    bribes, kickbacks & other illegal payments, 15-31
    exclusions, 15-30
    foreign base company income, 15-28–15-31
      foreign base company oil-related income, 15-30
      foreign base company sales income, 15-29
      foreign base company services income, 15-29–15-30
      foreign base company shipping income, 15-30
      foreign personal holding income, 15-28–15-29
  types of distributions, 4-36–4-38
Controlled groups, 3-26–3-34
  avoiding controlled group status, 3-38
  brother-sister controlled groups, 3-28–3-30
  combined controlled groups, 3-30–3-31
  compared to affiliated groups, 8-4–8-5
    differences between definitions, 8-5
  consolidated tax returns, 3-32–3-34
    advantages of filing, 3-33–3-34
    disadvantages of filing, 3-32–3-34
    who can file, 3-32–3-33
  controlled group test, application of, 3-32
  definition of, 3-27
  parent-subsidiary controlled groups, 3-27–3-28
  special election, to allocate reduced tax rate benefits, 3-35–3-37
  special rules for, 3-26–3-27, 3-32, 8-5
Controlled subsidiary corporations
  liquidation of, 6-9–6-12
    basis of property received, 6-12
    cancellation of stock, 6-10–6-11
    exception to gain/loss recognition rules, 6-14–6-17
    insolvent subsidiary, 6-11
    minority shareholders receiving liquidating distributions, 6-11–6-12
    recognition of gain or loss, 6-11–6-12
    requirements, 6-10–6-11
    stock ownership, 6-10

subsidiary debt obligations, satisfaction of, 6-12
Control requirements
  acquisitive Type D reorganizations, 7-24–7-25
  Sec. 351(a), 2-13–2-17
    immediately after the exchange, 2-16–2-17
    transferors of both property and services, 2-14–2-15
    transfers to existing corporations, 2-15–2-16
  Sec. 355, 4-38
Corporate elections, 3-2–3-6, 11-11–11-12, 11-42
  accounting methods, 3-4–3-5, 11-11–11-12
    accrual method, 3-5
    cash method, 3-5
    hybrid method, 3-5
  tax year, selection of, 3-2–3-4, 11-12, 11-42
Corporate form
  disregard of, 2-9–2-10
Corporate nonliquidating distributions
  See Nonliquidating distributions
Corporate property
  bargain purchase of, 4-14
  shareholder use of, 4-14
Corporate requirements, S corporations, 11-4–11-5
Corporate stock, exchange of partnership interest for, 10-22
Corporate taxable income
  capital gains/losses, tax treatment, 3-9
  compared to individual taxable income and, 3-6–3-8
    deductions/losses, 3-6–3-8
    gross income, 3-6
  deductions, 3-10–3-22
    accrued compensation deductions, limitation on, 3-22
    charitable contributions, 3-12–3-15
    deduction calculations, sequencing of, 3-20–3-22
    dividends-received deduction, 3-15–3-19
    net operating losses (NOLs), 3-19–3-20
    organizational expenditures, 3-10–3-12
    start-up expenditures, 3-13
  sales/exchanges of property, 3-9–3-10
    net capital gain, 3-9
    net capital losses, 3-9
    tax benefit recapture rule, 3-9–3-10
Corporate taxation, 3-1–3-46
  compliance/procedural considerations, 3-38–3-46
  election, 11-43
  filing requirements, 3-38
  paying taxes, 3-38
  tax returns
    schedules, 3-39–3-42
    types of, 3-38–3-39
    when to file, 3-39
  controlled group rules, 3-26–3-34
  corporate elections, 3-2–3-5
  tax formula/tax rates, 3-5–3-8, 3-24–3-26

taxable income, computation of, 3-6–3-24
tax liability, computation of, 3-24–3-26
See also C corporations, personal service corporations, S corporations
Corporations
  accumulated earnings tax, 5-25–5-35
  as agent of shareholders, 2-10
  alternative minimum tax (AMT), 5-2–5-14
    computation of, 5-2–5-14
    minimum tax credit, 5-12
    tax credits and, 5-12–5-13
  capital contributions, 2-32–2-34
    by nonshareholders, 2-32–2-34
    by shareholders, 2-32
  charitable contributions, 3-12–3-15
  compared to partnerships, 2-8–2-9
  definition of, 2-8–2-10, 3-1
  disregard of corporate entity, 2-10
  dividends-received deduction, 3-15–3-19
  estimated taxes, 3-42–3-46
  extensions of due date, 16-15
  filing requirements, 3-38
  formation of, 2-1–2-40
    legal requirements, 2-10
    tax considerations, 2-10–2-12
  liquidating distributions, 6-1–6-32
  net operating losses, 3-19–3-22
  nonliquidating distributions, 4-1–4-49
  organization forms, 2-2–2-8
    C corporations, 2-5–2-7
    partnerships, 2-4–2-5
    S corporations, 2-7–2-8
    sole proprietorship, 2-2–2-3
  tax liability computations, 3-24–3-26
    accumulated earnings tax, 5-25–5-35
    alternative minimum tax, 5-2–5-14
    personal holding company (PHC) tax, 5-15–5-25
    regular tax, 3-24–3-26
    superfund environmental tax, 5-14
  tax payment requirements, 3-38
  tax return
    schedules, 3-39–3-42
    type of, 3-38–3-39
    when to file, 3-39
  tax year, selection of, 3-2–3-4
  transactions between shareholders and, 3-22–3-23
    different accounting methods used, 3-23
    gains on sale/exchange transactions, 3-22–3-23
    losses on sale/exchange transactions, 3-23
  See also C corporations; Acquisitions; Incorporation; Liquidating distributions; Nonliquidating distributions; S corporations
Correspondence audit, 16-7
Court system, overview of, 1-17–1-19
Creditable taxes, foreign tax credit, 15-4
Credits
  accumulated earnings credit, 5-33–5-34
  and alternative minimum tax, 5-12–5-14
  estates, 14-12
  fiduciary accounting, tax calculation formula, 14-12

Credits (*continued*)
  foreign death tax credit, estate tax, 13-30
  foreign tax credit, 15-4–15-8
  minimum tax credit, 5-12
  trusts, 14-12
  See also specific types of credits
Criminal fraud penalties, 16-27–16-28
  burden of proof, 16-27
  criminal fraud investigations, 16-27–16-28
  penalty provisions, 16-28
    Sec. 7201, 16-28
    Sec. 7203, 16-28
    Sec. 7206, 16-28
Crummey trust, 12-20
Cumulative Bulletin (C.B.), 1-13, 1-20, 1-27, 1-34
Current earnings and profits (E&P), 4-3–4-7
  adjustments to taxable income, 4-5–4-6
  compared to accumulated earnings and profits (E&P), 4-7–4-9
  computation of, 4-4
  income deferred to later period, 4-5
  income excluded from taxable income, 4-4–4-5
  nondeductible expenses/losses in computing taxable income, 4-6–4-7
  unallowable deductions from, 4-6
Curtesy rights, gross estate, 13-11

Daily compounding, of penalty interest, 16-17
Data bases, 1-39
Date-of-death valuation, 13-6–13-9
  annuities, 13-8–13-9
  interests in firms whose stock is not publicly traded, 13-8
  listed stocks, 13-7–13-8
  real estate, 13-8
  remainders, 13-8–13-9
  reversions, 13-8–13-9
  terms for years, 13-8–13-9
Death of partner, 10-19–10-22
  payments
    basis, 10-21–10-22
    goodwill, 10-19, 10-21
    partnership property, 10-19–10-21
    unrealized receivables, 10-19, 10-21
Death taxes, stock redemptions to pay for, 4-27–4-29, 13-34–13-35
Debt
  capital, 2-29–2-30
  issuance of debt, 2-30
  unsecured debt obligations, 2-35–2-37
  when indebtedness is satisfied, 2-30
  when interest is paid, 2-30
  worthlessness of, 2-34–2-35
  See also Equity capital
Debt-financed stock, corporations, dividends-received deduction, 3-19
Deductions
  alternative minimum tax, 5-3–5-7
  corporate taxable income
    accrued compensation deductions, limitation on, 3-22
    charitable contributions, 3-12–3-15
    dividends-received deduction, 3-15–3-19
    net operating losses (NOLs), 3-19–3-20
    organizational expenditures, 3-10–3-12
    sequencing of deduction calculations, 3-20–3-22
    start-up expenditures, 3-12
  current earnings and profits (E&P), 4-6
  estate tax, 13-4
    administration expenses, 13-21–13-22
    charitable contribution deduction, 13-23–13-24
    debts, 13-21–13-22
    funeral expenses, 13-21–13-22
    losses, 13-22–13-23
    marital deduction, 13-24–13-27
  foreign-earned income, housing cost deduction, 15-12–15-13
  foreign source income, allocable to, 15-7
  gift tax
    charitable contributions, 12-24–12-25
    marital deduction, 12-21–12-23
  See also Dividends-paid deduction; Dividends-received deduction
Deductions in respect of a decedent (DRD), 14-37
Deemed liquidation election, 6-4, 6-20–6-27
  allocation of basis, 6-22–6-25
    allocable basis, 6-22–6-24
    to individual assets, 6-24–6-25
  deemed purchase, basis of assets following, 6-22–6-25
  deemed sale, 6-22
  eligible stock acquisitions, 6-20–6-21
  grossed-up basis for stock, 6-23
  liabilities of target corporation, 6-24
  liquidation of target corporation, 6-26–6-27
  Sec. 338 election, 6-21–6-22, 6-31
  tax accounting elections for new corporation, 6-25–6-26
  valuation of stock, 6-22–6-24
  See also Liquidation
Deemed paid credit, calculation of, 15-23–15-24
Deferral privilege
  foreign corporations, 15-22
  income ineligible for deferral privilege, 15-27–15-31
Deferred intercompany transactions, 8-11–8-16
  basis and holding periods, 8-11–8-12
  deferred gain or loss, amount/character of, 8-11
  inventory adjustments, 8-15
  investment tax credit recapture, 8-12
  restored gain/loss, determination of, 8-12–8-15
  See also Intercompany transactions
Deficiency dividends, 5-23–5-24
De minimis rules, gift tax and, 12-31–12-32
Depletion
  tax preference, 5-4
Depreciation
  alternative minimum tax, 5-5–5-6
  corporate formation
    computation of, transferee corporation, 2-26–2-27
    recapture of, 2-25–2-26
  earnings and profits, 4-5–4-6
  fiduciary accounting, 14-7–14-8
  recapture of, reorganizations, 7-8–7-9
Device requirement, Sec. 355, 4-38
Dickman ruling, gift tax and, 12-30 *fn*
Direct foreign tax credit, 15-4
Disallowed losses, alternative minimum taxable income (AMTI), 5-7
Disclaimers
  estate tax and, 13-38–13-39
  qualified disclaimers, 12-11
Discriminant function (DIF) program, audits and, 16-6
Dissolution, compared to liquidation, 6-5
Distributable net income (DNI)
  computation of, 14-14–14-15
  definition of, 14-13–14-14
  significance of, 14-12–14-13
Distributing corporations
  distribution of stock of controlled subsidiary
    earnings and profits (E&P), effect on, 4-44
    recognition of gain or loss, 4-43–4-44
  nontaxable stock dividends, effect on, 4-15–4-16
  property distributions, consequences of, 4-10–4-11
    earnings and profits, effect on, 4-10–4-11
    recognition of gain or loss, 4-10
  stock redemptions
    recognition of gain or loss, 4-29
    earnings and profits, effect on, 4-29–4-30
    questions for, 4-18
Distribution deduction
  complex trusts/estates, 14-11
  determination of, 14-23–14-24
  estates, 14-10–14-11
  fiduciary accounting, calculation formula, 14-10–14-11
  trusts, 14-10–14-11
    complex trusts, 14-11
    simple trusts, 14-10–14-11
Distribution requirement, Sec. 355, 4-39
Distributions
  C corporations
    nonliquidating, 4-9–4-14
    definition of, 4-2
    timing, of 4-48–4-49
  stock dividends & stock rights, 4-14–4-17
  stock of controlled corporations, 4-36–4-44
  stock redemptions, 4-17–4-36
  partnerships, liquidating, special adjustments
    to transferree partners, 10-38–10-40
  partnerships, nonliquidating, special adjustments
    optional adjustments on, 10-35–10-38
    allocation of, 10-37–10-38
    amount of, 10-36–10-37
  S corporations, 11-27–11-32
    with accumulated earnings/profits, 11-29–11-32
    with no earnings/profits, 11-27–11-28
  tax-free reorganizations, 7-9–7-13

shareholders and security holders, 7-10–7-13
target corporations, 7-9
See also Dividends; Stock distributions
Dividends
as gross income, 4-2
capital gain dividends, 4-3
constructive dividends, 4-12–4-14
  corporate payments for shareholder's benefit, 4-14
  corporate property, 4-14
  definition of, 4-12
  intentional avoidance of dividend treatment, 4-12
  loans to shareholders, 4-12–4-13
  shareholder property, excessive compensation paid for, 4-13
  shareholders-employees, excessive compensation to, 4-13
  unintentional constructive dividends, 4-12
definition of, 4-2
distributing corporation, 4-10–4-11, 4-17
from foreign corporations, 3-18
nonliquidating distributions, 4-14–4-17
  effect on distributing corporation, 4-10–4-11, 4-17, 4-29–4-30, 4-43–4-44
  nontaxable stock dividends, 4-14–4-17
  stock of controlled subsidiary, 4-36–4-44
  stock redemptions, 4-17–4-36
  taxable stock dividends, 4-17
  taxable stock rights, 4-17
  tax-free stock dividends, 4-15–4-16
  tax-free stock rights, 4-16–4-17
personal holding company income (PHCI) and, 5-17
personal holding company tax (PHC)
  consent dividends, 5-21–5-23
  current year dividends, 5-21–5-22
  deficiency dividends, 5-22–5-24
  dividend carryovers, 5-23
  liquidating dividends, 5-22–5-23
  throwback dividends, 5-21–5-22
stock redemptions treated as, 4-17–4-36
See also Constructive dividends
Dividends-paid deduction, 5-32–5-33
accumulated earnings tax, 5-32–5-33
preferential dividends and, 5-22, 5-32
Dividends-received deduction
affiliated groups, 8-18–8-19
computed on consolidated basis, 8-18–8-19
corporations, 3-15–3-19
  affiliated group members, 3-18
  debt-financed stock, 3-19
  dividends from foreign corporations, 3-15, 15-25
  general rule for, 3-16
  limitation, 3-16
    exception to, 3-16–3-18
  stock held 45 days or less, 3-18
Divisive reorganizations, 7-7, 7-29–7-32
Type D reorganizations, 7-29–7-31
  asset transfer, 7-30
  business adjustments accomplished by, 7-30
  distribution of stock, 7-30–7-31
Type G reorganizations, 7-31–7-32

See also Acquisitive reorganizations; Reorganizations
Divorce
community property laws, 12-6
  innocent spouse provision, 16-33–16-35
property settlements, gift tax and, 12-10–12-11
Domestic corporations, definition of, 3-2
Domestic international sales corporations (DISCs), 15-21, 15-39–15-40, 15-48
filing requirements, 15-48
requirements, 15-39
taxable income, 15-39
taxation of distributions, 15-39–15-40
Domestic subsidiary corporations, 15-21
Donor-donee allocation of income
family partnerships, 9-38–9-39
requirements for, 9-38–9-39
Double taxation
C corporations, 2-6
estates, 14-36
fiduciary accounting and, 14-4–14-5
liquidating distributions, exemption from, 6-29–6-30
Dower rights, gross estate, 13-11
Due dates, 16-14–16-20
corporate tax returns, 3-39, 16-14
estate tax returns, 13-41, 14-46
extensions, 16-15
  corporations, 3-39, 11-42, 16-15
  estate tax return, 13-41
  fiduciaries, 14-46, 16-15
  gift tax returns, 12-34
  individuals, 16-15
fiduciary returns, 14-46, 16-15
gift tax returns, 12-34
interest on tax not timely paid, 16-16–16-17
  daily compounding, 16-17
  determination of rate, 16-16–16-17
  period for which interest is imposed, 16-17
for payment of tax, 16-15–16-16
partnerships, 9-41, 16-15
penalties, 16-17–16-20
  failure to file, 16-17–16-18
  failure to pay, 16-18–16-20
S corporations, 11-42–11-43

Earned income exclusion, *See also* foreign earned income exclusion
Earnings and profits (E&P), 4-2–4-9
accumulated earnings and profits, 4-3
current E&P, 4-3–4-7
current versus accumulated E&P, 4-7–4-9
distributing corporation, 4-44
stock redemptions, effect of, 4-29–4-30
Economic Recovery Tax Act (1981), gift tax and, 12-3
Educational organization, definition of, 12-9
"Effectively connected" test, 15-18–15-19
Election by Small Business Corporation to Tax Corporation Income Directly to Shareholders (Form 2553), 11-42
Employment-related expenses, foreign-earned income exclusion and, 15-13–15-14

Employment-related retirement benefits, gross estate, 13-16
Enforcement of tax law, Internal Revenue Service, role of, 16-2–16-3
Entity attribution, 4-21
Equity capital, 2-31–2-32
partnership interests, 9-3–9-4
stock
  multiple classes of, 2-31
  tax advantages of, 2-31, 2-33
  tax disadvantages of, 2-31, 2-33
  worthlessness of, 2-34–2-35
See also Debt capital
Estate Planning, 1-29
Estates, income taxation of
administration expenses deduction, 14-40, 14-45
beneficiary, tax treatment of, 14-24–14-28
capital losses, 14-28
credits, 14-12
distributable net income (DNI), 14-23–14-24, 14-26
  computation of, 14-23–14-24
  definition of, 14-13–14-14
  significance of, 14-21
distribution deduction, 14-23–14-24
documents to be furnished to IRS, 14-46–14-47
due date, 14-46
estimated taxes, 4-46
expense deductions, 14-9–14-10, 14-22–14-23
filing requirements, 14-45–14-46
gross income, 14-9, 14-22–14-23
inception of, 14-3
income in respect of a decedent (IRD), 14-35–14-38
  common examples, 14-35–14-36
  deductions in respect of a decedent, 14-37
  definition of, 14-35–14-36
  double taxation, 14-36
  no step-up in basis, 14-37–14-38
  Sec. 691(c) deduction, 14-36–14-37
  significance of, 14-36–14-38
net operating losses, 14-28
personal exemption, 14-11–14-12, 14-23
tax liability, 14-8–14-12
timing of distributions, 14-43–14-44
year-end, choice of, 14-44–14-45
See also Trusts
Estate tax, 13-1–13-42
administrative expenses, where to deduct, 13-40
alternate valuation date, 13-9–13-10
  election of, 13-41
annuities and, 13-15–13-16
calculation formula, 13-2–13-6
  adjusted taxable gifts, 13-4–13-5
  deductions, 13-4
  gross estate, 13-2–13-4
comprehensive illustration, 13-30–13-33
deductions, 13-21–13-27
  administration expenses, 13-21–13-22
  charitable contribution deduction, 13-23–13-24
  debts, 13-21–13-22
  funeral expenses, 13-21–13-22

K-8 • *Subject Index*

Estate Tax (*continued*)
  losses, 13-22–13-23
    marital deduction, 13-24–13-27
  deferral of tax payments, 13-33–13-34
    interests in closely held businesses and, 13-33–13-34, 13-39–13-40
    reasonable cause, 13-33
    remainder interests, 13-33
    reversionary interests, 13-33
  disclaimers, 13-38–13-39
  documents to be included with return, 13-41–13-42
  due date, 13-41
  exemption equivalent, 13-37
  filing requirements, 13-40
  flower bonds, 13-40
  generation-skipping transfer tax (GSTT), 13-35–13-36
  inter vivos gifts, 13-37
  life insurance, 13-19–13-20, 13-39
  liquidity, 13-33–13-35
  post-1976 gift taxes, reduction for, 13-5–13-6
  prepayments, gifts tax and, 12-33–12-34
  qualifying for installment payments, 13-39
  special use valuation, of farm realty, 13-35
  stock redemptions, to pay death taxes, 13-34–13-35
  tax base, tentative tax on, 13-5
  tax liability
    computation of, 13-27–13-30
    credit for pre-1977 gift taxes, 13-29
    credit for tax on prior transfers, 13-29–13-30
    foreign death tax credit, 13-30
    state death tax credit, 13-28–13-29
    taxable estate and tax base, 13-27
    tentative tax and reduction for post-1976 gift tax, 13-27–13-28
    unified credit, 13-28
  unified credit, 13-6
  valuation, need for documentation, 13-41
  See also Gross estate
Estate Tax Return (Form 706), 13-41–13-42
Estate tax returns, substantial omissions, 16-30–16-31
Estimated taxes
  affiliated groups, 8-37–8-38
    consolidated or separate basis, 8-38
    short-period return, 8-38
    underpayment rules, 8-38
  C corporations, 3-42–3-56
    annualized income exception, 3-45
    paying remaining tax liability, 3-46
    payment rules/dates, 3-43–3-44
    penalty provisions, exceptions to, 3-44–3-45
    seasonal income exception, 3-45–3-46
    underpayment penalties, 3-44–3-45
  estates, 14-46
  individuals, 16-20–16-23
    exceptions to, 16-22–16-23
    underpayment penalties, 16-21–16-21
    withholding and, 16-21
    payment requirements, 16-20–16-21
  partnerships, 9-42
  S corporations, 11-40–11-41
  trusts, 14-46

Excess loss account, 8-10
Excess net passive income tax, as special S corporation tax, 11-15
Exclusions
  foreign-earned income, 15-8–15-14
    amount of, 15-11–15-12
    election not to use, 15-44–15-45
    housing cost exclusion/deduction, 15-12–15-13
    reporting of, 15-47
  gift tax, 12-18–12-20
    amount of, 12-18–12-19
    Crummey trust, 12-19–12-20
    definition of, 12-18
    present interest requirement, 12-19–12-20
    trust for minors, 12-20
  See also Annual exclusion
Exemption equivalent, 12-7
  estate tax and, 13-37
Expenses
  estates, 14-9–14-10
    fiduciary accounting, calculation formula, 14-9–14-10
  trusts, 14-9–14-10
  See also Deductions
Extensions
  of due date, 16-15
    C corporations, 3-39, 11-42, 16-15
    estate tax return, 13-41
    fiduciaries, 14-46, 16-15
    gift tax return, 12-34
    individuals, 16-15
    partnerships, 9-41, 16-15
  See also Due date

Failure-to-file penalty, 16-17–16-18
Failure-to-pay penalty, 16-18–16-20
Fair market value (FMV)
  definition of, 13-7
  property distributions and, 14-44
Family attribution, 4-20–4-21
  complete termination of interest and, 4-44–4-45
Family partnerships, 9-37–9-39
  capital ownership, 9-37–9-38
    donor retained control, 9-38
    minor donees, 9-38
  donor-donee allocation of income, 9-38–9-39
  requirements for, 9-38–9-39
  See also Partnerships
Family S corporations, 11-20–11-21
  See also S corporations
Farm realty, special use valuation of, 13-35
Federal Court System, 1-17–1-26
  Appeals court procedures, 1-23–1-24
  District court procedures, 1-23–1-24
  Overview of court system, 1-17–1-18
  Precedential value of various decisions, 1-24–1-26
  Supreme Court, appeals to, 1-24
  Tax Court procedures, 1-19–1-22
    IRS acquiescence policy, 1-20
    Small cases procedures, 1-20
Federal estate tx, *See also* estate tax
Federal gift tax, *See also* gift tax
Federal income tax, *See also* tax law
Federal Income Taxation of Estates and Beneficiaries (Ferguson et al.), 14-12 fn

Federal Reporter, Second Series, 1-23
Federal Supplement (F. Supp.), 1-22
Federal Taxation: Research, Planning, and Procedures (Norwood), 16-10 fn
Federal Taxation of Income, Estates, and Gifts (Bittker), 16-24 fn, 16-26 fn
Federal Taxes 2d (Prentice Hall tax service), 1-29–1-30
  organization of, 1-30
  updating of, 1-30
Fiduciaries, 14-1–14-47
Fiduciary accounting, 14-1–14-12
  calculation formula, 14-8–14-12
    credits, 14-12
    distribution deduction, 14-10–14-11
    expense deductions, 14-9–14-10
    gross income, 14-9
    personal exemption, 14-11–14-12
  principles of, 14-5–14-8
    depreciation, 14-7–14-8
    expenditures, 14-7
    income and principal, identification of, 14-5–14-6
    income receipts, 14-6–14-7
    principal receipts, 14-7
    state law, effects of, 14-6
    terms of trust instrument, effects of, 14-6
    Uniform Act, 14-6–14-7
  See also Accounting
Fiduciary taxation, 14-1–14-47
  basic principles of, 14-4–14-5
    conduit approach, 14-5
    no double taxation, 14-4–14-5
    similarity to rules for individuals, 14-5
    trusts/estates as separate taxpayers, 14-4
Field audit, 16-7
Filing requirements
  accumulated earnings tax, 5-40
  affiliated groups, 8-2
  aliens, 15-47–15-48
  corporations, 3-48
  domestic international sales corporations (DISCs), 15-47
  estates
    estate tax returns, 13-41–13-42
    income tax returns, 14-45–14-46
  foreign corporations, 15-47–15-48
  foreign sales corporations (FSCs), 15-48
  gift tax returns, 12-34–12-35
  personal holding company (PHC) tax, 5-39–5-40
  S corporations, 11-42–11-43
  trusts, 14-45–14-46
Final regulations, 1-15
Finance Committee, U.S. Senate, tax law and, 1-13
Fiscal year
  C corporation, 3-2–3-4
    personal service corporations (PSCs), 3-3–3-4
  estates, 14-44–14-45
  partnerships, 9-15, 9-17–9-19, 9-41–9-42
  S corporations, 11-11–11-12, 11-42
  trusts, 14-44–14-45
Flower bonds, estate tax and, 13-40
Foreign base company
  foreign personal holding company income, 15-31
  oil-related income, 15-30

sales income, 15-29
services income, 15-29–15-30
shipping income, 15-30
Foreign branches, 15-21
  definition of, 15-21
Foreign corporations
  alternative minimum tax, 15-24–15-25
  branch profits tax, 15-25
  controlled foreign corporation, 15-26–15-34
  filing requirements, 15-47–15-48
  regular tax, 15-24–15-25
  special foreign corporation forms, 15-34
  U.S. activities, taxation of, 15-24–15-25
Foreign death tax credit, estate tax, 13-30
Foreign-earned income exclusion
  bona fide resident test, 15-9–15-10
  disallowance of deductions/credits, 15-13–15-14
    employment-related expenses, 15-13–15-14
    foreign income taxes, 15-14
  earned income definition, 15-9–15-10
  election not to use, 15-44–15-45
  exclusion, 15-8–15-14
    basic exclusion, 15-11–15-12
    housing cost exclusion/deduction, 15-12–15-13
  physical presence test, 15-10
  reporting of exclusion, 15-47
  U.S. citizens/resident aliens employed abroad, 15-9
Foreign personal holding company (FPHC), 15-34
Foreign personal holding company income (FPHCI), 15-28–15-34
Foreign-related transactions
  special treatment of income, 15-3–15-4
  U.S. taxation of, 15-1–15-48
    jurisdiction to tax, 15-2–15-4
    of nonresident aliens, 15-15–15-20
    of U.S. citizens/resident aliens, 15-4–15-15
    of U.S. persons doing business abroad, 15-20–15-42
Foreign risks, insurance of, 15-27–15-28
Foreign sales corporations (FSCs), 15-21, 15-34–15-39
  administrative transfer pricing rules, use of, 15-37–15-38
  advantages of, 15-35
  determination of foreign trade income, 15-36–15-37
  exemption of FSC dividends from taxation, 15-38–15-39
  filing requirements, 15-47
  foreign tax credit, 15-36
  investment income, taxation of, 15-36
  requirements, 15-35
  taxation of activities, 15-35–15-36
  transfer pricing rules, 15-37–15-39
    administrative transfer pricing rules, 15-37–15-38
    arm's-length transfer pricing rules, 15-38
Foreign tax credit
  affiliated groups, 8-35
  alternative minimum tax (AMT), 5-13–5-14
  creditable taxes, 15-4
  definition of, 15-4

earned income exclusion, loss of credit, 15-14
eligibility for, 15-4
foreign corporations, 15-22–15-24
  deemed paid credit calculation, 15-23–15-24
  translating dividend/foreign taxes into U.S. dollars, 15-24
limitation, 15-5–15-8
  carrybacks/carryovers, 15-7
  determining income amount, 15-6–15-7
  formula for, 15-41
  general limitation calculation, 15-5–15-6
reporting of, 15-46–15-47
special limitations, 15-7–15-8
translation of payments, 15-4–15-5
Foreign taxes
  deduction versus credit for, 15-42
  election to accrue, 15-42–15-44
  special election for cash basis taxpayers, 15-42–15-44
  translation into U.S. dollars, 15-24
Foreign trade income, foreign sales corporations (FSCs), determination of, 15-35–15-36
Foreign trading gross receipts, 15-36–15-37
Form 706, 13-40–13-41
Form 709, 12-34
Form 709A, 12-34–12-35
Form 712, 13-41
Form 851, 8-39
Form 966, 6-30
Form 1040, Schedule E, 11-43
Form 1040–NR, 15-47
Form 1041, 14-45–14-46
Form 1041–ES, 14-46
Form 1065, 9-41–9-40
Form 1065, Schedule K-1, 9-41
Form 1099–DIV, 6-30–6-31
Form 1120, 3-38–3-42, 8-39
Form 1120–IC–DISC, 15-48
Form 1120–A, 3-38–3-40
Form 1120–F, 15-48
Form 1120–FSC, 15-48
Form 1120, Schedule PH, 5-39
Form 1120S, 11-42–11-43
Form 1120S, Schedule K-1, 11-43
Form 2555, 15-47
Form 2688, 16-15
Form 2758, 14-46
Form 4626, 5-38–5-39
Form 4868, 16-15
Form 7004, 3-39, 8-39, 11-42, 16-15
Form 8023, 6-31
Form 8716, 9-41–9-42
Form 8752, 9-42
Form 8820, 7-45
Forum shopping, precedential value of decisions and, 1-26
Fraud
  when fraud is proven, 16-31–16-32
  criminal provision, 16-32
  deficiency and civil fraud penalty, 16-31–16-32
  See also Civil fraud penalty
Fringe benefits
  C corporations, 2-6
  S corporations, treatment of, 11-34–11-35
  tax planning device, 3-35

Funeral expenses, as estate tax deduction, 13-21–13-22
Future interest, definition of, 12-19

General Agreement on Tariffs and Trade (GATT), 15-34
General business credit
  affiliated groups, 8-34–8-35
  alternative minimum tax (AMT), 5-13
General Explanation of the Economic Recovery Tax Act of 1981 (U.S. Congress), 12-10 *fn*
General partner, definition of, 9-3
General partnerships
  partner's share of liabilities and, 9-27–9-29
  rights/restrictions of, 9-3
  See also Partnerships
General power of appointment, 12-17
  estate tax and, 13-17–13-18
  gift tax consequences, 12-17
  gross estate, 13-17–13-18
General Utilities doctrine, 11-16 *fn*, 11-16
Generation-skipping transfer tax (GSTT), 13-35–13-36
Gift tax, 12-1–12-37
  below market loans, 12-30–12-32
  calculation formula, 12-4–12-8
    deductions, 12-6
    determination of gifts, 12-5
    exclusions, 12-6
    gift-splitting election, 12-6
  comprehensive illustration, 12-27–12-28
  cumulative nature of, 12-6–12-7
  deductions, 12-20–12-25
    charitable contribution deduction, 12-20, 12-24–12-25
    marital deduction, 12-20–12-23
  definition of, 12-2
  determination of value, 12-35–12-36
  due date, 12-34
  exclusions, 12-17–12-20
    amount of, 12-17–12-18
    present interest requirement, 12-19–12-20
  filing requirements, 12-34
  gift-splitting election, 12-6, 12-25–12-26, 12-35
  inter vivos gifts, 12-32–12-33
  liability computations, 12-26–12-8
    previous taxable gifts, effect of, 12-26–12-27
    unified credit, 12-27
  lifetime giving plan, basis considerations, 12-28–12-30
  negative aspects of gifts, 12-33–12-34
  revocable trusts, 12-12
  retained powers, 12-12–12-13
  short-form gift tax return, 12-35
  statute of limitations, 12-36–12-37
  statutory exemptions from, 12-9–12-11
    medical expenses payments, 12-9–12-10
    property settlements from divorce, 12-10–12-11
    qualified disclaimers, 12-11
    transfers to political organizations, 12-10
    tuition payments, 12-9–12-10
  tax liability, 12-35
  transfer consequences, 12-15–12-18

Gift tax (*continued*)
  general power of appointment, exercise of, 12-17
  joint bank accounts, 12-15–12-16
  joint tenancies, 12-16
  life insurance policies, 12-16–12-17
  net gifts, 12-17–12-18
  transfers subject to, 12-8–12-18
    cessation of donor's dominion/control, 12-11–12-13
    inadequate consideration, 12-8–12-9
  transfer taxes
    concept of, 12-2–12-3
    history/purpose of, 12-2–12-3
  unified credit, 12-4, 12-7–12-8
  unified transfer tax system, 12-3–12-4
    death tax base, impact of taxable gifts on, 12-4
    unified rate schedule, 12-3–12-4
  valuation of gifts, 12-13–12-15
    general rules, 12-13
    life estates/remainder interests, 12-13–12-14
    special valuation rules - estate freezes, 12-15
  See also Exclusions; Grantor trusts; Revocable trusts; Transfer taxes; Trusts
Gift tax returns, substantial omissions, 16-30–16-31
"Good faith" belief requirement, certified public accountants (CPAs), 16-37–16-38
Goodwill payments, at death/retirement of partner, 10-19–10-20
Grantors, 14-2
Grantor trusts
  provisions, 14-38–14-42
    administrative powers, retention of, 14-41
    Clifford trusts, 14-39–14-40
    economic benefits, retention of, 14-41–14-42
    effect of, 14-38–14-39
    post-1986 reversionary interest trusts, 14-40–14-41
    purpose, 14-38–14-39
    revocable trusts, 14-39
Grey areas, tax research, 1-4
Grossed-up basis for stock, deemed liquidation election and, 6-23
Gross estate
  calculation formula for estate tax, 13-2–13-6
  compared to probate estate, 13-10
  estate tax calculation, 13-2–13-6
  inclusions, 13-10–13-21
    annuities, 13-15–13-16
    consideration offset, 13-19–13-20
    curtesy rights, 13-11
    dower rights, 13-11
    employment-related retirement benefits, 13-16
    general powers of appointment, 13-17–13-18
    jointly owned property, 13-16–13-17
    life insurance, 13-18–13-19
    property in which dedecent has interest, 13-10–13-11

recipient spouse's interest in QTIP trust, 13-20–13-21
transferor provisions, 13-11–13-15
valuation, 13-6–13-10
  alternate valuation date, 13-9–13-10
  date-of-death valuation, 13-6–13-9
Gross income
  estates, 14-9
  fiduciary accounting, calculation formula, 14-9
  substantial omission of, 16-30–16-31
  trusts, 14-9
Guaranteed payments
  partnerships, 9-35–9-37
    determination of, 9-36
    guaranteed minimum, 9-36
    tax impact of, 9-36–9-37

Hedge agreements, 4-46–4-47
Hobby loss rules, S corporation shareholders, 11-23
Holding period
  for acquired properties, 7-10
  for corporate formations, 2-20–2-21
  deferred intercompany transactions, 8-11–8-12
  partnership interest, 9-9
  property contributions, partnerships, 9-11
Housing cost exclusion/deduction, foreign-earned income, 15-12–15-13
100% dividends-received deduction election, 8-37
Hybrid method of accounting,

Illegal payments, as foreign base company income, 15-31
Inadequate consideration
  gift tax and, 12-8–12-9
    bargain sales, 12-9
    transfers in normal course of business, 12-9
Includible corporation
  affiliated groups, 8-4
  controlled gruop, definition of, 3-32 *fn*
Includible gain, Sec. 644 tax, trusts, 14-34–14-35
Inclusions
  gross estate, 13-10–13-21
    annuities, 13-15–13-16
    comparison with probate estate, 13-10
    consideration offset, 13-19–13-20
    curtesy rights, 13-11
    dower rights, 13-11
    employee-related benefits, 13-16
    general powers of appointment, 13-17–13-18
    jointly owned property, 13-16–13-17
    life insurance, 13-18–13-19
    property in which decedent had interest, 13-10–13-11
    recipient spouse's interest in QTIP trust, 13-20–13-21
    transferor provisions, 13-11–13-15
Income allocations
  S corporation, 11-18–11-20
  partnerships, 9-38–9-39
Income beneficiary, *See* Beneficiary
Income in respect of a decedent (IRD), 14-35–14-38

common examples, 14-35–14-36
deductions in respect of a decedent, 14-37
definition of, 14-35–14-36
double taxation, 14-36
no step-up in basis, 14-37–14-38
Sec. 691(c) deduction, 14-36–14-37
significance of, 14-36–14-38
Income splitting
  corporations and, 3-26–3-27
  lifetime gifts and, 12-32–12-33
Income tax returns, substantial omissions, 16-30–16-31
Incorporation
  deferring gain/loss upon, 2-12–2-28
    control requirement, 2-13–2-17
    property requirement, 2-13
    stock requirement, 2-17
  exchange of partnership interest, 10-22–10-23
  requirements for, 2-10
Individual taxable income
  compared to corporate taxable income, 3-6–3-8
  deductions/losses, 3-6–3-8
  gross income, 3-6
Information releases, tax law, 1-28
Innocent spouse provision, 16-33–16-35
  community property laws, effect of, 16-35
  no basis in fact or law, 16-34–16-35
  relief from tax liability, conditions to be met for, 16-34
  test for substantial understatement of tax, 16-34
Insolvent subsidiary, liquidation of, 6-11
Installment obligations, shareholder, liquidating distributions, 6-12
Installment payments, qualifying an estate for, 13-39–13-40
Insurance
  estate tax consequences, 13-18–13-19, 13-39
  gift tax consequences, 12-16–12-17
Intercompany transactions, 8-11–8-16
  deferred intercompany transactions, 8-11–8-15
    amount/character of deferred gain/loss, 8-11
    basis and holding period, 8-11–8-12
    inventory adjustments, 8-15
    investment tax credit recapture, 8-12
    restored gain/loss, determination of, 8-12–8-15
  other intercompany transactions, 8-16
Interest
  complete termination of, 4-23–4-24, 4-44–4-45
  continuity of interest doctrine
    reorganizations, 7-35
    Sec. 355, 4-40
  debt capital, 2-29–2-30
  on late payment of tax, 16-16–16-20
    determination of rate, 16-16–16-17
    period for which interest is imposed, 16-17
  on personal holding company (PHC) tax, 5-40
  qualified terminable interest property (QTIP), 13-20–13-21

split-interest transfers, 12-24–12-25
   charitable contribution deductions and, 12-24–12-25
   definition of, 12-24
   estate tax and, 13-23–13-24
   example of, 12-24
   gift tax and, 12-23–12-24
   See also Partnership interest
Interest income, personal holding company income (PHCI) and, 4-17–4-18
Internal Revenue Bulletin (I.R.B.), 1-20
Internal Revenue Code, 1-12–1-14
   divisions of, 1-14
   history of, 1-13–1-14
   organizational scheme, 1-14
   tax law and, 1-13–1-14
Internal Revenue Service
   audits
      field office procedure, 16-8
      office audit procedure, 16-8
      selecting returns for, 16-5–16-7
   Discrimination Function (DIF) system, 16-5
   organization of, 16-3role of, 16-2–16-3
      enforcement/collection, 16-2–16-3
      interpretation of statute, 16-3
   Taxpayer Compliance Measurement Program (TCMP), 16-6
Interpretations, tax law, 1-12, 16-3
Interpretative regulations, 1-15–1-16
Inter vivos gifts, 12-32–12-33
   annual exclusion, use of, 12-32
   estate tax and, 13-37
   gift in contemplation of donee-spouse's death, 12-33
   gift tax amount, removal from transfer tax base, 12-32
   income splitting, 12-32–12-33
   income tax savings, charitable gifts, 12-33
   lessening state transfer tax costs, 12-33
   post-gift appreciation, removal from tax base, 12-32
Inter vivos trusts, 14-2
Inventory
   donation of, 3-13–3-14
   partnerships, basis, 9-10
   substantially appreciated inventory, 10-7–10-18
Inventory adjustments, deferred intercompany transactions, 8-15
Investment income
   foreign sales corporations (FSCs), 15-36
   nonresident aliens, 15-16–15-17
Investment interest limitation rules, S corporation shareholders, 11-23
Investment tax credit (ITC) recapture, 2-26
   deferred intercompany transactions, 8-12
IRS Letter Rulings (CCH), 1-27
IRS Service Centers, location of, 16-3 *fn*

Joint bank accounts, gift tax consequences, 12-15–12-16
Jointly owned property
   estate tax and, 13-16–13-17
      ownership involving only spouses, 13-17
      ownership involving persons other than spouses, 13-16–13-17
   gross estate, 13-16–13-17

Joint returns
   tax liability, 16-33–16-35
      innocent spouse provision, 16-33–16-35
      validity of, 16-33
Joint tenancies, transfers of, gift tax consequences, 12-16
Joint tenancy with right of survivorship, definition of, 13-16 *fn*
Journal of Corporate Taxation, The, 1-29
Journal of Partnership Taxation, The, 1-29
Journal of Real Estate Taxation, The, 1-29
Journal of Taxation, The, 1-29
Judicial decisions
   importance of facts, 1-5–1-12
   tax law, 1-17–1-26
      Circuit Court of Appeals, 1-23–1-24
      court system, overview of, 1-17–1-19
      precedential value of decisions, 1-24–1-26
      Supreme Court, 1-24
      U.S. Claims Court, 1-22–1-23
      U.S. district courts, 1-22
      U.S. Tax Court, 1-19–1-22
Judicial doctrines
   reorganizations, 7-34–7-37
      business purpose requirement, 7-36
      continuity of business enterprise, 7-35–7-36
      continuity of proprietary interest, 7-35
      step transaction doctrine, 7-37
Judicial interpretations, tax law, 1-12, 1-17–1-26
   citations, 1-21–1-26
      primary cite, 1-22
      secondary cite, 1-22
      unreported decisions, 1-22
   Federal court system, 1-17–1-20
   precedential value, 1-24–1-26

Kickbacks, as foreign base company income, 15-31

Late payment of tax
   interest on, 16-16–16-17
      determination of rate, 16-16–16-17
      period for which interest is imposed, 16-17
   See also Penalties
Law of Federal Income Taxation (Callaghan & Co.), 1-31–1-32
Lawful resident test, 15-16
Legal data bases, 1-39
Legislative process, steps in, 1-12–1-13
Legislative reenactment doctrine, 1-16
Legislative regulations, 1-15–1-16
Letter rulings
   requests for, 16-12–16-14
   tax law, 1-27
LEXIS data base, 1-39
Life insurance
   estate tax and, 13-18–13-19, 13-39
   incidents of ownership in policies, 13-18–13-19
   transfer of policies, gift tax consequences, 12-16–12-17
Lifetime giving plan
   basis considerations, 12-28–12-30
      property received at death, 12-30
      property received by gift, 12-29–12-30

Limitations
   accrued compensation deductions, 3-22
   acquisitions, tax attributes, 7-38–7-41
   at-risk loss limitations, partnerships, 9-31–9-32
   dividends-received deduction, exception to, 3-16–3-18
   foreign tax credit, 15-4–15-8
      carrybacks/carryovers, 15-7
      determining income amount, 15-6–15-7
      general limitation calculation, 15-5–15-6
   investment interest limitation rules, 11-21
   partnerships
      partner loss limitation, 9-30–9-34
      passive activity limitation rules, 9-33–9-34
   S corporations
      shareholder loss limitations, 11-21–11-23
   Sec. 382 loss limitation, 7-38–7-41, 8-24–8-28
   statute of, 16-28–16-33
Limited partner, definition of, 9-3–9-4
Limited partnerships
   exchange of interest, 10-22
   partner's share of liabilities and, 9-27–9-29
   rights/restrictions of, 9-3–9-4
   as tax shelter, 10-40–10-41
   See also Partnerships
Liquidating corporations
   distributions to related persons, 6-15
   effects of liquidating on, 6-13–6-19
   general liquidation expenses, 6-17–6-18
   liabilities assumed or acquired by shareholders, 6-13–6-14
   net operating losses (NOLs), treatment of, 6-18
   property distribution in redemption of stock, recognition of gain/loss, 6-13–6-17
   property distribution in retirement of debt, recognition of gain/loss, 6-17
   sales with tax-avoidance purpose, 6-15–6-17
   subsidiary corporation, 6-14–6-15
   tax attribute carryovers, 6-18–6-19
Liquidating distributions, corporations, 6-1–6-32
   compared to dissolution, 6-5
   complete liquidation, definition of, 6-5
   compliance/procedural considerations, 6-30–6-32
      general liquidation procedures, 6-30–6-31
      Sec. 332 liquidations, 6-31
      Sec. 338 deemed liquidations, 6-31
   controlled subsidiary corporations, 6-9–6-12
      basis of property received, 6-12
      cancellation of stock, 6-10–6-11
      debt obligations, satisfaction of, 6-12
      insolvent subsidiary, 6-11
      minority shareholders receiving liquidating distributions 6-11–6-12
      recognition of gain or loss, 6-11–6-12

K-12 • Subject Index

Liquidating distributions, corporations (*continued*)
  requirements, 6-10–6-11
  stock ownership, 6-10
  deemed liquidation election, 6-20–6-27
  effects of, 6-3–6-19
    on corporation, 6-4, 6-13–6-19
    on shareholders, 6-3, 6-5–6-12
    expenses of, 6-17–6-18
  installment obligations received by shareholders, 6-12
  liquidating dividends
    accumulated earnings tax, 5-23
    personal holding company (PHC) tax and, 5-38
  plan of liquidation, 6-31–6-32
  tax attributes of liquidating corporation, 6-4
  tax consequences, to the corporation, 6-3–6-4
    expenses of liquidation, 6-17–6-18
    net operating losses, 6-19
    recognition of gain or loss on retirement of debt, 6-17
    recognition of gain or loss on retirement of stock, 6-13–6-17
    exceptions, 6-14–6-17
    tax attributes, 6-19–16-20
  tax consequences, to the shareholder
    accounting method, effect of, 6-6
    basis of property received, 6-7
    open versus closed transactions, 6-8–6-9
    partially liquidating distributions, 6-6–6-7
    recognized gain/loss
      amount of, 6-6
      character of, 6-7
    stock acquisition, 6-6
    subsequent assessments against shareholders, 6-7–6-8
  tax-planning considerations, 6-28–6-30
    avoiding Sec. 332 nonrecognition rules, 6-30
    double tax exemption, 6-29–6-30
    recognition of ordinary losses when liquidation occurs, 6-28–6-29
    timing the liquidation transaction, 6-28
  See also Deemed liquidation election
Liquidating distributions, partnerships, 10-11–10-16
  basis in assets received, 10-12–10-14
  effects on partnership, 10-15–10-16
  gain/loss recognition by partner, 10-11–10-12
  Sec. 751 effects, 10-14–10-15
  as tax-planning consideration, 10-42–10-43
  termination of partnership interest and, 10-26–10-27
Liquidation-reincorporation transactions, 7-25 *fn*
Listed stocks, date-of-death valuation, 13-7–13-8
Litigation
  audits, 16-11–16-12
    appeal of lower court's decision, 16-11–16-12
    district court, 16-11

    Tax Court, 16-11
    U.S. Claims Court, 16-11
Loans to shareholders, as disguised dividends, 5-42
Loss corporation, 7-38
Losses
  C corporations
    affiliated groups, 8-20–8-28
    nonaffiliated, 3-19–3-24
    Sec. 382 limitation, 7-38–7-42
  estates, 14-19
  partnerships, 9-30–9-34
    at-risk loss limitations, 9-31–9-32
    at-risk rules and current distributions, 9-32–9-33
    passive activity limitations, 9-33–9-34
  S corporations, 11-21–11-24
    allocation of loss, 11-21
    at risk loss limitation, 11-23–11-24
    hobby loss rules, 11-23–11-24
    investment interest expense limitation, 11-23–11-24
    passive activity limitations, 11-23–11-24
    post-termination loss carryovers, 11-23–11-24
    shareholder loss limitations, 11-21–11-23
  trusts, 14-19
Marital deduction
  estate tax, 13-24–13-27
    passing requirement, 13-25
    property in gross estate, 13-24–13-25
    QTIP transfers, 13-26–13-27
    size of deduction, 13-37–13-38
    terminable interest rule, 13-25–13-26
    tests for, 13-24
  gift tax, 12-20–12-23
    amount of, 12-21
    nondeductible terminable interests, 12-21–12-22
    QTIP provisions, 12-22–12-23
Medical expenses, gift tax and, 12-9–12-10
Medical care, definition of, 12-9
Memorandum decisions, U.S. Tax Court, 1-19
Mergers
  partnerships and, 10-28
  Type A reorganizations, 7-14–7-21
    requirements for, 7-14–7-15
    reverse triangular mergers, 7-21
    tax consequences, 7-19
    triangular mergers, 7-19–7-21
Mertens, *See Law of Federal Income Taxation* (Callaghan & Co.)
Minimum tax credit, alternative minimum tax (AMT), 5-12
Minority shareholders, liquidating distributions and, 6-12
Minors, present interest, special rule for trusts, 12-19–12-20
Modified Accelerated Cost Recovery System
  alternative minimum tax, 5-5, 5-8–5-9
  corporate formations, 2-25–2-26
  earnings and profits, 4-5–4-6

Negligence penalty, 16-23–16-24
Net accounting income, definition of, 14-6

Net capital losses
  complex trusts/estates, 14-28–14-29
  C corporation, 3-9
  simple trusts, 14-19–14-20
Net gifts, 12-17–12-18
  gift tax consequences, 12-17–12-18
Net operating losses (NOLs)
  affiliated groups, 8-20–8-29
    carrybacks/carryforwards, 8-21–8-24
    carryback to separate return year, 8-22–8-23
    carryforward to separate return year, 8-24
    current year NOLs, 8-20–8-21
    Sec. 382 limitation, 8-26–8-28
  alternative minimum tax, 5-7
  C corporations, 3-19–3-20
  complex trusts/estates, effect of, 14-19
  consolidated tax returns, 8-20–8-28
  earnings and profits, 4-6
  liquidating corporation, treatment of, 6-18
  simple trusts, 14-19
Net Sec. 1231 gain/loss, 8-30 *fn*
New loss corporation, 7-39
"New" Sec. 1374 tax, *See* Built-in gains tax
90-day letter, 16-10–16-11
"No basis in fact or law", innocent spouse relief and, 16-34–16-35
Nonabusive tax shelters, definition of, 10-40
Nonbusiness bad debts, advances to corporation, 2-35–2-37
Nondeductible terminable interests
  estate tax, 13-25–13-26
  gift tax, 12-21–12-22
Nonliquidating distributions
  active conduct of trade or business, definition of, 4-45–4-46
  complete termination of interest, 4-23–4-24, 4-44–4-45, 4-49
  constructive dividends, 4-12–4-14
  controlled corporations, stock of, 4-36–4-44
    tax consequences
      distributing corporation, 4-43–4-44
      shareholders and security holders, 4-40–4-43
  not essentially equivalent to a dividend, 4-24–4-25
  partnerships, 10-2–10-6
    basis effects of distributions, 10-4–10-5
    character of distributed property, 10-6
    holding period, 10-6
    recognition of gain, 10-3
    with Sec. 751, 10-6–10-11
  preferred stock bailouts, 4-30–4-33
  property distributions, 4-9–4-14
  spinoffs, 4-40–4-41
  split-offs, 4-41–4-42
  split-ups, 4-41–4-42
  stock dividends, 4-14–4-17
    effect on distributing corporation, 4-17
    taxable stock dividends, 4-17
    taxable stock rights, 4-17
    tax-free stock dividends, 4-15–4-16
    tax-free stock rights, 4-15–4-16

stock redemptions, 4-17–4-30
    attribution rules, 4-20–4-21
    bootstrap acquisitions, 4-47–4-48
    complete termination of shareholder's interest, 4-23–4-24, 4-44–4-45, 4-49
    effect on distributing corporation, 4-29–4-30
    effect on shareholder, 4-18–4-20
    not essentially equivalent to a dividend, 4-24–4-25
    partial liquidations, 4-25–4-27
    preferred stock bailout, 4-32
    related corporation redemptions, 4-33–4-36
    substantially disproportionate redemptions, 4-21–4-23
    to pay death taxes, 4-27–4-29
    stock rights, 4-14–4-17
        taxable stock rights, 4-17
        tax-free stock rights, 4-16–4-17
    timing of distributions, 4-48–4-49
Nonrecognition of gain/losses
    avoidance under Sec. 351, 2-37–2-39
    partnerships, formation of, 9-7
    tax-free reorganizations, 7-7–7-37
Nonrecourse loans
    definition of, 9-28
    partner's share of liabilities and, 9-27–9-29
Nonresident aliens
    definition of, 15-3, 15-16
    "effectively connected" test, 15-18–15-19
    filing requirement, 15-47–15-48
    investment income, 15-16–15-18
    lawful resident test, 15-16
    ordinary income/capital gains earned by, 15-17
    real estate investors, special election for, 15-18
    special resident alien elections, 15-45–15-46
    substantial presence test, 15-16
    taxation of, 15-15–15-20
    tax calculation, 15-19
    trade/business income, 15-18–15-19
Nonshareholders, capital contributions, 2-32–2-34

Office audit, 16-7
Oil-related income, foreign base company, 15-30
Old loss corporation, 7-39
"Old" Sec. 1374 tax, *See* Capital gains tax
One class of stock requirement, S corporations, 11-4, 11-35–11-37
Open-fact situations, client-oriented tax research and, 1-3
Open transaction doctrine, 6-8–6-9
    liquidating distributions, 6-8–6-9
Optional basis adjustments
    partnerships, Sec. 754 election, 10-2, 10-29–10-40
Option attribution, 4-21
Oral conclusions, tax research, 1-5
Ordinary gross income (OGI), 5-16
Ordinary income/loss
    partnerships, 9-22
    S corporations, 11-12–11-15
        carrybacks/carryforwards when status changes, 11-13–11-15

compared to C corporation treatment, 11-14
    deductions that cannot be claimed, 11-14
Ordinary income property
    corporation
        deducting contributions of, 3-13–3-14
        definition of, 3-13
Ordinary loss
    versus capital loss, 2-34–2-39
    debt obligations, 2-35–2-37
    Sec. 1244 stock, 2-34–2-35, 2-39
    Securities, worthlessness, 2-34–2-39
Organizational expenditures
    alternative minimum tax, 5-10
    as corporate taxable income deductions, 3-10–3-12
    definition of, 3-11
    partnerships, 9-14–9-15
    S corporations, 11-14
Organization forms
    corporations
        C corporations, 2-5–2-7
        S corporations, 2-7–2-8
    partnerships, 2-4–2-5
    sole proprietorships, 2-2–2-3
Original issue discount, 2-30

Parent corporation, as agent for affiliated groups, 8-39–8-40
Parent-subsidiary corporation redemptions
    definition of, 4-35
    stock redemptions
        treated as dividends, 4-35
        treated as sales, 4-35–4-36
Partial liquidations
    stock redemptions, 4-25–4-27
        determination made at corporate level, 4-25–4-26
        effect on shareholders, 4-26–4-27
        safe harbor, 4-26
Partially liquidating distributions, liquidation rules, 6-7
Partner, definition of, 9-3
Partnership agreement, 9-22–9-23
Partnership interest
    exchange of, 10-22–10-23
        for another partnership interest, 10-22
        for corporate stock, 10-22
        incorporation, 10-22–10-23
    gift of, 10-23
    holding period for, 9-9
    income recognition of, 10-23–10-25
    optional adjustments on, 10-29–10-40
        allocation to assets, 10-32–10-33
        amount of, 10-31–10-32
        effects of, 10-33–10-35
    sale of, 10-16–10-19
        impact on partnership, 10-19
        liabilities, 10-17–10-19
        Sec. 751 properties, 10-16–10-17
    transfers of, 10-23–10-25
Partnership item, definition of, 9-42
Partnership liabilities
    effect of, 9-27–9-29
        increases/decreases in, 9-27
        partner's share of, 9-27–9-29
Partnership property, payments at death/retirement of partner, 10-19–10-20

Partnerships, 2-4–2-5
    compared to corporations, 2-8–2-9
    contribution of service, 9-12–9-14
        allocation of expense deduction, 9-13
        basis adjustment, 9-13–9-14
    definition of, 2-4, 9-2–9-4
    division of, 10-29
    elections, 9-15–9-20
        partnership's taxable year, 9-15–9-19
    estimated taxes, 9-42
    family partnerships, 9-37–9-39
    Form 1065, 9-41
    formation, 9-1–9-43
        tax implications of, 9-6–9-15
    general partnerships, 9-3
    IRS audit procedures, 9-42–9-43
    limited partnerships, 9-3–9-4
    liquidating distributions, 10-11–10-16
        basis in assets received, 10-12–10-14
        effects on partnership, 10-15–10-16
        gain/loss recognition by partner, 10-11–10-12
        Sec. 751 effects, 10-14–10-15
        as tax-planning consideration, 10-43
    loss limitations, 9-30–9-34
        at-risk loss limitation, 9-31–9-32
        at-risk rules and current distributions, 9-32–9-33
        passive activity limitation rules, 9-33–9-34
    loss recognition, timing of, 9-40–9-41
    nonliquidating distributions, 10-2–10-6
        basis effects of distributions, 10-4–10-5
        character of distributed property, 10-6
        holding period, 10-6
        recognition of gain, 10-3
        with Sec. 751, 10-6–10-11
    operation, 9-1–9-43
        effects of, 9-29–9-30
        loss limits, 9-30
    optional basis adjustments, 10-29–10-40
        on distributions, 10-35–10-38
        election to make adjustments, 10-30, 10-42–10-43
        special adjustments on distributions to transferee partners, 10-38–10-40
        on transfers, 10-30–10-35
    organizational expenditures, 9-14–9-15
    partner/partnership transactions, 9-34–9-37
        guaranteed payments, 9-35–9-37
        sales of property, 9-34–9-35
    partner reporting of income, 9-22–9-26
        distributive share, 9-22
        partnership agreement, 9-22–9-23
        special allocations, 9-23–9-26
        varying interest rule, 9-23
    partnership interest, 9-26–9-30
        beginning basis, 9-26–9-27
        partnership liabilities, effect of, 9-27–9-29
    partnership reporting of income
        ordinary income, 9-22
        ordinary loss, 9-22
        separately stated items, 9-21–9-22
        taxable income, 9-20–9-22
    property contributions, 9-6–9-12
        alternatives to, 9-40
        holding period for property, 9-11

Partnerships (*continued*)
  holding period for partnership interest, 9-9
  liabilities, 9-7–9-9
  nonrecognition of gains/losses, 9-7
  partner's basis in partnership interest, 9-9
  partnership's basis in property, 9-9–9-11
  recapture provisions, 9-11–9-12
  recognition of gains/losses, 9-7
publicly traded partnerships, 10-41
reporting to IRS/partners, 9-41
  retroactive allocation of losses, 9-39–9-40
Sec. 732(d) election, 10-43
Subchapter K, election out of, 9-3 *fn*
syndication expenditures, 9-14–9-15
tax advantages, 2-4–2-5
taxation, 9-4–9-6
  distributions, 9-6
  overview of, 9-4–9-6
  partner's basis, 9-5–9-6
  partnership profits/losses, 9-4–9-5
tax disadvantages, 2-5
tax shelter partnerships, 10-40–10-41
termination of, 10-25–10-28
  effects, 10-26–10-28
  events causing termination, 10-25
  liquidating distributions and contributions, 10-26–10-27
  no business operated as partnership, 10-25
  sale/exchange of 50% or more interest, 10-25–10-26
  timing of termination, 10-26
terminating partnership interest, 10-11–10-29
  consolidations, 10-28
  division of partnership, 10-29
  exchange of interest, 10-22–10-23
  gift of interest, 10-23
  income recognition of interest, 10-23–10-25
  liquidating distributions, 10-11–10-16
  mergers, 10-28
  retirement/death of partner, 10-19–10-22
  sale of interest, 10-16–10-19
  termination of partnership, 10-25–10-28
  transfers of interest, 10-23–10-25
See also Family partnerships; Publicly traded partnerships; Special partnership issues
Party to a reorganization, definition of, 7-44
Passive activity limitation rules
  alternative minimum tax, 5-7
  closely held C corporations, 3-24
  estates, 14-9
  partnerships/partners, 9-33–9-34
  S corporation/shareholders, 11-23
  trusts, 14-9
Passive foreign investment company (PFIC), 15-34
Passive income requirement
  personal holding company (PHC) tax, 5-16–5-20
  S corporations, 11-40–11-41

Passive losses
  alternative minimum tax, 5-7
  closely held C corportions, 3-24
  estates, 14-9
  partnerships, 9-33–9-34
  S corporations, 11-23
  trusts, 14-9
Payment of taxes
  C corporations, 3-42–3-46
  estates, 14-46
  S corporations, 11-43
  trusts, 14-46
  withholding, nonresident aliens and foreign corporations, 15-19
Penalties
  civil fraud penalty, 16-26–16-27
  criminal fraud penalties, 16-27–16-28
    burden of proof, 16-27
    criminal fraud investigations, 16-27–16-28
    penalty provisions, 16-28
  for failure to file, 16-17–16-18
  for failure to pay, 16-18–16-20
  negligence penalty, 16-23–16-24
  personal holding company (PHC) tax, 5-40
  substantial understatement penalty, 16-24–16-26
    substantial authority, 16-25–16-26
    tax shelters, 16-26
    understatement versus underpayment, 16-24–16-25
  for underpaying estimated taxes, 16-21–16-22
    exceptions to, 16-22–16-23
Penalty taxes
  accumulated earnings tax, 5-25–5-34, 5-38, 5-40
  personal holding company tax, 5-15–5-25, 5-37–5-40
Periodicals, tax research, 1-28–1-29
Permanent differences, definition of, 3-40
Personal exemption
  estates, 14-11–14-12
  fiduciary accounting, calculation formula, 14-11–14-12
  trusts, 14-11–14-12
Personal holding company income (PHCI)
  definition of, 5-17
  determination of, 5-17–5-20
  personal service contracts exclusion, 5-20
  rent exclusion, 5-18–5-20
  See also Undistributed personal holding company income (UPHCI)
Personal holding company (PHC)
  definition of, 5-15
  foreign personal holding company (FPHC), 15-34
Personal holding company (PHC) tax, 5-15–5-25, 5-37–5-38
  avoidance of, 5-37–5-38
    changing stock ownership, 5-37
    changing income earned by corporation, 5-37
    liquidating the corporation, 5-38
    making dividend distributions, 5-38
    S corporation election, 5-38
  dividend distributions, use of, 5-21–5-24
    carryovers, 5-23
    consent dividends, 5-21–5-23

current year dividends, 5-21–5-22
deficiency dividends, 5-22–5-24
liquidating dividends, 5-22–5-23
throwback dividends, 5-21–5-22
types of, 5-21–5-22
excluded corporations, 5-15
filing requirements, 5-39
interest on underpayment, 5-40
liquidation of corporation, 5-38
passive income requirement, 5-16
payment of tax, 5-40
penalties on underpayment, 5-40
penalty tax, 5-20–5-21
stock ownership requirement, 5-15–5-16
tax calculation, 5-24–5-25
Personal service contracts, exclusion from PHCI, 5-20
Personal service corporations (PSCs)
  fiscal year, 3-3–3-4
  passive activity limitation, 3-24
  regular tax liability, 3-24–3-25
  Sec. 444 and, 3-3–3-4
  tax rates, 3-24–3-25
PHINet legal data base, 1-39
PH TC Memorandom Decisions, 1-21–1-22
Physical presence test, foreign-earned income and, 15-10
Plan of liquidation, 6-31–6-32
Plant replacement, as reasonable business need, 5-28
Policy-oriented tax research, 1-2
Political organizations, transfers to, gift tax and, 12-10
Pooled income fund, definition of, 12-24 *fn*
Portfolio obligations
  definition of, 15-17 *fn*
  "effectively connected" test and, 15-18–15-19
Possessions corporations, 15-40–15-42
Post-1976 gift taxes, reduction for, 13-5–13-6, 13-27–13-28
Post-gift appreciation, *inter vivos* gifts, removal from tax base, 12-32
Post-termination loss carryovers, S corporations, 11-23–11-24
Power of appointment, 12-17
  See also General power of appointment
Practical merger transactions, *See* Type C reorganizations
Pre-1977 gift tax, credit for, 13-29
Pre-acquisition losses, offsetting of, 7-38–7-41
Pre-ACRS depreciation, ACE adjustment, 5-9
Preadjustment year, definition of, 16-34
Precedential value of decisions, 1-24–1-26
  Circuit Court of Appeals, 1-23–1-24
  forum shopping, 1-26
  Tax Court, 1-19–1-22
  U.S. District Court, 1-22
Preferential dividends, dividends-paid deduction and, 5-22, 5-32
Preferred stock bailouts, 4-30–4-33
  nonliquidating distributions, 4-30–4-33
  Sec. 306 stock
    definition of, 4-31
    dispositions of, 4-31–4-32
Prentice Hall citator, 1-34–1-39
  abbreviations used in, 1-37

excerpt from, 1-38
information included in, 1-34–1-36
Present interest
  Crummey trust, 12-20
  definition of, 12-20
  special rule for trusts for minors, 12-19–12-20
Primary cites, 1-22–1-24
Principal partner, definition of, 9-17
Principal receipts, fiduciary accounting, 14-7
Private letter ruling, 1-27
Private Letter Rulings (Prentice Hall), 1-27 *fn*
Private nonoperating foundation, 3-14
Probate estate, compared to gross estate, 13-10
Profits interest, 9-12
Property
  definition of, 4-2
  Sec. 317(a) definition, 4-9
  Sec. 351 definition, 2-13
Property distributions, 4-9–4-14
  C corporations
    consequences to distributing corporation, 4-10–4-11, 4-29
    consequences to shareholders, 4-9–4-14
  estates, 14-44
  partnerships
    without Sec. 751, 10-2–10-6
    with Sec. 751, 10-6–10-11
  S corporations
    with E&P, 11-29–11-32
    without E&P, 11-27–11-28
Property requirement, Sec. 351, 2-13
Proposed regulations, 1-15
Proprietary interest, continuity of, reorganizations, 7-35
Protest letters, 16-8–16-10
  contents of, 16-8–16-10
Publicly traded partnerships (PTPs), 10-41
  definitions, 10-41
  exceptions to classification as, 10-41
  passive losses, 10-41
  See also Partnerships
Published opinions, U.S. Tax Court, 1-20–1-22

Qualified disclaimers, gift tax and, 12-11
Qualified joint interest, 13-17
Qualified Subchapter S trusts (QSSTs), 11-3 *fn*, 11-3
Qualified terminable interest property (QTIP)
  estate tax
    marital deduction and, 13-26–13-27
    recipient spouse's interest in, 13-21
    transfer of, 13-21
  gift tax
    definition of, 12-22
Qualified transfer, definition of, 12-9

Real estate
  alien investors in U.S. property, special election for, 15-18
  alternative minimum tax
    as adjustment, 5-5
    as tax preference item, 5-5
  corporate sales, recapture, 3-9–3-10
  date-of-death valuation, 13-6–13-9

Reasonable business needs
  evidence of, 5-27–5-31
    Bardahl formula, 5-28–5-31
    business contingencies, 5-28
    business enterprise acquisition, 5-28
    business expansion, 5-28
    no specific time limitations, 5-28
    plant replacement, 5-28
    specific, definite, and feasible plans, 5-27–5-28
    stock redemptions, 5-28
    subsequent events, impact of, 5-28
  stock redemptions as, 5-28
Reasonable cause, for deferral of estate tax payments, 13-33–13-35
Reasonable compensation, determination of, 3-35
Reasonableness of earnings accumulation, accumulated earnings tax and, 5-26–5-31
Recapitalization, 7-32–7-34
  definition of, 7-32
Recapture
  affiliated groups
    depreciation, 8-13–8-15
    investment tax credit, 8-12
  corporate formation, 2-25–2-26
  corporate sales of real estate, 3-9–3-10
  partnerships
    property contributions, 9-11–9-12
  tax benefit recapture rule, 3-9–3-10
Recognition of gain/loss
  C corporations
    acquiring corporation, 7-9–7-10
    controlled subsidiary corporations, liquidation of, 6-10–6-12
    corporate formation, 2-21–2-25
    distributing corporation, 4-10–4-11, 4-29, 4-43–4-44, 6-13–6-17
    stock distributions, reorganizations, 7-9
    when property is distributed in redemption of stock, 6-13–6-17
  estates, 13-44
  partnerships
    liquidating distributions, 10-11–10-16
    property contributions, 9-6–9-7
Recourse loans
  definition of, 9-27–9-28
  partner's share of liabilities and, 9-27–9-29
Refund claims, statute of limitations, 16-32–16-33
Regional commissioner, IRS, 16-2
Regular corporation, 2-5
  See also C corporations
Regular decision, U.S. Tax Court, 1-19
Regular tax liability
  affiliated groups, 8-28–8-29
  alternative minimum tax, 5-3, 5-13
  C corporations, 3-24–3-26
  foreign corporations, 15-24–15-25
Related corporations
  affiliated groups, 3-32–3-34, 8-3–8-5
  controlled groups, 3-26–3-32
  stock redemptions by, 4-33–4-36
    brother-sister corporations, 4-33–4-35
    parent-subsidiary corporations, 4-35–4-36

Related party transaction rules
  expense transactions, 3-23, 11-34
  liquidations, exceptions to recognition of gain/loss rules, 6-14–6-17
  partnerships, 9-34–9-35
  sales or exchanges, 3-22–3-23, 8-12, 8-14, 11-33–11-34
  S corporations, 11-33–11-34
Remainder interest, and deferral of estate tax payments, 13-33
Remainderman, 14-7
Remainders, date-of-death valuation, 13-8–13-9
Rental income expenses, adjusted ordinary gross income (AOGI) and, 5-17
Rents, exclusion from PHCI, 5-18–5-20
Reorganizations
  acquiring or transferee corporation, 7-9–7-10
    basis of acquired property, 7-10
    holding period for acquired properties, 7-10
    recognition of gain or loss, 7-9–7-10
  acquisitive reorganizations, 7-7, 7-14–7-29
    Type A reorganizations, 7-14–7-21
    Type B reorganizations, 7-26–7-29
    Type C reorganizations, 7-21–7-24
    Type D reorganizations, 7-24–7-25
    Type G reorganization, 7-29
  divisive reorganizations, 7-7, 7-29–7-32
    Type D reorganizations, 7-29–7-31
    Type G reorganization, 7-31–7-32
  judicial restrictions on, 7-34–7-37
    business purpose requirement, 7-36–7-37
    continuity of business enterprise, 7-35–7-36
    continuity of proprietary interest, 7-35
    step transaction doctrine, 7-37
  party to a reorganization, 7-44
  plan of reorganization, 7-44
  reporting requirements, 7-45
  ruling requests, 7-44–7-45
  shareholders and security holders, 7-10–7-13
    basis of stocks/securities received, 7-12
    character of recognized gain, 7-11–7-12
    holding period of stocks/securities, 7-13
    recognition of gain or loss, 7-10
  target or transferor corporation
    asset transfer, recognition of gain or loss on, 7-8
    assumption of liabilities, 7-9
    depreciation recapture, 7-8–7-9
    distribution of stock/securities, recognition of gain or loss on, 7-9
    recognition of gain, amount and character of, 7-8–7-9
  tax attributes, 7-37–7-41
    assumption of, 7-37–7-38
    limitation on use of, 7-38–7-41
  tax consequences of, 7-8–7-13
    acquiring or transferee corporation, 7-9–7-10
    shareholders and security holders, 7-10–7-13

Reorganizations (*continued*)
   target or transferor corporation, 7-8–7-9
   tax-free reorganizations, types of, 7-7–7-8
   tax-planning considerations, 7-41–7-44
      avoiding reorganization provisions, 7-43–7-44
      consideration used in reorganizations, 7-42–7-43
      taxable transactions versus reorganizations, 7-41–7-42
   Type E reorganizations, 7-32–7-34
   Type F reorganizations, 7-34
   See also Acquisitive reorganizations; Divisive reorganizations
Repetitive audit examinations, special relief rule, 16-7–16-8
Research
   client-oriented research, 1-2
   closed-fact situations, 1-2–1-3
   definition, 1-2
   open fact situations, 1-3
   steps in research process, 1-3–1-5
   tax planning research, 1-3
Resident aliens
   definition of, 15-3
   foreign-related transactions
      foreign-earned income exclusion, 15-8–15-14
      foreign tax credit, 15-4–15-8
   special resident alien elections, 15-45–15-46
Restoration of basis
   S corporation debt, 11-26–11-27
   S corporation stock, 11-27
Restored gain/loss, deferred intercompany transactions, determination of, 8-11–8-16
Retained life estate, transfers with, 13-13–13-14
Retroactive allocation of losses, partnerships, 9-39–9-40
Return of capital distributions, 4-2–4-3
Returns, due dates for filing, 16-15
Revenue agent, meeting with for audit, 16-8
Revenue procedures, tax law, 1-27
Revenue rulings, tax law, 1-26–1-27
Reverse triangular mergers
   Type A reorganizations, 7-21
   See also Triangular mergers
Reversionary interests
   and deferral of estate tax payments, 13-33
   definition of, 13-14 *fn*
   as gross estate inclusion, 13-14
Reversions, date-of-death valuation, 13-8–13-9
Review of Taxation of Individuals, The, 1-29
Revised Uniform Principal and Income Act, *See* Uniform Act
Revocable trusts
   creation of, 14-4
   definition of, 14-4
   gift tax and, 12-12
   grantor trust rules, 14-39
   as gross estate inclusion, 13-14–13-15
Royalty income, personal holding company income (PHCI) and, 5-18

Rule Against Perpetuities, definition of, 14-3 *fn*
Rulings
   letter rulings, definition of, 16-12
   request for, 16-12–16-14
      information included, 16-12–16-13
      IRS decision to rule, 16-13–16-14
      when rulings are desirable, 16-14
   tax law, 1-26–1-27

Salary payments, closely held corporations, compensation planning and, 3-34–3-35
Sales/exchanges of property
   corporate taxable income and, 3-9–3-10
      net capital gain, 3-9, 3-22–3-23
      net capital losses, 3-9, 3-23
      tax benefit recapture rule, 3-9–3-10
   partnerships
      gain sales, 9-35
      loss sales, 9-34–9-35
   S corporations
      tax benefit recapture rule, 11-14
Sales income, foreign base company, 15-27
Schedule K-1 (Form 1041), 14-47
Schedule K-1 (Form 1065), 9-41
Schedule K-1 (Form 1120S), 11-41
Schedule L (of Form 1120), 3-39
Schedule M-1 (of Form 1120), 3-40–3-42
Schedule M-2 (of Form 1120), 3-42
Scientific research property, deducting contributions of, 3-13
S corporations, 2-7–2-8, 11-1–11-45
   with accumulated earnings/profits, 11-29–11-32
      built-in gains tax, 11-15
      excess net passive income tax, 11-15–11-17
      money distributions, 11-29–11-31
      post-termination transition period, 11-32
      prior rules, 11-29
      property distributions, 11-31
      termination of election, 11-8
   administrative audit rules, 11-44–11-45
   alternative minimum tax (AMT) adjustments, 11-32
   basis adjustments, 11-25–11-27
      to S corporation stock, 11-25–11-26
      to shareholder debt, 11-26–11-27
   definition of, 2-7
   distributions, 11-27–11-32
      corporations with accumulated earnings/profits, 11-29–11-32
      corporations with no earnings/profits, 11-27–11-28
   election of status, 11-5–11-11
      making the election, 11-5–11-7, 11-42
   estimated tax payments, 11-43–11-44
   filing requirements, 11-42–11-43
   fringe benefits paid to shareholder-employees, 2-7, 11-34–11-35
   operations, 11-11–11-18
      accounting method elections, 11-12
      ordinary income/loss, 11-12–11-15
      special S corporation taxes, 11-15–11-18
      taxable year, 11-11–11-13, 11-42–11-43
   purposes of S corporation rules, 11-2

   recapture of LIFO benefits, 11-18
   related party transaction rules, 11-33–11-34
   requirements, 11-3–11-5
      corporate requirements, 11-4–11-5
      shareholder requirements, 11-3–11-4
   sample S corporation tax return, 11-45
   second class of stock requirement, 11-35–11-37
   shareholder taxation, 11-18–11-25
      family S corporations, 11-20–11-21
      income allocation procedures, 11-18–11-20
      loss/deduction pass-through to shareholders, 11-21–11-25
   special taxes
      built-in gains tax, 11-15–11-17
      capital gains tax, 11-17–11-18
      excess net passive income tax, 11-15
   tax-planning considerations, 11-37–11-42
      advantages of S corporation treatment, 2-7–2-8, 11-37–11-38
      disadvantages of S corporation treatment, 2-7–2-8, 11-38–11-39
      income allocation based on S corporation's accounting methods, 11-39
      increasing the benefits from S corporation losses, 11-39–11-40
      passive income requirements, 11-40–11-41
      using an S corporation when liquidating, 11-41–11-42
   tax preference items, 11-32–11-33
   termination of election, 11-7–11-11
      allocation of income, 11-8–11-9
      avoidance of, 11-10–11-11
      inadvertent termination, 11-9–11-10
      new election following termination, 11-10
      post-termination transition period, 11-32
      revocation, 11-7–11-8
   See also C corporations; Corporations; Ordinary income/loss; Special S corporation taxes
Seasonal income, exception to corporate estimated taxes, 3-45–3-46
Secondary cites, 1-22
Sec. 1231, gains/losses, 8-30
Sec. 1244 stock, worthlessness of, 2-34–2-35, 2-39
Sec. 1245
   corporate formation, 2-25–2-26
   partnership formation, 9-11
Sec. 1250
   corporate formation, 2-25–2-26
   partnership formation, 9-11
Sec. 1374 tax, *See* Built-in gains tax
Sec. 1375 tax, *See* Excess net passive income tax
Sec. 306 stock
   definition of, 4-31
   dispositions of, 4-31–4-32
   exceptions to treatment, 4-32–4-33
   redemptions of, 4-32
   See also Preferred stock bailouts
Sec. 332 liquidations, 6-9–6-12, 6-14, 6-29–6-31

Sec. 338 deemed liquidations, 6-20–6-28, 6-31
Sec. 351, 2-12–2-28
  assignment of income doctrine, 2-27
  avoidance of, 2-37–2-39
    nonrecognition of gain, 2-37–2-39
    nonrecognition of losses, 2-37
  boot, receipt of, 2-18
  computing depreciation, 2-26–2-27
  effect on transferee corporation, 2-21–2-22
  effect on transferors, 2-17–2-21
  reasons for and procedures for obtaining rulings, 2-40
  recapture of depreciation, 2-25–2-26
  reporting requirements, 2-39–2-40
  requirements for complete deferral of gain and loss under, 2-12–2-13
  shareholder's basis, computation of, 2-19–2-20
  transfer of multiple assets, computation of gain, 2-18–2-19
  transferor's holding period, 2-20–2-21
  transferor's liabilities, assumption of, 2-23–2-25
  See also, Corporate formation; Incorporation
Sec. 355
  requirements of, 4-38
    active conduct of trade or business requirement, 4-39
    business purpose requirement, 4-39
    continuity of interest requirement, 4-40
    control requirement, 4-38
    device requirement, 4-38
    distribution requirement, 4-39
  tax consequences to distributing corporation, 4-43–4-44
  tax consequences to shareholders, 4-40–4-43
  See also Nonliquidating distributions; controlled corporations
Sec. 381, tax attributes, 7-37–7-38
Sec. 382, tax attributes
  loss limitation
    affiliated groups, 8-26–8-28
    reorganizations, 7-38–7-41
    stock ownership change, 7-39–7-40
Sec. 383, tax attributes, 7-41
Sec. 384, tax attributes, 7-41
Sec. 644 tax, trusts/estates, 14-46
Sec. 721, nonrecognition of gain, partnerships, 9-6–9-7
Sec. 732(d) election, partnerships, 10-43
Sec. 751
  nonliquidating distributions with, 10-6–10-11
    exchange of assets and other property, 10-8–10-11
    substantially appreciated inventory, 10-7–10-8
    unrealized receivables, 10-6–10-7
Sec. 754 election
  distributions, 10-35–10-40
  election, 10-42–10-43
  revocation of election, 10-43
  transfers, 10-31–10-35
Sec. 7872, gift tax and, 12-30–12-31
Securities
  reorganizations, recognition of gain/loss on distribution of, 7-9
  worthlessness of, 2-34–2-35
Security holders
  definition of, 7-8 *fn*
  distribution of controlled subsidiary stock
    basis of property received, 4-42–4-43
    recognition of gain, 4-40–4-42
Separate return limitation year (SRLY) rules, 8-25–8-26
Separate return year, definition of, 8-7 *fn*
Separate share rule, trusts, 14-27
Separate taxable income, 8-7
Service companies
  Bardahl formula and, 5-30–5-31
  See personal service companies
Services income, foreign base company, 15-29–15-30
Shareholder debt
  basis adjustments to, S corporations, 11-25–11-27
Shareholder-employees
  compensation planning for, 3-34–3-35
    avoidance of unreasonable compensation, 4-46–4-47
    determination of reasonable compensation, 3-35
    fringe benefits, 3-35
    salary payments, 3-34–3-35
Shareholder requirements
  S corporations, 11-3–11-4
    alien individuals, 11-4
    eligible shareholders, 11-3–11-4
    35-shareholder limit, 11-3
Shareholders
  capital contributions, 2-32
  consent to S corporation election, 11-6–11-7
  consequences of property distributions to, 4-9–4-10
  corporation as agent of, 2-10
  disregard of corporate form by, 2-10
  distribution of controlled subsidiary stock
    basis of property received, 4-42–4-43
    recognition of gain, 4-40–4-42
  dividend distributions, 4-9–4-10
  dividends - received deduction, 3-15–3-19
  liquidating distributions, 6-5–6-13
  partial liquidations, effect on, 4-25–4-27
  reorganizations, tax consequences, 7-10–7-13
  stock redemptions
    complete termination of interest, 4-23–4-24
    effect of redemption on, 4-18–4-20
    questions for, 4-18
Shareholder taxation
  S corporations, 11-18–11-25
Shipping income, foreign base company, 15-30
Short-form gift tax return, 12-35
Short tax period, 3-3
  short-period tax return, 3-3
Short-term trusts, *See* Clifford trusts
Simple trusts
  distribution deduction, 14-10–14-11
  taxable income
    allocation of expenses to tax-exempt income, 14-16–14-17
    comprehensive illustration, 14-20–14-22
    distributable net income (DNI), determination of, 14-17
    distribution deduction, determination of, 14-17
    net capital loss effect, 14-19–14-20
    net operating loss effect, 14-19
    tax treatment for beneficiary, 14-17–14-18
  See also Complex trusts/estates; Trusts
65-day rule, estate tax, 14-44
Small cases procedures, U.S. Tax Court, 1-20
Solely-for-voting-stock requirement
  Type B reorganizations, 7-26–7-29
  exceptions to, 7-27
  timing of transaction, 7-27–7-28
Sole proprietorships, 2-2–2-4
  as business form, 2-2–2-4
  definition of, 2-2
  tax advantages, 2-3
  tax disadvantages, 2-3–2-4
Special agents, criminal fraud investigations, 16-27–16-28
Special allocations
  partnerships
    contributed property, 9-24
    substantial economic effect, 9-24–9-26
Special foreign corporation forms, 15-34
Special limitations, foreign tax credit, 15-7–15-8
Special loss limitations
  consolidated NOLs
    consolidated return change of ownership (CRCO) rules, 8-24 *fn*
    Sec. 382 loss limitation, 8-26–8-28
    separate return limitation year, 8-25–8-26
Special relief rule, for repetitive audit examinations for same item, 16-7–16-8
Special resident alien elections, 15-45–15-46
Special S corporation taxes, 11-15–11-18
  built-in gains tax, 11-15–11-17
  capital gains tax, 11-17–11-18
  excess net passive income tax, 11-15
Specific, definite, and feasible plans, reasonable business needs and, 5-27–5-28
Spinoffs, 4-37, 4-40–4-41
  illustration, 4-37
  recognition of gain by shareholders, 4-40–4-41
Split-interest transfers
  charitable contribution deductions and, 12-24–12-25
  definition of, 12-24
  estate tax and, 13-23–13-24
  gift tax and, 12-24–12-25
  example of, 12-24
Split-offs, 4-36–4-37, 4-41–4-42
  illustration, 4-37
  recognition of gain by shareholders, 4-41–4-42
Split-ups, 4-37–4-38, 4-41–4-42
  illustration, 4-39
  recognition of gain by shareholders, 4-41–4-42
Sprinkling trust, 14-44

S short year, 11-8
Standard Federal Tax Reporter (CCH), 1-30, 1-34
Start-up expenditures
  as corporate taxable income deduction, 3-12
  examples of, 3-12
State death tax credit, estate tax, 13-28–13-29
State law, fiduciary accounting and, 14-6
Statements on Responsibilities in Tax Practice (SRTP), 16-35–16-36
State transfer tax costs, lessening of, 12-33
Statute of limitations, 16-28–16-33
  general three-year rule, 16-29–16-30
    carrybacks, 16-31
    extension of three-year period, 16-31
    when fraud is proven, 16-31–16-32
  gift tax purposes, 12-36–12-37
  refund claims, 16-32–16-33
  six-year rule for "substantial" omissions, 16-30–16-31
    gift and estate tax returns, 16-30–16-31
    income tax returns, 16-30
  when no return is filed, 16-31
Statutory exemption amount, alternative minimum tax, 5-3
Statutory Notice of Deficiency, 16-10–16-11
Statutory regulations, 1-15–1-16
Step transaction doctrine, reorganizations, 7-37
Step-up in basis, loss of, 12-33
S termination year, 11-8
Stock
  debt-financed stock, 3-19
  dividends-received deduction, 3-15–3-19
  multiple classes of, 2-31
  tax advantages of, 2-31, 2-33
  tax disadvantages of, 2-31, 2-33
  worthlessness of, 2-34–2-35
  See also Sec. 306 stock
Stock acquisitions, 7-6–7-7
  basis of stock/securities received, 7-12
  holding period, 7-13
  recognition of gain/loss, 7-10
    character of, 7-11–7-12
  See also Acquisitions
Stock distributions
  of controlled corporations, 4-36–4-44
    active conduct of trade or business requirement, 4-39
    business purpose requirement, 4-39
    continuity of interest requirement, 4-40
    control requirement, 4-38
    device requirement, 4-38
    distributions requirement, 4-39
    requirements of Sec. 355, 4-38
    tax-free distributions, 4-36–4-38
  dividends
    taxable stock dividends, 4-17
    taxable stock rights, 4-17
    tax-free stock dividends, 4-15–4-16
    tax-free stock rights, 4-16–4-17
  reorganizations
    corporate recognition of gain/loss on, 7-9
    shareholder recognition of gain or loss, 7-10–7-13

Stock dividends
  taxable dividends, 4-17
  tax-free dividends, 4-15–4-16
  allocation of basis, 4-15
Stock-for-bond exchange, Type E reorganizations, 7-34
Stock-for-stock exchange
  Type B reorganizations, 7-26–7-31
  Type E reorganizations, 7-32–7-33
Stock losses, ordinary loss deduction for, 2-33–2-34, 2-39
Stock redemptions, 4-17–4-30
  attribution rules, 4-20–4-21
    entity attribution, 4-21
    family attribution, 4-20–4-21
    option attribution, 4-21
  by brother-sister corporations, 4-33–4-35
  by related corporations, 4-33–4-36
    brother-sister corporations, 4-33–4-35
    parent-subsidiary corporations, 4-35–4-36
  complete termination of interest, 4-23–4-24
  definition of, 4-17
  distributing corporation
    effect on, 4-29–4-30
    questions for, 4-29
  E&P, effect on, 4-29–4-30
  equivalency to dividend, 4-24–4-25
  liquidating distributions, 6-13–6-17
    exceptions to gain/loss recognition rules, 6-14–6-17
    liabilities assumed/acquired by shareholders, 6-13–6-14
  nonliquidating distributions, 4-17–4-30
  partial liquidations, 4-25–4-27
    determination made at corporate level, 4-25–4-26
    effect on shareholders, 4-26–4-27
  as reasonable business need, 5-28
  reasons for, 4-17–4-18
  Sec. 306 stock, 4-32
  shareholders
    effect of redemption on, 4-18–4-20
    questions for, 4-18
  substantially disproportionate redemptions, 4-21–4-23
  to pay death taxes, 4-27–4-29
Stock requirement, Sec. 351, 2-17
Stock rights
  tax-free rights, 4-14–4-17
    allocation of basis, 4-16
    holding period, 4-16–4-17
  taxable rights, 4-17
Subchapter J, purposes of, 14-6
Subchapter K, election out of, 9-3 *fn*
Subpart F income, 15-26–15-31
Subsidiary corporation stock, distributions/sales of, 6-14
Substantial authority, concept of, 16-40–16-41
Substantially all requirement, Type C reorganizations, 7-21
Substantially appreciated inventory, 10-7–10-8
Substantial omissions, income tax returns, 16-30
Substantial presence test, 15-16
Substantial understatement penalty, 16-24–16-26
  substantial authority, 16-25–16-26

tax shelters, 16-26
  understatement versus underpayment, 16-24–16-25
Substantial understatement of tax, joint returns, test for, 16-34
Superfund environmental tax, corporations, 5-14
Supreme Court
  appeal of lower court's decision, 16-11–16-12
  tax law decisions, 1-24
Supreme Court Reporter (S.Ct.), 1-24
Syndication expenditures, partnerships, 9-14–9-15

"Tainted" income, 15-26
"Tainted" stock, 4-30
Target corporation
  acquisitions, tax consequences for, 7-3
  definition of, 7-8 *fn*
  liquidation of, 6-26–6-27
  shareholders, tax consequences for, 7-3–7-5
  tax accounting elections for, 6-25–6-26
  tax consequences for, 7-3
Taxable estate, 13-27
Taxable income
  accumulated earnings tax and, 5-31–5-34
    accumulated earnings credit, 5-33–5-34
    dividends-paid deduction, 5-32–5-33
    negative adjustments, 5-32
    positive adjustments, 5-32
  complex trusts/estates, 14-22–14-29
    distributable net income (DNI), determination of, 14-23–14-24
    net capital loss effect of, 14-28–14-29
    net operating loss effect of, 14-28
    tax treatment for beneficiary, 14-24–14-28
  corporations
    affiliated groups, 8-6–8-8
    compared to individual taxable income and, 3-6–3-8
    deductions, 3-10–3-22
    reconciliation of book income items to, 3-40–3-42
    sales/exchanges of property, 3-9–3-10
  partnerships, 9-20–9-22
  S corporations, 11-12–11-15
  Simple trusts, 14-15–14-22
    allocation of expenses to tax-exempt income, 14-16–14-17
    comprehensive illustration, 14-20–14-22
    distributable net income (DNI), determination of, 14-17
    exemption, 14-16
    net capital loss, effect of, 14-19–14-20
    net operating loss, effect of, 14-19
    short-cut approach to proving, 14-18–14-19
    taxation to beneficiary, 14-17–14-18
  See also Corporate taxable income
Taxable versus tax-free acquisitions, 7-3–7-5
  accounting for the acquisition, 7-5
  tax consequences, 7-3–7-5
    for acquiring corporation, 7-3
    for target corporation, 7-3

for target corporation's shareholders, 7-3–7-5
Tax Adviser, The, 1-29
Taxation for Accountants, 1-29
Tax attributes
  acquisitions, 7-37–7-41
    assumption of, 7-37–7-38
    limitation on use of, 7-38–7-41
  carryovers, 6-18–6-19
Tax benefit recapture rule (Sec. 291), 3-9–3-10
Tax Coordinator (Research Institute of America), 1-31
Tax Court, *see* U.S. Tax Court
Tax Court of the United States Reports, 1-21
Tax credits
  affiliated groups, 8-34–8-35
    foreign tax credit, 8-35
    general business credit, 8-34–8-35
  alternative minimum tax (AMT), 5-12–5-14
  foreign tax credit, 15-4–15-8
Taxes—the Tax Magazine, 1-29
Tax-free reorganization summary, 7-16–7-17
Tax-free reorganizations, 7-3–7-5, 7-7–7-45
Tax-free stock distributions, 4-14–4-17, 4-36–4-44
Tax-haven sales subsidiary, illustration of use of, 15-26
Tax law
  administrative interpretations, 1-26–1-28
    announcements, 1-28
    information releases, 1-28
    letter rulings, 1-27
    revenue procedures, 1-27
    revenue rulings, 1-26–1-27
    technical advice memoranda, 1-28
  definition of, 1-2, 1-12
  Internal Revenue Code, 1-13–1-15
  judicial decisions, 1-17–1-26
    circuit court of appeals, 1-23–1-24
    court system, overview of, 1-17–1-19
    precedential value of decisions, 1-24–1-26
    Supreme Court, 1-24
    U.S. Claims Court, 1-22–1-23
    U.S. district courts, 1-22
    U.S. Tax Court, 1-19–1-22
  legislative process, 1-12–1-13
  sources of, 1-12–1-29
  Treasury Department regulations, 1-15–1-17
    authoritative weight, 1-16
    citations, 1-16–1-17
    final regulations, 1-15
    interpretative regulations, 1-15–1-16
    proposed regulations, 1-15
    statutory regulations, 1-15–1-16
    temporary regulations, 1-15
Tax Law Review, 1-29
Tax liability
  accumulated earnings tax, determination of, 5-31–5-34
  affiliated groups, 8-32–8-34
    alternative minimum tax liability, 8-33–8-34
    regular tax liability, 8-32–8-33
    consolidated tax returns, 8-32–8-34
  corporations, 3-24–3-26

accumulated earnings tax, 5-25–5-26
personal holding company (PHC) tax, 5-15–5-25
regular tax, 3-24–3-26
superfund environmental tax, 5-14
estates
  estate tax, 14-8–14-12
    computation of, 13-27–13-30
    credit for pre-1977 gift taxes, 13-29
    credit for tax on prior transfers, 13-29–13-30
    foreign death tax credit, 13-30
    post-1976 gift tax, reduction for, 13-27–13-28
    pre-1977 gift tax, credit for, 13-29
    prior transfers, credit for, 13-29–13-30
    state death tax credit, 13-28–13-29
    taxable estate, 13-27
    taxable estate and tax base, 13-27
    tentative tax computation, 13-27–13-28
    tentative tax and reduction for post-1976 gift tax, 13-27–13-28
    unified credit, 13-28
  foreign corporations, 15-24–15-25
  gift tax, 12-26–12-28, 12-35
    previous taxable gifts, 12-26–12-27
    unified credit, 12-27
  joint returns, 16-33–16-35
    innocent spouse provision, 16-33–16-35
    validity of, 16-33
  nonresident aliens, 15-15–15-20
  partnerships
    distributions, 9-6
    overview of, 9-4–9-6
    partner's basis, 9-5–9-6
    partnership profits/losses, 9-4–9-5
  S corporations
    special S corportion taxes, 11-15–11-18
  transferee liability, 16-35
  trusts, 14-8–14-32
    simple trusts, 14-8–14-22
    complex trusts, 14-22–14-32
  See also Regular tax liability
Tax Management Portfolios (Bureau of National Affairs), 1-32
Tax matters partner, definition of, 9-42
Tax Notes, 1-29
Taxpayer Compliance Measurement Program (TCMP), audits and, 16-6
Tax periodicals, 1-28–1-29
Tax-planning situations, 1-2–1-3
  client-oriented tax research and, 1-2–1-3
Tax practice, 16-35–16-40
  statements on responsibilities in, 16-35–16-38
  statutory provision concerning tax return preparers, 16-38–16-39
Tax preference items, alternative minimum taxable income (AMTI), 5-3–5-5
Tax Reform Act (1976), gift tax and, 12-3
Tax research, 1-1–1-40
  citators, 1-33–1-39
    Commerce Clearing House Citator (CCH citator), 1-34–1-35
    Prentice Hall citator, 1-34–1-39
  client-oriented tax research, 1-2–1-3
  computers as research tool, 1-39–1-40
  definition of, 1-2

end product of, 1-2–1-3
grey areas, 1-4
overview of, 1-2–1-3
policy-oriented tax research, 1-2
sample work papers and client letter, 1-40
steps in process, 1-3–1-5
tax advisors' conclusions, 1-5
tax periodicals, 1-28–1-29
tax services, 1-29–1-33
tax treaties, 1-28
Tax results
  case examples, 1-6–1-11
    comparison of winning/losing cases, 1-11
    taxpayer loses, 1-8–1-10
    taxpayer wins, 1-6–1-8
  designing factual situation favoring taxpayer, 1-11–1-12
  importance of facts to, 1-5–1-12
Tax services, 1-29–1-33
  Bender's Federal Tax Service, 1-32–1-33
  Federal Taxes 2d, 1-29–1-30
  Law of Federal Income Taxation, 1-31–1-32
  research of tax questions, 1-33
  Standard Federal Tax Reporter (CCH service), 1-30
  Tax Coordinator, 1-31
  Tax Management Portfolios, 1-32
Tax shelter partnerships, abusive tax shelters, 10-40–10-41
Tax shelters, substantial understatement penalty, 16-26
Tax treaties, 1-29
  objectives of, 15-45
Tax year
  affiliated group elections, 8-8–8-9
  C corporations
    annual accounting period, change in, 3-4
    personal service corporations, 3-3–3-4
    restrictions on adoption of, 3-3–3-4
    selection of, 3-2–3-4
  partnerships, 9-15–9-19, 9-41–9-42
  Sec. 706 restrictions, 9-15–9-19
  S corporations, 11-11–11-12, 11-42
Technical advice memoranda
  audits and, 16-8
  tax law, 1-28
Temporary differences, definition of, 3-40–3-41
Temporary regulations, 1-15
Tenancy by the entirety, definition of, 13-16 *fn*
Tentative minimum tax, definition of, 5-3
Term certain interest, 12-14 *fn*
Terminable interest rule, marital deduction and, 13-25–13-26
Terminable interests
  definition of, 12-21
  nondeductible terminable interests, characteristics of, 12-21
  qualified terminable interest property (QTIP), 12-22
Termination
  affiliated groups, 8-9–8-10
    effect on former members, 8-10
    good cause request to discontinue status, 8-10
  of partnership interest, 10-25–10-28

K-20 • Subject Index

Termination (*continued*)
  of S corporation election, 11-7–11-11
    allocation of income, 11-8–11-9
    avoidance of, 11-10–11-11
    inadvertent termination, 11-9–11-10
    new election following termination, 11-10
    post-termination loss carryovers, 11-23–11-24
    revocation, 11-7–11-8
  stock redemption
    complete termination of interest, 4-23–4-24
      definition of, 4-44–4-45
      family attribution rules and, 4-44–4-45
Testamentary transactions, 13-2
Testamentary trust, 14-2–14-3
Thirty-five-shareholder limit, S corporations and, 11-3
Thirty-day rules, consolidated taxable income, 8-7–8-8
Throwback dividends, 5-21–5-22, 5-32–5-33
Throwback rules, *See* Accumulation distribution rules
Tier-1 beneficiaries, 14-25–14-27
Tier-2 beneficiaries, 14-25–14-27
Transferee corporation
  effect of Sec. 351 on, 2-21–2-22
    basis for property, 2-22
    gain or loss recognized by, 2-21–2-22
  reorganizations, 7-9–7-10
Transferee partners
  special adjustments on distributions to, 10-38–10-40
    calculation of, 10-39
    Sec. 732(d) and 751, 10-39–10-40
Transferor corporation, definition of, 7-8 *fn*
Transferor provisions
  estate tax, 13-11–13-15
    gifts made within 3 years of death, 13-11–13-12
    gross-up rule, 13-12–13-13
    reversionary interests, 13-14
    revocable transfers, 13-14–13-15
    transfers with retained life estate, 13-13–13-14
  gross estate, 13-11–13-15
Transferor's liabilities
  assumption of, 2-23–2-25
    general rule (Sec. 357(a)), 2-23
    liabilities in excess of basis (Sec. 357(c)), 2-24
    liabilities of taxpayer using cash method of accounting (Sec. 357(c)(3)), 2-24–2-25
    tax avoidance (Sec. 357(b)), 2-23–2-24
Transfer pricing rules
  foreign sales corporations (FSCs), 15-37–15-39
  administrative transfer pricing rules, 15-37–15-38
  arm's-length transfer pricing rules, 15-38
  exemption of FSC dividends from taxation, 15-38–15-39
Transfers of partnership interest
  optional basis adjustment, 10-30–10-35

types of transfers, 10-22–10-25
Transfer tax base, removal of gift tax amount from, 12-32
Transfer taxes
  estate tax, concept of, 13-2–13-6
  generation-skipping transfer tax (GSTT), 13-35–13-36
  gift tax
    concept of, 12-2–12-3
    history/purpose of, 12-2–12-3
  unified transfer tax system, 12-3–12-4
    death tax base, impact of taxable gifts on, 12-4
    unified credit, 2-4
    unified rate schedule, 12-3–12-4
Translation of payments, foreign tax credit, 15-4–15-5
Treasury Department Circular 230, rules of, 16-39–16-40
Treasury Regulations 1-15–1-17
  authoritative weight, 1-16
  citations, 1-16–1-17
  forms of, 1-15–1-16
  interpretative and statutory regulations, 1-15–1-16
Triangular mergers, 7-19–7-21
  advantages of, 7-20–7-21
  substantially all requirement, 7-20
  Type A reorganizations, 7-19–7-21
  See also Reverse triangular mergers
  Type B reorganizations, 7-29
  Type C reorganization, 7-24
Trustees, 14-2
Trusts
  accumulation distribution rules, 14-32–14-34
  administration expense deduction, 14-46
  classification rules/size of exemption, 14-15–14-16
  compared to associations, 2-9
  credits, 14-12
  definition of, 2-9, 14-2
  distributable net income (DNI), 14-12–14-15
    computation of, 14-14–14-15, 14-17, 14-23–14-24
    definition of, 14-13–14-14
    significance of, 14-12–14-13
  distribution deduction, 14-10–14-11, 14-17, 14-23–14-24
    property distributions, 14-44
    65-day rule, 14-44
    timing of distributions, 14-43–14-44
  distributions from, personal holding company income (PHCI) and, 5-18
  expense deductions, 14-9–14-10
  filing requirements, 14-45–4-46
    documents to be furnished to IRS, 14-46–14-47
    due date, 14-46
  grantor trust provisions, 14-38–14-42
    administrative powers, retention of, 14-41
    Clifford trusts, 14-39–14-40
    control of other's enjoyment, 14-42
    economic benefits, retention of, 14-41–14-42
    effect of, 14-38–14-39

  post-1986 reversionary interest trusts, 14-40–14-41
  purpose, 14-38–14-39
  revocable trusts, 14-39
gross income, 14-9
inception of, 14-2–14-3
income in respect of a decedent (IRD), 14-35–14-38
  common examples, 14-36
  deductions in respect of a decedent, 14-37
  definition of, 14-35–14-36
  double taxation, 14-36
  no step-in basis, 14-37–14-38
  Sec. 691(c) deduction, 14-36–14-37
  significance of, 14-36–14-38
nontax aspects of, 14-4
personal exemption, 14-11–14-12
reasons for creation of, 14-3–14-4
sample simple/complex trust returns, 14-47
Sec. 644 tax, 14-34–14-35
  computation of, 14-34–14-35
  purpose, 14-34
  when applicable, 14-34
shifting income, ability to, 14-43
sprinkling trust, 14-44
taxable income, 14-18–14-12
  allocation of expenses to tax-exempt income, 14-16–14-17
  comprehensive illustration, 14-20–14-22, 14-29–14-32
  distributable net income (DNI), determination of, 14-12–14-15, 14-17, 14-23–14-24
  distribution deduction, determination of, 14-10–14-11,14-17, 14-23–14-24
  net capital loss, effect of, 14-19–14-20, 14-28–14-29
  net operating loss, effect of, 14-19, 14-28
  short-cut approach to proving correctness of, 14-18–14-19
  tax treatment for beneficiary, 14-17–14-18, 14-24–14-28
taxation, 14-1–14-47
tax liability, 14-8–14-12
tax-saving aspects of, 14-3–14-4
tax year, 14-45–14-46
See also Accumulation distribution rules; Complex trusts/estates; Grantor trusts; Simple trusts; Voting trust
Tuition payments, gift tax and, 12-9–12-10
Type A reorganizations, 7-14–7-21
  consolidations, 7-14–7-15
  definition of, 7-14
  requirements for, 7-14–7-15
  mergers, 7-14–7-21
  requirements for, 7-14–7-15
  reverse triangular mergers, 7-21
  tax consequences, 7-19
  triangular mergers, 7-19–7-20
Type B reorganizations, 7-26–7-29
  advantages of, 7-28
  disadvantages of, 7-28–7-29
  solely-for-voting-stock requirement, 7-26–7-28
  control, 7-27
  exceptions to, 7-27

timing of transaction, 7-27
tax consequences of, 7-28
triangular Type B reorganizations, 7-29
Type C reorganizations, 7-21–7-24
  advantages of, 7-23
  consideration used to effect reorganization, 7-22–7-23
  disadvantages of, 7-23
  stock distribution, 7-21–7-22
  substantially all requirement, 7-21
  tax consequences of, 7-23–7-24
Type D reorganizations, 7-24–7-25
  acquisitive Type D reorganizations, 7-24–7-25
    control requirements, 7-24–7-25
    tax consequences of, 7-25
  divisive Type D reorganization, 7-29–7-31
    requirements, 7-29
    tax consequences of, 7-29–7-31
Type E reorganizations, 7-32–7-34
  bond-for-bond exchange, 7-33
  bond-for-stock exchange, 7-33
  stock-for-bond exchange, 7-34
  stock-for-stock exchange, 7-32–7-33
Type F reorganizations, 7-34
Type G reorganizations
  acquisitive form, 7-29
  divisive form, 7-31,

Underpayment of estimated taxes
  penalty, 16-21–16-22
    exceptions to, 16-22–16-23
    Understatement versus underpayment, 16-24–16-25
Understatement of taxes, penalties for aiding/abetting, 16-38–16-39
Undervaluation
  of estate tax, 13-41
  of gift tax, 12-35–12-36
Undistributed personal holding company income (UPHCI), 5-20–5-21
  calculation of, 5-21
    negative income adjustments, 5-21
    positive income adjustments, 5-21
  See also Personal holding company income
Unified credit, 12-4, 12-7–12-8, 12-27, 13-6, 13-28
  estate tax, 13-6, 13-28
  gift tax, 12-4, 12-7–12-8, 12-27
Unified rate schedule, 12-3–12-4
Unified transfer tax system, 12-3–12-4
  death tax base, impact of taxable gifts on, 12-4
  unified credit, 12-4, 12-7–12-8
  unified rate schedule, 12-3–12-4
Uniform Act, fiduciary accounting and, 14-6–14-7
Uniform Gifts to Minors Act, 4-44
Uniform Limited Partnership Act (ULPA), 2-8, 9-4
Uniform Partnership Act (UPA), 2-8, 9-4
Unintentional constructive dividends, 4-12
United States Board of Tax Appeals Reports, 1-21
United States Reports, Lawyers' Edition (L. Ed.), 1-24

United States Supreme Court Reports (U.S.), 1-24
Unrealized receivables
  partnerships, basis, 9-10
  payments for, at death/retirement of partner, 10-19–10-20
  as Sec. 751 assets, 10-6–10-8
    substantially appreciated inventory, 10-7–10-8
Unreasonable compensation
  hedge agreements, use of, 4-46–4-47
  See also Compensation planning
Unreported decisions, U.S. district courts, 1-22
Unsecured debt obligations, 2-35
U.S. Circuit Court of Appeals, 1-23–1-24
  precedential value of decisions, 1-26
  primary cites, 1-23
  secondary cites, 1-23
U.S. citizens
  foreign-related transactions, 15-4–15-15
    employment in Puerto Rico/U.S. possessions, 15-14–15-15
    foreign-earned income exclusion, 15-8–15-14
    foreign tax credit, 15-4–15-8
U.S. Claims Court, 1-22–1-23
  precedential value of decisions, 1-26
  primary cites, 1-23
  secondary cites, 1-23
U.S. district courts, 1-22
  precedential value of decisions, 1-25
  primary cites, 1-22
  secondary cites, 1-22
  unreported decisions, 1-22
Use valuation, farm realty, 13-35
U.S. Income Tax Return for an S Corporation (Form 1120S), 11-42
U.S. jurisdiction for taxation, 15-2–15-4
  country of citizenship, 15-2
  country of residence, 15-2
  location where income is earned, 15-2
  type of income earned, 15-2
U.S. persons doing business abroad
  controlled foreign corporations, 15-25–15-34, 15-43
    constructive distributions of income, 15-27–15-31
    definition of, 15-27
    disposition of stock, 15-32
    distributions from, 15-31–15-32
    investments in U.S. property, 15-31
    prior to Subpart F rules, 15-25–15-26
    Sec. 482 rules, 15-33–15-34
    under Subpart F rules, 15-26–15-27
  domestic international sales corporations (DISCs), 15-39–15-40, 15-43
    requirements, 15-39
    taxable income, 15-39
    taxation of distributions, 15-39–15-40
  domestic subsidiary corporations, 15-21, 15-43
  foreign branches, 15-21
  foreign corporations, 15-21–15-25, 15-43
    deferral privilege, 15-22
    foreign personal holding company, 15-34
    foreign tax credit, 15-22–15-24

    passive foreign investment companies, 15-34
    taxation of U.S. activities, 15-24–15-25
  foreign sales corporations (FSCs), 15-34–15-39, 15-43
    advantages of, 15-35
    determination of foreign trade income, 15-36–15-37
    requirements, 15-35
    taxation of activities, 15-35–15-36
    transfer pricing rules, 15-37–15-39
  possessions corporations, 15-40–15-43
  tax breaks, 15-20–15-21
U.S. risks, insurance of, 15-27–15-28
U.S. shareholder, definition of, 15-27
U.S. Tax Cases (USTC), 1-22
U.S. Tax Court, 1-19–1-25
  acquiescence policy, 1-20
  history of, 1-19
  language of, 1-19–1-20
  memo decisions, 1-19
  precedential value of decisions, 1-24–1-25
  published opinions and citations, 1-20–1-22
  regular decisions, 1-19
  small cases procedures, 1-20

Valuation
  of gifts, 12-13–12-15
    general rules, 12-13
    life estates, 12-13–12-15
    penalty for undervaluation, 12-35–12-36
    remainder interest, 12-13–12-15
  of estates
    adjusted taxable gifts, 13-4–13-5
    alternate valuation date, 13-9–13-10
    date-of-death valuation, 13-6–13-9
    estate tax returns, 13-41
    gross estate, 13-6–13-10
    penalty for undervaluation, 13-41
  of stock, deemed liquidation election and, 6-22–6-24
Voting trust, definition of, 11-3 *fn*

Ways and Means Committee, U.S. House of Representatives, tax law and, 1-12–1-13
WESTLAW legal data base, 1-39
Working capital, reasonable need of business and, 5-28–5-31
Worthlessness
  advances to corporation, 2-35
  ordinary loss deduction, 2-34–2-35
  of stock/debt obligations, 2-34–2-35
  securities, 2-34–2-35
  unsecured debt obligations, 2-35
Worthless securities
  losses from, 2-34–2-35, 2-39
  ordinary loss, 2-34–2-35, 2-39
Writ of certiorari, 1-18–1-19
Written conclusions, tax research, 1-5

Year-end, choice of
  C corporation, 3-2–3-4
  partnership, 9-15–9-19
  S corporation, 11-11–11-12
  trust's/estate's, 14-44–14-45

1991 *Tax Rate Schedules*

ESTATES AND TRUSTS

If Taxable Income Is:		The Tax Is:	
Over—	But Not Over—		Of the Amount Over—
$0	$ 3,450	15%	$0
3,450	10,350	$ 517.50 + 28%	3,450
10,350		2,449.50 + 31%	10,350

CORPORATIONS

If Taxable Income Is:	The Tax Rate Is:
$0 to $50,000	15%
50,000 to 75,000	25%
75,000 to 100,000	34%
100,000 to 335,000	39%
335,000 and above	34%

UNIFIED CREDIT AMOUNT FOR ESTATE AND GIFT TAX

Year of Gift/ Year of Death	Amount of Credit	Exemption Equivalent
January through June, 1977	$ 6,000	$ 30,000
July through December, 1977	30,000	120,666
1978	34,000	134,000
1979	38,000	147,333
1980	42,500	161,563
1981	47,000	175,625
1982	62,800	225,000
1983	79,300	275,000
1984	96,300	325,000
1985	121,800	400,000
1986	155,800	500,000
1987 and later years	192,800	600,000